INTERNATIONAL

MARKETING

6TH EDITION

SUBHASH C. JAIN
THE UNIVERSITY OF CONNECTICUT

SOUTH-WESTERN
™
THOMSON LEARNING

Australia · Canada · Mexico · Singapore · Spain · United Kingdom · United States

International Marketing, Sixth Edition by Subhash C. Jain

Publisher: Dave Shaut
Senior Acquisitions Editor: Pamela Person
Developmental Editor: Mardell Toomey
Senior Marketing Manager: Joseph A. Sabatino
Media Technology Editor: Kevin von Gillern
Media Production Editor: Robin Browning
Production Editor: Amy S. Gabriel
Manufacturing Coordinator: Sandee Milewski
Cover Design: Tinbox Studio Inc., Cincinnati
Cover Image: © PhotoDisc, Inc.
Production House: Pre-Press Company, Inc.
Compositor: Pre-Press Company, Inc.
Printer: West Group

Printed in the United States of America
1 2 3 4 5 03 02 01 00

For more information contact South-Western, 5101 Madison Road, Cincinnati, Ohio, 45227 or find us on the Internet at http://www.swcollege.com

For permission to use material from this text or product, contact us by
• **telephone: 1-800-730-2214**
• **fax: 1-800-730-2215**
• **web: http://www.thomsonrights.com**

Library of Congress Cataloging-in-Publication Data
Jain, Subhash C., 1942–
    International marketing/Subhash C. Jain.—6th ed.
      p. cm.
    ISBN 0-324-06370-9 (alk. paper)—ISBN 0-324-10086-8 (international : alk. paper)—ISBN 0-324-06373-3 (cases v. : alk. paper)—ISBN 0-324-10085-X (cases v. : international : alk. paper)
    1. Export marketing—Management. 2. Export marketing—Management—Case studies.   I. Title.

HF1416 .J35 2001
658.8'48—dc21   00-059565

To Aarti and Amit

BRIEF CONTENTS

CONTENTS

After decades of resting comfortably at the top of the global marketplace, U.S. business has awakened to fierce competition. As more countries become industrial powerhouses and their companies seek larger marketplaces, international marketing as a discipline of study achieves greater significance than ever before. Japan, the most potent of all the new competitors, is pushing into such American strongholds as biotechnology and super-computers. Western Europe is coming up fast in aeronautics and office equipment. The newly industrialized countries of China, Taiwan, South Korea, Malaysia, Singapore, India, and Brazil are establishing themselves as low-cost producers of everything from steel to television sets. In addition, the U.S. faces new competition in Canada and Mexico as a result of the North American Free Trade Agreement (NAFTA).

At the same time that American supremacy is being challenged, the powerful force of technology is driving the world toward a converging commonality: the emergence of global markets. Millions worldwide want all the things they have heard about, seen, or experienced via new communication technologies. To capitalize on this trend, American companies must learn to operate and compete globally, as if the world were one large market, ignoring superficial regional and national differences.

Global markets offer unlimited opportunities. Corporations geared to this new reality can benefit from enormous economies of scale in production, distribution, marketing, and management. By translating these benefits into reduced world prices, they can dislodge competitors who still operate with the past perspectives. Today, only companies capable of becoming global will achieve long-term success.

As more business battles cross borders, managers must broaden their view of markets and competition. Doing business in a global economy requires a lot of new learning—including how to find the right country in which to build a plant, how to coordinate production schedules across borders, and how to absorb research wherever it occurs. They must learn what sort of people to hire, how to inculcate a global mentality in the ranks, and when to sell standardized products instead of customizing them for local markets.

Only a few managers are capable of handling the competitive rigors of the new global marketplace. Even in companies long accustomed to doing business overseas, managers find it difficult to look beyond their own domain to consider the capabilities and needs of the company as a whole to serve the global marketplace. Business schools across the country face a similar problem in producing global strategists. They must focus on the development of business education programs that explain how to function effectively in today's global business environment.

During the 1980s the American Assembly of Collegiate Schools of Business (AACSB) had offered seminars emphasizing how business schools might internationalize their curriculum. The U.S. Department of Education continues to provide funding for enhancing international business education. These kinds of support have helped many schools in adding international components to their existing courses, and in developing new international courses. Despite these efforts, in most business education programs insufficient attention is paid to the international dimension of business. A study commissioned by AACSB on the future of management education and development summarizes the problem:

International business is an area of the curriculum where we found a considerable amount of, at worst, lip service, and, at best, serious concern on the part of deans and faculty (but, we should point out, *not* on the part of most corporate-sector respondents). It was one of the four specific areas most often mentioned in both interviews and on the surveys as needing more emphasis in the curriculum. The problem, as most acknowledged, is how to implement this—whether to do it through adding more specific courses on international business, international finance, international marketing and the like, or by putting more emphasis on international issues in courses already in the curriculum. This whole area has been the object of much discussion within the business school community, and we probably cannot shed much additional light on the curriculum aspects of the matter except to say this: Although there seems to be an increasing awareness among business school deans and faculty that more ought to be done to emphasize this area, this awareness of sensitivity so far does not appear to us to have been translated into a great deal of action. More is being done now than ten years ago, and this seems clearly demonstrable by an examination of curricula and in interviews with knowledgeable observers, but much more needs to be done.*

As business schools globalize their curriculum, various specific international courses are being added to give students a worldwide perspective. Because of the deep impact of local customs and business practices on marketing, marketing requires separate exposure in the international context, more so than any other area of business. Many business schools now have international marketing courses at the undergraduate level, and some even at the graduate level. Many more schools are rapidly adding such courses.

Skills Developed Through Study of the Sixth Edition

The sixth edition of *International Marketing* has been developed based on the methodological and theoretical underpinnings developed in various social sciences. This book also integrates major marketing paradigms and frameworks. In each case, the cultural, legal, political, and institutional implications of international operations are properly analyzed. The text aims to make the reader an "informed observer" of the global marketplace. In addition to covering all important frameworks of marketing, concepts from other disciplines (for example, finance and accounting) are touched upon, since those must be grasped to fully understand the perspective of conducting marketing across national boundaries.

This book is designed to enable readers to develop skills for making marketing decisions in the global context, addressing issues like the following:

- *Finding new markets to replace saturated markets.*
- *Customizing products for the demands of new markets.*
- *Determining which products are in demand by world customers.*
- *Determining how to best reach the customers.*
- *Applying the pricing strategies that are most appropriate.*
- *Determining which distribution channels are adequate to serve the world customers.*
- *Overcoming barriers that hinder implementation of marketing programs.*

Retained Features of the Sixth Edition

Throughout the book, a *variety of examples* are used to illustrate the points made. Important frameworks and theories are explained with quotes from original sources. *Learning objectives* are found at the beginning of each chapter. Included at the end of the text material are *30 cases* that describe unique decision-making situations in international market-

---

*Lyman W. Porter and Lawrence E. McKibbin, *Management Education and Development: Drift or Thrust into the 21st Century?* (New York: McGraw-Hill Book Company, 1988), p. 8.

ing. The cases provide adequate information for an intelligent and lively discussion, and should enhance the learning experience.

New to the Sixth Edition!

The sixth edition has been prepared based on the feedback received from over 100 colleagues who responded to a survey on the content and structure of an international marketing course. Based on their thoughtful feedback substantial changes were made resulting in the following distinguishing features in this edition:

- *New topics* covering recent developments like the European Monetary Union, Asian Currency Crisis, economic liberalization among developing countries and other issues.

- *Expanded discussion* of entry strategies, international trade, U.S. exports, and marketing planning and strategy.

- An in-depth look at the role played by *international agreements and institutions in formulating global marketing strategies*, including discussion of the progress of the European Monetary Union.

- "*International Marketing Highlights*" boxed articles describing interesting ideas, stories, and factual information relevant to marketing decisions; Over 100 of these boxes appear throughout the book, describing real-world episodes in international marketing decision-making.

- *New and interesting examples*, both from industrialized and developing nations, to illustrate underlying concepts.

- Discussion of the latest round of *GATT talks* (i.e., the Uruguay Round) and *NAFTA*.

- *Substantial revision of chapters* on economic analysis of global trade and business, multinational sales management and foreign sales promotion, export management, and marketing planning and strategy for international business.

- *Updated* statistics, illustrations, and references to provide the most current perspectives on the subject.

- *Complete revision of the 15 cases* included from the previous edition, plus *15 new cases*. These 30 short and long cases involve such well-known companies as Colgate-Palmolive, Gillette, FedEx and UPS, Kodak and Fuji, Carvel, Seagram, IKEA, Nestlé, PSA Peugeot Citroën, ABB, Hewlett-Packard, Outback Steak House.

- Positioned at the end of each chapter, *creative questions* challenge the students on their understanding of concepts and theories presented in the text and lead to lively discussion.

- *Improved organization* of the material within the chapters for a better flow of ideas.

- Condensed coverage to keep the text to a *semester length* without compromising thoroughness.

Supplements

Instructor's Resource Kit on CD-ROM (ISBN 0-324-06371-7) includes a variety of pedagogical aids such as answers to end-of-chapter discussion questions, true-false and multiple-choice examination questions, transparency masters, solutions to cases, suggestions for further reading, and a listing of additional cases. Also included is a *PowerPoint Slide Presentation* with over 100 slides to complement classroom lectures. All cases in the back of the book are available as a stand-alone book, *International Marketing Cases* (ISBN 0-324-06373-3) suitable for students with relatively little background in marketing.

Personal Attention by the Author

I am personally available by phone, e-mail, or during conferences to discuss and advise colleagues on the structure of their international marketing course.

Acknowledgements

A project like this cannot be completed without help and advice from different sources. I have been fortunate in having the counsel of many scholars who contributed comments and criticism on previous editions. Although it is impossible to recognize them all here, I would like to thank Sanjeev Agarwal, Iowa State University; Lyn S. Amine, St. Louis University; S. Tamer Cavusgil, Michigan State University; Claude Cellich, International University, Geneva; John R. Darling, Louisiana State University at Shreveport; Roberto Friedman, University of Georgia; Pervez N. Ghauri, University of Groningen; Thomas Greer, University of Maryland; Andrew C. Gross, Cleveland State University; Erdener Kaynak, Pennsylvania State University at Harrisburg; Vinay Kotharis, Stephen Austine State University; James C. Nicholas, Connecticut World Trade Association; C.P. Rao, Kuwait University; Ravi Parameswaran, Oakland University; Ronald J. Patten, DePaul University; John K. Ryans, Jr., Kent State University; Saeed Samiee, University of Tulsa; Albert Stähli, Graduate School of Business Administration, Zurich; and Attila Yaprak, Wayne State University.

I also want to thank the following individuals for their permission to include cases written by them: Jacqueline M. Abbey, Georgetown University; Mohammed Ali Alireza, University of San Diego; Bill Bambara, University of Connecticut; Michel Berthelier, Group EM Lyon; Grady D. Bruce, California State University; Fullerton; Roland Calori, Group EM Lyon; Ellen Cook, University of San Diego; Golpira Eshghi, Bentley College; Madelyn Gangelbad, University of Missouri at Kansas City; Philip Hunsaker, University of San Diego; Michael Lubatkin, University of Connecticut; Gordon H. G. McDougall, Wilfrid Laurier University; Franklyn A. Manu, Morgan State University; Karen L. Newman, Georgetown University; Stanley D. Nollen, Georgetown University; Francese Parés, IESE, University of Navarra; George M. Puia, Indiana State University, Krishnan Ramaya, University of Southern Indiana; Lluis G. Renart, IESE, University of Navarra; José Antonio Segarra, IESE, University of Navarra; Ven Sriram, Morgan State University; Marilyn L. Taylor, University of Missouri at Kansas City; Suzanne Uhlem, Lund University; Philippe Very, Group EM Lyon; and Andrew Zacharakis, Babson College. I am indebted to Stephen M. Walsh, State University of New York College at Oneonta, for contributing 125 objective questions to the *Instructor's Manual*.

A special mention of appreciation must go to my doctoral student, Piotr Chelminski, for library search, for coordinating various revision chores and for computer work. I would like to thank the staff of our International Programs Office, especially Associate Director, Kelly Dunn, Graduate Assistant, Jay Chhatbar, and staff assistants, Amy Hotsko, Will Flynn, and Nicole Terry, for their administrative support. I am thankful to many writers and publishers for granting me the permission to include excerpts from their works.

The talented staff at South-Western deserves praise for their role in shaping the sixth edition. Team director, Dave Shaut, offered excellent advice and direction on the structure of the sixth edition and the acquisitions editor, Pamela Person, took the initiative in getting the project off the ground. Development editor, Mardell Toomey, did a superb job of coordination, and production editor, Amy S. Gabriel, did an excellent job of managing the manuscript to completion. I am indebted to them for their help. Thanks are due to Jennifer Carley of Pre-Press Company, Inc., for the fine job of production.

I want to thank my dean, Thomas G. Gutteridge, for his encouragement and support in this endeavor, and my former professor, Stuart U. Rich of the University of Oregon, who continues to influence my thinking through his writings.

Finally, my thanks go to my wife and our children, Aarti and Amit, who have put up with me through the hectic times of book revision. They provided the time, support, and inspiration so necessary to complete a project of this nature.

Subhash C. Jain

PART I

Framework of International Marketing

CHAPTER 1

Aspects of International Advertising

CHAPTER FOCUS_____

After studying this chapter, you should be able to

■ Explain the growing importance of international business.

■ Describe how international marketing differs from domestic marketing.

■ Discuss the significant role of multinational corporations in the expansion of business on an international scale.

■ Compare alternative entry routes into foreign markets.

One of the most significant economic developments since World War II is the increasing internationalization of business. Although business has been conducted across national boundaries for centuries, during the last four decades business dealings have escalated on a global scale. Leading corporations around the world have increasingly turned their attention to international business in order to maintain a competitive edge in today's dynamic economic scene.

This increase of international business affects the world economic order profoundly. It is a change with an impact comparable to that of the Industrial Revolution. In fact, today's global activity has been described as the second Industrial Revolution. Today's market provides not only a multiplicity of goods, but goods from many places. It is not surprising if your shirt comes from China, your jeans from Mexico, and your shoes from Italy. You may drive a Japanese car equipped with tires manufactured in France, nuts and bolts manufactured in India, and paint from a U.S. manufacturer (see International Marketing Highlight 1.1).

Consider McDonald's emerging MacWorld. Big Macs are on sale in 100 countries. By 2005, more than half of all the firm's restaurants are expected to be abroad. Business outside the United States is lucrative. In 1995 the 38 percent of McDonald's restaurants outside the United States accounted for 47 percent of its $29.9 billion in worldwide sales and 54 percent of its $2.6 billion operating profit. In 1995 the average sales at each of the company's restaurants abroad rose from $2.25 million to $2.42 million. Yet in America aaverage sales fell from $1.58 million to $1.54 million. Operating profit margins show a similar trend.[1]

International Marketing Highlight 1.1

Do You Know Where Your Ford Was Made?

The 1992 Ford cars get controllers for their antilock brakes from Germany, engine computers from Spain, shock absorbers from Japan, and key axle parts from England. Windshields, instrument panels, seats, and fuel tanks are made in Mexico.

Source: Fortune, June 17, 1992, p. 53

Worldwide consumers, particularly those in the developed countries, truly live in a global village. Young Europeans, Americans, and Japanese alike sport Benetton sweaters made in Italy, covet Japanese compact disc players, and haunt similar hangouts.

And America is irrevocably enmeshed in this global business (see International Marketing Highlight 1.2). We export some 20 percent of our industrial production, and we sell two out of five acres of our farm produce abroad.

In 1999 U.S. exports of goods and services supported a total of 14.4 million U.S. jobs. From 1993 to 1999, exports accounted for approximately 80 percent of U.S. real economic growth. The U.S. Department of Commerce estimates that over 38,000 U.S. manufacturing companies export, slightly more than one-third of all U.S. firms.[2] Almost one-third of U.S. corporate profit derives from international trade and foreign investment. The share of trade in the gross national product has more than doubled in the past decade. Considering our potential exposure to import penetration, more than three-fourths of U.S. goods are now effectively in international competition, and more than half the supplies of 24 important raw materials, ranging from petroleum to cobalt, come from foreign sources.

International Marketing Highlight 1.2

Globalization of Dollar Demand

There are now $422 billion of U.S. currency in circulation worldwide. More than two-thirds of this currency circulates abroad. So it is no wonder that when the United States rolled out redesigned, hard-to-counterfeit bills in 1996, the Treasury planned on spending $31 million over five years on brochures in 23 languages to convince people around the world to accept the new bills. The dollar has clout even in Iran, Iraq, and Cuba. It can pay your way even in remote villages.

Source: USA Today, March 15, 1996, p. 1.

Global marketing for U.S. companies makes sense when we realize that about 95 percent of the world's population and two-thirds of its total purchasing power are currently located outside this country. Even for relatively small companies, the global business activity has become irresistible. The U.S. Department of Commerce reports that 60 percent of American firms exporting today have fewer than 100 employees.[3]

A Conference Board study showed that a commitment to the international marketplace is important to sustained growth and superior profitability. Sales for firms with no foreign activities grow at half the average, whereas those for firms with international activities grow faster in every industry and in most size categories. Profitability as well rises for firms with a broad global scope. Companies with foreign plants in all three major global regions (North America, Europe, and the Pacific Rim) significantly outperform companies with more restricted international activities, both in return on assets and return on equity.[4]

Briefly, a worldview based on outmoded concepts of nationality and traditional antagonisms among nations and ethnic groups is not useful in today's global business environment. In fact, the first conceptual leap toward a pragmatic and productive businessperson's worldview would be to dismiss such a view outright and instead consider the inhabitants of different countries as a single race of consumers with shared needs and aspirations. Attaining this concept is critical, because recognition of new opportunities requires an awareness of new realities.

Doing business is a creative enterprise. Doing business outside one's own country is a much more demanding, complicated enterprise. Consider advertising. In the United States television advertising of consumer products is taken for granted. However, in many countries, such as the Netherlands, commercials are not permitted on television. In other countries television advertising is permitted only on a limited scale. In Switzerland, commercials are broadcast between 6:30 AM and 8:00 AM on weekdays. As another example of cultural differences, consider alcohol use in Japan, where drinking is widely considered part of the work ethic. Many businessmen openly talk about getting drunk. Whiskey is advertised abundantly on television. Beer is sold from vending machines on the street. All this would be unthinkable in the United States.

Similarly, the retailing industry structure varies dramatically across nations. In the United Kingdom, France, and Germany, an everincreasing percentage of total retail sales is made through large national retailing chains. In Italy, China, and Brazil, the retail industry is made up essentially of independent "mom and pop" stores. Still other countries have strong cooperative retailing or buying groups.

Just from this limited consideration of marketing perspectives, it is clear that international business necessitates an awareness of the clash of cultural standards among countries. These differences require analytical abilities and business acumen of the international marketers.

Overview of the Book

In this chapter we will examine what international marketing is, how it differs from domestic marketing, and why international marketing must be studied as a separate subject. Chapter 2 analyzes the rationale behind worldwide economic activity.

Chapters 3 and 4 provide the perspectives of the international marketplace. Chapters 5 through 7 in Part Three review the international institutions and agreements that continually create the conditions of the worldwide economic scene in which international marketing is conducted. Part Four, Chapters 8 through 11, explores the economic, cultural, political, and legal environments that affect business decisions. Chapters 12 through 16 are devoted to marketing decisions about products and their price, distribution, and promotion. Chapter 17 examines exporting.

The two final chapters deal with marketing planning and control. Chapter 18 discusses corporate organizational arrangements for international marketing management. Chapter 19 introduces the formulation of marketing strategy within the context of international business and provides a foundation for the advanced study of international marketing.

After establishing an understanding of the state of the art of international business, we will discuss the crucial role of the marketing function in conducting business across national boundaries, present a framework for making international marketing decisions, explore the reasons firms engage in foreign business, and describe the various modes of entry. Finally, we will consider the pivotal importance of the multinational corporation in global business.

International Business

The term *international business* refers to a wide range of activities involved in conducting business transactions across national boundaries. Taking a comprehensive approach to operations of both large and small firms engaged in business overseas, we will consider international marketing as it has developed and as it must, in the author's opinion, change in the future.

Perspectives of U.S. Business Overseas

Although many U.S. firms had long engaged in international business ventures before World War II, greater impetus to overseas expansion came after the war. While the U.S. government was helping to reconstruct war-torn economies through the Marshall Plan, by providing financial assistance to European countries, the postwar American economy emerged as the strongest in the world. America's economic assistance programs, in the absence of competition, stimulated extensive U.S. corporate interest overseas.

In recent years, overseas business has become a matter of necessity from the viewpoint of both U.S. corporations and the U.S. government. Many U.S. industries face increasing foreign competition. Take the shoe industry for example. The share of U.S. producers plunged from 50 percent in 1981 to 28 percent in 1985 to 19 percent in 1997.[5] The bicycle industry provides another example: the import share of bike sales jumped to 62 percent in 1997 from 40 percent in 1993.[6]

Faced with saturated markets at home, U.S. corporations have been forced to look for new markets. The flat growth rate of the beer industry in the early 1980s necessitated Anheuser-Busch's exploration of the huge overseas beer market. The company estimates that by the year 2003, foreign operations will account for almost one-fourth of its earnings.[7]

Other companies have similar stories. In brief, whereas in the 1950s and 1960s international business was a means of capitalizing on new opportunity, today's changing economic environment has made international business dealings vital for survival.

Essentially, there are two aspects of international business: direct investment and trade.

Direct Investment At the end of 1998, according to a U.S. Department of Commerce report, the U.S. direct investment abroad stood at $981 billion, up from $716 billion in 1996.[8] Over 65 percent of U.S. direct investments overseas have traditionally been in developed countries, with Europe accounting for over 47 percent of the total. Canada took a 10 percent share, while Japan, Australia, and New Zealand collectively represented 8 percent of the total. Latin America's share was 22 percent. The rest of Asia accounted for just under12 percent of the total.[9] It is interesting that, although, for cultural, political, and economic reasons, the most viable opportunities were found in Western Europe, Canada, and to a lesser extent Japan, many developing countries provided a better return on direct U.S. investments. According to a U.N. study, for example, in 1998 the profitability of U.S. investment in Africa was 25.5 percent, in Asia and the Pacific 20.4 percent, in Latin America 15.0 percent, in Canada 5.7 percent, and in Europe 9.4 percent.[10]

Direct foreign investment in the United States has come traditionally from Europe and Canada. Almost $652 billion of the $813 billion in book value of direct foreign investment in the United States at the end of 1998 came from the Netherlands, the United Kingdom, Canada, Germany, Japan, and Switzerland. By contrast, about $2.5 billion came from the 13 nations of the Organization of Petroleum Exporting Countries (OPEC).[11]

Foreign investments in the United States have taken the form of both wholly owned subsidiaries and stock ownership. For example, Bic Pen Corporation (a French company), BMW (a German company), Lever Brothers (an English company), Nestlé S.A. (a Swiss company), and Toyota Motor Corporation (a Japanese company) operate U.S. subsidiaries as part of their worldwide operations. Other foreign investments are in the form of stock ownership in U.S. corporations. For example, a Swiss-Swedish company, ASEA Brown Boveri (Holding) Ltd., bought a controlling interest in Combustion Engineering Inc. and Westinghouse Electric Corporation's smaller electrical-transmission equipment unit. Likewise, a Dutch company, Royal Ahold, maintains about two-third's ownership in Stop & Shop, a large food chain.

Trade (Goods and Services) The other aspect of international business is trade. In 1999 the United States exported an estimated $958.5 billion in goods and services. Imports during the same year amounted to $1,229.8 billion, resulting in a balance-of-trade deficit of $271.3 billion. The subject of trade will be explored in detail in Chapter 17, but it is important to note here that the U.S. share of the world exports in 1999 for manufactured goods—measured by value—comes to about 13 percent, slightly higher than it was in the mid1990s.[12]

The traditional view of foreign trade as an exchange of tangible goods is increasingly giving way to the realization that trade encompasses both goods and services. As the economies of more and more countries have become service-oriented, foreign sales of engineering, consulting, banking, transportation, motion pictures, insurance, tourism, franchising, construction, advertising, and computer services are gaining recognition as significant factors in the foreign trade position of many nations. The importance of such exported U.S. services is borne out by the fact that deficits in merchandise trade have been partially balanced by growing services exports. Services exports and their income from overseas U.S. affiliates reached an estimated $275.5 billion in 1999, compared with $225 billion in 1997. Services imports in 1999 were estimated at $199.7 billion, giving a favorable balance of $75.8 billion.[13]

Why Go International?

Traditionally, the major focus of U.S. business has been on its large and expanding domestic market. In recent years, however, new factors have made international business the more desirable alternative for growth. These factors are expected to persist and to have even greater impact in the future.

Whether or not a company conducts international business, its competitors are likely to hail from all over and challenge its position in its own home market. For example, foreign manufacturers, including many from the Third World, have created problems for such established U.S. firms as USX, LTV, and other stay-at-home steelmakers.

Market Saturation Markets for a variety of goods in the United States, as is true of other industrialized countries, are becoming saturated far faster than new markets are being found. Staple consumer goods such as cars, radios, and TVs already outnumber U.S. households, and other products are fast approaching the same level. The slowing growth of the U.S. population means that the number of households is likely to grow at less than 1.6 percent per year to the year 2005, and demand for consumer goods is unlikely to grow any faster. This point is illustrated by the baby food market, in which Gerber Products Company has 70 percent of the U.S. market yet nonetheless, has trouble growing—it loses 10,000 customers a day as tots start taking grownup's food. The U.S. birth rate is declining, making it harder to replace Gerber consumers. Moreover, infants are eating less baby food on average these days.[14]

Thus, companies in many industries must develop new markets to continue to operate successfully. International markets, especially those where market saturation is a distant threat, provide an attractive alternative. Consider the cigarette industry. Sales have stagnated in the United States, but Third World countries offer rich markets. In Indonesia, per capita cigarette consumption quadrupled in the last 10 years. Kenya's consumption has been rising 10 percent annually. And Third World markets are unburdened by many of the restraints imposed in the United States and other industrialized nations. Firms generally can advertise freely on radio and television, and packages need not carry health warnings.

To transform global challenges into new opportunities, smart companies seek markets across national borders (see International Marketing Highlight 1.3). For example, Disney's theme park in France, following its entry in Japan, shows how important it is for a company to expand overseas in the wake of market saturation at home. Some United States hospitals, facing tighter health care budgets and dwindling occupancy rates, have started seeking foreign patients.[15]

International Marketing Highlight 1.3

Coors Brews Big Plans for Korea

Coors is going where the growth is. With Korean beer sales expanding 15 percent a year, compared with a puny 2 percent in the United States, Coors Brewing Co. has formed a joint venture with Jinro, Korea's largest producer of alcoholic beverages, to build a 1.8 million-barrel Coors brewery in Seoul. Coors expects to capture 20 percent of the Korean market before long.

This is Coors's first plant outside the United States, part of an international expansion program for America's third-largest brewer, which wants to be in 25 markets outside the United States by 2003. Coors beer is now available for sale in nine foreign countries.

Source: Company records of Coors Brewing Co.

U.S. Trade Deficit American industry grew up in a climate of private enterprise—nationwide markets without trade barriers to hamper the full development of economic efficiency. Most decisions could be made without considering how they would affect world market position. But such is no longer the case. U.S. business faces a declining share of world-manufactured exports and a continuing trade deficit. Just as an individual family should not, and cannot in the long run, live beyond its means, neither should a nation.

Therefore, the staggering U.S. trade deficit has to be balanced—That means the United States must make a strong attempt to increase exports.

Foreign Competition In many industries U.S. firms face fierce and intense competition from foreign manufacturers. For example, foreign competitors are invading what was once Xerox Corporation's undisputed turf by offering low-priced, high-quality copying machines. Xerox no longer can take industry leadership for granted. In a crowded field, with some 14 competitors from Japan alone, the battle resembles the one being fought by U.S. automakers against foreign importers.

Another example of intense foreign competition is the $82 billion textile industry. Garment imports increased threefold between 1985 and 1995, to $32 billion a year. Some 300 textile mills have been closed since 1980, and over 200,000 jobs have vanished. Industry experts think that textile apparel imports will continue to grow 15 percent annually. At this pace, imports will have 85 percent of the U.S. market by the year 2003.[16]

For still anohter example, we can return to the auto industry, where Japan is once again offering U.S. markets a new level of competition. In 1999, the Toyota Camry and the Honda Accord emerged as the two best-selling cars in America. (Germany's Volkswagen Passat was the third best-selling car.) Japanese invasion of the U.S. auto market shows how foreign competition can harm the local industry (see International Marketing Highlight 1.4).

The truth of the matter is that the United States' ability to compete in the world market has eroded significantly during the past 25 years. Most of this decline has occurred in such traditional industries as steel, automobiles, consumer electronics, apparel, and machine tools. Recently, even high-tech industries have become susceptible. Competition has forced some companies to shift their consumer electronics manufacturing to the Far East, which explains why the high-tech industry is losing its edge.[17] Even this measure did not succeed for General Electric, which in 1986 sold 80 percent of its consumer electronics business (including the RCA brand acquired in late 1985) to Thomson, France's state-owned leading electronics manufacturer. The last American-owned television maker, Zenith, has lost money on operations since the mid 1980s, and finally sold out to Lucky Goldstar of Korea. Thus in the color television business the United States completely gave up, yielding the market to Japanese, European, and Korean companies.[18]

━━━━━━━━━━━   **International Marketing Highlight 1.4**   ━━━━━━━━━━━

How Japanese Automakers Invaded the U.S. Market

During the late 1960s Japanese car manufacturers wanting to enter the U.S. market looked for a niche and found one at the low end of the market: students and other consumers who wanted no-frills transportation. The small-and-cheap car market, as it so happened, was a niche that did not interest the Detroit auto companies. (Even relatively small American-made cars, such as Ford's Falcon and Fairlane, were essentially family cars.) The only formidable presence in this market was Volkswagen. Even so, VW could not fill the wide-open, small-car market fast enough. The Japanese companies responded by following a time-tested military strategy: taking uncontested ground first.

Toyota and Honda first began to introduce their cars into the United States around 1967. U.S. automakers paid little attention to the newcomers; they derided the Japanese cars as cheap models suitable only for a market that did not interest them in the first place. Essentially, the American automakers' attitude was to let Volkswagen fight it out with Datsun and Honda. Meanwhile the Japanese focused on providing low-cost products, built up a following (and, more important still, a low-cost, high-quality manufacturing base), then gradually introduced larger, better, higher-priced models.

Now Toyota, Nissan, Honda, Mitsubishi, and other major Japanese manufacturers have established themselves as a permanent, formidable presence in the U.S. automobile market. These companies have moved beyond their initial niche to satisfy America's demands for a wide variety of high-quality cars. The Detroit automakers have had an increasingly difficult time competing effectively against them.

The declining international position of the United States in the high-tech area is a matter of serious concern. More troubling is the fact that many of these high-tech products derive from technology developed in the United States. Phonographs, color televisions, audiotape recorders, and videotape recorders were all invented here, yet U.S. companies have practically no business left in these products (see International Marketing Highlight 1.5).

One way for U.S. companies to meet the challenge from foreign companies is to enter the home markets of their foreign competitors. Just as Japanese cars gained favor with American consumers in the early 1980s, there may be Japanese car buyers interested in U.S. cars now and in the future—but not if these cars have their steering wheels on the wrong side.

■■■■■■■■■■■■■ International Marketing Highlight 1.5 ■■■■■■■■■■■■■

There Goes Another One

In recent years U.S. companies have conceded one homegrown industry after another to more aggressive and competitive foreign rivals. First came cameras, then televisions, tape recorders, stereo equipment, and semiconductors. Recently, Cincinnati Milacron, the last independent U.S. producer of heavy industrial robots, agreed to sell the business to a subsidiary of Switzerland's Asea Brown Boveri.

Milacron retreated from the $4 billion market after 13 years because its share of the business had dwindled from a commanding 75 percent to just 10 percent, and its losses from robotics had been mounting since the mid 1980s.

Source: Business Week, September 24, 1990, p. 71.

Emergence of New Markets The world is changing fast, resulting in the emergence of new markets. In the 1990s new business opportunities developed from the European Community, enhanced by the reunification of Germany, and the thriving economies in the Pacific Rim countries. In the next century, China, Latin America, and the emerging market-based economies in Eastern Europe promise new opportunities. Elsewhere in developing countries, momentum toward *privatization* (the transfer of business ownership from government to private citizens or institutions) and liberal policies are promising signs as well see International Marketing Highlight 1.6).

For U.S. marketers, despite the recent currency crisis, the Pacific countries hold great promise. A market of more than 2 billion potential consumers is emerging. In the last 25 years, as the Pacific region began its time-bending leap into the twentieth century, millions of Asians began an equally rapid transition from rural to urban, from agrarian to industrial, from feudal to contemporary society. With more of the Pacific region's rural population traveling to the cities to shop every day, the demand for goods and services—from the most basic household commodities to sophisticated technical devices—is soaring. The growing importance of Asia for the United States is supported by the fact that the share of America's exports that goes to Europe has fallen from 31 percent to 20 percent over the past 20 years, while the share going to Asia has risen from 20 percent to 30 percent.[19] Asia is the fastest growing market for most of the West's top brands. Those in the luxury-goods and fashion businesses reckon that roughly a third of their sales are now to Asia (including Japan), and by 2005 this region will make up half of the world's luxury-goods market.[20]

International Marketing Highlight 1.6

Gerber Locates a Niche in India

Gerber Products Company has undertaken extensive market research in India. Despite India's predominantly poor population, the country has a prosperous middle class and a small but wealthy upper class that Gerber considers a promising market.

Until recently, most Indians have been unlikely to show any interest in Western-style baby foods. Lately, though, the convenience of such products, plus their status appeal, has heightened consumers' curiosity and openness. Initial focus groups show that baby foods have high potential for success in certain areas of the subcontinent.

According to PepsiCo, early in the next century China is expected to be the second-largest market after the United States. The Chinese soft-drink market accounted for just 700 million cases last year, or about 13 servings a person, compared with about 8 billion cases, or nearly 800 servings a person, in the United States, showing the huge potential for growth. As another example, each year the average Chinese household shoots a little less than half a roll of film. If only it could be persuaded to snap a full roll, that would be the equivalent of adding an entire American market to the world film business. If Eastman Kodak could coax the Chinese not just to take those extra shots but to take them using Kodak film, the company would double its global sales. [21]

The emerging markets in developing countries can help many U.S. corporations counter the results of demographic changes in the Western nations. In most advanced nations of the world, birth rates are declining, whereas population in the developing countries is growing. Consider the automobile industry. The people-per-car ratio is 725 in India, 680 in China 431 in the Philippines, 270 in Thailand, 114 in Brazil, 89.5 in Mexico, 47 in South Korea, and 36 in Poland. In the United States, Europe, and Japan, the respective figures are 1.7, 2.5, and 3, showing the tremendous potential in the developing countries.[22] Similarly, the number of people per television set is 1.2 in the United States compared with about 30 in developing countries, again showing significant market potential among the latter. Nike reckons that its domestic sales averaging $20 for each American may be nearing a ceiling. By contrast, the per capita Nike sales in Japan are $4, in Germany $3, and in China and India just over two cents. It is the developing countries where Nike looks for growth[23] (see International Marketing Highlight 1.7).

International Marketing Highlight 1.7

DVDs Real Market: China

The most promising market for the digital videodisks is not in the United States, but in China. In 1997 more DVD players were shipped in China than the United States It makes sense: after all, China is a land of 1.2 billion people. There are nearly 300 million TV sets, but broadcast programming is limited, and the average household does not have a VCR. China is a video tabula rasa, ready and willing to go digital with the latest hardware.

Source: Fortune, December 29, 1997, P. 62.

Globalization of Markets Theodore Levitt asserts that technology has homogenized worldwide markets and that, companies should therefore produce globally standardized products and market them in the same way to people everywhere.[24] All the principal barriers to the growth of such markets have weakened in the last decade. Tariffs have been reduced by the world trade agreements. Transportation costs have declined with the use of containerization and larger-capacity ships. Many products have emerged that pack very high value into very small packages. Consumer needs in the industrialized nations have become increasingly similar, and purchasing power in many countries has increased sharply. In consequence, a multitude of distinct national markets is beginning to coalesce into a true world market for a number of products in different industries. This development can be a source of competitive advantage for companies that plan their strategies accordingly.

A few examples will suggest how extensive the global product phenomenon has already become. Kids everywhere play on Nintendo and listen to music on a Sony Walkman. The videocassette recorder (VCR) market took off simultaneously in Japan, Europe, and the United States, but the most extensive use of VCRs today is probably in places like Riyadh and Caracas. Shopping centers from Dusseldorf to Rio sell Gucci shoes, Yves St. Laurent suits, and Gloria Vanderbilt jeans. Siemens and International Telephone & Telegraph (ITT) telephones can be found almost everywhere in the world. Mercedes-Benz and the Toyota Corolla are as much objects of passion in Manila as in California.

Just about every gas turbine sold in the world has some General Electric technology or component in it, and what country doesn't need gas turbines? How many airlines around the world could survive without Boeing or Airbus equipment? Developing country markets for high-voltage transmission equipment and diesel-electric locomotives are bigger than those in the developed countries. Today's new industries—robotics, videodiscs, fiber optics, satellite networks, high-technology plastics, and artificial diamonds—seem to be global at birth.

Opportunities via Foreign Aid Programs Although in recent years U.S. foreign aid programs for developing countries have declined gradually, in the 1950s and 1960s they provided billions of dollars to developing countries to undertake programs of economic buildup. Most of these programs required that aid recipients spend U.S. money on goods and services from U.S. corporations, except in cases where the desired goods were available only from non-U.S. sources. In either circumstance, the aid money created new markets in developing countries. Even more recent aid programs, small as they were ($15.3 billion in 1999—$8.9 billion in economic support and $6.4 billion for military hardware), provided opportunities for some businesses to go abroad.

Other Reasons A variety of other reasons make conducting business across national boundaries profitable and attractive. One is the possibility of achieving economics of scale. In industries where economies of scale are feasible, a large market is essential, so if the home market is not large enough, entering foreign markets may be an attractive alternative. Polaroid Corporation, a dominant force in the U.S. photographic industry, claims to have achieved economies of scale by entering foreign markets.

Another reason for engaging in international business is that it provides a safety net during business downturns. Usually a recession starts in one country and takes several quarters to move into other countries. It is said that European economies are affected by a U.S. recessionary trend after about six months. Thus, firms that do business internationally can shift their emphasis from U.S. to foreign markets during the recession. For example, during the U.S. recession of 1991, multinational companies were able to shift their marketing focus to Europe and Asia, where an economic boom was in progress.[25]

In many industries, labor constitutes a major proportion of costs. Since labor cost in developing countries is much lower than in the United States, it is economically attractive for the companies to expand foreign operations. For example, electronics companies depend on hundreds, sometimes thousands, of young women to do the painstaking job of assembling tiny parts that are shipped to the United States for use in computers and other products. Labor sometimes represents as much as half of the cost of these parts, so the cheaper the labor, the higher the profit. Thus, a number of U.S. companies—Hewlett-Packard, Intel, National Semiconductor, and ITT, among a dozen others—have gone as far as Malaysia to save on labor cost.

Some nations offer tax incentives to attract foreign businesses to their countries. An important motive for extending such tax incentives is to increase scarce foreign exchange and create jobs at home. Typically, a company finding such tax concessions viable will establish a plant in the low-tax country and then sell the manufactured goods locally, as well as exporting from there to its primary markets.

Many companies find it more desirable to develop and/or test new products outside the United States This practice avoids exposure to competitors and, to some extent, keeps new development information secret until the product is ready for full introduction. Ford Motor Company, for example, did much of its world-car development in Germany.

Some international markets are less competitive than the U.S. market; several are still in an embryonic stage. Further, in some instances, governments will give companies a monopoly or quasi-monopoly position if they assemble and produce their products there. Many companies follow their customers at home abroad. Take the case of steelmakers. They are following their customers—automakers and manufacturers of appliances, heavy equipment, and machine tools—all over the world. For example, Whirlpool Corporation decided in the early 1990s to go global. It now manufactures in 13 countries, including China and India. Its steel suppliers are now catching up in these emerging markets.[26]

Finally, international presence provides expanded access to advances in technology, worldwide raw materials, and diverse international economic groups. For example, European auto manufacturers led the way in fuel injection technology. An active U.S. auto company presence in Europe provided earlier insights into this technology.

International Marketing and Its Growing Importance

Stage of International Involvement

The term *international marketing* refers to exchanges across national boundaries for the satisfaction of human needs and wants. The extent of a firm's involvement abroad is a function of its commitment to the pursuit of foreign markets. A firm's overseas involvement may fall into one of several categories:

1. *Domestic*: operating exclusively within a single country.
2. *Regional exporter*: operating within a geographically defined region that crosses national boundaries. Markets served are economically and culturally homogeneous. If activity occurs outside the home region, it is opportunistic.
3. *Exporter*: operating from a central office in the home region and exporting finished goods to a variety of countries. Some marketing, sales, and distribution is outside the home region.
4. *International*: operating regionally in a somewhat autonomous fashion, but with key decisions made and coordinated from the central office in the home region. Manufacturing and assembly, marketing, and sales are decentralized beyond the home region. Both finished goods and intermediate products are exported outside the home region.
5. *International to global*: operating with independent and mainly self-sufficient subsidiaries in a range of countries. While some key functions, such as research and de-

velopment (R&D), sourcing, and financing are decentralized, the home region is still the primary base for many functions.

6. *Global*: operating as a highly decentralized organization across a broad range of countries. No geographic area (including the home region) is assumed a priori to be the primary base for any functional area. Each function (including R&D, sourcing, manufacturing, marketing, and sales) is performed in the location(s) around the world most suitable for that function.

Typically, the journey begins at home. Companies operating exclusively within a single country reach the limits to growth in their home market and face the need to expand to achieve further growth. The time that it takes to reach this outer growth limit depends almost entirely on the size of the home market. North American companies will take longer to reach the outer limit than will companies in Singapore, South Korea, Taiwan, and Japan, whose home markets are substantially smaller and provide less room to grow. Once the domestic barrier is reached, companies evolve into an export modality, either on a limited, regional basis where markets are still economically and culturally homogeneous, or on a broader basis where finished goods are exported to a variety of countries. Regional exporters and export companies continue to run operations from a central office in the home market, though some marketing, sales, and distribution functions begin to crop up elsewhere.

As companies become more successful in their export operations, they reach that critical point where the need to achieve greater proximity to overseas markets becomes paramount. At this point, such companies begin to replicate their business systems in new markets by creating relatively autonomous regional operations. Manufacturing and assembly, marketing, and sales are decentralized, and both finished goods and intermediate products are exported outside the home region, but key decisions are made, or at least coordinated, by a head office in the home region. Companies that have reached this stage of evolution may be characterized as "international" companies. The replication of a company's business system in various locations around the world does not, however, represent a long-term formula for profitable growth, so ultimately international companies face the need to optimize their businesses globally by adopting a global model of operation. For global companies, no one geographic area is assumed to be the primary base for any function—R&D, sourcing, and manufacturing are situated in the most suitable locations worldwide.

Why Study International Marketing?

We have already examined the factors that make international business an important field of endeavor from the viewpoint of a businessperson. How does this importance extend to marketing? Marketing is more significant, both for doing business abroad and for analyzing the impact of international happenings on business at home, than other functions of a business—such as manufacturing, finance, and research and development—because marketing responds to the local culture and to the business's multiple interrelationships with the local environment. Growing internationalization of business brings about changes in the positioning of competitors and the appropriate competitive strategies. "You can't sell what people won't buy" is a truism. Consumers overseas have different needs and expectations than those in America.

The only way to guarantee long-term competitive success is to provide better value to customers. Consider the Japanese market. American companies and U.S. government agencies complained that restrictions, in the form of tariffs and visible (and invisible) nontariff barriers and constraints, excluded much U.S. business from Japanese markets. However, an unbiased analysis showed that American business had not made a great effort to enter the Japanese market. As has been remarked,

> Americans still are going to have to practice the marketing methods they preach if they are going to exploit the opportunities that are opening up in Japanese markets. In short, U.S. businesses

still must find out what the Japanese consumers want, tailor products to fit the Japanese market, and put these products into suitable distribution channels.[27]

A U.S. Chamber of Commerce report indicated that U.S. business had fallen short of success in Japan because it failed to keep track of changes in Japan's marketing environment. Certain U.S. consumer goods such as automobiles, watches, cigarette lighters, and whiskey had been regarded in Japan as status symbols and were consumed by a limited number of wealthy buyers. Distribution of such products had been organized emphasizing the exclusiveness of the products and brand prestige. This traditional mode of marketing luxury items was inadequate to substantially increase exports to Japan or to develop a mass market. In brief, if imports were to become a part of Japanese daily life, rather than just status symbols, U.S. manufacturers had to reexamine pricing policies and distribution channels and then develop products that better fit Japanese consumers' needs.[28]

In other words, U.S. companies frequently fumble overseas because they fail to respond to the peculiarities of the markets. Apple Computer, Inc., had the market to itself when it became the first company to sell a personal computer in Japan. But the company began to lose ground for failing to do the right things. Apple didn't provide Japanese manuals. The computers arrived with keyboards that didn't work, and the packaging was shoddy.[29] Similarly, American automakers would like the Japanese to buy their cars, but they do not manufacture cars with steering on the right side to accommodate Japanese driving.

Another mistake by U.S. corporations is to pursue the short-term strategy of selling luxury goods to the affluent classes in developing countries instead of securing mass markets that would provide long-term benefits. For example, malnutrition is a common problem in a number of developing countries. Therefore, vitamin pills are important. But U.S. firms sell the same vitamin at about the same price in poor countries as they do in the United States. Only the minority upper class in those countries can afford the pills.

Mass markets are ready for U.S. products, but American businesses have not responded to the opportunities with responsible marketing. To cash in effectively on the opportunities these markets represent, in developing countries and elsewhere, U.S. corporations must become more sophisticated marketers.

Domestic versus International Marketing

The basic nature of marketing does not change when it extends beyond national boundaries, but international marketing, unlike domestic marketing, requires operating simultaneously in more than one kind of environment. Operations in the different environments must be coordinated, and the experience gained in one country used for making decisions in another country. The demands are tough, and the stakes are high. International marketers not only must be sensitive to different marketing environments internationally, but also must be able to balance marketing moves worldwide to seek optimum results for the company.

The impact of environment on international marketing can be illustrated by the watch industry. New technology, falling trade barriers, and changing cost relationships have affected the competitive patterns of the industry worldwide. Only companies with global perspective are operating successfully. A few *world companies* sell *world product*s to increasingly brand-conscious consumers. This multinationalization of the watch industry has resulted in four producers—Switzerland, Japan, Hong Kong, and the United States—dominating the scene by emphasizing brand names. Their manufacturing operations are specialized by country according to costs of specific processes, components, and subassemblies.

To successfully compete globally, rather than simply operate domestically, companies should emphasize: (1) global *configuration* of marketing activities (i.e., where activities such as new product development, advertising, sales promotion, channel selection, marketing research, and other functions should be performed), (2) *global coordination* of marketing activities (i.e., how global marketing activities performed in different countries should be coordinated); and (3) *linkage* of marketing activities (i.e., how marketing activities should be linked with other activities of the firm).[30]

Many marketing activities, unlike those in other functional areas, must be dispersed in each host country to make an adequate response to the local environment. Not all marketing activities need to be performed on a dispersed basis, however. In many cases, competitive advantage is gained in the form of lower cost or enhanced differentiation if selected activities are performed centrally as a result of technological changes, buyer shifts, and evolution of marketing media. These activities include production of promotional materials, sales force and service support organization training, and advertising. Further, international marketing activities dispersed in different countries should be properly coordinated to gain competitive advantage. Such coordination can be achieved by (1) performing marketing activities using similar methods across countries (2) transferring marketing know-how and skills from country to country, (3) sequencing marketing programs across countries, and (4) integrating the efforts of various marketing groups in different countries.

Finally, a global view of international marketing permits marketing to be linked to upstream and support activities of the firm. As a result, marketing can unlock economies of scale and learning in production and R&D by (1) providing the information necessary to develop a physical product design that can be sold worldwide—a universal product; (2) creating demand for more universal products even if historical demand has been for more varied products in different countries; (3) identifying and penetrating segments in many countries that will buy universal products; and (4) providing services or local accessories that effectively tailor the standard universal product to local needs.

Framework of International Marketing

Marketing decisions relative to product, price, promotion, and distribution must be made whether business is conducted in the United States, France, Japan, or Mexico. But the environment within which these decisions are made is unique to each country. This differential of environment distinguishes international marketing from domestic marketing.

Typically, a firm should make domestic marketing decisions only after considering internal and external environments. *Internal environment* factors primarily refers to corporate objectives, corporate organization, and resource availability. *External environment* factors include competition, technological change, the economic climate, political influences, social and cultural changes, pertinent legal requirements, current ethical business standards, and changes among marketing channels.

A U.S. firm will face the same internal and external factors doing business in a foreign market as it faces domestically, but from an entirely different environmental perspective. Consider the following factors: Economic conditions vary from one country to another. The antitrust laws in the United States are much tougher than those in some countries, such as Japan. The United States has a two-party political system; many countries, such as Mexico, do not. Women have an important decision-making role as consumers in the United States and in other Western countries, but this is not the situation among the Islamic nations. As a matter of fact, business environments vary tremendously even among countries that are geographically in the same region or that have the same cultural heritage. For instance, it would be wrong to assume that the United States and England have common marketing environments. There may be some similarities, but overall the two are very different.

Exhibit 1.1 depicts the marketing decisions and environments of international marketing. The nature of decision making in international business is essentially the same as in domestic business. Consideration of environment, however, is more philosophically abstract. The internal and external environmental aspects listed previously combine to

EXHIBIT 1.1   Decisions and Environments of International Marketing

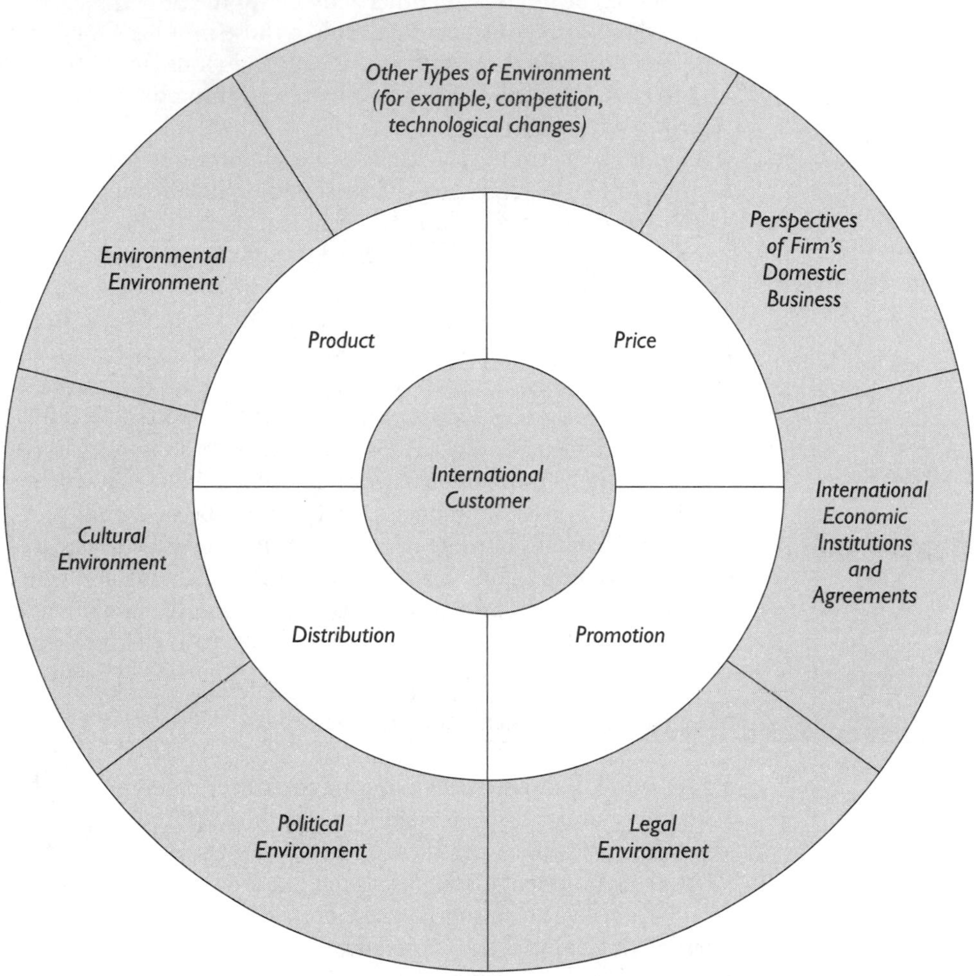

create a unique environmental reality for each individual country that the international marketer must perceive. The economic, cultural, political, and legal aspects of each environment must be understood by the international marketer, along with the effect of international economic institutions such as the International Monetary Fund (IMF) and agreements such as the World Trade Organization (WTO) Accord and the North American Free Trade Agreement (NAFTA).

Also, an international marketer must be sensitive to certain aspects of the domestic environment, such as competition and technological changes, included in Exhibit 1.1 under "Other Types of Environments". Marketing decisions to serve the international customer require consideration of the firm's domestic business as well—its objectives and strategies, commitments and resources, and organization structure.

Multinational Corporations

The *multinational corporation (MNC)* is the principal instrument in the expansion of business on an international scale. In barely four decades, it has become, by all accounts, the most formidable single factor in world trade and investment. The MNC plays a decisive role in the allocation and use of the world's resources by introducing new products and services, creating or stimulating demand for them, and developing new modes of manufacturing and distribution. Current rates of energy consumption, for example, would be unthinkable without the role of MNCs in the development and expansion of the automobile and electrical appliance industries. Indeed, MNCs largely set the patterns and pace of industrialization in today's capitalist economies.

Dimensions of MNCs

The MNC represents the highest level of overseas involvement and is characterized by a global strategy of investment, production, and distribution. According to a U.N. estimate, some 60,000 MNCs were in operation in 1997, controlling more than 500,000 foreign affiliates. Worldwide assets accumulated from past *foreign direct investment* (FDI) stood at $4.2 trillion at the end of 1998. The largest 100 MNCs controlled about 75 percent of the foreign assets of all MNCs and accounted for about 22 percent of their sales.

Most of these large companies were in a handful of industries: 40 percent of their foreign assets were in electronics, followed by petroleum and mining (24 percent), motor vehicles (19 percent), and chemicals and pharmaceuticals (15 percent). Together the largest 200 MNCs control about one third of the world's gross domestic product (GDP).

An important dimension of MNCs is the predominance of large firms. Typically, an MNC's annual sales run into hundreds of millions of dollars. In fact, more than 500 MNCs have annual sales of over $1 billion. The largest 100 MNCs have sales ranging between $10 billion and $178 billion.[31]

Many MNCs derive a substantial portion of their net income and sales from overseas operations. As shown in Exhibit 1.2, the non-U.S. earnings of many large companies exceed 50 percent of the total earnings.

The economic strength of these corporations as compared with other economic entities, including the economies of many nations, suggests an important source of global power. Exhibit 1.3 shows that many MNCs have a higher annual revenue than the gross national product (GNP) of various countries. For example, General Motors generates more revenue annually than the GNP of Denmark or Greece. Similarly, General Electric's annual sales exceed the GNP of New Zealand or Singapore.

EXHIBIT 1.2
Nondomestic Earnings, Sales, and Assets of Selected U.S. Firms: 1998

Company	Percent of Net Earnings	Percent of Sales	Percent of Assets
Avon	65	65	59
Cable & Wireless	83	70	64
Texas Instruments	93	61	44
Coca-Cola	77	67	60
Colgate-Palmolive	78	76	64
Dow Chemical	61	56	58
Gillette	64	63	63
Goodyear	77	47	49
McDonald's	58	58	56
Hewlett-Packard	53	56	53
IBM	66	61	51
Smithkline Beecham	94	78	73
Johnson & Johnson	50	49	41
Xerox	61	50	54

Source: Compiled from various annual reports

EXHIBIT 1.3
GNP of Various
Countries Ranked
with Sales of Selected
Corporations: 1998

Country	Billions of U.S. Dollars
Switzerland	$284.8
Sweden	226.9
Austria	217.2
General Motors	161.3
Denmark	156.4
Ford Motor Company	142.7
Exxon	127.8
Greece	122.9
General Electric	100.5
Colombia	100.1
Singapore	95.1
IBM	81.7
New Zealand	55.8
Mobil	53.5
Sears Roebuck	41.3
Texaco	31.7
Chevron	29.9
Dupont	25.7

*Figures in billions of U.S. dollars.
Source: The World Bank, 1999. Sales figures of corporations taken from the various companies' annual reports for 1999.

Another important feature of MNCs is their predominantly oligopolistic character; that is, they operate in markets that are dominated by a few sellers. Their technological leads, their special skills, and their ability to differentiate their products through advertising are all factors that help to sustain or reinforce their oligopolistic nature. Most MNCs have a sizable number of foreign branches and affiliates: 200 of the largest have affiliates in 25 or more countries.

MNCs are mainly the product of developed countries. However, the relative importance of MNCs from different home countries has changed in the last 15 years—that of Japanese and Western European companies has increased and that of U.S. companies has declined. The available evidence suggests that these shifts are due primarily to changes in the international competitiveness of companies based in different home countries.

MNCs have made significant positive contributions to economic and social progress throughout the world. Through their technological and managerial capabilities, they have helped to develop the material and productive resources of many nations and have worked to meet the world's growing needs for good and services. Their investments have stimulated the diversification of local national economies. Their capital input has helped host governments to fulfill nationally defined economic development goals. They have provided jobs and helped to raise living standards in many areas. Yet MNCs have been strongly criticized in recent years using cheap-labor factories in developing nations[32] (see International Marketing Highlight 1.8).

■■■■■■■■■■   **International Marketing Highlight 1.8**   ■■■■■■■■■■

Pangs of Conscience

The marketing pizzazz of Nike Inc.'s "Just Do It" U.S. campaign is nowhere evident in the 12 Indonesian factories run by the company's Taiwanese, South Korean, and Indonesian subcontractors. Although these are some of the most modern factories in the industry, they are drab and utilitarian. Vast sheds house row upon row of mostly young women, who will glue, stitch, press, and box 70 million pairs of Nikes this year. Here a pair of Pegasus running shoes, which retails for $75, costs just $18.25 to put together and ship to the United States Indonesia's military police deal harshly with those workers who rebel, and independent unions are outlawed.

The stark contrast between the tens of millions of dollars that Nike icon Michael Jordan earns and the $2.23 basic daily wage in Indonesia paid by the company's subcontractors has helped make Nike a lightning rod for concern about overseas manufacturing standards. Although Nike claims it is a leader in improving conditions, its Indonesian subcontractors secured an exemption from a minimum-wage increase that would have forced them to pay $8.92 a month extra to each worker at a time when Nike has reported record profits.

Source: Business Week, July 29, 1996, p. 46.

Multinationals from the Third World

The Birla Group of India, United Laboratories from the Philippines, and Autlan of Mexico are among the several hundred MNCs from the Third World whose overseas subsidiaries have increased from dozens in about 1960 to a few thousand today. They are successfully competing for a share of world markets.

These MNCs have gone abroad following the *international product life cycle* concept (see Chapter 2). They began by seeking export markets. When tariffs, quotas, or other barriers threatened overseas markets, they started assembling abroad. Their initial move, and greatest impact so far, has been in neighboring developing countries.

The strength of Third World MNCs comes from their special experience with manufacturing for small home markets. Using low technology and local raw materials, running job-shop kinds of plants, and making effective use of semiskilled labor, they are able to custom-design products best suited to host countries. For example, a Philippines paper company has managed projects in countries ranging from Indonesia to Nigeria. Its managers have drawn on their ability to make paper from inexpensive, locally available materials. In addition, they run a very efficient job-shop operation with printing, folding, and cutting machinery selected or built in-house to make very short runs of a wide range of cigarette, candy, and other packages. These are the types of skills that the Western MNCs have usually forgotten.[33]

Although small-scale manufacturing remains their unique strength, these companies also are moving in other areas that are particularly suited to local conditions. For example, a Thai company uses rice stalks for paper and plantain products for glue. A Brazilian company has developed sunfast dyes and household appliances that resist high humidity and can survive the fluctuating voltages common in the developing world.

The rapid growth of Third World MNCs provides both a threat and an opportunity to the MNCs from the advanced countries. The Third World MNCs can be tough competitors in seeking contract work for building plants that do not require high technology such as steel plants and chemical complexes. But these MNCs also offer profitable opportunities to Western companies for joint operations. Lacking in marketing skills, for example, they may share their special know-how with traditional MNCs in exchange for brand names and skills in promoting new lines.[34] Moreover, as Third World MNCs become visible and viable economic entities, their governments may well become more sympathetic to the needs of MNCs from the developed world.

Entry Strategies

Five different modes of business offer a company entry into foreign markets: exporting, contractual agreement, joint venture, strategic alliance, and wholly-owned subsidiary.

Exporting

A company may minimize the risk of dealing internationally by exporting domestically manufactured products either by minimal response to inquiries or by systematic development of demand in foreign markets. Exporting requires minimal capital and is easy to initiate. Exporting is also a good way to gain international experience. A major part of the overseas involvement of large firms is through export trade.

Contractual Agreement

There are several types of contractual agreements: patent licensing agreement, turnkey operation, coproduction agreement, management contract, and licensing.

Patent Licensing Agreement The *patent licensing agreement* is based on either a fixed-fee or a royalty-based agreement and includes managerial training.

Turnkey Operation The *turnkey operation* is based on a fixed-fee or cost-plus arrangement and includes plant construction, personnel training, and initial production runs.

Coproduction Agreement The *coproduction agreement* was most common in the Soviet-bloc countries, where plants were built and then paid for with part of the output.

Management Contract Currently widely used in the Middle East, the management contract requires that an MNC provide key personnel to operate the foreign enterprise for a fee until local people acquire the ability to manage the business independently. For example, Whittaker Corporation of Los Angeles operates government-owned hospitals in several cities in Saudi Arabia.

Licensing A variety of contractual agreements are encompassed in *licensing,* whereby an MNC marketer makes available intangible assets such as patents, trade secrets, know-how, trademarks, and company name to foreign companies in return for royalties or other forms of payment. Transfer of these assets usually is accompanied by technical services to ensure proper use.[35]

Some of the advantages of licensing are as follows:

1. Licensing requires little capital and serves as a quick and easy entry to foreign markets (see International Marketing Highlight 1.9).
2. In some countries licensing is the only way to tap the market.
3. Licensing provides life extension for products in the maturity stage of their life cycles.
4. Licensing is a good alternative to foreign production and marketing in an environment where there is worldwide inflation, skilled-labor shortages, increasing domestic and foreign governmental regulation and restriction, and tough international competition.
5. Licensing royalties are guaranteed and periodic, whereas shared income from investment fluctuates and is risky.
6. Domestically based firms can benefit from product development abroad without research expense through technical feedback arrangements in a licensing agreement.
7. When exports no longer are profitable because of intense competition, licensing provides an alternative.
8. Licensing can overcome high transportation costs, which make some exports noncompetitive in the target markets.
9. Licensing is immune to expropriation.
10. In some countries, manufacturers of military equipment or any product deemed critical to the national interest (including communication equipment) may be compelled to enter licensing agreements.

■■■■■■■■■   **International Marketing Highlight 1.9**   ■■■■■■■■■

Starbucks Steams Ahead in Asia

After Starbucks opened its first Asian store as a joint venture in Japan in 1996, it changed tactics and struck tailor-made licensing deals in seven other countries. Though Starbucks prefers the degree of control joint ventures offer, it had shied away from the capital commitments such a strategy demands. Less than 5 percent of global revenue currently funds international expansion, and the coffee brewer is unwilling to pay for half of every branch it opens in Asia. Franchising would circumvent this problem, but Starbucks is not comfortable having a franchise partner select sub-franchisers, as is typical. Licensing lets the firm maintain control over expansion while limiting financial exposure. The local partner funds the capital costs of expansion—and bears the business risks.

Moreover, secondary benefits accrue from partnering with local outfits, such as instantly gaining valuable regional expertise. For example, Rustan Coffee has operated supermarkets and retail outlets in the Philippines for 45 years, giving Starbucks a head start with distribution and possible supermarket sales. Local partners also help the U.S. company navigate tricky local regulations, such as local content laws in the Philippines or strict quality testing procedures in Japan.

Detailed licensing agreements give the local partners exclusive rights to develop and operate Starbucks retail stores. However, the agreements also stipulate that Starbucks remains involved in every aspect of planning, operations, design and training. Parent-company consultants visit each foreign store at least once a month. Store managers are sent to Seattle for an intensive training course of 12–14 weeks and all menu changes must be discussed with headquarters before being implemented.

Source: Crossborder Monitor, April 26, 1999, p. 12

Some disadvantages of licensing are as follows:

1. To attract licensees, a firm must possess distinctive technology, a trademark, and a company or brand name that is attractive to potential foreign users.
2. The licensor has no control over production and marketing by the licensee.
3. Licensing royalties are negligible compared with equity investment potential. Royalty rates seldom exceed 5 percent of gross sales because of host government restrictions.
4. The licensee may lose interest in renewing the contract unless the licensor holds interest through innovation and new technology.
5. There is a danger of creating competition in third, or even home, markets if the licensee violates territorial agreements. Going to court in these situations is expensive and time consuming and no international adjudicatory body exists.

Joint Venture

Joint venture represents a higher-risk alternative than licensing because it requires various levels of direct investment. A joint venture between a U.S. firm and a native operation abroad involves sharing risks to accomplish mutual enterprise. Joint ventures, incidentally, are the next most common form of entry once a firm moves beyond the exporting stage to a more regular overseas involvement.

One example of a joint venture is General Motors Corporation's partnership with Egypt's state-owned Nasar Car Company to establish a plant to assemble trucks and diesel engines. Another example of a joint venture is between Matsushita of Japan and IBM to manufacture small computers. The alliance between Coca-Cola Co. and Nestlé S.A. to develop and sell ready-to-drink coffees and teas is still another example of a joint venture. Joint ventures normally are designed to take advantage of the strong functions of the partners and supplement their weak functions, be they management, research, or marketing.

Joint ventures provide a mutually beneficial opportunity for domestic and foreign businesses to join forces. For both parties, the ventures are a means to share both capital and risk and make use of each other's technical strength. Japanese companies, for example, prefer entering into joint ventures with U.S. firms because such arrangements help ensure against possible American trade barriers. American firms, on the other hand, like the opportunity to enter a previously forbidden market, to utilize established channels, to link American product innovation with low-cost Japanese manufacturing technology, and to curb a potentially tough competitor.

As a case in point, General Foods Corporation tried for more than a decade to succeed in Japan on its own and watched the market share of its instant coffee (Maxwell House) drop from 20 to 14 percent. Then, in 1975 the firm established a joint venture with Ajinomoto, a food manufacturer, to use the full power of the Japanese partner's product distribution system and personnel and managerial capabilities. Within two years, Maxwell House's share of the Japanese instant coffee market recovered reached close to 25 percent.[36]

Joint ventures, however, are a mixed blessing, with their main problem stemming from one cause: there is more than one partner, and one of the partners must play the key, dominant role to steer the business to success. Obviously, conflicts can arise in the management process.

Joint ventures should be designed to supplement each partner's shortcomings, not to exploit them. It takes as much effort to make a joint venture a success as to start a grassroots operation and eventually bring it up to a successful level. In both cases, each partner must be fully prepared to expend the effort necessary to understand customers, competitors, and himself or herself. A joint venture is a means of resource appropriation and of easing a foreign business's entry into a new terrain. It should not be viewed as a handy vehicle to reap money without effort, interest, or additional resources.

Joint ventures are a popular mode to seek entry in a foreign country. There is hardly a Fortune 1000 company active overseas that does not have at least one joint venture. Widespread interest in joint ventures is related to

1. *Seeking market opportunities*. Companies in mature industries in the industrialized countries find joint venture a desirable entry mode for new markets overseas.
2. *Dealing with rising economic nationalism*. Often host governments are more receptive to or even require joint ventures.
3. *Preempting raw materials*. Countries with raw materials such as petroleum or extractable material usually do not allow foreign firms to be active there other than through joint venture.
4. *Sharing risk*. Rather than taking the entire risk, a joint venture allows the risk to be shared with a partner, which can be especially important in politically sensitive areas.
5. *Developing an export base*. In areas where economic blocs play a significant role, joint venture with a local firm smoothes the entry into the entire region, such as entry into the European Union (EU) market through a joint venture with a French company.
6. *Selling technology*. Selling technology to developing countries becomes easier through joint ventures.

Although joint venture is an attractive entry mode, it poses a potential for failure. When either partner in a joint venture concludes that the venture is a failure, there are five alternatives to resolve the problem. First, the joint venture may be continued even after it is seen as a failure if the circumstances force the partners to do so—for examples. Both partners may be temporarily dependent on the venture for some critical resource, or one party may have legal basis for forcing continuation. A second option is for one partner to continue the business. A third is for another entity to acquire all or a major portion of the joint venture. A fourth is to create a new organization, independent of the original partners, to run the business. This option is usually relevant for joint ventures that have achieved some measure of success but are no longer useful to the founding partners. Finally, the joint venture may be liquidated.

The choice of which termination strategy to use depends on a number of factors. If either partner is dependent on the joint venture for some critical resource, the preservation of that resource will be a critical consideration in selecting a strategy. Another factor is whether the joint venture could survive as an independent entity. If the joint venture is not dependent specifically on the founding partners, it may be able to shift its association to some other business organization.

If the owners decide not to continue the joint venture, the outcome will depend on whether the venture is worth more as a going concern than its liquidation value. New joint ventures will be less visible and less attractive to potential buyers than old ones. Small joint ventures are unlikely to have the necessary resources to survive as independent organizations. All of these factors suggest that new and small ventures will be liquidated. Larger and longer-established ventures have a greater opportunity for survival.

Strategic Alliance

In recent years, a new type of collaborative strategy in international business has gained popularity. Commonly called strategic alliance, leading firms, particularly in high-tech industries, have used this route for their mutual benefit. Strategic alliances are short of complete merger, but deeper than arm's length market exchanges. They involve mutual dependence and shared decision making between two or more separate firms. Strategic alliances differ from joint ventures in that they encompass select activities and often are formed for a specific period. Strategic goals pursued through strategic alliances are product exchange or supply alliances (aimed to reduce transaction costs by establishing a mutual commitment between the supplying and buying firms); learning alliances (aimed to develop new capabilities through technology transfer or joint research); and market positioning alliances (aimed to develop demand for a product, spread technology, or develop a dominant standard in the market).

Strategic alliances make sense for the following reasons:[37]

1. Their flexibility and informality promote efficiencies.
2. They provide access to new markets and technologies.
3. They all the creation and disbanding of projects with minimum paperwork.
4. Multiple parties share risk and expenses.
5. Partners can retail their independent brand identification.
6. Partners possessing multiple skills can create major synergies.
7. Rivals can often work harmoniously together.
8. Alliances can take multifarious forms, from simple R&D deals to huge projects.
9. Ventures can accommodate dozens of participants.
10. Antitrust laws can shelter cooperative R&D activities.

Strategic alliances are especially useful for seeking entry into emerging markets. MNCs look to emerging markets for growth. Companies in emerging markets look for ways into the burgeoning global economy. Strategic alliances are the obvious solution for both sides. Given this pattern of mutual benefit, it is not surprising that strategic alliances account for at least half of market entries into Latin America, Asia, and Eastern Europe.[38]

Wholly-Owned Subsidiary

MNCs may also establish themselves in overseas markets by direct investment in a manufacturing or assembly subsidiary. Because of the volatility of worldwide economic, social, and political conditions, these *wholly-owned subsidiaries* are the most risky form of overseas involvement. An example of a direct investment situation is Chesebrough-Pond's operation of overseas manufacturing plants in Japan, England, and Monte Carlo. An example of the risk involved in such arrangements is India's Bhopal disaster, in which a poisonous gas leak in a Union Carbide Corporation plant killed over 2,000 people and permanently disabled thousands—in the worst industrial accident that has ever occurred. It has been suggested that MNCs not manufacture overseas where a mishap could jeopardize the survival of the whole company. As a matter of fact, in the wake of the Bhopal accident, many host countries tightened safety and environmental regulations. For example, Brazil, the world's fourth-largest user of agricultural chemicals, restricted the use of the deadly methyl isocyanate.

Conclusion

A firm interested in entering the international market must evaluate the risk and commitment involved with each entry and choose the entry mode that best fits the company's objectives and resources. Entry risk and commitment can be examined by considering the following five factors:

1. Characteristics of the product.
2. The market's external macroenvironment—particularly economic and political factors, and the demand and buying pattern characteristics of potential customers.
3. The firm's competitive position—especially the product's life cycle stage as well as various corporate strengths and weaknesses.
4. Capital budgeting considerations, including resource costs and availabilities.
5. Internal corporate perceptions, which affect corporate selection of information and the psychic distance between a firm's decision makers and its target customers, as well as control and risk-taking preferences.

These five factors combined indicate the risk to be reviewed vis-à-vis a company's resources before determining a mode of entry.[39]

It is useful to remember that a company may use different modes of entry in different countries. For example, McDonald's Corporation deemed it sufficient to license three restaurants on the small Caribbean island of Aruba, but in Japan it has had a joint venture since 1971. The local partner helped McDonald's blanket the Japanese market to such an extent that there are now over 600 outlets across the country, the largest number of McDonald's restaurants in any country outside the United States

Summary

In today's environment even firms that do not seek to do business outside their national boundaries have no choice but to be aware of the international business scene. The U.S. economy, as is true of the economies of other industrialized nations, is so intricately linked to international economics that even strictly domestic business is affected by what takes place in other countries. Thus, all students of business should be thoroughly familiar with the perspectives of international business.

International marketing instruction in particular is required because, of all the functional areas of a business, marketing problems are the most fundamental and the most frequent. Although basic marketing decisions do not change as marketers expand their business from the domestic field to the international field, the environments they must consider while making those decisions can be profoundly different. The major aspects of the international marketing environment include the economic, cultural, and legal and political environments.

International marketing is also affected by international institutions such as the International Monetary Fund and agreements such as NAFTA.

A firm aspiring to enter the international scene may choose from the various entry modes—exporting, contractual agreement, joint venture, strategic alliance, and wholly-owned subsidiary. Each entry mode provides different opportunities and risks.

Today's thrust for growth in international business comes from MNCs. In recent years some of the tactics of the MNCs have become a subject of intense discussion, particularly with reference to their operations in developing countries. The MNC will continue to be an institution of great significance, but leaders of these companies will require an increasing awareness of the needs of host countries in the environment in the future.

Review Questions

1. Why should a business operating entirely in the U.S. domestic market be concerned with happenings in the international business environment?
2. Why should international marketing be considered as a separate field of study even though marketing decisions in both domestic and international markets are basically the same?
3. What are the different modes of entry into the international market? What are the relative advantages and disadvantages of each mode?
4. How can a firm's overseas involvement be categorized?
5. Why do a very large proportion of U.S. firms confine themselves to domestic markets?
6. Why should a firm enter international business? Give examples of each reason.

Creative Questions

1. Usually, MNCs are associated with a particular country—thus, there are U.S. MNCs, Japanese MNCs, etc. Inasmuch as MNCs do business globally, and their stockholders are spread all over the world, is it conceivable that MNCs in the future would be characterized under the authority of an international agency and become stateless? What are the pros and cons of such a move?
2. What is the difference between a joint venture and a strategic alliance? What are the key issues in the successful management of strategic alliances?

Endnotes

1. "Mac World," *The Economist*, June 29, 1996, p.61.

2. See National Trade Data Bank, U.S. Department of Commerce, updated First Quarter 2000.

3. "It's a Small (Business) World," *Business Week*, April 17, 1995, p. 96.

4. *U.S. Manufacturers in the Global Marketplace* (New York: The Conference Board, Inc., 1994, p. 35.

5. U.S. Department of Commerce.

6. Ibid.

7. See Subhash C. Jain, "Global Competitiveness in the Beer Industry: A Case Study," Working Paper (Storrs, CT: Food Policy Center, The University of Connecticut, 1994).

8. The direct investment position is the net book value of U.S. companies and other investors' equity in and outstanding loans to foreign affiliates.

9. Joseph P. Quinlan, "Europe, Not Asia, Is Corporate America's Key Market," *The Wall Street Journal*, January 12, 1998, p. A20.

10. *Transnationals*, October 1995, p. 10.

11. *Statistical Abstract of the United States: 2000* (Washington, D.C.: U.S. Department of Commerce, 2000), p. 682.

12. U.S. Department of Commerce, International Trade Administration.

13. Ibid.

14. Ibid.

15. See "No Smoking Sweeps America," *Business Week*, July 27, 1987, p. 40. Also see James S. Hirsch, "U.S. Liquor Makers Seek Tonic in Foreign Markets," *The Wall Street Journal*, October 24, 1989, p. B1.

16. See Edmund Faltermayer, "Is 'Made in U.S.A.' Fading Away," *Fortune*, September 24, 1990, p. 62.

17. "America's High-Tech Crisis," *Business Week*, March 11, 1985, p. 56. Also see Bernard Wysocki, Jr., "American Firms Send Office Work Abroad to Use Cheaper Labor," *The Wall Street Journal*, August 14, 1991, p. 1.

18. "The Angry Angels at Zenith," *Business Week*, August 12, 1996. P. 32.

19. *The Economist*, February 19, 1994, p. 21.

20. "Asia's Brand Barons Go Shopping," *The Economist*, August 10, 1996, p. 45.

21. "Kodak in China; smile, please," *The Economist*, March 28, 1998, p. 60.

22. *World Almanac*, 2000.

23. Roger Thurow, "In Global Drive, Nike Finds Its Brash Ways Don't Always Pay Off," *The Wall Street Journal*, May 5, 1997, p. A1.

24. Theodore Levitt, "The Globalization of Markets," *Harvard Business Review*, May–June 1983, pp. 92–102.

25. Ibid.

26. Chris Adams, "Steelmakers Scramble in a Race to Become Global Powerhouses," *The Wall Street Journal*, August 1997, p.1.

27. Frank Meissner, "Americans Must Practice the Marketing They Preach to Succeed in Japan's Mass Markets," *Marketing News*, October 17, 1990, p.5.

28. *See* Kenichi Ohmae, *Beyond National Borders* (Homewood, IL: Dow Jones-Irwin, 1987), Chapter 3.

29. Stephen K. Yoder, "Apple, Loser in Japan Computer Market, Tries to Recoup by Redesigning Its Models," *The Wall Street Journal*, June 21, 1985, p. 30.

30. Hirotaka Takeuchi and Michael E. Porter, "Three Roles of International Marketing in Global Strategy," in Michael Porter, ed., *Competition in Global Industries* (Boston: Harvard Business School Press 1986), pp. 111–116.

31. *World Investment Report 1999* (New York: United Nations, 1999).

32. See Rajib N. Sanyal and Turgut Guvenh, "Relations Between Multinational Firms and Host Governments: The Experience of American-owned Firms in China," *International Business Review*, 9 no. 1 (2000): 119–134.

33. See *World Investment Report*.

34. Francis H. Ulgado, Chwo-Ming J. Yu, and Anant R. Negandhi, "Multinational Enterprises from Asian Developing Countries: Management and Organizational Characteristics," *International Business Review* 3, no. 2 (1994): 123–134.

35. See Farok J. Contractor, "Strategic Perspectives for International Licensing Managers: The Complementary Roles of Licensing— Investment and Trade in Global Operations," Working Paper no. 90.002, Rutgers University Center for International Business Education and Research.

36. Kenichi Ohmae, *Triad Power* (New York: The Free Press, 1985), p. 116.

37. "Partness-Partners," *Business Week*, October 25, 1999, p. 106.

38. Ashwin Adarkar, Asif Adil, David Ernst and Paresh Vaish, "Emerging Market Alliances: Must They Be Win-Lose? *The Mckinsey Quarterly*, November 4, 1997, pp. 120–137.

Economic Rationale of Global Trade and Business

CHAPTER FOCUS_____

After studying this chapter, you should be able to

■ Give the rationale for global trade and business.

■ Describe the barriers that nations impose to restrict free trade.

■ Explain the role of the General Agreement on Tariffs and Trade (GATT) in liberalizing world trade.

■ Describe U.S. trade liberalization endeavors.

■ Discuss how a multinational corporation participates in global markets.

Commerce is older than recorded history. Archaeological discoveries provide us with evidence of the antiquity of trade. Thousands of ancient commercial documents indicate that a considerable commercial class existed many centuries before any European or Mediterranean city attained a high degree of civilization. In the ancient world, there had even developed a system of payment of precious objects for traded goods—a forerunner of the modern monetary system.

Trading has evolved through the ages in response to altering needs spurred by changes in technology and philosophy. Growth in trade was particularly stimulated by the discovery and use of metals and by the global horizons provided by advances in transportation and later in communication. As a result of those advances, trade evolved from exchanges among isolated peoples to trade through conquest, then to trade among friendly neighbors, and then to a system of silent barter among both adversaries and friends. In brief, although world trade as we know it today is very different from ancient trading practices, groups of people have always traded.

As civilization progressed around the world, trading became more organized and productive. For example, ancient seaborne commerce was inefficient and, proportionately, insignificant. Piracy and raiding of ships were commonplace. Such hazards discouraged trade expansion and required that harbors be fortified for protection. In modern times, although nations still go to war, piracy and raiding have been virtually eliminated by a variety of treaties, arrangements, and other international laws.

World trade requires that nations be willing to cooperate with each other. Countries naturally trade with those nations with whom they are on friendly terms. Nonetheless, trading often goes on among nations even when political relations are not amicable. For example, the United States and China are on many issues politically opposed, yet the two nations trade with each other. The mutual benefits, or economic advantages, of U.S.–China trade outweigh political differences.

Economic advantage has historically been the most important consideration that trading nations share. This chapter examines and discusses the nature of that advantage and also deals with the political and economic hindrances that produce economic disadvantage and tend to discourage trade, particularly among developed and developing countries.

In the post–World War II period, world trade has multiplied tremendously and has added new dimensions to global economic activity. An example is presented here to depict the emergence of the MNC as the basic institution of present international economic activity. Current international economic activity is much wider in both scope and activity than the traditional importing and exporting trade described by classical economists.

Theory of Comparative Advantage

The classical economists—Adam Smith, David Ricardo, and John Stuart Mill—are credited with providing the theoretical economic justification for international trade. In simple terms, modern trade takes place because a foreign country is able to provide a material or product cheaper than native industry can. For example, if the landed cost of a Japanese-made television set is less than the cost of an American-made one, it makes economic sense to import television sets from Japan. Likewise, if U.S. computers can be sold at cheaper prices in Japan than computers manufactured in Japan, Japanese businesses will find it economically desirable to import U.S. computers.

David Ricardo advanced the concept of *relative or comparative costs* as the basis of international trade. He emphasized labor costs more than other aspects of production. Such aspects as land and capital, in Ricardo's view, either were of no significance or were so evenly distributed overall that they always operated in a fixed proportion, whereas labor did not. In sum, his *theory of comparative advantage* states that even if a country is able to produce all its goods at lower costs than another country can, trade still benefits both countries, based on comparative, not absolute, costs. In other words, countries should concentrate efforts on producing goods that have a *comparative* advantage over other countries, and then export those goods in exchange for goods that command advantage in their native countries.

To illustrate this point, let us assume the following information about the United States and Italy:

Labor Costs per Unit (in Hours)

Country	Hand Calculator	Bottle of Wine
United States	6	8
Italy	30	15

Although these figures show that the production cost of both hand calculators and wine is lower in the United States than in Italy, according to the theory of comparative advantage, the United States is better off specializing in hand calculators and exchanging them for Italian wine. This way, it can obtain from Italy a bottle of wine for only six hours of labor instead of the eight hours that would be required at home. Italy would also gain from the exchange by concentrating on producing wine and exchanging it for hand calculators at the cost of 15 instead of 30 hours of labor. The key to this concept is in the word "comparative"—which implies that each and every country has both definite "advantage" in producing some goods and definite "disadvantage" in producing other goods. But, further, the advantage for some goods may be greater than for others (e.g., hand calculators versus wine for the United States).

The following example quantitatively demonstrates the benefits derived from free trade. Consider two countries, Japonia and Latinia. Japonia has a clear competitive advantage over Latinia in producing both radios and TVS, as follows:

Worker Hours per Unit

	Japonia	Latinia
Radio	1	4
Television Sets	4	8

It follows that 48 worker hours of production will result in 24 radios and 6 television sets in Japonia. The same number of worker hours produces six radios and three television sets in Latinia. Therefore, the two countries can produce a total of 30 radios and 9 television sets with 96 worker hours of effort.

Now suppose Japonia and Latinia choose free trade and tear down the barriers they have erected against each other's products. With the same worker-hour requirement per unit and the same number of worker hours devoted to production, their combined output will change to 32 radios and 10 televison sets.

This is not really a miracle; it simply is *division of labor* based on *comparative advantage*. Under free trade, Latinia is induced to withdraw resources it had devoted to radio production and concentrate entirely on television sets. Consequently, Latinia produces 6 television sets and no radios in 48 hours. Japonia is likewise induced to reallocate some resources and devote 32 worker hours to radios, where its comparative advantage is greatest, leaving the remaining 16 hours for television sets. Thus, 32 radios and 4 television sets are produced with every 48 worker hours of effort.

As a result, the world has more radios and television sets, but are Japonia and Latinia better off individually? To find out, we have to introduce the price system. In doing that, we must realize that price relationships are more important than the prices themselves. Differences in price relationships are what people act upon.

Here is the lineup of prices (we'll use the same prices both before and after free trade):

	Japonia	Latinia
Radios	24,000 yen	600 pesos
Television sets	96,000 yen	1,200 pesos

After free trade, the Japonian retailer can choose a television set at 96,000 yen or 1,200 pesos, corresponding to an exchange ratio of 80:1. The retailer will want to buy pesos whenever they can be obtained for less than 80 yen apiece. The Latinian retailer can choose a radio at 24,000 yen or 600 pesos, corresponding to a ratio of 40:1. This retailer will be in the market for yen whenever more than 40 yen can be exchanged for a peso.

The differential in price relationships between television sets and radios in the two countries has created an entrepreneurial opportunity: buying and selling currencies. Price differentials on many products—and many other factors, including people's expectations concerning the relative economic outlook of the countries involved—play a part in establishing exchange rates. But the Japonian and Latinian marketers in this case should be satisfied if the yen/peso rate falls somewhere between 40:1 and 80:1.

We could choose any number, but let us say that the exchange rate becomes 60:1—right in the middle. Before free trade, a Japonian retailer could buy a shipment of 20 radios and 5 television sets for 960,000 yen. A Latinian retailer could buy the same shipment for 18,000 pesos. After free trade, the Japonian and Latinian retailers, each acting in his or her own self-interest, do their buying. Here is the result:

Japonian Retailer		
20 radios × 24,000 yen		= 480,000 yen
5 TVs × 1,200 pesos × 60 yen		= 360,000 yen
	Shipment	840,000 yen
Savings: 120,000 yen		

Latinian Retailer		
20 radios × 24,000 yen / 60 pesos		= 8,000 pesos
5 TVs × 1,200 pesos		= 6,000 pesos
	Shipment	14,000 pesos
Savings: 4,000 pesos		

In both countries, purchasing power has been increased. Both can afford to buy more of the same things or to buy new things they could not afford before. Both are wealthier.

Possibly you aren't convinced until you can see it "in dollars and cents." So why not create a world price in dollars for radios and television sets, and redo the arithmetic? At a 60:1 yen/peso exchange rate, the dollar price of a TV is $240, since 300 yen equals 5 pesos equals $1. You will find that Japonia will have enough extra radios to sell at $80 each to buy from Latinia the television sets it stopped producing, and it will still have some dollars to spare. Latinia will have dollars left over after selling extra television sets to buy all of the radios it no longer makes.

Rationale for Seeking Comparative Advantage

Every nation seeks to increase the material standard of living of its people, and that living standard increases as a function of *productivity*. With greater productivity, the same amount of labor yields more goods and services. As productivity increases, greater material wealth results. Thus, the rationale for seeking comparative advantage is increased productivity.

Different countries enjoy productivity gains in different ways. Sweden has made a choice of longer vacations; the United States prefers increased material possessions. In both cases, increased productivity yields the desired benefits.

Productivity is enhanced—and the living standard raised—by the *specialization* of production, whereby countries do not try to produce all the goods they require but only those they can produce efficiently. The rest are imported. *Sheltered* businesses—the ones chosen to provide certain goods and services nationally—include health care, government administration, goods distribution, and manufacturers of special goods such as pharmaceuticals and essential military goods.

Businesses included in the sheltered category are influenced by consideration of economic feasibility, national security, and self-sufficiency. Sheltered manufacturing businesses include those in which increased production scale is not great enough to offset the costs of distributing the product to a larger geographic area. This category includes products that, for one reason or another, are expensive to transport, such as milk or sulfuric acid.

For a nation to have a high standard of living, it must export enough goods to balance the import of the goods it cannot efficiently produce itself. Exports are especially important for maintaining the living standard in a country whose resources are limited and whose imports, in balance, are relatively high. Consider Japan, which built a viable export market and in return developed an invulnerable position in many industries. South Korea, Taiwan, and Brazil appear to be following Japan's example by developing export markets.[1]

Exhibit 2.1 presents a hypothetical comparison of two countries whose only export is oil. If the market absorbs the production of both countries, the price is usually set according to the cost of the labor hours required by the least efficient producer, in this case Country B. Country A may set a price slightly lower in order to guarantee the sale of all its output. Regardless, Country A's per-hour income will be much higher than that of Country B. This greater income can be used for higher wages, for reinvestment to support a free health care system for everyone in the country, or for whatever the country desires. In brief, specialization profits Country A and leads it to a higher standard of living.

EXHIBIT 2.1
Relative Productivity: A Hypothetical Example

	Labor Hours per Barrel	
	Country A	Country B
Operating	1	3
Capital cost amortization	1	2
Total	2	5
World price (in labor-hour equivalents)	5.0	5.5
Income (per labor hour)	2.5	1.1

Business Specialization and Trade

The *economic law of comparative advantage* states that every nation benefits when specialization and trade take place. Even when one nation cannot produce any good more efficiently than another can, it is still in the economic interest of both nations for each to specialize. Regardless of its productivity relative to other suppliers, every nation has comparative advantage in producing certain goods rather than others. The specialization and the advantage are achieved on the basis of one or more production factors—natural resources, technology, capital, managerial know-how, and labor.[2]

Classical economists considered labor the chief delineating factor of comparative advantage between two trading nations. In modern days, however, other factors besides labor may be more important in equipping a country for specialization. As a matter of fact, wage levels for blue-collar workers are becoming increasingly irrelevant in world competition. This is because blue-collar labor no longer accounts for enough of total costs to give low wages much competitive advantage. For example, blue-collar costs in U.S. manufacturing account for 18 percent of total costs, but they are down from 23 percent only a few years ago, and they are dropping fast.[3]

In addition to being influenced by the preceding production factors, a country's leverage may change with time and with changes in the political, social, cultural, and economic environment. For example, Japan has a comparative advantage relative to the United States in producing steel. Japan's leverage in steel is based on managerial ability and technology. Even though Japan must import the raw material of iron ore, other factors provide enough leeway to ensure comparative advantage. This does not mean that its current comparative advantage in steel is everlasting. The supplier of Japan's iron ore could stop supplying for political reasons, or another country could develop a technology superior to Japan's and supersede its advantage. Thus, leverage must be not only developed but also maintained for long-term gains.

Natural Resources Nature randomly endowed different regions of the world with natural resources. The natural riches of a place bestow upon it unique economic advantages. But nations are groups of communities arbitrarily organized, usually without regard to such economic considerations as the abundance or lack of natural resources.

The most outstanding example of the possession of a resource providing economic leverage is the abundance of oil in the Middle East. In raw-material exchanges based on natural resources, even if both nations have the same natural resource, one country may be better off than the other because of various physical characteristics of the resource. For example, certain economic considerations—such as seam thickness, depth, and purity of ore bodies or the number of hours required to pump a barrel of oil—come into play. Saudi Arabian oil from a shallow well is a richer resource than Iranian oil from a deep well.

Mineral trade is based on the natural availability of minerals in different countries. The aircraft industry is crucially dependent on cobalt, which is used in jet engine blades. Zambia and Zaire produce two-thirds of the world's cobalt and thus have a natural advantage in this area. Since the metal is important for an essential industry, the random distribution of the natural resource leads to world trade. In brief, the natural resources of a country can permit it to engage in international trade from an advantageous position.

Technology Manufacturers in different countries have different production costs as a result of the unevenness of technological advances. Differences in production scale, run lengths, distribution structure, product mix, and technological development capability, among other things, often determine productivity differences among producers. For example, some Japanese companies can assemble a television set in one-third the time required by their European or American competitors. This advantage is derived from product designs that use fewer components, machines that automate some of the board assembly, and equipment that reduces labor in the handling of materials.

As another example, Japan's technological advantage in manufacturing steel leads it to surpass India in the world markets. This happens despite the facts that (1) Japan must import iron ore from India and (2) Indian labor is much less expensive than Japanese labor.

Managerial Know-How People who bring capital, labor, and resources together to fashion them into a productive organization—one that faces the risks of an uncertain world—occupy strategic positions. Thus, given the same inputs, a country with superior management will likely do better than one with weak management. The importance of managerial know-how can be illustrated by the airlines industry. Most airlines of the free world use the same planes and offer essentially the same services while charging common prices. Yet some carriers outperform others. The difference must be management. Singapore Airlines does better than any other airline, partly because of its lower labor costs, but mainly because of superior management.[4]

Obviously, an explanation of world business involves many elements. However, with a basic understanding of the elements covered so far—comparative advantage and specialization—we can now consider other reasons for nations to engage in international business.

Product Life Cycle and International Trade

The theory of comparative advantage is a classic explanation of world trade. In the late 1960s researchers at the Harvard Business School provided a new explanation of international trade and investment patterns.[5] The new approach uses the *product life cycle model,* which gives significant insight into how MNCs evolve. The product life cycle model states that U.S. products go through four stages:[6]

Phase I, in which U.S. export strength for a product builds.
Phase II, in which foreign production of the same product starts.
Phase III, in which foreign production becomes competitive in export markets.
Phase IV, in which import competition begins in domestic U.S. markets.

During Phase I the product is manufactured in the United States for a high-income market and afterward introduced into foreign markets through exports. At that point, the United States usually holds a monopoly position as the only country able to supply the product. The product continues to be manufactured only in the United States, since business acumen dictates that operations be located close to markets where the demand exists. Overseas customers, however, import the U.S. product in response to their own market demands and thus create a program of export of the U.S. product.

During Phase II, as the product becomes popular, entrepreneurs in other advanced countries, perhaps in Western Europe, venture into producing the same product. The technology involved is by then fairly routine and easily transferred from the United States. Subsequently, the overseas-manufactured product begins to outsell the U.S. export in selected markets because the overseas product benefits from lower labor costs and savings in transportation. The stage where overseas manufacturers are able to compete effectively against U.S. exports has been reached.

In the third phase, the foreign producers begin to compete against the U.S. exports in developing countries. Consequently, the market for the U.S. exports declines further. Between Phases I and II, the U.S. firms begin to consider making direct investments abroad to sustain or regain their original market position.

Phase IV occurs when the foreign firms, strong in their home and export markets, achieve economies of scale and then begin to invade the U.S. home market. Presumably, the foreign firms have lower costs so that, despite ocean freight and U.S. customs costs, they are able to compete effectively against the domestically produced U.S. products.

These four phases complete the product life cycle and describe how American firms that once commanded a monopoly position in a product find themselves being pushed out of their home market.

The product life cycle theory applied to world trade holds that advanced countries like the United States play the innovative role in product development, and then, later on, other relatively advanced countries such as Japan or Western European countries take over the market position held by the innovative country. The second-stage countries go through the same cycle as did the innovative country and in turn lose their markets to the next group of countries, say, emerging countries. In other words, a product initially produced in the United States might eventually be produced only in developing countries, with the result that the United States, Western Europe, and Japan would meet their needs for that product through import from the developing countries.

The product life cycle model has been helpful in explaining the history of a number of products, particularly textiles, shoes, bicycles, radios, television sets, industrial fasteners, and standardized components for different uses. These products, first available only in the United States, Western Europe, and Japan, are now being imported from Korea, Taiwan, Hong Kong, Brazil, Mexico, Malaysia, India, and other emerging countries. South Korea in particular has made enormous strides out-competing Japan in a number of consumer products. Abandoning years of prejudice, Japanese are snatching up low-priced goods from newly industrialized countries. For example, in 1998 an imported 20-inch color television set was available for $475 while a similar Japanese-made set was priced at $730.[7]

Despite its apparent validity in the manufacturing field, the product life cycle model does not provide a complete answer to the growth activities of MNCs.[8] We now turn to some concepts that apply there.

Production Sharing

In the late 1970s Peter Drucker introduced a new concept of international business and trade, *production sharing,* which he described as

> the newest world economic trend. Although production sharing is neither "export" nor "import" in the traditional sense, this is how it is still shown in our trade figures and treated in economic and political discussions. Yet it is actually economic integration by stages of the productive process.[9]

Production sharing arose as a solution to an economic problem in developed countries posed by the fact that higher levels of education there create higher levels of personal expectation, leading to a gradual disappearance of the semiskilled and unskilled labor so necessary to labor-intensive manufacturing. As a result, developed countries turn to developing countries where the availability of labor is a major asset, in order to "share" production of products requiring such labor. This concept also covers the U.S. tariff-schedule advantage of U.S. companies whereby American components made by American labor can be further processed or assembled abroad and then returned to the U.S. market for further work or sale, with duty paid only on the value added.

Drucker describes the process as follows:

> Men's shoes sold in the United States usually start out as the hide on the American cow. As a rule the hide is not tanned, however, in the United States, but shipped to a place like Brazil for tanning—highly labor-intensive work. The leather is then shipped—perhaps through the intermediary of a Japanese trading company—to the Caribbean. Part of it may be worked up into uppers in the British Virgin Islands, part into soles in Haiti. And then uppers and soles are shipped to islands like Barbados or Jamaica, the products of which have access to Britain, to the European Common Market (now European Union), and to Puerto Rico, where they are worked up into shoes that enter the United States under the American tariff umbrella.

Surely these are truly transnational shoes. The hide, though it's the largest single-cost element, still constitutes no more than one quarter of the manufacturer's cost of the shoe. By labor content these are "imported shoes." By skill content they are "American-made." Raising the cow, which is capital-intensive, heavily automated, and requires the greatest skill and advanced management, is done in a developed country, which has the skill, the knowledge, and the equipment. The management of the entire process, the design of the shoes, their quality control and their marketing are also done entirely in developed countries where the manpower and the skills needed for these tasks are available.[10]

Currently, production sharing seems to be quite prevalent, and growing at a rapid pace. It is a new phenomenon for which there are no classic or neoclassic explanatory theories. Strictly speaking, production sharing is different from the traditional idea of international trade. It is a transnational business integration—a new relationship made possible by technological and business forces.[11] Production sharing offers both the developed and developing countries of the world a chance to share their resources and strengths for mutual benefit.

Internalization Theory

A multinational firm can serve a market across national boundaries either by (1) exporting from a production facility located in the country of the parent company or from a third country subsidiary or (2) by setting up production facilities in the market itself. The sourcing policy of the firm is the result of the firm's decisions as to which of its production facilities will service its various final markets. Thus, the firm establishes an international network linking production to markets. Such a network enables the firm to grow by eliminating external markets in intermediate goods and subsequently by *internalizing* those markets within the firm. When international markets are internalized, the internal transfers of goods and services occur. The incentives to internalize intermediate-goods markets are strongest in areas where research inputs and proprietary technology are an important part of the manufacturing process.

Many intermediate-product markets, particularly for types of knowledge and expertise embodied in patents and human capital, are difficult to organize and costly to use. In such cases, the firm has an incentive to create internal markets whenever transactions can be carried out at a lower cost within the firm than they can through external markets. This internalization involves extending the direct operations of the firm and bringing under common ownership and control the activities of the market.

The creation of an internal market permits the firm to transform an intangible piece of research into a valuable property specific to the firm. The firm can exploit its advantage in all available markets and still keep the use of the information internal to the firm in order to recoup its initial expenditures on research and knowledge generation.[12]

The internalization theory assumes that the firm has a global horizon, and it recognizes that the enterprise needs a competitive advantage or a unique asset to expand. However, the underlying thesis of internalization is the firm's desire to extend its own direct operations rather than use external markets. The internalization approach rests on two general axioms: (1) firms choose the least-cost location for each activity they perform; and (2) firms grow by internalizing markets up to the point where the benefits of further internalization are outweighed by the costs.

The internalization theory provides an economic rationale for the existence of MNCs. The sourcing decision rests on the costs and benefits to the firm, taking into consideration industry-specific factors (e.g., nature of the product), region-specific factors (e.g., geographic location), nation-specific factors (e.g., political climate), and firm-specific factors (e.g., managerial ability to internalize).

The internalization theory primarily focuses on the motives and decision processes within the MNC but pays little attention to the host country's policies or other external factors that may affect internalization cost/benefit ratio.

Trade Barriers and Trade Liberation

No matter how we look at it, the internationalization of business and trade appears to perpetuate worldwide prosperity.[13] Despite that fact, not a single country permits international business dealings at will. All impose some sort of barriers to restrict trade and business across national boundaries. But there are reasons for trade barriers as well as for the efforts that have been made internationally to liberate trade. The U.S. effort to promote free trade is particularly interesting.

Trade Barriers

There are two types of barriers that governments impose to restrict foreign trade: tariff and nontariff.

Tariff Barriers *Tariffs* refer to taxes levied on goods moved between nations. The most important of these is the tax usually called the *customs duty* that is levied by the importing nation. But a tax may also be imposed by the exporting nation, and that is called an *export tax*. In addition, a country through which goods pass on the way to their destination may impose a *transit tariff*. The real purpose behind trade barriers is to protect national interest. Exhibit 2.2 lists the major reasons that countries advance for such protection.

Different nations handle tariff barriers differently. A country may have a single tariff system for all goods from all sources. This is called a *unilinear* or *single-column tariff*. Another type of tariff is the *general-conventional tariff*, which applies to all nations except those that

EXHIBIT 2.2
Arguments for Protection

- *Keep-money-at-home argument:* To prevent national wealth from being transferred in exchange with another nation for goods.
- *Home-market argument:* To encourage home industry to perpetuate.
- *Equalization-of-costs-of-production argument:* To make local goods compete fairly against imports that might otherwise be cheaper because of technological advantages or other similar reasons.
- *Low-wage argument:* To protect home industry against competition from imports from low-wage countries.
- *Prevention-of-injury argument:* To safeguard against potential trade concessions that may have to be made in response to multinational trade agreements.
- *Employment argument:* To preserve level of home employment.
- *Antidumping argument:* To prevent dumping of foreign products.
- *Bargaining-and-retaliation argument:* To seek reduction of tariffs by other countries or to retaliate against another country.
- *National security argument:* To be on one's own for national security reasons such as war or natural calamities.
- *Infant-industry argument:* To encourage new industry in the country.
- *Diversification argument:* To promote a broad spectrum of industries in the country.
- *Terms-of-trade argument and the optimum tariff:* To compensate the country for loss in revenue when price elasticity of import demand is greater than zero.
- *The theory of the second-best:* This argument is based on the fact that free trade, while the best alternative, cannot be pursued optimally because of a variety of distortions. As an alternative, new distortions of tariffs may be utilized to neutralize the existing distortions.

Source: Modified from Franklin R. Root, *International Trade & Investment*, 3rd ed. (Cincinnati, OH: SouthWestern Publishing Co., 1983), pp. 306–322.

have tariff treaties (or a convention to that effect) with a particular country. A tariff may be worked out on the basis of a tax permit, called *specific duty*, or as a percentage of the value of the item, referred as *ad valorem* duty. Sometimes both specific and ad valorem duty may be levied on the same item as a combined duty.

Nontariff Barriers *Nontariff barriers* include quotas, import equalization taxes, road taxes, laws giving preferential treatment to domestic suppliers, administration of antidumping measures, exchange controls, and a variety of "invisible" tariffs that impede trade. A. D. Cao has summarized the principal nontariff barriers in the following categories:[14]

1. *Specific limitation on trade.* This category includes the measures that limit the allowable amount of imports, such as *quotas*, referring to quantity or value allowed for specific imported products during a specific period; *licensing requirements*, which obligate exporters and importers of specific products to obtain licenses before trading; *proportion restrictions of foreign to domestic goods*, which limit the quantity of imports to a specified proportion of domestic production; *minimum import price limits*, which require adjustment of import prices to equal or surpass domestic prices; and *embargoes*, which prohibit import of specific products from specific origins.

2. *Customs and administrative entry* **procedures.** This category includes procedural requirements comprising *valuation of imports* (i.e., enforcing a varying valuation process on imported goods that is often left at the discretion of customs officials and is highly arbitrary and discriminatory); *antidumping practices* (i.e., measures against imported goods sold at prices below those in the home market of the exporting country to injure the importing country industry); *tariff classifications* (i.e., arbitrary classification of imported products into a high-tariff category); *documentation requirements* (i.e., enforcing unnecessary and time-consuming bureaucratic requirements); and *fees* (i.e., imposing fees for different services to boost the price of imported goods).

3. *Standards.* This category includes unduly discriminatory health, safety, and quality standards such as *standard disparities* (i.e., imposing higher standards on imported goods than on domestic products); *intergovernmental acceptance of testing methods* (i.e., using tougher testing methods than those used for domestic products to determine the wholesomeness of products); and applying *packaging, labeling, and marketing standards* of the country to imported goods in an unduly stringent and discriminatory way (see International Marketing Highlight 2.1).

4. *Government participation in trade.* This category includes government involvement in trade through *procurement policies* favoring domestic products over the imported ones; *export subsidies* (i.e., providing tax incentives, export credit terms, or direct subsidies to domestic firms); *countervailing duties* (i.e., taxes levied to protect domestic products from the imported products that had been given export subsidy by the exporting country's government); and *domestic assistance programs* (i.e., other forms of assistance given to domestic products to strengthen their position against the imports).

5. *Charges on imports.* This category consists of various types of charges levied on imports to make them less competitive against the domestic goods, including *prior import deposit requirements* (i.e., requiring domestic importers to deposit a percentage of import value with the government before importing); *border tax adjustment* (i.e., levying various taxes on imported products that have been charged to domestic products); *administrative fees* (i.e., making an extra charge for processing import-related requirements); *special supplementary duties* (i.e., unusual charges levied on imports); *import credit discriminations* (i.e., providing credit accommodation to domestic producers); and *variable levies* (i.e., taxing imports at a higher rate than domestic goods). (see International Marketing Highlight 2.2).

6. *Other categories.* These categories include recent measures employed by importing countries to discourage imports such as *voluntary export restraints*, whereby an exporting country, often at the request of the importing country, agrees to limit its exports of a specific product to a particular level, and *orderly marketing agreements*, which refer to explicit and formal agreements negotiated between exporting and importing countries to restrict imports.

■■■■■■   International Marketing Highlight 2.1   ■■■■■■

Nontariff Barriers in Japan

Japanese standards are said to be written in a way that often excludes foreign products from the Japanese market. The Japanese standardsetting process is not easily understood, making participation—and even access to information—by foreigners difficult. Other problems include nonacceptance of foreign test data, lack of approval for product ingredients generally recognized as safe worldwide, and the nontransferability of product approval.

America's food processing industry, for example, maintains that these standards are deliberately discriminatory. Unlike the United States and most other countries, whose governments issue lists of additives generally safe for human consumption and a comparable list of substances banned, the Japanese have only one list. A specific additive can be used only for a specific purpose and only in a prescribed amount. Foods containing additives not on the so-called "positive" list may not be imported into Japan, even if those additives are not considered unsafe. The explicit policy of the Ministry of Health and Welfare is against adding ingredients to the positive list.

Regarded as an even more exasperating problem is the fact that Japan does not accept the results of certain testing and certification procedures conducted outside Japan for certain products such as drugs. The United States, on the other hand, generally accepts foreign data from testing done in accordance with appropriate U.S. standards and test procedures.

Furthermore, foreign manufacturers cannot apply directly to Japanese ministries for product approval. Only an approved Japanese entity can hold approval rights. Until recently, if foreign exporters wanted to change agents, their new agents had to reapply for product approval unless their formerly "approved" agents were willing to give up their rights. Of course, American firms could circumvent this constraint by establishing a subsidiary in Japan, but this option is not necessarily open to all manufacturers.

Subsidies, quotas, and monetary barriers are the most common nontariff barriers. Many nations provide *subsidies,* direct payments to select industries to enable them to compete effectively against the imports. For example, since 1980 the U.S. government has been providing a kind of subsidy for the sugar industry to strengthen its position against imports.[15]

Quotas impose a limit on the quantity of one kind of good that a country permits to be imported. A quota may be applied on a specific country basis or on a global basis without reference to exporting countries.[16] The United States, for example, has established quotas for textile imports from particular countries.

Monetary barriers are exchange controls of which there are three widespread types: blocked currency, differential exchange rate, and government approval to secure foreign exchange. *Blockage of currency* totally cuts importing by completely restricting the availability of foreign exchange. This barrier is often used politically against one or more nations. The *differential exchange-rate barrier* refers to the setting of different rates for converting local currencies into the foreign currency needed to import goods from overseas. A government can set higher conversion rates for items whose import it wishes to restrict, and lower rates for imports it does not wish to restrict. Finally, a country may require specific *government approval* before allowing the import of any goods. Most developing countries working toward maintaining a secure foreign exchange position strictly enforce the requirement of obtaining government approval for imports and grudgingly grant it only accompanied by a variety of hindrances and bureaucratic headaches.

■■■■■■■■   International Marketing Highlight 2.2   ■■■■■■■■

Old Russian Customs

One of the earliest and most educational experiences western managers have in Moscow comes when their possessions pass through Russian customs. Unlike almost any other country, Russia levies import duties—sometimes to the tune of several thousand dollars—on ordinary household removals.

But the latest move by the Russian customs service is making even hardened expatriates blench. In the past, foreign business offices were allowed to import cars, computers, and so forth duty-free, on the understanding that they would eventually reexport them. As of April 1, 1999, this has been cancelled—in a way which leaves foreign companies with potential costs of tens of millions of dollars.

Nor does the customs regime make any allowance for depreciation. In other words, a foreign representative office which has already imported a 1995 Land Rover will now have to pay duty on it—and at its original price ($29,000), rather than its current value (about $12,000). The tariff on new cars is a cool 100 percent. In addition, if any item on a customs declaration is missing, then the whole document becomes invalid. Woe betide the company that has imported, say, an old fax machine and subsequently thrown it away—it risks having to pay additional penalty duties on every other piece of office equipment imported with it. Those who clear their goods late will pay double or treble the usual duties (plus interest, at sky-high Russian rates, from the moment the shipment entered Russia). Even the slightest past infringement leads to the highest category of penalty. Fines of $100,000 and more are, in principle, quite possible on just one car.

Rather than pay the duties, you decide to destroy your imported car? You still pay duty. You arrange to have it stolen? Same result. Even reexporting them may not be possible. Simply removing temporary imports physically from Russia is not enough; the paperwork must be done too.

But for those who know the ropes, theory and practice in Russia are of course different. One western bank has used the services of a security agency run by a well-connected ex-KGB general. For the unfastidious, a corrupt customs officer will charge a few thousand dollars for setting—you hope—everything straight.

Despite squawks of protest, the Russian government—which claims to like foreign investors—has refused to bend. The best offer so far is that, maybe, western companies will be allowed to avoid duties if they donate the goods in question to charities (including those favored by the government, of course).

Source: The Economist, May 8, 1999, p. 68.

Tariff Reduction Programs

Internationally, systematic tariff reduction programs started after World War II. In 1947 the United States and 22 other major trading countries got together in Geneva to find ways to reduce tariffs and remove trade barriers. The **General Agreement on Tariffs and Trade (GATT)** resulted.[17] Since then, eight major efforts to reduce trade barriers have been undertaken under GATT's auspices (see Exhibit 2.3).

The first two rounds, Geneva 1947 and Annecy (France) 1949, are considered significant, both for tariff reduction and for structuring GATT's organization. The Torquay (England) 1951 and Geneva 1956 rounds are regarded as less significant. Insurmountable differences arose among nations over the issue of tariff disparities—that is, the difference between the high tariff of one country and low tariff of another. Next, the Dillon Round in 1962 resulted in further reduction of average world tariff rates. But it fell short of its goals: an across-the-board 20 percent reduction of tariffs and the settlement of problems unresolved since the 1956 meeting, especially those involving trade agreements with less-developed countries.

The Kennedy Round, sixth in the negotiation series, was the most comprehensive round of negotiations in terms of the number of participating countries, the value of the world trade involved, and the size of tariff reductions. The negotiations were concluded in 1972, with tariffs reduced on some 60,000 commodities valued at $40 billion in world trade. Despite its success, the Kennedy Round did not quite meet all the ambitious goals set for it. A major goal was a 50 percent across-the-board reduction in tariffs on industrial products. Overriding national interests forced exceptions to that reduction for such commodities as chemicals, steel, aluminum, pulp, and paper.

The question of tariff disparities, linked with the 50 percent goal, also yielded to exceptions because many Western European countries raised objections. Overall, the Kennedy Round negotiators agreed to tariff cuts on industrial products that averaged about 35 percent. The round was also meant to resolve the problem of nontariff barriers, but the results were rather modest except for the adoption of an antidumping code.

The principal objective of the Tokyo Round in 1973, seventh in the negotiation series, was the expansion and greater liberalization of world trade. The Tokyo Round recognized that the scope of exceptions should be limited and supported the general feeling that the special interests of the developing countries should be borne in mind during the tariff negotiations. This Tokyo Round, concluding in 1978, was the most complex and comprehensive trade negotiating effort attempted to that point. It tried to develop a substantially freer world trading system with balanced opportunities for countries with different economic and political systems and needs. Although the actual achievements fell short of the goals, the overall results of the Tokyo Round were very encouraging.

In the almost 40 years of its existence, GATT can claim some successes: Average tariffs in industrial countries in the mid 1980s tumbled to around 5 percent from an average of 40 percent in 1947. The volume of trade in manufactured goods multiplied twentyfold. GATT's membership increased fivefold. In the 1980s, however, the growing protectionism fostered by the economic difficulties that beset the world in the 1970s served to un-

EXHIBIT 2.3
Dimensions of Agreements under GATT

Major Agreements	Number of Contracting Parties	Value of World Trade Involved (Billions of Dollars)	Percent of Average Tariff Reduction
1947 Geneva	23	$10.0	n.a.*
1949 Annecy, France	33	n.a.*	n.a.*
1951 Torquay, England	37	n.a.*	n.a.*
1956 Geneva	35	2.5	4
1962 Geneva (Dillon Round)	40	4.9	7
1967 Geneva (Kennedy Round)	70	40.0	35
1973 Tokyo (Tokyo Round)	85	115.0	50
1986 Punta del Este (Uruguay Round)	117	530.0	55

*n.a. = not available

dermine the credibility of GATT and threatened the open trading system it upheld. Cars, steel, videos, semiconductors, and shoes followed textiles and clothing into "managed trade." In agriculture, where the United States, the European Union, and Japan were spending a total of $70 billion a year on subsidies, GATT rules proved unworkable. GATT did not cover services (nearly 30 percent of all world trade) or investment abroad or intellectual property (patents, copyrights, and so on), which have been of growing importance to the rich countries as the centers of manufacturing increasingly shift to the developing countries.

It was under such circumstances that in November 1985, 90 countries unanimously agreed to a U.S. proposal to launch a new round of global trade talks, eighth in the negotiation series, in September 1986 in Punta del Este, Uruguay, named the *Uruguay Round*. The focus of this round was on agricultural exports, services, intellectual properties, and voluntary trade limits.

The timing for another round of trade talks could not have been more appropriate. Protectionist forces had been gaining momentum, particularly in the United States. In Europe, where half of all economic activity relates to trade, America's protectionist sentiments had created uneasiness. The Europeans had warned that they would retaliate if the United States adopted protective measures. The developing economies did not know what to do, since the Western nations constituted a big market for their limited exportable products. Individual efforts of different nations to meet the protectionist threat did not succeed. One of the achievements of 40 years of trade liberalization had been the expansion of world trade, which was being challenged in the 1980s. What countries could not accomplish unilaterally, however, they might, it was hoped, be able to accomplish under the GATT umbrella.

The Uruguay Round had generally been acknowledged to be a make-or-break affair for GATT. The intention was to strengthen GATT rules in its traditional areas, especially in agriculture, where the rules were ambiguous; improve its enforcement powers; and extend its scope of neglected areas such as services. But after four years of talks, the Uruguay Round was suspended in December 1990 without an agreement. The talks stumbled over the refusal of various nations to make concessions demanded by various others.

Finally, in December 1993, after tortuous negotiations, trade officials from 117 nations wrapped up a trade pact that slashed tariffs and reduced subsidies globally. It was intended to reduce barriers to trade in goods, including tariffs and such nontariff barriers as quotas, export subsidies, and anti-import regulations. It also was intended to extend the 47-year-old GATT, which functioned as a rule book for international trade, to agriculture, financial, and other services, as well as serving to protect intellectual property such as patents. The Uruguay Round agreement met some of these goals, but negotiators jettisoned several controversial issues at the last minute. Following are its key results.[18]

Tariffs The United States, Europe, and other major industrial powers agreed to eliminate tariffs altogether on pharmaceuticals, construction equipment, medical equipment, paper, and steel. In all, the share of goods imported by developed countries without tariffs should more than double, to 43 percent from 20 percent; for developing countries it should rise to 45 percent from 22 percent. Tariffs also are to be cut substantially on chemicals, wood, and aluminum. Most tariffs on microprocessors would remain at zero, but those on memory chips and others would drop to 7 percent from 14 percent. Industrial tariffs, which now average 4.7 percent of the value of the products traded, would be reduced to an average of 3 percent.

Dumping The agreement provided for tougher and quicker GATT actions to resolve disputes over use of antidumping laws, invoked by the United States and Europe to impose penalties on foreign producers that sell goods abroad below cost. Developing nations, often the subject of such antidumping laws, sought to curtail their use. Nonetheless, the final compromise is closer to the U.S. and European position.

Textiles and Apparel Textiles and clothing are the most important export for many developing countries, accounting for nearly a quarter of their industrial exports. A system of quotas that limited imports of textiles and apparel to the United States and other developed countries, the Multi-Fiber Arrangement, will be phased out over 10 years. Most U.S. textile tariffs would be reduced by about 25 percent.

Intellectual Property The pact provides for 20-year protection of patents, trademarks, and copyrights. However, it allows developing countries at least 10 years to phase in patent protection for pharmaceuticals.

Agriculture Countries that export farm goods will reduce the volume of subsidized exports by 21 percent over 6 years. Bans on rice imports in Japan and South Korea will be lifted. Quotas for imports of sugar, dairy, and peanuts to the United States will be phased out and replaced by tariffs. Initial access to previously closed markets would equal at least 3 percent of domestic consumption; Japan agreed to allow the share of imported rice to increase to 4 percent in 1995 and 8 percent over six years. The largest tariff cuts are for cut flowers; the smallest, for dairy products.

Service Trade in services among GATT members amounts to more than $900 billion a year but has not previously been covered by GATT rules. Developing countries agreed to open their markets in legal services, accounting, and software. However, U.S. negotiators failed to secure access to foreign markets that are largely closed to U.S. banks and securities firms such as Japan, several Southeast Asian nations, and many developing countries. The United States agreed to open its doors to foreign financial-services firms but asserted the right to limit access to firms from nations that fail to reciprocate.

Audiovisual Services Among the very last remaining issues was a dispute between the United States and the European Union, France especially, over European limits on foreign programming shown on European television and the use of taxes on movie tickets and blank videocassettes to subsidize the French film industry. Unable to resolve this thorny issue, negotiators agreed to drop it altogether.

Subsidies The agreement limited government subsidies for research in such goods as computer chips to 50 percent of applied research (that which leads to the first prototype) and 75 percent of basic research, and allowed governments to average the limits for research that was a combination of the two.

Multilateral Trade Organization The agreement created a *World Trade Organization (WTO)* to replace the GATT secretariat. The WTO has more authority to oversee trade in services and agriculture than GATT did.[19]

Estimates by the World Bank and the Organization for Economic Cooperation and Development (OECD) suggest that the Uruguay Round agreement could eventually be worth some $213–$274 billion each year to the world economy.[20] Such numbers, at best sophisticated conjecture, are almost certainly conservative because they do not take into account benefits from strengthening GATT's rules and from liberalizing investment and trade in services. The gains are likely to accrue as follows: European Union, $82 billion, China $38 billion, Japan $29 billion, United States $25 billion, EFTA $15 billion, Latin America $9 billion, other Asian nations $6 billion, and other nations $8 billion (see International Marketing Highlight 2.3).

With the Uruguay Round behind them, at the behest of the United States the WTO members met in Seattle in December 1999 to launch another round of trade talks. The Seattle talks agenda included setting a timetable for global negotiations to lower tariffs, eliminate export subsidies, consider the link between trade rules and labor standards, and initiate talks on trade in agriculture and services. Unfortunately, the talks collapsed, but the delegates from 135 nations agreed to assemble in Geneva for further haggling in a year or two.[21] The main reason for the breakdown of the talks even before getting underway were the protests by more than 35,000 activists who aggressively demonstrated against further globalization. Included among them were the members of the U.S. trade unions and companies who had lost their jobs or businesses to developing countries, as well as those concerned about protection of the environment. But the breakdown of these talks should not be viewed as the end of trade liberalization. Rather, it shows the need for a greater sensitivity to the victims of globalization, wherever they may be (see International Marketing Highlight 2.3).

Despite the problem in Seattle, trade cooperation among nations continues to progress. A noteworthy event has been China's entry into the WTO. In May 2000, the U.S. Congress approved the Chinese deal leading China to joint the WTO as a member. Most of the opposition to China was based on the notion that bringing China into the WTO would make it impossible to get labor and environmental standards incorporated into global trade rules, since China is too big a country to be pushed around.[22] But, under heavy pressure from corporate America, Congress voted for letting China in.

███████████████   **International Marketing Highlight 2.3**   ███████████████

Trade and Development: Rich Countries versus Poor Countries

In 1993, when the Uruguay Round, was completed, it was said that poor countries would benefit most. Six years on, that claim sounds rather hollow.

Developing countries have three big complaints. First, they are being forced to open their markets too far, too fast. Second, rich countries are conspiring to keep their markets closed. And third, they lack the resources and information to negotiate effectively, to implement trade agreements, and to exploit world trade rules to their advantage.

The first complaint is wide of the mark. Although developing countries agreed to make deep tariff cuts in the Uruguay Round, that is a gain not a loss. Poor countries benefit from opening their markets, even unilaterally, since consumers can buy cheaper imports, and foreign competition spurs domestic producers to greater efficiency.

But there is a good deal of truth in their other two charges. Rich countries cut their tariffs by less in the Uruguay Round than poor ones did. Since then, they have found new ways to close their markets, notably by imposing antidumping duties on imports they deem "unfairly cheap." Rich countries are particularly protectionist in many of the sectors where developing countries are best able to compete, such as agriculture, textiles, and clothing. As a result, rich countries' average tariffs on manufacturing imports from poor countries are four times higher than those on imports from other rich countries. This imposes a big burden on poor countries. It has been estimated that they could export $700 billion more a year by 2005 if rich countries did more to open their markets.

Poor countries are also hobbled by a lack of know-how. Many had little understanding of what they had signed up to in the Uruguay Round. That ignorance is now costing them dear. A study had indicated that implementing commitments to improve trade procedures and establish technical and intellectual property standards can cost more than a year's development budget for the poorest countries.

Moreover, in those areas where poor countries could benefit from world trade rules, they are often unable to do so. On the whole, poor countries are justified in feeling they get a raw deal.

Source: The Economist, September 25, 1999, p. 89.

U.S. Trade Liberalization

Liberalization of U.S. foreign trade began with the enactment of the Reciprocal Trade Agreement Act of 1934. With that act, Congress authorized the president to reduce then-existing tariff duties by 50 percent. A noteworthy aspect of the act was the inclusion of the *most-favored-nation clause,* which limited discrimination in trade by extending to third parties the same terms provided to contracting parties. This clause has become a fundamental principle of U.S. trade policy.

The Reciprocal Trade Agreement Act of 1934 encouraged bilateral agreements that would increase U.S. exports as long as the exports did not adversely affect domestic industry. In effect, the injury to domestic industry could not take place because of highly protective tariff rates and an item-by-item approach to negotiations that would allow certain commodities to be excluded if a decrease in rates would result in an increase in imports.

The Reciprocal Trade Agreement Act was extended every three years, and by 1945 the United States had concluded negotiations with 29 countries. Overall, the act helped in reducing the average rate of tariffs on taxable imports into the United States from 47 percent in 1934 to 28 percent in 1945. In 1945 Congress authorized the president to cut rates by an additional 50 percent. While the act has been successful in reducing tariff barriers, it did little to reduce such nontariff barriers as quotas and internal taxes.

The second phase in U.S. trade liberalization efforts came in 1947. At that time the United States and 22 other major trading nations negotiated simultaneously for both reduction of tariffs and removal of trade barriers. These efforts, as previously discussed, resulted in the establishment of GATT. GATT institutionalized multilateral tariff negotiations by promoting the unconditional most-favored-nation principle—that is, a tariff reduction given to one trading nation had to apply to all other trading nations that were signatures to the GATT.

The Trade Expansion Act of 1962 marked another phase in U.S. foreign trade policy. This act authorized the president to (1) reduce tariffs up to 50 percent of the rates existing as of July 1, 1962, (2) eliminate tariffs on products in which the United States and Common Market (now European Union) countries together accounted for at least 50 percent of world trade, and (3) eliminate rates that did not exceed 5 percent.[23]

The Trade Expansion Act empowered the president to negotiate across-the-board tariff reductions (rather than item-by-item reductions) and modify the safeguard provisions of the old trade agreements program. As a matter of fact, this act was designed to stimulate not only U.S. exports, but also world trade in general, so that benefits would accrue to all nations as a result of international specialization and trade. When the United States entered trade negotiations for the Kennedy Round, the authority of the Trade Expansion Act of 1962 was in effect.

In the 1970s, despite the urgency for a new international trade perspective, no effective trade legislation was passed by Congress. As a matter of fact, in the 1970s a variety of U.S. government measures hindered rather than helped trade. The Trade Act of 1974 barred export-import credit via the Export-Import Bank, which was established to finance "big-ticket" item exports like aircraft or nuclear power technology. The Foreign Corrupt Practices Act of 1977 imposed jail terms and fines for overseas payoffs by U.S. companies. The Carter administration's human rights legislation denied export-import credit to rights violators. Loans were withheld from South Africa, Uruguay, and Chile. U.S. trade embargoes banned exports to Cuba, Vietnam, Rhodesia, and other countries.

In the 1980s the Reagan administration took a variety of ad hoc measures to deal with emerging crises. In 1982 President Reagan signed the Export Trading Company Act, which was designed to attract manufacturers, export-management companies, banks, freight forwarders, and other export services into joint efforts to gain foreign markets (see Chapter 17). In the fall of 1985, to avert a possible trade war stemming from mounting protectionist pressures in Congress and elsewhere in the nation, the Reagan administration committed itself to join England, France, Germany, and Japan in pressuring the world's financial markets to lower the dollar's value. This action was planned to help the United States reduce its trade deficit. The U.S. government also unveiled a "fair trade" program built around the threat of retaliation against nations that refused to drop barriers to U.S. goods.

A hallmark of the Reagan era was the passage of the Omnibus Trade and Competitiveness Act of 1988 as a long-term solution to the problem of the U.S. trade deficit. This act was the product of a three-year effort involving Congress, the administration, and the business community. It maintained the U.S. commitment to free trade but also provided better trade-remedy tools for judicious use in opening foreign markets.

During the Bush administration, the major emphasis had been on extending the United States–Canada Free Trade Agreement into a truly North American free trade agreement, and on helping Eastern Europe, the former Soviet States, and Latin America toward greater reliance on market forces. Progress continued to be made in implementing the United States–Canada Free Trade Agreement that went into force in 1989, and Congress authorized the president to pursue a similar agreement with Mexico, with the North American Free Trade Agreement (NAFTA) resulting during the Clinton administration.

Early in his administration, President Clinton announced a new export strategy to massively upgrade the U.S. government's trade promotion efforts, in line with the direction set out by Congress in the Export Enhancement Act of 1992. The strategy comprised creating one-stop shops for consolidating federal programs traditionally handled by 19 different agencies, developing a strategic plan for each major country, providing higher-level U.S. government support for foreign government procurement (for example, wooing Saudi Arabia into buying $6 billion worth of Boeing and McDonnell civilian aircraft); increasing the Overseas Private Investment Corporation (OPIC) project limit from $50 million to $200 million (for providing insurance coverage for U.S. companies in developing countries), liberalizing high-tech exports (previously restricted in many nations), and tying foreign aid to American exports.[24] A Trade Promotion Coordinating Committee (TPCC) was established to oversee the implementation of the new export strategy.

In putting together the National Export Strategy, the administration had several assumptions in mind. First, predictions for the American economy, made it clear that no national priority, with the exception of military security, would rank higher than the creation of more and better jobs. To realize this goal, the United States would have to sell more into the marketplace beyond its shores. Second, competition for markets abroad was increasingly brutal. The United States needed to be aggressive and strategic. Traditional competitors such as Japan, France, and Germany, as well as newcomers such as South Korea and Taiwan, had been actively and skillfully seeding new markets and cementing their role as the main supplier of goods and services to countries around the globe. This activity would have to be competed against. Third, many dramatic new opportunities were opening in the world marketplace. In Asia and Latin America, economic growth was healthy, and everywhere governments were turning to open markets, making them significant for U.S.

sales. Fourth, the United States was performing far below its potential. Some 50 firms accounted for nearly half of all exports of goods. Ten states accounted for 64 percent of merchandise exports. There seemed to be tremendous room for export expansion merely if more firms began to think globally.

MNCs and World Markets

Within the last 30 years MNCs have become the most formidable single factor in world trade and investment. They play a decisive role in the allocation and use of the world's resources. They conceive new products and services, create and stimulate demand for them, and develop new modes of manufacture and distribution (see International Marketing Highlight 2.4). Consider the example of Gillette and how it participates in world markets as an MNC.

The Gillette Company

Gillette is the leading manufacturer of blades and safety razors in the world. Its products are sold in more than 200 countries and territories. Although the company's market position varies from country to country, Gillette plays an important role in most blade/razor markets.

The company so dominates shaving worldwide that its name has come to mean a razor blade in some countries. It is the leader in Europe, with a 73 percent market share, and in Latin America, with 91 percent. (In the United States, the company holds a 68 percent share of the net shaving market compared with 13 percent for closest rival Shick.[25]) Indeed, for every blade it sells at home, Gillette sells five abroad, a figure likely to grow as recent joint ventures in China, Russia, and India expand.

The company holds a dominant position in many markets, and in select markets, this dominance extends to its other product lines, such as grooming aids, toiletries, and writing instruments. According to company management, its success in international markets is based on continual efforts at product innovation and improvement, strict quality control, aggressive marketing, and able management worldwide.

In addition to U.S. and Canadian plants, Gillette has manufacturing plants in a number of countries abroad. Shaving products plants are located in Isleworth (United Kingdom), Berlin, Annecy (France), Rio de Janeiro, Buenos Aires, Cali (Colombia), Mexico City, Melbourne, and Seville. These plants serve the host country as well as other countries in the region.

███████████   **International Marketing Highlight 2.4**   ███████████

How to Become a Global Company

There is no handy formula for going global, but any company serious about joining the race will have do most or all of the following:

- Make yourself at home in all three of the world's most important markets—North America, Europe, and Asia.
- Develop new products for the whole world.
- Replace profit centers based on countries or regions with ones based on product lines.
- "Glocalize," as the Japanese call it: Make global decisions on strategic questions about products, capital, and research, but let local units decide tactical questions about packaging, marketing, and advertising.
- Overcome parochial attitudes such as the "not invented here" syndrome. Train people to think internationally, send them off on frequent trips, and give them the latest communications technology such as teleconferencing.

- Open the senior ranks to foreign employees.
- Do whatever seems best wherever it seems best, even if people at home lose jobs or responsibilities.
- In markets that you cannot penetrate on your own, find allies.

Source: Jeremy Main, "How to Go Global and Why," *Fortune*, August 28, 1989, p. 76.

During 1999 Gillette derived over 70 percent of its sales and 74 percent of its income from markets outside the United States (excluding Canada)! The company concentrates on three main product areas: shaving, stationery, and small electrical appliances. Razors and blades account for one-third of its sales, but two-thirds of its operating profits.[26]

Organization   Traditionally, Gillette International, a division of Gillette Company, was responsible for overseas manufacturing and marketing, which affects almost all of Gillette products including blades and razors, toiletries and grooming aids, and writing instruments. A few years ago, the company restructured its international operations into two groups: Gillette North Atlantic and Gillette International. Gillette North Atlantic integrates the U.S., Canadian, and most of the European operations. Gillette International is responsible for the rest of the world.

Gillette North Atlantic's organization structure integrates European and U.S. operations according to different product groups: blade and razor group, personal care group, and stationery products group. Each group has a North American Division and a European Division, the latter organized into five areas each under the leadership of a general manager as follows: Northern Europe, Western Europe, Southeast Europe, Central Europe, and Iberia.

The integration of European operations within the U.S. organization indicates Gillette's move toward becoming a truly global company. This helps the company take advantage of the European Market integration program.

Gillette International, located at company headquarters in Boston, is organized into three groups: (1) Latin American, (2) Asian-Pacific, and (3) African, Middle Eastern, and Eastern European. Each of the three groups is headed by a group general manager. In addition, there is a staff group called the Gillette International Marketing Department (GIMD), located in Boston and led by a marketing director assisted by individual specialists in each product field and by international coordinators in market research and advertising. These specialists give advice to marketing personnel worldwide.

The organization in each country revolves around a general manager to whom heads of manufacturing, marketing, personnel, and accounting report. Marketing people are employed in sales, market research, sales promotion, and brand management. The Gillette salesforce in each country handles a wide range of Gillette products, including shaving products, toiletries, and writing instruments. The salesforce is organized along the same line in each country and follows essentially the same selling technique.

Decision Making   Gillette's global decision-making system is mostly centralized. The recommendations of executives based overseas are sought and considered, but major marketing decisions, including those that concern strategic goals, the price structure, and global advertising, are made in Boston. However, both Gillette International and Gillette North Atlantic are responsible for operational decision making in their own regions.

Within Gillette International, key marketing decisions are generally made at the headquarters level in Boston, where management of the three component regions is also based. Implementation decisions, such as advertising placement and local distribution, are made at the country level.

Subsidiary executives have the authority to set their own prices as long as they stay within the centrally planned positioning strategy. Distribution strategy is similarly planned centrally and adjusted, when necessary, by the subsidiaries.

Advertising campaigns are sometimes fine-tuned at the local level. Promotion campaigns, although developed locally, must also support marketing goals established by headquarters.

Desired price relationships vis-à-vis competing brands and products are defined by product executives at headquarters. Within these parameters, subsidiary executives are responsible for setting prices in their own markets.

As part of its preparation for the post-1992 European Community, Gillette North Atlantic switched to a pan-European packaging strategy that relied less on words and more on symbols to make the same packaging usable in many countries.

Advertising Gillette International's advertising strategy is formulated at the regional level and Gillette North Atlantic's at the product group level. Each uses a single, though different advertising agency to create and coordinate its global campaigns. International retains McCann Erickson whereas North Atlantic primarily uses BBDO Worldwide Advertising Agency.

The decision not to use one agency throughout the world follows logically from the two-region organizational structure Gillette has adopted. Moreover, the company's senior management believes it is unwise to put all its international advertising eggs in one basket. These two agencies were chosen because they were deemed to be particularly strong in the operating region of the respective Gillette entity each is to serve.

Both North Atlantic and International centralize virtually all aspects of advertising. Ads are created at headquarters with only music on the basic soundtrack. Then the various messages to be used in the different countries are dubbed in with voice-overs. Consequently, ads are easily transferable from one market to the next.

In rare instances, when mandated by official regulation, overseas subsidiaries use local actors in locally shot commercials. Even then, however, the creative aspects, including the dialogue, theme, and slogan, are developed in Boston. The Gillette Sensor campaign, "Gillette, the best a man can get," is a good example of the company's global approach.

Foreign Staffing Gillette is firmly committed to staffing foreign subsidiaries with local citizens and third-country nationals. It attributes much of its international success to the strength of its overseas companies and management organizations. The company strives to be perceived as a local company in foreign markets rather than a locally established global company. For this reason, Gillette avoids filling executive openings at its subsidiaries, including those in marketing, with American expatriates.

Within Gillette International, no Americans hold group vice president positions. Latin America is headed by an Argentinean, the Africa/Middle East/Eastern Europe region by a Spaniard, and Asia/Pacific by a Briton. Most general managers are also local nationals or third-country nationals. Within Latin America, six of the seven key general managers are local nationals. Moreover, none of the eight general managers in the Asia/Pacific region is an American.

Gillette North Atlantic is similarly ethnically diverse: The general managers of the company's subsidiaries in Italy, Spain/Portugal, and Northern Europe are Italian, South African, and British, respectively.

Growth Strategy Tailoring its marketing to Third World budgets and tastes—from packaging blades so they can be sold one at a time, to educating the unshaven about the joys of a smooth face—has become an important part of Gillette's growth strategy. The company also tailors its marketing for pens, toiletries, toothbrushes, and other products in developing countries this way. Population trends favor its focus on Third World markets. The market for blades in developed countries is stagnant. Yet the Third World has a very high proportion of people under 15 years old who will be in the shaving population in a very short time. Gillette is in an excellent position to capitalize on this demographic.

Few U.S. consumer-products companies that compete in the Third World have expended as much energy or made as many inroads as Gillette. Since the company targeted the developing world in 1969, the proportion of its sales that come from Latin America, Asia, Africa, and the Middle East has doubled to 25 percent, and the dollar volume has risen eightfold.

In Latin America it began building plants in the 1940s, and Fidel Castro once told television interviewer Barbara Walters that he grew a beard during the Cuban revolution because he could not get Gillette blades while fighting in the mountains. The company's push into Asia, Africa, and the Middle East dates to 1969, when it dropped a policy of investing only where it could have wholly owned subsidiaries. That year, it formed a joint venture in Malaysia, which was threatening to bar imports of Gillette products. Since then it has added one foreign plant nearly every year in countries such as China, Egypt, Thailand, and India.

Gillette always starts with a factory that makes double-edged blades— still popular in the developing countries—and if all goes well, expands later into the production of pens, deodorants, shampoo, or toothbrushes. Only a few ventures have failed: A Yugoslav project never got off the ground, and Gillette had to sell its interests in Iran to its local partners.

Gillette sells familiar products in standardized form all over the world. But in some markets it customizes packaging. For instance, because many Latin American consumers cannot afford a seven-ounce bottle of Silkience shampoo, Gillette sells it in half-ounce plastic bubbles there. In Brazil, Gillette sells Right Guard deodorant in plastic squeeze bottles instead of metal cans (see International Marketing Highlight 2.5). In a few markets, Gillette has developed products exclusively for Third World buyers. The low-cost shaving cream is one. Another is Black Silk, a hair relaxer developed for sale to blacks in South Africa and now being sold in Kenya, Nigeria, and other African countries.

The Gillette case shows how MNCs can capitalize on opportunities far and wide the world over. Having won the loyalty of more than 700 million shavers around the world, from Kashmir to Tierra del Fuego, the company can amortize hefty development costs over fast-growing worldwide markets. Its technique is to establish shaving goods in a new market, then pour a steady stream of other Gillette products through the same retail pipelines. This is the classic approach of a successful MNC. In strictly theoretical terms, MNCs acquire raw materials and capital where they are most abundant, manufacture products where wages and other costs are lowest, and sell in the most profitable markets. In other words, MNCs seek to follow the economic law of comparative advantage—everyone benefits if each does its best work, *no matter where the work is performed.*

Summary

The classic explanation of world trade is provided by the theory of comparative advantage: when one country has an advantage over another in the production of more than one product, then it will enjoy a comparative advantage by producing only the product that provides its greatest advantage and importing the other products in exchange.

████████████   **International Marketing Highlight 2.5**   ████████████

How to Convince People to Shave

The hardest task for Gillette is convincing Third World men to shave. The company recently began dispatching portable theaters to remote villages to show movies and commercials that tout daily shaving. In South African and Indonesian versions, a bewildered bearded man enters a locker room where clean-shaven friends show him how to shave. In the Mexican version, a handsome sheriff, tracking bandits who have kidnapped a woman, pauses on the trail to shave every morning. The camera lingers as he snaps a double-edged blade into his razor. In the end, of course, the smooth-faced sheriff gets the woman.

In other places, Gillette agents with an oversized shaving brush and a mug of shaving cream lather up and shave a villager while others watch. Plastic razors are then distributed free and blades—which, of course, must be bought—are left with the local storekeeper. Such campaigns have a lasting impact.

Source: David Wessel, "Gillette Keys Sales to Third World Tastes," *The Wall Street Journal,* January 23, 1986, p. 35.

Significant world trade and investment patterns in recent years have been examined in various other ways than comparative advantage. Using the concept of product life cycle, Harvard researchers Raymond Vernon and Louis Wells observed that most products are first manufactured in the most developed countries like the United States, then exported to other advanced countries like Japan and those of Western Europe, which soon adapt the product and begin to manufacture it in their own countries. Subsequently, the first manufacturer faces tough competition from the advanced countries not only in its home market but also in the developing countries as well, where cheaper labor is available. This leads the first country to make direct investments in manufacturing in the second countries and thus counter their advantage. Despite this defensive measure, however, the first country may find it difficult to compete. This cycle continues with the result that the developing countries may eventually command the market everywhere.

In response to the limitations of the product life cycle theory, Peter Drucker advanced the concept of production sharing, which postulates splitting manufacturing into stages undertaken in different countries.

Still another theory, internalization, proposes that a firm establishes an international network linking production to its various markets and that this network enables the firm to grow by eliminating external markets in intermediate goods and thus internalizing those markets within the firm.

Two types of trade barriers, tariff and nontariff, have been erected to protect national economies and employment. Efforts at liberalizing international trade in a systematic fashion began after World War II with the establishment of GATT. In all, eight rounds of multilateral negotiations have been held under GATT toward this end. United States legislative efforts have both encouraged and hindered liberal trade with other nations.

Unquestionably, the MNC is the agent of modern day international business. The global business practices of the Gillette Company are illustrative of multinational trade and business in the next century.

Review Questions

1. Differentiate between absolute and relative advantage. Illustrate, with the help of an example, how comparative (relative) advantage encourages trade.
2. Despite the comparative advantage argument, nations continue to opt for self-sufficiency. How would you explain this behavior?

3. What are the limitations of the product life cycle theory of international trade?
4. Use an example to explain the concept of production sharing.
5. What factors lead countries to seek protection against imports?
6. What are the major types of tariffs that nations use against imports?
7. Discuss the major types of nontariff barriers.
8. What role have GATT agreements played in reducing trade barriers?
9. What is the World Trade Organization? What relationship does it have with GATT?

Creative Questions

1. Nontariff barriers continue to be a major deterrent to world trade. Could the forerunner of GATT, the WTO, be entrusted the task of enforcing the implementation of agreed upon rules to eliminate nontariff barriers? Will nations agree to specific rules relative to nontariff barriers? Will they let the WTO punish countries that break the rules?
2. What is the function of the U.S. Trade Representative's Office? How does it differ from that of the U.S. International Trade Commission? For more effective trade policy, should these two organizations be merged?

Endnotes

1. Value can sometimes be uncoupled from production hours, but typically only in cases of long-term scarcity (as with some precious metals) or when the quality of one producer's manufactured products is not matched by other suppliers. In these circumstances, virtual monopolies can develop.

2. See William W. Lewis, Hans Gersbach, Tom Jansen, and Koji Sakate, "The Secret to Competitiveness—Competition," *The McKinsey Quarterly*, November 4, 1993, pp. 29–44.

3. Peter F. Drucker, "Low Wages No Longer Give Competitive Edge," *The Wall Street Journal*, March 16, 1988, p. 23. Also see "Asia's Costly Labor Problems," *The Economist*, September 21, 1996, p. 62.

4. G. Todd Russell, "Business Travelers Rate Asia's Airlines as the World's Best," *The Asian Wall Street Journal Weekly*, November 18, 1985, p. 1.

5. Raymond Vernon, "International Investment and International Trade in the Product Cycle," *Quarterly Journal of Economics*, May 1966, pp. 190–207. Also see Raymond Vernon, *Sovereignty at Bay* (New York: Basic Books, 1971), pp. 65–112; Louis T. Wells, Jr., "Test of a Product Cycle Model of International Trade," *Quarterly Journal of Economics*, February 1969, pp. 152–162.

6. Louis T. Wells, Jr., "A Product Life Cycle for International Trade?" *Journal of Marketing*, July 1968, pp. 1–6. Also see J. F. Hennart, *A Theory of Multinational Enterprise* (Ann Arbor: University of Michigan Press, 1982).

7. James M. Lutz and Robert T. Green. "The Product Life Cycle and the Export Position of the United States," *Journal of International Business Studies*, Winter 1983, pp. 77–94. Also see Sak Onkvisit and John J. Shaw, "An Examination of the International Product Life Cycle and Its Application within Marketing," *Columbia Journal of World Business*, Fall 1983, pp. 73–78.

8. Alicia Mullor-Sebastian, "The Product Life Cycle Theory: Empirical Evidence," *Journal of International Business Studies*, Winter 1983, pp. 95–106.

9. Peter F. Drucker, "The Rise of Production Sharing," *The Wall Street Journal*, March 15, 1977, p. 24. Also see Martin K. Starr, "Global Production and Operations Strategy," *Columbia Journal of World Business*, Winter 1984, pp. 17–22.

10. Peter F. Drucker, "Economics Erases National Boundaries," excerpt ad from *Managing in Turbulent Times* by Peter F. Drucker (New York: Harper & Row, 1979), in *Industry Week*, April 28, 1980, pp. 63–64.

11. Joan Magretta, "An Interview with Victor Fung," *Harvard Business Review*, September–October 1998, pp. 102–117.

12. Peter J. Buckley, *Multinational Enterprises and Economic Analysis* (Cambridge, England: Cambridge University Press, 1982).

13. "The Never-Ending Question," *The Economist*, July 3, 1999, p. 68.

14. A. D. Cao, "Non-tariff Barriers to U.S. Manufactured Exports," *Columbia Journal of World Business*, Summer 1980, pp. 93–102. Also see Alan Bauerschmidt, Daniel Sullivan, and Kate Gillespie, "Common Factors Underlying Barriers to Export: Studies in the U.S. Paper Industry," *Journal of International Business Studies*, Fall 1985, pp. 111–124.

15. "Big Sugar May Be About to Take Its Lumps," *Business Week*, May 15, 1996, p. 45.

16. See: Tacho Bark and Jaime de Melo, "Export Quota Allocations, Export Earnings, and Market Diversification," *The World Bank Economic Review*, 2 (no. 3): 341–348, 1998.

17. At the time of the GATT negotiations, nations were also working toward setting up an international trade organization

(ITO), but the matter was dropped since the participating nations failed to come to an agreement.

18. "The Final Act of the Uruguay Round: A Summary," *International Trade Forum*, No. 1, 1994, pp. 4–21. Also see "Business Aspects of the Uruguay Round Agreements," *International Trade Forum*, No. 2, 1996, pp. 6–10.

19. Helene Cooper and Bhushan Bahrel, "World's Best Hope for Global Trade Topples Few Barriers," *The Wall Street Journal*, December 3, 1996, p. 1.

20. "The Eleventh Hour," *The Economist*, December 4, 1993, p. 23.

21. Helene Cooper et al., "WTO's Failure in Bid To Launch Trade Talks Emboldens Protesters," *The Wall Street Journal*, December 6, 1999, p. A1.

22. "Welcome To The Club," *Business Week*, November 29, 1999, p.34. Also see "China and the WTO: Prepare for Fireworks," *The Economist*, January 22, 2000, p.31.

23. *Future United States Foreign Trade Policy*, report to the president, submitted by the Special Representative for Trade Negotiations (Washington, DC: U.S. Government Printing Office, 1969). Also see Gordon O. Weil, *Trade Policy in the 70s* (New York: The Twentieth Century Fund, 1969).

24. The National Export Strategy," *Business America*, April 1994, pp. 5–10. Also see *Business America*, November 1997, pp. 6–14.

25. Mark Maremont, "Gillette Finally Reveals Its Vision of the Future...," *The Wall Street Journal*, April 14, 1998, p. A1.

26. See Gillette Company's annual report, 1999.

PART 2

Perspectives of International Markets

Global Marketing

CHAPTER FOCUS_____

After studying this chapter, you should be able to

■ Compare market opportunities in different parts of the world.

■ Discuss the dimensions of global markets.

■ Describe the forces behind market globalization.

■ Explain the rationale for segmenting the international market.

■ Evaluate different criteria for grouping countries.

There are over 200 countries in the world. It is difficult to imagine that a marketer would be interested in serving the entire global market. Granted, some companies such as Kodak and Coca-Cola are active in over 100 countries. However, such a vast coverage of market develops gradually. Initially, a company may enter just one country or a few countries. From there, the scope may broaden as the company brings other countries within its fold.

Obviously, the company must choose among the countries of the world in order to identify its target markets. Worldwide there is great contrast economically, culturally, and politically among nations. These contrasts mean that an overseas marketer cannot select target countries randomly, but must employ workable criteria to analyze the world market and choose those countries where the company's product or service has the best opportunity for success. While individual countries have peculiarities, they also have similarities that they share with other countries, and such bases render some grouping device feasible.

What are the characteristics of that global marketplace, the international market? What is the rationale for grouping countries into segments? What procedure would a company employ to segment the international market? How can in-country segmentation be achieved?

Global Market

The most basic information needed to appraise global markets concerns population, because the people, of course, constitute the market. The population of the world reached an estimated 6 billion in 1999. According to the latest estimates from the Population Division of the United Nations, this total is expected to increase to 7.2 billion by 2025. Current world population is growing at about 1.3 percent per year. This is a slight decline from the peak rate of 1.9 percent, but the absolute number of people being added to the world's population each year is still increasing. The figure is expected to peak by 2010, at about 75 million additional people per year.[1]

Population growth rates vary significantly by region. Europe has the lowest rate of population growth, at only about 0.3 percent per year. Several European countries are experiencing declining populations, including Austria, Denmark, Germany, Luxembourg, and Sweden. Growth rates are also below 1 percent per year in North America.

The regions with the highest population growth rates are Africa (3 percent per year), Latin America (2 percent per year), and South Asia (1.9 percent per year). China, the world's most populous country, is growing at only about 1.2 percent per year. Even so, that rate means that China's population increases by over 12 million each year. The world's second largest country, India, is growing at over 1.7 percent per year. It reached 998 million in 1999, and is expected to grow to 1.1 billion by about 2010 (see International marketing Highlight 3.1).

One striking aspect of population growth in the developing countries is the rapid rate of urbanization. The urban population is growing at less than 1 percent in Europe and North America, but it is growing at almost 3.5 percent in the developing world. Today 15 of the 20 largest urban agglomerations are in the developing world. By the year 2005, 17 of the 20 largest cities will be in the developing world. The only developed-country cities in the top 20 will be Tokyo, New York, and Los Angeles. The world's largest cities will be Mexico City (26 million), Sao Paulo (24 million), and Calcutta and Mumbai (both over 16 million).[2] These statistics show that the total markets in Europe and North America will not be increasing, because population will not add much to total market size. Of course, these populations are growing older, so that certain segments will have increasing numbers. For example, the total population of Europe increased only 1.6 percent from 1995 to 2000, but the over-65 population increased by 12 percent during the same period.

████████ ████ **International Marketing Highlight 3.1** ████ ████████

Babies Are Our Only Customers Worldwide

Gerber Products Co. is going global with a host of child-care products in an effort to break out of its mild-mannered, domestic baby-food niche.

The company has been fine-tuning its "superbranding" campaign for years. It feels it has developed a real following among mothers, and it is going to utilize its brand name to market products in three different categories: food and formula, baby-care products, and clothing.

Market research shows that moms around the globe recognize and trust the Gerber logo. The company's baby food already is sold in Mexico, Puerto Rico, Europe, and the Far East. Sales have expanded into Poland, Egypt, Russia, and Eastern Europe.

However, internationally, the company is an infant. About 95 percent of the babies born in the world are born outside the United States. Yet right now, international sales account for only about 5 percent of the company's total sales.

Gerber will introduce the baby-food lines in new international markets first, then follow with baby-care products and apparel.

Source: *Marketing News,* September 26, 1991, p. 22.

The population variable provides a snapshot of market opportunity in a country, but a variety of other factors must be considered to identify viable markets. For example, in the developing world, the increase in numbers does not necessarily mean increased market opportunity. The fastest growing region, Africa, is also experiencing low or negative rates of economic growth per capita. Much of Latin America is hampered by huge external debts that force those countries to try to limit imports while using their resources to generate foreign exchange for debt service. In most of these cases, the problem of foreign debt will have to be solved before the growing populations will translate into large markets, despite their economic liberalization programs.

Taking into account factors such as urbanization, consumption patterns, infrastructure, and overall industrialization, let us examine different parts of the global market.

Triad Market

The *triad market* refers to the United States and Canada, Japan, and Western European countries. They account for approximately 14 percent of the world's population, yet they represent over 70 percent of world gross product. As such, these countries absorb the major proportion of capital and consumer products and thus are the most advanced consuming societies in the world. Not only do most product innovations take place in these countries, but they also serve as the opinion leaders and mold the purchasing and consumption behavior of the remaining 86 percent of the world's population.

For example, over 90 percent of the computers worldwide are used by triad countries. In the case of numerically controlled machine tools, almost 100 percent are distributed in the triad market. The same pattern follows in consumer products. Triad accounts for 90 percent of the demand for electronic consumer goods. What these statistics point to is that a company that ignores the market potential of the triad does so at its own peril.[3]

An interesting characteristic of the triad market is the universalization of needs. For example, not too long ago manufacturers of capital equipment produced machinery that reflected strong cultural distinctions. West German machines reflected that nation's penchant for craftsmanship while American equipment was often extravagant in its use of raw materials. But these distinctions have disappeared. The best-selling factory machines have lost the "art" element that distinguished them and have become much more similar, both in appearance and in the level of skills they require to produce. The current revolution in production engineering has brought about ever-increasing global standards of performance. In an era when productivity improvements can quickly determine their life or death on a global scale, companies cannot afford to indulge themselves in a metallic piece of art that will last 30 years (see International Marketing Highlight 3.2).

At the same time, consumer markets have become fairly homogeneous. Ohmae notes,

> The Triad consumption pattern, which is both a cause and an effect of cultural patterns, has its roots to a large extent in the educational system. As educational systems enable more people to use technology, they tend to become more similar to each other. It follows, therefore, that education leading to higher levels of technological achievement also tends to eradicate differences in lifestyles. Penetration of television, which enables everyone possessing a television set to share sophisticated behavioral information instantaneously throughout the world, has also accelerated this trend. There are, for example, 750 million consumers in all three parts of the Triad (Japan, the United States and Canada, and the nations of Western Europe), with strikingly similar needs and preferences. . . . A new generation worships the universal "now" gods—ABBA, Levi's and Arpege. . . .Youngsters in Denmark, West Germany, Japan, and California are all growing up with ketchup, jeans, guitars. Their lifestyles, aspirations, and desires are so similar that you might call them "OECDites" or Triadians, rather than by names denoting their national identity.[4]

There are many reasons for the similarities and commonalities in the triad's consumer demand and lifestyle patterns. First, the purchasing power of triad residents, as expressed in discretionary income per individual, is more than 10 times greater than that of residents of developing countries. For example, television penetration in triad countries is greater than 94 percent, whereas in newly industrialized countries it is 25 percent, and for the developing countries less than 10 percent. Second, the technological infrastructure of triad countries is more advanced. Over 70 percent of households there have a telephone, making it feasible to use such products as facsimile, telex, and digital data transmission/processing equipment. Such is not the case outside the triad. Third, the educational level is much higher in triad nations than in other parts of the world. Fourth, the number of physicians per 10,000 in triad countries exceeds 30, which creates demand for pharmaceuticals and medical electronics. Fifth, better transportation infrastructure in the triad leads to opportunities not feasible in less-developed markets. For example, paved roads make rapid adoption of radial tires and sports cars possible.

▬▬▬▬▬ International Marketing Highlight 3.2 ▬▬▬▬▬

Who Sells What, Where?

There may be "global markets" out there, but "global brands" have not captured them yet. This was the finding of a survey of United States-based manufacturers of consumer nondurable goods. Of the 85 brands included in the survey, 29, or 34 percent, were not marketed outside the United States at all. Others were marketed only marginally abroad.

Companies surveyed showed a clear preference for selling their goods in markets culturally similar to the United States: Canada and the United Kingdom. While one might argue that Canada was targeted so frequently because of its geographical proximity to the United States, the choice of the United Kingdom cannot be so easily explained. It is as far away as many other foreign countries, and its population and economy are smaller than several other foreign markets.

Among the survey's other key findings:

• *Canada is the star.* Canada was the largest foreign market by far for U.S. brands (33 of the 56 sold abroad). In fact, for 13 brands, Canada is the only foreign market. The United Kingdom was a distant second, being the largest foreign market for five brands. Mexico was next, with four brands, followed by [the former] West Germany with three.

• *Few mega-brands exist.* There were only 14 "mega-brands," ones that could be termed truly global in that they were marketed in more than 50 countries. Those most internationalized were mainly soft drinks, cleaning products, and over-the-counter drugs. Food products rely less on standard branding worldwide.

• *Older products are more international.* An interesting finding was that a majority (57 percent) of the brands sold abroad were launched before 1960. This challenges the notion that new brands are more likely than older brands to be designed for global markets.

• *No name changes.* One might expect the limited distribution of U.S. brands overseas to be offset somewhat by foreign production of exports under different brand names, but this is not the case. Few survey respondents indicated that they sell similar items abroad under different brand names.

Source: International Marketing Review, 6 (1989): 7–19; and *Journal of Advertising,* 17 (1988): 14–22.

Pacific Rim

Despite the recent currency problems of South Korea, Indonesia, and Thailand, the Pacific Rim's growing power is the corporate challenge of the next century.[5] The long-anticipated emergence of the countries in the region (South Korea, Singapore, Taiwan, Hong Kong, Malaysia, Thailand, Indonesia, and the Philippines) as economic powerhouses is shaping up. Steel consumption in the region (including Japan) is higher than in the United States and in Europe. Similarly, demand in the Pacific Rim (again, including Japan) for semiconductors exceeds that of the European Union.

Some view Pacific Rim nations as a better business bet than Eastern Europe. According to them, Eastern Europe's embrace of free enterprise is just a shaky first step toward prosperity, and the hard part will be catching up with the work habits and entrepreneurship of an entrenched capitalistic system. These countries will find it difficult to shed the effects of 45 years of Marxism-Leninism to become "gung-ho" like the Japanese and citizens of the newly industrializing economies.

The Pacific Rim offers a variety of opportunities for American companies, from cars to telecommunications equipment, airline seats and banking services, and a host of other products. However, it is a very competitive market. Not only are potent Japanese companies active in this market, but so are aggressive, growing conglomerates from other countries in the region. Asian producers outside Japan have already gained 25 percent of the global market for personal computers.

Without the fanfare of a common market, the Pacific Rim is becoming an economically cohesive region. A new division of labor is taking place in manufacturing. Japan and the "four dragons"—Singapore, Hong Kong, Taiwan, and South Korea—provide most of the capital and expertise for the region's other nations, which have an abundance of natural resources and labor.

Unlike Japan, other countries in the region are more amenable to buying western products and forming manufacturing alliances with western companies. The point may be illustrated with reference to General Motors Corporation. The company owns a 30 percent stake in a $100 million plant in China that produces up to 60,000 light trucks annually. It has boosted distribution and marketing of Opels in Hong Kong and Singapore. In addition, it exports 14,000 U.S.–made cars to Taiwan annually and plans to assemble 20,000 Opels a year there. Further, it has set up auto assembly operations in Indonesia, Malaysia, and Thailand.[6]

Singapore in particular is promoting what it calls a "growth triangle," in which MNCs can offset the cost of high wages for Singapore's skilled workers by also using lower-paid, less-skilled workers in nearby Indonesia and Malaysia. With the lifting of the

19-year-old trade embargo on Vietnam, another potentially lucrative market has opened in Southeast Asia.

American investments in the region generally pay off handsomely. A U.S. Department of Commerce study showed average annual returns of 31.2 percent in Singapore, 28.8 percent in Malaysia, 17.9 percent in South Korea, 23.6 percent in Hong Kong, 22.2 percent in Taiwan, and 14.1 percent in Japan versus 15.2 percent for U.S. investments in all foreign countries.[7]

For all its burgeoning strength, however, the Pacific Rim faces risks. The region's economic and political stability in the long run could be shaken here and there as strong leaders hand over power, or as they economically overextend. The 1997–1998 currency crisis in the region is a case in point.

The risks of not tapping the region's potential are global. If U.S. companies do not establish a firm position in the region, competitors from Japan, Taiwan, and Korea will gain more strength at home and be prepared to make even bigger assaults on markets in America and Europe.

Postcommunist Countries

The pace of the political transformations that have swept Eastern Europe and the former Soviet Union is unprecedented. As the people of these communist countries toppled their governments, new markets took shape in those regions. The tattered nations are lurching toward a Western economic orbit, and when they reach it, Western Europe's focus will shift eastward. Europe's accent will become more Germanic and Slavic, and its potential economic might will grow to a staggering size—one nearly as large as the United States and Japan combined. As a result, the West stands to gain new markets as well as a labor supply that is well-trained and socially stable. It is a tantalizing prospect that Europe may produce the world's next economic miracle, harnessing the rich dynamism of the West to the untapped talent and energy of the East.[8]

Yet the immediate task of rescuing the backward economies of Eastern Europe is an enormous challenge. Unwinding the command economies without heaping too much pain on the populace is a herculean job. Privatizing industrial units, keeping inflation down, and coping with massive layoffs are some of the difficulties that await. So far, the biggest economies—Czechoslovakia, Hungary, and Poland—are making the most progress. Yugoslavia, racked by ethnic conflict, split into different, warring nations. Less developed Romania and Bulgaria are barely out from under their former rulers.

The challenges are huge, but if the East can forge new links with the West without inflaming the continent's old nationalistic passions, the world may well be headed for a "Pax Europa," with prosperity helping to ensure the peace.

At this time, Eastern Europe is more of a market for foreign investment and aid than for manufactured goods. Since communism crumbled in 1989, foreign investors have been looking hard at Eastern European countries. By the end of 1993 almost 15,000 foreign joint ventures had been established in Poland, Hungary, and former Czechoslovakia.[9] Once the changeover to the market economy is complete, these countries should offer attractive markets, but it is impossible to predict how long the process will take.

Experts claim that Eastern Europe's progress depends on two factors: its ability to attract adequate capital and the ability of the people to tolerate hardships during the changeover. According to one estimate, the cost of modernizing industry and infrastructure in Eastern Europe would be $500 billion over the next 15 to 20 years.[10] Considering the enormity of the task, it may be safe to say that Eastern Europe markets cannot evolve into mass markets on Western lines for another 20 years. In the interim, there will be an ad hoc opportunity for selling capital equipment, telecommunications, and, from time

Household-Equipment Ownership: Percent of Households, in Selected Countries

	Czech Republic	Hungary	Romania	Ukraine
CD players	27	18	8	3
Color television sets	94	89	70	84
Deep freezers	66	60	24	2
Microwaves	42	40	2	3
Mobile phones	12	18	4	1
Personal computers	15	16	6	1
Telephones (regular)	64	73	39	35
VCRs	40	46	15	16

Source: The Central and Eastern European Consumer, OECD, 1999.

to time, limited amounts of consumer goods. As Exhibit 3.1 shows, the household-equipment ownership in Eastern Europe is small except for color television sets. People are still making only modest changes in this respect.

The Commonwealth of Independent States poses similar problems. Russia is taking drastic steps to liberalize its economy quickly. The country is adopting a high-risk austerity program to stabilize its collapsed economy and integrate it with the rest of the world's. Russian leaders are convinced that only a radical reform program can save the country from a return to dangerous central control. However, many wonder if too much is being done too soon. Although prices have begun to increase at a slower pace, and more food is available in stores, enterprises around the country are hurting badly, and unemployment is increasing sharply. At the same time corruption is rampant.

Time is clearly of the essence. With economic pain stirring, Russia could become explosive. On the other hand, Russia could emerge as a healthy economy in the early years of the new century.

To westerners, Russia offers both a challenge and an opportunity. By and large, companies are optimistic about the country, and they are carefully watching its progress. If the economic measures succeed, Russia will offer all sorts of attractive opportunities.

Among other members of the commonwealth, the Baltics (Estonia, Latvia, and Lithuania) are expected to switch to market economies sooner than others. With a total population of less than 8 million, these countries are mere blips on the map of Europe, but they have a highly motivated, well-trained, and low-paid work force. Baltic workers are more productive than Russian workers, and the Baltic countries could emerge as a viable market if their goods could be sold for hard currency in Western Europe. But it is highly uncertain whether those goods could compete in today's European market, even at lower prices, considering the fact that those nations have been isolated from the West for more than 50 years, Even so, there are plenty of companies willing to wait several years until they can establish a manufacturing or service operation in the Baltics to take advantage of the emerging Russian market.

Opportunities in other former Soviet republics are hard to pinpoint at this time. Five of them (Azerbaijan, Uzbekistan, Turkmenistan, Kyrgyzstan, and Tajikistan) have joined Iran, Turkey, and Pakistan to become part of an Islamic common market. Presumably, their economic perspectives would be determined by the policies pursued by their Muslim brethren. Largely Christian Georgia and Armenia will stay closer to Russia in their endeavor to revamp their economies. The direction that Moldavia, Ukraine, and Byelorussia may adopt is uncertain. For example, Moldavia might link up with Romania, while Ukraine and Byelorussia may follow an independent course. In any event, considering their smaller populations, they are unlikely to offer any substantial market opportunity.

Latin America

As governments cut tariffs, welcome foreign companies, and unshackle their economies, market opportunities in Latin America abound. The severe miseries of the 1980s shocked the Latin countries into abandoning the statism, populism, and protectionism that had crippled their economies since colonial times. One after another in the late 1980s, governments in Latin America thrust their businesspeople into the free market, cutting tariffs, welcoming foreign investment, and unloading hopelessly unprofitable state enterprises. Debt is becoming manageable now, and incomes are growing.

The United States has a better opportunity in the region than other nations, since it has the inside track. Western European nations are largely occupied with Eastern Europe, and the Japanese remain focused mainly on developed countries.

Latin America is more attractive, especially to U.S. firms, than Eastern Europe. It can feed itself and has a business infrastructure, albeit rickety. U.S. trade with the region is already 15 times greater than with Eastern Europe. Indeed, Latin America holds the key to the U.S. trade deficit. Per capita consumption of basic foods and beverages in Latin America should continue to grow over the long term. The region's appealing demographics—notably, an expanding population segment of 15- to 50-year-olds and rising household incomes—bode well for U.S. companies in these sectors (see International marketing Highlight 3.3). But new entrants face two distinct challenges: brand loyalty and complex distribution demands. Well-established names and operations have a strong edge in Latin America, and some could endure for years despite growing competition. Foreign brands meet with greater acceptance where there are no home-grown equivalents. For instance, most countries have no local colas and few domestic snack-food brands. This fact accounts for the regionwide success of Coca-Cola and Sabritas, PepsiCo's snack unit.[11]

Latin America's distribution channels are fragmented, particularly in Mexico, where a large proportion of sales occur at mom-and-pop stores, in which shelf space is limited. The rise of supermarkets and hypermarkets, however, which carry many more brands, is facilitating distribution for new players.

International Marketing Highlight 3.3

Segmenting the Latin American Market

Gallup came up with four major categories of Latin American consumers and eight segments within those categories.

The "traditional elite" is 9 percent of the total population and 11 percent of the effective market base, the percentage of the total population excluding the 17 percent extreme poverty population. This segment's monthly income is equivalent to at least U.S. $1,800.

The "emerging professional elite" comprise 12 percent of the total population and 14 percent of the market base, with a monthly income of at least $1,800.

The middle class makes up 27 percent of the population and 33 percent of the market base with a monthly income of $800 to $1,800. The "progressive upper middle class" is 11 percent of the population and 13 percent of the market base. The "self-made middle class" is 9 percent and 11 percent respectively, and the "skilled middle class" is 7 percent and 9 percent, respectively.

The working class, which is 35 percent of the population and 42 percent of the effective market base has a monthly income of less than $800 and contains the "self-skilled working class" (11 percent, 13 percent), the "industrial working class" (12 percent, 14 percent), and the "struggling working class" (12 percent, 15 percent).

Gallup estimates there are 5.5 million traditional elites and 7 million emerging professional elites. Other segments and their estimated populations: progressive upper middle class, 6.5 million; self-made middle class, 5.5 million; skilled middle class, 4.5 million;

self-skilled working class, 6.5 million; industrial working class, 7 million; and struggling working class, 7.5 million.

Sixty-one percent of the self-made middle class and 54 percent of the industrial working class engaged in activities with children. The lowest participation was among traditional elites (34 percent) and emerging professional elites (35 percent).

Buying toys ranked highest among the industrial working class (43 percent bought them), self-made middle class (37 percent), and traditional elite (35 percent). The lowest interest was shown by the self-skilled working class (23 percent), the struggling working class (24 percent), and the emerging professional elite (27 percent).

Movie-going ranked highest among the emerging professional elite (63 percent attended movies), traditional elite (58 percent), and progressive upper middle class (55 percent). Only 29 percent of the self-skilled working class goes to the movies.

Fifty-three percent of the traditional elite, 49 percent of the progressive upper middle class, and 49 percent of the industrial working class buy perfume.

Buying records is most popular among the traditional elite (52 percent), emerging professional elite (48 percent), progressive upper middle class (48 percent), and industrial working class (40 percent).

Source: Marketing News, August 14, 1998. p.5.

Although opportunities beckon, Latin America still suffers from acute economic problems. For example, inflation continues to be high, and the debt problem still looms large. Slow or disappointing progress could turn the poor against free markets and back to a populist, anti-Yankee leader. Nonetheless, the rewards could outweigh the risks. Latin American consumers prefer U.S. products. Capital goods companies (e.g., telecommunications, transportation systems, mining and manufacturing equipment) have a special opportunity as these countries make investments to globalize their businesses.

China and India

China and India are by far the two most populous developing countries on earth. Notwithstanding the large differences in history, politics, and culture that separate them, the size of their populations and the vastness of their lands have stimulated similar responses to the changing global business environment. Both countries seek self-sufficiency, and at the same time are liberalizing their economies to link themselves to the global network.

Since the Tiananmen Square killings in 1989, China has become suspect in western capitals. Yet business opportunities in the country continue to grow. For example, Procter & Gamble launched its China efforts in the Guangzhou region in 1988, focusing on two products, Head & Shoulders shampoo and Oil of Olay skin cream. Both were quick hits. Avon started in 1990 and sold six months' worth of inventory in the first 30 days. Capital goods companies—for instance, Lockheed and Westinghouse—had similar experiences.

Despite communism, capitalistic values are slowly permeating certain parts of the country, particularly the delta area closer to Hong Kong. After the accession of Hong Kong to China, the level of business activity in the country, and hence the market opportunity, has accelerated. If a firm has the patience to endure endless negotiations and maddening bureaucratic tangles, China may provide it with a growing market.

It would be a mistake, however, to assume that the Chinese market will soon emerge on western lines. Only a few Chinese families have annual incomes approaching western standards. Chinese citizens who bring home more than Rm 40,000 ($4,800) constitute less than 0.2 percent of the total population. The average urban household headed by a state-sector employee sees just Rm 4,185 ($505) in disposable income annually; in wealthy cities like Beijing and Nanjing, this sum rises by about 45 percent. In economically robust Guangzhou, the average family makes about $1,250 annually.

Though the average person's cost of living is much lower in China, even urban residents continue to spend a large proportion of their income on food—about 46 percent in 1997. This leaves 12 percent for clothing, 10.7 percent for entertainment and education, 7.6 percent for household goods, and just 4.6 percent for the other purchases. Just 6 percent of families own a car[12] (see International Marketing Highlight 3.4).

■■■■■■■■■■   **International Marketing Highlight 3.4**   ■■■■■■■■■■

Not Quite a Billion

It is easy to overestimate the buying power of China's elite consumers. Together they represent no more than 30 million people in cities such as Beijing, Shanghai, Guangzhou and Shenzhen. And for the most part, they are not rich by world standards: according to the latest official government survey, the top 10 percent of city dwellers have an average annual disposable income of just $1,240 a person.

On the other hand, if GDP per head is adjusted for purchasing power, the incomes of the top 10 percent of city dwellers is probably closer to $10,000 a year. The prevalence of wide-screen televisions, fancy stereos, and home-karaoke machines in Shanghai apartments suggests that this new upper-middle class has more money than it admits to. Supposing that the real wealth of affluent Chinese lies somewhere between the two estimates, China's potential market must be somewhere between those of Belgium and Australia.

Put like that, China looks hefty, but not gigantic. But compare China today with China in 1985 (the first year the country conducted comprehensive consumer surveys), and it is clear that China's growth has been rapid.

Among urban households, fewer than one in five households had a color television in 1985; today the average such home has more than one. Then 7 percent had a refrigerator; now 73 percent do. Cameras are four times more common. Among richer urban households, more than half now have a VCR or video CD machine, a pager, air-conditioner and shower, and nearly a third of homes also own a mobile telephone. Every year, millions more Chinese join the ranks of this high-spending elite.

Source: The Economist, January 2, 1999, p.56

India's economic growth has occurred in a political culture that places a high value on national self-reliance and social equity. Thus, despite the fact that India is the world's largest democracy, in the realm of business it has pursued socialist policies. In recent years, however, dismayed by discouraging economic performance, India has started liberalizing the economy. In the early 1990s the government took drastic measures to encourage foreign investment and promote capital markets and exports. The current government aims to establish a worldwide economy through a large-scale liberalization by freeing foreign investment conditions, cutting down protection for Indian industry, and streamlining bureaucratic procedures, but the process is slow and uncertain.

Further, India is in the throes of a middle-class revolution that could transform its attitude toward business. The middle class accounts for some 200 million people and is growing rapidly. The rise of the middle class has sparked a boom in a variety of consumer products, durable and nondurable, a market once confined to a wealthy few. More and more foreign companies are taking advantage of the changing business conditions in India. Recently, such well-known corporations as Timex, Kellogg, and McDonald's have entered the Indian market, something that would have been impossible in the 1980s.

By and large, most Chinese and Indians have low incomes and thus lead spartan lives, as illustrated in Exhibit 3.2, showing standard of living comparisons between China, India, and the United States As incomes in the two giants go up, slowly market opportunities

EXHIBIT 3.2
Standard of Living
Comparisons for
China, India, and
United States: In
Percentages

Standard of Living Indicators	China	India	U.S.
Own an automobile	3	2	90
Have running hot water	1	4	98
Have access to sanitation	24	29	99
Have electricity	95	58	99
Have a telephone	9	7	97
Own a color television set	40	12	97
Own a refrigerator	25	12	97
Own a cat	6	6	31
Own a VCR	6	12	83

Source: Gallup India Pvt. Ltd.

will emerge. But which products to introduce, in what form, and when are the challenges that MNCs face in these frugal markets.[13]

**Developing
Countries**

A basic management reality in today's economic world is that businesses operate in a highly interdependent global economy, and the 100-plus developing countries are very significant factors in the international business arena. They are the buyers, suppliers, competitors, and capital users. In order to determine market opportunity in developing countries, it is important to recognize the magnitude and significance of these roles.

Traditionally, developing countries (including India and China, some Pacific Rim nations, and most Latin American countries) have provided a market for about one-third of all U.S. exports. The largest U.S. exports to developing countries are machinery and transport equipment, agricultural products, and chemicals, but all major product categories share in these markets (see International Marketing Highlight 3.5).

International Marketing Highlight 3.5

"Hmmm. Could Use A Little More Snake"

On any weekday morning, a dozen or so consumers take the elevator to the 19th floor of Cornwall House, a nondescript office building that's home to Campbell Soup Co.'s Hong Kong taste kitchen. There they split off into carrels and take their seats before bowls of soup and eager food scientists. Chosen carefully to get the right demographic mix, such groups are assembled to taste the offerings that Campbell hopes will ignite consumer interest in China and other parts of Asia.

The menu might include cabbage soup, scallop broth, or a local delicacy, such as pork, fig, and date soup. After up to an hour of tasting and observing, the technicians get their answers. Too much pork? Enough scallops?

Such insights are crucial to Campbell as it tries to create new products to whet regional appetites. Diet is a function of local culture, and Asia in particular puts huge demands on a western food company seeking to crack its exotic markets. Campbell opened the Hong Kong kitchen in 1991 to reach 2 billion Asian consumers.

Cooking up regional specialties isn't easy. Fewer than 1 in 20 varieties tested may hit the stores. Nonetheless, Campbell can score big if it gets the formula right. At an average of one bowl a day, the Chinese are among the highest per capita soup eaters in the world.

Campbell enters new markets gingerly. It typically launches a basic meat or chicken broth, which consumers can doctor with meats, vegetables, and spices. Then it brings out more sophisticated soups. The Hong Kong kitchen already has a couple of hits to its credit—new scallop and ham soups came out of the lab. Campbell has also discovered a few surprises. Among the company's biggest sellers across Asia are such U.S. standbys as cream of mushroom and cream of chicken, which researchers believe attract westernized Chinese. One Campbell breakthrough in China, watercress and duck-gizzard soup, was developed in the United States

Local ingredients may count, but Campbell draws the line on some Asian favorites. Dog soup is out, as is shark's fin, since most species are endangered. However, the kitchen staff keeps an open mind when it comes to other fare.

Source: Business Week, March 15, 1993. p. 53.

U.S. business with the developing countries follows closely the economic growth trends recorded in those countries. For example, U.S. exports declined sharply in the early and mid 1980s as purchasing power in those countries was reduced by debt-service problems, declining commodity prices, and the global recession. By 1987, however, these markets recovered more rapidly. U.S. exports to those countries showed a 16 percent gain over the preceding year, compared with increases of only 9 percent in sales to developed countries.[14]

Developing countries are likely to become more important in the global economy in the new century. Market opportunity in these countries rests on their ability to develop economically. That development will depend on two factors:[15] (1) their governments' willingness to encourage growth through liberal monetary and fiscal policies, and (2) the capacity of their managers to operate the productive apparatus in an efficient, effective, and equitable manner.

Traditionally, the U.S. trade focus has been on Europe and Japan. Whereas the industrial nations will continue to be our largest markets for decades to come, another category of country holds far more promise for large incremental gains in exports. These nations, the *"Big Emerging Markets" (BEMs),* comprise the Chinese Economic Area (China, Hong Kong, Taiwan), Indonesia, South Korea, India, Turkey, South Africa, Poland, Argentina, Brazil, and Mexico. The U.S. Department of Commerce estimates that nearly three-fourths of the growth in world trade in the next two decades is likely to take place in the developing countries. Most of this expansion will occur in the BEMs. The BEMs are likely to double their share of world GDP in that time, from today's 10 percent up to 20 percent. By the year 2010, their share of world imports is likely to exceed that of Japan and the European Union combined.

The BEMs will also be the competitive battleground of the future. Japan, Europe, and several developing countries can be expected to be fierce rivals in these markets.

Pursuing U.S. interests in these countries will require deft balancing of commercial and foreign policy considerations. It is in the BEMs that commercial opportunities coexist so closely with the complications of human rights, worker rights, nuclear nonproliferation, and violations of intellectual-property laws. The BEMs, moreover, have enough political influence and aspiration to often effectively challenge U.S. policies in multilateral organizations such as the International Monetary Fund (IMF), the WTO, and the United Nations.

Dimensions of the Global Market

Socioeconomic statistics can help international marketers segment the international market and thus formulate marketing strategy. This macro information is conveniently available from such international organizations as the United Nations, the World Bank, the IMF, and the Organization for Economic Cooperation and Development (OECD). The information relates to such economic aspects as population, income, trade, private consumption expenditures, total stock of durable goods (e.g., passenger cars, trucks, and buses), service facilities (e.g., telephone access lines), consumption of basic materials (e.g., cement, steel), average hourly wage rates, and other.

An example of useful macro information is the fact that per capita GDP of most Western European countries is over $15,000, while that of most Asian countries (except Japan, Hong Kong, South Korea, Taiwan, and Singapore) is less than $1,000. Per capita GDP of the two largest countries (China and India) is $750 and $430, respectively (1998 dollars). Moreover, in most developed countries, the average hourly wage is more than $5, while in most developing countries it is less than $1. In some countries (Sri Lanka, for example), it is as low as $0.19 an hour.

As can be expected, total private consumption expenditures are much higher in industrialized countries than those in the middle- and low-income brackets. By the same token, ownership of passenger cars and other durable goods, as well as consumption of energy and basic materials, is skewed in favor of advanced countries. As a matter of fact, it is the low level of energy consumption and meager use of such materials as steel and cement that characterize less developed countries.

Based on this kind of information, *Crossborder Monitor* has identified the 12 largest markets in the world (see Exhibit 3.3). Interestingly, 5 of these 12 markets are the developing countries of Russia, Mexico, China, Brazil, and India. Obviously, it would be foolhardy for a company to treat all developing countries alike. Some developing countries offer a better market opportunity than the industrialized countries.

EXHIBIT 3.3
Size, Growth, and Intensity of World's 12 Largest Markets

	Market Size (% of World Market)		Market Intensity (World = 0)		Cumulative Five-Year Market Growth (%)
	1991	1996	1991	1996	1996
Major Markets					
United States	19.55	20.46	5.13	5.60	7.61
Japan	9.85	10.09	4.98	5.82	8.33
China	9.38	8.80	0.23	0.23	36.29
Germany	4.62	5.66	4.65	4.96	15.65
India	4.87	5.04	0.13	0.12	33.39
France	3.50	3.73	4.05	4.60	2.77
Italy	3.57	3.60	4.15	4.38	2.59
United Kingdom	3.11	3.42	3.64	4.13	0.48
Russia	—	2.75	0.96	0.95	−25.08
Brazil	2.53	2.58	0.85	0.98	31.07
South Korea	1.53	2.10	—	2.66	55.45
Canada	1.96	1.95	4.66	4.32	9.04

Market intensity measures the richness of the market, or the degree of concentrated purchasing power it represents. Taking the world's market intensity as 1, the EIU has calculated the intensity of each country or region as it relates to this base. The intensity figure is derived from an average of per capita ownership, production, and consumption indicators. Specifically, it is calculated by averaging per capita figures for automobiles in use (double weighted), telephones in use, TVs in use, steel consumption, electricity production, private consumption expenditure (double weighted) and the percentage of population that is urban (double weighted).
Market size shows the relative dimensions of each national or regional market as a percentage of the total world market. The percentages for each market are derived by averaging the corresponding data on total population (double weighted), urban population, private consumption expenditure, steel consumption, electricity production and ownership of telephones, passenger automobiles and televisions.
Market growth is an average of cumulative growth in several key economic market indicators: population; steel consumption; electricity production; and ownership of passenger automobiles, lorries, buses, and TVs.
Source: *Crossborder Monitor*, November 4, 1998, p. 12.

An interesting characteristic of global markets is their emerging universality. In other words, a one-world market exists for products ranging from cars to consumer electronics to carbonated drinks. Firms today are engaged in world competition to serve consumers globally (see International Marketing Highlight 3.6). It must be cautioned, however, that each nation still has its own cultural peculiarities. Thus, a firm cannot assume that in each case what is good for the home country is good for the world.

A number of broad forces have led to growing globalization of markets:

1. *Growing similarity of countries.* Because of growing commonality of infrastructure, distribution channels, and marketing approaches, more and more products and brands are available everywhere. This fact proves that similar buyer needs exist in different countries. Large retail chains, television advertising, and credit cards are just a few examples of once isolated phenomena that are rapidly becoming universal.

2. *Falling tariff barriers.* Successive rounds of bilateral and multilateral agreements have lowered tariffs markedly since World War II. At the same time, regional economic agreements such as the European Union have facilitated trade relations among member countries.

3. *Strategic role of technology.* Technology is not only reshaping industries, but contributing to market homogenization. For example, electronic innovations permit the development of more compact, lighter products that are less costly to ship. Transportation costs themselves have fallen with the use of containerization and larger-capacity ships. Increasing ease of communication and data transfer make it feasible to link operations in different countries. At the same time, technology leads to an easy flow of information among buyers, making them aware of new and quality products and thus creating demand.

Global markets offer unlimited opportunities. However, competition in these markets is intense. To be globally successful, companies must learn to operate and compete as if the world were one large market, ignoring superficial regional and national differences. Corporations geared to this new reality can benefit from enormous economies of scale in production, distribution, marketing, and management. By translating these benefits into reduced world prices, they can dislodge competitors who still operate with the perspectives of the past. Thus, companies willing to change their perspectives and become global can attain sustainable competitive advantage (see International Marketing Highlight 3.7).

Segmenting the Global Market

A *market segment* refers to a group of countries that are alike in respect to their responsiveness to some aspect of marketing strategy. *Market segmentation* may be defined as a technique of dividing different countries into homogeneous groups. The concept of segmentation is based on the fact that a business cannot serve the entire world with a single set of policies, because there are disparities among countries—both economic and cultural. An international marketer, therefore, should pick out one or more countries as the target market. A company may not find it feasible to do business immediately with the entire spectrum of countries forming a segment. In that case, the firm may design its marketing programs and strategies for those countries it does enter and draw upon its experience with these countries in dealing with new markets.

■■■■■■■■■■■ **International Marketing Highlight 3.6** ■■■■■■■■■■■

Global Disorientation

She arrives on her British Airways flight, rents a Toyota at the Hertz desk in the terminal, and drives to the downtown Hilton hotel. She drops into a chair, flips on the Sony television, and gazes glassily at this week's scandal on "Dallas." Room service delivers dinner along with the bottle of Perrier and the pack of Marlboro cigarettes she ordered. While eating dinner she catches herself nodding off, but is brought back to consciousness by a sudden feeling of disorientation. Is she in Sydney, Singapore, Stockholm, or Seattle? Her surroundings and points of reference over the past few hours have provided few clues.

With the expansion of the international economy and the growth of international business in the post–World War II era, the marketplace has taken on a recognizably similar face in countries around the globe. No longer is the overseas traveler surprised to see a familiar logo flashing from a neon sign or to find a favorite brand from home on sale in a foreign location. The most interesting phenomenon is not just that MNCs have entered the foreign markets. Increasingly, it has become evident that the same few companies compete against each other for leadership positions in numerous national markets worldwide. In automobiles, construction equipment, consumer electronics, cameras, office copiers, airframes, computers, and a variety of other industries, not more than half a dozen MNCs dominate the major markets worldwide.

Source: From a note entitled "Global Competition and MNC Managers," by Christopher A. Bartlett, Harvard Business School, 1985.

International Marketing Highlight 3.7

Why Go Global?

The rules for survival have changed since the beginning of the 1980s. Domestic markets have become too small. Even the biggest companies in the biggest countries cannot survive on their domestic markets if they are in global industries. They have to be in all major markets. That means North America, Western Europe, and the Pacific Rim countries.

Take, for example, the pharmaceuticals business. In the 1970s, developing a new drug cost about $16 million and took four to five years. The drug could be produced in Britain or the United States and eventually exported. Now, developing a drug costs about $250 million and takes as long as 12 years. Only a global product for a global market can support that much risk. No major pharmaceuticals company is in the game for anything other than global products. That helps explain a series of mergers of major drug companies, most recently the marriage of Bristol-Myers and Squibb.

Source: Fortune, August 1989, p. 70.

The importance of segmentation can be illustrated by reference to Massy-Ferguson Ltd., a Toronto-based farm equipment producer. As far back as 1959, this company decided to concentrate on sales outside North America and thus avoid competing head-on with Ford Motor Company, Deere & Company, and International Harvester Company. It took the company years to implement successfully its segmentation strategy before reaching a point where it derives almost 70 percent of its sales outside North America. As a matter of fact, as the market matured in North America, Massey continued to grow and earn substantial income, since demand overseas accelerated while it slowed down in North America. Whereas Ford, Deere, and International Harvester struggled hard to maintain profitability, Massey-Ferguson, because of its decision to avoid the North American segment, showed a fine performance.

To survive and prosper in the increasingly competitive global marketplace many companies are learning to find and dominate "niche markets." For companies of all kinds and sizes, nichemanship is rapidly becoming the new business imperative.

Simply defined, a *niche* is a relatively small segment of a market that the major competitors or producers may overlook, ignore, or have difficulty serving. The niche may be a narrowly defined geographic area, or it may relate to the unique needs of a small and specific group of customers, or it may target some, highly specialized aspect of a very broad group of customers. In some cases, the niche market may actually be very large in numbers of customers even though it is a small percentage of a company's total customer base, particularly if the company operates globally.

The possibilities for niche marketing are virtually endless. So too are the opportunities, as effective niche strategies can be extremely profitable. By focusing on a niche market, companies often develop an excellent understanding of their customers' operations—and how those customers make money. This understanding, in turn, provides an edge when it comes to identifying opportunities for new products and marketing programs. Emphasis on a niche provides a very clear focus for the development of business strategies and action plans.

The importance of niche strategy may be illustrated by the experience of Linear Technology, a Canadian firm.[16] It successfully carved out a niche in the world integrated circuit ("chip") business. Although this market, as a whole, is dominated by major Japanese and American firms, Linear Technology dominates the global market for one narrow segment—audio amplifier chips for hearing aids. Even in Japan, it has achieved more than a 50 percent market share in competition with companies like NEC. By having a broad product line within its specialized area and by focusing on the needs of one set of customers, it has managed to beat all competitors.

A basic problem in market segmentation is choosing the right criteria. Traditionally, geography has been employed to divide the world. However, segmentation based on geography is often less useful than that based on economic and cultural differences among countries.

For example, the countries of the Middle East in no way constitute a homogeneous market. Iran, Iraq, Kuwait, the United Arab Emirates (UAE), Saudi Arabia, Egypt, and Lebanon are all very different. Lebanon has had special problems, while all the others have different legal and political systems. The UAE has no formal business laws at all, Saudi Arabia has fairly new and sophisticated statutes; Egyptian law has a long history and is based on French law. Lately, the Middle Eastern countries have attempted to present a common economic posture through tariff regulations, duties, and the like. But a foreign company cannot take full advantage of these measures because the natural fragmentation of Middle Eastern markets is reinforced by the inherent nationalist tendencies. Therefore, it is not possible for a company simply to go into the cheapest or most liberal country and expect to maximize its profit by trading into the whole area from that base.

The Middle East situation illustrates the point that world markets need to be grouped judiciously for effective market segmentation, and this requires evaluation of culture, law, and politics in order to identify the dimension(s) to be employed in classifying the countries.

Segmentation Process

Five procedural steps should be followed to determine the segmentation criteria for world markets:

1. Develop a market taxonomy for classifying the world markets.
2. Segment all countries into homogeneous groups—that is, groups having common characteristics with reference to the dimensions of the market taxonomy.
3. Determine theoretically the most efficient method of serving each group.
4. Choose the group in which the marketer's own perspective (its product or service and its strengths) is in line with the requirements of the group.
5. Adjust this ideal classification to the constraints of the real world (existing commitments, legal and political restrictions, practicality, and so forth).

A company interested in expanding business overseas can utilize this procedure by first deciding on a criterion for classifying the countries for its product. Not all countries should be analyzed, but only those that appear to offer real potential.

For example, a machine tool manufacturer might segment countries based on need: those requiring simple machines (first-generation machine tools), those requiring medium-size machine tools (say, second-generation machines), and those requiring large, sophisticated machines. The company may find it is well placed to serve the second segment, where medium-size machine tools are needed. Let us assume the following countries fall into this segment: Malaysia, Brazil, Thailand, Indonesia, Philippines, Mexico, and Turkey. To serve this targeted segment, the company might establish three assembly plants, one in Turkey, one in Brazil, and one in Malaysia (assuming other countries in the geographic area would be served through exports from these three countries). However, because the machine tool industry often encounters a lack of scientific personnel in such foreign countries, the company might choose to establish an assembly plant in India (instead of Malaysia), which has a large pool of scientific talent, to serve the Asian part of its segment. It might do so even though the Indian market is highly competitive. This is what is meant by adjustment of the ideal system to the real world.

Criteria for Grouping Countries

As is true in domestic market segmentation, countries of the world can be grouped using a variety of criteria. For example, a company could group world markets (countries) based on a single variable such as per capita GNP or geography. Similarly, religion or political system might serve as a criterion. Alternatively, a combination of a few selected variables. could be used—such as political system, geography, and economic status (GNP per capita)—or a large number of variables could be used, similar to what is done in establishing lifestyle or psychographic segments in domestic marketing.

Following is a discussion of economic status grouping, geographic grouping, political system grouping, grouping by religion, cultural grouping, multiple-variable grouping, and intermarket grouping. The discussion ends with a recommended scheme for country classification called the *portfolio approach.*

The choice of an appropriate grouping method depends on the nature of the product. For example, a defense equipment manufacturer would classify countries based on their political systems, whereas an appliance company would look at their economic status.

Economic Status Grouping The simplest way to form economic groups is to classify countries on the basis on GNP per capita. For example, countries with GNP per capita of more than $12,000 might be classified as high-income countries, those with GNP of $1,000 to $7,500 as middle-income, and those with GNP of less than $1,000 as low-income. If we follow this scheme, about 55 countries will fall in the low-income category, 50 in the middle-income category, and 23 will be considered high-income.[17] (Economic status groupings should be differentiated from regional market agreements, discussed in Chapter 7, which are formed using more than strictly economic considerations.)

There is no empirical study showing the economic status classification of countries by GNP per capita to be a viable system. Furthermore, based on domestic marketing experience, it is questionable if a single variable should be used to group countries into homogeneous categories. For example, GNP per capita of Kuwait, UAE, and Hong Kong would put them in the category of industrialized countries, but these countries by no means constitute the same market as industrial countries such as the United States, Germany, Italy, and so on. Additionally, emphasis on economic status alone in classifying countries misses the crucial impact of cultural differences among nations.

The grouping of countries based on GNP per capita assumes, like other economic criteria for segmentation, that market behavior is directly related to income. In domestic marketing, a number of studies have questioned the relevance of income as a discerning variable. In the international arena as well, sole reliance on GNP per capita for international comparisons is considered inadequate. For example, in 1998 Pakistan had a per capita GNP of $480 versus India's $430. However, if the purchasing power of a dollar in the two countries is considered, the per capita GNP for Pakistan comes out to $1,560 in U.S. dollars while that for India is $1,700.[18]

Geographic Grouping One popular way of grouping nations is to classify them along regional lines. Many MNCs organize their worldwide operations into such regions as Western Europe, Latin America, Far East (including Australia and New Zealand), Middle East, and Africa. Geographic grouping of countries has several advantages. First, geographic proximity makes it easier to manage countries blocked together. For example, all countries in Latin America can be managed, say, from a regional headquarters in Brazil. Both transportation and communication are easier to handle on a regional basis. Consider the difficulties of ignoring geographic proximity: Suppose Argentina is grouped with Italy, Spain, and New Zealand, while Brazil is grouped with South Korea, Taiwan, and India (assuming some viable basis). One can see the challenges in managing these far-flung countries as one market.

Moreover, nations in the same geographic region often share cultural traits. And another factor that supports regional classification of countries is the post–World War II organization of countries into trading groups, such as the European Union (EU), MERCOSUR and NAFTA. These organizations are regional in character; that is, countries in the same geographic region decided to join with each other to become large economic entities. Typically, members of a group agree to trade freely with each other without any barriers. In fact, the EU countries go even further and levy common external tariffs. From the point of view of an international marketer, the existence of common economic arrangements among nations by means of groups means that entry into one country will automatically smooth entry into another country belonging to the same group; the same marketing strategy perspective can be applied to one or all. Thus, geographic division of countries appears sound.

Despite these reasons, geographic lumping of countries to form market segments is not always sound. Geographic proximity of countries does not automatically guarantee the same market opportunity for international business. For example, the Philippines and Thailand do not provide as viable markets as Singapore, Malaysia, South Korea, Taiwan, and Hong Kong, even though all these countries are in the same geographic region. Similarly, Mexico is geographically part of the same continent as the United States and Canada, but Mexico obviously differs culturally and economically from the other two.

Political System Grouping Another way of grouping countries is to classify them by their political perspective—For example, democratic republic, dictatorship, communist dictatorship, or monarchy. These categories are used simply to facilitate discussion. As appropriate to a marketer's purposes, they may be refined further. For example, the two-party system of the United States, the multiparty systems of Italy, Israel, and Germany; and the single-party system of Mexico could be used. Dictatorships could be classified as either military or civilian.

Once a suitable set of political categories has been worked out, countries in each group can be considered as homogeneous for purposes of developing marketing strategy. In other words, one marketing strategy would be relevant for the firm's international business with all the countries in a particular political group.

Using politics as the segmentation criterion for grouping countries, Nigeria, Bangladesh, and Argentina would have belonged in the same category in 1988. All then had military dictators, with inclinations toward holding free elections to establish democratic governments. However, from the vantage point of the multinational marketer, their political closeness did not render them potentially similar markets. Argentina was economically much closer to the Western European countries. Nigeria's economic potential is linked with oil prices. And highly populated Bangladesh, ranked among the low-income countries of the world. The differing economic perspectives of the three countries would obviously negate the validity of their grouping according to political environment for marketing purposes.

Grouping by Religion Religion constitutes an important element of society in most cultures. It greatly influences lifestyle, which in turn affects marketing. Following this logic, religion could work out to be a viable criterion for marketing segmentation. What has been said of Latin America, for example, applies to many other parts of the world in regard to different religions.

> The life of the family and of the individual is greatly and continuously involved with the Church. One must not exaggerate the implications of this relationship of the individual, the family, and the community to the Church. But one should also be careful not to underestimate it. It gives the life a certain quality and adds something to the meaning of daily activities which is lacking in the United States.[19]

Religion can be defined as the quest for the values of the ideal life and as involving three components: the ideal itself, the practices for attaining the ideal, and the theology or worldview relating the quest for the ideal to the surrounding universe. This definition relates religion to virtually all aspects of a country's life—its aesthetics, its material culture, its social organization, its language, and even its politics and economics.

Animism, Buddhism, Christianity, Hinduism, Islam, and Judaism are the major religions of the world. Religion as an aspect of cultural environment is discussed in Chapter 9. Briefly, however, animism is a prehistoric form of religion—ancient religion without religious texts. Animism today is found all over the world but is practiced most obviously in African countries. Some Latin American religious practices have animistic tendencies as well.

Hinduism, defined more as a way of life than a religion, is practiced mostly in India. Considered to be 4,000 years old, it reflects a complex set of tenets and beliefs but lacks a common creed or dogma.

Buddhism sprang from Hinduism in India in the sixth century B.C. Buddhists are found mainly in Southeast Asia and Japan. In Burma, Sri Lanka, Thailand, Laos, and Kampuchea it is the dominant religion. There are some Buddhists in western countries, and, presumably, in the People's Republic of China as well.

Judaism is the monotheistic religion of the Jewish people, tracing its origin to Abraham, having its spiritual and ethical principles embodied chiefly in the Bible and the Talmud. Jews do not belong to one race of people. The term *Jew* applies correctly to anyone who is a member of the Jewish faith. Nationally speaking, Jews are Germans, Arabians, Americans, and almost everything else.

Islam is practiced by over 500 million people, living in about 30 countries. The Islamic countries are located mainly in the Middle East, Northern Africa, and South Asia. Islam defines a total way of life. It includes legislation that organizes all human relationships.

Christianity, sometimes referred to as the religion of the Western World, is found all over the globe. With the Protestant Reformation, Christianity increased its emphasis on individuality. Although marked differences exist between the two major divisions of Christianity, Roman Catholicism and Protestantism, both stress similar values such as achievement and thrift. Interestingly, the Protestant countries in particular rank economically among the highest in the world in terms of GNP per capita.

The effect of religion on lifestyle makes it a relevant criterion for grouping countries. Yet the formulation of a common marketing strategy for a group of countries following Islam, or any one religion, may not suffice. Both Pakistan and Saudi Arabia are strong adherents of Islam. However, the economic differences between the two countries would invalidate lumping them together for marketing decision making. Saudi Arabia, with a per capita GNP of $7,740 (1998 estimate), is a customer for a variety of consumer and industrial products. On the other hand, Pakistan, with its per capita GNP of $480 (1998 estimate), offers a very low potential for international marketers. Similarly, France and the Philippines, both primarily Catholic countries, cannot be served by following the same marketing perspective. In brief, while religion via culture plays an important role in determining lifestyle, by itself it may not serve as a viable criterion for grouping countries.

Cultural Grouping Presumably, countries of similar cultures should be amenable to the same marketing strategy. To an extent, cultural groupings make sense, since lifestyle is affected strongly by culture. The problem lies in determining what constitutes a cultural category. Unless we use a variable like religion to serve as a surrogate for culture, it will not be easy to establish cultural categories.

One way to divide countries into homogeneous country groups is to use Geert Hofstede's approach. According to him, the way people in different countries perceive and interpret their world varies along four dimensions: power distance, uncertainty avoidance, individualism, and masculinity.[20]

Power distance refers to the degree of inequality that the population of a country considers acceptable (i.e., from relatively equal to extremely unequal). In some societies, power is concentrated among a few people at the top who make all the decisions. People at the other end simply carry these decisions out. Such societies are associated with high power-distance levels. In other societies, on the other hand, power is widely dispersed, and relations among people are more egalitarian. These are cultures of low power distance.

Uncertainty avoidance concerns the degree to which people in a country prefer structured over unstructured situations. At the organizational level, uncertainty avoidance is related to such factors as rituals, rules orientation, and employment stability. As a consequence, organization personnel in less structured societies tend to face the future as it takes shape without experiencing undue stress. Risk-avoidance behavior is less common in these societies. Their managers abstain from creating bureaucratic strictures that would make it difficult to respond to unfolding events. In contrast, managers in cultures of high uncertainty avoidance engage in activities like long-range planning to establish protective barriers to minimize the anxiety associated with future events.

Individualism denotes the degree to which people in a country are encouraged to act as individuals rather than as members of cohesive groups (i.e., from collectivist to individualist). In individualistic societies, people are self-centered and independent. They seek the fulfillment of their own goals over the group's goals.

Managers belonging to individualistic societies are competitive by nature and show little loyalty to the organizations they work for. In collectivistic societies, members have a group mentality. They subordinate their individual goals to work toward the group goals. They are interdependent and seek mutual accommodation to maintain group harmony. Collectivistic managers have high loyalty to their organizations and subscribe to joint decision making.

Masculinity refers to the degree to which "masculine" values emphasizing assertiveness, performance, success, and competition prevail over "feminine" values emphasizing the quality of life, personal relationships, service, care for the weak, and solidarity. Masculine cultures exhibit different roles for men and women, and tend to perceive "big" as "important." People in such societies are more likely to have a need to be ostentatious than those in feminine societies. Feminine cultures value "small as beautiful," and stress quality of life and environment over purely materialistic gains.

Although the four variables identified by Hofstede for discerning cultural categories appear reasonable, they would require dividing countries into 12 groups—an enormous task of questionable value.

Multiple-Variable Grouping A number of studies in marketing literature have used a large number of variables to form country clusters (cluster analysis).[21] The argument behind the use of multiple variables has been that countries relate to each other in accordance with their cultural, religious, socioeconomic, and political characteristics. Therefore, all of these characteristics should be considered in forming international segments, not just geographic proximity or economic status.

An important grouping study by S. Prakash Sethi used 29 variables to cluster 91 countries.[22] First, a large number of variables were collapsed into smaller, more meaningful groups, or clusters, called *variable clusters* or *V-clusters.* These were discriminatory variables such as GNP, cars, and single-family homes per capita. Second, countries were scored on the basis of each V-cluster. *O-analysis,* meaning *object analysis,* was used, with each country considered an "object" and a large number of countries classified into subgroups called *O-clusters* or *O-types.* The scores were used to identify O-types with similar characteristics.

The multiple-variable approach attempts to combine countries with similar social-economic-political perspectives into segments, but it falsely assumes that countries are indivisible, heterogeneous units.

Intermarket Grouping In recent years, a refined approach for segmenting the market has been suggested in which groups of customers who are alike in different countries form homogeneous segments. In other words, each country's market consists of different segments, and each segment consists of customers from different countries.[23] These segments are called *intermarket segments* (see International Marketing Highlight 11.6).

Assume a U.S. chemical manufacturing company is interested in foreign expansion. The company manufactures different types of chemicals such as pharmaceuticals, fine chemicals, and fertilizers. In its attempts to segment the world market, the company may find small farmers in developing countries a segment worth serving. These customers, whether from Pakistan, Indonesia, Kenya, or Mexico, appear to represent common needs and behavior patterns. Most of them till the land using bullock carts and have very little cash to buy agricultural inputs. They lack the education and exposure to appreciate fully the value of using fertilizer, and they depend on government help for such things as seeds, pesticides, and fertilizer. They acquire their farming needs from local suppliers and count on word-of-mouth to learn and accept new things and ideas. Thus, even though these farmers are in different countries continents apart, and even though they speak different languages and have different cultural backgrounds, they may represent a homogeneous market segment.

Take the case of Mercedes-Benz. It has a worldwide market niche among the well-to-do. Even in Japan, Mercedes is considered the most popular foreign luxury car. Similarly, a designer of men's clothing may find that elites of different countries compose a single market segment. For another company, the teenagers of different countries may work out to be a viable segment (see International Marketing Highlight 3.8). In Exhibit 3.4 the behavioral traits of two intermarket segments: global elite and global teenagers, illustrating the significance of forming segments across nations.[24]

A recent study showed that the following four major types of consumers dominate the world, and their purchase decisions are heavily influenced by the wealth of their nations.[25]

EXHIBIT 3.4   Behavioral Aspects Related to the Identification of Global Consumer Segments

	Global Elites	Global Teenagers
Shared Values	Wealth; success; status	Growth; change; future; learning; play
Key Product Benefits Sought	Universally recognizable products with prestige image; high-quality products	Novelty; trendy image; fashion statement; name brands/novelty
Demographics	Very high income; social status, and class; well-traveled and well-educated	Age 12–19; well-traveled; high media exposure
Media/Communications	Upscale magazines; social-selective channels (i.e., cliques); direct marketing; global telemarketing	Teen magazines; MTV; radio; video; peers; role models
Distribution Channels	Selective (i.e., upscale; retailers)	General retailers with name brands
Price Range	Premium	Affordable
Targeted by Global Firms	Mercedes Benz, Perrier, American Express, and Ralph Lauren's Polo, etc.	Coca-Cola Co., Benetton, Swatch International, Sony, PepsiCo, Inc., etc.
Related Microsegments/Clusters	Affluent women; top executives; highly educated professionals; professional athletes	Preadolescents; female teens; male teens
Factors Influencing Emergence of Segment	Increased wealth, widespread travel	Television media; international education

Source: Salah S. Hassan and Lea Prevel Katsanis, "Identification of Global Consumer Segments," *Journal of International Consumer Marketing*, 3 (2): p. 24. 1994

1. "Deal makers": 29 percent of 37,743 respondents from 40 countries concentrate on the process of buying. This is a well-educated group, median age 32, with average affluence and employment.
2. "Price seekers": 27 percent place primary value on the product. This group has the highest proportion of retirees, the lowest education level, mostly female, and has an average level of affluence.
3. "Brand loyalists": 23 percent of the respondents and the least affluent are brand loyalists. The group is mostly male, median age 36, who hold average education and employment.
4. "Luxury innovators": 21 percent seek new, prestigious brands and are the most educated and affluent shoppers, with the highest proportion of executives and other professionals. The group is mostly male with a median age of 32.

In the United States, 37 percent are deal makers, 36 percent price seekers, 17 percent luxury innovators, and 11 percent brand loyalists. Deal makers predominate in Asia, Latin America, and the Middle East. Price seekers dominate in Europe and Japan.

Price seekers exist mainly in competitive, developed markets like Europe and Japan where shoppers generally cannot haggle or negotiate. Deal makers are more often in developing markets that have less brand competition and a tradition of bazaars and open-air markets, where the process of buying is half the fun. The United States straddles the two styles because of its heterogeneous culture and also because shoppers can bargain at many retail outlets and even large category-killer stores.

The concept of intermarket segmenting is relevant not only on a worldwide basis, but especially within a region. For example, it would be a mistake to suppose that women all over the world have similar cosmetic-usage behavior patterns. Like other lifestyle behavior, cosmetic use is deeply affected by culture. Muslim women are supposed to veil in public so cosmetic use among them is likely to be very low. Some Latin women consider excessive cosmetic usage as self-indulgence. Others do not —depending on the specific region. Thus, from the viewpoint of a cosmetic company, stereotyping people globally could prove unproductive. Instead, grouping people in a region where culture and economic conditions do not vary substantially from country to country may represent a viable segment.

Applying the concept of intermarket segmentation in Europe, many companies are pursuing the idea of a *Eurobrand,* that is, a product or brand designed for a market consisting of niches in different Western European countries. The development of satellite communication makes it feasible to simultaneously reach customers in different countries, which would not have been possible through the traditional television channel.

International Marketing Highlight 3.8

The Global Teen Segment

In the world divided by trade wars and tribalism, teenagers, of all people, are the new unifying force. From the steamy playgrounds of Los Angeles to the stately boulevards of Singapore, kids show amazing similarities in taste, language, and attitude. African Americans, Asians, Latinos, and Europeans are zipping up Levi's, dancing to the Red Hot Chili Peppers, and punching the keyboards of their IBM PCs. Propelled by mighty couriers like MTV, trends spread with sorcerous speed. Kids hear drumbeats a continent away, absorb the rhythm, and add their own licks. For the Coca-Colas and the Nikes, no marketing challenge is more basic than capturing that beat. There are billions to be earned.

Teens almost everywhere buy a common gallery of products: Reebok sports shoes, Procter & Gamble Cover Girl makeup, Sega and Nintendo videogames, PepsiCo's new Pepsi Max. They're also helping pick the hits in electronics, from Kodak cameras to Motorola beepers. Teen choices are big business. Last year America's 28 million teenagers spent $57 billion of their own money. In Europe, Latin America, and the Pacific Rim, a swath of over 200 million teens are converging with their American soul mates in a vast, free-spending market that circles the globe.

Source: Shawn Tully, "Teens—The Most Global Market of All," *Fortune,* May 16, 1994, p. 9. ©1994 Time Inc. All rights reserved.

Portfolio Approach The *portfolio approach,* as shown in Exhibit 3.5, proposes dividing countries on a three-dimensional basis according to country potential, competitive strength, and risk. Following this method, 18 country segments are obtained.

Country potential in the portfolio approach refers to the market potential for a firm's product or service in a given country and is based on such factors as population size, rate of economic growth, real GNP, per capita national income, distribution of population, industrial production and consumption patterns, and the like. Both internal and external factors determine *competitive strength.* In a given country, the *internal factors* include the firm's market share; its resources; and facilities, including knowledge of the unique features of that country and the skills and facilities it owns to match these features. *External factors* include strength of competitors in the same industry, competition from industries of substitute products, and the structure of the industry locally and internationally. *Risk*—that is, political risk, financial risk, and business risk (like change in consumer preferences)—is any factor that causes variation in profit, cash flow, or other outcomes generated by involvement in a country.

This approach has the following advantages:

- It is three-dimensional, which implies greater representativeness of the multinational environment.
- Its dimensions are relevant to marketing.

EXHIBIT 3.5   International Market Taxonomy Matrix for Classifying Countries

Competitive Strength

	Strong	Average	Weak	
High				High
				Medium
Risk				Low → **Country Potential**
Low				High
				Medium
				Low

- It treats risk as a separate dimension, which makes it close to the real-world situation, since many countries of the world could have high potential and be attractive if not for a high degree of risk.
- Each of the dimensions is a composite measure of a variety of subfactors. For example, neither GNP nor income level, by itself, is adequate as a descriptor of overall country potential.
- It uses an 18-cell matrix with three levels each of the country-potential and competitive strength dimensions, and two levels of risk. This feature is important, because the world contains not only highs and lows, but middle positions as well.

The portfolio approach requires an abundance of information, both internal and external to the firm, which may not be easy to collect and analyze. Additionally, this approach is more relevant for use at a product or market level than at a headquarters level. Thus, a company involved in marketing a number of products or services abroad would have to work out a number of segmentation schemes. The scheme, however, makes strategic sense and provides an important framework for analyzing opportunities for chosen products in select markets that appear to be potentially viable.

In-Country Segmentation

So far the discussion has dealt with grouping the countries of the world, but the concept of segmentation also is relevant *within* a particular country. Just as markets are segmented in the United States, so can they be segmented in other countries, using simple demographic and socioeconomic variables, personality and lifestyle variables, or situation-specific events (such as use intensity, brand loyalty, attitudes).

For example, a U.S. food company segmented the French market into modern and traditional segments, defining the modern French consumer as liking processed foods while the traditional type looks upon them with disfavor. A leading industrial manufacturer discovered that the critical variable for segmenting the Japanese market was the amount of annual usage per item, not per order or per any other variable. A toiletries manufacturer used geographic criteria—urban versus rural markets in South Africa. Exhibit 3.6 provides an inventory of different bases for market segmentation. Most of these bases are covered in any principles of marketing text.

Besides products and customers, a market can also be segmented by level of customer service, stage of production, price-performance characteristics, credit arrangements with customers, location of plants, characteristics of manufacturing equipment, channels of distribution, and financial policies.

The key is to choose a variable or variables that will divide the market into segments of customers who have similar responsiveness to some aspect of the marketer's strategy. The variable (or variables) should be measurable; it should represent an objective value such as income, rate of consumption, or frequency of buying, not simply a qualitative viewpoint such as the degree of customer happiness. Also, the variable should create segments that could be responsive to promotion. Even if it were possible to measure happiness, for instance, segments based on a happiness variable cannot be reached by a specific medium. Thus, happiness cannot serve as an appropriate criterion because it is not easily manipulated.

Once segments have been formed, the next strategic issue is deciding which ones should be targeted. Criteria are as follows:

1. The segment should be one in which the maximum differential in competitive strategy can be developed.

EXHIBIT 3.6
Bases for Segmentation

1. Demographic factors (age, income, sex, etc.)
2. Socioeconomic factors (social class, stages in the family life cycle)
3. Geographic factors
4. Psychological factors (lifestyle, personality traits)
5. Consumption patterns (heavy, moderate, and light users)
6. Perceptual factors (benefit segmentation, perceptual mapping)
7. Brand and loyalty patterns
8. Product attributes

2. The segmentmust be capable of being isolated so that competitive advantage can be preserved.
3. The segment must be valid, even though imitated.

Summary

Worldwide there are over 6 billion people living in about 200 countries. Not all people, however, are potential consumers. The global market may be divided into different regions, affording different market opportunities, such as the triad market, Pacific Rim market, postcommunist countries, Latin America, China and India, and developing countries. The richest and most advanced among these is the triad market.

An interesting aspect of today's international business is the globalization of markets. World markets are slowly becoming homogeneous, requiring companies to develop marketing programs to serve consumers across national boundaries. A company interested in marketing abroad needs to decide which countries to enter and how those countries could be grouped together in homogeneous categories. The use of categories limits the need for developing marketing programs for each country separately and permits countries in each group to be served through a common marketing program.

Countries may be classified by such criteria as their economic status, geographic location, cultural traits, religious perspective, political system, socioeconomic-political characteristics, or common intermarket characteristics. In addition, a new approach for grouping countries, the portfolio method, recommends grouping countries based on three factors: competitive strength, risk, and country potential.

The concept of segmentation in the context of international marketing can be carried to another level, that is, segmentation of the in-country market. Just as the U.S. market is segmented in different ways, it may be desirable to segment the market within each country and choose one or more segments to be served. The process of accomplishing in-country segmentation is essentially the same in international marketing as in domestic marketing.

Review Questions

1. What factors make the triad market most attractive?
2. What forces account for the growing globalization of markets?
3. Does the Pacific Rim market (excluding Japan) or the Eastern European market appear to offer better market opportunities?
4. What is the rationale for grouping countries for marketing strategy?
5. Even countries that appear to be the same in so many ways—the United Kingdom and Canada, for example—can nevertheless be very different. Thus, does grouping of countries really help in making sound marketing decisions?
6. Discuss the following: "Philosophical imposition of political boundaries as the starting point in the matter of segmenting the world market is superfluous and dysfunctional. Why should we segment countries? We should rather segment the customers of the world. After all, it may be hypothesized that high-income people, whether living in the United States, France, Brazil, India, Nigeria, Egypt, Sweden, or Mexico, provide a similar potential for a product. If this is true, then it is customer segmentation on a worldwide basis that should be sought and not country classification. Income, education, geography, political views, age, and a host of other demographic and socioeconomic criteria may be used to segment the world market."
7. What are the variables used in the portfolio approach to classify countries? What problems do you anticipate in adapting the portfolio approach in practice?

Creative Questions

1. According to the U.S. government, the most growth in the next century will be in 10 nations called the Big Emerging Markets (comprising China, Indonesia, South Korea, India, Turkey, South Africa, Poland, Argentina, Brazil, and Mexico). Should this list be refined? Which countries should be added to this list? Why? Which countries should be dropped?

2. Often a case is made for making investments in developing countries on the basis that their long-run business potential is high. However, the term "long run" usually is not defined. Should the MNCs invest money in developing countries on the assumption that long-run benefits are assured? If not, should these countries be ignored until they present sustainable business opportunity?

Endnotes

1. *Time*, November 2, 1999, p. 86.

2. *The Futures Group Reports*, March 1989.

3. Kenichi Ohmae, *Triad Power* (New York: The Free Press, 1985).

4. Ibid., p. 23.

5. Rob Norton, "Why Asia's Collapse Won't Kill The Economy," *Fortune*, February 2, 1998, p. 26.

6. See "U.S. Automakers in Asia," in Subhash C. Jain, *International Marketing Management*, 6th ed. (Storrs, CT: Digital Publishing Co., 1999), pp. 824–831.

7. Louis Kraar, "The Rising Power of the Pacific," *Fortune*, Pacific Rim Issue, 1990, p. 80.

8. "Ready to Shop Until They Drop," *Business Week*, June 22, 1998, p. 104.

9. Paul Hofheinz, "Yes, You Can Win in Eastern Europe," *Fortune*, May 16, 1994, p. 110. Also see "Partners-Partness," *Business Week*, October 25, 1999, p. 106.

10. Shawn Tully, "What Eastern Europe Offers," *Fortune*, March 2, 1990, p. 51.

11. Malt Moffett and Helene Cooper, "In Backyard of the U.S., Europe Gains Ground in Trade, Diplomacy," *The Wall Street Journal*, September 18, 1997, p. 1.

12. *Country Monitor*, September 29, 1999, p. 8.

13. "How Not to Sell 1.2 Billion Tubes of Toothpaste," *The Economist*, December 3, 1994, p. 79.

14. *The Global Century: A Source Book on U.S. Business and the Third World* (Washington, D.C.: National Cooperative Business Association, 1989).

15. "Africa: A Flicker of Light," *The Economist*, March 5, 1994, p. 21.

16. Federal Industries (a Canadian firm) Annual Report, 1986.

17. *World Development Report*: 1999 (New York: Oxford University Press, 1999).

18. Ibid.

19. Lane Kelley and Reginald Worthley, "The Role of Culture in Comparative Management: A Cross-Cultural Perspective," *Academy of Management Journal* 1 (1981): pp. 164–173.

20. Geert Hofstede, *Cultural Consequences: International Differences in Work-Related Values* (London: Sage Publications, 1980).

21. See Ellen Day, Richard J. Fox, and Sandra M. Huszagh, "Segmenting the Global Market for Industrial Goods: Issues and Implications," *International Marketing Review*, Autumn 1988, pp. 14–27.

22. S. Prakash Sethi, "Comparative Cluster Analysis for World Markets," *Journal of Marketing Research*, August 1971, pp. 348–354. *Also see* Kenneth Matsuura, *A Classification of Countries for International Marketing*, Master's thesis, University of California, Berkeley, 1968.

23. "Citibank in Indonesia: Targeting the Affluent," *Crossborder Monitor*, July 13, 1994, p. 8.

24. Salah S. Hassan and Lea Prevel Katsanis, "Identification of Global Consumer Segments," *Journal of International Consumer Marketing* 1994 3 (no. 2): p. 24.

25. Kelley Shermach, "Portrait of the World," *Marketing News*, August 28, 1995, p. 20. Also see: Tom Miller, "Global Segments from 'Strivers' to 'Creatives,'" *Marketing News*, July 1998, p. 11.

Appendix

International Consumer Markets

Provided here is statistical information on markets for different kinds of goods and services in select countries. Although consumers around the world are driven by similar needs and desires, their behavior in the marketplace is distinctly influenced by their culture. Cultural differences lead to different tastes, habits, and customs, preventing people from universally preferring the same product attributes, advertising messages, packaging, or presentation.

Culture has a profound impact on how individuals perceive who they are, and what their role is as a member of society. These perceptions are often so thoroughly internalized that they are difficult to express explicitly, but they are revealed through behavior such as consumption. Thus, business success requires aligning the marketing activities to the cultural traits of the society. This approach may be less efficient in terms of standardization but more efficient in terms of creating value for the consumers and thereby resulting in higher returns.

Gross Domestic Product

As noted in Exhibit 3A.1, China's GDP, measured at purchasing power parity (PPP), was $3.8 trillion. This makes it the second-biggest economy in the world, ahead of Japan's GDP of $3.1 trillion, but only roughly half of America's GDP of $7.8 trillion. Most emerging-market economies look relatively larger when measured on a PPP basis, because their exchange rates tend to be undervalued relative to the U.S. dollar. Indeed, 7 of the world's 15 biggest economies are in the emerging world.

Overall Consumption

As Exhibit 3A.2 shows, America's private consumption spending was $5.5 trillion, more than that of any other country. As a percentage of GDP, however, spending by households and firms in Argentina, Egypt, the Philippines, Greece and Turkey was greater than in the United States. For instance, 82 percent of Argentina's GDP was devoted to private consumption in 1997, compared with 68 percent of GDP in America. Consumption by companies and households in Scandinavia was generally lower than in the rest of Europe: in Sweden, for example, it accounted for only 53 percent of GDP. But Sweden looks positively spendthrift compared with Singapore, where private consumption was only 41 percent of GDP. This is partly thanks to the city-state's mandatory savings schemes that discourage private spending. Private consumption is usually the

EXHIBIT 3A.1   GDP / World GDP at PPP

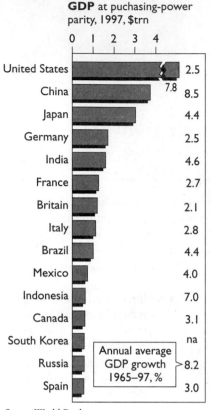

GDP at puchasing-power parity, 1997, $trn

United States	2.5
China	7.8 / 8.5
Japan	4.4
Germany	2.5
India	4.6
France	2.7
Britain	2.1
Italy	2.8
Brazil	4.4
Mexico	4.0
Indonesia	7.0
Canada	3.1
South Korea	na
Russia	8.2
Spain	3.0

Annual average GDP growth 1965–97, %

Source: World Bank

World GDP at PPP*
by region, 1997, as % of total

Total: $36.4trn

- North America 23
- Euro-11 16
- Other EU 5
- Other East Asia 15
- Japan 8
- South Asia 6
- Latin America 9
- Africa/Middle East 6
- Other 12

*At purchasing-power parity

Source: World Bank
* At purchasing-power parity

largest single component of a country's GDP. Investment, government spending and net exports make up the rest.

Breakdown of Consumer Spending

As is well known, poor countries spend a greater proportion of their income on food, beverages, and tobacco. Thus, in both China and India expenditure on this category exceeds 50 percent, whereas it is less than 20 percent in the United States, European Union, and Japan (see Exhibit 3A.3).

Hot Drinks

World hot-drink sales reached $53 billion in 1997, 23 percent more than in 1993. Patterns of coffee and tea consumption vary greatly. Most nations, though, drink more coffee than tea. The biggest coffee drinkers are the Swiss, who consume 8.7 kg of coffee each a year (see Exhibit 3A.4). The Irish are by far the biggest tea drinkers: they brew 3.6 kg each a year, far more than the second-place British. Tea is also popular in Turkey, Egypt, Hong Kong, and Russia. Coffee is becoming more popular in many tea-drinking countries, such as Britain. Nevertheless, health concerns are encouraging people to switch to decaffeinated coffee and herbal tea.

EXHIBIT 3A.2   Private Consumption, as % of GDP

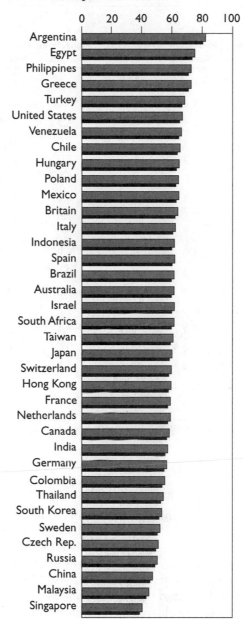

Source: Merrill Lynch

Coca-Cola's Penetration

In the United States, the per capita consumption of Coca-Cola products is 376 eight-ounce servings compared to 6 servings in China and 3 in India. Assuming there are no economic and cultural barriers to drinking Coke, eventually China and India should emerge into large markets (see Exhibit 3A.5).

▬▬▬▬▬▬▬▬▬   **EXHIBIT 3A.3**   Consumer Spending by Category, as Percent of Total: 1994

	Food, Beverages, Tobacco	Clothing, Footwear, Textiles	Household Fuels	Household Goods	Housing	Health	Leisure and Education	Transport and Communications	Other
Argentina	30.3	11.8	5.4	9.1	11.7	8.8	9.4	13.5	0.0
Australia	21.2	5.4	2.2	6.6	18.2	7.8	10.4	14.8	13.4
Brazil	36.4	4.4	5.4	4.5	25.0	4.6	4.4	8.0	7.4
Canada	18.7	5.1	3.4	8.6	20.5	4.5	11.0	14.0	14.2
China	56.2	8.2	0.0	5.3	10.7	2.9	6.7	3.2	6.9
Colombia	33.5	9.6	2.2	5.7	7.8	4.7	7.8	18.5	10.2
Eastern Europe	36.5	9.4	4.8	6.2	6.2	5.1	8.7	7.3	15.7
European Union	19.1	7.1	3.7	7.9	16.0	6.6	9.2	11.5	18.9
India	51.4	9.7	4.1	2.7	5.6	2.3	3.5	13.7	7.1
Indonesia	40.3	3.9	3.0	9.9	11.7	0.0	1.4	3.7	26.0
Israel	23.7	6.5	3.7	9.8	21.3	8.9	8.5	13.0	4.8
Japan	19.5	5.5	0.0	5.8	21.1	11.3	10.8	9.4	16.6
Mexico	32.4	6.3	0.0	9.6	13.9	4.5	5.8	12.7	14.8
Nigeria	46.1	5.5	0.0	3.4	13.1	0.0	0.0	2.2	29.7
Singapore	19.8	7.0	0.0	9.5	16.5	5.2	15.4	17.3	9.3
South Korea	27.5	3.9	4.0	6.7	12.0	6.2	12.3	13.0	14.4
Thailand	26.7	10.1	1.3	8.4	4.5	8.0	17.1	12.6	11.3
United States	17.2	5.3	2.7	5.0	14.3	15.7	11.3	11.6	16.8

Source: International Marketing Data and Statistics 1996 (London: Euromonitor, 1996), table 2515.

Beer Consumption

The Czechs drink more beer than any other nation. Retail sales there topped 179.5 liters in 1996—almost half a liter a day. Elsewhere sales are stagnant or falling in most beer-drinking countries. In second-place Ireland, sales per head were 136 liters in 1997, only 1.6 percent more than five years earlier. Sales per person fell in 11 of the top 20 beer-drinking countries between 1992 and 1997. Only two notched up double-digit percentage gains: Poland (26 percent) and Slovakia (15 percent). Outside the top 20, sales per head also rose sharply in Colombia (up by 25 percent), Britain (24 percent), Chile (16 percent) and Argentina (10 percent). Sales per head fell most, by 25 percent, in Romania (see Exhibit 3A.6).

Alcohol Consumption

Germans drank an average of 100 liters of alcoholic drinks each in 1998 (Exhibit 3A.7). But that was down from 104 liters per person in 1994. Australians drink almost as much alcohol as the Germans. Egypt, which is mostly Moslem, is the driest country in the chart. Egyptians sipped a mere half-liter of alcoholic drink each in 1998. And that was two and a half times what they drank in 1994.

EXHIBIT 3A.4   Coffee and Tea Consumption, kg per Person, 1997

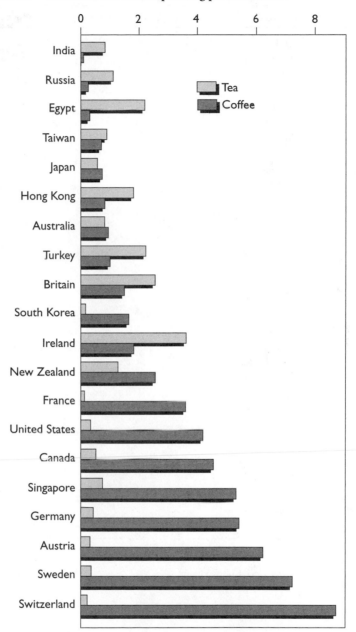

Source: Euromonitor

EXHIBIT 3A.5   Per Capita Consumption and Market Populations for Coca-Cola

Market	Population in Millions	Per Capita*
China	1,244	6
India	960	3
United States	272	376
Indonesia	203	10
Brazil	163	134
Russia	148	21
Japan	126	150
Mexico	94	371
Germany	82	203
Philippines	71	130
Egypt	64	28
France	59	88
Thailand	59	69
Great Britain	57	118
Italy	57	95
Korea	46	71
South Africa	43	155
Spain	40	201
Colombia	37	116
Argentina	36	207
Benelux/Denmark	32	196
Canada	30	196
Morocco	28	61
Romania	23	57
Venezuela	23	219
Australia	18	276
Chile	15	325
Zimbabwe	12	69
Hungary	10	153
Israel	6	267
Norway	4	272

* Eight-ounce servings of company beverages per person per year (excludes products distributed by The Minute Maid Company).
Source: Coca-Cola Company.

Chocolate Consumption

Britain is the most chocaholic nation in the G7. In 1998 Britons consumed an average of 9.5 kg of chocolate each, nearly a third more than German consumers, and two-thirds more than Americans. Chocolate accounted for two-thirds of the average British's total consumption of confectionery—which, at 14 kg per head, means that the British lead the world in "sweet teeth" as well as "stiff upper lips". British chocolate consumption grew steadily in 1993–98, in contrast to Germany, where consumption has leveled off, and in America, where it has actually fallen (see Exhibit 3A.8).

EXHIBIT 3A.6   Beer Sales, 1997

Source: Euromonitor

EXHIBIT 3A.7 Alcoholic-Drinks Consumption, Litres per Person, 1998

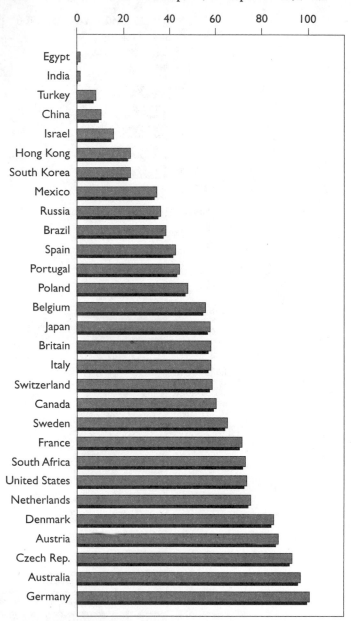

Source: Euromonitor

Health-Care Expenditures

Worldwide sales of over-the-counter health-care products were worth $75 billion in 1998 (see Exhibit 3A.9). Vitamins and dietary supplements make up one-third of the total; cold and allergy remedies account for just under a fifth. Although they still represent only a small share of the overall market, sleeping aids and products to help people give up smoking are the two fastest-growing segments of the market. Richer countries tend to spend

EXHIBIT 3A.8   Chocolate Consumption: Average Sales, 1998, kg per Head

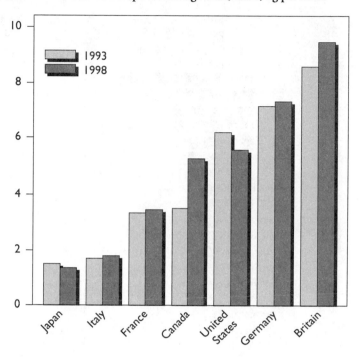

Source: Euromonitor

more on over-the-counter health care than poorer ones. But there are wide disparities, even so. At an average of $135 per person per year, the Japanese spend the most on over-the-counter health care. Americans are second, at $76 per head. At the other extreme, Indians spend an average of only 55 cents.

Videocassette Recorders Ownership

Almost 25 percent of the world's 317 million households with a videocassette recorder (VCR) are in the United States, where an astonishing 82.9 percent of homes now owns one (Exhibit 3A.10). Of the world's television-owning homes, 37.1 percent own a VCR. The popularity of VCRs, a technology now in its 20th year, may be some guide to the prospects for other new media hardware. From market inception, VCRs took between 7 and 11 years to achieve 20 percent penetration of households with television sets in European countries. Other media technologies are unlikely to be taken up much faster. A VCR has an average retail value of $200 in the United States but around $430 elsewhere.

Telephone Use

As a rule, the wealthier a country, the more telephone lines it tends to have. In 1995 rich countries averaged more than one main telephone line for every two people. Poor regions still have relatively underdeveloped telephone networks. South Asia, for example, has only 13 main lines for every 1,000 people, while sub-Saharan Africa has only 11. Hong Kong,

EXHIBIT 3A.9   Health-Care Products*

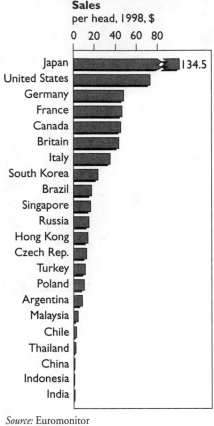

Sales
per head, 1998, $

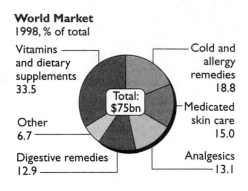

World Market
1998, % of total

Vitamins and dietary supplements 33.5

Cold and allergy remedies 18.8

Other 6.7

Total: $75bn

Medicated skin care 15.0

Digestive remedies 12.9

Analgesics 13.1

Source: Euromonitor
* Over-the-counter

on of the richest emerging markets, has 530 main telephone lines for every 1,000 people. This is more than in Britain or Germany, but fewer than America's 627 lines per 1,000. Greece is not far behind, with 493 per 1,000 people. At the other extreme, India, the poorest country in the chart, has only 13 lines for every 1,000 people (see Exhibit 3A.11).

Recorded Music Sales

Global recorded-music sales rose by 3 percent in 1998, to $38.7 billion. But unit sales fell by 1 percent, to $4.1 billion units. A rise in CD sales of 6 percent was offset by a 10 percent fall in cassette purchases and an 11 percent decline in singles. Sales in America, which made up 34 percent of the world market in 1998, jumped by 11 percent to $13.2 billion (Exhibit 3A.12) Sales in the European Union were up by 3 percent, to $11.6 billion. But Japanese sales fell by 4 percent, to $6.5 billion. Sales in crisis-hit Asia plunged: in Indonesia they were down by 56 percent.

Gold Purchases

Demand for gold has steadied, after slumping in early 1998 in the wake of the Asian crisis. Demand in the 25 main markets totaled 1,712 tonnes in the first nine months of

EXHIBIT 3A.10   VCR Penetration, % of TV Households with a Video Recorder

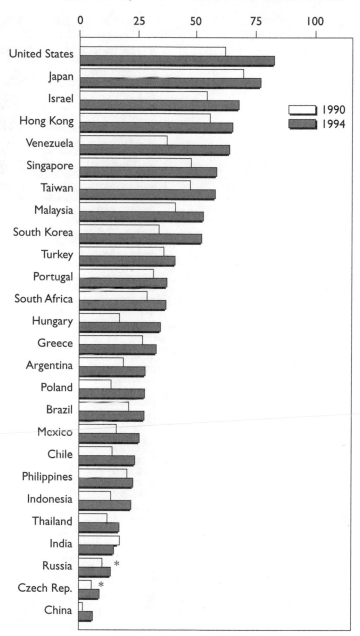

Source: Screen Digest
* 1993

1998, 20 percent down on the same period in 1997 (see Exhibit 3A.13). But whereas gold consumption in the first quarter was 46 percent below the 1997 level, gold use in the three months to September was only 1 percent lower than in the same period in 1997. The world's two biggest gold markets are leading the recovery. Gold consumption in the first nine months of 1999 was up by 19 percent in India and by 17 percent in the United States compared with the same period in 1997. Gold use has risen by 8 percent in Saudi Arabia

EXHIBIT 3A.11   Main Telephone Lines, per 1,000 Persons, 1995

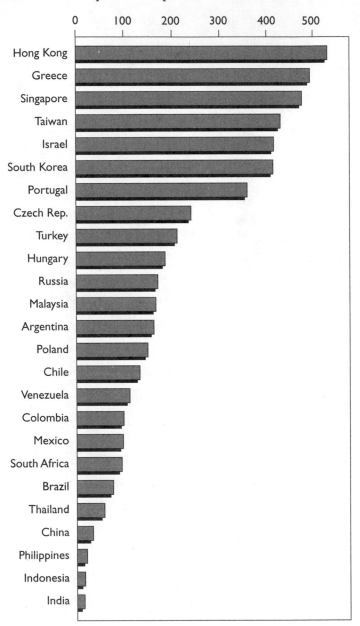

Sources: World Bank, ITU

and by 5 percent in the Gulf states, mainly the United Arab Emirates. But despite the pickup in demand, the price of gold continues to fall. An ounce of gold cost over $400 in early 1996. It cost less than $300 in 1998.

EXHIBIT 3A.12   World Music

Sales, 1998, $bn

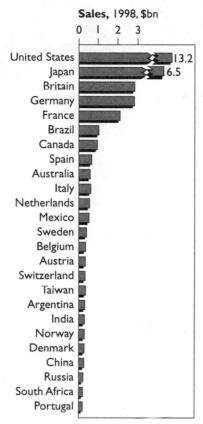

% of Total Sales 1998

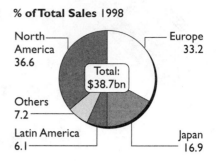

North America 36.6

Europe 33.2

Others 7.2

Latin America 6.1

Japan 16.9

Total: $38.7bn

Source: International Federation of the Phonographic Industry

EXHIBIT 3A.13   Gold, Largest Consumer Markets, Net Demand Tonnes

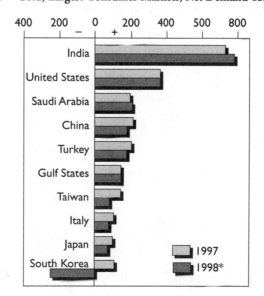

Source: World Gold Council
* First nine months at annual rate

International Marketing Research

CHAPTER FOCUS _____

After studying this chapter, you should be able to

■ Explain the importance of marketing research in the context of international business.

■ Discuss the procedure for undertaking marketing research across national boundaries.

■ Identify sources of secondary data both in the United States and abroad.

■ Describe the problems of conducting primary research overseas.

■ Discuss the perspectives of an international marketing information system.

The prime function of marketing research is to determine what buyers *want* so that companies can produce and sell those items rather than simply selling whatever can be most easily made. This role of marketing research is the same in domestic and international marketing.

The worldwide marketing research industry had a value of about $10.5 billion in 1999. Of this, the largest single market was the United States, accounting for some $4.9 billion or about 47 percent of the total. Europe accounted for $3.7 billion, 35 percent of the total global marketing research expenditures. Japan, Australia, and New Zealand added another 8 percent. Canada accounted for 5 percent.

The remaining $525 million, about 5 percent of the world total, came from developing countries. Half of that amount was spent in Latin and South America, mainly Mexico, Brazil, Argentina, and Venezuela. The Far East, excluding Japan, accounted for $185 million. The African total would have been very small if not for the $27 million of the $30 million total spent by South Africa. The Middle East, with Saudi Arabia the main market, contributed about $13 million and is a growth area, but one that has slowed in recent years. India, Pakistan, and Sri Lanka added a further $35 million.[1]

The top 25 firms account for almost 70 percent of the industry's worldwide revenue. Global market research is a booming industry, growing at more than 15 percent a year. With competition among retailers and manufacturers intensifying, speedy, accurate research can be crucial to the success of products, particularly new ones. The top 10 marketing researchers are ACNielsen Corp.(U.S.), IMS Health Inc.(U.S.), The Kantar Group Ltd.(U.K.), Taylor Nelson Sofres plc.(U.K.), Information Resources Inc.(U.S.), NFO Worldwide Inc.(U.S.), Nielsen Media Research(U.S.), GfK Group AG(Germany), IPSOS Group S.A.(France), Westat Inc.(U.S.).[2]

The differences in international environments make marketing research more difficult there than in a domestic environment. Consider the research information needed by these potential international marketers:

- A manufacturer of a specialized industrial product, iron fitting, believes that there is potentially a good market for export and wants to begin to develop it. Neither the company's management nor any of its salesforce, however, has knowledge of possible markets or of the nature of the competition.

- A large U.S. corporation is contemplating building a factory in Western Europe. Management wonders if its product should be changed to suit the new market.

- A pharmaceutical company has to decide how to price a prescription drug item manufactured in its factory in Brazil for the Latin American market. Should the same pricing schedule used in the United States be followed? If not, what criteria should be used to set the price?

- A soft drink company must determine how effective its U.S. advertising strategy will be in promoting its product in Southeast Asia.

Such situations are examples of international marketing problems that require marketing research. In each case, the firm's past experience cannot provide an adequate basis for decision. In fact, the information necessary to support management action is more likely to be found outside the organization. Specialized trade journals or government studies or discussions with professional-level personnel who have special industry expertise are likely to be helpful. If all these fail, it may finally become necessary to conduct a customer survey.

This chapter examines the meaning of marketing research and provides a framework for conducting such research. The two types of research, primary and secondary, are differentiated and their procedures discussed. Alternative ways of organizing international marketing research are presented, and the need for establishing an international marketing information system is explained.

Meaning of Marketing Research

The term *marketing research* refers to gathering, analyzing, and presenting information related to a well-defined, specific problem or a project with a beginning and an end. In contrast, *marketing intelligence* is information gathered and analyzed on a continual basis. Unlike marketing research, marketing intelligence is evaluated information whose credibility, meaning, and importance have been established.

Often the term *marketing research* is used interchangeably with the term *market research*, but the latter is conceptually narrower in scope, focusing on current and potential customers—who they are; why they buy a product or service; and where, when, and how they buy it. Both marketing research and market research deal with *marketing mix variables*—product, price, distribution, and promotion—as well as marketing organizational matters and the marketing environment. A *marketing information system* consists of market research, marketing research, and marketing intelligence.

The procedures and methods of conducting marketing research are conceptually the same for both domestic marketing and international marketing. For example, in both cases, before collecting data the researcher must have a clear idea of the research problem or focus. Likewise, only an appropriate sample will yield valuable results in either domestic or international research. But international marketing research differs from domestic marketing in three major ways:

1. The effects of the international environment on the whole company as a profit-oriented unit are considered. For example, the marketing research project concerned with the ramifications of a substantial price hike in a particular foreign country must consider questions that do not apply to the domestic market, such as whether the company's subsidiary will be nationalized if prices are increased beyond a certain level (see International Marketing Highlight 4.1).
2. Many concepts and frameworks (e.g., market segmentation), which constitute the core of marketing decision making in the domestic arena, may be unusable in international marketing, not because the concept cannot be transferred, but because the information necessary to make such a transfer is not available. For example, if there is a lack of current income distribution data on a country, any analysis of the demand for a product will assume incorrect income categories and therefore be invalid.
3. Finally, the ethnocentric nature of marketing makes cultural differences among nations a significant factor. Whereas the culture in a domestic market is already understood, in international marketing the culture must be fully investigated.[3]

To illustrate this last point, consider a recent study that explored the effect of a monetary incentive on the questionnaire response rate. Receipt of one U.S. dollar increased the response rate from Japanese business people but decreased the response from Hong Kong business people. The author of that study noted,

> In this study, Japanese business executives were more compliant than Hong Kongese in general, and the monetary incentive was successful in more than doubling the response from Japan but decreased the response from Hong Kong. These findings may be biased because of the small sample, the sampling frame, or the questionnaire content. However, the results may imply a cultural difference either toward responding to questionnaires, or toward monetary incentives. The cross-cultural researcher should be aware of such problems, and explore the effect of monetary incentives prior to the mass mailing of surveys. Theoretically, monetary incentives may increase response rates in any culture or country; however, the type (local or foreign currency) and amount may be important factors.[4]

Such factors raise a variety of conceptual, methodological, and organizational issues in international marketing research relating to[5]

1. The complexity of research design, caused by operation in a multicountry, multicultural, and multilinguistic environment.
2. The lack of secondary data for many countries and product markets.
3. The high costs of collecting primary data, particularly in developing countries.
4. The problems associated with coordinating research and data collection in different countries.
5. The difficulties of establishing the comparability and equivalence of data and research conducted in different contexts.
6. The intrafunctional character of many international marketing decisions.
7. The economics of many international investment and marketing decisions.

█████████████   **International Marketing Highlight 4.1**   ██████████

Local Culture and Market Potential

The chairman of a large American soft drink company decided that the firm should target Indonesia for sales of its most popular beverage. @TX2:With a population of nearly 180 million people, Indonesia is the fifth most populous country in the world. Management considered this huge potential market irresistible and worked out a bottling and distribution arrangement to serve the country. The company sold the soft drink syrup to a bottler, who then bottled the drink and distributed it.

Unfortunately, sales were terrible. The drink simply didn't sell. The marketing campaign flopped despite predominantly good initial research, including research into the local competition and government attitudes, because the chairman and his project directors forgot to consider two major factors. First, Indonesia does have 180 million inhabitants, but most of them live in rural areas, still functioning within a preindustrial economy. Most Indonesians simply don't have much money. Second, many of them prefer sweet coconut-based drinks; they are unaccustomed to American-style carbonated beverages. A market for American drinks does exist, but almost exclusively in the major cities. That market—consumers with western tastes and sufficient disposable income to purchase foreign-style beverages—totals only about 8 million people.

Framework for International Marketing Research

Most marketing research studies proceed through a common series of major tasks:

- Define the problem and specify the information needed for support of management's decision-making process.
- Identify alternative sources of information.
- Plan and execute data collection.
- Analyze the data and prepare a report.

Defining the Problem

The first task, defining the problem, sounds deceptively simple but, may be the pivotal task in the entire study. In defining the problem, two important considerations are market structure and product concept. *Market structure* refers to the size of the market, its stage of development, the number of competitors and their market shares, and the channels through which the market is approached.

The importance of market structure in problem definition is shown by a 1963 *Reader's Digest* study, which reported that French and German consumers ate significantly more spaghetti than Italians.[6] This finding was wrong. The study had concerned itself with only packaged, branded spaghetti, and not *total* spaghetti consumption. Because much of the spaghetti sold in Italy is unpackaged and unbranded, the results of the study were totally invalid. The *Reader's Digest* researchers should have clearly defined the kind of spaghetti consumption to be studied in each of the different countries (see International Marketing Highlight 4.2).

████████████████   **International Marketing Highlight 4.2**   ████████████████

Health Clubs in Singapore

A widely franchised health club opened a facility in Singapore. With its young, urban population and a widespread appreciation of western culture, Singapore seemed a site destined for success. Moreover, the club's physical appearance and stock of equipment equaled or surpassed that of comparable facilities in the U.S.

Yet the club couldn't sign up enough members. Despite the Singaporeans' interest in sports, the club attracted few of them and ended up catering to the relatively small expatriate community instead. Citizens of Singapore felt little enthusiasm for the American-style health club; they were more attracted either to western competitive sports or to Chinese calisthenics and other traditional Asian forms of exercise.

Source: Charles F. Valentine, *The Arthur Young International Business Guide* (New York: John Wiley & Sons, 1988), p. 74.

In addition, a product may be viewed differently in different cultures. Thus, even before attempting to define the marketing research problem for study, exploratory research may be necessary to understand the ***product concept***, that is, the meaning of the product in a particular environment.

Berent points out that milk-based products are viewed very differently in the United Kingdom and Thailand.[7] In England, they are usually consumed at meals and bedtime for their sleep-inducing, soothing, relaxing properties. In Thailand, the same products are consumed on the way to work and often away from home, for they are considered invigorating, energizing, and stimulating.

Let us assume a multinational marketer is interested in finding out the potential market for a brand of yogurt in England and Thailand. The problem definition in the two countries will have to be stated differently. In the United Kingdom, the yogurt might be primarily perceived by the consumers as a healthful and relaxing product to be used prior to retiring. In Thailand, the research problem would determine if yogurt would be considered mainly an energy food used to start the day.

Identifying Alternative Information Sources

After the problem has been defined, where the necessary information may be found and how to obtain it must be determined. In some cases, the study may be confined to *secondary data*, that is, published information that has been collected elsewhere. Such data may be available free (for example, government statistics), for a price (for example, syndicated research findings), or through restricted distribution sources (for example, trade association statistics).

Let us assume that Ford Motor Company is interested in assembling its new world car in India in collaboration with an Indian company. Before committing itself to the joint venture, Ford would like to study the car's market potential in India over a 10-year period. Fortunately, the Indian government collects a variety of socioeconomic-demographic information on a regular basis. This information is conveniently available. Ford, therefore, can use with confidence such secondary information as population projections, income data, consumer expenditure patterns, and rural-urban population shifts to assess the market potential.

Sometimes internal data are also useful. Existing files, in fact, can often provide important insights into the question at hand. In the preceding example, Ford might have found that it already had sufficient information on population trends in India gathered when the company had earlier negotiated for the assembly of tractors there. Thus, there would be no need for another source of information.

In cases where no amount of investigation of secondary sources or of internal data provides the required information, *primary data* must be compiled through interviews and other direct collection of information. Primary data may be gathered in various ways (to be discussed later), from trade association representatives, governmental experts, managerial personnel, or the buying public.

For example, a company may be interested in introducing its prefabricated houses in Latin America. The company would have to study house-buying behavior in the target countries, information that may not be conveniently available from secondary sources. Consequently, primary data gathering may be necessary. The importance of such information for decision making is revealed in a study on the subject done in the United Kingdom.

> Home ownership in different countries could also have completely different implications. The proverb that "a man's home is his castle" is far more applicable in the United Kingdom (where castles can in fact be found) than in the United States, where the geographic and social mobility of the population means that the regular exchange of homes is a commonplace experience during the life cycle of most families. Therefore, the decision-making patterns of husband and wife, and the amount of effort spent in making a home-buying decision, should be quite different between these two countries.[8]

Thus, before entering the market with prefabricated houses in Latin America, the company has to learn through primary research in which ways houses might mean "home" in various locales.

Data Collection

The actual collection of data, which will be discussed at length in later sections of this chapter, must be planned and executed carefully. Tracking down reliable, usable data sources can be time-consuming. This is particularly so when a variety of sources are pursued concurrently. In fact, the search can go on with decreasing returns unless a person with knowledge of the country appraises the progress being made.

Interview questions must be tested for their appropriateness so that they produce the desired results. A sound approach is to conduct professional-level interviews in two phases: (1) collect basic data and (2) explore interview questions not anticipated at the start of the project.

Once basic data have been collected, the process of cross-checking can begin. This step requires that all information be examined critically for its relevance. Cross-checking establishes the reliability of data by comparing one source with another. It is important to document the criteria used by the project team to determine the reliability of collected data.

Analysis, Interpretation, and Report Preparation

For the final step, the preparation of the report, the data must be analyzed and interpreted. Here also, attention should be paid to a country's cultural traits. For example, in an examination of the beer market it was found that beer was perceived as an alcoholic drink in Northern European countries but as a soft drink in Mediterranean countries. Thus, other products listed with beer as alternative drinks would influence the research findings. Similarly, in Japan noncarbonated fruit juices are often substituted for bottled soft drinks, a practice rare in the United States. In brief, *the significance of different concepts of the product in various countries must be taken into account.*

Reports must be complete, factual, and objective. It is particularly important to communicate the reliability as well as the limitations of the facts presented. Particular attention should be given to the following aspects of a report:

1. Data sources must be identified. Different sources of data warrant varying degrees of confidence. For example, information on a developing country obtained from the

United States Agency for International Development is probably more reliable than the information available from the government of that country.

2. Data projection must be explained and the statistical computations simplified as much as possible.

3. The identity of all those interviewed should be included as well as their titles or qualifications. (This rule does not apply to consumer research.) This requirement may have to be relaxed when anonymity has been guaranteed.

4. The alternative courses of action developed from analysis and interpretation of the data must be labeled as such, clearly reserving to management the responsibility for selecting the appropriate course of action.

Information Requirements of International Marketers

The nature of marketing decisions does not vary from country to country, but the environment differs from country to country. For this reason, the sort of information required to complete a marketing study may vary from one country to another. For example, in a situation where a marketer is free to set prices based on competition, a detailed analysis of competition should be made. However, in a country where the price is set by government, information on governmental cost analysis would be of greater importance. The fact that environment determines what kind of information is needed makes international marketing research efforts quite different from domestic marketing research work.

Exhibit 4.1 shows the types of marketing studies a company may want to conduct in the different areas of promotion, distribution, price, product, or market. Each of these area studies requires a different form of information, as the following discussion makes clear.

Market Information

Market research is required for testing, entering, or leaving a market and deals with market performance, market shares, and sales analysis and forecasting. *Marketing performance research* involves market measurements, either to compare a company's performance against specified standards or to project a possible future outcome. *Market potential* refers to the total market demand under optimal conditions, whereas *market forecast* shows the expected level of market demand under the given conditions. To illustrate, when Pizza Hut decided to expand its business into certain Middle Eastern countries like Saudi Arabia, it conducted beforehand market-potential research for five years in each country.

Market share refers to a company's proportion of total sales in an industry during a set time, usually a year. The market shares held by competitors shape marketing strategy for a company. The competitor with a respectable market share will have a cost advantage over its rivals. This cost advantage can be passed on to the customers through lower prices, which in turn strengthen the company's hold on the market. Because of the strategic importance of market share, business corporations keep constant watch on its fluctuations. Data supplied by industry associations, if properly analyzed, usually show respective market shares.

Past *sales information* can be analyzed in different ways: by amount of profit from different products, by productivity of sales territory (for example, Latin America or Western Europe), or by customer type. Sales analysis can pinpoint problems.

Sales forecasts refer to estimates of future sales of a product during a specific period. The sales forecast is the single most important basis for preparing budgets.

Product Information

Product research means both product-line research and individual product research. This kind of research bears on when to add, delete, or change the product.

A company operating overseas must often decide which product lines it should add, drop, or rejuvenate. These decisions require a variety of information. Consider this exam-

FIGURE 4.1 Types of Marketing Studies Required for Doing Business Abroad

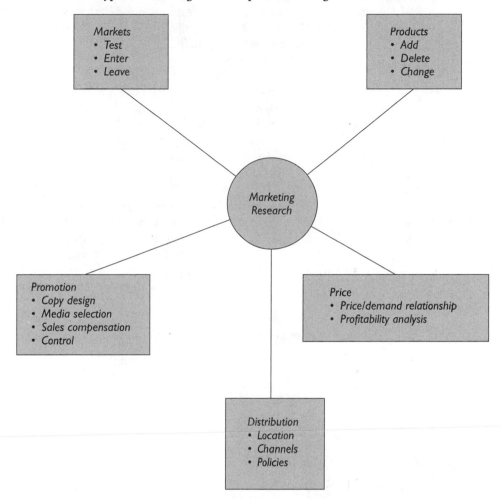

ple. A large paper products company manufactured an expensive line of writing paper, as well as other kinds of paper products. The company had about a 30 percent market share in Latin America, but the demand had been constant for a number of years. As part of a program for simplification of product lines, the company conducted marketing research to see if there had been changes in the office environment in Latin countries that made the use of expensive paper obsolete. and thus warranted dropping that product line.

A manager may also seek marketing research on an individual product as it passes through its life cycle, since different marketing programs must be developed for every stage. It is important to identify the stage a product is in so as to choose the appropriate marketing program. Marketing research can be of real value in plotting a product's life cycle in different countries.

Promotion Information

Promotion research is designed specifically for application in advertising and personal selling. Companies consult this research in order to select appropriate advertising copy and make the best media selection. A trading stamp company operating in Europe, for example, redeemed stamps saved by consumers in two ways, either in merchandise or in travel. Over the years, it was found that more and more customers preferred overseas travel to merchandise. For the company, however, merchandise was more profitable; so the company considered starting an ad campaign to entice consumers into redeeming their stamps in merchandise. As a part of this campaign, a merchandise catalog emphasizing the virtue of material acquisitions as status symbols would be marketed in Europe. The production of the catalog would cost about 2 million dollars. Obviously, the catalog's market effectiveness had to be tested beforehand.

As applied to personal selling, promotion research is designed to solve problems such as that expressed by the sales manager of a U.S. pharmaceutical company: "My salespeople in Italy are not productive enough, even though we pay them a lot more than the industry average there." Marketing research can provide insights into this kind of problem by answering questions about how many salespeople to hire, how much to pay them, how to form sales territories, and how much time to spend on retaining old customers versus developing new accounts.

Distribution Information

Distribution research consists of channel research and location research. As its name implies, *channel research* provides information on the availability of channels and their relative desirability. A water systems manufacturer, for instance, traditionally used manufacturer's representatives for the distribution of its water pumps in the Canadian market. The company, however, was becoming dissatisfied with manufacturer's representatives and wanted to use its own salesforce. A marketing research firm was asked for a study of the effect on sales of making such a change.

Location research concerns decisions about warehousing, inventory, and transportation. For example, the decision to own a warehouse in Germany or to use a public warehouse there requires marketing research.

Price Information

A company sets the prices of its products to meet both short-term and long-term objectives. To set prices, information about the ability of consumers to pay, about dealer reaction, and about the effect of price on demand is necessary. Studies that measure the public perception of a product's quality in relation to price also help in making pricing decisions.

Environment Information

No matter which sort of international marketing study is planned, the researchers must take into account the foreign country's environment in all its aspects: legal, political, social, cultural, and attitudinal, as shown by both the buying habits of its consumers and the business practices of its enterprises. Naturally, familiarity with the environment is equally important in domestic marketing, but in that case most of the necessary knowledge has already been obtained from personal experience. For example, if a U.S. company is interested in doing business in China, it must learn about the political system there, whereas little or no money or effort need be expended on investigating the U.S. political system.

General Research Information

In addition to the specific categories of marketing research discussed thus far, general research information is necessary on the following:

1. *Community-type conditions* (for example, political happenings such as campaigns and elections; cultural events such as county fairs and special annual ethnic or religious celebrations; and national events such as sports, championships, and holidays).
2. *Business conditions* (for example, business ethics and traditional associations).
3. *Lifestyles and living conditions,* that is, social and cultural customs and taboos (for example, marriageable age for men and women and the role of women in society)[9] (see International Marketing Highlight 4.3).
4. General economic conditions (for example, the standards of living of various groups of people and the economic infrastructure—transportation, power supply, and communication).

Also required is

1. Industry information about government decisions affecting the industry.
2. Resource availability (for example, labor and land).
3. Current or potential competitors (that is, general information about their markets and their problems).
4. Competition from U.S. companies, local companies, and third-country companies.
5. Industry policy, concerted actions in the industry, and so forth.

In addition, study-related information is desirable on specific subjects. For example, a study concerned with market potential needs information on supply and demand in market areas of current and potential interest (capacity, consumption, imports, exports). A study concerned with the introduction of a new product requires information about existing products, the technical know-how available in the country, sources of raw material, and leads for joint ventures.

■■■■■■■■■■■   **International Marketing Highlight 4.3**   ■■■■■■■■■■■

Hands-on Market Research

When Sony researched the market for a lightweight portable cassette player, results showed that consumers wouldn't buy a tape player that didn't record. Company chairman Akio Morita decided to introduce the Walkman anyway, and the rest is history. Today it is one of Sony's most successful products.

Morita's disdain for large-scale consumer surveys and other scientific research tools isn't unique in Japan. Matsushita, Toyota, and other well-known Japanese consumer goods companies are just as skeptical about the western style of market research. Occasionally, the Japanese do conduct consumer attitude surveys, but most executives don't base their marketing decisions on them or on other popular techniques.

Of course, Japanese corporations want accurate and useful information about their markets as much as U.S. and European companies do. They just go about it differently. Japanese executives put much more faith in information they get directly from wholesalers and retailers in the distribution channels. Moreover, they track what's happening among channel members on a monthly, weekly, and sometimes even daily basis.

Japanese-style market research relies heavily on two kinds of information: "soft data" obtained from visits to dealers and other channel members, and "hard data" about shipments, inventory levels, and retail sales. Japanese managers believe that these data better reflect the behavior and intentions of flesh-and-blood consumers.

Source: Reprinted by permission of *Harvard Business Review*. An excerpt from "Market Research the Japanese Way" by Johny K. Johansson and Ikujiro Nonaka, May–June 1987, p. 16. Copyright (c) 1987 by the President and Fellows of Harvard College; all rights reserved.

The amount of information to be gathered in a given case depends on the cost/benefit relationship of such information. For example, let us assume a company has an opportunity to export machinery to Kenya. Although normally the company checks on the credit rating of an importer before making a shipment, such a delay might ruin a particular transaction. The company figures out that if the importer does not make the payment as stipulated, it stands to lose $2,000 after accounting for the advance from the importer. On the other hand, the company could have a market research firm do a study on the creditworthiness of the importer for $3,000 in a very short time. So the cost exceeds the benefit, making the study not worth its expense. This example, though oversimplified, illustrates the importance of relating the cost to benefit in terms of time and money before undertaking a marketing research project.

Finally, the nature of information required will vary based on the objective of research. To illustrate this point, Exhibit 4.2 lists the types of information a firm needs to determine export potential. The firm must examine different types of environments as well as undertake market and product research.

EXHIBIT 4.2   Information Needs for Determining Export Potential

Stage One: Preliminary Screening

Preliminary screening involves defining the physical, political, economic, and cultural environment.

Demographic/Physical Environment
- Population size, growth, density
- Urban and rural distribution
- Climate and weather variations
- Shipping distance
- Product-significant demographics
- Physical distribution and communications network
- Natural resources

Political Environment
- System of government
- Political stability and continuity
- Ideological orientation
- Government involvement in business
- Government involvement in communications
- Attitudes toward foreign business (trade restrictions, tariffs, nontariff barriers, bilateral trade agreement)
- National economic and developmental priorities

Economic Environment
- Overall level of development
- Economic growth: GNP, industrial sector
- Role of foreign trade in the economy
- Currency, inflation rate, availability, controls, stability of exchange rate
- Balance of payments
- Per capita income and distribution
- Disposable income and expenditure patterns

Social/Cultural Environment
- Literacy rate, educational level
- Existence of middle class
- Similarities and differences in relation to home market
- Language and other cultural considerations

The export marketer will eliminate some foreign markets from further consideration on the basis of this preliminary screening. An example would be the absence of comparable or linking products and services, a deficiency that would hinder the potential for marketing products.

Stage Two: Analysis of Industry Market Potential

Market Access
- Limitations on trade: tariff levels, quotas
- Documentation and import regulations
- Local standards, practices, and other nontariff barriers
- Patents and trademarks
- Preferential treaties
- Legal considerations; investment, taxation, repatriation, employment, code of laws

Product Potential
- Customer needs and desires
- Local production, imports, consumption
- Exposure to and acceptance of products
- Availability of linking products
- Industry-specific key indicators of demand
- Attitudes toward products of foreign origin
- Competitive offerings
- Availability of intermediaries
- Regional and local transportation facilities
- Availability of manpower
- Conditions for local manufacture

Stage Three: Analysis of Company Sales Potential

The third stage of the screening process involves assessing company sales potential in those countries that prove promising based upon the earlier analyses.

Sales Volume Forecasting

- Size and concentration of customer segments
- Projected consumption statistics
- Competitive pressures
- Expectations of local distributors/agents

Landed Cost

- Costing method for exports
- Domestic distribution costs
- International freight and insurance
- Cost of product modification

Cost of Internal Distribution

- Tariffs and duties
- Value-added tax
- Local packaging and assembly
- Margins/commission allowed for the trade
- Local distribution and inventory costs
- Promotional expenditures

Other Determinants of Profitability

- Going price levels
- Competitive strengths and weaknesses
- Credit practices
- Current and projected exchange rates

Source: S. Tamer Cavusgil, "Guidelines for Export Market Research," *Business Horizons,* November–December 1985, pp. 30–31.

Gathering Secondary Data at Home

There are two kinds of data—primary and secondary. *Primary data* are gathered by the researcher. *Secondary data* are data that have been collected by someone else, either an individual or an organization. Exhibit 4.3 characterizes the two kinds of data. Research based on secondary data may be conducted either at home or abroad. This section discusses secondary research in the United States

U.S. Sources of Data

There are five sources of information in the United States: international agencies, U.S. government, consulting firms, foreign government offices, and banks.

International Agencies The United Nations (UN), the World Bank, and the International Monetary Fund (IMF) gather a variety of economic and social information on different countries of the world. This information is available to the public. For example, the

EXHIBIT 4.3   Characteristics of Primary and Secondary Data

Primary Data

- From knowledgeable individuals
- May be costly in time and travel
- May tend to be subjective
- Must be pilot-tested
- Can be very specific to problems
- Cannot require disclosure of proprietary information

Secondary Data

- From published sources or at the professional level collected by others
- Usually free or low cost
- Can be collected quickly
- May be biased or incomplete
- May be out of date at hand
- Requires careful analysis of limitations

UN Yearbook provides information on worldwide demographics. Also, the World Bank's *The World Development Report* summarizes information on living patterns comprising such indicators as daily calorie supply, life expectancy at birth, and school enrollment. The IMF provides historical information on national economic indicators (GNP, industrial production, inflation rate, money supply) of its member countries. This information is available on computer tapes.

The information available from these international organizations, however, has two drawbacks. First, the information is based on data supplied by each member country, and is difficult to determine what criteria and means have been used. In some cases, the reliability of the data should be questioned because various bureaucrats may have slanted it for their own purposes. Second, the information is dated. It takes time for an international organization to gather information from all over the world, analyze it, and make it available to the public in summary form.

Most university libraries and public libraries in major cities carry the UN and the World Bank publications. The IMF information may be available only in more specialized libraries.

U.S. Government The U.S. Department of Commerce is the single most important source of secondary information. Forty-eight international trade administration district offices and 19 branch offices of the U.S. Department of Commerce in cities throughout the United States and in Puerto Rico provide information and professional export counseling to business people. Each office is headed by a director, supported by trade specialists and other staff. These professionals can help a company's decision makers gain a basic understanding of profitable opportunities in exporting and assist them in evaluating the company's market potential overseas.

Each district office can give information about

- Trade and investment opportunities abroad.
- Foreign markets for U.S. products and services.
- Services to locate and evaluate overseas buyers and representatives.
- Financing aid for exporters.
- International trade exhibitions.
- Export documentation requirements.
- Foreign economic statistics.
- U.S. export licensing and foreign national import requirements.
- Export seminars and conferences.

Most district offices maintain an extensive business library containing the department's latest reports.

The U.S. Department of Commerce information is obtained in two ways: on a regular basis from periodicals such as *Export America* (formerly *Business America*) and on an ad hoc basis from special reports prepared on opportunities for American companies, for example, in Saudi Arabia.

The U.S. Department of Commerce informs businesses not only about international business conditions abroad, but also about events and happenings in Washington and their impact on international business. Information is available on all phases of marketing.

Useful information may also be available from other departments or agencies of the federal government such as the U.S. State Department's Agency for International Development (USAID) or the U.S. Department of Agriculture. Most of these organizations issue newsletters and other publications. An international marketer could subscribe to those pertinent to particular products or markets. Currently, all U.S. government information, entitled *National Trade Data Bank* (NTDB), is available on CD rom, updated every three months. The NTDB information can also be accessed on the internet.

U.S. Consulting Firms Many management consulting firms (including accounting firms) specialize in services for U.S. business abroad. Some of these firms conduct original research. Their findings are available to the international marketer. One such firm is Business International Corporation, a division of *The Economist*. It puts out a number of publications (newsletters issued periodically, studies issued on a regular basis, and ad hoc studies). Another firm that specializes in providing secondary data is Predicasts of Cleveland, Ohio. Similarly, major accounting firms and major banks issue a variety of finance- and accounting-related information on different countries of the world. For example, Price Waterhouse regularly publishes booklets on select countries, providing perspectives on doing business there. Bank of America offers a service entitled World Information Services, which tracks, analyzes, and forecasts economic and business conditions in 100 countries.

U.S. Foreign Government Offices Almost all countries maintain embassies in Washington, D.C. In addition, these countries have consulates and UN mission offices in New York City. A country may have more than one consulate office in the U.S. For example, the government of Brazil maintains consulate offices in New York, Chicago, Dallas, and Los Angeles, in addition to their embassy in Washington, D.C. Usually, an embassy has a commercial attaché who may be a good source of secondary information on the country. The consulate and the UN mission usually have basic information on their country to offer the researcher. For example, let us assume research is being done to prepare a market-potential study in order to decide whether a company should assemble television sets in Nigeria. Import data on this product in Nigeria for the past five years are needed. The Nigerian consulate in New York might have a government publication that quickly and easily provides such information.

Other units of a foreign government in the United States can serve as important sources of data. For example, a hotel chain interested in constructing a hotel on the Caribbean island of St. Lucia may find the St. Lucian government tourist office in New York City an important source of information on tourist trade there.

Many governments maintain special offices in the United States for the purpose of promoting trade and business with U.S. companies. For example, the Indian government's India Investment Center in New York City offers all sorts of business-related information. If the center does not have the information, it can guide the researcher to the proper source.

U.S. Multinational Banks Both U.S. banks active worldwide (e.g., Citicorp, BankAmerica Corp., Chase Manhattan Bank), and branches of foreign banks in the U.S. are additional sources of secondary information. Many of these banks maintain libraries. They usually offer free access to customers, present and prospective. In some instances, however, a bank may have information a researcher seeks in one of its reports, but the data may not be made available. It is worthwhile, nevertheless, to contact a multinational bank for secondary data.

Advantages of Secondary Research at Home

Secondary research conducted in the United States is less expensive and less time-consuming than research abroad. The research at home keeps the financial commitment to projects at a low level: no contacts have to be made overseas, and no high-level decisions have to be made on exploring markets outside the United States. Research in the home environment affords easy communication with sources of information. In addition, requests for certain kinds of information are often more favorably received by foreign sources located in the United States where political pressure and business customers do not inhibit response. Furthermore, research undertaken in the United States about a foreign environment gains objectivity. The researcher is not constrained by overseas customs or mores and can apply the same standards of quality and analysis as would be used for a project related to domestic business.

Disadvantages of Secondary Research at Home

Secondary research undertaken in the United States has various limitations. First, current information may be scarce in the United States. After all, there is a time lag between data gathering in a foreign country and its transmission here. Further, certain things may be uncovered in the foreign environment that ultimately will bear on the project. For example, a company may be exploring the feasibility of establishing a plant in Saudi Arabia to manufacture air conditioners. Research done in the United States is likely to reveal good potential there for air conditioners based on secondary data such as high per capita income, hot climate, low rate of air conditioners per 100 households, and encouragement by the Saudi government. However, these data omit an important fact about Saudi living: a large proportion of the people live in mud houses. Additionally, there are regions without electricity. Such facts would become immediately obvious to a researcher on the spot.

Secondary Research Abroad

An alternative to doing secondary research in the United States is undertaking secondary research abroad. It should be recognized that the abundance of information available in the United States from both government and private sources is not found in most countries of the world, including the developed ones. Since World War II, however, interest in collecting socioeconomic information has greatly increased throughout the world. As countries have progressed economically, it has become more important to collect and publish statistical information on commercial matters on a regular basis. Indeed, the availability of reliable secondary data appears directly related to the level of economic development of a country. Even among developing countries, data-gathering activity has greatly improved since the 1970s. This trend may be attributed partly to the UN's efforts to impress upon countries the desirability of keeping national statistical information accurate and current.

Foreign Sources of Information

Following are the major sources of secondary information for an international marketer:

Government Sources The single most important source of secondary information in a country is the national government. The quality and quantity of information will vary from country to country, but in most cases information on population statistics, consumption standards, industrial production, imports and exports, price levels, employment, and more is conveniently available from its government. (Data on retail and wholesale trade, however, may be found only in certain countries.) The government data are usually available through a government agency or major publishers in the country. In many countries, marketing-related information gathered by the government is not separated from other sorts of information. Thus, the researcher must go through a plethora of information to choose what is relevant.

Private Sources In many countries there are private consulting firms (like Gallup Research, Business International Corporation of New York City; and Predicasts of Cleveland, Ohio) that gather and sell commercial information (see International Marketing Highlight 4.4). Information from private sources may, in fact, have been collected by the government originally, but the consulting firms analyze and organize it in such a manner that business executives can more easily make sense of it.

The commercial attaché at the U.S. embassy should be able to provide the names and addresses of local consulting firms. For example, International Information Services Ltd. (IIS), a global product pickup service located in Sussex, United Kingdom, provides answers to such specific issues as the most popular pizza flavors in France and retail pricing structure for shampoos in Venezuela compared with its neighbors Colombia and Brazil. Each day over 400 IIS shoppers visit supermarkets in 120 countries searching for information requested by clients such as Coca-Cola, General Foods, Procter & Gamble, Nestlé, and Unilever. The information gathered by IIS shoppers is stored, along with data from the company's comprehensive library of foreign trade publications, in a computerized database, enabling IIS to offer clients continuous updates on new food, household, and pharmaceutical products introduced worldwide. IIS uses these data to compile bimonthly indexes of the new products.[9]

Research Institutes, Trade Associations, Universities, and Similar Sources Although not every country in the world has trade associations or research institutes, in both developed and developing countries (like India, Brazil, South Korea, Egypt) such organizations could be important sources of secondary data. In some countries, they are set up with the help of international agencies or the government. Information on these sources should be sought from the appropriate U.S. embassy.

Local Businesses A U.S. company may be in contact with one or more businesses in a foreign country. These contacts can serve as important sources of secondary data. Even if these businesses have collected no data on their own, they could gather and communicate data available through other local sources such as those mentioned earlier.

International Marketing Highlight 4.4

Direct Mail Responders Love to Shop

The 1990 Target Group Index (TGI) survey by the British Market Research Bureau found that people who respond to direct-response advertising are less brand-loyal and more likely to experiment in their purchasing behavior.

The TGI is a national product and media survey. It measures the use of over 3,000 brands in more than 200 product areas and the use of 450 other services. The survey can be used to link responsiveness data with geographic and demographic information to more accurately target cold mailings.

Although the traditional image of the direct mail respondent is someone who doesn't like to shop, the response to the TGI survey contradicts this notion.

People who respond to direct mail enjoy their shopping more than anyone else, even though they are also the busiest people. They also hunt for bargains more enthusiastically, and are more likely to try new brands.

The TGI also found that in the past 12 months, at least 62 percent of the adult population (over age 15) in the U.K. purchased goods through a mail order catalog or responded to a direct-response advertisement, or did both.

Seventeen million adults (39 percent) responded to direct-response ads, and 19.5 million (43 percent) made purchases through mail order companies.

Source: Direct Mail Information Service, 14 Floral Street, Covent Garden, London WC2E 9RR, United Kingdom.

U.S. Embassies The U.S. embassy (including the resources of other U.S. government agencies abroad such as the Agency for International Development) may also provide secondary data on the country. Sometimes embassy personnel have gathered information on a particular industry in a country in order to understand its impact on U.S. business at home (for example, the impact of the Japanese auto industry on U.S. automobile companies might be better understood with information from the U.S. embassy in Japan). Embassy appointees can be requested to be mindful of U.S. trade prospects for particular raw materials (for example, the U.S. embassy in Colombia would be aware of Colombian coffee bean trade). In addition, the embassy may be able to lead the marketing researcher to other sources of secondary data in the country such as trade associations or research institutes.

Problems with Foreign Secondary Data

Researchers should be aware of the problems and deficiencies that exist in interpreting foreign secondary data.

The Underlying Purpose of Data Collection As mentioned earlier, the single most important source of marketing-related secondary data in a country is the government, and the government as a political institution may not approach data collection with the same objectivity as a business researcher. This problem is particularly severe in developing countries where governments may enhance the information content in order to paint a rosy picture of economic life in the country. Political considerations may well compromise the reliability of the data.

It is worth noting that the United States as a society is more open than other countries. No matter how embarrassing data may appear to be for the government or the nation, the free flow of information is considered desirable. Such, however, is not the case elsewhere. It is not surprising, therefore, that the plight of the poor in the United States seems exaggerated when measured by standards of poverty in developing countries. The researcher should ascertain that the data available from such countries are not distorted in this manner.

Currency of Information Information gathering is an expensive activity, so in governments where it is assigned a lower priority, it is not conducted as frequently as desirable. Consequently, information from overseas is often outdated to the point of being useless. For example, a sensible decision about a housing project in Indonesia could not be made on the basis of 1960s' house prices.

Reliability of Data As mentioned, political considerations may affect the reliability of data. In addition, the reliability of data may be affected by data collection procedures. For example, the sample may not be random, in which case the results cannot be assumed to reflect the behavior of the total population. Even when a good sampling plan has been laid out, it may not be properly adhered to (e.g., the interviewers might substitute subjects when those required by the sampling plan cannot be reached). Numerous other factors may affect the reliability of foreign data.[10]
Researchers should judge for themselves how far to accept such data on the basis of inputs from different contacts in the country about their own experiences with secondary data there. Possibly researchers would be better off undertaking primary data gathering.

Data Classification Another problem has to do with the classification scheme of the available data. In many countries, data are too broadly classified for use at the micro level. For example, in Malaysia the category "construction equipment, machinery, and tools" includes large bulldozers as well as hand-operated drills. Thus, a company interested in manufacturing heavy construction machinery in Malaysia cannot get a clear idea about the current availability of such equipment in the country from the information given under such a category.

Fortunately, the problem of data classification is in the process of being solved. The international trading community has for years been frustrated by the lack of a standardized goods classification system for products. The use of diverse systems has complicated the preparation of documents and the analysis of trade data. Uncertainty in the negotiation and interpretation of trade agreements has slowed the movement of traded goods. However, as countries adopt the Harmonized Commodity Description and Coding System, an international goods classification system designed to standardize commodity classification, information across countries will be similarly classified, eliminating many of the problems that arise from the use of a nonstandardized system. In the United States, the Harmonized System (HS) was adopted on January 1, 1988, requiring all U.S. exporters and importers to conform to the revised classification.

The HS assigns all products a six-digit code to be used by all countries for both imported and exported goods. It is more detailed and contains many new subdivisions to reflect changes in technology, trade patterns, and user requirements.

The HS replaces the Tariff Schedules of the United States Annotated (TSUSA) and Schedule B. The U.S. import and export schedules under the HS will be nearly identical and completely compatible. The only differences will occur with regard to level of detail; in some areas such as textiles, the import schedule will need to be subdivided in much finer detail than is necessary for exports. In addition, both the U.S. import and export schedules will be identical through the first six digits with those of trading partners adopting the HS. Under the current system, a product may be given one code when it is imported, a separate code when it is exported, and various other codes in foreign countries. If the HS is applied on a worldwide basis, any single product will bear the same six-digit base code anywhere in the world. National subdivisions beyond the six-digit level are possible for tariff and statistical purposes.

This system will also provide U.S. exporters with information concerning the tariff classification of their goods in other countries as well as a procedure for bringing goods classification disputes before an international customs council.

Use of a common system would accelerate the movement of goods and associated paperwork. International traders would no longer have to redescribe and recode goods as they move through the international marketplace. Elimination of such obstacles would save both time and money.

The HS consists of 5,019 six-digit headings and subheadings. Developing countries will be able, under certain circumstances, to adopt the system at the four-digit level; developed countries, however, will have to use all six digits. The first two digits represent the chapter in which the goods are found, the next two digits represent the place within the chapter where the goods are described, and the final two digits represent the international subdivisions within the heading.

The United States will further subdivide the 5,019 six-digit international headings and subheadings into approximately 8,800 eight-digit rate lines, or classification lines, and into approximately 12,000 ten-digit statistical reporting numbers. This represents an increase in rate lines of about 1,500 and a decrease of about 2,000 in the statistical reporting numbers from the present system.

Another noteworthy development in making international economic information more useful is a new framework for national-income accounting, the new System of National Accounts (SNA).[11] The new SNA takes into account changes in both the world's economy and in accounting practices in the past 25 years. Its guidelines on accounting for inflation have been beefed up, and the way it measures trade flows has been improved. The new SNA will account for trade in the same way as the IMF's balance-of-payments statistics. Imports of goods will now be valued "free on board" (FOB), that is, at the point of export. (The old system incorrectly lumped in cost, insurance, and freight.) The system will also adopt the IMF's approach to the return on foreign direct investment, treating retained profits of foreign-owned businesses as though they had been repatriated. The new SNA is a joint effort by the UN, the IMF, the World Bank, the OECD, and Eurostat, the Statistical Office of the European Union.

Comparability of Data Multinational corporate executives often like to compare information on their host countries about such matters as review of market performance, strategy effectiveness in different environments, and so on. Unfortunately, the secondary data obtainable from different countries are not readily comparable. Keegan reports, for example, that in Germany television purchases are considered expenditures for recreation and entertainment, while in the United States they are in the category of furniture, furnishing, and household equipment.[12] These discrepancies make brand-share comparison nearly impossible.

Availability of Data Finally, in many developing nations, secondary data are very scarce. Information on retail and wholesale trade is especially difficult to obtain. In such cases, primary data collection becomes vital.

Primary Data Collection

An alternative to secondary data is primary data collection. Primary data presumably provide more relevant information because they are collected specifically for the purpose in mind. However, the collection of primary data is an expensive proposition in terms of both money and time. Thus, the underlying purpose must justify the effort. For example, when a company has to make a decision about appointing a dealer for the occasional sale of its product in a developing country, it is not necessary to have primary data on the long-term market potential. On the other hand, if the company is considering the establishment of a manufacturing plant in the country, it may be important to undertake a market-potential study.

Problems of Primary Data Collection

Primary data collection in a foreign environment poses a variety of problems not encountered in the United States. These problems are related to social and cultural factors and the level of economic development. They can be grouped under three headings: (1) sampling problems, (2) questionnaire problems, and (3) the problem of nonresponse.

Sampling Problems A good piece of research should reflect the perspectives of the entire population. This is feasible, however, only when the sample is randomly drawn (see International Marketing Highlight 4.5). Unfortunately, in many countries it is difficult to get completely representative information on the socioeconomic characteristics of the population. Such information is so incomplete that most samples in the end are biased. Cateora adds,

> In many countries, telephone directories, cross-index street directories, census tract and block data, and detailed social and economic characteristics of the universe are not available on a current basis, if at all. The researcher then has to estimate characteristics and population parameters, sometimes with little basic data on which to build an accurate estimate. To add to the confusion, in some cities in South America, Mexico, and Asia, street maps are unavailable; and in some large metropolitan areas of the Near East and Asia, streets are not identified nor houses numbered.[13]

Limitations aside, directories are available to help the international marketing researcher draw an adequate sample, especially in the industrial marketing area. *Boltin International*, for example, provides names and addresses of more than 300,000 firms in 100 countries, under 1,000 product classifications, by trade and by country.[14] Another source is *Kelly's Manufacturers and Merchants Directory*, which lists firms in the United States and other major trading countries in the world.[15]

Even if a workable random sample is drawn, inadequate means of transportation may prevent interviewing people as planned. For example, in developing countries, many areas, especially rural ones, are quite inaccessible. Thus, data gathering may have to be confined to urban areas. Further, only a small percentage of the population has telephones. The World Bank statistics indicate that there are only 4 telephones per 1,000 population in Egypt, 6 in Turkey, and 32 in Argentina. In many countries, the postal system is so inefficient that letters may not be delivered at all or may reach the addressee only after a long delay. In Brazil an estimated 30 percent of the domestic mail is never delivered.[16] In brief, it may be extremely difficult to obtain a proper random sample, especially in developing countries.

International Marketing Highlight 4.5

Who Drinks More Wine?

According to a recent study, the Italians drink the most wine of any country—about 116 liters per capita a year, compared with 77 for the French and just over 9 for the British. But another study disagrees. It gives the French first place in the wine-drinking competition, finding that annual per capita intake in France is 70 liters and that the Italians drink only 62 liters a year. (The difference may well be in the way the population is defined or the way the questions were asked.)

No matter what the reason, the study by the French Inter-Professional Office of Wine (ONIVINS) says that the French have cut their wine consumption. More than half of the 12,400 people interviewed in this study said they abstain from drinking wine.

In 1980, according to ONIVINS, nearly one-third of the French drank wine daily, compared with only 18 percent in 1990. Families spend less time together and eat together less often, forcing wine to take a back seat to other options such as mineral water and soft drinks. The ONIVINS study also found that the French are choosing to drink higher-quality, when they choose to drink wine.

Source: The European, August 10–12, 1990.

Questionnaire Problems In many countries, different languages are spoken in different areas. Thus, the questionnaire has to be in different languages for use within the same country. In India, for example, 14 official languages are spoken in different parts of the country, although most government and business affairs are conducted in English. Similarly, in Switzerland, German is used in some areas and French in others. In the Republic of Congo, the official language is French, but only a small part of the population is fluent in French. Unfortunately, translating a questionnaire from one language to another is far from easy. In the translating process many points are entirely eclipsed, because many idioms, phrases, and statements mean different things in different cultures. For example, in Spanish there is no word that means "value" as we define it in English. Therefore, a U.S. restaurant chain conducting marketing research in Spain had to ask guests such questions as, "Do you think the quality of the food was equal to the price you paid?"[17] A Danish executive observed,

> Check this out by having a different translator put back into English what you've translated from the English. You'll get the shock of your life. I remember "out of sight, out of mind" had become "invisible things are insane."[18]
>
> This translation problem may be partially averted with the help of computers, but only partially; experience with computers shows that they cannot fathom the subtleties of language.[19]

Problem of Nonresponse Even if the interviewee is successfully reached, there is no guarantee that he or she will cooperate in furnishing the desired information. There are many reasons for nonresponse. First, cultural habits in many countries virtually prohibit communication with a stranger, particularly for women. For example, a researcher simply may not be able to speak on the phone with a housewife in an Islamic country to find out what she thinks of a particular brand. Second, in many societies such matters as preferences for hygienic products and food products are too personal to be shared with an outsider. In many Latin American countries, a woman would be embarrassed to talk with a researcher about her choice of a brand of sanitary pad or even, hair shampoo or perfume. Third, respondents in many cases may be unwilling to share their true feelings with interviewers because they suspect the interviewers may be agents of the government, perhaps seeking information for imposition of additional taxes. Fourth, middle-class people, in developing countries in particular, are reluctant to accept their status and may make false claims in order to reflect the lifestyle of wealthier people. For example, in a study on the consumption of tea in India, over 70 percent of the respondents from middle-income families claimed they used one of the several national brands of tea, a finding that could not be substantiated since over 60 percent of the tea sold nationally in India is unbranded, generic tea sold unpackaged.

Fifth, many respondents, willing to cooperate, may be illiterate, so that even oral communication may be difficult. In other words, their exposure to the modern world may be so limited and their outlook so narrow that the researchers would find it extremely difficult to elicit adequate responses from them. Sixth, in many countries, privacy is becoming a big issue. In Japan, for example, the middle class is showing increasing concern about the protection of personal information. Information that people are most anxious to protect includes income, assets, tax payments, family life, and political and religious affiliation.

Finally, the lack of established marketing research firms in many countries may force the researcher to count on ad hoc help for gathering data. How far such temporary help may be counted on to complete a job systematically can only be guessed.

Resolving the Problems

No foolproof methods exist for solving all the problems just discussed. Some suggestions, however, have been advanced: First, it has been proposed that the international marketing research effort be undertaken in conjunction with a reputable local firm. Such a firm could be a foreign office of a U.S. advertising firm like J. Walter Thompson, a U.S. accounting firm like Price Waterhouse, or a locally owned firm belonging to a third country, like a Japanese advertising agency in Italy. The resources of the cooperating firm would be invaluable—for example, its knowledge of local customs, including things like the feasibility of interviewing housewives while husbands are at work; its familiarity with the local environment, including modes of transportation available for personal interviews in smaller towns; and its contact in different parts of the country as sources for drawing a sample.

From the beginning, a person fully conversant with both sound marketing research procedures and the local culture should be involved in all phases of the research design. Such a person can recommend the number of languages the questionnaire should be printed in and what sort of cultural traits, habits, customs, and rituals to keep in mind in different phases of the research. A U.S.–educated marketer could serve in this function or anyone or with good business education or experience, preferably in marketing.

The questionnaire can first be written in English, then translated into the local language(s) by a native fluent in English. A third person should retranslate it back into English. This retranslated version can then be compared with the original English version. The three people involved should work together to eliminate differences in the three versions of the questionnaire by changing phrases, idioms, and words. Ultimately, the questionnaire in the local language should accurately reflect the questions in the original English questionnaire.

The persons hired to conduct the interviews should have prior experience if possible. A local cooperating firm could be helpful here. In any event, complete instructions and training should be given before work starts, the conducting of interviews should be practiced. Ways to ensure that the interviewers follow the instructions must be found for proper sampling control. For example, the researcher might accompany the interviewer sporadically.

Finally, the researcher should draw the best possible sample. If the sample is not random, the researcher should employ appropriate statistical techniques in analyzing the collected information so that the results reflect the reality of the situation.

Organization for International Marketing Research

International marketing research can be carried out at U.S. headquarters and in the host country. Marketing research at U.S. headquarters is useful both for short-term planning and budgeting and for strategy formulation. For example, yearly forecasts of sales for different products in different countries will be a part of the annual budget. But a study undertaken to determine if a new product successfully sold in the United States should be introduced in international markets would have a strategy focus.

Marketing research studies in host countries are concerned mainly with day-to-day operations, tactics to achieve designated goals, and short-term marketing planning. Thus, a study might examine the factors responsible for poor sales performance in the previous quarter. Or research might be undertaken to decide if a concentrated 6- or 10-week advertising campaign is preferable to spreading advertising over the whole year. Naturally, sales forecasting will be done to develop budgets. As mentioned earlier, the headquarters may also make sales forecasts. Thus, for discussion of annual plans and budgets, the host country manager would use his or her forecasts as the basis for resource allocation, while the headquarters' people use their forecasts to negotiate and approve the country budgets.

Marketing research is unquestionably an important function both at headquarters and in the host countries. The persons to take charge at the two different locations would vary from company to company. For example, at NCR a staff assistant reporting to the vice president of international marketing is responsible for marketing research at the corporate headquarters. The marketing research function for NCR in host countries is performed at different levels according to the importance of each country to the parent company. In Japan, in the U.K., and in Germany, NCR has large marketing research departments simply because the company is extremely active in these markets. On the other hand, in a country like South Korea, where NCR commitment is meager, marketing research study might be assigned to an outside consultant.

In addition to undertaking marketing research at the corporate level and in the host countries, in many companies marketing research is also conducted at the regional level. A company may divide its international operations into regions; for example, Western Europe, Far East, Latin America, Middle East, Africa, and South Asia. Each country manager in a region would report to the regional executive. Under such arrangements, the regional executive may seek marketing research information to formulate regional marketing strategy or to develop the marketing perspective of a country within the region. There may be a specific person responsible for marketing research in the region, or one of the staff persons may carry this responsibility.

What is important to recognize is that the process of gathering, analyzing, and reporting market-related information, which is in fact marketing research, may not necessarily be *called* marketing research. Moreover, marketing research responsibility may not necessarily be assigned to a marketing person. Of course, the extent of marketing research that a company undertakes would vary according to the style of management and the importance of a particular foreign country for a given product.

International Marketing Information System

Earlier in this chapter, three terms were introduced: *market research, marketing research,* and *marketing intelligence.* An international marketing information system is a formal way of structuring the information flow through these three modes. Large, complex organizations may do business in a great number of countries with any number of products and services. This complexity, combined with today's difficult and demanding business environment, makes it particularly important for international marketers to have adequate and timely information available in order to make the right moves.

The following mishap illustrates the critical need for information:

"I never dreamed this would happen to us," exclaimed the chairman of the American drug firm G.D. Searle & Co. (sales over $600 million) in an interview published in *Business Week*. The company was apparently unaware that it would be investigated by a Senate subcommittee on health involving charges that the company mishandled research data on two of its best selling products. It is obvious that this company—like many others—did not have an adequate "early warning" capability or intelligence system that could have enabled management to anticipate the crisis. One result of the threat: a corporate committee of social scientists was established to study economic and political trends and their potential effect on the company.

Another recent example of an intelligence mishap involved Westinghouse Corporation's agreement to sell utility companies 80 million pounds of uranium at an average contracted price of $10 a pound over a period of 20 years. At the time the agreement was signed, Westinghouse owned only about 20 percent of the contracted amount of uranium. Since then, its price rose to $40, so if the company would have fulfilled the terms of the agreement it could have lost about $2 billion. Obviously, top management was unaware that such an agreement was being negotiated, an intelligence failure concerning internal operations.[20]

Steps for Establishing an Information System

Exhibit 4.4 shows the essential steps for developing and maintaining an international marketing information system: determining information needs, identifying information sources, gathering information, analyzing information, and disseminating information.

Information will be needed at corporate headquarters, regional offices, and country locations. Some of it will be strategic information, and some will be operational information. It could also be grouped in the categories of market information, competitive information, foreign-exchange related data, resource information, prescriptive information (e.g., foreign taxes), and general-conditions information.

No generic framework for classifying information needs is suitable for all companies. Every company should work out its own information categories, based on its marketing information needs and the attitude of top management toward systematic information management. Whatever the ultimate system is—highly structured, computerized, primitive, unstructured, manual—it must be sophisticated enough and comprehensive enough to meet the information needs of that particular company.

Aspects of System Use

The information sources may be internal or external, international or domestic, secondary or primary. The information may be gathered by mail, telephone, or computer terminal through remote entry. Some information may be gathered regularly, and some may be collected on an ad hoc basis. Also, information may be gathered in a structured fashion or an open-ended one. In gathering information, duplication should be avoided, as it is wasteful in most cases to gather the same information from different sources. In certain cases, though, duplication can be used as a control device. The gathered information must be analyzed for use in the most convenient form and disseminated to all designated users. Some information may be made widely available to all managers. Other information may

EXHIBIT 4.4   Components of an International Marketing Information System

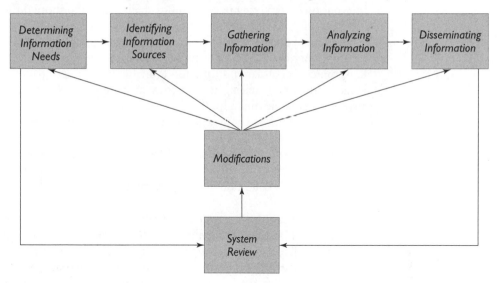

be restricted for senior people in the organization. Information may be disseminated on a regular basis or irregularly, or in some cases be available only on request.

The system design should be reviewed from time to time to ensure it still meets the demands placed on it. The review should also evaluate the cost/benefit relationship of the entire system. The review may recommend modifications in any one or more of the system components.

Most large, multimarket, multiproduct companies have some sort of multinational marketing information system in operation. It is difficult to say, however, how many of these systems can be labeled "sophisticated" or "advanced." The increasing popularity of the international data networks made available by such companies as Data Research Inc. and Predicasts indicates a trend toward the establishment of computerized information systems. These systems may serve information needs of marketing and of other functional areas of the business as well, in the following manner:

1. To aid in decisions relating to international market expansion, for example, whether new countries are potential candidates for market entry or whether existing products might be carried into new markets
2. To monitor performance in different countries and product markets based on criteria such as return on investment and market share. This way, existing or potential future problems can be detected and marketing tactics or strategies changed accordingly.
3. To scan the international environment in order to assess future world and country scenarios and to monitor emerging and changing environmental trends
4. To assess strategies with regard to the allocation of corporate resources and effort across different countries, product markets, target segments, and modes of entry to determine whether changes in this allocation would maximize long run profitability.

Summary

The techniques and tools of international marketing research do not vary according to whether research is done in the United States or abroad. An international marketing research project essentially follows domestic procedures: problem definition, research design, data collection, analysis, and report preparation. However, several factors make international marketing research more challenging and more difficult, one being cultural differences.

Data are obtained from either secondary or primary sources. The United States offers a variety of secondary sources. Foremost among them is the U.S. Department of Commerce. Secondary information available in host countries may be plagued by problems of timeliness, reliability, and comparability. The collection of primary data abroad also poses possible difficulties such as the inability to draw a random sample, the unwillingness of the sample population to cooperate, and the inability to develop an adequate questionnaire.

Despite the inherent problems, a researcher can adopt measures to solve some, if not all, of the difficulties involved. Two helpful measures are the involvement of talented individuals in data collection and cooperation with respectable foreign marketing information sources.

The international research activity may be formally organized at home or in the host country, or at both locations. Further, the marketing research organization may be just a one-person department or a large entity in accordance with the scope of marketing activity in a country. A company deeply involved in business around the globe should establish an international marketing information system with formal structuring to determine information needs, to identify information sources, and to gather, analyze, and disseminate information.

Review Questions

1. What factors make conducting international marketing research more difficult than domestic marketing research?
2. What are the principal sources of secondary data in the United States?
3. What difficulties are associated with secondary data on marketing in host countries?
4. Discuss the problems a researcher may face in primary data collection overseas.
5. What factors account for the unreliability of secondary data in foreign countries?
6. What steps can be taken to resolve the problems of primary data collection in the developing countries?
7. What kind of companies should consider developing an international marketing information system?
8. What help can be expected from international agencies in the search for secondary data?

Creative Questions

1. Pizza Hut is interested in surveying consumers in France, Singapore, and Mexico. A consultant suggests conducting a telephone survey using the same questionnaire (initially written in English but duly translated into local languages). Evaluate the consultant's recommendation. Do you have any alternative recommendation for conducting the survey?
2. The U.S. government collects and disseminates an abundance of foreign trade data. Yet the marketing-related data is commonly not available. If you were to make a case to the U.S. government that it should provide data readily usable by marketers, indicate what type of data it should provide, in what format, and how current it should keep that data.

Endnotes

1. Jack Honomichl, "Research Growth Knows No Boundaries," *Marketing News,* August 17, 1998, p. 142. These 1999 figures have been extrapolated based on 1997 data. Also see "Market Research-Data Wars," *The Economist*, July 22, 1995, p. 60.

2. Ibid. Also see Cyndee Miller, "Research Firms Go Global to Make Revenue Grow," *Marketing News*, January 6, 1997, p. 1.

3. Earl Naumann, Donald W. Jackson, Jr. and William G. Wolfe, "Examining the Practices of United States and Japanese Market Research Firms," *California Management Review*, Summer 1994, pp. 49–69.

4. Charles F. Keown, "Foreign Mail Surveys: Response Rates Using Monetary Incentives," *Journal of International Business Studies*, Fall 1985, p. 153.

5. Susan P. Douglas and C. Samuel Craig, *International Marketing Research* (Englewood Cliffs, NJ: Prentice-Hall, Inc., 1983), p. 16.

6. *European Market Survey* (Pleasantville, NY: Reader's Digest Association, 1963).

7. Paul H. Berent, "International Research Is Different: The Case for Centralized Control," in *International Marketing Research: Does It Provide What the User Needs?* (Amsterdam: European Society for Opinion and Marketing Research, 1986), pp. 110–111.

8. Charles S. Mayer, "The Lessons of Multinational Marketing Research," *Business Horizons,* December 1978, p. 9.

9. "Product Pick-up Firm Samples International Supermarkets," *Marketing News*, March 1, 1985, p. 10.

10. *See* Ravi Parameswaran and Attila Yaprak, "A Cross-National Comparison of Consumer Research Measures," *Journal of International Business Studies*, Spring 1987, pp. 35–50.

11. "Grossly Distorted Picture," *The Economist*, February 5, 1994, p. 71.

12. Warren J. Keegan, *Multinational Marketing Management*, 4th ed. (Englewood Cliffs, NJ: Prentice-Hall, 1989), p. 223.

13. Philip R. Cateora, *International Marketing*, 5th ed. (Homewood, IL: Irwin, 1983), pp. 267–268.

14. *Boltin International* (Los Angeles, CA: Boltin International, an annual publication).

15. *Kelly's Manufacturers and Merchants Directory* (New York: Kelly's Directories Ltd., an annual publication).

16. Susan P. Douglas and C. Samuel Craig, *International Marketing Research* (Englewood Cliffs, NJ: Prentice-Hall, Inc., 1983), p. 224. Also see David Jobber and John Saunders, "An Experimental Investigation into Cross-National Mail Survey Response Rates," *Journal of International Business Studies*, Fall 1988, pp. 483–490.

17. Wallace Doolin, "Taking Your Business on the Road Abroad," *The Wall Street Journal*, July 25, 1994, p. A14.

18. Ferdinand F. Mauser, "Losing Something in Translation," *Harvard Business Review*, July–August 1987, p. 14.

19. J. Terence Gallagher, "A Problem of Translation," *The Asian Wall Street Journal Weekly*, September 30, 1985, p. 11c.

20. E. D. Jaffee, "Multinational Marketing Intelligence: An Information Requirements Model," *Management International Review* 19, no. 2 (1979): 53–60.

Appendix

Sources of Secondary Data

The following represents selected sources of information for international marketing purposes.

A. Information Available from International Agencies

1. *The United Nations.* United Nations publications can be obtained from
United Nations Publications
Sales Office
New York. NY 10017

    a. *Statistical Yearbook of the United Nations* (annual). A major source of world economic data, including information on population, manpower, agriculture, manufacturing, mining, construction, trade, transport, communications, balance of payments, consumption, wages and prices, national accounts, finance, international capital flows, housing, health, education, and mass communications.

    b. *Economic Survey of Europe* (annual). Review of current developments in the European economy. *Economic Bulletin for Europe,* issued twice annually; supplements *Survey.*

    c. *Economic Survey of Asia and the Far East* (annual). Review of current situation concerning agriculture, transport, trade, and balance of payments. *Economic Bulletin for Asia and the Far East,* issued three times annually; supplements the *Survey.*

    d. *Economic Survey of Latin America* (annual). Review of regional economic developments. *Economic Bulletin for Latin America,* issued twice annually; supplements the *Survey.*

    e. *Economic Developments in the Middle East* (annual). Review of developments concerning agriculture, industry, loom foreign trade, and balance of payments.

    f. *World Economic Survey* (annual). World economic report. A comprehensive review of world economic trends and issues.

    g. *World Trade Annual.* Information from the 24 principal trading countries of the world, providing statistics of trade by commodity and country.

    h. GATT publications (available from UN Publications Sales Office).

        i.   Analytical Bibliography—Market surveys by products and by countries

        ii. *Guide to Sources of Information on Foreign Trade Regulations*

      iii. Compilation of Basic Information on Export Markets
      iv. *Compendium of Sources: International Trade Statistics*
      v. *Manual on Export Marketing Research for Developing Countries*
      vi. *World Directory of Industry and Trade Associations*
      vii. *Directory of Product and Industry Journals*

2. Organization for Economic Cooperation and Development (OECD) publications can be obtained from

    OECD Publications Office, Suite 1305
    1750 Pennsylvania Avenue, N.W.
    Washington, D.C. 20006

    a. OECD Economic Surveys. Each title in this series of economic studies is a booklet published annually by the OECD and pertaining to one of the 21 OECD member countries. Each booklet has information concerning recent trends of demand and output, prices and wages, foreign trade and payments, economic policy, and prospects and conclusions.

    b. *OECD Economic Outlook* (semiannual). Survey of economic trends and prospects in OECD countries, examining the current situation and prospects regarding demand and output, employment, costs and prices, and foreign trade for OECD as a whole and in some of the major countries. Trends of current balances, monetary developments, and capital movements as factors affecting international monetary developments are also considered.

    c. *Monthly Statistics of Foreign Trade.* This bulletin is intended to serve as a timely source of statistical data on the foreign trade by OECD member countries. The data cover not only overall trade by countries, but also a number of seasonally adjusted series, volume and average value indices, and trade by SITC sections.

3. International Monetary Fund (IMF) publications can be obtained from

    International Monetary Fund
    Washington, D.C. 20431

    a. *International Financial Statistics* (monthly). Statistical information on such financial matters as international liquidity, interest rates, prices, and money supply.

4. World Bank publications can be obtained from

    The World Bank
    1818 H Street, N.W.
    Washington, D.C. 20433

    a. *World Bank: Annual Report* (annual).

    b. *World Development Report* (annual). Reviews economy, assesses the impact of external factors on development, and considers future scenarios.

    c. *World Tables* (annual). Presents annual data for most of the World Bank's members in a four-page table for each economy.

    d. *Publications Update* (monthly). Lists various research publications of the World Bank. For example: William W. Ambrose, Paul R. Hennemeyer, and Jean-Pat, *Privatizing Telecommunications Systems: Business Opportunities in Developing Countries,* 1990.

5. International Chamber of Commerce (ICC) publications can be purchased at the following address

    The ICC Publishing Corporation, Inc.
    801 Second Avenue, Suite 1204
    New York, NY 10017

    a. *ICC/E.S. O. M.A.R. International Code of Marketing and Social Research Practice.* This code provides individuals and organizations with a set of rules so that marketing and opinion research can be conducted in accordance with accepted principles of integrity and fair competition.

    b. *International Code of Direct Mail and Mail Order Sales*

    c. *International Uniform Definitions for the Distributive T.* List of current definitions that permit international standardization of types of establishments, outlets, and selling methods.

    d. *Marketing: Discipline for Freedom*

    e. *Media Information for Advertising Planning*

    f. *Advertising Agencies: Their Services and Relationship with Advertisers and Media*

B. Information Available from U.S. Government Sources

    1. *U.S. Department of Commerce.* The following publication can be purchased by writing to

        The Superintendent of Documents
        U.S. Government Printing Office, Room 1617
        Publications Sales Branch
        Washington, D.C. 20402
        or:
        U.S. Department of Commerce
        Washington, D.C. 10130

        a. *A Basic Guide to Exporting.* Provides step-by-step approach to exporting; It is especially useful for firms with little or no export experience.

        b. *Foreign Trade Report FT410* (monthly). Provides a statistical record of shipments of all merchandise from the United States to some 100 countries.

        c. *International Economic Indicators* (quarterly). Lists trade trends for the United States and seven principal industrial countries.

        d. *International Demographic Data* (updated periodically). Details demographic profiles of developing countries and Eastern European economies.

        e. *Market Share Reports* (annual). Shows U.S. participation in foreign markets during the last five years. Covers 88 countries for 1,000 manufactured products.

        f. Overseas Business Reports (yearly). Some 60 percent of the reports are issued with background data on both developed and developing countries.

        g. *Foreign Economic Trends and Their Implications for the United States* (yearly). Some 150 reports are issued with country-by-country trade and economic statistics and trends.

        h. Global Market Surveys. Market research studies conducted in selected countries for specific U.S. products.

    i.   Country Market Sectoral Surveys. Reports showing the most promising export opportunities for U.S. firms in selected countries.

    j.   Trade Lists. Provide names and addresses of potential buyers, distributors, and agents for different industries in selected countries.

    k.   *Business America* (biweekly). Covers domestic and international news.

    l.   Country Studies. Each study classifies and analyzes the country's economic, military, political, and social systems and institutions, as well as the impact that cultural factors have on the country's lifestyle.

    m.   *European Trade Fairs: A Guide for Exporters.* Provides expert advice on participating in trade fairs.

    n.   *Custom Statistical Service for Exporters.* Includes current data and market trends on thousands of products in more than 200 nations. Data are arranged by time frames from one month to five years, and by dollar and unit value, quantity, growth rate, and market-share percentages.

2.   Other Government Sources

    a.   *Aids to Business* (overseas investment). Explains how the Agency for International Development can assist U.S. firms interested in developing nations.

    b.   *Export Marketing for Smaller Firms.* Small Business Administration publishes guidelines for how small business firms can expand either their export or import market.

    c.   *Export-import Bank of the United States.* Describes U.S. export financing program.

    d.   *Agricultural Economy and Trade.* Published by the U.S. Department of Agriculture. Describes overseas business opportunities in the agricultural sector.

C.   Information Available from Commercial Publishers

1.   Books

    a.   Bartels, Robert. *Global Development and Marketing.* Columbus, OH: Grid Inc., 1981.

    b.   Buzzell, Robert D., John A. Quelch, and Christopher Bartlett. *Global Marketing Management: Cases and Readings,* 2nd ed. Reading, MA: Addison-Wesley Publishing Co., 1992.

    c.   Cateora, Philip C. *International Marketing,* 7th ed. Homewood, IL: Richard D. Irwin, Inc., 1990.

    d.   Cundiff, Edward W., and Marye Tharp Hilger. *Marketing International Environment.* Englewood Cliffs, NJ: Prentice-Hall, Inc., 1984.

    e.   Czinkota, Michael R., and Ilkka A. Ronkainen. *International Marketing,* 2nd ed. Chicago: Dryden Press, 1990.

    f.   Douglas, Susan P., and C. Samuel Craig. *International Marketing Research.* Englewood Cliffs, NJ: Prentice-Hall, Inc., 1983

    g.   Jain, Subhash C., and Lewis R. Tucker, Jr., eds. *International Marketing: Managerial Perspectives,* 2nd ed. Boston: Kent Co., 1986.

    h.   Jeannet, Jean-Pierre, and Hubert D. Hennessey. *International Marketing Management: Strategies and Cases.* Boston: Houghton Mifflin Co., 1988.

    i.   Kahler, Ruel. *International Marketing,* 5th ed. Southwestern Publishing Company, 1983.

j. Kaynak, Erdner. *Transnational Retailing.* Hawthorne, NY: de Gruyter, Inc., 1988.

k. Keegan, Warren J. *Global Marketing Management,* 4th ed. Englewood Cliffs, NJ: Prentice-Hall, Inc., 1989.

l. Kirpalani, V. H. *International Marketing.* New York: Random House, Inc., 1984.

m. Peebles, Dean M., and John K. Ryans, Jr. *Management of International Advertising.* Newton, MA: Allyn & Bacon, Inc., 1984.

n. Robock, Stefan H., and Kenneth Simmonds. *International Business and Multinational Enterprises,* 4th ed. Homewood, IL: Richard D. Irwin, Inc., 1990.

o. Terpstra, Vern. *International Marketing,* 4th ed. Hinsdale, IL: Dryden Press, 1987.

p. Thorelli, Hans B., and Helmut Becker, eds. *International Marketing Strategy,* rev. ed. New York: Pergamon Press, 1982.

q. Vernon, Raymond, and Louis T. Wells, Jr. *Manager in the International Economy,* 5th ed. Englewood Cliffs, NJ: Prentice-Hall, Inc., 1986.

2. Reference Material

a. *Business International Weekly Report.* New York:

Business International Corporation, weekly issue. Reports important events of interest to managers of worldwide operations.

b. Doing Business in Different Nations series. New York: Business International Corporation.

c. *Encyclopedia of Geographic Information Sources.* Detroit: Gale Research, 1990.

d. *European Markets: A Guide to Company and Industry Information Sources.* Washington, D.C.: Washington Researchers, 1989.

e. *European Statistics: 1987–88* and *International Marketing Statistics: 1989–90.* Detroit: Gale Research. Designed for market planners and researchers, provides information on social, economic, and consumer trends in 140 countries.

f. *International Marketing Data and Statistics* (annual). London: Euromonitor Publications, Ltd. Presents statistical information on all basic marketing parameters for over 100 countries.

g. *Exporter's Encyclopedia* (annual). Import regulations and procedures required for shipping to every country in the world, as well as information on preparing export shipments. Lists world ports, steamship lines, airlines, government agencies, trade organizations. Special sections on packing, marine insurance, export terms, and many other areas of foreign trade. Price includes twice-monthly supplementary bulletins and newsletters. Available from Dun and Bradstreet International, P.O. Box 3224, Church Street Station, New York, NY 10008.

h. *Multinational Business, Retail Business, Special Industry Reports.* New York: The Economist Intelligence Unit.

i. *Predibrief.* Cleveland, OH: Predicasts. Industry news reports for thirty-five countries.

j. *Reference Book for World Traders.* Loose-leaf handbook covering information necessary for planning exports to and imports from all foreign countries, as well as market research throughout the world. Kept up to date by monthly supplements. Available from Croner Publications, Inc., 211–213 Jamaica Avenue, Queens Village, NY 11428.

k. *Sources of European Economic Information,* 4th ed. Cambridge, England: Gower Publishing Co., Ltd., 1989.

l. *The World in Figures,* 5th ed. London: The Economist Newspaper Limited, 1990.

m. *World Advertising Expenditures,* 1990 edition. New York: Starch INRA Hooper Group of Companies, 1991.

n. *Worldcasts.* Cleveland, OH: Predicasts. These are short-term and long-term economic forecasts in select industries for different countries.

o. *The Europa Year Book,* vol. 1 and vol. 2 (annual). London: Europa Publications, Ltd. An authoritative reference work providing a wealth of detailed information on the political, economic, and commercial institutions of the world.

p. *The Statesman's Year-Book* (annual). London: The Macmillan Ltd. A statistical and historical annual of the states of the world.

3. Magazines and Newspapers
    The Wall Street Journal
    The New York Times
    Nihom Keizai Shimbun, Japan
    Financial Times, England
    Frankfurter Algemine, Germany
    Business Week
    Fortune
    Forbes
    The Asian Wall Street Journal Weekly

4. Service Organizations

    An important source of foreign market information are service organizations such as banks and consultants. Most large international banks have periodicals and special reports on international market developments.

International Marketing Research: Internet Addresses

A. U.S. Government

1. Agency for International Development
    http://www.usaid.gov
2. Customs Service
    http://www.customs.ustreas.gov
3. Department of Agriculture
    http://www.usda.gov
4. Department of Commerce
    http://www.doc.gov
5. Department of State
    http://www.state.gov

6. Department of the Treasury
http://www.ustreas.gov

7. Federal Trade Commission
http://www.ftc.gov

8. International Trade Commission
http://www.usitc.gov

9. Small Business Administration
http://www.sba.gov

10. World Trade Centers Association
http://www.wtca.org

11. Export-Import Bank of the United States
http://www.exim.gov

12. National Trade Data Bank
http://www.stat-usa.gov

13. Office of the U.S. Trade Representative
http://www.ustr.gov/index.html

B. United Nations

1. All listings at
http://www.un.org

2. Industrial Development Organization
http://www.unido.org

C. Other

1. International Bank for Reconstruction and Development (World Bank)
http://www.worldbank.org

2. International Monetary Fund
http://www.imf.org

3. Inter-American Development Bank
http://www.iadb.org

4. Asian Development Bank
http://www.asiandevbank.org

5. European Community Information Service
http://www.europa.eu.int

6. Organization for Economic Cooperation and Development
http://www.oecd.org (France)
and
http://www.oecdwash.org (Washington, D.C.)

7. Organization of American States
http://www.oas.org

8. Commission of the European Union to the United States
http://www.eurunion.org

D. Periodic Reports, Newspapers, Magazines

1. Advertising Age
http://www.adage.com

2. Business Week
http://www.businessweek.com

3. The Economist
http://www.economist.com

4. Forbes
http://www.forbes.com

5. Fortune
http://pathfinder.com/fortune

6. Wall Street Journal
http://www.wsj.com

E. Indexes to Literature

1. New York Times Index
http://www.nytimes.com

2. Public Affairs Information Service Bulletin
http://www.pais.org

3. Wall Street Journal Index
http://www.wsj.com

PART 3

The Field of International Business

International Monetary System

CHAPTER FOCUS_____

After studying this chapter, you should be able to

■ Describe the development of today's international monetary system.

■ Explain how foreign exchange transactions are conducted.

■ Identify the problems associated with exchange rate fluctuations.

■ Discuss the balance-of-payments perspectives of the United States.

■ Examine current global monetary issues.

This chapter examines the subject of international business and trade in monetary terms. Trade settlements involve topics such as determination of foreign exchange rates, balance of payments, foreign exchange transactions, international financial flows, and international financial and trade institutions.

Each country has its own currency through which it expresses the value of its goods. For international trade settlements, however, the various currencies of the world must be transformed from one into the other. This task is accomplished through foreign exchange markets.

Periodically, a country must review the status of its economic relations with the rest of the world in terms of its exports and imports, its exchange of various kinds of services, and its purchase and sale of different types of assets and other international payments or receipts and transfers. Such an overall review is necessary to ascertain whether the country has a favorable or unfavorable monetary balance in relation to the rest of the world. In the post–World War II period, a number of institutions came into existence to monitor and assist countries in this endeavor. As a result of the establishment of these institutions, a new system of international monetary relations emerged in the late 1950s, one that went a long way toward increasing international trade. In the early 1970s, however, the weakening of the U.S. dollar caused the system to falter.

The all-important commitment of the United States to the monetary system of the 1950s and 1960s deserves mention here. In order to encourage worldwide monetary stability, the U.S. government agreed to exchange the dollar at the fixed price of $35 for an ounce of gold. With the value of the dollar stabilized, countries could deal in dollars without being constrained by currency fluctuations. Thus, the dollar became the common denominator in world trade. Because of the subsequent weakening of the dollar, and other related issues, the monetary stability of the world was disturbed and remained unsettled in the 1970s and early 1980s.

As the 1980s advanced, the U.S. economy stabilized, and the value of the dollar, against other currencies, climbed to an all-time high, adversely affecting the U.S. trade balance. In the fall of 1985 leading industrialized countries joined in the U.S. effort to intervene in the foreign exchange markets to decrease the value of the dollar. The dollar continued to stay weak in the remaining years of the 1980s and in the early 1990s. At the beginning of the year 2000, it appreciated a little bit and is expected to remain stable for the next few years.

Development of Today's International Monetary System

Post–World War II financial developments had long-range effects on international financial arrangements and on the role of gold. Moreover, this period saw problems of disequilibria brought about by adjustment of balance of payments. Following World War II, a keen awareness of the need to achieve economic prosperity grew among nations. The war years had shattered the economies of Europe and Japan, which therefore needed reconstruction. A number of countries were wresting political freedom from colonial rulers, particularly from Britain, and soon realized that political freedom alone was not sufficient. Economic prosperity was not only necessary for existence but mandatory for long-term survival and growth.

Countries realized that planned international cooperation fostered economic development and prosperity. Thus, immediately after the war, they agreed to a framework of international rules—a code of behavior—to maintain monetary discipline and to ensure that dissenting nations would not frustrate economic development efforts through counteractions.

Bretton Woods Conference

Negotiations to establish the postwar international monetary system took place at Bretton Woods, New Hampshire, in 1944. The general feeling at that time was that the economically disastrous interwar period and, to an extent, the precipitation of World War II resulted from a failure to include economic factors as a major consideration in post–World War I planning. Aiming to avoid the mistakes of the past and to set goals for economic prosperity the negotiators at Bretton Woods made the following recommendations:

- Each nation should be at liberty to use macroeconomic policies for full employment.
- Free-floating exchange rates were to be abandoned, as their ineffectiveness had been demonstrated during the 1920s and 1930s. The extremes of both permanently fixed and free-floating rates were to be avoided.
- A monetary system was needed that would recognize that exchange rates were both a national and an international concern.

International Monetary Fund

After long and careful deliberations, a monetary system was agreed upon at Bretton Woods. Member countries agreed to control the limits of their exchange rates in a predetermined way. Under the original agreement, exchange rates were permitted to vary by 1 percent above or below par. As a country's rate of exchange attained or approached either limit, called *arbitrage support points,* its central bank intervened in the market to prevent the rate from passing the limit. Market intervention required a nation to accumulate international reserves, composed of gold and foreign currencies, above normal trading requirements. The ***International Monetary Fund (IMF)*** was established at Bretton Woods to oversee the newly agreed upon monetary system.

In addition to the IMF, the *World Bank* was established to help developing countries in their economic development efforts. The World Bank family consists of the International Bank for Reconstruction and Development (IBRD); its concessional window, the International Development Association (IDA); the International Finance Corporation (IFC); the Inter-American Development Bank and its Fund for Special Operations (IDB/FSO); the Asian Development Bank and Fund (ADB/F); and the African Development Bank and Fund (AFDB/F). The World Bank makes loans to assist the growth of less developed countries around the globe, while the regional banks focus on the development needs in their geographic area.

More and more nations joined the original 55 IMF signatories, so that today there are over 150 members. With the passage of time, various changes have been made in the IMF system to ameliorate the difficulties that nations face. For example, if a nation's fixed parity ceases to be realistic, it can overvalue or devalue its currency. In such cases, the IMF agreed on orderly and reasonable changes in parity based upon the initiative of the country concerned. Such a system of alterable pass is often termed the *adjustable peg.*

The IMF has several major accomplishments to its credit:

- It sustained a rapidly increasing volume of trade and investment.
- It displayed flexibility in adapting to changes in international commerce.
- It proved to be efficient (even when there were decreasing percentages of reserves to trade).
- It proved to be hardy (it survived a number of pre–1971 crises, speculative and otherwise, and the down-and-up swings of several business cycles).
- It allowed a growing degree of international cooperation.
- It established a capacity to accommodate reforms and improvements.[1]

To an extent the fund served as an international central bank to help countries during periods of temporary balance-of-payments difficulties by protecting their rates of exchange. Because of that, countries did not need to resort to exchange controls and other barriers to restrict world trade.

As time passed, it became evident that the fund's resources for providing short-term accommodation to countries in monetary difficulties were not sufficient. To resolve the situation, the fund, after much debate and long deliberations, created *special drawing rights (SDRs)* in 1969. Sometimes called *paper gold*, SDRs special account entries on the IMF books designed to provide additional liquidity to support growing world commerce. Although SDRs are a form of fiat money not convertible to gold, their gold value is guaranteed, which helps to ensure their acceptability. Initially SDRs worth $9.5 billion were created. By the end of 1998 the IMF resources stood at $81.7 billion SDRs, of which $58.4 billion had been issued to member countries.[2]

Participant nations may use SDRs in a variety of ways: as a source of currency in a spot transaction, as a loan for clearing a financial obligation, as security for a loan, as a swap against currency, or in a forward exchange operation. A nation with a balance-of-payments need may use its SDRs to obtain usable currency from another nation designated by the fund. A participant also may use SDRs to make payments to the fund, such as repurchases. The fund itself may transfer SDRs to a participant for various purposes, including the transfer of SDRs instead of currency to a member using the fund's resources.

By providing a mechanism for international monetary cooperation, working to reduce restrictions to trade and capital flows, and helping members with their short-term balance-of-payments difficulties, the IMF makes a significant and unique contribution to human welfare and improved living standards throughout the world.

In the post–World War II period, in addition to IMF and the World Bank, a variety of other institutions came into existence to strengthen global trade and business and to promote economic development. These included the General Agreement on Tariffs and Trade (GATT) and the Organization for Economic Cooperation and Development (OECD). GATT (replaced by a new World Trade Organization) governed the trade of its member countries. OECD was organized for mutual cooperation in implementing the Marshall Plan and now promotes economic growth of its member countries.

The IMF and the Debt Crisis

In the 1970s developing nations all over the world found their efforts to manage their economic affairs swamped by a unique combination of adverse circumstances: dramatically increased oil prices, followed by worldwide inflation, a collapse in commodity prices, the worst world recession since the 1930s, and historically high interest rates. When oil prices shot up, these countries borrowed heavily at high interest rates to stave off economic dislocation.

Between 1974 and 1982 the two oil price shocks created a temporary savings surplus in high-income oil-exporting countries. Their surplus funds were recycled to developing countries. In addition to increasing their development aid, high-income oil-exporting countries placed much of their surplus oil revenue with international commercial banks in the form of short-term deposits. This action contributed to raising liquidity in the international banking system, because credit demand in the industrialized countries had been depressed by the oil price shocks. The liquidity drove real interest rates down. It prompted the banks in the industrialized countries to compensate for the slack in their traditional markets by lending more to developing countries.

Commercial lending to developing countries—along with official lending and aid—grew very rapidly during this period. As a result, the total medium- and long-term debt of developing countries rose fourfold in nominal terms, from about $140 billion at the end of 1974 to about $560 billion in 1982. By the end of 1998 their indebtedness had reached $2.4 trillion.[3] Developing countries were happy to take advantage of this unaccustomed access to cheap loans with few strings attached. They stepped up their commercial borrowing, which enabled them to maintain domestic growth and to finance major public investment programs, especially in the energy sector. With hindsight, it is clear that lending and borrowing decisions were often imprudent and resulted in excessive indebtedness in a number of countries. New funds were often channeled into low-yielding investments. In a number of countries, borrowings fueled a flight of capital that drained the pool of resources for investment even as the burden of foreign debt mounted.[4]

The debt crisis has had a profound impact on the economic performance of developing countries. One of the most urgent tasks facing the international community is to find ways of reducing the drag exerted by the continuing debt overhang on economic growth in the developing world. A framework to reduce the burden of debt must have two elements. First, the debtors need to grow faster and export more. Second, the cost of debt service must fall. With the right policies in both industrial and developing countries, these elements can go hand in hand.

While long-term solutions to the debt crisis are being examined, most countries have sought IMF assistance for debt relief. In the debt crisis, the fund assumed a new role as financial organizer for the troubled debtor nations. For example, the fund worked out a two-year program of austerity, currency devaluations, and domestic economic restructuring designed to produce sustained economic health for Brazil. It helped Brazil emerge from a $16 billion balance-of-payments deficit in 1982 to a $530 million surplus in 1984. The devaluations stopped capital flight and spurred exports, mainly of steel, shoes, textiles, and alcohol. In addition, steps to conserve energy slashed oil imports. Since then, Brazil has been able to service its debt of more than $100 billion.[5]

International Monetary Crisis in the 1970s

Toward the end of the 1960s the American economy began to deteriorate. Inflation continued to increase, and unemployment became widespread. Subsequently, President Nixon announced on August 15, 1971, that the United States would not redeem dollars officially held in gold. In addition, the dollar was devalued in 1971 and again in 1973. Thus, starting with 1971, the dollar's link with gold was broken. Without any attachment to gold, the U.S. dollar began to float. The United States hoped this would force its trading partners to revalue their currencies. It was commonly held that many strong foreign currencies were undervalued, giving them a substantial advantage against the dollar. Revaluation would have the effect of making the exports of revaluing countries like Japan and the then West Germany more expensive and their imports less expensive, thus reducing the U.S. balance-of-payments deficits.

Fixed versus Floating Rates

In the 1960s, most monetarists considered fixed exchange rates to be the backbone of international financial cooperation and the stability of the international monetary system. Floating, or "flexible," exchange rates were considered impractical. Today, however, all major nations have floating currencies.

In 1976, at an IMF meeting in Kingston, Jamaica, over 100 member nations reached consensus on amendments to the IMF Articles of Agreement that in effect accepted floating rates as the basis for the international monetary system.[6] The amended agreement, while reaffirming the importance of international cooperation and exchange rate stability, also recognized that such rate stability can be achieved only as the result of stability in underlying economic and financial conditions. Exchange rate stability of any lasting duration cannot be imposed externally by adoption of the pegged exchange rates and heavy official intervention in the foreign exchange market.

However, the merits attributed to floating exchange rates were not borne out. For example:

- When the floating exchange rates were introduced, it was said that balance-of-payments adjustments would be facilitated, but not only have imbalances not disappeared, they have become worse.

- It was thought that speculation would be curtailed. On the contrary, never has it assumed such proportions nor had such destabilizing effects as today.

- It was believed that market forces, left at last to their own devices, would determine the correct exchange-rate balance. But never have imbalances been so great, nor fluctuations so wide and erratic and so little justified by economic fundamentals.

- It was hoped that autonomy in economic and monetary policy would be preserved, allowing each country free choice of its monetary policy and rate of inflation. Facts have completely belied this prediction.

In the mid 1980s, the countries with primary responsibility for the world economy recognized the need for renewed international cooperation on monetary matters. Subsequently, in early 1987 the United States, Japan, France, Britain, Canada, Italy, and what was then West Germany concluded an accord called the *Louvre Agreements* on two complementary aspects: coordination of economic policy and more stable exchange rates. The seven signatories agreed to policies aimed at reducing their internal and external imbalances. For example, they agreed to intervene in exchange markets when necessary.

Since then, the Louvre Agreements have been reconfirmed and adjusted as required by economic and market developments. Economic policy commitments have been adapted and strengthened, including those of central banks. Thus, a first milestone was reached on the road to rebuilding an international monetary order, though it rested on the will and ability of governments to impose self-discipline.[7]

The IMF and the Mexican Debacle

In 1995 Mexico ran into deep economic problems, since the Mexican leaders pushed the country's borrowing too far ahead of its economic growth. The value of the peso went down 30 percent within a week, as foreign investors lost confidence in the country's economy.

How did Mexico get into a mess? Consider a person whose business is doubling every year but whose debt is tripling. When his creditors wake up and ask for some money back, he does not have the cash. It might take him a couple of years to raise it. Meanwhile he needs some more credit to keep his business going. This scenario fits Mexico well. Mexico has been growing consistently for half a dozen years, and its government finances were solid; the federal budget had been balanced three years running. So Mexico looked like a great place to invest. But foreign lenders, mainly American banks, pension, and mutual funds, overdid it. From 1991 through 1993 they loaned to Mexican enterprises and to the government $15 billion to $25 billion a year more than what Mexico was earning from its exports. Toward the end of 1994 these creditors recognized the problems and asked for some money back. But Mexico had no way to pay. The reason was that Mexico had $28 billion in dollar-denominated Treasury notes becoming due in 1995, of which $16 billion was owned by Americans.[8]

Most of the Mexican loans were owned by thousands of U.S. mutual and pension funds and retirement accounts. They had legal obligations to pay benefits to tens of millions of Americans, mostly small savers. There was no practical way to demand new loans from them. Therefore, the IMF and the U.S. government had to come to their rescue.

The IMF committed $17.8 billion to help Mexico in her currency crisis, while the U.S. government provided $40 billion in loan guarantees. The IMF help came with stringent measures to restore the country's economic health.

The IMF and the Asian Crisis

In the fall of 1997 the so-called growth economies of Southeast Asia, one after the other, ran into deep financial crisis. These included Thailand, Indonesia, South Korea, Philippines, and Malaysia. Particularly in the first three nations, the situation became serious enough for the IMF to come to the rescue. The collapse in their asset prices, the extent of financial and corporate insolvency, and the slowdown in the economic growth across the region showed no sign of abating.

The IMF put together a package of $57 billion for South Korea, $43 billion for Indonesia, and $17 billion for Thailand (see International Marketing Highlight 5.1). As a result of the vast sums of money that the IMF applied to the Asian problem, and the strict financial discipline that it required (tight government budgets, high interest rates, and liberalizing economic reforms), the Asian economies at the time of preparing this book had started to come back. Noteworthy are (1) important role that the IMF has come to play in rescuing nations in financial mess and (2) the need for nations to work together, since in a global economy problems are contagious. If one nation fails, others may not be far behind.

The world is undergoing tremendous changes in its economic and political spheres. In the midst of such changes, further adjustments and amendments are necessary to reform the international monetary system in future years (see International Marketing Highlight 5.2). For example, many nations argue that to cope with modern financial crisis, the IMF needs more cash. More cash can be obtained either by doubling members' subscriptions or by issuing new SDRs, the IMF's artificial currency. Alternatively, the IMF can borrow from international capital markets. But the merit of these ideas depends on the answer to a more fundamental question: What is the purpose of IMF intervention in a financial crisis?[9]

Apparently, there is a need for a new international monetary system, especially in light of the problems that Mexico and then the Southeast Asian nations faced. Perhaps a new system will emerge in the new century, based on the spirit of the Louvre Agreements. In their 1999 annual meeting in Washington, the IMF members reaffirmed their commitment to exchange rate stability. The members called for the creation of a representative committee of ministers from developing and industrialized countries to consider the reform and improvement of the international monetary system. In the not too distant future, a true international monetary system may emerge with a standard unit of value, automatic mechanisms, and sanctions that would be beyond the control of the countries involved. The time is ripe for dispassionate consideration of this issue.

International Marketing Highlight 5.1

The Fund's Sums

After committing $17.8 billion to rescue Mexico, how much money does the IMF have left in its coffers? The question sounds simple. But the answer is not, for the IMF's financial structure is fiendishly complex. For a start, its internal accounts are calculated in terms of SDRs—artificial assets created by the IMF and made up of a weighted basket of the world's top five currencies. At present, one SDR is worth $1.47.

The IMF's main source of capital is the subscriptions, or "quotas," that all its members pay. A country's quota depends on the size of its economy. The total amount of IMF quotas is 145 billion SDRs. But since countries pay part of their quota in their own currencies, and many of these are not freely convertible, the IMF's liquid resources stand at only 62.5 billion SDRs after its efforts to help the Mexicans. As some of these liquid resources have already been committed to countries in trouble, the IMF has an adjusted measure for what it calls "uncommitted usable resources." These total 48 billion SDRs.

The usual way to top-up the IMF's resources is to increase members' quotas, but this takes time. So in emergencies there are other potential sources of cash. Under a special agreement, the IMF can borrow up to 17 billion SDRs from industrialized countries and another 1.5 billion SDRs from Saudi Arabia. In extremis, it could sell some of its 104m ounces of gold, which are probably worth around $39 billion.

The IMF has some liabilities too. Every one of its members is entitled to receive a portion of its quota (the so-called "reserve tranche") with no questions asked. The IMF must always be in a position to honor these tranches, which add up to around $29 billion SDRs.

The reality, then, is that it is almost impossible to calculate how much the Fund could safely lend to a troubled country.

Source: The Economist, February 11, 1995, p. 67.

Foreign Exchange

An international marketer needs to transact financial transfers across national lines in order to close deals. The financial transfers from one country to another are made through the medium of foreign exchange. This section examines the framework for dealing in foreign exchange, with its problems and complexities.

The Meaning of Foreign Exchange

Foreign exchange is the monetary mechanism by which transactions involving two or more currencies take place. It is the exchange of one country's money for another country's money (see International Marketing Highlight 5.3). Assume a Mexican representative imports a machine from Cincinnati Milacron, a U.S. manufacturer. The machine costs $1.2 million in U.S. dollars. Commercial exchanges take place in Mexico in pesos, but Cincinnati Milacron wants to be paid in U.S. dollars, not pesos. The Mexican importer, therefore, must buy U.S. dollars against pesos, that is, obtain foreign exchange—or, more specifically, *dollar exchange*—to pay Milacron.

■■■■■■■■■■■■   **International Marketing Highlight 5.2**   ■■■■■■■■■■■■

Cooperation Remains the Watchword

The Louvre Accord may constitute the most important watershed in the post–Bretton Woods era. The major industrialized countries agreed not only to cooperate closely in foreign exchange markets but also to coordinate their macroeconomic policies toward commonly agreed goals—sustainable noninflationary growth and the elimination of external imbalances.

Monetary policy has been managed broadly within the framework of such international policy coordination. Fiscal policy, however, has been managed more independently, owing partly to domestic political constraints. As a result, monetary policy has been overburdened and its independence called into question.

We are confronted with a most difficult policy problem: how to incorporate fiscal policy discipline within the framework of international macroeconomic policy coordination. We have not solved this problem under either the Bretton Woods regime or the managed floating system.

Here, we should consider the issue of structural adjustment. It is, of course, important to promote more efficient resource allocation through structural reform, which may in turn contribute to achieving the aims of macroeconomic policy. At the same time, however, we should keep in mind that structural reforms are basically support measures, and not a substitute, for demand management policy. It is also important to understand that such reforms take time. This is what Japan has told the United States repeatedly in recent meetings and on other occasions. There may be no policymakers nowadays who have not become keen advocates of international policy coordination. We should be prepared to subordinate national interests to international objectives when necessary.

Source: Takeshi Ohta, "Beyond Bretton Woods," *Speaking of Japan,* March 1990, p. 18.

Terminology in Foreign Exchange

Transacting foreign exchange deals presents two problems. First, each country has its own methods and procedures for effecting foreign exchanges—usually developed by its central bank. The transactions themselves, however, take place through the banking system. Thus, both the methods of foreign exchange and the procedures of the central bank and commercial banking constraints must be thoroughly understood and followed to complete a foreign exchange transaction.

A second problem involves the fluctuation of rates of exchange that occurs in response to changes in the supply and demand of different currencies. For example, back in the 1960s a U.S. dollar could be exchanged for about five Swiss francs. In the early 1990s, this rate of exchange went down to as low as 1.3 Swiss francs for a U.S. dollar. Thus, a U.S. businessperson interested in Swiss currency has to pay much more today than in the 1960s. In fact, the rate of exchange between two countries can fluctuate from day to day. This produces a great deal of uncertainty, as a businessperson cannot know the exact value of foreign obligations and claims.

To appreciate the complexities of foreign exchange, several terms must be understood: gold standard, gold exchange standard, gold bullion standard, inconvertible currencies, hard and soft currencies. Understanding these terms also will provide a historical perspective on the making of payments across national boundaries.

Gold standard refers to using gold as the medium of exchange for effecting foreign commercial transactions. Before World War I, most countries followed the gold standard. Private citizens were permitted to own gold, and it could be shipped in and out of the country by individuals or banks without government interference. After World War I, the gold standard was abandoned because gold holdings were concentrated in a few countries, which made international trade difficult to manage.

After the gold standard was established, many countries adopted the *gold exchange standard,* which means that the foreign exchange rate of a currency was set in relation to that country's gold holdings. A country on the gold exchange standard is able to buy in the free market its own currency when it falls in value and to sell it when it increases beyond a predetermined point. This mechanism minimizes the effects of fluctuations in foreign exchange value.

Another way of maintaining a parity with gold is to be on the *gold bullion standard,* which amounts to holding an adequate quantity of gold in reserve in bar or bullion form to settle international transactions at the level of government. Under the gold bullion standard, private individuals are prohibited from possessing gold and it is no longer in coinage, but a government may deal in gold by buying and selling it.

After World War II, most nations prohibited conversion of currency into gold, hence the term *inconvertible currencies.* The phrase also refers to currencies that cannot be conveniently exchanged for other currencies. For example, currencies of a number of developing countries are inconvertible to U.S. dollars.

Currencies may also be labeled as *hard currencies* or *soft currencies:* hard currencies are those in great demand; soft are relatively easy to obtain. The currencies of the majority of developing countries are described as soft currencies as far as international transactions are concerned, whereas those of developed nations are hard currencies.

International Marketing Highlight 5.3

Foreign Exchange Market

Generally exporters prefer to be paid for their goods and services either in their own currency (Japanese in yen and Germans in marks, for example) or in U.S. dollars, which are accepted all over the world. For example, when the French buy oil from Saudi Arabia, they may pay in U.S. dollars, not French francs or Saudi dinars, even though the United States in not involved in the transaction.

The foreign exchange market is where the buying and selling of different currencies takes place. The market comprises a worldwide network of traders, connected by telephone lines and computer screens—there is no central headquarters. The three major centers of trading which handle more than half of all foreign exchange transactions are Great Britain, the United States and Japan. The transactions in Singapore, Switzerland, Hong Kong, Germany, France and Australia account for most of the rest of the market. Trading goes on 24 hours a day; 8 A.M. in London, the trading day is ending in Tokyo, Singapore, and Hong Kong. At 3 P.M. in London, the New York market opens for business. When it is 10 P.M. in London, the Tokyo market is already active.

The foreign exchange market is fast-paced, volatile and enormous. In fact, it is the largest market in the world. In 1996 an estimated $1 trillion was traded every day, roughly equivalent to every person in the world trading $190 per day.

Source: The Basics of Foreign Trade and Exchange (New York: The Federal Reserve Bank, 1997).

Exchange Rates

When countries were on the gold standard, the value of two currencies was determined on the basis of the gold content of each currency. (The technical term used to describe this procedure of determining relationship between two currencies is *par of exchange*.) For example, in the 1920s a U.S. dollar had 23.22 grains of pure gold, while the British pound sterling had 113.0016 grains. Since the latter currency had 4.8665 times more fine gold than the American dollar, it was worth $4.8665.

For those countries off the gold standard, exchange rates are regulated by the central banks. Most countries, however, attempt to maintain a steady exchange rate, which is necessary to promote foreign trade. The base price of a currency is determined by the supply and demand of a currency (see International Marketing Highlights 5.4).

The supply and demand of a currency is influenced by a variety of factors. For example, if a country continues to buy, year after year, more from other nations than it exports, the supply of its currency increases. Likewise, if a country spends overseas—say, to fight a war—its currency supply increases. Such increases adversely affect currency value, which is the base, or market, price.[10] (Exhibit 5.1 lists the factors affecting the supply and demand of the U.S. dollar.)

International Marketing Highlight 5.4

Big MacCurrencies: Can Hamburgers Provide Hot Tips about Exchange Rates?

The Big Mac index is based on the theory of *purchasing-power parity (PPP)* the notion that a dollar should buy the same amount in all countries. In the long run,

EXHIBIT 5.1	The Following Factors Increase the Supply of U.S. Dollars in World Markets	The Following Factors Increase the Demand for U.S. Dollars in World Markets
Factors Affecting the Supply and Demand of U.S. Dollars	1. Imports of merchandise 2. Imports of gold and silver 3. Payments to foreign ships for freight and passenger service 4. American tourist expenditures abroad 5. Banking and all other financial charges payable to foreigners 6. Interest and dividends due on American securities held abroad 7. New purchases of foreign securities 8. Repurchase and redemption of American securities held abroad 9. Transfer of American balances to foreign banks 10. U.S. government grants and loans	1. Exports of merchandise 2. Exports of gold and silver 3. Foreign payments to U.S. shippers 4. Foreign tourist expenditures in the U.S. 5. Banking and other financial charges receivable from foreigners 6. Interest and dividends due on foreign securities held here 7. New sale of American securities abroad 8. Repurchase and redemption of foreign securities held here 9. Transfer of foreign balances to American banks

according to this theory, currencies should move toward the rate that equalizes the prices of an identical basket of goods in each country. Our "basket" is a McDonald's Big Mac, which is now produced in over 100 countries. The Big Mac PPP is the exchange rate that would leave hamburgers costing the same in America as abroad. Comparing actual exchange rates with PPP provides one indication of whether a currency is under- or overvalued.

Massive discounting in America by McDonald's might have distorted the PPP calculations, except for the fact that the discounts did not include the Big Mac. So the annual burgernomics-fest can be served.

The first column in the table on page 141 shows local currency prices of a Big Mac; the second converts them into dollars. The average American price (including tax) is $2.42. China is the place for bargain hunters: a Beijing Big Mac costs only $1.16. At the other extreme, Big Mac fans pay a beefy $4.02 in Switzerland. In other words, the yuan is the most undervalued currency (by 52 percent) and the Swiss franc the most overvalued (by 66 percent).

The third column calculates Big Mac PPPs. For example, dividing the German price by the American price gives a dollar PPP of DM 2.02 (2.02 deutsche marks). The actual rate on April 7th was DM 1.71, implying that the deutsche mark is 18 percent overvalued against the dollar. But over the past two years the dollar has risen nearer to its PPP against most currencies. The yen is now close to its PPP of ¥121. Two years ago the Big Mac index suggested that it was 100 percent overvalued against the dollar.

Some critics find these conclusions hard to swallow. Yes, we admit it, the Big Mac is not a perfect measure. Price differences may be distorted by trade barriers on beef, sales taxes, or large variations in the cost of nontraded inputs such as rents. All the same, the index tends to come up with PPP estimates that are similar to those based on more sophisticated methods.

The Hamburger Standard

	Big Mac Prices		Implied PPP* of the Dollar	Actual Dollar Exchange Rate 7/4/97	Local Currency Under (-)/ Over(+) Valuation,† by Percent
	In Local Currency	In Dollars			
United States	$2.42	—	—	—	—
Argentina	Peso 2.50	2.50	1.03	1.00	13
Australia	A$ 2.50	1.94	1.03	1.29	220
Austria	Sch 34.00	2.82	14.0	12.0	117
Belgium	BFr 109	3.09	45.0	35.3	128
Brazil	Real2.97	2.81	1.23	1.06	116
Britain	£ 1.81	2.95	1.34	1.63	122
Canada	C $2.88	2.07	1.19	1.39	214
Chile	Peso 1,200	2.88	496	417	119
China	Yuan 9.70	1.16	4.01	8.33	252
Czech Republic	CKr 53.0	1.81	21.9	29.2	225
Denmark	DKr 25.75	3.95	10.6	6.52	163
France	FFr 17.5	3.04	7.23	5.76	126
Germany	DM 4.90	2.86	2.02	1.71	118
Hong Kong	HK $9.90	1.28	4.09	7.75	247
Hungary	Forint 271	1.52	112	178	237
Israel	Shekel 11.5	3.40	4.75	3.38	140
Italy	Lire 4,600	2.73	1,901	1,683	113
Japan	¥ 294	2.34	121	126	23
Malaysia	M $3.87	1.55	1.60	2.50	236
Mexico	Peso 14.9	1.89	6.16	7.90	222
Netherlands	Fl 5.45	2.83	2.25	1.92	117
New Zealand	NZ$ 3.25	2.24	1.34	1.45	27
Poland	Zloty 4.30	1.39	1.78	3.10	243
Russia	Rouble 11,000	1.92	4,545	5,739	221
Singapore	S$ 3.00	2.08	1.24	1.44	214
South Africa	Rand 7.80	1.76	3.22	4.43	227
South Korea	Won 2,300	2.57	950	894	16
Spain	Pta 375	2.60	155	144	17
Sweden	SKr 26.0	3.37	10.7	7.72	139
Switzerland	SFr 5.90	4.02	2.44	1.47	166
Taiwan	NT $68.0	2.47	28.1	27.6	12
Thailand	Baht 46.7	1.79	19.3	26.1	226

* Purchasing power parity: local price divided by price in the United States.
† Against dollar
Source: McDonald's.

The base, or market price, however, may not be the real value of a currency, since the central bank may set a different price in order to realize a stated set of objectives. For example, the value of the U.S. dollar was slowly deteriorating in the market in the 1980s, but President Regan refused to devalue it.

Many countries set a lower value on their currency to encourage exports or to seek balance-of-payment adjustments. In other words, long-term objectives may lead a country to set a different value on its currency than the current market value. Incidentally, the IMF assists nations in arriving at a realistic value for their currency in relation to long- and short-term goals. Frequently, the IMF pressures a country to value its currency at what seems to be an acceptable level. For example, it persuaded the Philippines to devalue its currency, the peso, in 1986 and India to devalue its rupee in 1991.

Conducting Foreign Exchange Transactions

Foreign exchange transactions may be conducted by governments via their central bank, brokers, commercial banks, or business corporations. Described here is the process that corporations follow. Assume Boeing wishes to buy $300 million worth of Rolls Royce (British) jet engines for use in its new series of airplanes. Boeing needs to buy the equivalent of $300 million in British pounds sterling to pay Rolls Royce for the engines. Boeing may buy the British currency either in the spot or forward market. In the spot transaction, the purchase is effected right away; forward buying is finalized at a predetermined future date. If the payment is to be made right away, Boeing will have no choice but to buy British pounds sterling on the spot. However, if payment is to be made at a future date, Boeing may transact a forward deal. A forward deal will be preferable if British currency is currently available at a rate that is expected to increase by the time the payment is due. The forward deal will enable Boeing to buy British pounds sterling at a future date at a currently agreed upon price.

Whether the purchase is to be made on the spot or in the future, Boeing Company will contact a number of commercial banks to seek price quotations for British pound sterling in terms of the U.S. dollar. Usually, different banks will quote different prices. For example, a multinational bank like the CitiGroup might have acquired British pound sterling balances when British currency was priced very low. That bank would be able to offer a better price to Boeing than, say, Bank of America, which might not have British pounds sterling on hand and would then have to buy them on the open market to satisfy Boeing's needs. The market might contain customers interested in exchanging British pounds sterling for another currency, or a British bank might be willing to lend the local currency.

Even when the British pounds sterling must be bought from the market, one bank might quote a better price than the other. It all depends on the size of the transaction, the importance of the customer to the bank, the direction of the currency market, future prospects of the currency, and the bank's present financial position.[11] Other things being equal, Boeing would choose the bank providing the best price.

Many MNCs pointedly seek the foreign currencies of the countries in which they are active by making deals at advantageous times.[12] For example, a U.S. corporation with excess cash on hand might buy a currency whose price is low in expectation of the price going up when the corporation needs U.S. dollars again. This way a corporation can make money dealing in foreign exchange transactions (see International Marketing Highlight 5.5).

■■■■■   **International Marketing Highlight 5.5**   ■■■■■

Shock from the Rise in Yen's Value

Sony's annual report for 1986 published an enviable listing of business achievements— new products, sales gains in major ranges, production and distribution rationalization, and strong performances by overseas subsidiaries. Yet the same report broke the bad news that net sales were down 7 percent, operating income had plummeted 75 percent, and net income had fallen 43 percent.

Where did the shock come from? Why the miserable results? Sony was the victim of a 40 percent rise in the yen's value against the dollar. Business excellence—doing all the right things, including protecting the value of revenues through forward currency contracts—had failed to shield the company from the ravages of foreign exchange rate turbulence.

Sony is not alone in having to inform its shareholders of disastrous results following adverse movements in exchange rates. Many other companies that are heavily dependent on international markets are also at the mercy of exchange rates. The auto industry is an obvious example. In 1987, Honda reported that "the strong yen . . . [made] it impossible to raise prices sufficiently to keep pace with currency movements . . . leading to significant declines in earnings." In 1986 Swedish forest products group MoDo cited the falling dollar's lead role in inducing a severe displacement of competitiveness in North American pulp markets. Volvo, Sanyo, Nissan, Matsushita, Philips, and Porsche have all suffered. Losses can come quickly and be painful.

Source: Staffan Hertzell and Christian Caspar, "Coping with Unpredictable Currencies," *The McKinsey Quarterly*, Summer 1988, p. 12.

Balance of Payments

The *balance of payments* of a country summarizes all the transactions that have taken place between its residents and foreigners in a given period, usually a year. The word *transactions* refers to exports and imports of goods and services, lending and borrowing of funds, remittances, and government aid and military expenditures. The term *residents* includes all individuals and business enterprises, including financial institutions, permanently residing within a country's borders, as well as government agencies at all levels. In other words, the balance of payments reflects the totality of a country's economic relations with the rest of the world: its trade in goods, its exchange of services, its purchase and sale of financial assets, and such important governmental transactions as foreign aid, military expenditures abroad, and the payment of reparation. Certain forces determine the volume of these transactions, how they are brought into balance, what problems arise when they fail to balance, and what policies are available to deal with those problems.

Recording Balance-of-Payments Transactions

Exhibit 5.2 highlights the U.S. balance-of-payments position for the year 1998. The transactions are recorded in three categories: current account, capital account, and addendum. The balance-of-payments record is made on the basis of rules of debit and credit, similar to those in business accounting. For example, receipts are entered as credits and payments as debits. Thus, exports, like sales, are entered as credits; imports, like purchases, as debits. All transactions affecting increases in assets, like direct investment abroad, or decreases in indebtedness, like the repayment of external debts, are recorded as credits. However, decreases in assets, like liquidation of foreign securities, and increases in liabilities, like borrowing abroad, are treated as debits.

The *current account* shows U.S. trade in currently produced goods and services. The positive or negative sign preceding each figure indicates whether the transaction represents a gain (+) or a loss (-) of foreign currency. In merchandise transactions, there was a negative balance (of trade) in 1998, meaning the import of goods exceeded the export of goods by $247.0 billion. Line 4 shows the net effect of expenditures incurred by U.S. military installations abroad and the amount of foreign currency earned by selling armaments. Line 5 shows that in 1998 America spent $78.3 billion less on services (tourism, shipping,

EXHIBIT 5.2

U.S. Balance-of-Payments Accounts: 1998 (in Billions of U.S. Dollars)

Current Account

(1) Balance of trade		−247.0
(2) Merchandise exports	+670.2	
(3) Merchandise imports	−917.2	
(4) Net military transactions		−4.4
(5) Net services		+78.3
(6) Net income from investments		−12.2
(7) Balance on goods and services (Lines 1 plus 4 plus 5 plus 6)		−176.5
(8) Unilateral transfers		−44.1
(9) Private	−26.7	
(10) U.S. government (nonmilitary)	−17.4	
(11) Balance on current account (Lines 7 plus 8)		−220.6

Capital Account

(12) Net private capital flows		+238.7
(13) Change in U.S. assets abroad	−285.6	
(14) Change in foreign assets in the U.S.	+524.3	
(15) Net governmental capital flows		+28.2
(16) Change in U.S. government assets	−7.2	
(17) Change in foreign official assets in the U.S.	−21.0	
(18) Balance on capital account (Lines 12 plus 15)		+210.5

Addendum

(19) Sum of Lines (11) and (18)	−10.1
(20) Statistical discrepancy	+10.1

Source: Statistical Abstract of the United States: 1998 (Washington, DC: U.S. Department of Commerce), pp 788–789.

other) than foreigners spent in the United States. Line 6 focuses on another major source of our foreign earnings, return on U.S. investments abroad.

The net result of all trading in goods and services is shown on Line 7. Lines 8–10 describe *unilateral transfers*, comprising private gifts to foreigners and official foreign aid. The current account balance ($220.6 billion in 1998) is shown on Line 11.

Lines 12–18 summarize transactions in the *capital account*. Line 12 shows that, on balance, Americans bought $238.7 billion more in assets abroad than private foreign investors bought in the United States (see the difference between Line 13 and 14).

The current-account deficit combined with the surplus in the capital account left the United States with a fairly large balance-of-payments deficit (see Line 19).

Since the two accounts should balance as a simple matter of arithmetic, the difference is considered a *statistical discrepancy* (Line 20). Although part of this discrepancy is attributable to errors in data collection and computation, the major portion reflects the U.S. balance-of-payments deficit.

The balance-of-payments record may not strictly follow double-entry bookkeeping in that not every transaction gives rise to equal and thus offsetting debit and credit entries. Discrepancies will occur when particular balance-of-payments entries do not represent the movement of funds, but rather the movement of a document or other proof of obligation. Further, some international payments are unilateral (one-sided), such as gifts, grants, and transfer payments. Payments of this type are entered as debits, and receipts as credits.

Finally, instead of using the T account of standard accounting, the U.S. Department of Commerce posts all balance-of-payments transactions in a single column, with debits preceded by minus signs and credits by no sign at all.

"Surplus" or "Deficit" Balance-of-Payments

In Exhibit 5.2, with the help of the statistical-discrepancy item, the entries added up to zero. This is the usual way of striking the balance.

In the case of the United States, however, it is extremely difficult to compute the true balance-of-payments figure for two reasons. First, the U.S. dollar plays a key role in international trade and finance even after its devaluation. For this reason, a number of transactions take place in U.S. dollars between other nations exclusive of the United States. Second, foreign central banks, as well as the IMF, hold U.S. dollars as investments and as working balances to finance international trade and payments. With the complexities produced by these numbers, no single number can adequately describe the international position of the United States during any given period.

To illustrate the difficulty involved in compiling the "true" balance-of-payments figure for the United States, consider the following case. Official government statistics reveal that the United States has had continuous trade deficits since 1977. The trade deficit for 1999, for example, reached $271 billion. Further, with the exception of a very small surplus in 1980, the current account, a broader measure, has also been in deficit since 1977. Traditionally, nations with continuing balance-of-trade and current-account deficits experience a drop in the international value of their currencies. Indeed, this is the basic adjustment mechanism in a floating exchange rate system. Yet, the U.S. dollar continues to be strong.

U.S. Balance-of-Payments Position

Since World War II, the international transactions of the United States have shown enormous growth. In 1950 total receipts came to $10,203 million. Such transactions in 1960 amounted to $19,650 million; in 1970 to $42,969 million; in 1980 to $100,110 million; in 1990 to $143,000 million, and in 1999 to an estimated $242,000 million. Even after adjusting for inflation, these figures reflect a vast growth in international dealings by the United States with the rest of the world, as evidenced by the upsurge in U.S. private foreign investment, the rise in U.S. government expenditures abroad, and the emergence of the U.S. dollar as the world's principal reserve and trading currency.

In recent years the U.S. industry and government have adopted a variety of measures to improve its balance-of-payments position. U.S. exports have been encouraged at all levels. The U.S. economy has been restructured via new investments and technology, facilitating a rise in productivity that makes U.S. products more competitive abroad. Similarly, efforts have been made through persuasion and negotiations to limit Japanese exports. Finally, efforts to bring the value of U.S. dollar down by intervening in the financial markets has made U.S. products more competitive in export markets.[13]

Current and Emerging Issues

This section briefly examines the current strains on the world monetary system and attempts to project forthcoming events as we enter the next century. Although the world has overcome the crisis created by the 1973–1974 oil price increase, OPEC has lately shown an increase in its surplus, and if it takes measures to maintain this position, we might see a further increase in the price of oil and a need to recycle funds from oil exporters to the rest of the world. If, on the other hand, the price of oil declines, many oil-producing countries such as Nigeria and Mexico will face new difficulties on that account.

A large number of countries lived through the 1970s by means of heavy borrowing. At the same time, their ability to repay debts declined. International bankers in the last few years were stunned by the inability of these countries to service and repay their debts. Although IMF assistance has helped many nations (for example, Mexico, South Korea, Thailand, Indonesia), in meeting the immediate crisis, the debt problem is likely to linger for many years.

The private international bankers are already overcommitted, especially in developing countries. These institutions may be unwilling to accommodate the growing needs of the developing countries in the new millennium.

Lessons from the Asian Crash

The Asian companies and, in general, companies in the developing world will find it difficult to borrow money because of their past inability to repay loans. They must pay stiff risk premiums until lenders are confident that the money will not be frittered away and that no currency crisis will occur to destroy their ability to repay. The consolidation in the corporate sector is likely to spur the rise of a newer breed of Asian company—one that is smaller but more focused. Its forerunners are found among exporters that already have adjusted to the new rules of the global marketplace. In other words, the enterprises in developing countries need to abandon the favored practice of diversifying into a broad range of new industries. They should stay with a few core sectors and sell off the rest.[14]

Furthermore, the companies should not rely only on cheap labor. They must improve logistics, design, and inventory management to be globally competitive. Finally, they should team up with foreign partners to better understand the marketplace in the industrialized countries and serve the customers better and thus gain competitive strength.

Summary

After World War II, the nations of the world came to an important realization: for a secure future, national economies would have to be rebuilt or developed, and such a feat could be accomplished only through worldwide cooperation. Subsequently, a historic meeting of 55 nations took place at Bretton Woods, New Hampshire, to develop a monetary system that would ensure stable conditions for a healthy growth of the world economy. The IMF was originated to oversee the system. Essentially, the system controlled the limits on exchange rate movements in its member countries in a predetermined way. The exchange rates were permitted to vary by only 1 percent above and below par. As a country's rate of exchange attained or approached either limit, the country's central bank intervened in the market to prevent the rate from passing the limits.

The IMF not only reviews the status of different economies, but also gives advice on how a nation can achieve monetary stability.

In times of temporary balance-of-payments deficits, countries can approach the IMF for short-term loans to weather the difficult period. The IMF's short-term accommodation, however, has proved insufficient, and, therefore, SDRs have been created to provide additional liquidity.

The United States at one time guaranteed to convert the U.S. dollar into gold at a fixed rate of $35 per ounce of gold. This guarantee helped countries to trade. Indeed, many countries linked their national currencies to the U.S. dollar. In the early 1970s, however, the value of the U.S. dollar began to decline. Eventually, the United States devalued its dollar twice and abandoned the fixed parity between its dollar and gold. Since then, all currencies have floated free, and their values fluctuate on the basis of supply and demand.

A system of foreign exchange is necessary for transacting payments in foreign trade. When people import something, they must make payment to the exporter for it. Since the exporting country ordinarily has a different currency than the one used in the importing country, the importer must obtain the exporter's currency in order to pay for the imported good. The importer obtains the exporter's currency from its central bank. The central bank of the country sets an exchange value on its currency for the other currency. In this way, it is possible to determine how much the importer needs in local currency to pay the bank in order to receive the requisite amount of the exporter's currency.

The balance-of-payments concept refers to a systematic record of the economic transactions of a nation during a given period between its residents and the rest of the world. In general, if a nation exports more than it imports, it will have a favorable balance of payment; if the reverse is true, the nation will have an unfavorable balance of payment.

Review Questions

1. What reasons led nations to seek international monetary stability? How does such stability help promote world trade?
2. How did the Bretton Woods agreement provide a stable monetary environment?
3. What are special drawing rights (SDRs)? Why were they created?
4. What led the United States to devalue its dollar?
5. Why is it desirable for a country to maintain a stable foreign exchange rate for its currency?
6. Define *balance of payment*. How does it differ from balance of trade? How accurate are the U.S. balance-of-payment records?

Creative Questions

1. Has the role of the IMF (for example, maintenance of fixed exchange rates) in the world economy become less important since that organization was birthed at the Bretton Woods Conference? What new role might the IMF play to continue to be a viable institution?
2. In the interest of increasing its exports, can a country devalue its currency indiscriminately? Is there a point at which it may be counterproductive to devalue the currency? If so, explain why. Also, why don't the Japanese devalue the yen to help Japanese companies keep their export tempo?

Endnotes

1. *IMF Economic Reviews*, January–April 1999.

2. *The Economist*, February 21, 2000, p. 78.

3. *World Development Report* (Washington, DC: The World Bank, 1996).

4. "East Asia: Which Way to Safety?" *The Economist*, January 10, 1998, p. 62.

5. See *World Development Report 1999, Op. Cit.*

6. "Sisters in the Wood: A Survey of the IMF and the World Bank," *The Economist*, October 12, 1991, pp. 5–48.

7. See Edward Balladur, "Rebuilding an International Monetary System," *The Economist*, February 23, 1988, p. 28.

8. Rich Thomas, "How to Save Face—And Trade," *Newsweek*, February 6, 1995, p. 34.

9. "Why Can't a Country be Like a Firm?" *The Economist*, April 22, 1995, p. 79.

10. Robert G. Ruland and Timothy S. Doupink, "Foreign Currency Translation and the Behavior of Exchange Rates," *Journal of International Business Studies*, Fall 1988, pp. 461–476.

11. Arvind D. Jain and Douglas Nigh, "Politics and the International Lending Decisions of Banks," *Journal of International Business Studies*, Summer 1989, pp. 349–359.

12. Timothy A. Luehrman, "Exchange Rate Changes and the Distribution of Industry Value," *Journal of International Business Studies*, Fourth Quarter 1991, pp. 619–649.

13. "Exports: 'This Show Has Legs,'" *Business Week*, September 19, 1994, p. 48.

14. "What to Do About Asia," *Business Week*, January 26, 1998 p. 26.

CHAPTER 6

International Finance and Accounting

CHAPTER FOCUS_____

After studying this chapter, you should be able to

■ Explain the implications of financial decisions for international marketing strategy.

■ Describe the dimensions of international money management.

■ Discuss how international investment decisions are made.

■ Compare U.S. accounting practices with those of other nations.

Today's multinational enterprises must deal with an international monetary system full of complexities, challenges, and risks. Finance managers and treasurers in particular play a key role in managing worldwide money matters. It is important for international marketers to possess insight into multinational finance and accounting functions, because these functions usually have a significant impact on marketing. For example, without such an understanding of the financial side of international business, a marketing manager for an airplane manufacturer that is supplying 10 planes to a Mexican airline might accept routine negotiation for payment over three years in Mexican pesos. In contrast, a manager with international financial insight would foresee the depreciation of Mexican currency and opt for payment in U.S. dollars. The impact of the finance function on international marketing decisions can spell success or failure with each decision.

The financial objectives of a corporation typically constrain the latitude of a marketing manager. Marketers are affected by all aspects of their company's money management—the raising of money, the investing of money, the maintenance of liquidity, and even lesser factors like the repatriation of funds from subsidiaries to parent corporations. The decisions of marketing managers also are affected by accounting considerations.

Implications of Financial Decisions for Marketing

A discussion of the financial aspects of multinational business in a marketing text is entirely relevant in view of the fact that an enterprise ultimately ventures across national boundaries for the enhancement of its long-term profitability. Therefore, financial commitments and their results deeply affect the marketing perspective of a business. The close relationship between finance and marketing functions has long been recognized, but in the realm of international business, it is of heightened significance. Consider, for example, the effect on marketing of the parent corporation's *transfer pricing* policy (transfer pricing will be discussed thoroughly in Chapter 13). Decisions in setting prices for the transfer of goods, services, and technology between related affiliates in different countries are inevitably affected by fund positioning, income taxes, tariffs, and quotas; managerial incentives and evaluation; antitrust prosecution; the interest of joint venture partners; and corporate bargaining power with suppliers or financial institutions. Many of these sometimes conflicting considerations have both financial underpinnings and a direct or indirect impact on marketing.

Eventually, all marketing decisions that involve capital investment or other types of long-term financial commitment on the part of the parent corporation must be reviewed in the context of corporate international financial policy. For example, marketing wisdom might suggest improving the provision of after-sale services, which might entail manufacturing parts locally. But local manufacturing might require substantial investment and transfer of technology. In the context of overall financial goals, the parent may find it undesirable to invest in manufacturing spare parts and supplies in a host country. Or the parent may learn that another affiliate recently expanded capacity to manufacture the same parts, or that the political situation in the host country is discouraging to additional investments, and so on. In the end, the decision, which appeared potentially desirable based on marketing considerations, may be postponed or dropped when reviewed from the financial angle.

The financial strength of a company deeply affects marketing, particularly in the company's ability to maintain inventories. Making timely deliveries to customers could provide important competitive leverage in international business, particularly if inventory replenishment involves great distances and time. Similarly, marketing is affected by the company's ability to make economical bulk purchases of merchandise. Marketing decisions on promotional efforts in the mass media to strengthen the brand, commitment of resources to research and development for the timely introduction of new and improved products, and investment in developing cordial relationships with channels of distribution are all influenced by financial decisions. This intimate relationship between the two functions of finance and marketing means that marketers, especially international marketers, need a basic knowledge of financial matters (see International Marketing Highlight 6.1).

Few companies today, small or large, can afford to disregard the growing importance of overseas markets as a source of corporate growth. Increasingly interdependent trade flows and growing government involvement in economic affairs make financial management a complex function. The volatility of exchange rates adds to the complexity. Given the difficulties posed by these factors, plus the recent turbulent economic environment in a number of Asian nations in 1997–1998, setting global marketing strategies without the benefit of financial inputs is like looking through a pair of binoculars with one eye closed (see International Marketing Highlight 6.2).

The competitive challenges for all businesses have never been more daunting. There is enormous pressure to develop compelling products, services, and solutions for highly demanding customers while generating profitable growth. Three forces are converging to create both opportunities and risks for companies of all sizes:

- Globalization.
- Highly liquid capital markets.
- Shorter business life-cycles.

This pace of intense change is expected to continue. More than ever, cutting-edge strategy and superior execution separate the leaders from the laggards. Leading companies are transforming finance from a support function into a strategic weapon, creatively applying resources to those areas most critical to business performance. A well-equipped finance organization is a powerful strategic weapon that helps the enterprise generate growth and sustain shareholder value.

International Marketing Highlight 6.1

How Volkswagen Lost It All

To illustrate the impact of exchange rate changes, which is a financial impact on marketing, consider the case of Volkswagen (VW). In the 1960s VW experienced phenomenal growth. During 1960–1970, its annual sales increased from DM (deutsche mark) 4 billion to DM 15 billion and its exports increased manyfold. In the early 1960s exports represented half of total sales; toward the end of the decade, exports had become two-thirds of its total sales. VW emerged as the largest automobile exporter in the world.

Volkswagen's success in the U.S. market was highly remarkable. Since their introduction in the U.S. market in the early 1950s, VW's vehicles (particularly the Beetle) had filled an important market niche, catering to price-sensitive consumers. To many Americans, the Beetle was the ideal economy vehicle.

Volkswagen's commitment to the U.S. market was never in doubt. With service support and corporate commitment, annual sales increased from 200,000 vehicles in 1960 to 600,000 vehicles by the end of the decade. In the early 1960s the United States was VW's largest foreign customer, accounting for 30 percent of VW's exports; the U.S. market for imported cars was increasing; and VW was getting an increasing share of a growing market. By 1970, when imported cars constituted 14 percent of the U.S. car market, VW's market share in the U.S. was 6 percent, compared with 3 percent in 1960.

Then came the decline, and by 1973 the losses were huge. In October 1969 the DM was revalued, and its full effect was felt in 1970. The revaluation of the DM weakened the competitive position of VW in all the export markets. Volkswagen's net earnings dropped from DM 330 million in 1969 to DM 190 million in 1970. In some European countries, considerable losses in market share were experienced. The DM was again revalued in 1971 and 1972, and by 1972 its revaluation amounted to 40 percent over the 1969 figure. To partially offset currency change effects, VW prices were increased in the United States, and as a result VW lost its market share. In 1971 alone, the losses in the United States because of currency changes were estimated to be DM 200 million.

The early 1970s saw the gradual and regular strengthening of the DM and, with it, the weakening of VW's position. VW's fortunes were inextricably linked with those of the DM: as the DM rose, VW's profits fell. A strong currency clearly weakens the position of the country's exporters; this is particularly true if they are catering to price-sensitive markets. As its annual report of 1972 poignantly recorded, "Exports account for more than two-thirds of the Volkswagen AG's total sales. Of all the world's leading automobile manufacturers, VW is therefore the one most affected by variations in exchange rates."

Stuart Perkins, the chief executive of VW's American subsidiary, was so frustrated and exasperated by the havoc currency changes were playing on his sales that he exploded: "I used to call the sales people and ask how sales were doing. Last quarter, my first move was to call the financial people and ask how the D-mark-to-dollar exchange rate was doing."

The final collapse came in 1973, when VW incurred a loss of DM 807 million. Cash flow plunged from DM 1,671 million in 1972 to DM 618 million in 1973. Equity dropped to 24 percent of assets, from 31 percent the previous year. There was a steady decline in sales in the U.S. market, from a high of 570,000 vehicles in 1968 to 200,000 vehicles in 1976. VW ended 1975 in the red, with losses of DM 160 million.

Currency changes affected VW in three ways. First, the DM revaluation vis-à-vis the dollar made VW's position very uncompetitive in the United States, its biggest market. Second, the DM's revaluation in relation to other Western European currencies such as the pound sterling, the lira, and the French franc resulted in similar effects in those markets. VW found it increasingly difficult to compete in the United Kingdom, France, and Italy. Third, within the [former] West German market, VW had to face increasing import competition, especially from Renault and Fiat. Because of the weakening of the French and Italian currencies, these automobiles became very competitive on the German market.

■■■■■■■■■■■■■ International Marketing Highlight 6.2 ■■■■■■■■■■■■■

Marketing Transaction Example

Suppose that J.T. Enterprises, a small manufacturer of wooden block sets, discovers an opportunity to sell 1,000 cases of blocks to a toy company in France. Under the terms of the sale agreement, the company will export the blocks to France and receive payment in French francs in approximately 60 days. The company must then sell the francs in exchange for U.S. dollars.

The French company has agreed to pay all shipping costs as well as the going rate of $100 per case of blocks. On the day of the sale agreement (September 4, 1992) the exchange rate between U.S. dollars and French francs is .20777, which means that one franc is worth 20.777 cents U.S. Or, put another way, it takes 1/.20777 or 4.813 francs to equal one dollar. Thus, the French toy company agrees to pay J.T. Enterprises 481.3 francs per case (4.813 × 100) or 481,300 francs for the entire order (481.3 × 1,000).

The company enters into the agreement with great confidence. The actual cost of manufacturing and packing the blocks for sale is $75 per case. Thus, the company expects to realize a profit of $25,000 ($100 − $75 × 1,000). But will the company actually realize this amount? Three possible situations could occur. First, the exchange rate could hold for the next 60 days. Second, the dollar could "weaken" in relation to the French franc within the next 60 days. And third, the dollar could "strengthen" in relation to the French franc in the next 60 days.

1. If the exchange rate between U.S. dollars and French francs holds at .20777, the company will indeed realize a profit of nearly $25,000. When it receives payment for the order, it can exchange 481,300 francs for $100,000 U.S. (with a slight amount of transaction costs).
2. If the dollar weakens relative to the French franc, then it takes less French francs to equal one US. dollar. This situation would be favorable to J.T. Enterprises. If, for example, the exchange rate was .26316 in 60 days, it would take only 1/.26316, or 3.800, francs to equal one U.S. dollar. Thus, the company could exchange 481,300 francs for $126,658 (481,300/3.800), and the profit realized would be approximately $51,658.
3. If, however, the dollar grows stronger relative to the French franc in the next 60 days, there will be a negative impact on the profit realized by J.T. Enterprises. For example, if the exchange rate fluctuates to .17241 on the day that the company receives its payment for the shipment, it will take 1/.17241, or 5.800 francs, to equal one U.S. dollar. Thus, when the company makes the currency exchange, it will receive only $82,983 (481,300/5.800), and profit realized will be approximately $7,893.

The company would be prudent to take measures to protect its anticipated profitability of $25,000 on the transaction. When a company fails to protect its profitability, it has what is known as an "open" position, meaning it is open, or exposed, to exchange rate risk. When a company ensures that it will receive the profit anticipated at the time of the sale agreement, it is said to have "covered" the exchange risk of the transaction.

Multinational Financial Management

The finance function has two principal aspects: (1) to provide the monetary wherewithal to do business and (2) to ensure an adequate financial return on the assets of the company commensurate with its objectives. Even in a strictly domestic business, the able management of funds and investment means solving all sorts of problems related to issues such as what financial return is adequate, how should the return be defined, what sources of funds should be tapped, when should funds be raised, and where should funds be used. In the international arena, the problems multiply. Finance management must not only deal with different currencies and their fluctuating rates, but also allow for the vagaries of the economic and political environments of nations with varying perspectives. This section briefly examines various facets of the finance function and relates them to conducting business across national boundaries.

Financial Objectives

Consider the financial objectives of an MNC that manufactures different types of parts and accessories for the automotive industry and related markets. The corporation's measure of performance is the return on capital employed. *Capital employed* is the sum of all assets plus the accumulated reserves for depreciation. In its financial goals, the corporation recognizes that not all operations are directly comparable, and states that targets for individual profit centers and operations will take into account the nature of the operation, its performance plans, and its record of achievement against them.

Target profit performance is stated to consist of

1. A competitive return on capital employed with a basic minimum pretax return of 15 percent, which shall be inflation-adjusted from time to time.
2. An annual growth rate of pretax profits of at least 12 percent.

New projects and further capital commitments are subject to a minimum hurdle rate of 25 percent return on capital unless deemed otherwise necessary or desirable by the corporation in view of legal requirements or the corporation's best long-term interest.

Emphasis on asset management at all levels will include annual targets for cash generation, capital expenditures, and balance sheet items, including inventory and receivables management. Particular attention is drawn to the differences between actual cash-generating capacity and book results. Each group and profit center is expected to develop not only net cash-generating capacity for its own requirements, but also sufficient funds for the corporation to meet its high-priority investment commitments and opportunities.

Thus, the company may require its subsidiaries to repatriate surplus funds to the corporate headquarters. As a guideline, the corporation intends each of its non–U.S.-dollar organizations to remit as dividends, or otherwise, an amount of its annual after-tax earnings equal to the same percentage that the corporation is currently paying from its consolidated after-tax income to its stockholders. Deviations from this policy may be expected when host country restrictions exist or when it is in the corporation's best long-term interest.

Financial limitations are identified as follows:

1. Investment in net working capital of less than 35 percent of annual sales; investment in net fixed assets of less than 25 percent of annual sales.
2. Dividend payments of approximately 40 percent of earnings.
3. No significant dilution of shareholders' ownership.

This company has nicely blended the financial objectives for both domestic and international business. From every business deal it expects a minimum inflation-adjusted pretax return of 15 percent, a minimum annual growth of 12 percent in pretax profits, and a 25 percent return on capital from new projects—the hurdle rate. The company intends to regularly repatriate profits and duly provide for exchange rate fluctuations. The objectives clearly recognize the legal/political constraints that may be imposed by host governments, and the company is willing to accept deviations from its objectives to comply with the local environment.

The financial limitations, stated as a part of the objectives, provide guides for sources and uses of funds. The company wants to make rather substantial, regular dividend payments of approximately 40 percent. This means internal funds in the form of retained earnings will be limited for investment in growth. Also, the company wants no significant dilution of shareholder's equity. It is possible, then, that equity capital will have to be considered as a last resort for raising money.

Financial objectives constitute the foundation for making financial decisions for a company. For example, in order to protect itself against exchange rate fluctuations, it might require managers in overseas subsidiaries to forecast regularly the exchange rates month-by-month for the upcoming six months. On the basis of those forecasts, corporate funds in a currency likely to be substantially depreciated would be utilized before funds in stronger currencies.

To illustrate this point, consider that in 1998 the Thai currency, the bhat, continued to decline, and all indications pointed toward a further depreciation of the currency. At the same time, the U.S. dollar continued to strengthen. Thus, in 1998 international financial managers had good reason to spend their bhat accumulations and save dollars.

Likewise, the goal to repatriate profits suggests that a financial manager in a foreign subsidiary can plan on meeting future investment needs only partially from retained earnings. According to the financial objectives, a new project proposed in a subsidiary outside the United States need not be put through the channels for final approval by the corporate management if it is not expected to meet the hurdle rate. Thus, financial objectives affect investment decisions as well.[1]

Money Management

Money management deals with sources and uses of funds, involving such considerations as how funds should be obtained (equity versus debt), in which currency a corporation or subsidiary should be responsible for raising funds, how the transfer of funds from one subsidiary to another or between a subsidiary and corporation should be handled, and in which financial instrument the funds should be invested as well as in which market. Prudent international money management requires minimizing the cost of funds and maximizing the return on investment over time by means of the best combination of currency of denomination and maturity characteristics of financial assets and liabilities. Such money management requirements are very complex in the international context. They require (1) the formulation and revision of capital structure decisions for different entities and (2) budgets for intracompany funds transfer.

Typically, a multinational enterprise is susceptible to three risks related to money management:[2] (1) the *political risk* of assets being taken over by the host country; (2) the *exchange risk* whereby the value of the U.S. dollar changes with reference to the host country currency; and (3) the *translation risk* whereby the corporate financial statements are required by the U.S. Securities and Exchange Commission (SEC) regulations to be based on historical costs rather than current value.

The goal of an international money manager is to obtain finances for foreign projects in a way that minimizes after-tax interest costs and foreign exchange losses. The *exchange rate parity theory* suggests that international differentials in interest costs are offset by changes in foreign exchange rates; that is, the expected value for net financing costs will be equal for all currencies over any given time period, provided foreign exchange markets are efficient. Thus, it makes no difference which currency is used to finance a foreign project.

Assuming the exchange rate parity theory holds, a number of considerations, such as tax policies, favor the use of host country financing. Many countries—Australia, Indonesia, South Africa, and Germany, for example—have no taxes on gains or losses arising from most long-term exchange transactions.[3] In some countries, gains and losses from long-term exchange transactions are subject to preferential capital gains tax rates or reserves treatment.[4] Furthermore, most countries apply some kind of surtax on foreign interest payments. These taxes are generally of the withholding sort and are usually available for rebate. A few countries—Argentina, for example—even impose a separate tax on foreign interest payments. These taxes increase the cost of borrowing in U.S. dollars or other foreign currency. Such policies encourage MNCs to prefer the use of host country financing. As a matter of fact, many firms require that all foreign projects be financed in the currency of the host country.[5]

The use of host country currency for financing limits the foreign exchange exposure and hence the risk.[6] Experience in India is relevant here.[7] Traditionally, foreign investors did not think that India provided an opportunity for raising capital locally. However, Honda Motor Company's issue was oversubscribed 165 times within a span of 72 hours. Similarly, Burroughs Corporation's stock and debenture issue was oversubscribed 30 times. In brief, even in many developing countries there is no shortage of local capital.

Translation risk still arises from foreign financing decisions. On the whole, however, such translation risk is less severe because, whereas exchange risk leads to a realizable gain or loss, translation risk is a paper gain or loss. Besides, the former is taxable, whereas the effects of translation risk rarely are.[8] Thus, an effective argument can be made for host country financing. But the argument is based on a variety of assumptions, both economic and noneconomic and if these assumptions fail, a company may be forced to seek funds in other markets than the host country.[9] In many developing countries, for example, the government may make it virtually impossible to raise money locally. In other situations, the local currency may be unusable.

Of course, money management involves many more facets than just host country financing. For our purposes here, however, such limited treatment of the subject is sufficient to provide a bird's-eye view of international money management.

Repatriation of Funds

In domestic business, an important financial decision made by a corporation is the establishment of *dividend policy,* that is, the amount of earnings to be distributed to the owners, the stockholders. Likewise, a multinational firm needs to formulate a strategy on remission of dividends from overseas affiliates to headquarters. According to Eiteman, Stonehill, and Moffett, the international dividend policy is determined by the following six factors:[10]

1. Tax implications.
2. Political risk.
3. Foreign exchange risk.
4. Age and size of affiliate.
5. Availability of funds.
6. Presence of joint venture partners.

Many countries—Germany, for example—tax retained earnings, which yields higher dividend payouts. Countries that levy withholding taxes on dividends paid to a foreign parent, on the other hand, discourage distribution of earnings in the form of dividends.

Taxes aside, in the case of countries exhibiting higher political risk, the parent might require the remission of all earnings minus funds needed for working capital and approved capital projects planned for the next few months. Such a perspective would more often apply to developing countries. Where political risk may not be an important factor, the dividend policy will be based on availability and use of funds. For example, if funds are needed in the United Kingdom, headquarters might decide to transfer its retained earnings from a German subsidiary to the United Kingdom rather than transferring funds from the United States. An alternative to this action would be the investment of funds in German marks.

Another factor that affects international dividend payment is foreign exchange risk. If the value of the host country currency is expected to decline substantially, other things being equal, common business wisdom will direct conversion of funds into a strong currency. Age and size of affiliates also influence the dividend policy. Research on the subject has showed that older affiliates provide a larger proportion of their earnings to the parent since their reinvestment needs decline with time. By the same token, recently established affiliates provide only marginal dividends. As far as size is concerned, larger firms usually have a formal policy for dividend payout, but small firms depend on ad hoc decisions.

Finally, if a foreign affiliate is formed as a joint venture, the interests of local stockholders force the company to follow a more stable dividend policy, because the worldwide corporate perspective cannot be pursued at the cost of valid claims by local investors who do not necessarily benefit from the global dividend strategy of the parent.

On the basis of the six factors just listed and discussed, a multinational firm may follow either a pooled strategy or a flexible strategy for distribution of earnings generated by foreign affiliates. The *pooled strategy* refers to a stated policy of remittance of profits to the parent on a regular basis. The *flexible strategy* leaves the decision on dividends to factors operating at the time. The flexible strategy permits the parent to make the most viable use of funds vis-à-vis its long-term global corporate objectives. Overall, the flexible approach in foreign earnings permits better utilization of the total financial resources available and eventually leads to a higher level of inflow of funds to the parent company in all forms—dividends, royalties, and various fees.

Making International Investments

Successful international companies continue to be interested in growth prospects, evaluating a variety of proposals from different sources that potentially could lead to investments abroad. These sources include company employees, unknown host country firms, licensees, distributors, and joint venture partners. Essentially, two processes of an investment proposal determine its fate: the selling of the proposal and its review. Proposal selling and reviewing go through a variety of formal and informal human interactions. The processes are significantly affected by the firm's internal politics—that is, factors such as who is backing the proposal, what the company's organization is, how company personalities interact—and by factors outside the firm. Ultimately, the winning strength of a proposal depends on the diligent work of those who prepare it (see Exhibit 6.1).

EXHIBIT 6.1
Checklist for
Preparing
International
Investment Proposal

1. Check with all the people whose approval is needed.
2. Check with all the people *they* will call on for advice.
3. If possible, determine who is most important for which aspects of the proposal (but be careful not to categorize people too narrowly).
4. Sell at the highest possible level—there's nothing like having the president's office behind you from the opening whistle.
5. Establish "people priorities"—who, in descending order, is most important for passing on the project. (This will by no means necessarily be in order of rank.)
6. Set up a flexible "people timetable"—who should be won over in what order.
7. Think ahead as to what each person is going to want to know about the project, and program that into the project analysis. (As one executive put it, you should "do *their* homework" for *them*.)
8. Measure your proposal against *all* stated corporate policy objectives; although sales and profit objectives are the easy ones, don't forget others.
9. Identify any potential enemies to your project and any points of potential resistance, and then establish strategies, or at least mental contingency plans, for dealing with them.
10. Make sure that the investment proposal format corresponds exactly to that used for domestic proposals so as to avoid having it appear to be exotic and thereby attract special detailed scrutiny regarding risk.
11. Give careful thought to any objections that may be raised against your proposal.
12. Be sure you know where your allies stand at all times.
13. In terms of the proposal itself, check carefully that you have not overlooked any obviously important details. Then check for more subtle omissions, and be particularly aware of problem areas and weak points. Have a good idea of the margin of error in the estimates.
14. Anticipate as many objections as possible, but don't be defensive and show your refutations of the objections too hastily.
15. At all times, carefully monitor the pulse of the project's momentum. Momentum can change abruptly. Be ready to facilitate steady progress and to forestall hitches.
16. Be particularly wary of dangerous "parabusiness" environmental criticism of overseas projects, that is, qualitative or essentially subjective, negative social and political judgments. (A domestic officer wishing to shoot down an international proposal may revert to the very thing that is seldom, or rarely, considered for domestic investment proposals, namely, a careful analysis of the political and social climate.)
17. Try to keep the project moving forward at a deliberate speed. Don't let it get stalled in excessive reviewing.

Selling Investment Proposals

Depending on the organizational arrangements of the company, the selling job begins at the middle-management level in the division or department responsible for the country where investment is being considered. When an opportunity arises that seems worthwhile, the manager involved, usually the manager of international development, begins checking with colleagues in manufacturing, marketing, and legal departments in a very informal fashion on such matters as sales projections, manufacturing estimates, patents, and taxes. The manager would also apprise superiors of the forthcoming proposal.

Throughout the early investigatory period that leads up to a formal presentation of the proposal to an international executive, it is important to concentrate on the really critical matters involved. Although these vary somewhat from industry to industry, the overriding emphasis should be put on marketing, because it is in this area that major problems occur. Once the investigation has been completed, a formal proposal is developed and submitted to the head of the section or department.

The section or department head will make a more detailed study of the proposed project with the objective of strengthening the proposal. The location of the investment, market estimates and sales forecasts, equipment costs, total capital required, sources of funding, raw materials availability, and human resources are examined.[11] On the basis of this examination, the proposal is completed for submission to the senior management. Accompanied by a letter, the final proposal includes an appropriations request, an engineering report, the project proposal, and financial analysis. The letter activates the formal review procedure, first through the finance committee, then through the board of directors.

Reviewing Investment Proposals

The review process of a investment proposal is shaped by the perspectives of a company's top management. Often the process and philosophy behind the review of investment opportunities change dramatically with a new person at the helm. In any event, most companies have a comprehensive system for reviewing investment proposals,[12] and all strive to determine whether the investment will provide long-term, lasting benefits for the owners. It is important that the chief executive or another top officer participate actively in the review process of individual major investment decisions in order to assess its value to the long-term strategic posture of the company.

The checklist in Exhibit 6.2 indicates the type of information needed for review of an international investment project. With this information, a framework for evaluation can be laid out. In the final analysis, the evaluation should provide the cost/benefit effects of the project for the host country, parent corporation, and foreign subsidiary.

International Accounting

Global economic interdependence and the existence of large, multinational enterprises create needs for measurement, information transfer, and evaluation of microinformation and macroinformation on an unprecedented scale. International accounting must address these issues. Traditionally, the flow of information between the parent and its subsidiaries was limited. In the last 20 years or so, however, the communication of accounting data across national boundaries has increased enormously. The rapid development of computer capability, as well as achievements in the field of air travel and telecommunications, has made it possible for an MNC to assemble detailed data from its worldwide operations on short notice. But, a challenge arises in determining exactly what information—out of the overwhelming abundance of information available—a parent corporation should request to serve both internal and external needs.

An international accounting system serves the same two basic purposes as domestic accounting. It provides information on the business conducted during a certain period

EXHIBIT 6.2
Checklist for
Reviewing
International
Investment Proposal

1. Carefully examine the record and predilections of the individual most directly responsible for the proposal. Is she chronically optimistic? Does she usually underestimate costs or overestimate future sales?
2. Who has been won over to her side? Why do certain managers support the proposal? Why do others oppose it?
3. Determine as best you can the politics of the situation, and try to discount each aspect in your analysis.
4. Systematically review all the estimates and projections of the proposal.
5. Look at the details, but also sit back and broadly scrutinize the project. Does it hang together, not only in its details but also as a whole? Does it fit in with the company's long-term objectives?
6. Give particularly close attention to the most crucial elements in your industry—marketing, manufacturing, technical know-how, or financing.
7. Look for holes. Errors of omission are sometimes harder to spot than outright mistakes.
8. Probe the weak or questionable assumptions that lie behind the figures.
9. Make sure you don't overlook anybody on the corporate staff, or elsewhere in the company, whose advice would be useful and who should see the proposal.
10. Don't let the proposal get "railroaded" through the process without sufficiently careful analysis.
11. Make sure that the difficulties—present and future—of doing business in the country and region in question are not minimized. What about the future effects of nascent regional trade groups? Any serious chance of low-price competition from new sources, for example, in the Pacific Rim or Eastern Europe?
12. Take a hard look at the broad political, social, and financial prospects of the country involved. Can you foresee the possibility of anything like an Iraqi attack on Kuwait or the currency turmoil in Southeast Asia?
13. Look at the overall conditions of doing business in the country involved. What are the chances of price controls, nationalization of retail outlets (such as pharmacies are in Sweden), greater mandatory fringe benefits, new labor legislation, work permit problems (as exist in Switzerland)?
14. Test the key assumptions of the proposal by subjecting them to a test of their elasticity, and test the overall flexibility of the project by projecting the effects of changes on the project. Suppose, for example, that the sales forecast is off by 10 percent. What will that do to profitability?

and the results obtained. The first purpose is achieved through the *income statement*. The second purpose is accomplished through the *balance sheet*, which shows the position of a business, its assets, and its liabilities at a particular time.

Accounting information is needed for the internal workings of the organization and to satisfy the requirements and expectations of the external community.

The internal contexts of an international corporation are obviously more complex and larger in scope than the external ones. For internal purposes, accounting information must meet the decision-making and control needs of *both* the parent company and its foreign subsidiary. Again, a challenge lies in determining how much of what information a corporation should compile in its internal accounting system. The external interest of corporate publics (e.g., stockholders, governments, financial communities, labor, customers, creditors, and employees) in *both* the parent and host country must also be served through accounting information. The external use of information creates the company image that will be presented to current and potential investors.[13]

International Accounting Reports

The income statement and the balance sheet are used all over the world. The emphasis placed on these statements, however, varies from country to country. In the United States the income statement is of primary interest. This is so because most large U.S. corporations are publicly owned, and stockholders" wealth depends primarily on stock market prices, which in turn are greatly affected by earnings per share. In Europe, as well as in Latin America and Asia, the major concerns are the ownership of wealth (rather than the generation of income) and the position of the firm in regard to its assets and the claims against them. This view makes the balance sheet of primary importance.

The format of an income statement and a balance sheet also varies among countries.[14] In the United States balance sheet liabilities appear on the right and assets on the left. In most European countries, the order is reversed. Along the same lines, non–U.S. balance sheets usually show fixed assets and stockholders' equity sections at the top, and current assets and current liabilities near the bottom. Such variations in format do not make a substantial difference in the information presented. But there are significant differences in the amount of information disclosed by various countries. By and large, U.S. companies disclose much more information than companies elsewhere.[15] This is largely due to the requirements of the SEC, as well as the listing requirements of the stock exchanges, particularly those of the New York Stock Exchange (NYSE) (see International Marketing Highlight 6.3).

▬▬▬▬▬   International Marketing Highlight 6.3   ▬▬▬▬▬

Let the Investor Beware

So you want to invest overseas? That makes sense. After all, foreign stock markets often outperform the U.S. market. Now all you have to do is figure out what you're investing in.

It won't be easy. Disclosure and accounting rules overseas differ sharply from those in the United States—and also differ significantly among the foreign countries.

Only companies in the United States and Canada, for example, issue reports quarterly on profits and other key financial data. Most companies in Japan and Germany don't consolidate the financial data of majority-owned subsidiaries.

In some nations, the lack of a strong enforcement body like the Securities and Exchange Commission permits overseas companies to be more footloose and fancy-free with disclosures. Insider trading is often greeted with a wink by government regulators. In Holland, Spain, and France, where stock exchanges are relatively small, government regulation and oversight of company disclosures are very relaxed.

Source: The Wall Street Journal, September 22, 1989, p. R30.

Harmonization of International Accounting

Recent years have seen growing interest in facilitating the comparison of accounting information provided by multinational firms. Authorities on the subject, while rejecting the goal of complete standardization with totally uniform accounting, nevertheless recommend *harmonization,* which implies a reconciliation of different methods of presenting information to enhance international communication.[16]

Multinational firms raise capital in different countries. It is desirable, therefore, that investors and creditors be provided common information on which to base their investment decisions. The principal force behind the accounting profession's attempt at harmonization to facilitate the generation of common information has been the International Congress of Accountants (ICA). In its tenth meeting in Sidney in 1972, the ICA established the International Coordination Committee for the Accounting Profession (ICCAP) to provide leadership in the harmonization effort. One of the outcomes of ICCAP's efforts was the 1973 formation of the International Accounting Standards

Committee (IASC), which was formed to (1) develop basic standards to be observed in presenting audited financial statements and (2) promote worldwide acceptance and observance of these standards.

Very much in the manner of the Financial Accounting Standards Board (FASB) in the United States, the IASC issues international accounting standards. By 1992, the IASC had issued 44 standards.

The IASC has had only an indirect effect on the external financial reporting practices of U.S. multinational enterprises. The American Institute of CPAs (AICPA), for example, has pledged its best efforts to promote IASC standards. Yet the FASB, not the AICPA, presently sets U.S. accounting standards, and that organization has done little to harmonize its standards with those of the IASC, nor has the IASC attempted to harmonize its pronouncements with those of the FASB. As U.S. firms are bound by FASB, not IASC, standards, they are not presently required to disclose whatever differences exist between these two sets of standards.

The IASC appears to have more influence with financial institutions in other countries. For example, the World Federation of Stock Exchanges has asked member exchanges to require compliance with IASC standards. In addition, the London Stock Exchange requires that listed companies conform with IASC standards.

The ultimate success of the IASC in its harmonization effort depends primarily on the kinds of standards it issues. To be successful, it must issue statements that either develop broad accounting principles acceptable to most countries, including the United States, or gain the authority to require disclosures that would enable users to make valid comparisons of multinational enterprises.

America's accounting standards are among the world's most rigorous. The FASB claims that (1) the IASC standards are too flexible, giving firms too much discretion over what they report; (2) their meaning is often ambiguous; and (3) there are big uncertainties about how they will be enforced.[17] Thus, IASC standards are not likely to be accepted in the United States in the near future.[18]

Consolidation of Accounts

Most MNCs consolidate the accounting information from their different entities to present a single income statement and balance sheet for both parent and affiliates. The consolidation process is based on legal requirements of the parent company, information available from subsidiaries, and the practice established over time within the corporation. In the United States, MNCs are generally required by law to consolidate the accounts of a subsidiary if the parent owns 50 percent or more of the affiliate. In order to publish consolidated financial statements within a reasonable time after the end of the parent corporation's financial year, the U.S. multinationals usually require the affiliates to prepare their accounts earlier. For example, if the parent's financial year ends on December 31, the subsidiaries may end their financial year on October 31. This way subsidiaries' financial accounts will be available to the parent by December 31 for consolidation with its own.

Most corporations have standard procedures for the subsidiaries to report their accounting information. Thus, the management of subsidiaries must not only satisfy the legal accounting requirements of their host countries, but also make the information available in the format required by their corporate headquarters. Usually U.S. multinationals require their subsidiaries to submit quarterly accounts, comparing actual results against the standards. But some corporations request monthly accounts. Review meetings are held to examine the future outlook of the business on the basis of such periodic information. The recent trend has been to seek as much detailed information on the subsidiaries' activities as feasible, including, in addition to accounting information, data on markets, industry, climate, and economic environment.

National differences and delayed international standardization make it necessary for each multinational enterprise to deal individually with the issue of adequate reporting (see International Marketing Highlight 6.4). Unfortunately, varying national approaches to inflation accounting, new regional requirements for consolidation, demands for social accounting data, and uncoordinated actions by international "standardizing" organizations create additional problems. Consequently, there is a great need for new developments in accounting theory and practice to provide adequate multinational information.

■ International Marketing Highlight 6.4 ■

A Computer Comparison

To illustrate how tough it is to compare profit performance in different nations, three accounting professors at Rider College in Lawrenceville, New Jersey, set up a computer model of an imaginary company's financial reports in four countries. Starting with the same gross operating profit of $1.5 million, the company had net profit of $34,600 in the United States, $260,600 in the United Kingdom, $240,600 in Australia, and $10,402 in Germany—all because of varying accounting rules in each country.

Although many companies have worldwide operations, their financial results in different countries aren't comparable. This is a serious problem for accountants who may be called upon to analyze a foreign company's financial statements.

The results of companies in Japan, Germany, Switzerland, and Spain are among the most difficult to compare with those of their U.S. counterparts. In Japan and Germany, many corporations don't consolidate results of their majority-owned subsidiaries; in Switzerland and Spain, some concerns set up hidden reserves, which result in lower reported profits.

Investing in Korean companies can also be tricky. Some Korean companies create "special gains and losses" that sometimes don't relate to company successes or failures.

Source: The Wall Street Journal, September 22, 1989, p. R30.

Summary

International marketing decisions are profoundly affected by the finance and accounting function; therefore, a brief review of their conduct in the international business field is in order. Essentially, international finance deals with the management of financial resources such as the sources and uses of funds and the remission of profits from subsidiaries. The underlying force behind financial decisions is a corporation's financial objectives. These objectives usually are defined in terms such as desired return on investment or assets, desired profit growth, hurdle rate (for accepting new projects), and proportion of earnings desired to be paid in the form of dividends.

After setting its financial objectives, a corporation can decide how to raise funds—whether to borrow money or to make a stock offering, where to raise money (in the United States or in another capital market) and who should trigger certain actions, the parent or a subsidiary. Two of the factors influencing international finance decisions are: (1) the varying and fluctuating exchange rates of different currencies, and (2) the restrictions imposed by host countries on the transfer of funds. Thus, before the source of funds can be settled, the exchange rates of the countries where the funds are to be raised must be predicted. Then funds can be raised to avoid exchange losses on the one hand and to minimize the cost of capital on the other.

Another factor that must be dealt with in money management is the political climate of the host country. If problems that may jeopardize the ownership of corporate funds appear likely, it might be desirable to transfer funds out of the country while there is still time, even at a substantial exchange loss.

Remission of profits from one country to another is determined by such factors as tax implications, political risk, foreign exchange risk, age and size of affiliate, availability of funds, and presence of joint venture partners. MNCs pursue either a pooled or flexible strategy in the matter of profit transfer from a subsidiary to the parent or to another subsidiary. The pooled strategy spells out profit to the parent by each subsidiary on a predetermined basis. The flexible strategy leaves the decision on remission of profits to the circumstances of the critical moment.

Marketing is affected by financial decisions in many ways, one being transfer pricing—the price that a subsidiary charges to another subsidiary belonging to the same parent for its goods, services, and technology. Another way that financial decisions affect marketing is that approval of projects that seem crucial from a marketing standpoint may be denied because they conflict with overall corporate financial objectives.

Most multinationals have a systematic procedure to receive, evaluate, and approve projects requiring capital expenditures. The selling of an investment project is followed by its review, in which the cost/benefit effects on the host country, parent corporation, and foreign subsidiary are evaluated.

In international accounting differing emphasis is placed on the income statement versus the balance sheet in different countries. For example, in the United States the income statement is considered of prime importance. In Europe, Asia, and Latin America, the balance sheet has greater significance.

Accounting systems and procedures, although essentially following the double-entry system, differ worldwide in various ways. Therefore, it is difficult to make comparisons. Efforts at harmonization of international accounting information are being spearheaded by the IASC.

Review Questions

1. Describe the meaning of money management in the international context.
2. What risks does a multinational enterprise sometimes face in international money management?
3. What are the arguments for and against raising capital in host country currency?
4. What factors determine international dividend policy?
5. What is transfer pricing, and what factors affect it?
6. What sorts of reports usually are included with a project proposal?
7. Explain why the income statement is considered more important than the balance sheet in the United States, whereas the reverse is true in Europe.
8. Why is more information usually disclosed by U.S. firms in their financial accounts than by their counterparts in Europe?

Creative Questions

1. The format of an income statement and a balance sheet in the United States varies from the conventions followed elsewhere in the world. What difference would it make if U.S. companies followed the practices of other nations? Would this practice make it easier for U.S. MNCs to consolidate their subsidiaries' accounts and interpret their performance?
2. What is a euro? Can a company raise money in euro? What are the pros and cons of such a decision?

Endnotes

1. *Crossborder Monitor*, December 16, 1998, p. 12.

2. Kwang Chul Lee and Cluik C. Y. Kwok, "Multinational Corporations vs. Domestic Corporations: International Environmental Factors and Determinants of Capital Structure," *Journal of International Business Studies*, Summer 1988, pp. 195–218.

3. *Investment, Licensing and Trading Conditions Abroad* (New York: Business International Corporation, no date).

4. See Alan C. Shapiro, *Multinational Financial Management*, 4th ed. (Boston: Allyn & Bacon, 1995).

5. J. S. Ang and Lai Tsong-Yue, "A Simple Rule for Multinational Capital Budgeting," *Global Finance Journal*, Fall, 1989, pp. 71–75.

6. Jongmoo Jay Choi, "Diversification, Exchange Risk, and Corporate International Investment," *Journal of International Business Studies*, Spring 1989, pp. 145–156.

7. "Indian Shares—Oversensitive," *The Economist*, February 9, 1994, p. 80.

8. Thomas G. O'Brien, "Accounting Versus Economic Exposure to Currency Risk," *The Journal of Financial Statement Analysis*, Summer 1997, pp. 21–28.

9. John D. Daniels and Lee H. Radebaugh, *International Business Environments and Operations*, 8th ed. (Reading, MA: Addison-Wesley, 1998), chapters 3–6.

10. David Eitemann, Arthur I. Stonehill, and Michael M. Moffett, *Multinational Business Finance*, 7th ed. (New York: Addison Wesley, 1995), chapter 19.

11. Joshua Mendes, "Go Abroad for Bigger Returns," *Fortune*, 1993 Investor's Guide, p. 88.

12. J. J. Pringle, "Managing Foreign Exchange Exposure," *Journal of Applied Corporate Finance* 3, (1991): pp. 73–82

13. William M. Abdallah and David E. Keller, "Measuring the Multinationals' Performance," *Management Accounting*, October 1985, pp. 25–30.

14. Timothy S. Doupink and Stephen B. Salter, "An Empirical Test of a Judgemental International Classification of Financial Reporting Practices," *Journal of International Business Studies* 24, no. 1 (1993): 41–60.

15. A. M. Agami, "Global Accounting Standards and Competitiveness of U.S. Corporations," *Multinational Business Review*, Spring 1993, pp. 38–43.

16. "MNCs Home Competitive Edge With Activity-Based Costing," *Business International*, January 29, 1991, p. 37.

17. Jeffrey E. Garten, "Global Accounting Rules? Not so Fast," *Business Week*, April 5, 1999, p. 26

18. "Accounting Standards: America v. the World," *The Economist*, January 17, 1998, p. 58.

CHAPTER 7

Regional Market Agreements

CHAPTER FOCUS_____

After studying this chapter, you should be able to

■ Present the rationale behind regional market agreements.

■ Discuss how market agreements affect international marketing.

■ Understand the historical perspectives of market agreements.

■ Discuss the European Community and its various aspects such as the Europe 1992 program and the Monetary Union.

■ Describe other agreements, especially the North American Free Trade Agreement.

A previous chapter discussed the worldwide postwar efforts to restore free trade. These efforts included the elimination of tariff barriers through the General Agreement on Tariffs and Trade (GATT) and stabilization of currencies through the International Monetary Fund (IMF). At the same time these efforts went forward on the international level, an interest in economic cooperation at the regional level also developed, resulting in different forms of market agreements. Regional economic cooperation is based on the premise that nations in a region connected by historical, geographic, cultural, economic, and political affinities may be able to strike more intensive cooperative agreements for mutually beneficial economic advantages than those in a more wide-ranging group.

An outstanding example of regional economic cooperation is today's **European Union (EU)**. Originally called the European Economic Community (EEC), in 1958, or simply the European Common Market, the name was changed in 1980 to European Community (EC), and then in 1992 to European Union. At the time of development of the Marshall Plan, the United States urged European nations to seek economic integration in coping with the problems of reconstruction. Such economic integration was expected to bring forth a Western European market as large as the U.S. market, one that would allow economies of scale via mass production. The self-interest of the United States was also involved in the push for European economic integration. The creation of a large, and to some extent homogeneous, market was certainly beneficial to U.S. corporations.

Economic cooperation has an effect on international marketing, varying according to the different forms of market agreements among nations. The international marketer should be aware of early attempts at regional cooperation and economic integration like that which led to the European Union, and of the cultivation of existing market agreements in different parts of the world.

Effects of Market Agreements on Marketing

Market agreements affect international marketing in a variety of ways. *First, the scope of the market is broadened.* For example, after the formation of the Common Market, the French market ceased to be just a French market; it became a part of the larger Common Market. Such an expanded market provides a *flexibility* that would not be feasible dealing with individual countries. For example, under one type of market agreement called a *free trade area agreement,* internal trade barriers among member countries are abolished and a company may move products from one country to another freely. This permits economies of scale not only in production but also in product promotion, distribution, and other aspects of business. Thus, the establishment of the Common Market allowed the Ford Motor Company to integrate its operations in Germany and Britain, and, as described in *Forbes,*

> A new management organization was created to make all the critical decisions for both the British and German companies. There were obvious operating economies in the arrangement—the duplicate dealer organizations in third markets could be eliminated, and responsibility went where the skill was: body development work was concentrated in Germany, power train development concentrated in Britain. The pooling cut the engineering bill in half for each company, provided economies of scale with double the volume in terms of purchase—commonization of purchase, common components—and provided the financial resources for a good product program at a really good price.[1]

Another company that benefited from the Common Market was Elizabeth Arden International. This global cosmetics and perfume company owned by Unilever recognized the need for pan-European integration early in the 1990s. At that time management created a project-team structure, with eight teams of 10–50 people (300 in all), led by a project director and reporting to a steering committee. The company spent two years on the effort, pursuing three specific objectives: build a pan-European business, not only to harmonize operations but to defend Arden against the activities of parallel importers and consolidation of the retail trade; optimize the business's tax position; and minimize indirect expenses, which at 30 percent of sales were unduly high.

The problem of excessive indirect costs stemmed mainly from duplication of processes within individual countries. But another cause was supply chain defects like the use of third-party distributors and stock movements that looked fine from a national standpoint but were blatantly inefficient when viewed at the pan-European level. Indeed, where inventories were concerned, poor information led to an increase in stock levels along the supply chain and high holding costs.

Marketing was also out of control, as national subsidiaries acted with little regard for coordination, resulting in high marketing costs and conflicting brand messages. Levels of customer satisfaction varied by country. Management decided that the time had come to take advantage of economies of scale and scope and to focus resources on the critical aspects of maintaining and expanding business. It decided that the answer would be to develop regionwide shared services.[2]

Since the formation of the EU, U.S. business activity in the region has grown significantly. U.S. investment in the EU increased fourfold during the 1970s. In 1998 U.S. investment in the EU was almost $420 billion, while EU investments in the United States amounted to nearly two-thirds of all foreign investments, about $380 billion.

A second way that market agreements affect international marketing is that they change the nature of competition. For example, before the formation of the Common Market, many American MNCs found little local competition in Western Europe, but afterward local companies were encouraged to expand quickly. They became factors in the market, through mergers and such, with the encouragement of member governments. In the computer field, for example, Siemens A.G. (German), Compagnie International pour L'Informatique (French), and Philips N.V. (Dutch) entered into a joint venture to compete effectively against IBM.

Despite IBM's best efforts, in 1985 the EU denied IBM the opportunity to join European firms for basic research to close Europe's technology gap with the United States and Japan. This research was sponsored to (1) use Esprit, a $1 billion program focusing on basic information technology and (2) encourage Britain's ICL, France's Bull, Italy's Olivetti, former West Germany's Nixdorf, and the Netherlands' Philips to cooperate with each other competing against giants such as IBM.[3] Such cooperation among businesses need not necessarily be among companies of different nations. In Italy, for example, Montecatini and Edison companies merged to form Montedison.

Third, market-agreement firms expand through mergers and acquisitions and thereby become highly competitive outside their market area as well. For example, after the formulation of the Common Market, French and German companies were able to compete aggressively against U.S. and Japanese multinationals worldwide. Consider Airbus Industrié, a consortium of French, German, English, and Spanish companies formed in 1970. This company grabbed 40 percent of newcraft orders in 1997 in a short span at the cost of American airframe manufacturers.[4]

Finally, market-agreement countries are able to make decisions favorable to all member-country companies. An individual country could never enforce certain measures that are desirable for the group. For example, Common Market antitrust policies could adversely affect an American company and its subsidiaries or licensees that previously had been given exclusive rights in, say, Italy and the Netherlands.

It is important to mention also that economic integration, while leading to a variety of benefits, can create some problems. Consider, for example, the potential for trouble with the freedom-of-labor movement within the EU. With relatively poor countries like

Greece and Portugal having joined the group, controversy over guest workers from these countries, in Germany in particular, has arisen. What is more, free entry for Spanish and Portuguese agricultural products has worsened the EU's agricultural problems, boosting output of such products as olive and citrus fruit and thus depressing prices. The lower prices are likely to put further pressure on the EU's budget, two-thirds of which is already spent on farm subsidies.

Another problem is the jeopardy into which existing agreements of a nation are thrown when it joins a market group. Entry into the EU caused Great Britain's commitments to the Commonwealth to diminish. Agricultural overproduction and inefficiencies are always potentially troublesome among member countries since no nation wants its output outpriced by cheap imports. Agricultural exports have been a chief issue of conflict between the United States and the EU, and to a large extent have been responsible for the delay in concluding the Uruguay Round deadlock, as was discussed in Chapter 2.

Many marketers erroneously thought that with the establishment of the Common Market, Western Europe would present a single homogeneous market. Instead, the market was simply enlarged. Within this enlarged, heterogeneous market, however, homogenous segments can be identified for the development of effective marketing strategy—each segment to be served by a unique marketing mix. These smaller markets are the ones that must be recognized and targeted.

Early Attempts at Regional Economic Integration

Current efforts toward regional economic integration among the nations of the world began with the creation of the *European Economic Community (EEC)* in 1958, born through a long history of trial and deliberation. In 1948 the *Organization for European Economic Cooperation (OEEC)* was established to administer the Marshall Aid program. Very soon it became obvious to all concerned that European nations would have to seek some form of economic cooperation in order to emerge as a large, autonomous market.

The drive toward European economic unity continued to gain momentum in the early 1950s, although many leaders doubted that perpetual cooperation, other than on an ad hoc basis, would ever be feasible. The proponents of the movement met with their first success with the establishment of the *European Coal and Steel Community (ECSC)* in 1952. The ECSC was created to develop a common market in coal, steel, and iron ore. The six countries participating in this effort were France, West Germany, Italy, Belgium, the Netherlands, and Luxembourg.

The success of the ECSC led these six nations to venture into the 1957 establishment of the EEC by the Treaty of Rome. Initially, the EEC was established as a *customs union* (discussed later in this chapter) that was gradually to include both industrial and agricultural goods and to lead to the abolition of restrictions on trade among member nations and the creation of common external tariffs. The EEC's organizers expected eventual economic union among the member countries to enable free movement of people, services, and capital, and gradual development of common social, fiscal, and monetary policies.

Simultaneously with the formation of the EEC, the *European Free Trade Association (EFTA)* was established in 1960 by the United Kingdom, Denmark, Sweden, Norway, Switzerland, Austria, and Portugal. These seven nations had been unable to come to agreement with the EEC.

With Europe as an example, regional agreements have come into existence all over the world—in Africa, in the Arab world, in Latin America, and in Asia. Communist countries also have made their own regional cooperative arrangements.

**Bases of
Economic
Cooperation**

Economic cooperation among nations is mainly dictated by economic, political, geo-graphic, and social factors. Nations often cooperate with each other simply as a matter of economic necessity.[5] For example, 77 countries located distantly around the world have joined in a group called the *New International Economic Order (NIEO),* which negotiates concessions from richer countries for the purpose of enhancing NIEO member trade.

Nations also may cooperate for political reasons. The *Commonwealth* is an interesting example of a political union of nations. Commonwealth countries are economically far apart from each other. For example, Australia is among the developed nations, while Pakistan is a developing country. Geographically, the Commonwealth countries are spread over different continents. Canada is in North America, Great Britain in Europe, Nigeria in Africa, and In-dia in Asia. Even some political similarities of the past have vanished as these nations pursue different political modes: Burma is a military dictatorship; New Zealand, a democracy. The commonality of these nations is their historical partnership in the British Empire.

Geographic proximity is another factor that facilitates economic cooperation and in-tegration among nations. Presumably countries in the same geographic region have a bet-ter appreciation of each other's strengths and weaknesses, and together they may come to realize synergies that would make them economically stronger. For example, a mass mar-ket is necessary for mass production. Nations located near each other are better able to de-velop a mass market. A notable example of such cooperation among nations in geographic proximity to one another is the EU.

Finally, countries also may associate with each other on the basis of social customs, traditions, taboos, and culture. Arab countries, for example, share a long Islamic heritage. Such bonds favor economic union.

**Factors in
Successful
Economic
Cooperation**

What factors make for successful economic integration? Briefly, economic cooperation is likely to flourish when member countries have diverse products and raw materials. The most successful case of economic integration has been the EU. Nations belonging to the EU have more or less complementary economies, diverse industries, different natural resources, and varying agricultural bases. Further, it is desirable that member nations be of compatible eco-nomic status in terms of balance-of-payments position and level of development.

Types of Market Agreements

There are five principal forms of market agreements among nations: free trade area, cus-toms union, common market, economic union, and political union. Such agreements are differentiated on several bases, as follows.

Free Trade Area

The *free trade area* type of agreement requires nations to remove all tariffs among the members. Let us assume three nations—A, B, and C—agree to a free trade area agreement to abolish all tariffs among themselves and permit free trade. Beyond the agreement, these nations may impose tariffs as they choose. For example, if Nation X trades extensively with Nation B, Nation B may have very low tariffs for goods imported from Nation X, while Nations A and C impose high tariffs on goods from Nation X. Under this type of agree-ment, Nation B is free to continue its *preferred* relationship with Nation X while Nation A and Nation C are at liberty to decide their own external tariff policies. *The European Free Trade Area (EFTA)* and the *Latin American Free Trade Area (LAFTA)* illustrate the free trade area type of agreement.

Customs Union

A *customs union,* in addition to requiring abolition of internal tariffs among members, fur-ther obligates the members to establish common external tariffs. To continue with the ex-ample of Nations A, B, and C, under a customs union agreement (instead of a free trade area agreement), Nation B would not be permitted to have a special relationship with Nation X. Nations A, B, and C would have to have a common tariff policy toward Nation X. A customs union agreement exists among Caribbean countries. Their cooperative effort started as a free trade area and later developed into a customs union. As mentioned earlier, the EU began as a customs union.

Common Market

In a *common market* type of agreement, members not only abolish internal tariffs among themselves and levy common external tariffs, but they also permit the free flow of all factors of production (capital, labor, technology) among themselves. In our illustration, Nations A, B, and C, under a common market agreement, not only would remove all tariffs and quotas among themselves and impose common tariffs against other countries such as Nation X, but also would allow capital, labor, and technology to move freely within their boundaries as if they were one nation. This means, for example, a resident of Nation A is free to accept a position in Nation C without a work permit. Likewise, an investor in Nation B is at liberty to invest money in Nation A, B, or C without restriction from either home or host government when transferring funds for investment.

Economic Union

Under the *economic union* arrangement, common market characteristics are combined with harmonization of economic policy. Member countries are expected to pursue common monetary and fiscal policies. Ordinarily this means synchronizing taxes, money supply, interest rates, and regulation of capital market, among other things. In effect, the economic union calls for a supranational authority to design an economic policy for an entire group of nations. The EU, to a great extent, can be called an economic union. This designation is justified by the fact that the union has a common agricultural policy and shares the European monetary system.

Political Union

A *political union* is the ultimate market agreement among nations. It includes the characteristics of an economic union and requires, in addition, political harmony among the members. Essentially, it means nations merging with each other to form a new nation.

In its pure form, an example of the political union does not exist. In the 1950s, however, Egypt, Syria, and Yemen formed a short-lived political union. To an extent, the Commonwealth of Nations and perhaps the newly formed Commonwealth of Independent States can be characterized as politically based agreements. In the future, in a very limited sense, the EU, with the European Parliament in place, could be considered a political union.

Market Agreements in Force

Most current market agreements are organized by geography. Some agreements are not formed according to region, however, but extend over different geographic areas of the world.

Europe

European nations have been by far the most aggressive in seeking economic integration. They have formed the EU, the EFTA, and the now defunct Council for Economic Assistance.

European Union (EU) Often called the *European Common Market*, the EU agreement came into existence in January 1958. Its purpose was to abolish over a 12-year period all customs, tariffs, and other economic barriers among the six member countries of the former: West Germany, France, Italy, the Netherlands, Belgium, and Luxembourg. In 1973 the United Kingdom, Denmark, and Ireland joined the EU. Greece became a full member in 1982. Spain and Portugal joined as full members on January 1, 1986. Austria, Finland

and Sweden became full members on January 1, 1995. As it stands today, the 15-member EU is the world's largest exporter, producing over one-fourth of world exports.

The EU represents a true customs union, having abolished all customs duties and restrictions on trade in industrial goods within the community while imposing common external tariffs and supporting free internal movement of labor and capital. In the area of agriculture, the EU has developed a protective common agricultural policy that consists of a support system designed to promote domestic agricultural production and guaranteed farm incomes.

The European Community's 1957 *Rome Treaty* called for the eventual formation of an economic union. Although some progress has been made toward this end in the form of a common antitrust policy, complete economic and monetary union, not to mention political union, has a long way to go. However, the name change from European Economic Community to European Community in 1980 and to European Union in 1992 indicated the broadened economic and political role this group was likely to play in the later years.

A number of other countries are linked with the Common Market as associate members. Turkey is one. The EU also has preferential trade agreements with a number of Mediterranean countries and with the countries in the EFTA.

Following the *Lomé* (capital of Togo) *Convention* in 1975 and its latest extension in 1990 (the fourth Lomé Convention), the EU agreed to a trading program with 66 *African, Caribbean, and Pacific (ACP)* countries that was valid for five years (1990–1995). The fourth Lomé agreement consolidated and built on the earlier Lomé agreements, and provided, in particular, trade opportunities and development aid to selected Third World countries from EU members.[6] It established a vast, privileged domain of cooperation among multiform (economic, commercial, and even cultural) northern (the members of the EU) and southern (the associated states of Africa, the Caribbean, and the Pacific) countries. At the time of preparing this book, a new agreement was in the works to replace the *Lomè IV* agreement that ended at the end of February 2000.

Today the EU is a viable world economic force with as large a market as that of the United States If the present trend continues, the EU will continue to grow as other countries join. In its meeting at Luxembourg in 1997, the EU decided to next offer membership in the group to the Czech Republic, Estonia, Hungary, Poland, Slovenia, and Cyprus.[7] At the Helsinki meeting in 1999, the EU invited another six countries, Bulgaria, Latvia, Lithuania, Malta, Romania, and Slovakia, to start negotiating for membership. Turkey, which has been waiting to join the group since 1969, was added to the official list of prospective members during the Helsinki deliberations.[8]

Because of the EU program, Western European nations are doing more together than ever. The Common Market is expanding, both in members and in terms of trade, after settling a protracted dispute over budgetary share. New agreements on matters important in future European development—space, broadcasting, and computer research—have been negotiated among countries and companies. But expanding trade has been, and continues to be, the greatest achievement of the Common Market.

The rate of expansion in European trade during the 1990s was seven times the rate of economic growth. This means several things. First, trade is acting as a propellant to Europe's overall economy—exactly what the continent's leaders had in mind when they launched the Common Market more than 42 years ago. The key provision of the treaty, the elimination of tariffs among member states, touched off a trade boom that continues to this day despite the severe recession of the 1990s.

Despite the tremendous achievements of the EU, in the mid-1980s the organization faced a variety of problems (see International Marketing Highlight 7.1). A critical examination showed that the EU had never really become a common market. After the first heady years, various kinds of nontariff barriers had once again begun to choke off trade among member nations. A common currency, even a single free capital market, remained little more than a goal for the distant future. Less soaring aims, like harmonizing economic policies and standardizing member countries' value-added taxes, also appeared remote. Freedom of trade in services hardly existed at all, and there was little consensus on how to bring it about. The EU's *common agricultural policy (CAP),* which guarantees farmers high prices without limiting production, had produced huge surpluses that disrupted international markets and strained the EU budget. Yet farmers were not happy; their gripes about prices and market share erupted in violence.

The most disappointing failure was a lack of progress in creating a true common market in manufactured goods, the EU's original reason for existence. Before the EU's birth, Europe was a maze of protectionism. Tariffs and quotas were the most visible and significant barriers, backed by a host of regulations and other protectionist devices, some more than 100 years old. After the tariffs and quotas were eliminated, much of their protectionist function was gradually taken over by the nontariff barriers, many of which have proliferated over the years (see International Marketing Highlight 7.2).

International Marketing Highlight 7.1

Crazy Quilt of Regulations

If a commercial truck driver left New York and drove the 5,000 or so kilometers to Los Angeles, respecting all the applicable work and rest rules, he could drive the entire distance at an average speed of 60 kilometers per hour. If that same rule-obeying driver in the same heavy lorry were to leave the Midlands in the United Kingdom, pass by London, and drive down to Athens, also a distance of some 5,000 kilometers, he would be able to average only 12 kilometers per hour. It is worth noting that 12 kilometers per hour happens to be the speed of a horse and cart.

International Marketing Highlight 7.2

How Nontariff Barriers Hindered European Growth

A recent study by the EC Commission listed no fewer than 56 different categories of nontariff barriers, ranging from discrimination in government procurement contracts through national health and technical regulations to sheer customs chicanery at national borders. Many customs restrictions, such as taking currency in or out of France and Italy, are more stringent now than they were in the past. The time wasted getting goods through borders adds significantly to European industry's costs—as much as $1 billion a year. The total cost to industry of complying with all of the customs formalities is estimated at more than $10 billion, or between 5 percent and 10 percent of the value of the goods traded. This amounts to a substantial hidden tariff. In 1983, several truckloads of West German freezers were turned back at the French border for failing to have new certification documents in French, a requirement that had been introduced almost overnight. At the Italian border, customs officials often are simply unavailable, which halts truck traffic. Moreover, Italy still requires, as it did before 1958, that any pasta sold there must be made of durum wheat, not the soft wheat normally used for pasta-type products elsewhere. In Germany, a law whose origins go back several centuries specifies that beer sold there may be made only of barley malt, hops, and water. Since brewers in France, Belgium, and the Netherlands, like those in the United States, now use other grains or additives, this means that not a single bottle of Kronenbourg, Stella Artois, or Heineken can be sent across the Rhine.

Governments take action under many guises that discriminate against foreign products. France and Italy, for instance, impose disproportionately heavy taxes on big, powerful cars, which suits their automobile manufacturers, whose output is concentrated in the small-car end of the line. As buyers of goods and services—telecommunications equipment, for example, or pharmaceuticals for national health services—governments can be decidedly protectionist.

Source: European Community Press and Information Service, New York, March 1985.

The EU members realized that as markets and industries globalize, those constraints—physical, technical, and fiscal—are no longer endurable. Further, as the forces of globalization increased, the influence of European countries, both political and economic, had weakened. During the first half of the 1980s, Europe lost jobs at a rate of 0.5 percent per year, while its economy, roughly the same size as that of the United States, grew at 1.5 percent per year. At the same time, the unemployment rate in Europe climbed from 4 percent to around 6 percent. These numbers pointed to a troubling decline in the international competitiveness of European companies.

Thus, to create jobs, restore international competitiveness, and boost the value to European customers of the goods and services available to them, the EU members were led to adopt a new course, that is, *Europe 1992,* or the *Internal Market Program.*

In this program, the 12 member countries of the EU committed to integrating into a single internal market by the end of 1992. The result was to be a $4 trillion market of 340 million people. This Internal Market Program proposed sweeping changes in virtually every aspect of business life that were to greatly alter the way U.S. firms did business in Europe.

Initially described in a 1985 EU Commission White Paper, the Internal Market Program (or "Europe 1992") consisted of 285 legislative directives intended to eliminate present barriers to the free movement of goods, people, and capital among the 12 EU member states. Internal Market directives reached into every aspect of commercial activity, from eliminating border controls and duplicative customs documents, to setting uniform product standards, to establishing guidelines for company mergers.

The program concluded on time, although there have been a variety of hindrances relative to the national interests of member nations. For example, a German law discourages the import of parallel pharmaceuticals (drugs bought cheaply in one market and exported to where they are expensive) by requiring them to bear a certificate proving they meet German standards. The EU Commission, however, is getting tougher as it seeks to ensure that national governments effectively administer EU rules. To resolve the German pharmaceutical problem, the commission persuaded Germany to tell its customs offices to ignore the law.[9] By 1997, 85 percent of all regulations affecting business in the EU were EU regulations and directives instead of national laws.

European officials believe that the integration of the EU market has increased economic growth and employment, and led to greater consumption and imports. A study by the EU Commission predicted that the removal of existing barriers would result in a 5 percent increase in EU gross domestic product (GDP), more than $260 billion, through more economies of scale and greater economic efficiency.[10]

European industry has benefited most from the program. The ability to compete in a continental scale market and to avoid duplication of administrative procedures, production, marketing, and distribution systems has offered great advantages. In addition, a unified EU market offers tremendous opportunities to U.S. companies, both those located in Europe and those exporting. Of course, it also poses tougher competition, for U.S. companies, particularly in such industries as financial services, pharmaceuticals, telecommunications, electronics and computers.[11]

U.S. company sales in the 12-nation EU are over $650 billion, almost four times greater than sales to Japan. Achieving a single EU internal market should mean greater economic growth for Europe, which, in turn, should bring increased demand for American products. The uniformity of trade and financial regulations has allowed U.S. companies easier access to all the EU countries by eliminating the need to meet national registration requirements in each country. In other words, a product or service that meets the EU requirements in one member state can be freely marketed throughout the EU. U.S. industries are thus able to reach a greater number of European consumers at a lower cost.

The 1992 program dealt with three general objectives: the removal of physical barriers, the removal of technical barriers, and the removal of fiscal barriers through standardization of *value-added tax (VAT)* rates and excise taxes.

The removal of physical barriers meant eliminating the regulations and procedures that gave rise to such border controls as vehicle safety checks or animal and plant inspections. One important aspect of the program, and one with an immediate impact, was the adoption as of January 1, 1988, of a *Single Administrative Document,* which eliminated the need for duplicative customs documents for goods shipped to and within the EU.

Perhaps the most significant aspect of the program from the point of view of U.S. industry is the directives related to the removal of technical barriers. EU directives mandate the creation of uniform EU industrial standards, the opening of public procurement procedures, the removal of restrictions on trade in services and capital movements, and stricter guidelines against barriers to competition.

Another achievement of the EU is its 1991 historic accord on monetary and political union, the *Maastricht Treaty.* This treaty a milestone that will transform the way Europe does business. Exhibit 7.1 summarizes its main points. Like its precursor, the 1986 *Single Europe Act,* which paved the way for free trade within the EU after 1992, the accord promises to become a powerful force for even closer economic and political integration. The new *European Currency Unit,* to be called the *euro* (previously called the *ECU*), has the potential to become a strong rival to the dollar in international finance and trade.[12]

As per the Maastricht Treaty, EU created a *European Monetary Union (EMU)* on January 1, 1999. Of the 15 EU nations, 11 joined the union (see International Marketing Highlight 7.3). Britain, Sweden, Denmark and Greece have stayed out of it for the time

---

EXHIBIT 7.1

Major Points of Maastricht Treaty

Monetary Union: The EU would form a central bank by 1999 that would issue a single EU currency. Britain could opt out of monetary union.

Political Union: The EU states would forge common foreign and security policies, generally by consensus. In 1996 the EU reviewed political cooperation and formed a defense arm with a common defense policy.

New Policies: By replacing unanimity with majority voting at EU meetings, the EU gets more say in education, public health, culture, consumer protection, research and development, environment, and development cooperation. Britain had the right to opt out of decisions on social affairs.

European Parliament: The EU's 518-member assembly, primarily a consultative body, *would get some legislative say,* notably in internal trade, environment, education, health, and consumer protection.

Immigration: The EU would set goal of *common rules on immigration from outside* the EU, movement of immigrants within the community, and increased immigration-law enforcement. Decisions would require unanimity.

Citizenship: The EU would introduce "Citizen of the Union" guaranteeing free movement within the community, *granting after 1994 the right to vote and run in municipal elections in any EU nation.*

---

being. The currencies of member countries have been linked with fixed exchange rates, and the *European Central Bank (ECB),* headquartered in Frankfurt, Germany, runs the monetary policy for the entire Monetary Union.[13] The ECB is independent from governments, with a strict mandate of price stability.

To sum up, from January 1, 1999, the euro became the official EU currency. Starting from January 1, 2002, euro bills and coins will start circulating. Until July 2002, the curencies of individual countries—franc, gilder, lira, and so forth—will be simultaneously used along with euro. Thereafter those individual currencies will be phased out, and the euro will become the only currency in 11 of the 15 EU countries.[14]

■■■■■■■■■■　International Marketing Highlight 7.3　■■■■■■■■■■

Sex and the Single Currency

No one loves Europe's prospective single currency more than the Italians. Three-quarters are "very happy" about monetary union, say opinion pollsters. This year they uncomplainingly paid a hefty "tax for Europe" so that they could join it. There is even a prime-time television program, Maastricht Italia, devoted to extolling the euro. They love it, all right, but do they know what it is?

Not if you believe a survey recently published in *Il Mondo.* The newspaper said that only 21 percent of Italians know that the future single currency is called the euro. Slightly fewer get half-credit for identifying it as the ECU, a basket-currency that is the forerunner to the euro; and 59 percent haven't a clue what the object of their desire is called. They have even less idea where its headquarters will be. Only 0.2 percent managed to identify Frankfurt as the site of the future European central bank. Quite a few Italians, according to another poll, think the euro is a nickname for the European Union or a satellite television program.

Do Italians know less than other Europeans? Apparently. Though Eurobarometer, the EU's pollster, does not ask Europeans what the single currency is called "as widespread knowledge of the name euro is now taken for granted."

There is other evidence that ardor and ignorance go together. According to Eurobarometer, the countries that deem themselves well informed about monetary union (cool-headed northerners like Denmark, Finland, Germany and Britain) are the most euro-skeptic. The enthusiast (Italy, Greece, Spain) admit to being ill-informed. So eager are they nevertheless to join the euro that, according to OECD, Italy and Spain will have squeezed their budgets enough this year to qualify. These hot-blooded southerners are about to discover what happens when curbside seductions turn into lifelong commitments.

Source: The Economist, December 20, 1997, p. 74.

European Free Trade Association (EFTA) In 1959 EFTA was formed in Stockholm after a series of negotiations among those Western European countries that for one reason or another did not join the EEC. (Great Britain, for example, had certain arrangements with Commonwealth countries that hindered its joining the EEC.) Austria, Denmark, Norway, Portugal, Sweden, Switzerland, and the United Kingdom were the original seven members of the EFTA. Finland (as an associate) and Iceland joined later. Denmark and the United Kingdom ceased to be members in 1973, after joining the EU. That left EFTA with seven members: Austria, Finland, Iceland, Norway, Sweden, Switzerland, and tiny Liechtenstein.

The 12-nation EC, the world's largest trading bloc, and the seven-member EFTA agreed in October 1991 to form a new common market, the *European Economic Area (EEA).* The agreement (after it was approved by each of the 19 national parliaments) allowed for the free flow of most goods, services, capital, and people among its 19 member nations. It went into effect just as a single regional market was formed by the EU on January 1, 1993.[15]

The EEA, with the exception of Switzerland, consists of those countries whose voters narrowly rejected membership of the giant free trade area. The agreement also paved the way for several new countries to seek full membership in the EU, which is rapidly moving toward social and political as well as economic integration.

Of the seven members of EFTA, the two Nordic countries (Sweden and Finland) and Austria have joined the EU as full members in 1995. Switzerland and Norway by referendum on EU membership have decided to stay out. Iceland and Liechtenstein are still undecided. Thus for all intents and purposes, EFTA has splintered.

Council for Mutual Economic Assistance (CMEA) In 1949 communist countries, led by the Soviet Union, formed the *Council for Mutual Economic Assistance(CMEA)*, (sometimes called the *Council of Mutual Economic Cooperation COMECON)*, to coordinate trade and promote economic cooperation. Before it was disbanded on January 1, 1991, CMEA's membership included Bulgaria, Czechoslovakia, East Germany, Hungary, Mongolia, Poland, Romania, the Soviet Union, Cuba, and Vietnam. It was formed more as a political group than an economic association and was organized and tightly controlled by the Soviet Union.

Although some trade gains were recorded among its member nations, CMEA did not promote economic integration through product specialization in any significant way. This may be partly attributed to the fact that foreign trade among the centrally planned economies had been looked upon as a means of balancing shortages and surpluses generated by the domestic sector.[16]

Africa

Influenced by the EU, a number of African countries have attempted to draw up market agreements in order to benefit from economic integration and cooperation. There are several major African market groups. The *Afro-Malagasy Economic Union* was formed in 1974 with Cameroon, Central African Republic, Chad, Congo-Brazzaville, Dahomey, Ivory Coast, Mali, Mauritania, Niger, Senegal, Togo, and Burkina as members. The *East Africa Customs Union* was formed in 1967 with Ethiopia, Kenya, Sudan, Tanzania, Uganda, and Zambia as members. The *West African Economic Community (WAEC)* was established in 1972 with Ivory Coast, Mali, Mauritania, Niger, Senegal, and Burkina as its member countries. Another agreement has been the *Maghreb Economic Community* consisting of Algeria, Libya, Tunisia, and Morocco. The *Economic Community of West African States (ECOWAS)* was created with Benin, Cape Verde, Gambia, Ghana, Guinea, Guinea-Bissau, Ivory Coast, Liberia, Mali, Mauritania, Niger, Nigeria, Senegal, Sierra Leone, and Burkina as members.

Despite the fact that there are many market agreements in force in Africa, they have had no significant effect in promoting trade or economic progress, because most African nations are small and have no economic infrastructure to produce goods to be traded among themselves.

The *Economic Community of West African States (ECOWAS)* is a recent attempt by 15 African countries to seek economic cooperation for their mutual advantage. The agreement called for complete economic integration by 1992. However, Nigeria accounts for almost two-thirds of the community's exports, and its economic woes hindered smooth achievement of the goal of full integration.[17] Nevertheless, and despite the unique set of difficulties that the member countries have been going through, ECOWAS has survived. In 1994 the ECOWAS nations relaunched their efforts at economic reforms and trade liberalization. Although there have been problems, the regional economy ECOWAS covers offers significant opportunities for international marketers.

A recent development in the region is a 1996 trade protocol that provided for the establishment, within eight years, of a free trade area composed of all 14 Southern African countries. So far, only four—Botswana, Mauritius, Tanzania and Zimbabwe—have ratified the protocol. To speed things up, South Africa has proposed a system in which some 75 percent of current exports would enter the free trade area duty-free immediately and 87.6 percent within five years.[18]

Enormous scope exists to increase trade among the 14 states. Currently only 20 percent of trade is intraregional—compared with more than 50 percent in Asia and 70 percent in the EU—and even that is highly concentrated among a few nations.

Another hope is that the free trade area will result in increased capital flows, especially from South Africa to its smaller, poorer neighbors, where costs are significantly lower. Perhaps the most important attraction is a linkage to the EU that could help them gain improved access to the world's largest single market.

The snags are enormous, though. Because South Africa accounts for 75 percent of regional output, other partners want increased access to South Africa, yet are reluctant to offer reciprocity out of fear of killing their nascent manufacturing industries. Above all, political disputes continue to prevent economic union.

Latin America

Of all the developing areas of the world, Latin America has struggled the longest for the benefits of economic integration and cooperation. Market agreement attempts have been made to have certain countries specialize in certain industries, such as textiles, metal working, or shoe manufacturing, in order to derive benefits of scale and experience. The United States has played a major role in helping Latin American countries with market agreements. Unfortunately, the low level of economic activity and the political instability in the region have repeatedly been stumbling blocks.

Five major market agreements operate in Latin America: (1) the Latin American Integration Association (LAIA), (2) the Central American Common Market, (3) the Andean Common Market, (4) the Caribbean Community Common Market, and (5) Mercado Comun del Sur (Mercosur).

The *Latin American Free Trade Association (LAFTA),* originally formed in 1960, was renamed the *Latin American Integration Association (LAIA)* via the *Treaty of Montevideo* in August 1980. Its members are Argentina, Brazil, Chile, Mexico, Paraguay, Peru, Uruguay, Colombia, Ecuador, Venezuela, and Bolivia. LAFTA was the first attempt at economic cooperation among Latin American counties, but its large membership hampered its effectiveness. The fact that some member countries (Argentina, Brazil, Chile, Mexico, and Venezuela) are economically more advanced than others, like Uruguay and Bolivia, has made it difficult to make agreements for free trade among themselves. Even so, over the years the member-nations have lowered duties on select products and have taken steps to encourage trade in the region by keeping nontariff barriers under control.

The *Central American Common Market,* comprising Costa Rica, El Salvador, Guatemala, Honduras, and Nicaragua, was established in 1960. Its scope was more limited than that of LAFTA, and the countries, which are essentially on the same level of economic development, found the agreement mutually beneficial. However, it collapsed in 1969, when war broke out between Honduras and El Salvador after a riot at a soccer match involving the two countries. The members decided in 1992 to reestablish the Central American Common Market by 1995,[17] but even in 2000 the progress to date has been insignificant.

The *Andean Common Market* was created in 1969 by Bolivia, Chile, Colombia, Ecuador, Peru, and Venezuela as a subgroup of LAFTA. Chile is no longer a member, while Panama holds associate status in the group. The group decided to form a customs union by 1996 and work toward joining NAFTA or MERCOSUR (discussed later) by the year 2000.

The *Caribbean Community and Common Market (CARICOM)* was formed in 1968 with Barbados, Guyana, Jamaica, Trinidad and Tobago, Antigua, Dominica, Grenada, Montserrat, St. Kitts-Nevis-Anguilla, St. Lucia, St. Vincent, and Belize as the members. CARICOM countries have worked out a common external tariff structure and are continuing their efforts to establish a single-market economy. The group has negotiated trade concessions from the United States under the auspices of the *Enterprise for Americas Initiative (EAI)*.

MERCOSUR originated with a trade agreement signed in March 1991 by Uruguay, Brazil, Argentina, and Paraguay. It was officially launched on January 1, 1995 with a combined income providing an internal market of $500 billion.[19] MERCOSUR represents the beginning of the process of integration of 200 million consumers into one single market accounting for 75 percent of South America's GDP.[20]

MERCOSUR is a full- fledged customs union. The agreement allows for the free movement of goods and services and production factors among member countries and establishes a *common external tariff (CET)* for third countries. The maximum CET on most imported goods is 20 percent.[21] (See International Highlight 7.4.)

Of the aforementioned agreements, LAIA has been the least effective and indeed is almost defunct, while MERCOSUR offers that most hope for integration in the area. The ultimate dream of most Latin American countries is to join, together or alone, with the *North American Free Trade Area (NAFTA)* of Mexico, Canada, and the U.S.

International Marketing Highlight 7.4

What MERCOSUR Has Done

The Free Trade Area In a transition phase between 1991 and 1994, MERCOSUR's members cut tariffs sharply on trade with each other; today most goods go tariff-free inside MERCOSUR, though there are some far from trivial exceptions: cars and sugar (which are subject to special arrangements) and groups of products considered sensitive by each member, 950 items for Uruguay, 427 for Paraguay, 221 for Argentina and 29 for Brazil. Internal tariffs on these products are to be cut progressively to zero by 2000 (1999 for Brazil and Argentina), by which time cars and sugar are supposed to be brought into the free trade scheme. But, unlike NAFTA, MERCOSUR as yet lacks agreements to achieve eventual free trade in services, or to deal with such issues as intellectual property and government procurement.

The Customs Union Against most expectations, at the end of 1994 MERCOSUR agreed to embark on the second stage of its integration project: to create a customs union in which, as in the European Union (but not in NAFTA), members apply a *common external tariff (CET)* to imports from third countries. From January 1, 1995, a CET set at 11 different levels, from zero to 20 percent, was applied to most imports. In this case, a larger group of products has been temporarily excluded: each country was allowed to exempt 300 items (299 for Paraguay) whose tariffs will converge (through annual increases or decreases) at the CET by January 2001 (2006 for Paraguay, which will have to raise its tariffs). A second group of products also is subject to special arrangements: tariffs on imported capital goods are to converge by 2001 at a CET of 14 percent, and on computers and telecommunications equipment at 16 percent by 2006. During 1995 two further changes were made. To support its anti-inflation plan, Brazil was allowed temporarily to cut tariffs below CET levels on 150 products (since reduced to ten), while the others were allowed to do this for 50 products. Secondly, because of global financial markets' concern over fiscal and balance-of-payments deficits in developing countries after the Mexican crisis, Argentina imposed a general 3 percent duty on imports from outside MERCOSUR, besides raising its tariffs on capital goods and telecoms equipment, while Brazil increased its list of CET-exempt products by 150 for a year, and raised tariffs on consumer electronics and cars.

Toward a Common Market In December 1995 MERCOSUR agreed on a five-year program under which it hopes to perfect the free trade area and customs union. This involves standardizing many trade-related rules and procedures, and moving toward harmonizing its members' economic policies. But since there is no commitment to allow free movement of labor, creating a true common market remains a fairly distant aspiration.

Free Trade Agreement with Chile During 1996 tariffs on most MERCOSUR/Chilean trade will be cut on both sides by 30 percent; from 2000 they will then fall to zero over four years. A small group of Chile's food and agricultural imports from MERCOSUR will have special treatment: tariffs on most of these will start falling in 2006 and reach zero by 2011, though wheat, flour, and sugar will retain their existing tariffs (from zero to 31 percent, depending on world prices) until at least 2014. To qualify for tariff preferences, goods must have MERCOSUR or Chilean content of at least 60 percent.

Source: The Economist, October 12, 1996

Asia

Asia is a vast continent with a large population. In the past, meager industrial development combined with the diversity and size of the region gave little reason for market arrangements. Nonetheless, many years ago Japan and the Pacific countries, Australia and New Zealand, along with the United States and Canada, created the *Pacific Basin Economic Council* to encourage intraregional trade, but it failed to develop into a market agreement.

In Southeast Asia, though, the emerging countries of Indonesia, Malaysia, the Philippines, Singapore, and Thailand have made a first attempt at establishing a market agreement. With these countries as members, the *Association of South East Asian Nations (ASEAN)* became operational in 1978. Brunei and Vietnam became members later. Cambodia, Laos, and Myanmar have become associate members and participate in such functional programs of the group as science and technology, tourism, and human resources development.

The association seeks closer economic integration and cooperation through the establishment of complementary industries and investment incentives to nonmember countries. Although the group initially had setbacks in meeting its goals, it now shows slow progress. To further integrate their economies, the ASEAN members in 1993 signed an agreement to establish *ASEAN Free Trade Area (AFTA)* by 2003. This agreement calls for lowering of tariffs and elimination of nontariff barriers over a 15-year period.[22] AFTA is on track to become the most populous free-trade zone in the world by 2003, easily surpassing the EU and NAFTA.

When ASEAN was first established, it was an unlikely partnership of five underdeveloped economies—Indonesia, Malaysia, the Philippines, Thailand, and Singapore. The main raison d'etre for the organization was to act as a regional buttress against communism. Now, nearly two decades later, ASEAN has grown beyond its preoccupation with the political conflict in Indochina. AFTA is the linchpin of its members' ambitions to form an economic bloc.[23]

An interesting development in Asia is the emergence of a new group called *Asia-Pacific Economic Cooperation (APEC)* among 18 nations, who had their first meeting in 1993. APEC, whose membership includes China, Japan, Australia, New Zealand, Brunei, Canada, Chile, Hong Kong, Indonesia, South Korea, Malaysia, Mexico, Papua New Guinea, the Philippines, Singapore, Taiwan, Thailand, and the United States had a combined GDP of

$15.1 trillion in 1998, nearly equal to the $16.2 trillion GPD of the *Group of Seven (G-7)*—(United States, United Kingdom, Germany, France, Italy, Canada, and Japan. By the year 2003 APEC will be larger than the G-7 and will dominate U.S. trade; 40 percent of U.S. foreign commerce will by then be with APEC nations, twice that with Europe.

APEC is committed to pursue free and open trade and investment, as well as economic and technical cooperation within the region. Developed countries in APEC seek to provide free access to their markets by 2010. Although the agreement is not binding, the developing countries are expected to fulfill its requirements by 2020.[24]

The Indian subcontinent region, with a population of over 1 billion people, provides another possibility for a regional market group. In December 1985, seven nations of the region (India, Pakistan, Bangladesh, Sri Lanka, Nepal, Bhutan, and Maldives) put aside their differences and launched the *South Asian Association for Regional Cooperation (SAARC)*. SAARC's initial purpose has been limited to cooperation in noncontroversial areas such as agriculture, rural development, telecommunications, postal services, transport, science and technology, meteorology, tourism, and sports. Important elements like the formation of a common market or a free trade zone have been omitted. Unfortunately, the chronic enmity between India and Pakistan makes the trade agreement difficult. In spite of this, there are hopeful signs that some sort of trade agreement in South Asia may occur in the next few years. This optimism is based on the fact that seven nations in the region (Bangladesh, Bhutan, India, Maldives, Nepal, Pakistan, and Sri Lanka) entered into a *South Asian Preferential Trade Arrangement* (SAPTA) in December 1995. SAPTA may lead to a full-fledged trade agreement once the nations realize the benefits of market cooperation. As a large nation in the region, India must take the lead if ever a South Asian free trade agreement is to become a reality.[25]

Countries in the Arab region have already made some progress in making market agreements. Several market groups are operating there. One of these is the *Arab Common Market (ACM)* formed in 1964 with Egypt, Iraq, Kuwait, Jordan, and Syria as members. This group planned to achieve free internal trade within 10 years, but it has not yet achieved this goal. External tariffs are likely to be regulated sometime early in this century.

U.S.–Canada Free Trade Agreement

On January 2, 1988, President Reagan and Prime Minister Mulroney of Canada signed the U.S.–Canada *Free Trade Agreement (FTA)*. This historic agreement represents the culmination of efforts stretching back more than 100 years. FTA was designed to strengthen an already extensive trading relationship and enhance economic opportunity on both sides of the common border.

Each year the United States and Canada exchange more goods and services than any other two countries in the world. Bilateral trade in goods and services exceeded $325 billion in 1999. The elimination of tariffs and most other barriers to trade between the two countries under the FTA has increased economic growth, lowered prices, expanded employment, and enhanced the competitiveness of both countries in the world marketplace.

Although the FTA does not eliminate all trade problems between the two nations, it does provide a consultative framework for managing these problems before they create serious economic and political friction. Predictably, industries in both the United States and Canada have undergone some structural readjustment to adapt to changing market conditions. The less restricted trade permitted by the FTA has spurred both economies to higher growth rates, increased efficiency, and improved competitiveness with other trading partners.[26]

The agreement came into force one year after it was signed, on January 1, 1989. The two governments have established a joint Canada–U.S. Trade Commission to oversee its implementation. A secretariat in each capital (Washington, D.C., and Ottawa) is the principal government office responsible for that country's implementation of the agreement.

North American Free Trade Agreement (NAFTA)

On January 1, 1994, the U.S.–Canada–Mexico free trade agreement emerged as the *North American Free-Trade Agreement (NAFTA).* NAFTA created the largest market in the world: 370 million consumers and $7 trillion in output. It bodes well for U.S. and Canadian marketers, who stand to gain much in meeting the long pent-up demands of newly affluent Mexicans. The Mexicans have been able to attract a variety of manufacturing to their country. Following are NAFTA's key provisions.[27]

- America and Canada are to phase out tariffs on *textiles and apparel* over 10 years. Mexico is to eliminate many tariffs in this sector immediately.

- All tariffs on *cars and car parts* are to be eliminated over 10 years.

- In *agriculture,* Mexico and America phased out 57 percent of trade barriers immediately, 94 percent will be eliminated after 10 years, and 100 percent after 15 years. Similarly, Mexico and Canada would phase out tariffs. The U.S.–Canada FTA remains unchanged.

- Pemex, Mexico's state oil company, will keep its constitutional monopoly over most of the country's *oil industry.* However, foreigners could invest in petrochemicals, electricity generation, and coal mines. Procurement contracts for Pemex and Mexico's state electricity commission are opened for foreigners.

- Foreign *banks and securities brokers* are to have unrestricted access to Mexico from the year 2000 on. Some restrictions remain on sales of policies in Mexico by American and Canadian *insurers,* but with gradual freeing of direct investment.

- *Lorry-drivers* are able to cross the Mexican border freely beginning in 1999.

- Most of Mexico's trade barriers on *telecommunications equipment* have been eliminated. Basic voice services remain protected, but with foreigners authorized to provide value-added telephone services.

- Modest agreement has been reached to open *central-government procurement* to competition. However, this provision need not bind lower layers of government.

- *Intellectual property* is protected to U.S. standards.

- NAFTA *investors* generally receive national treatment, with freedom to seek binding arbitration from an international forum. However, special protection is given to Mexican energy and railway industries, American airline and radio communications industries, and Canadian culture.

- Each country applies its own *environmental standards,* provided such standards have a scientific basis. Lowering of standards as a lure to investment is "inappropriate."

- Two *commissions* have been established with power to impose fines and remove trade privileges (as a last resort) when environmental standards or legislation involving health and safety, minimum wages, or child labor have been ignored. Governments pay the fines, and only after a long bureaucratic process.

The way the three economies (U.S., Canadian, and Mexican) complement each other allows for greater room for growth and efficiency gains from free trade. Increased economic ties through NAFTA have resulted in net growth for the three partners. Nevertheless, at the time of this writing, there has been a fierce debate in the United States about the usefulness of NAFTA. The critics argue that NAFTA has led to huge U.S. trade deficits with Mexico and Canada. For example, in 1993 before NAFTA went into force, the United States had a trade surplus with Mexico amounting to $1.7 billion and a trade deficit of $11.0 billion with Canada. Since then, the United States has regularly incurred trade deficit with Mexico, while the deficit with Canada hit high, the worst showing since 1986. In 1997 the United States had a trade deficit of $16 billion and $13 billion with Canada and Mexico, respectively. In addition, NAFTA, it is claimed, has cost over 300,000 U.S. jobs, and has depressed wages and caused the flight of industry and investment to Mexico.[28]

On the other hand, according to NAFTA supporters, the accord prompted a major increase in U.S. exports to Canada and Mexico, stimulated domestic industrial production, and helped cushion the blow of Mexico's economic collapse. NAFTA proponents acknowledge the trade deficits, but blame them on a slow-growing Canadian economy and the 1994 peso crisis that plunged Mexico into economic turmoil.

At the time NAFTA was signed, the United States had expected to extend the agreement to include additional countries and ultimately to create a hemispheric trade pact, the *America Free Trade Agreement,* which would attempt to meld five separate free trade pacts involving countries in North and South America. Chile has been talked about as the first country to be invited into NAFTA. To move ahead, the Clinton administration needed the fast-track authority by which Congress votes yes or no on trade pacts but cannot change the terms. Unfortunately, in 1997 the Congress declined to grant the fast-track authority. Contrary to expectations, President Clinton did not make another attempt to seek the congressional authority, so during his term Chile might not become a member of NAFTA. Meanwhile, both Mexico and Canada have separately made trade agreements with Chile without waiting for the United States.

Regional trade agreements have promoted growth for the EU, Mexico, and others. Even when trade agreements occur among economies with different levels of development, the net result has been positive. The accession of Greece, Spain, and Portugal to the EU did not depress real wages within the EU. In fact, during the 1980s, real manufacturing wages rose in the Federal Republic of Germany, France, and the United Kingdom by at least 20 percent. EU programs have resulted in the continued lowering of barriers to trade and investment and have prompted a renewal of economic and job growth. Similarly, NAFTA, which concluded in 1996, has powered the region's economic growth, productivity, and global competitiveness into the twenty-first century.[29] (See International Marketing Highlight 7.5.)

■ International Marketing Highlight 7.5 ■

Rush Hour Replaces Siestas

The U.S. has a new "New South." It's called Mexico.

Four decades ago, U.S. industry migrated to Georgia, Alabama and other Southern states in search of cheap land and labor, eventually transforming what was once a largely rural backwater into one of the country's most economically vibrant regions. In a single generation, millions of Southerners vaulted from poverty to the middle class, and the South became an important market for the very goods it was producing. A similar process is now unfolding in Mexico. In the five years since the passage of NAFTA U.S. manufacturers have hired 600,000 new workers in Mexico, a pace of job creation almost identical to what took place in the U.S. Southeast in the 1960s and the 1970s. Once-sleepy towns are turning into cities, with malls and multiplexes reminiscent of the U.S. Sun Belt. And laborers, who once sought a better life across the border, are now settling in the arid north of Mexico to work in factories that have become critical to the global production plans of U.S. firms.

Source: The Wall Street Journal, October 29, 1999, p. A1

Other Forms of Agreements

We have discussed the important types of market agreements extant among nations in different regions of the world. In addition to these, various nations have made a variety of other arrangements for their economic benefit. For instance, four different forms of agreement are the Commonwealth of Nations, the Commonwealth of Independent States, commodity agreements, and producer cartels. Although the *Commonwealth of Nations* was mentioned in relation to political union, it is not, strictly speaking, a political union. The only political bond among the Commonwealth nations existed in the past when they constituted part of the British Empire. On the economic front, the member nations accord one another preferential treatment by agreeing to import from each other on a selective basis. Still, this situation has changed greatly since its beginnings in the post–World War II period, partially on political grounds and partially in response to individual economic interest.

The *Commonwealth of Independent States (CIS)* is a confederation of 11 countries that were previously part of the Soviet Union.[30] The shape that this agreement will ultimately take is difficult to say since its scope is not clear, but there is little doubt that it would be dominated by Russia, which has half of the former superpower's people and most of its resources and industrial base. Some people are skeptical that the CIS will survive long. Most of the member republics, especially Ukraine, are deeply suspicious of Russian intentions.

Another significant type of market agreement is the ***commodity agreement***. Some of these agreements have been entered into under the auspices of GATT to stabilize the price of commodities such as textiles, coffee, olive oil, sugar, tin, cocoa, and wheat. The underlying purpose of commodity agreements, which are made between producing and consuming countries, has been to prevent excessive price fluctuations that would be detrimental to the developing countries.[31]

The term *producer cartel* refers to a unilateral agreement among producers of a commodity, or suppliers of a natural resource, to deal collectively as a group with the buyers for purposes of trading the commodity. The producer cartel became a popular mode of economic cooperation among producers of strategic commodities after the success of the OPEC petroleum cartel. Since 1975 a number of producer cartels have been organized by countries exporting bauxite, phosphate, chromium, rubber, and copper. However, it is unrealistic to expect other cartels to duplicate OPEC's record.

Summary

In the post–World War II period, nations came to realize that the task of economic reconstruction and expansion could be achieved more smoothly through cooperation among nations. The cooperation took two forms: global and regional. Global cooperation was reflected in steps such as the establishment of the World Bank, the IMF, and the GATT. Chapters 2 and 5 examined these efforts.

Regional cooperation took the form of economic integration through market agreements among nations in geographical proximity to each other. Five types of market agreements are free trade area, customs union, common market, economic union, and political union. Market agreements are based on commonality of interest among nations. For example, developing countries share the common objective of economic development. Likewise, political systems and culture may influence nations to enter into economic cooperation. However, geographic proximity turns out to be the basis for market agreements more often than any other reason for cooperation. Other things being equal, nations located in the same region are usually influenced by common social and economic environments.

Historically, the economic cooperation among nations that influences governments today first emerged in Europe. Six European countries—former West Germany, France,

Italy, the Netherlands, Belgium, and Luxembourg—agreed to form what is now called the EU. Its example was followed by the establishment of market agreements in other parts of Europe and elsewhere throughout the world.

From the marketing viewpoint, the importance of market agreements lies in the potential generation of markets. Inasmuch as mass production can be justified only by mass markets, market agreements boost industrial development and economic activity. For example, the EU is about equal in size to the U.S. market. Thus, certain economies of scale that previously could not be achieved in Western Europe are now feasible as a result of the formation of the EU.

Review Questions

1. What factors lead nations to work toward economic integration?
2. What role did the United States play in the establishment of the EEC?
3. Why did Great Britain not join the EEC at the time of its creation, but did so later?
4. List the differences between the arrangements of a free trade area and a customs union.
5. Is economic integration workable among developing countries?
6. Explain why Japan might be hindered in establishing a market agreement in the Pacific region based on your general knowledge of the factors that promote such arrangements.
7. In what way has the unification of the European market in 1992 benefited U.S. business and industry?

Creative Questions

1. Do regional market agreements contradict multilateral agreements? Why do we need the regional agreements if we have the latter? Are there any major provisions in NAFTA that have not been covered by the Uruguay Round agreement?
2. Is a market agreement among the Indian Ocean countries (i.e., India, Pakistan, Iran, South Africa, and others) feasible? What problems discourage such an agreement? How can these problems be resolved?

Endnotes

1. "Common Marketing for the Common Market," *Forbes,* July 1, 1972, p. 23. Also see John Drew, "European Markets: A Business Overview," *Europe,* July–August 1984, pp. 18–19.

2. "Elizabeth Arden Whips up a New Formula," *Country Monitor,* July 7, 1999, p. 12.

3. "IBM Finds a Club that Doesn't Want It as a Member," *Business Week,* February 11, 1985, p. 42.

4. "Up, Up and Away: At Last for Airbus?," " *Business Week,* February 9, 1998, p. 58.

5. See Bela Balassa, *The Theory of Economic Integration* (Homewood, IL: Irwin, 1961), pp. 1–21.

6. "Lomé IV Convention," *Development Forum,* May–June 1989, p. 20.

7. "The Luxembourg Rebuff," *The Economist,* December 20, 1997, p. 17. Also see "Turkey and the EU," *The Economist,* December 20, 1997, p. 74.

8. "The European Union Decides It Might One Day Talk Turkey," *The Economist,* December 18, 1999, p. 42. Also see "EU Enlargement," *The Economist,* December 18, 1999, p. 148.

9. Francine Lamoriello, "Completing the Internal Market by 1992: The EC's Legislative Program for Business," *Business America,* August 1, 1988, pp. 16–18.

10. *Business International,* November 27, 1989, p. 365.

11. *The Economist,* April 10, 1993, p. 74. *Also see Crossborder Monitor,* August 17, 1994, p. 3.

12. "A Little EMU Enlightenment," *The Economist,* February 22, 1997, p. 88.

13. "A Common Currency in Europe will Bring Big Changes to Many," *The Wall Street Journal,* March 24, 1997, p. A1. Also see: "Is Europe's Currency Coming Apart?," *The Economist,* June 7, 1997, p. 13.

14. Thomas Kamm, " As the Euro's Arrival Nears, Europe Braces For Lots of Headaches," *The Wall Street Journal,* November 30, 1998, p. A1. Also see: *Talking About Euro* (Brussels, Belgium: Information Program for the European Citizen, 1997).

15. Alan Riding, "Europeans in Accord to Create Vastly Expanded Trading Bloc," *The New York Times,* October 23, 1991, p. A1. Also see "Tearing Down Even More Fences in Europe," *Business Week,* November 4, 1991, p. 50.

16. "COMECON's Crumbling Credit-Worthiness," *The Wall Street Journal,* September 18, 1985, p. 31.

17. Thomas V. Greer, "The Economic Community of West African States," *International Marketing Review,* Vol. 9. No. 3, 1992, pp. 25–39.

18. "Free Trade Accord?," *Crossborder Monitor,* December 2, 1998, p. 10.

19. "Growing Markets Lure Companies to Mercosur Region," *Crossborder Monitor,* June 8, 1994, p. 1.

20. "Remapping South America," *The Economist,* December 12, 1996.

21. MERCOSUR and Beyond: The Imminent Emergence of the South American Markets (Austin, TX: CIBER - University of Texas, 1996).

22. *The Asian Free Trade Area* (Singapore: Intercedent, 1997).

23. *Crossborder Monitor,* July 23, 1994, p. 8. Also see: Minoru Murofushi, "A Business Agenda for APEC," *Asia–Pacific Review,* vol. 3, Nov. 2, Fall/Winter 1996, pp. 21-36.

24. *APEC Means Business* (Singapore: Asia Pacific Economic Cooperation Secretariat, 1996).

25. Subhash C. Jain, "Prospects for a South Asian Free Trade Agreement: Problems and Challenges," *International Business Review,* 8 (Nov. 4, 1999), pp. 1-15.

26. Alan Freeman, "Free-Trade Pact Creates Winners, Losers," *The Wall Street Journal,* February 7, 1989, p. A20.

27. "Depending on the View, NAFTA Glass Half Full or Half Empty," *The Wall Street Journal,* March 9, 1997, p. A13. Also see: "Singing the NAFTA Blues," *Business Week,* December 9, 1996, p. 54; and Sidney Weintraub, "Extend the Benefits of Free Trade," *The Wall Street Journal,* February 26, 1998, p. A16.

28. "The Americas: The Free-Trade Winds Die Away," *The Economist,* November 22, 1997, p. 35.

29. Joel Millonan, "What Southeast was to U.S. companies, Mexico is Becoming," *The Wall Street Journal,* October 29, 1999, p. A1.

30. "How Long Can Yeltsin Hold It All Together?" *Business Week,* January 13, 1992, p. 49.

31. Steve Mufson, "Third World Pleas on Commodity Prices Get No Sympathy in Developed Nations," *The Wall Street Journal,* October 2, 1985, p. 34.

PART 4

Environmental Factors Affecting International Marketing

CHAPTER 8

Economic Environment

CHAPTER FOCUS

After studying this chapter, you should be able to

◼ Describe the macroeconomic and microeconomic environment.

◼ Explain the effect of the economic environment on international marketing strategy.

◼ Analyze the components of the economic environment of a country.

◼ Describe the emerging opportunities in developing countries.

This chapter deals with the phenomenon of economic environment. In most cases, economic environment can be viewed from two different angles: the macro view or the micro view. From a macro view, people's wants and needs and the economic policy of a country establish market scope and economic outlook. A microenvironmental view focuses on a firm's ability to compete within a market.

Different countries provide varying market potential based on their population. However, "potential" does not guarantee a realizable opportunity for any given firm. For example, a low level of economic activity in a country may force most of its people to live modestly. In such a country, many foods and services taken for granted in the industrialized countries are considered luxuries and would be marketable only to the elite. In addition, even if there is a market for a given product or service, the competition from both existing and other potential businesses may make it difficult for a new firm to establish itself.

Not only does the economic environment of a country, both from the macro and micro viewpoints, largely define the marketing opportunity in that country, but the economic environment of a firm's home country, to an extent, also influences marketing overseas. Hence the economic situation of the United States at any given time will affect the international activity of U.S. firms.

This chapter begins with an examination of the factors that compose macro- and microeconomic environments. This explanation is followed by an illustration of the economic environment's impact on international marketing strategy. Finally, a framework for measuring economic potential and conducting opportunity analyses is furnished.

Macroeconomic Environment

A country's economy is based on its sources of domestic livelihood and the allocation of those resources. Because not all of the world's economies operate at the same level of efficiency, it is necessary to form a clear idea of the economic situation of a particular host country in order to make good marketing decisions. Such economic perspectives of a country refer to its macroeconomic environment.

Population and Income

The most basic information to be considered is that which describes the nature of the population, because the people, of course, constitute the market. Exhibit 8.1 shows the population of different countries of the world, but population figures alone provide little information useful for marketing, since people must have an adequate income to become viable customers. Thus, Exhibit 8.1 also shows population combined with per capita GNP, providing an estimate of *consuming capacity.* An index of consuming capacity depicts the absolute, or aggregate, consumption for different countries. The consumption can be satisfied either domestically or through imports.

The information in Exhibit 8.1 should be interpreted cautiously because it makes no allowances for differences in the purchasing power of different countries. This point may be illustrated with reference to Thailand. Although its per capita GNP is lower than that of the United States, the Thai bhat goes much further than the U.S. dollar. A few years ago, for example, one dozen eggs cost only $.79 in Bangkok, while in New York they cost $1.15; an apartment rented for $950 in Bangkok, while the rent for an equivalent apartment in New York was $1,680; the taxi fare for a five-mile ride in New York and Bangkok came to $8.12 and $1.83, respectively.[1]

Two conclusions are obvious, however: (1) aggregate consuming capacity depends on total population as well as per capita income, and (2) advanced countries dominate as potential customers. In Chapter 1, it was noted that the U.S. MNCs are mainly active in

EXHIBIT 8.1
Consuming Capacities
of Selected Countries

Country	Population (in Millions)	Per Capita GNP (in U.S. Dollars)	Index of Consuming Capacity
United States	270	29,340	7,921,800
Japan	126	32,380	4,079,880
Germany	82	25,850	2,119,700
France	59	24,940	1,471,460
United Kingdom	59	21,400	1,262,600
Italy	58	20,250	1,174,500
Brazil	166	4,570	758,620
Canada	31	20,020	620,620
India	980	430	421,400
Netherlands	16	24,760	396,160
Australia	19	20,300	385,700
Mexico	96	3,970	381,120
Argentina	36	8,970	322,920
Switzerland	7	40,080	280,560
Belgium	10	25,380	253,800
Turkey	63	3,160	199,080
Denmark	5	33,260	166,300
Thailand	61	2,200	134,200
South Africa	41	2,880	118,080
Israel	6	15,940	95,640
Philippines	75	1,050	78,750
Peru	25	2,460	61,500
New Zealand	4	14,700	58,800
Ecuador	12	1,530	18,360
Paraguay	5	1,760	8,800
Uganda	21	320	6,720

Source: World Bank Report 2000 (Washington, DC, The World Bank, 2000).

Western Europe, Japan, and Canada—advanced countries with high population and high per capita income. In contrast, despite a large population, Bangladesh does not offer a realizable market potential. This is true also of other developing countries.

It must be noted that many developing countries are slowly emerging from their traditional poverty. Thus, it would be shortsighted to write them off. As a matter of fact, there is an interesting development taking place in the economic arena as far as the United States is concerned: Western Europe and Japan are becoming more competitive with the United States, while developing countries are becoming potential markets. Indeed, U.S. exports to developing countries as a group already substantially exceed exports to its traditional trading partners.

Structure of Consumption

Nations' overall patterns of consumption can be viewed not only on the basis of potential but also on the basis of structure. In other words, it is important not only to measure the volume of consumption among various nations, but to note the characteristics of that consumption, which reveal its structure. Particularly conspicuous in this respect are differences in emphasis. Depending on economic factors, a country may have to emphasize producer goods over consumer goods. Also, what are considered necessities in one economy may be luxuries in another. In addition, consumption in most advanced countries is characterized by a higher proportion of expenditures devoted to capital goods than consumption in developing countries, where substantially more is spent on consumer goods.

When a less developed economy decides to become technically and economically more advanced, an extraordinary percentage of national income must be diverted to capital goods, especially if that economy is unable to attract substantial amounts of foreign currency in the form of direct investment, loans, or other aid. This is one important reason why less developed countries find the transition period to economic advancement so difficult.

The structural differences with regard to expenditures among nations can be explained by a theory propounded by the German statistician Engel. The *law of consumption (Engel's law)* states that poorer families and societies spend a greater proportion of their incomes on food than well-to-do people.[2] Exhibit 8.2 substantiates Engel's law on a global scale. Shown is the percentage of per capita income spent for food, housing, clothing, and other purposes in selected countries. Developing countries like the Philippines and Sri Lanka spend a larger percentage on food than countries like the United States. Further, in any country, rural people spend a larger percentage on food than urban dwellers (not shown in the exhibit). Housing, in particular, receives a much smaller share of income in developing countries than in the advanced nations (see International Marketing Highlight 8.1).

The structure of consumption varies among developed countries, too. While the average American home covers 1,583 square feet and the typical European dwelling is more than 1,050 square feet, Japanese families manage with 925 square feet. The U.S. nuclear

EXHIBIT 8.2   Consumption Expenditures of Selected Countries

Country (Base Year)	Food & Beverage	Clothing & Footwear	Housing & Operations	Household Furnishings	Medical Care & Health	Transportation	Recreation	Other*
Industrial Market Economies								
Belgium	19.7	6.8	17.7	10.7	10.6	13.1	6.6	14.8
Canada	16.2	5.7	22.4	9.7	4.2	15.8	11.3	14.7
France	19.4	6.2	17.8	8.2	10.5	6.8	8.1	13.0
Japan	20.8	6.1	18.6	6.3	10.4	10.7	10.6	16.5
Sweden	22.3	8.4	23.5	6.8	2.7	17.9	10.5	8.0
United Kingdom	21.1	6.7	18.4	7.2	1.3	18.3	10.1	17.0
United States	13.3	7.7	17.4	6.3	12.4	16.4	11.7	14.8
[Former] West Germany	23.6	8.6	19.8	9.7	3.1	16.4	10.7	8.2
Middle-Income Countries								
Mexico	37.4	8.2	12.6	12.4	4.0	9.1	5.6	10.8
Philippines	60.0	5.3	3.1	13.5	n.a.	2.3	n.a	15.8
Republic of Korea	36.8	4.7	9.9	6.1	7.2	11.2	11.9	12.3
Low-Income Countries								
India	53.5	13.1	11.1	4.9	2.4	7.5	3.2	4.3
Sri Lanka	52.7	10.1	4.2	5.5	1.3	18.3	4.1	3.9

Other includes expenditures for personal care, restaurants, and hotels.
Note: The expenditures are expressed as percentages of total consumption in constant prices.
Source: United Nations Statistical Yearbook, 1993-1994.

family boasts 2.2 cars on average; comparable households in the European community average 1.3 cars. In Japan, the average is 0.88. And while food costs absorb 26 percent of the typical Japanese household's income, the amount is less than 15 percent for the average American family, and about 20 percent for the Europeans.[3] As shown in Exhibit 8.3, while the average person in England eats 13 pounds of cereal a year, per capita consumption in France is just 1 pound, and in Japan less than one-fourth of a pound. Americans eat about 10 pounds of cereal each per year.

■■■■■■■   International Marketing Highlight 8.1   ■■■■■■■

Acquiring a Vacation Spot

One CEO visited North Africa and fell in love with Morocco. Imagining frequent trips to this desert kingdom, he established a Marrakesh subsidiary for his firm, which manufactures kitchen cabinets. Unfortunately, he neglected to notice that most Moroccans don't have indoor kitchens, much less kitchen cabinets. The branch operation was a total failure. The lure of exotic climes had distorted this executive's previously sound business judgment.

Source: Charles F. Valentine, *The Arthur Young International Business Guide* (New York; John Wiley & Sons, 1988), p. 22.

Other Economic Indicators

Population, income, and expenditure data provide basic insights into the economies of different nations. For a certain point in time, however, a variety of other aspects of economic environment may be pertinent in a given case. This economic information may be found in categories such as

- Production indicators (such as the production of raw steel, automobiles, trucks, and electric power; crude-oil refinery runs, coal production, paper-board production, lumber production, and rail freight traffic).

EXHIBIT 8.3
Food Consumption Differences among Nations: 1995

Country	Food Market and Habits		
	Per Capita Cereal Consumption (in Pounds)	Per Capita Frozen-Food Consumption (in Pounds)	Percent of Homes with Microwave Ovens
United States	9.8	92.4	80
Britain	12.8	48.2	43
[former] West Germany	2.0	33.4	21
Denmark	4.6	53.9	—
Sweden	—	51.7	—
France	1.1	40.5	16
Norway	—	38.3	—
Netherlands	—	34.8	8
Switzerland	—	33.2	—
Spain	0.4	—	13
Ireland	15.4	—	—
Australia	12.3	—	—
Canada	8.7	—	—
Belgium	—	—	10
Italy	—	—	3
Japan	0.2	18.6	—

Source: Kellogg Co. Annual Report, 1996.

- Prices (such as the price of gold, finished steel, aluminum, wheat, cotton, industrial raw materials, and foodstuffs).
- Finance (such as corporate bond yield, prime commercial paper, value of local currency with reference to U.S. dollars, money supply).
- Other indicators (such as index of industrial production, retail sales, installment credit debt, and wholesale and retail inventories).

It is neither necessary nor possible for a marketer to gather information about and review all these indicators from each country.[4] At any given time, the choice of economic indicators to be examined is determined by the purpose of the project at hand. For example, a company contemplating manufacturing tires abroad needs to look into the foreign country's automobile and truck production data for a number of previous years as well as the data for those countries that are likely to import tires from the foreign country. A processed-food manufacturer, on the other hand, would be interested in such information as inflation rate, foodstuff prices, and retail sales data. In brief, marketers should examine only those economic indicators that are relevant to their marketing decisions. Relevancy can be determined in part by the marketer's domestic operations but should also reflect the new situation in the foreign country.

Concept of Economic Advancement

Developing countries are becoming important markets as their economies advance. According to the concept of *international product life cycle* examined in Chapter 2, more and more developing countries may become significant markets. It would be desirable for a marketer, therefore, to keep informed about countries slowly reaching the point where market potential will become worthwhile. GNP per capita, adjusted for purchasing power parity, may be relied on as a measure of the economic viability of a market. It provides a reasonable estimate of the market in cases where detailed analysis is not feasible.

Economic advancement is characterized by such factors as comparatively small allocation of labor force to agriculture; energy available in large amounts at low cost per unit; high level of GNP and income; high levels of per capita consumption; relatively low rates of population growth; complex modern facilities for transportation, communication, and exchange; a substantial amount of capital for investment; urbanization based on production as well as exchange; diversified manufacturing that accounts for an important share of the labor force; numerous tertiary occupations; specialization of both physical and mental labor; surpluses of both goods and services; and a highly developed technology that includes ample media and methods for experiment. These factors can be utilized to examine economic standing. Needless to say, a large variety of information is needed to categorize countries on an economic development scale. For many characteristics, hard data may not be available, in which case judgment becomes the determining factor.[5]

Generally, the conditions in underdeveloped economies are the reverse of those that characterize economic advancement. This fact raises an interesting question. Can poor countries be converted into advanced countries by reversing the conditions that hamper economic progress? The answer, however, is not a simple yes, because economic development is not a simple, discrete process. Many historical, geographic, political, and cultural factors are intimately related to the economic well-being of a nation. For example, no wars have been fought on U.S. soil in the last 100 years, a fact contributing to this counry's present economic greatness.

Economic Systems

The economic system of a country is another important factor that a marketer must understand. Traditionally, there are two types of economic systems: state-owned and capitalist. The state-owned, or Marxist, system is pursued in communist countries, where all activities related to production and distribution are controlled by the state. The capitalist system predominates in the Western World, but no country exhibits a pure form of capitalism today. The "invisible hand" of the marketplace propounded by Adam Smith is not given completely free reign, even in the United States, where some laws and conditions are imposed on various businesses. (The nature of some of these laws and controls are examined in Chapter 11. Most countries have mixed economic systems in which certain industries are allowed to run freely while others are strictly or partially controlled. The nature of the economic system affects the political/regulatory control of the economy.

An interesting development of the recent past is an economic system that is new to the modern world and links economic life with religion.[6] Some Muslim countries have adopted a national economic perspective based on Islam. This trend, led by Iran, is still emerging, and it is difficult to say how far it will go or what impact it will have on marketers (see International Marketing Highlight 8.2).

▬▬▬▬▬ International Marketing Highlight 8.2 ▬▬▬▬▬

Turning the Prophet's Profits

Islamic banks and investment funds are increasingly popular with Muslim savers. Can they continue to grow?

There are now more than 100 specialized institutions that invest money according to strict Islamic principles, ranging from mass-market savings banks in Geneva. Even some western banks are embracing the concept: last month the Citibank opened the first western-owned Islamic bank. Based in Bahrain, Citi Islamic Investment Bank has startup capital of $20 million.

Islamic banks are still puny by international standards. Taken together, their assets are somewhere between $25 billion and $30 billion. But they are growing fast. Some of the biggest, such as Kuwait Finance House and Pakistan's Muslim Commercial Bank are growing their assets by about 10 percent a year. The potential market—1 billion or so Muslims—is huge.

Islam's religious revival is the industry's motor. True believers obey *sharia*, Islam's holy law. This places several demands on Muslim savers. They must not finance activities prohibited by the Koran, such as gambling and the consumption of alcohol. Nor are they allowed to receive interest. ("Those who benefit from interest," warns the Koran, "shall be raised like those driven mad by the touch of the devil.")

To abide by those strictures, Islamic banks have developed alternative financial contracts. The most common of those is *murabaha*, a form of so-called "cost-plus" financing. This works as follows. Say a company wants to purchase $100 million of equipment. Instead of lending it the money for three months at 2% interest, an Islamic bank will buy the equipment itself. It will then sell it to the firm for $102 million, with payment deferred for three months. The bank will then claim that it is charging a profit mark-up rather than an interest rate.

Source: The Economist, August 24, 1996, p. 58.

Mutual Economic Dependence   The U.S. economy is profoundly related to the economies of other nations, particularly those of the advanced countries. The U.S. market is so large that despite its ability to supply most of its needs from domestic output, it is also deeply embroiled in international trade. Thus, what happens in Western Europe cannot be ignored by the United States. Although there may be a time lag, happenings there are bound to ultimately affect the U.S. economy. It has been estimated that a recession in Western Europe affects the United States after a lag of about six months. Thus, when performing an economic analysis of a country, an international marketer needs to consider the economic perspectives of the overall world economy, particularly those of its major trading partners and the host country.

The depth of economic analysis needed varies from case to case. For example, if the enterprise concerns Saudi Arabia, economic development in the Pacific region can be discounted. In contrast, if a project is related to Japanese industries, the economic environment in emerging countries of Southeast Asia must be reviewed.

Microeconomic Environment

Microeconomic environment refers to the environment surrounding a specific product or market rather than a country's overall economic environment. An examination of a microenvironment indicates whether a company can successfully enter a specific market. Essentially, then, the microeconomic environment concerns competition.

Sources of Competition

A U.S. company may face competition in an international market from three different sources: local business, other U.S. corporations, and foreign companies.[7] For example, if Ford Motor Company were to consider entering the German market, it would compete against General Motors, Volkswagen, and Honda Motors of Japan. Different competitors, however, might aim to satisfy different types of demand: existing, latent, or incipient. *Existing demand* refers to a product bought to satisfy a recognized need. *Latent demand* applies in a situation where a particular need has been recognized, but no products have been offered. *Incipient demand* describes a projected need that will emerge when customers become aware of it sometime in the future.

Consider demand in the computer industry. Overall, IBM may be strong in, let us say, Spain. But a firm like Dell Computers may choose to enter the Spanish market to serve latent demand there. As a result, Dell avoids direct confrontation with IBM, which is serving existing, not latent, demand, at least in the short run. Competition can also be analyzed according to the characteristics of products: breakthrough, competitive, and improved. A *breakthrough product* is a unique innovation that is mainly technical in nature, such as the digital watch, VCR, and personal computer. A *competitive product* is one of many brands currently available in the market and has no special advantage over the competing products. An *improved product* is not unique but is generally superior to many existing brands.

The nature of the competition that a company faces in entering an overseas market can be determined by relating the three types of products to the three types of demand. Upon examining the competition, a company should be able to ascertain which product or market it is most capable of pursuing.

For example, let us assume Procter & Gamble is interested in manufacturing hair shampoo in Egypt and seeks entry into the emerging Arab market. The company finds that in addition to a number of local brands, Johnson & Johnson's baby shampoo and Helene Curtis Industries' Suave Shampoo are the *competitive* products in the market. Gillette has recently entered the market with its Silkience brand, which is considered an *improved* product. Most of the competition appears to be addressing the *existing* demand. No attempts have been made to satisfy *latent* demand or *incipient* demand.

After reviewing various considerations, Procter & Gamble may decide to fulfill latent demand with an improved offering through its Head & Shoulders brand. Based on market information, the company reasons that a hair problem most consumers face in that part of the world is dandruff. No brand has addressed itself to that problem. Even Gillette's new entry mainly emphasizes silkiness of hair. Thus, analysis of the competition with reference to product offerings and demand enables Procter & Gamble to determine its entry point into the Arab market.

Competitive Advantage

The [preceding analysis—according to type of product (breakthrough, competitive, or improved) and type of demand (existing, latent, or incipient)—is sufficient to reveal an open space in the market for entry. But competitors might follow right on the heels of Procter & Gamble's entry steps. Thus, further analysis is needed to figure out the *competitive advantage* the company has over rivals, existing and potential. The following questions could be raised to analyze the competition:

- Who is the competition now, and who will it be in the future?
- What are the key competitors' strategies, objectives, and goals?
- How important is a specific market to the competitors, and are they committed enough to continue to invest?
- What unique strengths do the competitors have?
- Do they have any weaknesses that make them vulnerable?
- What changes are likely in the competitors' future strategies?
- What are the implications of competitors' strategies on the market, the industry, and one's own company?

The best way to examine the competition is to draw up a demographic profile of the industry. Markets dominated by small, single-industry businesses or small national competitors differ significantly from those dominated by multi-industry companies, and those in turn are different from markets controlled by multinational or foreign companies.

A simple listing of major competitors is not enough information. Their goals, and if possible, their total financial situations should be learned, including their serious problems as well as their advantages and opportunities—that is, their relative strengths and weaknesses. Exhibit 8.4 lists areas to be assessed for competitive strengths and weaknesses. Note that most areas of strength either are related to the excellence of personnel or are resource-based. Not all factors have the same significance for every product or market. Therefore, it is desirable first to recognize the critical factors that could directly or indirectly bear on a product's performance in a given market. Adequate distribution might be critical in a

---

EXHIBIT 8.4
Assessing Competitor's Areas of Strength

1. Excellence in product design and/or performance (engineering ingenuity).
2. Low-cost, high-efficiency operating skill in manufacturing and/or in distribution.
3. Leadership in product innovation.
4. Efficiency in customer service.
5. Personal relationships with customers.
6. Efficiency in transportation and logistics.
7. Effectiveness in sales promotion.
8. Merchandising efficiency—high turnover of inventories and/or of capital.
9. Skillful trading in volatile price movement commodities.
10. Ability to influence legislation.
11. Highly efficient, low-cost facilities.
12. Ownership or control of low-cost or scarce raw materials.
13. Control of intermediate distribution or processing units.
14. Massive availability of capital.
15. Widespread customer acceptance of company brand name (reputation).
16. Product availability and convenience.
17. Customer loyalty.
18. Dominant market share position.
19. Effectiveness of advertising.
20. High quality of salesforce.

developing country with inadequate means of transportation and communication, whereas development of new products through research and development might be strategic to gain the competitive edge in Western Europe.

An example of strength is provided by the BMW car company. It is commonly known that selling foreign cars in Japan is not easy. Yet BMW sells almost 100,000 cars annually to the Japanese, and that number is expected to be four times as high by the year 2010. With Japanese consumers' increasing interest in luxury cars, a new market segment had been emerging but was not being tapped by the Japanese companies. BMW took advantage of the situation. Avoiding the pitfalls that make doing business in Japan difficult, it established a comfortable niche for itself. After establishing its own dealer network and expanding it, the company advertised heavily, set up a service-and-parts system, and lowered interest rates to a single digit (5 percent) when the consumer interest rates were 15 percent. In brief, despite the fact that Japan is a difficult market to enter, analysis of the microeconomic environment showed that BMW could successfully seek entry.[8]

Japanese auto companies, in turn, have captured a major share (in 1998, approximately 31 percent) of the U.S. auto market. Let us assume Ford Motor Company decides to retaliate by exploring the possibility of entering the Japanese market. Despite all its strengths and experience in international business, Ford may find itself greatly constrained in its endeavors. In the past, cost was a major factor in U.S. auto competition with Japan. Because of U.S. wage-price and managerial efficiency differentials, the Japanese companies were able to build a car and ship it to the United States for $2,000 to $2,300 less than it would cost Detroit to produce an equivalent vehicle. Now, because of (1) the appreciation of the yen against the dollar and (2) U.S. companies' attempts to overhaul their operations, cost differential is not significant anymore. Yet U.S. companies may find it difficult to match Japanese selling methods—one-half the cars sold there are peddled by door-to-door salesmen. Such sales tactics, coupled with high-quality vehicles, stack the odds against Ford Motor Company.[9] Thus, even if Ford were to assemble cars in Japan, other things being equal, it would still be severely handicapped in its lack of selling experience in Japan. In this instance, analysis of the microeconomic environment paints a discouraging picture for Ford's entry into the Japanese market.

Economic Environment and Marketing Strategy

The overall macroeconomic climate of the host country as well as the microeconomic environment surrounding the product or market has a significant effect on marketing strategy. The macroeconomic environment sets the limit of activity in different sectors of the economy. Thus, when the economy is booming, there will be plenty of jobs, consumers will be optimistic, and cash registers will ring often. In a booming economy situation, the international marketer will have more opportunity in the marketplace, although marketplace opportunities may attract new competition. However, when an economy is down, unemployment may rise, interest rates may go up, sales could be more difficult to generate, and the international marketer's decisions will take a different shape.

Impact of Macroeconomic Environment

Brazil, one of the countries emerging into a developed economy, provides a case where there should be ample opportunities for U.S. international marketers. Yet, at the dawn of the new century, the Brazilian economy was beset by a variety of problems that restricted the realization of opportunities there. The turmoil in the financial markets makes the outlook for 2000–2002 risky. If the government avoids a devaluation, the austerity measures required to support the national currency, the real, and to cut the fiscal deficit will have a negative impact on consumer confidence. The economy may not grow more than 2 percent to 3 percent annually. The private consumption and investment are likely to be hurt. Moreover, Brazilian exports to the United States and other markets have been noncompetitive in price.

But the monetary reforms that the country introduced in the past few years should help. For example, the launching of the new currency, the real, helped slash inflation from 50 percent a month in June 1994 to just under 5 percent in 1997. The revival of consumer credit could trigger a spending surge, giving new strength to many industrial sectors.[10]

Betting on Brazil's recovery, U.S. investors have sent billions of dollars flowing into that nation's stock market. At the end of 1997 Brazil had received more U.S. direct investment than any other country, amounting to $18.0 billion against Mexico's $16.4 billion. Thus, the long-run economic outlook for Brazil may be promising.

The health of an economy affects consumer confidence, which is then reflected in consumer buying plans. A favorable economic climate generates a spirit of optimism that makes consumers more willing to spend money. The reverse occurs when economic conditions are unfavorable. In Brazil's case, 1998–1999 was not an exciting period. Although inflation has been under control, the credit restrictions have had a negative impact on consumption. Things might stabilize in a year or so, and then opportunities should develop. A recent survey by Price Waterhouse confirmed that 93 percent of the company's U.S. clients consider Brazil to be Latin America's most attractive investment target.[11]

Although economic climate affects all businesses, some are affected more deeply than others. International marketers should calculate the extent to which their business is susceptible to economic conditions. For example, in a booming economy, consumers tend to buy durable goods. Thus, the economic environment in Brazil during 2000 seemed unattractive for consumer goods manufacturers interested in entering the market.

It should be noted, however, that current economic environment is just one variable. Even if the short-run economic environment is not conducive to profits, a company might wisely enter an overseas market based on good long-term economic prospects in that country and such other favorable factors as growing political stability or the existence of low wage scales. The long-run perspective is the most important one, provided a firm has sufficient resources to endure waiting for the future favorable environment. From that standpoint, Brazil is an attractive market to enter.

Impact of Microeconomic Environment

The following example shows how the microeconomic environment of a product/market affects marketing strategy: A very successful U.S. company, for many years a leader in its field, launched a cheaper version of its traditional product almost simultaneously in the United States and in Europe. The product design, pricing, and advertising copy—in fact, the whole marketing approach—were quite similar in both areas. The strategy was very successful at home, but in Europe sales fell far below expectations. What was the cause of the trouble? The company had neglected several significant differences between the two market areas:

1. In the United States it had a major share of the market, while in Europe it was an insignificant factor.
2. At home, the company's product concept was in the mature phase of its life cycle, while in Europe it was at its beginning.
3. In the United States roughly 85 percent of all households knew the company and its products, whereas in Europe the awareness level was barely 5 percent, and few customers understood the nature of this innovative product.
4. As a result, the advertising copy that featured a low price without explaining the product concept was meaningful to most U.S. consumers but unsuitable for most of the European market.

It is evident from this illustration that the U.S. company got into problems in Europe because its competitive strength there was meager (small market share), the product, relatively speaking, was new to the market (starting life cycle position), and the product presented an unfamiliar concept. In other words, the company did not orient its marketing program with the product/market environment existing in Europe.

Impact of Domestic Economic Environment

Although international marketers should be concerned with economic environment overseas, they should also be sensitive to economic perspectives of the home market, just as the reverse is true for domestic marketers. Indeed, firms react to changing domestic and international economic environments and can be expected to shift their relative emphasis in promoting domestic versus foreign trade. During 1990, as the recession deepened in the United States, U.S. companies appeared to put greater stress on foreign markets than on U.S. markets. Similarly, in 1993, as the dollar fell, companies became more anxious to tap export markets.[12] During slack conditions in the U.S., overseas markets provide a realistic alternative for maintaining business tempo.[13] However, to develop perpetual foreign markets, firms cannot simply shift gears in favor of overseas markets when something goes wrong in the domestic market and then abandon foreign markets once the domestic economy picks up again. Such tactics are harmful to long-term market development abroad, plus they damage the reputation of the business.

Analysis of Economic Environments

Given the perspectives of macro- and microeconomic environment, an opportunity analysis may be performed to determine if it is worthwhile to seek entry into a foreign country's market. A conceptual scheme is helpful for analyzing economic environment in practice in order to assess marketing opportunities. The conceptual scheme requires consideration of such variables as those shown in Exhibit 8.5. With the use of these variables, analysis of marketing opportunity centers on two sets of criteria: cost/benefit criteria and risk/reward criteria.*

Cost/Benefit Criteria Analysis

Cost-benefit criteria answer a series of questions that stress markets, competition, and the financial implications of doing business in a foreign country.

Markets Will people want our products? More importantly, will they want them enough to pay a price that will yield us a profit? Is the market large enough for the firm?

Competition What kind of competition will we have to face, and will the rules apply equally to all? Concern about equal treatment within a market arises from the *altered marketplace competition* that exists in many countries because of host governments that own or subsidize competitors. In such cases, the foreign business usually is at a disadvantage even when it is pitted against inefficient local business.

Financial Examination How many resources (and how much of each type of resource) must be committed, and what will they cost? What return may be expected, and how long might it take to recover the investment?

---

* Inasmuch as this chapter deals with economic environment only, the risk/reward criteria will be examined here solely with reference to economic situation. The risk/reward analysis should be extended by relating it to cultural environment (Chapter 9) and the political environment (Chapter 10).

EXHIBIT 8.5
Considerations
in the Evaluation
of Economic
Environments

Financial Considerations

1. Capital acquisition plan
2. Length of payback period
3. Projected cash inflows (years one, two, and so forth)
4. Projected cash outflows (years one, two, and so forth)
5. Return on investment
6. Monetary exchange considerations

Technical and Engineering Feasibility Considerations

7. Raw materials availability (construction/support/supplies)
8. Raw materials availability (products)
9. Geography/climate
10. Site locations and access
11. Availability of local labor
12. Availability of local management
13. Economic infrastructure (roads, water, electricity, and so forth)
14. Facilities planning (preliminary or detailed)

Marketing Considerations

15. Market size
16. Market potential
17. Distribution costs
18. Competition
19. Time necessary to establish distribution/sales channels
20. Promotion costs
21. Social/cultural factors affecting products

Economic and Legal Considerations

22. Legal systems
23. Host government attitudes toward foreign investment
24. Host attitude toward this particular investment
25. Restrictions on ownership
26. Tax laws
27. Import/export restrictions
28. Capital flow restrictions
29. Land-title acquisitions
30. Inflation

Political and Social Considerations

31. Internal political stability
32. Relations with neighboring countries
33. Political/social traditions
34. Communist influence
35. Religious/racial/language homogeneity
36. Labor organizations and attitudes
37. Skill/technical level of the labor force
38. Socioeconomic infrastructure to support families

In addition to these cost/benefit criteria, the level of training and skills of a national workforce are important considerations. So is the availability of educated, experienced local managers. Most MNCs have learned the value of having local or regional executives in host countries. For example, Sperry Rand Corporation in Japan shares a joint venture that is manned entirely by Japanese workers and executives.[14] Furthermore, transportation, the communications system, and the availability of local resources (especially energy) should be considered. This list could go on and on, but enough has been said to illustrate some of the assessable conceptual factors influencing market-entry decisions.

Risk/Reward Criteria Analysis

Risk/reward criteria emphasize the overall constantly changing mix of situations in the social, political, and economic climates of a host country. In terms of economics, the macro-economic characteristics of a nation will almost always affect the specific economics of business. The national economic objectives of the country, therefore, also figure in a firm's decision to explore entry there.

For example, the firm needs to know how *fiscal policy* (control of the nation's economy through taxes) translates into business taxation, and how *income policy* (wage/price guideposts) may affect wage and price controls. The firm also needs to know about a country's *monetary policy* (control of the nation's economy through increasing or decreasing interest rates by the central bank). Does the country's policy place restrictions on international cash transactions, such as the repatriation of profits? What is the outlook, for example, for the cost and availability of credits? Is the currency strong, and, more important, what is the inflation situation?

Social/Cultural and Political Factors Although it is convenient to categorize a country's environment into social/cultural, political, and economic aspects, they each overlap, and they all influence the intelligent analysis of any one aspect.

In the social area, the demographic characteristics of the population should be taken into account. The general level of education is an important indicator of the society's development, the likelihood of its accepting new ideas, and possibly its attitude toward a foreign investor. The standard of living and the general expectations of the country tell marketers a great deal. Is the society a progressive one or a static one? Does it aspire to development, or is it frozen into old social patterns and mores? Are its expectations pragmatic or unrealistic? Class structure, where it exists, also yields useful information.

The political area reflects both the social and economic situations, and vice versa. However, some political aspects are particularly relevant to economic analysis:

- What kind of political system does the country have? Is it a democratic/parliamentary society? Or is it authoritarian and possibly repressive?
- Is the national leadership popular or unpopular? The answer might indicate the probability of radical change.
- By our standards, are the national policies successful or unsuccessful?
- What is the level of insurgency, if any? It might range all the way from random, occasional violence to organized guerrilla warfare or foreign-supported insurgency. One of the biggest changes in international business has been the necessity of physical and ideological defense in foreign countries.

If there is a common denominator of both the cost/benefit and risk/reward equations, it is the desirability of stability. That is not to suggest that business should want some imposed stability at the price of reduced performance. Rather, what is desired is a reasonable level of stability already existing in all of the areas just discussed. The aim should be to ensure that capital investment is recovered over a reasonable period, generates a satisfactory profit, and provides a base for the further expansion of international business.

An Illustration

Decisions related to foreign market entry, expansion, and conversion, as well as phasing out from foreign markets, call for a systematic framework for analysis, as discussed previously. Various approaches are available to assess international marketing opportunities.[15] Illustrated here is one method of putting a framework into practical use, consisting of three phases:

1. Appropriate national markets are selected by quickly screening the full range of options without regard to any preconceived notions.
2. Specific strategic approaches are devised for each country or group of countries based on the company's specific product technologies.
3. Marketing plans for each country or group of countries are developed, reviewed, revised, and incorporated into the overall corporate concept without regard to conventional wisdom or stereotypes.

Phase One: Selecting National Markets There are over 180 countries in the world; of these the majority may appear to offer entry markets. Many countries go out of their way to attract foreign investment by offering lures ranging from tax exemptions to low-paid, amply skilled labor. These inducements, valid as they may be in certain individual cases, have repeatedly led to hasty foreign market entry.

A good basis for decision is arrived at through a comparative analysis of different countries, with long-term economic environment having the greatest weight. First, certain countries, on account of their political situations (for example, Libya under Qadhafi) would be considered unsuitable for market entry. It might help to consult an index that rates different countries for business attractiveness. The final choice should be based on the company's own assessment and risk preference.

Next, markets that are either too small in terms of population and per capita income or economically too weak should be eliminated. For example, a number of countries with populations of less than 20 million and annual per capita incomes below $2,000 are of little interest to many companies because of limited demand potential.

The markets surviving this screening are then assessed for strategic attractiveness. A battery of criteria should be developed to fit the specific requirements of the corporation. Basically, the criteria should focus on the following five factors (industry/product characteristics may require slight modifications):

1. Future demand and economic potential of the country in question.
2. Distribution of purchasing power by population groups or market segments.
3. Country-specific technical product standards.
4. "Spillover" from the national market (via standards, regulations, norms, or economic ties) to other markets (for example, the MERCOSUR Pact provides for duty-free exports from Brazil to Uruguay).
5. Access to vital resources (qualified labor force, raw materials sources, suppliers).

There is no reason to expand the list, since additional criteria are rarely significant enough to result in useful new insights. Rather, management should concentrate on developing truly meaningful and practical parameters for each of these five criteria, so that the selection process does not become unnecessarily costly and the results are fully relevant to the company concerned. For example, a German flooring manufacturer, selling principally to the building industry, selected the following yardsticks:

1. *Economic potential:* new housing needs; GNP growth.
2. *Wealth:* per capita income; per capita market size for institutional building or private dwellings (the higher the per capita income, market volume, and share of institutional buildings, the more attractive the market).
3. *Technical product standards:* price level of similar products—for example, price per square meter for floor coverings (the higher the price level, the more attractive the market tends to be for a technically advanced producer).
4. *Spillover:* area in which the same building standards (especially fire safety standards) apply (for example, the U.S. National Electrical Manufacturers' Association standards are widely applicable in Latin America, and British standards apply in most of the Commonwealth countries).
5. *Resource availability:* annual production volume of PVC (an important raw material for the company).

Using these criteria, the German manufacturer in our example based its analysis of economic potential on two factors: housing needs and economic base (see Exhibit 8.6). In specifying these criteria, the company deliberately confined itself to measures that (1) could readily be developed from existing sources of macroeconomic data, (2) would show trends as well as current positions, and (3) would match the company's particular characteristics as closely as possible.

Since German producers of floor covering employ a highly sophisticated technology, it would have been senseless to give a high ranking to a country with only rudimentary pro-

EXHIBIT 8.6   Assessing Country Economic Potential:
The Case of a Building Industry Flooring Supplier

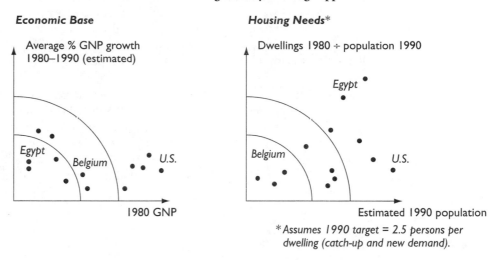

Economic Base

Average % GNP growth
1980–1990 (estimated)

Egypt   Belgium   U.S.

1980 GNP

*Housing Needs**

Dwellings 1980 ÷ population 1990

Egypt

Belgium   U.S.

Estimated 1990 population

*Assumes 1990 target = 2.5 persons per
dwelling (catch-up and new demand).*

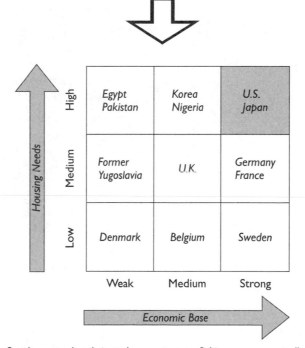

	Weak	Medium	Strong
High	Egypt Pakistan	Korea Nigeria	U.S. Japan
Medium	Former Yugoslavia	U.K.	Germany France
Low	Denmark	Belgium	Sweden

Housing Needs

Economic Base

Examples: Sweden—needs only in replacement sector, Pakistan—economically too weak to meet needs.

duction technology in this particular facet. Companies in other industries, of course, would have to consider other factors—auto registrations per thousand population, percentage of households with telephones, density of household appliance installations, and the like.

The resulting values are rated, for each criterion, on a scale of 1 to 5, so that by weighing the criteria on a percentage basis, each country can be assigned an index number indicating its overall attractiveness. In this particular case, the result was that, out of the 49 countries surviving the initial screening, 16 were ultimately judged attractive enough—on the basis of market potential, per capita market size, level of technical sophistication, prevailing regulations, and resource availability—to warrant serious attention.

Interestingly, the traditionally German-favored markets of Austria and Belgium emerged with low rankings from this strategically based assessment because the level of potential demand was judged to be insufficient. Some new markets such as Egypt and Pakistan were also downgraded as offering an inadequate economic base. Likewise, even such high-potential markets as Italy and Indonesia were eliminated for objective reasons (in the latter case, the low technical standard of most products).

Phase Two: Determining Marketing Strategy After a short list of attractive foreign markets has been compiled, the next step is to group these countries according to their respective stages of economic development. Here the criterion of classification is not per capita income, but the degree of market penetration by the generic product in question. For example, the floor covering manufacturer already mentioned grouped the countries into three categories—developing, take-off and mature—as defined by these factors (see Exhibit 8.7):

EXHIBIT 8.7   **Grouping Countries by Phase of Development**

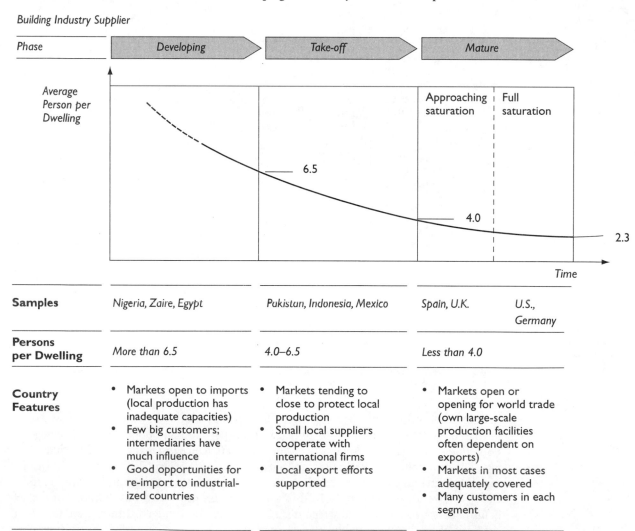

	Developing	Take-off	Mature	
Samples	Nigeria, Zaire, Egypt	Pakistan, Indonesia, Mexico	Spain, U.K.	U.S., Germany
Persons per Dwelling	More than 6.5	4.0–6.5	Less than 4.0	
Country Features	• Markets open to imports (local production has inadequate capacities) • Few big customers; intermediaries have much influence • Good opportunities for re-import to industrialized countries	• Markets tending to close to protect local production • Small local suppliers cooperate with international firms • Local export efforts supported	• Markets open or opening for world trade (own large-scale production facilities often dependent on exports) • Markets in most cases adequately covered • Many customers in each segment	

1. *Accessibility of markets:* crucial for the choice between export and import production.
2. *Local competitive situation:* crucial for the choice between independent construction, joint venture, and acquisition.
3. *Customer structure:* crucial for sales and distribution strategy.
4. *Re-import potential:* crucial for international product/market strategy.

The established development phases and their defining criteria must be very closely geared to the company situation, since it is these factors, not the apparent attractiveness of markets, that will make or break the company's strategic thrust into a given country.

This being the case, for each country or group of countries on the short list, management should formulate a generic marketing strategy with respect to investment, risk, product, and pricing policies—that is, a unified strategic framework applicable to all the countries in each stage of development. This step should yield a clear understanding of what the respective stages of economic development of each country entail for the company's marketing strategies (see Exhibit 8.8).

Companies are too often inclined to regard "overseas" as a single market, or at least to differentiate very little among individual overseas markets. Another common error is the assumption that product or service concepts suited to a highly developed consumer economy will work as well in any foreign market. This is rarely true. Different markets demand different approaches.

Across-the-board strategic approaches typically result in ill-advised and inappropriate allocation of resources. In less developed markets that could be perfectly well served by a few distributors, companies have in some cases established production facilities that are doomed to permanent unprofitability. In markets already at the take-off point, companies have failed to build the necessary local plants and instead have complained about declining exports only to finally abandon the field to competitors. And in markets already approaching saturation, companies have often sought to impose domestic technical standards where adequate standards and knowledge already exist or tried to operate like minireplicas of parent corporations, marketing too many product lines with too few salespeople.

Again and again, product-line offerings are weighted toward either cheaper or higher-quality products than the local market will accept. Clearly, the best insurance against such errors is to select strategies appropriate to the country.

Phase Three: Developing Marketing Plans In developing detailed marketing plans, it is first necessary to determine which product lines fit local markets and to allocate resources accordingly. A rough analysis of potential international business, global sales, and profit targets based on the estimates worked out in Phase One will help in assigning product lines. A framework for resource allocation can then be mapped out according to rough comparative figures for investment quotas, management needs, and skilled-labor requirements. This framework should be supplemented by company-specific examples of standard marketing strategies for each group of countries.

Exhibit 8.9 illustrates the resource allocation process. Different product lines are assigned to different country groups, and for each country category different strategic approaches are specified, for example, support on large-scale products, establishment of local production facilities, cooperation with local manufacturers.

The level of detail in this resource allocation decision framework will depend on a number of factors: company history and philosophy, business policy objectives, scope and variety of product lines, and the number of countries to be served. Working within this decision framework, each product division should analyze its own market in terms of size, growth, and competitive situations; assess its profitability prospects, opportunities, and risks; and identify its own current strategic position on the basis of market share, profit sit-

EXHIBIT 8.8   Developing Standard Strategies

Phase	Developing	Take-Off	Mature
Basic strategy	Test market; pursue profitable individual projects and/or export activities	Build base; allocate substantial resources to establish leading position in market	Expand/round off operations allocate resources selectively to develop market niches
Elements of Strategy			
Investment	Minimize (distribution and services)	Invest to expand capacity (relatively long payback)	Expand selectively in R&D, production, and distribution (relatively short payback)
Risk	Avoid	Accept	Limit
Know-how transfer (R&D)	Document know-how on reference projects	Use local know-how in product technology and/or production engineering	Transfer know-how in special product lines; acquire local know-how to round off own base
Market share objective	Concentrate on key projects possibly build position in profitable businesses with local support	Extend base with new products, new outlets, and/or new applications	Expand/defend
Cost leadership objective	Minimum acceptable (especially reduction of guarantee risks)	Economies of scale; reduction of fixed costs	Rationalize; optimize resources
Product	Standard technology; simple products	Aim for wide range, "innovator" role	Full product line in selected areas; products of high technical quality
Price	Price high	Aim for price leadership (at both ends)	Back stable market price level
Distribution	Use select local distributors (exclusive distribution)	Use large number of small distributors (intensive distribution)	Use company salesforce (selective distribution)
Promotion	Selective advertising with typical high-prestige products, aiming at decision makers	Active utilization of selective marketing resources	Selected product advertising

uation, and vulnerability to local risks. Each product division will then be in a position to develop country-specific marketing alternatives for servicing each national market.

Top management's role throughout is to coordinate the marketing strategy development efforts of the various divisions and constantly monitor the strategic decision framework.

This three-phase approach exhibits a number of advantages.

- It allows management to set up, with a minimum of planning effort, a strategic framework that gives clear priority to market selection decisions, thus making it much easier for the divisions to work out effective product-line strategies, unhampered by the usual "chicken or egg" problem.

EXHIBIT 8.9   Specimen Framework for Resource Allocation

Phase	Specimen Countries	Resource Allocation by Product Division					
		PVC Floor Coverings	Carpeting	Suspended Ceilings	Wall Paneling	PVC Tubes	Plastic Coated Roof Insulation
Developing: "test marktet"	Nigeria	Intensive	None	Moderate	None	Intensive	Intensive
(Share of total resources: 20%)		Specific Plans: • Develop own plastics-processing facilities • Acquire plastics processors					
Take-off: "Build base"	Indonesia	Moderate	None	None	None	Moderate	Moderate
(Share of total resources: 50%)		Specific Plans: • Give support in key projects • Cooperate with state-owned construction organization					
Mature: "Expand/round off operations"	Spain	Moderate	Moderate	Intensive	Intensive	None	None
(Share of total resources: 30%)		Specific Plans: • Develop local facilities for tufting and paneling • Acquire/cooperate with suppliers using unique product and production technology • Develop own distribution channel • Extend range to provide complete interior equipment program (system concept)					

- Division managers can foresee, at a fairly early stage, what reallocations of management, labor, and capital resources are needed and what adjustments may have to be imposed from the top because of inadequate resources.

- The company's future risk profile can be worked out in terms of resource commitment by country group and type of investment.

- The usual plethora of "exceptional" (and mostly opportunistic) product/market situations is sharply reduced. Only the really good opportunities pass through the filter; exceptions are no longer the rule.

- The dazzling-in-theory but unrealistic-in-practice concept of establishing production bases in low-wage countries, buying from the world's lowest-cost sources, and selling products wherever the best prices can be had is replaced by a realistic country-by-country market evaluation.

- Issues of organization, personnel assignment, and integration of overseas operations into corporate planning and control systems reach management's attention only after the fundamental strategic aspects of the company's overseas involvement have been thoroughly prepared.

This three-phase approach enables management to profitably concentrate resources and attention on a handful of really attractive countries instead of dissipating its efforts in vain attempts to serve the entire world.

Opportunities in the Developing World

The framework just discussed is applicable for analyzing the economic environment in both developed and developing countries. However, further examination of opportunities in developing countries is appropriate for two reasons. First, more and more developing countries are pursuing a growth path. South Korea, Taiwan, Singapore, and Hong Kong were first; Brazil and China followed. Now India and Eastern European countries have been opening up (see International Marketing Highlight 8.3). Several other nations are following suit as well. The developing world is beginning to rely on the market mechanism to attract investment and technology and become industrialized.

The second reason why opportunities in developing countries should be even more closely examined than those in advanced countries is that government plays a bigger role in business decisions in developing countries. This necessitates dealing with the bureaucrats approach foreign investment with much less sophistication and confidence than do private-sector executives.

These characteristics suggest that in analyzing opportunities in developing countries, a company should place more emphasis on long-term potential than on short-term gains (see International Marketing Highlight 8.4). In addition, extra attention should be paid to political and social variables since they will greatly influence the scope and nature of the market and are likely to differ in at least some respects from those of the home country. Business conditions vary so much from one country to the other that a comparative (i.e., multicountry) analysis may be difficult. Moreover, reliable and timely information is less available in developing countries than in advanced ones; thus, there is no way to systematically evaluate such factors as sociopolitical conditions. Instead, broad guidelines and a general feel for the situation are necessary, for which a trusted native could be of immense help.

For example, it has been estimated that basic packaged-foods sales take off when GDP per head increases to $5,000.[16] Based on this guideline, only a few Asian countries qualify for packaged foods. However, many of these nations are already more affluent than the aggregate figures imply. In countries such as Indonesia and Thailand, a rising middle class can afford to indulge itself. Besides, Asia has a higher percentage of younger people, a trend likely to continue for the next 30 years or so. That is important, because young people are more willing to change their living habits than older ones.

■■■■■■■   **International Marketing Highlight 8.3**   ■■■■■■■

Scents and Sensibility

Avon Products is increasingly focusing on what its CEO calls "Avon Heaven," the developing countries that in 1995 accounted for 38 percent of the firm's sales and 49 percent of its pretax profits. Developing countries might have been designed for Avon. First, the retailing infrastructure tends to be underdeveloped—and, apart from a very basic distribution network, Avon needs no infrastructure. Second, the products sold by local vendors tend to be of poor quality. And, third, women in most developing countries are eager to work to supplement the family income: they call on three or four times as many clients as their western counterparts.

But what really appeals to Avon is how little cash it has to spend to generate big profits. In Russia, the firm has invested less than $500,000 but its 16,000 representatives sold a net $30 million of products in 1996, up from nothing in 1993. From this, Avon skims an operating profit margin of around 30 percent. Avon imports all the products it sells in Russia from its British operations. When net sales hit about $50 million a year, the firm may manufacture locally.

Source: The Economist, July 13, 1996, p. 57

In general, many U.S. firms' overall approach to foreign-investment decision making regarding developing countries is much less sophisticated than that for developed countries. The former is often characterized by a lack of breadth in consideration of important variables, a biased perspective, and inadequate preparation. The key to future improvement of opportunity analysis in developing countries may lie in the motivation generated by the inevitable increase in competition. In the past, for example, the sheer power, dynamism, and momentum of U.S. business virtually ensured its success in almost any developing nation. As competition, particularly from Japan, becomes more significant, the recognition of shades of difference and finer distinctions with regard to opportunities becomes more important as well.

███████████   **International Marketing Highlight 8.4**   ███████████

Procter & Gamble's Foreign Formula

The day after a 34-year-old Peruvian became manager of Procter & Gamble Co.'s Peru subsidiary in September 1988, the economy hit the skids. By the end of the year, inflation had soared to 2,000 percent. Key managers fled. Leftist terrorists kidnapped or murdered business leaders. The P&G subsidiary's sales plunged more than 30 percent, and the unit posted a loss. Money became tight. But while many MNCs pulled out of Peru. P&G remained. Now, the consumer-products company is expanding there.

Throughout Latin America, P&G is shaking the stranglehold of government controls and its own strict U.S. culture. The Latin American division began as a fledgling detergent company but now is a $1 billion business that contributes 15 percent of P&G's international sales. The company expects the division, which has subsidiaries in 9 countries and sells in 10 others through distributors, to double its revenue again in five years. The division's profit margins exceed its international average.

P&G's success is attributed to an important lesson: U.S. management and marketing plans often don't work outside the United States. For example, Ace detergent, launched in Mexico in the early 1950s, was clobbered by local competitors. Developed for U.S. washing machines, the product had a low-suds formula. But at that time, many Mexicans washed their clothes in the river or in a basin of water, and they judged detergent by its suds.

Eventually, the formula was changed. Similarly, P&G switched from cardboard boxes to plastic bags, which kept the detergent drier and were cheaper. Besides, many consumers shop every day and can afford only small amounts of detergent each time. Now, one top seller throughout Latin America is the 100-gram bag, enough to wash just one basket of clothes.

Source: The Wall Street Journal, June 5, 1990, p. 1.

Summary

The economic environment of a foreign country must be examined before an international marketer decides to enter its market. A country burdened with economic problems may lack stability and become vulnerable to political radicalism. On the other hand, a growing and burgeoning economy usually stimulates business activity and offers new opportunities. Thus, a careful review of economic conditions, both short-and long-term, is a prerequisite for a decision about entering an overseas market.

The economic environment can be divided into macro- and microeconomic aspects. Macroenvironment describes the overall economic situation in a country and is analyzed using economic indicators such as population, GNP per capita, index of industrial production, rate of economic growth, inflation rate, balance-of-trade surplus (deficit), interest rates, unemployment data, and the like. The economic system of a country is also part of the macroenvironment. Two extreme types of economic systems are the capitalist system and state control. The latter is mainly found in socialist countries; most western countries pursue a mixed form of capitalism.

Microenvironment refers to economic conditions relevant to a particular product or market. Analysis of microeconomic environment is largely performed with reference to competition. A firm should properly identify different sources of competition and examine its own strengths and weaknesses relative to major competitors. Equipped with a competitive advantage over its rivals, a firm will be able to develop a workable marketing mix.

International marketers should examine not only the economic environment of a country, both macro- and micro-, before preparing to enter its market, but should also take into account the impact of the economic environment of their own country. For example, many U.S. firms enter the international market during a recession to sustain their business, only to withdraw as the domestic scene improves.

Conceptual schemes or frameworks are helpful for analyzing economic environment. Analysis can be performed with reference to cost/benefit and risk/reward criteria. Cost/benefit criteria include markets, competition, and financial implications of doing business in a country. Risk/reward criteria include the broad social, economic, and political climates of a nation. The successful application of a conceptual scheme yields a marketing strategy that will foster the development of market plans appropriate to a particular foreign market at a particular time. The conceptual scheme can be used to analyze opportunities in developed and developing economies. In many cases, however, lack of adequate information on developing countries may require decision makers to depend more on the "feel" of the situation than on actual data.

Review Questions

1. Should all the different types of economic indicators be used to examine the macroeconomic environments of different countries? Discuss what should be used and why.
2. Discuss the following statements: "Although advanced countries offer an immediate market opportunity, the competitive activity is excessively keen there. It may, therefore, be more advantageous for a firm to gain a permanent foothold in one or more developing countries, since often there is no competition to reckon with."
3. Present a scheme for analyzing the economic environment of Mexico from the viewpoint of an appliance manufacturer.
4. What relevance does Engel's law have in the analysis of economic environment for overseas business?
5. How can a firm determine its competitive advantage overseas?
6. Illustrate how the economic perspectives of different countries are related.

Creative Questions

1. A company is interested in selling telecommunications equipment (telephone exchanges, etc.) to India, which has 990 million people and only 7 million phone lines. What kind of economic analysis would you conduct to determine the viability of this opportunity in India?
2. The product life cycle theory alleges that the nature and number of competitors vary at different stages. During the early stages (introduction, growth) of the product life

cycle the product has little or no competition, whereas at later stages (maturity, decline), the competition becomes tougher. Does this mean that if a company enters a growth market overseas, it need not undertake competitive analysis?

Endnotes

1. "A Snapshot of Living Standards," *Fortune*, July 31, 1989, p. 92.

2. Gunnar Myrdal, *The Asian Drama: An Inquiry into the Poverty of Nations* (New York: Pantheon, 1968).

3. Bill Saporito, "Where the Global Action is," *Fortune*, Autumn–Winter 1993, p. 63.

4. *The Economist*, April 2, 1994, p. 100. Also see "The Myth of the Japanese Middle Class," *Business America*, September 12, 1988, p. 49.

5. The most up-to-date statistics on a worldwide basis are available from the World Bank. See *World Development Report—2000* (New York: Oxford University Press, 2000).

6. Benjamin R. Barber, "Jihad vs. McWorld," *The Atlantic*, March 1992, pp. 53–56, 58–63.

7. See Jonathan Friedland, "U.S. Phone Giants Find Telmex Can Be a Bruising Competitor," *The Wall Street Journal*, October 23, 1998, p. A1.

8. Information was obtained from BMW Marketing Division in Germany.

9. Valerie Reitman, "In Japan's Car Market, Big Three Face Rivals Who Go Door-to-Door," *The Wall Street Journal*, September 28, 1994, p.1.

10. "Upbeat in Brazil," *Country Monitor*, February 9, 2000, p. 1.

11. *Crossborder Monitor*, January 21, 1998, p. 2.

12. "U.S.-Based MNCs say Weak Dollar Is Nothing to Cry About," *Crossborder Monitor*, July 20, 1994, p. 1.

13. C.P. Rao, M. Krishna Erramilli, and Gopala K. Ganesh, "Impact of Domestic Recession on Export Marketing Behavior," *International Marketing Review* 7, no. 2 (1990): 54–65.

14. See Jeremy Main, "How to Go Global and Why," *Fortune*, August 28, 1989, p. 70.

15. V. Kumar, Antonie Stam, and Erich A. Joachimsthaler, "An Interactive Multi-Criteria Approach to Identifying Potential Foreign Markets," *Journal of International Marketing* 2, no. 1 (1994): 29–52. Also see Marie E. Wicks Kelly and George C. Philippatos, "Comparative Analysis of the Foreign Investment Evaluation Practices by U.S.–Based Manufacturing Multinational Companies," *Business Studies*, Winter 1982, pp. 19–42; Robert Weigand, "International Investments; Weighing the Incentives," *Harvard Business Review*, July–August 1983, pp. 146–153; and Philip Kotler and Liam Fahey, "The World's Champion Marketers: The Japanese," *Journal of Business Strategy*, Summer 1982, pp. 3–13.

16. "Adam Smith and the Wok," *The Economist*, December 4, 1993, p. 15.

CHAPTER 9

Cultural Environment

CHAPTER FOCUS

After studying this chapter, you should be able to

- Explain the meaning of culture, and describe its various aspects.

- Describe the impact of culture on product, price, promotion, and distribution decisions.

- Analyze cultural implications for a product or market.

- Discuss cultural adaptation.

- Explain the process of cultural change.

Doing business across national boundaries requires interaction with people nurtured in different cultural environments. Values that are important to one group of people may mean little to another. Some typical U.S. attitudes and perceptions are at striking variance with those of certain other countries. These cultural differences deeply affect market behavior. International marketers, therefore, need to be as familiar as possible with the cultural traits of any country they want to do business with. International business literature is full of instances where stereotyped notions of countries' cultures have led to insurmountable problems. More than any other function of a business, marketing perhaps is most susceptible to cultural error, since marketing by definition requires contact with the people of the country concerned. Practically all marketing decisions are culture-bound.

The effect of culture on international marketing ventures is multifaceted. The factoring of cultural differences into marketing mix decisions to enhance the likelihood of success has long been a critical issue in overseas operations. With the globalization of worldwide commerce, cultural forces have taken on additional importance. Naïveté and blundering in regard to culture can lead to expensive mistakes. And although some cultural differences are instantly obvious, others are subtle and can surface in surprising ways.

This chapter begins by examining the meaning of culture and goes on to explore its profound effect on marketing outside the U.S. Various elements of culture are discussed. A framework for analyzing culture is introduced. The impact of the sociocultural fabric of the host nation on different marketing decisions is explored. Following this, a procedure for cultural adaptation overseas is recommended. Finally, the impact of foreign business on local culture as an agent of cultural change in the host country is examined.

The Concept of Culture

It was the middle of October, and a marketing executive from the U.S. was flying to Saudi Arabia to finalize a contract with a local company to supply hospital furnishings. The next day, he met the Saudi contacts and wondered if they would sign the deal within two or three days, since he had to report the matter to his board the following Monday. The Saudi executive made a simple response: "Insha Allah," which means "if God is willing." The American felt completely lost. He found the carefree response of the Saudi insulting and unbusinesslike. He felt he had made an effort by going all the way to Saudi Arabia in order for them to question any matter requiring clarification before signing the contract. He thought that the Saudi executive was treating a deal worth over $100 million as if it meant nothing.

During the next meeting the American was determined to put the matter in stronger terms, emphasizing the importance of his board's meeting. But the Arabs again ignored the issue of signing the contract. "They were friendly, appeared happy and calm, but wouldn't sign on the dotted lines," the American later explained. Finally on orders from the president of his company, he returned home without the contract.

Why did the Saudi executives not sign the sales contract? After all, they had agreed to all the terms and conditions during their meeting in New York. But in Riyadh they did not even care to review it, let alone sign it.

Unfortunately, the U.S. executive had arrived at the wrong time. It was the time of Ramadan, holy month, when most Muslims fast. During this time, everything slows down, particularly business.[1] In western societies, religion is for most people only one aspect of life, and business goes on as usual most of the time. In the Islamic countries, religion is a total way of life for the majority of people. It affects every facet of living. Thus, no matter how important a business deal may be, it will probably not be conducted during the holy month. This U.S. executive was not aware of Muslim culture and its values and therefore scheduled a business meeting for the one time of year when business was not likely to be conducted.

Culture includes all learned behavior and values that are transmitted to an individual living within the society through shared experience. The concept of culture is broad and extremely complex. It involves virtually every part of a person's life and touches on virtually all human needs, both physical and psychological. A classic definition is provided by Sir Edward Tylor: "Culture is that complex whole which includes knowledge, belief, art, morals, law, custom, and any other capabilities and habits acquired by [individuals as members] of society."[2]

Culture, then, develops through recurrent social relationships that form patterns that are eventually internalized by members of the entire group. It is commonly agreed that a culture must have these three characteristics:

1. It is *learned*, that is, people over time transmit the culture of their group from generation to generation.
2. It is *interrelated*, that is, one part of the culture is deeply connected with another part, such as religion with marriage, or business with social status.
3. It is *shared*, that is, the tenets of the culture are accepted by most members of the group.[3]

Another characteristic of culture is that it continues to evolve through constant embellishment and adaptation, partly in response to environmental needs and partly through the influence of outside forces.[4] In other words, a culture does not stand still, but slowly, over time, changes.

A nation may embody more than one culture, each exhibiting fundamental differences. Canada has a dual culture: English-speaking and French-speaking. Two distinctive cultures also exist in Israel: a so-called western group consisting of European and U.S. immigrants, whose culture corresponds to their backgrounds, and a so-called Oriental group consisting of immigrants from Asian and African countries, most of them Arab-speaking Muslim societies. The contrasts between the two groups have been described this way by Abraham Pizam and Arie Reichel:

> The Oriental set of values corresponds to the values generally attributed to traditional societies described as: compulsory in their force, sacred in their tone and stable in their timelessness. They call for fatalistic acceptance of the world as is, respect for those in authority, and submergence of the individual in collectivity.
>
> In contrast to this, the norms and values of Israelis of western ancestry can be described as stressing acquisitive activities, an aggressive attitude toward economic and social change, and a clear trend toward a higher degree of industrialization. The oriental Israeli immigrants, having arrived later than the western immigrants, were expected to be absorbed in a western society, having a strong emphasis on specificity, universalism, and achievement.[5]

Cultural Field

Knowledge of a culture can be gained by probing its various aspects—but which aspects? Since culture is such a vast concept, it is desirable to develop a field for cultural understanding. From the viewpoint of a marketer, one way of gaining cultural understanding is to examine the following cultural elements within a country: material life, social interactions, language, aesthetics, religion and faith, pride and prejudice, and ethics and mores.[6]

Material Life

Material life refers to economics, that is, what people do to derive their livelihood. The tools, knowledge, techniques, methods, and processes that a culture utilizes to produce goods and services, as well as their distribution and consumption, are all part of material life. Thus, two essential parts of material life are knowledge and economics.

Material life reflects the standard of living and degree of technological advancement. Suppose a large proportion of a hypothetical population is engaged in agriculture. Agricultural operations are mainly performed by manual labor; mechanization of agriculture is unknown. Modern techniques of farming such as use of fertilizers, pesticides, and quality seeds are unfamiliar. The medium of exchange is a barter system, markets are local, and living is entirely rural. Such a composite description suggests that the society is primitive. Opportunities for multinational business in a primitive environment will be limited.

By contrast, consider a society in which the manufacturing industry serves as the major source of employment, and agriculture supports about one-tenth of the population. People live in urban centers and have such modern amenities as television, cars, VCRs, newspapers, and so on. Money is the medium of exchange. In such a culture, business across national boundaries would make sense.

The material life of any given society will fall on a continuum between traditional and industrialized poles. That position indicates a society's overall way of life and can be analyzed to determine opportunities for an international marketer. For example, Brazil and Pakistan are both developing countries, but the study of material life in the two countries would show that Brazil is ahead of Pakistan, offering market opportunities for electrical appliances, stereos, and television sets. In Pakistan, which is still emerging from total dependence on farming, agricultural tools would be more important.

Social Interactions

Social interactions establish the roles that people play in a society and their authority/responsibility patterns. These roles and patterns are supported by society's institutional framework, which includes, for example, education and marriage.

Consider the traditional marriage of a Saudi woman. The woman's father chooses the husband-to-be. After agreeing on a small payment for the bride, the two men hold hands in front of a judge to finalize the marriage. The woman sees her husband for the first time when he comes to consummate the marriage. The social role assigned to women in the strict Islamic world is one of complete dependency on men, whose authority and command cannot be questioned. A woman's place is always in the home. Outside the home, if women are seen at all, they are veiled. Karen Elliott House described the Islamic male and female ways this way:

> Moslems [sic] believe in the segregation of men and women, with the exception of husbands and wives and close family members. Men who are strangers to the family are not even supposed to see a man's female relatives. Moslems are not receptive to the western concept of liberation of women. Males are more privileged. It is not uncommon, as an example, to witness some Moslem males traveling by air in the first-class section of an airliner and their wives in the back, flying economy.[7]

Social roles are also established by culture. For example, a woman can be a wife, a mother, a community leader, and/or an employee. What role is preferred in different situations is culture-bound. Most Swiss women consider household work (e.g., washing dishes, cleaning floors) as their primary role. For this reason, they resent modern gadgets and machines.

Behavior also emerges from culture in the form of conventions, rituals, and practices on different occasions such as festivals, marriages, informal get-togethers, and times of grief or religious celebration.

Likewise, the authority of the aged, the teacher, and the religious leader in many societies is derived from the culture (see International Marketing Highlight 9.1). The educational system, the social settings (celebrations and festivities), and customs and traditions prescribe roles and patterns for individuals and groups. A good example is the caste system in India. A person's social and occupational status is determined by birth in a certain family or community. Such is the strength of social heritage that, despite caste discrimination being declared unconstitutional and legally punishable, the system still prevails, especially in rural areas.

With reference to marketing, social interactions influence family decision making and buying behavior and define the scope of personal influence and opinion. In Latin America and Asia the extended family is considered the most basic and stable unit of social organization. It is the center for all economic, political, social, and religious life, providing companionship, protection, and a common set of values with specifically prescribed means for fulfilling them. In contrast, the nuclear family (husband, wife, and children) is the focus of social organization in the U.S.

An empirical study by Chin Tiong Tan and James McCullough showed how cultural differences affect the husband-wife influence in buying decisions.[8] A Singapore husband, it was discovered, played a more dominant role than his U.S. counterpart in family decision making. Similar results were obtained in a study of Dutch and U.S. housewives.[9] The U.S. wife played a more autonomous role than the Dutch wife in family decision making. Thus, social roles vary from culture to culture and are likely to affect buying behavior.

■■■■■■   **International Marketing Highlight 9.1**   ■■■■■■

"The Flower Day"

Although professors in Thai universities receive very low salaries, they are greatly respected, at least in part because until around 1900, all educators were Buddhist monks. One day a year, there is a ceremony at each Thai university called "The Flower Day," which an American Fulbright professor describes this way: "Today students paid homage to their professors—a symbolic celebration of rather common significance to them. I found it an astonishing phenomenon. In a large auditorium, student representatives from each department crawled up, in the manner of Asian supplication, and gave beautiful floral offerings to their *Aacaan* (professors). Their choral chants asked for blessing and showed gratitude. Their speeches asked for forgiveness for any disrespect or nonfulfillment of expectation. They promised to work diligently. In a moment of paradox, I remembered I must not forget to pay the premium on my professional liability insurance this year."

Language

Language as part of culture consists not only of the spoken word, but also symbolic communication of time, space, things, friendship, and agreements. Nonverbal communication occurs through gestures, expressions, and other body movements.

The many different languages of the world do not literally translate from one to another, and understanding the symbolic and physical aspects of different cultures' communication is even more difficult to achieve. For example, a phrase such as "body by Fisher" translated literally into Flemish means "corpse by Fisher." Similarly, "Let Hertz put you in the driver's seat" translated literally into Spanish means "Let Hertz make you a chauffeur."[10] Nova translates into Spanish as "it doesn't go." A shipment of Chinese shoes destined for Egypt created a problem because the design on the soles of the shoes spelled "God" in Arabic. Olympia's Roto photocopier did not sell well because "roto" refers to the lowest class in Chile, and "roto" in Spanish means "broken."[11]

In addition, meanings differ within the same language used in different places.[12] The English language differs so much from one English-speaking country to another that sometimes the same word means something entirely opposite in a different culture. "Table the report" in the U.S. means postponement; in England it means "bring the matter to the forefront."

Language differences can affect all sorts of business dealings, contracts, negotiations, advertising, and labeling. A dentist's store sign in Hong Kong read, "Teeth extracted by the latest methodists." A tailor's store sign in Jordan advised, "Order your summer suits.

Because in big rush we will execute customers in strict rotation."[13] Coca-Cola Co., gained some important language information that warned it not to use the diet name in France: the word "diet" suggests poor health there. Instead, the company called its Diet Coke Coca-Cola Light.

Symbolic communication poses some cross-cultural dangers, too. To be on time for an appointment is an accepted norm of behavior in the U.S. A person is looked down upon if he or she fails to be on time. But in many other cultures, people are not particular about time and an appointment for 11 AM means *about* that time (see International Marketing Highlight 9.2). Greetings vary from culture to culture, encompassing the handshake, hug, nose rub, kiss, and placing the hands in praying position. In Chile, women typically greet everyone, even strangers, with a kiss on one cheek. In Brazil, it is kisses on both cheeks. In Spain, in business circles, one had better become friends before kissing or even patting someone on the shoulder.[14] Lack of awareness concerning a country's accepted form of greeting can lead to awkward encounters and sometimes offended feelings.

<hr>

International Marketing Highlight 9.2

Being on Time

Attitudes toward punctuality vary greatly from one culture to another and unless understood can cause confusion and misunderstanding. Romanians, Japanese, and Germans are very punctual, while many of the Latin countries have a more relaxed attitude toward time. The Japanese consider it rude to be late for a business meeting, but it is acceptable, even fashionable, to be late for a social occasion. In Guatemala, on the other hand, a luncheon at a specified time means that some guests might be 10 minutes early while others may be 45 minutes late.

<hr>

Aesthetics

Aesthetics include the art, drama, music, folkways, and architecture endemic to a society. These aspects of a society convey its concept of beauty and modes of expression. For example, different colors have different meanings worldwide. In western societies, wedding gowns are usually white, but in Asia, white symbolizes sorrow.

The aesthetic values of a society show in the design, styles, colors, expressions, symbols, movements, emotions, and postures valued and preferred in a particular culture. These attributes have an impact on the design and promotion of different products.

Likewise, space, and the way that a person occupies it, communicates something about social position in the terms of each culture. A large office on the top floor of a building in the U.S. means that the person occupying that office is important in an organizational hierarchy. Such a conclusion elsewhere would not always be right. Japanese executives usually share an office.

In the U.S., worldly possessions and material things are often used as symbols of success. A Lincoln Continental or a Mercedes automobile signifies achievement. However, in many countries, owning such expensive automobiles would not command respect. Particularly in the Islamic countries, an emphasis on material possessions is frowned upon.

In many situations the symbolic language of communication is more important than the actual words, and people respond accordingly. Therefore, an international businessperson must understand nonverbal cultural differences to avoid communicating the wrong message.

Religion and Faith

Religion influences a culture's outlook on life, its meaning and concept. Islam considers emphasis on material wealth ignoble. In Christianity, particularly in western cultures, the ideal of people taking dominion of the earthly environment has combined with the Calvinist ethic of hard work and success to promote the idea of the acquisition of wealth as a measure of achievement. Hinduism, while it places no sanction on the acquisition of wealth, is fatalistic about the acquisition of riches. In general, the religion practiced in a society influences the emphasis placed on material life, which in turn affects the attitudes toward owning and using goods and services. Religious traditions may even prohibit the use of certain goods and services altogether.[15] For example, Hinduism prescribes vegetarianism, with special stress on abstinence from beef. Islam forbids the eating of pork.

A fatalistic belief leads Asians to choose an auspicious time to buy a car or to plan a wedding. Car salespeople in Japan deliver a car to a consumer on a lucky day; contractors check for an auspicious day before breaking ground; and insurance salespeople are careful to pick a good day for obtaining a customer's signature on a life insurance policy.[16]

Religion also influences male-female roles, as well as societal institutions and customs such as marriage and funeral rites. Islam assigns women an inferior role and restricts their activities to the household. Whereas a Muslim man may have more than one wife, a woman must practice monogamy.

Religion affects patterns of living in various other ways. It establishes authority relationships, an individual's duties and responsibilities both in childhood and as an adult, and the sanctity of different acts such as hygiene. In the name of religion, Iranians in 1979 disrupted their whole country.[17] The Catholic church officially continues to prohibit the use of birth control devices. Animism, a religion emphasizing magic and practiced in many parts of Africa, demands human sacrifices.

In general, organized religion and faith inevitably motivate people and their customs in numerous ways. The impact of religion is continuous and profound (see International Marketing Highlight 9.3). Consequently, international marketers must be sensitive to the religious principles of each host country (see International Marketing Highlight 9.4).

International Marketing Highlight 9.3

Cultural Diversity

When a manager from the dominant U.S. culture saw two Arab-American employees arguing, he figured he had better stay out of it. But the employees *expected* a third-party intermediary, or *wasta* in Arabic, and without one the incident blew up.

The expectation goes back to the Koran and Bedouin tradition. While the dominant American culture is likely to take an individualistic, win-lose approach and emphasize privacy, Arab-Americans tend to value a win-win result that preserves group harmony but often requires mediation.

A Latino manager starts a budget-planning meeting by chatting casually and checking with his new staff on whether everyone can get together after work. His non-Latino boss frets over the delay and wonders why he doesn't get straight to the numbers. Latino culture teaches that building relationships is often critical to working together, while the dominant American culture encourages "getting down to business."

Source: The Wall Street Journal, September 12, 1990, p. B1.

International Marketing Highlight 9.4

Laziza Rises Again

The Arab world is not a good place to sell beer. Islam, the main religion in all Arab countries, prohibits alcohol, and many states—Saudi Arabia, Kuwait, and several of the United Arab Emirates, among others—ban it outright. Elsewhere, booze is sold only in windowless bars in posh hotels, or by bureaucratic state-owned firms. Even Lebanon, the country with the loosest living and freest markets in the region, consumes a mere 3.5m cases of beer each year. Big western exporters have little time for the area. So why is Laziza, a long-defunct Lebanese beer brand, relaunching itself with plans for a grand expansion?

The answer lies in a clever marketing ploy. From its founding in 1931 until stray civil-war shells peppered the company's brewery and forced a halt in production in 1990, Laziza was Lebanon's foremost brand of beer. Many of the Gulf Arabs who poured into Beirut in the 1960s and 1970s for a spot of debauchery acquired a taste for it. Their successors, who have taken to visiting Lebanon again since the end of the civil war in 1991, are doubtless also succumbing to the charms of Lebanese beer. But they could not indulge the habit at home until Georges Khawam, grandson of Laziza's founder, hit on the idea of relaunching the brand with a nonalcoholic line for export.

Laziza reappeared in Beirut's stores and bars in May, where it has quickly captured a third of the market, according to Mr. Khawam. Within a year, he hopes to be selling in Saudi Arabia, Bahrain, Qatar, Syria, Jordan and the UAE. He is also shipping to Britain and France, where the Arabic name (meaning delicious or delightful) and Lebanese pedigree should appeal to expatriate Arabs. Since he has subcontracted local production to Bavaria, a Dutch-owed brewery, his investment has been small; but if the Arabs get a taste for Laziza he might even consider spending the $15m needed to refurbish the old shell-scarred brewery in Beirut.

Source: The Economist, June 26, 1999.

Pride and Prejudice	Even the culture most backward in the eyes of a westerner will foster a certain pride in its people about its traits and ways. Indeed, developing countries sometimes evince more pride—and prejudice— than developed countries. The Chinese are jealous of their cultural heritage, and they speak of it with great emotion. So do the Egyptians of their heritage. In contrast, many Americans express feelings of being deprived of cultural history in a country so young and diverse by nature (see International Marketing Highlight 9.5).

Cultural pride and prejudice make many nations reject foreign ideas and imported products. But the reverse also occurs: a perception of greatness attributed to another culture may lead to the eager acceptance of things reflecting that culture. For example, the Japanese are proud of their culture and economic achievement and prefer to buy Japanese manufactures. Yet the words *Made in the U.S.A.* marked on a product communicate quality and sophistication to the Japanese as well as to people in many developing countries. The Japanese respond to names. They like dealing with people of standing. It is for this reason that Mead Corporation, which has successfully operated in Japan for 35 years, had Nelson Mead, the son of the founder, handle that business.

--------------------------------■ **International Marketing Highlight 9.5** ■--------------------------------

Cultural Islands

Japan: Boasts the strongest work ethic, exhibits the greatest concern about the work ethic of employees from other nations, and strongly supports free trade.

South Korea: Strongly favors protectionism, puts country ahead of company, encourages a corporate responsibility toward employees, and expresses optimisim about the future.

India: Expresses optimism about the future and strongly favors protectionism.

Hungary: Favors a different corporate organization than that found in other countries and emphasizes economic regeneration.

Source: Rosabeth Moss Kanter, "Transcending Business Boundaries: 12,000 World Managers View Change," *Harvard Business Review,* May–June 1991, p. 153.

Ethics and Mores   The concept of what is right and wrong is based on culture.[18] To be straightforward and openly honest are considered morally right in the U.S., even if feelings are hurt. In Latin cultures, however, people avoid direct statements that would embarrass or make another uncomfortable. Thus, even if a Latin businessman does not mean to do business, he would appear to participate, only later to excuse himself from the transaction process.

In an empirical study of U.S., French, and German managers substantial differences were noted on ethical issues. On an issue that may benefit the firm at the expense of the environment, the French and German managers were more likely to side with their employers and participate in what they perceived as a relatively minor infraction of environmental law. The American managers were less likely to approve a production run that would result in illegal air pollution.[19]

The differences in mannerisms between the Japanese and the Koreans also illustrate this point. The Japanese are formal and reserved; the Koreans informal and outgoing. A Korean saleswoman puts her hand on a customer's shoulder as she walks him to the door; a Korean executive invites a business acquaintance home to meet the family. Such acts of familiarity would be very unusual in Japan.[20]

John L. Graham noted that culture has significant influence on the process of business negotiations conducted by the executives in the U.S., Japan, and Brazil.[21] His study revealed substantial differences in bargaining style across the three cultures. Brazilians made fewer commitments and more demands. Their first offers were more greedy. Americans were more apt to offer a fair price, one that was closer to the eventual solution. Japanese consistently asked for higher profit solutions when making the initial offer in a negotiation. (see International Marketing Highlight 9.6).

Culture and Marketing

Culture influences every aspect of marketing. Exhibit 9.1 illustrates the linkages between culture and marketing action. A marketing-oriented firm makes decisions based on customer perspectives which determine customers' actions and are shaped by customers' lifestyles and behavior patterns. The products that people buy, the attributes that they value, and the principals whose opinions they accept, are all culture-based choices. It is not an overstatement to say that a person's perspectives or resources, problems, and opportunities to a considerable extent are generated and conditioned by culture (see International Marketing Highlight 9.7).

███████   **International Marketing Highlight 9.6**   ███████

Why Can't People Do Things the American Way?

Bill Hastings, the assistant director of marketing for a small American manufacturing company, visited Bangkok to investigate the possibility of distributing the company's products in Southeast Asia. Bill traveled with Cheryl Acosta, field director for the company's international operations. Neither of them had any prior experience in Asia. Bill, in fact, had never traveled outside the U.S. Both executives felt mildly apprehensive about being neophytes in the field, but they felt great excitement, too, as if they were the first explorers in an uncharted area. (Neither acknowledged that their counterparts in other companies probably had had years of international experience and had developed a mastery of Southeast Asian business practices.)

Bill and Cheryl attempted to complete a 12-country marketing study in six weeks. Bill figured that once he obtained the facts and made a quick decision on how to proceed, sales would start rolling in. But they found the environment baffling and made little head-

EXHIBIT 9.1   Impact of Culture on Marketing Decisions

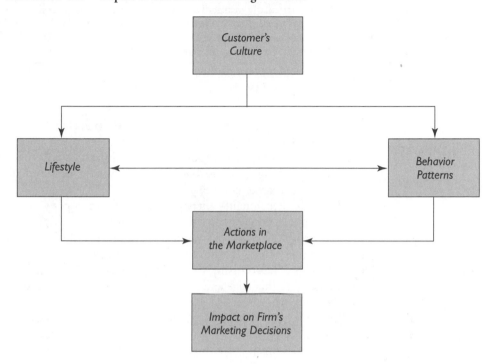

way. Frustrated, they impulsively recommended a plan to headquarters that ended in a fiasco one year later.

"I can't understand what happened," Bill reflected in the aftermath. "The same method worked just fine when we started operations in Los Angeles."

A good example of cultural impact is found in the foods that people prefer. Of all the universals that constitute "culture," few, if any, are so ingrained and consistently reinforced as food habits. The daily physiological requirement of nutrition in some form exists for every human inhabitant in any society or culture—there is no escape from eating for an extended period. Food consumption, acquisition, and preparation also are interrelated with many of the other universals of the culture, including religious observances and ceremonies, feasting, folklore, and the division of labor.

International Marketing Highlight 9.7

Embarrassment in the Air

United Airlines' experiences in the Pacific market show how embarrassing cultural mistakes can be. One of the airline's officials reported the following:

> The map we inserted into our sales promotion brochure left out one of Japan's main islands. Our magazine ad campaign, "We Know the Orient," listed the names of Far Eastern countries below pictures of local coins. Unfortunately, the coins didn't match up with the countries.
>
> I leave to your imagination how Chinese businessmen felt taking off from Hong Kong during the inauguration of our concierge services for first-class passengers. To mark the occasion, each concierge was proudly wearing a white carnation . . . a well-known Oriental symbol of death.
>
> Perhaps the most embarrassing mistake was our in-flight magazine cover that showed Australian actor Paul Hogan wandering through the Outback. The caption read, "Paul Hogan Camps It Up." Hogan's lawyer was kind enough to phone us long distance from Sydney to let us

know that "camps it up" is Australian slang for "flaunts his homosexuality." The Paul Hogan story is particularly instructive. Americans often assume that the folks Down Under are just like Americans because we all speak English. This does not make for happy customers. Australians expect real cream in their coffee—not artificial whitener. And the American hand gesture for "thumbs up" has quite a different meaning Down Under. It does *not* mean "OK."

Source: John R. Zeeman, "Service—The Cutting Edge of Global Competition: What United Is Learning in the Pacific," a presentation before the Academy of International Business, Chicago, Illinois, November 14, 1987.

The human perception of edibile desirability has little to do with actual nutritional fulfillments. Culture creates the system of communication among humans about edibility, toxicity, and repleteness in regard to food. Cultural pressures easily overrule physiological necessities, making it impossible for an individual from one culture to predict the food preferences of another culture.

Consider McDonald's entry into India. The company had to deal with (1) a market that is 60 percent vegetarian, (2) an aversion to either beef or pork among the minority meat eaters, (3) a hostility to frozen meat and fish, and (4) the general Indian fondness for spice with everything. To satisfy such tastes, McDonald's had to do more than provide the right burgers. The company serves vegetarian burgers as well as chicken and fish burgers, and makes sure that vegetarian burgers are cooked in a separate area in the kitchen using separate utensils. Sauces like *McMasala* and *McImli* are on offer to satisfy the Indian taste for spice. The company also introduced a spiced version of its fries.[22]

Although the trend is slowly shifting, drink preferences vary markedly across Europe: Germans still consume six times as much beer per capita as Italians, and the French six times as much wine per capita as the British.[23] And despite their geographic closeness, Japan and Korea couldn't have more different coffee markets. The average Japanese drinks 800 cups of coffee a year, a Korean about a quarter of that.[24] Marketing is also influenced by cultural customs in gift giving, which likewise vary from country to country. As explained by Kathleen Reardon, customs concerning gift giving are extremely important to understand. In some cultures, gifts are expected, and failure to present them is considered an insult, whereas in other countries, offering a gift is considered offensive. Business executives also need to know when to present gifts—on the initial visit or afterward; where to present gifts—in public or in private; what type of gift to present; what color it should be; and how many to present.

Gift giving is an important part of doing business in Japan. Exchanging gifts symbolizes the depth and strength of a business relationship to the Japanese. Gifts are usually exchanged at the first meeting. When presented with a gift, companies are expected to respond by giving a gift.

In sharp contrast, gifts are rarely exchanged in Germany and are usually not appropriate. Small gifts are fine, but expensive items are not a general practice.

Gift giving is not a normal custom in Belgium or the U.K., either, although in both countries flowers are a suitable gift if invited to someone's home. Even that is not as easy as it sounds. International executives must use caution to choose appropriate flowers. For example, avoid sending chrysanthemums (especially white) in Belgium and elsewhere in Europe since they are mainly used for funerals. In Europe, it is also considered bad luck to present an even number of flowers. Beware of white flowers in Japan where they are associated with death, and purple flowers in Mexico and Brazil.[25]

These descriptions are merely summaries; they do not encompass all trends, etiquettes, and traditions observed in the respective cultures. Each country warrants an in-depth report to provide meaningful data for planning a thorough marketing strategy.

Cultural differences always affect decision making when it comes to the product and its price, as well as to the way it is distributed and promoted. Lack of familiarity with the business practices, social customs, and etiquette of a country can weaken a company's position in the market, prevent it from accomplishing its objectives, and ultimately lead to failure.[26]

The Product

Two similar products are introduced into a country. One does extremely well; the other flops. Why? Although the performance of a product/market depends on a variety of factors, in many cases *failure is directly traceable to cultural blunders*. For example, Kentucky Fried Chicken was received well in France (as in Germany and the U.K.), but McDonald's stumbled.[27] The British prefer a wood handle on their umbrella while we in the U.S. find the plastic handle satisfactory, a fact that umbrella manufacturers have learned to heed. Procter & Gamble's Head & Shoulders shampoo did well in the U.K., the Netherlands, and Germany, but flopped in France because in France dandruff is a socially embarrassing problem that nobody wants to admit having.

A product that has been highly profitable in the U.S. may not achieve the same success elsewhere, because the product attributes desired in the U.S. may not be desired in another part of the world. The Campbell Soup Company found out the hard way that the condensed soups so popular and acceptable in the U.S. were not liked in England. Accustomed to ready-to-eat soups, the English consumer found it hard to believe that water or milk could be added to soup without spoiling the taste.[28] Phillip Morris ran into difficulties because of taste differences among nations. One of its popular brands was a dismal flop in Canada despite adequate promotion. Canadians have a preference for Virginia-type tobacco blends, which are different from what the popular brand had to offer.[29]

Sometimes a product that is unacceptable in its U.S. form may succeed if it is adapted to the culture of the new market. Mister Donut's success in Japan is the result of a series of minute but sensible modifications. Their coffee cup is smaller and lighter, to fit the finger size of the average Japanese consumer. Even their donuts are a little smaller there than those in the U.S. Similarly, Japanese mothers found the Beechnut babyfood jar too big. After the jar was made smaller, the sales increased. After years of painstaking market research, P&G finally realized that Japanese parents are very concerned with keeping their babies clean, and they change their children's diapers far more often than Americans do. In response, P&G devised Ultra Pampers, a more-absorbent diaper that keeps the child drier and makes frequent changing a less-messy task. P&G also discovered that in land-starved Japan, shelf and closet space is almost as precious to housewives as their children, so it made the diapers thinner so the same number fit in a much smaller box. The popularity of the new diapers spread rapidly, and today Ultra Pampers is the market leader in Japan.[30]

Another good example is the Barbie doll of cultural adaptation. This all-American best-seller did not do very well in Japan for a long time. Finally, Mattel Toys, its creator, gave the manufacturing license to Takara, a Japanese company. Takara's own survey revealed that most Japanese girls—and their parents—thought the doll's breasts were too big and the legs unrealistically long. After correcting these minor defects, and converting the Barbie doll's blue eyes to dark brown, Takara started selling the same doll under the same brand name and concept, and found that its production could not keep up with the demand. Takara sold some 2 million Barbie dolls in just two years. According to a Takara executive, dolls in Japan are a reflection of what girls want to be. With the target customer group in Japan being eighth-graders, the doll had to look more Japanese than the original version.[31]

In India, the Barbie doll had a slightly different problem. In a conservative country like India, the concept of a boyfriend was unacceptable, so Ken did not accompany her. However, since brothers and sisters in India are much closer than in Western societies, Mattel created Mark as Barbie's brother for the Indian market.

The positioning of a product in different countries should be in line with the cultural traits of each society[32] (see International Marketing Highlight 9.8). Renault's strategy in different countries illustrates the point. In France, the Renault car was introduced as a little "supercar" that was fun to drive both on highways and within the city. In Germany, where auto buying is viewed as a serious matter, the emphasis was put on safety, modern engineering, and interior comfort. In Italy, road performance—road-handling capacity and acceleration—was stressed. In Finland, the focus was on solid construction and reliability. For Holland, the Renault car had to be redesigned, because the Dutch consider a small car cheap and mechanically inferior.[33] The same principle about positioning and culture applies to the personal computer. American computer companies learned early on that they could not simply target Europe as one market, but must court each country market separately, acknowledging cultural differences. The French, for example, are very nationalistic, looking for more French-made parts in the product. The German market focuses mostly on high quality.[34]

Cultural attitudes toward risk sometimes require different marketing tactics. In Mexico, where consumers are influenced by fatalism, the belief that humans have little control in life events, the use of product warranties to reduce the risk of negative outcomes associated with purchases is less effective than in the U.S.[35]

International Marketing Highlight 9.8

The Marlboro Man

What do college students in different countries think when considering Marlboro cigarettes? A researcher at Northwestern University posed this question and put it to the test by researching college students in five countries: Brazil, Japan, Norway, Thailand, and the U.S. Small samples of students in each country participated in a word-association test by responding to the statement: "Smoking a Marlboro cigarette . . ."

Responses were sharply mixed. Thai students considered smoking a Marlboro cigarette to be relaxing. Norwegian students most closely linked smoking Marlboros to disease, and Brazilians associated the brand with pollution. U.S. students responded to "Smoking a Marlboro cigarette . . ." with words like "cowboy," "horse," and "macho"—all relating directly to Marlboro's longstanding advertising campaign. The Japanese associated smoking Marlboros with social occasions.

These different images point out that products and brands mean different things around the world because the cultural contexts in which they are interpreted vary greatly. This means that creative advertising needs to be adjusted to accommodate the specific cultural context in which it is placed. For example, because Japanese consumers associate Marlboro cigarettes with being sociable, it would be best for Marlboro advertisements in Japan to show the cowboy with other cowboys rather than by himself. In Thailand, where consumers perceive cigarettes to be suggestive of relaxation, it would be most effective to show the cowboy in a subdued context rather than chasing wild horses.

Source: Lenore Skenazy, "How Does Slogan Translate," *Advertising Age*, October 12, 1987, p. 84.

Distribution   The cultural dimensions of a nation make certain distribution arrangements more viable. For example, in the U.S., Sears, Roebuck & Co. merchandises a big percentage of products under its own brand name. In Mexico, however, Sears has done two things differently in order to respond to pride aspects in the local culture. First, it buys over 90 percent of its items from national manufacturers. Second, it carries U.S. national brands made in Mexico to cater to well-to-do customers who like to distinguish themselves by using U.S. brands.

Channels of distribution may need to be modified to suit local conditions. Avon uses door-to-door and other direct-selling methods in the U.S. with great success. Americans appreciate the opportunity to make buying decisions in the privacy of their homes or workplaces. Such arrangements, however, did not work abroad. European women considered calls by Avon representatives to be intrusions on their privacy, and the representatives felt uncomfortable as well.[36] The company faced a similar problem in Japan. To solve the problem, it had to reassign each saleswoman to her own neighborhood and social group, a milieu in which she already knew her customers or could get to know them easily.[37]

Another case of culture affecting the mapping of sales territories involved a French company in Africa. It decided to divide the sales territories based on market potential (respecting local administrative boundaries), something it had done successfully in the Western European market. This type of territory structure, however, did not allow for the fact that the African countries contained a number of tribes, each with a particular person authorized to buy in the community. The territory arrangements overlapped with these tribal areas and created a great deal of confusion in the assignment of sales responsibilities.[38]

Promotion

Promotion practices, particularly advertising, are perhaps most susceptible to cultural error. Examples abound where advertising copy and design were culturally repugnant and therefore totally ineffective. In Thailand the Warner-Lambert Company used its U.S. ad for Listerine showing a boy and a girl being affectionate with each other. This type of appeal was ineffective since the boy-girl relationship shown was ultra-modern and hence against the cultural norms of Thailand's conservative society. A slight modification—two girls talking about Listerine—had a positive effect on sales.[39]

Colgate Palmolive Company introduced its Cue toothpaste in France only to find out later that *cue* in French is a pornographic word.[40] Pepsi ran into difficulties in Germany for using its U.S. ad, "Come alive, you're in the Pepsi generation," which in German meant "Come alive out of the grave."[41] Pepsodent's promise of white teeth backfired in Southeast Asia, where betel nut chewing was an acceptable norm, and therefore, yellow teeth were taken for granted.[42] A P&G soap commercial showed a Japanese husband in the room as his wife was bathing. The Japanese considered it an invasion of privacy and distasteful.[43] An airline ad campaign urged Hispanics to fly *en cuero*. It is hard to figure out what the airline had in mind, given that the phrase means stark naked.[44]

Ajax's white tornado was not perceived as a symbol of power in many countries, Ultra Brite's sexy girl throwing kisses was ineffective in Belgium, and the company was forced to drop the theme "Give your mouth sex appeal."[45] Carlsberg had to add a third elephant to its label of Elephant beer for an ad in Africa since two elephants are a symbol of bad luck there.[46]

Usage of color in ads must be attuned to cultural norms as well. In Japan, as in many Asian countries, the color white is for mourning; purple is associated with death in many Latin American countries; and brown and gray are disliked in Nicaragua[47] (see International Marketing Highlight 9.9).

■■■■■■■■   **International Marketing Highlight 9.9**   ■■■■■■■■

Taboos Around the World

- Never touch the head of a Thai or pass an object over it, as the head is considered sacred in Thailand. Likewise, never point the bottoms of the feet in the direction of another person in Thailand or cross your legs while sitting, especially in the presence of an older person.

- Avoid using triangular shapes in Hong Kong, Korea, or Taiwan, as the triangle is considered a negative shape in those countries.

- Remember that the number seven is considered bad luck in Kenya, good luck in Czech Republic, and has magical connotations in Benin.

- Red is a positive color in Denmark but represents witchcraft and death in many African countries.

- A nod means "no" in Bulgaria, and shaking the head from side to side means "yes."

Source: Business America, Vol. 112, no. 2 (Special Edition 1991): 26–27.

Pricing

The price that a customer is willing to pay for a product may depend more on its perceived than its actual value. Since the value of goods imported from a western country is often perceived as much higher than that of domestic products in developing countries, the imported goods often command an inflated price. A story is told of an East Indian who on a trip to England bought an expensive sweater for his wife from a London department store. He was disappointed to find, on closer inspection, after returning home, that the sweater had been manufactured in India. What had seemed a reasonable price for an English product was too high for a domestic one. Perceived value, not actual value, was the determinant of acceptable price.

An empirical investigation by Philippe Cattin and his colleagues showed that U.S. and French purchasing managers attached varying degrees of importance to products manufactured in different countries.[48] For example, *Made in England* appeared to be favorably perceived by the French, promising more luxurious and more inventive products, than *Made in the U.S.A.* On the other hand, *Made in Germany* products were more highly regarded by American than French consumers.

It would appear that in countries where the image of the exporting country is high, a premium price can be charged. However, where a national image is weak, an international business could do well to deemphasize "made in" information and perhaps seek market entry through a joint venture or some other form of close association with a domestic firm.

Cultural Analysis—The Primacy-of-Host-Country Viewpoint

The analysis of cultural differences is necessary for the formulation of international marketing strategy. Conceptually, cultural analysis may be based on any of the following three approaches: ethnocentrism, assimilation, and primacy-of-host-country viewpoint.

The *ethnocentrism approach* assumes, "We are the best." Many U.S. companies assume that what is good at home will work in foreign markets as well. The examples discussed in the previous section illustrate how ethnocentrism can lead to costly mistakes. The *assimilation approach* is somewhat similar, assuming that since the U.S. is a cultural melting pot, the cultural traits demonstrated in U.S. society are relevant anywhere. The third viewpoint, the *primacy-of-host-country approach*, bases decisions on the cultural traits of the host country. This approach considers domestic information inappropriate to successful operation in markets outside the U.S. The discussion that follows assumes the primacy-of-host-country viewpoint.

Assessment of Culture

An assessment of a country's culture for marketing's sake involves analyzing the people's attitudes, motivations, perceptions, and learning processes. Exhibit 9.2 summarizes more specifically the cultural determinants. The information contained in this exhibit attempts to relate cultural traits to marketing decisions. For example, simply knowing about the religion or morality of a culture is not enough. What must be analyzed is whether or not

▆▆▆▆▆▆▆▆▆▆▆▆▆   **EXHIBIT 9.2**   Outline of Cross-Cultural Analysis of Consumer Behavior

1. **Determine relevant motivations in the culture.** What needs are fulfilled with this product in the minds of members of the culture? How are these needs presently fulfilled? Do members of this culture readily recognize these needs?

2. **Determine characteristic behavior patterns.** What patterns are characteristic of purchasing behavior? What forms of division of labor exist within the family structure? How frequently are products of this type purchased? What size packages are normally purchased? Do any of these characteristic behaviors conflict with behavior expected for this product? How strongly ingrained are the behavior patterns that conflict with those needed for distribution of this product?

3. **Determine what broad cultural values are relevant to this product.** Are there strong values about work, morality, religion, family relations, and so on, that relate to this product? Does this product connote attributes that are in conflict with these cultural values? Can conflicts with values be avoided by changing the product? Are there positive values in this culture with which the product might be identified?

4. **Determine characteristic forms of decision making.** Do members of the culture display a studied approach to decisions concerning innovations or an impulsive approach? What is the form of the decision process? Upon what information sources do members of the culture rely? Do members of the culture tend to be rigid or flexible in the acceptance of new ideas? What criteria do they use in evaluating alternatives?

5. **Evaluate promotion methods appropriate to the culture.** What role does advertising occupy in the culture? What themes, words, or illustrations are taboo? What language problems exist in present markets that cannot be translated into this culture? What types of salespeople are accepted by members of the culture? Are such salespeople available?

6. **Determine appropriate institutions for this product in the minds of consumers.** What types of retailers and intermediary institutions are available? What services do these institutions offer that are expected by the consumer? What alternatives are available for obtaining services needed for the product but not offered by existing institutions? How are various types of retailers regarded by consumers? What alternatives are available for obtaining services needed for the product but not offered by existing institutions? How are various types of retailers regarded by consumers? Will changes in the distribution structure be readily accepted?

Source: James F. Engel, Roger D. Blackwell, and David T. Kollat, *Consumer Behavior,* 3rd ed. (Hinsdale, IL: Dryden Press, 1978), p. 90.

the product slated to be introduced into the country has any direct or indirect connotations that conflict with the cultural patterns of the society. Similarly, an examination of advertising themes, phrases, words, or expressions should confirm viability of promotional decisions.

The cultural values of a nation may be studied through either observation or fieldwork. *Observation* requires living in a culture over a long period in order to become deeply involved in its pattern of living. *Fieldwork,* on the other hand, involves gathering information on a set of variables relative to the culture. Although the observation method may be more desirable for a fuller understanding of the culture, from the standpoint of business it is impractical. The study of culture in the realm of international marketing must be based on fieldwork.

One way to conduct the cultural analysis of a country for the purpose of making marketing decisions is to answer the specific marketing-related questions raised by Engel and his colleagues in Exhibit 9.2.

A different way of understanding foreign cultures is recommended by Edward T. Hall.[49] His framework, which he calls a *map of culture,* is a two-dimensional matrix containing different human activities, which he calls *primary message systems.* These activities are interaction, association, subsistence, bisexuality, territoriality, temporality, learning, play, defense, and exploitation. Exhibit 9.3 explains briefly the 10 primary message systems.

■■■■■■■■■■■■   **EXHIBIT 9.3**   Primary Message System of Edward Hall's Map of Culture

1. *Interaction.* The interaction with the environment through different modes such as speech and writing.
2. *Association.* The structure and organization of society and its various components.
3. *Subsistence.* The perspective of activities of individuals and groups that deal with livelihood and living.
4. *Bisexuality.* The differentiation of roles and functions along sex lines.
5. *Territoriality.* The possession, use, and defense of land and territory.
6. *Temporality.* The division and allocation of time and its use for various activities.
7. *Learning.* The patterns of transmitting knowledge.
8. *Play.* The process of enjoyment through relaxation and recreation.
9. *Defense.* The protection against natural and human forces in the environment.
10. *Exploitation.* The application of skills and technology to turn natural resources to people's needs.

Source: Excerpt from *The Silent Language* by Edward T. Hall, © 1959 by Edward T. Hall. Used by permission of Doubleday, a division of Bantam, Doubleday, Dell Publishing Group, Inc.

A person interested in learning about a culture need not study all 10 aspects, but by examining any one of them fully can gain an adequate understanding of the culture. Hall explains it this way:

> Since each [aspect] is enmeshed in the other, one can start the study of culture with any of the 10 and eventually come out with a complete picture. For example, to understand buyer behavior, a marketer could analyze the culture by examining the association aspect; association intersects with all other nine aspects just as they intersect with association. With each intersection, a variety of questions can be raised to gain cultural understanding. To illustrate the point, the intersection of association with learning may be examined by seeking answers to such questions as: How do different groups of the society learn about new things? Whose opinions are respected in each group? Similarly, the intersection of learning with association would be revealed in connection with such problems as how learning takes place through different sources in different groups.

The use of Hall's framework for international marketers is shown in Exhibit 9.4 in an analysis of the play activity for a toys and games company. Presumably, perspectives of play vary from one culture to another. To suit the marketing program to the cultural traits of the local market, Hall's framework creates 18 categories of questions (see Exhibit 9.4). For example, categories 13 and 14 deal with learning as it emerges in play and play as it leads to learning.

Hall's approach provides an overall perspective on the culture through analysis of one or two primary message systems. In relation to the needs of business, this system works well, because the time and expense for a comprehensive cultural perspective are not required. Only the particular element of the culture directly related to a particular international marketing decision needs to be analyzed.

Cultural Adaptation

Cultural adaptation refers to the making of business decisions appropriate to the cultural traits of the society. In other words, decision makers must ensure that native customs, traditions, and taboos will offer no constraint to implementation of the marketing plan.

Although the necessity for cultural adaptation is widely recognized, its practice is hindered by the tendency to use a ***self-reference criterion*** (SRC), i.e.: Whenever people are faced with unfamiliar situations, their own values are the measure for their understanding and response to the circumstances. For example, if someone in the U.S. is late for an appointment, that person will most likely feel guilty about it and apologize for being late—

██████████████   **EXHIBIT 9.4**   Business Application of Edward Hall's Map of Culture

Intersections of Play and Other Primary Message Systems	Sample Questions Concerning Cultural Patterns Significant for Marketing Toys and Games
1. Interaction/play	How do people interact during play as regards competitiveness, instigation, or leadership?
2. Play/interaction	What games are played involving acting, role playing, or other aspects of real-world interaction?
3. Association/play	Who organizes play, and how do the organization patterns differ?
4. Play/association	What games are played about organization—for example, team competitions and games involving kings, judges, or leader-developed rules and penalties?
5. Subsistence/play	What are the significant factors regarding people such as distributors, teachers, coaches, or publishers who make their livelihood from games?
6. Play/subsistence	What games are played about work roles in society such as doctors, nurses, firemen?
7. Bisexuality/play	What are the significant differences between the sexes in the sports, games, and toys enjoyed?
8. Play/bisexuality	What games and toys involve bisexuality—for example, dolls, dressing up, dancing?
9. Territoriality/play	Where are games played, and what are the limits observed in houses, parks, streets, schools, and so forth?
10. Play/territoriality	What games are played about space and ownership—for example, Monopoly?
11. Temporality/play	At what ages and what times of the day and year are different games played?
12. Play/temporality	What games are played about and involving time—for example, clocks, speed tests?
13. Learning/play	What patterns of coaching, tuition, and training exist for learning games?
14. Play/learning	What games are played about and involving learning and knowledge—for example, quizzes?
15. Defense/play	What are the safety rules for games, equipment, and toys?
16. Play/defense	What war and defense games and toys are utilized?
17. Exploitation/play	What resources and technology are permitted or utilized for games and sport—for example, hunting and fishing rules, use of parks, cameras, vehicles, and so forth?
18. Play/exploitation	What games and toys about technology or exploitation are used—for example, scouting, chemical sets, microscopes?

Source: Stefan H. Robock and Kenneth Simmonds, *International Business and Multinational Enterprises*, 4th ed. (Homewood, IL: Irwin, 1989), p. 426.

the value of punctuality and the importance of time have been instilled. The same person visiting an Arab country will be unhappy and angry with an Arab businessperson who arrives late and fails even to apologize. But punctuality is not given the same priority in the Arab world as in the U.S. To the Arab, a 9:00 AM meeting means *about* 9:00 AM. Indeed, it may mean simply some time in the morning. This is only one example of how the tendency toward SRC acts as a stumbling block to cultural adaptation.

Framework for Adaptation

A four-step procedure is recommended for checking the influence of SRC in business adaptation:

- *Step 1.* Define the business problem or goal in terms of the cultural traits, habits, or norms of the U.S.
- *Step 2.* Define the business problem or goal in terms of the foreign cultural traits, habits, or norms. Make no value judgments.
- *Step 3.* Isolate the SRC influence in the problem, and examine it carefully to see how it complicates the problem.
- *Step 4.* Redefine the problem without the SRC influence, and solve for the optimum business goal situation.

To illustrate the implementation of this four-step procedure, consider this hypothetical question: What automobile would be appropriate for the Pakistani market?

Step 1. In the U.S., the automobile is a necessity for most people. Two cars per family is an accepted concept. Highway systems are designed for speeds of up to 80 miles per hour, but the legal limit for many highways is 65 miles per hour. Gasoline of high octane without lead is conveniently available. Consumers look for comforts in the automobile such as air conditioning, AM/FM radio, cruise control, and leg room. Manufacturing techniques are sophisticated, and foreign exchange problems are unknown. Purchasers have a choice of buying either domestic or foreign-made automobiles. Introduction of yearly models of different cars is an accepted practice. Imports have achieved a significant share of the U.S. market and continue to challenge the viability of the domestic industry.

Step 2. Pakistan is a developing country. Over 60 percent of the people are illiterate and live in villages with muddy roads. Even in urban areas, the lack of modern roads restricts speed to 35–40 miles per hour. Gasoline is very expensive—the equivalent of almost $5 for a U.S. gallon—and it is only 60 octane. The country is committed to a thoroughly Islamic way of life. Islamic thinking is finding its way into economic, political, educational, and family life. The western attitude toward acquisition of goods and toward materialistic life is frowned upon. The rich have to live inconspicuously. The bicycle is the major mode of individual transportation and may be compared to having a good used car in the U.S. Some people, a little more well-to-do, drive scooters, smaller versions of the motorcycle. Automobile ownership is a symbol of status and achievement. Ownership of an imported car is the equivalent of owning a Mercedes in the U.S. With per capita GNP of $480 (1998 estimate), discretionary income is minimal.

Step 3. Review of Steps 1 and 2 brings out the significant differences between the two countries. Even the cheapest American car, say, a Geo, would not match Pakistan's needs. In brief, an automobile manufacturer interested in entering Pakistan may not be able to successfully penetrate the market simply by modifying a U.S. model. Pakistan's needs call for a new product concept.

Step 4. The company seeking to enter the Pakistan market will be obliged to design an entirely new car. Such a car should be simple in all aspects: lightweight; few, if any, castings; and no compound body design; capable of giving very high mileage, say, 80–100 miles per gallon, with cruising speeds up to 40 miles per hour. The car could simply be made of scrap iron with a low-powered engine and no frills. Such a car should be manufactured using local materials with minimum dependence on imported technology or parts. In other words, foreign exchange requirements of the project should be minimal. Overall, the price for the car would have to be around $4,000.

Pakistan is not the only country that needs such a car. A large majority of developing countries offer potential opportunities for a product of this type. Unfortunately SRC criteria, so deeply ingrained among western auto manufacturers, have interfered with the development of an automobile for poorer nations.

Areas of Adaptation

Essentially, there are three areas of foreign business adaptation: product, institutional, and individual. The *product* may be marketed abroad as is; or it may be modified to fit the foreign country's climate, electrical specifications, color preferences, and the like; or it may be completely redesigned to match local requirements—a $5,000 automobile for the developing countries would be an example. *Institutional* behavior includes adaptation of the organization and business interactions to match the host's perspective. Thus, the U.S. firm in Spain might allow the workers time for a siesta during the day.

Most important, the adaptation of *individuals'* responses to foreign situations should strive to be free of SRC. Such adaptation may be required in all regards—the meaning of time, social behavior, play behavior, family interactions, and more. For example, adaptation may require that the female spouse of a U.S. executive not accompany him to a dinner party in an Islamic country. Unfortunately, in international situations, each culture is so deeply imbued with its own values that only what is normally seen and done appears appropriate and right.

Appropriate adaptive behavior is necessary to the successful conduct of foreign business, but adaptation should not be misinterpreted to mean that a person should adopt the foreign country's attitudes and traits for his or her own. Rather, one should, by inhibiting SRC, gain understanding and develop a spirit of tolerance and appreciation of different cultures. Neglect of cultural factors will at best limit marketing success and at worst lead to failure.

Cultural Change

International marketers must not only become familiar with the culture of a prospective market and then orient the marketing mix accordingly, they must also be prepared for the fact that over time *cultures do change*.

This characteristic of culture brings up interesting possibilities. Products and services that were at one time acceptable may become unacceptable at a later time because of cultural change. For example, back in the 1950s the filter cigarette was rejected in many Southeast Asian countries because its basic for-health's-sake promotion over regular cigarettes made no sense in countries where the average life span was 30 years. After 10 years, the filter cigarette slowly began to gain more acceptance. To an extent, the shift in attitude toward this product may be attributed to cultural change.

Basis of Cultural Change
Different anthropologists specify different reasons for cultural change. Although it may be disputed, one way of looking at cultural change is through economic development linked to Maslow's hierarchy-of-needs theory. Maslow ranked five human needs from lowest to highest, with lowest needs being the ones that people try to satisfy first: *physiological needs* (food, water, shelter, sex); *safety needs* (protection, security, stability); *social needs* (affection, friendship, acceptance); *ego needs* (prestige, success, self-esteem); and last, *the need for self-actualization* (self-fulfillment).[50]

Maslow's theory as applied to cultural change goes this way: As a country begins to move from a subsistence economy, where fulfillment of physiological needs has been the major goal, to a situation where basic needs are easily achievable, new needs take precedence. This change forces cultural adjustments. In other words, as the economic well-being of a society satisfies one level of needs, it gives rise to new needs whose satisfaction requires cultural change.

Consider the role of an Asian homemaker. In a village economy, she would be fully confined to her home. However, a job for her husband in a factory in a nearby city enables the family to move to town. This move assures the family of basic needs fulfillment. There will be no more dependence on the farm for survival, but instead a weekly check. At this time, safety needs become important. Safety requires buying groceries at the factory store as soon as they are available. In many developing countries items such as cooking oil, sugar, and bar soap are often in short supply. Thus, while the husband is at work, the wife must shop. This new role for the wife represents a cultural change that results from economic prosperity. No longer are her activities confined within the home; now she can go out alone to shop, something that would have been culturally prohibited before.

Whether all aspects of a culture change when a single aspect changes is a question that may be answered by referring to Hall's classification of cultural aspects into formal, informal, and technical.[51] *Formal* aspects constitute the core of a culture. They are the most deeply rooted and are extremely difficult to change. Formal aspects are taught as absolute rights and wrongs. Nonobservance of formal aspects cannot be forgiven.

Informal aspects are traits that one learns by being a member of the society. Everyone is supposed to be aware of these aspects. If an informal aspect is not adhered to, an expression of disapproval or concern would be shown, but accommodation is feasible in relation to informal aspects.

Technical aspects are transmitted in the form of instruction and have reasons behind them. Change can be most easily accomplished in technical cultural aspects. So long as change can be reasoned in a logical fashion, no emotions stand in the way.

The definition of formal, informal, and technical cultural aspects will vary from country to country. For example, take the case of cigarette smoking among middle-class teenage girls. In India this matter would be concerned with a formal aspect of the culture and completely rejected. In Latin America it would be in conflict with an informal aspect of the culture. While parents might not like their daughters smoking, they might tolerate it after registering their disapproval. In Germany and Sweden a young girl's smoking could be categorized as a technical aspect. Parents might, on technical grounds, oppose smoking for health reasons. Once it is agreed that the cigarettes will be low-tar, there might be no objection to the girl's smoking.

MNCs as Agents of Change

A family's move from village to town, from farm work to factory work, illustrates how industrialization forces cultural change. A country may industrialize by exploiting its indigenous resources. But in the modern era, an important source of industrialization is the MNC. An MNC rapidly and effectively transfers features of one cultural society to certain sectors of another, perhaps very different society. In this process, it is uniquely capable of forcing cultural change.

MNCs transmit home country values in two ways: (1) through the vast network of affiliates, which introduce, demonstrate, and disseminate new behaviors while increasing and shaping the manufacturing sector of host countries, and (2) through the business service structure, including advertising and business education.

Millions of people in host countries work for foreign affiliates of MNCs. In early 1998 50 million people were directly employed by MNC affiliates in other countries. Today that number is even higher. These people, while living in their own culture, spend their working lives in a foreign environment. Foreign affiliates are in most cases highly integrated with the parent corporation. They are subject to close headquarters control through a variety of mechanisms, notably majority equity ownership, managerial control in key decision areas, and the presence of expatriate managers among the senior employees of the affiliate. Thus, the working life of the affiliate to a large extent reflects the values common in the corridors of the parent corporation. These affiliate employees may initiate, learn, and internalize new values and become channels to further diffuse these values in the host country culture at large.

The advertising media of MNCs is another avenue of transmitting cultural values in host countries. The move of manufacturing companies to foreign countries is frequently accompanied by a simultaneous move by advertising agencies. Of the top six advertising agencies in the world, five are based in the U.S. Therefore, MNC affiliates in their marketing efforts abroad have easy access to the agencies handling parent company business. These foreign agencies transmit and reinforce attitudes that fit nicely with the requirements of the MNCs. Change in the acceptance of advertising has been influenced by American practices. Today most European countries permit commercials on their broadcasting networks.

The role of advertising in the context of international marketing was summarized well by Paul C. Harper, Jr.:

It should be noted that advertising does more than merely sell products and form consumption patterns; it informs, educates, changes attitudes, and builds images. For purposes of illustration, we may quote the statement of a marketing manager who answered the basic marketing question, "What do we sell?" in the following way: "Never a product, always an idea." In other words, the function of advertising agencies is to seek "to influence human behavior in ways favorable to the interests of their clients," to "indoctrinate" them.[52]

Another interesting development is the spread worldwide of U.S. business education. Business schools, especially the Harvard Graduate School of Business Administration, have trained thousands of foreign students through professional education in business. Additionally, many U.S. business schools have aided in the establishment of similar institutions in host countries. The Harvard Business School alone has helped Switzerland, Japan, France, Turkey, India, the U.K., and a number of other countries in creating institutions for offering advanced education in business. In all these schools, staff and alumni from Harvard are an influential, if not dominant, group within the faculty, and in most cases, teaching and reading reflect a decidedly U.S. business philosophy. The coming generation of top managers in Europe, all more or less similarly trained to put the commercial interests of their enterprises above other considerations, are increasingly divorced from their particular national framework and reflect to various degrees the business philosophy of the top U.S. schools.[53]

These students, whether actually instructed in the U.S. or their homeland, generate and support ideas, values, and viewpoints that conform to the cultural traits revered in U.S. business circles. At the product/market level, they demand products and services in market categories where international marketers have traditionally had more experience. Included is a range of products from nutritious and more hygienically packaged goods to various kinds of household furnishings, appliances, and entertainment-oriented products. Also, new products are more easily accepted by people who have been educated by U.S. institutions.

Summary

The cultural traits of a country have a profound effect on people's lifestyle and behavior patterns, and these are reflected in the marketplace. *Culture* is a complex term, and its precise definition is difficult. Broadly defined, it refers to all learned behavior of all facets of life and living transmitted from generation to generation. Cultural differences among countries can be striking or subtle and should be zealously examined by the international marketer.

The study of culture includes material life (the means and artifacts people use for livelihood); social interactions between individuals and groups in formal and informal situations; language (spoken/written words, symbols, and physical expressions that people use to communicate); aesthetics (art, drama, music); religion and faith; pride and prejudices; and ethics and mores. Cultural traits account for such differences among nations as color preferences, concept of time, and authority patterns. For example, in western countries a bride's gown is usually white, but in the Far East women wear white during mourning.

Cultural differences have impact on marketing decisions regarding product, price, distribution, and promotion. One framework for analyzing culture is provided by Engel's questions used to seek information on the cultural differences of national societies. Another is Hall's cultural map, with its two-dimensional matrix using 10 human activities to generate a cultural analysis.

To conduct business successfully across national boundaries, marketers must adapt their products and promotion to local cultures. A four-step process for facilitating cultural adaptation guides the international marketer to avoid the influence of self-reference criteria (SRC). The tendency toward SRC reinforces the idea that what is good at home is good—and relevant—anywhere else as well. This type of thinking poses a big stumbling block to cultural adaptation.

A discussion of culture must also deal with cultural change. Cultures do change, though change is usually slow. Industrialization is an important factor behind cultural change. MNCs, through involvement in the industrialization process, serve as change agents in foreign cultures. Their worldwide networks of affiliates transmit the values of the parent corporation's culture. Cultural change also takes place as a result of advertising media and the internationalization of business education.

Review Questions

1. What elements of culture may be most relevant to marketing? Why?
2. How might a marketer of cosmetics assess significant cultural traits for his or her business in the Muslim world?
3. Americans share a variety of common traits with the English. Based on this assumption, will it be safe to conclude that the two societies have a more or less common culture?
4. Illustrate how an international marketer can use Hall's map of culture.
5. How has the spread of professional education in business affected local culture?
6. Describe how MNCs influence host country culture through their network of affiliates.
7. How could aesthetics, as an element of culture, affect marketing decisions in the international context?
8. Should an international marketer deliberately attempt to seek cultural change in a society?
9. Discuss this statement: "It is economic not cultural differences that count. Given the economic environment and income levels of the U.S., people in any country, Muslim or Christian, would follow the U.S. lifestyle and materialistic living."

Creative Questions

1. China has a large population, and its economy is booming. However, in 1998 cola consumption in the country was only 10 servings (8 oz. per serving) per capita. For a comparison, the consumption in the U.S. in the same year was 360 servings per capita. Apparently, there is a huge potential for soft drinks in China. Are there any cultural barriers that may become hurdles in realizing this potential? Discuss the nature of these barriers, and explain how they could affect cola consumption.
2. What cultural adaptations are required to make U.S. cars more acceptable in Japan?

Endnotes

1. "Making Do During Ramadan," *Business Week*, April 8, 1991, p. 18A.

2. Edward B. Tylor, *Primitive Culture* (London: John Murray, 1871), p. 1.

3. Edward T. Hall, *Beyond Culture* (Garden City, NY: Anchor Books, 1977), p. 16. *Also see* Edward T. Hall, "Learning the Arabs' Silent Language," *Psychology Today*, August 1979, p. 54.

4. Subhash, C. Jain and Lewis R. Tucker, "The Influence of Culture on Strategic Constructs in the Process of Globalization: An Empirical Study of North America and Japanese MNCs." *International Business Review*, 4, no. 1 (1995): 19–37.

5. Abraham Pizam and Arie Reichel, "Cultural Determinants of Managerial Behavior," *Management International Review* 2 (1977): 66.

6. Martin J. Gannon, *Understanding Global Cultures* (Thousand Oaks, CA: 1994), pp. 3–18.

7. Karen Elliott House, "Saudi Marriage Mores Are Shaken as Women Seek a Stronger Voice," *The Wall Street Journal*, June 8, 1981, p. 1. *Also see* "Marriage-Minded Japanese Turn to Mama," *The Asian Wall Street Journal Weekly*, August 24, 1981, p. 13.

8. Chin Tiong Tan and James McCullough, "Ethnicity and Family Buying Behavior." Paper presented at the Annual Meeting of

the Academy of International Business, Cleveland, Ohio, October 1984.

9. Robert T. Green, Bronislaw J. Verhage, and Isabell C. M. Cunningham, "Household Purchasing Decisions," *Working Paper* (Austin, TX: Univ. of Texas, 1993).

10. David A. Ricks, "How to Avoid Business Blunders Abroad," *Business*, April–June 1984, pp. 3–11.

11. David A. Ricks, "International Business Blunders: An Update," *B&E Review*, January–March 1988, p. 11.

12. Vern Terpstra, *International Marketing* (Hinsdale, IL: Dryden Press, 1983). *Also see* Robert Howells, "Culture Clash: An American's Guide to English," *The Wall Street Journal*, October 30, 1984, p. 34.

13. Ricks, "International Business Blunders," p. 12.

14. Susan Barciela, "Know the Customs of the Country," *The Hartford Courant*, March 14, 1994, p. 7.

15. Gillian Rice, "Philosophy and Practice of Islamic Ethics: Implications for Doing Business in Muslim Countries," Working Paper #96-5 (Glendale, AZ: The American Graduate School of International Management, no date).

16. "Before Buying Insurance, Consult This Calendar," *The Asian Wall Street Journal Weekly*, October 10, 1988, p. 8.

17. *See* Youssef M. Ibrahim, "Revolutionary Islam of Iran Is Neutralized by Policies of Bahrain." *The Wall Street Journal*, August 11, 1987, p. 1; and Karen Elliott House, "Rising Islamic Fervor Challenges the West, Every Moslem Ruler," *The Wall Street Journal*, August 7, 1987, p. 1.

18. Fred Seidel, "Comparative Business Ethics in Europe," Working Paper, E.M. Lyon, France, 1999. Also see: Alexander L. Nill, "Marketing Ethics in a Cross-Cultural Environment: A Communicative Approach," Discussion Paper series No. 99–1, Thunderbird Research Center, 1999.

19. Helmut Becker and David J. Fritzsche, "A Comparison of the Ethical Behavior of American, French and German Managers," *Columbia Journal of World Business*, Winter 1987, pp. 87–96.

20. Lee Smith, "Korea's Challenge to Japan," *Fortune*, February 6, 1984, p. 94.

21. John L. Graham, "The Influence of Culture on Business Negotiations," *Journal of International Business Studies*, Spring 1985, pp. 81–96.

22. "Spice with Everything," *The Economist*, November 22, 1997, p. 81.

23. *The McKinsey Quarterly*, No. 4, 1991, p. 6. *Also see* Philip R. Harris and Robert T. Moran, *Managing Cultural Differences*, 2nd ed. (Houston, TX: Gulf Publishing Co., 1987).

24. Damon Darlin, "Coke, Nestlé Launch First Coffee Drink," *The Wall Street Journal*, October 25, 1994, p. 42.

25. *See* Kathleen Reardon, *International Business Gift-Giving Customs* (Jamesville, WI: The Parker Pen Company, 1981). *Also see* Michael Lynn, George M. Zinkham, and Judy Harris, "Consumers Tipping: A Cross-Country Study," *Journal of Consumer Research* 20 (1993): 478–488.

26. Tevfik Dalgic and Ruud Neijblom, "International Marketing Blunders Revisited—Some lessons for Managers," *Journal of International Marketing* 4, no. 1 (1995): 81–92.

27. Susan Douglas and Bernard Dubois, "Looking at the Cultural Environment for International Marketing Opportunities," *Columbia Journal of World Business*, Winter 1977, p. 102. *Also see* Ian R. Wilson, "American Success Story—Coca-Cola in Japan." in Mark B. Winchester, ed., *The International Essays for Business Decision Makers* (Dallas: The Center for International Business, 1980), pp. 119–127.

28. "The $30 Million Lesson," *Sales Management*, March 1967, pp. 31–38. *Also see* Henry Lane, "Systems, Values, and Action: An Analytic Framework for Intercultural Management Research," *Management International Review* 3 (1980): 61–70.

29. Robert D. Buzzell, "Can You Standardize Multinational Marketing?" *Harvard Business Review*, November–December 1968, pp. 102–113.

30. *Fortune*, November 6, 1989, p. 86. *Also see* Patriya Tansuhaj, et al., "Across National Examination of Innovation Resistance," *International Marketing Review* 8, no. 3 (1991): 7–20.

31. Kenichi Ohmae, *Triad Power* (New York: The Free Press, 1985), pp. 102–104.

32. Jennifer L. Aaker and Bernd Schmitt, "The Influence of Culture on the Self-Expressive Use of Brands," CIBER Working Paper, No. 98-27. Anderson Graduate School of Management, UCLA.

33. Susan Douglas and Bernard Dubois, "Looking at the Cultural Environment for International Marketing Opportunities," *Columbia Journal of World Business*, Winter 1977, pp. 106–107.

34. L. Erik Calonius, "As a Market for PCS, Europe Seems as Hot as the U.S. Is Not," *The Wall Street Journal*, August 19, 1985, p. 1.

35. Robert J. Hoover, Robert T. Green, and Joel Saegart, "A Cross-National Study of Perceived Risk," *Journal of Marketing*, July 1978, pp. 102–108.

36. Susan Douglas and Bernard Dubois, "Looking at the Cultural Environment for International Marketing Opportunities," *Columbia Journal of World Business*, Winter 1977, p. 107. *Also see* Erdener Kaynak and Lionel A. Mitchell, "Cultural Barriers to the Full-Scale Acceptance of Supermarkets in Less-Developed Countries," a paper presented at the Annual Meeting of the Academy of International Business, New Orleans, October 1980.

37. Gary A. Knight, "International Marketing Blunders by American Firms in Japan—Some Lessons for Management," *Journal of International Marketing* 3, no. 4 (1995): 107–129.

38. Douglas and Dubois, "Looking at the Cultural Environment."

39. R. S. Diamon, "Managers Away From Home," *Fortune*, August 15, 1969, p. 50.

40. Howe Martyn, *International Business—Principles and Problems* (New York: Collier-Macmillan, 1964), p. 78.

41. *Advertising Age*, May 9, 1960, p. 75.

42. Matt Miller and Sundeep Chakravarti, "For Indians, a 2,000 Year-Old Habit of Chewing Red Goo Is Hard to Break," *The Wall Street Journal*, May 12, 1987, p. 28.

43. *Fortune*, November 6, 1989, p. 86.

44. "Catch As Catch Can," *World* 2 (1992): 2.

45. S. Watson Dunn, "Effect of National Identity on Multinational Promotional Strategy in Europe," *Journal of Marketing*, October 1976, pp. 54–55.

46. J. Douglas McConnell, "The Economics of Behavioral Factors on the Multinational Corporation," in Fred C. Allvine, ed., *Combined Proceedings* (Chicago: American Marketing Association, 1971), p. 264. *Also see* Arndt Sorge and Malcom Warner, "Culture, Management and Manufacturing Organization: A Study of British and German Firms," *Management International Review* 1 (1981): 35–48.

47. Charles Winick, "Anthropology's Contribution to Marketing," *Journal of Marketing*, July 1961, p. 59. *Also see* D. E. Allen, "Anthropological Insights into Customer Behavior," *European Journal of Marketing* 5 (1971): 45–47.

48. Philippe Cattin, Alain Jolibert, and Colleen Lohnes, "A Cross-Cultural Study of 'Made-in' Concepts," *The Journal of International Business Studies*, Winter 1982, pp. 131–142. *Also see* Victor V. Cordell, "Competitive Context and Price as Moderators of Country of Origin Preferences," *Journal of the Academy of Marketing Science*, Spring 1991, pp. 123–128.

49. Edward T. Hall, *The Silent Language* (Garden City, NY: Doubleday, 1959), pp. 61–81.

50. *See* Abraham H. Maslow, *Motivation and Personality* (New York: Harper & Row, 1954).

51. Hall, *The Silent Language.*

52. Paul C. Harper, Jr., "The Agency Business in 1980," *Advertising Age*, November 29, 1978, p. 35.

53. *See* Robert S. Greenberger and Ian Johnson, "Chinese Who Studied in U.S. Undercut Dogmas at Home," *The Wall Street Journal*, November 3, 1997, p. A24.

CHAPTER 10

Political Environment

CHAPTER FOCUS _____

After studying this chapter, you should be able to

■ Describe how political situations affect international marketing decisions.

■ Identify sources of political problems.

■ Discuss different ways that governments may intervene in the affairs of foreign firms.

■ Explain how the political perspectives of a country can be examined.

■ Compare alternative strategies a company may pursue in response to political intervention.

A thorough review of the political environment of a country must precede commitment to a new market there. A rich foreign market may not warrant entry if the political environment is characterized by instability and uncertainty. Political changes and upheavals may occur after an international marketer has made a commitment and has an established business. The revolution in Iran, for instance, exposed U.S. companies to potential losses of $1 billion and drove home the lesson that the political situation in a country must be reviewed on a continuing basis.

Political environment connotes diverse happenings such as civil difficulties (for example, the conflict between the rival tribes in the African country of Sudan); acts of terrorism against businesses (for example, kidnappings and arson); and conflicts between countries in a particular region, which may be one-time occurrences like the war between India and China or perennial problems like the enmity between the People's Republic of China and Taiwan.

Political stability has been found to be one of the crucial variables that companies weigh when considering going overseas. If risks of violence, expropriation, restriction of operations, or restrictions on repatriation of capital and remittances of profits are high in a particular country, it is necessary to know how to monitor that country's ongoing political situation. This chapter examines the effects of political conflicts and difficulties in foreign countries on overseas business and discusses ways to analyze politics and measure risk. Strategic responses to political change available to multinational marketers also are covered.

Politics and Marketing

A few years ago the French president François Mitterrand invited Apple Computer executives to lunch at his residence, Élysée Palace. The Apple executives jumped at the invitation, since for months they had been trying to sell their personal computers to the French government. The French government had authorized a $156 million purchase of teaching computers for the French school system, but Apple's foreign citizenship had hindered its efforts to get a piece of the order.

During the private, two-hour lunch, with a translator present, the Apple executives praised the government's computer program and offered to help in any way they could. But President Mitterand rebuffed them. Later one aide said that the president had invited the Apple executives to discuss technological cooperation with French companies, not the educational computer purchase program.[1]

How Apple tried, and failed, to get a significant share of the computer order is a revealing tale of international marketing and politics. The total order, for 120,000 microcomputers, was the biggest single purchase of educational computers in Europe and part of an ambitious campaign to teach almost everybody in France how to use computers. Although Apple at that time was the largest vendor of professional microcomputers in France, when the list of suppliers for the new program was announced, Apple received no order.

The head of Apple's subsidiary near Paris, a Frenchman, blamed the company's exclusion on lobbying by competitors and Apple's U.S. nationality: "The color of our passport is wrong."

On hearing about Apple's difficulties, the U.S. government complained to France about what it considered the unfair handling of the microcomputer order, raising the possibility of retaliatory moves in U.S. government contracting procedures. Other than registering its annoyance, the U.S. government did not pursue the matter, perhaps for political reasons.

Whether such nationalistic buying got French students the best equipment is a matter of debate. Yet this event clearly brings out the political underpinnings of international marketing.

The political perspectives of both home and host countries are inextricably involved in marketing decisions.[2] Certainly U.S. politics have significantly affected the U.S. automotive industry. Stringent requirements such as fuel efficiency standards have burdened the industry in several ways. On the other hand, governments around the world help the competitiveness of their domestic industries through various fiscal and monetary measures. Such political support can play a key role in an industry's search for markets abroad.

The U.S. auto industry would benefit from U.S. government concessions favoring U.S. automotive exports. European countries rely on *value-added taxes (VATs)* to help their industries. These taxes are applied to all levels of manufacturing transactions up to and including the final sale to the user, unless the final sale is for export, in which case the taxes are rebated, thus effectively reducing the price in international commerce. Japan imposes a *commodity tax* on selected lines of products, including automobiles. In the event of export, the commodity tax is waived. The U.S. has no corresponding arrangement. Thus, when a new automobile is shipped from the U.S. to Japan, it receives no rebate or relief of its U.S. taxes upon export and also must bear the cost of the Japanese commodity tax (15 or 20 percent depending on the size of the vehicle) when it is sold in Japan[3] (see International Marketing Highlight 10.1).

The competition facing U.S. manufacturers, therefore, both at home and in international markets, is potent and resourceful. Moreover, a number of these overseas competitors are wholly or partly state-owned and thus respond to the direction of their governments, which depend heavily on their export business for the maintenance of employment and the earning of foreign exchange. This fact makes politics profoundly important.

The ways in which politics may affect international marketing are varied. For example, in January 1985, Ford Motor Company divested itself of its auto operations in South Africa to take a 40 percent minority position.[4] At about the same time, Japan liberalized tobacco imports by lifting restrictions on price, distribution, and the number of retail outlets that can handle their products, thus encouraging foreign suppliers to intensify their marketing efforts.[5] In July 1985, Mexico approved the long delayed, once rejected, 100 percent IBM-owned microcomputer plant to encourage more foreign investment.[6] After waiting for several years, toward the end of 1988, PepsiCo got the Indian government's approval for a joint venture there.[7] In 1991, after much politicking, the French government permitted IBM to link up with France's state-owned computer maker, Groupe Bull, to develop high-speed RISC computer technology.[8]

■■■ International Marketing Highlight 10.1 ■■■

Politics of Smoking

The federal government officially discourages cigarette smoking in the U.S. But if people in other countries are going to smoke anyway, why shouldn't they puff away on American tobacco?

Armed with this logic, the Reagan administration strong-armed Japan, South Korea, and Taiwan to dismantle their government-sanctioned tobacco monopolies. This opened lucrative markets and created such growth for U.S. cigarette makers that skyrocketing Asian sales did much to offset the decline at home.

However, Thailand, with a government tobacco monopoly of its own, has been fighting U.S. pressure to open up, and U.S. tobacco companies approached the Bush administration to take up trade sanctions against the Thais. That raises many questions about U.S. trade policy, including: Should Washington use its muscle to promote a product overseas that it acknowledges is deadly? Are trade disputes to be decided by lawyers and bureaucrats on the basis of commercial regulations, or should health and safety experts get into the act? Should the U.S. use trade policy to make the world healthier, just as it does to save whales, punish Cuba, or promote human rights?

Source: Business Week, October 9, 1989, p. 61.

Conceptually, multinational enterprises are affected by politics in three areas: (1) the pattern of ownership in the parent company or the affiliate, (2) the direction and nature of growth of the affiliate, and (3) the flow of product, technology, and managerial skills within the companies of the group. Take the case of China. The impact of politics on the strategies adopted by MNCs there leads to one important conclusion: the strategic choices made by MNC affiliates are a response more to political environment than to the interaction of market forces or to technological innovation. In other words, the government can substantially influence the strategy of MNC affiliates in ways that were thought impossible even a few years ago.

In India many MNC affiliates had to diversify into areas where neither the parent company nor the affiliate had the core capabilities. Competence ceased to be an important factor in strategy formulation compared with the need to comply with political directives and regulations. In general, the transfer of product and technology from the parent company in order to exploit new markets in the host country meets with obstruction from the government unless the technology is in the areas specified by regulation.

Sources of Political Problems

Exhibit 10.1 shows that the two main sources of political problems for firms doing business in foreign countries are political sovereignty and political conflict.

Political Sovereignty

Political sovereignty refers to a country's desire to assert its authority over foreign business through various sanctions. Such sanctions are regular and evolutionary, and therefore predictable. An example is increases in taxes over foreign operations. Many of the developing countries impose restrictions on foreign business to protect their independence (economic domination is often perceived as leading to political subservience). These countries are jealous of their political freedom and want to protect it at all costs, even if it means going at a slow economic pace and without the help of MNCs. Thus, the political sovereignty problem exists mainly in developing countries.

The industrialized nations, whose political sovereignty has been secure for a long time, require a more open policy for the economic realities of today's world. Today governments are expected simultaneously to curb unemployment, limit inflation, redistribute income, build up backward regions, deliver health services, and avoid abusing the environment. These wide-ranging objectives make developed countries seek foreign technology, use foreign capital and foreign raw materials, and sell their specialties in foreign markets. The net result is that these countries have found themselves exchanging guarantees for mutual access to one another's economies. In brief, among the developed countries, multinationalism of business is politically acceptable and economically desirable.

Political Conflict

Many countries in different parts of the world undergo *political conflict* of various sorts—turmoil, internal war, and conspiracy that can be irregular, revolutionary, and/or discontinuous. *Turmoil* refers to instant upheaval on a massive scale against an established regime (for example, the Islamic fundamentalists' mass protest against the shah of Iran). *Internal*

EXHIBIT 10.1   Politics and Foreign Business

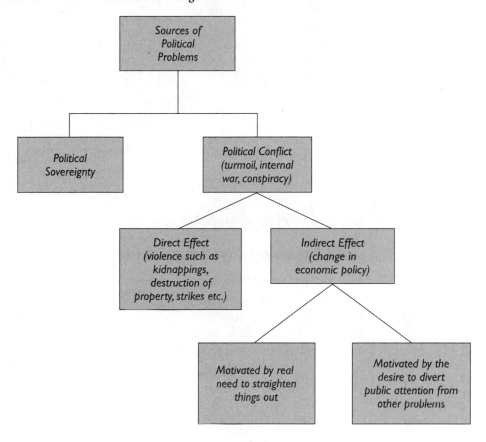

war means large-scale, organized violence against a government, such as guerrilla warfare (for example, Vietnam's actions in Cambodia). *Conspiracy* represents an instant, planned act of violence against those in power (for example, the assassination of Egyptian President Anwar Sadat).

Political conflict may or may not have an impact on business. For example, while the ouster of the shah of Iran incurred heavy losses for U.S. business there, the murder of Anwar Sadat made no difference to international business in Egypt at that time.

Political change sometimes leads to a more favorable business climate. For example, after the Peronist regime was overthrown in Argentina, the new government's policy was so favorable toward multinationals that the previously nationalized firms were returned to their owners. Similarly, Sukarno's departure from the Indonesian scene improved the business climate there, as did Nkrumah's absence from Ghana. After the assassination of Prime Minister Rajiv Gandhi in 1991, India's policy became highly favorable for international business. Suddenly U.S. multinationals found India an attractive place to do business.

It is important to make a distinction between political risk and political conflict. Political conflict in a country may lead to unstable conditions, but those conditions may or may not affect business. Therefore, political risk may or may not result from political unrest. Businesses must analyze each occurrence of political conflict and assess the likelihood of its impact on business.[9] Consider the case of the Philippines. During 1988 Communist threats posed insurmountable problems for foreign companies, although the economy had been doing well. For example, Dole's banana plantation there was attacked and two ware-houses destroyed. Yet, in the interest of long-term opportunity, Dole officials refused to take any drastic steps.[10]

Sometimes the conflict is in response to a particular political event that subsides with time, such as when disgruntled French farmers ransacked a Coca-Cola plant in a series of demonstrations brought on in part by U.S. pressure on Europe to reduce agricultural subsidies.[11]

The effect of political conflict on business may be direct or indirect. *Direct effects* would be violence against the firms in such forms as kidnapping an executive, damaging company property, striking, and the like. Overall, direct effects are usually temporary and do not result in huge losses (see International Marketing Highlight 10.2). *Indirect effects* occur because of changes in government policy. Such changes may come from a new atti-tude on the part of an existing government or from a new government. The changes may be motivated by a sincere desire to straighten things out or simply to divert public atten-tion from other domestic problems plaguing the country.

International Marketing Highlight 10.2

Executives in Peru Don't Leave Home without It

Herbert Dunn, a former police officer and SWAT-team member in the U.S., came to Peru in 1984 as a security consultant. He now teaches local executives how to defend them-selves in a terrorist attack—a common occurrence in Peru.

With two major terrorist groups and a variety of smaller ones carrying out bombings, killings, and kidnappings, security is an obsession here. In 1990 alone, political violence claimed 3,384 lives—more than were lost in Lebanon's civil war in 1990—and caused ma-terial damage estimated by one research firm at $3 billion. That's about 15 percent of Peru's gross domestic product.

Many top businesspeople, some journalists, and even usually sedate political scientists don't leave home without a revolver. Visitors to corporate headquarters routinely check their guns, along with IDs, upon entering. Factories are fortified bunkers, surrounded by high walls and barbed wire, with armed guards looking out from watchtowers.

Even some of Lima's Kentucky Fried Chicken outlets have three armed guards at the entrance—not, as one resident jokes, to guard the quality of the product, but to keep the stores standing after two bomb attacks this year. Terrorists "seem to have an obsession about fried chicken," says Bustavo Gorriti, a journalist. "They must think it's the food of choice of the American plutocracy."

Source: The Wall Street Journal, April 10, 1991, p. 1.

It is important to understand the nature of political conflict in foreign countries and the motivation behind government actions. If a change in government policy is merely for symbolic purposes, it represents less risk to foreign businesses. Also, when new policy is expressed through the imposition of certain constraints, requirements, or controls on for-eign businesses, it is important to assess the host government's administrative ability. Does that government have the capacity to promulgate and enforce the new policy? If such ca-pabilities are lacking, the new policy will remain a well-intentioned effort that produce no actual affects on foreign businesses.

Political Intervention

Carefully chosen overseas markets provide substantial opportunity but often with the risk of intervention by host governments seeking to further their own interests. Nations are not monolithic, or even bipartisan. Rather, they are composed of different groups, each of which is intent on maximizing its individual interests. In countries where foreign investment plays a significant role in the economy, the goals of special interests frequently bring on interference in the operations of foreign firms. If a foreign company is prominent in the economy of such developing countries as Zambia, Guinea, Iran, and Tanzania, the possibilities of government intervention are relatively great. Although such intervention is certainly not limited to developing countries, it is more likely there than in developed countries, which generally respond to foreign enterprise by establishing their own multinationals to challenge the foreign firms both on the home front and abroad. Developing countries may have to intervene directly in the operations of MNCs operating in their lands in order to pursue their own special interests.

Political intervention can be defined as a decision on the part of the host country government that may force a change in the operations, policies, and strategies of a foreign firm. The intervention may range from some sort of control to complete takeover, or annexation, of the foreign enterprise. The magnitude of intervention would vary according to the company's business in the country and the nature of the intervention.

There are different forms of intervention: expropriation, domestication, exchange control, import restrictions, market control, tax control, price control, and labor restrictions. The likely effects of these on marketing mix variables comprise the following:[12]

- **Product:** local content law, technology content, restrictions on the sale of some products, products' functional range, design of products, useful life, adaptability to local conditions, patent life, local manufacturing and assembling.

- **Place:** territory assigned, type of dealership, minority representation, payments to agents, products handled by different outlets.

- **Price:** transfer pricing, price ceiling and price floor, price paid for local raw materials, price contracts, price paid for imported raw materials.

- **Promotion:** local production of commercials, local artists, type of message, type of copy, availability of media, time restrictions on the use of certain media.

Expropriation

Of all the forms of political intervention, *expropriation* is most pervasive. As defined by Eitemen and Stonehill, it is

> Official seizure of foreign property by a host country whose intention is to use the seized property in the public interest. Expropriation is recognized by international law as the right of sovereign states, provided the expropriated firms are given prompt compensation, at fair market value, in convertible currencies.[13]

Other terms used interchangeably with expropriation are nationalization and socialization. *Nationalization* refers to a transfer of the entire industry within that country from private to public ownership, with no discrimination as to foreign ownership or local ownership. *Socialization*, also referred to as communization, differs from nationalization in that it is a transfer of all the industries within the country. *Confiscation* means expropriation without compensation.

Traditionally, patterns of expropriation have been differentiated according to industry, geographic region, type of ownership, technology, degree of vertical integration, asset size, and politicoeconomic situation. In an older study, Latin America accounted for 49 percent of all expropriations between 1960 and 1976, followed by the Arab countries with 27 percent, black Africa with 13 percent, and Asian nations with 11 percent.[14] A study by the United Nations of foreign firm takeovers between 1960 and 1974 showed that two-thirds of all takeovers were accounted for by just 10 nations, including Argentina, Chile, Cuba, Peru, Algeria, Libya, and Iraq.[15]

For a long time it was believed that ownership shared with host nations through joint ventures was advantageous. This belief has been proved wrong. For example, David G.

Bradley found that joint ventures with host country governments, as opposed to wholly-owned foreign subsidiaries, have a greater rate of expropriation.[16]

Technology can serve as the defense against expropriation, if the technology of the enterprise cannot be duplicated by the host country or cannot be made operable by the expropriators. Further, if a firm is vertically integrated with the parent firm so that the parent controls either the supplies for production or the market for the product, the firm is then an unlikely target for expropriation. Asset size also makes a difference here. A firm with total assets in excess of $100 million has a 50 times greater chance of being expropriated than a firm with assets of less than $1 million.[17]

The politicoeconomic backdrops against which expropriations have taken place have been associated with sweeping and violent upheavals that transformed the basic government structure and politicoeconomic ideologies of the nations involved. Signs of such upheavals being imminent should serve as a warning of expropriations being likely.

Recent trends show that expropriation activity has decreased over time. Many developing countries now protect foreign direct investors from expropriation. This change reflects their governments' shift away from an emphasis on ideologies and politics to a more functional need for economic development. In light of this trend, expropriations have become more selective, directed toward those foreign-owned enterprises whose policies or aspirations have collided with the economic plans and priorities of the developing nation. A recent study on the subject supports the conclusion that expropriation is unlikely to resurface in the near future as a source of MNC–developing country contention.[18] The broad-scale movement in developing countries to privatize state-owned enterprises also indicates that governments will not be eager to replace private-sector activity with state ownership. In sum, for the near future, significant expropriation activity is unlikely.

Domestication

Domestication, which can be thought of as *creeping expropriation*, is a process by which controls and restrictions placed on the foreign firm gradually reduce the control of the owners. Although domestication may lead ultimately to expropriation, in a way it offers a compromise to both parties. The MNC continues to operate in the country while the host government is able to maintain leverage on the foreign firm through imposing different controls. Domestication involves several measures, including

- Gradual transfer of ownership to nationals.
- Promotion of a large number of nationals to higher levels of management.
- Greater decision-making powers accorded to nationals.
- More products produced locally rather than imported for assembly.
- Specific export regulations designed to dictate participation in world markets.

From the viewpoint of the host country, domestication is preferable to expropriation. It provides the host country enough control to carefully scrutinize and regulate activities of the foreign firm. In this way, any truly negative effects of the MNC's operations in the country can be discovered and prompt corrective action taken, either through negotiations or through legislation and decree for further control.

Other Forms of Intervention

In addition to expropriation and domestication, there are various other means of government intervention in foreign enterprise, usually in the form of legislative action or a decree enacted in the best national interest. Although such intervention usually applies to both domestic and foreign businesses, a deeper probe often reveals that certain aspects of the law or decree are irrelevant for domestic business and are meant specifically to control foreign business. For example, a clause in a decree restricting repatriation of profits to stockholders outside the country would be meaningless for native companies. Following is a discussion of exchange control, import restrictions, market control, tax control, price control, and labor restrictions.

Exchange Control Countries having difficulties with the balance of trade often impose restrictions on the free use of foreign exchange. For example, import of luxuries from outside the country may be restricted. Similarly, restrictions may be placed on the remittances from the country involving hard currency. This type of *exchange control* may also be an effort to encourage domestic industry.

Exchange-control measures affect foreign business in two ways. First, profits and capital cannot be returned to the parent company at will. Second, raw materials, machinery, spare parts, and the like cannot be liberally imported for operating purposes.

Many developing countries utilize exchange control to regulate their hard-currency balances. The need for such regulations is one important reason for restrictions on imports of consumer goods (for example, cars, appliances, clothing, perfumes) in most emerging countries. Sometimes even developed countries may resort to exchange control. One example is France in 1981 after the socialist government took over.[19]

Import Restrictions Another type of government intervention, *import restrictions,* is primarily for the support of native industries. Consider a foreign pharmaceutical company traditionally importing certain compounds and chemicals from the parent company. If the host country places restrictions on imports, the company may be forced to depend on local sources of supply for these new materials. Such dependence on local supply can create two types of problems for the foreign firm. First, the local product may be of inferior quality, which would affect the quality of the finished product. Second, locally the product may be in such short supply that the pharmaceutical manufacturer cannot acquire it in adequate quantity.

Presumably, governments legislate import restrictions with the total industry and not a particular company in mind. Thus, the difficulties likely to be faced by a foreign company do not figure in the discussion. Further, when a country wants to encourage domestic industry as a matter of industrial policy, import restrictions are adopted with the realization that the local product will be inferior, at least initially. Strictly from the point of view of the government, import restrictions seem reasonable, but they ordinarily jeopardize the functions of foreign business.

Market Control The government of a country sometimes imposes *market control* to prevent foreign companies from competing in certain markets. For example, until recently Japan prohibited foreign companies from selling sophisticated communications equipment to the Japanese government. Thus, AT&T, GTE-Sylvania, and ITT could do little business with Japan.

The Arab boycott of companies doing business with Israel was an interesting example of market control. The Arab states had not accepted Israel's right to exist and hoped that the boycott eventually would bring about its collapse. Although many companies had given in to Arab demands, the U.S. government adopted strict laws to prevent companies from becoming susceptible to the Arab blackmail.

As another example of market control, in April 1998 China ordered all direct-sales operations to cease immediately. Alarmed by a rise in pyramid schemes by some direct sellers and uneasy about the big sales meetings that direct sellers hold, Beijing gave all companies that held direct-selling licenses six months to convert to retail outlets or shut down altogether. The move threatened Avon's China sales, of about $75 million a year, and put Avon, Amway, and Mary Kay's combined China investment of roughly $180 million at risk. It also created problems for Sara Lee Corp. and Tupperware Corp., which had recently launched direct-sales efforts in China.[20] (China withdrew the order after a little arm-twisting from Washington, and also because over 20 million Chinese were involved in direct sales, with more turning to the business as unemployment rose.)

Tax Control Governments may also impose *tax control* by means of excessive and unconventional taxes on foreign business. For example, a new form of excise tax for which there is no precedent may be placed on the output of a foreign firm. Such taxes are imposed for three reasons. First, an out-of-the-way burden on foreign companies is an indirect way of warning them that they are not wanted in a country any longer. Second, when a country is in dire need of new revenues, an additional tax burden on foreign companies appears not only politically prudent but economically convenient. And third, taxes can be retaliatory when a government learns that foreign corporations have abused differences in international taxation and have deprived the country of due revenue.

Taxes per se do not hinder foreign enterprise. However, problems do arise over excessively discriminatory taxes or taxes imposed at variance with the company's agreement with the government. For example, the host government may have agreed to give a tax holiday to a company—say, for five years—to establish its operations in the country. Three years later, though the government may choose to reverse its position for some reason, such as a new government's refusing to live with the agreement entered into by its predecessor.

Price Control For the sake of the public interest in difficult economic times, countries often resort to *price controls*. Even in the U.S., the price-control weapon has been used many times. President Nixon imposed price controls in the early 1970s to fight inflation. Likewise, many states control the price that a vendor may charge for milk. Until recently the price of gasoline was regulated.

Countries use price-control devices in various ways to improve their economies, by setting an official price on essential products such as drugs, heating oil, sugar, and cereals. Price control becomes a special problem if it is imposed randomly—for example, if a price limit is placed on a company's finished product, but the prices of the raw materials used in the production of that product are left to market forces. If the product of a particular foreign company has been singled out for price control without any economic rationale, such a measure amounts to undesirable intervention in the working of a foreign firm.

Labor Restrictions In many nations, labor unions are very strong and have great political clout. In these countries *labor restrictions* are an effective form of government intervention. Using its strength, labor may be able to talk the government into passing very restrictive laws that support labor at heavy cost to business. Traditionally, labor unions in Latin America have been able to prevent layoffs, plant shutdowns, and the like, even when business could not afford to meet such demands. Labor unions are gradually becoming strong in Western Europe. Germany and a number of other European nations require labor representation on boards of directors.

Foreign firms may find it difficult to accommodate labor demands transformed into laws. Even where there are no labor laws to comply with, there may be labor problems. Problems can reach such a level that the foreign enterprise is left with no other choice but to leave.

Political Perspectives

Given today's climate of global economic and political change and the experience of widespread nationalizations and expropriations in the 1960s and 1970s, there is a growing recognition in the business world of the need for a company to "look before it leaps" when considering entry into a foreign country. Any multinational marketer would be well-advised to make a thorough analysis of political risks as well as risks peculiar to the company's industry in foreign settings.

History shows that far and away the riskiest ventures are those in developing countries, where appeals to nationalism are most damaging to multinationals. On the other hand, these countries cannot simply be ignored by international marketers. For the U.S., the developing countries are increasingly important both economically and politically. They are major suppliers of raw materials, including, of course, oil; moreover, they constitute the most rapidly growing U.S. export markets. From 1994 to 1999 U.S. exports of capital goods to developing countries almost doubled, from less than $72 billion to more than $145 billion. In fact, taken as a group, developing countries (excluding OPEC countries) now account for more U.S. exports than the Western European countries.

During the recessionary period of the early 1990s, while U.S. exports to industrial countries stagnated or declined, exports to developing (including oil-exporting) countries continued to expand. Without that demand for U.S. goods, unemployment and production figures would have been far worse. In 1998 about 28 percent of $860 billion in direct overseas U.S. investments was in developing countries. The developing countries also accounted for around 42 percent of the $637 billion in U.S. bank claims on foreigners. Profits and interest from these investments and loans play an important role in offsetting U.S. trade deficits.

The political perspectives of a nation should be examined according to

- Type of government.
- Stability of government.
- Quality of host government's economic management.
- Change in government policy.
- Host country's attitude toward foreign investment.
- Host country's relationship with the rest of the world.
- Host country's relationship with parent company's home government.
- Attitude toward assignment of foreign personnel.
- Extent of anti-private-sector influence or influence of state-controlled industries.
- Fairness and honesty of administrative procedures.
- Closeness between government and people.

The importance of these factors varies from country to country. Nevertheless, it is desirable to consider them all to ensure a complete knowledge of the political outlook for doing business in a particular country.

Type of Government

World governments can be grouped in four categories: democratic republics, communist dictatorships, dictatorships, and monarchies. In each category there is a spectrum of variation. *Democratic republics* are formed through regular elections and have party systems. In the U.S. and England, two major political parties are active. Italy and France have several political parties. In Mexico, one dominant party controls. Although economic policies are an important issue in democracies, different parties hold different views on how the country's economy can be strengthened. In England, the two major parties. Labour and Conservative (or Tory), have different economic approaches. A Labour government usually seeks greater government control, while a Tory government stands for programs similar to those of the Republican party of the U.S.

Communist dictatorships control all business activity. Such governments exist in Cuba, the People's Republic of China, Vietnam, North Korea, and Burma. Communist countries maintain various types of ties with foreign business. Because China desires to achieve economic progress through using western technology and skills, the business climate there has been favorable. On the other hand, Myanmar (formerly Burma) has totally isolated itself from the rest of the world. The attitude of the Chinese government swings with changing events. It is convinced that the best way for the country to survive is to keep the screws on political dissent while it energizes the economy with free-market reforms.

Dictatorships are authoritarian regimes. These governments are run either by military dictators as in Pakistan or by civilian dictators as in Libya. Military dictators often eventually adopt a civilian posture, usually by holding an election that gives the appearance of a government elected by popular vote.

Authoritarian governments can be further categorized according to economic philosophy. They may be left-wing or Marxist-oriented, or right-wing and directed toward free enterprise. Angola and Nicaragua reflect, for instance, left-wing characteristics, whereas both Pakistan and Nigeria follow right-wing policies.

Finally, *monarchies* are governments in which the ruler derives power through inheritance. A country may have a monarchy and yet be democratic such as Great Britain, whose Queen Elizabeth II is titular head of the country but not head of the British government. But in many countries, the government is actually run by the monarch. Saudi Arabia and Jordan have monarchies. The shah of Iran was a reigning monarch. A monarch may have political inclinations to either the left or the right.

Any review of a country's political system and its impact on foreign business must remain free of stereotyped notions. Political philosophies change over time. Thus, what a government or a party stood for in the 1980s may not hold true in the year 2000. Both current and emerging perspectives need to be analyzed.

Government Stability

Many countries have frequent changes of government. In such a climate, a foreign business may find that by the time it is ready to implement an agreement, the government with whom the initial agreement was arranged has changed to one that is not sympathetic to the commitments made by its predecessor. Consequently, it is important for international marketers to examine, before making agreements, whether the current government is likely to continue to be in office for a while (see International Marketing Highlight 10.3). In a democratic situation, the incumbent party's strength or the alternative outcomes of the next election can be weighed to assess the likelihood of change. In other situations, a variety of symptoms could point toward governing instability:

- Public unrest (demonstrations, riots, or other demonstrations of social tension).
- Government crises (opposition forces trying to topple the government).
- Armed attacks by one group of people on another, or by groups from a neighboring country.
- Guerrilla warfare.
- Politically motivated assassinations.
- Coup d'état.
- Irregular change in top government leaders.

A report covering these points should be prepared to present evidence of a government's stability or instability.

Government Economic Management

Another factor to examine is the quality of the host government's economic management. A country that manages its economic affairs according to sound economic principles, whether through free economics or socialist policies, will, all things being equal, provide a more favorable environment than a country governed by political emotions and abrupt practices. The economic environment of a country should be studied in the political context with reference to

- The ability of the government to sustain its internal and external debt.
- The country's pursuit of stable and diversified economic growth.
- The country's ability to generate an adequate amount of foreign exchange.
- The nature of the various fiscal and monetary means used to steer the economy.
- The quality of the long-term planning of economic policy and its implementation.

As an example, a country that continues to live on borrowed funds, either from private sources or international agencies like the IMF, and frequently defaults on payments demonstrates poor economic management.

International Marketing Highlight 10.3

Change in Command

Sam Parry was the assistant director of a corporate team investigating the prospects of a manufacturing venture in a small Caribbean country. After six weeks in the field, the team received a request from the government to address the head of state and his cabinet about their proposal. The team spent several days preparing a presentation. At the last minute, however, the project director was called away; she assigned Sam to address the assembled leaders in her place.

Sam had spent enough time helping to prepare the presentation that he felt comfortable with it. He even practiced his introduction to the prime minister—the honorable Mr. Tollis—and to the prime minister's cabinet. Finally, the day arrived for the address. Sam and the team were received at the governmental palace.

Once settled into the prime minister's meeting room, Sam opened the presentation. "Honorable Mr. Tollis," he began, "and esteemed members of the cabinet. . . ."

Abruptly, the prime minister interrupted Sam. "Won't you please start over?" he asked with a peeved smile.

Sam was taken aback. He hadn't expected his hosts to be so formal. They always seemed so casual in their open-necked short-sleeved shirts while Sam and his team sweated away in their suits. But Sam soon regained his composure. "Most honorable Mr. Tollis and highly esteemed members of the cabinet. . . ."

"Be so kind as to begin again," said the prime minister, now visibly annoyed.

"Most esteemed and honorable Mr. Tollis—"

"Perhaps you should start yet again."

Shaken, Sam glanced desperately at his team, then at the government officials surrounding him. The ceiling fans rattled lightly overhead.

One of the cabinet ministers nearby took pity on Sam. Leaning over, the elderly gentleman whispered, "Excuse me, but Mr. Tollis was deposed six months ago. You are now addressing the honorable Mr. Herbert."

Source: Charles F. Valentine, *The Arthur Young International Business Guide* (New York: John Wiley & Sons, 1988), p. 400.

Change in Government Policy

More than anything else, MNCs dislike frequent policy changes by host countries. Policy changes may occur even without a change in government. It is important, therefore, for the foreign business to analyze the mechanism of government policy changes. Information on the autonomy of legislatures and study of the procedures followed for seeking constitutional changes can be crucial.

Attitude Toward Foreign Investment

Many nations look upon foreign investment with suspicion. This is true of both developed and developing countries. Take, for example, Japan, where it is extremely difficult for a foreign business to establish itself without first generating a trusting relationship that enables it to gain entry through a joint venture. Developing countries are usually afraid of domination and exploitation by foreign business. In response to national attitudes, these nations legislate a variety of laws and regulations to prescribe the role of foreign investment in their economies.[21] It is appropriate, therefore, to review a host country's regulations and identify underlying attitudes and motivations before deciding to invest there. Indirectly, the success of other multinational businesses in a country indicates a favorable climate.

International Stance of Government

Countries that maintain amicable political relationships with the rest of the world and have respect for international law and order show political maturity. These countries can be expected to behave in a responsible fashion. Iran serves as a negative example: in the post-shah period the government behaved erratically, without regard for international treaties and obligations. Uganda during Dada's regime did the same. Usually, extreme cases can be easily identified. For less spectacular situations, membership in regional and international organizations as well as adherence to bilateral and multilateral principles and agreements provides evidence of a country's relationship with other nations.

Relationship with Parent Company's Home Government

In theory, MNCs have no political alignment. Yet a company originating in the U.S. will continue to be known as a U.S. company even though it may derive a major portion of its revenues and profits from operations outside the U.S. Nestlé, for example, generates close to 50 percent of its revenues in the U.S. and only 4 percent in its home country, Switzerland. Nevertheless, it is identified as a Swiss company.

Thus, the relationship between the host country government and the parent company government will affect, either directly or indirectly, the MNC. International marketers should therefore trace the history of the relationship between the host country's government and the home country government before deciding to enter a market. Do the two governments agree on issues debated in international agencies? Are there any points of discord? Are there reasons to believe that relations between the two countries will improve or deteriorate in the future? (see International Marketing Highlight 10.4).

Attitude Toward Foreign Managers

A company making an investment in a foreign country needs to make sure that its business there is managed effectively. Among other factors, a crucial determinant of success in overseas operations is the assignment of experienced persons to key positions. But in a country where appointment of local nationals to key positions is a requirement, and where qualified nationals are in short supply, there are bound to be difficulties.

Anti-Private-Sector Influence

An interesting development of the post–World War II period has been the increased presence of government in a wide spectrum of social and economic affairs that were previously ignored by government. In the U.S., concern for the poor, the aged, minorities, consumers' rights, and the environment has spurred government response and the adoption of a variety of legislative measures. In a great many foreign countries, such concerns have led governments to take over businesses to be run as public enterprises. Sympathies for public-sector enterprises, successful or not as businesses, have rendered private corporations suspect and undesirable in many countries. Also, public-sector enterprises are not limited to developing countries. Great Britain and France have many government corporations, from airlines to broadcasting companies to banks and steel mills. An example is Airbus Industrié, a civilian aircraft manufacturer owned by the British, French, German, and Spanish governments.

Obviously, in nations where there is an ongoing bias against home-grown private businesses, an MNC cannot expect a cordial welcome. In such a situation, an MNC must contend with the problems that arise because of it being a private business as well as a foreign one. Sound business intelligence and familiarity with the industrial policy of the government and related legislative acts and decrees should provide clarification of the role of the private sector in any given economy.

███████████   **International Marketing Highlight 10.4**   ███████████

Copyright Struggle in New York

A copyright squabble in 1988 between two small companies in New York's Chinatown over videotapes of Taiwanese soap operas illustrates how a relationship between governments could erupt into a political problem. U.E. Enterprises Inc., accused of pirating the Taiwanese television programs, claims that Taiwanese nationals no longer are entitled to copyright protection as a result of the decision by the U.S. to recognize the People's Republic of China as the "sole legal government" of China in 1979. That decision, the defendants claim, negated the U.S.–Taiwan Friendship, Commerce and Navigation Treaty of 1948, which is the legal framework for trade as well as copyright agreements between the U.S. and Taiwan. The defendant's case relies on a complex argument that a law passed by Congress in 1979, purporting to maintain normal trade relations with Taiwan after recognition of the People's Republic, is constitutionally invalid because it effectively amended the treaty by changing the parties from the Republic of China to the "governing authorities of Corp., E-II Holdings Inc.'s Samsonite Unit, Walt Disney Co., and many others from the pirating of their products in Taiwan. Because of this the case received wide publicity.

Although the judgment was against U.E. Enterprises, the case highlights the significance of political relations between countries.

Source: The Wall Street Journal, October 25, 1988, p. B8.

Administrative Procedures

Every country has its own unique administrative scheme. The scheme emerges from such factors as experience, culture, the system of reward and punishment, availability of qualified administrators, and style of leadership. Additionally, the availability of modern means of transportation and communication helps to streamline government administration. Businesses often complain about the U.S. federal bureaucracy and its states' agencies, but if they were to compare U.S. administration with other nations', they would be pleasantly surprised to learn that government in the U.S. is far more efficient than elsewhere. It is not extraordinary in many African countries for administrators to be altogether unavailable, the telephones not to work, or files to be forever lost. Similar difficulties would not be unusual in either Asia or Latin America. Such hindrances, in addition to the usual red tape, make business dealings uncomfortable and unpleasant. Although a company would probably not bypass an overseas opportunity solely because of this factor, knowledge about the inefficiency of administrative machinery might warn its managers to lengthen schedules and perhaps engage the services of a local broker or an agent.

Closeness of Government to People

Iran's 1979 crisis suggests that economic development cannot be imposed on a nation; rather, it must evolve over time. The breakneck speed with which the shah of Iran invested billions of dollars in development in the late 1960s and early 1970s created a fragile society. The shah imposed a modern infrastructure, an industry dependent on foreign technology, and a western lifestyle on a Muslim society that was opposed to change. This swift modernization, with GNP per capita increasing from $200 to over $2,000 in a decade's time, triggered a reaction that led to the shah's fall. The people, in other words, could not absorb modernization quickly enough to adapt their lives accordingly, and they revolted. Religious priests became the leaders of a people disillusioned by western living and material progress.

The Islamic revolution in Iran provides a classic case of how the distance between government and people can lead to the total disruption of a country. Many political scientists have noted the similarities between Saudi Arabia's modernization and Iran's. There also, a tribal nomadic society is being transformed seemingly overnight into an industrial society with modern amenities and facilities.[22] To an extent, South Vietnam presented a similar problem. The government kept developing programs, with U.S. aid, that widened the distance between the government and its people.

It is sometimes difficult to ascertain whether the people and the government of a country are in accord. The U.S. government, despite all its resources, failed to foresee that the shah would fall. However, contact with journalists, religious leaders, and the intelligentsia of a country can provide some insights into the feelings of ordinary citizens toward their government and its programs. In traditional societies, where a windfall such as oil revenues suddenly offers an opportunity for multinational business, it would be prudent to investigate the sentiments of the people before making major commitments.

Political Models

On the basis of the factors discussed so far, a country can be categorized as having one of the following political slants: state-centric international politics, pluralistic national politics, bureaucratic organizational politics, or transnational politics. Each of these political model systems presents different kinds of risk for doing business.

The *state-centric model* of international politics assumes that national governments seek power and status in relation to one another, that they do so in the context of a competitive, decentralized international political system, and that they utilize whatever internal political resources are available in pursuit of their international objectives. National governments' actions are thus assumed to be functions of the officials' desire for international power and status and of their reactions to political pressures exerted by other national governments.

The *pluralistic model* of national politics assumes that national governments are responsive to the diverse and conflicting interests and pressures of multiple interest groups within a political system. Group interests and pressures are expressed through electoral processes but are especially important in legislative and administrative processes, where they take the form of lobbying activities. National governments' actions are thus assumed to be functions of the officials' desire to remain in office or of their reaction to internal political pressures.

The *bureaucratic organizational politics behavior model* assumes that national governments' actions are the result of organizational processes within government bureaucracies. Intragovernmental conflicts, then, are generated by the differing policy preferences of individual officials and agencies. These variances arise from conflicting organizational interests, differences in career experiences, differences in ties to domestic clientele groups, and other factors. This model also suggests that government policies are slow to change because of bureaucratic inertia.

The *transnational politics model* emphasizes the increasingly important role played in world politics by organizations other than those of national governments. Thus, not only MNCs but also international organizations and nongovernmental associations such as transnational interest groups are all assuming greater influence, often at the expense of national governments.

Each model contains numerous variables and and is based on propositions about relationships among these variables. Each one is also evident in an abundance of impressionistic case studies, systematic quantitative studies, and historical narratives. Even this abbreviated discussion suggests the utility of these models in political risk assessment, for they can be used to develop a lengthy and systematic list of potential sources of political risk.

Political Risk Assessment (PRA)

Political risk assessment (PRA) is useful for three reasons:

1. To identify countries that may turn out to be the Irans of tomorrow. (PRA should sound a warning signal of mounting political risks so that a firm can protect itself by minimizing its exposure.)
2. To identify countries unnecessarily discounted as politically unsound, for example, Cambodia, and to identify countries where political conditions have changed for the better, for example, Vietnam and Haiti.
3. To provide a framework to identify countries that are politically risky, but not so risky as to be automatically ruled out. (Most developing countries fall into this category.)

PRA Methods

Corporations utilize any number of methods to analyze political risk. The currently favored approaches are (1) qualitative ones known as the grand-tour approach, old-hand approach, and delphi technique, and (2) quantitative methods.

Grand Tour In the *grand-tour approach,* an executive or a team of executives visit the country in which investment is being considered. Usually, prior to the visit, there is some preliminary market research. Upon arrival, there are usually meetings with government officials and local businesspersons. The results of this type of visit can be very superficial, representing only selected pieces of information and therefore possibly camouflaging undesirable aspects of the market.

Old Hand The *old-hand approach* relies on the advice of an outside consultant or a person deemed to be an expert. Usually such persons are seasoned educators, diplomats, local politicians, or businesspersons. The capability and experience of the advisor is the factor determining the quality of this report.

Delphi Technique In the *delphi technique,* a group of experts are asked to share their opinions independently on a given problem, in a form that can be scored in order to produce a statistical distribution of opinion. The experts are shown the resulting distribution and given the chance to alter their original views. The process is repeated several times. For some problems, it has been found that the average opinion of the group at the last round is usually more nearly correct than any of the individual views in the beginning.

To use this method, a group of experts would be asked to rate different political factors, for example, the stability of government, the role of its armed forces, and its political conflicts. Based on the final expert opinion, a go or no-go decision can be made.

Quantitative Methods In addition to the foregoing qualitative methods, many businesses have tried *quantitative methods* to judge political risk. A quantitative method involves developing a mathematical relationship among a series of quantifiable factors in order to predict (within specified probability ranges) the likelihood of certain events. Banks have utilized this technique before granting loans to foreign countries. This technique requires collection of different forms of quantitative data, complex analysis of data using an appropriate computer program, and expert interpretation of the results.

PRA Models

PRA has become a fact of U.S. corporate life. The surge of interest in PRA began with the unexpected fall of the shah's regime in Iran and was reinforced by the overthrow of apparently secure governments in Nicaragua and South Korea. Several independent PRA consultants are available to help corporate clients develop general PRA summaries or provide studies of specific countries. The best-known risk raters are the Economist Intelligence Unit (EIU), a New York–based subsidiary of The Economist Group, London; BERI S.A.'s Business Risk service (BRs); and Bank of America's Country Risk Monitor.

EIU's Country Risk Service (CRS) assesses composite country risk through four types of risk to investors: political risk (22 percent of the composite), economic policy risk (28 percent), economic structure risk (27 percent), and liquidity risk (23 percent). The *political risk* component includes two subcategories: (1) political stability, represented in five indicators—war, social unrest, orderly political transfer, politically motivated violence, and international disputes—and (2) political effectiveness, with six indicators—change in government orientation, institutional effectiveness, bureaucracy, transparency/fairness, corruption, and crime.

Economic policy risk is determined with 27 variables in five categories: monetary policy, fiscal policy, exchange rate policy, trade policy, and regulatory environment. Economic structure risk incorporates global environment, growth, current account, debt, and financial structure groupings with 28 variables. *Liquidity risk* employs 10 variables. In each of the four categories, numerical scores are converted to letter grades ranging from A to E.

BERI provides a complete picture of country risk based on a set of quantitative indices developed and refined over a 25-year period. A comprehensive *Profit Opportunity Recommendation (POR)* is an average of three ratings, each on a 100-point scale. *The Political Risk Index (PRI)* is composed of ratings on 10 political and social variables. The *Operations Risk Index (ORI)* includes weighted ratings on 15 economic, financial, and structural variables. The third index is the *R Factor,* also a weighted index, covering the country's legal framework, foreign exchange, hard currency reserves, and foreign debt. The POR thus represents all aspects of country risk. Risk is calculated for the present, as well as one-year and five-year time frames.

In its *Country Risk Monitor,* Bank of America evaluates country risk on the basis of economic ratios. For 80 countries, an ordinal ranking is created for each of the ratios. A rank of 1 indicates the least difficulty or problem; a rank of 80 is associated with the most difficulty. The ranks are then averaged across the 10 variables, and a comprehensive ranking of the averages is created to provide a picture of relative risk. The *Country Risk Monitor* provides rankings for the current year, historical data for the previous four years, and projections for the next five years.

Consider Brazil's ratings in 1999. BERI gave Brazil an overall score of 74 (out of 100), ranking it 42nd out of 147 countries, a significant improvement over 1997, when the score was 62. Bank of America, however, expressed a rather dim view of Brazil in its 1999 forecast. EIU put Brazil in category C, giving it a total score of 58 (which is a slight improvement over the 1997 score of 54).[23] The reason behind this improved showing is easy to see. Inflation is down and the country has liberalized the economy to become attractive to foreign investors.

Too often, consultants' reports are of dubious usefulness to subsidiary managers, since they are mainly oriented to corporate headquarters. The objectives of a good PRA system should not be limited to collecting and evaluating information but rather should aim to select the best political intelligence for decision making. Toward this end, a specific study tailored to a particular purpose is more useful than a general one. Although there is some debate about the usefulness of the indexing services, their client lists include a number of Fortune 500 companies.

Strategic Response

When a company has become susceptible to political risk or has been politically victimized, it must make an effort to salvage its position. Whereas there is little a company can do to ward off internal violence or political instability in the host country, it can employ a number of tactics to discourage expropriation or to generally strengthen its position (see International Marketing Highlight 10.5). As one author has stated,

> In sum, host governments should not be seen by MNC top managers exclusively as an impediment to global strategic freedom, to be avoided at all cost. Occasionally they may provide enough of a helping hand—through privileged market access, export credits, and subsidies—for smaller MNCs to face global competition, to make it worthwhile for those smaller, often weaker, MNCs to relinquish wholeheartedly some strategic freedom to gain competitive strength through government support. Host governments can thus either hamper or help global strategies, depending on their policies and on the strategic options of the affected firms. It is important, therefore, to make an analysis of host government goals, policies, and actions an integral part of the strategy formulation process in a global business.[24]

International Marketing Highlight 10.5

How Big Mac Kept from Becoming a Serb Archenemy

During most of the 78-day air war against Yugoslavia, while NATO kept the bombs dropping, McDonald's kept the burgers flipping.

Vandalized at the outset by angry mobs, McDonald's Corp. was forced to temporarily close its 15 restaurants in Yugoslavia. But when local managers flung the doors open again, they accomplished an extraordinary comeback using an unusual marketing strategy: They put McDonald's U.S. citizenship on the back burner.

To help overcome animosity toward a quintessential American trademark, the local restaurants promoted the McCountry, a domestic pork burger with paprika garnish. As a national flourish to evoke Serbian identity and pride, they produced posters and lapel buttons showing the golden arches topped with a traditional Serbian cap called sajkaca (pronounced shy-KACK-a). They also handed out free cheeseburgers at anti-NATO rallies. The basement of one restaurant in the Serbian capital even served as a bomb shelter.

Now that the war is over, the company is basking in its success. Cash registers are ringing at prewar levels. In spite of falling wages, rising prices and lingering anger at the U.S., McDonald's restaurants around the country are thronged with Serbs hungry for Big Macs and fries. And why not, ask 16-year-old Jovan Stojanovic, munching on a burger. "I don't associate McDonald's with America," he says. "Mac is ours."

Source: The Wall Street Journal. September 3, 1999, p. B1

Strategic Choices

Essentially, a company has three strategic responses to political difficulties in a host country: to *adapt*, to *withdraw*, or to take *counteractive measures*.[25] For example, in the 1970s IBM completely withdrew from India because the company could not live with the restrictions imposed by the government on freedom of strategy in product development, pricing, and other areas. Nestlé, on the other hand, accepted India's infringements in return for continued presence in the market. CPC International, du Pont, and Brown Boveri (a European company) likewise seek market presence rather than complete withdrawal.

The third choice, counteractive response, amounts to making a new move to gain a competitive advantage based on company strengths and the needs of the host government.

For example, Honeywell merged its French subsidiary, Honeywell Bull, with the French government company, Compagnie International pour L'Informatique, which was losing money. This arrangement gave Honeywell access to the French market and qualified it to receive French government grants for R&D (see International Marketing Highlight 10.6). Thus it may be perfectly rational to stay in the country even if, or perhaps because, the competitors have left. In the long run, staying, but with a minimum commitment, may provide greater freedom of operation once the political situation stabilizes.[26]

■■■■■■■■■■■   **International Marketing Highlight 10.6**   ■■■■■■■■■■■

Managing Government Intervention

Bristol-Myers pursued the counteractive strategy in Indonesia. It had successfully marketed one of its nutritional products in Indonesia, which was centrally obtained from its Nijmegen facility in Holland. This worked well for Bristol-Myers, since the Indonesian market wasn't developed enough to justify the cost of building a plant there to service this market. The problem started when the Indonesian government decided to close its borders to the "finished product" that Bristol-Myers had introduced so successfully into the market. Bristol-Myers had to decide whether to find an alternative that could circumvent the new regulation or withdraw from the Indonesian market. Bristol-Myers decided to follow the former route. The concerned product was composed of a highly sophisticated powder that was blended with a heat-sensitive key raw material and canned. Bristol-Myers solved the problem by ascertaining what the Indonesian government really meant by "finished product." It worked closely with the ministry of health and the ministry of economics in Indonesia to come up with a mutually acceptable solution: Bristol-Myers was permitted to import a "base" powder that it would blend with an indigenous raw material. Bristol-Myers successfully subcontracted with an Indonesian company to produce and blend the raw material with the base. The "finished product" was subsequently canned, carried the Bristol-Myers label, and continued to be sold in Indonesia.

Keep in mind, however, that no single strategy works best in a single country or even in a single industry. If the MNC's managers are flexible and imaginative in responding to government demands, the consequences could be surprisingly favorable. Encarnation and Vachani found that new product lines and markets, risk diversifications, and higher earnings were among the benefits MNCs operating in India enjoyed in the wake of that country's "hostile" equity laws. Some, for example, negotiated for manufacturing licenses and other concessions in exchange for "Indianization." Others successfully sought entry to new markets, hitherto forbidden.[27] The choice, of course, among the three options of adapting, withdrawing, or taking counteractive measures depends on the bargaining power of the company in respect to the bargaining power of the host government.

MNCs' Bargaining Power

The bargaining power of MNCs stems from such factors as technology, economies of scale, and product differentiation. Companies with *technology* badly needed by the host country and unobtainable on comparative terms elsewhere can bargain from a leverage position. For example, in the late 1970s Indonesia desperately sought to boost its oil exploration activity. This goal required sophisticated technology, and Indonesia was willing to go to any length to get it. In other words, oil companies negotiated with the Indonesian government on very favorable terms since they had the necessary technology.[28]

Similarly, Mexico willingly permitted IBM to establish a wholly owned microcomputer plant because the Mexican government was concerned that without a major microcomputer plant, the local market would consists of outmoded and overpriced products. If a company like IBM entered the market, it could pull other companies in the production chain along with it. Technology can provide effective bargaining power.

Economies of scale, which a foreign firm might realize through its worldwide production and distribution arrangements, can also yield a unique bargaining strength. If the low cost of the local multinational firm's output is directly related to its worldwide network or vertical integration (via the establishment of specialized plants in various countries and the transfer of components or end products among them), the host country will hesitate to intervene out of fear that any intervention would cancel out the benefits that the firm derives from being a part of the network. In the case of Marcona Mining's iron milling operation in Peru, such intervention did just that. The firm signed long-term supply agreements with its customers stipulating that in the event of nationalization, the contracts with its Peruvian subsidiary would be considered void and Marcona Mining would supply its customers from its other milling operations. When the firm was expropriated, the Peruvian government found it had no outlet for iron ore concentrate. As the trade in this commodity is based almost entirely on long-term controls, there was no well-developed spot market to which the Peruvian government could turn.

Product differentiation (i.e., differentiation based on the nature of the product and product quality/performance attributes, and not on consumer perceptions) can serve as another area of strength in foreign firms' bargaining with the host governments. For example, a firm producing high-quality agricultural machinery will have greater leverage in dealing with a host government than will a cosmetics manufacturer.

To sum up, firms with technical, operational, and managerial requirements that are within the reach of the abilities of the host nation will have little bargaining power. Such firms are more likely to experience intervention than those in complex fields. Hence, there is considerable local pressure on governments in Kenya, Indonesia, Brazil, and India to restrict such areas as consumer goods manufacturing, retailing, importing and exporting, and distribution to nationals only.

Bargaining Power of Host Country

The bargaining power of the host country mainly depends on two factors: control of market access and inducements. The host country controls access to the market by restricting entry for other competitors or by opening up rights to restricted markets. For example, Spain attracted Ford Motor Company by making it feasible for the company to sell enough cars there. Similarly, Japan has permitted foreign companies to sell communications-related products to its government, which may serve as an incentive for such firms as Western Electric to become more active in that market.

In addition, host countries may offer such inducements as R&D funds, tax holidays, market information, land subsidies, and financial concessions (repatriation arrangements) to attract the businesses sought. For example, ITT's European units have received large government grants to develop communication equipment tailored to local conditions.

Strategic Response

The strategic response a company makes to intervention by the host country should depend on the bargaining power on each side. The following strategies are recommended for improving the odds in international investing:

- Seek joint ventures with local private parties.
- Concentrate proprietary research, product development, and process technology in the home country.
- Ensure that each new investment is economically dependent on the parent corporation in the U.S. (For example, establish the parent as the sole supplier of essential materials.)

- Avoid local branding or establish a single global trademark.
- Adopt a low-profile, multiplant strategy, with a number of investments in different countries.

To conclude, the major benefits to a host country from a foreign investment usually appear at the beginning. Over time, the incremental benefits become smaller and the costs more apparent. Unless the firm continually renews these benefits by introducing more products, say, or by expanding output and developing export markets, it is likely to be subject to increasing political risks. The common government attitude is to ignore the past and instead ask what will be done for it in the future. In a situation where the firm's future contributions are unlikely to evoke a favorable government reaction, the firm is advised to concentrate on protecting its foreign investments by striking a balance between the company's goals and those of its host. For example, a company may introduce higher technology products and thereby foster the government's economic plans.

Summary

An international marketer needs to examine carefully the political environment of a country before making major commitments in that country. The political situation of a country may or may not be conducive to profitable business there.

Political problems related to foreign business occur mainly because of political sovereignty, a country's desire to assert its authority, and political conflict—either internal conflicts such as civil war or external ones with another country. Such troubles may lead a country to intervene politically in the affairs of private business, particularly those of foreign firms. Intervention may range from some form of control to complete takeover, or expropriation, which is the official seizure of foreign property by a host country. Other forms of intervention include exchange control, import restrictions, market control, tax control, price control, and labor restrictions. At one time, political intervention mainly occurred in developing countries. Now, even industrially developed countries seek to control foreign enterprises in various ways.

The possibility of political intervention makes it necessary for a foreign marketer to carefully analyze the political situation of a country before investing there. This analysis can be made through study of the country's type of government (republic, dictatorship, and so forth); stability of government; economic management by government; frequency of changes in government policy; attitudes toward foreign investment, other governments, the parent company's home government, foreign managers, and private business; viability of administrative procedures; and closeness between the government and its people. On the basis of the preceding factors, the foreign firm can determine the political risk of doing business with a given country. Various methods or models can be employed for political risk assessment.

In theory, a company should not enter a politically unsafe country. However, situations sometimes change within a country after entry has been made. For example, traditionally Iran provided a workable environment, but beginning in 1978 it became an extremely high-risk country. What can a company do if problems arise after it has entered a market? Three strategic responses to political intervention are (1) adapt, accepting infringements and molding the business operations to suit the foreign government's requirements; (2) withdraw and call it quits even if this means suffering a loss of property; or (3) attempt counteractive measures such as proposals to provide the government with what it wants and at the same time allow the company a few concessions.

In the final analysis, the host government's willingness to grant concessions to the foreign enterprise would depend on the MNC's bargaining leverage. For example, a host government would be willing to concede to the terms of a multinational enterprise involved in business that is of strategic national importance and that cannot be replaced. On the other hand, a company manufacturing consumer goods such as bar soaps and shampoo may not have much bargaining power with the host government.

Review Questions

1. Why is it necessary for international marketers to study political environment? How can foreign politics affect marketing decisions?
2. What are the underlying causes of political unrest? Discuss.
3. Discuss different ways in which a host government may intervene in the affairs of a multinational firm.
4. Define *expropriation*. What can a company do to counteract expropriation?
5. What factors should a company study to gain insight into a country's politics?
6. Why is it desirable to undertake political risk assessment?
7. What responses can a company make to government intervention in a foreign country?

Creative Questions

1. In 1999 the Clinton administration extended "most favorite nation" (MFN) trading status to China despite that country's poor record in respecting human rights. What political factors influenced this decision? Should America have compromised its policy on human rights for economic gains? What influence is this decision likely to have on other nations with questionable records on maintaining human rights?
2. According to *The Economist*, causes of war have not disappeared from the face of the earth. One possibility is a general war between Islamic nations and the West. Such a war would have three potential ignites: ideology, skin color, and conflict of interest. Examine this proposition, suggesting ways such a war could be averted.

Endnotes

1. Richard L. Hudson, "Apple Computer vs. French Chauvinism: Politics, Not Free Trade, Wins in the End," *The Wall Street Journal*, February 22, 1985, p. 34.

2. *See* Roberto Friedmann, "Political Risk and International Marketing," *Columbia Journal of World Business*, Winter 1988.

3. "Toyota's Fast Lane," *Business Week*, November 4, 1985, p. 42. *Also see* "Asian Auto Makers Find a Back Door to the U.S. Market," *Business Week*, December 9, 1985, p. 52; "Import or Die," *The Economist*, February 19, 1983, pp. 11–12.

4. "The Screws Are Tightening on U.S. Companies," *Business Week*, February 11, 1985, p. 38.

5. "Foreign Cigarette Makers Aim for Bigger Share of Japan Market," *The Asian Wall Street Journal Weekly*, October 28, 1985, p. 23.

6. Steve Frazier, "Mexico Hopes Its Approval of IBM Plant Encourages More Foreign Investment," *The Wall Street Journal*, July 25, 1985, p. 25.

7. Anthony Spaeth and Amal Kumar Naj, "PepsiCo Accepts Tough Conditions for the Right to Sell Cola in India," *The Wall Street Journal*, September 20, 1988, p. 44.

8. *Business Week*, February 10, 1992, p. 43.

9. See "Mr. Tatum Checks Out, " *The Economist*, November 9, 1996, p. 78.

10. Lynne Reaves, "U.S. Marketers Fend Off Turmoil in Philippines," *Advertising Age*, May 16, 1988, p. 10.

11. *Fortune*, November 2, 1993, p. 18.

12. Humayun Akhtrer and Robert F. Lusch, "Political Risk and the Evolution of the Control of Foreign Business: Equity, Earnings and the Marketing Mix," *Journal of Global Marketing*, Spring 1988, p. 117.

13. David K. Eiteman and Arthur I. Stonehill, *Multinational Business Finance* (Reading MA: Addison-Wesley, 1979), p. 186.

14. David G. Bradley, "Managing Against Expropriation," *Harvard Business Review*, July–August 1977, pp. 75–84.

15. *Transnational Corporations in World Development: Third Survey* (New York: United Nations, 1983).

16. David G. Bradley, op. cit.

17. Ibid.

18. Michael S. Minor, "The Demise of Expropriation as an Instrument of Old LDC Policy, 1980–1992," *Journal of International Business Studies* 25, no. 1 (1994): 177–188.

19. "Europe's Economic Malaise," *Business Week*, December 7, 1981, p. 74.

20. "Ultimatum for the Avon Lady," *Business Week*, May 11, 1998, p. 33.

21. "Indian Tobacco: Raj Pickle," *The Economist*, April 1, 1995, p. 56.

22. Douglas Jehl, "Saudis' Heartland is Seething with Rage at Rulers and U.S.," *The New York Times*, November 5, 1996, p. 1A.

23. *The Economist*, January 10, 2000, p. 48.

24. C. K. Prahalad and Yves L. Doz, *The Multinational Mission* (New York: The Free Press, 1987), p. 68.

25. Yves L. Doz and C. K. Prahalad, "How MNCs Cope with Host Government Intervention," *Harvard Business Review*, March–April 1980, pp. 149–157.

26. Amjad Hadjikhari and Jan Johanson, "Facing Foreign Market Turbulence: Three Swedish Multinationals in Iran," *Journal of International Marketing*, no. 4 (1996): 53–74.

27. D. J. Encarnation and Sushil Vachini, "Foreign Ownership: When Hosts Change the Rules," *Harvard Business Review*, September–October 1985, pp. 152–160.

28. "Foreign Countries Offer Wide Range of Incentives to Invest," *The Asian Wall Street Journal Weekly*, August 24, 1981, pp. 12–14.

CHAPTER 11

Legal Environment

CHAPTER FOCUS

After studying this chapter, you should be able to

■ Describe two types of legal systems.

■ Discuss jurisdiction of laws.

■ Compare some relevant host country laws, U.S. laws, and international laws and conventions.

■ Explain how companies may use arbitration to resolve conflict in a foreign environment.

Multinational enterprise in its global exercise must cope with widely differing laws. A U.S. corporation not only has to consider U.S. laws wherever it does business, but also must be responsive to the host country's laws.[1] For example, without requiring proof that certain market practices have adversely affected competition, U.S. law nevertheless makes them violations. These practices include horizontal price fixing among competitors, market division by agreement among competitors, and price discrimination. Even though such practices might be common in a foreign country, U.S. corporations cannot engage in them. Simultaneously, local laws must be adhered to even if they forbid practices that are allowed in the U.S. For example, in Europe a clear-cut distinction is made between agencies and distributorships. Agents are deemed auxiliaries of their principal; distributorships are independent enterprises. Exclusive distributorships are considered restrictive in European Union (EU) countries. The foreign marketer must be careful in making distribution arrangements in, say, France, so as not to violate the regulation concerning distributorship contracts.

Worldwide, different countries pursue legal systems of varied complexity and dimension. In some countries, laws provide only a broad guide, and the interpretation is left to the courts. In other countries, laws spell out virtually every detail. A foreign enterprise, therefore, has to be scrupulous in learning and heeding all local laws and regulations.[2] From the marketing standpoint, a U.S. company should be especially careful in obeying laws pertaining to competition, price setting (such as price discrimination, resale price maintenance), distribution arrangements (such as exclusive dealership), product quality (such as wholesomeness, packaging, warranty and service, patents and trademarks), personal selling (such as white-collar employment/labor laws), and advertising (such as media usage, information provision).

In addition, there are both host country and U.S. laws concerned with taxes, tariffs, licensing, and other areas related to business that should be understood and complied with, along with certain international laws and conventions that affect marketing decision making in the global context. The international marketer should also understand the use of arbitration as an alternative to legal recourse.

The impact of law on marketing is illustrated by an Italian law allowing wine coolers to be sold there. Although Italy had been producing wine coolers for export for years, existing law had prohibited wine from being mixed with other ingredients, basically to protect consumers from tampered wine. The new law prevents the beverage from being called a wine cooler. Instead, it is to be described as a wine-based "fantasy" beverage with a minimum of 75 percent wine and grape juice. The Italian word *fantasia* also means multicolored. No artificial flavors, sugar, or water are allowed. Both Riunite and Cantina Sociale di Foggia launched their wine beverages in Italy within days of official publication of the laws.[3]

International Legal Perspectives

Two important aspects of international legal systems are pertinent to marketing: the philosophical bases of the laws and the jurisdiction of these laws.

Common Law versus Code Law

Philosophically, two types of legal systems may be distinguished: common law and code law. *Common law* is based on precedents and practices established in the past and interpreted over time. Common law was first developed in England, and most of the countries that at one time or another formed a part of the British Empire follow this system. *Code law* is based on detailed rules for all eventualities. Code law was developed by the Romans and is popularly practiced by a number of free world countries. Most countries of the free world may be divided into those that follow common law, as do Great Britain, U.S., Australia, India, and Kenya, and those that have code law, as do Italy, France, Germany, Mexico, and Switzerland.

It is important for an international marketer to be familiar with the genesis of a country's law, for it frequently has far-reaching effects on all kinds of decisions. For example, the *right to a property* (which would cover such things as trademarks) in a common-law country would depend on the history of use of the property—that is, in the case of a trademark dispute which party actually used the trademark on its package and in its advertising campaign. According to code law, however, the right of property would be based on which party actually registered the trademark. Assume two companies, say Alpha and Beta, are claiming rights to a trademark. Alpha registered the trademark but never used it. On the other hand, Beta has been using it all along in various commercial ways without ever bothering to register it. In a common-law country, the trademark would belong to Beta Company. In a code-law country, it would be the property of the Alpha Company.

Similarly, so-called *acts of God* in contractual obligations are interpreted differently in the two legal systems. Consider a Japanese company that enters into contracts with firms in England and Italy to deliver certain electronic equipment on a specified date. When a hurricane on the high seas destroys the Japanese shipment, the company cannot fulfill the contract. In both England and Italy, this is considered an act of God, and the Japanese company is not held liable for not meeting the contractual terms. But now assume the shipment is destroyed by a breakdown in the air conditioning of the building where the goods are stored. In this case, the common law might not release the Japanese exporters from noncompliance, because air conditioning failure during summer heat can be expected and therefore is not an act of God. Under code law, however, both circumstances would most likely be considered acts of God.

The division between code-law and common-law countries, broad in nature, narrows in actual practice. Some common-law countries also have specific codes, particularly in the area of commerce, that must be followed. Furthermore, although two countries follow the same system, the interpretation in a particular case may differ based on the experiences and precedents in the two environments. Thus, air conditioning failure might be considered an act of God in Kenya, even though it is a common-law country, because air conditioning is limited there and the climate is sultry most of the year.

Jurisdiction of Laws

Remarkably enough, although business across national boundaries is an accomplished fact, there is no international body to make rules and oversee their fulfillment by different parties. Thus, a business incorporated in a particular country carries the burden of complying with the laws of both the incorporating nation and the host country. A large U.S. manufacturer with subsidiaries incorporated or registered in different parts of the world is liable to the laws of all the nations where it does business.

Major problems can occur when laws of more than one country must be respected and these laws have conflicting values. If a contract contains a *jurisdiction clause* stipulating which country's legal system should be used to settle disputes, the matter can be settled accordingly; but in the absence of such a clause, legal and counterlegal actions, presumably in different courts, perhaps in different countries, may follow. Should the laws of the country where the agreement was made prevail, or the laws of the country where the contract has to be fulfilled? Each party naturally would like to settle the issue according to the legal system that favors its position. Sometimes arbitration, which will be discussed in a later section, can settle the dispute.

Consider the Bhopal tragedy, in which over 2,000 people died from a gas leakage accident in a Union Carbide plant in India in 1984. The Indian government would have liked the question of compensation to survivors settled in the U.S. courts, because the U.S. courts have been more liberal than the Indian courts in granting compensation to victims in such cases. Union Carbide would have preferred that the case be settled in the Indian courts, in the hope that its liability would be reduced substantially. In the end, the case was settled in India (for readers' interest, it was an out-of-court settlement).

Host Country Laws

Countries enact laws to control foreign businesses in their economies, and some of these laws are discriminatory against foreign goods and businesses. On the other hand, laws are sometimes designed to allow reciprocity with nations on good trading terms with the country. Extremely favorable laws may be passed to attract foreign investment.

In general, the legal environment of a country for foreign commerce depends on that country's economic objectives and its obligations and position in relating to worldwide commerce. In some situations, though, the laws have political aims as well. For example, a government may decide to restrict all imports in order to promote a feeling of national unity among the people and their political supporters. Or different political considerations may cause a country to liberalize its laws pertaining to foreign business. In 1988, in the wake of a high U.S. trade deficit and under pressure from Washington, Taiwan reduced tariffs on some 3,500 items by an average of 50 percent, including telecommunications, medical equipment, pharmaceuticals, sophisticated electronic equipment, forest products, agricultural goods, and cigarettes.[4] South Korea and Japan, other trading partners of the U.S. with whom it had a substantial negative trade balance, have been similarly tilting their trade policy toward the U.S. Japan has finally scrapped its Staple Food Control Act that restricted free trade in rice. As a result, U.S. rice should be easy to sell in Japan. Also, the freer competition should bring down the price for the Japanese consumers, which has been roughly nine times the world market price.[5]

Laws that bear on entry into foreign markets take several forms, including tariffs, antidumping laws, export/import licensing, investment regulations, legal incentives, and restrictive trading laws.

Tariffs

A *tariff* is a tax that a government levies on exports and imports. The tax on exports is called *export duty*. The tax on imports is called *import duty* or *customs duty*. The purpose of export duty is to discourage selling overseas to maintain adequate supply at home.

The import duty is levied for different reasons: to protect home industry from being outpriced by cheap imports, to gain a source of revenue for the government, and to prevent the dilution of foreign exchange balances through consumer goods purchased by a few privileged people. In developing countries, where new industries cannot compete with imports from the Western World and resources are limited, the import duty serves as an important measure to promote economic development. Although the usual reasons for levying import duties do not apply for the U.S. and other industrialized countries, the influx of Japanese imports, particularly automobiles, has led many concerned groups to recommend heavy import duty on Nissans, Toyotas, and Hondas.

An import duty may be assessed either according to the value of the product (called *ad valorem*), or on a unit basis (called *specific duty*), or both. Computation of a specific duty is easier because the price factor does not come into the picture as it does in ad valorem duty.

A related term, *subsidy,* is relevant here. A subsidy is a reverse tariff. Many countries provide a subsidy for local manufactures for export abroad. For example, South Korea provides a subsidy to its steel manufacturers to compete effectively in the world market. A subsidy may also be provided to local products to make them competitive against imports. The U.S. government subsidizes certain types of steel to protect the U.S. industry against imports.

Antidumping Laws

Dumping is a type of pricing strategy for selling products in foreign markets below cost, or below the price charged to domestic customers. Dumping is practiced to capture a foreign market and to damage rival foreign national enterprises. In the 1980s foreign car manufacturers were charged with dumping cars in the U.S. Japanese television manufacturers and steel companies have been similarly charged. In recent years the U.S. government has accused India, France, and Brazil of dumping stainless steel wire rods and forged stainless steel flanges.[6]

Host governments often pass laws against dumping with a view to protecting local industries. Dumping can be a problem for developed and developing countries alike. The U.S. Treasury Department found that 23 of 28 foreign automakers had been dumping cars in the U.S. It demanded that the foreign manufacturers increase their car prices. Subsequently, Volkswagen, for instance, raised its car price an average of 2.5 percent.

In the same way, on the recommendation of the International Trade Commission, under the provisions of the 1974 Trade Act, the Treasury Department set minimum steel import price levels to enable U.S. manufacturers to compete against Japanese steelmakers.[7] Among the developing countries, Brazil has passed antidumping legislation against imports from the U.S. and Japan. Similar laws exist in South Korea, Taiwan, India, and Nigeria (see International Marketing Highlight 11.1).

In theory, the practice of dumping cannot be criticized. A business should be free to set any price it finds would be beneficial in the long run; thus, different prices may be set in different markets, based on the demand and the competition. The argument against dumping, however, is that price differentials are intended strictly to weaken competition and over the long run hurt everyone. Particularly in international business, dumping inhibits the orderly development of national industry. From this viewpoint, attacks on rival markets by dumping amount to destructive as well as unscrupulous means of securing market position. It is for this reason that countries pass *antidumping laws.*

■■■■■■■■■■   **International Marketing Highlight 11.1**   ■■■■■■■■■■

Dump, Counterdump

The United States is the terror of the memory-chip industry. Over the years its trade officials have charged Japan, South Korea, and Taiwan with dumping, sparking trade wars, disrupting the industry, and, according to some, exacerbating shortages that have at times kept prices artificially high. Now, for the first time, Taiwan's semiconductor industry association is charging America's Mircron, along with the American subsidiaries of South Korea's LG and Samsung, with selling these chips, known as DRAMS, below cost in the Taiwanese market.

The Taiwanese allege that Micron is damaging local producers by selling chips more cheaply in Taiwan than at home. So far Taiwan has produced little evidence that this is so—and Micron denies it. But then again Taiwan's law is such that not much evidence is needed; there is, for instance, no requirement to prove a link between alleged dumping and injury. If the semiconductor association prevails, Taiwan could impose special tariffs on Micron and the American arms of the two South Korean firms, much as America has done to Japanese and South Korean producers in the past. In fact, things will probably not get so far; instead, most analysts see this Taiwanese action as a retaliation for the antidumping case against Taiwan that America started last year. If America dropped those charges, no doubt Taiwan would drop its charges against the U.S.

Source: The Economist, May 15, 1999, p. 66.

Export/Import Licensing

Many countries have laws on the books that require exporters and importers to obtain licenses before engaging in trade across national boundaries. For example, Singapore requires importers of video games to obtain an import permit from the Board of Film Censors to distribute their product in Singapore.[8] The purpose of an *export license* may be simply to allow for the statistical tracking of export activities. Licensing may also help to ensure that certain goods are not exported at all, or at least not to certain countries. Chapter 17 discusses U.S. government prohibition of exportation of certain high-tech and defense-related goods to certain countries. Readers may recall the debate in the Congress in 1993 about the sale of Cray's super computers and nuclear power plants to China, which finally was approved.[9]

Import licensing is enforced to control the unnecessary purchase of goods from other countries. Such restraints save foreign exchange balances for other important purposes like the import of pharmaceuticals, chemicals, and machinery. India, for example, has strict licensing requirements against the import of cars and other luxury goods.

Foreign Investment Regulations

One of the primary aims of laws and regulations on foreign investment is to limit the influence of MNCs and to achieve a pattern of foreign investment that contributes most effectively to the realization of the host country's economic objectives. There are several broad areas of legislation concerned with foreign investment: administration of the investment process, screening criteria, ownership, finance, employment and training, technology transfer, investment incentives, and dispute settlement.

General Motors (GM) Corporation's problems in Germany show how varying investment laws can pose difficulty. GM sold its unprofitable Terex subsidiary, which made earthmoving equipment, to IBH Holding AG of Mainz in 1980. Over the next two years, before IBH declared bankruptcy in 1983, GM made four equity investments in the increasingly troubled German holding company. In return, the automaker received immediate repayments of millions owed to it by IBH. Such a maneuver, called "round-tripping," is generally considered illegal, unless properly disclosed, in Germany—though not in the U.S. The Germans contend that this round-tripping could hide a company's true financial condition and thus mislead investors and creditors.

Criminal investigation was launched against GM and its chairman Roger Smith. It took two years for the problem to be settled and GM to be exonerated of any wrongdoing. Before making a routine visit to Germany in 1986, Mr. Smith directed GM attorneys to seek assurances from a German prosecutor's office that he would not be arrested. He further requested the audit committee of the GM board to conduct its own review to satisfy itself that he had acted properly.[10]

Legal Incentives

Investment incentives enacted to attract foreign investment are an important part of government policy in most developing countries. In a few cases, incentive schemes are still the only significant regulation of foreign investment. Also, in certain countries foreign private investment is the main or sole beneficiary of incentives, because local capital and entrepreneurship cannot undertake the kind of investment encouraged by the incentives. On the other hand, other countries restrict incentives to local enterprises, joint ventures, or enterprises with a minority foreign participation.

Depending on the basic approach to investment regulation, incentives may be awarded automatically to all enterprises meeting the conditions specified in the relevant legislation, or incentives may be granted for a specific performance or contribution to the host country's economy such as export promotion and diversification, the development of a backward area, the transfer of modern technology, the encouragement of applied research in the host country, and so forth. Incentives also are often awarded on the basis of case-by-case negotiation in accordance with ad hoc criteria.

The main incentive to the establishment of an enterprise is ordinarily an income-tax holiday of several years' duration. Some governments are inclined to reduce the length of such tax holidays when they involve important tax revenue losses. Tax measures such as accelerated depreciation (often used in developed countries as a stimulant to investment) have proved less effective for various reasons as incentives in the economic environment of developing countries, where the main interest is in new investment rather than the encouragement of expenditure on plant replacement. Other fiscal incentives obtainable in developing countries include the waiver of import duties on equipment and materials essential for production, exemptions from property taxes, and numerous minor tax concessions granted by the provinces or localities where the enterprise is located.

Restrictive Trading Laws

In addition to the tax incentive laws, many governments adopt measures that restrict imports or artificially stimulate exports. Usually such laws are referred to as *nontariff barriers* to international trade. There are several major types:

- *Government participation in trade:* subsidies, countervailing duties, government procurement, and state trading.
- *Customs and entry procedures:* valuation, classification, documentation, and health and safety regulations.
- *Standards:* product standards, packaging, and labeling and marking.
- *Specific limitations:* quotas, exchange controls, import restraints, and licensing.
- *Import charges:* prior import credit restrictions for imports, special duties, and variable levies.

    For example, suppose Germany imposes an 11 percent value-added tax on a domestic product and a 13 percent tax adjustment at the border on a product of identical price and quality imported from the U.S. German buyers would choose the German product over the U.S. import because the tax is 2 percent lower. If a German exporter were given a rebate of 13 percent, he would be able to sell at 2 percent below U.S. price levels and would benefit from an equivalent export subsidy.[11]

- *Other measures:* voluntary export restraints whereby agreement is made between two trading countries to limit the exports of a specific product to a particular level, such as the agreement between Japan and the U.S. in the 1980s to limit Japanese car exports to the U.S.; and orderly marketing agreements, which are specific agreements between trading partners to negotiate trade restrictions (see International Marketing Highlight 11.2).

■■■■■ **International Marketing Highlight 11.2** ■■■■■

Tough Move on Gum Control

Like spitting, public chewing may wind up on the wrong side of the law in the sternly ruled island republic of Singapore. The government has banned the manufacture, sale, and importation of chewing gum. Mere possession of the stuff is not illegal yet, but offending sellers face fines of up to $1,200, and importers could get a year in jail. Gum, explains a government spokesman, "causes filthiness to our public facilities."

Singapore's subway trains have been halted several times recently when wads of chewing gum jammed their doors. The gum lobby argues that gum does not clog doors, people do. The government is unmoved.

Gum fanciers arriving from abroad must declare any gum they have with them on their customs forms. They will be allowed to bring in small amounts for their personal use, but the government reserves the right to define how much that may be.

Source: Time, January 13, 1992, p. 31.

U.S. Laws

Both U.S. corporations and their U.S. officers working abroad remain liable to the laws of the U.S. For instance, individuals must comply with U.S. Internal Revenue Service (IRS) laws, and corporations are bound by U.S. antitrust laws. One application of the U.S. antitrust laws to an American company overseas is the Gillette Company case. Many years ago, the Justice Department sought an injunction against Gillette for its acquisition of shares in Braun AG of Germany. The Justice Department held that Gillette's acquisition of Braun would restrict competition in shaving devices in the U.S., given the fact that Braun makes electric razors and that Braun had previously relinquished to a third company its rights to sell in the U.S. market until 1976.[12] (For readers' interest, Gillette acquired Braun AG in late 1980s.)

Some laws, however, have been specially enacted to direct multinational marketing activities, such as the Foreign Corrupt Practices Act (FCPA) of 1977. Basically, the intention of these laws is to protect American economic interests, ensure national security, maintain recognized standards of ethics, and promote fair competition.

Laws Affecting Foreign Trade

The U.S., relative to other nations, has a liberal attitude toward exports and imports. Nevertheless, there are many regulations that a U.S. exporter must be aware of in the conduct of business. First of all, the government prohibits trading with some nations, for example, Iran, Cuba, and, until recently, Vietnam. Also, exportation of several products, among them defense-related equipment, must be cleared with the U.S. Department of Commerce by obtaining a license permitting shipment (licensing requirements will be discussed in Chapter 17). The Omnibus Trade and Competitiveness Act of 1988 affects U.S. exporters in many ways, as discussed in Chapter 2.

The U.S. government imposes some restrictions, via the IRS, on pricing for intracompany foreign transactions. The IRS ensures that prices are not underestimated to save U.S. taxes. For example, a U.S. corporation may export certain goods to its subsidiary, say, in Germany, at a very low price. This would reduce the corporation's U.S. taxes. It is for this reason that the IRS is authorized to review pricing and demand change, if necessary, in such company-to-company overseas transfers.

In regard to imports, the U.S. markets traditionally are open to all nations with few restrictions. For health and safety reasons, food products from many developing countries are usually the subject of those restrictions. For example, in 1985 the Food and Drug Administration detained Sri Lankan tea imports for special testing following terrorist threats to contaminate that nation's black tea with cyanide. Sri Lanka provides about 11 percent of U.S. tea imports, or about 21 million pounds of black tea annually. As another example, for several weeks in 1989, Chilean grapes and other fruits were prohibited from entering the U.S., since some of these products had been poisoned.

Although the federal government basically subscribes to free trade and has supported through GATT (now WTO) the worldwide effort toward this goal, various leg-

islative and nonlegislative measures have been adopted to protect domestic U.S. industry. Protectionism increased in the 1970s when more and more U.S. companies showed
signs of crumbling, often from an inability to compete in the world market. The textile,
tire, and auto industries cut production or closed down entire factories, largely because
U.S. consumers purchased imports. Consequently, workers and industries applied continuing pressure for tougher tariffs and trade quotas. Thus, for some products, like automobiles, import duties were increased. For other products, like textiles, quotas were
imposed on imports from various countries. For steel, the government set minimum
prices on imports to make domestic steel competitive.

Antitrust Laws

As noted earlier, the U.S. antitrust laws apply to U.S. corporations in their international dealings as well as in their domestic transactions. More specifically, U.S. businesses must carefully ascertain if antitrust laws would be violated in any way in the
following situations:

- When a U.S. firm *acquires* a foreign firm.
- When a U.S. firm *engages in a joint venture* abroad with another American com-
  pany or a foreign firm.
- When a U.S. firm *enters into a marketing agreement* with a foreign-based firm.

The Justice Department has become very strict in the application of U.S. antitrust
laws on foreign operations of U.S. corporations. Justice Department enforcement takes
several forms.

- In 1980 it initiated criminal grand jury probes into allegations that U.S. and
  foreign competitors illegally set the prices of uranium, phosphate, and ocean
  shipping rates.
- In 1985 it reviewed the overseas licensing agreements of some two dozen multinationals to see whether their prices or territorial arrangements unreasonably prevented overseas producers from selling in the U.S.
- In 1990 it investigated oil company reactions to the new two-tier pricing system
  for foreign crude oil along with other aspects of their relations with oil-producing
  countries.
- In 1997 it examined the "marketing" merger between Texaco and Shell Oil and its
  impact on U.S. gasoline prices.

The antitrust laws are being legislated outside the U.S. as well, especially in EU
countries. In 1999 Italy's competition authority nailed Coca-Cola for its anticompeti-
tive practices. It has been claimed that Coca-Cola and CCBI, its affiliated bottler, along
with six other local bottlers, not only dominate the Italian market, but have also abused
this power to damage their competitors. One prong of Coke's strategy targets wholesalers. They are bound in by a complicated system of exclusivity bonuses and discounts,
which are designed less to boost sales of Coke than to oust Pepsi from the market. To illustrate, a Roman wholesaler was lured into a 4 percent extra discount for exclusively
carrying Coke by ousting Pepsi.[13] At the time of preparing this book the matter was still
pending.

**Foreign Corrupt
Practices Act
(FCPA)**

The FCPA, passed by Congress in 1977, has stringent antibribery provisions prohibit-
ing all U.S. companies on file with the Securities and Exchange Commission (SEC)
from making any unauthorized payments. These payments include those made to foreign
officials, political parties, or candidates. The law prescribes a $1 million penalty to a

corporation for violation of the law. Corporate officers connected with illegal payments may be fined $10,000 or be subjected to a five-year imprisonment, or both.

How FCPA can create hindrances is illustrated by the Coca-Cola Company's deal with the former Soviet Union. In 1986 Coca-Cola signed a $30 million six-year agreement to expand its business in the U.S.S.R. Until then, Coke was sold only in Moscow shops for tourists, and the company's Fanta orange soda was available in only a few other cities. Published reports indicated that the Coca-Cola Company paid bribes to people in the Soviet Union to crack the Soviet market. Subsequently, a federal grand jury initiated an investigation to determine if the allegations of wrongdoing were correct. Although the company was finally proved innocent, it had to endure subpoenas of its documents and other inconveniences to prove its innocence.[14]

In part, the FCPA is an effort to extend American moral standards to other countries. The act also seeks to enlist U.S. MNCs as instruments of U.S. foreign policy. The FCPA, therefore, marks a major attempt by the U.S. government to enforce a series of noneconomic foreign policy objectives through private enterprise, which has traditionally been considered to have only economic purposes. The FCPA places American corporations doing business abroad in an awkward position. On the one hand, they must comply with the U.S. law, and on the other, they have to compete with other foreign countries whose governments do not prohibit such payments. In some nations where American business is conducted, bribery is commonplace; the FCPA could weaken the competitive position of U.S. corporations in such countries (see International Marketing Highlight 11.3).

In addition to the fact that the FCPA adversely affects U.S. trade, critics of the act argue that the U.S. should not try to force its moral principles and concepts of right and wrong on the whole world. Questionable practices such as bribery will continue in certain countries whether U.S. corporations participate or not. The best that can be hoped is that in the future, international bribery perhaps might be controlled through an international agreement effected through WTO.

The Omnibus Trade and Competitiveness Act of 1988 was passed to limit the scope of the FCPA. The primary change concerned the FCPA's prohibition against payments to third parties by a U.S. firm "knowing or having reason to know" that the third party would use the payment for prohibited purposes. Under the new law, the U.S. firm must have actual knowledge of or willful blindness to the prohibited use of the payment.

The act also clarifies the types of payments that are permissible and would not be considered bribery.[15] For example, under the FCPA as originally enacted, payments to low-level officials who exercise only "ministerial" or "clerical" functions were exempt. Unfortunately, this provision provided little guidance to companies in determining whether a given foreign official exercised discretionary authority: special problems arose in countries in the Middle East and Africa, where foreign officials can be employed part-time. The trade act provides a U.S. business with better guidance by specifying the types of payments that are permissible rather than which individuals can receive them. The act specifies that a payment for a routine government action such as processing papers, stamping visas, or scheduling inspections may be made without criminal liability. These changes to the FCPA make it easier for U.S. companies to do business in foreign countries by removing concerns about inadvertent violations.

■■■■■■■   International Marketing Highlight 11.3   ■■■■■■■

A World of Greased Palms

A secret Commerce Department study prepared with the help of U.S. intelligence agencies catalogs scores of incidents of bribery, of aid with strings attached, and other improper inducements by America's trading partners. In the case of strings-attached foreign aid, the deals may violate international trade pacts. And the cost of such practices to the U.S. economy appears enormous. In 1994 alone, U.S. intelligence tracked 100 deals worth a total of $45 billion in which overseas outfits used bribes to undercut U.S. rivals, the study says. The result: foreign companies won 80 percent of the deals. Among the main culprits are some of America's staunchest political allies: France, Germany, and Japan. The corporations involved are not cited by name in the study, but government sources identify premier European high-tech companies—including Germany's Siemens, France's Alcatel Alsthom, and the European airframe consortium Airbus Industrie—as among the major practitioners.

Foreign governments and companies, of course, gripe that the Clinton administration has been doing lots of aggressive advocacy of its own to win deals for U.S. business. "Each time we win a deal, it's because of dirty tricks," says an Airbus official with bitter sarcasm. "Each time Boeing wins, it's because of a better product." Indeed, many officials overseas view the U.S.'s holier-than-thou attitude about shady business practices as naïve and hypocritical.

Source: Business Week, November 6, 1995, p. 36.

Antiboycott Laws

From time to time nations attempt to put pressure on each other through programs of economic boycott. The early 1980s Arab boycott of companies doing business with Israel is an example of such a tactic. Most Arab states did not recognize Israel and hoped that an economic boycott would contribute to Israel's collapse. The oil fortunes of these Arab countries gave them significant economic clout to implement the boycott. Companies that dealt with Israel were blacklisted with the intention of squeezing Israel from all directions and forcing the country into economic isolation.

The U.S. government adopted various measures to prevent U.S. companies from complying with the Arab boycott. For example, the Tax Reform Act of 1976 included a measure that denied foreign income tax benefits to companies that subscribed to the boycott. The law preempts any state or local regulations dealing with boycotts fostered or imposed by foreign countries.[16]

The Arab boycott crumbled toward the end of the 1980s, making it easier for U.S. companies to continue their operations in Israel and at the same time seek out business in Arab states. For example, Coca-Cola Company began making inroads into the Gulf, Lebanon, Jordan, and Saudi Arabia as the boycott became ineffective.[17]

Laws to Protect Domestic Industry

The U.S. government has legislated many laws to protect domestic industry. From time to time, the government sets quotas on imports. For a number of years the sugar import quotas were set so as to preserve about half the market for U.S. producers. Often quotas are split among several countries interested in exporting to the U.S. Such allocation is partly influenced by political considerations. Thus, a certain proportion of a quota may be assigned to a developing country even though its price is higher than that of other exporters. For a few years early in the 1980s, the U.S. government had imposed quotas on Japanese car imports. Recently, a debate has been going on in the federal government about limiting Japanese textile exports to the U.S. by establishing quotas for different categories of textiles.

Quotas, usually provide only temporary relief to domestic industry. In the long run, a domestic industry must stand on its own. If it is inherently inefficient, quotas amount to a support of inefficiency. However, sometimes quotas are appropriately and productively used to buy time so an infant industry can mature and compete effectively.

Laws to Eliminate Tax Loopholes

Many federal laws are designed to eliminate tax loopholes. A prominent example is legislation against *tax havens,* countries that provide out-of-the-ordinary privileges to multinationals in order to attract them to their lands. Tax havens make it more profitable for companies to locate there than in the U.S. There are four types:

1. Countries with no taxes at all, such as the Bahamas, Bermuda, and the Cayman Islands.
2. Countries with taxes at low rates, such as the British Virgin Islands.
3. Countries that tax income from domestic sources but exempt income from foreign sources, such as Hong Kong, and Panama.
4. Countries that allow special privileges, which generally are suitable as tax havens only for limited purposes.

Tax havens offer corporations a legal way to save on taxes. However, a country must offer more than tax benefits to be a good market. Political stability, availability of adequate means of communication and transportation, economic freedom for currency conversion, and availability of professional services are important criteria for evaluating a tax haven.

Tax Treaties

Tax treaties are arrangements between nations that prevent corporate and individual income from being double-taxed. The U.S. has tax treaties with over 56 nations. Thus, foreigners who own securities in U.S. corporations and who are from countries with which there is a tax treaty pay a withholding tax of about 15 percent, while those from non–tax treaty countries pay a 28 percent tax.

The tax treaties are meant to provide a fair deal to individuals and corporations from friendly countries and thus encourage mutually beneficial economic activity. Usually, under a tax treaty, the country where the primary business activity takes place is provided the right to be the principal receiver of tax revenue. A small proportion of the tax may accrue to the other nation. Take, for example, the case of a Pakistani exporter with a business in the U.S. Since there is a tax treaty between the U.S. and Pakistan, the income of the Pakistani businessman, as far as his U.S. operations are concerned, would be taxable under the U.S. IRS rules. However, he would pay only a negligible tax in Pakistan.

Businesses, particularly the MNCs, use tax treaties in various ways to seek maximum benefits. Consider the following situations:

- A tax treaty between the U.S. and England requires a 15 percent withholding tax on dividends.
- A tax treaty between the U.S. and the Netherlands specifies a 5 percent withholding tax.
- A tax treaty between the Netherlands and Great Britain calls for a 5 percent withholding tax. Additionally, dividends from foreign sources are not taxed in the Netherlands.

According to these arrangements, a U.S. company could establish a holding company in the Netherlands that might receive dividend income from a British subsidiary. Moreover, the dividends could be remitted to the parent company in the U.S. The combined tax in the whole process would amount to 10 percent rather than 15 percent.

Tax treaties between the U.S. and different countries are reviewed from time to time. This permits periodic changes in treaty agreements to accommodate changes in the country's monetary and fiscal policies. Usually, a treaty spells out the procedure for consultation and negotiation between officials of the two countries, should disagreements occur.

U.S. Government Support

Nations provide many kinds of support to their companies to enable them to compete successfully for foreign business. Companies belonging to EU countries are often eligible for such government support as low-cost or no-cost bank guarantees, low-cost or no-cost working capital loans, and protection from price escalation.

Traditionally, this type of support has not been available from the U.S. government. In the fall of 1985, however, the U.S. government established a program of bank guarantees similar to those of EU countries.[18] Congress approved the creation of a "war chest" of $300 million to allow the Export-Import Bank to match or beat competitors' subsidies for the benefit of U.S. exporters (see International Marketing Highlight 11.4). In 1992, under pressure from the U.S. during President Bush's trip to Japan, the Japanese automakers promised to increase their purchases of U.S. parts from $9 billion annually to $19 billion in four years and import an estimated 20,000 more U.S. cars per year.[19] For various reasons, this program did not go far.

■■■■■■■■■■   **International Marketing Highlight 11.4**   ■■■■■■■■■■

U.S. Subsidizes Big Food Companies in Their Search for Foreign Markets

McDonald's got $465,000 from the U.S. Agriculture Department in 1991 for ads, paper tray liners, and counter displays promoting Chicken McNuggets to customers around the world.

Campbell Soup Co. spent part of the $450,000 it got from the government to remind the people of Japan, Korea, Argentina, and Taiwan to have a V8 juice. Joseph E. Seagram and Sons touted its Four Roses whiskey in Europe and the Far East with $146,000 from the department.

The three companies are among dozens of well-known corporate giants that have collected money under a U.S.D.A. program to find new overseas market for U.S. food, candy, bourbon, wine, ginseng, cotton, mink pelts, and bovine semen. The $200-million-a-year Market Promotion Program is supposed to help U.S. farmers by promoting exports of products that contain at least 50 percent U.S. agricultural commodities. Two-thirds of the grants in 1991 went to industry associations that conduct promotions for products such as strawberries, kiwis, or cling peaches. The remainder went to a long list of companies to advertise their brand-name products. Those brands include Burger King, M&M-Mars, Hershey Foods, Del Monte, Welch's, Ocean Spray Cranberries, Nabisco, and Quaker Oats.

Source: Marketing News, March 2, 1992, p. 7.

Then, in October 1994 the U.S. and the Japanese governments made four new trade deals.[20] Two of these deals made it easier for Americans (and other foreigners) to sell telecom equipment to the Japanese government and to NTT, Japan's biggest telephone firm, which is 65 percent state-owned. The third deal helped foreign firms to seek government's contracts to supply medical equipment. The fourth deal clarified regulations in the Japanese insurance market, permitting companies to change premium and introduce new products without permission from regulators.

International Laws

International law is a huge area of study, impossible to cover here, even perfunctorily. We will focus on certain areas of international law that are of particular relevance to the marketer.

GATT, IMF, and the World Bank were discussed in Chapter 3. Agreements under these institutions compose international laws of sorts that influence business in different ways. The WTO regulations are particularly relevant for marketers since they deal with trade restrictions and barriers that affect market potential.

To give the reader an idea of other areas covered by international law and the agencies that administer these laws, a brief discussion follows of those relating to property protection, UN treaties and conventions, metric transition, UN consumer protection, and regional laws.

Protection of Property

"Property" here refers to patents, trademarks, and the like. In the U.S., businesses seek protection of their property under U.S. laws. For example, a trademark can be registered. In an overseas situation, a multinational enterprise runs the risk of piracy. Stories are told of jeans manufactured in Hong Kong being given the Calvin Klein brand name and sold in Europe at half the usual price. Computer pirates in Taiwan incur the wrath of IBM Corporation. IBM-compatible computers are sold widely in Taiwan by scores of small companies, who manufacture counterfeit machines in violation of IBM's copyrights.[21] The U.S. Patent Trademark Office estimates that intellectual-property losses for U.S. industry, measured in terms of lost licensing opportunities and cost of enforcement, totaled at least $30 billion in 1988 alone[22] (see International Marketing Highlight 11.5).

Companies spend millions of dollars to establish trademarks and brand names. Consider, for example, Coca-Cola, Tide, and Corningware's cornflower pattern. If a foreign firm steals a company's established brand name and uses it on a locally conceived and manufactured product, not only are potential markets lost, but often that company's reputation is hurt if the imitated product is of inferior quality, as it frequently is.

In Ciudad del Este, Paraguay, which borders Argentina and Brazil, counterfeit goods from Asia spill onto the streets, at corners, near bus stops—even in the middle of a four-lane highway. As in the street markets of Mexico City, the shirt with a Nike logo is not a Nike-authorized product. Nor are the Guess watches, the music cassettes, or the video games legitimate.

The Paraguayan border city is just one example of Latin America's informal economy, or *gray market*. Seldom thought of in the context of the logistics chain, this market robs transport companies of cargo to carry, warehousers of freight to store, and insurers of traffic to cover. And, of course, trademark, patent, and copyright violations cost companies in the U.S. and other industrialized countries billions of dollars in lost sales.[23] Yet, many governments in Latin America are willing to close their eyes to the informal economy because it provides needed employment.

U.S. companies are particularly susceptible to piracy because of their lead in many technologies and number of household brand names. In 1992 a federal jury ordered Minolta Camera Co. to pay Honeywell Inc. $96 million for infringing on two Honeywell patents in its autofocus cameras.[24] The intellectual-property protection problem, however, is not limited to U.S. companies. Multinationals from other parts of the world face similar problems. For example, Hitachi Ltd. has accused Korea's Samsung Electronics Co. of using its technology to make dynamic random access memory chips. Hitachi also has sued the U.S.'s Motorola, Inc., charging that its MC88200 chip infringes on a Hitachi patent.[25]

The traditional way of protecting property outside the home country is by obtaining parallel protection in each host country. This process is cumbersome and expensive. It cost one large company almost $2 million to obtain foreign patents. In addition, this process is replete with risks that the patent will not be granted because the standards for patentability in some countries are not compatible with accepted practices in other countries.[26]

There are international conventions and agreements that can make it easier to secure property rights. But overall, international arrangements for property protection are insufficient and inadequate, and brand name/trademark piracy is not actually alleviated. The real problem arises when the question of copyright infringement is not clear-cut. Consider the fight between Lego System (a Danish company), the world's leading maker of children's building blocks, and a U.S. company, Tyco, popularly known for its model trains. Tyco spotted Lego's lack of competition and launched its own high-quality Lego copies called Super Blocks at retail prices 25 percent below Lego's. Thanks in part to its hard-hitting advertising campaign ("If you can't tell the difference, why pay the difference?"), in 1986 Tyco captured more than one-fifth of the $100 million U.S. market for blocks. Lego sued Tyco for copyright infringement in Hong Kong, where Tyco's blocks were made before production was shifted to Taiwan. Following a trial in 1986 that cost each company $2 million, the Hong Kong lower court decided in favor of Lego. However, the appeals court reversed parts of the decision, and both toy makers have appealed to the London Court of Arbitration. In early 1987 the London court upheld the decision of the appeals court.[27]

Interestingly, owing to philosophical differences between code law and common law, sometimes injured parties lose in legal dispute. For example, under common law, the right to property is established by actual use, while under code law the right emerges from legal registration. Thus, if a pirate registered a well-known brand (say, Colgate) in a code-law country (say, Italy), in a legal dispute the actual owner (the Colgate Palmolive Company) may lose to the pirate, at least in Italy. Of course, if the country in question happens to be a friendly country, the U.S. government may be willing to help.

International Marketing Highlight 11.5

Rounding Up Counterfeiters

Levi Strauss & Co. touts its trousers as "America's original jeans." But these days, so do a lot of others. The famous apparel maker is fighting an unprecedented explosion of counterfeit pants. In 1991 Levi seized 1.3 million pairs of knockoffs, more than five times as many as it usually confiscates in a year. But the new knockoffs, most of which are made in China, differ from the crude copies the company has seen in the past.

Counterfeiters have crossed the threshold. The typical consumer would not be able to detect that they are buying counterfeits. The fakes bear labels saying that they're made in the U.S. and proclaiming that their colored-tab and stitched-pocket design are registered trademarks to help you identify garments made only by Levi Strauss & Co.

Only someone well-versed in the "construction and engineering" of Levis could tell the difference. There are a few identifying marks on the real McCoys, but Levi doesn't want to tell consumers what they are for fear of tipping its hand to counterfeiters. (One difference is that real Levi labels note that they are "made from recycled paper.")

Though the fake Levis look nearly identical, the company contends they may fall apart at the seams. After a few washes, belt loops fall off, rivets rust, and shrinkage control is not what it should be. Levi contends that poor-quality jeans will hurt its reputation.

Counterfeiters are trying to cash in on the huge demand for Levi jeans overseas. Though fakes have been seized in 31 countries, most are destined for the booming European market, where Levis are a status symbol, commanding up to $100 a pair. In 1990 alone, the company's sales in Europe, where Levi sells mostly jeans, rose 55 percent. But Levi can't meet worldwide demand for its best-selling button-fly "501" jeans, most of which are manufactured in the U.S.

Counterfeiters are eager to take up the slack. To combat them, Levi has spent about $2 million on more than 60 investigations, relying on a network of informants in Asia and Europe and trying to build paper trails on the middlemen who drive the market.

Source: The Wall Street Journal, February 19, 1992, p. B1.

Following is a description of the important international conventions for property protection.

International Bureau for the Protection of Industrial Property. This bureau was established by the Paris Convention, to which over 50 nations including the U.S. subscribed. Currently the membership includes some 94 countries. Under this convention, once a company has filed for a patent in one country, it has priority for 12 months in seeking the patent in all other member countries. Further, the convention requires each member country to extend to the nationals of other member countries the same rights it provides to its own nationals.

The Inter-American Convention. Most Latin American countries and the U.S. are parties to this convention. It provides its members protection similar to that of the Paris Convention for inventions, patents, designs, and models.

Madrid Arrangement for International Registration of Trademarks. This forum has 26 members in Europe. The U.S. is not a member of the Madrid Convention. Under the Madrid arrangement, the member countries grant automatic registration in all countries through registration in one of the countries upon payment of the required fee. For example, if a company registers a trademark in Spain, a member country, registration is simultaneously ensured in the other 25 member countries after the appropriate payments are made.

The Trademark Registration Treaty. In the early 1970s, 16 European nations signed a convention to establish a European patent office. Under this convention, the patent office makes one grant for all the member countries under a single European patent law. The European patent office became operational in 1978 in Munich, Germany (see International Marketing Highlight 11.6).

■■■■■■■■ **International Marketing Highlight 11.6** ■■■■■■■■

Wanted: One Patent for One Market

When it comes to patent applications in Europe, companies have two choices: to take a national route or opt for a "European" solution. The first entails the process of applying for a patent in each member state—a drawn-out, expensive process requiring separate translations, procedures, lawyers, agents, and fees for each state.

On completion, the company will have a number of patents, each of which varies in scope and conditions, and each open to separate interpretations in each national court.

The alternative is to take the "European" route. This involves filing an application at Munich's European Patent Office (EPO). However, the EPO does not grant an EU patent but only a bundle of national patent rights whose terms and conditions will differ according to the respective national laws of the contracting countries—the 15 EU member states plus Switzerland, Liechtenstein, Monaco and six Eastern European states. Once the grant is made, a "national phase" follows that entails a full translation of the filing for each state in which a firm has applied for patent rights. The applicant has to pay for translations, filings and attorney fees.

Source: Crossborder Monitor, September 1998. p.1.

Intellectual-property protection has improved in several problem countries in recent years, particularly Taiwan, Indonesia, and China.[28] This improved protection has largely been the result of political pressure from the U.S. (see International Marketing Highlight

11.7). In the Uruguay Round of GATT negotiations, intellectual-property rights was a new issue deliberated by the nations. The members agreed to a negotiating framework that allowed for conclusion of a comprehensive agreement to govern the *trade-related aspects of intellectual property (TRIPs)*. The Uruguay Round supports the concept of *reciprocity* in the matter of intellectual-property rights (i.e., rights available to nationals are extended to foreigners as well), and applies the concept of "most favored nation" to the area of intellectual-property rights.[29]

Following is a checklist for intellectual-property protection:[30]

- Find out how the country protects intellectual property, if at all.
- Register your copyrights and trademarks in countries in which you do business.
- Clearly spell out dispute-resolution procedures in contracts.
- Explore entering into licensing contracts with likely problem competitors, especially in countries without strong intellectual-property laws.
- Consider distributing only older material overseas, especially in countries where the state of technology is somewhat less advanced.
- Establish relations and cooperate with local customs officials and police.
- Hire a private investigator to gather evidence of piracy and work with local officials.

UN Treaties and Conventions

The United Nations (UN) has established a number of autonomous bodies and agencies to encourage worldwide economic cooperation and prosperity, as follows.

World Health Organization. (WHO): works to improve health conditions. WHO deals with such matters as drug standardization, epidemic control, health delivery systems, and related programs.

International Civil Aviation Organization (ICAO): promotes safe and efficient air travel through regulating flow of air traffic, air-worthiness standards, airport operations, and related communications.

■■■■■■■■■■■■■■■   International Marketing Highlight 11.7   ■■■■■■■■■

Saudi Copyright Law

Saudi Arabia passed a copyright law to curb widespread piracy of such material as videotapes and computer software. The law, approved by King Fahd in December 1989, was in response to pressure from the U.S., where the Motion Picture Association of America has claimed industry losses of about $200 million a year due to piracy of videotapes in Saudi Arabia alone. The new law strictly forbids piracy, but diplomatic sources said much will depend on how the Saudis enforce the law.

Source: The Wall Street Journal, January 18, 1990, p. A16.

International Telecommunications Union (ITU): regulates international communications via radio, telephone, and telegraph. For example, ITU controls and allocates radio frequencies and facilitates intercountry telegraph and telephone communications.

Universal Postal Union (UPU): facilitates postal communication. For example, UPU conducts settlements among nations related to revenue sharing.

International Labor Organization (ILO): protects workers' rights, promotes worker welfare, and enhances the effectiveness of their organizations.

International Telecommunications Satellite Consortium (INTELSAT): deals with matters of telecommunication. INTELSAT's work mainly concerns new satellite communications technology.

International Standards Organization (ISO): another specialized UN agency, ISO is particularly important because its administration bears directly on marketing. ISO promotes standardization of different products and processes. The ultimate purpose is to encourage world trade and business without hindrance from design/style/feature variations among nations.

As an example, the ISO has over 100 committees that are actively engaged in developing uniform international standards in various fields. In 1987 the ISO issued *ISO 9000,* a series of documents that provide guidance on the selection and implementation of an appropriate quality management program for a supplier's operations. The purpose of the program is to document, implement, and demonstrate the quality assurance systems used by companies that supply goods and services internationally.

The impact of these agencies on international business varies. For example, an airframe industry is affected by the ICAO regulations; a WHO agreement might apply to a pharmaceutical company. But the importance of the need for standardization does not vary. A grinding machine still usable in the U.S. might be unsuitable in England for such reasons as differences in electric current and weight measures (in England, power is normally supplied at 220 volts and the metric system is used). Thus, in order to sell a U.S.–made grinding machine, the tolerance measurement may have to be varied to conform to measurements commonly used in Great Britain. Similarly, the electrical wiring may require change for the machine to operate with a different supply power.

Consider the European telecommunications industry: In Spain, the busy signal is three pips a second; in Denmark it is two. Telephone numbers within French cities are seven digits long; in Italy they're almost any length. German phones run on 60 volts of electricity; elsewhere, on 49. Only about 30 percent of the technical specifications involved in phone systems are common from one country to the next.[31]

Needless to say, standardization in the European telecommunications industry is overdue.

Metric Transition

The differences in standards are among the major hindrances to world trade and business development and have led to market opportunity losses for U.S. companies in many nations. International cooperation is overdue in this area. Traditionally, U.S. industry and government have played almost no role in seeking common standards worldwide. This indifference may be attributed to the fact that the overseas business of U.S. firms is proportionately small. In the future, however, U.S. businesses are more likely to participate actively in the standardization effort.

The U.S. Department of Commerce's National Institute of Standards and Technology (NIST), previously known as the National Bureau of Standards (NBS), has been given several new assignments to boost U.S. industry in the world marketplace by seeking standardization. The assignments result from the 1988 Omnibus Trade and Competitiveness Act, which addresses the problem by moving the U.S. closer to the metric system, now used by most of the world's population. The "inch-pound" system of measurement used in the U.S., known as the *customary* or *English* system, was abandoned even by the English when the U.K. switched to the metric system in the early 1970s. Only the U.S. continues to use it.

The 1988 act states that the metric system is "the preferred system of weights and measures for U.S. trade and commerce." It directs the federal government to provide leadership in metric conversion and calls for a preference in government purchasing for metric products. The act requires federal agencies to use the metric system wherever it is practical to do so in procurements, grants, and other business-related activities. The agencies have notified grantees, contractors, and suppliers of the new requirements and of time schedules for meeting the government's deadline.

The act specifies that the federal government has a responsibility to develop procedures and techniques to assist industry, especially small business, as it voluntarily converts to the metric system. Nevertheless, individual groups and industries are still free to decide whether to convert and to determine conversion timetables according to their own needs.

The trade act requires government and industry to use metric units in documentation of exports and imports as prescribed by the International Convention on the Harmonized Commodity Description and Coding System *(Harmonized System).* This system is designed to standardize international commodity classifications for all major trading nations. The international metric system (SI) is the official measurement system of the Harmonized System.

Congress spelled out in the act the reasons it believes the U.S. would benefit from converting to the metric system:

- World trade is increasingly geared toward the metric system of measurement.
- Industry in the U.S. is often at a competitive disadvantage when dealing in international markets because of its nonstandard measurement system, and is sometimes excluded when it is unable to deliver goods that are measured in metric system.
- The inherent simplicity of the metric system of measurement and standardization of weights and measures has led to major cost savings in certain industries that have converted to that system.
- The metric system of measurement can provide substantial advantages to the federal government in its own operations.[32]

The EU is proceeding aggressively with plans to standardize differing national specifications and testing and certification procedures into a single EU-wide body of uniform standards and regulations. Such standardization can offer real advantages to U.S. businesspeople interested in a large market for their goods. A U.S. product that meets the EU requirements in one member state can be freely marketed throughout the EU.

UN Guidelines on Consumer Protection

After more than six years of work, in April 1985 the UN General Assembly adopted by consensus a set of guidelines on consumer protection. The guidelines cover the following basic consumer principles:[33]

- Insurance of the physical safety of consumers and their protection from potential dangers caused by consumer products.
- Protection of consumers' economic interests.
- Consumers' access to the necessary information to make informed choices according to their individual wishes and needs.
- Availability of effective consumer redress.
- Freedom to form consumer groups or organizations and the opportunity of such organizations to be consulted and to have their views represented.

These guidelines are important because without acceptance of such principles and strong information links on products that have been banned or severely restricted in various countries, sales could continue unabated. In other words, profit motive may override consideration for the harm many products may induce. Implementation of these guidelines by countries currently lacking adequate consumer protection will help make up for that lack.

Regional Laws

Regional laws pertain to specific areas involving a group of countries tied together through some kind of regional economic cooperation. (Chapter 7 examined different forms of regional groupings.) Market groups may legislate laws applicable to MNCs conducting business within the member countries. The most progressive market agreement is represented by the EU. The EU has adopted a variety of directives that deeply affect multinational enterprises. For example, the head offices of MNCs with European-based subsidiaries are required to make disclosures of their global operations to local labor unions twice a year, obliging them to inform and consult with the labor unions on any major decision affecting workers.

Another directive requires MNCs to consolidate the accounts of European subsidiaries. A third directive relates to product-liability standards, effectively eliminating the need for plaintiffs to show negligence to justify injury claims. Under a fourth one, workers would sit on the boards of all public companies. Most radical of all is a directive that makes corporate directors *personally* liable for damages should minority stockholders or creditors, or even employees, of a subsidiary suffer as a result of a corporate headquarters' decision favoring the interests of the parent company and its stockholders.

These kinds of directives are not accepted quickly; the EU lawmaking process is cumbersome. The directives to harmonize the national laws of the 15 members of the EU must first be endorsed by a majority of the 19 European commissioners (two each from Britain, France, Germany, and Italy, one each from the rest, and all appointed for four-year terms by their governments). Draft-stage directives then go to the 520-member European Parliament in Strasbourg, whose main role is to propose amendments for the commissioners' consideration. After receiving the parliament's views, the commission prepares a final draft of the directive and submits it to the Council of Ministers, composed of the appropriate cabinet-level officers from each national government. With the council's consent, a proposal becomes a legally binding EU directive, but even then it does not become law automatically. Enacting legislation to fulfill the intent of EU directives remains a prerogative of national parliaments. For example, in 1985 an EU product-liability directive was adopted by the Council of Ministers after more than eight years of talks. The directive allows consumers to collect damages for injuries from defective products without showing that the manufacturer was at fault. Member nations were directed to pass laws that would comply with the directive within three years, which they did.

Arbitration

Despite their best efforts, U.S. businesspeople working at the international level run into difficulties from time to time with people, companies, or organizations in foreign countries. The conflict may be with the host country government; a native firm, either in the public or private sector; or a multinational firm belonging to a third country. The source of the difficulty may arise from differing interpretations of the contractual terms or because of opposing positions on an ad hoc issue that was not anticipated at the time the contract was made.

There are three ways for an international firm to resolve conflicts. First, the two parties mutually agree to settle the differences. Second, the firm decides to sue the other party. Third, the conflicting parties agree to arbitration. Of the three alternatives, the first one is the best. Usually, however, the conflicting parties cannot realistically be expected to resolve their differences between themselves. Legal action, the second alternative, may not, for a variety of reasons, be in the best long-term interest of the international marketer. Legal action against a native firm would surely affect the reputation of the foreign enterprise, no matter how strong its case. Further, there is no guarantee that the court would make a fair, unbiased decision. Moreover, the legal route can be messy, time-consuming, and expensive.

For example, taking legal action in a trade case can range from an average of $54,700 for a Section 301 violation (an unfair foreign trade practice) to $715,000 or more for a Section 337 case (an infringement or theft of intellectual property rights such as patents, trademarks, and copyrights.) Similarly, legal costs in a dumping case may range from $151,000 to $553,000. An import threat to national security may cost $181,300 to $537,500.[34]

Usually the best recourse of a multinational firm to resolve conflict in a foreign environment is *arbitration,* which can be defined as a process of settling disputes by referring the matter to a disinterested party for a review of the merits of the case and for a judgment. The judgment may or may not be binding on the conflicting parties—hence the term *binding arbitration.* Traditionally, the disputing parties resorted to ad hoc arrangements for arbitration, because prior to 1966 there was no international authority to serve as arbitrator between an international marketer and a host country party. Currently, a number of arrangements are available for arbitration, as follows:

1. The *International Center for Settlement of Investment Disputes (ICSID)* was established in 1966 by the World Bank convention to enable private investors to obtain redress against a foreign state for grievances arising out of an investment dispute. The convention established strict rules for arbitration that may explain in part why it is seldom used:

The Convention provides that, where both parties have consented to arbitration under the auspices of the Center, neither may withdraw its consent unilaterally; and should either party refuse to submit to the jurisdiction of the Center thereafter, an award can nevertheless be entered which will be final, binding, and enforceable without relitigation, in all nations that are members of the Convention. To facilitate the enforcement of awards, each member nation is obliged to designate a domestic court or other authority responsible for enforcement of awards made.

ICSID has not been able to play the role expected by the signatories who created the convention. The problem is that large developing countries, important prospects for direct foreign investment, are not ICSID members. Most of Latin American countries are among the nonsignatories; they subscribe to the *Calvo doctrine* for representation of their position. Named after an Argentine jurist, this doctrine provides that a foreign investor, by virtue of making an investment, implicitly agrees to be treated by the host government as a national and gives up the right to involve any outside agency or home government in the resolution of a dispute. ICSID has received lukewarm support from host countries as an arbitrator of disputes.

2. The *Inter-American Commercial Arbitration Commission* serves to arbitrate disputes for businesses of 21 Western Hemisphere countries, including the U.S.

3. The *International Chamber of Commerce (ICC)* is an association of chambers of commerce worldwide. It has established a court of arbitration that has set rules used in conducting arbitration proceedings. Perhaps of all the arrangements for arbitration, ICC is the most successful. Of the over 200 decisions that the ICC Court of Arbitration made in recent years, only about 24 were questioned by the disputants. Of these 24 decisions, 21 were upheld in the courts when further legal action was pursued.

The ICC arbitration procedure is rather simple. In the first instance, it tries to settle the dispute through mutual conciliation. If that fails, each party is allowed to choose one member of the Court of Arbitration from its current list of distinguished lawyers/ jurists/judges. The third member is appointed by ICC. The Court of Arbitration schedules hearings and, after reviewing the facts presented by the plaintiff and the defendant, makes a decision.

4. The *American Arbitration Association (AAA)* is basically a U.S. tribunal originally established to conduct arbitration among businesses in the U.S. More recently, the AAA extended the scope of its activities beyond the U.S.

5. The *Canadian-American Commercial Arbitration Commission (CACAC)* serves as arbitrator between U.S. and Canadian businesses.

6. The *London Court of Arbitration* has jurisdiction that is restricted to cases that should legally be arbitrated in the U.K. The decisions of this court are legally binding on the parties in dispute under the English law.

A number of other agencies and organizations arbitrate in disputes about foreign direct investment. One of these is the *International Court of Justice (ICJ)*, also sometimes referred to as the *World Court,* a special judicial UN agency. ICJ can be approached for the arbitration of disputes between sovereign nations. Thus, if the U.S. government decides to take up a matter on behalf of a U.S. company that is in a conflict with a government overseas, the dispute can be referred to ICJ for decision. Needless to say, the federal government would pursue the matter only if it involved a national issue. Since ICJ deals only with disputes between nations, and not those between individuals or their companies, and since the government would involve itself only if the matter is of national importance, ICJ has not been extensively used for the settlement of investment disputes.

Another agency is the *Permanent Court of Arbitration (PCA)*. Established by the Hague Conventions of 1899 and 1907, the PCA consists of a small bureau at the Hague and a panel of arbitrators, four from each member country. The arbitrators are chosen from the panel members whenever a case must be examined. PCA has played an insignificant role in connection with international investment disputes. Like the ICJ, use of PCA for arbitration in international investment disputes comes only through the U.S. federal government.

Finally, arbitration may also be conducted by an *International Claims Commission (ICC)*. The ICC is an ad hoc arbitration arrangement. When a substantial number of claims between two countries accumulate, an ICC arbitration tribunal may be established by agreement between the interested nations. ICC's use requires that the U.S. government espouse and raise the MNC's claim against the other nation. To invoke the jurisdiction of any of the last three bodies, the foreign nation in question must consent to arbitration.

Summary

A U.S. corporation involved in international marketing should comply not only with U.S. laws but also with host country laws. Worldwide, different countries follow different sets of laws. An international marketer should be particularly familiar with host country laws pertaining to competition, price setting, distribution arrangements, product liability, patents and trademarks, and advertising.

To fully grasp a country's laws, it is essential to understand the legal philosophy of the country. Countries may follow common law or code law. Common law is based on precedents and practices; England, for example, is a common-law country. Code law is based on detailed rules; Mexico is a code-law country. The legal basis of a country can affect marketing decisions in multifaceted ways.

Another important legal environment aspect is the jurisdiction of laws. The question of which laws will apply in which particular matters must be known. In some instances, those of the country where the agreement was made apply; in others, those of the country where the business was conducted apply. It is desirable to have a jurisdictional clause in agreements. If there is none, when a conflict of interest occurs, it may either be settled through litigation or be referred for arbitration.

In addition to heeding both U.S. and host country laws, international marketers must be aware of treaties and international conventions. By and large, the relevant laws of the host country would be those concerning tariffs, dumping, export/import licensing, foreign investment, foreign investment incentives (provided by the government to attract foreign business), and restrictions on trading activities. The relevant U.S. laws would be those affecting foreign trade, antitrust laws, antiboycott laws, laws to protect domestic industry, laws to prevent loopholes in the existing tax laws (tax haven laws), tax treaties, and laws that pertain to U.S. government support of U.S. business abroad.

Some international treaties and conventions are concerned with the protection of property such as patents, trademarks, models, and the like, in foreign countries. Some international laws have provisions for the encouragement of both worldwide economic cooperation and prosperity and standardization of international products and processes.

If a legal conflict occurs between parties from different countries, one way of resolving it is through arbitration. A number of organizations are available for arbitration of disputes: the International Center for Settlement of Investment Disputes, the Inter-American Commercial Arbitration Commission, the International Chamber of Commerce, the American Arbitration Association, the Canadian-American Commercial Arbitration Commission, and the London Court of Arbitration.

Review Questions

1. Distinguish between code law and common law. Illustrate how the differences between the two may affect marketing decisions.
2. Explain how one might determine which of two different countries' laws would be applicable in the event of a dispute.
3. Define *dumping*. Why do countries pass antidumping laws?
4. Do U.S. antitrust laws apply to U.S. corporations in their international dealings? If so, how does this affect the competitive position of U.S. corporations?
5. What sort of support could the U.S. government provide to help U.S. corporations compete effectively against non–U.S. multinationals?
6. What is arbitration? Discuss the role of the ICC as an arbitration agency.

Creative Questions

1. Internationally adequate protection of intellectual-property rights is important for the U.S. since we as a nation have a higher stake than others in the matter. The WTO agreement provides 20 years of protection for patents, trademarks, and copyrights in the book, software, film, and pharmaceutical industries. Developing countries were given 10 years to phase in patent protection for pharmaceuticals. Is this enough to protect U.S. interests? If not, what additional measures should be adopted?
2. In developing countries, governments have large procurement programs. Often multinational corporations outside the U.S. have high-level government support to

successfully compete for these programs. Should the U.S. provide such help to its companies? What if such help leads to government interference in other business matters?

Endnotes

1. Gillian Rice, " Philosophy and Practice of Islamic Ethics: Implications for Doing Business in Muslims Countries," *Discussion Paper Series*, No. 90–5, The American Graduate School of International Management.

2. Shoshana B. Tancer, " Strategic Management of Legal Issues in the Evolving Transnational Business," *Discussion Paper Series*, No. 99-5, The American Graduate School of International Management.

3. *Advertising Age*, April 2, 1988, p. 34.

4. Ford S. Worthy, "Tightwad Taiwan Starts to Spend," *Fortune*, December 5, 1988, p. 177.

5. "Japanese Rice: The End of An Era," *The Economist*, August 20, 1994, p. 52.

6. Aziz Haniffa, "India Accused of Dumping Steel," *India Abroad*, August 6, 1993, p. 24.

7. Warren J. Keegan, *Multinational Marketing Management*, 3rd ed. (Englewood Cliffs, NJ: Prentice-Hall, 1984), p. 346.

8. *Asia Wall Street Journal Weekly*, February 21, 1994, p. 8.

9. "President Pitchman," *Business Week*, December 6, 1993, p. 42.

10. Doron P. Levin and Thomas F. O'Boyle, "GM's Chairman Runs into Bizarre Problem Under German Law," *The Wall Street Journal*, June 10, 1987, p. 1.

11. A. O. Cao, "Nontariff Barriers to U.S. Manufactured Exports," *Columbia Journal of World Business*, Summer 1980, p. 95.

12. Raymond Vernon, "Antitrust and International Business," *Harvard Business Review*, September–October 1968, p. 86. *Also see* Robert H. Brumley, "How Antitrust Law Affects International Joint Ventures," *Business America*, November 21, 1988, pp. 2–4.

13. "Going for Coke," *The Economist*, August 14, 1999, p. 51.

14. "Coke Said to Face Inquiry Over Sales in Soviet Union," *The Wall Street Journal*, June 12, 1988, p. 22.

15. "Doing Business Abroad with Few Restraints," *The Wall Street Journal*, June 5, 1990, p. B1.

16. Sandra MacRae Huszagh, "Exporter Perceptions of the U.S. Regulatory Environment," *Columbia Journal of World Business*, Fall 1981, pp. 22–31; Samuel Rabino, "An Examination of Barriers to Exporting Encountered by Small Manufacturing Companies," *Management International Review*, No. 1 (1980), pp. 67–74.

17. "A Red Line in the Sand," *The Economist*, October 1, 1994, p. 86.

18. "The New Trade Strategy," *Business Week*, October 7, 1985, p. 90.

19. Allan T. Demaree, "What Now for the U.S. and Japan," *Fortune*, February 10, 1992, p. 80.

20. "U.S.–Japan Trade: Big Deal," *The Economist*, October 8, 1994, p. 76.

21. "IBM Hints for Taiwanese Pirates," *The Wall Street Journal*, October 16, 1984, p. 32. *Also see* Gunter Hauptamn, "Intellectual Property Rights," *International Marketing Review*, Spring 1987, pp. 61–64.

22. *Business International,* May 29, 1989, p. 166.

23. "Gray Market Blues," *Crossborder Monitor*, April 29, 1998, p. 2.

24. "From the Mind of Minolta—Oops, Make that 'Honeywell'," *Business Week*, February 24, 1992, p. 34.

25. "Japanese Reverse Tack on Patent Protection," *The Wall Street Journal*, October 24, 1989, p. B1. *Also see* Thomas J. Maronick, "European Patent Laws and Decisions: Implications for Multinational Marketing Strategy," *International Marketing Review*, Summer 1988, pp. 31–40.

26. See "How U.S. Firm won Patent Suit in China," *Crossborder Monitor*, August 6, 1997, p. 8.

27. Erik Bjerager, "Denmark's Lego Challenges Imitators of Its Famous Toy Blocks Across Globe," *The Wall Street Journal*, August 5, 1987, p. 18.

28. John D. Mittelstaedt and Robert A. Mittelstaedt, "The Protection of Intellectual Property: Issues of Origination and Ownership," *Journal of Public Policy & Marketing*, Spring 1997, pp. 14–25.

29. Subhash C. Jain, "Problems of International Protection of Intellectual Property Rights," *Journal of International Marketing* 4, no. 1 (1996): 9–32.

30. Ibid.

31. Richard L. Hudson, "European Officials Push Idea of Standardizing Telecommunications—But Some Makers Resist," *The Wall Street Journal*, April 10, 1985, p. 32.

32. *Business America*, August 1, 1988, p. 9.

33. "U.N. Rallies to Consumers," *Development Forum*, July–August 1985, p. 14.

34. Virginia M. Citrano, "So, Sue Me," *Northeast International Business*, May 1989, p. 38.

PART 5

International Marketing Decisions

Product Policy and Planning

CHAPTER • 12

CHAPTER FOCUS_____

After studying this chapter, you should be able to

■ Discuss the perspectives of international product planning.

■ Debate the pros and cons of standardization versus customization of products in overseas markets.

■ Describe various aspects of new-product introduction in international markets.

■ Explain the factors that affect global adoption and diffusion of new products.

■ Compare various branding alternatives for international markets.

■ Describe the role of international product warranties and services.

The product decision is among the first decisions that a marketing manager makes in order to develop a marketing mix. Traditionally, the product decision in international marketing simply has meant exporting products already produced and marketed in the U.S. Now such a simple perspective on product policy will not work. U.S. companies today face strong competition from European and Japanese companies, as well as from newly industrialized countries and emerging nations. At the same time, foreign markets have become more sophisticated, and an American product cannot count on success simply because it is an American product.

Thus, the product decision must be made on the basis of careful analysis and review. The nature, depth, and breadth of the product line; the possibilities of new-product development and innovation; the importance attached to product design (the adaptation and customization of products to suit local conditions vis-à-vis standardization); the decision on foreign R&D; and a planned screening and elimination of unsuccessful products bear heavily on success in foreign markets.

This chapter examines these product-related issues and suggests conceptual approaches for handling them. Also discussed are international packaging and labeling matters, international brand strategy, and warranty and service policies.

Meaning of Product

Products are all around us, and yet it is not always easy to define precisely what a product is. The difficulty lies in the fact that the same product may have a different significance for people in different countries. A refrigerator is a necessity in the U.S. because people tend to depend on a variety of frozen foods and weekly shopping. In Mexico, however, as in other developing countries, food shopping most commonly occurs on a daily basis. A refrigerator there is a luxury for the rich to store either leftovers or perishable foods for a short time.

A definition of *product*, thus, must be comprehensive enough to cover both necessities and luxuries. One way to define it as a bundle of attributes that satisfies a customer demand. It may be offered in the form of a tangible item, a service, or an idea. For example, the attributes of a wine are flavor, taste, consistency, and its quality as a thirst quencher or cool refreshment. Different wines have different attributes, and each brand is intended to meet the demands of a particular set of target customers. The attributes of a corporate jet plane are width of cabin, fuel economy, flight range, speed, and noise level. Businesspersons around the world would prefer different sets of attributes in choosing a plane for their use.

Putting it differently, customers do not simply buy products in the physical sense, they buy *satisfaction*, which is derived from the product's attributes, various features, and characteristics. This fact has important ramifications in defining product objectives.

A company can offer different versions of the same product and thus broaden its product line by catering to the needs of heterogeneous segments of the market. In the U.S., the Coca-Cola Company is a *full-line* soft drink manufacturer producing Classic Coke, Diet Coke, Sprite, Minute Maid, and other soft drinks to cater to the needs of different target groups. Outside the U.S., the company offers just Coca-Cola in most countries. Thus, the Coca-Cola Company is considered a full-line manufacturer at home, but a *limited-line* manufacturer internationally.

International Product Planning

International product planning involves determining which products to introduce into which countries; what modifications to make in the products; what new products to add; what brand names to use; what package designs to adopt; what guarantees and warranties to give; what after-sales services to offer; and finally, when to enter the market. All these are crucial decisions requiring a variety of informational inputs. Chapter 4 on marketing research specifies different ways and sources for gathering appropriate information. Basic to these decisions are three other considerations: (1) product objectives, (2) coordination of product planning activities between headquarters and subsidiary, and (3) foreign collaboration.

The process of product planning in the international context is diagrammed in Exhibit 12.1. A company interested in an international market should first define its business intent based on the objectives of both the corporation and the host country. The product objectives of a company should flow from the definition of its business. Ultimately, the offering should provide satisfaction to the customer, which will be reflected in the realization of the goals of both the corporation and the host country.

Product Objectives

Product objectives emerge from host country and corporate objectives combined via the business definition. The company's goals usually are *stability*, *growth*, *profits*, and *return on investment*. Stated differently, the corporate objectives may be defined in terms of *activities* (the manufacture of a specific product, or export to a particular market), *financial indicators* (to achieve a targeted return on investment), *desired position* (to gain market share and relative market leadership), and all these in combination with each other. Host country objectives vary depending on the country's economic, political, and cultural environment. For example, the typical goals of a less developed country would be to seek faster economic growth, to build a balanced industrial sector, to create employment opportunities, and to earn foreign exchange. On the other hand, the objectives of an oil-rich country might be to provide a modern living standard to its masses in a short time without disrupting the cultural structure of its society and/or to diversify its economy to reduce its dependence on oil over the long term.

Obviously, the objectives of the host country and the company are poles apart. In any market worldwide, however, no company can hope to succeed without aligning itself with the national concerns of the host country. There are no models to use in seeking a description of such an alignment. Conceptually, though, a macroanalysis of a country's socioeconomic perspectives should provide insights into its different concerns and problems. The company can then figure out if its business would help the country in any way, directly or indirectly. The business definition should be developed accordingly.

For example, the shortage of foreign exchange might be a big problem for a country. A multinational marketer's willingness to pursue a major effort of export promotion in the country would amount to an objective in line with the country's need. But a company focused simply on manufacturing and selling such consumer goods as toiletries and canned foods in a nation that is interested in establishing a basic infrastructure for industrial development in the country may not be serving the national interest.

As stated, the definition of product objectives should emerge from the business definition. Product objectives can be defined in physical or marketing terms. "We sell instant coffee" is an example of defining objectives in physical terms. In marketing terms, the objective statement would emphasize the satisfaction of a customer need. The latter method is preferred because it reinforces the marketing concept.

To illustrate the point, assume that Maytag is interested in establishing a plant for manufacturing washing machines and dryers in Egypt. The product objectives may be defined in the following manner:

- *Maytag corporate objective:* Earn a minimum of 25 percent return on investment in any developing country.
- *Egypt's national concerns:* Create employment opportunities and build up faltering foreign exchange balances.

EXHIBIT 12.1   Perspectives of International Product Planning

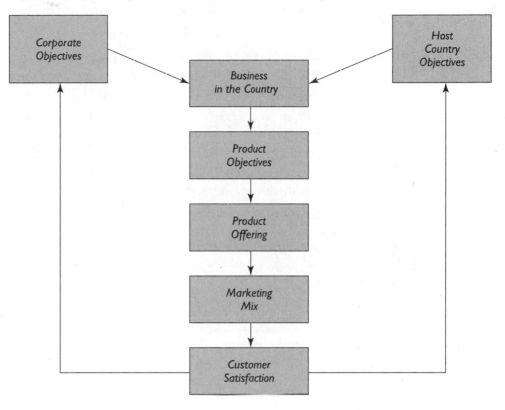

- *Business definition:* Establish a large appliance plant in Egypt to compete effectively in the Middle East.
- *Product definition:* Meet the laundry needs of the masses.

Product Planning

The perspectives of international product planning can be categorized as issues of day-to-day concern on the one hand and strategic issues on the other. The *day-to-day issues* arise in implementing decisions already made. Suppose, in regard to the Maytag example, an issue arises concerning the need for extra precautions to protect working washers and dryers from dust. This issue applies only to the Middle East market, where the climate requires that windows be open all the time, and where the winds carry a lot of dust into the houses. The issue should be handled by local managers. If any specific technological help is needed, it would be sought from the parent corporation on an ad hoc basis.

Strategic issues require major commitments, which must be taken up with the parent corporation. Using the Maytag illustration again, the question might be raised whether motors for the appliances should be imported from Maytag in the U.S. or from a relatively new Japanese subsidiary located in Egypt. Another strategic question could arise with reference to trading with a country that is not on friendly terms with the U.S. Let us assume Egypt does a lot of trade with Libya, but the U.S. has a trade embargo against Libya. Should the Maytag subsidiary in Egypt export the appliances to Libya in view of the U.S. government's trade embargo? Strategic questions cannot be handled by subsidiary management alone; they must be referred to the parent organization.

It is difficult to accumulate an inventory of decisions to label as day-to-day or strategic. It all depends on the individual situation. The subsidiary management must decide if the matter involved is strategic enough to require input from or a decision by the parent. At the risk of overgeneralization, an issue/matter/decision can be considered strategic if:

- The U.S. government comes into the picture.
- Substantial investment needs to be made.
- Previously agreed-upon arrangements would be overturned by a decision.
- Long-term financial interests of the parent are affected.
- The host government appears to be imposing regulations that might affect the long-term survival of the company.
- Technical problems have arisen that cannot be handled locally.
- Certain accusations have been made against the subsidiary that could flare up in labor trouble or have other ramifications.

In addition to ad hoc problems that may be day-to-day or strategic, the parent should require inputs in the form of the subsidiary's plans. Product planning for established product lines and plans for the development and marketing of new product lines would then be prepared by each host country or geographic area and separately submitted to corporate management for approval.

Foreign Collaboration/ Investment

Often international businesses seek foreign collaboration in order to enter world markets. Such collaboration may take shape in a licensing agreement or in a joint venture with a business in the host country. Traditionally, the concept of foreign collaboration has been explained with reference to the *international product life cycle*. As discussed in Chapter 2, essentially this cycle has meant that U.S. exports dominate the world market at first, but then the producers from other developed countries become increasingly competitive—first in their markets, next in third-country markets, and finally in the U.S. market. The cycle may be repeated with successive challenges from producers in developing countries.

In theory, a U.S. corporation should seek foreign collaboration in the third and fourth stages of the international product life cycle, that is, when it is competitively more desirable to produce abroad and compete effectively in foreign markets, as well as in the U.S., through importing from the foreign source. The theory would work if worldwide markets were perfect, which, of course, they are not. Host governments insist on establishing plants even when the plants are not good economic propositions in the international context. For example, a country may opt for a steel mill even though it can import steel from a neighboring country much more economically.

In brief, market imperfections brought about by tariff and nontariff barriers intrude upon the practical application of the theory. In some industries, such as the automobile industry, the theory may fail because investment requirements at the third and fourth stages are tremendous. For this reason, we should not expect auto industries to move from Japan and Europe to emerging developing countries.

An international marketer can also seek foreign collaboration by producing a specialized product in another country in order to take advantage of the peculiar strengths of that country. For example, labor in some nations is cheap, particularly in most developing countries. Other countries have a big pool of scientific talent—India, for example. By collaborating with a foreign company to produce or distribute a product based on an advantage in that company's country, a multinational marketer can gain competitive leverage.

Coca-Cola Company's recent collaboration with Nestlé S.A. of Switzerland illustrates the point. The two companies undertook a multimillion-dollar effort to market canned coffee, either warm or cold in South Korea.[1] The effort was quite successful, leading the Coca-Cola Nestlé Refreshments Co. to roll out Nescafé canned coffee throughout Asia.

Product Design Strategy: Standardization or Customization

An important question that multinational marketers need to answer is whether the product approach successful at home will be equally successful in foreign markets. In other words, a decision must be made about which is the more appropriate of two product design strategies—standardization or customization. *Standardization* means offering a common product on a national, regional, or worldwide basis. *Customization* means adapting a product, that is, making appropriate changes in it, to match local perspectives.

The environmental differences among nations abroad are sometimes great. The degree of difference determines whether product customization, or adaptation, should be chosen over standardization in order to cater to the unique situation in each country. Yet, there are potential gains to consider in product standardization, as will be discussed shortly.[2] International marketers must examine all the criteria in order to decide the extent to which products should vary from country to country.[3]

Decision Criteria   Whether to standardize or to customize is a vexing question with which international marketers have long wrestled. It is simple enough to figure out the rationale for standardization: nothing new needs to be done to make the offering ready for any market, resulting in a significant cost saving. The literature, however, is full of illustrations showing how standardization has led to complete market failure. General Electric Company's debacle in the small-appliance field in Germany and Polaroid's difficulties with the Swinger camera in France are classic examples. At the same time, Volkswagen's success worldwide with the Beetle supports standardization.

Excessive concern with local customization can be troublesome, too. Holland's Philips Company learned the hard lesson that it cannot afford to customize television sets for each European market separately. Standardization became necessary to obtain R&D and manufacturing efficiencies.[4] Because neither strategy—customization or standardization—is superior to the other on its merits, certain criteria should be used to determine which would be desirable in a particular market for a particular product or service and to what extent that strategy should be taken.[5]

Nature of Product Research on the subject shows that foreign product design strategy varies with the nature of the product. More standardization is feasible in the case of industrial goods than consumer goods. Among consumer goods, nondurables require greater customization than durables, because nondurable consumer goods appeal to tastes, habits, and customs. These traits are unique to each country; therefore, adaptation becomes significant. An alternative to customization, is to limit the target market to a small, identifiable segment.

Market Development Different national markets for a given product are in different stages of development. A convenient way of explaining this phenomenon is through the product life cycle concept. Products go through several life cycle stages over a period of time, and in each stage different marketing strategies are appropriate. The four stages are usually identified as introduction, growth, maturity, and decline.

If a product's foreign market is in a different stage of market development than its U.S. market, appropriate changes in the product design become desirable in order to make an adequate product/market match. The claim is that Polaroid's Swinger camera failed in

France because the company pursued the same strategy there as in the U.S. at a time when the two markets were in different stages of development. The U.S. market was in the mature stage, while the French market was in the introductory stage.[6]

Even within a country one segment may be ready for a standardized product while others require that the product be adapted. For example, John S. Hill and Richard R. Still found that products targeted to urban markets in less developed countries need only minimal changes from those marketed in developed countries, but the rural markets in LDCs require greater adaptation[7] (see International Marketing Highlight 12.1).

International Marketing Highlight 12.1

United Distillers Face Venezuelan Squeeze

With the recent economic decline in Venezuela, overall liquor sales plummeted from 9m cases in 1994 to an estimated 7.3m cases in 1995 and stagnated at that level in 1996. Sales of premium products were hit hardest because of changing demographics as well as falling incomes.

United Distillers, over the past two years, refocused its marketing, advertising, and distribution strategies to counteract the plunge in consumer purchasing power. The goal has been to cut costs, bolster long-term competitiveness and prepare for the economy's turnaround while maintaining brand loyalty and image.

The company took control of its Dewar's White Label, Old Parr, and Black Label brands, which had been licensed out. It shipped its product mix to account for consumers' switch from premium scotches and whiskeys to rum, white spirits, and whiskey-flavored dry spirits. In addition, United Distillers introduced some new products in the value-for-money category, including Gordon's gin and vodka, both of which were made locally. Although these products were cheaper to produce, their correspondingly lower prices cut into profit margins. Despite this drawback, their overall profit potential has been great because the lower prices expand the company's customer base. The key, of course, is to sell high volumes.

New market niches also figure in United Distiller's strategy. A good example is whiskey-flavored dry spirits, such as Country Club, a relatively inexpensive whiskey substitute the company introduced. This market, virtually nonexistent several years ago, now accounts for 500,000 cases per year—roughly equal to Venezuela's whiskey sales.

Source: Crossborder Monitor, February 26, 1997, p. 9.

Cost/Benefit Relationship Product adaptation to match local conditions involves costs. These costs may relate to R&D; physical alteration of the product's design, style, features, or changes in packaging, brand name, performance guarantee, and the like. In contrast, with standardization no R&D is required, since manufacturing technology and quality control procedures have been established, and performance has been tested and improved. Thus, standardization brings certain cost savings. The only big cost that standardization may involve, and it is difficult to quantify, is *opportunity cost*. If a product is customized, presumably it will have greater appeal to the mass market in the host country. The question is, how much greater appeal? Enough to make it worth the cost of customizing? A cost/benefit analysis is necessary to determine what it would cost to customize and what benefits might be expected in the form of market growth. The results of that analysis should then be compared with the same analysis applied to standardization. The net difference indicates the relative desirability of the two strategies.

Legal Requirements Different countries have different laws about product standards, patent laws, and tariffs and taxes. These laws may require product adaptation. For example, in Europe the 220-volt electrical system is used. As a result, European governments set stringent safety standards for such products as irons—cord connections must be stronger, radio interference must be shielded, and so on. Likewise, foreign auto manufacturers must adapt their cars for export to the U.S. because of the U.S. government safety standards and emission control requirements (see International Marketing Highlight 12.2).

Competition In the absence of current or potential competition, a company may continue to do well in a market overseas without ever changing its standard product. But many firms from the newly industrializing countries of Asia are successfully competing against MNCs from the industrialized countries by rapidly adapting their products to changing markets and continually applying more innovative product strategies. In these situations, product customization is essential if a company is to have any chance of maintaining market share.

Traditionally, Kodak could get away by selling a standard film globally because it was so rich, efficient, and powerful. However, with changing competitive conditions, Kodak cannot succeed with parochial attitudes. It is not the only company in the market anymore. Now, for instance, Kodak sells film in Japan with the ruddier flesh tones preferred by the Japanese.[8]

■■■■■■   International Marketing Highlight 12.2   ■■■■■■

Oh, How Life Would Be Easier If We Only Had a Europlug

Those of you who have traveled Europe know of the frustration of electrical plugs, different electrical voltages, and other annoyances of international travel. But consider the cost to consumers and the inefficiency of production for a company that wishes to sell electrical appliances in the European "common" market.

Philips, the electrical appliance manufacturer, has to produce twelve kinds of irons to serve just its European market. The problem is that Europe does not have a universal standard. The ends of irons bristle with different plugs for different countries. Some have three prongs, others two; prongs protrude straight or angled, round or rectangular, fat, thin, and sometimes sheathed. There are circular plug faces, squares, pentagons, and hexagons. Some are perforated and some are notched. One French plug has a niche like a keyhole; British plugs carry fuses.

Europe's plugs and sockets are balkanized partly because different countries have different voltages and cycles. But the variety of standards also has other causes, such as protecting local manufacturers. The estimated cost of the lack of universal standards is between $60 billion and $80 billion a year, or nearly 3 percent of the EC's total output of goods and services.

Source: The Wall Street Journal, August 7, 1985, p. 1.

Note: EC (now EU) has set common standards for many products for the entire union and is expected to make further progress in this matter.

Support System The *support system* refers to institutions and functions that are necessary to create, develop, and service demand. These include retailers, wholesalers, sales agents, warehousing, transportation, creditors and media. The availability, performance, and cost of the support system profoundly affect the product design strategy. For example, frozen foods cannot be marketed in countries where retailers do not have facilities with freezers. When Lever Brothers attempted to introduce frozen vegtables in developing countries, the lack of refrigeration facilities at the retail level (as well as in homes) prevented implementation of the plan. The company therefore developed a line of dehydrated vegetables such as peas, carrots, and beans for countries like India, Pakistan, Kenya, and the Philippines.

Physical Environment The physical conditions of a country (i.e., climate, topography, and resources) may also require product adaptation. For example, air conditioners in a very hot climate, as in the Middle East, require additional features for satisfactory performance. Differences in the size and configuration of homes in some countries affect product design for appliances and home furnishings. European kitchens are usually smaller than U.S. kitchens, and, European homes generally do not have basements. Thus, compactness of design in washers and dryers is a necessity, since they must be accommodated within a crowded area.

Examples, of customized products and marketing include GE's European washing machines, which are designed vertically to conserve water; P&G's Tide detergent and Pantene shampoo, packaged in small, low-priced packets in India, and Whirlpool's Asian International Room Air Conditioner, a lightweight air conditioner.

Market Conditions Cultural differences, economic prosperity, and customer perceptions in the foreign country should also be considered in the deciding whether to adapt a product. Even where tastes are converging, significant national differences will likely persist for many years. In the drinks industry, for example, consumers in heavy beer-drinking countries (the U.K., Germany) are shifting toward wine, and consumers in heavy wine-drinking countries (France, Italy), toward beer. The trend is real. But the Germans still consume six times as much beer per capita as the Italians, and the French six times as much wine per capita as the British. And these numbers will change very slowly indeed. [9]

The British prefer a slightly more bitter taste in soup than Americans do. The taste difference required the Campbell Soup Company to modify soup ingredients in Britain. To cater to local taste in Japan, Domino's offers pizza with such toppings as chicken teriyaki, apple, rice, and corn.[10]

The masses in many countries cannot afford the variety of products that U.S. consumers consider essential. To bring such products as automobiles and appliances within the reach of the middle class in developing countries, the products must be appropriately modified to cut costs without reducing functional quality.

Foreign products in many cultures are perceived as high-quality products. In such cases, standardization is desirable. On the other hand, if the image of a country's products is weak, it is strategically desirable to adapt those products so that they can be promoted as different, rather than typical, of the country. For example, U.S. automobiles are considered substandard. Thus, success by American auto manufacturers Japan would require a changed product.[11]

Standardization: A Common Practice

Other things being equal, companies usually opt for standardization. A recent study on the subject lends support to the high propensity to standardize all or parts of marketing strategy in foreign markets. For example, an extremely high degree of standardization appears to exist in brand names, physical characteristics of products, and packaging. John S. Hill and Richard R. Still observed,

> More than half the products that MNCs sell in less developed countries originate in the parent companies' home markets. Of the 2,200 products sold by the 61 subsidiaries in the sample, 1,200 had originated in the U.S. or the U.K.[12]

The benefits of standardization are realization of cost savings, development of world-wide products, and achievement of better marketing performance. Standardization of products across national borders eliminates duplication of such costs as R&D, product design, and packaging. Further, standardization permits economies of scale.

Standardization also makes it feasible to achieve consistency in dealing with customers and in product design. The consistency in product style—features, design, brand name, packaging—should establish a common image of the product worldwide to help increase overall sales. A person accustomed to a particular brand is likely to buy the same brand overseas if it is available. The global exposure that brands receive these days as a result of extensive world travel and mass media requires the consistency feasible through standardization.

Finally, standardization may be urged on the grounds that a product that has proved successful in one country should do equally well in other countries that present more or less similar markets and similar competitive conditions. For example, Gillette's Sensor razor, launched in 1989 at a cost of $200 million, is the same razor throughout the world, sold with the same advertising[13] (see International Marketing Highlight 12.3).

Rewards of Adaptation

Although standardization offers benefits, too much attachment to standardization can be counterproductive. Marketing environment varies from country to country, so a standard product originally conceived and developed in the U.S. may not really match the conditions in each and every market (see International Marketing Highlight 12.4). In other words, standardization can lead to substantial opportunity loss.

Pond's cold cream, Coca-Cola, and Colgate toothpaste have been cited as evidence that a universal product and marketing strategy for consumer goods can win worldwide success. However, the applicability of a universal approach for consumer goods appears to be limited to products that have certain characteristics, such as universal brand-name recognition (generally earned by huge financial outlays), minimal product knowledge requirements for consumer use, and product advertisements that demand low information content.

Clearly, Coca-Cola, Colgate toothpaste, McDonald's, Levi jeans, and Pond's cold cream display these traits. Thus, whereas a universal strategy can be effective for some consumer products, it is clearly an exception rather than the general rule. Those who argue that consumer products no longer require market tailoring because of the globalization of markets brought about by today's advanced technology are not always correct.

An MNC that intends to launch a new product into a foreign market should consider the nature of its product, its organizational capabilities, and the level of adaptation required to accommodate cultural differences between the home and host country. An MNC should also analyze factors such as market structures, competitors' strategic orientations, and host government demands.[14]

The successful companies realize a simple truth: all consumers are not alike. Take the case of Domino's Pizza delivery. In Britain, customers don't like the idea of Domino's delivery man knocking on their doors—they think it is rude. In Japan, houses aren't numbered sequentially, so finding an address means searching among rows of houses numbered willy-nilly. And in Kuwait, pizza is more likely to be delivered to a waiting limousine than to someone's front door.

Other differences have been noted in making cars, selling soap, and packaging toilet paper. International marketers must understand that just because a product plays in Peoria, it will not necessarily be a hit in Helsinki.

Companies are therefore adapting products to local situations. To satisfy local tastes, products ranging from Heinz ketchup to Cheetos chips are tweaked, reformulated, and reflavored. Fast-food companies such as McDonald's Corp., popular for the "sameness" they offer all over the world, have discovered that to succeed, they also need to offer some local appeal—like selling beer in Germany and adding British Cadbury chocolate sticks to their ice-cream cones in England.

The result is a delicate balancing act for international marketers: how does a company exploit the economies of scale that can be gained by global marketing while at the same time making its products appeal to local tastes? The answer is, "Be flexible," even when it means changing a tried-and-true recipe.

The international marketplace is far more competitive today than in the past, and most likely will remain so. Thus, some sort of adaptation might provide a better match of the product with local conditions for competitive advantage. Sushil Vachani and Louis T. Wells Jr., report that, based on a study of the product decisions of Indian subsidiaries of five multinationals, there remain important consumer segments that have special needs that are not met by global products.[15] Kenichi Ohmae's charges against American companies for not adapting their products to Japanese needs are also revealing:[16] American merchandisers, Ohmae points out, still push such products as oversized cars with left-wheel drive, devices measuring in inches, appliances not adapted to the lower voltage and frequencies necessary in Japan, office equipment without *kanji* capabili-ties, and clothes not cut to smaller Japanese dimensions. Although most Japanese like sweet oranges and tart cherries, the U.S. sends them the opposite. As Japanese consumers compare imported oranges with domestic *mikans* (very sweet tangerines) and cherries with plums (somewhat tangy and sour), they are dissapointed in the American offerings.

International Marketing Highlight 12.3

Gillette Tries to Nick Schick in Japan

For Gillette Co., the leading razor maker in most parts of the world, Japan has always been a sore spot. The company, which averages a 65 percent market share in 70 percent of its markets, hobbles along with a 10 percent share of the razor and blade market in Japan.

What has barred the giant Gillette from growing in Japan is not a closed market, unfair Japanese customs, or anything else Japan is accused of. It is rival American Warner-Lambert Co., owner of the Schick brand name. Although Schick trails Gillette in the U.S., it has gained 62 percent of Japan's "wet-shaving" razor and blade market by using the Japanese style of marketing.

Now the battle is heating up as both sides promote new products worldwide. Armed with its popular Sensor brand, Gillette is launching a new strategy. While Schick stresses its Japanese way of marketing, Gillette is emphasizing its "Americanness." It is airing the same ads it runs in the U.S. and selling Sensor in the same packages, with the brand name in bold English letters and a Japanese version of it only in tiny letters in a corner. The company vows to double market share in Japan in the next three to five years. Previously, Gillette had TV ads made just for the Japanese market, although it did use foreign models and sports personalities.

Source: The Wall Street Journal, February 4, 1991, p. B1

International Marketing Highlight 12.4

Taking on Japanese Flavor

Fast-food outlets in Japan are trying to become more Japanese, offering burgers dipped in teriyaki sauce and making buns out of rice. McDonald's Japanese subsidiary, the country's biggest fast-food chain, has added a sandwich of fried chicken soaked in soy sauce to its menu. The company tested the 320-yen ($2.25) item, called Chicken Tatsuta, and found that it sold nearly as well as the Big Mac.

Japanese-style burgers appeal to consumers because they seem more healthful. Moreover, tastes are changing. When U.S. chains first entered Japan two decades ago, what Japanese consumers were looking for in a hamburger was America. But now, consumers say they've gotten the American taste down, and they're asking if we have something else. Wendy's restaurants in Japan offer sandwiches with deep-fried pork cutlets—usually served with a bowl of rice—as well as a version of the teriyaki burger.

Source: The Wall Street Journal, June 19, 1991, p. B1.

There are several patterns and various degrees of differentiation that firms can adopt to do business on an international scale. The most common of these are obligatory and discretionary product adaptation. An *obligatory*, or minimal, product adaptation implies minor changes or modifications in the product design that a manufacturer is forced to introduce for either of two reasons. First, it is mandatory in order to seek entry into particular foreign markets. Second, it is imposed on a firm by external environmental factors, including the special needs of the foreign market. In brief, obligatory adaptation is related to safety regulations, trademark registration, quality standards, and media standards. An obligatory adaptation requires mostly physical changes in the product.

Discretionary, or voluntary, product adaptation reflects a sort of self-imposed discipline and a deliberate move on the part of an exporter to build stable foreign markets through a better alignment of product with market needs or a cultural alignment of the product. An empirical study on the subject showed that product adaptation is most directly influenced by two factors: cultural aspects and legal requirements. Th former is discretionary, and the other is obligatory.

Swiss-based pharmaceutical maker Ciba-Geigy's efforts in adapting its products to local conditions are noteworthy. Basic to the company's adaptation program are its quality circles. These circles include local executives with line responsibilities in packaging, labeling, advertising, and manufacturing. They are responsible for determining if Ciba-Geigy's products (1) are appropriate for the cultures in which they are sold and are meeting the users' needs, (2) are promoted in such a way that they will be used correctly for the purposes intended, and (3) when used properly, will present no unreasonable hazards to human health and safety.[17] (see International Marketing Highlight 12.5).

International Marketing Highlight 12.5

A Car for the Emerging Markets

Suzuki is the car maker to the developing world. The style of the company and its president—a self-described "loan shark" in his early days who married into the Suzuki family and adopted its name—sets them apart from their rivals.

Though Suzuki is a bit player in the U.S., its small, rugged vehicles rule the roads in India and are popular in Eastern Europe and China, markets that U.S. automakers only recently began targeting.

Down-and-dirty vehicles geared to low-tech economies are a Suzuki specialty. In Vietnam, Suzuki engineers observed jerri-built vehicles bouncing through congested Ho Chi Minh City, then cobbled up the Super Carry, $7,000 pint-sized cross between a pickup and a van. The vehicle's backend comes with benches that can seat 12 or tote pigs and rice sacks. Vinyl pull-down shades substitute for glass windows in back.

Suzuki vehicles are fuel-efficient and inexpensive. That is important in nations where annual per capita income is measured in hundreds rather than thousands of dollars and where gasoline costs as much as $4 a gallon. The tiny subcompact Suzuki produced at its Indian joint venture sells for $5,200 and commands 80 percent market share in India. Ford Motor Co.'s new made-in-India Escort costs $17,500. With recession ravaging incomes in once promising markets such as Thailand and Indonesia, Suzuki's leanness is its strength. Suzuki's low-cost plants, simple car models, and frugal operating style enable it to offer rock-bottom prices and still scratch out a profit.

Source: Valerie Reitman, "Frugal Head of Suziki Drives Markets in Asia," *The Wall Street Journal*, February 26, 1998, p. A12.

Developing an International Product Line

Continued success in overseas markets requires the individual designing of a viable product line for each country. To achieve this viability, the composition of the product line may need to be periodically reviewed and changed. Such environmental changes as customer preferences, competitors' tactics, host country legal requirements, and a firm's own perspectives (including its objectives, cost structure, and spillover of demand from one product to another) can all render a product line inadequate. Thus, it may become necessary to add new products or eliminate existing products.

Additions to the product line may take different forms. A firm may simply extend additional domestic products abroad. Alternatively, certain specific products may be sought for a particular foreign country, either locally abroad or in the home country. Finally, new products may be developed for international markets. Also, products may be either eliminated or selectively cut from a line in some countries. There are various ways of obtaining an optimum product line for different international markets.

Extension of Domestic Line

The extension of domestic products to foreign markets follows the logic of the concept of the international product life cycle. Companies develop products for the home market that prove successful and lead to some export orders. As the exports grow, the firm considers setting up a warehouse, a sales branch, or a service center in the foreign locale. Later, the firm finds it more economical to assemble or manufacture the product in the host country.

Relating this process to product-line extension, a firm may initially market a few products overseas. As those markets grow or change, an opportunity may emerge to extend the line by selecting additional products from the domestic line for overseas distribution. A TRW subsidiary in the 1960s, for example, exported fractional horsepower motors to Egypt, Nigeria, India, and a number of other developing countries. In the 1970s many of these countries started manufacturing sophisticated equipment that required large horsepower motors. This change at the customer level made the company's international division choose additional motors for export to these countries.

Another example of product-line extension is provided by the Coca-Cola Company. It began marketing Coca-Cola in Japan in 1958, and as the market developed, it introduced additional beverages: Fanta in 1968, and Sprite in 1970. By 1983 those other products were outselling Coke.[18]

Introducing Additional Products to the International Line

Products may be added to the line for two reasons: (1) to serve an unfulfilled customer need in a particular market overseas or (2) to optimize the existing marketing capacity. For example, a chemical company selling fertilizer and pesticides overseas in developing countries may discover a dire need for good-quality seeds and thus may add such seeds to its line. Alternatively, the same company may feel it has established a good distribution network to serve rural customers but that the network is not being fully utilized. The company may therefore consider products that could be successfully distributed to their rural customers. Such products may or may not be related to the company's business.

For example, in Japan Coca-Cola markets two fruit-drink products, a canned coffee-flavored noncarbonated drink, and a carbonated orange fruit drink that it does not sell in the U.S. Similarly, Coca-Cola markets potato chips in Japan, a business unknown to the company at home.[19] Campbell Soup Company sells gourmet cookies in Europe and Japan but not in the U.S.[20]

Implementation of this strategy alternative can be illustrated with reference to Colgate Palmolive Company's experience. Colgate distributes internationally a variety of products that belong to other companies. For example, Colgate sold Wilkinson razor blades for their British manufacturer. Colgate did the same for Henkel's (a German company) Pritt Glue Stick.[21]

MNCs often add products differently to their parent country market than to the international market, where product-line strategy alternatives are pursued in response to the needs and opportunities of world markets. The products for addition to the line are determined according to inputs or product specifications received from different markets abroad. Insofar as possible, attempts are made to develop one standardized product to serve customers worldwide.

The decision to add a product to the line is influenced by compatibility considerations regarding marketing, finances, and environment. *Marketing compatibility* involves the match between the new addition and the current and potential marketing compatibilities of the parent company and its foreign subsidiary in matters such as product, price, promotion, and distribution. The closer the proposed product is to current marketing perspectives, the easier it would be to market the product successfully. A low compatibility may affect profitable marketing. Thus, in the earlier example, the chemical company may find adding seeds to its line more compatible than offering leased agricultural machinery.

Sound business judgment requires a full examination of the financial risks and opportunities relative to the product addition under consideration. The common criteria for use in determining the *financial compatibility* of the proposed addition are profitability and cash flow implications.

Environmental compatibility includes concern for the customer, competitive action, and legal or political problems. The inclusion of a product in the line should not pose any problem for either existing or potential customers. At the same time, the competitive reactions to the company's product addition should be projected and evaluated. If the legal or political problems are likely to become a big stumbling block, it might be best to cancel plans to add the product.

Introducing New Products to a Host Country

For the purposes of this discussion, a "new product" is defined as one that is new to the host country but not new to the international market. For example, when Kodak started distributing its pocket camera in Asia in 1982, it was a new product to Sri Lanka, Pakistan, Thailand, and other countries in the region, though not to the U.S., Western Europe, and Japan. Many decisions are required for the introduction of new products in foreign markets. These include decisions about (1) which products to introduce in which different foreign markets, (2) timing and the sequence of introduction, and (3) whether to introduce the product as it is marketed in the U.S., that is, in the standardized form, or to adapt it to the peculiar requirements of the host country.

An empirical study on new-product introductions overseas showed that U.S. corporations frequently introduced new products first to countries culturally similar to the U.S.[22] Thus, Great Britain, Canada, and Australia were the leading recipients of new U.S. international offerings, accounting for almost half of all new-product introductions, and other developed countries accounted for more than one-third. Only one-sixth of new-product introductions were made in developing countries.

New-product introductions to foreign markets also varied by industry. Those in the category of office machines, computers, and instruments were introduced across national boundaries in less than half the cases. On the other hand, textiles, paper, and fabricated metal innovations were entered in foreign markets in 85 percent of the cases.

As far as timing is concerned, U.S. corporations have been introducing new products to overseas markets faster than before. The percentage of foreign introductions within one year of domestic introduction went up from 5.6 percent of all innovations in the period of 1945–1950 to 38.7 percent in 1971–1975. This statistic testifies to the growing importance of new products for successful competition in international markets. Although no empirical evidence is available, in the wake of increasing competition this percentage is probably higher for the 1980s and higher still for the 1990s.

Alternative Ways of Seeking New Products for Foreign Markets A company can develop a new product for a foreign market either internally or by acquisition of another company. Internally, new products are developed through R&D. R&D may be conducted in either the home or the host country. For example, Colgate-Palmolive developed in the U.S. a manual washing device—an all-plastic, hand-powered washer for developing countries. IBM developed IBM 2750 and 3750 electronic private business telephone exchanges within the U.K. For most companies, however, R&D is centralized at home. (A later section will examine the role of foreign R&D in international product policy in detail.)

Many companies add new products through acquisitions. Gillette acquired Braun AG of Germany in order to add electric shavers to its line. Similarly, Gulf Oil acquired Shawinigan Chemical of Canada to enter the field of carbon black. International Telephone and Telegraph (ITT) acquired Rimmel Ltd. of England to enter the cosmetics field.

Rationale for New Products A firm may introduce new products in foreign markets as either a defensive or an offensive measure. Defensively, the new product is expected to help the company compete effectively. For example, a well-established company may be challenged by new competition. In response to this, introduction of a new product may appear to be the most desirable course against the competition. For this reason, with coffee drinking gaining in popularity over tea, the Brooke Bond Tea Company, a British company, decided to introduce its own brand of coffee in a number of Asian countries.

Alternatively, a new product may be introduced to satisfy host government requirements for business related to national development. Thus, Union Carbide, a chemical company, seriously considered adding men's shirts to its portfolio of businesses in India.

A new product may also be developed to evoke local identity. During the 1999 air war against Yugoslavia, McDonald's restaurants, in order to overcome animosity toward a quintessentially American trademark, introduced a domestic pork burger with paprika garnish called McCountry. It was a great success.[23]

New products may also be added because the corporation had earlier licensed its company/brand name to someone else. Union Carbide had to develop a new product/brand for Europe because a German firm had the license for Eveready.

When introduced as an offensive weapon, new products are designed to stimulate growth. Polaroid Corporation sought growth by developing a conventional film because the instant photography market had matured and showed no signs of survival. Branded as Polaroid Super Color, the film was introduced in Spain and Portugal in 1986. In 1988 the company entered it in several other markets.[24] Coca-Cola Company introduces dozens of new products every year to keep up with local competition. In Japan, the company's product line includes a Ginseng-based still drink (Real Gold) and a milk-based drink (Ambassa) as well as a honey-and-lemon flavored juice (Mone).[25] For the Japanese market, Anheuser-Busch has developed a new beer branded as Buddy: a low-malt brand with more alcohol that sells for two-thirds the price of Budweiser. The smaller price and bigger alcohol content are a potent combination that suits Japanese consumers.[26]

The rationale for new-product introduction can take three shapes: (1) to serve a segment hitherto ignored, (2) to satisfy an unfulfilled need, or (3) to adapt a domestic product for better product/market match. Often there is no single reason, but rather a number of considerations figuring into a new-product decision (see International Marketing Highlight 12.6).

■ **International Marketing Highlight 12.6** ■

B.A.T. Gambles in Uzbekistan

U.K. tobacco giant B.A.T. is one of Uzbekistan's few successful foreign investors. The firm bought into a tobacco factory in Tashkent in 1994 in one of Uzbekistan's biggest foreign investments. It was intended to counter the presence of USA's Phillip Morris in neighboring Kazakhstan.

All consumer goods marketers in Uzbekistan face a tricky problem: how to pitch their products in a market wherein "West is best" ideas still prevail but where purchasing power is painfully low. There is, however, money to be made both by serving the rich elite and by selling low-price goods to the mass market.

The U.K. firm turned industry practice on its head right from the start: while the other international producers either pushed their global brands or took over cherished Soviet-era lines, B.A.T. gambled on launching two completely new low-priced local cigarette brands—Saraton and Khan—to fill what the company's executives saw as a viable market niche.

Saraton is a cheap, strong, no-filter cigarette that costs Som 20 ($0.33), and Khan is a marginally more upscale filtered cigarette costing Som 30. In comparison, international brands sell for Som 125. B.A.T. has unsentimentally dropped the country's flagship Soviet-brand cigarette, Uzbekistan.

The launch of Khan was remarkably successful. Within a year, it became Uzbekistan's top-selling cigarette, with over 1 billion packets sold. The key, say B.A.T. managers, was the emphasis on TV advertising, particularly commercials specifically made for the Uzbek market (as opposed to recycled Russian material).

Source: Crossborder Monitor, January 7, 1998, p. 8.

Overall, new products are appearing more frequently because so-called product life cycles (from drawing board until the last is sold) are getting shorter as companies cut their development times and reorganize their factories to build new things more quickly (see International Marketing Highlight 12.7). Products survive for a shorter time in the market because they are rapidly outdated by products from rivals who are speeding up their operations, too. The incentive for successful innovation is great. Premium prices can be charged for novel things, particularly if they create new markets. IBM did this with its personal computers. America's Compaq then stole some of IBM's market by developing the next generation of IBM-compatible computers before IBM.[27]

To illustrate the way in which new product opportunities can develop in overseas markets, consider the lives of devout Muslims, who must face Mecca and pray five times each day. Because the proper time for each prayer is measured from either sunrise or sunset, it changes from day to day and greatly from place to place. In addition, the Koran specifies that the body face Mecca within two and one-half degrees. The Muslim faithful can obtain charts of every part of the globe that show the direction to Mecca, but attaining the proper accuracy can be tough, even with a compass. Therefore, Sensortron Technology Ltd. brought high technology to bear on the problem. The company, which was founded in Monaco by an American, Romm Doulton, developed two pocket-sized aids. One points to Mecca; the other emits an electronic *Hadan,* or call to prayer. Both have microprocessors that calculate the direction of Mecca based on a person's proximity to one of 11,000 programmed locations. Sensortron figured its potential market is 10 percent of the one-half billion Muslims.[28]

■■■■■■■■   **International Marketing Highlight 12.7**   ■■■■■■■■

Japanese Passion for New Products

The Japanese system rests, in large part, on the dynamic that drives its consumer products companies perpetually to create and introduce new products. This "product churning" reflects, of course, the Japanese consumer's well-known passion for new products. It also reflects, among manufacturers, the speed-to-market in new product development, in which the Japanese completely outclass their American and German rivals.

In the soft drink industry, for example, more than 700 new products and brands are marketed each year, but about 90 percent of them disappear after only one year in the market. This is a common pattern. Ajinomoto, the largest packaged-foods company in Japan, launched between 20 and 35 new frozen-food brands each year between 1986 and 1989. Only about half survived for one year, and most have gone entirely from today's market. Such product churning activity is not limited only to packaged goods, but applies as well to consumer electronics. Sony launched 182 new products in 1990, almost one new product per business day.

Source: Tatsuo Ohbora, Andrew Parsons, and Hajo Riesenbeck, "Global Marketing," *The McKinsey Quarterly*, 3 (1992): 59.

New-Product Development Process Usually six steps are involved in new product development: idea, screening, evaluation, prototype product, market testing, and entry. Organizations spend varying amounts of time on each step. At each step, management must make a go or no-go decision. As a product progresses from one step to the next, it requires a greater commitment of resources.

Ideas derive from different sources, the principal ones being the host government, customers, subsidiary employees, and international agencies such as the World Health Organization. The ideas received go through a *screening* process to select the promising one for detailed consideration. Screening begins by matching the product idea with the overall objectives of the subsidiary in the host country. Next comes a determination of product feasibility in regard to the resources of both the subsidiary and the parent company, including finances, raw materials, energy, past experience, management skills, patents (for example, the ownership of a technical design/process), and the like.

Product ideas that seem feasible are carried on through the *evaluation* step. Evaluation mainly concerns total market-potential and demand analysis. At this time, accounting information such as fixed costs, unit variable cost, and likely price is used to conduct the break-even analysis—that is, to figure out the point at which the company would be at a no-profit/loss situation in terms of either volume or dollar sales.

Once the evaluation step has been completed, the management must make the go or no-go decision. If it is *go*, the idea is next given physical shape in the form of a *prototype product.* Engineering and production groups work jointly in this task. Marketing astuteness demands *market testing* before final commitment to full-scale commercialization. Testing the market helps in two ways: (1) it furnishes information on the chances of product acceptance and (2) it indicates an appropriate strategy. If the market tests are encouraging, the company will go ahead with *entry* of the product into the market.

Conceptually, the whole process appears to be logical and sequentially possible. However, a variety of difficulties can arise that might require accepting shortcuts or even omissions of certain things. For example, the test marketing may be rendered difficult for lack of a marketing research firm specializing in market testing in the host country. Similarly, if the product-development effort is located outside the host country, the coordination between engineering/production and the host country marketing group would prove difficult. Further, the host government requirements can delay the product-development procedure. For example, the target date for full-scale introduction may have to be altered. Finally, internal organization and management style may hinder smooth and timely development of new products.

Difficulties aside, new products provide a viable route for growth as much in foreign markets as at home (see International Marketing Highlight 12.8).

Management of Product Line

Based on the experiences of successful companies, a few generalizations can be made about profitably managing an international product line. These suggestions relate to market segmentation, product design, product quality, product innovation, and economies of scale.

First, any product added to the line, whether entirely new or extended overseas from the home country, must be directed toward a well-defined target group. For example, at one time Riunite became the largest-selling imported wine in the U.S. through advertising itself as a beverage drink for young consumers: "More than a wine, it's a beverage. It can be drunk by anybody who is legal, anywhere, at any time of day. Its real competitors are soft drinks, beer, vodka and tonic, and iced tea."[29]

Second, it is helpful to distinguish products according to aesthetic appeal and functional design. This principle holds true for both consumer and industrial goods. Additionally, well-made, long-lasting products obtain a permanent place in the market that competitors find difficult to challenge. Inasmuch as foreign markets vary, a novel product created to match the characteristics of a particular market can be an extremely useful step to gain an advantage over competition selling "me-too" products extended from the parent company.[30]

Product innovation is especially helpful for mature industries with static demand. And, a cost advantage over the competition provides a strong, enviable position. Thus, realization of economies of scale in managing the product line is a desirable objective. For example, before the value of the yen hit the ceiling, the Japanese automakers occupied an unbeatable position in the U.S. market, based largely on a cost advantage of almost $2,000 over an equivalent U.S.–built car.

Overseas R&D

R&D is essential to originating new products. U.S. corporations spend billions of dollars annually on R&D. In 1999, they spent over $280 billion over and above the amount supported by the federal government. Although U.S. companies make significant investments in R&D, their performance is now lagging behind that of the Japanese. In 1980, of the top ten patent winners in the U.S., seven were U.S. companies (GE, RCA, U.S. Navy, AT&T, IBM, Westinghouse, and General Motors), two were European, and one was Japanese. In 1990, five were Japanese companies and only three were U.S. (GE, Kodak, and IBM), and two were European.[31]

■■■■   **International Marketing Highlight 12.8**   ■■■■

Better Than the Best

Getting the Lexus out of Toyota, whose forte is rolling out wheels for the world's million-aires, is like producing beef Wellington at McDonald's. Toyota had to target its customer precisely, create all-new management organizations, rethink components down to the tiniest screw, and invest more time and money—six years and over $500 million—than anyone had originally imagined.

Toyota set out to do what nobody else had done: design a sedan that would travel 150 mph while carrying four passengers in relative quiet, comfort, and safety—and without incurring the American gas-guzzler tax. Even though 65 mph is the legal limit in the U.S., Toyota figured Lexus owners would want to brag about outrunning radar.

Those specifications dictated breakthroughs in aerodynamics, noise dampening, suspension, and, most of all, the engine. The company devised a nine-stage process to reach each design target. It included the following: discussing how goals would be met, making continual follow-ups, and trying wherever possible to have it both ways. For example, the company wanted the optimum solution—the biggest engine with the least noise—even though the two objectives are difficult to reconcile. Compromise was unacceptable. "We had to push the engineers to achieve the vision we wanted to create," said the chief engineer. Despite obstacles aplenty, the product looks like a stunning success.

Source: Fortune, August 14, 1989, p. 63.

Most of the R&D activity of MNCs is centralized in the U.S. The overseas R&D is concentrated mainly among the large multinationals, just as domestic R&D is highly concentrated among the large industrial corporations.

The following reasons lead companies to centralize R&D in the home country:

- *Critical mass and economies of scale.* By expanding R&D in the home country, a company can realize economies of scale rather than incur initial costs.

- *Easier communication.* Social and cultural barriers such as language differences are avoided.

- *Better protection of know-how.* A company finds it easier to protect its research output and patents at home than abroad.

- *More leverage with host government.* The host country's interest in seeking R&D would make the overseas company more vulnerable to foreign government action.

- *Ease of control of coordination.* R&D activity can be controlled better by centralization of the entire program in one country; centralization permits better coordination with marketing and production.

Although U.S. multinationals and those of other nations centralize the major portion of R&D in their home countries, companies do undertake some R&D abroad as well. Foreign R&D is undertaken for the following reasons: adaptation of home products abroad, response to subsidiary pressures, response to host government incentives for local R&D, use as a public relations tool, capitalizing on local professional talent, realizing cost savings, providing broader base for new product ideas, offering proximity to markets, and serving as a continuation of R&D activities of a firm acquired abroad.

In the future, more and more companies are likely to initiate or enlarge their R&D activity abroad. This prediction is based on the known fact that the foreign marketplace is becoming highly competitive as host countries become very aggressive in seeking technology. Today U.S. MNCs have to compete against non–U.S. MNCs not only from Europe but also from the developing countries. The sharing/transferring of technology serves as an effective tool for entry into many countries. An obvious form of *technology transfer* takes place when the parent company engages in R&D activities abroad.

In June of 1997 Haagen-Dazs began serving a new flavor called *dulce de leche* at its ice cream shop in Buenos Aires. Named after the caramelized milk that is one of the most popular flavors in Argentina, the locally developed line was an immediate hit. Within weeks, the super-sweet, butterscotch-like confection was the store's best-seller.

Just one year later, consumers from Boston to Los Angeles to Paris can find *dulce de leche* at the supermarket or in one of Haagen-Dazs's 700 retail stores. In Miami, *dulce* sells twice as fast as any other flavor. In the U.S., it does $1 million a month in revenue. And in Europe, it will soon move up from a seasonal flavor to year-round status.

The dessert is just the latest example of an emerging two-way trend among American marketers. No longer does the shrinking of the globe mean simply that U. S. companies pump out hamburger, sneakers, and movies for the world to consume—or that Asian and European companies readily sell their goods in the U.S. In globalization's latest twist, American companies from Levi Strauss & Co. to Nike Inc. are lifting products and ideas from their international operations and bringing them home. Although U.S. companies have long exported their products, a few have now begun using their international operations as incubators for the next big hit. As the world becomes smaller—relentlessly, if slowly—the interchange and exchange of ideas is becoming much more commonplace.[32]

Procter & Gamble's (P&G's) experience illustrates how R&D is becoming an international process for more and more companies. A few years ago P&G introduced Liquid Tide, which, by drawing on ideas and technology from around the world, has a distinctly international R&D connection. A new ingredient that helps suspend dirt in wash water came from the company's research center near P&G's Cincinnati headquarters; the formula for Liquid Tide's surfactants, or cleaning agents, was developed by P&G technicians in Japan; and the ingredients that fight the mineral salts present in hard water came from P&G's scientists in Brussels.[33] By pooling its research and development strength worldwide, P&G was able to develop a successful product that would not have been possible if it had relied only on its R&D in the U.S. Certain technologies are more advanced in particular countries because of endemic needs and conditions. The best R&D takes advantage of those advancements.

Unilever, a company whose core products include soaps and detergents, as well as margarine and other inexpensive edible oils, provides another example of an MNC that has globalized its R&D. The company has four major laboratories that conduct basic research: one in the Netherlands, one in India, and two in the U.K. It also has some 40 applied-research centers in foreign subsidiaries, 24 of which are in developing countries. Unilever makes a practical organizational distinction between basic research and applied research, granting subsidiaries responsibility for the latter.[34]

Product Elimination

In international marketing, primary attention is usually given to developing, adding, and modifying new products rather than deleting existing products. This section discusses the importance of international product deletion and its strategic implications.

In recent years, global competitive pressures have caused many MNCs to reappraise their product mixes. The scarcities of raw materials, price controls in some countries, increasing entry difficulties, tariffs, and the fear of a global energy crunch have forced multinational companies of every size, shape, and kind to reexamine their overseas product mix and make appropriate changes. Very often a small proportion of a company's products, say, 20 to 30 percent, accounts for a large percentage, say, 60 to 80 percent, of its profits. The majority of the products, accounting for most of the losses or a smaller proportion of profits, should be examined very carefully. In many cases, the breadth and depth of the worldwide product line is greater than that of the domestic line. Weak products, on the basis of estimated future contribution to the product line, must be phased out to prevent dispersion and fragmentation of effort.

There are many reasons for failure of overseas products. Honeywell, Inc., decided to sell a substantial part of its 47 percent interest in its French subsidiary, Honeywell Bull, because of continuing losses. J.C. Penney decided to pull out of Belgium when economic and political conditions made it impossible to operate profitably there. For example, Belgium's strict price controls made it difficult for the company to pass along cost increases to customers. Volkswagen AG closed its U.S. manufacturing operations under pressure from Japanese competitors and poor U.S. sales, which had been linked to an image problem that hurt the company's U.S.–produced cars. ITT Corporation closed most of its telecommunications in Argentina primarily because of unstable economic conditions causing delays in payments from the government-owned telephone company and a lack of new orders. In 1999 Nestlé pruned its sprawling broad portfolio to realize cost savings and synergy for growth.[35]

Another important reason for product deletion overseas is customer rejection of the product. After three years and an advertising campaign of $2 million, the Campbell Soup Company decided to close its Brazilian canned soup operation. Campbell had failed to interest Brazilian cooks, who felt they could serve only soup that they could call their own.[36] Campbell's offerings—mostly vegetable and beef combinations packed in extra large cans bearing a variant of the familiar red and white label—failed to catch on. Brazilian cooks preferred the dehydrated products of competitors such as Knorr and Maggi, which they could use as soup starters and add ingredients of their own. Campbell's soup was considered only an emergency solution when cooking time was short.

Like the Campbell Soup Company, Gerber Products Company decided to leave the Brazilian market. The company had failed to convince mothers to use baby food as an everyday feeding item despite an award-winning advertising campaign telling mothers they would have more time to show affection to their infants if they were not bent over a sink preparing food. The company underestimated a cultural factor. Brazilian mothers are not willing to accept that prepared baby food is a good substitute for food freshly made by themselves—or, more likely, by their live-in maids, since most women in Brazil who can afford to buy prepared baby food can afford to have a maid.[37] In general, Brazilian women like to use prepackaged baby food only for convenience, when visiting friends and relatives or going to the beach.

All in all, appropriate organizational procedures for systematic review of products must be established. Specific criteria to evaluate product performance such as minimum level of sales, market share, profitability, and condition of the product line should be set. The criteria can be established by local organizational units relative to specific market conditions, by headquarters' management, or by both, depending on the organizational structure. Some coordination of these criteria is ordinarily desirable. The review of products based on these criteria can be carried out on a market-by-market, regional, or global basis depending on the uniformity of the product mix in different markets. Typically, however, some informational input from local organizational units is necessary.

Adoption and Diffusion of New Products

Of paramount concern in the introduction of new products is acceptance by the customers. One way of determining whether a new product will be accepted by a sufficient number of customers is through an analysis of expected product adoption and diffusion in the foreign market.

Adoption   Customers do not instantly buy new products. They usually go through a step-by-step mental process of adoption, or accepting a new product. Typically, this process occurs in sequential stages:

- *Awareness:* Being exposed to a new product, consumers become aware of it.
- *Knowledge:* Consumers develop enough interest in the product to seek additional information.
- *Evaluation:* An attitude forms, negative or positive, about the product.
- *Trial:* Consumers buy the product to see if it indeed meets their needs.
- *Adoption:* The product is accepted for continuing use after satisfactory experience during trial.

Not all customers pass through all these stages in their adoption of new products. Some move straight from awareness to evaluation to adoption. Also, different customers take varying amounts of time to move from stage to stage. The time lapse between stages varies with the nature of the product as well. The whole process may involve only a few minutes for an inexpensive product, but months for an expensive one.

A classic study on the subject showed how a new product is accepted by people over time. Initially, only a small percentage of people accept it. A little larger percentage follows. Eventually the product is accepted by the masses. The adoption over time can be represented by a *bell-shaped curve.* Based on this conceptualization, five categories of customers can be identified: innovators, early adopters, early majority, late majority, and laggards. Innovators constitute a small proportion. The real market develops when early and late majority consumers enter the market.

Although in practice adoption might not pattern itself so neatly, it is reasonable to expect a tendency toward the bell-shaped distribution. Assuming this, the adoption framework can be utilized to forecast the initial demand for a new product in a foreign country and how the demand would mature with time. Thus, even where economies of scale are important for a product to achieve satisfactory performance, a company may not establish production facilities if customers cannot be expected to enter the market for several years.

Diffusion In international marketing, the concept of *diffusion* refers to how a new product captures a target market. Whereas the adoption process is concerned with acceptance by individuals, the diffusion process emphasizes the aggregate of individual decisions to adopt a new product. Thus, an analysis of the diffusion process in a country or culture indicates if the new product would be acceptable.

Research on the subject shows that diffusion is influenced by a number of organizational factors, such as effectiveness of communication between the parent and the subsidiary. In addition, a variety of product-related and market-related characteristics facilitate diffusion. The product-related characteristics are relative advantage, compatibility, complexity, divisibility, and communicability. The market-related characteristics include innovativeness of target customers and their clearer perception of need and economic ability.

Product-Related Characteristics

Relative Advantage The degree of superiority of a new product compared with current offerings is its relative advantage. If the new product is perceived as more beneficial, that is, if it appears to make a stronger promise of need fulfillment, it is likely to diffuse more quickly. One of the major causes of faster diffusion of superior products is word-of-mouth from the innovator, or initial adopter, to other customers.

Compatibility The higher the compatibility of the new product to the current ones, the more rapidly it will diffuse. *Compatibility* refers to social/cultural perspectives and the consistency of the product with existing tastes, values, and behaviors. Socially, a product requiring little change will be more readily accepted. Change is painful because it necessitates adjustments, both physical and mental, in established patterns. New products, or innovations, can be classified into three categories in order to judge compatibility. They may be labeled continuous innovations, dynamically continuous innovations, or discontinuous innovations.

A *continuous innovation* has the least disrupting influence on established patterns. Alteration of a product is involved, rather than the establishment of a new product. Examples would be fluoride toothpaste, new-model automobile changeovers, and menthol cigarettes.

A *dynamically continuous innovation* has more disrupting effects than a continuous innovation, although it still does not generally alter established patterns. It may involve the creation of a new product or the alteration of an existing product. Examples would be electric toothbrushes and Touch-Tone telephones.

A *discontinuous innovation* involves the establishment of a new product and the establishment of new behavior patterns. Examples would be television, computers, and the VCR.[38]

A product representing continuous innovation would diffuse more rapidly than those in the other two categories. The diffusion of products in the last category, discontinuous innovation, would require the longest time.

Complexity A product that is easy to comprehend and use would be diffused relatively quickly. A *complex* product requires detailed instructions for customer use. A customer must not only be made aware of the new product but also be educated in its use; the more complex the product, the slower the learning process. Nestlé baby formula ran into difficulties in many African countries because mothers in rural sections of Africa watered down the baby formula, making it inadequate for proper nutrition.

Divisibility If a product is available for trial on a limited basis, it diffuses far more rapidly. Customers can try it without making major commitments. In other words, divisibility reduces the risk to the customer, because a product can be sampled or used on a returnable basis—for example or, 10 days' free trial.

Communicability A product with attributes that can be conveniently communicated to the target customers and so distinguish it from other products can be more readily diffused. In other words, the degree to which the benefits of a product are obvious to potential customers dictates the pace of diffusion. By the same token, if a product is visible in a culture, it tends toward fast diffusion.

Market-Related Characteristics

Customer Innovativeness Wherever customers by virtue of their social/cultural traits are open to accepting new things, diffusion becomes easier. Thus, diffusion occurs more rapidly in western societies than in eastern ones. Within the same country, different cultural groups show different tendencies toward acceptance of a new product. For example, in Israel most Arab Jews would be less inclined to accept new innovations than would most European Jews.

Need Perception In situations where customers have a clear perception of their needs, new products are more likely to be diffused rapidly, because it is easier to determine if the product matches the need. Where customers do not know whether they need the product or not, diffusion is rather slow, even if the product is desirable. For example, in many developing countries birth-control–related products are not diffused since customers are not convinced of the need, or aware of the option, to limit family size. In such situations, even when birth-control devices are offered free, they are not accepted.

Economic Ability Despite the presence of all the characteristics favorable to rapid diffusion, a new product may fail if the customers are unable to afford it. Thus, the economic ability of the customers is another determining factor in the rate of diffusion. Many developing countries failed in their family planning campaigns because couples could not afford birth-control pills.

Impact of Diffusion Process on New Products

The characteristics that affect the diffusion process can be added up for an estimate of the length of diffusion time. Although the exact time of product spread cannot be predicted, the approximate length of time can. If the diffusion time is longer than anticipated or desirable, it may become necessary to make some changes in the new product to achieve more rapid diffusion. For example, the product design may have to be simplified to make it convenient for the customers to understand and use the product. Likewise, new features added to the product could provide an advantage to users over competing products.

In fact, adjustments may have to be made in the entire marketing mix to increase the pace of diffusion. However, the variable most related to diffusion, other than the product variable, is promotion. Promotional perspectives may have to be reoriented to provide customers an opportunity to try the product before making a commitment.

Foreign Product Diversification

Diversification refers to seeking unfamiliar products or unfamiliar markets, or both, for the purpose of expansion. Every company is at its best offering certain familiar products; diversification requires substantially different and unfamiliar knowledge, thinking, skills, and processes. Thus, diversification is at best a risky strategy, and a company should choose this path only when current product/market orientation seems to provide no further opportunities for growth.

Most large multinationals are already diversified and have no need to undertake product diversification solely for international business. In other words, their diversification is usually planned in the home market, and once the diversified product succeeds there, it can be introduced in foreign markets as well.

For a variety of reasons, though, a company may decide to diversify in a particular market overseas. First, in a particular country, government pressure may force a foreign company into unrelated areas. As mentioned earlier, Union Carbide considered entering the field of men's dress shirts in India to fulfill a government regulation.[39] Second, a special opportunity in a field may lead a company to diversify in that country. For example, a U.S. hotel chain might enter the car rental business in Latin America but not in the U.S., where there is fierce competition in the car rental business. Third, a strictly one-product international company may diversify overseas if its main business has reached maturity. Take the case of the Hoover Company. In the U.S., it is basically a vacuum cleaner company, In Europe, the company has long been active in washing machines as well. The European business at one time accounted for more than 50 percent of Hoover's sales. In the late 1970s and early 1980s the European business slowed down because of recession and aggressive, low-priced continental competitors, causing chronically depressed earnings. The company, therefore, decided to adopt a new strategy that included diversifying into a new line of cleaners and washing machines just for the European market, particularly Britain.[40]

Similarly, Unilever has diversified into different fields to strengthen its position in the U.S. market. In 1987 the company paid $3.1 billion to acquire Chesebrough-Pond's, which sells personal-care items and cosmetics including Pepsodent, Vaseline, Pond's, Q-tips, and Fabergé. In August 1989, for a total of $1.5 billion, Unilever acquired Elizabeth Arden, whose products include Visible Difference cosmetics, Elizabeth Taylor's Passion perfume, Erno Laszlo skin-care products, and Red Door salons. Subsequently, the company acquired Calvin Klein Cosmetics, which sells Eternity and Obsession fragrances.[41]

Brand Names and Trademarks

Corporate identification is a valuable asset in marketing, in both domestic and international markets. Firms face the choice of linking the company closely with its products and brands or of establishing market strength for each individual product line or brand. In the context of international business, the factors that usually determine policy on identification are further complicated by problems of nationalism, language and cultural differences, and customer preferences that vary with the distinctive characteristics in each market. Despite these difficulties, a company must make decisions on multinational identification about the use of brand names, trademarks, and names of subsidiaries.

Brand Strategy Alternatives

An overseas marketer has several choices in regard to brand names:

- Use one name with no adaptation to local markets.
- Use one name but adapt and modify it for each local market.
- Use different names in different markets for the same products.
- Use the company name as a brand name under one house style or the corporate umbrella approach.

One Brand Name Worldwide This strategy is useful when the company primarily markets one product that is widely distributed, and the brand name does not seem to conflict with local cultures of different societies. Coca-Cola, for example, is marketed around the globe under the brand name Coke without any adaptation to local markets.

The worldwide use of one brand name provides a greater identification of the product with the company on an international basis. It helps to achieve greater consistency and coordination of advertising and promotion on a worldwide basis. It permits clear identification of a brand with a company noted for quality or technical superiority. It eliminates confusion with products of other companies. Finally, a great sense of consumer familiarity through customer identification of trademarks is realized. (see International Marketing Highlight 12.9).

━━━━━━━━━━━ **International Marketing Highlight 12.9** ━━━━━━━━━━━

Power Brands

What would happen if you tried to compare the world's best-known brand with those held in the highest esteem? To find out, Landor Associates, a San Francisco design consulting firm, assembled a list of what it calls "brands with global image power."

Landor surveyed 10,000 consumers in the U.S., Western Europe, and Japan, asking them to judge 6,000 brands by both measures. The top 10: Coca-Cola (a U.S. brand);

Sony (Japanese); Mercedes-Benz (German); Kodak (U.S.); Disney (U.S.); Nestlé (Swiss); Toyota (Japanese); and McDonald's, IBM, and Pepsi Cola (all U.S.).

Source: Landor Associates, San Francisco, 1991.

Modifying Brand Names for Each Market Some factors overseas may lead a company to adapt a brand name to suit local conditions. Nestlé, for example, introduced several new products in Europe by modifying the brand name for each country. Its soluble coffee was introduced in Germany under the name Nescafé Gold and in Britain under Nescafé Gold Blend.

Very often when a company leaves its home market, it tries to shake its so-called foreignness. When the Campbell Soup Company entered the British market on a national scale, it attempted to take advantage of its Scottish-origin name. Each of its brands of soups was introduced at a tasting party for the press with a number of Campbell families living in Britain, including the Duke of Argyll, head of the Campbell clan, and Donald Campbell, the racing motorist. To add further to the name, some 5,000 Campbells in the London telephone directory were sent a sample can of Campbell's soup. Today, Campbell Soup is thought to be a British company by a large portion of its consuming public in Britain.[42]

The adaptation of the parent brand name to local conditions is also affected by media considerations. For example, Unilever sold one of its detergents in Germany under the brand name Radion, but for special reasons it was sold under another name in Austria. For a few years this worked out well. Then a great majority of Austrians began to watch German TV programs and read German magazines. Thus, German advertisements gained importance among Austrians. In the case of Radion detergent, however, this was a problem since it was sold under a different brand name in Austria. The company finally decided to substitute Radion for the Austrian brand name.

Different Brands for Different Markets Local brands are often used when the brand name cannot be translated into the local language; when a product is manufactured, sold, and consumed locally; when it is a leading selling brand and part of a new local acquisition; or when the company wants to play down its foreignness and be thought of as a local company. Unilever has different brand names for its fabric softener in the U. S. and France. It is called Snuggle in the U.S., while in France it is marketed as Cajoline. The reason behind this decision, according to company sources, is that the word *snuggle* does not communicate the intended meaning in French.

A local brand name is necessary when a product has no local manufacturer and the imported international brand is too expensive for the typical local consumer. The British American Tobacco Company has a number of markets where it caters to the full range of purchasing power. It provides cigarettes at the lowest possible prices for the mass consumer (through purely local brands, unheard of elsewhere), as well as international brands for the relatively wealthy minority who can afford them.

Individual brand names permit greater identification of the product by consumers with a name more suited to the local language or jargon. For example, in the U.S., Frigidaire was synonymous with the word "refrigerator," but this was obviously not the case in non-English-speaking markets. When a local brand name has a strong market following, an acquiring company may retain it, perhaps linking it with the corporate name. For example, the local name on the package could be underscored with the caption, "A Product of XYZ Company." A local brand name or trademark can support a general campaign by the company to "go local" in its total approach to the market. Moreover a local trademark or brand name lessens the impact on other company products and the total corporate image if the new product proves to be a failure.

Company Name as Brand Name Many companies use standard trademarks for all their products but are flexible in the case of brand names, taking into consideration local consumer motivation, language and translation problems, and other market factors. Some use both worldwide brands and local brands according to each market situation and thus avoid the major disadvantage of a worldwide brand policy—inflexibility.

Scott Paper Co. had local brand names in 80 foreign countries where the company generated almost 50 percent of its $3.8 billion in sales. Starting in 1995 the company started phasing out the local brand names with Scott. The company claims that global branding, which allowed for common advertising messages around the world, has proved to be more important than local sentiments for brands.[43]

Trademarks in the form of symbols, logos, letters, and initials have all become forms of corporate identification. A brand name is identified with the product, but a trademark goes further, identifying both the product and the company. The double task carries a much stronger corporate message back to the consumer. Whereas the brand name may contend with the company name for first place, the trademark usually complements and reinforces it.

Some companies can benefit from the double impact of a trademark that is the same as or similar to the company name. Levi Strauss & Company has profited from Levi's jeans identity. However, success in the foreign markets has brought with it the problem of keeping others from using the same name, because as international sales have increased, so have the infringements upon Levi trademarks. (The problem of infringements will be discussed in a later section.)

The dilemma of brand name versus company name is a contested issue. Even the largest international companies, such as Unilever, Shell, and Imperial Chemicals Industries (ICI), differ on this point. Shell and ICI promote products under the company name and are heavy corporate advertisers. Unilever promotes brands and products and does not emphasize its corporate name, especially in areas outside its home territory.

The 3M Company (Minnesota Mining and Manufacturing) is an example of a firm that has successfully taken the umbrella approach and has created a family look around its products. Faced with an ever-growing number of new products and a constant need for new brand names, 3M decided on a corporate packaging theme for all its products. Previously, names and packaging had not conveyed the impression of one versatile company offering products to industry, to commercial business, and to the home consumer. The new corporate design system consists of three rectangular elements. One rectangle always carries the 3M logo, another the product identification, and the third the divisional identification, such as the Scotch$^{(TM)}$ plaid of the retail tape and gift wrap division. 3M considers the one look worldwide more important internationally than in the U.S., since identity and packaging problems had become quite difficult internationally as a result of multiple sources of supply, different languages, and various modes of distribution.

Three trends are pushing companies into increasingly making their corporate names more noticeable on their products. First, product proliferation; second, product commoditization; and third, eternal values. With regard to the first two, the proliferation of brands and the fact that product differences are usually copied within six months mean that consumers will look to the company behind a brand to simplify the buying decision. As for the third, consumers are redefining brand loyalty as a two-way street: if a firm wants them to be loyal to its brands, then it must show them a commitment as well. Trust, integrity, reputation—such values will provide the emotional connection consumers seek and the necessary reassurance that they are making the right product choices.

Exhibit 12.2 summarizes strategic/tactical considerations in choosing brand names.

Brand Piracy

One persistent problem that well-known brands face in foreign markets is counterfeiting. Consider the irritation it would cause P&G to find out that its Crest brand name is being used falsely on a toothpaste sold for one-fifth the P&G price in various markets abroad. Unfortunately, the laws pertaining to brand piracy in many countries are loose, with little punishment for shady practices.[44]

Of the many factors that encourage brand piracy, two stand out. First, a variety of U.S. brands are held in high esteem, particularly those of long standing, such as Singer sewing machines. In the developing countries, goods from industrialized countries, especially the luxury goods, serve as status symbols and most of the time are in short supply. Thus, a ready-made market exists for imported brands that the counterfeiter likes to exploit. Second, the technological knowledge required to produce a counterfeit product is readily available. For example, a person in Taiwan interested in counterfeiting a Seiko watch will encounter little difficulty in acquiring the know-how and parts required.

As U.S. companies do more manufacturing offshore, developing countries acquire the technology to produce bogus goods. But not all offenders are foreign. According to a *Business Week* report, 20 percent of the world's fakes are made in the U.S., mostly by marginal producers who cannot make a profit legally.[45] This report went on to say that no one knows the exact number of shoddy goods being traded, but experts estimate that up to $60 billion in annual world trade are in fakes.

EXHIBIT 12.2
Strategic/Tactical Recommendations in Choosing Brand Names

Unique Feature	Strategic/Tactical Recommendation
Selecting Corporate and Brand Names	
Ideographs	Choose brand name with desirable connotations.
Homonyms	Choose name with desirable sound associations.
Multiple tones	Choose name with desirable tonal associations.
Writing as art	Present name in attractive calligraphy.
Multiple writing systems	Use writing system appropriate for product category.
Lucky names	Choose name associated with luck based on stoke number and *yin-yang*.
Establishing the Right Image	
Prestige	Create prestigious associations, promote the image of the corporation, and leverage corporate image in brand extensions.
Mysticism	Check for mysticism and *feng-shui*.
Aesthetics	Focus on complexity, balance and naturalism.
Enhancing Quality Perceptions	
Collectivism	Use reference groups as influencers.
Societal role of company	Engage in community projects and sponsorships.
Personal service	Customize service elements.
Service rituals	Attune to movement, gestures, and rituals.

Source: Bern H. Schmitt and Yigang Pan, "Managing Corporate and Brand Identities in the Asia-Pacific Region," *California Management Review*, Summer 1994, pp. 32–48.

Three forms of piracy can be labeled: imitation, faking, and preemption. *Imitation* amounts simply to copying an established brand. For example, a manufacturer in Italy may produce cheap jeans and put on the Calvin Klein label for sale as a genuine Klein product. *Faking* refers to identifying the fraudulent product with a symbol, logo, or brand name that is very similar to the famous brand. For example, in Europe several companies have sold jeans under the brand names of "Lewis" (in France) and "Levy's" (in Germany), which are pronounced very similarly to Levi's. A Hong Kong firm advertises its blue jeans under its own brand name, but displays the figure of the Levi Strauss trademark, "The Levi's Saddleman," with the only difference being that the branding iron in the hand of saddleman is replaced by a horsewhip.[46]

Here is another example: Recently, McDonald's filed a request for a temporary injunction against McDavid's, a Tel Aviv hamburger outlet. The restaurant looks distinctly American—from the plastic counters and beeping digital cash registers to the Uncle Sam hat atop the McDavid's symbol. The owner of McDavid's was quoted as saying that he had McDonald's 120-page manual for its franchise owners translated into Hebrew.[47]

Piracy through *preemption* of brand names is feasible in those countries where the law permits wholesale registration of brand names. In such countries, a person may register in his or her name a large number of well-known brand names, and then either sell these names to those interested in counterfeiting or, better still, to the multinational when it is ready to move into the country. In Nigeria, for example, one person registered 300 famous brand names such as Chase Manhattan, Bankers Trust, du Pont, Sears, Texaco, NBC, and CBS.

Needless to say, brand piracy can cause unfair competition to multinational enterprises in many markets. Sometimes the counterfeit product is even exported to the home market. This practice causes worse damage to an MNC. For example, while the loss of a particular country as a market may not cause much worry to P&G, a fake product in the U.S. sold at a meager price would create a real problem.

Unfortunately, MNCs have little protection in the form of international laws to protect their brands overseas. Some conventions, such as the Paris Convention and the Madrid Convention, discussed in Chapter 11, make it convenient to obtain registration of the brand simultaneously in member countries, but other than that, the international marketer can do little against brand piracy. Legal recourse overseas may be ill-advised if the foreign court cannot ensure an unbiased decision. Besides, legal action is expensive and can result in adverse publicity in the foreign market (see International Marketing Highlight 12.10). Thus, the only option of the international firm to protect its brand is either to withdraw from the market where it must compete against imitations and fakes or to promote its product in such a way as to make the customer aware of false brands.

The best defense for business victimized by brand piracy is to strike back rather than to rely on government agencies. In this regard, the experience of Paris-based Cartier is illuminating. Despite Cartier's best efforts, Mexican officials were uncooperative about pursuing a Mexico City retail store owner who was selling fake Cartier products, even with 49 legal decisions against him. So Cartier opened its own store directly across the street and forced the retailer to strike a deal: in return for not selling forgeries, he would become Cartier's sole local distributor.[48]

In recent years, the protection of intellectual properties has figured prominently in multilateral talks. For example, in the Uruguay Round members agreed to a negotiating framework that allowed for conclusion of a comprehensive agreement to govern the trade-related aspects of intellectual property (TRIPS). The Uruguay Round supports the concept of *reciprocity* in the matter of intellectual property rights (i.e., rights available to nationals are extended to foreigners as well), and applies the concept of "most favored nation" to the area of intellectual-property rights.

■■■■■■■■■■■■■ **International Marketing Highlight 12.10** ■■■■■■■■■■■■■

Drug Push

Egypt is defying foreign drug makers as it creates a home-grown pharmaceuticals industry. Local companies, insignificant before the 1980s, now supply two-thirds of the nation's medicines. Their profit margins run as high as 26 percent, and their executives ride in limousines.

But some of their most lucrative products are knock-off versions of drugs, such as Glaxo Wellcome PLC's Zantac ulcer medicine and Pfizer Inc.'s Cefobid anti-infection drug, that are still under patent in most countries.

It's piracy, Pfizer and Glaxo say, but it's legal under Egyptian law, which provides only weak patent protection for drugs. The wrangling that produced the 1994 General Agreement on Tariffs and Trade (GATT) gave poorer countries 10 years to strengthen their drug-patent laws and the U.S. a similar period to lift quotas protecting its textile industry.

Source: Daniel Pearl, "Big Drug Makers Push Egypt, " *The Wall Street Journal*, December 13, 1996, p. 1.

Identifying Country of Origin

A related question here is whether a company should identify the country of origin on a product. For example, should a U.S. company use the *Made in the USA* label on its product? The answer to this question depends on the market for which the product is destined. There was a time when U.S. products were held in high esteem worldwide. Traditionally, therefore, as far as U.S. companies were concerned, identifying the country of origin was considered very desirable. A recent study, though, showed that perceptions of U.S. product quality are no longer high in every instance. Also, perceptions vary across product perspectives: i.e., U.S.–branded/U.S.–made, U.S.–branded/foreign-made, foreign-branded/U.S.–made, and foreign-branded/foreign-made. Nevertheless, the sourcing country stimuli came out stronger than brand name in this study when the consumers evaluated bi-national products.[49]

Although the USA label is no longer the sole mark of prestige, technical advancement, and innovativeness, names that connote "America" or, more specifically, the American West, are hot in many countries today, particularly in Asia.[50] From Beijing to Bombay, American brands are commanding big premiums over inferior hometown competitors.[51] In many other countries, nationalist sentiments favor locally produced products, so the decision to use the "made in" attribute must be evaluated for each market and each product. Where laws require such identification, the company has no choice. For example, goods entering the U.S. must be identified by their origin. In countries where there are no such legal requirements, the "made in" identification should be used only if research findings and business acumen indicate that the identification would benefit the company (see International Marketing Highlight 12.11).

Private Branding for Foreign Markets

Private branding is a common practice whereby large retailers sell a variety of products under their house brand. For example, products sold under stores' labels (private brands) comprise 30 percent of supermarket sales in Britain and are rising in France, Switzerland, and Italy.[52] The question is to what extent this practice is relevant in international marketing.

An essential requirement for private branding is the existence of a developed distribution system in the market, particularly at the retail level. Thus, only industrialized societies qualify for successful private branding outside the U.S. In other words, U.S. businesspersons may find it advantageous to enter a country, say, England, by producing private brands for a large retailer there. The danger with such a decision is that the U.S. exporter is entirely at the mercy of the English retailer. The manufacturer's name is not known. As product becomes popular, the retailer might want to strike such a hard bargain that the U.S. producer is caught in an unfavorable cost/profit situation and must end the association. This is likely to happen because the retailer can easily find alternative sources of supply for the product both in the U.S. and elsewhere.

International Marketing Highlight 12.11

American Cars

What makes an American car? Nowadays it is notoriously hard to tell. Chrysler's Stealth sports car is imported from Japan, and its popular minivans come from Canada. General Motor's latest Cadillac luxury car is assembled in Europe by its Opel subsidiary. Some of Ford's Escorts are assembled in Mexico, while its Aspire minicar is imported from South Korea. On the other hand, Japan's Honda produces most of its best-selling Accord cars in Marysville, Ohio. In all, Japanese car makers will build more than 2m vehicles in America this year at nearly a dozen "transplant" assembly lines; imports are less than half their sales.

Source: The Economist, September 24, 1994, p. 67.

It is for such reasons that H.J. Heinz Co. opposed the retailers' big push into private labels in Britain. Although Heinz's major competitors, Campbell Soup and Nestlé, succumbed to pressure from the food chains, Heinz decided against private branding. To compete with private-label brands, which retail up to 15 percent less than its own products, Heinz is depending on brand loyalty, hoping that consumers will continue to consider its products superior and demand them despite higher prices. If this happens, the retailers eventually will lose their leverage.[53]

Even in nonfood areas, private branding at the international level is slowly becoming popular. For example, Polaroid agreed to let Minolta Camera Co. of Japan sell the Spectra Pro, its most expensive consumer instant camera, in the U.S. as the Minolta Instant Pro. Polaroid considers the agreement to be a logical move to find new ways to grow through private branding.[54] Private branding for U.S. retailers by foreign companies is also prevalent. For example, J.C. Penney has an array of its electronic products and appliances (radios, toasters) manufactured in Southeast Asia under the J.C. Penney brand.

International Packaging

Good marketing practice requires that products be offered to customers in serviceable shape and pleasing form. Therefore, packaging plays an important role that can be described basically in two ways—physical and psychological. Physically, the packaging should be sturdy enough to undergo all the strain involved in shipment. The psychological aspect involves the package as a promotional tool. In general, international packaging decisions ought to take into account the requirements of four groups of people: customers, shippers, distributors, and host governments.

Customer Requirements

Packaging requirements for the customer vary from country to country, based on socioeconomic-cultural factors. Customer characteristics should be examined in order to make sound packaging decisions. The aesthetics of the package is the first important consideration. The shape of the package and the logo, symbols, and figures used on it; the words and phrases describing the product; and the color scheme must all be appropriately attuned to the cultural traits of the host country.

Whereas in developed countries the major emphasis in packaging is on visual aesthetics, in developing countries the overall physical quality of the package is important because the package will most likely be kept and used as a container. Thus, the package itself may become a selling point. The higher the quality of the package, however, the higher the cost. If package costs substantially increase product price, demand will be adversely affected.

Another aesthetic factor to reckon with is size. An eight-ounce jar of coffee may sell well in the U.S. but not at all in a tea-drinking nation where coffee is used infrequently.

Climate is another consideration in a foreign packaging decision. The package may have to be redesigned for shipping to zones of high temperature, such as Saudi Arabia. Package failure would mean that customers would be buying a stale product, and the brand name would earn a bad image.

Finally, packaging should be safe in every way, both when it is used to house the product and during after-use. It is particularly important that after-use not lead to any bad side effects, including ecological ones. The disposal of the package should not be hazardous to humans or pets and should not create any pollution of the environment.

Shipper Requirements

Regardless of the mode of transportation, the main concern of shippers involved in international marketing is getting goods to their destination without damage, theft, or loss, and doing that with the least possible cost. The key to accomplishing this feat is in efficient packing and packaging methods. The major questions to answer in order to design proper packaging for international shipment are as follows: Where is the shipment going? Will it be stacked? For how long and where (in a warehouse or in an open space)? What are the handling requirements (net weight and type of load)? Are there any unusual or additional requirements? When these questions are difficult to answer, a consulting firm with expertise in packaging for international shipments can be helpful.

Distributor Requirements

The distribution channels for dispersion and conversion of products for worldwide markets require that theft, pilferage, and damage of shipped goods be avoided through proper packaging. For example, advertising the company or product on the shipping case is inadvisable. Not only does it involve unnecessary printing cost, but it is also an invitation to pilferage. Most of the requirements of channels of distribution in international marketing are similar to those of domestic marketing channels. For example, the package should not waste shelf space, should handle easily, and should permit easy and efficient price marketing and labeling. Foremost, the package should protect the contents and be aesthetically attractive to promote the product at the point of purchase.

Government Requirements

Government requirements in the area of packaging are mainly related to labeling and marking. Labeling applies to retail packages and is intended to provide consumers with essential information about the contents of the package in order to assure them that both the package and its contents conform to the regulations in force within the market. Marking regulations concern only the transport container and normally do not affect the labeling on the retail package inside.

Many countries with two common languages require bilingual labeling. Likewise, nations on the metric system require provision of information on weight and measure in metric designation. Canada's law pertaining to labeling illustrates the point. It requires

1. That the identity of the product by its common or generic name or its function be shown on the principal display panel in English and French.
2. That the net quantity of the product be declared in metric units and in the French and English languages.
3. That the person by or for whom the product was manufactured be identified sufficiently for postal purposes.

Special "other information" requirements are set forth for food products related to the use of artificial flavorings.

International Warranties and Services

Customers buy not only the physical product but also the benefits that the product provides. Warranties and service agreements are included in these benefits.

Warranties

A *warranty* is a guarantee from the manufacturer that the product will perform as stipulated. Warranties are common in industrialized countries, and companies are grappling with the question of whether they should be extended internationally. There are various reasons for companies to give warranties. First, a warranty serves as a competitive tool. A good warranty policy tends to differentiate the product in the marketplace. It enhances the customer's confidence in the product. Second, a warranty sometimes helps in gaining additional business. For example, the warranty may hold good only if the product is regularly serviced. Thus, to keep the warranty viable, the customer might contract with the company for servicing. To illustrate the point, in 1990 Boeing sold six jet airliners to Moroccan Airways for $300 million. Along with the sale went a service contract for $20 million for training personnel and servicing the airliners.

Another advantage of warranties is that an explicit warranty limits the liability of the company should the product fail to meet the expectations of the buyer.

The design of a warranty policy raises an important managerial question: Should a standard warranty be provided worldwide, or should the warranty be customized for each country or region? For example, on most electronic toys, manufacturers provide one-year guarantees in the U.S. Whether this one-year warranty should be extended to toys sold outside the U.S. is a question that must be investigated.

The answer to this question would involve a variety of considerations. First among these considerations is the nature of the market. If the international market is represented as one market, such as the EU, where goods move freely within the market, it is desirable to offer a standard warranty.

Competition within international markets would be another consideration. For example, the company may not have an elaborate warranty policy at home, but in an international market it might be forced into matching the warranty offered by competitors. In 1986 Ford Motor Company did not offer extensive warranties on most of its cars in the U.S. However, outside the U.S., Ford continued its two-year-or-60,000-kilometer warranty.

The warranty may have to be different if the conditions of the use of the product vary in different markets. A warranty may have to be made much more restrictive if wear and tear on the product because of, say, climatic conditions is likely to be excessive. For example, in the dusty conditions and hot climate of Saudi Arabia, equipment such as air conditioners would wear out in a shorter period than in Switzerland. A company may need to offer a more liberal warranty in Switzerland than in Saudi Arabia.

Another consideration is the nature of the product. Conventionally, a warranty on certain products is limited to basic performance. In such cases, a standard warranty could be offered worldwide. For example, Allis Chalmers, Bell & Howell, Brunswick (bowling equipment), Caterpillar, AB Dick, Parker Pen, Sunbeam, and Volkswagen offer a basic performance warranty common to all markets.

A final consideration in deciding between a standard and localized warranty is the ability of the company to service the product under warranty. Servicing requires servicing facilities. If it is not feasible to have facilities in all the markets and countries the company sells in, it may offer different warranties to fit the situation.

Service

Service constitutes an offer to maintain the original product through overhauling, replacement of parts, adjustments, and the like. Most industrial products and many consumer durables require servicing on a regular basis. Provision of service on an international basis is important on two accounts. First, service must be provided to comply with the warranty policy. For example, if a piece of equipment carries a year's warranty on certain parts and functions, the manufacturer should make arrangements to ensure that the terms of the warranty are adequately fulfilled by providing appropriate service facilities. Second, service ranks as a promotional tool. When a product by its very nature periodically requires after-sale service, the company that provides such a service has an edge over a competitor who does not offer service.

International customer service has received far less attention from U.S. firms than domestic customer service. Typically, U.S. exporters delegate the responsibility for service to third parties such as importers. Consequently, the service needs of foreign customers often are handled ineffectively.[55]

The formulation of a service policy requires an objective assessment of needs. The need may vary by country, depending on such factors as intensity of use, climatic conditions, and the technical skills of the people using the product. For example, in the U.S. higher labor costs mean that various industrial machine tools are used much more intensively than in Japan. In an extreme climate, a product is very likely to require greater care. Also, when the people using the product have marginal skills, the need for service escalates.

A prerequisite to an offer of service is an adequate supply of spare parts. Companies often fail in this regard and thereby earn a bad reputation among their customers. The problem in supplying parts is that many products come in different models, and parts frequently vary from model to model. Furthermore, a product may have a large number of parts, some of which are exorbitantly expensive, and a service facility has to carry all of them. There is no easy solution to this problem. Usually, companies consult their own past experience to work out a list of parts that often need replacing and then carry these parts in the inventory.

Providing service necessitates training the personnel to perform the service. Most companies either train the native service personnel in their own country by one or more technicians from the U.S. or bring them to the U.S. for training. Usually training involves on-the-job experience as well as classroom instruction. Training of high-technology products is rendered on an ongoing basis. Many companies have teams of trainers who visit country after country to update local personnel on new materials, processes or parts related to the product.

In conclusion, a good service program is helpful, directly and indirectly, in getting feedback from customers on various aspects of the marketing mix. The service organization, based on customer inputs, can serve as a catalyst to generate ideas on product improvement. Similarly, this information can shed light on other aspects of the marketing mix.

Summary

Decisions about products involve such issues as what products and product lines to introduce in various countries, to what extent a product should be adapted to local customs and characteristics, whether new products should be introduced, where the R&D effort should be concentrated, whether the firm should diversify into unrelated areas, which products should be eliminated, how products should be packaged, what brand policy to pursue, what after-sale services to offer, and what warranties the company should provide on various products.

Product means a bundle of attributes put together to satisfy a customer need. The product objectives for each country or market should be defined separately and be based on (1) overall corporate objectives and (2) the concerns of the individual national governments. Product planning decisions, both immediate and strategic, are based on product objectives.

Product design is a major strategic issue. A company can either offer a standard product worldwide or adapt it to local requirements. Adaptation can be prompted by physical requirements (for example, changes made in the electrical wiring system of a machine to match voltage requirements of a country) or cultural requirements (for example, a color change in response to a cultural preference). The decision to standardize or adapt is dictated by the nature of the product, market development, cost/benefit considerations, legal requirements, competition, support system, physical environment, and market conditions. Generally, companies try to market a standardized product internationally. Although this helps in cost savings, standardization can also lead to missed opportunities.

To operate overseas successfully, periodic review of the product line is necessary. Product-line development essentially involves three alternatives: (1) extending the domestic line, which refers to the introduction of domestic products to overseas markets; (2) adding products to the overseas line even if the company does not carry those products domestically; and (3) adding new products. New products for international markets can be either developed internally or acquired. Decisions involving the addition of new products and the procedure for undertaking new-product development are complex. Product review may result in product elimination as well as product improvement. There are several reasons for product elimination and different ways of implementing elimination decisions.

Some companies undertake R&D across national boundaries, but companies largely centralize R&D activity at home for a variety of reasons. More recently, R&D effort in host countries has been initiated by some companies. There are relative pros and cons of centralization versus decentralization of R&D.

The diffusion of innovations in overseas markets involves adoption and diffusion processes that are affected by a series of factors. In fact, the diffusion process itself may have an impact on new products.

There are four alternatives for formulating an international brand strategy: using one name worldwide, using one name with adaptations for each market, using different names in different markets, and using the company name as a family name for all brands.

An important problem that companies face in brand management is that of brand piracy, the illegal use of famous brand names in various ways. In the absence of any international law to protect the brands, each company must independently guard its brand from invaders. Whether to identify the country of origin on the product and whether to employ private branding for international markets are decisions that must be made in relation to specific situation.

International packaging is influenced by such considerations as customers, distribution channels, shippers, and host governments. The service/warranty component provides a company with an important opportunity to differentiate its product from the competition.

Review Questions

1. What are the advantages of product standardization worldwide?
2. Under what circumstances should the product be adapted to local conditions?

3. Distinguish between obligatory and discretionary adaptation. Give examples.
4. Illustrate the logic behind the extension of the domestic product line to overseas markets.
5. What factors influence a decision to add products to the overseas product line?
6. Discuss the rationale behind the introduction of new products across national boundaries.
7. What factors help in the successful management of the international product line?
8. Why do MNCs mainly centralize R&D at home?
9. What alternative strategies can a company adopt to brand its international products?
10. What factors enhance the diffusion of innovations overseas?

Creative Questions

1. Academic research confirms that the country of origin of a product affects its perception and evaluation by the consumers. Consumers in developed countries tend to attach lower value to products from developing countries. What strategies might be adopted to successfully sell products with developing-country origins in industrialized nations?

2. The powerful force of technology is driving the world toward a converging commonality: the emergence of a global market. To serve the global market, one school of thought recommends adopting a common marketing mix worldwide. This way, companies can benefit from enormous economies of scale. By transferring these benefits into reduced world prices, they can gain competitive leverage. On the other hand, experience shows that socioeconomic, legal/political, and cultural differences among nations do not permit complete marketing standardization. Accepting the latter viewpoint, divide products into these categories: (a) where more or less complete standardization is desirable, (b) where complete customization is necessary, and (c) where at least one aspect of the marketing mix must be adapted to local conditions.

Endnotes

1. Samon Darlin, "Coke, Nestlé Launch First Coffee Drink," *The Wall Street Journal*, October 25, 1991, p. B1

2. Subhash C. Jain, "Standardization of International Marketing Strategy: Some Hypotheses," *Journal of Marketing*, January 1989, pp. 70–79.

3. See: David A. Aacker and Eric Joachimsthaler, "The Lure of Global Branding," *Harvard Business Review*, November–December 1999, pp. 137–146.

4. Donald S. Henley, "Evaluating International Product Line Performance: A Conceptual Approach," in *Multinational Product Management* (Cambridge, MA: Marketing Science Institute, 1976), pp. II-1–II-19.

5. *See* Saeed Samiee and Kendall Roth, "The Influence of Global Marketing Standardization of Performance," *Journal of Marketing*, April 1992, pp. 1–17; David M. Szymanski, Sundar G. Bharadwaj, and P. Rajan Varadarajan, "Standardization Versus Adaptation of International Marketing Strategy: An Empirical Investigation," *Journal of Marketing*, October 1993, pp. 1–17; and, George S. Yip, "Patterns and Determinants of Global Marketing," CIBER Working Paper Series—NO. 96-5, The John E. Anderson Graduate School of Management at UCLA.

6. Jose De La Torre, "Product Life Cycle as a Determinant of Global Marketing Strategies," *Atlantic Economic Review*, September–October 1975, pp. 9–14.

7. John S. Hill and Richard R. Still, "Effects of Urbanization on Multinational Product Planning: Markets in Lesser-Developed Countries," *Columbia Journal of World Business*, Summer 1984, pp. 62–67.

8. Seth Luboro, "Aim, Focus, and Shoot," *Forbes*, November 26, 1990, p. 67.

9. Hajo Riesenbeck and Anthony Freeling, "How Global Are Global Brands?" *The McKinsey Quarterly* 4 (1991): 6.

10. Yumiko Ono, "Pizza in Japan Is Adapted to Local Tastes," *The Wall Street Journal*, June 4, 1993, p. B1.

11. Allan T. Demaree, "What Now for the U.S. and Japan," *Fortune*, February 10, 1992, p. 90

12. John S. Hill and Richard R. Still, "Adapting Products to LDC Tastes," *Harvard Business Review*, March–April, 1984, pp. 93–94. *Also see* John S. Hill and William L. James, "Product and Promotion Transfers in Consumer Goods Multinationals," *International Marketing Review* 8, no. 2 (1991): 6–17.

13. "Blade-Runner," *The Economist*, April 10, 1993, p. 68.

14. W. Chan Kim and R. A. Manborgue, "Cross-Cultural Strategies," *Journal of Business Strategies*, Spring 1987, p. 31. *Also see* M. P. Kacker, "Export-Oriented Product Adaptation—Its Patterns and Problems," *Management International Review*, No. 6 (1976): 61–70.

15. Sushil Vachani and Louis T. Wells, Jr., "How Far Should Global Products Go?" *Vikalpa*, April–June 1989, pp. 3–10.

16. Kenichi Ohmae, *Triad Power* (New York: The Free Press, 1985), pp. 101–102.

17. W. Chan Kim and R. A. Manborgue, "Cross-Cultural Strategies," *Journal of Business Strategies*, Spring 1987, p. 30.

18. Ian R. Wilson, "American Success Story—Coca-Cola in Japan," in Mark B. Winchester, ed., *The International Essays for Business Decision Makers*, 5 (Dallas: The Center for Business, 1980), p. 121.

19. Ibid.

20. "Campbell Soup Unit's Cookies Will Be Sold in Japan by Meiji Seika," *The Asian Wall Street Journal Weekly*, September 30, 1985, p. 22.

21. Vern Terpstra, "International Product Policy: The Role of Foreign R&D," *Columbia Journal of World Business*, Winter 1977, p. 25.

22. William H. Davidson and Richard Harrigan, "Key Decisions in International Marketing: Introducing New Products Abroad," *Columbia Journal of World Business*, Winter 1977, pp. 15–28.

23. Robert Block, " How Big Mac Kept From Becoming a Serb Archenemy," *The Wall Street Journal*, September 3, 1999, p. B1.

24. "A New Focus for Polaroid: Conventional Film," *Business Week*, July 25, 1988, p. 36.

25. "Fizzing," *The Economist*, September 4, 1993, p. 63.

26. Yumiko Ono, "Anheuser Plays on Tipsiness to Sell Japan Strong Brew," *The Wall Street Journal*, November 17, 1998, p. B1.

27. "Another Day, Another Bright Idea," *The Economist*, April 16, 1988, p. 82.

28. "Computers That Point Moslems Toward Mecca," *Business Week*, March 25, 1985, p. 46.

29. Charles G. Burck, "The Toyota of the Wine Trade," *Fortune*, November 30, 1981, p. 155.

30. X. Michael Song and Mark E. Parry, "A Cross-national Comparative Study of New Product Development Processes: Japan and the United States," *Journal of Marketing*, April 1997, pp. 1–18.

31. Thomas A. Stewart, "The New American Century," *Fortune*, The New American Century Issue, 1991, p. 12.

32. "It Was a Hit in Buenos Aires—So Why Not Boise? *Business Week*, September 7, 1998, p. 56.

33. Paul Ingrassia, "Industry Is Shopping Abroad for Good Ideas to Apply to Products," *The Wall Street Journal*, April 29, 1985, p. 1.

34. W. Chan Kim and R. A. Manborgue, "Cross-Cultural Strategies," *Journal of Business Strategy*, Spring 1987, pp. 28–35.

35. Ernest Beck, "Nestlé Sticks to Strategy of Broad Categories of Brands, "*The Wall Street Journal*, September 24, 1999, p. B4.

36. "Campbell Soup Fails to Make It to the Table," *Business Week*, October 12, 1981, p. 66.

37. "Gerber Abandons a Baby-Food Market," *Business Week*, February 9, 1982, p. 45.

38. Thomas S. Robertson, "The Process of Innovation and the Diffusion of Innovation," *Journal of Marketing*, January 1964, pp. 15–16.

39. Yves L. Doz and C. K. Prahalad, "How MNCs Cope with Host Government Intervention," *Harvard Business Review*, March–April 1980, p. 149.

40. "Hoover: Revamping in Europe to Stem an Earnings Drain at Home," *Business Week*, February 15, 1982, p. 144. *Also see* Sushil Vachini, "Distinguishing Between Related and Unrelated International Geographic Diversification: A Comprehensive Measure of Global Diversification," *Journal of International Business Studies*, 22, no. 2 (Second Quarter 1991): 307–322.

41. "The New, Improved Unilever Aims to Clean Up in the U.S.," *Business Week*, November 27, 1989, p. 102.

42. *Choosing Corporate, Product, and Brand Names for Worldwide Marketing* (New York: Business International Corporation, no date), pp. 24–32.

43. "Scott Rolls out a Risky Strategy," *Business Week*, May 22, 1995, p. 48.

44. *See* "Dead Men Tell No Tales," *The Economist*, December 18, 1999, p. 87.

45. "The Counterfeit Trade," *Business Week*, December 16, 1985, p. 64.

46. *Choosing Corporate, Product, and Brand Names for Worldwide Marketing.*

47. Jack A. Kaikati and Raymond LaGrace, "Beware of International Brand Piracy," *Harvard Business Review*, March–April 1980, p. 54.

48. "The Counterfeit Trade," *Business Week*, December 16, 1985, p. 64.

49. C. Min Han and Vern Terpstra, "Country-of-Origin Effects for Uni-National and Bi-National Products," *Journal of International Business Studies*, Summer 1988, pp. 235–256. *Also see* Graham J. Hooley and David Shipley, "A Method for Modeling Consumer Perceptions of Country of Origin," *International Marketing Review*, Autumn 1988, pp. 67–76.

50. "U.S. Locations Make Hot Brand Names Abroad," *Business International*, April 6, 1992, p. 101.

51. Patricia Sellers, "Brands: It's Thrive or Die," *Fortune*, August 23, 1993, p. 52.

52. "The Eurosion of Brand Loyalty," *Business Week*, July 19, 1993, p. 22.

53. "Heinz Struggles to Stay at the Top of the Stack," *Business Week*, March 11, 1985, p. 49.

54. "Polaroid and Minolta: More Developments Ahead," *Business Week*, July 16, 1990, p. 32. *Also see* Ron Suskind, "Minolta Puts Name on Polaroid," *The Wall Street Journal*, August 29, 1990, p. B1.

55. Martin Christopher, Richard Lancioni, and John Gattorna, "Managing International Customer Service," *International Marketing Review*, Spring 1985, pp. 65–70.

CHAPTER 13

International Pricing Strategy

CHAPTER FOCUS_____

After studying this chapter, you should be able to

■ Explain the importance of the pricing decision in the international context.

■ Describe the parent company's role in pricing.

■ Discuss factors that should be considered in setting prices.

■ Compare the cost approach versus the market approach for price setting.

■ Name the factors that affect transfer pricing.

■ Discuss the issues of dumping and leasing.

Pricing is a particularly critical and complex variable in overseas marketing strategies. The pricing decision ultimately affects an organization's ability to stay in the market. Yet the uncertainties of entirely unpredictable forces such as costs, competition, and demand pose numerous pitfalls for international pricing. This chapter develops a framework for understanding the international pricing process and describes the problems and tactics of international marketers. A variety of concerns are addressed, including intrafirm pricing, dumping, and leasing.

Importance of Pricing

Pricing is an important decision in any business, be it domestic or international, because it directly affects revenue and thus profitability. Furthermore, appropriate pricing aids growth, as development of a mass market depends to a large extent on price. For businesses dependent on acquiring business contracts through competitive bidding, such as the construction and mining industries and drilling companies, a poor pricing decision threatens survival. Too high a price may mean no business, while a lower price may lead to an unprofitable operation. In many cases, the price indicates a product's quality.[1] If the Mercedes car, for example, were priced in the same range as the Oldsmobile, the Mercedes would lose some of its quality image. Finally, price affects the extent of promotional support to be allocated to a product.

Parent Company's Role in Pricing

One question in overseas pricing pertains to the role of the parent corporation. The parent company must decide how much say it wants to reserve for itself in international pricing, including whether the pricing decision will be made centrally or delegated to foreign subsidiaries. To an extent, the pricing role of the parent company is determined by the emphasis put on price competition in the total marketing mix.

Strategic Significance of Pricing

The role assigned to the pricing variable in developing the marketing mix depends on its strategic significance. Traditionally, U.S. companies have relied more on nonprice competition than on pricing. They generally avoided price competition and more often went after competitive leverage through advertising, selling, and product differentiation. This sort of behavior can be attributed to the fact that U.S. manufacturing costs were usually high, which made it difficult to compete pricewise. Further, the quality of U.S. goods had been considered high, which permitted targeting the product for a segment in which price did not matter.

In the last few years, however, price competition has been stressed more than before. Sales promotion, presale and postsale service, advertising and product differentiation, and product quality are no longer depended upon exclusively. This change has been necessitated partly by the importance of focusing on mass markets overseas, particularly in Western Europe. A small decrease in price can be an effective way of increasing penetration in many foreign markets, especially wherever there is considerable price consciousness and where products are not highly differentiated. For example, the Italian appliance industry made significant inroads in the Western European markets through price competition. Furthermore, costs in many countries, Germany for example, have been rising faster than in the U.S. Thus, price competition is feasible in some cases.

Leff makes an interesting case for penetrating developing-country markets through judicious use of pricing. The high elasticity of demand for consumer products and the highly skewed income distribution in developing countries lead him to recommend making changes in the pricing/output strategy. In this way, mass markets can be developed, enabling the MNC to achieve higher profits and larger growth, and enabling the host country to enhance the rate of economic development.[2]

Uniform versus Differentiated Pricing

To what extent the setting of uniform prices is desirable in worldwide markets is a question that MNCs perpetually face. Some international marketers argue for uniform prices. Others, however, observe that the obvious differences in the markets of various countries favor the use of an internationally differentiated pricing policy. In brief, pricing in overseas markets is a controversial issue involving legal, economic, governmental, and marketing aspects, both in the practice of differentiated pricing and in price uniformity.

In theory, it is desirable on economic grounds to set different prices in different markets, because demand and supply differ from country to country. This occurs under any form of imperfect competition such as pure monopoly, oligopoly, and monopolistic competition.

> In evaluating each foreign market, the firm may find that there exist different demand elasticities than those encountered in the home market. Hence it behooves the firm to take advantage of these different demand elasticities by charging the appropriate price in each market.[3]

Thus, it makes economic sense for the multinational firm to vary prices from market to market. Such a strategy, however, may cause the firm to be charged with dumping in the host country. So from a legal standpoint, it may be desirable to set a uniform price globally. The host country may frown upon differentiated pricing since it may expose the domestic firm to foreign competition. Such an argument would even be economically justified in the case of an infant industry.

Empirical research on the subject corroborates the conceptual framework. Boddewyn found that over two-thirds of consumer-nondurable marketers and almost 50 percent of industrial-good manufacturers among U.S. MNCs adapted pricing to local conditions. This adaptation is justified on the grounds that manufacturing costs, competitor's prices, and taxes all vary from country to country, making local market considerations a critical factor in pricing.[4]

Despite the importance of differentiated pricing, some firms try to standardize at least the relative price level. As a matter of fact, some sort of uniformity in international pricing ensures adequate product positioning and control.

All in all, the decision between uniform and differentiated pricing would be dictated by such factors as competitive conditions, life cycle position of the product, product diffusion process, regulatory considerations, channel structure, company objectives, and consumer price perceptions. If the competitive position of the firm does not vary from market to market, it may be worthwhile to pursue a uniform pricing strategy. A firm essentially in a monopoly or differentiated oligopolistic situation may price its product uniformly on a global scale. For example, Boeing sells a highly differentiated jetliner. To all intents and purposes, therefore, it charges the same price for its planes everywhere, whether they are sold in the U.S. or Europe. Even the developing countries pay the same price. In the introductory product stage when the product is not highly diffused, markets are limited to a few daring or innovative customers. These customers constitute homogeneous segments even though they may be geographically apart. Thus, a new product may initially be priced uniformly throughout the world. Further, if the diffusion process of an innovation has a similar pattern worldwide, standardized pricing will make sense. The perspectives of pricing—uniform versus differentiated—are also affected by local laws. Even when other conditions favor a standard price worldwide, local taxes, for example, may oblige a company to price the product higher in a particular country than elsewhere.

The wholesale and retail distribution structure of a country also influences the price decision. A *Business International* study, although dated, found, for example, that radios and TVs were priced lowest in Germany; prepared foods were more expensive in Italy and least expensive in the Netherlands. Such differences were attributed to retail structure.[5] Thus, where the channel structure is inefficient, additional distribution costs will be incurred, which must be absorbed through accelerating prices, resulting in nonuniformity of price worldwide.

The corporate objectives in a country may vary. Such differences in objectives would make standardized pricing ineffective. For example, a company may enter one market to develop a mass market through penetration and plan to be there for a long time. On the other hand, its entry in another country may be considered an ad hoc opportunity, expected to last a few years until the domestic industry, currently in its infancy, matures. Such a difference in objectives would suggest the development of different pricing strategies in the two countries. In the latter case, skimming the cream off the top of the demand curve will make sense. In the first case, however, a penetration pricing strategy would be in order.

████ ████ **International Marketing Highlight 13.1** ████ ████

Standardization vs. Customization

It is an illusion to believe that a globally identical brand can be sold in different countries at prices which differ substantially relative to costs of arbitrage. This problem has been largely neglected. A global product and local price are incompatible. One answer to international pricing problems may be to introduce different brands in high-price, high-income countries and in low-price, low-income countries. This would make the products less suitable for arbitrage, and much larger price differentials could be established. Of course, this runs counter to economies of scale and global branding. A conscious tradeoff had to be made.

Source: Hermann Simon, "Pricing Problems in a Global Setting," *Marketing News*, October 9, 1995, p. 4.

Finally, the price perceptions of customers may vary from country to country, requiring differentiated pricing. For example, in the competitive environment of Western Europe, an American product may be perceived as the equivalent of local products and hence must be competitively priced. However, the same product in a developing country might be perceived as superior in quality, and a low standard price would disturb the customer.

Responsibility for Price Setting

The corporate headquarters should spell out who is responsible for price setting. Three ways to allocate price-setting responsibility are (1) headquarters only decides, (2) each overseas subsidiary decides independently, and (3) decisions are jointly made between the parent and the subsidiary. Because of differences in local manufacturing and market situations, it would appear impractical for the parent organization to set the price for foreign markets. Many companies assign pricing responsibility exclusively to country managers.

Most frequently, however, companies follow some sort of joint decision-making procedure. The parent company specifies a basic framework for pricing, leaving considerable leverage for overseas affiliates to set actual prices. The framework may consist of a formula to be adopted for figuring out base price or simply a few guidelines. The following is an example of a price guideline issued by one headquarters to each of its foreign affiliates.

Our products should command a premium price, although not necessarily the top price in the market, and therefore should appeal to the consumer to whom superiority . . . is important.[6]

Pricing Factors

The factors to consider in international pricing exceed those in strictly domestic marketing not only in number, but also in ambiguity and risk. Domestic price is affected by such considerations as pricing objectives, cost, competition, customer, and regulations. Internationally, these considerations apply at home and in the host country. Further, multiple currencies, trade barriers, and longer distribution channels make the international pricing decision more difficult. Each of these considerations comprises a number of components that vary in importance and interaction in different nations. This section reviews pricing factors and looks at their influence on pricing in international business operations.

Pricing Objectives

Pricing objectives should be closely aligned to marketing objectives, which should in turn be derived from overall corporate objectives. Essentially, objectives can be defined in terms of profit or volume. The profit objective may take the shape of either a percentage markup on cost or price or a target return on investment. The volume objective is usually specified as a desired percentage of growth in sales or as a percentage of the market share to be achieved. Sometimes businesses define their pricing objectives in such general terms as *image building* (that is, pricing should project a certain image of the product/company), *stability,* (that is, pricing should realize a stable level of sales and profits), and *ethics* (that is, the setting of a price should meet the ethical standards of good and fair business.[7]

Two questions must be answered in setting price objectives: (1) Who should set the pricing objectives in different countries (the parent organization or the host country subsidiary)? (2) Should there be common objectives worldwide, or should objectives vary by country? (These questions will be examined in later sections.) Suffice it to say here that, inasmuch as market conditions differ in each country, it would be dysfunctional to set common pricing objectives globally. Further, no matter who sets the final price, both parent/regional and subsidiary inputs should be properly reviewed before making the decision. For example, what price the market will bear should be properly related to the parent corporation's profit goal.

Cost Analysis

Cost is one important factor in price determination. Of all the many cost concepts, fixed and variable costs are the most relevant to our discussion. *Fixed costs* are those that do not vary with the scale of operations, such as number of units manufactured. Salaries of the managerial staff, office rent, and other office and factory overhead expenses are examples of fixed costs. On the other hand, *variable costs,* such as costs of material and labor used in the manufacture of a product, bear a direct relationship to the level of operations.

It is important to measure costs accurately in order to develop a cost/volume relationship and to allocate various costs as fixed or variable. Measurement of costs is far from easy. Some fixed, short-run costs are not necessarily fixed in the long run; therefore, the distinction between variable and fixed costs matters only in the short run. For example, in the short run, the salaries of the marketing staff in the home office would be considered fixed. However, in the long run, the sales staff could be either increased or cut, making sales salaries a variable instead of fixed expense.

Moreover, some costs that initially appear fixed may be viewed as variable when properly evaluated. A company manufacturing different products can keep a complete record of the sales manager's time spent on each product and thus may treat this salary as variable, However, the cost of that record keeping will far exceed the benefits to be derived from making the salary a variable cost. Also, no matter how well a company maintains its records, some variable costs cannot be allocated to a particular product or line of business. In the final analysis, allocation of costs must be examined on the merit of each particular case.

The impact of costs on pricing strategy can be studied by considering the following three relationships: (1) the ratio of fixed costs to variable costs, (2) the economies of scale available to a firm, and (3) the cost structure of a firm vis-à-vis competitors. If the fixed costs of a company in comparison with variable costs form the higher proportion of its total costs, adding sales volume will be a great help in increasing earnings. Consider, for example, the case of an airline with fixed costs as high as 70 percent to 80 percent of total costs. Once fixed costs are recovered, the additional tickets sold add greatly to earnings. Such an industry would be termed *volume sensitive.* There are some industries, such as the paper industry, where variable costs constitute the higher proportion of total costs. Such industries are *price sensitive,* because even a small increase in price adds much to earnings (see International Marketing Highlight 13.2).

■■■■■■■■   **International Marketing Highlight 13.2**   ■■■■■■■■

Pricing at Replacement Cost

Why did gas prices go up so fast? It's hard to blame consumers for wondering why gas should increase by 10 to 20 cents a gallon just five days after Iraqi tanks rolled into Kuwait City—the oil companies were selling gasoline from old, cheap crude, weren't they?

The real answer is a combination of accounting and price-setting practices for crude oil. The last-in first-out method of accounting for inventory that most U.S. oil companies use causes them to price products according to the cost of replacing them, not according to historical cost. Reason: When it's time to figure profits for a given quarter, the cost of the most recently purchased oil is what gets subtracted from revenues. Since that cost went up quickly, oil companies must increase revenues quickly as well to maintain profit margins.

Source: Joel Drefuss, "Gas Pump Economics 101," *Fortune,* September 10, 1990, p. 42.

If substantial economies of scale are obtainable through a company's operations, market share should be expanded. In considering prices, the expected decline in costs should be duly taken into account—that is, prices may be lowered to gain higher market share in the long run. The concept of obtaining lower costs through economies of scale has often been referred to in the literature as *experience effect,* which means that all costs go down as accumulated experience increases. Thus, if a company acquires a higher market share, its costs would decline, enabling it to reduce prices. If a manufacturer is a low-cost producer, maintaining prices at competitive levels will earn additional profits. The additional profits can be used to promote the product aggressively and increase the overall scope of the business. If, however, the costs of a manufacturer are high compared with other competitors, prices cannot be lowered in order to increase market share. In a price-war situation, the high-cost producer is bound to lose.

Competition   The nature of competition in each country is another factor to consider in setting prices. The competition in an industry can be analyzed with reference to such factors as the number of firms in the industry, product differentiation, and ease of entry. In addition, competitive environment can be categorized as privileged position, leadership, chaotic, or stabilized competition, as shown in Exhibit 13.1. The *privileged position* amounts to a monopoly situation. The supply of spare parts is one example in this category, particularly in industrial markets. The *leadership position* refers to oligopolistic competition in which

EXHIBIT 13.1   Competitive Environment

Points of Differentiation	Privileged Position	Leadership Position	Chaotic Situation	Stabilized Competition
Definition	Lack of significant direct competition.	Leader has ability to set price level; leader affects degree of variation from basic level.	Price level and variation are unpredictable and frequently changing.	Firms have pricing latitude; price levels and variations adjust smoothly to each firm's strategy.
Characteristics	High degree of technical/service differentiation; high cost of entry; good customer, competitor intelligence; considerable latitude in pricing.	Few competitors; high cost of entry; leader has high market share; leader has recognized technical and marketing leadership, and generally is low-cost producer; leader has reputation for good pricing decisions; leader is able to communicate its policies; leader's actions are predictable.	Price is the major competitive tool; "commodity" products—everybody viewed the same; customers are price sensitive, or made to be price sensitive; tendency to excess capacity; no recognized leader and no restraint.	No recognized industry price leader; no firm has dominant market share; firms employ product differentiation and market segmentation; competition based on technology, service and delivery, not on price; infrequent price changes.
Implications	High margins and profits; responsibility for market development.	Good margins and profits for leader; acceptable margins for profits for followers; customers are satisfied.	Nobody making even acceptable profits; customer probably dissatisfied.	Good or acceptable margins for all; customers are satisfied.

Source: Donald S. Henley, "Evaluating International Product Line Performance: A Conceptual Approach," in *Multinational Product Management* (Cambridge, MA: Marketing Science Institute, 1976), pp. II-13–II-16.

the leader reaps high margins while the followers receive only adequate margins. The *chaotic situation* also operates in oligopoly. Only long-run programs can rescue a company from chaos. Finally, *stabilized competition* applies to a monopolistic situation where a high degree of product differentiation prevails.

The impact of market structure on pricing is illustrated by Raphael Elimelech's comments on the Japanese market:

The oligopolistic structure of Japanese industry is the main reason for widespread price coordination. In most branches of industry, many company or industrial groups exist, each of which has strong connections in the financial sector, in the Diet and in the bureaucracy. Any attempt by one of these companies to engage in heavy price competition could provoke such a powerful negative reaction from the others that it would probably produce more harm than benefit. Furthermore, price coordination and resale price maintenance (RPM) have various advantages for manufacturers. In the Japanese market, with its overwhelming number of small retail outlets, RPM also serves to protect the small retailers. When prices are uniform, consumers do not have much incentive to prefer large outlets (which can cut prices as a result of economies of scale) over small, more expensive shops. Thus, price coordination and RPM are strongly supported by small retailers, who in sheer numbers are a politically visible segment of the population.

Examples of price coordination and industrial cooperation are clearly evident. In the summer, electric fans that are identical in color, shape, quality, and price are on the market—but are produced by several different companies. Even discount prices tend to be coordinated. In Akihabara, Tokyo's largest consumer electrical goods shopping area, numerous outlets will offer identical models of vacuum cleaners at discount prices. Although each shop sells the products of different manufacturers, the discount prices are all at the same level.[8]

Customer Perspective

Customer *demand* for a product is another key factor in price determination. Demand is based on a variety of considerations, among which price is just one. These considerations include the ability of customers to buy, their willingness to buy, the place of the product in the customer's lifestyle (whether a status symbol or a daily-use product), prices of substitute products, the potential market for the product (whether there is an unfulfilled demand in the market or if the market is saturated), the nature of nonprice competition, consumer behavior in general, and consumer behavior in segments in the market. All these factors are interdependent, and it may not be easy to estimate their relationships accurately.

Demand analysis involves predicting the relationship between price level and demand, simultaneously considering the effects of other variables on demand. The relationship between price and demand is called **elasticity of demand,** or *sensitivity of price,* and it refers to the number of units of a product that would be demanded at different prices. Price sensitivity should be considered at two different levels: the industry and the firm.

Industry demand for a product is elastic if it can be substantially increased by lowering prices. If lowering price has little effect on demand, it would be considered inelastic. Environmental factors, which vary from country to country, have a direct influence on demand elasticity. For example, when gasoline prices are high, the average U.S. consumer seeks to conserve gasoline. If gasoline prices should go down, people are willing to use gas more freely, thus, in the U.S., the demand for gasoline can be considered somewhat elastic. In a developing country like Bangladesh, where only a few rich people own cars, no matter how much gasoline prices change, the total demand would not be greatly affected, making it inelastic.

When the total demand of an industry is highly elastic, the industry leader may take the initiative to lower prices. The loss in revenues from a decrease in price will presumably be more than compensated for by the additional demand generated, thus enlarging the total dollar market. Such a strategy will be highly attractive in an industry where economies of scale are possible. Where demand is inelastic and there are no conceivable substitutes, prices may be increased, at least in the short run. In the long run, however, the government may impose controls, or substitutes may develop (see International Marketing Highlight 13.3).

An *individual firm's demand* is derived from the total industry demand. An individual firm seeks to find out how much market share it can command in the market by changing its own prices. In the case of undifferentiated, standardized products, lower prices should help a firm in increasing its market share, as long as competitors do not retaliate by matching the firm's prices. Similarly, when business is sought through bidding, lower prices should help. In the case of differentiated products, however, market share can actually be improved by maintaining higher prices (within a certain range).

The products may be differentiated in various real and imagined ways. For example, a manufacturer in a foreign market who provides adequate warranties and after-sale service might maintain higher prices and still increase market share. Brand name, an image of sophistication, and the impression of high quality are other factors that can help in differentiating a product and hence afford an opportunity to increase prices and not lose market share. Of course, other elements of the marketing mix should reinforce the image suggested by the price. In brief, a firm's best opportunity lies in differentiating the product. A differentiated product offers more opportunity for increasing earnings through higher prices.

■■■■■■■ International Marketing Highlights 13.3 ■■■■■■■

Pricing Protest Blocks Hungarian Highway Plan

A major foreign-invested infrastructure project has been blown off course by political storm. Three months after opening, Hungary's new M5 toll motorway is in trouble as drivers have flocked to back roads to avoid paying tolls. The headache for western investors is how the government will refinance the project.

Local residents are up in arms as cost-conscious truckers bring traffic jams to their doorsteps. The common denominator for both residents and motorists is a demand for toll reductions. The government has caved in to public protests. This development is a worrying lesson for western concession operators, as it undermines the rationale behind the "build-operate-transfer" scheme used to finance new roadways.

Hungary has one of the region's most ambitious motorway programs, covering over 500km. Under 35-year operating concessions, construction consortia finance new roads, then levy tolls to recoup costs. The first segment, from the northern Hungarian city of Gyor to the Austrian border, was built by Elmka, a consortium led by Transroute International (France).

Toll rates calculated to cover construction costs are fixed in the concession agreements. A Budapest court has ruled that the Ft1,000 ($5.90) toll for passenger cars on the M5—the second-highest toll per kilometer in Europe—should be halved. Elmka has appealed, arguing that the M5 stretch was built entirely from private sources, whereas the European routes cited by the court enjoyed state subsidies. Meanwhile the consortium has halted work on another segment of the motorway.

Source: Crossborder Monitor, March 26, 1997, p.1.

Government and Pricing

Government rules and regulations pertaining to pricing should be taken into account in setting prices. Legal requirements of both the host government and the U.S. government must be satisfied.

Chapter 11 discusses legal aspects that affect marketing decisions. In brief, the provisions of U.S. antitrust laws (for example, the Robinson-Patman Act related to price discrimination) would apply to any foreign pricing decision that would adversely affect competition in the U.S. Suppose an electronics company exports integrated circuits (ICs) to South Korea at a price lower than the one it charges U.S. customers. Suppose further that the Korean importer uses these ICs to assemble computer terminals that are exported to the U.S. to compete against U.S.–made terminals. If the Korean company gets an advantage over the U.S. terminal manufacturers because of the lower price it pays for the ICs bought form the U.S., the IC manufacturer could be charged with price discrimination.

A host country's laws concerning price setting may range from broad guidelines to detailed procedures for arriving at prices, amounting to virtual control over prices. But government regulations evolve over time and may change during a firm's operation. For example, relatively new antitrust laws have been enacted in the European Union (EU). These laws may be even more stringent than those of the U.S. The first company cited for viola-

irly stable prices. It has two
ts can become troublesome.
ariable costs? What propor-
ould costs related to R&D
ded? The answers to these
brings an element of in-
ost.

of pricing. On the other
otherwise lost. Exhibit
le to conduct its foreign
the full-costing method
he opportunity to add

simply be a markup
may represent a de-
ent in a business i
rs) is $25,000,000
. Multiplying th
ercent, would giv
s

desired return
ent

ce-up is
a problem.
on invest-
client cost of
air return.
of Chile 8 per-
ed to the
ion.
performs.
alternate is
ts in price mine
ed cost increaher
estimated prodicd
Japanese firm first
cost necessary for via
the target cost. When
set a target price of $1,000
old for several thousand dolla
ve given Canon the radical pric
challenged to reinvent a cheaper
allenge was met by substituting a
anism used in other copiers.[10]
sider common factors in determin-
roaches involves the core concern in
from the viewpoint of the customer.

'ng bananas at lower prices in the Netherlands
gle currency, the euro, will impact pricing
Marketing Highlight 13.4).

keting Highlight 13.4

e easily comparable, without exchange risks and
ore crossborder buying, as customers shop around
d compare and review their own prices in euros to
continue with current prices, modify their product
overall price strategies, i.e., aggressive or defensive.

o heighten domestic pressures for harmonization of value-
xcise tax. Industries that find themselves at commercial dis-
ley are based in a country with high VAT rates will pressure the
ice them. Even before EMU, UK brewers had complained about
French suppliers because of lower excise taxes across the Channel.

pressure. Harmonization and rationalization across Europe will cre-
ard pressure on prices, which will hit low-margin business especially
main challenge is to anticipate the change and prepare for a more price-
future within the euro zone.

gical thresholds. Prices are often set just below rounded financial values,
M 100, or _10, because they "feel" like a better consumer value. When a
.99 price is converted to E 10.26, the supplier may have to consider how
offer the product at E 9.99. These price changes may mean sacrificing mar-
ing package size.

pricing. Trading during the transition period imposes additional
eting departments because dual-currency pricing, if used, will be
not therefore appear to justify the costs of implementation.
ularly serious one for retailers.

, 1998, p. 3.

cing decision depends on various factors, such as pricing
mer demand, and government requirements, an empiri-
otal costs to be the most important factor.[9] The com-
ext important factor, followed by the company's out-
licy, and the customer's ability to pay.

emand conditions, competition, and
in by following a particular pricing
entations and discusses export price
re also considered.

rientation: the cost approach and
omputing all relevant costs and
price. The cost approach is popular

because it is simple to comprehend and use and leads to f...
drawbacks, though. First, definition and computation of cos...
Should all (both fixed and variable) costs be included or only...
tion of fixed costs should be included, if any? Particularly, sh...
and parent corporation administrative overhead costs be inclu...
questions are far from easy to determine. Second, this approac...
flexibility into the pricing decision, because of the emphasis on ...

A conservative attitude would favor using *full costs* as the basis...
hand, an *incremental-cost* pricing could allow for seeking busines...
13.2 illustrates this point. The Natural Company would not be ab...
business if it insisted on recovering the full unit cost of $11.67. If ...
were the decision criterion, the company would actually pass up t...
$3,000 to profit.

The profit markup applied to the cost to compute final price ma...
percentage arbitrarily decided upon. Alternatively, the profit markup...
sired percentage return on investment. For example, if the total invest...
$16,000,000, and the total cost of annual output (averaged over the ye...
the *capital turnover ratio* would be $16,000,000/$25,000,000, or 0...
capital turnover ratio, 0.8, by the desired return on investment, say, 20 p...
a markup of 16 percent (0.8×0.20) ... standard cost. It can be shown ...

$$\text{Percentage markup on cost} = \frac{\text{Total invested capital}}{\text{Standard cost of annual normal produ...}} \times \text{Percentag... on investm...}$$

This method is an improvement over the pure cost-plu...
rived more scientifically. Nonetheless, the determination of ra...hod sin...
Academically, the rate of return should be based on the minim...*turn*...
ment. In other words, rate of return has to be equal to, or more t...
capital. In actual practice, a certain amount usually comes to be ac...
Thus, 15 percent is considered a normal return in manufacturing...
cent to 10 percent suffices in services industries. In this method, ...
total investment and therefore does not consider changes in price...

Under the *market approach,* pricing starts in a reverse fas...
made of the acceptable price in the target segment. An analysis ...
if this price would meet the company's profit objective. If not, ...
give up the business or increase the price. Additional adjustme...
to cope with competitors, host country government, expec...
eventualities. The final price is based on the market rather tha...

Market approach is widely used in Japan. For example, o...
likely competitors and their products, then estimates the uni...
into the market. The engineers try to design a product to me...
set out to challenge Xerox in the personal copier business, it...
home copier. At that time, Canon's least expensive copier ...
Trying to reduce the cost of existing models would not h...
improvement it needed. Instead, Canon engineers were ...
copier, without compromising quality standards. The c...
disposable cartridge for the complex image transfer mech...

Both the cost and market approaches essentially co...
ing the final price. The difference between the two ap...
setting prices. The market approach focuses on pricing...

EXHIBIT 13.2
Full Costing versus
Incremental Costing

Following is an illustration of the full-costing and incremental-costing methods. The Natural Company has a production capacity of 20,000 units per year. Presently the company is producing and selling 15,000 units per year. The regular market price is $15.00 per unit. The variable costs are as follows:

Material	$5/unit
Labor	$4/unit
Total Variable Cost	$9/unit

The fixed cost is $40,000 per year
The income statement reflecting the preceding situation would appear as follows:

Income Statement

Sales (15,000 @ $15.00)		$225,000
Cost: Variable Cost (15,000 @ $9.00)	$135,000	
Fixed Cost	40,000	175,000
Profit		$ 50,000

Now suppose the company has the opportunity to sell an additional 3,000 units at $10.00 per unit to a foreign firm. This is a special situation that would not have an adverse effect on the price of the product in the regular market.

If Natural Company uses the full-costing method to make its decision, the offer would be rejected. The reasoning behind this rejection is that the price of $10.00/unit does not cover the full cost of $11.67/unit ($175,000 ÷ 15,000 = $11.67). By using the full-costing method as a decision criterion, the company would actually be giving up $3,000 in additional profits.

If the incremental-costing method is used, the offer would be accepted, and thus a gain of $3,000 in profits would be realized. The incremental-costing method compares additional costs to be incurred with the additional revenues that would be received if the offer is accepted.

Additional Revenue (3,000 @ $10.00)	$30,000
Additional Costs (3,000 @ $9.00)	27,000
Additional Income	$ 3,000

The difference between the two decision methods results from the treatment of fixed costs. The full-costing method includes the fixed cost per unit calculation. The incremental-cost method recognizes that no additional fixed costs will be incurred if additional units are produced. Therefore, fixed costs are not considered in the decision process.

Following is an income statement comparing the results of the company with and without the acceptance of the foreign offer:

Income Statement

	Rejecting the offer	Accepting the offer
Sales (15,000 units @ $15.00)	$225,000	$225,000
(3,000 units @ $10.00)	—	30,000
Total Sales	$225,000	$225,000
Costs: Variable (@ $9.00/unit)	$135,000	$162,000
Fixed	40,000	40,000
Total Cost	$175,000	$202,000
Net Income	$ 50,000	$ 53,000

NOTE: An important factor in such a decision is considering what the effects of accepting the offer will be on regular market price. If the additional sales were made in the regular market at the $10.00 price, it could depress the regular market price below $15.00. This would severely hamper operations in the future.

Unfortunately, in many countries it may not be easy to develop an adequate price-demand relationship, and therefore implementation of the market approach may occur in a vacuum. It is this kind of uncertainty that forces marketers to opt for the cost approach (see International Marketing Highlight 13.5).

In theory, pricing may be based on either of the two pricing approaches, but in practice the cost approach usually turns out to be the best because of the difficulty of gaining adequate knowledge of the foreign market and the need to ensure a satisfactory profit on export transactions.

Export Pricing

Export pricing is affected by three factors:

1. The price destination (that is, who it is that will pay the price—the final consumer, independent distributors, a wholly owned subsidiary, a joint venture organization, or someone else).
2. The nature of the product (that is, whether it is raw or semiprocessed material, components, finished or largely finished products: or services or intangible property—patents, trademarks, formulas, and the like).
3. The currency used for billing (that is, the currency of the purchaser's country, the seller's home country currency, or a leading international currency).

The *price destination* is an important consideration since different destinations present different opportunities and problems. For example, pricing to sell to a government may require special procedures and concessions not necessary in pricing to other customers. A little extra margin might be called for. On the other hand, independent distributors with whom the company has a contractual marketing arrangement deserve a price break. Wholesalers and jobbers that shop around have an entirely different relationship with the supplier than the independent distributors.

As products, raw materials, and commodities give a company very little leeway for maneuvering, there is usually a prevalent world price that must be charged, particularly when the supply is plentiful. However, if the supply is short, the seller may be able to demand a higher price. When it is a sellers' market, the seller can make the buyer pay for adverse exchange fluctuations, and vice versa.[11]

■■■■■■■■■■ **International Marketing Highlight 13.5** ■■■■■■■■■■

Approach to Price Setting

Seiko Epson, the Japanese computer peripherals manufacturer, sets floor prices at headquarters after considering costs, recommendations from executives in the company's various manufacturing divisions and country markets, and a corporate profit markup target for the particular product. Starting from this figure, product division presidents at headquarters establish flexibility parameters. The low-end products, such as Epson's LQ-500 series printer, are usually restricted to a variability range of less than 5 percent, while the prices charged for high-end products like computers and laser-jet printers can range from 10 percent to 25 percent above or below the base price. Salespeople in headquarters are allowed to negotiate prices within these parameters with country-level sales affiliates. In view of the rapid technological change and rapid entry of new products in that industry, this sort of price flexibility is considered essential by marketing staff.

Source: Marketing Strategies for Global Growth and Competitiveness (New York: Business International, no date), p. 64.

A company must decide whether to set a common price or different prices for exports to domestic and international markets. Although some companies have common prices,

tions in the EU was United Brands, for selling bananas at lower prices in the Netherlands than in other countries. Similarly, the EU's single currency, the euro, will impact pricing decisions in the future (see the International Marketing Highlight 13.4).

■■■■■■■■■   International Marketing Highlight 13.4   ■■■■■■■■■

Pricing Impact of the Euro

- **Price transparency.** Prices will be easily comparable, without exchange risks and other costs. This will lead to more crossborder buying, as customers shop around for the best deal. Firms should compare and review their own prices in euros to decide whether they should continue with current prices, modify their product offerings or rethink their overall price strategies, i.e., aggressive or defensive.

    One effect may be to heighten domestic pressures for harmonization of value-added tax (VAT) and excise tax. Industries that find themselves at commercial disadvantage because they are based in a country with high VAT rates will pressure the government to reduce them. Even before EMU, UK brewers had complained about a loss of trade to French suppliers because of lower excise taxes across the Channel.

- **Competitive pressure.** Harmonization and rationalization across Europe will create downward pressure on prices, which will hit low-margin business especially hard. The main challenge is to anticipate the change and prepare for a more price-competitive future within the euro zone.

- **Psychological thresholds.** Prices are often set just below rounded financial values, such as DM 100, or _10, because they "feel" like a better consumer value. When a DM 19.99 price is converted to E 10.26, the supplier may have to consider how he can offer the product at E 9.99. These price changes may mean sacrificing margins or reducing package size.

- **Dual-currency pricing.** Trading during the transition period imposes additional expenses on marketing departments because dual-currency pricing, if used, will be temporary. It may not therefore appear to justify the costs of implementation. This issue is a particularly serious one for retailers.

Source: Crossborder Monitor, February 4, 1998, p. 3.

Although, international pricing decision depends on various factors, such as pricing objective, cost, competition, customer demand, and government requirements, an empirical study on the subject has shown total costs to be the most important factor.[9] The competitors' pricing policies rank as the next important factor, followed by the company's out-of-pocket costs, return-on-investment policy, and the customer's ability to pay.

Aspects of International Price Setting

The impact of such factors as differences in costs, demand conditions, competition, and government laws on international pricing is figured in by following a particular pricing orientation. This section examines different pricing orientations and discusses export price setting. Perspectives of price setting in foreign markets are also considered.

Pricing Orientation

Companies mainly follow two different types of pricing orientation: the cost approach and the market approach. The *cost approach* involves first computing all relevant costs and then adding a desired profit markup to arrive at the price. The cost approach is popular because it is simple to comprehend and use and leads to fairly stable prices. It has two drawbacks, though. First, definition and computation of costs can become troublesome. Should all (both fixed and variable) costs be included or only variable costs? What proportion of fixed costs should be included, if any? Particularly, should costs related to R&D and parent corporation administrative overhead costs be included? The answers to these questions are far from easy to determine. Second, this approach brings an element of inflexibility into the pricing decision, because of the emphasis on cost.

A conservative attitude would favor using *full costs* as the basis of pricing. On the other hand, an *incremental-cost* pricing could allow for seeking business otherwise lost. Exhibit 13.2 illustrates this point. The Natural Company would not be able to conduct its foreign business if it insisted on recovering the full unit cost of $11.67. If the full-costing method were the decision criterion, the company would actually pass up the opportunity to add $3,000 to profit.

The profit markup applied to the cost to compute final price may simply be a markup percentage arbitrarily decided upon. Alternatively, the profit markup may represent a desired percentage return on investment. For example, if the total investment in a business is $16,000,000, and the total cost of annual output (averaged over the years) is $25,000,000, the *capital turnover ratio* would be $16,000,000/$25,000,000, or 0.8. Multiplying the capital turnover ratio, 0.8, by the desired return on investment, say, 20 percent, would give a markup of 16 percent (0.8 × 0.20) on standard cost. It can be shown as

$$\frac{\text{Percentage markup}}{\text{on cost}} = \frac{\text{Total invested capital}}{\text{Standard cost of annual normal production}} \times \frac{\text{Percentage desired return}}{\text{on investment}}$$

This method is an improvement over the pure cost-plus method since markup is derived more scientifically. Nonetheless, the determination of *rate of return* poses a problem. Academically, the rate of return should be based on the minimum fair return on investment. In other words, rate of return has to be equal to, or more than, the current cost of capital. In actual practice, a certain amount usually comes to be accepted as a fair return. Thus, 15 percent is considered a normal return in manufacturing industries, while 8 percent to 10 percent suffices in services industries. In this method, markup is linked to the total investment and therefore does not consider changes in price of cost components.

Under the **market approach,** pricing starts in a reverse fashion. First, an estimate is made of the acceptable price in the target segment. An analysis is performed to determine if this price would meet the company's profit objective. If not, the alternatives are to either give up the business or increase the price. Additional adjustments in price may be required to cope with competitors, host country government, expected cost increase, and other eventualities. The final price is based on the market rather than estimated production costs.

Market approach is widely used in Japan. For example, one Japanese firm first examines likely competitors and their products, then estimates the unit cost necessary for viable entry into the market. The engineers try to design a product to meet the target cost. When Canon set out to challenge Xerox in the personal copier business, it set a target price of $1,000 for a home copier. At that time, Canon's least expensive copier sold for several thousand dollars. Trying to reduce the cost of existing models would not have given Canon the radical price improvement it needed. Instead, Canon engineers were challenged to reinvent a cheaper copier, without compromising quality standards. The challenge was met by substituting a disposable cartridge for the complex image transfer mechanism used in other copiers.[10]

Both the cost and market approaches essentially consider common factors in determining the final price. The difference between the two approaches involves the core concern in setting prices. The market approach focuses on pricing from the viewpoint of the customer.

EXHIBIT 13.2
Full Costing versus
Incremental Costing

Following is an illustration of the full-costing and incremental-costing methods. The Natural Company has a production capacity of 20,000 units per year. Presently the company is producing and selling 15,000 units per year. The regular market price is $15.00 per unit. The variable costs are as follows:

Material	$5/unit
Labor	$4/unit
Total Variable Cost	$9/unit

The fixed cost is $40,000 per year
The income statement reflecting the preceding situation would appear as follows:

Income Statement

Sales (15,000 @ $15.00)		$225,000
Cost: Variable Cost (15,000 @ $9.00)	$135,000	
Fixed Cost	40,000	175,000
Profit		$ 50,000

Now suppose the company has the opportunity to sell an additional 3,000 units at $10.00 per unit to a foreign firm. This is a special situation that would not have an adverse effect on the price of the product in the regular market.

If Natural Company uses the full-costing method to make its decision, the offer would be rejected. The reasoning behind this rejection is that the price of $10.00/unit does not cover the full cost of $11.67/unit ($175,000 ÷ 15,000 = $11.67). By using the full-costing method as a decision criterion, the company would actually be giving up $3,000 in additional profits.

If the incremental-costing method is used, the offer would be accepted, and thus a gain of $3,000 in profits would be realized. The incremental-costing method compares additional costs to be incurred with the additional revenues that would be received if the offer is accepted.

Additional Revenue (3,000 @ $10.00)	$30,000
Additional Costs (3,000 @ $9.00)	27,000
Additional Income	$ 3,000

The difference between the two decision methods results from the treatment of fixed costs. The full-costing method includes the fixed cost per unit calculation. The incremental-cost method recognizes that no additional fixed costs will be incurred if additional units are produced. Therefore, fixed costs are not considered in the decision process.

Following is an income statement comparing the results of the company with and without the acceptance of the foreign offer:

Income Statement

	Rejecting the offer	Accepting the offer
Sales (15,000 units @ $15.00)	$225,000	$225,000
(3,000 units @ $10.00)	—	30,000
Total Sales	$225,000	$225,000
Costs: Variable (@ $9.00/unit)	$135,000	$162,000
Fixed	40,000	40,000
Total Cost	$175,000	$202,000
Net Income	$ 50,000	$ 53,000

NOTE: An important factor in such a decision is considering what the effects of accepting the offer will be on regular market price. If the additional sales were made in the regular market at the $10.00 price, it could depress the regular market price below $15.00. This would severely hamper operations in the future.

Unfortunately, in many countries it may not be easy to develop an adequate price-demand relationship, and therefore implementation of the market approach may occur in a vacuum. It is this kind of uncertainty that forces marketers to opt for the cost approach (see International Marketing Highlight 13.5).

In theory, pricing may be based on either of the two pricing approaches, but in practice the cost approach usually turns out to be the best because of the difficulty of gaining adequate knowledge of the foreign market and the need to ensure a satisfactory profit on export transactions.

Export Pricing   Export pricing is affected by three factors:

1. The price destination (that is, who it is that will pay the price—the final consumer, independent distributors, a wholly owned subsidiary, a joint venture organization, or someone else).
2. The nature of the product (that is, whether it is raw or semiprocessed material, components, finished or largely finished products: or services or intangible property—patents, trademarks, formulas, and the like).
3. The currency used for billing (that is, the currency of the purchaser's country, the seller's home country currency, or a leading international currency).

The *price destination* is an important consideration since different destinations present different opportunities and problems. For example, pricing to sell to a government may require special procedures and concessions not necessary in pricing to other customers. A little extra margin might be called for. On the other hand, independent distributors with whom the company has a contractual marketing arrangement deserve a price break. Wholesalers and jobbers that shop around have an entirely different relationship with the supplier than the independent distributors.

As products, raw materials, and commodities give a company very little leeway for maneuvering, there is usually a prevalent world price that must be charged, particularly when the supply is plentiful. However, if the supply is short, the seller may be able to demand a higher price. When it is a sellers' market, the seller can make the buyer pay for adverse exchange fluctuations, and vice versa.[11]

■■■■■■   International Marketing Highlight 13.5   ■■■■■■

Approach to Price Setting

Seiko Epson, the Japanese computer peripherals manufacturer, sets floor prices at headquarters after considering costs, recommendations from executives in the company's various manufacturing divisions and country markets, and a corporate profit markup target for the particular product. Starting from this figure, product division presidents at headquarters establish flexibility parameters. The low-end products, such as Epson's LQ-500 series printer, are usually restricted to a variability range of less than 5 percent, while the prices charged for high-end products like computers and laser-jet printers can range from 10 percent to 25 percent above or below the base price. Salespeople in headquarters are allowed to negotiate prices within these parameters with country-level sales affiliates. In view of the rapid technological change and rapid entry of new products in that industry, this sort of price flexibility is considered essential by marketing staff.

Source: Marketing Strategies for Global Growth and Competitiveness (New York: Business International, no date), p. 64.

A company must decide whether to set a common price or different prices for exports to domestic and international markets. Although some companies have common prices, more often, for reasons discussed in the previous section, a firm develops two price lists, one for the domestic and one for the foreign market. The salesperson or distributor for a particular foreign market receives the foreign price list, which is used in discussing price with customers. Usually, a company charges the same price to a given customer even if a product is supplied from various plants.

For example, a Brazilian order might be filled from either a U.S. plant or a plant in Italy. Normally, the Brazilian market would be served from the U.S., and the U.S. price list would be used. In an emergency, if the order must be filled from Italy, the parent company would absorb the extra cost of shipping the product from Italy in order to maintain stable prices.

Often, a margin is built into the price list so that, if necessary, prices can be easily adjusted to local market conditions. Such conditions include overall competitiveness based on production and related costs, the export incentives other governments give their manufacturers, and the actual margin another product has in a given country.

Price lists are periodically reviewed for adjustments. With increasing competition, such reviews are becoming more frequent. For example, a chemical MNC reviewed prices every three months instead of semiannually, mostly because of world supply/demand conditions. Usually, exporting firms give anywhere between 30 to 90 days' notice of an impending price increase, depending on the nature of the product.

As far as currency conditions are concerned, the appropriate strategy would depend on the currency used and its relative strength. For example, if domestic currency is used, S. Tamer Cavusgil recommends alternative strategies depending on whether it is weak or strong (see Exhibit 13.3).

A company may make sales on a spot basis or for future delivery. For sales on a *spot basis,* prices are determined according to the daily exchange rate at the time of the order. On orders for *future delivery,* a company may either quote at the current rate or use a forward rate. The final decision on the use of the exchange rate will depend on the company's overall export exposure and its past experience with exchange losses.

Escalation in Export Prices

The retail price of exports is usually much higher than the domestic retail price for the same product. This escalation in foreign price can be explained by such costs as transportation, customs duty, and distributor margins, all associated with exports. The geographic distance that goods must travel results in additional transportation cost. The imported goods must also bear the import taxes in the form of customs duty imposed by the host government. In addition, the completion of the export transaction may require the passage of the goods through many more channels than in a domestic sale. Each channel member must be paid a margin for services it provides, which naturally increases cost. Also, a variety of government requirements, domestic and foreign, must be fulfilled, incurring further costs.

The process of price escalation is illustrated in Exhibit 13.4. It is evident that the retail price for exported goods is about 60 percent more than the domestic retail price. For example, about $80 more is spent on transportation alone. An additional $90 is accounted for by the import tariff. Finally, the agent costs for the exported goods amount to about $371, compared with $194 for domestic distribution.

The price escalation could raise the final price to the foreign customer so much that demand drops. An exporter has various means to counteract such a problem:

1. Ship modified or unassembled products, which might lower transportation costs and duties.
2. Lower the export price at the factory, thus reducing the multiplier effect of all the markups.

EXHIBIT 13.3
International Pricing Strategies under Varying Currency Conditions

When Domestic Currency Is Weak	When Domestic Currency Is Strong
Stress price benefits.	Engage in nonprice competition by improving quality, delivery, and after-sale service.
Expand product line and add more costly features.	Improve productivity and engage in vigorous cost reduction.
Shift sourcing manufacturing to domestic market.	Shift sourcing and manufacturing overseas.
Exploit export opportunities in all markets.	Give priority to exports to countries with relatively strong currencies.
Use a full-costing approach, but employ marginal-cost pricing to penetrate new or competitive markets.	Trim profit margins and use marginal-cost pricing.
Speed repatriation of foreign-earned income and collections.	Keep the foreign-earned income in host country; slow down collections.
Minimize expenditures in local or host country currency.	Maximize expenditures in local or host country currency.
Buy needed services (advertising, insurance, transportation, etc.) in domestic market.	Buy needed services abroad and pay for them in local currencies.
Bill foreign customers in their own currency.	Bill foreign customers in the domestic currency.

Source: S. Tamer Cavusgil, "Pricing for Global Markets," in *Marketing Strategies for Global Growth and Competitiveness* (New York: Business International, no date), p. 61.

EXHIBIT 13.4
An Example of Price Escalation: Export from U.S. to Middle East

	Domestic Transactions	Middle East Transactions
Manufacturing price in the U.S.	$362.00	$362.00
Transportation to wholesaler/point of shipment	18.00	23.00
	$380.00	$385.00
Export documentation (i.e. bill of lading, counselor's invoice)		4.00
Handling for overseas shipping		2.50
Overseas freight and insurance		58.50
		$450.00
Import tariff: 20 percent of landed cost		90.00
		$540.00
Handling at foreign port of entry		3.00
		$543.00
Transportation from port of entry to importer		17.00
		$560.00
Importer margin (on sale to wholesaler): 10 percent		56.00
		$616.00
Wholesale margin: 8 percent	30.40	49.28
	$410.40	$665.28
Real margin: 40 percent	164.16	266.12
Final retail price	$574.56	$931.40

3.   Get its freight and/or duty classifications changed for a possible lowering of these costs.

4.   Produce within the export market to eliminate the extra steps.

Export Price Quotation

An export price may be quoted to the overseas buyer in any one of several ways. Every alternative implies mutual commitment by exporter and importer and specifies the terms of trade. The price alters according to the degree of responsibility that the exporter undertakes, which varies with each alternative.

There are five principal ways of quoting export prices: ex-factory, free-alongside-ship (F.A.S.), free-on-board (F.O.B.), cost, insurance, and freight (C.I.F.), and delivered duty-paid. The *ex-factory* price represents the simplest arrangement. The importer is presumed to have bought the goods right at the exporter's factory. All costs and risks from thereon become the buyer's problem. The ex-factory arrangement limits the exporter's risk. However, an importer may find an ex-factory deal highly demanding. From another country, it could prove difficult to arrange for transportation and to take care of the various formalities associated with foreign trade. Only large companies, such as Japanese trading companies can handle ex-factory purchases in another country smoothly.

The *F.A.S.* contract requires the exporter to be responsible for the goods until they are placed alongside the ship. All charges incurred up to that point must be borne by the seller. The exporter's side of the contract is completed on receiving a clean wharfage receipt indicating safe delivery of goods for foreign embarkation. The F.A.S. price is slightly higher than the ex-factory price since the exporter undertakes to transport the goods to the point of shipment and becomes liable for the risk associated with the goods for a longer period.

The *F.O.B.* price includes actual placement of goods aboard the ship. The F.O.B. price may be the F.O.B. inland carrier or F.O.B. foreign carrier. If it is the former, then the F.O.B. price will be slightly less than the F.A.S. price. However, if it is an F.O.B. foreign carrier, then the price will include the F.A.S. price plus cost of transportation to the importer's country.

Generally, U.S. companies prefer quoting export prices as F.O.B. This limits their responsibility to activities in the U.S. In fact, companies usually favor F.O.B. inland carrier over F.O.B. foreign carrier.

Under the *C.I.F.* price quotation, the ownership of the goods passes to the importer as soon as they are loaded aboard the ship, but the exporter is liable for payment of freight and insurance charges up to the port of destination.

Finally, the *delivered duty-paid* alternative imposes on the exporter the complete responsibility for delivering the goods at a particular place in the importer's country. Thus, the exporter makes arrangements for the receipt of the goods at the foreign port, pays necessary taxes/duties and handling, and provides for further inland transportation in the importer's country. Needless to say, the price of delivered duty-paid goods is much higher than the goods exported under the C.I.F. contract.

Price Setting in Foreign Markets

The pricing decision of an MNC for a foreign market is essentially based on the same considerations as those affecting pricing in the domestic market. As discussed earlier in this chapter, these considerations include the overall parent company objectives, competition, customer, costs, and government regulations. In the international field, however, there is a range of additional factors to be examined before finalizing the price. First, the price in various regions of the world should be kept fairly uniform. Such parity prevents unrelated dealers in home markets from competing with the overseas company units. For example, if a firm in Europe makes and sells products identical to those it makes and sells in the U.S., a customer in Europe would not have any reason to prefer one source over another except for a significant price differential. If the price for a given product sold in Europe goes up substantially above the selling price in the U.S., the European customer will very likely import the U.S.–made product and undercut the U.S. firm's European manufacturing subsidiary.

Here's another example: At the Treats snack and sandwich bar in central London, store manager Rehan Iqbal could stock up on Coca-Cola produced an hour's drive away. Instead, his cooler is filled with Coke bottles from Bratislava, Slovakia. The Coke labels are in Slovak, even though it is illegal to sell food and drink in the U.K. without English labels. Mr. Iqbal's Slovakian Coke passed through more than four hands on its 850-mile journey, as middlemen took advantage of prices at least 25 percent lower than Coke produced in England. The Slovak bottling operation is operated by Coca-Cola Beverages PLC, London, which is 50 percent-owned by Coke. But local bottlers don't force customers to sell Coke to local retailers exclusively, giving middlemen the chance to take advantage of regional price differences.

Even after shipping, a half-liter (0.53 quart) bottle of Slovakian Coke can be bought from a British wholesaler for less than 30 pence (47 cents), compared with the U.K. bottler's price of 39.5 pence. Shops then sell the bottles for as much as 85 pence.

It is almost impossible to measure the size of Britain's gray market, but people involved in the industry estimate anywhere from 5 percent to 20 percent of Coke sold in the U.K. originates outside the country.[12]

Enormous price differentials exist between countries, with prices sometime deviating 30 percent to 150 percent. A certain drug costs exactly five times more in Germany than in Italy. A person living in France can save substantially by buying a car in a neighboring country: 24.3 percent on a Citroen, 18.2 percent on a Peugeot, or 33 percent on a Volkswagen Jetta.[13] Coca-Cola (1.5 liter bottle) cost 82 cents in Amsterdam and $2.04 in Copenhagen; Levi's 501 jeans sold for $50 in London while the price in Madrid was $76.65; and the Bosch 500-2 power drill was priced at $70.94 and $99.34 in Brussels and Milan, respectively.[14]

Second, ethical considerations in the foreign market sometimes differ from those in the domestic market. For example, a pharmaceutical company may find it ethically desirable to sell drugs in developing countries at a lower margin despite the feasibility of realizing a higher profit.

Third, price segmentation becomes more significant in the foreign market. The nomads of the Sahara, although they are extremely poor, need expensive clothes because of harsh conditions and extreme temperatures. In fact, a small market for expensive products always exists anywhere in the world.

Fourth, U.S. businesspersons characteristically like to maximize short-term performance. In foreign markets, however, it may be preferable to seek long-term gains, even if less-than-optimum profits are earned in the initial years. Thus, pricing to realize a designated rate of return may have to be staggered over several years. In this way, the return would be lower in the first few years but much higher in the later years, averaging out overall to a figure considered satisfactory by the parent corporation (see International Marketing Highlight 13.6).

Finally, government plays a much more prominent role in pricing in almost all countries outside the U.S. In many countries, prices are strictly controlled and all price changes have to be cleared with the government before taking effect. And price control is not limited to developing countries. In recent years, a number of European countries (Belgium, France, Ireland, the Netherlands, Spain, Sweden, and the U.K.) instituted price controls.

Ordinarily, price control means that an application to increase price must be filed with the government, together with supporting data of cast increases. Government approval may take several months, and often the price increase only takes effect after an additional several months.[15] In other words, a future price increase is publicly announced several months ahead of time. This practice leads to obsessive buying to beat the price increase. The price-control problem can eventually force a company to leave a country. The following case is an illustration:

Gerber Products Co. had been operating in Venezuela since 1960. Unprofitable operations forced the firm to sell out in 1979. The company blamed price controls as a major factor in losses. Some of Gerber's products were still being sold at prices set in 1968. The government had refused repeated requests for price increases. The price squeeze forced Gerber to cut output from 88 varieties to as low as 12.[16]

Transfer Pricing

Transfer pricing refers to the pricing of goods or services among units within the corporation. It serves as a measure of the economic performance of profit centers within the enterprise. It differs from *market price,* which measures exchanges between a company and the outside world, for the net effect of transfer pricing is borne by the same organization.

The determination of transfer prices in MNCs is an important issue because a substantial proportion of international exchanges consists of transactions between a parent corporation and its affiliates. For example, in the case of the U.S., 55 percent of 1999 exports and 50 percent of 1999 imports were within related firms. Similarly, in the case of OECD countries, about one-third of merchandise imports and exports represented transfers among affiliated enterprises.

■■■■■■ **International Marketing Highlight 13.6** ■■■■■■

Giveaway Pricing

Japanese companies definitely conduct business differently. Consider Japan's number one computer maker, Fujitsu Ltd., which won a contract to design a computer system for the city of Hiroshima by bidding 1 yen, or 0.7 cents. Fujitsu's strategy is simple: give away the design job, which, it is hoped, will lead to the company receiving the city's equipment orders. Japanese companies hope that once they get the inside track, they will enjoy a lifetime of orders. Such lowball pricing is a common practice in Japan. In the past, Fujitsu and NEC Corp. had both submitted a 1 yen bid to design a library computer system. They drew straws, and Fujitsu won. Earlier, Fujitsu had won a contract to design a telecommunications system in Wakayama Prefecture by bidding 1 yen.

The lowball pricing highlights Japanese companies' managerial philosophy: Shoot for the long term. They don't mind giving away business in the short run and dividing up the bidding with their Japanese competitors to ultimately hype the market share, the end-game of Japanese business strategy.

Giveaway pricing shows how difficult it is to break into the Japanese market. Even if other structural barriers to trade, i.e., distribution system, exclusionary business practices, and land-use policies, are eliminated, the rigged bids would be an insurmountable hurdle for U.S. companies to cross.

Another kind of price distortion practiced in Japan is the government's price-floor enforcement, applicable in such industries as airlines, insurance, agriculture, and fertilizer, whereby the business is divided up in cartels. This way competitors are prevented from entering the market.

Source: Business Week, November 20, 1989, p. 50.

Factors Affecting Transfer Pricing   Economic theory holds that price reflects demand and supply. For intracompany transactions, however, the parent corporation can control transfer pricing, because the exchange is little more than an accounting entry between units of the same corporation. The principal objective of the parent corporation in setting intrafirm prices is to maximize the long-term economic interests of the total corporation. In this endeavor, one or more affiliates of the company may often end up losing, which leads to conflicts that must be resolved. Essentially, transfer pricing decisions are affected by the following factors:

1. Income tax liability within the host country.
2. Income tax liability within the U.S.
3. Tariffs and/or customs duties within the host country.
4. Exchange controls within the host country.
5. Profit repatriation restrictions within the host country.
6. Quota restrictions within the U.S.
7. Credit status of the U.S. parent firm.
8. Credit status of the foreign subsidiary or affiliate.
9. Joint-venture constraints within the host country.

The importance of these factors varies from company to company and according to the location of affiliates. An older study, indicated that income tax liability was the most important variable influencing transfer pricing.[17] This conclusion was based mainly on research conducted to investigate MNCs' experiences vis-à-vis industrialized countries. In the case of developing countries, however, Seung H. Kim and Stephen W. Miller ranked profit repatriation restrictions, exchange control constraints, and joint venture constraints within the host country as the three most important factors affecting the pricing decision.[18] Despite the importance of different factors in different parts of the world, the motivation behind transfer pricing is the same: to maximize overall corporate performance.[19]

Transfer Pricing Methods

For setting transfer prices, companies usually use guidelines like the following:

- All domestic and foreign units are profit centers, and transfers must be set at levels that yield a reasonable profit to both the selling and buying units.
- Profit is divided according to functions performed in producing and marketing goods to unrelated buyers.
- *Gross margins* (the spread between production and distribution costs and the sale to an unrelated buyer) are divided more or less evenly between domestic producing and foreign marketing units.
- Overall impact on consolidated profit is the paramount consideration, and profit is taken where it is best for the total corporation.

Such guidelines are meant to provide a broad perspective for arriving at prices. The actual price is left to the discretion of the manager concerned, as differences in corporate objectives and environmental conditions may not permit a uniform method. For instance, in order to cover certain costs, transfer prices may be raised in countries that limit or refuse to allow royalties as a deductible business expense for a local subsidiary or in countries with exchange controls on dividends that delay remittances. Prices to high-tariff countries may be kept as low as legal requirements permit. A company that is attempting to enter a foreign market or to expand its share of a market will frequently suppress initial administrative, research, or other expenses when establishing costs in its transfer price. Since the transfer price has a variety of repercussions both at home and in host countries, many governments have developed rules for setting transfer prices following the *"arm's length" principle,* which more or less means arriving at the price based on competitive conditions.

Government involvement in the setting of transfer prices is understandable. In addition to profit shifting and tax avoidance in tax havens, transfer pricing can also affect the international price structure in critical areas, thereby possibly fueling the inflationary process or creating a balance-of-payments problem (see International Marketing Highlight 13.7).

In many industries, the products planned for transfer from the parent or another affiliate are commonly available from sources outside the corporate family. In such cases, many companies let their contracting units negotiate the transfer price. The negotiated price may be based on market price or landed cost plus an agreed-upon profit markup.

Handling Interdivisional Conflicts

Decentralized units of a corporation usually are profit centers. Each profit center's rewards and benefits depend on its bottom-line performance. Thus, if the transfer pricing system affects the profits of a unit, it is likely to lead to a conflict among the units involved. Interdivisional conflict because of transfer pricing is unhealthy and should be avoided or at least minimized by setting the transfer price in such a way that a balance exists between each division's perception of the other's advantage in the transfer situation. If one of the divisions is perceived to enjoy an advantage, the performance of the other division may be adversely affected.

Experience shows that where either the supplier or the customer division is seen as making excessive profits from transfer pricing transactions, interdivisional conflict is increased; that is, conflict results not only from the real impact of a transfer price on a unit's performance, but also from the perception about the impact on the divisions involved. It is necessary, therefore, to provide adequate information to both the affiliates to prevent misconceptions about impact. Further, arrangements should be made through some sort of organizational setup at headquarters to handle any conflict. The thrust of the conflict-handling effort should be to remove the imbalance that may favor one unit over the other.

Dumping

Dumping refers to the practice of pricing exports at levels lower than the domestic price. Strictly as a business strategy, dumping is a way of setting differential prices to achieve certain objectives. Thus, if a product is sold in the U.S. in two different markets at different prices (assuming this is feasible within the Robinson-Patman Act), there is nothing wrong with that practice. However, in the context of the international market, if this strategy is used intentionally to destroy a domestic industry, it becomes a matter of concern for the host country government on behalf of the greater interest of its nation. It is for this reason that many nations have antidumping laws on the books.

An international marketer must make sure that pricing decisions are free from liability for dumping in the host country. Countries usually levy a heavy penalty against dumping, which may cause the imported goods to be much higher than the market price.

Actually, the problem of dumping is more prevalent in developed markets. It is in these markets that exporters find the best opportunity for growth. Dumping is one way to render the domestic industry noncompetitive. If carried to its extreme, dumping can force the domestic manufacturers out of business. Once that happens, the price of imported goods can be increased. Thus, an exporter may practice dumping with lower profits in the short run but will face extremely high profits in the long run.

As an example, the U.S. is a large market. Overall, U.S. tariff barriers are very low. Exporters from Japan, South Korea, Brazil, and even from Europe find it a lucrative market to expand in. Dumping provides an opportunity to exporters to undercut the price of U.S.–manufactured goods. Accordingly, in the past, many exporters have been charged with dumping, particularly the Japanese (especially television manufacturers and steelmakers). Responding to the steel industry's pleas, the Treasury Department established minimum prices for different types of imported steel, with prices below the minimum automatically initiating an investigation of possible dumping.

■■■■■■■■   International Marketing Highlight 13.7   ■■■■■■■■

Two Ways to Skin the Cat

To reduce exposure to significant tax and penalty costs in the area of transfer pricing, an MNC has only two choices: rely on self-compliance or obtain an *advance pricing agreement (APA).* Self-compliance involves a consistent, documented effort to report "arm's-length" results from intercompany transactions. An APA is an agreement between the MNC and the IRS in advance covering the transfer-pricing methods that will apply in the future—a period of three to five years—to the MNC's transactions with its affiliates.

MNCs should consider the following factors in choosing among transfer-pricing alternatives:

- **Protection against IRS adjustments and penalties.** With self-compliance, there is a risk of IRS-imposed adjustments and penalties because the area is so fact-specific and complex. An APA offers more reliable protection against an unforeseen tax bite.

- **Protection against double taxation.** With self-compliance, there is the risk that the foreign country will not agree to an MNC's method and will tax the same income that the IRS taxes. With a binational APA, as an extension of the one in the USA, this risk is eliminated.

- **Practical pricing policies.** An APA allows for negotiation of a pricing method that best suits the company. Under self-compliance, the MNC must fit into the IRS cookbook of rules.

- **Up-front costs.** The initial costs incurred in satisfying self-compliance procedures may be less than those involved in obtaining an APA.

- **Ongoing costs.** There may be significant costs under self-compliance in trying to comply with all the rules. With an APA, yearly costs entail only the time and effort needed to comply with the agreement.

- **Best earnings results for MNCs.** IRS agents' responsibility is to make adjustments favorable to the government, whereas the APA division's job is to reach reasonable agreements with taxpayers. Thus, savings are more likely to result from an APA than from an audit of self-compliance methods.

Source: Crossborder Monitor, July 20, 1994, p. 12.

Meeting the Import Challenge

Many firms face competition from imports. Foreign goods are often sold at prices that seem so ridiculously low that they can only be explained as dumping. A company can consider the following strategic options to protect its markets from imports and possibly develop new opportunities for its products.

- Evaluate underlying competitive position and that of foreign competitors.

- Assess whether it is feasible to drive the domestic value-added component down to the same level as that of the import.

- Look at import competition in the context of changes in world production and trade factors. Adopting this approach will help differentiate between the short- and long-run impact of imports.

- Clearly understand the impact of changes in either its own or the foreign competitor's value-added and raw-material components. Be aware that the basis for import competition will vary with the country of origin. European imports require a different response than Japanese imports, and these, in turn, will require still a different response than that for, say, Korean or Taiwanese imports.

- When there are fundamental differences in cost that cannot be eliminated, attempt to change the product. The domestic producer should ensure, however, that value-added additions to its products result in differences in real value in the marketplace and that the foreign producer cannot emulate them. If the foreign competitor can follow with relative ease, the foreign competitor's leverage is actually increased.

- Segment the market so that efforts are concentrated where competitive leverage is greatest. Attempting to match imports across a wide spectrum of products can often be disastrous. The domestic producer should be both thoughtful and explicit in the method of segmentation.

- Fully assess the impact of volume on value added. If this impact is significant, and if reasonable changes in volume can be made, then those changes, combined with the ability to purchase raw material at internationally competitive prices, can bring about significant reductions in total cost. As a result, the domestic producer could possibly become competitive with imports. The remaining domestic producers may then face an abrupt change in both their at-home and foreign strategies.

Leasing

In domestic marketing, leasing has long served as an important alternative to outright buying, especially in the area of industrial marketing. Now leasing has emerged in international marketing as well. TAW Company founded TAW International Leasing Inc., to rent different types of heavy equipment, especially in Africa. Similarly, Clark Equipment Company leases equipment overseas through its Clark Rental Corporation subsidiary.[20] Actually, leasing strategy is employed by essentially all capital goods and equipment manufacturers active in foreign markets today.

Conditions that make leasing a viable pricing strategy to pursue in foreign markets are capital shortage, the need for maintenance and servicing, customers' unwillingness to make a long-term commitment because of the prospect of intermittent need or technological obsolescence, and investment incentives, including tax advantages, for leasing.

Capital shortage may make it difficult for customers to buy certain equipment, particularly in developing countries. Leasing provides a way to procure use of the equipment. By the same token, leasing permits the international marketer an entry into a market that otherwise might be closed because of capital shortage.

Furthermore, many kinds of equipment require regular *maintenance and service.* Customers may shy away from buying equipment because they fear a lack of adequate servicing. Leasing transfers the burden of maintenance and service onto the lessor and relieves the customer of this worry.

In many situations, a customer may be unwilling to buy a product out of concern about the need for the product being intermittent or about possible technological obsolescence. In such cases of *customer unwillingness to buy,* leasing provides a solution. The customer can use the equipment for as long as desired without being stuck with it should the need for it end or if better equipment becomes available. In many leasing arrangements, the customer is given an option to buy the product at a specified price after having the opportunity to use it for some time.

Finally, many countries offer *investment incentives* that are available for both outright purchase and leased equipment/plant. Where capital shortage becomes a hindrance to an outright purchaser, the incentive still can be sought through leasing. To the U.S. marketer, leasing offers an additional advantage: the entire lease price or rental may be written off as an income tax expense. The marketer may even be willing to pass on a portion of this tax benefit to the overseas customer.

Advantages aside, leasing poses two problems. First, how should the leasing price be set? Second, what can a lessor do if the customer overseas abruptly calls the deal off? For example, in the U.S., an attempt is usually made to recover the total cost of the leased equipment in about half its useful life. Thus, the leasing charge/rental during the second half of life would be strictly profit. However, the life of the equipment may be longer or shorter in a foreign setting, depending on the intensity of use and the conditions under which the use takes place. Establishing the useful life of the product might therefore be problematical. Additionally, it would be difficult to compute the monetary value of risks involved in a long-term foreign transaction. Finally, the inclusion of foreign inflation factors in setting the lease price poses problems, because forecasts of inflation rates are usually unreliable.

A still greater problem occurs when a foreign party backs out of a deal. For example, in 1984 the Zambian government canceled its contract with TAW to rent 330 tractors and 400 trailers. TAW had gone out of its way to manufacture the equipment custom-designed for heavy-duty usage on inferior roads at a time when U.S. business was good and parts were short. The Zambian government's decision created a big problem for TAW. How was it to dispose of the equipment?[21]

Despite the problems that leasing may pose, in the years to come it is likely to become more popular. Recently, many governments have facilitated marketing overseas through leasing plans. For example, the French government tried to establish a market for its Concorde, the supersonic jetliner, through backing a leasing program.[22] Similarly, the U.S. Export-Import Bank provides guarantees on foreign leasing by U.S. companies. Such support helps companies venturing into new foreign markets through leasing.

Summary

Prices determine the total revenue and to a large extent the profitability of any business. Because of the crucial importance of pricing, top management often plays a significant role in making pricing decisions. Top management must decide the strategic significance of pricing in the marketing mix. For example, U.S. companies traditionally have competed overseas based on nonprice factors. Lately, however, more and more companies emphasize price competition. Further, top management's goals must determine the extent to which uniform versus differentiated prices are set worldwide. It is argued usually that dissimilar conditions in overseas markets favor differentiated prices. Yet standardized pricing is believed to increase overall corporate effectiveness. Finally, top management assigns the pricing responsibility either to headquarters or to subsidiaries, or jointly between them.

In making any pricing decision, the following factors deserve consideration: pricing objectives, cost, competition, customer, and government regulations. In international marketing, these factors must be examined both at home and in the host country. Each factor comprises a number of components that vary in each nation, both in importance and in interaction.

Prices in overseas business are set by following either a cost approach or a market approach. The cost approach involves computing all relevant costs and adding a profit markup to determine the price. The market approach examines price setting from the customer's viewpoint. If the price that appears satisfactory to the potential customer does not meet the company's profit goal, either the business is given up or the price is increased. Thus, either approach brings a viable decision on price.

Export pricing is affected by three additional considerations: the price destination, the nature of the product, and the currency used in completing the transaction. Usually companies prepare separate price lists for different overseas markets. The price list contains a profit margin that the price to be adjusted to local market conditions, including competitive price, the government's export incentives in some countries, and the flexibility for competitive reduction of the price.

Price escalation is an important consideration in export retail pricing. The retail price of exports usually is much higher than the domestic retail price for the same good. This difference can be explained by the added costs associated with exports, such as transportation, customs duty, and distributor margin. To counteract the excessive escalation of export prices, a variety of strategic alternatives is available to management.

Price setting is one strategy. Multinational marketers in foreign markets follow essentially the same procedure for price setting as practiced in domestic markets. Internationally, however, a few additional factors become important. The price in various regions of the world should be kept relatively uniform to avoid competition for company units from unrelated dealers in the home market. Especially in developing countries, the ethics of pricing requires careful examination. Also price segmentation acquires more significance in foreign markets. Further, it may not always be desirable to pursue short-term pricing goals in foreign markets. Finally, governments outside the U.S. play a significant role in pricing.

An important topic in international marketing concerns pricing intracompany transfer of goods and services, that is, prices for goods and services exchanged within the corporate family. When transactions between units of the same enterprise take place across national frontiers, and the units are subject to different environmental factors such as customs duties, tax rates, and currency risks, adjustments in transfer prices can be used to advance various corporate goals and increase overall corporate profits. Since the transfer price has repercussions for both the home and host countries, many governments have rules to monitor such prices. In the U.S., for example, the IRS requires setting transfer prices according to the arm's-length principle, which more or less means arriving at the price based on competitive conditions.

Two important issues in international pricing are dumping and leasing. Dumping refers to the practice of pricing exports at lower levels than the domestic price for the same goods. As dumping may adversely affect domestic industry, many nations have legislated antidumping laws. As an alternative to outright purchase, leasing is slowly emerging in importance in international marketing. While setting leasing prices presents difficulties for various reasons, it nevertheless provides a good entry into markets otherwise inaccessible because of capital shortage.

Review Questions

1. What role does corporate management play in price setting for international markets?
2. What arguments favor a strategy of differentiated pricing in international markets?
3. Under what circumstances may uniform prices make sense?
4. Briefly discuss various factors that affect the pricing decision internationally.
5. Differentiate between the cost and market approaches to pricing.
6. What is meant by price escalation? What strategic options are available to international marketers to counteract escalation in export prices?
7. Under what circumstances might dumping be useful to the people of the importing country? Explain.
8. What advantage does leasing offer in international markets?

Creative Questions

1. U.S. steel manufacturers feel that Korean steel companies are dumping their products into the U.S. steel market. What recourse do the U.S. companies have to this practice? Does the U.S. government have any rules to punish foreign companies dumping goods in the U.S. market? How do the U.S. companies go about establishing their claim against the Koreans?
2. Since demand and supply conditions vary from market to market, setting uniform prices on a global basis is unrealistic. Do you agree? Are there conditions under which uniform pricing would make sense? What kinds of products are more amenable to uniform pricing?

Endnotes

1. Bill Saporito, "Why the Price Wars Never End," *Fortune*, March 23, 1992, p. 68. *Also see* Johny K. Johansson and Gary Erickson, "The Price-Quality Relationship and Trade Barriers," *International Marketing Review*, Autumn 1985, pp. 52–63.

2. Nathaniel H. Leff, "Multinational Corporate Pricing Strategy in the Developing Countries," *Journal of International Business Studies*, Fall 1975, p. 55.

3. Peter R. Kressler, "Is Uniform Pricing Desirable in Multinational Markets?" in Subhash C. Jain and Lewis R. Tucker, Jr., eds., *International Marketing Managerial Perspectives* (Boston: CBI Publishing Company, Inc. 1979), p. 389.

4. J. J. Boddewyn, "American Marketing in the European Common Market, 1963–1973," in *Multinational Product Management* (Cambridge, MA: Marketing Science Institute, 1976), pp. VII-1–I-25.

5. "Why Common Market Does Not Mean Common Prices," *Business International*, February 2, 1993, p. 47.

6. Sharon V. Thach and Catherine N. Axinn, "Pricing and Financing Practices of Industrial Exporting Firms," *International Marketing Review* 8, no. 1 (1991): pp. 32–46.

7. S. Tamer Cavusgil, "International Pricing Decision," *Columbia Journal of World Business*, Winter 1996, pp. 66–78.

8. Raphael Elimelech, "Pricing for the Japanese Market," in Subhash C. Jain and Lewis R. Tucker, Jr., eds., *International Marketing: Managerial Perspectives*, 2nd ed. (Boston: Kent Publishing Co., 1986), pp. 285–297.

9. "Factors that Influence Pricing Decisions, *International Management*, June 1991, p. 3.

10. "MNCs Home Competitive Edge With Activity-Based Costing," *Business International*, January 28, 1991, p. 37.

11. Sharon V. Thach and Catherine N. Axinn, "Pricing and Financing Practices of Industrial Exporting Firms," *International Marketing Review* 8, no. 1 (1991): pp. 32–46.

12. Mathew Rose and Ernest Beck, "Coke's Public-Relations Trouble was Worsened by Gray Trade," *The Wall Street Journal*, July 6,1999, p. A12.

13. Hermann Simon, "Pricing Problems in a Global Setting," *Marketing News*, October 9, 1995, p. 4.

14. *Financial Times*, July 9, 1990, p. 4.

15. Venkatakrishna V. Bellur, Radharao Chagauti, Rajeswarnrao Chagauti, and Saraswati P. Singh, "Strategic Adaptions to Price Controls: The Case of the Indian Drug Industry," *Journal of the Academy of Marketing Science*, Winter–Spring 1985, pp. 143–159.

16. Vern Terpstra, *International Dimensions of Marketing* (Boston, MA: Kert Publishing Co., 1982), p. 151

17. Jeffrey S. Arpan, "Multinational Firm Pricing in International Markets," *Sloan Management Review,* Winter 1973, pp. 1–9.

18. Seung H. Kim and Stephen W. Miller, "Constituents of the International Transfer Pricing Decisions," *Columbia Journal of World Business,* Spring 1979, pp. 69–77.

19. Mohammad F. Al-Eryani, Pervaiz Alam, and Syed H. Akhter, "Transfer Pricing Determinants of U.S. Multinationals," *Jour-* *nal of International Business Studies,* no. 3 (Third Quarter 1990): 409–426.

20. *Business Abroad,* May 13, 1986, p. 15.

21. "Zambia: The TAW Truck Deal Runs Out of Gas," *Business Week,* April 27, 1984, p. 56.

22. *See* "Collision Course in Commercial Aircraft: Boeing-Airbus-McDonnell Douglas-1991 (A)," A Case Study, Harvard Business School, 1989.

CHAPTER 14

International Channels of Distribution

CHAPTER FOCUS

After studying this chapter, you should be able to

■ Compare the merits of alternative international channels of distribution.

■ Explain the international channel selection process.

■ Describe wholesaling and retailing in foreign environments.

■ Discuss international franchising and physical distribution.

As in domestic marketing, the distribution process for international programs involves all activities related to time, place, and ownership utilities for industrial and ultimate consumers. The selection, operation, and motivation of effective channels of distribution are often crucial factors in a firm's differential advantage in international markets. The diverse activities and culturally differentiated roles of channel intermediaries make the formulation of distribution strategies a challenge for any firm entering foreign markets.

The channels of distribution available in a country are the result of culture and tradition. For example, in Japan there are usually too many channels involved in the distribution of a product. In the developing countries, channels of distribution are scattered, small in scope, inefficient, and insufficient. An international distribution system must be adapted to the country's established practices. Channel innovations ought to emerge from customer need rather than an arbitrary attempt to streamline the distribution system.

This chapter describes the alternative channels of distribution for an international marketer to consider. Examples of different types of intermediaries, both domestic and foreign, for distribution across national boundaries are presented. Guidelines are provided for selecting, motivating, and controlling the channels most appropriate for a firm's distribution mix. In addition, wholesale and retail patterns in overseas markets are examined. Also explored is the rationale of overseas franchising relationships along with their patterns of development. Finally, the perspectives of international physical distribution are discussed.

International distribution, which requires special knowledge of complex rate structures and tariffs, presents many unique problems. These call for an adequate management information system. Throughout the chapter, examples are given to illustrate how to achieve an effective distribution system in international markets.

Perspectives of International Distribution Channels

Distribution channels are the link between producers and customers. As Exhibit 14.1 shows, there are various ways of creating this link. Basically, an international marketer distributes either directly or indirectly. *Direct distribution* amounts to dealing with a foreign firm. *Indirect distribution* means dealing through another U.S. firm that serves as an intermediary. The choice of a particular channel link will be founded on considerations to be discussed in a later section of this chapter.

Channel Theory   It has long been held that the channels of distribution available in a country depend on its stage of economic development, which is reflected in the per capita real income and the sociopsychological, cultural, or anthropological environment. From this premise, it can be concluded that

- The more developed countries have more levels of distribution, more specialty stores and supermarkets, more department stores, and more stores in the rural areas.
- The influence of the foreign import agent declines with economic development.
- Manufacturer-wholesaler-retailer functions become separated with economic development.
- Wholesaler functions approximate those in North America with increasing economic development.
- The financing function of wholesalers declines and wholesale markups increase with increasing development.

EXHIBIT 14.1   Selected Channels of Distribution in International Marketing

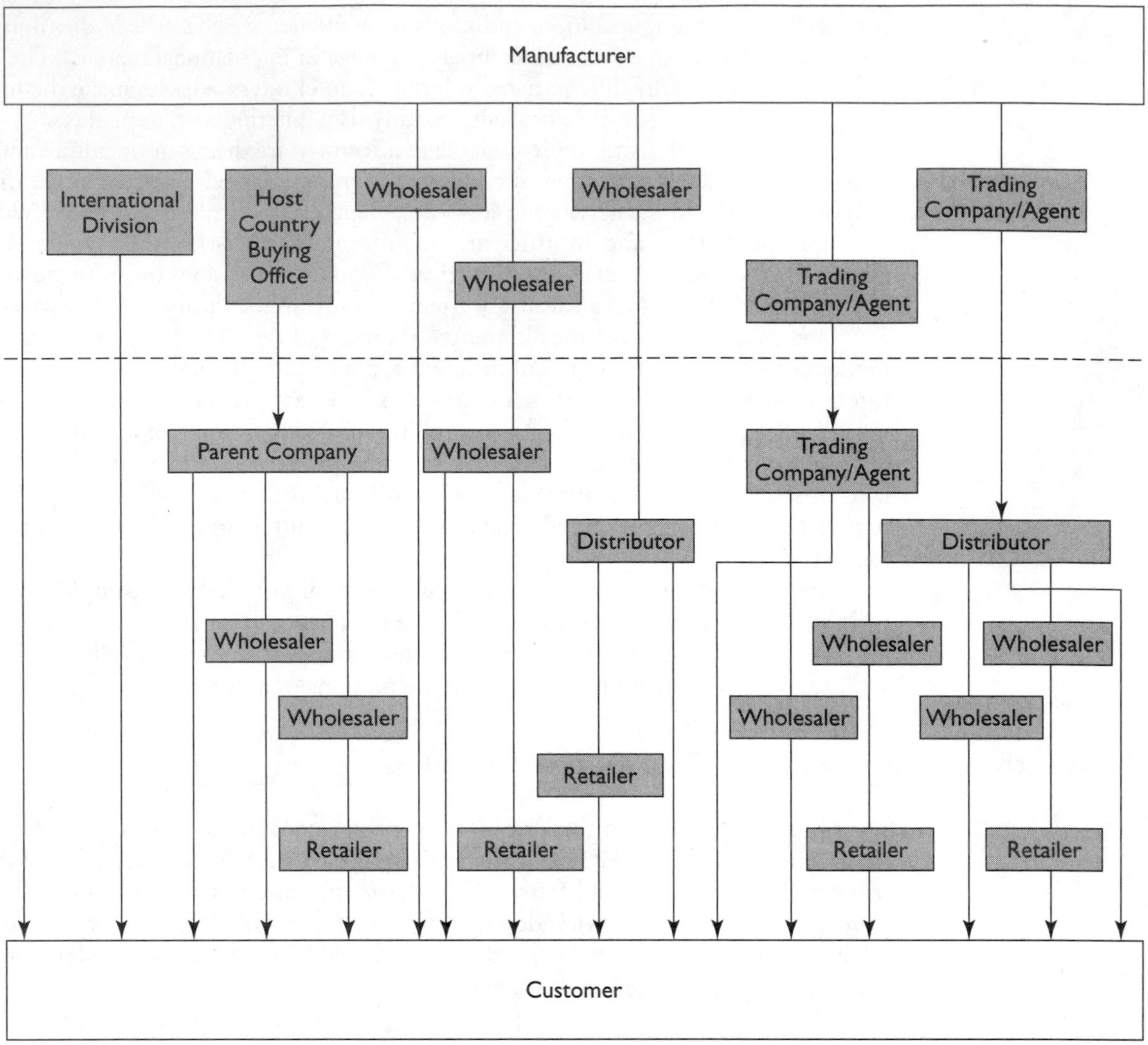

Note: Middle agents above the dotted line are U. S.–based. Those below the dotted lien are foreign channels.

- The number of small stores declines and the size of the average store increases with increasing development.
- The role of the peddler and itinerant trader and the importance of the open-garden-fair decline with increasing development.
- Retail margins improve with increasing economic development.[1]

According to this theory, changes in the channel structure of a country can be introduced only in response to changes in its economic and other environments. Channel changes cannot be enforced from without. At the risk of oversimplification, consider the fact that a supermarket distribution would not work in poor countries such as Egypt, Kenya, Sudan, and Pakistan because the economy and other environments operating in those countries are not conducive to such a form of distribution.

One empirical study cast doubts on the viability of this theory. Results showed little evidence to support the idea that the development of a distribution system in a country is determined by the limits of its social, economic, technological, and cultural environments. For example, it was found that channel structure and relationships mainly depend on the relative size of the firms at different channel stages rather than on the country's level of development.[2]

Apparently, the relationship between a country's channel structure and its environment remains undefined. How else to explain the channels of distribution in a country is a matter of speculation. All that can be said, given the current state of the art, is that distribution channels, like any other socioeconomic phenomenon, evolve slowly from a multitude of factors, some direct and some indirect. We do not quite know what these factors are, let alone their relationships.

Distribution Channels in Japan: An Example

Each country, rich or poor, has its own unique distribution system, evolved over time. International marketers must carefully examine the various aspects of a country's established distribution system to determine how to obtain distribution for their goods.

Despite the fact that Japan is the second economic power in the world today, its distribution system has been labeled outmoded, complex, cumbersome, and inefficient. The purpose of focusing this discussion on Japan is to emphasize that distribution structure is country-specific, and it would be naive for international marketers to enforce their own new distribution system on a country. Distribution channels must be used as they are, and efforts should be made to fit into the country through the established patterns.

In general, the Japanese system encompasses a wide range of wholesalers and other agents, brokers, and retailers, differing more in number than in function from their American counterparts. There are myriad tiny retail shops. An even greater number of wholesalers supplies goods to them, layered tier upon tier, many more than most U.S. executives would think necessary. For example, soap may move through three wholesalers plus a sales company after it leaves the manufacturer, before it even reaches the retail outlet. A steak goes from rancher to consumer in a process that often involves a dozen middle agents. Furthermore, Japan's distribution channels have traditionally been segregated by product type, with the consequent development of many specialized marketing routes.[3]

The Japanese distribution system is built into the fabric of its society. It is a sort of welfare system—it provides a living for so many people that the government does not have to pay welfare. In this way, the seemingly inefficient distribution system serves an important social function. It has been a flexible make-work device, acting as a buffer to absorb excess workers, particularly those on the verge of retirement. Many observers expect this social role to increase as the current slowdown in Japan's economic growth shrinks employment in manufacturing.[4]

Another reason for the longevity of Japan's distribution system is that it serves most companies well. Some suppliers, for instance, keep their inventories at or near their customers' headquarters to ensure rapid deliveries. Foreign companies, of course, cannot compete with such service unless they maintain substantial stockpiles and facilities in Japan.

Consumers are also served well. Lacking much storage space in their small homes, most Japanese homemakers shop several times a week and prefer convenient neighborhood shops. The little shops often strengthen their position by doing more for customers than just selling goods.

In brief, Japanese distribution channels are more complex than comparable channels in the U.S. However, the dominant view in Japan is that the system suits the needs of Japanese consumers. For example, while furniture stores in the U.S. may take up to 10 weeks for delivery, Japanese consumers usually receive delivery within a week.

Moreover, statistics indicate that the Japanese distribution system is not likely to change soon. According to government figures, the number of mom-and-pop retailers employing 4 or fewer workers increased almost 60 percent between 1975 and 1990 to 2 million outlets. During the same period, the number of similar-size wholesalers rose to more than 413,000 from about 250,000.[5] The papa-mama stores control 56 percent of Japan's retail sales (versus 3 percent for U.S. mom-and-pops and 5 percent in Europe).[6]

Japan has one retailer for every 74 people, compared with one for every 144 Americans. The U.S. has 145,000 food stores to serve a nation of 250 million; Japan has more than 620,000 to serve a population one-half the size.[7]

Similarly, Japan has 1 million bars and restaurants, more than three times as many per person as in the U.S. More than one-half of these establishments are independent operators, so they need frequent deliveries in small quantities. Wholesalers of perishable foods make as many as three drop-offs a day. Campbell Japan Inc.'s typical delivery of soup to a retailer is minuscule by U.S. standards: six cans. Campbell's average shipment to wholesalers is three to five 24-can cases. That and a 19 percent duty increase the price of a can of tomato soup in Tokyo to $1.45 compared with $.39 in New York.[8]

It costs U.S. and German retailers about $25 to deliver a market basket of groceries to a customer, but in Japan the cost to retailers is about $35. This means the average Japanese must work 40 percent longer than his or her German or American counterpart to buy a weekly supply of groceries.[9]

In conclusion, the way the Japanese distribution channels are structured and managed presents one of the major reasons for the failure of foreign firms to establish major market position in Japan. Despite the fact that the Japanese channels are obviously inefficient and cumbersome, they seem to serve the customer well (see International Marketing Highlight 14.1).

International Marketing Highlight 14.1

Customer Service—The Japanese Way

My husband and I bought one souvenir the last time we were in Tokyo—a Sony compact disk player. The transaction took seven minutes at the Odakyu Department Store, including time to find the right department and to wait while the salesman filled out a second charge slip after misspelling my husband's name on the first.

My in-laws, who were our hosts in the outlying city of Sagamihara, were eager to see their son's purchase, so he opened the box for them the next morning. But when he tried to demonstrate the player, it wouldn't work. We peered inside. It had no innards! My husband used the time until the Odakyu would open at 10:00 to practice for the rare opportunity in that country to wax indignant. But at a minute to 10:00 he was preempted by the store ringing us.

My mother-in-law took the call and had to hold the receiver away from her ear against the barrage of Japanese honorifics. Odakyu's vice president was on his way over with a new disk player.

A taxi pulled up 50 minutes later and spilled out the vice president and a junior employee who was laden with packages and a clipboard. In the entrance hall the two men bowed vigorously.

The younger man was still bobbing as he read from a log that recorded the progress of their efforts to rectify their mistake, beginning at 4:32 PM the day before, when the sales-clerk alerted the store's security guards to stop my husband at the door. When that didn't work, the clerk turned to his supervisor, who turned to his supervisor, until a SWAT team leading all the way to the vice president was in place to work on the only clues, a name and an American Express card number. Remembering that the customer had asked him

Commission Agent Foreign customers interested in buying U.S. products are represented by *commission agents*. They serve as so-called finders for their principals, locating desired goods at the lowest price. The commission agents receive their commission from their foreign clients.

Country-Controlled Buying Agent The *country-controlled buying agent* is an official buyer of a foreign government, seeking to buy designated goods for his or her country. Many developing countries, for example, maintain supply missions in the U.S. with a number of officers who are entrusted with the task of procuring different goods for their countries.

American Trading Company (ATC) The *American Trading Company (ATC)* is a relatively new form of indirect channel that can be formed under the Export Trading Company Act of 1982 (also see Chapter 17). The goal of this act is to increase U.S. exports by encouraging more efficient provision of export trade services to producers and suppliers alike, by improving the availability of trade finance, and by removing the antitrust disincentive to export activities.[11] Before the Export Trading Company Act, U.S. firms were handicapped in forming trading companies because of the fear of antitrust prosecution and inadequate capitalization. Since the passage of this legislation, however, there has been an increasing interest among businesses of all sizes to form trading companies.

Although the act provides a legal basis for the development of ATCs, the shape of their operating characteristics (i.e., type of product exported, the export role adopted—agent or merchant—services provided, etc.) is left in the hands of private business. Because the whole concept of trading companies is new to the U.S., it is too early to say what products they normally will handle, how they will be managed, and what services they will concentrate on. Thus far, agribusiness firms are taking more interest in trading companies than are any other types of business.[12]

Empirical research on the subject indicates that ATCs are more diversified both in handling products and in geographic coverage. In addition, unlike the EMCs, the ATCs have the potential to be much larger in size and operations. By the same token, decision making in ATCs is diversified, since the membership is shared by firms (e.g., banks, manufacturers, EMCs) with different backgrounds and cultures.[13]

Indirect Distribution Through Merchant Intermediaries

Merchant intermediaries located in the U.S. serve as middle agents for manufacturers in their export endeavors. Export merchants, other manufactures, export vendors, overseas military market representatives, MNCs, and the U.N. principally fill this role.

The merchant intermediaries invariably take title to the goods and deal in their own names. They may or may not undertake delivery of the goods, and the services they provide vary. Likewise, the authority exercised by these intermediaries differs. For example, the export merchant usually has pricing authority, but a cooperative exporter does not.

Export Merchant The *export merchant* buys directly from manufacturers according to their specifications, taking title to the goods. These merchants have overseas contacts through which the goods are sold either to wholesalers or retailers. They assume all the risks and sell in their own names. Their compensation consists of a markup percentage that is based on market conditions. In general, an export merchant resembles a domestic wholesaler.

Cooperative Exporter The *cooperative exporter* is any company that has an established system of handling exports for its own goods and distributes products overseas for other

---

about using the disk player in the U.S., the clerk called 32 hotels in and around Tokyo to ask if a Mr. Kitasei was registered. When that turned up nothing, the Odakyu commandeered a staff member to stay until 9 PM to call American Express headquarters in New York. American Express gave him our New York telephone number. It was after 11 PM when he reached my parents, who were staying at our apartment. My mother gave him my in-law's telephone number.

The younger man looked up from his clipboard and gave us, in addition to the new $280 disk player, a set of towels, a box of cakes, and a Chopin disk. Three minutes after this exhausted pair had arrived they were climbing back into the waiting cab. The vice president suddenly dashed back. He had forgotten to apologize for my husband having to wait while the salesman had rewritten the charge slip, but he hoped we understood that it had been the young man's first day.

My Tokyo experience contrasts sharply with treatment I've received at home. In late July, without explanation or apology from Bloomingdale's, a credit of $546.66 appeared on my American Express statement for china ordered January 12, paid for April 17, and never received.

Source: Hilary Hinds Kitasei, "Japan's Got Us Beat in the Service Department Too," *The Wall Street Journal,* July 30, 1985, p. 30.

International Channel Members

The previous section mentioned two forms of distribution: direct and indirect. While a direct distribution channel may appear more effective, in practice it is better only if the customers are geographically homogeneous, have similar buying habits, and are limited in number. Indirect channel is preferable when customers and buying habits are heterogeneous.[10]

Either way, a company may go through one or more agents or merchant intermediaries. The essential difference between them concerns the legal ownership of goods. An agent, without taking title to the goods, distributes them on behalf of the principal, the manufacturer. Merchant intermediaries do business in their own names and hold title to the goods they deal in. Exhibit 14.2 identifies important types of intermediaries. The type of intermediaries and their names vary from country to country and from industry to industry in the same country. For this reason, the discussion here is limited to certain intermediaries popularly used worldwide for distribution across industries.

Indirect Distribution Through Agents

Important among these types of agents are export management companies (EMCs), manufacturers' export agents (MEAs), cooperative exporters, Webb-Pomerene associations, foreign freight forwarders, commission agents, and country-controlled buying agents and trading companies. Although these agents do not take title, they do take possession of goods. However, they have different duties in respect to continuation of relationship with the principal (long-term versus ad hoc); degree of control maintained by the principal (complete versus slight versus none); pricing authority accorded to the agent (full versus partial versus advisory); affiliation with buyer or seller; number of principals served at a time (few versus many); involvement or noninvolvement with shipping or handling of competitive lines; provision of promotional support (continuous versus one-time versus none); extension of credit to principal (regularly versus occasionally versus rarely versus never); and provision of market information (good versus fair versus poor).

Export Management Company (EMC) An *export management company (EMC)* is an independent export organization that serves different companies in their export endeavors.

EXHIBIT 14.2   Intermediaries in International Distribution

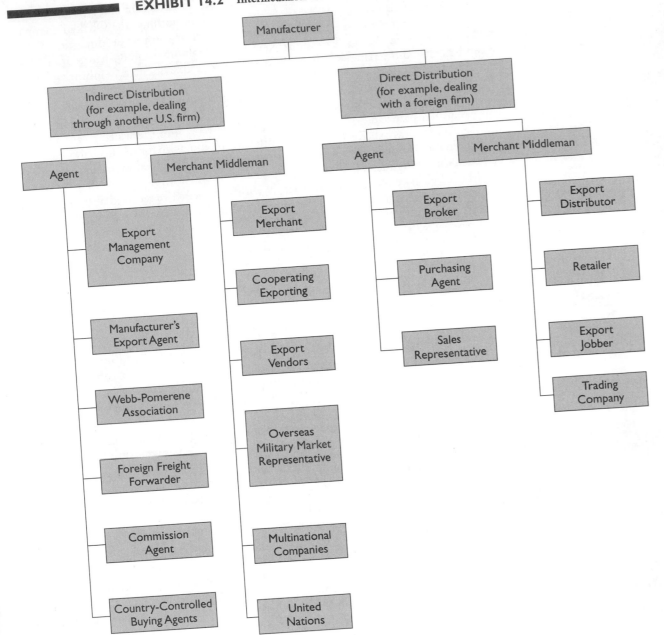

The EMC regards the exporter as a client, not as an employer. It deals in a number of allied but noncompetitive lines and usually handles the entire export function for a manufacturer. In all contacts and communications overseas, the EMC operates under the client's name, using client stationery and promotional materials such as catalogs.

EMCs differ in the scale of their operations. Some handle export sales for as few as four or five manufacturers; others serve as many as 50 companies. A typical firm represents 10 manufacturers. EMCs are especially helpful to small companies that are unable to af-

ford experienced and skilled export managers. EMCs understand foreign cultures. They are up to date on international politics, logistics, taxation, and legal problems. They provide a viable alternative for small firms to launch themselves in the export business.

An EMC may be just a one-person operation, or it may employ as many as 100 people. Some firms are relatively new, while others have decades of experience. Large export management firms often maintain overseas offices in strategic locations. Senior executives of these firms frequently travel overseas to seek orders and develop relationships with the customers.

There are about 1,200 EMCs in the U.S. Most are located in the larger seaport cities. The important sources for locating an EMC are the U.S. Department of Commerce, port authorities, and banks handling foreign trade. The National Federation of Export Management Companies, based in Washington, DC, and local chambers of commerce are also good sources. An exporter should attempt to find an EMC that specializes in its product type, has in place a well-organized and controlled worldwide distribution system, is well-financed and managed, and is willing and eager to devote significant amounts of managerial effort and money to launching its product.

EMCs generate their income either from commissions or from discounts on goods they buy for resale overseas. The commission or discount varies from 10 percent or less to 30 percent or more, based on the services provided and the difficulty of the marketing task.

EMCs are used by both large and small companies, simply because they can undertake exporting more effectively and generally at a lower cost than other channels. Further, it is quite common for exporters to use multiple EMCs. A single EMC may not be able to reach all world markets. In addition, EMCs usually come to specialize by product. Hence, a company that deals in diverse products may use several EMCs.

Manufacturer's Export Agent (MEA) The *manufacturer's export agent (MEA)* provides services similar to those provided by the EMC, but the MEA covers limited markets and the contractual relationship is short-term only, from a few months to a year or two. Sometimes the contract applies only to a particular transaction as well. MEAs act under their own names and receive a commission for services. Whereas an international marketer might deal with only one EMC, it would be represented by several MEAs. Because MEAs do not serve the export department of the principal as an EMC does, they cannot be relied upon to perpetuate business for an export-minded company.

Webb-Pomerene Association A *Webb-Pomerene association* is formed among competing U.S. manufacturers especially and exclusively for the purpose of exports according t the Webb-Pomerene Act of 1918. An agreement in the form of a Webb-Pomerene associ tion is exempt from antitrust laws.

The members of a Webb-Pomerene association can engage in different internation marketing activities to their mutual advantage. For example, they can set prices, comb shipments, jointly undertake marketing research, or share information with each oth and allocate orders among different members of the association. It is estimated that th are currently over 30 active Webb-Pomerene associations.

Foreign Freight Forwarder The *foreign freight forwarder* specializes in handling seas shipping arrangements. Its services can be utilized for handling goods from a port to the foreign port of entry. Occasionally, it may handle inland shipments as w foreign freight forwarder receives a discount or fees from the shipping company. For services such as packing, it would be paid additional fees.

manufacturers on a contractual basis. For example, several years ago Colgate-Palmolive Company distributed Wilkinson blades in many international markets. Recently, Colgate and Kao Corporation of Japan formed a joint venture to manufacture toiletry products in the U.S. The products of this venture would be distributed worldwide through the former's distribution network.[14] Similarly, Sony Corporation serves as a distributor in Japan for different U.S. and European companies. Kao Corporation of Japan, a diversified chemical and detergent company, markets Dow Chemical Co.'s corrosion-resistant vinyl ester resin, a type of fiberglass-reinforced plastic used in industry.[15] Whirlpool used Sony in Japan, Perrier marketed the Swiss chocolate Lindt in the U.S., Breck Shampoo used Schick in Germany, and Champion Spark Plug used a Nanjing spark plug manufacturer to distribute its products in China.[16]

These cooperative arrangements are also called *piggybacking*. The cooperative exporter may assume the role of an EMC or may just serve as a commission agent for a short period in select markets. The principal asset of cooperative exporters is their experience in dealing overseas as manufacturers themselves. Therefore, they are more aware of and sympathetic toward the problems of the manufacturer interested in developing export markets.

Export Vendor The *export vendors* are companies that specialize in buying poor-quality and overproduced goods for distribution overseas. These companies buy the goods outright, taking title to them. They ship the goods to one or more countries and sell them through their established contacts. Such intermediaries are useful in times of depressed business conditions in the U.S. or when a company for some reason gets stuck with certain unwanted products. For example, many small U.S. manufacturers used such intermediaries to get rid of goods they produced for the 1980 Olympic Games in Moscow. Since the U.S. did not participate in the games, these goods could not be sold in a normal way.

Overseas Military Market Representatives These are representatives who specialize in selling to US. military *post exchanges (PXs)* and commissaries. More than $5 billion annually in consumer goods, not all of them made in the U.S., are sold to U.S. military PXs and commissaries overseas. The bulk of this market is made up of the joint Army–Air Force PX system. PX managers abroad decide what to buy. Commissary managers are restricted by a "brand name contracts" list but still have considerable discretion. All PX and commissary orders are placed through central headquarters in the U.S.

The PX and commissary system primarily serves young consumers, among whom ethnic products are popular. Usually these products are purchased in bulk at top discounts. These representatives generally work for a commission but on occasion will buy on their own for resale. Some representatives handle all types of consumer products; others are specialized.

Multinational Companies Some 3,000 U.S. companies, through overseas subsidiaries, have overseas operations including factories, branch and regional offices, and in some countries elaborate residential compounds for American personnel. (American compounds with more than 1,000 residents are not unusual in the Middle East.)

Not all of these companies are committed to buy products from the U.S. Usually they do, however, for three important reasons: (1) their staff is familiar with products from the U.S., (2) purchasing of major items can be done in the home office, and (3) it is cheaper to consolidate purchasing and buy the same brand for all subsidiaries.

The MNC market generates massive demand for plant machinery, supplies, testing equipment, vehicles, spare parts, process control systems, training equipment, computer systems, appliances, office machines, furniture, and other goods. Residents of the compounds require all types of household appliances, fixtures, foods and other consumables, educational equipment and materials, and entertainment and leisure products.

United Nations The UN's purchasing is spread out among a number of agencies. Some have headquarters in the U.S., others in Europe. Any member nation can compete for this business. Each agency is specialized.

The UN agencies themselves do not purchase goods in the same quantities as do projects financed by organizations such as the World Bank. The UN agencies often act as advisors rather than actual buyers.

A good example is UNESCO (the United Nations Educational, Scientific, and Cultural Organization). A $50 million educational development project in Zaire, for instance, may be jointly financed by the government of Zaire, the African Development Bank, and the World Bank, but designed (including product specifications) by UNESCO advisors. Purchasing and contracting will be done by the Ministry of Education of Zaire, probably with advice from the same UNESCO team who helped write the specifications.

Other UN agencies operate in much the same manner. A notable exception is UNICEF (the United Nations Children's Fund). UNICEF maintains in Copenhagen a large warehouse with substantial stocks of basic equipment and teaching aids for primary schools in developing countries. UNICEF ships from Copenhagen and issues replacement orders as stocks are depleted.

In the U.S. all UNICEF buying is done through the UN's New York headquarters. To qualify as a vendor, one must submit catalogs and specifications, and sometimes samples for evaluation. UNICEF has very strict requirements governing the types of products included on its basic list and carried in its regular inventory.

Direct Distribution Through Agents

A company may deal with different types of agent intermediaries overseas. These agents do not take title to the goods and usually work for a commission. The product involved, and the way it is marketed in the U.S., will provide a clue as to who might be employed to undertake overseas distribution—sales representatives, purchasing agents, or export brokers.

Sales Representative The *sales representative* resembles a manufacturer's representative in the U.S. A manufacturer supplies the sales representatives with literature and samples to conduct sales in a predesignated territory. These representatives usually work on a commission basis, assume no risk or responsibility, and are under contract for a definite period. They may operate on either an exclusive or nonexclusive basis, and they do not handle competing lines. They serve as a good source of market information.

Purchasing Agent The *purchasing agent* is also referred to as a *buyer for export, an export commission house*, or an *export confirming house*. These agents are active in U.S. markets, seeking goods of interest to their foreign principals. Their product quality and price demands stem from the requirements of the principals.

Usually, foreign purchasing agents represent governments or big contractors, either for a specified time or for a particular task. In any event, they do not provide continual service and stable volume to vendors. For example, a foreign government might authorize a purchasing agent to buy designated goods in the U.S. for the completion of a large mill or plant. Once the mill or plant is constructed, the purchasing agent ceases to be active.

Purchasing agents receive commissions from their principals. A transaction with a purchasing agent is completed, as in domestic marketing, with the agent handling all packing and shipping details. A purchasing agent may represent several principals requiring the same goods and may deal with different competing vendors.

Export Broker The *export broker* brings the foreign buyer and U.S. seller together. Usually export brokers receive a commission or fee from the seller for their services. They take neither title nor possession of goods and assume no financial responsibility relative to the export transaction. Export brokers generally are used in the export of commodities such as grain and cotton. Only rarely is the export broker involved in the export of manufactured goods.

Direct Distribution Through Merchant Intermediaries

The foreign merchant intermediaries take title to the goods and sell them under their own names. They may or may not take possession of the goods. They render services similar to a domestic wholesaler. Major types of foreign merchant intermediaries are export distributors, foreign retailers, export jobbers, and trading companies.

Export Distributor The *export distributors* purchase goods from a U.S. manufacturer at the greatest possible discount and resell them for a profit. They are especially active in distributing products that require periodic servicing. They commit themselves to providing adequate service to the customers through carrying a sufficient quantity of spares and parts, maintaining facilities, and providing technicians to perform all normal servicing operations.

Export distributors buy in their own names and usually maintain an ongoing relationship with the exporter. They have exclusive sales rights in a country or region and receive easy payment terms from exporters.

Foreign Retailer In some cases, U.S. manufacturers deal directly with *foreign retailers,* particularly in the case of consumer goods. For example, Campbell Soup Co. sells its Pepperidge Farm Cookies in Japan by directly dealing with a 3,300-store 7-Eleven chain throughout Japan.[17] The contact may be made either through a traveling salesperson or by mail using catalogs or brochures. In many countries, large retailers perform dual roles. While they sell directly to consumers through their own outlets, they also distribute imported goods to smaller retailers. Thus, exports handled by the retailer may receive wide coverage.

Export Jobber The *export jobbers* determine customer needs overseas and fill them by making purchases in the U.S. Some jobbers reverse the process, filling needs of U.S. customers by supplying imported products. The jobbers mainly deal in staples, openly traded products for which brand names have little importance.

Trading Company In modern times, the so-called *trading companies* usually are associated with Japan. Actually, the concept of the trading company is much older. During colonial times many European countries, particularly Britain and France, used trading companies to develop trade with other nations. For example, the East India Company was England's major means to enter India. Similarly, the French trading companies Cie Française de l'Afrique Occidentale and Ste Commerciale de l'Ouest Africain were active in Africa.

In Japan the trading company originated as a commodity dealer that outgrew its wholesale functions. When the country was opened to the West, the trading company primarily served as a buffer between Japanese merchants and foreign businesses. Then Japan began to industrialize. Having neither raw materials at home nor an empire to exploit, the new industry needed imports. Rather than depend on foreigners, they adapted their trading companies to the task of acquiring the raw materials in addition to moving Japanese goods overseas.

Japanese trading companies have been very successful in promoting Japan's exports. They offer a broad range of services, from marketing research to financing, and present a relatively inexpensive way for the small or medium-size firm to do international marketing.

Some major functions of trading companies include trading and distributing, risk-hedging in exchange rates and commodity price fluctuation, domestic and overseas marketing of exported and imported technology, management consulting, participation in manufacturing, joint ventures abroad in resource developments and urban and rural development, and organizing new industries. The only functions that trading companies do not perform are production and retailing, but they may become involved even in these activities through joint ventures.

There are approximately 7,000 trading companies in Japan today, but only about 300 of them engage in foreign trade. The six largest trading companies in Japan, referred to as the Big Six, are Mitsui Bussan, Mitsubishi, Sumitomo, Marubeni, Itochu and Nissho Iwai. They had a combined sales of around $1 trillion, equivalent to a quarter of Japan's GDP. They are responsible for bringing in about 68 percent of Japan's imports and shipping out about 40 percent of its exports. These six companies have over 500 offices outside Japan, employing over 15,000 people.[18]

The big trading companies control 56 percent of Japan's foreign trade. Together they are the main exporters of almost every product (except cars and electrical appliances) exported from Japan. Japanese trading companies have expert knowledge about the lures most attractive to distributors of Japanese exports in all major foreign countries. By contrast, foreign exporters cannot compete so easily in Japan, because they will usually have to sell through a trading company that is part of a Japanese group probably making a competing product.

In addition to privately controlled trading companies such as those in Japan, many countries have state-controlled trading companies. Such companies are active in countries like those in Eastern Europe where business is conducted by a few government-sanctioned and government-controlled trading outfits. (Currently, attempts are in progress, especially in Poland and the Czech Republic, to privatize their trading companies.) In many countries, the state-controlled trading companies may be the only means of doing business. In many other nations, however, trading companies bridge the gap between western business style and local cultural practices for conducting business.

Dealing with Intermediaries

After an exporter successfully locates prospective intermediaries, terms of agreement must be defined between them. A detailed, written agreement often avoids later disputes and misunderstandings. However, some companies prefer a simple agreement, leaving details to be settled when and as questions arise. As long as the intent of both parties is good, it is feasible to work without spelling out every detail in a written document. Yet, it is still considered wise to prepare a written contract after the manufacturer has investigated the channel member's overall integrity, financial soundness, community standing, share of the market, and other product lines carried. Exhibit 14.3 shows the items included in a typical agreement.

In addition to the items shown in the sample agreement, it is desirable to specify that the intermediary will not deal in competing lines, disclose confidential information, or make agreements that bind the exporting firm in any way. Further, the place and time for the title to the merchandise to pass from the seller to the buyer should be clearly stated because of tax implications in the countries of both the exporter and the interme-

EXHIBIT 14.3
Items to Include in an Agreement with Foreign Intermediaries

- Names and addresses of both parties.
- Date when the agreement goes into effect.
- Duration of the agreement.
- Provisions for extending or terminating the agreement.
- Description of product lines included.
- Definition of sales territory.
- Establishment of discount or commission schedules and determination of when and how to be paid.
- Provisions for revising the commission or discount schedules.
- Establishment of a policy governing resale prices.
- Maintenance of appropriate service facilities.
- Restrictions to prohibit the manufacture and sale of similar and competitive products.
- Designation of responsibility for patent and trademark negotiations or pricing.
- The assignability or nonassignability of the agreement and any limiting factors.
- Designation of the country (not necessarily the U.S.) and state (if applicable) of contract jurisdiction in the case of dispute.

diary. Finally, the contract should avoid articles that directly or indirectly conflict with U.S. antitrust laws.

Company-Owned Distribution

An alternative way for a company to arrange for distribution in other countries is to establish its own distribution instead of going through intermediaries. An exporter may choose this alternative for three reasons: to enhance coverage with the objective of increasing sales, to maintain complete control over foreign distribution, and to seek distribution when channels are unavailable.

Foreign company-owned channels not only take a long time to establish, but also may not always provide the desired sales results. Difficulties are likely to occur, especially when a change is made in channel arrangements. For example, if an exporter drops existing channels in favor of company-owned distribution, it will face tough competition from them. Moreover, in many countries it may not be easy to find qualified individuals to serve as salespersons. Indeed, many nations, Japan for example, a company may face insurmountable problems in seeking distribution of its own.

Occasionally, a joint venture with a host country business is preferable to a strictly company-owned distribution. The host country business may already have a distribution setup. The joint venture route provides the exporter an opportunity to enhance control and market coverage without the problems of building channels from scratch (see International Marketing Highlight 14.2).

■■■■■■ **International Marketing Highlight 14.2** ■■■■■■

Harnessing the Hustle

Coke has engineered what looks like a masterstroke in its quest for better distribution: it has hooked up with China's famous busybodies, the street committees. Although the traditional role of these self-important old people—as "spies" and petty enforcers of laws and community norms—is being eroded, they still retain much of their privileged status. They come and go pretty much as they please and do as they like.

And what they like, say Coke managers, includes pushing sales carts of cold Coke around the traffic-and-vendor-restricted areas of downtown Shanghai. The company has signed up enough street committees to warrant a fleet of 150 pushcarts plus 300 tricycles.

The pushcart vendors keep their Coke vehicles in the local street committee lockups, where they usually also have room for a large ice-making machine. Each committee is contracted to store, chill, and sell Coke on its turf on an exclusive basis.

The cola giant will not reveal the volume the street committees are turning over. Clearly it varies, with the vast bulk of sales coming during the hot summer months. Company executives will only say that they are more than satisfied with the progress to date.

Source: Crossborder Monitor, July 30, 1997, p. 9.

Gray Market

The *gray market* refers to distribution through unauthorized channels. The term is derived from *black market,* the infamous underground economy for goods and services. However, where a black market typically deals with illegal goods and services (or the illegal trading of otherwise legal goods), the line between proper and improper is not as clear in a gray market. The pipeline in a gray market is legal, but somewhat controversial. Many consider it unethical. Others argue that it is economically unsound because it often involves purchasing goods and selling them at a profit without adding any value.

Typically, a gray-market transaction would work as follows: A broker buys goods from a distributor overseas, where wholesale prices are low, then diverts them to the U.S., where he or she undersells domestic distributors who have paid a higher wholesale price. The usual scenario involves four steps:

1. *Authorized sale:* This is usually direct from a manufacturer or exporter to a distributor.
2. *Diversion:* This is the critical step in a gray-market transaction. The distributor diverts the shipment to another storage site, where it is either held or transported to a free-trade port (such as Panama).
3. *Import:* Discounters learn of the stored products through brokers and purchase huge quantities at the lower overseas wholesale prices.
4. *Retail sale:* The discounter sells the product in the U.S. at below-market prices, but still makes a profit.

Gray markets are especially prevalent in the trading of luxury goods (such as autos, furs, jewels, and upscale clothing and perfumes) and high-tech goods (disk drives, computers, and computer chips). Considering the price differences between the U.S. and Japan for the following products, it is conceivable for gray market to develop.[19]

	Price	
Item	U.S.	Japan
Hermes Silk Scarf	$245	$ 398
Parada Nylon Backpack	470	750
Louis Vuitton Drawstring Bag	795	1060

A specific example helps to illustrate the problems facing a company caught in gray market trading: A customer of a certain computer company buys components (such as disk drives) at a volume discount. The contract calls for "adding value," but instead, the customer resells the "raw" drives to major dealers, systems houses, and *original-equipment manufacturers (OEMs)*. In doing so, the customer can undercut the prices set by the manufacturer's authorized distributors. These distributors become angry and, more important, they are now unmotivated to highlight and sell the manufacturer's product. The company is caught in a real trap—it risks losing the loyalty of a valuable distributor base, but satisfying this base hurts the company's salesforce, which may depend on gray-market sales for a good portion of its quotas.

High-tech industries are particularly susceptible to gray markets because their products usually involve short life cycles, which translate into a short shelf-life. Salespeople become willing to sell to anybody, anxious to avoid holding outdated or obsolete products. A vicious circle is created: the salesforce is pressured to move products, which forces sales to the gray market, which erodes prices, which causes further pressures to move products.

It is the manufacturers who are on the defensive. Some are simply absorbing profit losses to the gray market as an acknowledged cost of doing business. Others are taking a more aggressive stand, through privately funded fraud investigations, litigation, and even corporate guerrilla tactics.

One key step for companies determined to fight the gray market is self-examination. The perfume industry is a classic example. Wholesale prices charged to U.S. retailers can be 25 percent higher than the currency-adjusted wholesale prices charged in Europe. Such price discrepancies are meant to guarantee that U.S. perfume distributors limit their distribution network to select dealers and upscale stores. Yet, it is exactly this type of discrepancy among markets that allows the gray market to flourish through "underground distribution systems."

One would think that perfume manufacturers would be somewhat hesitant to ship huge quantities of their priciest potions to such questionable havens of the rich such as Poland, Egypt, and Panama. A few years ago, for example, French perfume exports directly to Panama totaled $40 million—theoretically making that country's per capita consumption of perfume 35 times that of the U.S.[20] Critics argue that the perfume companies know full well that such shipments are heading directly for major gray-market trans-shipment points, but a company's financial results and product positioning simply take priority. Stated another way, the companies attempting to fight the gray-market system become their own worst enemies. They regularly sell to known gray-market diverters to meet sales targets, and they have allowed their own distribution systems to spin out of control.

Channel Management

Channel management means selecting appropriate channels of distribution and making them work. The selection process requires decisions on distribution structure and choice of specific channel members. Once the selection is made, the goal is to make the channel arrangements work adequately. This requires maintaining cordial relationships and minimizing conflicts.

Channel Selection

The channel selection process in international marketing is similar to the one for a domestic situation. Usually, the selection process involves establishing channel objectives and feasible channel alternatives, evaluation of alternatives, and the choice of appropriate channels.

Establishing Objectives The objectives of an international channel of distribution derive from total marketing objectives in the foreign market. These objectives are concerned with a clear-cut definition of the target customers. Implicit in the definition of target customers is the decision about whether the company wants intensive, selective, or exclusive distribution. *Intensive distribution* is an attempt to reach the mass market, and it requires a broad-based channel structure. *Selective distribution* refers to distributing the goods through a few so-called elite outlets. *Exclusive distribution* means letting a designated channel undertake distribution on a monopoly basis.

Objectives should not only designate the target customers but also specify the type of service to be rendered to each group of customers. For example, the acceptable time lag between the receipt of an order and delivery of goods should be clearly defined. Similarly, an OEM should state not only the types of services the company intends to make available but also with what frequency.

Establishing Feasible Channel Alternatives The characteristics of customers, product, intermediaries, competitors, marketing environment, and company's strengths and weaknesses determine the various possible alternatives for the distribution of a line of products.[21] If the number of customers is large or geographically widespread rather than concentrated, and if they make their purchases in smaller quantities at frequent intervals, the company will have to opt for intensive distribution, that is, a large number of channel outlets. Another factor to be considered here is the desire of the customer to deal with a particular type of channel. For example, the customer in a country may dislike the idea of buying groceries from large supermarkets. In other words, a customer's susceptibility to different selling methods is an important factor to be considered.

A variety of product characteristics have an effect on the selection of channels of distribution. Perishable goods require direct channels. Bulky but inexpensive products can use long channels. Shorter channels are employed when the unit value of a product is high, as in the case of computers or when the product has to be custom-made, like air-conditioning equipment for a large building. Proximity to the customer helps in cutting down costs as well as in rendering good service. Also, products requiring installation and regular maintenance call for shorter channels of distribution. Most capital equipment falls into this category.

The kinds of channels available constrain channel selection. The company should consider the terms demanded by different channel constituents and evaluate them in comparison with services and benefits provided, including factors such as channel location, credit granted, quality of the sales force, warehousing facilities, reputation in the market, outlay on advertising, and overall experience. Consideration must also be given to the demands of the intermediaries from the company (i.e., what the channels expect from suppliers in such matters as decision-making authority, services, and financial assistance). Depending on other factors such as customer and product characteristics, the company will choose those channels that make the maximum impact in the market at minimum cost.

Host country trade practices concerning the distribution of a particular product is another influential variable. For example, innovations may not be easily accepted in all countries. Even today, many Swiss homemakers prefer buying groceries from mom-and-pop-type outlets. Over 80 percent of U.K. retail sales are still conducted in towns, despite a crusade by food superstores, mall developers, and other big retailers who want to locate outside downtown. In the U.S., only 4 percent of the retail market is still in downtown.[22]

The environment of the host country constitutes another variable to weigh in making a channel selection decision. For example, the economic structure affects the suitability of a particular channel. In free economies, it is common practice to use private agents or distributors who buy and resell at a markup. Most agents or distributors function as parts of local companies that deal in a large number of product lines ranging from candy to sophisticated machine tools. In state-controlled markets, like those of Jordan and Syria, international marketers must do business with state-owned trading companies operating on very low margins that cover physical distribution costs but usually no other necessary marketing activities. In such countries, international marketers often retain the services of private agencies to promote their products to the final consumers. Poor economic conditions may not justify committing the company to excessive fixed costs, and thus distribution through wholesalers may be deemed the best alternative. A depressed economy may also demand cutting down on nonessential services.

The final factor in evaluating channel alternatives is the company's own strengths and weaknesses in the overseas market. A well-known company of long standing in the market will tap channels more easily than the new entrant. A financially strong company need not necessarily opt for channels that absorb a part of the distribution costs of inventory, transportation, advertising, or training. Similarly, a company with a large number of products for the same market could deal directly with the customers.

All these factors serve as a basis for determining the feasible alternative channels of distribution. Generally, the company would have three channel alternatives: selling direct to the customers, selling through intermediaries based in the U.S., and selling through foreign distributors. In practice, however, channels in international marketing can be a labyrinth of complicated relationships. For example, the company might sell directly in some countries while employing U.S.–based distributors in another country and utilizing overseas distributors in still other cases.

Evaluation of Alternative Channels Each channel alternative should be evaluated on the basis of three factors: coverage, control, and cost. *Coverage* refers to both qualitative and quantitative coverage of customers and is determined by an analysis of customers, including such factors as their geographic locations, sales potential, and service requirements. Usually customers are grouped into homogeneous categories. Each channel alternative can then be evaluated for different customer segments according to geographic coverage, coverage of big accounts, meeting the needs of different segments, and the like. If deemed necessary, different weights can be assigned to these factors. Often, it will be found that no one channel provides optimum coverage for each segment. Thus, to cater to different segments, the company may be obliged to choose more than one channel.[23]

Control refers to the discretion that the company has, or wants to have, in seeing the goods through to the customers. Dealing with some intermediate agents leaves the company in better control of various activities such as establishing prices, recommending cooperative advertising, and suggesting inventory level. On the other hand, other intermediaries will demand flexibility in pricing, the right to refuse to enter into cooperative advertising, freedom in deciding how much inventory they would like to carry, and so forth. Going through the agent or distributor usually necessitates sharing control. If a company wants complete control, it must develop company-owned distribution. Direct distribution, however, requires patience and ingenuity (see International Marketing Highlight 14.3).

A third factor in evaluating channel alternatives is *cost*. Direct distribution by the company is usually more costly if the sales base is small, but it gives the company full control over distribution.

In the final analysis, a balance has to be struck between cost, coverage, and control. No one factor can be considered in isolation. Probably a composite index should be utilized to measure each channel. The channel with optimum coverage and control at minimum cost would be the obvious choice.

Choosing the Channels After alternative channels have been evaluated, the one most appropriate to the stated objective should be chosen. Unfortunately, it is often difficult to state the objective in concrete terms for clear matching with alternatives. Thus, subjective judgment becomes important in the final decision. Management should not only consider the implications of the short run, but also allow sufficient flexibility to meet changing requirements. Sometimes a channel is chosen as a stopgap arrangement that will allow for a new alternative in the future.

■■■■■■   International Marketing Highlight 14.3   ■■■■■■

"Boutique" Marketing System

Fieldcrest Mills' bed and bath division decided in 1976 to export its "boutique" marketing system to Western Europe and Japan. "It seemed an obvious thing to do," the president explains. "Department stores in those countries were decades behind the United States. They still looked on towels and sheets as mundane products with no fashion pizzazz whatever. And just like our stores decades ago, they were selling unattractive products at virtually no profit, sort of like a public service to customers."

The firm embarked on a campaign to convince department stores in Europe and Japan that they could, like their U.S. counterparts, make money by selling high-fashion (that is, high markup) towels and sheets. At first there was considerable resistance to Fieldcrest's selling efforts. The owner of a Stuttgart department store flatly rejected the offer of a written guarantee that installation of a Fieldcrest boutique would double the profits generated on that floor space within two years.

But Fieldcrest eventually succeeded in convincing a number of overseas department stores to take a fling. Stores in Hamburg, Munich, London, and Tokyo agreed to install boutiques in especially favorable locations—usually on the main floor near the cosmetics counters, where customer traffic is heavy. Fieldcrest provided the design and even the lighting systems at its own cost. Foreign consumers are now developing a taste for those fashionable U.S. bed and bath products. At London's famed Harrods, the Fieldcrest boutique has become one of the most successful profit centers. As a result of its boutique concept, Fieldcrest's exports jumped in 1980 by a most respectable 58 percent.

Source: Herbert E. Meyer, "How U.S. Textiles Got to Be Winners in the Export Game," *Fortune*, May 5, 1980, p. 261.

Pros and Cons of Using Intermediaries

Independent intermediaries play a significant role in the total global marketing effort of many companies. Although even some large companies use intermediaries for seeking distribution in smaller foreign markets or for distribution of certain product lines in larger markets, the distribution through intermediaries is especially important for smaller companies, which generally do not have the scale of operations, financial resources, or experience to operate more directly in foreign markets.

The popularity of this mode of distribution has been attributed to the many advantages that intermediaries provide in foreign markets. A distributor brings immediate new assets to the multinational marketer by providing local market know-how, knowledge, and contacts with little expenditure on the part of the exporter. In the case of selling computers in the Middle East, a computer executive noted:

> Although you know more about the product, inevitably the local guy will know more about the market. And make no mistake—market knowledge is more important than product knowledge in getting sales in the Middle East.

Further, the overseas distributor adds to the effective capital available for a company's worldwide marketing efforts, because distributors have funds of their own, as well as local borrowing power that a firm located in another country may not have. What is more, intermediaries afford an opportunity for the stocking and sale of a company's product in a new market at negligible cost. The cost of a company-owned local operation, involving support staff, office space and equipment, overhead, and the like is worthwhile only when a certain volume of business and a certain operating margin are achieved. A distributor may be able to do a good job with a smaller volume by spreading his costs among many lines of products.

The point can be illustrated with this example. A chemical company charges its distributors of textile fibers F.A.S. price less 3 percent. That 3 percent would never cover the costs of maintaining a sales force, local travel expenses, or overhead. But the distributor handles other noncompetitive products—such as textiles machinery—with larger margins. The irregularity of this machinery business is balanced by the steadiness of the fiber sales. Spreading the costs makes it possible for the distributor to carry economically and profitably both lines of goods where neither might be viable separately (see International Marketing Highlight 14.4).

On the other hand, there are some serious disadvantages to using independent distributors. First, the manufacturer has less direct control over an independent distributor than over its own employees. Second, there is a risk of violation of U.S. or EU antitrust laws when a distributor is being directed, particularly in the area of pricing. Third, the manufacturer may have little contact with, or knowledge of, the retail outlets used by the distributor. Fourth, the manufacturer has little or no control over the sales techniques, and credit policies of the distributor. Finally, in some cases, it may be very difficult and costly for the manufacturer to cancel an agreement.

In conclusion, then, a company should use distributors in markets where sales volume would not justify its own distribution or when it does not have the staff and know-how to set up its own operations. A firm may or may not change a satisfactory distributor arrangement when local volume could pay the costs of a company's own operation. In some markets, such a volume may never be reached, but in others when it is reached, the distributor relationship is retained for any of a host of reasons. Alternatively, the company may acquire or just continue to use the distributor as an adjunct to its own operations in the market.

■■■■■■■ International Marketing Highlight 14.4 ■■■■■■■

Schick versus Gillette in Japan

In Japan, a product's success often depends on how widespread the distribution network is. And that is a classic strength of Schick. After entering the market along with Gillette and other foreign makers in 1962, when Japan liberalized the razor market, Schick decided to leave distribution to Seiko Corp. Seiko imports Schick razors from the U.S. and now sells them to 150,000 wholesalers nationwide.

Gillette, meanwhile, flopped when it tried to crack the market on its own and never caught up with Schick. Instead of going through a sole Japanese agent like Seiko, Gillette mainly tried to sell razors through its own salespeople, a strategy that failed because Gillette didn't have the distribution network available to Japanese companies—which was crucial. In 1998, Gillette is making another try on its own. It has doubled salespeople in Japan to 40, and for the first time held lavish parties last year for wholesalers.

Selecting Intermediaries   Finding reliable distributors is a major challenge for firms entering markets in other countries. There are a number of potential sources of overseas distributors ranging from local trade and banking houses to chambers of commerce, officials of foreign embassies in the U.S., and various state departments of commerce plus the federal department. Of all of these, the U.S. Department of Commerce provides the most thorough information. It offers several aids to assist U.S. exporters, which are described in Chapter 17. One important service, titled Agent/Distributor Service (A/DS), is designed exclusively to help U.S. firms identify suitable representatives abroad for a fee. Exporters can obtain the names of agents or distributors abroad who have indicated an interest in handling specific products from the U.S. from this service.

The following four criteria could be employed to identify suitable intermediaries: financial strength, good connections, the number and kinds of other companies represented, and the quality of local personnel, facilities, and equipment.

Financial Strength Sales in foreign markets take time to mature. Yet, the distributor must invest in personnel and equipment ahead of the actual business activity if the organization is to have an effective beginning. Thus, the prospective distributor must be financially sound and should have the strength and will to take the risks involved. Financial strength involves both credit standing and cash flow position.

Good Connections In a large number of countries, business is conducted on a personal basis. In many cases, the government is deeply involved in business. Thus, for agents and distributors to be effective, they should be well connected both in private and in government circles. They should be regarded as respectable businesspersons by all concerned and follow established traditions and practices.

Other Business Commitments Information should be gathered on other commitments that the potential intermediary is involved in. For example, someone currently dealing in noncompeting goods and enjoying a good reputation for providing service, handling complaints and problems, and carrying inventory might be a viable candidate. Information on performance can be sought from the companies he or she has been representing. In addition to an encouraging reputation, any experience gained through handling complementary goods would be advantageous in representing the firm's products. However, sound business practice prohibits distributors from handling competing lines.

Personnel, Facilities, and Equipment The number and quality of the representative's employees, equipment, and facilities should be examined. After all, the reputation of the foreign firm in the host country depends on the activities and behavior of the people representing it. The people should not only be skilled and qualified in their trade, but also have good public relations. Further, the distributor's facilities and equipment should be adequate, as well as properly located. If certain equipment is lacking, the distributor should be willing to make additions. Often potential representatives are willing to hire more people and purchase additional facilities and equipment, if selected. To ensure that the distributor lives up to such promises, these provisions should be specified in the agreement.

To sum up, the selection of intermediaries is dictated by the following considerations:

- Capability to provide adequate sales coverage.
- Overall positive reputation and image as a company.
- Product compatibility (synergy rather than conflict).
- Pertinent technical know-how at staff level.
- Adequate infrastructure in staff and facilities.

- Proven performance record with client companies.
- Positive attitude toward the company's products.
- Mature outlook regarding the company's inevitable progression in market management.

Channel Control and Performance

Distribution in foreign locales through intermediaries always entails compromise. The compromise involves loss of some control over the company's foreign marketing operations in exchange for relatively low-cost representation. Although some control must be relinquished to intermediaries even in domestic markets, in foreign markets it is more significant because the firm has no permanent presence abroad. A distributor, the only means of accomplishing all the related tasks—selling, servicing, providing market information—often falls short of the manufacturer's expectations. The independent distributor represents an entity separate from the exporter, and their goals may not match exactly. Despite the fact that the exporter/manufacturer lacks full control of foreign distribution, it still wants adequate information. This raises the dilemma of how to encourage high performance by channels that are not a part of the firm's own network.

No matter how one looks at it, companies using independent distributors will have great difficulty in controlling them. It is difficult for the exporter to make sales forecasts, set sales targets, and develop customer-contact plans when there is no access to the distributor's books, sales reports, or other records. Thus, rather than depending on controls to optimize distributor performance, the manufacturer should use motivational methods.

A distributor wants to do the best possible job for each of his manufacturers, but he really cannot. So he concentrates on (1) where he makes the most money and (2) where he has the least aggravation or the greatest personal pull. The following are some thoughts on how the company may build loyalty:

1. Build the distributor with the company; bring her into your picture; discuss future plans as they affect her area with her; seek her advice.
2. Give the distributor an attractive profit margin; try to keep in mind that the company wants to be in business with him for several years; make him want to continue the relationship.
3. Be sure the distributor has credit terms which make her competitive, or more so, in amount and length of payment.
4. Maintain regular correspondence with the distributor, and make sure he can clearly understand the company's viewpoint.
5. Make a point of commenting to the distributor on other, successful distributors in whatever communication the company uses in her area (advertising, publicity, house organs, sales bulletins, and so on).
6. Keep the obvious control to a minimum; as his performance improves, the supervision can be reduced.
7. If financing is needed locally and the company has the ability to help, do so if her situation justifies this.
8. Bring the distributor to the U.S. on occasion and let him see what goes on.
9. Offer a college scholarship to the children of a successful distributor.
10. Establish a recognition system: recognition certificates, cash prizes, trips, and so on.
11. Make available remembrance items: giveaways with the company name—perhaps, if warranted, with the distributor's name too.

An empirical study on the subject notes that the performance of an overseas distributor is affected by such relational factors as formalization, standardization, reciprocity, intensity, and conflict.[24] *Formalization* refers to the extent to which the relationship is agreed upon and made explicit. *Standardization* indicates the extent to which the established roles and trading routines are followed. *Reciprocity* means the extent to which the manufacturer and distributor are *both* involved in decision making, despite the traditional domains of each part. *Intensity* is the level of contact and resource exchange between the parties. Finally, *conflict* refers to the level of tension and disagreement between the two parties. The findings of this study strongly recommend that high performance is associated with certain relational characteristics. High performance requires that the two parties

- Adapt their roles and routines (or make them less standardized).
- Display a commitment to developing business in the market in question (or focus on contact and resource intensity).
- Exhibit lower levels of intercompany tension and disagreement (or conflict).

In addition, the manufacturer should demonstrate (1) a genuine interest in the foreign market and in the overseas distributor, (2) a willingness to adapt his or her ways of doing business to be an effective competitor abroad, and (3) an ability to minimize disagreements with the overseas distributor.[25]

Modification of Channel

Environmental forces, internal or external, may force a company to modify existing channel agreements. A shift in the trade policy or practice of a country, for instance, may render distribution through a state trading organization obsolete. The experience of companies in Europe is relevant here. MNCs in the EU area, in response to the 1992 single internal market program, have been changing their distribution channels from covering only one national market to covering two or more national markets and serving areas reflecting natural rather than national boundaries. Similarly, technological changes in product design may require service calls to customers more frequently than the current channels can manage, and thus require the company to opt for direct distribution.

Ordinarily, a company new to the international market starts distribution through intermediaries. As the company's home managers have little, if any, knowledge of the conditions overseas at this point, they lack the insight necessary to deal with the vagaries of the foreign market. For good reasons, therefore, intermediaries are patronized. With their knowledge of the market, they play an important role in establishing demand for a company's products. Once the company attains a foothold in the market, it may discover that it does not have enough control of distribution to make further headway. At this time, modification becomes essential.

Managerial astuteness requires that the company do a thorough study before deciding to change existing channel arrangements. No matter how long a U.S. company has been engaged in business with other countries, there are customs and conditions that may interfere with a non-native firm's establishment of its own distribution system. Hurried measures could create insurmountable problems, resulting in loose control and poor communications.

The affected intermediary agents should be taken into the company's confidence about future plans and compensated for any breach in terms. Any modification of channels should tally with the total marketing system. Therefore, the effect of a modified plan on various ingredients in the marketing mix, such as pricing, promotion, and so on, must be assessed. The managers in different departments (as well as the customers) should be informed so that the change does not come as a surprise. In other words, care must be taken to ensure that a modification in channel arrangements causes no distortion in the overall distribution system.

Wholesaling in Foreign Environments

An international marketer interested in overseas distribution must acquire complete knowledge of the existing wholesale and retail patterns of the host country. Such knowledge is essential to determine what sort of distribution is feasible; what economic, social, and cultural factors influence the distribution structure of the country; and what legal and political requirements must be followed. The following two sections examine different aspects of wholesaling and retailing in foreign markets.

Overall, wholesalers worldwide perform such functions as purchasing, selling, transportation, storage, financing, information gathering, production planning, risk management, and even management consulting. However, in certain countries, some of the functions are reserved for manufacturers or retailers, or both. In other words, functions performed by wholesalers vary from country to country. Exhibit 14.4 provides statistical information on wholesaling in foreign markets.

Status and Role of Wholesalers

The status and role of wholesalers vary from country to country. In developing countries, wholesalers play a crucial role by handling imports as well as products of small, domestic manufacturers and by financing the flow of goods between the producers and retailers. Despite their importance in many developing countries, wholesalers are held in low esteem for two reasons. First, the major economic emphasis in developing countries is on production since goods are scarce in virtually all sectors. Second, wholesale trade, like retail, in many countries is dominated by foreigners. The local population, therefore, looks down upon wholesalers, considering them to be getting rich by exploiting consumers. For example, in many African countries like Kenya and Sierra Leone, people of the Indian subcontinent control the trading sector of the economy. About 75 percent of Kenya's retail

EXHIBIT 14.4   Wholesaling in Selected Countries

Country	Number of Wholesaler	Number of Wholesale Employees	Employees per Wholesaler	Retailers per Wholesaler	Population per Wholesaler
United States	416,000	5,355,000	13	5	564
Ireland	3,073	42,100	14	11	1,139
Austria	12,890	148,900	12	3	582
Sweden	27,913	193,900	7	3	145
(The former) Soviet Union	1,000	120,000	120	481	174,922
Belgium	57,079	177,400	3	2	174
United Kingdom	80,104	1,087,000	14	3	698
Israel	4,862	36,900	8	8	782
Japan	429,000	4,091,000	10	4	278
India	116,000	—	—	32	5,612
Turkey	24,592	87,200	4	20	1,923
Chile	561	15,900	28	42	20,856
Brazil	46,000	442,000	10	61	2,820
South Korea	45,568	173,200	4	21	878
Italy	120,366	547,000	5	8	473
Egypt	1,766	42,300	24	1	25,595
Yugoslavia	1,110	138.100	124	70	20,000

Source: United Nations Statistical Yearbook, 1993–1994, pp. 889–890.

and wholesale business even today is controlled by Asians. Similarly, the Chinese have been dominant in the Philippines and Indonesia. And European companies control a large proportion of Hong Kong's and Singapore's trade.

The size of wholesaling operations differs significantly from country to country. In Finland, four wholesaling houses handle the major portions of all trade. One of these four houses, Kesko, controls over 20 percent of the market.[26] On the other hand, Japan is known for its myriad wholesalers linked to each other in a multilevel arrangement.

Services Offered by Wholesalers

Services provided by wholesalers are related to competition. In a country like India, where there are virtually hundreds of wholesalers, the margins are low and the competition is fierce. In such an environment, wholesalers provide a variety of services from financing to inventory maintenance. On the other hand, the large trading companies usually provide a good service mix, but at a substantial cost to the manufacturer or retailer. In most industrialized countries, the merging trend toward vertical integration has squeezed the wholesaler from both sides. The wholesalers, therefore, have tried to streamline by carefully limiting the areas of operation and strictly controlling them. For example, wholesalers continue to be a major factor in Western Europe in food products. Thus, even though Kraft distributes in Germany through company-owned channels, it must provide the wholesalers their commission without receiving any services.[27]

Merchandising Policies

Smaller wholesalers usually limit their business to handling a particular family of goods. Whenever they expand, they venture only into related goods. Large wholesalers, however, deal in different products without any underlying relationship among them. For example, Hamashbir Hamerkazi, a large wholesale group in Israel, handles different kinds of products and has interests in 12 large manufacturing firms.[28]

Margins and Efficiency

The margins and efficiency of wholesalers depend on the services they provide and the competition they face. Where competition is lacking, wholesalers run an inefficient operation. The wholesaling function simply amounts to an intermediate function for the flow of goods; the inefficiency of operations has no relationship to margins. When the business develops into a monopoly and the goods are in short supply, margins are rather high, despite the low level of services (related to credit, storage, shipping, and market research information). Keen competition, however, raises the level of services that wholesalers provide without simultaneous improvement in either the margins or efficiency. In brief, wholesaling worldwide is not marked by efficiency; with poor efficiency and keen competition, the margins are meager.

Retailing in Overseas Markets

Diverse retailing patterns can be observed from country to country, even more than in wholesaling. Retailing in many respects is a localized activity, deeply influenced by prevailing social and cultural norms and government controls. An international marketer should gain as much insight into the retailing practices of the host country as necessary for marketing endeavors.

Worldwide Retailing Patterns

Retailing operations vary widely in size. Some countries have large stores comparable to those in the U.S. In other nations, retailing is a small family business. Harrods of England, Mitsukoshi of Japan, and Au Printemps of France are well known names in retailing. These stores have a large clientele and carry an extensive line of merchandise along the lines of a typical department store in the U.S. For example, Mitsukoshi serves over 100,000 customers every day. Contrast this with retailing in Pakistan and Nigeria, where retailers in a large city number in the thousands and carry one or two lines of goods, serving a very few customers.

The relative size of retail patterns is illustrated in Exhibit 14.5. Relatively speaking, not only is the number of retail stores in the developing countries much greater than in the industrialized nations, but also, by contrast, the number of customers served is low. Even among developed countries, retailing patterns vary significantly. For example, in 1991 the average sales volume per store was $695,000 in the U.S., $532,000 in Great Britain, and $182,500 in Japan.[29]

The level of services that retailers provide to manufacturers varies according to their size. Large retail houses generally carry inventory, render financial help, display and promote merchandise, and furnish market information. Smaller retailers depend entirely on the manufacturer or wholesaler. On their own, they would carry a limited quantity of products (which might lead to out-of-stock items) and would expect the vendor to provide credit. Promotion and merchandise display material would have to be handled by the manufacturer or the wholesaler.

The smaller retailers carry limited lines of goods in limited variety. Usually their operations are run inefficiently, and their margins are low. On the other hand, large-scale operations are able to achieve economies of scale and infuse professionalism into the operations. Their margins are relatively high, but so are their services.

An international marketer would have difficulty dealing directly with smaller retailers. Thus, in nations where retailing is a mom-and-pop business, the wholesaler becomes important. By the same token, new ideas and innovations overseas at the retail level can be successfully introduced only in countries that have large retail houses.

Theory of International Retailing

Any institutional framework in a country is a function of its environment. Evidence suggests that efficiency in distribution channels, and consequently in retailing, depends largely on a country's infrastructure and the level of economic development.[30] In the area of international retailing, this thesis is supported by empirical studies. For example, supermarkets were found to be more common and retail outlets much larger in countries with relatively higher GNPs per capita. Time lags in the development of retailing innovations and improvements appeared similar in length to lags in environmental development.[31]

EXHIBIT 14.5
Retailing in Selected Countries

Country	Retail Outlets (In Thousands)	Population per Outlet	Employees per Outlet
Argentina	787.0	40	3
Canada	134.5	185	9
South Korea	716.8	60	2
Australia	160.2	100	6
India	3,140.0	259	—
Malaysia	148.3	124	9
Mexico	825.0	109	3
Philippines	118.5	531	29
U.S.A.	1,872.5	228	11
Japan	1,821.0	68	3

Sources: International Marketing Data and Statistics, 18th ed. (London: Euromonitor Publications, 1994); and "Indicators of Market Size for 117 Countries," *Crossborder Monitor*, August 31, 1994.

In brief, it can be theorized that the retailing structure (that is, the number of inhabitants per retail establishment and sales per retail establishment) emerges from the environmental characteristics of the country. The environmental determinants of retail structure are personal consumption expenditures per capita, passenger car ownership, and geographical concentration of population.

The theory of retailing propounded here has some implications for multinational marketers. Western capital-intensive mass-market technology clearly is ill-suited to serve low- and middle-income consumers in the Third World. Instead, the traditional labor-intensive food retailer is more suitable for marketing staples to the bulk of the world's population—that is, neither so primitive as to offer no escape from low production and low income, nor so highly sophisticated as to be out of the reach of poor people.

Until recently the transfer of capital-intensive marketing technology was recommended as a solution to Third World problems. The horizontally and vertically integrated systems surrounding institutions known as supermarkets were considered generators of substantial benefits as a result of economies of scale, self-service, and a shortened distribution channel. Supermarkets supposedly help to bypass the public wholesale markets; replace the crowded, old-fashioned, noisy, disorderly, dirty but picturesque food stands in municipal retail bazaars; and do away with street vendors, who cause health and safety hazards in busy downtown areas. In short, the small, limited-line retailers of consumer staples—plus the long, labor-intensive, and haphazardly coordinated distribution chain—have been arrogantly brushed aside as inadequate, inefficient, and irrelevant.

The experience of the past 25 years, however, shows that western marketing technology is too big and too expensive for developing countries. It does not create the jobs needed to absorb the rapidly expanding labor force in these countries, and it is not appropriate for the small firms and businesses that make up the bulk of the economic activity in developing countries.

Global Retailing Trends

Worldwide, various trends are emerging in the retail scene, some limited to advanced nations, extending to developing countries, and still others peculiar to developing countries.

Adoption of U.S. Retailing Innovations Such U.S. retailing innovations as self-service supermarkets, discount houses, and suburban shopping centers gradually are finding their way everywhere (see International Marketing Highlight 14.5). The growth of *discounting* in Germany illustrates the point. Starting with the first discount store in 1953, the number of discounters exceeded 1,000 by 1991. The new discount houses, called *verbraucher markte* (consumer markets), are in some cases larger than a typical discount store in the U.S.

Similarly, discounting has taken off in France, where 1960s supermarkets have evolved into *hypermarkets,* selling not just food but furniture, clothing, and hardware. Their size allows hypermarkets to pass on savings from economics of scale to consumers: cat food costs 2.80 francs at a hypermarket compared with 5.30 francs at a neighborhood shop.

Incidentally, hypermarkets did not succeed in the U.S. Wal-Mart Stores Inc. established four hypermarkets in different cities to penetrate suburban markets, but the company had trouble in running them profitably. Similarly, Kmart Corporation's hypermarket failed to meet expectations.[32]

Discounting is becoming popular in Japan as well. Daiei Inc. has 204 stores that conduct American-style discounting business. Its cut-rate stores are shaking up Japan's protective distribution system, where manufacturers tend to dictate prices to retailers.[33] For example, in a Tokyo department store, a pair of designer jeans costs $63, while in a suburban discount store the same product costs $39. A can of Coors costs 240 yen in a neighborhood liquor store, 178 yen in a supermarket, and 139 yen in a discount store.[34]

Certain American retailing innovations are also finding their way to developing countries. McDonald's, Kentucky Fried Chicken, Pizza Hut, Burger King, Ponderosa, and Wendy's are thriving in many Southeast Asian nations, including China.

International Marketing Highlight 14.5

The Mall, The Merrier

On August 21, 1993, the largest shopping mall in Asia threw open its glass and chrome doors to Bangkok's overeager shoppers. Set by a dusty suburban highway, Seacon Square incorporates all the latest tricks of the mega-mall trade: a vast fountain-filled atrium, a 14-screen cinema complex, an amusement park complete with roller coasters—and miles and miles of shops.

The arrival of Seacon Square is the latest symptom of Asia's retailing revolution. The mall craze is driven by demographics. Residents of Bangkok now earn on average around $4,000 a year. The number of households is growing by a steady 2–3 percent a year. The expanding middle class has more than enough disposable income to make a trip to the mall a feasible alternative to a visit to a pollution-choked park. As Thais find new ways to spend their money, the landscape of Bangkok is rapidly changing. The dowdy shophouses that have lined the city's commercial districts for a century are giving way to mega-malls, out-of-town hypermarkets and 24-hour convenience stores.

Source: The Economist, August 27, 1994, p. 59.

Even mail-order business is catching up.[35] At one time, the mail-order business had a shoddy image in Japan. Only such products as contraceptive devices and aphrodisiacs, which reputable stores refused to sell, were convenient to channel through the mail. With more Japanese women working and with mail-order houses trying hard to improve their image, the mail-order business has begun to boom. Well-known companies have begun selling jewelry, kitchen utensils, fur coats, baby clothes, and even automobiles by mail and electronically. This trend extends to other countries as well[36] (see International Marketing Highlight 14.6.)

The share of business for the large retailers has been increasing as retailing becomes concentrated in fewer hands throughout Western Europe, with the exception of Italy.[37] In Japan large department stores have captured about 10 percent of domestic retail sales. However, their strong market position has been overtaken by so-called *supers,* or general merchandise stores, which handle about 15 percent of retail sales. *Self-service* and *convenience chain stores* have also grown rapidly and together hold another 15 percent of the market.[38]

International Marketing Highlight 14.6

Electronic Shopping Finds Market in India

After a successful three-year campaign to develop the market, Telebrands Corp., Fairfield, NJ, has introduced electronic shopping and marketing to India.

A vast and difficult-to-penetrate marketplace, India presents both opportunities and obstacles for international direct marketers. Telebrands has invested financial and managerial resources to help develop the market, firmly establishing itself in India's industry of direct response to retail marketers. It now is positioned to introduce infomercial and direct response companies into the marketplace.

With a population nearing 1 billion and a booming gross domestic product, India holds an impressive potential for direct marketers. However, trade barriers affecting duties and taxes placed on imports can render foreign products unattractive to local consumers.

To overcome the trade barrier obstacle, Telebrands has built its own manufacturing facility in India, where production and labor costs are low. The generation of jobs also gives the company a favorable status with the government. In addition to the company's manufacturing facilities, Telebrands maintains its own warehouse, telemarketing, and distribution options in Bombay. Telebrands also has developed a close relationship with the post office and customs areas of the government to assure speedy delivery of all parcels within two weeks of order placement.

Through its manufacturing facilities in India, Telebrands produces a number of high-profile products in such categories as licensed eye wear, kitchen equipment, personal hygiene, cosmetics, chemicals, and exercise/fitness.

Numerous U.S.-based infomercial marketers are looking to Telebrands for representation in the emerging market. In addition to the inroads mentioned above, Telebrands maintains media buying and management teams in the country.

Source: Marketing News, September 23, 1996, p. 40.

Internationalization of Retailing The growing interest among large retailers of industrialized countries in expansion overseas is exemplified by Sears, Roebuck & Company venturing into Mexico, South America, and Spain; J.C. Penney Company moving into Mexico and Italy; Safeway entering Great Britain, Germany, and Australia; and Federated Department Stores finding its way into Madrid. Likewise, Avon representatives and Tupperware parties have become common in a number of countries. Since 1984, Toys 'R' Us Company has opened megastores in Canada, Britain, Singapore, Germany, France, Italy, and Japan.[39]

Wal-Mart has made a major commitment to the Canadian market. It acquired 120 Woolco discount department stores from Woolworth and plans to build additional outlets of its own.[40] Wal-Mart has also expanded into Argentina and Brazil.[41]

The internationalization of retailing is not limited to U.S. business. Harrods, Britain's best-known department store, has branched out into Japan. France's Au Printemps department store opened stores in Japan, Singapore, Saudi Arabia, South Korea, and Turkey. In 1987, it opened its first U.S. store in Denver and plans to open many more in the future. Chilean food retailer Santa Isabel has moved into a number of less developed countries, Peru, Paraguay, Ecuador, in the region. Dutch food giant Royal Ahold has been actively buying U.S. supermarket chains. It has become the fourth-largest food retailer in the U.S. after acquiring Giant Food, Stop & Shop, BI-LO, Edwards Super Foods Stores and Tops markets. Ahold derives 60 percent of its annual revenues in the U.S.[42] Exhibit 14.6 lists the world's top retailers.[43]

Internationalization aside, it will be wrong to assume that successful retailers at home can conveniently make it abroad. A number of well-known retailers (Lane Crawford, Hong Kong; Kmart, U.S.; and Galleries Lafayette France) had to shut down their stores in Singapore after running up massive losses. Similarly, Wal-Mart could not survive in Hong Kong.

According to retail analysts, the companies fall into the trap of assuming that a winning formula in one country will automatically work in another.[44] They seem to have presumed that since Kowloon and Arkansas are both home to 2.5 million people, the same products will appeal equally well. However, basketball sets and garden games are not much use to people living in tower blocks in the densely populated Hong Kong.[45]

Social Marketing An interesting trend in the developing countries has been the retailers' entry into *social marketing,* marketing that reinforces government programs. Retailers in

EXHIBIT 14.6
The Retail Elite:
The World's Top
Retailers, by Sales

	Main Type of Trade	Home Country	Sales 1993 $bn	Number of Stores
Wal-Mart	Discount	United States	68.0	2,540
Metro Int.	Diversified	Germany	48.4	2,750
Kmart	Discount	United States	34.6	4,274
Sears, Roebuck	Department	United States	29.6	1,817
Tengelmann	Supermarket	Germany	29.5	6,796
Rewe Zentrale	Supermarket	Germany	27.2	8,497
Ito-Yokado	Diversified	Japan	26.0	12,462
Daiei	Diversified	Japan	22.6	5,920
Kroger	Supermarket	United States	22.4	2,208
Carrefour	Hypermarket	France	21.7	647
Leclerc, Centres	Hypermarket	France	21.1	524
Aldi	Supermarket	Germany	20.9	3,435
Intermarché	Supermarket	France	20.7	2,890
J.C. Penney	Department	United States	19.6	1,766
Dayton Hudson	Discount	United States	19.2	893
American Stores	Supermarket	United States	18.8	1,695
Edeka Zentrale	Supermarket	Germany	17.9	11,670
Promodès	Hypermarket	France	16.0	4,676
J. Sainsbury	Supermarket	Britain	15.9	514
Jusco	Diversified	Japan	15.8	2,452
Price/Costco	Warehouse club	United States	15.5	200
Safeway	Supermarket	Unites States	15.2	1,078
Koninklijke Ahold	Supermarket	Holland	14.6	2,152
Otto Versand	Mail Order	Germany	14.4	n.a.
Tesco	Supermarket	Britain	12.9	430

Source: Management Horizons, 1995

Kenya, Jamaica, and India willingly display and sell contraceptives to support their governments' efforts to popularize family planning. This shows the awareness of even small businesses and retailers in developing countries toward the need for social programs and their willingness to participate. It seems that the primitive distribution networks in developing counties can be counted on for delivery of medically and socially oriented products, ideas, and services. In other words, psychologically, physically, and economically, the retailers are accessible for distribution of such products as health-related foods, over-the-counter medicines, and nutrition and hygiene information, even though each of them may run a small, inefficient operation.

Cooperative Retailing The emergence of consumer retail cooperatives is another trend that deserves mention. Traditionally, consumer cooperatives have been popular in Europe. For example, consumer cooperatives control almost one-fourth of food sales in Switzerland. Presumably, the two largest Swiss cooperatives have over one-third of Swiss households as members. In Japan, consumers' cooperative union stores, which are non-profit institutions, are fast emerging as a viable force in food retailing.[46]

The cooperative movement at the retail level, however, is spreading much faster in the developing countries of Asia and Africa. In many countries (for example, Mexico and India), government-sponsored cooperative societies have been formed to undertake distribution of essential products. The presence of the cooperatives reduces the volume of trade handled by private retailers and increases the government's control over trade. Interestingly, cooperatives do not succeed in many nations because, in an economy of scarcity, cooperatives are often out of stock of the most-needed goods and products. This situation forces consumers to depend on private sources for their crucial purchases, even though it means paying a higher price.

International Franchising

Expansion into international markets represents a major growth opportunity for domestic franchise operations. This section focuses on the entry motivations, ownership practices, marketing strategies, and problems associated with U.S. franchise operations abroad.

The term **franchising** has many connotations; therefore, its meaning must be delineated in the context of private enterprise, where it refers to a form of marketing or distribution in which a parent company customarily grants an individual or relatively small company the right or privilege to do business (for a consideration from the franchisee) in a prescribed manner over a certain period of time in a specified place. An important aspect of a franchise arrangement is the continuing relationship between the parties. The current growth of the franchise industry is of recent origin and is strictly an American phenomenon.

Perspectives of International Franchising

Companies are primarily motivated by three factors in the expansion of their franchising operations internationally: market-growth opportunities, profit potential, and the desire to be known as an international firm. Companies usually initiate franchising in other countries on a limited scale—one or two countries with a few outlets in key locations. Initial success then leads to further expansion.

As with the international expansion of U.S. business in general, foreign franchising operations usually start with Canada, Western Europe, and Japan. Canada has the largest number of U.S. franchise operations, followed by England and Japan.[47] In Australia, U.S. fast-food chains—McDonald's, KFC, and Pizza Hut—and the convenience store chain 7-Eleven are included within the top 25 retailers.[48] Fast foods and business services account for over 50 percent of international franchising operations of U.S. firms. In 1987, 354 U.S. franchisers operated 32,000 outlets in foreign countries, and their gross sales amounted to almost $6 billion.[49]

Marketing Strategy

Firms entering overseas markets by establishing franchising operations must determine if they will follow a standardized or differentiated strategy with reference to product, price, and promotion. Most firms follow a standardized approach, particularly the soft drink and business services organizations. However, some fast-food companies have made adaptations in their overseas operations in response to particular cultural habits and customs of different nations. For example, in Japan Denny's serves ginger pork, curried rice, and dishes flavored with soy sauce. McDonald's offers tomato and beet-root in Austria; in France it serves wine with meals. Dairy Queen is attempting to penetrate the Middle East market by adding *roti*, a type of bread, and a fried vegetable and meat dish to the fare.

Similarly, price is duly adjusted to local competition. Promotion also varies, depending on media availability. For example, television in some foreign markets is a much less popular means of promotion than radio.

Future Trends

For numerous reasons, the international franchising operations of U.S. corporations should grow at a fast pace in the twenty-first century. First, as the people in Western Europe and Japan move away from downtown areas into suburbs, and as more and more women start working, the fast-food industry should prosper. Second, there has been a gradual break in the tradition of going home for lunch in France, Germany, England, and the Scandinavian countries. This change is attributed to tightening of working hours, forced by the need to increase productivity. Third, the rise in discretionary income in Europe and Japan has enhanced the need for convenience foods. For example, companies like McDonald's and Kentucky Fried Chicken are showing annual sales increases of 50 percent a year.

Fourth, franchising permits a substantial involvement of the local entrepreneur (for example, in the franchisee-owned ownership arrangement) right from the beginning. This arrangement makes entry into the country easier. Fifth, even among developing countries, franchising has a great potential because it permits mass distribution, involves native businesspersons, and offers a standard product or service at a price trimmed by economies of scale. In conclusion, the future of franchising operations in the international markets appears promising, and more and more companies may seek foreign market entry through franchising.

International Physical Distribution

International *physical distribution (PD)* encompasses the logistics, or movements, of goods across countries from the sources of supply to the centers of demand. In other words, it is concerned with getting the right product to the right place at the right time, in good condition and at reasonable cost. Warehousing, transportation, and inventory are the major components of physical distribution. The final purpose of physical distribution activity is to provide adequate service to the customer. For satisfactory performance of this function, the various components of PD should be properly integrated for worldwide distribution.

Importance of International Physical Distribution

The importance of international PD is illustrated by Japan. Two large metropolitan areas in Japan, Tokyo and Osaka, consume approximately 85 percent of all gasoline sold in Japan. The PD system for a particular oil company serving Japan is made up of four different levels of intermediary agents—a national wholesaler, a regional wholesaler, a local wholesaler, and a retailer. The gasoline is physically delivered to the national wholesaler, who then has it delivered to the regional one, then on to the local one, and finally the retailer.

There is nothing odd about this PD system until one stops to consider that all channel members are located within the same metropolitan area. It would be considerably more convenient and far cheaper to ship the gasoline directly from the oil company's tanks to the retailer. However, the cultural environment in Japan demands this unwieldy PD. As explained earlier, all the middlemen provide needed employment, so it would be unfeasible to streamline the system. Nevertheless, the example serves to indicate that, by evaluating and implementing an alternative system, the delivery cost of the gasoline could be lowered. One American manufacturer trying to penetrate the Japanese consumer goods market satisfied the cultural requirements by routing the paperwork through various levels of appropriately compensated intermediaries while distributing the product itself directly.

Distribution is a marketing area that management might have a tendency to view as a so-called *cost sink* without realizing that considerable savings can be achieved by proper analysis and revision.

Management of International Physical Distribution

The three important aspects of physical distribution are warehousing, transportation, and inventory management. The basic decisions to be made concerning *warehousing* are how many warehouses of what size a company needs (if any at all) and in which country they should be located. Information is needed on where the firm's customers, both current and potential, are geographically located around the world; what is the pattern of their current demand; what demand pattern is likely to emerge in the future; and what level of customer service should be followed. The last item refers to the number of days within which the customer order would be filled. Often customers are categorized based on their importance to the company. The service level is varied in different categories. All this information needs to be analyzed before making the warehousing decision is made.

The *transportation* decision mainly involves the choice of a mode of transportation for shipping the goods both internationally and locally within a foreign nation. This decision is affected by such factors as the availability of transportation, nature of product, size of shipment, distance to be traveled, type of demand (routine versus urgent demand), and cost of different shipping alternatives.

Inventory management deals with stocking inventory to fill customer orders. It involves two decisions—how often to order in a given period and how much to order. The costs involved with these decisions are inversely related. For example, if too many orders are placed in a year, the ordering costs go up. On the other hand, if large quantities are bought at a time, the total number of orders is reduced and hence the total ordering cost, but the costs of carrying large purchases goes up. Thus, an optimum point must be found for the number of orders and the size of each order. This optimum can be figured by using different forms of informational inputs and an appropriate mathematical formula (information beyond the scope of this book.)

So far the three aspects of physical distribution have been discussed separately, but for an integrated decision on international physical distribution, they must be considered simultaneously. Such an evaluation amounts to considering PD as a system with three components: warehousing, transportation, and inventory management.

The logic of applying a systems approach to PD is based on the fact that the costs involved in administering warehousing, transportation, and inventory functions are interrelated. For this reason, they must be considered simultaneously for effective decision making. Suppose the number of warehouses is increased. Transportation costs will decrease in that event, but inventory costs will increase, because—inventory will have to be duplicated at more places. Or suppose an attempt is made to decrease inventory costs by cutting down inventory levels. In that event, transportation costs will go up. Obviously, an optimum decision mandates that all relevant costs be considered in an integrated fashion and in relation to the desired service level.

International Physical Distribution: An Example

Illustrated here are the highlights of Eastman Kodak Company's international physical distribution arrangements as an example of how a large MNC moves goods internationally. For Kodak, proper distribution means getting the right product to the right place at the right time, in good condition, and at a reasonable cost. To achieve this, Kodak developed a highly integrated worldwide distribution system.

International Organization Sophistication, coordination, and cooperation are required in order for Kodak to provide a wide range of products manufactured in both the U.S. and foreign factories to all of its corporate installations around the world. The center of Kodak's organization in this important area is the International Distribution Operations Committee. The committee provides a focal point for the Distribution Division's interface with the International Photographic Division and also develops and evaluates new ideas in the export area.

Inventory Management Kodak's inventory management system consists of two subsystems. The automatic replenishment subsystem determines the timing and amount of an order to be placed with one of the manufacturing companies. If stock is below a predetermined reorder point, the system prepares a replenishment order that is reviewed by the local planning department, thereby eliminating the time the stock planner usually spends in clerical review of the product line and leaving more time for true planning. In addition, the system automatically establishes control points used in the reorder cycle, which is the second part of the inventory management process. This system provides each of Kodak's computerized foreign facilities with an effective and efficient means of maintaining properly balanced inventories.

The results of the dual process are replenishment orders sent to Kodak manufacturing plants from one location to another. Transmission of computerized information is relayed over telephone lines in Northern Europe among six nonmanufacturing companies. One large computer in Sweden services smaller computer systems in Denmark, Norway, Finland, Belgium, the Netherlands, Mexico, Singapore, Brazil, Japan, and Spain. Each night, replenishment orders from these 10 Kodak companies are transmitted from Sweden to New York and then to Rochester. By reducing lead time, inventories at the ordering locations can also be reduced. In attempting to maintain a proper worldwide balance of inventories, the main considerations are efficiency, accuracy, and timing.

Shipping Kodak's General Transportation group coordinates product movement from Rochester to foreign markets. Kodak's goods are shipped to New York City by truck and then by either ocean or air freight. In-transit time accounts for the majority of time between the issuance and receipt of an order by a foreign company. Therefore, the General Transportation group must try to make this time as short as practical, and the product as safe as possible, during the in-transit time interval. Also, it must schedule the timing and method of shipment so that Kodak gets the best possible rates for the service it uses.

Warehousing Kodak's international distribution system is based on the assumption that the supplying factory has sufficient inventory in its distribution center to fill the order. This is the most important link in the entire chain of events. Along with its marketing and manufacturing divisions, Kodak's Distribution Division is responsible for ensuring that the factory distribution centers will have the product when it is needed. To accomplish that goal, Rochester must maintain close contact with the international marketplace to see that sales requirements for the foreign market are properly incorporated into the marketing, distributing, and manufacturing chain of events.

This function is performed by International Estimating, and an international information system has been developed to aid them in the task. This information system consists of three parts. First, weekly information is provided to International Estimating for a select number of key items. Second, monthly stock and product sales data are generated in card format from each of the international companies to the supplying factory. The final portion of the system operates on a quarterly basis and is involved with medium-term forecasting. The last step helps International Estimating establish sales estimates to present to marketing as the first step in the production scheduling process.

Summary

Once opportunities in other countries have been determined, arrangements must be made to get the product to the market. Essentially, a company has two options concerning foreign distribution: establish company-owned channels or deal with different types of intermediaries. Initially most companies use an existing system of distribution rather than attempting to build their own channels.

An important consideration in channel selection for overseas distribution is the availability of appropriate channels. Theory has it that the channel structures of a country reflect the stage of its economic development. According to this concept, channels of distribution in developed countries would be similar to those in the U.S., while in developing countries channels would be fragmented, smaller in operation, and inefficient. Unfortunately, the limited research that exists on the subject fails to support this theory. Presumably, the contradiction occurs because the channel structure of a country is more complex than has previously been suggested. For example, Japan is an advanced country, yet the Japanese channels of distribution are labeled by some as outmoded, complex, cumbersome, and inefficient.

Different types of intermediaries are active in the field of international distribution. Essentially, they can be categorized either as domestic agents and merchant intermediaries who provide channels of indirect distribution, or as foreign agents and merchant intermediaries who make it feasible to distribute directly. An essential difference between agents and merchant intermediaries is that the agents do not take title to the goods and operate only on behalf of their principals. The merchant intermediaries take title to the goods and conduct business on their own.

An international marketer should select appropriate channels and make them work. The selection process includes the establishment of channel objectives, feasible alternatives, and the choice of appropriate channels.

Once the distribution channel is determined, reliable foreign distributors must be found. The U.S. Department of Commerce provides different forms of services in this area. The actual selection of an intermediary is based on criteria such as the candidates' financial strength, their connections, the number and kind of other companies they represent, and the quality of their local personnel, facilities, and equipment.

Overall, independent intermediaries play a crucial role in international marketing. Their knowledge of the market and of the relevant business customs and practices adds to the strength of the manufacturer or exporter. They are especially important for smaller companies. Even some large companies with particular products prefer distributors over company-owned channels.

Use of intermediaries necessitates that manufacturers relinquish part of the control of the channel. It is important, therefore, for the manufacturer to design and implement an appropriate program to motivate channel members for effective performance.

An international marketer should gain knowledge of the host country's wholesale and retail patterns. Such knowledge will provide insights into the social, economic, political, and cultural factors that will affect distribution. Wide variations exist in the wholesaling and retailing characteristics of developed and developing countries. Even among the advanced countries, channels differ significantly.

A discussion on physical distribution concludes the chapter. Physical distribution concerns the flow of goods from the manufacturer to the customer. Essentially, there are three aspects of physical distribution—warehousing, transportation, and inventory management—and they are related to each other. For an optimum decision, they should be considered as a system. Physical distribution is one area where cost savings through efficiency are feasible provided the decision is systematically made.

Review Questions

1. What accounts for the differences in available channels in developed and developing countries?
2. Describe the distinguishing characteristics of Japanese distribution channels.
3. Discuss the role played by an export management company in international distribution.
4. Why do MNCs undertake distribution for other multinationals? What are the pros and cons of such piggybacking?
5. Discuss the importance of trading companies in foreign trade. Why are there no U.S. trading companies comparable in size and scope to the Japanese trading companies?
6. What criteria should an international marketer adopt in channel selection?
7. What factors weigh heavily with international firms in the selection of particular distributors/dealers?
8. What steps can a firm take to motivate the channel members to perform effectively?

Creative Questions

1. Gradually, U.S. retailing innovations are being adopted in other nations. Even some U.S. retailers like J.C. Penney, Toys 'R' Us, and Sears have selectively gone overseas. Yet, we don't find U.S. department stores venturing into foreign markets. What rationale do they have for not seeking overseas expansion? What conditions might attract them to operate stores outside the U.S.?
2. Trading companies have played a key role in helping small Japanese companies to export. In the U.S., although small companies are being encouraged to export, the trading company distribution route has been neglected. Why have trading companies not been considered important in the U.S.? Are there any cultural reasons that prevent us from preferring trading companies for distribution in export markets?

Endnotes

1. George Wadinambiaratchi, "Channels of Distribution in Developing Economies," *The Business Quarterly,* Winter 1965. *Also see* Leon V. Hirsch, *Marketing in an Underdeveloped Economy: The North Indian Sugar Industry* (Englewood Cliffs, NJ: Prentice-Hall, 1962); and George Wadinambiaratchi, "Theories of Retail Development," *Social and Economic Studies* (a publication of the University of West Indies), December 1972, pp. 391–403.

2. Susan P. Douglas, "Patterns and Parallels of Marketing Structures in Several Countries," *MSU Business Topics,* Spring 1971, p. 48.

3. L. Joseph Rosenberg, "Cultural Background: Implication 3.and Effects on Japanese Distribution Channels," in Michael G. Harvey and Robert F. Lusch, eds., *Marketing Channels: Domestic and International Perspectives* (Norman, OK: Center for Economic and Management Research, School of Business Administration, The University of Oklahoma, 1982), pp. 52–58. *Also see* Michael R. Czinkota and Jon Woronoff, "Import Channels in the Japanese Market," *International Trade Forum* 1 (1997): 8.

4. *See* Robert E. Weigand, "Japan's Changing Marketing Channels," Working Paper, The University of Illinois at Chicago, 1988.

5. "Selling in Japan Gets Less Befuddling," *Business Week,* February 20, 1989, p. 122D.

6. Damon Darlin, "Papa-Mama Stores in Japan Wield Power to Hold Back Imports," *The Wall Street Journal,* November 14, 1988, p. 1.

7. *The McKinsey Quarterly* 3 (1992): 52–62.

8. "Selling in Japan Gets Less Befuddling," *Business Week,* February 20, 1989, p. 122D.

9. Yumiko Ono, "As Discounting Rises in Japan, People Learn to Hunt for Bargains," *The Wall Street Journal,* December 31, 1992, p. A1.

10. *See* Bruce Seifert, "Export Distribution Channels," *Columbia Journal of World Business,* Summer 1989, pp. 15–22.

11. Donald G. Howard and James M. Maskulka, "Will American Export Trading Companies Replace Traditional Export Management Companies?" *International Marketing Review,* Winter 1988, pp. 41–50.

12. Don Stow, "Export Trading Companies: An Update," *Business America,* January 20, 1994, p. 9.

13. Daniel C. Bello and Nicholas C. Williamson, "The American Export Trading Company: Designing a New International Marketing Institution," *Journal of Marketing*, Fall 1985, pp. 60–69.

14. "Colgate-Palmolive, Kao Join to Create Hair Products Line," *The Asian Wall Street Journal Weekly*, January 24, 1983, p. 22.

15. "Kao Takes Over Sales of Dow Chemical Vinyl Ester in Japan," *The Asian Wall Street Journal Weekly*, October 7, 1985, p. 21.

16. Vern Terpstra and Chow-Ming J. Yu, "Piggybacking a Quick Road to Internationalization," *International Marketing Review* 7, no. 4 (1990): 52–63.

17. "Campbell's Taste of the Japanese Market is MM-MM Good," *Business Week*, March 28, 1988, p. 42.

18. "Japan's Trading Companies: Sprightly Dinosaurs?" *The Economist*, February 11, 1995, p. 55.

19. "Dollar Days for the Cartier Crowd," *Business Week*, August 21, 1995, p. 53.

20. Dale F. Duhan and , Mary Jane Sheffet, "Gray Markets and the Legal Status of Parallel Importation," *Journal of Marketing*, July 1988, p. 75.

21. *See* Bert Rosenbloom and Trina L. Larsen, "International Channels of Distribution and the Role of Comparative Marketing Analysis," *Journal of Global Marketing* 4, no. 4 (1991): 39–54.

22. Dana Milbank, "Guarded by Greenbelts, Europe's Town Centers Thrive," *The Wall Street Journal*, May 3, 1995, p. B1.

23. *See* Saul Klein, "Selection of International Marketing Channels," *Journal of Global Marketing* 4, no. 4 (1991): 21–37.

24. Philip J. Rosson and I. David Ford, "Manufacturer-Overseas Distributor Relations and Export Performance," *Journal of International Business Studies*, Fall 1982, pp. 571–572. *Also see* Gary L. Frazier, James D. Gill, and Sudhir H. Kale, "Dealer Dependence Levels and Reciprocal Actions in a Channel of Distribution in a Developing country," *Journal of Marketing*, January 1989, pp. 50–69.

25. Philip J. Rosson, "Success Factors in Manufacturer-Overseas Distributor Relationships in International Marketing," in Erdener Kaynak, ed., *International Marketing Management* (New York: Praeger Publishers, 1984), pp. 91–107. *Also see* Constance L. Hays, "In Japan, What Price Coca-Cola?" *The New York Times*, January 26, 2000, p. C1.

26. Vern Terpstra, *International Marketing*, 4th ed. (Hinsdale, IL: Dryden Press, 1987), p. 388.

27. Ibid., p. 390.

28. Philip R. Cateora, *International Marketing*, 7th ed. (Homewood, IL: Irwin, 1990), p. 589.

29. *United Nations Statistical Yearbook*, 1993–94.

30. *See* Saeed Samie, "Retailing and Channel Considerations in Developing Countries: A Review and Research Propositions," Working Paper, College of Business Administration, University of South Carolina, 1992.

31. Erdener Kaynak, *Transnational Retailing* (Hawthorne, NY: Walter de Gruyter, Inc., 1988).

32. "Wal-Mart Gets Lost in the Vegetable Aisle," *Business Week*, May 28, 1990, p. 48.

33. "A Retail Rebel Has the Establishment Quaking," *Business Week*, April 1, 1991, p. 39.

34. Yumiko Ono, "As Discounting Rises in Japan, People Learn to Hunt for Bargains," *The Wall Street Journal*, December 31, 1993, p. 1. *Also see* "Bargain Hunters: Retailing in South Korea," *The Economist*, April 26, 1997, p. 65.

35. "Otto the Great Rules in Germany," *Business Week*, January 31, 1994, p. 70.

36. "The Japanese Go on a Mail-Order Shopping Spree," *Business Week*, September 7, 1987, p. 44; and "Next, a Mail-Model," *The Economist*, January 16, 1988, p. 65.

37. Vern Terpstra, *International Marketing*, 4th ed. (Homewood, IL: Irwin, 1987), p. 391. *Also see* Brenda Sternquist, *International Retailing* (New York: Fairchild Publications, 1997).

38. Kaoru Kobayashi, "Marketing in Japan," *Tradepia International*, Winter 1980, pp. 22–23.

39. "Guess Who's Selling Barbies in Japan Now," *Business Week*, December 9, 1991, p. 72; and "Toy Joy," *The Economist*, January 4, 1992, p. 62.

40. *Business Week*, January 31, 1994, p. 38.

41. "Wal-Mart's Not-So-Secret British Weapon," *Business Week*, January 24, 2000, p. 132.

42. "Now, For Its Next Course...," *Business Week*, January 24, 2000, p. 62.

43. Javier Castrillo, Ramon Forn and Rafael Mira, "Hypermarkets May Be Losing Their Appeal for European Consumers," *The Mckinsey Quarterly* 4, (1997): 194-207.

44. "Chilean Chain Moves into Ecuador," *Crossborder Monitor*, January 14, 1998, p. 9.

45. "The Lesson the Locals Learned a Little too Quickly," *The Economist*, September 28, 1996, p. 71.

46. Bradley K. Martin, "Japan's Mom-and-Pop Stores Cooped Up," *The Wall Street Journal*, September 18, 1985, p. 23.

47. *Business America*, May 9, 1988, p. 27.

48. Madhav Kacker, "Australia Retailing Offers Growth for U.S. Marketers," *Marketing News*, April 12, 1993, p. 22.

49. *Business America*, May 9, 1988, p. 27. *Also see* "Franchising Is Still Proving Its Validity as a Marketing Method," *Business America*, March 16, 1987, p. 18.

(continued)

Country	Total	Print	TV	Radio	Cinema	Outdoor Advertising	Direct Transit	Miscellaneous
Italy	5,709.7	2,466.9	2,908.1	91.7	—	243.0	—	—
Japan	38,433.6	11,971.1	11,164.4	1,612.7	—	4,347.7	3,628.7	5,709.0
Kenya	20.5	9.6	3.0	4.0	0.6	1.2	0.2	1.9
Korea, South	2,826.2	1,370.0	845.2	134.7	—	476.3	—	—
Malaysia	321.6	153.5	130.7	5.5	1.1	26.2	—	4.6
Malta	14.6	9.5	4.0	0.2	—	0.6	0.3	—
Mexico	2,199.3	314.4	1,649.1	235.8	—	—	—	—
Netherlands	4,334.6	2,232.4	331.7	59.9	7.1	80.7	1,277.9	344.9
New Zealand	624.5	281.2	210.1	83.6	—	—	—	49.6
Norway	1,233.4	730.9	20.0	8.0	9.6	17.6	447.3	—
Oman	11.9	6.9	5.0	—	—	—	—	—
Pakistan	89.6	39.9	39.2	2.5	0.2	4.6	—	3.2
Panama	54.0	16.0	32.0	3.5	0.5	2.0	—	—
Portugal	415.6	154.9	181.7	32.6	—	46.4	—	—
Qatar	10.7	7.3	3.4	—	—	—	—	—
Saudi Arabia	139.7	89.4	50.3	—	—	—	—	—
Singapore	314.7	200.3	95.4	6.6	1.9	8.3	—	2.2
Spain	10,348.3	4,051.8	2,393.8	784.9	58.9	363.0	1,299.9	1,396.0
Sri Lanka	21.0	12.7	3.8	2.5	0.1	1.9	—	—
Sweden	2,729.3	1,706.8	39.9	—	11.8	78.9	891.9	—
Switzerland	4,098.0	1,895.3	162.7	41.0	22.3	299.5	1,677.2	—
Taiwan	1,569.2	710.4	458.1	84.7	5.5	35.3	44.5	230.7
Trinidad and Tobago	23.4	7.4	0.4	5.2	0.2	0.8	0.4	—
United Arab Emirates	69.4	47.9	21.5	—	—	—	—	—
United Kingdom	15,726.0	9,055.6	4,149.4	200.9	69.6	503.3	1,747.2	—
United States	128,640.0	42,174.0	28,405.0	8,726.0	—	1,084.0	23,370.0	24,881.0
Venezuela	439.2	136.5	285.7	8.5	—	8.5	—	0.2
Zambia	4.1	3.3	0.4	0.2	—	—	—	—
Zimbabwe	26.3	17.9	4.6	3.0	0.5	0.3	—	—

Source: World Advertising Expenditures (New York: Starch, INRA, Hooper and International Advertising Association, 1992), pp. 36–37.

Advertising is a key tool in international marketing. Whereas the rationale for advertising may vary from country to country and among industries within a country, its overall relevance remains beyond question. Like any other tool, of course, advertising can be misused. For this reason, many firms have ethics codes for advertising.

Advertising is important for the following reasons. First, it involves a significant commitment of funds—the cost of effective and ineffective advertising varies little; both are expensive. An effective advertising campaign represents a tangible resource, transferable from one market to another. Obviously, every effort must be made to achieve effective advertising performance and so create a durable asset.

Second, advertising is the sole representative internationally for many companies. If advertising succeeds in establishing and maintaining a desired market image, it can pave the way for expansion. Third, advertising can establish the desired position for a product in a market. Once this position has been achieved, any local disturbances and changes, such as price-related effects, are less significant. Fourth, global advertising requires a certain degree of centralization, which in itself becomes a measure of control over global activities. And finally, advertising provides the most cost-effective method for communicat-

---

CHAPTER • 15

International Advertising

CHAPTER FOCUS

After studying this chapter, you should be able to

■ Compare the pros and cons of using standardized versus localized advertising.

■ Discuss the development and availability of international media.

■ Describe the steps in an international advertising program.

■ Discuss global advertising regulations.

■ Explain the role of advertising agencies internationally.

Promotion is the fourth and final decision about marketing mix. Promotion means communication with the customer. The creation of awareness, interest, desire, and action is the universal aim of the promotion mix. Coordinating promotion with other aspects of a marketing strategy is often quite difficult to achieve in overseas markets. The quality, availability, and scheduling of promotional tools all influence the degree of success realized by a product or service.

Promotion includes advertising, personal selling, sales promotion, and publicity. *Advertising* refers to the corporate-sponsored messages transmitted through the mass media. *Personal selling* involves person-to-person contact with the customer. *Sales promotion* consists of different techniques (for example, samples, trading stamps, point-of-purchase promotion, coupons, contests, gifts, allowances, and displays) that support and complement advertising and personal selling. *Publicity* includes seeking favorable comments on the product or service and/or the firm itself through a write-up or presentation in mass media for which the sponsor is not charged. The focus of this chapter is on advertising. Personal selling and other forms of promotion will be examined in Chapter 16.

There are several important considerations in the design of international advertising and what it communicates. One important strategic consideration is whether to standardize advertising worldwide or to adapt it to match the environment of each country. Another consideration is the availability of media, which varies around the world. The development of advertising programs for foreign markets should take these differences, as well as advertising regulations in international markets, into account. The expertise of international advertising agencies can be valuable.

Perspectives of International Advertising

Worldwide, advertising plays a crucial role. In the case of many products and markets, a successful advertising campaign is the critical factor in achieving sales goals. Indeed, more and more companies are considering successful advertising requisite to profitable international operations.[1]

Global advertising expenditures were estimated to be $335 billion in 1998 and projected to increase to $362 billion by the year 2002. Outside the U.S., advertising expenditures could rise from $195 billion in 1998 to $215 billion by 2002.[2] These are impressive projections.

Marketers abroad are increasingly emulating U.S. advertising practices, which changed significantly around 1960. From that year to 1995, the total amount of money spent for advertising rose from a little less than $12 billion to more than $105 billion, more than a sevenfold increase. During the same period, the economy of the U.S. also increased approximately six times.

Advertising as a percentage of GNP should rise in many countries as their media and marketing practices move increasingly in directions pursued in the U.S. Certainly such is the case in China, where the advertising industry has been growing at a rate of 50 percent a year[3] (see International Marketing Highlight 15.1).

■■■■ International Marketing Highlight 15.1 ■■■■

Television Advertising in Asia

Commercial television in Asia has emerged and expanded, stimulating fresh marketing efforts. Japan, the most mature television advertising market in Asia, has seen its market almost double between 1990 and 1995. Additionally, two of the largest potential consumer markets on the continent, China and India, have opened their doors to commercial television by expanding western programming. General evening viewing in India has climbed to 500 million people by 1995.

Television ad expenditures in Asia do not come close to matching those Europe, but the pace of growth has been more dramatic. Between 1990 and 1 ad expenditures climbed 58.5 percent versus 27.5 percent in Europe.

The signs of change can be discerned in advertising data for selected Asian

- **Japan:** Japanese adore television. They spend an average of four and one-hours a day in front of television and make up the world's largest advertisi market after America—$14.5 billion in 1995.
- **China:** The Chinese ad market quadrupled to $3 billion over 1992–1995 expected to soar to $22 billion early in the next century.
- **India:** India's advertising business is growing at 35 percent a year, amounti $1.2 billion in 1995.

Source: Business Week, October 23, 1995; *The Economist,* July 15, 1995; and *Business Week,* November 18, 199

Exhibit 15.1 summarizes advertising expenditures during 1990 in selected cou As might be expected, advanced countries accounted for a greater proportion of t penditures than developing nations. In fact, it may be postulated that advertising exp tures are significantly related to economic development.

■■■■ EXHIBIT 15.1   Distribution of Advertising Expenditure in 1990: By Media and Selected Countries (in Millions of U.S. Dollars)

Country	Total	Print	TV	Radio	Cinema	Outdoor Advertising	Direct Transit	Miscellaneous
Argentina	829.1	262.3	250.9	72.4	27.7	79.6	58.4	7
Australia	3,548.0	1,869.7	1,057.9	335.2	63.3	221.9	—	—
Austria	1,012.0	566.0	264.7	119.3	—	62.0	—	—
Bahrain	11.0	6.1	4.9	—	—	—	—	—
Belgium	1,223.5	527.4	321.4	21.5	13.8	134.5	204.9	—
Bolivia	64.6	14.0	46.8	2.7	0.5	0.6	—	—
Brazil	3,186.5	1,121.8	1,825.9	153.0	—	63.6	—	22.2
China People's Republic	523.1	159.7	117.4	19.1	0.5	—	126.0	100.4
Colombia	476.4	103.3	283.4	89.7	—	—	—	—
Costa Rica	67.9	26.1	32.7	—	9.1	—	—	—
Cyprus	4.8	1.6	2.2	0.9	—	—	—	0.1
Denmark	1,377.2	897.1	129.3	22.6	12.1	19.6	—	296.5
Dominican Republic	58.5	11.3	37.6	7.4	0.2	1.9	—	0.1
Ecuador	45.8	9.4	27.4	3.9	0.1	0.7	0.4	3.9
Finland	1,800.2	1,167.3	210.3	62.5	1.3	40.8	318.0	—
France	12,891.9	3,627.0	2,523.3	619.8	84.5	1,138.6	—	4,898.7
Germany Federal Republic	13,944.4	8,429.8	1,708.2	550.8	136.2	420.9	2,698.5	—
Greece	526.2	232.8	221.1	35.6	1.3	35.4	—	—
Guatemala	16.3	4.8	10.5	1.0	—	—	—	—
Hong Kong	861.3	363.0	421.9	37.9	11.2	27.3	—	—
India	895.8	599.9	177.1	22.9	4.6	91.4	—	—
Indonesia	286.9	172.2	26.1	53.5	4.1	31.0	—	—
Ireland	321.1	168.8	84.9	35.2	—	22.1	—	10.1
Israel	587.9	415.3	20.0	30.1	4.5	42.0	20.6	55.4

(continued)

ing with potential buyers and creating markets in other countries (see International Marketing Highlight 15.2).

Determining Advertising Strategy: Standardization versus Localization

An important strategic decision for international marketers to make is whether the basics of an advertising campaign developed at home can be transferred to other nations simply by translating them into local languages. Many marketers strongly believe that a successful advertising concept will do well anywhere. Critics of standardization in advertising argue however, that cultural differences require a campaign to be tailored to each country. This section examines the arguments for and against global transferability of advertising and proposes an analytical approach for the formulation of advertising strategy.

Standardized Approach

Many practitioners and scholars believe that universal advertising can work. Often it does. A Swedish executive found that savings bank promotions were successfully transferable all over Scandinavia.[4] Similarly, Fatt supports a standardized approach, believing that "the desire to be beautiful is universal. Such appeals as 'mother and child,' 'freedom from pain,' and 'glow of health,' know no boundaries."[5]

Empirical research on the subject and the experiences of many marketers confirm that such sentiments abound among advertisers. In their study sample of Fortune 500 firms, Donnelly and Ryans discovered that 90 percent of the firms to at least some degree extend their U.S. advertising approach to nondomestic situations.[6]

International Playtex, Inc.'s efforts in developing a standardized campaign for its Wow bra are all the more revealing. The company traditionally ran 43 versions of its ads worldwide, employing different ad agencies in various countries. For Wow, the company assigned the entire global business to Grey Advertising, Inc. The ad theme was based on a single feature: Wow provides the extra support features of underwire bras without using uncomfortable wires. The company used a plastic that took three years to develop. Beyond the basic theme, however, the commercial for each market had to be fine-tuned to meet local requirements. For example, the most noticeable change in the commercial had to be made for South Africa, where television standards don't allow women to be shown modeling bras. In this market, fully clothed models hold up the bra on a hanger, while in other countries the models wear the bras. Further, some commercials had to be 29 seconds long, while others had to be 30 seconds long, because some countries want one second of silence at the beginning of the ad, while others do not. Certain national preferences in taste also had to be observed: the French like lacy bras, while Americans prefer plainer, opaque styles.

Creating a global commercial that meets government regulations and industry standards in different countries requires good logistics. Grey Advertising, for example, showed Playtex foreign managers videotapes of potential models for ads. Three models were selected by consensus from over 50 prospects. Overall, the standardized approach did pay off. The Wow campaign allowed Playtex to present one unified message and save money. Grey was able to produce the Wow ad for a dozen countries for $250,000; the average cost of producing a single U.S. ad had been $100,000.[7]

■■■■■■■■ **International Marketing Highlight 15.2** ■■■■■■■■

International Coffee War

When you think of coffee, what country do you think of? When researchers asked that question in 1959, most U.S. consumers replied, "Brazil." The National Federation of

Coffee Growers of Colombia found to their dismay that the country of Colombia received almost no mention.

Obviously, Colombian coffee growers felt a major awareness campaign was needed. They also wanted U.S. consumers to identify brands with 100 percent Colombian coffee as quality, or "premium." This might sound like an impossible mission. Who, after all, cares which country grows the coffee beans?

The Colombian coffee growers federation accepted the challenge. It developed the slogan, "The Richest Coffee in the World," and the character of Juan Valdez as a spokesperson who taught consumers how to identify brands that contain 100 percent Colombian coffee. The Valdez character also explained the unique properties of Colombia that enabled it to grow the best coffee in the world.

DDB Needham ads established the premium image by featuring upscale settings with discriminating consumers enjoying 100 percent Colombian coffee. For example, one ad featured a businessman sitting in a lush grand parlor in front of a fireplace reading *The Wall Street Journal* and drinking a cup of Colombian coffee. The copy featured only the headline, "50 percent Tax Bracket, 100 percent Colombian coffee," the Juan Valdez logo, and the campaign slogan.

By the mid 1980s, unaided awareness of Colombia as a coffee-producing country reached an all-time high of 96 percent. Additionally, 62 percent of consumers believed that Colombia grows the best coffee. In the great coffee war, Colombia took the offensive away from Brazil. In 1983 only 35 coffee brands featured the Colombia logo. Today, 640 brands are in the program. People are willing to pay 15 percent more for the Colombian coffee compared with the blends.

Source: "The Richest Coffee in the World," DDB Needham Case Study, unpublished document.

Unilever, a British-Dutch consumer goods maker, has a crossborder advertising campaign for the Impulse line of fragrances that serves as another good example of the standardized approach. Impulse was developed as a spray-on perfumed deodorant by Unilever's South African subsidiary. The parent company decided that the line had pan-European potential. Subsequently, a crossborder campaign was based on a simple but powerful advertising idea: When a woman wears Impulse, men cannot help but give her flowers. It did what every campaign, whether national, regional, or global, should do—it tapped into a really provocative consumer insight. It brought together the impulsiveness of the male-female interaction and created an embodiment of that. The earliest campaigns varied because of the way relationships are conducted from country to country. For example, in Italy the boy plucked flowers from a garden, while in France he bought the flowers.[8]

There is an apparent trend toward standardization. A number of companies, including A.T. Cross Pencil company, Deere & Co., and Nike, have been reported as favoring standardization.[9] Proponents of the standardized approach advance various reasons to support their viewpoint. First, there is the cost savings. Once an advertising concept is developed, it can be transferred to other nations with minor additional cost. Second is the realization of economies of scale made possible by the centralization of worldwide advertising authority to the home office. Third, standardization permits full utilization of home office advertising expertise. Fourth, it prevents the generation of disparate messages in different nations that eventually may blur the established image of the product. Fifth, the common approach to advertising ensures proper concern for corporatewide objectives in promoting the product. Finally, similarities in the usage of media among specific segments across nations justify the standardized approach.

For example, Christine D. Urban's study on the subject showed that French and American women belonging to the same socioeconomic groups revealed similar media usage behavior.[10] Culture aside, this means that a particular type of segment in one country exhibits behavior comparable to that of a similar segment in another country. Thus, businesspeople in France may not differ from those in the U.S., Egypt, or Singapore. Presumably, then, a standard advertising strategy can be employed to reach businesspeople in many different countries (see International Marketing Highlight 15.3).

International Marketing Highlight 15.3

Gillette's Panregional Approach

Gillette has organized its advertising plans according to regional and cultural clusters: pan-Latin America, pan–Middle East, pan-Africa, and pan-Atlantic. This is the result of what Gillette calls *convergence,* which is based on the belief that the company can identify the same purchase incentives and needs among consumers in regions or in countries that are linked by culture, consumers' habits, and development of the company's market for products.

For example, Gillette may use the same European-style advertising for Australia, New Zealand, and South Africa. In Asia the company will link the less economically developed countries of Malaysia, Thailand, the Philippines, and Indonesia. It will market Singapore, Hong Kong, and Taiwan together but handle Japan, China, and India separately.

The overall objective of Gillette's panregional strategy, which sells some 800 products in 200 countries, is to approximate a global marketing strategy while remaining sensitive to regional and national differences. Every two years, Gillette conducts research on brand usage of its products and those of competitors in most major markets.

Source: Business International, February 20, 1989, p. 51.

Localized Advertising

Customization of advertising for each nation is justified on the grounds of cultural differences among countries. The international marketing literature is full of examples illustrating how efforts at standardization have backfired. Consider the following example:

A worldwide leader in the toilet goods field built up one of its toothpaste brands to a leadership position in its home market with a promise of decay prevention. Given this success, the same promise was used to introduce the product in Latin American markets. The company was well-established in that part of the world, and together with its advertising agency developed on-site a new advertising campaign to carry the decay-prevention message—an execution tailored to those markets in every detail. At the end of one year of broad-scale advertising and selling effort, the product was withdrawn. It had achieved only a 3 percent share of market instead of the 15 percent achieved in the U.S.

A leading producer of farm equipment was particularly pleased with the success of a North America advertising campaign that was built around the testimonials of small farmers. The manufacturer felt that this campaign combined the traditional virtues of an endorsement by actual users with the added element of those customers to whom economy of use was a vital factor in their purchase decision. For these reasons, the testimonial campaign was introduced into Europe. The advertising vice president was dismayed to receive an urgent Telex from the largest distributor organization demanding that the campaign be withdrawn after only two weeks. The distributor had been flooded with telegrams from his dealers. They all found the campaign to be insulting and described it like this: "Most of our farms in Europe are small to begin with. When you stress 'smallness' so much, our customers think you are talking about peanuts. And who likes advice from them?"[11]

As these examples show, product-related attributes sometimes influence buyer behavior differently around the globe. More examples follow: General Motors' Nova car did not do well in Latin America, because *no va* translated into Spanish means "doesn't go." Emphasis on "whiteness" from a laundry detergent will not work in Brazil, because Brazilians do not wear white clothes. Chileans buy their coffee strictly on the basis of price, but for Germans good coffee is a must for which they will pay any price.[12] Kentucky Fried Chicken is viewed as an ordinary meal in the U.S., while the Japanese consider it to be a treat. A television candy commercial for South Africa with a circus elephant had to be changed since the animal is sacred to the Venda people, the segment to which the ad was directed. Besides, the royal title of the wife of the king of neighboring Swaziland is "she-elephant," and it was feared the ad might offend that country.[13]

Students of West African culture recommend against printing an advertisement on white paper there. In West Africa, white is associated with death and it might be perceived as a death notice. Grammatical errors in copy annoy the French. The macho image of a model wearing a hard hat does not excite Latin Americans. They prefer their macho men in suits suitable for executives. Testimonial advertising is considered "pushy" and "phony" among the Japanese.[14] Gillette, in its efforts to introduce its Trac II razor to Europe, found that products in the toiletries category are geared to cultural traits and lifestyles and thus the U.S. advertising approach would fail abroad. In its attempt to develop localized advertising, the company changed the Trac II name to G II in some nations, since marketing research showed that *trac* in some of the Romance languages meant "fragile." Similarly, the copy design was adapted to match the local perspective. The U.S. copy showed builders constructing a new and unique razor. In Europe a sports analogy made sense, emphasizing synchronization of two moves to score a goal, or the closest shave through G II.[15]

Although product attributes and functions are generally similar in different countries, the perception of these attributes varies from nation to nation. Thus, the common needs of people belonging to different nations do not necessarily mean that the same products will be appreciated in the same ways. Thus, standardized advertising will not always work globally. As Jacob Hornik explains,

> Product [need] universality cannot imply global message appeal. . . . [Israeli and American women] might manifest the same need for cosmetics (i.e., preservation of beauty), but this certainly does not mean that an Israeli woman perceives the American cosmetic ad the same way it is perceived by the American. Therefore, understanding consumer wants, needs, motives, and behavior is a necessary condition to the development of an effective promotional program.[16]

A standardized advertising approach seems particularly unsuited in developing countries, where marked differences in lifestyle, level of wealth, market structure, and various other aspects of the environment exist compared with advanced nations. Amine and Cavusgil, for example, found localized advertising advisable for Morocco, since knowledge of local environment and campaign targeting are essential for effective advertising.[17]

Strategy Selection

The determination of international advertising strategy is not a simple matter of choosing between standardization and localization. Conditions differ from nation to nation. Further, even though one campaign may have been successfully transferred, another campaign might flop in the same country.[18] Yet, when localization appears best, marketers struggle with the desire to enjoy the benefits of standardization.

To decide between standardization and localization, the following procedure is recommended: (1) apply choice criteria, (2) analyze advertising transferability, and (3) make organizational arrangements.

Choice Criteria The extension of the home country advertising program to a host country is affected by the following factors: host country environment, advertising objectives relative to the host country, target market, product characteristics, media availability, and cost-benefit relationship. Although it may not be feasible to combine all these influencing factors into a quantitative model, an international advertiser will find even a qualitative, sequential examination of these criteria helpful.

Environmental Factors A variety of environmental factors affect advertising transferability across national boundaries:

> Rate of economic growth of country.
> Per capita income and distribution of income.
> Average size of household.
> Level of literacy.
> Level of education.
> Vocational training.
> Social class structure.
> Attitudes toward authority.
> Attitudes toward the U.S.
> Degree of nationalism in country.
> Attitudes toward achievement and work.
> Attitudes toward risk taking.
> Attitudes toward wealth and monetary gain.
> Similarity of ethical and moral standards to U.S. standards.
> Availability of time on commercial broadcast media.
> Adequacy of coverage of market by broadcast media.
> Availability of satisfactory outdoor media.
> Availability of satisfactory print media.
> Independence of media from government control.
> Political organization and stability.
> Import/export perspectives.
> Legal restraints on advertising within the country.
> Availability of prototype campaigns.
> Relative importance of visual versus verbal in ad message.
> Experience and competence of personnel in foreign subsidiary and distributor's staff.
> Experience and competence of personnel in foreign agency or branch of U.S. agency.
> Eating patterns and customs.
> Importance of self-service retailing.
> Import duties and quotas in country.
> Development and acceptance of international trademark or trade name.
> Applicability of product's theme or slogan to other markets.

Not all these factors would be relevant in every case. It is desirable, therefore, to diagnose and identify the most salient environmental concerns for a product/market.

For example, factors considered important from the viewpoint of consumer goods companies in developed countries might comprise level of education; level of literacy; attitudes toward risk taking, achievement, work, wealth, and monetary gain; experience and competence of personnel in foreign agency or branch of U.S. agency, foreign subsidiary, or distributor; degree of nationalism in the country and attitudes toward the U.S.; rate of economic growth of country; per capita income and distribution of income; import duties and quotas in the country; development and acceptance of international trademark and trade name; eating patterns and customs; importance of self-service retailing; attitudes toward authority; social structure; applicability of product or slogan to other markets; independence of media from government control; and availability of satisfactory media. Clearly, a different set of factors would be applicable to developing countries. Similarly, relevance of environmental factors would vary based on the type of goods. However, if the overall perspectives of the environmental factors vis-à-vis the host country are similar to those of the U.S., standardization might be feasible. A significant difference in the environment, however, would suggest localized advertising (see International Marketing Highlight 15.4).

Advertising Objectives   Advertising objectives vary from market to market. Advertising does not lead directly to sales. A sale is a multiphased phenomenon, and advertising can be used for transferring the customer from one phase to the next. Advertising attempts to move consumers from unawareness of a product or service—to awareness—to comprehension—to conviction—to action. Presumably, customers in the host country may not be at the same point in the product adoption cycle as those in the home country. If this is so, the advertising objectives of the two markets would differ, and thus the home-country advertising concept might not work in the host country.

For example, a VCR manufacturer's advertising objectives for Mexico would have to be different from those for the U.S.,, because in the U.S. the VCR is in the maturity stage of its product life cycle, while in Mexico it is in its growth stage. In Mexico, the major focus of advertising may be to move the customer from awareness to comprehension, whereas in the U.S. it would be from conviction to action. Thus, the U.S. advertising concept for marketing VCRs would not be effective in Mexico.

Target Market   If the proposed ad campaign for another country is aimed toward a segment that is more or less similar in characteristics to the segment served in the home country, standardized advertising would appear satisfactory. However, if the target segment differs, a localized campaign would be desirable. To make the point, assume there are three target segments:

- *International sophisticates:* a select group of well-to-do and successful people who are mainly in the developed countries and who have international exposure because of travel, education, responsibility and the like.

- *Semisophisticates:* a large group of middle-and high-income individuals who are largely in developed countries and who have substantial discretionary income.

- *Provincials:* people who have a narrow outlook and ethnocentric orientation.

Of the three groups, the first one would be most receptive to standardized advertising. The provincial group can effectively be reached through localized advertising. The semisophisticates may or may not be convinced by the standardized approach, depending on the nature of the product.

■■■■■■   International Marketing Highlight 15.4   ■■■■■■

The Euroteens (and How to Sell to Them)

For years, marketers have been heralding the arrival of the Global Teen, a new breed of youth who share universal tastes in food, fashion, and attitude. However, despite the rise of global media, differences still abound, making life complicated for marketers.

Take Levi Strauss & Co. It sells a key part of the international teen uniform but found that European teens reacted negatively to the gritty urban realism of its U.S. ads, which evoked a side of America that makes them uncomfortable. So Levi's European ads draw on a mythical America. One example: a mini-Western of two girls traveling by covered wagon who stop to watch a young man bathe in a creek wearing nothing but his Levi's.

Marketers say European kids are also starting to look toward Central and Eastern Europe for music and fashion clues. The hottest cities on teens' travel itineraries are not Los Angeles and New York but Berlin, Prague, and Budapest. It's cool to look to America, but there's a deep-seated need and pride for one's own roots and heritage.

Research underscores the difference among kids. Compared with Yanks, European teens enjoy closer relationships with their parents, and—except for Britons—don't watch as much television, according to a 1993 study by Yankelovich Partners Inc. A study by Paris-based Martine Thiesse of Research International found that teens in such recession-wracked countries as Germany, Denmark, and Belgium worry that they'll never match the living standards of their parents. Europe's teens also prefer a more irreverent style of ad. A British spot aimed at 15-year-old boys, for example, urges them to buy the snack food Nik Naks, not because they taste good but because they're revolting. Two cartoon characters in the macabre ads torture one another into misshapen forms.

Source: Business Week, April 11, 1994, p. 84

Product Characteristics The characteristics of a product involved also determine whether standardized advertising would be appropriate. These characteristics include purchase and usage patterns, psychological attributes, (e.g., attitude); and cultural factors associated with the product. The following questions should be raised for each characteristic to determine the appropriate advertising approach.

Product Patterns Is the product or service purchased by relatively the same consumer income group from one country to another? Do the same family members motivate the purchase in all target countries? Do the same family members dictate brand choices in all target countries? Do most consumers expect the product to have the same appearance? Is the purchase rate the same regardless of the country? Are most purchases made at the same kind of retail outlet? Do most consumers spend the same amount of time making the purchase? Do most consumers use the product for the same purpose or purposes? Is the product or service used in different amounts from one target area or country to another? Is the method of preparation the same in all target countries? Is the product or service used along with other products or services?

Psychological Attributes Is brand loyalty the same throughout target countries for the product or service under consideration? Will past advertising strategies conflict with the projected standardized approach? Are the media of the target countries suitable for a common advertising strategy? Are the basic psychological, social, and economic factors motivating the purchase and use of the product or service the same for all target countries? Are the advantages and disadvantages of the product or service in the minds of consumers basically the same from one country to another? Does the symbolic content of the product or service differ from one country to another? Is the cost of purchasing or using the product or service the same, whatever the country? Does the appeal of the product or service for a cosmopolitan market differ, thus crossing national boundaries? Is the brand name equally known and accepted in all target countries? Are customer attitudes toward pricing basically the same?

Cultural Factors Does society restrict the purchase or use of the product or service to a particular sex, age group, religious group, or education level? Is there a stigma attached to the product or service—the brand name, advertising content, or type of artwork in one or more of the target countries? Does usage of the product or service as suggested by advertising interfere with tradition in one country and not the others?

Although it may not be feasible to specify a definite "yes" or "no" answer to all the aforementioned questions, a sense of direction can be gained by considering the questions—the use of standardized advertising or localized advertising.

Media Availability Media availability is another consideration that determines the feasibility of using standardized advertising. For example, a U.S. television ad would not be suitable in India where commercial advertising on television is limited. Because of legal restrictions in France, the International Playtex Company could not use coupons and door-to-door samples as it could in the U.S. for a promotion campaign for its Jhirmack line of hair-care products. The company was therefore obliged to launch in-store demonstrations.[19]

Cost/Benefit Relationship In the final analysis, the choice between the standardized approach and localization should be based on a careful consideration of cost versus benefit. If the cost of local adaptation exceeds the benefit that an adaptation might provide, it is desirable to opt for standardized advertising. On the other hand, it would be reasonable to incur costs, as a form of investment, if the localized advertising could open up new opportunities that might be lost by sticking to the standardized advertising concept.

Transferability Analysis There are two aspects to consider in advertising propositions for international transfer: the buying proposal and the creative presentation. The *buying proposal* refers to the content, not the form, of the advertisement. Its focus is on the most persuasive and most relevant elements of the advertisement. The *creative presentation* assists in transferring the buying proposal into an advertising message, which consists of the headline idea and all the visual and verbal elements of the advertisement.

The difference between the two aspects can be illustrated with reference to toothpaste: the buying proposal would be cosmetic benefits; the creative presentation, cavity prevention. A buying proposal is far easier to transfer across national boundaries than a creative presentation, because certain needs are basic worldwide and customer motivations for such products do not vary much. For example, expectations for a laundry detergent may not differ from nation to nation. Similarly, emphasis on punctuality by an airline would be considered important by businesspersons who fly frequently, regardless of their nationality.

The creative presentation, on the other hand, is difficult to transfer in its original form. The following barriers limit an intact transfer of creative presentation:

- *Cultural barriers:* In most Anglo-Saxon countries, women are accepted without question as family spokespersons, but much less so in Latin America and seldom in Muslim countries.

- *Communication barriers:* Something accepted as funny in one country might be considered silly in another. Exxon's tiger ad, putting a cartoon character in the gas tank, did not make sense to the Swedes.

- *Legislative barriers:* Laws and regulations imposed on the advertising industry differ among nations.

- *Competitive barriers:* Competition for a product varies from one national market to another and sometimes necessitates changes in advertising viewpoint for proper positioning.

- *Implementation barriers:* such barriers might include poor printing and reproduction because of (1) the level of facilities available and (2) the necessity of using local landscapes and models to avoid negative connotations.

It would be naive to expect that a standardized creative presentation could succeed globally. Therefore, appropriate marketing research must be conducted to determine which elements of the creative presentation can be retained, which must be eliminated or replaced, and what should be added. Then, once the creative presentation has been reworked, it should be tested in the prospective market before becoming final.

Organizational Support Whatever strategy is selected, its successful implementation requires appropriate organizational arrangements. If the standardized approach is adopted, the company should establish and adequately staff the international advertising office. For example, Deere & Company has organized its international advertising at a central office at its headquarters that develops yearly several hundred pieces of advertising in as many as 12 languages with the assistance of one advertising agency.

Similarly, if a localized strategy is decided upon, then communication links must be established to coordinate the advertising efforts of far-flung subsidiaries. Such a coordination not only would serve as a control device, but also should be shared with subsidiary advertising people to avoid the necessity of reinventing the wheel, so to speak, for each operation.

In conclusion, it should be noted that no particular strategy is appropriate for all companies at all times. In fact, two companies in the same industry may well pursue different strategies (see International Marketing Highlight 15.5). Some companies adhere to a policy of standardization. This group includes such multinationals as International Playtex Company, British Airways, and Philip Morris, Inc. For example, Philip Morris has used the Marlboro-country concept and has kept the basic Marlboro look in all its ads worldwide. Traditionally, British Airways had decentralized advertising arrangements and its local managers enjoyed a great deal of autonomy. However, the decentralized arrangement led country managers to position British Airways in different markets differently. Therefore, British Airways introduced a widely publicized global advertising campaign to present a common image worldwide. The campaign included the well-known 90-second Manhattan Landing television commercial created by the Saatchi & Saatchi advertising agency, one of the leading proponents of global advertising.[20]

At the other end of the spectrum are those companies that have delegated almost the entire advertising responsibility to locals. Nestlé S.A., for example, utilizes 130 different ad agencies in over 40 countries and has given near autonomy to country managers. There are companies in between the British Airways and Nestlé styles that pursue a patterned approach, establishing basic guidelines for global advertising centrally and leaving development of individual campaigns to locals.

In the final analysis, whatever the advertising strategy, a company must consider local factors. Even products that had been considered sure winners have been hurt by a failure to reckon with local realities. General Food's Maxwell House was dismayed to find that the great American coffee had gained little respect among the Germans. Similarly, Procter & Gamble's Crest fluoride appeal did not mean much to English customers.[21] A recent study of Japanese advertisements, featuring products and services in a home setting showed an emphasis on status rather than personal efficacy, which was more prominent in the U.S. ads[22] (see International Marketing Highlight 15.6). The theory that people are alike and that they have the same generic needs and preferences is continually being disproved in international advertising.

■■■■■■■■■   **International Marketing Highlight 15.5**   ■■■■■■■■■

Nike versus Reebok: Marching to Different Drummers

Nike, the worldwide sports and fitness company, has created a global advertising program and tailored it regionally to local markets. The basic vehicle is the popular "Bo

Knows" commercial that was used in the company's U.S. campaign. In that ad, Bo Jackson, an American professional football and baseball star, was seen taking part in a wide variety of other professional sports, such as tennis and basketball while wearing Nike shoes and apparel. Well-known professional athletes from other sports exclaimed that "Bo knows" their sports as well.

For international use, Nike used Jackson in a similar ad while including athletes whose names were well known in the target countries such as cricket star Ian Botham for ads that ran in the U.K. and soccer star Ian Rush for ads that ran in France, Sweden, Denmark, and Norway. The ads ran in the local European language without subtitles.

In contrast, another leading U.S. athletic shoe producer, Reebok, bases its international ad strategy on addressing the individual needs and national brand identities of each country while remaining under a global umbrella theme. Individual strategies may differ from country to country and are designed to capitalize on international talents and unique country differences, but the common thread of a global brand identity remains consistent.

For the most part, Reebok's foreign advertisements feature actors and athletes famous in each country, who promote the company's shoes in campaigns devised locally. However, U.S. commercials and print ads are often adapted for foreign use. For example, Reebok's new brand image campaign, "It's Time to Play," is in use in France, but with a revised edit that is more in tune with the demographics of that market.

Source: Marketing News, December 4, 1989, p. 10.

Media

The global growth of the advertising industry is directly related to the development and availability of mass media. Mass media are most highly developed in the U.S., followed by Britain, Germany, France, Japan, and Italy. In the less developed countries, where a majority of the world population lives, the mass media are far behind. This is evident in the information contained in Exhibits 15.2 and 15.3.

Exhibit 15.2 shows the number of newspapers (local and regional/national) and magazines (consumer/trade and technical) for selected countries. Although the number of newspapers is one indicator of the media resources of a country, the extent of their circulation also matters. For example, in 1990 Pakistan had as many as 168 local and regional newspapers, but their total circulation was rather small, limited to about 5.3 million (figure not given in the exhibit). On the other hand, that same year, Japan achieved a circulation of over 16.5 million (figure not given in the exhibit) with 79 local and regional newspapers. Thus, in many countries, the lag is not in overall numbers of newspapers published, but in the extent of the circulation.

In some countries, however, poor media development is a factor, as typified by such a large country as South Korea with only 68 newspapers in 1990. In others, such as Mexico, the problem is media inefficiency. In 1990, 317 magazines achieved a circulation of 6 million there. By comparison, Sweden, with 239 magazines, had a circulation of 7 million in 1990 (see International Marketing Highlight 15.7).

Exhibit 15.3 examines the broadcasting media of radio and television. In the U.S. and many other industrialized countries, television constitutes the most important medium for advertising, accounting for anywhere from 15 percent to 27 percent of advertising expenditures.[23] In the developing countries, television is still in its primitive stages. In many poor countries, it cannot be considered a mass medium; even if it is available, commer-cials are more or less prohibited. Overall, though, worldwide demand for television is expanding at

EXHIBIT 15.2
1990 Media
Information:
Newspapers and
Magazines for
Selected Countries

Country	NEWSPAPERS			MAGAZINES		
	Total	Local & Regional	National	Total	Consumer	Trade & Technical
Argentina	255	—	255	850	450	400
Austria	197	164	33	129	59	70
Belgium	17	—	17	64	64	—
Brazil	1,939	1,939	—	45	195	550
China	773	—	773	751	?	?
Colombia	32	30	2	110	52	58
Costa Rica	4	—	4	31	6	25
Cyprus	13	—	13	21	7	14
Dominican Republic	10	1	9	36	34	2
Ecuador	41	37	4	26	20	6
Greece	225	195	30	540	30	510
Guatemala	6	2	4	25	15	10
Hong Kong	43	43	—	613	—	613
Indonesia	109	107	2	109	104	5
Ireland	73	60	13	90	30	60
Israel	147	135	12	—	—	—
Japan	84	79	5	3,889	—	—
Kenya	8	3	5	70	45	45
Korea, South	68	35	33	145	97	48
Malaysia	41	21	20	165	115	50
Malta	8	—	8	26	16	10
Mexico	332	332	10	17	120	197
Netherlands	78	70	8	1,200	—	1,200
New Zealand	133	127	6	500	—	—
Pakistan	180	168	12	1,640	1,630	10
Panama	7	2	5	4	3	1
Portugal	51	15	36	8	54	34
Singapore	14	—	14	3,700	3,700	—
Spain	120	110	10	3,200	200	3,000
Sri Lanka	86	—	86	—	—	—
Sweden	157	152	5	239	30	209
Switzerland	220	220	—	2,050	50	2,000
Taiwan	226	—	226	193	193	—
Trinidad & Tobago	6	—	6	—	—	—
United Kingdom	1,680	1,660	20	6,667	2,373	4,304
United States	1,622	1,620	2	15,350	11,050	4,300
Zambia	9	3	6	3	2	1
Zimbabwe	16	14	2	38	18	20

Source: World Advertising Expenditures (New York: Starch, INRA, Hooper and International Advertising Association, 1992) pp. 48–49.

EXHIBIT 15.3
1987 Media
Information: TV Sets
and Radio Receivers
for Selected Countries

Country	TV SETS		CABLE	RADIO		Cinemas
	Total (Millions)	Per 1,000 Population	Subscribers (Thousands)	Total (Millions)	Per 1,000 Population	
Argentina	9.8	310.7	600	10.4	329.5	511
Australia	7.0	429.8	—	26.2	1,619.3	514
Austria	1.9	252.7	447	—	—	470
Bahrain	—	—	—	—	—	—
Belgium	3.5	355.0	2,950	—	—	371
Bolivia	0.3	36.8	—	0.6	87.6	45
Brazil	27.8	196.8	—	59.5	421.3	1,423
Canada	9.1	351.9	—	—	—	—
Chile	3.2	253.6	80	5.6	446.7	180
China, People's Republic	90.0	84.2	—	300.0	280.7	—
Colombia	5.0	169.5	200	9.0	305.1	—
Costa Rica	0.3	92.3	90	0.4	147.6	35
Cyprus	0.2	243.0	—	0.2	316.6	20
Denmark	2.1	411.4	—	3.8	744.4	315
Dominican Republic	4.9	732.6	100	6.0	893.4	79
Ecuador	—	—	—	—	—	350
El Salvador	0.4	76.4	20	1.2	241.3	30
Finland	2.6	525.6	345	—	—	328
France	—	—	—	—	—	2
Germany, Federal Republic	23.4	384.7	3,800	—	—	3,281
Greece	3.5	349.9	—	—	—	220
Guatemala	0.9	110.8	80	2.5	291.5	50
Hong Kong	1.6	295.9	—	4.8	873.9	110
India	16.0	20.1	10	50.0	62.7	12,400
Indonesia	9.0	53.0	—	—	—	2,115
Ireland	1.0	276.9	320	1.8	498.5	101
Israel	1.0	228.6	—	1.1	251.5	250
Italy	19.0	331.3	—	14.3	248.6	5,500
Jamaica	0.4	170.1	—	1.4	582.7	33
Japan	83.0	679.6	4,935	153.0	1,252.8	2,109
Jordan	—	—	—	—	—	—
Kenya	1.0	45.3	—	4.2	190.1	67
Korea,	9.3	221.2	—	9.8	233.5	676
Kuwait	—	—	—	—	—	—
Lebanon	0.5	181.2	—	0.6	235.5	50
Malaysia	2.0	120.8	—	2.2	132.9	205
Malta	1.2	3,333.3	—	0.2	611.1	14
Mexico	11.9	144.7	152	12.9	157.4	1,000
Morocco	3.0	130.6	—	—	—	250
Netherlands	—	—	—	—	—	—
New Zealand	0.9	282.3	—	3.5	1,046.1	154
Nigeria	5.3	49.2	—	84.0	787.0	147
Norway	—	—	—	—	—	—
Oman	—	—	—	—	—	—

Country	TV SETS		CABLE	RADIO		Cinemas
	Total (Millions)	Per 1,000 Population	Subscribers (Thousands)	Total (Millions)	Per 1,000 Population	
Pakistan	1.5	14.6	—	12.5	122.0	—
Panama	0.2	105.6	3	0.4	155.8	22
Peru	3.1	148.1	—	—	—	—
Philippines	4.1	70.4	25	8.0	137.3	940
Portugal	2.4	237.4	—	—	—	324
Puerto Rico	1.5	448.3	225	1.7	508.1	115
Qatar	—	—	—	—	—	—
Saudi Arabia	—	—	—	—	—	—
Singapore	0.5	206.5	—	0.6	247.1	42
South Africa	—	—	—	—	—	400
Spain	13.0	334.5	—	—	—	2,083
Sri Lanka	0.6	39.7	—	3.0	183.4	200
Sweden	3.3	388.9	—	—	—	1,236
Switzerland	2.3	353.8	1,100	—	—	431
Taiwan	4.3	219.1	—	2.8	145.8	600
Thailand	6.3	117.1	—	8.2	153.2	262
Trinidad & Tobago	0.3	265.8	—	0.4	344.2	20
Turkey	8.5	160.8	—	7.0	132.5	88
United Arab Emirates	—	—	—	—	—	—
United Kingdom	33.0	580.5	—	—	—	1,252
United States	87.4	359.1	39,700	482.3	1,981.7	8,600
Venezuela	3.1	169.7	500	3.2	176.6	436
Zambia	0.2	29.2	—	0.9	127.8	22
Zimbabwe	0.2	21.4	—	0.8	83.3	92

Source: *World Advertising Expenditures* (New York: Starch, INRA, Hooper and International Advertising Association, 1988), pp. 52–53.

a breathtaking pace. By 1995 over 800 million households around the world had television, 56 percent of the total. This statistic is expected to rise to 60 percent or almost 1 billion households, by 2005. [24] Thus, slowly, television should emerge as the dominant media globally. Thanks to the development of transistor technology, radio is also becoming a popular mass medium worldwide.

◼◼◼◼◼◼   International Marketing Highlight 15.6   ◼◼◼◼◼◼

Is Global Branding More Myth Than Reality?

Despite the prominence of some well-known global brands, a recent study indicated that most U.S.–based MNCs do not seriously pursue the ideas of global branding. According to the survey, which examined U.S.–based manufacturers of consumer nondurable goods, "global markets" may be out there, but global brands have not yet captured them. Of 85 brands included in the survey, 29 (or 34 percent) were not marketed outside the U.S. at all, and many of the remaining brands were only minimally marketed abroad (see the following table).

Largest Foreign Markets for U.S. Brands

	Number of Brands for which Listed Country Is Largest Foreign Market	Number of Brands for which Listed Country Is Second-Largest Foreign Market
Canada	33	2
United Kingdom	5	9
Mexico	4	0
Germany	3	5
Japan	2	4
Australia	2	4
France	1	1
Italy	1	2
Nigeria	1	1
Norway	1	0
Missing	3	14
Total	56	42

Companies surveyed showed a clear preference for selling their goods in markets culturally similar to the U.S. market, i.e., Canada and the U.K. (see above table). Although one might argue that Canada was targeted so frequently because of its geographic proximity to the U.S., the choice of the U.K. cannot be so easily explained. It is as far away as many other foreign countries, and its population and economy are smaller than those of several other foreign markets.

Source: Marketing Strategies for Global Growth and Competitiveness (New York: Business International Corp., October 1990), p. 36.

Advertising and Mass Media

Advertising is the principal source of revenue for most commercial mass media throughout the world. Although the dependence of media on advertising revenues is generally considerable, cross-national comparisons show some variations. In the case of most developed countries, including the U.S., television relies heavily on advertising revenues. In those countries where television is subsidized or owned by the government, as in Western European countries, the high costs of transmission require considerable support from commercial advertising. However, in those countries where the television owner pays an annual fee to the government for viewing, as in Italy, Finland, and Sweden, advertising revenues are not so significant.

Newspapers and magazines are not dependent on advertising revenues to the same degree in every country, either. In some countries, the reader pays most of the cost, while in others the advertiser does. The dependence of radio on advertising revenues also varies by country and is lowest in Western Europe.

Throughout the world, a trend toward commercialization of mass media is apparent. In the printed media, this trend is reflected in the substantial increase in the commercial content of newspapers and magazines. In the case of television, the amount of time devoted to advertising is not very significant compared with the proportional amount of space in newspapers and magazines. This is partly because the amount of advertising time allowed on television is regulated in most countries. In Mexico, for example, a maximum of 15 percent of total broadcasting time can be used for advertising, and individual advertisements cannot exceed two and one-half minutes in length.

Nevertheless, worldwide there has been a tendency toward the commercialization of television. In Colombia, where the control of television was originally in the hands of the state, the system was modified to allow for the sale of time to commercial interests. Israel commercialized its system in 1976. Even in Europe, the traditionally strong state-owned systems have shifted one by one to allow some commercial support. Italy has become one of the world's most commercial and competitive television markets. The U.K. opened a commercial channel in 1955, which claims to have taken away more than half of the BBC's viewers. Switzerland, which long held out against television advertising, finally yielded to commercial support. In France and the Netherlands, television became commercial in 1968.

Although in many countries, including Belgium, Denmark, Sweden, and Norway, government broadcasts still carry no television advertising, deregulation is sweeping the television industry in Europe. Guided by free market policies, governments are selling their own stations or letting entrepreneurs into the game. Cable networks covering as many as 18 countries have started broadcasting programs from different countries.[25]

The demand for time to broadcast commercials and increased programming costs have led to a dramatic rise in the cost of television advertising. To begin with, compared to the U.S., media costs are much higher in foreign markets, and as a recent study of nine major global markets shows, the costs are increasing at a rate of 10 percent to 15 percent annually. In part, the increase can be explained by shortages of advertising time. In the U.K., for example, instead of paying fixed rates, companies bid for television time, which escalates the prices. Moreover, stations follow a preempt system. Even though a company has booked a spot at $57,000, another company that is willing to pay more will get it.[26]

Relative Importance of Different Media for Advertising

A comparison of advertising expenditures by media category around the world reveals that print is still the most important: 40 percent of the reported expenditures by 53 countries in 1990 were made in newspapers and magazines. Television is second with 24 percent, and radio is third with 7 percent. The remaining expenditures go to media such as outdoor posters and transit advertising, cinema, direct mail, exhibits, sales promotion, and reference publications.[27]

Of course, patterns and levels of expenditures vary from country to country and from region to region (see Exhibit 15.1). Differences in media expenditures do not always reflect the preferences of advertisers, since in several countries, particularly in Europe, there are restrictions on television and radio advertising. Thus, print advertising is relatively high in Western Europe and Australia and relatively low in Latin America. On the other hand, television advertising is well above average in Latin America and Asia and below average in Western Europe and the Middle East/Africa. The use of television as an advertising medium continues to expand proportionately faster than the use of other media, with the most pronounced increases occurring among the developing countries. Radio advertising is very popular in Latin America, but less so in Western Europe, where commercial radio is even more limited than commercial television.[28] Despite variations among regions and countries, a trend has emerged: advertising expenditures on television are increasing, while expenditures on print and radio advertising are decreasing in relative terms.

▬▬▬ International Marketing Highlight 15.7 ▬▬▬

24,629 Journals—In 92 Languages

Despite the low literacy rate of around 40 percent, perhaps no country matches India in the number of newspapers published in an incredible variety of languages, shapes, sizes, and opinions.

Newspapers and periodicals are published in 92 languages—the 16 main languages recognized by the constitution, 76 others, and a few foreign languages. At the end of 1987 the total of newspapers and magazines was 24,629, of which 2,151 were dailies, 7,501 weeklies, 3,366 biweeklies, 8,123 monthlies, and the rest quarterlies and annuals. In contrast, the U.S. has 1,642 dailies and about 8,000 weeklies.

Although English is the mother tongue of fewer than 250,000 people in India, the overall circulation of the English-language press is second only to that of Hindi. The Hindi press had a total readership of 14 million; English was next with 10 million, followed by Malayalam with 6 million.

Hardly any major urban center in India is without at least two English papers. New Delhi alone has six English dailies, compared to two in Washington and five in London. About 30 percent of newspapers published in the country are concentrated in the four metropolises of Delhi, Bombay, Calcutta, and Madras. Among multiple-edition dailies, *The Indian Express,* published in 11 centers in English, leads, with a circulation of 632,199, followed by another English daily, *The Times of India,* with a circulation of 573,552 in six editions.

Source: India Abroad, August 25, 1989, p. 12.

The growing importance of television advertising is due largely to the continuing increase in the number of television sets throughout the world. For example, China now has about 150 million homes with television. Seven years ago, the figure was 30 million.[29]

Mention must be made of two emerging television media, cable and satellite, which are having significant effects on advertising. Consider Germany. Back in 1990 there were only three television channels—all state-owned. In 1994 there were more than 20 channels on cable, 15 of which were privately owned. Cable is available in more than three-quarters of all households in Germany.[30] In other European countries, the situation is similar.

It is predicted, for example, that by the year 2005, 175 million European families will watch the same cable programs, despite the cultural impediments.[31] The European communications satellite (ECS-1), used by major pan-European television stations in the U.K., Germany, France, Italy, the Netherlands, and the U.S., has a range of coverage beyond the EU, including some parts of Eastern Europe and the former Soviet republics. With the market for satellite television growing, Europe's broadcasting regulators have accepted that national monopolies on television transmissions are no longer defensible. For example, the arrival of pan-European satellite broadcasting has breached the long-standing barrier to television advertising in Sweden. Subsequently the expected that Swedish television went commercial in 2000.

Cable and satellite television are not limited to Europe. The number of cable subscribers is rising by over 20 percent in Latin America. This growth is expected to continue for many years since 90 percent of Latin households have a television (only half have a telephone), but only 16 percent were hooked up to cable.[32] Developing countries are experimenting with satellite broadcasts to reach the masses. India, for example, has launched a satellite to reach people in remote villages, making broadcasts of the same program in different languages. Currently such broadcasts are limited to social programs such as family planning, but may eventually be opened for commercial advertising.

International Advertising Program

The development of an international advertising program depends on the advertising strategy that a company pursues. For the sake of discussion, let us assume that a company has decided to decentralize its advertising and let its overseas subsidiaries play a major role in determining their advertising program. The parent corporation maintains sufficient control through periodic review and approval authority over the final budget. The advertising program essentially includes nine steps:

1. Provision of guidelines by headquarters
2. Definition of advertising goals

3. Preparation of a campaign plan
4. Review and approval of plan
5. Copy development and testing
6. Media planning
7. Budget approval
8. Campaign implementation
9. Measurement of advertising effectiveness

Basically, an advertising program, in both domestic and international advertising, involves decisions concerning the media, the message, and the budget allocation. However, differences in number and types of media in conjunction with cultural and other environmental aspects necessitate tailoring themes, messages, presentations, and illustrations to the target market. As an advertising executive remarked, "It is the advertising environment embracing language, culture, and socioeconomic conditions that changes from one country to another, not the approach taken to plan and to prepare effective advertising campaigns."

Head Office Guidelines

The head office guidelines should include procedural, discretionary, and format guidelines.

Procedural Guidelines These may include what should be done, and when. For example, the guidelines may specify that no commitments be made to the media except with budget approval. Likewise, subsidiaries may be required to prepare a minimum of four different ads and market test them to single out the final copy. Essentially, procedural guidelines are requirements that must be followed. Their purpose is to bring about global consistency in advertising. These guidelines essentially draw upon the parent corporation's past experience.

Discretionary Guidelines These are bits of advice that a subsidiary may or may not choose to accept. The following is an example of such a guideline: "Experience in the U.S. and elsewhere supports the usage of testimonial advertising. You may, therefore, consider using a local model to promote the product."

Format Guidelines These define any form, design, or procedure that should be followed in planning the campaign. These guidelines also include dates that must be adhered to. The major purpose of format guidelines is to make it easy for the corporation to impose and maintain control over the advertising activities of the subsidiaries.

Advertising Goals

Advertising goals should be appropriately related to product/market objectives. Thus, a subsidiary serving two markets (business customers and household consumers) may have different advertising goals in the two markets. Because advertising produces changes in attitudes, advertising goals should be defined in order to influence attitudinal structures. Accordingly, advertising may be undertaken to (1) affect those forces that strongly influence the choice criteria used for evaluating brands belonging to the product class; (2) add characteristic(s) to those considered salient for the product class; (3) increase or decrease the rating for a salient product class characteristic; (4) change perception of the company's brand with regard to some particular salient product characteristic; and (5) change perception of competitive brands with regard to some particular salient product characteristic. Based on these additional perspectives, advertising objectives may be defined as:

- Increasing consumers' or buyers' *awareness* of the product, either generally or comparatively.
- Improving the product's *image* among consumers or buyers, either generally or comparatively.

- Increasing a target group of opinion leaders' or consumers'/buyers' *awareness* of the company, either generally or comparatively.
- Increasing the company's *image* among a target group of opinion leaders or consumers/buyers, either generally or comparatively.
- Increasing the product's *sales* or market share among consumers or buyers, either generally or comparatively. (These objectives are more appropriate for retail or direct-response advertising.)[33]

A good definition of objectives aids in writing appropriate copy and in selecting the media. The firm's headquarters should make sure that the objectives have been defined by the proper managerial person.

Establishing Campaign Plan

The campaign plan outlines what sort of advertising the subsidiary has in mind. It spells out the dimensions of strategy and media and estimates the preliminary budget. For example, a subsidiary might plan along the following lines:

- Develop ad copy using a female model to promote the product, and run it simultaneously in six different magazines every other month for one year.
- Estimate the impact of the campaign by twice exposing 60 percent of the target customers to the new version of the product.
- Remember that the rationale behind this campaign is to reinforce the product's image among customers and counteract the competitor's recent entry into the market with a product similar to ours.
- Measure the effectiveness of the campaign by having an ad agency do a recognition test with a sample of women in the third, sixth, and ninth months of the campaign.
- Continue to position the product among women between 20 and 40 years of age from middle-income families.
- Estimate that the costs of this campaign during the first year will be $2 million.
- Decide that, for implementation of this plan, approval is needed by December 15.

Review and Approval of Plan

Headquarters should review each subsidiary's advertising schemes to ensure that they will contribute to the realization of the subsidiary's marketing goals and to assess that the planned campaign is realistic and entails a proper use of resources. In the review process, it is important to judge matters from the viewpoint of the individual subsidiary's business and related environments. In other words, headquarters' managers should avoid using *self-reference criteria* (discussed in an earlier chapter). Where insufficient information has been provided by the subsidiary, further information should be requested. Finally, reviewers at corporate headquarters should remember that events do not move at the same pace in every country. Thus, every effort should be made to meet the deadline set by the subsidiary.

Copy Development and Testing

Copy refers to the content of an advertisement. In advertising, the term is used in a broad sense to include words, pictures, symbols, colors, layout, and any other ingredients of an ad. Copywriting is a creative job, and its quality depends to a large extent on the creative genius of persons in the advertising agency or the company. However, creativity alone may not produce good ad copy. The marketing managers should provide their conception of the copy and furnish adequate information on the product, objectives, target customers, competitive activity, and legal aspects. The copywriter uses these facts as well as talent and imagination to develop ad copy. Before copy is finalized, it should be screened and revised as necessary. Sometimes several versions of the copy are developed and tested simultaneously, and the final version is chosen on the basis of test results.

Often subsidiaries have available various ads used in the U.S. and elsewhere in the world. If the copy of one of the available ads appears basically appropriate, it may well be worthwhile to use it. But such "foreign" copy should be adapted for local conditions. This point is especially noteworthy when expatriate managers have to make ad copy decisions.

To avoid snarls, it is best for subsidiary management to work closely with their advertising agency. The task of adaptation becomes easier if the agency that initially worked on the campaign has an office in the subsidiary's country. Multinational ad agencies have global experience and contacts that facilitate locating and using the best talent for adapting the ad to local conditions. Interestingly, often local native-born managers are as bad as expatriate managers in the localization of ad copy. Long accustomed to the outside world, they may be quite divorced from the realities of life in their home countries and may approach the task with imported ideas.

The final test of the appropriateness of copy is the marketplace. Three or four different versions should be sample-tested using appropriate statistical procedures. Unless a subsidiary is very well equipped, the copy-testing task should be assigned to the agency. The final copy should be selected based on test results. In some cases, it may become necessary to develop yet another entirely new copy if none of the original ones appears sufficiently effective.

Media Planning

The decision on media is made simultaneously with the copy decision. It is influenced by media availability, media coverage, and media cost. *Media availability* elsewhere in the world is more restricted than in the U.S. Even in developed countries like Switzerland, commercial advertising is permitted only during certain hours. In Germany, Europe's richest and largest national market, television spots are kept to barely 40 minutes a day and none on Sunday.[34] Many countries ban the advertising of certain products. For example, Venezuela bans foreign cigarette and liquor advertising. In England, the government once questioned the high expenditures budgeted by Unilever and Procter & Gamble for advertising detergents. In brief, in media planning, careful analysis is necessary to figure out which media are practical to use before making the actual selection among them.

Media coverage varies from country to country. The average is affected by the range of exposure and ownership of receivers. Ownership is a problem in the developing countries, where only a small percentage of the population owns radios and/or television sets. Printed media present similar problems. The masses may be illiterate, may not have enough income to subscribe to newspapers and magazines, or may live beyond circulation centers. In addition, the heterogeneity of a country with different languages or cultural and religious groups may make it difficult to reach enough people through a single campaign (see International Marketing Highlight 15.8).

A related problem here is the availability of coverage statistics. In many countries, the sole source of such information is the government, whose figures may be overstated for political reasons, besides being haphazardly gathered or outdated. In other countries, absolutely no information may be available on the coverage of different media, except the best guesses of bureaucrats. In other words, Starch's coverage data and Nielson's ratings are not widely known outside the U.S. In any event, subsidiary management should gather as much information on media coverage as possible in order to select the media focus.

The final consideration is *media cost*. In many countries, media prices are subject to negotiation. Thus, the cost could be affected by the bargaining abilities of the subsidiary management. In some cases, media rates are arbitrarily set and increased without any market justification. This often happens where media are government-controlled and do not depend solely on advertising revenues to operate.

Further, in developing countries, media costs are relatively high compared with industrialized nations. In newspaper advertising, the most popular medium worldwide, the rates are much higher in the developing countries in proportion to circulation than in advanced ones. The real cost of reaching potential buyers with advertising messages may be even higher because the media are not readily available and a large proportion of the population is scattered in rural areas. The subsidiary management should consider all these potential problems in selecting the best media available for its purposes.

Budget Approval

Budget approval is generally granted during the review process, but some companies keep budget approval pending until the copy has been developed and tested and the media planning completed. Although it may seem odd that subsidiaries proceed to develop and test copy as well as undertake media selection without budget approval, it may be necessary to do so. Changing business environments, as a result of political situations like threatened nationalization or business conditions that are declining because of competition, may make it essential to postpone commitments.

Campaign Implementation

Once budget approval has been received, the campaign should be undertaken as planned. Contingency plans are also necessary in case of unexpected difficulties. For example, one company in Pakistan had planned an ad using a female model to promote a brand of bar soap. Everything seemed fine during the planning stages. As release time approached, the Pakistani government banned all use of female models in ads. In such eventualities, contingency plans can save the day.

■■■■■■   **International Marketing Highlight 15.8**   ■■■■■■

Reaching Consumers in Rural India

U.S. personal-care products maker Colgate-Palmolive has a long history in India and is the leader in the toothpaste market, with a claimed share of 62 percent. It expects rural sales of its toothpaste to reach more than 50 percent of its earnings in the country by 2003. The firm aims to turn millions of rural Indians into customers by promoting both oral hygiene and the Colgate brand. The target groups are consumers in rural villages who use no oral hygiene products at all and those who now use toothpowder.

The challenge of creating awareness has proved a tough job. Illiteracy is high (60 percent) in rural areas, and only one-third of the people live in homes with television. This means people in a number of villages have never heard of either toothpaste or toothbrushes. They tend to use traditional tooth cleaners such as charcoal and salt.

To reach its sales targets, Colgate-Palmolive is using a variety of techniques. One key initiative is to send promotion vans equipped with videos, educational materials and samples to rural areas and then follow up with monthly visits. The program covered 16,000 villages and more than 10 million people in 1996, up from 6,000 villages and 9 million people in 1995.

Another element of the marketing campaign is to offer 10-gram sachets costing Rs1 (two U.S. cents). The sachet launch has now been supported by television and radio ads, posters and other publicity.

In addition, the company has introduced new-look toothpowder cans (200g, 100g and 50g) with labels in seven regional languages. It holds dental clinics in vans or on trains in villages all across India, covering all age groups. It puts a high priority on superstockists, who appoint stockists in rural areas who in turn visit the villages to ensure product availability. Finally, Colgate-Palmolive holds programs jointly with prestigious government organizations and dental associations to promote oral hygiene.

Source: Crossborder Monitor, November 19, 1997, p. 5.

The thrust of the program may also require change if initial feedback on the campaign is discouraging. In any event, a certain amount of flexibility can accommodate changes for an effective campaign.

Measuring Effectiveness

Advertising effectiveness may be measured both before and after an ad is run (see International Marketing Highlight 15.9).

International Marketing Highlight 15.9

U.S. Brands Trail Japanese in China Study

Despite U.S. marketers' push into China, a new study shows that brand-name recognition for U.S. products lags woefully behind Japanese brands. Six of the 10 companies with the most brand recognition were from Japan,. Only Coca-Cola, Walt Disney's Mickey Mouse products and Philip Morris' Marlboro cigarettes scored in the top 10, at numbers 2, 7, and 8, respectively. Coke was recognized by 62 percent of those surveyed, Mickey Mouse by 54 percent, and the Marlboro man by 51 percent.

The brand name with the most recognition was Hitachi, the Japanese consumer-electronics company. The top 10 also included one Chinese brand, Tsing Tao beer at number 5, with 56 percent recognition.

The study by the Gallup Organization is the first nationwide consumer survey taken in China and was conducted among 3,400 households in nearly every province. Gallup representatives traveled by foot, bicycle, motorbike, and even camel to conduct the study.

The U.S. does exceed other countries in two distinct and predictable categories: fast food and soft drinks. KFC, the chicken chain, is the most recognized, followed by McDonald's, Grand Metropolitan's Burger King and Pizza Hut. Coca-Cola is followed by PepsiCo's Pepsi-Cola and by 7Up.

Source: The Wall Street Journal, February 16, 1995, p. B8.

Pretesting measures include

- Opinion and attitude ratings gathered by questioning a sample of the prospective audience.
- Projective techniques, which are indirectly elicited responses from the audience using motivation research techniques.
- Laboratory testing, gathered by exposing a sample of customers to the ad and asking their reactions.

Post-testing measures include

- Recognition and recall.
- Changes in attitude ascribable to the ad.
- Inquiries and sales measures—for example, the return of a card included with the ad.

The methods discussed thus far are the same as those utilized in the U.S. However, their utilization may not be feasible in every nation. The facilities, talent, and resources needed for advertising effectiveness studies may be lacking.

Conclusion

Many problems can arise overseas to hinder the smooth development of an advertising program. Some countries lack facilities for fine printing. In other nations, government restrictions on advertising cause difficulties. In still other cases, illiteracy and language differences within the same country have an adverse effect. Mostly these problems arise in developing countries.

There are no easy answers for these problems. In some cases, advance planning and patience may help. For example, if an ad must be approved by the country government beforehand, enough time should be allocated so that, if a delay occurs in the process, the prompt release of the ad is assured. Similarly, if some printing or recording must be done in the home country for lack of facilities in the host country, advance planning is vital. Beyond that, an advertiser must accept the problems as an environmental constraint in doing business internationally.

Global Advertising Regulations

Most countries impose some regulations on advertising. The purpose behind these regulations is twofold: (1) to protect the consumers against misleading advertising and their own gullibility and (2) to protect smaller businesses from the competitive threats of large corporations. It is interesting to note that advertising regulation is more common in developed societies than in developing countries. This difference may be explained by the fact that the advertising industry is still in its infancy in most developing countries and therefore is ignored as yet. Besides, not all developing countries have the administrative machinery to enforce regulations.

Exhibit 15.4 illustrates the types of issues that lead to regulation in different parts of the world. For example, while France and Mexico resist the use of foreign language, the Muslim countries regulate the use of foreign material themes and illustrations. Essentially, advertising regulation is focused on specific areas (see International Marketing Highlight 15.10):

- Certain classes of product/service, such as alcoholic beverages, tobacco, non-prescription pharmaceuticals, and financial and real estate deals.
- Mail-order distribution.
- Ads targeted toward children.
- Foreign ownership of advertising agencies.
- Comparative advertising.
- "Puffery" or superlative claim—for example, "This brand is *the* best."
- Use of foreign language/words, models, backgrounds, and illustrations.
- Media—for example, time limits for advertising.
- Sexism in advertising.

■■■ International Marketing Highlight 15.10 ■■■

War on Smoking

While cigarette smoking is declining in the U.S., it is a growth industry in many countries overseas. Nonetheless, these are protective markets not open to outsiders. Consider Thailand's $744 million cigarette market, which was finally open to imports under heavy pressure from U.S. trade negotiators only after Thailand imposed high import duties, a cumbersome customs-clearance procedure, and stiff restrictions on cigarette advertising.

What is interesting about Thailand's efforts to curb American tobacco imports is that it relied heavily for help on an alliance of local and international antismoking activists. As a spokesperson from the American Cancer Society, an alliance member, notes, "The Thais complained to us that your government is trying to force U.S. cigarettes down our throats." Now these antismoking groups are actively campaigning against smoking throughout Asia, and have seriously hurt the U.S. tobacco industry.

As U.S. companies stepped up their efforts to develop the Asian markets, the antismoking activists intensified their efforts to keep them away. For example, a 14-nation group called the Asian Consultancy on Tobacco Control met in Hong Kong to formulate a four-year strategy to prevent smoking in the area. The group's aim is to persuade Asian countries to adopt uniform tobacco-control regulations and thus prevent U.S. companies from making inroads in the region.

Source: "Asia: A New Front in the War on Smoking," *Business Week,* February 25, 1991, p. 66.

Regulations affecting advertising in various regions of the world have grown both in number and stringency over the years. Some examples of advertising regulations include

- China, the world's largest and potentially most lucrative cigarette market (with nearly 1.2 billion people and one out of every three smokers) has banned tobacco advertising.

- India announced an upper limit of $10,000 for advertising expenses for all companies doing business in India; expenditures over that limit were to be taxed at the rate of 50 percent. Widespread cancellation of advertising in reaction to this law, however, caused the withdrawal of this tax, as the government was concerned with effects that the cancellation of advertising might have on employment.

- In Costa Rica, a law provides for the national majority ownership of the media and the agencies.

- In Germany, television advertising on the commercial stations is restricted to 20 minutes per day in blocks of 5 to 7 minutes between 5:00 PM and 8:00 PM with

---

EXHIBIT 15.4
Taboo on TV

Egypt	Sex; anything more than a little kiss.
Poland	References to the Church or sex.
Hong Kong	Indecent matter; obscene or vulgar language.
Iran	Women whose heads, arms, and legs are not covered; drinking.
Most Arab Countries	Nudity, sex, enthusiastic necking; criticism of the head of state; criticism of any religion.
Brazil	Explicit sex and violence during prime time; references to government repression.
Mexico	Criticism of the government.
Thailand	Anything remotely critical of the royal family.
Japan	Criticism of the imperial family or religious sects.
Israel	Any shot of a political candidate; terrorists' opinions.
Turkey	Ethnic problems.
Indonesia	Anything offending religion.
South Africa	Any reference to Jesus Christ; all expletives containing the word "God," including "Oh, God!"

Source: John Lippman, "Television Is Fast Changing the Way the World Works, the Way It Plays, the Way It Goes to War and Makes Peace," *The Milwaukee Journal,* December 20, 1992, J1, J3.

no advertising on Sundays and holidays. In the Netherlands, television commercials must be confined to 5-minute blocks in the evenings.

- In Turkey, the state-owned commercial television station carries 12 minutes of noncommissionable advertising each evening in 3-minute blocks.
- In Denmark, Germany, and Italy, medical-product advertising must be supervised as to content.
- In Germany, France, Belgium, Austria, Italy, and the Netherlands, restrictions on comparative advertising are enforced.
- A French law forbids the use of foreign words and expressions when French equivalents can be found in the official dictionary.[35]

Despite the regulations, many companies find alternative ways to outmaneuver ad bans. As has been noted by Fara Warner,

> It is against the law to advertise cigarettes in Malaysia. But watch television or step into the street in Kuala Lampur, the capital, and it's hard to miss the commercials and billboards pitching the Benson & Hedges Bistro, Camel clothing, and Salem music stores.
>
> As governments across Asia clamp down on cigarette advertising in an attempt to stem the increase in smoking in the region, tobacco companies worldwide are building powerful marketing arsenals by licensing their cigarette brands to noncigarette products.
>
> Once limited to promotional T-shirts and baseball caps, the trademark diversification has become high art. For instance, in Malaysia, Rothmans of Pall Mall has put its Peter Stuyvesant cigarette brand name on travel agencies, which then sponsored broadcasts of the smoke-free Olympics. Trademark diversification, called "alibi marketing" by industry critics, started in Europe more than a decade ago, as cigarette companies searched for ways to get around ad bans there. Now, more than 1,000 Marlboro Classics stores dot Europe and Asia, selling everything from leather vests to wool barn blankets and lizard-skin cowboy boots. (In the U.S., cigarette companies have yet to license their brand names to specific products, but they have extended their name recognition with programs like Marlboro Country Store and Camel Cash, where smokers earn points to receive products ranging from kayaks to pool tables.)
>
> In Asia, companies have expanded their brands into music, travel and restaurants. Malaysia has become a proving ground for some of the newest innovations, including the world's first Benson & Hedges Bistro, a restaurant where the walls are almost the same shade of gold as the cigarette brand's packaging.[36]

Industry Self-Regulation

The growing trend toward government action has led the advertising industry to attempt self-regulation in order to prevent further, undesirable government regulations. Self-regulation also shields the industry from unfair internal competition. Standards are set, and objective arbitration settles complaints and disputes outside the framework of government. The degree of self-regulation throughout the world varies from country to country according to each country's cultural and social values and level of development.

Most self-regulation measures are spearheaded by advertising industry associations. In many countries, Belgium for one, specialized self-regulatory bodies have been formed to deal with the problems related to advertising. Large advertising agencies, and even the mass media in some countries, have set their own standards or codes of conduct.

Advertising Agencies

Advertising agencies serve advertisers. As MNCs have circled the globe, their advertising agencies, as well as involved banks and accounting firms, have followed suit. The principal reason that advertising agencies go international has been to serve their clients both at home and abroad. Chapter 1 examined the domination of the multinational scene by U.S. corporations. This domination is even more apparent in the case of advertising agencies. Of the ten largest advertising agencies in the world, all but two are U.S.–based.

Globally, the major thrust of the advertising agencies' business is in the developed countries. Their principal clients focus most of their activities in these countries. It has been estimated that over 85 percent of their income is derived from activities in developed countries. The major portion of their income from developing countries originates in the Pacific Rim, followed by Latin America.

Advertising agencies use various modes of foreign entry. One form of foreign entry is the opening of a local office. Such an arrangement permits complete control over the nature and size of the foreign office. However, it is a costly alternative, as it takes eight to ten years for a new office to generate enough clients to become financially self-sufficient. Another alternative is to acquire full or partial interest in existing agencies. This offers an ongoing business with a trained staff and a roster of clients. However, in practice, it is difficult to impose control over an acquired business that has established procedures of its own.

A third alternative is to form a joint venture that may later develop into full ownership. A fourth is to form a holding company. The choice of mode of entry would depend on the captive business, availability of a viable firm for acquisition, future prospects, financial resources of the agency, and national regulations.

Usually, a multinational firm prefers using a home-based advertising agency in order to achieve and maintain control. Even when strategy decisions are delegated to nationals, if a subsidiary works with the same agency that the MNC uses in the U.S., then there is sufficient assurance that the overall advertising function will be performed satisfactorily.

Often multinational enterprises retain the same agency for both U.S. and international advertising. One problem with this practice is a lack of cultural insight into the market. Sometimes, the foreign agency will have local employees, but nations where the dearth of local talent may force an agency to depend entirely on expatriate managers, chances are there is no local agency, leaving the MNC no choice but to use the foreign agency.

Overall, the trend to employ one agency worldwide, rather than a separate agency in each country is particularly strong in businesses such as personal computers where markets are similar around the world. For example, IBM has put its worldwide advertising business including the U.S., into a single agency, Ogilvy & Mather.[37] By using a single agency, the company aims to avoid diverse advertising approaches, which its management believes would result in a loss of overall advertising effectiveness. But not everybody thinks in the same way: in 1991 Coca-Cola decided to change from using just one firm and instead spread its business among 30 or more agencies.[38]

As in the U.S., a foreign advertising agency (unless prohibited by the national law) receives a 15 percent discount from the media on the business it places. This constitutes the main source of revenue for ad agencies. In some countries, there is a movement away from the 15 percent compensation plan to a schedule of fees. Further, in many countries, local agencies aggressively compete against the multinational agencies by passing along a portion of their discount to their clients. Fifteen percent is a standard charge for a routine advertising job. In cases where a client requires help beyond the simple work of creating copy and scheduling the media, the agency normally charges more.

Summary

The promotion of goods and services is an important part of the marketing mix. The purpose of promotion is to inform, persuade, and remind the customer that certain goods and services are available. The four ingredients of promotion are advertising, personal selling, sales promotion, and publicity.

Advertising is an American institution born of U.S. economic progress. However, the rest of the world is catching up fast. World advertising expenditures, other than those of the U.S., are likely to rise from $195 billion in 1998 to $215 billion in 2002.

An important decision for international advertisers to make is whether the advertising campaign should be standardized worldwide or localized. Arguments for standardized advertising are (1) a successful campaign in one country is likely to be effective in another nation as well and (2) standardized advertising is economical. The argument against standardization is that advertising campaigns effective in some countries are not always effective in others, because of differences in cultural traits, language, economic life, and the like. For example, a female ad model is not likely to be acceptable in a Muslim country. In the final analysis, the choice between standardized and localized advertising should be based on such environmental considerations as levels of education, experience and competence of personnel in the foreign agency, degree of nationalism and rate of economic growth in the country, eating patterns and customs of the country, attitudes toward authority, and independence of media from government control. If overall environmental differences are significant, then advertising should be localized. Besides the environment, other criteria to be weighed before using a standardized campaign overseas are advertising objectives relative to the host country, target market, product characteristics, media availability, and cost/benefit relationship.

The growth of global advertising is directly related to media development. However, in many countries, media have not yet developed adequately. Besides, many nations strictly regulate media availability. Statistical information reflects worldwide media differences. Unlike those in the U.S., overseas media do not derive revenues solely from advertising.

The steps to follow to build an international advertising program are provision of headquarters guidelines, definition of advertising goals, preparation of a campaign plan, review and approval of plan, copy development and testing, media planning, budget approval, campaign implementation, and measurement of advertising effectiveness.

Overseas countries impose different regulations on advertising. While the thrust of the regulations varies from nation to nation, the essential focus is on certain classes of products/services, mail-order distribution, ads targeted toward children, foreign ownership of advertising agencies, comparative advertising, superlative claims in ads, use of foreign language/words, and media. Many U.S. advertising agencies have expanded outside the U.S.

Review Questions

1. What factors argue for an internationally standardized approach to advertising?
2. Is the fact of cultural differences among nations strong enough to justify localized advertising?
3. Define the terms *buying proposal* and *creative presentation*. How do they affect the decision for standardized versus localized advertising?
4. In the U.S., advertising is the principal source of revenue for the media. Is this true in other countries? If not, how do media derive their incomes?
5. List the various steps for developing an international advertising program.
6. Illustrate with examples the types of regulations that countries overseas impose on media.
7. Why is it desirable for a U.S. company to use a U.S.–based advertising agency in other countries?

Creative Questions

1. An MNC is interested in standardizing its advertising worldwide. However, advertising rules and regulations vary from country to country, which means in each nation, some form of adaptation will be necessary. In view of this, the company must decide whether it should hire a large ad agency with contacts in most major markets or let each subsidiary hire a local ad agency. What are the pros and cons of hiring a global agency versus local agencies? Should the company make separate arrangements for concept and tactical advertising?

2. Critically examine the impact of technological changes on global advertising through electronics media.

Endnotes

1. *See* Tom Griffin, *International Marketing Communications* (Oxford, U.K.: Buttersworth-Heinemann Ltd., 1993).

2. *The Economist,* January 2, 1999, p. 88.

3. "China Is Planning to Hold Its First Advertising Parley," *The Asian Wall Street Journal Weekly,* December 2, 1985, p. 11.

4. Erik Elinder, "How International Can Advertising Be?" in S. Watson Dunn, ed., *International Handbook of Advertising* (New York: McGraw-Hill, 1964), pp. 59–71.

5. Arthur C. Fatt, "The Danger of 'Local' International Advertising," *Journal of Marketing,* January, 1976, p. 61. *Also see* Gordon E. Miracle, "Internationalizing Advertising Principles and Strategies," *MSU Business Topics,* Autumn, 1968, pp. 29–36.

6. James H. Donnelly, Jr., and John K. Ryans, Jr., "Standardized Global Advertising: A Call as Yet Unanswered," *Journal of Marketing,* April, 1969, pp. 57–60. *Also see* George Fields, "How to Scale the Cultural Fence," *Advertising Age,* December 13, 1982, pp. 4–11.

7. "Playtex Kicks Off a One-Ad-Fits-All Campaign," *Business Week,* December 16, 1985, p. 48.

8. *Crossborder Monitor,* August 17, 1994, p.7.

9. Dean M. Peebes and John K. Ryans, Jr., *Management of International Advertising: A Marketing Approach* (Rockleigh, NJ: Allyn & Bacon, 1984), p. 73. *Also see* Ken Wells, "Global Ad Campaigns, After Many Missteps Finally Pay Dividends," *The Wall Street Journal,* August 27, 1992, p. 1.

10. Christine D. Urban, "A Cross-National Comparison of Consumers' Media Use Patterns," *Columbia Journal of World Business,* Winter, 1977, pp. 53–64.

11. James Killough, "Improved Payoffs from Transnational Advertising," *Harvard Business Review,* July–August, 1978, p. 103.

12. B.G. Youovich, "Maintain a Balance of Planning," *Advertising Age,* May 17, 1982, p. M-7.

13. *Washington Post,* January 11, 1982, p. 38.

14. Ann Helming, "Pitfalls Lie Waiting for Unwary Marketers," *Advertising Age,* May 17, 1982, p. M-8.

15. Jamie Talan, "Gillette Company on Track with Sharp Marketing for GII," *Advertising Age,* May 17, 1982, p. M-14.

16. Jacob Hornik, "Comparative Evaluation of International vs. National Advertising Strategies," *Columbia Journal of World Business,* Spring 1980, p. 43.

17. Lyn S. Amine and S. Tamer Cavusgil, "Mass Media Advertising in a Developing Country," *International Journal of Advertising,* 2 (1983): 317–330.

18. Roger Blackwell, Riad Ajami, and Kristina Stephan, "Winning the Global Advertising Race: Planning Globally, Acting Locally," *Journal of International Consumer Marketing,* 3, no. 2 (1991): 97–120.

19. "Playtex Conditions Its Strategies," *Advertising Age,* May 17, 1982, p. M-16.

20. John A. Quelch, "British Airways," a Harvard Business School case.

21. S. Watson Dunn, "Effect of National Identity on Multinational Promotion Strategy in Europe," *Journal of Marketing,* October 1976, pp. 50–57.

22. Russell W. Belk and Richard W. Pollay, "Materialism and Status Appeals in Japanese and U.S. Print Advertising," *International Marketing Review,* Winter 1985, pp. 38–47.

23. *See World Advertising Expenditures* (Mamaroneck, NY: Starch INRA Hooper, Inc., 1989) pp. 32–33.

24. Scott Beardsley, Alan Miles and John S. Rose, "A Bouquet of Choices: The Future of Direct-to-Home Television," *The McKinsey Quarterly* 1 (1997): 56–81.

25. Ibid.

26. Tim Harper, "U.K. Eyes New Channel to Ease Demand Prices," *Advertising Age,* May 16, 1988, p. 68.

27. *World Advertising Expenditures* (New York: Starch, INRA, Hooper and International Advertising Association, 1992), pp. 36–37.

28. *See* Cynthia Webster, "The Effect of Nationality on Media Usage Patterns: A Study of Consumers From Countries of Various Levels of Development," in James E. Littlefield and Magdolna

Csath, eds., *Marketing and Economic Development* (Budapest, Hungary: Karl Marx University of Economic Sciences, 1988), pp. 238–241.

29. Lynn Elber, "U.S. television Networks Expand Interests Overseas," *Marketing News,* November 7, 1994, p. 7.

30. Tutsuo Ohbora, Andrew Parsons and Hajo Risenbeck, "Alternate Routes to Global Marketing," *The McKinsey Quarterly* 3 (1992): 52–74.

31. S. Tamer Cavusgil and Karl Hutchinson, "Pan-Europe television Opens up New Multinational Markets," *Marketing News,* March 27, 1987, p. 8. *Also see* "The Battle for Europe's Telly Addicts," *The Economist,* April 22, 1995, p. 63.

32. "Yo Quiero mi MTV," *The Economist,* February 25, 1995, p. 67.

33. Dean M. Peebes and John K. Ryans, Jr., *Management of International Advertising* (Rockleigh, NJ: Allyn & Bacon, 1984), p. 25.

34. "The Media Barons Battle to Dominate Europe," *Business Week,* May 25, 1987, p. 158.

35. Based on information reported in various issues of *Advertising Age* during 1996–1998.

36. Fara Warner, "Tobacco Brands Outmaneuver Asian Ad Bans," *The Wall Street Journal,* August 6, 1996, p. B1.

37. *Crossborder Monitor,* August 10, 1994, p. 3.

38. "So What Was the Fuss About?" *The Economist,* June 22, 1996, p. 59.

CHAPTER 16

Multinational Sales Management and Foreign Sales Promotion

CHAPTER FOCUS_____

After studying this chapter, you should be able to

- Describe the role of personal selling in international business.

- Discuss the problems of expatriates and third country nationals.

- Explain the formulation and implementation of policy guidelines regarding the transfer of people from nation to nation.

- List the steps in building foreign sales promotion and public relations programs.

417

Personal selling, sales promotion, and public relations are all devices of a company's total promotional scheme, but each one has certain characteristics that assign it a unique role. When a company begins selling in export markets, switches from export selling to international marketing, launches a new product line or service in a new foreign market, or takes an established line of products into a new country or region, it invariably has more promotion tasks to undertake than funds available. In other words, marketers' aspirations with respect to foreign marketing almost always exceed their ability or willingness to allocate funds.

Therefore, this chapter highlights the significance of different types of promotion and examines their relevance in different foreign situations. Unfortunately, no ready-made formulas are available to prioritize different forms of promotion. However, the discussion here identifies considerations that may help in determining where and how to begin.

Sales Personnel and Personal Selling Abroad

Sales personnel in international business can be classified in two ways: by the task they perform or by their nationality. In regard to the task they perform, there are three categories of selling tasks: sales generation, sales support, and missionary work. *Sales generation* is the creative task of helping the customer to make a purchase decision. *Sales support* is concerned with after-sale service. *Missionary work* is undertaken by a manufacturer's salespersons to stimulate demand to help the distributors.

By nationality, sales personnel can be categorized as expatriates, natives, or third country nationals. *Expatriates* are home-country employees on deputation in the host country. For example, a GE sales manager from the U.S. assigned to launch the GE sales effort in Spain would be considered an expatriate. *Natives* are employees belonging to the host country. A Spanish national working for GE as a salesperson in Spain is a native. *Third-country nationals* are employees transferred from one host country to another. A French national transferred to Spain would be defined as a third country national.

For the most part, MNCs do not transfer selling personnel abroad. There are two reasons for this. First, selling requires deep familiarity with the local culture, which an expatriate cannot be expected to have. Selling strategies cannot usually be transferred from a home market to one in a different cutlure. Second, it is extremely expensive to assign expatriates to selling positions. For these reasons, most companies—IBM as an example—depend mainly on nationals for selling jobs. Unilever is another company that employs nationals of a country only for marketing jobs in other countries.[1]

There are occasions, however, when companies may assign expatriates to work, usually for short periods, in the selling area. Such a practice is more commonly followed in the marketing of big-ticket items. The expatriate who has a proven track record at home can be quite helpful in resolving difficult foreign situations, in serving as a catalyst for the natives.

For example, Otis Elevator had to assign a sales engineer from the home office to provide after-sale service for its elevators in a large office complex in Singapore for a year. This became necessary because the native salesforce had failed to ensure smooth functioning of its elevators. Likewise, NCR Corporation uses expatriates to provide on-the-job training to natives. As a matter of fact, the company has a cadre of seasoned salespeople who travel from country to country assisting native salesforces in selling the company's products.

Many big-ticket items require selling directly from the home office, which usually involves expatriates. Boeing bids for selling airliners to foreign airlines from its headquarters in Seattle. Its salespeople, mainly expatriates, travel extensively worldwide to call on its customers. In 1993 Saudi Arabia decided to rejuvenate its air force by buying 100 new fighter bombers. This amounted to over $4 billion worth of business. Therefore, a number of U.S. aircraft companies and European companies sent sales personnel to Riyadh to make sales presentations and contacts.

The management of a native salesforce is a local matter to be handled according to business practices in the host country. From the viewpoint of parent corporations, therefore, the major concern is with expatriates and third country nationals. Foreign sales positions are demanding assignments that require long hours of hard work, perseverance, and self-sacrifice. Developing the long-term relationships necessary for successful selling in a foreign environment takes tremendous effort.

Expatriates

The recruitment, transport, and risks connected with sending expatriate salespeople overseas are time-consuming and expensive, ranging from two-and-a-half to three times the costs involved with an equivalent domestic salesperson. In addition, an MNC risks a loss of time and money if the salesperson fails to stay the length of the assignment. Productivity may suffer, too, if the person becomes a so-called brownout—someone who stays on the foreign assignment but becomes inefficient because either he or she or the family is unhappy. Also, an expatriate's lack of knowledge or disregard for the host country's cultural practices may damage a company's reputation or cause the loss of a critical contact. Finally, the MNC should be concerned with the repatriation of expatriates in order to reassimilate them into the stream of domestic corporate activity without the loss of efficiency. (see International Marketing Highlight 16.1).

In addition to using expatriates for sales positions overseas for limited periods, many companies place expatriates in foreign subsidiaries for reasons that may be hard to accept. A study by O. Jay Galbraith and Anders Edstrom offers four reasons for using expatriates: (1) to fill a position, (2) to utilize managerial talent, (3) to give an executive international experience, and (4) to facilitate coordination and control with the parent company.[2] Although the study deals with foreign placement in general, it has equal application for the assignment of salespeople overseas.

The first reason usually involves a technical position becoming vacant in a subsidiary located in a developing country with a lack of technically qualified personnel. One example is the recruitment of engineers for high-paying positions in the Middle East. According to the study, this reason accounted for 60 to 70 percent of all transfers.

The second reason, to utilize managerial talent, is explained by the authors as follows: "A job opportunity and a promotable individual do not always occur in the same subsidiary." This situation complements the first. An absence of opportunity at home and a need overseas would encourage the transfer of a talented individual to a subsidiary outside the U.S.

The third reason, to provide international experience for executives, was cited by U.S. firms in the study as the second most important criterion for foreign assignment. This consideration, however, is not independent of the need to fill a position. If there are qualified local managers and the transfer occurs, then the probable reason is valuable international experience and exposure. Knowledge gained during the assignment would increase the firm's global perspective in relation to existing markets. Firsthand information is always preferable. This leads to the fourth reason, coordination and control, which is particularly crucial in situations where the firm is initiating large efforts to crack a local market, where the organization is implementing policy changes, or where the firm lacks confidence in developing countries.

It is quite logical to bring in expatriates for specific so-called firefighting assignments (for example, to supervise or train locals) or for a developmental assignment, that is, to expose a promising executive to multinational experience. The problems occur when people are sent overseas for historical, egocentric, or nationalistic reasons like, "But we've always had an expatriate do that job. No one can manage that operation except an American." Political maneuvering within a company can also cause problems, like sending an employee overseas to clear the way for another person to take up an emerging position. Retreading the path of least resistance—that is, figuring that the best solution is always to bring in an American whenever there is any problem—can be counterproductive. Changing lifestyles and expectations are creating new categories of expatriates—and sounding the death knell for huge overseas allowances. Following are some of the types of managers being sent abroad by multinational companies:[3]

- *Go-it-aloners.* These executives have spouses who don't want to move. They are willing to spend two to three years overseas alone, with frequent trips home. In Japan, where getting children into good schools has become an obsession, this approach is common.

- *In-betweenies.* Some executives will go if the company helps find their spouses' jobs. Some personnel professionals now spend more time helping spouses find jobs than worrying about how the new transfers will manage in a foreign location.

- *Trailing husbands.* An increasing number of husbands are forgoing their careers to advance their wives' careers. But with many high-tech or service-business skills easily transferable, many of these men can work as consultants and advisers in the foreign location.

- *The over-50s.* Older individuals, with spouses who like to travel, are glad to represent the organization for a few years, while boosting their retirement benefits. An added bonus is that in places such as Asia, Africa and the Middle East, age is highly respected. These managers are often ideal ambassadors for companies, especially at the start-up stage.

- *Short-term soloists.* The globalization of operations often requires technical and specialized professionals to be on-site for weeks or months rather than years. So people will increasingly be sent abroad on a series of short-term assignments.

■■■■■■■■■   **International Marketing Highlight 16.1**   ■■■■■■■■■

Indifference at Home

In a survey of personnel managers at 56 MNCs based in the U.S., the following responses were tallied:

1. 56 percent say a foreign assignment is either detrimental to or immaterial in one's career.
2. 47 percent say their returning expatriates aren't guaranteed jobs with the company upon completion of their foreign assignments.
3. 65 percent say their expatriates' foreign assignments are not integrated into their overall career planning.
4. 45 percent view returning expatriates as a problem because they are so hard to fit back into the company.
5. 20 percent consider their company's repatriation policies adequate to meet the needs of their returning expatriates.

Source: Moran, Stahl & Boyer, New York.

Third Country Nationals

In recent years, a new trend has been to assign employees at all levels from one host country to another. This trend has arisen for two reasons. One, in many countries of the world there is a surplus of workers, while other countries lack adequate workforces. For example,

Singapore's population is about 3 million people. If a company is developing fast there, it may need a large salesforce yet find it difficult to find suitable natives to fill sales positions. Singapore is therefore forced into accepting salespeople from other developing countries, like the Philippines, India, or South Korea. Too, a company often needs a salesperson with certain experience for a subsidiary. Looking around, the company may discover that the most appropriate person for the job is a third country national (see International Marketing Highlight 16.2).

<hr>

■ International Marketing Highlight 16.2 ■

Wooing Third-Country Nationals

Multinational firms are tapping more third-country nationals (TCNs) for overseas posts. Nationality matters less as businesses race to enlarge their ranks of global managers. These TCNs—neither Americans nor local nationals—often win jobs because they speak several languages and know an industry or foreign country well. The average number of TCNs per U.S. company rose to 46 in 1989 from 33 in 1988.

Pioneer Hi-Bred International employs 29 TCNs in key jobs abroad, triple the number five years ago, partly because they accept difficult living conditions in Africa and the Middle East. Raychem has a dozen such foreigners in top European posts, up from eight in 1986. The numbers are going to increase as Europe's falling trade barriers ease relocation. A French citizen runs the company's Italian subsidiary, a Belgian is a sales manager in France, while a Cuban heads the unit in Spain.

Scott Paper, whose TCN managers have increased to 13 from 2 in 1987, will step up recruitment of young foreigners willing to move around Europe or around the Pacific.

<hr>

Source: The Wall Street Journal, September 16, 1990, p. B1.

Third country individuals face unique organizational problems (see Exhibit 16.1). For example, third country employees naturally want to know to which organization—the parent corporation or the host country company—they belong in regard to promotion and benefits and their feeling of identity. To manage third country employees effectively, both headquarters and host country management should study their special problems. An appreciation of their needs enhances performance for the benefits of the corporation. Although the episode in International Marketing Highlight 16.3 concerns an executive, it is equally relevant for salespersons. The story illustrates the type of management thinking and planning that ought to precede actual transfer of people across national boundaries. Cultural biases, financial interests, and individual preferences all play a role in a person's life. A person's success in one environment doesn't guarantee success elsewhere. A company needs a sound policy for moving people from country to country.

<hr>

■ International Marketing Highlight 16.3 ■

Managing Third-Country Nationals

The scene is the West Coast headquarters of a worldwide high-technology company. It is late in the afternoon, and an all-day conference involving the personnel director and the vice president of international operations is in progress.

What is the problem? The problem is Pierre. Who is Pierre? He is not just another militant employee off the assembly line. Pierre is a key executive, two levels from the top of the organization, and heretofore regarded as a comer headed for a key top management position in the U.S. upon conclusion of his current assignment.

How did Pierre get in this fix? He was hired in Paris and managed the French subsidiary until it achieved significant market penetration in France. One day Pierre woke up and found that the job had lost challenge. There was nowhere for him to go. He was a big fish in a small pond. About the same time, the company was beginning operations in Australia. What was better logic than to send Pierre from France to Australia to utilize his flair for building up the business? After he had opened up operations in Australia, there were vague plans to move him back to headquarters.

Pierre was a task-oriented man. For six months, he left his family in Paris, took a flat in Sydney, and worked day and night, making only two brief return trips to France. Then he moved his family to Australia and the trouble began.

The problems started simply enough. How did he get paid? The French subsidiary wanted him off their books. "No problem," said the personnel director, "we will pay you like an American. After all, you work for an American company, so we will pay you in U.S. dollars." Pierre received his first paycheck and could not believe it. When transferred to the U.S. scale, he made less money than in France. (Top management salaries in parts of Western Europe have reached parity and in many cases have surpassed their U.S. counterparts—this is not even considering benefits, which have historically been much better in Europe than in the U.S.)

Pierre took the salary reduction in stride, primarily because he was too involved in building up the market and did not have time to worry about it then. After his family had been there one month, the U.S. dollar was devalued and the Australian dollar revalued. Since Pierre used U.S. dollars to buy Australian dollars, his purchasing power was cut.

The problems then increased in intensity. There was the matter of taxes. He was in Australia and legally responsible for Australian taxes. But Pierre's Australian taxes were more than he would have paid had he stayed in Paris. The first of many cables was sent to corporate headquarters.

"What about my salary and taxes?"

"Pay him like an American, tax him like an American," said the personnel director.

The next round of cables soon followed. "But I am not an American; I am a Frenchman. I want a French salary and French tax levels, and while I'm at it, what about my French profit sharing? Do I lose this while in Australia?" (In France, many companies set aside, at least by U.S. standards, a rather liberal amount of money for profit sharing.) "What about my company car?" (Having a company car is another European custom for top management.) "How about vacation?" (Holidays in France are longer.) "How about home leave? When can I go back to France?"

As if this were not enough, further cables kept rolling in "What about housing? I pay more for housing in Sydney than I did in Paris." Then there was education. Who would pay the fee for correspondence courses to keep Pierre's children involved in the French education system?

The crowning blow was when Pierre asked for a cost-of-living allowance. "It couldn't cost him more to live in Sydney than in Paris!" shouted the vice president of international operations. "What's happened to Pierre? He has turned into a greedy, me-first employee. Is this the kind of manager we want representing us overseas? Get him back here; let's talk this out now!"

Pierre gladly caught the next plane. How did all this happen? What caused Pierre's metamorphosis? It was another common fault of multinational companies engaging in the movement of people across borders. In the heat of battle, decisions are made to move people without being thoroughly thought out. Moreover, these decisions are made without an underlying philosophy and plan.

Source: David M. Neor, *Multinational People Management* (Washington, D.C.: Bureau of National Affairs), pp. 9–11.

EXHIBIT 16.1
Problems Faced by
Third-Country
Nationals

- *Blocked promotions.* The tendency of MNCs to reserve top positions at headquarters for parent country managers.

- *Transfer anxieties.* The third-country managers' anxieties caused by uncertainty about the timing of their next transfers, the countries to which they will be transferred, the positions to which they will be assigned, and the extent of managerial autonomy involved in their next assignments.

- *Income gaps.* The tendency of third-country managers to feel deprived in terms of income in comparison to parent country managers, and the tendency of host country managers to feel deprived in comparison to third country managers.

- *Unfamiliarity and adaptability difficulties.* The natural tendency of newly arrived third-country managers to make mistakes and their compulsion to cover them up.

- *Avoidance of long-range projects.* The tendency of third-country managers to concentrate on short-range, non-risk, and demonstration-type projects.

- *Inappropriate leadership style.* The tendency of third country managers to imitate the managerial style prevalent at headquarters.

- *Nonparticipative decision making and screening of information.* The tendency of third country managers to adopt a detached leadership style because of their perception of headquarters as their positive reference group.

- *Insufficient authority in industrial relations.* The tendency of MNCs to delegate insufficient authority to third country managers in top positions for dealing with critical industrial relations issues in their subsidiaries.

- *Lack of commitment of top-ranking third country managers to the perpetuation of the host country organizations.* The conviction of host country managers that third country managers are less committed to the perpetuation of the host country organization and to the welfare of their host country subordinates.

Formulating Policy Guidelines

The high rate of expatriate failure among U.S. multinationals is a matter of great concern. It stems from several factors: the family situation, lack of cross-cultural relational abilities, the short duration of overseas assignments, problems of repatriation, overemphasis on the technical competence criterion to the disregard of other important attributes such as relational abilities, and inadequate training for cross-cultural encounters.

Companies can no longer afford to transfer people from nation to nation without having an appropriate policy for a guide. Too many people and too much money are involved. Although the common practice is to hire natives for sales positions, the number of short-term specific assignments for solving ad hoc problems is on the increase, which requires bringing in expatriates or third country nationals.

The policy should cover determination of the most appropriate nationality, the selection of the nonnative salesperson, plans for repatriation and reassignment, work assignments, and the development of native salespersons by the nonnative selected. In actuality, companies may not have a thoroughly articulated policy for expatriates and third country nationals that covers all these points. Nonetheless, increasingly, companies attach importance to the problems that occur when people work in different cultures. The following procedure for assignment, repatriation, and reassignment of international employees is recommended to help prevent problems.

**Check
Background**

The long-term interest of the corporation is best served by limiting international assignments to those management and professional employees who have an established record of competence. International assignments can be a valuable supplement to the normal training and development programs for the high-potential employee.

Management and professional people with international experience are an invaluable corporate asset, and every effort should be made to assure that experience gained by employees through such assignments is retained and properly utilized. Consequently, all companies assigning personnel internationally should develop specific plans for the selection, assignment, and repatriation of management and professional employees. Consistent with the needs for international staffing, organization units should identify competent employees who have the desire and potential to successfully undertake an assignment abroad.

**Develop
Guidelines**

Guidelines are needed for pre-assignment, repatriation, and assignment.

Pre-Assignment A pre-assignment orientation program should be planned and implemented on a timely basis to assure that candidates and their dependents are fully prepared to undertake international assignments. Companies assigning personnel internationally should define in writing all known conditions of assignment, including but not limited to the employee's salary, allowances, duration of assignment, etc. The employee should be provided copies of all applicable policies and procedures.

Repatriation and Reassignment Companies should periodically review the status of their international assignees and develop specific repatriation plans for each employee. Where performance continues to be satisfactory, it is the responsibility of the company to assure that personnel selected for international assignments will have upon return a position at least equivalent to the level held by the employee prior to accepting the international assignment. For coordination reasons, it is also the responsibility of the company to keep key personnel services advised of their repatriation plans or problems.

Abroad as at home, poor supervision and inappropriate policies produce negative results. Deficiencies in management away from home can be costly. More and more attention, therefore, is likely to be given to recruiting, selecting, developing, and motivating managers for overseas assignments, however brief the assignment.

Rosalie L. Tung suggests that to enhance expatriate success and minimize failure, U.S. multinationals (1) adopt a longer-term orientation with regard to expatriate assignments and provide support mechanisms at corporate headquarters to allay concerns about repatriation, (2) develop a more international orientation, and (3) provide more rigorous training programs to prepare expatriates for cross-cultural encounters.[4]

Implementing Policy

The first step after formulating a policy for the management of both expatriates and third country nationals is the pursuit of this policy to administer adequately the selection, orientation and training, compensation, and placement procedures inaugurated for salespeople for positions away from home.

Selection

Employee selection is crucial to the success of overseas appointments. It is important to establish adequate selection criteria and to adapt the criteria carefully to ensure that the right person is chosen. Selection criteria include motivation, health, language ability, family considerations, resourcefulness and initiative, adaptability, career and financial planning. Potential candidates can be rated as either satisfactory or unsatisfactory on each of the criteria listed. The person showing the highest satisfactory ratings overall is the final choice.

In addition, the candidate's spouse should be involved in the selection process right from the start. Many failures stem from a spouse's initial reluctance to transfer or inability to adapt to host country conditions. Conversely, an expatriate rated as having a marginal chance of success might do very well because of a supportive spouse. It is therefore crucial to consider spouse evaluation in an expatriate selection system.[5]

Further, before accepting the assignment, the candidate and his or her spouse should be given an opportunity to see the country. An advance trip of a week or two cannot give anyone a thorough understanding of a country's culture, but if properly done, it enables the prospective expatriate to make a more intelligent decision (see International Marketing Highlight 16.4).

Orientation and Training

Sales personnel slated for foreign assignment should be oriented to the new job and provided relevant training. Essentially, orientation and training should cover the terms and conditions of the assignment, language training, and cultural training[6] (see International Marketing Highlight 16.5). Empirical research has shown that many MNCs fail to provide adequate training or social support during the international assignment.[7]

International Marketing Highlight 16.4

Spouses Must Pass Test Before Global Transfers

Employees' families are playing a bigger role in international transfers. The inability of spouses or children to adapt to their new surroundings is the number one cause of failure in overseas transfers, including premature returns, job-performance slumps, and other problems. With overseas postings costing an average of $225,000 to $250,000 a year, companies are trying to smooth the way.

Many companies include spouses in the screening process for overseas assignments, including a formal assessment of such qualities as flexibility, patience, and adaptability. Ford Motor interviews spouses before the move. Exxon also meets with the spouses and sometimes children. Minnesota Mining & Manufacturing offers spouses educational benefits and uses electronic mail to introduce employees' children to peers in the target country. The 3M Company recently found new housing for one Japanese executive in the U.S. so his 65-pound dog could rejoin the family.

The programs are largely a response to pressure from employees. As many as 75 percent of international transfers end in such family problems as marital discord or adjustment problems in children. Companies are finding that it's difficult to get someone to go unless they address those issues.

Source: The Wall Street Journal, September 6, 1991, p. B1.

Terms and Conditions of the Assignment The employee should be provided with a clear and concise overview of the company's expatriate policies, procedures, and compensation system; information on housing, transportation, and schools in the host country; and information on moving arrangements.

Language Training Language training is perhaps the most basic type of knowledge that a foreigner needs for a productive life in a host country. Language is the key to a country's culture. It permits one to understand the subtleties of the country and the reasons why certain things are done certain ways.

A language can be learned in different ways: in a language school with a regular program lasting several months; through a short, intensive program offered either by a commercial school or a local university, or at home through a self-study program. Do-it-yourself kits are available for home study programs in the form of records, cassette recordings, books, telephone conversations with instructors, and different combinations of these alternatives. Regardless of the method, the one central ingredient in learning a language is proper motivation on the part of the employee and family. It is incumbent upon the multinational employer to emphasize the need for language training.

■■■■■■■■■   **International Marketing Highlight 16.5**   ■■■■■■■■■

Colgate-Palmolive Global Marketing Training Program

Few companies pour as much money and management expertise into training marketing managers as New York-based Colgate-Palmolive. Although much smaller than Lever Brothers and Procter & Gamble, Colgate derives 60 percent of its revenue from abroad. The company prides itself in its ability to penetrate new markets (sometimes before its giant competitors arrive) and maintain good profitability. To retain its position as one of the world's preeminent consumer products companies, Colgate decided years ago to develop a program to ensure itself of a steady supply of superior marketers with the skills to operate almost anywhere.

The "Global Marketing Training Program" Colgate created, which gives its participants a two-year immersion in global marketing, has acquired considerable prestige since its establishment. Admission is highly competitive and is sought by some of the brightest B.A.'s and M.B.A.'s from the world's best colleges and business schools. Successful applicants must have not only excellent academic credentials but also leadership skills, fluency in at least one other language in addition to English, and some international-living experience, for example, a year of study in a country other than the applicant's own.

The program itself consists of assignments in various departments at Colgate, with a strong emphasis on marketing functions. A typical rotation includes some time in finance and manufacturing and larger blocks of time at Colgate's ad agency, in market research, and in product management. The trainees serve for seven months as field salespeople in the U.S., and they actually perform the job rather than merely accompanying regular salespeople on their rounds.

The program gives trainees the basic skills global marketing managers need. The participants learn to use computers, devise budgets, formulate sales promotion strategies, manage work groups, and so on. They also begin to develop relationships that will help them when they start to operate in the international environment.

Most of Colgate's new marketing "graduates" are sent to markets in developing countries. Some are initially assigned to work in the U.S., but they, too, are soon posted overseas. Because non–U.S. markets are so important to Colgate, it does not automatically bring its international marketers back to the U.S. after a foreign assignment, as do many other MNCs. Often, the marketers go directly from one overseas post to another, in essence, career internationalism.

Source: Business International, September 10, 1990, p. 306.

Cultural Training Both academic and interpersonal cultural training should be given. *Academic training* includes the provision of things like books, maps, brochures, films, and slides. *Interpersonal training* consists of making arrangements for candidate and family to make a trip to the host country, in addition to meeting with host country natives living in the U.S. and people who have lived previously in the host country.[8]

Compensation

Salespeople away from their home base cost more. They must be paid extra compensation, first, as a premium for climatic conditions in the host country, separation from friends and relative, cultural shock, and subjection to situations of political instability and economic risk in conditions of unstable currencies. Second, they need an allowance for housing, children's schooling, return trips home on a periodic basis, income tax, and overall cost-of-living expenses. Third are certain perquisites common in host countries for particular positions, like car and driver, servants, and club memberships.[9]

The elements of compensation and the amount paid under each heading differ from country to country depending on the living costs. According to *The Economist,* giving New York an index of 100, the cost-of-living index in Tokyo would be 150, Hong Kong 125, London 115, Beijing 100, Singapore 95, Buenos Aires 90, Moscow 80, Mexico City 75, Bangkok 65, and Delhi 45.[10]

Exhibit 16.2 illustrates a typical expatriate compensation package. Note that the total additional compensation is over three times more in the U.K. than in the U.S. Even in a developing country, an expatriate may cost more depending on demand and supply conditions relative to different elements of compensation. In a city like Tokyo, housing would be very expensive since suitable apartments are very scarce. In many developing countries, housing is expensive because western-style accommodations are difficult to

---

EXHIBIT 16.2
The Price of an Expatriate

Following are an employer's typical first-year expenses of sending a U.S. executive to Britain, assuming a $100,000 salary and a family of four.

Direct Compensation Costs:	
Base salary	$100,000
Foreign-service premium	15,000
Goods and services differential	21,000
Housing costs in London	39,000*
Transfer Costs:	
Relocation allowance	$5,000
Air fare to London	2,000
Moving household goods	25,000
Other Costs:	
Company car	$15,000
Schooling (two children)	20,000
Annual home leave (four people)	4,000
U.K. personal income tax	56,000*
Total:	$302,000

Note: Additional costs often incurred aren't listed above, including language and cross-cultural training for employee and family, and costs of selling home and cars in the U.S. before moving.

* Figures take into account payments by employee to company based on hypothetical U.S. income tax and housing costs.
Source: Organizational Resource Counselors Inc., New York.

locate, and a high premium must be paid for the few that are available.[11] Similarly, if taxes are very high in a country and if the foreigner is taxed like a native, the company must bear the tax burden over and above what the employee would have paid in the U.S. or other home country.

Placement

Once a salesperson accepts an overseas position, the company should provide adequate information to prepare for the departure to the host country. This information includes advice on such matters as how to apply for a passport, how to obtain necessary visas and immunizations, how expenses should be handled for reimbursement, how to obtain transportation and arrange accompanied baggage and unaccompanied baggage shipment, tax matters, and current status under the various company benefit, pension, stock, and insurance plans. Information is also needed on obtaining an international driver's license, making financial arrangements, deciding what clothing to take, and even reminding the salesperson to notify correspondents of a change of address. Some of these arrangements and details are quite complicated, and generous advice and counsel for each individual can smooth the passage of personnel and their families to transfer assignments.

Repatriation and Reassignment

Traditionally, salespeople have welcomed overseas assignments. It has meant taking extra compensation and seeing the world at company expense; besides, going abroad was considered to be a route to the executive suite. More recently, however, fewer jobs are opening up in Euro-capitals. The Middle East and the developing countries are the new foreign-assignment destinations, where "hardship pay" lives up to its name and the experience offers little beyond just that—experience. A returning salesperson faces a severe penalty for being out of the home office working environment and a severe shock when confronted with the domestic real estate market.

Fewer salespeople are willing to accept overseas positions, particularly those personnel who perceive the risk of an inferior position upon return. On a number of occasions, there has been no job for a returning expatriate, who has then spent months in a holding pattern. Many companies lose good marketing people for lack of job vacancies in the U.S. when their time comes to return.

Returning home amounts to facing previously familiar surroundings. Yet, as the following quotes show, expatriates have found the reentry into the home environment more of a problem than going abroad.[12]

> Repatriating executives from overseas assignments is a top management challenge that goes far beyond the superficial problems and costs of physical relocation . . . the crux of the matter is the assumption that since these individuals are returning home—that is, to a familiar way of life— they should have no trouble adapting to either the corporate or the home environment. However, experience has shown that repatriation is anything but simple.

> Managers know that there is always a risk of being stuck, at least temporarily, in a mediocre job when they return.

> Few, if any, executives ever come out ahead financially in a transfer back to the U.S. . . . An even more serious shock [than the financial shock], because it can have a long-range impact on the executive's career, is the re-adaptation to corporate life . . . a foreign assignment [tends to] . . . keep the executive out of the mainstream of advancement. . . . In some respects the more outstanding a performer the executive was overseas, the more uncomfortable his return will be.[13]

The returning executives themselves have made these comments:

Going home is a harder move. The foreign move has the excitement of being new . . . more confusing, but exciting. Reentry is frightening. . . . I'll be happy to be home . . . I wonder if I can adjust back.

There's some kind of traumatic reaction to it. It evidenced itself in my insomnia. There was something there . . . waking me up at 4 AM

Career . . . it didn't help. I got personal learning. I lost time. My career stopped when I left and started again when I returned.

Colleagues view me as doing a job I did in the past. I had the experience before going . . . they don't view me as gaining while overseas.

The organization has changed . . . work habits and norms and procedures have changed and I have lost touch with all that. . . I am a beginner again.

Colleagues are indifferent to my international assignment.

Before going overseas I thought that it might help my career. Within the home organization, international is more remote from domestic. You are visible only within international.

I have no specific reentry job to return to . . . I want to leave international and return to domestic . . . Working abroad magnifies problems while isolating effects . . . i.e., you deal with more problems, but. . . [the home office] does not know the details of the good or bad effects . . . managerially, I'm out of touch with financial policies. . . I'll be less confident in managing . . . If this job had been in North America, . . . my old management style would have worked.[14]

The repatriation problem is not limited to U.S. expatriates. Even Japanese returnees find it hard to assimilate their own culture after having spent a few years in the U.S. Because most Japanese white-collar workers have a negative attitude toward overseas assignments, many returnees end up taking jobs with the U.S. subsidiaries in Japan.[15]

To alleviate the reluctance of personnel to be recruited for foreign assignments, companies are providing prospective expatriates with written guarantees on company foreign personnel policy. These repatriation agreements are really no more than general promises in writing that include a limit of a two to five-year maximum on time spent abroad and assurances of return to a mutually acceptable job. Union Carbide assigns senior executives to act as sponsors for overseas managers, including salespeople. Sponsors scout six months prior to the expatriates' return to locate a suitable position. The Dow Chemical Company has 10 full-time counselors who visit with each of the company's expatriate employees, including those in sales, once a year. The counselors let the expatriates know that they have not been forgotten and act as advocates for possible promotion considerations. Also, repatriation supervisors are assigned to expatriates to monitor compensation, performance, and potential career paths.[16]

Sales people with international experience are an invaluable corporate asset. Repatriation agreements should ensure that the experience gained by personnel through such assignments is retained and properly utilized.

International Sales Negotiations

Face-to-face negotiation with the customer is the heart of the sales job. Negotiations are necessary to reach an agreement on the total exchange transaction, comprising such aspects as the product to be delivered, the price to be paid, the service agreement, the payment schedule, and other issues. In other words, negotiations are the means of deciding the terms of sales.

International sales negotiations have many characteristics that distinguish them from negotiations in the domestic setting. First and foremost, the cultural background of the negotiating parties is different, which may inhibit understanding of each other's viewpoint.[17] Second, political factors often complicate and delay international business negotiations. Third, in many cases, the host government must be involved in bringing the negotiations to a conclusion.

Sales negotiations may involve such issues as product features, service, price, delivery date, mode of payment, training of buyer personnel, and financing. Although these issues are usually negotiated between buyer and seller in domestic situations as well, they assume greater importance in international marketing for a variety of reasons. Consider service. In the U.S. a company selling a product that requires periodic servicing will presumably have adequate service facilities and parts inventory. If the product sale is negotiated in, say, Thailand, and the company's closest service facilities in the area are located in Japan, the customer would want certain assurances about timely servicing at a reasonable cost. The customer may demand that the company establish facilities in Thailand itself. But the company may not find it financially feasible to do so. In such a situation, negotiations become essential. The Thai government may even step in and refuse to grant foreign exchange for the purchase of the product until the company agrees to make local service arrangements.

Negotiating Process

The objective of a negotiating process is to reach an agreement of mutual benefit. The process begins from a situation of *contention,* meaning each party has its own agenda to strike the deal. It ends with *conclusion,* whereby a mutually satisfying agreement has been reached. The distance from contention to conclusion is covered through the stages of (1) clarification and comprehension, (2) confidence and credibility, (3) convergence, and (4) conciliation and concession. The first stage, *clarification and comprehension,* involves seeking information to form a better idea of each other's position on significant issues.[18] The second stage *confidence and credibility,* refers to the formation of attitudes among the parties based on an appreciation of each other's requirements and the reasons behind them. At the conclusion of this stage, the two parties reach a *convergence* of views on many aspects of the deal. The third stage, *concession and conciliation,* requires the parties to reach a compromise on the remaining unsettled issues through give and take. This fourth stage leads to the conclusion of negotiations.

The shape of the negotiated agreement depends on the bargaining power of the two parties, which in turn is determined by the importance of the deal for each of them. For example, if the product involves substantial business for the seller now and potential additional sales later, the buyer would be in a relatively strong bargaining position. Conversely, if the product is not readily available from another source, the seller will approach negotiations from a point of leverage.

In addition to the bargaining power of the two parties, negotiations are considerably affected by the negotiating skills of the people involved in the process. Issues such as how people perceive each other, how they interact, how the ambience of negotiations can be altered, how confidence and trust can be established, and how they threaten and intimidate each other will significantly influence the outcome.[19] These issues, along with the fact that the negotiating parties come from different economic, political, and cultural backgrounds and may speak different languages, make international negotiating a complex exercise. It is for this reason that many scholars consider international negotiating an art.

Negotiating Strategies

Basic to negotiating well is the ability to put yourself in the other person's shoes, understand his or her way of thinking, recognize his or her perspective, and allocate sufficient time for the task. Even when you start from a point of weakness, there are strategies that a salesperson can pursue to negotiate to his or her advantage. Here are some adapted suggestions from Thomas C. Keise:

1. *Increase your variables, and know your alternatives.* Price is not the only flexible factor. Consider every aspect of the deal—R&D, specifications, delivery, and payment arrangements. The more options you have, the greater your chances of success.
2. *When attacked, listen.* Keep the customer talking and you will learn valuable things about his or her business and needs.
3. *Pause often to summarize.* To reduce frustration and assure the customer that you're hearing what he or she is saying, pause often to summarize your progress.
4. *Assert your own company's needs.* Too much empathy for the customer can reduce the emphasis on problem solving and lead to unnecessary concessions.
5. *Urge a commitment.* Try to make your customer commit to the outcome of the whole negotiation. Make sure the full solution works for both parties.
6. *Save the hardest issues for last.* Begin with issues that can be quickly settled in order to set a mood of success and relaxation.
7. *Start high, concede slowly, and keep your expectations high.* Remember that every concession has a different value for buyer and seller. One with a high value for your side may not be that high for the other, so do not compromise more than you need to.
8. *Never give in to emotional blackmail.* If the customer loses his temper, don't lose yours. Withdraw, postpone, dodge, sidestep, listen. As a last resort, declare the attack unacceptable, but always refuse to fight.[20]

Negotiating style varies from culture to culture, and often involves differences in language, cultural conditioning, approaches to problem solving, implicit assumptions, gestures and facial expressions, and the role of ceremony and formality.[21] In preparing for and analyzing a negotiation, it is useful to review these dimensions fully. As has been said: "The negotiator must enter into the private world or cultural space of the other, while at the same time, sharing his or her own perceptual field."[22]

Foreign Sales Promotion

Sales promotion devices aim to stimulate new attitudes toward the promoted product. The lure of getting something for nothing can be successful in creating desire for a product among buyers no matter which country or region they belong to. Although historically sales promotion is a uniquely American phenomenon, it is used today to supplement advertising and personal selling throughout the world (see International Marketing Highlight 16.6).

Besides increasing sales at the retail level, sales promotion helps in building the morale of the salesforce. Some companies use sales promotion simultaneously with sales incentive schemes so they can complement each other. For example, Hoover Company promoted its vacuum cleaners in England by providing a packet of one dozen throw-away vacuum bags as a lure. At the same time, the company organized a sales contest for its dealers and salesforce for a vacation in the U.S.

Sales promotion also acts as a "push-through" device by creating a demand for a product among customers, who then compel dealers and retailers to stock it. For example,

Coca-Cola Company introduced its orange soda, Fanta, in many developing countries through free gifts of ballpoint pens and pencils and the like. Because of the resulting consumer demand, even the very small retailers were forced to carry Fanta.

Devices of sales promotion can be classified on the basis of the function to be performed and the target to be reached. Three main types of sales promotion can be distinguished according to function: introducing a new product, encouraging increased use of a product, and directly enticing customers at the retail level. Free samples, price-off coupons, and refund offers are the devices used for introducing new products. Price-off deals, premiums, contests, and sweepstakes are methods for encouraging greater use of a product. Trading stamps, retailer coupons, and point-of-purchase demonstrations are used at the retail level.

Sales promotion techniques may be consumer-oriented or dealer- and distributor-oriented. That is, the *targets* of promotion may be consumers or dealers and distributors. Sampling, demonstrations, or instructions; premium offers or temporary price reductions; and contests and sweepstakes are consumer-oriented promotion devices. Intermediary or agent-oriented techniques include assistance in store layout, assistance in planning and developing strategy such as accounting and inventory instructions, cooperative advertising, dealers' sales training, provision of point-of-purchase materials, and money and merchandise allowances.

International Marketing Highlight 16.6

Globalization of Coupons

International coupon use is on the rise, a trend that will continue through the 1990s, according to a recent study. "Coupon Distribution and Redemption Patterns Report," released by NCH Promotional Services, Chicago, examines the couponing and promotion trends in major world markets including the U.S., Canada, the U.K., Spain, Italy, and Belgium.

Although the U.S. remains the world's leading coupon market, with over 279.4 billion coupons issued in 1990, several other markets around the world are beginning to experience the same couponing growth that occurred in the U.S. during the early 1980s. The European Community's recent gains in political and economic freedoms have given marketers the opportunity to use more creative promotional techniques. The European market has enormous, untapped promotional possibilities.

As distribution methods standardize and multinational firms introduce tried-and-true coupon promotion practices on a large scale, the barriers to couponing will begin to dissolve.

The study said consumers in the U.K. and Belgium are the EU's most active coupon users. In 1990 an average of 17 coupons per household were redeemed in the U.K., and 18 coupons per household were redeemed in Belgium. The U.K., Europe's largest coupon market, has had redemption growth of 21 percent since 1989, the largest increase in the world.

The study also reported that the U.K.'s coupon industry outlook is bright, since 7 out of 10 consumers already use coupons regularly. Newspapers and magazines are the most popular means of distribution in the U.K. Spain and Italy rely heavily on in- or on-pack promotions for their coupon distribution. In several European markets, door-to-door coupon distribution is common, although this technique is virtually unheard of in the U.S. In other parts of Europe, couponing has had relatively stagnant growth. In Spain, distribution has declined over the past few years, and Italy's couponing has shown only modest increases. In both countries, an average of 3 coupons were redeemed per household, compared with 77 in the U.S. and 26 in Canada.

Although couponing has just become legal in Denmark, other European countries have limited access to coupons. In Holland and Switzerland, major retailers refuse to accept them.

Source: "Global Coupon Use Up; U.K., Belgium Tops in Europe," *Marketing News,* August 5, 1991, p. 6. Copyright 1991 by the American Marketing Association.

The preceding categorization is based on U.S. practices. The marketing environment in a foreign market may require making appropriate adaptations in sales promotion offerings. In some nations, a marketer may be forced to invent an entirely new sales promotion idea that is in line with the country's environment. Poor economic conditions in developing countries may prompt a greater emphasis on the economic value of the offering, assuming the product is directed at the mass market. Legal restrictions in many countries call for adaptation. In Germany, giveaways (other than items of insignificant value such as calendars and diaries) are legally prohibited. A sales promotion campaign should not create conflict in the marketplace that could have political ramifications. Inasmuch as some sales promotion campaigns must be implemented through wholesalers and retailers, their structure and practices would also be a consideration in planning a sales promotion campaign. For example, retailers in most developing countries are small, scattered, and disorganized. They may not be able to handle the equivalent of a cents-off type of sales promotion.

Above all, the sales promotion offering should be culturally acceptable. The need for customizing of sales promotion to match the perspectives of a country is well illustrated by Ford Motor Company's efforts in Brazil. In the midst of high inflation, banks in Brazil were not willing to finance purchases of big-price items by low-income families. Ford Motor Company, therefore, established car-buying clubs of 60 members in each. Each member made 60 monthly payments toward a car. A drawing was held each month, and the member whose name appeared on the drawing received the car that month. This way the low-income Brazilian families continued to buy the cars without being burdened with high interest costs. The company in turn generated a guaranteed number of customers each month.

Management of sales promotion requires (1) a clear definition of *objectives* (for example, introducing a new product, increasing sales of an existing product, reducing seasonal declines in sales, countering competitor's gains, and registering new customers); (2) making *budget* allocations (which must be done in the context of a total promotional budget including advertising and personal selling); (3) drawing a *plan of action* covering such points as length of the campaign, details of sales promotion offerings, instructions required for the salesforce and middle agents, coordination needed with other departments of the company, media announcements, and cost estimates; and (4) an *evaluation* of the campaign to determine its viability for future use in the same country, and in other nations.

Public Relations Overseas

Public relations are a useful device for establishing a foothold or strengthening existing position in an overseas market. The public relations activity is directed toward an influential, though relatively small, target audience of editors and journalists who work for publications or in broadcasting aimed at a firm's customers and prospects. Since the target audience is small, it is relatively inexpensive to reach.

To do an effective public relations job overseas, an international marketer needs to hire an established public relations firm, one with relevant experience and adequate resources if possible. If the U.S. public relations firm of the company has an office in the host country, it may be retained there too. Alternatively, one may have to choose from among the local firms.

After the public relations firm is recruited, the company should develop a *dossier,* that is, a package of information that editors can use for future reference. A typical dossier runs to 10 pages and includes information on the company's capabilities, its technologies, its preeminence, and why it operates in the host country. The dossier may be supplemented with a corporate *brochure,* preferably in the host country language, identifying worldwide manufacturing, research and development, and sales and service locations. Usually, the dossier is accompanied by a letter inviting editors to contact a designated person for further information. The letter may also state that articles and releases will be regularly issued by the company in the future.

The company should decide, in consultation with the public relations firm, how an initial contact should be made with the target audience, editors, and journalists. At this stage, the public relations firm is better known to the audience than its client. As a matter of fact, some public relations firms are so well accepted in a country that a release on the company's behalf signals editors that the story is newsworthy, factual, and worth publishing. Thus, the public relations firm should play a lead role in establishing initial contact for the firm.

Future announcements and releases may either be custom-developed for the host country or extracted from among those prepared for the domestic market. In other words, a firm entering an overseas market may reuse some of its U.S. news releases, application case histories, technical and feature articles, trends articles, and the like. The appropriateness of domestic material in an overseas market may be judged by the host country marketing management and the public relations firm. Wherever necessary, however, original releases should be produced and issued as desired.

Once a story or article on the firm appears in print, it will be read by only a small fraction of customers. Nonetheless, it is important to get all the promotional value one can from a good placement. One way of doing this is to send story or article reprints in quantity to the firm's salespeople and distributor salespeople for use in their sales calls and mailings. The reprints support sales training programs, too. New salespeople can learn much about the company's products and applications from a file of articles.

These activities help in establishing a good name for the company and its product during the startup period. For it to continue to generate news and be visible in the long run, a variety of techniques can be used. These include interviews and the publicizing of talks by area executives, publicity for new product designs or services developed in or for the overseas area, case histories from customers' experiences in the area, special activities for key media, invitations to the press to cover company-sponsored seminars, meetings, and workshops, and photographs to meet an editor's express needs. These techniques assist in *localizing* the company. Beyond that, as the company becomes fully established, the public relations activities may include sponsored speeches and seminars, as well as management leadership in professional associations (see International Marketing Highlight 16.7).

The role of public relations abroad does not differ greatly from that in the U.S., but somehow U.S. companies do not emphasize it overseas as thoroughly as at home. The public relations activity internationally should not be directly limited to market a product or service. Public relations programs should serve as a company's antenna, gathering and analyzing information on events, trends, and legislation, and as a contact point with the firm's various audiences.

■ **International Marketing Highlight 16.7** ■

Global Philanthropy

- American Express—developed an academic course to educate secondary school students on travel and tourism issues. Cost: $500,000.

- DuPont—sent 1.4 million water-jug filters to 8 nations in Africa. Their synthetic fabric removes debilitating parasitic worms from drinking water. Cost: $400,000.
- Alcoa—teamed up with local authorities in southern Brazil to build a sewage plant serving 15,000 rural residents. Cost: $112,000.
- H.J. Heinz—funded infant nutrition studies in China and Thailand through Heinz's Institute of Nutritional Sciences in Chengdu, China. Cost: $94,000.
- IBM—donated computer equipment and expertise to Costa Rica's National Parks foundation to develop strategies for preserving rain forests. Cost: $60,000.
- Hewlett-Packard Co.—donated computers to the University of Prague.

Source: Business Week, February 25, 1991, p. 91.

Summary

Personal selling is an important ingredient of any marketing program. The three sources of sales personnel are expatriates (e.g., U.S. nationals working in a host country, say, England), natives (an English national working in England), and third country nationals (a French citizen transferred by a U.S. company to work in England). In the realm of international business, most personal selling jobs are handled by the local management. The head office, however, can provide useful support to local management on such aspects as selection, training, supervision, compensation, and evaluation.

The chapter concentrates on the problems involved in managing expatriates and third country nationals. MNCs should have a well-defined policy for expatriates and third country nationals that deals with such matters as determining the most appropriate non-native nationality selection in host country personnel situations, employment upon repatriation, and plans for natives' development. Also covered are various aspects of managing expatriates and third country salespeople: selection, orientation, training (including terms and conditions of the assignment, cultural training, and language training), compensation, and placement, Finally, the process of international sales negotiations and strategies for successful negotiations are discussed.

In ways similar to domestic marketing, sales promotion and public relations are also relevant to international marketing. The role of sales promotion in other countries does not vary from what it is in the U.S. However, an appropriate sales promotion program for an overseas market should be geared to the local environment. For example, in a country where retailing organizations are small and scattered, it may be difficult to use the equivalent of cents-off coupons. Public relations provide a justification and an identity for the foreign enterprise in the economic sphere of the host country. It is desirable to hire the services of a public relations firm with relevant experience in order to get started on a solid program. Publicity programs, which give the firm and its products broad exposure to customers and prospects as well as third-party endorsement by the media, provide a cost-efficient use of a limited promotional budget.

Review Questions

1. Define *expatriate.* What problems are expatriates likely to face overseas?
2. Discuss the problems that pertain to the employment of third country nationals as salespeople.
3. What are the elements of policy guidelines for sales management overseas?

4. What precautions should be taken in selecting salespeople for overseas positions?
5. What type of training should be provided to expatriates?
6. Why do expatriate salespeople cost more? Illustrate with examples.
7. What steps may be adopted to adequately repatriate and reassign salespeople located abroad?
8. What role does a public relations firm play for an international marketer?

Creative Questions

1. Many developing countries have a surplus of skilled people who are willing to work at substantially lower wages than their counterparts in the industrialized countries. Despite this fact, should an MNC give hiring preference to nationals over third country workers in order to be a good corporate citizen?
2. Often it is said that marketing students interested in international business should be fluent in at least one foreign language. On the other hand, English is the commercial language of the world. Is the emphasis on learning a foreign language unnecessary? Even if one were to learn a foreign language, which language should be chosen? (Keep in mind that at this stage, the student cannot be sure in which part of the world he or she will be involved.)

Endnotes

1. W. Chan Kim and R. A. Manborgue, "Cross-Cultural Strategies," *Journal of Business Strategy,* Spring 1987, p. 29.

2. O. Jay Galbraith and Anders Edstrom, "International Transfer of Managers: Some Important Policy Considerations," *Columbia Journal of World Business,* Summer 1976, pp. 100–126.

3. "New Breed of Expatriates," *Crossborder Monitor,* August 20, 1998, p. 3.

4. Rosalie L. Tung, "Expatriate Assignments: Enhancing Success and Minimalizing Failure," *Executive* 2 (1987): 117–126.

5. Betty Jane Punnett, "Toward Effective Management of Expatriate Spouses," *Journal of World Business,* Fall 1997, pp. 243–257.

6. *See* Joann S. Lublin, "Younger Managers Learn Global Skills," *The Wall Street Journal,* March 31, 1991, p. B1.

7. Michael Harvey, "Dual Career Expatriates: Expectations Adjustment and Satisfaction with International Relocation.," *Journal of International Business Studies* 28, no. 3 (1997): 627–658.

8. *See* Cyndee Miller, "Growing Overseas Requires Marketers to Learn More Than a New Language," *Marketing News,* March 28, 1994, p.8. *Also see* Bob Hagerty, "Trainers Help Expatriate Employees Build Bridges to Different Cultures," *The Wall Street Journal,* June 14, 1993, p. B1.

9. *See* "The Fast Track Leads Overseas," *Business Week,* November 1, 1993, p. 64.

10. *The Economist,* June 16, 1999, p. 120.

11. "Up, Down, or Sideways," *Crossborder Monitor,* November 19, 1997, p. 1. *Also see* "Shell's Expat Pay: Dutch Treat," *Crossborder Monitor,* February 4, 1998, p. 8.

12. Susan Carey, "Expatriates Find Long Stints Abroad Can Close Doors to Credit At Home," *The Wall Street Journal,* May 17, 1993, p. B1. *Also see* Joan M. Inzinga, "The Perceived Learning Needs and Intercultural Experiences of Corporate Expatriates: American and Asian Pacifics," Ph.D. dissertation, The University of Connecticut, 1988.

13. "Successful Repatriation Demands Attention, Care and Dash of Ingenuity," *Business International,* March 3, 1978, p. 65.

14. Nancy J. Adler, "Re-Entry: Managing Cross-Cultural Transitions," paper presented at the Academy of International Business Meetings in New Orleans, October 1980.

15. Nan M. Sussman, "A Hard Homecoming for Japan's Expats," *The Asian Wall Street Journal Weekly,* January 13, 1986, p. 15.

16. *See* "How MNCs Ease Expatriates' Return to Home Countries," *Business International,* February 25, 1991, p. 65. *Also see* "Bringing Our Expatriates Home: A Fresh Look at Reentry," *Business International,* February 11, 1991, p. 49.

17. John L. Graham, Dong Ki Kim, Chi-Yuan Lin, and Michael Robinson, "Buyer-Seller Negotiations Around the Pacific Rim: Differences in Fundamental Exchange Processes," *Journal of Consumer Research,* June 1988, pp. 48–54.

18. Discussion in this section draws heavily on Claude Cellich, "Skills for Business Negotiations," *International Trade Forum,* October–November 1990, p. 8. *Also see* Claude Cellich, "Negotiations for Export Business: Elements for Success," *International Trade Forum,* 4 (1995): 20–31.

19. Nigel C. G. Campbell, John L. Graham, Alain Jolibert, and Hans Gunther Meissner, "Marketing Negotiations in France,

Germany, the United Kingdom and the United States," *Journal of Marketing,* April 1988, pp. 49–62. *Also see* Claude Cellich, "Contract Renegotiations," *International Trade Forum,* November 2, 1999, pp. 11–15.

20. Thomas C. Keise, "Negotiating With a Customer You Can't Afford to Lose," *Harvard Business Review,* November–December 1988, pp. 30–37.

21. John B. Ford, Michael S. LaTour, Scott J. Vitell and Warren A. French, "Moral Judgment and Market Negotiations: A Comparison of Chinese and American Managers," *Journal of International Marketing* 5, no. 2 (1997): 57–76.

22. Philip R. Harris and Robert T. Moran, *Managing Cultural Differences,* 2nd ed. (Houston: Gulf Publishing Co., 1987), p. 57.

CHAPTER 17

Export
Marketing

CHAPTER FOCUS

After studying this chapter, you should be able to

■ Discuss perspectives of U.S. export trade.

■ Explain how the U.S. government encourages and hinders exports.

■ Describe the steps in conducting export business.

■ Discuss duty-free zones and barter trade.

The U.S. is the world's largest exporter. Yet its exports are a meager percentage of it's GDP. The balance has shifted, however, to an extraordinary extent in the last decade. In 1970 the ratio of US. exports to GDP was 4.3 percent. Exports almost doubled to 7.5 percent of GDP in 1986, and increased to 12 percent of GDP in 1999. Still, in comparison with the exports of European nations and Japan, U.S. exports (as a percentage of GDP) are small. For Germany and the U.K., exports amount to roughly 20 percent of GDP.[1]

The international trade environment provides U.S. business with a variety of opportunities for export growth. First, the U.S. government is moving toward policies and procedures that encourage exports. Second, Western Europe and Latin America began to recover in 1997 from a long recession and are providing good markets now for U.S. goods. China also has been growing at a tremendous rate of 9 percent annually. Economic liberalization in developing countries provides an additional boost to world economies, and narrowing inflation differentials among nations always favor export growth. Thus, despite the Southeast Asian problems during 1997–1998, and the continuing recession in Japan, the U.S. exports are well poised for sustained growth.

Yes, prospects look good for U.S. export growth, but U.S. businesses need to make conscious efforts to boost exports if they are to realize their full export potential. In 1996, out of 690,000 manufacturing firms in the U.S., only 6 percent exported; only 5 percent of the nation's 770,000 wholesalers exported; and only 1/3 of 1 percent of all other types of U.S. companies—largely service-based firms—exported. Big MNCs account for the vast share of U.S. exports, indicating that most U.S. companies have neglected to explore export opportunities.

Why is this so? Some marketing managers do not fully explore potential sales abroad because of an uneasiness or lack of understanding about foreign credits and collections. Others shy away because of a fear that selling abroad involves too much red tape. Of course, selling abroad differs from selling in the domestic market, but it can be handled without much difficulty if management does the requisite research before making the attempt.

This chapter begins with an analysis of certain U.S. exports. Then the procedural details for conducting an export business are outlined. Significant export management issues are discussed, and the emerging area of barter trade is examined.

U.S. Export Trade

The U.S. imports more merchandise than it exports, resulting in a negative *balance of trade* (discussed in more detail later). To an extent, the negative trade balance is caused by excessive oil imports. During the 1950s U.S. exports amounted to 18 percent of world trade. This percentage declined to about 13.5 in 1970 during a period of indifference toward export trade. For example, either U.S. exports then were unique products that sold themselves—without significant competition from other countries—or export markets were used as last resorts to absorb periodic excess domestic inventories. Only a few companies were really committed to exporting. Moreover, in the recent past, the U.S. government had no clear-cut policy for the encouragement of exports. Not until the mid 1960s did the government become particularly concerned about the U.S. *balance of payments* (discussed again later in reference to the balance of trade).

During the 1970s two compelling reasons to expand exports emerged. First, U.S. economic growth had slipped to less than 2 percent annually from about 4 percent over the preceding 20 years. U.S. companies began to consider export markets as a way of sustaining their own growth rates. Second, the dramatic increase in the price and consumption of imported oil made it essential to boost exports to help offset the huge outflow of U.S. dollars paid for oil. The U.S. share of world exports climbed to as high as 20.6 percent in the early 1980s. It declined to 13 percent in 1990 and stood at 12.2 percent in 1999.[2]

The U.S. potential for export growth is enormous. Whereas the U.S. accounts for 22 percent of the world's wealth, it has only 4 percent of the world's consumers; 96 percent live outside this nation, representing a $3.0 trillion market. In 1999 exports supported over 11.5 million U.S. jobs. These jobs pay on average 13 percent more than jobs not related to exports. During 1995–1999, exports were responsible for nearly 3 million jobs.[3] A $10 billion increase in exports generates about 193,000 American jobs both directly and indirectly. A similar increase in imports eliminates about 179,000 jobs. Thus, the export job-generation effect is about 7.8 percent larger than the import job-loss effect.[4]

Thousands of U.S. companies offer products and services that could be competitive abroad. Entry into export markets should help domestic business as well, because as the market expands via exports, economies of scale should be realized in lower costs of products both for overseas shipment and for those to be sold in the U.S. Also, exports provide a cushion against slumps in the domestic market. And fully one-third of our economic growth is dependent on overseas trade.

Level and Direction of U.S. Export Activity

In the last few years, thousands of American companies have taken a fresh, aggressive approach to selling in the international markets. They are venturing into new markets, exporting goods and services that have never gone abroad before, using novel approaches to marketing products, and thinking up new ways to apply their technological know-how. This export vigor can be attributed to various factors. The fall of the dollar makes U.S. products cheaper for foreign buyers. Further, U.S. productivity has been rising since the late 1980s. Finally, U.S. labor costs have fallen since the 1990s.[5]

In 1999 U.S. industries exported $683 billion worth of goods to foreign customers; during the same year the U.S. imports amounted to $1,030 billion. (see Exhibit 17.1) This resulted in a trade deficit of $347 billion. For 20 years the U.S. continued to incur trade deficits; from $9.3 billion in 1976 to $169.8 billion in 1986 to $187 billion in 1996. In the 1990s exports increased faster than imports, but the trade deficit continued.

The U.S. continues to do well in trading services, generating a respectable trade surplus year after year. In 1999, for example, services exports amounted to $275 billion, while imports were $200 billion, leaving a surplus of $75 billion.

The *trade deficit,* refers to the U.S. balance of trade, and *not* to the balance of payments. The ***balance of trade*** is the difference between merchandise exports and imports. The ***balance of payments***, on the other hand, includes all international transactions such as merchandise exports and imports; transfers under U.S. military agency sales contracts; travel and transportation by U.S. citizens abroad and by foreigners in the U.S.; and direct investments, foreign aid, and other payments. Such international transactions (excluding mer-

EXHIBIT 17.1
U.S. Exports and Imports (in Billions of Dollars)

	Goods			Services		
	Exports	**Imports**	**Balance**	**Exports**	**Imports**	**Balance**
1990	394	495	(101)	120	81	39
1991	422	488	(66)	144	102	42
1992	448	532	(84)	160	110	50
1993	465	581	(446)	174	116	58
1994	502	668	(166)	199	139	60
1995	575	749	(174)	210	142	68
1996	612	79	(187)	224	151	73
1997	679	878	(199)	237	157	80
1998	670	917	(247)	264	181	83
1999	683	1,030	(347)	275	200	75

chandise exports and imports) usually are called *invisibles* in international commerce. Their significant role for the U.S. is borne out by the fact that at times our deficits in merchandise trade have been largely balanced or exceeded by growing positive "invisible" balances.

American exports consist primarily of agricultural products and ready-for-sale manufactured goods, as well as component parts and intermediate products used in manufacturing—in other words, from soybeans to computers and aircraft, and from blue jeans to machine tools. The U.S. import list includes oil, autos, television sets, and other consumer and industrial goods. Half the 10 key industries in U.S. foreign trade—aerospace, computer equipment, oil field machinery, medical equipment, and chemicals—enjoy export surpluses. The others—cars and trucks, textiles and apparel, electronics, steel, and machine tools—remain huge losers.

During the last 10 years, U.S. trade has undergone interesting changes. First, trade with Pacific Basin countries has registered a significant increase, while trade with Western Europe has relatively declined. According to GATT (now WTO) trans-Pacific trade overtook trans-Atlantic trade in value for the first time in 1984. Second, trade with developing countries has been increasing faster than with developed countries. Third, the role of manufactured products has increased in importance over basic products.

These shifts reflect the changes in the world economy. More nations today participate in trade than ever before. U.S. trade is moving away from its traditional markets of Canada and Western Europe toward a broader base of nations, indicating that U.S. business is truly becoming international in character (see International Marketing Highlight 17.1)

■■■■■■■■■   **International Marketing Highlight 17.1**   ■■■■■■■■■

America's Hottest Export: Pop Culture

There is good news for the U.S. these days on the export front: Around the globe, folks just can't get enough of America. They may not want our hardware anymore—our cars, steel, or television sets. But when they want a jolt of popular culture—and they want more all the time—they increasingly turn to American software, movies, music, TV programming, and home videos, which together now account for an annual trade surplus of some $8 billion. Only aerospace (aircraft and related equipment) outranks pop culture as an export.

Like it or not, Mickey Mouse, Michael Jackson, and Madonna—her overseas sales are two and a half times her domestic number—prop up what's left of our balance of trade.

Broaden the definition of pop culture to include licensed consumer products like Teenage Mutant Ninja Turtle bubble bath, throw in such culture-driven products as McDonald's burgers, Levi's jeans, and Coca-Cola's soft drinks, and you're looking at America's top seller abroad. Last year Walt Disney Co. sold $1.5 billion worth of consumer products—hats, watches, comic books—in Japan, where Coca-Cola earns more money than it does in the U.S.

In the past five years the overseas revenues of Hollywood studios doubled, and in a couple of years they should surpass domestic. The $20-billion-a-year American music business, basically rock & roll, collects 70 percent of its revenue outside the U.S. Sales of U.S. television programming to Europe are estimated at about $600 million a year. Almost everybody in the world watches Cosby, and everybody in the world watched Dallas. The most popular film of all time in Israel and Sweden is "Pretty Woman," which already has garnered more than $360 million worldwide at the box office and hasn't yet opened in the two biggest markets outside the U.S.—Japan and France.

Source: Fortune, December 31, 1990, P. 50 © 1990 Time Inc. All rights reserved.

Approximately two-thirds of U.S. goods exports are by U.S.–owned MNCs, with over one-third of these being exports by U.S. parent corporations shipped to foreign affiliates.

The affiliates usually include both local manufacturers and companies that market products from the U.S. parent. For example, General Motors, Ford, and IBM exported and sold over $1 billion of goods almost exclusively through foreign affiliates.

The direction of U.S. trade is indicated in Exhibit 17.2. The EU countries account for about 20 percent of U.S. exports. As a single country, Canada is the most important U.S. customer, followed by Japan. Moreover, almost one-third of U.S. exports are to developing countries. As far as U.S. imports are concerned, Canada was the U.S. leading import supplier, followed by Japan, and then by Mexico, China, Germany, Taiwan, and the U.K.

U.S. Export Problems

The U.S. export situation is adversely affected by various factors. Chief among these are that (1) many corporate managers consider exports to be only marginal business and (2) although the U.S. government pays lip service to the promotion of exports, it actually inhibits them through laws and regulations. Notably, the traditional business factors (high costs of labor and capital, or low productivity) that at one time were considered responsible for limiting U.S. exports are no longer influential; U.S. companies are now competitive. Instead, exports are hurt by an overall negative attitude. Sometimes agricultural exports are discouraged because of domestic price pressures; other times military exports are blocked for political reasons.

There are historical reasons for the U.S. indifference toward international trade. In the 1950s and 1960s the U.S. had little need of export markets because the home market was large enough to absorb mass production. However, today, to balance the cost of oil imports, the U.S. needs to generate additional exports in the tens of billions of dollars. The lack of activity in the export sector also costs jobs, corporate profits, and business growth. Consequently, it is likely to lead to slower economic growth and, ultimately, to a slower rise in living standards.

For nearly 20 years, the economies of overseas production, compared with high costs at home, encouraged U.S. companies to continue building plants abroad rather than exporting goods to serve foreign markets. Factors that at one time made that practice desirable no longer apply. For example, the percentage increase in unit labor costs in the U.S. since the early 1980s has been the lowest among the major industrial countries.[6] All that is needed to boost U.S. exports is determination among U.S. managers to export, and more help and less hindrance from the government.

Although the number of American firms exporting has grown, there are still thousands of companies that could sell in foreign markets but are not doing so. The resulting asymmetry in U.S. trade relations with the rest of the world is typified by the auto industry. Very few of the big cars that Detroit designs for the U.S. market are exported, while in contrast Europeans and the Japanese build smaller cars for world markets.[7] In 1999 those two nations combined shipped 3.4 million cars to the U.S. German cars have even found a niche in the Japanese market, something U.S. companies have failed to do. Japanese consumers are buying German cars for good reason. Over the past 15 years, German automakers have invested over $1 billion to build up dealer supply and service-support networks in Japan. They have adapted their cars to Japanese tastes. As a result, German carmakers have commanded more than 60 percent of the market for imported cars since 1991. American spending in Japan on support facilities has been estimated at just $120 million. Each of the German "big three"—Mercedes, BMW, and VW Audi—sells about 30,000 cars a year in Japan.[8]

At the same time, a number of countries impose barriers against U.S. exports (see International Marketing Highlight 17.2). These barriers comprise government laws, regulations, policies, or practices that either protect domestic producers from foreign competition or artificially stimulate exports of particular domestic products.

	Top 25 U.S. Markets	Leading U.S. Suppliers
EXHIBIT 17.2	1. Canada	1. Canada
U.S. Trade: 1999	2. Japan	2. Japan
	3. Mexico	3. Mexico
	4. United Kingdom	4. China
	5. South Korea	5. Germany
	6. Germany	6. Taiwan
	7. Taiwan	7. United Kingdom
	8. Singapore	8. South Korea
	9. Netherlands	9. Singapore
	10. France	10. France
	11. Hong Kong	11. Italy
	12. Belgium-Luxembourg	12. Malaysia
	13. Brazil	13. Venezuela
	14. Australia	14. Thailand
	15. China	15. Hong Kong
	16. Italy	16. Saudi Arabia
	17. Malaysia	17. Brazil
	18. Switzerland	18. Indonesia
	19. Saudi Arabia	19. Philippines
	20. Thailand	20. Switzerland
	21. Philippines	21. Sweden
	22. Israel	22. Belgium-Luxembourg
	23. Spain	23. Netherlands
	24. Venezuela	24. Israel
	25. Colombia	25. India

International Marketing Highlight 17.2

Prince for Sale or Rent

The biggest ripoff in the music industry—the widespread transfer to cassettes of compact discs (CDs) that people rent in Japan—looks like it is being outlawed. The Japanese authorities, who have hitherto turned a blind eye to the practice, had until the end of December 1991 to put a stop to piracy that cost foreign record companies upwards of $1 billion a year in lost sales. Record producers in America and Europe wanted the Japanese to ban the rental of new CDs for one year following their release.

At present, the Japanese CD rental stores are supposed to hold back new record releases for one to three weeks. Few bother. However, if Japan fails to come up with an answer soon, America will push ahead with the (rather fanciful) 50-year renting moratorium it has proposed at the GATT trade talks.

Under Japan's present copyright laws, record companies can ban the renting of CDs and records for up to a year after release, and demand a royalty fee from rental stores for 29 years thereafter. However, the agreement applies only to Japanese CDs and records, not foreign ones. The stores pay a one-time fee of 400 yen ($3) for the right to rent each new Japanese release. With foreign CDs and records accounting for a third of the rental market in Japan, western record companies understandably feel cheated.

Source: The Economist, December 21, 1991–January 3, 1992, p. 80.

EXHIBIT 17.3
Share of U.S. Market
Occupied by Imports
(in Percentages)

Product	1972	1999
Blowers and fans	3.6	38.0
Converted paper products	10.4	23.2
Costume jewelry	10.4	65.4
Dolls	1.8	62.4
Electronic computing equipment	0.0	17.5
Lighting fixtures	4.2	31.8
Precious metal jewelry	4.9	38.6
Primary zinc	28.4	64.6
Printing trade machinery	8.5	27.0
Radios and TVs	34.9	92.5
Semiconductors	12.3	46.8
Shoes	17.1	75.5
Luggage and personal goods	20.7	61.8
Men's and boys' outerwear	8.7	48.0
Men's and boys' shirts and nightwear	17.8	63.5
Musical instruments	14.9	26.0
Nitrogenous fertilizers	4.3	28.5
Power-driven hand tools	7.5	33.4
Sporting and athletic goods	13.0	41.6
Telephone and telegraph equipment	2.1	37.6
Tires and inner tubes	7.2	30.0
Women's blouses	14.9	60.8
Women's suits and coats	7.3	46.5
Wool yarn mills	6.1	26.8

Source: Different publications of the U.S. Department of Commerce.

Thus, the structure of international trade is moving further and further from the classical model of unimpeded commerce based strictly on comparative advantages. Eventually, the large reverse flow of foreign multinational investment now coming into the U.S. should help narrow the U.S. trade gap by substituting U.S.–made products for imports. Exhibit 17.3 shows how the U.S. is losing its markets to imports in industry after industry. This situation cannot be allowed to continue; U.S. businesspeople must learn to export aggressively.

Despite the gloomy picture that Exhibit 17.3 depicts, there are products such as pulp and wastepaper, electronic components and parts, and timber in which American companies maintain leads. If adequate encouragement is provided, these products offer an opportunity to offset the U.S. trade deficit.

U.S. Government Encouragement of Exports

Worldwide, governments play a vital role in encouraging exports. Traditionally, in the U.S. the issue of exports has not been given the status that issues such as tax reform, armaments, corporate corruption, the Arab boycott of Israel, and antitrust enforcement received. Nonetheless, the importance of balancing the trade deficit has led the government in the past few years to adopt programs to boost exports (see International Marketing Highlight 17.3).

Ask What Your Country Can Do For You

In principle, governments have four main methods at their disposal to help exporters, as follows.

Subsidize exporters. The crudest such measures—direct subsidies of exports—are outlawed under the rules of the WTO, which nearly all trading nations have promised to abide by. WTO members whose industries are damaged by others' industrial subsidies (even if these are not related to exports) can also bring a case before the trade club's dispute-settlement system: the result may be an end to the subsidy or compensation.

Even so, governments can still find channels down which to pump money for exporters. They can, for example, subsidize research and development. Under WTO rules, governments may pay up to 75 percent of a firm's industrial-research costs, or half the cost of product development. There is a respectable economic argument for this: a firm undertaking research may not secure all the benefits from it; these can accrue to everyone, say in the form of better-educated scientists.

Governments can also offer *tied aid,* in which the recipient promises to buy goods from companies in the donor country. This is often given for foreign-policy as much for commercial reasons, and might be categorized as "aid" not "trade." Or governments can finance exports through *export credit guarantees,* which insure exporters against the risk of default by their customers. In the past, governments have used these to subsidize exporters by guaranteeing loans at below market interest rates.

Boost exports by manipulating the exchange rate. By devaluing, a government makes exports cheaper in foreign-currency terms. This helps exporters in the short run, but not in the long. Devaluation raises import prices, and, if workers maintain the purchasing power of their wages, labor costs rise too. Eventually, much, if not all, of the initial gain is inflated away.

Information-gathering. Commerce departments and trade ministries spend lots of time and trouble gathering business information of every sort on foreign markets. Companies could do this for themselves singly (if big enough) or collectively—and many do. But firms, especially small ones, also get a sort of free ride from embassies set up for other reasons. Diplomats spend much of their time gathering information about local markets, showing the flag at trade fairs and arranging business meetings. These are skills at which the Americans and British are said to be conspicuously good—the Germans less so.

Trade Boosterism. This is exemplified by the high-profile, trade missions which governments sponsor to various nations.

Source: The Economist, February 1, 1997, p. 23.

The U.S. government aids exports through the Export-Import Bank, foreign sales corporations, the Overseas Private Investment Corporation, the U.S. Export Assistance Centers, and pressure on major trading partners to spur their economies. The Omnibus Trade and Competitiveness Act of 1988 has been hailed as landmark legislation intended to spur U.S. exports.

Export-Import Bank

The *Export-Import Bank (Eximbank)* was created by the U.S. government in 1934 to provide low-cost financing to encourage exports of aircraft, nuclear plants, and other "big-ticket" items. The bank's lending capacity is based on appropriations approved by Congress. The bank's subsidy supposedly helps U.S. businesses meet European and Japanese competition by means of their export-subsidy programs. For example, the bank might lend money equal to 45 percent of the price of the American goods to prospective buyers at low rates of interest. In some cases, the bank has financed up to 85 percent of the price. In at least one case—a proposed $16 million sale of gas turbines to Malaysia by United Technologies Corporation—the bank agreed to provide 100 percent financing.

Despite the bank's program, it is not easy to match Japanese and European competition. For example, in the Malaysian deal, a Japanese company won the sale with a government-backed 4-percent, 20-year loan. General Electric Co. lost the contract for Thailand's new power plant generators to Japan's Fuji Electric Co., since Japan's export-finance agency offered a highly subsidized, last-minute loan.

In the 1980s the bank's lending authority was vastly enhanced. For example, export credit programs were strengthened by increasing the level of the Eximbank ceiling on export guarantees. Further, in accordance with the provisions of the Export Trading Company Act (ETCA) of 1982, the bank's new ETCA Loan Guarantee Program was developed in a way that should be especially helpful to small and medium-size minority and agricultural exporters and producers. For example, exporters can obtain short-term, pre-export loans to be used to finance export-related activities when arrangements cannot be made in the private credit market.

In the 1990s the Eximbank redesigned and streamlined its loan, guarantee, and insurance programs to make them more accessible, especially to the small and medium-sized businesses with the greatest potential for increasing U.S. exports and improving the balance of trade. The bank also works with cities and states on a program to educate local officials about trade assistance available from the U.S. government.[9]

Foreign Sales Corporations (FSCs)

Before the creation of *foreign sales corporations (FSCs),* U.S. companies could establish *domestic international sales corporations (DISCs)* under the Revenue Act of 1971. The purpose behind the DISC legislation was to encourage businesses, especially small ones, to engage in export activity through the tax sheltering of income. A DISC could be established in any state with nominal capital of $2,500. To tax shelter the income, a minimum of 95 percent of the DISC sale had to be export-related and, whether the goods were grown, extracted, or manufactured in the U.S., they must have come from an organization other than the DISC. In other words, the DISC acted as a parent company and served as an export channel. DISCs ran into conflict with some of the fair-trade rules of GATT. After years of complaints from U.S. trading partners, GATT ruled in 1982 that DISCs are an illegal export subsidy. This ruling forced the U.S. government to abolish DISC legislation.

Thus, DISCs ceased after December 31, 1984. However, to continue to encourage U.S. businesses to export, the Deficit Reduction Act of 1984 replaced DISCs with FSCs. An FSC is a foreign corporation not located in the U.S. Customs Zone that is allowed to earn some exempt and nontaxable income on its exports from the U.S. In most cases, this partial exemption can result in U.S. tax savings of up to 7.4 percent of the profit on the export transaction for a manufacturer/exporter and 14.7 percent for a trading company/exporter. The FSC is required to pay U.S. tax on the balance of its nonexempt income. The FSC's trade income dividends to its U.S. corporate shareholders are not taxable to them.[10]

The FSC legislation has an advantage over the DISC legislation: it allows a permanent tax exemption to the U.S. corporate shareholders on dividend distributions that may be as frequent as the FSC desires and that may be invested anywhere. The DISC legislation required investing the proceeds in qualified foreign assets. Thus, U.S. farmers and agricultural cooperatives have benefited from the FSC whereas they did not benefit from the DISC. These benefits aside, overall, FSCs provide for limited tax exemption and are more costly to operate.[11] Even so, thousands of U.S. companies have created FSCs to take the tax advantage. Lately, the EU has once again complained that FSCs amount to an unfair export subsidy, since companies that use them pay less income tax on goods sent abroad than on those sold at home. American officials question the EU's reasoning. They argue that the law on FSCs was carefully crafted to comply with global trade rules. Furthermore, the law was introduced as a counterweight to trade-enhancing measures in Europe, such as the rebate of value-added tax on exported goods. But in 1999 the WTO panel decided that the FSC arrangement is in fact a subsidy. At the time of preparing this book, the U.S. has appealed the WTO decision.[12]

Overseas Private Investment Corporation (OPIC)

Established in 1969, the *Overseas Private Investment Corporation (OPIC)* has been the key agency of the U.S. government to encourage private business investment in developing countries and economies in transition. OPIC assists U.S. investors through three principal activities: financing of businesses through loans and loan guarantees, insuring investments against a broad range of political risks, and providing a variety of investor services. All of these activities are designed to reduce the risks associated with foreign investment.

Investment by OPIC clients may take many forms, including conventional equity investments, loans, service contracts, leases and various contractual arrangements such as licensing, franchising, and technical assistance agreements. The agency's assistance is available for new investments, privatization, and for expansion and modernization of existing plants controlled by U.S. multinationals.

OPIC supports, finances and insures projects that have a positive effect on U.S. employment, are financially sound, and promise significant benefits to the social and economic development of the host countries. OPIC does not support projects that could result in the loss of U.S. jobs, adversely affect the U.S. economy or the host country's development or environment, or contribute to violations of internationally recognized workers' rights.

Finally, OPIC provides insurance coverage for U.S. companies in countries where annual per capita income does not exceed $1,000. It offers 20-year coverage to U.S. companies abroad, compared with the 3-year policies typically available from private insurers. OPIC has been designed to be self-sufficient. It operates on its own profit without congressional funds. In 1999, the organization wrote $8.5 billion worth of insurance covering 140 countries.

In addition to these services, OPIC has special programs to meet specific needs of the investor involved in contracting and exporting, energy exploration, and development and leasing arrangements. Many developing countries require foreign firms to post performance or advance payment guarantees in the form of standby letters of credit. OPIC's *political risk insurance* for contractors and exporters protects against arbitrary or unfair drawing of these letters of credit. It also protects against confiscation of tangible assets or bank accounts and losses resulting from a government's failing to live up to contract provisions.

Energy programs are special insurance and finance programs geared toward U.S. investors involved in oil, gas, oil shale, geothermal, mineral, solar, and other energy projects. OPIC can provide a loan guaranty of up to $50 million to finance as much as 50 percent of a new project deemed commercially feasible.

Leasing programs provide specialized insurance and finance services for U.S. investors involved in international leasing. Political risk insurance is available for crossborder operating and capital leases running for at least 36 months. Loan guaranties to leasing companies can range from $500,000 to $30 million, with the fees paralleling OPIC's general finance programs. Direct loans are available to foreign leasing projects in which small U.S. businesses have significant interests.

Trade and Development Agency (TDA)

The *Trade and Development Agency (TDA)* of the U.S. develops feasibility studies of overseas markets for exports and investment in emerging markets. As an example, TDA completed a study detailing 26 projects valued at more than $500 million in Northern Ireland and the Republic of Ireland's border counties with the potential for U.S. exports and investment opportunities amounting to more than $500 million. The study included key contacts, market requirements, regulatory trends, and required steps for capitalizing on the export opportunities, including potential teaming partners and competitors. The study also reviewed financing options available through both U.S. and European sources, including the Eximbank and the Bank of Ireland.

U.S. Government Export Assistance Programs

The U.S. government helps exporters through the Commerce Department's *International Trade Administration (ITA)*. ITA's help to exporters is available both at home and abroad. Overseas, the help is provided through the *U.S. and Foreign Commercial Services (US/FCS)*. The US/FCS maintains 141 offices in 76 countries that are considered to be the principal U.S. trading partners. More than 200 commercial officers direct export promotion activities at these sites and manage promotional programs developed by ITA.

Commercial officers gather data on specific export opportunities, country trends affecting trade and investment, prospects for specific industries, and other commercial intelligence. They also identify and evaluate importers, buyers, agents, distributors, and joint-venture partners linked with U.S. firms; and they monitor and analyze local laws and practices that affect business conditions.

The domestic side of the U.S. government export assistance is provided by the U.S. Export Assistance Centers in 46 states with 104 offices. The *U.S. Export Assistance Centers (USEACs)* integrate U.S. government export marketing and trade finance assistance to provide a seamless delivery of these services to small and medium size exporters. USEACs combine the services and programs of the United States *Department of Commerce (DOC)*, the Eximbank, and the *Small Business Administration (SBA)*. Their services may be grouped in these categories:

Export Counseling The primary focus of the USEACs is to assist export-ready clients—those with the commitment and resources to establish or expand export operations. One-on-one counseling is available to small and medium size businesses with export potential. USEAC staff members evaluate the needs of clients and help them develop customized international business strategies based on the clients' experience and commitment to exporting (see International Marketing Highlight 17.4). The staff members work directly with clients by providing customized services and guiding them to other appropriate resources to help them meet their export objectives.

Trade Finance Assistance Trade finance assistance is available for U.S. businesses interested in selling their goods and services abroad. USEAC staff assist businesses in obtaining export credit insurance, pre-export financing through working capital loan guarantees, and medium- and long-term loans and guarantees to overseas buyers. This help allows small businesses to obtain needed capital through long-term, fixed-asset financing to establish or expand international markets. Guarantee programs that include short-term working capital loans and regular business loans are also available.

Other Assistance USEAC specialists are trained in all federal export promotion programs. In addition to the preceding services, they can also provide guidance to business on issues such as procurement opportunities and feasibility studies.

Publications That Assist Exporters A variety of publications are available to help exporters reach and expand foreign markets. The foremost of these are *Export America, Commercial News USA, A Basic Guide to Exporting, Market Share Reports, Global Market Surveys,* and *Overseas Business Reports* (see International Marketing Highlight 17.5).

■■■■■■■ International Marketing Highlight 17.4 ■■■■■■■

Obstacles Small Exporters Face

Small firms starting to export say the single largest source of information—the Department of Commerce—is also one of the biggest sources of frustration. They condemn trade-promotion programs throughout the federal government as unfocused, overlapping, and inefficient. Worse, U.S. commercial banks, citing too little profit and too much risk, routinely refuse to lend to small exporters. Talk of recession has amplified their concerns.

As more small companies search out business abroad, many say their two greatest needs, reliable trade information and trade financing, are in short supply. While N&N Contact Lens International Inc. of Lywood, Washington, began looking for information on overseas markets two years ago, the local Department of Commerce office was stumped by simple, specific questions. When asked who sells contact lenses in Caracas, Venezuela, it gave the company lists, many of which were outdated, of distributors of such broad categories as "medical devices."

Among major industrialized nations, the U.S. spends the least per capita to promote exports. Number 1, Canada, shelled out 18 times more in 1987, the latest year for which figures are available: $21.44 for each inhabitant versus $1.20 in the U.S. The U.S. government itself brands the services of the U.S. and Foreign Commercial Service, a unit of the Commerce Department's International Trade Administration, as unfocused and inefficient.

Source: Mark Robichaux, "Exporters Face Big Roadblocks at Home," *The Wall Street Journal*, November 7, 1990, p. B1.

■■■■■■■ International Marketing Highlight 17.5 ■■■■■■■

The Export Yellow Pages

Reaching out to the global marketplace became much easier in 1992 with the inaugural publication of *The Export Yellow Pages*. Produced as part of a public/private initiative with the U.S. Department of Commerce—which spearheads distribution of 50,000 copies worldwide—*The Export Yellow Pages* is uniquely designed to help

- Foreign firms buy U.S. products and services.
- U.S. executives locate export service providers.

Source: Business America, January 13, 1992, p. 34.

Export Assistance Programs ITA maintains a wide range of marketing programs to help U.S. companies in their export endeavors, as follows:

Programs to Identify Potential Markets Two programs are availabel to help firms identify potential markets. One is the *National Trade Data Bank (NTDB)*, a "one-stop" source of international trade data collected by federal agencies. It contains more than 200,000 trade-related documents, including market research reports, trade leads, trade contacts, statistical information, country reports, and much more. The NTDB is available at federal depository libraries, can be purchased on CD-ROM, or can be accessed through the Internet. Following is the kind of information available from the NTDB:

Market Statistics: The market statistics available include product import and export data, by country. This information indicates where your products are currently being exported.

Foreign Country Data: General economic and marketing background reports on virtually every country in the world are available, including the following:
Foreign government trade regulations, restrictions, and standards;
Best prospects for U.S. exports;

Economic and political country analysis;
U.S. and country contacts.

Market Research Reports: Over 10,000 market research reports developed by the Commercial Service are available covering a wide range of specific products and product lines in leading overseas markets. These reports cover topics such as: market size and outlook, characteristics, and competitive and end-user analysis.

The other program for identifying potential markets is the *Customized Market Analysis (CMA)*. The CMA report assesses the market for a specific product or service in a foreign market. The research provides information on sales potential, competitors, distribution channels, pricing of comparable products, potential buyers, marketing venues, quotas, duties and regulations, and licensing or joint venture interest. (Cost varies from $1,000 to $5,000 depending on country.)

Programs to Identify Potential Foreign Customers and Distributors   One program to identify potential customers and distributors is the *Agent/Distributor Service (ADS)*. The Commercial Service will conduct a customized overseas search for qualified agents, distributors, and representatives for U.S. firms. Commercial officers abroad identify up to six foreign prospects that have examined the U.S. firm's product literature and expressed interest in representing the U.S. firm's product. ($250 per country.)

The *World Traders Data Report (WTDRs)* is another service. Prepared by U.S. commercial officers abroad, WTDRs are business reports providing background information on potential foreign trade contacts. Each report also contains a general narrative prepared by the U.S. commercial officer conducting the investigation as to the reliability of foreign firm.

The *Trade Opportunities Program (TOP)* provides times sales leads from international firms seeking to buy or represent U.S. products or services. TOP leads are printed daily in leading commercial newspapers and distributed electronically via the Department of Commerce Economic Bulletin Board *(Globus)*.

Finally, the *Gold Key Service (GKS)* is a custom-tailored service that combines orientation briefings, market research, appointments with potential partners, interpreter service for meetings, and assistance in developing follow-up strategies. GKS is offered by the Commercial Service in export markets around the world. (Cost varies by country.)

Programs to Promote Products and Services Overseas   One program to promote products and services is *Commercial News USA*. Published 12 times annually and circulated by the Commercial Service's overseas posts to over 140,000 businesses in more than 155 countries and to 2 million electronic bulletin board users worldwide. Companies can advertise their U.S. products and services for as little as $495.

Trade missions also help. The Commerce Department conducts numerous U.S. trade missions to foreign countries each year. The "Matchmaker Trade Delegation" is a specialized mini mission that literally "matches" small and medium-sized U.S. firms with prescreened appointments in high potential overseas markets. (Participants are charged a prorated fee.)

The Commercial Service enables U.S. firms to participate in a variety of overseas *trade shows* by providing space and marketing assistance in selected foreign exhibitions or Commercial Service–sponsored events. (Participants are charged a prorated fee.)

The Commercial Service conducts *catalog shows* overseas that provide exposure of U.S. products to targeted business audiences and generate sales leads. U.S. companies send their catalogs to U.S. embassies, consulates, and trade centers abroad where potential buyers, agents, distributors, and end-users are invited to examine them.

Exporters' Licensing Services

Exporters licensing services are an ITA activity that assists U.S. firms in fulfilling their obligations under the Export Administration Act. The act helps to ensure U.S. national security and to further U.S. national foreign policies by controlling exports to certain destinations of certain kinds of sensitive, high-technology equipment and data. The exporters Licensing group gives speedy advice to business executives who need to determine whether their exports require advance, validated licenses or who need help in filing the requisite application.

Service Industries Development Program

The Trade and Tariff Act of 1984 mandates that the Commerce Department establish a *Service Industries Development Program*. An essential element of this program is an updated survey of the services sector, which includes statistics on exports and imports of services, receipts, employment, and wages paid by service firms. Improved data on service industries help analysis of this sector's contribution to the U.S. economy and advance the marketing of U.S. services abroad.

Foreign Requirements for U.S. Products and Services

U.S. companies wishing to sell abroad must know how to deal with foreign national requirements, standards, testing, and certification requirements. *The National Center for Standards and Certification Information (NCSCI),* a branch of the Commerce Department's National Bureau of Standards, is the government's central repository for standards-related information about foreign countries.

Foreign Metric Regulations

The *Office of Metric Programs* provides exporters with information about foreign metric import regulations. It also provides guidance and assistance on matters relating to U.S. transition to the metric system.

Pressure on Trading Partners

For many years, the U.S. government has tried to increase demand for U.S. products abroad by prodding foreign governments to stimulate their economies and thus draw in more U.S. goods. This idea is based on the assumption that recovery abroad would stimulate U.S. exports.

In addition, the U.S. government has been pressuring the Japanese to reduce barriers that restrict the sales of U.S. goods in Japan. For example, traditionally the Japanese government required purchase of telecommunications equipment from native sources only. Recent pressure, however, has led Japan to eliminate this restriction and thus has opened the door for U.S. firms such as Western Electric, a subsidiary of American Telephone and Telegraph, to explore export opportunities in Japan.[13] Similarly, pressure is being put on South Korea, Taiwan, and other trading partners to open their markets to American goods.

Export Trading Company Act, 1982

This act was the first major export expansion legislation in more than a decade. It encourages businesses to join together and form export trading companies. It provides antitrust protection for joint exporting, and permits banking institutions to own interests in these exporting ventures. The act makes exporting practical for small- and medium-size firms by permitting them to join forces and hire specialists to handle all the complicated details of exporting without fear of antitrust prosecution and inadequate capitalization.[14] Following are the highlights of the act's provisions.

Banking Provisions Bank holding companies and bankers' banks may invest up to 5 percent and loan up to 10 percent of their capital and surplus to an export trading company. Bank holding companies and bankers' banks may own up to 100 percent of the stock of an export trading company.

The *Federal Reserve Board (FRB)* must approve any proposed investment. Under this process, a bank need only notify the FRB of the intended investment. If no objection is made within 60 days thereafter, the bank may proceed with the intended investment. A bank is exempted from the collateral requirements contained in the Federal Reserve Act for loans to its export trading company.

Antitrust Certification Provisions The antitrust certification is provided by the Commerce Department. A certificate holder has complete immunity from U.S. antitrust laws, except for private party lawsuits for actual damages.

By the end of 1999 the Commerce Department issued 162 certificates providing antitrust protection to 71 firms and individuals. Small and medium-sized firms constituted a majority of the holders of these certificates. Interestingly, the agribusiness community is taking more interest in the *export trading company (ETC)* program than other industries. Further, by the end of 1999, a total of 88 bank ETCs had been formed with the approval of the FRB, and had invested $485 million in them.

Despite these achievements, the ETC program has received lukewarm support in the business community. Critics consider these achievements insignificant. Empirical research shows that such large companies as Sears, General Electric, Rockwell International, and General Motors would have formed ETCs with or without the ETC legislation. Banks and small and medium-sized manufacturers, which were supposed to benefit most from the legislation, have not responded well.

One reason for this lackluster support may be the ignorance of smaller companies about the act's relevance and usefulness to their business. The U.S. Department of Commerce's educational programs (e.g., conferences and publications) may encourage these firms to take advantage of the export opportunities furnished under the ETC Act.

Omnibus Trade and Competitiveness Act of 1988

On August 23, President Reagan signed the Omnibus Trade and Competitiveness Act of 1988. The major provisions of the act are discussed in Chapter 2. The act maintains U.S. commitment to free trade and provides better trade remedy tools to open foreign markets. It strengthens the ability of U.S. firms to protect their patented, copyrighted, and trademarked goods and ideas from international thievery.

Further, the act supported the Uruguay Round trade talks to adapt or expand GATT by improving existing rules with respect to agriculture and to dispute settlement, and by extending GATT discipline to new areas such as services, investment, and intellectual property.

The act also provides for the establishment of an interagency committee to assure the timely collection of accurate trade and economic data and to provide the private sector and government officials with efficient access to this data for policy-making and export promotion (see International Marketing Highlight 17.6).

International Marketing Highlight 17.6

Trade versus Environment

In the past few years, a new problem has arisen concerning trade barriers and environmental laws. In these trade-versus-environment conflicts, developing nations with an abundance of natural resources are pitted against industrialized nations. For example, fishermen in Mexico were harvesting yellowfin tuna by using nets that trap scores of dolphins in the process. As a result, tens of thousands of dolphins drowned. In 1988 the U.S. banned all imports of tuna caught using this technique. However, in response to a Mexican complaint, a GATT panel ruled that such a ban was an unfair trade barrier. The GATT panel ruled against a member country restricting imports of a product merely because it came from a country with different environmental policies than its own.

The Mexican government did not push the matter further despite the GATT ruling in its favor. However, if other countries transshipping Mexican tuna are banned from exporting, they may protest under the GATT ruling.

Concern for the environment is laudable. Nonetheless, the problem is that countries pursue trade protectionism in the name of a "safe" environment. For example, Canadians protect their prized Pacific salmon against overfishing by virtually counting the catch. Atlantic lobsters are safeguarded by New England states by banning sales of adolescent crustaceans. Europeans demand that imported beef must be untainted by artificial growth hormones. As world trade grows, such conflicts are likely and there is no easy way to resolve them. Resource-rich developing nations see imperialism in the efforts of industrialized nations to force environmental reforms on them. Rich nations, on the other hand, fear deterioration of the environment as a genuine concern.

Source: "Save the Dolphins—or Free Trade," *Business Week*, February 17, 1992, p. 130D.

U.S. Government Hindrance of Exports

Although the government encourages exports in various ways, several U.S. rules and regulations have acted as obstacles (although many of them are not as significant anymore as they used to be) to increasing exports:[15]

- The Foreign Corrupt Practices Act of 1977, which imposes jail terms and fines for overseas payoffs by U.S. companies.
- Limits on the sale and financing of nuclear plants (these restrictions have been designed to halt the spread of nuclear weapons).
- Human rights legislation, which denies credits to rights violators.
- U.S. trade embargoes, which ban exports to Cuba, Iran, Zimbabwe, and many other countries.
- Strategic control restrictions, which stop exports with potential military uses to many countries.
- Antitrust laws, which prevent U.S. companies from bidding jointly on major foreign projects.
- Super 301 trade law, which has been used against barriers in such countries as Japan, Brazil, and India.
- Imposition of U.S. environmental protection standards on trading partners.
- Restrictions on hi-tech exports to protect national security.

The U.S. policy in foreign trade matters continues to be based on *helping and reforming* other nations. Such a policy reinforces the view that major trading partners of the U.S. are so weak that they require very substantial U.S. concessions in trade and other economic matters, and that the U.S. is so strong that it is immune from economic injury no matter what concessions are made by its government. The validity of such an appraisal is questionable, as is the expectation that other nations will accept U.S. values and ethics as a basis for their exports.

Export Management

U.S. companies face a challenge to succeed in a time of growing protectionism and keen competition. Although, U.S. government programs are some help, the proper management of export activity at the company level is equally important. This section discusses select strategies to improve export performance.

Export markets offer a variety of opportunities. To capitalize on these opportunities, companies should develop an export focus and do a thorough job of identifying products and markets. Consider Japan. Often companies grumble about its closed markets, but they fail to realize that the new generation of Japanese crave U.S. goods and have plenty of purchasing power. Foreign products selling well in Japan are those not requiring much after-sale service, which foreign producers are relatively poor at providing, and those in which foreign producers maintain a competitive edge vis-à-vis their Japanese competitors in terms of either price or performance. These products are primarily nondurable consumer and specialty goods that satisfy individual tastes. Examples include black tea (market share of imports to the overall market equals 60 percent), canned soup (40 percent), neckties (25 percent), climbing ropes (90 percent), paper diapers (50 percent), skiing goods (30 percent), and fountain pens (35 percent).

Choosing Attractive Markets

A framework for selecting potential growth markets for exports is diagrammatically depicted in Exhibit 17.4. Market attractiveness may be based on company competencies, industry practices, and competitive conditions. A sustainable competitive position in selected foreign markets can be built if a company is able to reach a minimum level of size and effectiveness; that is, *critical mass.* Critical mass is determined by the ability of the company to match the product, price, distribution, and promotion requirements of the market relative to the competition.

Once different markets are located on the grid, the approximate allocation of resources for foreign market development may be made as follows: In the dark-shaded areas, at the upper right-hand corner of the grid, are found attractive markets where the company already has a strong position. In these markets, the appropriate strategy is usually to maintain that position or build it further. The light-shaded areas indicate attractive markets where the company is within reach of critical mass. Here the company can improve results by investing the necessary time and resources to gain the step-function benefits of crossing the threshold. The white areas of the grid are those markets with low attractiveness, or markets where it is unlikely that the company can reach critical mass. Here a strategy of careful opportunistic response and limited or reduced investment is probably called for.

Product Specialization

There was a time when U.S. products everywhere were considered superior across the board. In the past 20 years, however, other countries have achieved similar distinction in a variety of products. No longer are U.S. electronic goods considered the best. German machinery is often held superior to that of the U.S. Moreover, many developing countries are able to produce high-quality, low-technology products at significantly lower costs. In brief, U.S. corporations cannot just expect to do well overseas with all products. A careful choice of both products and market is essential.

High-technology products have provided a unique opportunity for U.S. business to acquire leverage in entering export markets. However, other industrialized nations are slowly challenging the U.S. position even in this area. U.S. companies need to be active in protecting their advantage in the export of high-technology products.

Appropriate Management Orientation

To compete effectively abroad and develop and expand foreign markets, U.S. businesspersons need to develop a particular management orientation. Different firms, depending on their experience, face different problems in the export arena. The management focus of each firm, therefore, should be directly related to its actual experience. For example, exporters may be divided into three categories: (1) exporters with only a partial interest in exporting, (2) exporters who export on an experimental basis, and (3) experienced exporters. The perspective of each type of export operation is significantly different from the others. Obviously, management style and strategy should vary accordingly.

To illustrate this point, experienced firms need to devote more attention to financial aspects and funds transfer, while new entrants should tackle packaging, funds transfer, document handling, and the mechanics of exporting. By the same token, as the dynamics of a firm's business change from the experimental to the experienced level, the nature of the problems changes, and then a different managerial emphasis is required.[16]

Appropriate Export Strategy

Finally, for a longer-term effective export performance, a company must develop an appropriate marketing strategy. For the foreseeable future, the global environment dictates

EXHIBIT 17.4   Setting Development Priorities in Overseas Markets

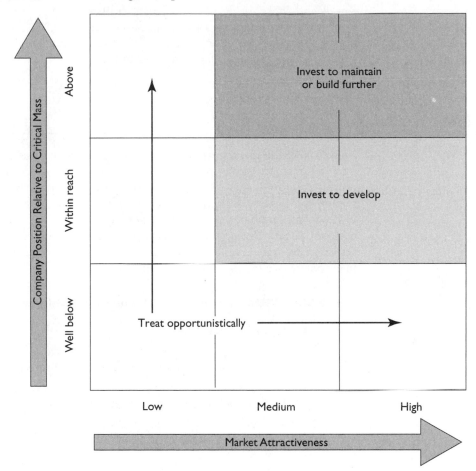

that U.S. export sales cannot be generated simply by repeating what a company does in the U.S. Overseas markets should be properly analyzed to search out and identify product/market niches where a certain company might have a particular opportunity. Next, adequate product, price, distribution, and promotion strategies need to be formulated to serve those target markets.

The textile industry's export performance during the late 1980s illustrates how a well-planned strategy can pay off.[17] U.S. textile exports (yarn, fabric, and carpeting) increased 50 percent, from $3.2 billion in 1980 to $4.8 billion in 1985. To accomplish this, the textile companies took three strategic measures.

First, they identified market segments that currently were not adequately served. For example, British carpetmakers mainly produced two types of carpets—woven wool carpet and synthetic carpet. The middle class could not afford the wool carpet because it was expensive; and the synthetic carpet looked cheap. To cater to the middle class, American mills introduced mid-priced carpeting in different shades, colors, and textures.

Second, riding on the tidal wave of enthusiasm for such U.S. fashions as blue jeans, U.S. textile producers started exporting denim and corduroy to European apparel makers. These foreign companies compete head-on with U.S. apparel makers such as Levi Strauss. Thus, the move to supply denim to a customer's competitors was risky. However, in the long run, the textile mills found it to be a sound strategy.

Third, the textile producers introduced new product concepts overseas. For example, towels and sheets in Europe and Japan had been stable, commodity-type products in standard shapes and designs, without fashion appeal. U.S. companies decided to introduce a "boutique" marketing system to develop an export market for bed and bath textile products. One company that stands out in the successful pursuit of this strategy is Fieldcrest Mills.

Export Procedure

Many marketing managers fail to explore fully potential business abroad because of their uncertainty about, or simply lack of understanding of, export mechanics. Although exporting is certainly more demanding than a strictly domestic business, by using the information provided by the U.S. Department of Commerce and employing agents and other professionals familiar with the formalities, export sales can be handled almost as easily as domestic sales.[18] One need not travel abroad and meet with customers in person to be successful in exports. As with most any undertaking, there are basic procedural tasks involved in exporting (see International Marketing Highlight 17.7).

■■■■■■■■■ **International Marketing Highlight 17.7** ■■■■■■■■■

Global Guidelines for Small Business

- **Look to existing customers.** Many companies can penetrate foreign markets by selling products or services to their domestic customers' units overseas.
- **Make a commitment.** Exporting is not a part-time effort. It requires extensive research. Foreign business should be run by seasoned managers.
- **Seek advice.** Universities often have MBA students who work as consultants on exporting. Some consulting firms, such as Arthur Anderson, provide free first-time consultation.
- **Use trade shows.** Trade promotions sponsored by U.S. and state agencies abroad draw big crowds. Cost-conscious companies can send a product without attending.
- **Pick markets carefully.** While potentially lucrative, fast-growing markets can tank unexpectedly. Consider customer quality, not just nationality.
- **Manage growth.** It takes time to line up financing and expand an organization to handle exports. Many small exporters are overwhelmed by big orders.
- **Use letters of credit.** Some first-time exporters ship a product and hope they get paid. A letter of credit protects against default by a weak or shady buyer.
- **Be patient.** Many foreign customers do business based on relationships. Small companies must spend time cultivating contacts before racking up export orders.
- **Choose partners carefully.** An experienced freight forwarder at home is crucial for handling customers paperwork. An inept distributor abroad can ruin a company's reputation.

Source: Business Week, April 17, 1995. p. 97.

Locating Customers

Overseas customers can be located in many ways. Large corporations have their established contacts. Firms new to exports can identify likely prospects overseas through the information available from the U.S. Department of Commerce. For example, as discussed earlier in this chapter, the *World Traders Data Reports (WTDRs)*, a service of the Commerce Department, provide detailed commercial information on foreign firms—background information on the organization, year established, number of employees, sales area, type of operation, products handled, name of contact officer, general reputation in trade and finance circles, names of other foreign firms the company represents, and even a U.S. foreign service officer's comment on the firm's suitability as a trade contact.

Before proceeding with a prospect, it is advisable to examine the socioeconomic-political-regulatory environment of the importing country. Such examination would indicate if an export can be successfully transacted For example, many countries prohibit the importation of certain products. Some require that an import license be obtained from the government. Other countries impose restrictions on the quantity imported. Thus, if an import license is required, the exporting firm should insist that the importer obtain it first. Similarly, if a government levies a heavy import duty, the exporter should remind the interested overseas party of the impact of such a barrier on the final cost of the product.

Obtaining Export Licenses

Exporters should be aware of U.S. government regulations affecting the export of certain strategic commodities to certain destinations. Essentially, all items intended for export require an export license. This rule is mandated by the need for national security and by the foreign policy and economic interests of the U.S. The rule, however, applies neither to U.S. territories and possessions nor, in most cases, to Canada.

There are two types of licenses: general and validated. A *general license* permits exportation within certain limits without requiring that an application be filed or that a license document be issued. A *validated license* authorizes exportation within specific limitations; it is issued only on formal application. Most goods can move from the U.S. to free-world countries under a general license. A validated license is required to export certain kinds of strategic goods regardless of the destination.

An exporter needs to know whether a general or validated license is necessary and which office to contact to obtain the license. For most commodities, the license is granted by the Commerce Department's *Office of Export Administration (OEA)*. For certain specific products and commodities, however, export licenses are provided by other U.S. government departments and agencies (see Exhibit 17.4). For example, in the case of arms, ammunition, and other war-related items, the license is given by the Department of State.

EXHIBIT 17.5
U.S. Export Licensing Authorities for Specific Commodities

Commodities	Commodity Licensing Authority
Arms, ammunition, and other war related products	Department of State
Atomic energy material (including fissionable materials and facilities for their manufacture)	Atomic Energy Commission
Gold and silver	Department of Treasury
Narcotic drugs	Department of Justice
Natural gas and electric energy	Federal Power Commission
Tobacco plants and seeds	Department of Agriculture
Vessels	Maritime Commission
Endangered wildlife	Department of the Interior

Source: U.S. Department of Commerce. *The Export Administration Regulations* (Washington, DC: U.S. Government Printing Office, 1993).

The type of license—general or validated—required for exporting is based on two considerations: country of destination and commodity to be exported. For export purposes, the U.S. government has classified countries (except Canada) into seven categories:[19]

Q   Romania
S   Libya
T   All countries of the Western Hemisphere except Canada and Cuba
W   Poland and Hungary
Y   Albania, Bulgaria, Czech Republic, the Commonwealth of Independent States, and several communist countries
Z   North Korea and Cuba
V   All other countries except Canada.

Exports to countries in the Z category are almost completely banned. There is a selective embargo, based on the type of commodity, on exports to countries in the Y group. In brief, different licensing requirements apply to countries in each category. Thus, exports to countries in the Y category would require a validated license; those in the T category, a general license.

Items requiring a validated license include, but are not limited to, certain chemicals, special types of plastics, sophisticated electronic and communication equipment, scarce materials, and related technical data. By referring to the commodity control list of the export administration regulations available from the U.S. Department of Commerce, a company can determine whether a validated export license is needed for a particular commodity to a particular country.

To obtain a validated export license, an application must be prepared following the procedures described in the export administration regulations. Where the value of the shipment is $5,000 or more and a validated license is needed, special forms generally must be completed by importers or their government to support the request for license.

A general license is a published authorization for the exporting of commodities that do not require a validated license. The majority of U.S. products exported require a general, not a validated, license. An exporter need not obtain formal authorization to ship products requiring a general license. Those products can be shipped by merely inserting the correct general license symbol or code on the export control document, that is, the shipper's export declaration. In other words, no formal application has to be made to export products for which a general license is needed.

Collecting Export Documents

Several documents are needed to complete an export transaction. The documents help to clear exported goods at shipping points and through customs, and to receive payment. Documentation requirements vary from country to country. The following documents are required most commonly.

Commercial Invoice A *commercial invoice* summarizes details of the sales contract and lists the names and addresses of the exporter, shipper, and consignee; date of order; shipping data; mode of shipment; delivery and payment terms; description of product; and prices, discounts, and quantities.

Some countries require additional information in the commercial invoice; for example, the invoice must be signed and notarized or countersigned by the exporter's chamber of commerce. Similarly, some countries require the invoice to be visaed by the resident consul of the importer's country. Details for the inclusion or attachment of additional information in the commercial invoice can be obtained from any of the U.S. export centers located in major cities across the nation.

Consular Invoice The *consular invoice* is a certificate pertaining to exports that should be obtained from the consulate office of the importer's country. A consular invoice is prepared on forms available from the consulate and often is in the language of the importing country. It is visaed by the resident consul, certifying the authenticity and correctness of the proposed shipment.

Certificate of Origin Many countries require a certificate *of origin,* either on a prescribed form or on the exporter's letterhead, specifying the origin of the merchandise. Usually such a statement is made on the commercial invoice, but some countries require an additional separate certificate. The certificate of origin makes it easier to establish possible preferential rates for import duties under a most-favored-nation arrangement.

Inspection Certificate An *inspection certificate* is an affidavit, either by the shipper or by an independent inspection firm, certifying the quality, quantity, and conformity of goods in relation to the order. Importers often request such a certificate to ensure the correctness of the shipment.

Shipper's Export Declaration The *shipper's export declaration* summarizes shipping information and contains a description of the merchandise in a special nomenclature, both in words and by commodity identifying number per export administration regulations. The reference to a specific validated or general export license also appears on this document.

Export Packing List The *export packing list* summarizes information about the merchandise and facilitates shipping. The list is also used by customs officials to check the cargo at both the point of shipment and the port of entry. The list helps the importer to inventory the merchandise received. It itemizes the material in each package; specifies the type of package (box, crate, drum); shows the package dimensions and weight; and provides the shipper's and buyer's references. The packing list is attached to the outside of one of the packages in a waterproof envelope marked "packing list enclosed."

Dock, or Warehouse, Receipt This *dock receipt,* or *warehouse receipt,* stipulates the receipt of goods at the pier or warehouse for further shipment abroad. This receipt is usually needed when the exporter has to deliver goods only to the U.S. port of export.

Insurance Certificate The *insurance certificate* specifies the type and amount of insurance coverage. Virtually all shipments overseas are insured to protect the goods against political risks and damage by natural causes. An exporter can obtain an open cargo policy to cover all foreign shipments or insure individual shipments.

Bill of Lading *This is the single most important export document.* A *bill of lading* establishes the ownership of goods, testifies to the carrier's obligation to ship the goods, and serves as a receipt of goods from the carrier. A bill of lading may be negotiable or nonnegotiable. The *nonnegotiable bill of lading* is usually used for air shipments; the goods are addressed to the named consignee. However, most shipments are made via *negotiable bills of lading.* The goods may be consigned to the consignee or to a third party but are delivered to the bearer of the bill of lading, that is, the party presenting the properly endorsed bill of lading.

Following commercial practice, a bill of lading, to be valid and acceptable, must be marked "Clean on Board." This amounts to a certificate by the carrier that the goods were received on board in good and satisfactory condition. Conversely, a bill of lading marked "Foul" by the carrier would mean that the goods were received on board either damaged or spoiled.

A bill of lading includes the name and address of the exporter, the forwarding agent, and the overseas consignee (both intermediate and ultimate); it identifies the carrier, the U.S. port of export, and the foreign port of unloading; and it includes the name of the party to be notified on arrival of the goods. It also contains details pertaining to the merchandise; nature of goods (e.g., "four boxes: textiles"), weight, value, and other pertinent information.

Packing and Marking

The importance of adequate packing for overseas shipment is discussed in Chapter 12 on product policy. Briefly, packing should be designed to prevent breakage and to protect against pilferage and exposure to moisture. Further, every effort should be made to keep package weight down to save on shipping costs, while ensuring that the package is sufficiently sturdy to withstand the violent handling, stocking, loading, and unloading so common to ocean shipping.

The package should be properly marked for easy identification. Legible and clear marking will ensure its shipment to the correct destination. Besides, it will help the consignee to identify the package without difficulty. Usually, overseas buyers specify special identification marks to be imprinted on the package. Frequently, exporters avoid showing trademarks or other clues that might reveal the contents of the shipment. Such precautions help to avoid pilferage.

Shipping Abroad

Shipping of merchandise to overseas destinations involves observing different formalities that not every exporter is able to handle independently. It is desirable, therefore, to enlist the services of a *foreign freight forwarder*, an agent who specializes in moving the cargo to overseas destinations. After the goods have been delivered to the port of export, the freight forwarder takes over to clear the goods through U.S. customs and delivers the cargo to the pier in time for loading aboard the selected vessel. In addition, a freight forwarder furnishes useful advice to the exporter relative to freight costs, port changes, consular fees, export documentation, and customs rules, both in the U.S. and the importer's country.[20]

The four leading U.S. freight forwarders are Air Express International, Expeditors International of Washington, Fritz Cos., and Harper Group. Air Express with $1.2 billion in sales is the largest among them with 600 offices in 123 countries. In contrast, Expeditors has 103 offices in different parts of the world with revenues amounting to about $600 million.[21]

Shipment may be made from the U.S. by either air or ocean carrier; in the case of countries accessible by land, such as Mexico and Canada, trucks can also be used. Carrier companies provide various types of contracts for overseas shipments. For example, three types of ocean service are available: conference lines, independent lines, and tramp vessels. The *conference* and *independent lines* operate on a predetermined schedule, while *tramp vessels* sail on ad hoc arrangements and usually carry bulk cargo. Conference lines are carriers who have formed an association to establish common freight rates and shipping conditions. Exporters who contract to deal exclusively with conference lines ship at lower rates than noncontract shippers. Independent lines price their services individually and aggressively compete for noncontract exporters, vying with the conference lines.

The shipping arrangement is finalized after a ***booking contract*** is obtained, reserving space for the cargo on a specified vessel.

Receiving Payment

There are various methods of receiving payment for export, such as cash in advance, open account, consignment sales, dollar draft, and letter of credit. The method of payment used and the terms and conditions agreed upon would depend on the credit standing of the importer, the exchange restrictions operating in the importer's country, and the competition the exporter faces. Usually, the international services of a commercial bank are used to receive payment.

Cash in Advance As far as the seller is concerned, *cash in advance* is the safest method. Payment received before shipping the goods relieves the seller of worry about collection. Besides, the money is available for use right away. From the buyer's viewpoint, thought this is not a preferred method for two main reasons. First, certain foreign exchange restrictions prohibit paying cash in advance. Second, there is no guarantee of shipment of the merchandise as specified.

Overall, this method of payment is not used frequently; trade conducted via cash in advance constitutes a small portion of the total trade.

Open Account With the *open account*, goods are shipped without any prior financial deal. This is a risky method of receiving payments unless the seller is dealing with a known party whose financial integrity is held in high esteem. Even where there is no danger of not receiving payment under this mode of payment, the trade practice in the buyer's country may be to pay only when the goods have actually been received. In developing countries, exchange problems may create an additional difficulty if the buyer fails to receive foreign exchange.

This method is most often used between organizations under the same corporate umbrella; for example one subsidiary of a company ships goods to another subsidiary in another country. Open-account shipments are also feasible between large organizations in industrialized countries; for example, General Motors may ship parts to Volvo in Sweden.

Consignment Sales In *consignment sales*, goods are shipped to the overseas party while the seller retains title to the goods. The consignee makes payment to the seller after the goods have been sold. The consignment arrangement, like the open account, is feasible if (1) the consignee's country provides a stable economic and political environment and (2) the consignee has a good reputation and offers a deal that is a sound business risk. Consignment sales are made mostly to exporters' overseas branches or affiliates.

Export Drafts An *export draft* is an unconditional order drawn by the exporter asking the importer to pay the designated amount either on presentation (sight draft) or at a future date mutually agreed upon (time draft). Usually the future date specified in the draft is 30, 60, 90, 120, or 180 days after presentation. The draft may name either the seller as the party to receive payment or a bank to handle collection.

If a bank is to handle payment, the exporter delivers the draft and shipping documents to the named bank. The bank then forwards them to its branch, affiliate, or correspondent bank in the importer's country. The branch contacts the buyer or the buyer's bank and demands immediate payment if it is a sight draft, or acceptance on the time draft. Once payment or acceptance is received, the shipping documents are delivered to the buyer.

An export draft can be drawn in U.S. dollars or in a foreign currency. A *payment-on-draft agreement* is usually used when the protection provided by a letter of credit (discussed next) is not necessary. This mode of receiving payment is less expensive, and, therefore, enhances the exporter's competitive position in seeking export business.

Letter of Credit A frequently used method of receiving payment for exports is through the *letter of credit*. This document is issued by a bank at the buyer's request in favor of the exporter. It promises to pay the specified sum of money in the designated currency within a specified time upon receipt by the bank of shipping documents (bill of lading).

Essentially, there are two types of letters of credit: revocable and irrevocable. An *irrevocable letter of credit*, once given to and accepted by the seller, cannot be altered in any way without permission of the seller. On the other hand, a *revocable letter of credit* may be declared invalid by the buyer, either personally or through a bank, for any discretionary reason. Except for cash in advance, the irrevocable letter of credit offers the exporter the highest degree of protection. Inexperienced exporters, particularly when dealing with unknown parties, and especially in developing countries, should find the letter of credit a safe way to secure themselves financially.

Duty-Free Zones

In order to encourage international trade despite import barriers, many countries have resorted to the opening of foreign-trade enclaves. There are different types of such enclaves. Among these, however, *duty-free zones* (also called *free-trade zones* or *foreign-trade zones*) are the most popular. The duty-free zones are unique because they let businesses store, process, assemble, and display goods from abroad without paying a tariff first. Once these products leave a zone and are delivered within the U.S., a tariff must be paid—but not on the cost of assembly, nor on profits. For example, a furniture maker will have to pay a duty only on the imported raw wood used, not on the cost of assembling the item or on the profits. Consider Timex Co. It used the Little Rock, Arkansas, free-trade zone to store machinery it had bought overseas. By storing the equipment in the duty-free zone, the company deferred import duties until it had decided in which U.S. plant to use the foreign machinery. Finished goods can be stored in free-trade zones for reasons other than deferring customs duties. One firm ages wine in the New Orleans duty-free zone and thus defers import duties for years.[22]

If a product is re-exported, a company never has to pay a tariff. That means a U.S. camera maker can assemble foreign parts in a Florida free-trade zone and ship the finished cameras to Latin America without paying U.S. duty.

Even if half the plants in these zones are foreign owned, it benefits the U.S. to have them because of the jobs created. Common for years in other countries, duty-free zones are becoming popular in the U.S. as the cost of doing business abroad rises. Currently, there are 149 foreign-trade zones in the U.S., in such large cities as New York, Boston, San Francisco, and Chicago; and in such remote places as Duluth, Minnesota; Little Rock, Arkansas; Bangor, Maine; and Burlington, Vermont. Warehousing and manufacturing activity combined, more than $171 billion worth of merchandise was processed in these zones in 1999, almost three times as much as in 1990. About 2,800 business firms employing over 315,000 persons were using these zones in 1997.[23]

The cost advantages of foreign-trade zones are exemplified by Berg Steel Pipe Co., a German-French joint venture in Panama City's zone.[24] Berg produces large-diameter pipe for, among others, the oil industry, importing some of the needed steel plate from Germany and Italy for about $450 to $500 a ton. Imported as materials, the plate normally would be taxed on 6 percent. However, with trade-zone status, Berg can convert the plate into pipe and move it into the U.S. market at the rate for finished products, 1.9 percent, or export it free of tariff.

With such savings, companies of all kinds are setting up in foreign-trade zones. The variety of goods processed runs from Ambrosia Chocolate Co.'s bulk chocolate in Milwaukee to Xerox Corp.'s copiers near Rochester, New York. General Motors Corp. has 11 plants in foreign-trade zones, Ford Motor Co., 12, and Chrysler Corp. 9. Other trade zones include Bethlehem Steel Corp.'s shipbuilding yard in Sparrows Point, Maryland, a Caterpillar Inc. engine plant near Peoria, Illinois, and three Eli Lilly & Co. plants in Indiana. Many foreign firms, such as Porsche, Nissan, and Mazda, are active, too. Although both the tonnage and dollar value are dominated by giant corporations, more small than big companies are involved in foreign-trade zones.

Barter

An interesting development in recent years has been the emergence of *barter,* whereby goods or services are exchanged for other goods or services without resorting to money-swapping. In other words, barter replaces money and credit as the medium of international exchange. Several types of barter deals are popular in the international market: counterpurchases, switch trading, clearing agreements, and buyback barter.

Counterpurchase (or Pure Barter)

Counterpurchase refers to a set of parallel cash agreements in which the supplier sells a service or product and orders unrelated products to offset the costs to the buyer. For example, a few years ago, Caterpillar Tractor sold tractors to a Latin American logger and sawmill operator and took coffins in exchange.[25]

In the past, countertrade was used primarily by the former Soviet Union and by Eastern European and foreign-exchange-poor developing economies. However, recently these practices have spread as countries such as Canada, Switzerland, Sweden, and even the U.S. have joined the trend. One example of a countertrade deal is the New Zealand Meat Board's agreement to sell $200 million worth of frozen lamb to the Iranian government in exchange for crude oil. Another example is General Electric's agreement to sell Swedish products in overseas markets in exchange for a contract to build engines for Sweden's JAS fighters.[26]

Switch Trading

In a *switch-trading* arrangement, additional parties are brought into the picture whereby part of the exchanged goods is shifted to the new party, often for cash. When one party has an unwanted balance of goods to be received from a second party, a third party in need of the goods offered by the first party is found to purchase the available goods, with the proceeds going to the second party. In one transaction, Mitsui, a Japanese company, bought tanning material in the former Soviet Union and delivered it to Argentina in return for plastic products. These Mitsui materials sold in the U.S. for cash.[27]

Clearing Agreement

The objective of the *clearing agreement* is to balance the exchange of products over time between two governments without having to transfer funds by using an agreed-on value of trade, tabulated in nonconvertible "clearing account units." The contracting parties establish an exchange ratio of their respective currencies to determine the amount of goods to be traded. Usually the exchange value is figured in U.S. dollars. An advantage of the clearing agreement is that flexibility is normally provided so that either side may accumulate a limited import/export surplus for the short term. The following example illustrates clearing agreements:

Morocco and the [former] Soviet Union agree to exchange capital equipment and fresh oranges for a new phosphate plant. Morocco might prefer to buy the equipment elsewhere, but it has little foreign exchange, so it buys from the country that will take oranges in payment rather than hard currency. But Morocco needs the equipment more than the Soviets need the oranges. At settlement date, Morocco corrects the deficit by either paying the difference in hard currency or hoping the Soviets will enter a new agreement and permit the deficit to be carried over to the next contract.[28]

Buyback Barter

Under *buyback barter,* one party's purchase of capital equipment (e.g., plant, process) is paid for through the output made feasible by the capital equipment. For example, a U.S. tire company may sell equipment to establish an auto-tire plant in Egypt and get paid for it through tires manufactured by the Egyptian plant.

The barter agreements are really a form of protectionism, because making any seller trade goods he or she would not otherwise buy eliminates part of free trade. Countries in the former Soviet bloc have been the chief practitioners of barter. In recent years, they have been joined by OPEC and other developing countries. As a matter of fact, more and more industrialized countries are following the same route to sell such big-ticket items as aircraft.

While Japanese and European companies have adapted themselves to barter, U.S. companies have not. Long accustomed to straight cash deals, they are being dragged very reluctantly into barter agreements. Because rival companies outside the U.S. are so accustomed to writing barter contracts, more and more U.S. companies are likely to be forced into the practice. How barter-type deals can hurt business is illustrated by General Electric's efforts to sell computerized axial tomographic (CAT) scanners to Austria. GE lost the deal for CAT scanners for Austrian hospitals after the German competitor, Siemens, agreed to step up production of unrelated electronic goods from an Austrian plant it operates, preserving 4,000 jobs.[29]

Barter trade is a wave of the future. It tends to complicate overseas sales agreements, but U.S. companies may have no choice but to engage in it. Stiff competition from European and Japanese companies, particularly in the case of high-value products, may force U.S. firms into barter deals.[30] More and more, U.S. companies are finding out that having a good product isn't enough. Countries with low hard-cash reserves now look as closely at an exporter's countertrade and financing terms as they do at its product. If competitors from Europe and Japan are willing to offer countertrade, the American companies must be, too. After all, barter accounts for over one-third of the world trade and appears to be increasing at a fast pace.[31]

Summary

The U.S. is the largest exporter in the world. Compared with other nations, however, U.S. exports constitute a small percentage of the GNP. Because the U.S. alone provided a large and growing market for labor-expensive American manufactured goods, export markets had not held much attraction for U.S. businesses. The situation changed in the 1970s. In particular, the high cost of oil imports made it necessary for the U.S. to put greater emphasis on exports and to seek a positive trade balance. Moreover, the devaluation of the U.S. dollar and wage increases overseas made U.S. goods competitive worldwide.

The U.S. government has a variety of programs to encourage exports. Through the Export-Import Bank, the government provides low-cost financing for overseas customers to buy American goods. An exporter can establish a foreign sales corporation to save taxes on his or her export earnings. The U.S. Department of Commerce's 48 district offices provide export-related information and counseling. The Overseas Private Investment Corporation, a federal government agency, insures U.S. business activity abroad in developing countries. Exporters are permitted to join together, without fear of antitrust prosecution, to form export trading companies under the 1982 Export Trading Company Act. Stronger tools to open foreign markets and help U.S. exporters are provided by the Omnibus Trade and Competitiveness Act of 1988. The 1994 National Export Strategy should significantly boost U.S. exports.

Although the government supports export growth in principle, many of its programs hinder export growth. For example, antitrust laws prevent U.S. companies from bidding jointly on major foreign projects.

Export markets provide a unique growth opportunity, but competition in these markets is fierce. Businesspersons, therefore, should adopt appropriate marketing strategies to conduct export trade profitably. They should be aware of attractive markets, specialize in the export of products where American business has a lead, adopt private measures (in addition to those available from the U.S. government) to strengthen their competitive position in relation to foreign competitors, and develop an appropriate orientation for managing export business.

Procedurally, exporting requires locating customers, obtaining an export license from the federal government (a validated or a general license), collecting export documents (such as bill of lading, commercial invoice, export packing list, insurance certificate), packing and marking products, shipping products abroad; and receiving payment. Methods of receiving payment include cash in advance, open account, consignment sale, dollar draft, and letter of credit. Of these, the latter two are most popular.

The provision of customs-privileged facilities, via the establishment of free-trade zones, is a recent trend that many countries have adopted to encourage and facilitate international trade. The U.S. government has approved 150 foreign-trade zones in different communities.

The age-old practice of barter, whereby goods are exchanged for other goods without money swapping, is recurring as a new force in international trade. Initiated by the former Soviet bloc, barter has spread to both the developing and industrialized nations. Currently, it accounts for 25–30 percent of world trade. Unaccustomed to noncash dealings, American companies have been reluctant to engage in barter. Since the practice is likely to become more important, more and more U.S. corporations could be forced into it in the future.

Review Questions

1. Traditionally, what are the reasons for America's meager interest in the export business?
2. Currently, why is it important for the U.S. to emphasize exports?
3. How does the Export-Import Bank help in enhancing U.S. exports?
4. Briefly, list the services of the U.S. Department of Commerce that assist exporters.
5. What is a foreign sales corporation? What role does it play in the context of U.S. exports?
6. What is a bill of lading? What functions does it serve?
7. Illustrate how a letter of credit helps in receiving payment for exports.
8. What is a free-trade zone? How does it help in increasing international trade?
9. Why is barter becoming important? What reasons account for U.S. companies' lack of interest in this activity?

Creative Questions

1. Currently Canada accounts for over one-fourth of U.S. exports. Potentially, in view of NAFTA, the importance of Canada should grow. Yet, Canada does not figure much in government export programs. By the same token, U.S. companies take the Canadian market for granted. To ensure that our largest export market is not jeopardized, what programs may the U.S. government develop to strengthen U.S. exports to Canada?
2. A mail-order sportswear company is interested in globalizing its business. It is planning to mail its monthly catalog to 18- to 30-year olds in select countries all over the world. What preparation does the company need to successfully take its business outside the U.S.?

Endnotes

1. Rob Norton, "Strategies for the New Export Boom," *Fortune*, August 22, 1994, p. 129. Information updated from the U.S. Department of Commerce.

2. U.S. Department of Commerce.

3. Ibid.

4. Richard S. Belous and Andrew W. Wyckoff, "Trade Has Job Winners Too," *Across the Board*, September 1987, pp. 53–55.

5. "Economy: Whoa, there!" *The Economist*, The World in 1999 issue, p. 20.

6. "Europe's Car Dynasties at a Crossroad," *The Wall Street Journal*, February 9, 2000, p. B1.

7. *A Business Guide to Federal Export Assistance* (Washington, DC; U.S. Department of Commerce, 1999).

8. "When in Japan, Do as the Germans Do," *Business Week*, July 3, 1995, p. 43.

9. Kenneth D. Brody, "Ex-Im Bank Marks World Trade Week With Reorganization," *Business America*, April 1994, p. 7.

10. "Forming an FSC in the U.S. Virgin Islands," *Business America*, September 17, 1984, p. 3.

11. B. E. Lee and Donald R. Bloom, "Deficit Reduction Act of 1984: Change in Export Incentives," *Columbia Journal of World Business*, Summer 1985, pp. 63–67.

12. "U.S. Exporters Get the Word: Guilty," *Business Week*, August 16, 1999, p. 42.

13. Rob Norton, "Clinton's High-Risk Trade Tactics," *Fortune*, May 16, 1994, p. 73. *Also see* "Talking to Japan," *The Economist*, February 12, 1994, p. 16.

14. *See* Joanne Hvala, Anne C. Perry, and Jean J. Boddewyn, "General Electric Trading Company: The Sogoshosha That Wasn't," *Journal of Global Marketing* 3, no. 4 (1990): 7–32.

15. "A Troubling Barrage of Trade Sanctions from all Across America," *Business Week*, February 24, 1997, p. 59.

16. "Ready to Take on the World," *The Economist*, January 15, 1994, p. 65.

17. *See* David A Ricks, Jeffrey S. Arpan, Andy H. Barnett, and Brian Toyne, "Global Changes and Strategies for Increasing the International Competitiveness of the U.S. Man-Made Fibers Industry," *Columbia Journal of World Business*, Summer 1986, pp. 75–84.

18. Daniel C. Bellow and David I. Gilliland, "The Effect of Output Controls, Process Controls and Flexibility on Export Channel Performance," *Journal of Marketing*, January 1997, pp. 22–38.

19. U.S. Department of Commerce, *Export Control Regulations* (Washington, DC: U.S. Government Printing Office, 1993).

20. See: Peter C. Burckhardt, Sharad Elhence and Marc E. W. Van Rooijen, "European Freight Forwarders: Which Way To Turn," *The Mckinsey Quarterly*, November 2, 1998, pp. 84–95.

21. "Greasing the Wheels of World Trade," *Fortune*, October 28, 1996, p. 228.

22. Peter Wright, "International Partnerships and Foreign Trade Zones: Strategies for Small Firms," *The Collegiate Forum*, Spring 1984, p. 4.

23. John J. Da Ponte, Jr., "The Foreign-Trade Zones Act: Keeping Up with the Changing Times," *Business America*, December 1997, pp. 22–25.

24. Ken Slocum, "Foreign-Trade Zones Aid Many Companies, But Stir Up Criticism," *The Wall Street Journal*, September 30, 1987, p. 1.

25. "Better Barter?" *Fortune*, February 18, 1985, p. 105.

26. Everett A. Martin and Thomas E. Ricks, "Countertrading Grows as Cash-Short Nations Seek Marketing Help," *The Wall Street Journal*, March 13, 1985, p 29.

27. Ibid.

28. Robert E. Weigand, "International Trade Without Money," *Harvard Business Review*, November–December 1977, p. 28.

29. "New Restrictions on World Trade," *Business Week*, July 19, 1982, p. 118.

30. Cyndee Miller, "Worldwide Money Crunch Fuels More International Barter," *Marketing News*, March 2, 1992, p. 5.

31. "Countertrade Increases Worldwide," *Development Forum*, March 1986, p. 16.

PART 6

Planning
and
Control

CHAPTER 18

Organization and Control in International Marketing

CHAPTER FOCUS

After studying this chapter, you should be able to

■ Describe alternative organizational designs for international marketing.

■ Specify criteria for choosing an appropriate organization structure.

■ Discuss delegation of authority to subsidiaries for marketing decisions.

■ Name some performance evaluation measures.

■ Identify possible conflicts and explain how they can be resolved between parent and subsidiaries.

Markets across national boundaries offer many opportunities for growth and expansion. In taking advantage of such opportunities, international marketers formulate diverse strategies to fit the various different markets and successfully compete in them. A basic requirement for the effective implementation of any strategy is appropriate organizational structure.

Theoretically, the structure of an organization should be commensurate to its task, technology, and external environment. In the context of international business, however, this concept is difficult to put into practice, since a multinational firm is faced with diverse external environments and various environmental constraints. Managers, for example, may follow a decision process of global coordination and integration, but the political demands of a particular host country may require a more diverse and locally responsive decision process. These simultaneous pressures for greater integration and greater diversity create strain in structuring the organization. Thus, the matter of choosing an ideal structure that fits the international marketing strategy and responds to international market demands is an important and complex issue.

This chapter reviews alternative organizational designs that companies use to manage their complex, far-flung operations effectively. The criteria for choosing an appropriate organization structure are examined. Conditions that require organizational changes are analyzed. The question of delegating authority to foreign affiliates is discussed. Finally, different ways of controlling foreign operations and measuring their profitability are considered.

Alternative Organizational Designs

This section discusses distinctive features of alternative organizational designs, relative advantages and disadvantages of each alternative, and the variables that influence the choice of a specific design.

Essentially, there are four organizational structure archetypes: (1) international division structure, (2) geographic structure, (3) product structure, and (4) matrix structure. A fifth type, the functional organization, is not considered here because few multinationals adopt this structure. Its biggest disadvantage is too much centralization. This makes coordination of functional decisions in an MNC difficult and equal interdependence between products and areas rare.

The company's selection of its organizational form has enormous implications for the marketing function. For example, if it is a matrix structure (discussed later), the director of international advertising may have dotted-line responsibility for all the country's advertising managers, who also must report to a local managing director. The director may not find this situation desirable but will have to accept it. The point is that the MNC is quite unlikely to let everything (finance, production, etc.) be organized on a geographic basis with the sole exception of marketing, an area that can choose whatever structure it desires.

Factors Affecting Organizational Structure

An MNC must choose an organizational structure that maximizes decentralization while still providing for the coordination of independent activities. The structure is mainly determined by the following factors.

Quality of Management The decentralization of authority to the local level can be limited when the quality of management varies from country to country.

Diversity of Product Lines Most firms with a high degree of product diversity decentralize on a product basis, rather than on an area basis. Firms producing a few similar products will not decentralize on a product basis because of the high degree of interdependence among their products. However, complete standardization is usually not practical or desirable for marketing decisions because of different market characteristics and consumers.

Size of Firm Firms that derive a substantial portion of business from foreign operations usually drop the international division structure in favor of a product or geographic structure, which facilitates growth. As long as its international business is small, a firm can operate effectively with an international structure.

Location of Subsidiaries and Their Characteristics A company that emphasizes local and regional variations will lean toward the geographic structure because specific geographic variations must be specifically catered to. On the other hand, a company whose subsidiaries are similar to those of the home country (as in the case of a Canadian subsidiary of a U.S. firm) is unlikely to favor a geographic structure because a good degree of standardization can be used in promoting products.

Economic Blocs Companies operating within a regional economic bloc usually integrate their subsidiaries within the bloc area to deal better with trade barriers and oversee these operations by establishing special regional organizational units. This way the unique economic characteristics of the bloc arrangement can be dealt with.

The ultimate decision on a firm's international organizational structure is based on specific factors unique to that company's operating environment. Hence, no two firms, even in the same industry, will exhibit exactly similar structures. In the computer industry, for example, IBM, Apple, and Compaq all use different organizational structures. Compaq operates with a product structure because of a diversified product line, while IBM, because of its large size, has an area organization. Apple's product line and international business have not expanded to the point where more decentralized decision making is necessary and can thus operate effectively with a functional structure.

International Division Organization

The *international division organization* is depicted in Exhibit 18.1. Under this structure, the firm's activities are separated into two units—one domestic and the other international. The main function of such an international division is a company's deliberate attempt to draw a distinction between its domestic and international business. Companies in a developmental stage favor this structure because they may not have enough trained executives to staff a worldwide organization effectively. Top management can thus be freed from foreign operations to work on domestic business (see International Marketing Highlight 18.1)

■■■■■ **International Marketing Highlight 18.1** ■■■■■

Organizing for International Success

Loctite, the engineering adhesives and sealants company, has consolidated all overseas activities under an International Group president based at corporate headquarters in Newington, Connecticut. Within the international group, operations are organized into three overseas regions, managed by a vice president and a secretary; Latin America is managed by the country manager of Brazil. Loctite allows its country managers to determine the product mix and design marketing programs, and to set pricing policy within the context of an annual business plan approved by headquarters.

Source: Winning in the World Market (New York: American Business Conference, Inc., 1989), p. 32.

...ept

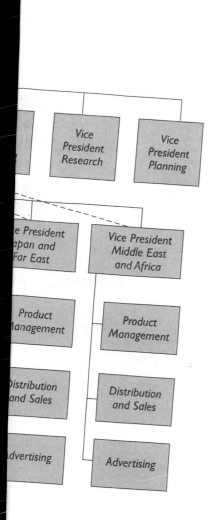

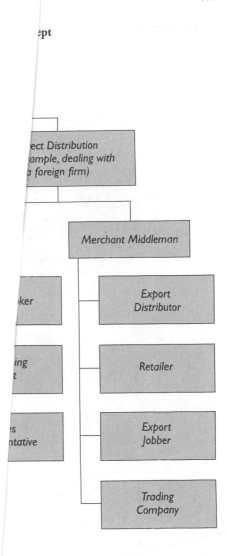

...blems associated with the in-
...d domestic operations are not
...not exist (see Exhibit 18.2).
...perational responsibility goes
...tains responsibility for world-

...e usually share the following

...els.

...ion of line authority and re-
...nufacturing is enhanced, and
...nificant disadvantage of this
...led to run the organization

... can easily grow too diverse for it. Further,
...ise of the two autonomous units. The isola-
...s like a blessing, can become a curse. Con-
...nd business overseas grows. Thus, when the
...onal division structure becomes ineffective.
... is that R&D cannot be easily decentralized
...ed. With the basic research domestically cen-
...d to only product modification.

EXHIBIT 18.2   Geographic Organization Concept

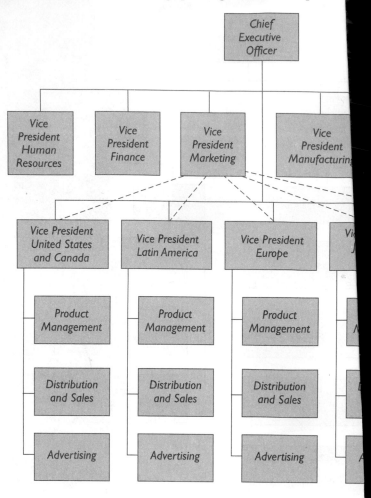

Geographic Organization

A worldwide *geographic organization* can overcome the pr[o]
ternational division structure. In this structure, foreign an[d]
isolated, but are integrated as if foreign boundaries did [not exist.]
Worldwide markets are segregated into geographic areas. C[...]
to area line managers, whereas corporate headquarters main[tains]
wide planning and control.

Companies that operate under a geographic structur[e...]
characteristics:

1. Their product lines are less diverse.
2. Their products are sold to end-users.
3. Marketing is the critical variable.
4. All of their products are marketed through similar chann[els.]
5. Products are changed for local consumer needs.

Geographic organization has many advantages. Delegat[ion of re-]
sponsibility is explicit. Coordination of product sales and ma[...]
overall there is a pooling of experience in problem areas. A si[...]
structure is that a large number of "super" executives are ne[...]

EXHIBIT 18.3   Product Organization Concept

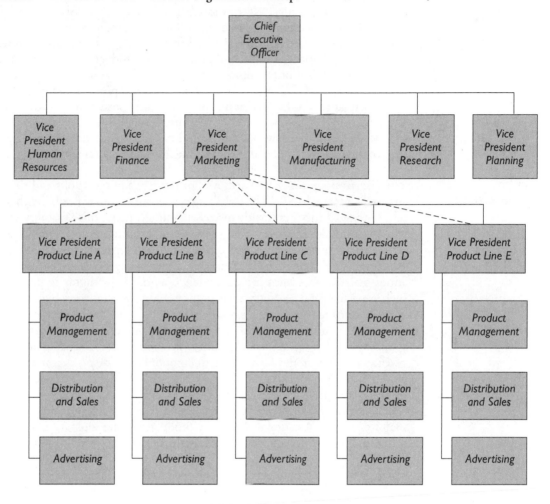

effectively. Another drawback is that individual products may suffer because there is no single executive responsible for the specific product activities. The use of product managers at corporate headquarters can alleviate this problem by ensuring that each product line has proper penetration in world markets.

Product Organization

A *product organization* assigns worldwide responsibility to product group executives at the line management level. The coordination of activities in a geographic area is handled through specialists at the corporate staff level. As shown in Exhibit 18.3, emphasis is placed on the product line rather than on geographic differences. The firm is segregated along product lines; each division is a separate profit center, with the division head directly accountable for profitability. Decentralization is critical in this structure. More decisions are likely to be left to the local manager, who is then usually more highly motivated.

Corporations that operate within the structure usually share the following characteristics:

1. They have a variety of end-users.
2. Their product lines are highly diversified and employ a high level of technological capability.
3. Shipping costs, tariffs, and other specific cost considerations dictate local manufacturing.

Decentralization of authority is a prime advantage of this structure. The motivation of division heads is high. New products can be added and old ones dropped with only marginal effect on overall operations. Another advantage of this structure is that the control of a product through the product life cycle can be managed more readily. Furthermore, MNCs do not have to abandon worldwide product division structure when the size of the foreign operations becomes large.[1]

A drawback of this structure is that coordination problems among various product divisions can arise. Product divisions must constantly be kept in check by top management. Also, division heads promoted to headquarters are likely to be biased in favor of their former product area. The possibility of neglect of certain product areas exists. Many companies employ area specialists who are assigned the responsibility for overcoming that problem.

Matrix Organization

The *matrix organization* first achieved prominence in the 1960s and since then has been adopted by many MNCs. The matrix structure offers greater flexibility than the single-line-of-command structures already discussed and reconciles this flexibility with coordination and economies of scale—the strength of large organizations. The main identifying feature of the matrix organization is that certain managers report to two bosses rather than to the traditional single boss; there is a dual rather than a single chain of command. Firms tend to adopt matrix forms when it is absolutely essential to be highly responsive to two sectors such as product and geography; when uncertainties generate very high information processing requirements; and when there are strong constraints on financial or human resources.

For the multinational firm, the matrix organization is a solution to the problem of responding to both economic and political environments. A matrix organization can include geographic- and product-management components. The *product-management component* would have worldwide responsibility for a given product line; the *geographic-management component* would be responsible for all product lines in a national setting. Because the responsibilities overlap at the national product/market level, both are brought into play for major decisions. A national subsidiary product division must be able to relate to both in order to operate adequately. As an example, GE operates in Asia with a matrix structure. Each unit manager is watched from two standpoints—how the unit contributes to the profit of the division globally and how it contributes to GE's profit at the country level.

In designing a matrix system, one has to be aware of its typical problems. Power struggles are a constant problem when the system is first applied. These struggles result from the dual command system, which has a tendency to create an imbalance of power as each side determines the limits of its influence. Besides tight control over the budgeting and evaluation systems, balance can be maintained by means of pay levels, job titles, and other means of increasing the status of the weaker side.

Another problem is the mistaken belief that matrix management is group decision making. It is not. Each matrix boss and his or her parallel in the other arm have separate functions that should seldom conflict. Their subordinates should work around any conflicting demands, coming to both bosses only as a last resort. The two bosses should rarely have to meet for decision making.

In conclusion, the matrix system is of great benefit to firms that have to react quickly to the environment Corporations generally evolve into matrix forms rather than starting with them from scratch. Besides geographic and product matrices, there can be geographic and functional, or functional and product, matrix systems. Exhibit 18.4 shows an example of how the matrix structure of a multinational corporation may look.

Empirical Evidence on Organizational Structure

Empirical work on organizational structures of multinational enterprises by Milton G. Halman shows that most firms have complex structures that include some sort of matrix structure with product/market on one axis and geography on the other.[2] In most cases the international division, or regional office serves as a buffer between top management and host

EXHIBIT 18.4 Matrix Organization Concept

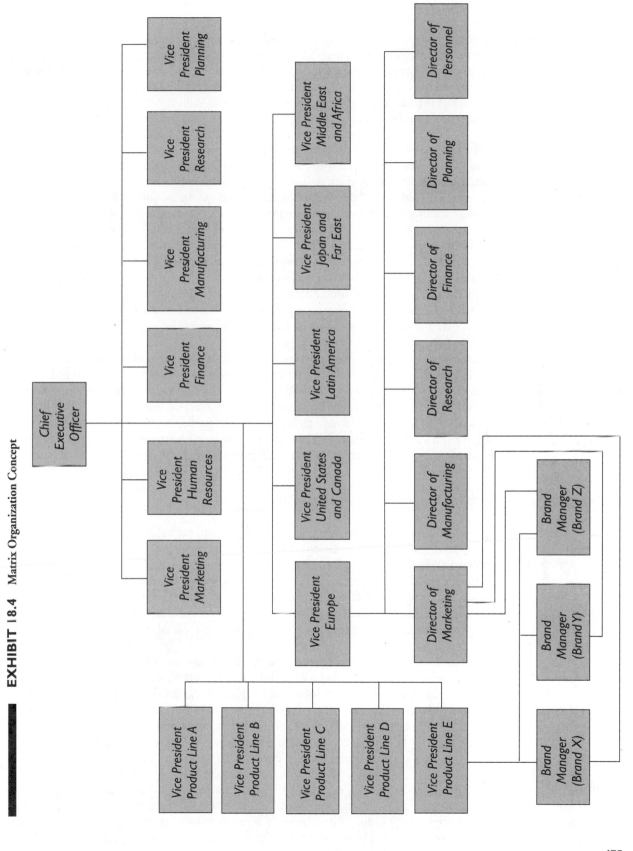

country management. This tendency can be explained by the fact that top management cannot take the time and energy to deal with the great diversity of operations abroad and the wide variety of laws, cultures, customs, and other international factors. Nor can operating subsidiaries or branches abroad be exposed for long to the monolithic perceptions and policies of top corporate officers. Thus, international divisions are created to translate and buffer the communication between foreign operations and headquarters policy.

Organization within Smaller Firms

Depending on the size of the firm, the responsibility for international marketing may be held by the president of the firm, be delegated to a line executive (for example, the vice president of sales), or be given to a staff person, like a marketing researcher or a strategic planner, as an additional duty. Occasionally, however, one person is appointed or hired to manage international operations in its entirety.

To illustrate the point, a chemical pump manufacturer in Ohio with annual sales of about $15 million handled its export business of about $3 million through the president's office. A high-technology firm in Boston (annual sales $16 million) with 50 percent of its business originating in Western Europe had a vice president of exports on par with the vice president of marketing (for domestic business). A precision instruments company in Connecticut traditionally filled export orders as received through the domestic sales organization. After a while, the company decided to expand aggressively overseas. It hired an MBA for this purpose who reported to the president.

Clearly, the organization of international marketing activity within a small firm depends on the extent of one's involvement in and commitment to overseas markets. Generally, initial international marketing activity is handled through the existing organization. As the interest in overseas business enlarges, a specific office is established for that purpose. That office may expand as the scope of business increases. It must be noted, however, that even one individual, if sufficiently committed and backed by top management, can make important strides in successfully launching or expanding a company's place in the international marketplace.

Choosing Appropriate Organizational Structure

The organizing goal of international marketing is a structure that helps the company to respond to differences in international market environments and at the same time enables it to extend valuable corporate knowledge, experience, and know-how from the home market to the entire corporate system. In other words, the structure must be compatible with the organization's task and technology and the relevant conditions of the external environment. Obviously, no one structure will meet the requirements of all corporations. The choice of an appropriate form of organization should be based on several criteria, as follows.[3]

Foreign Markets versus Domestic Markets

If a firm does a substantial proportion of business overseas, greater emphasis needs to be given in organizing foreign operations. If the major markets are at home, the foreign part of the business may simply be organized through an export department. For example, a company like Nestlé, which does over 96 percent of its business outside its home market of Switzerland, needs a global organization structure. In contrast, the major thrust of companies like Hershey Foods is on the domestic market; therefore, they would not attach the same importance to foreign markets as does Nestlé.

Evolution of Corporate Organization Structure

When an organization first expands to foreign markets, its foreign affiliates or subsidiaries report directly to the company president, or his or her delegatee, without assistance from a headquarters/staff group. As international business grows, however, the complexity of coordination and direction will extend beyond the scope of a single person. Assembling a staff group to take responsibility for growing international activities will become necessary. This evolutionary process dictates the choice of structure at any given point in time.

Nature of Business and Related Strategy

A company with minimum product diversity in different markets (both domestic and international) may effectively organize itself functionally. In other words, when the same products are sold worldwide for similar end-users, through similar channels of distribution and advertising themes, the functional domestic setup may be extended overseas as well. Where product lines are diverse, or where local expertise is requisite to adequately serving the market, a geographic organizational structure may be more appropriate.

Management's Orientation

The cultural attitude, or orientation, of a company's management toward different aspects of doing business overseas is another factor that affects the choice of an organization's structure.[4] Management orientation includes such considerations as attitudes toward foreigners and overseas environments, willingness to take risks and seek growth in unfamiliar circumstances, and ability to make compromises to accommodate foreign perspective. Three primary orientations identified among international executives are *ethnocentric,* or home country oriented; *polycentric,* or host country oriented; and *geocentric,* or world oriented.

An *ethnocentric orientation* considers home nationals more trustworthy and more reliable. Consequently, this orientation requires that home country methods and outlook be accepted overseas without question. The *polycentric orientation* acknowledges that host country cultures are different and believes that their people are difficult to understand. In line with this is the idea that local people know what is best for themselves and therefore local organizations should have local identities insofar as possible. The *geocentric orientation* views worldwide markets on an equal basis. Executives who subscribe to this global orientation seek the best personnel for key positions worldwide. The overseas affiliates, under this orientation, are considered an integral part of the corporation, rather than just satellites. The focus is on an amalgamation of worldwide objectives from local objectives with each part making its unique contribution from its particular competence. An organization operating with a world orientation is more complex and interdependent than it would be under either of the other two orientations.

Availability of Qualified Managers

The final criterion that determines the choice of organizational structure is the availability of internationally trained executives. If an adequate number of trained managers is not available, a company may be forced to accept a different structure for the short run than the one considered appropriate. In the long run, however, managers could be trained and the organization appropriately restructured. Of course, the investment needed for developing internationally trained executives would have to be justified in terms of future potential and foreign business expansion plans.

To evaluate a company's justifiable long-run development of management talent, it is helpful to consider the different conditions under which each of the four organization designs (international division, product division, area division, and matrix organization) appear to be suitable. The scheme presented in Exhibit 18.5 provides a generic framework for figuring out an appropriate organization for an international corporation. Particular schemes may have to be modified to accommodate company-specific factors.

Seeking Organizational Changes

Organizations operate in dynamic environments. Therefore, no organizational structure can remain static. As the environment undergoes changes, appropriate changes must be made in corporate strategy, and structure follows strategy.

Need for Reorganization

Essentially, reorganization becomes warranted as a result of one or more of the following four factors: (1) sales growth, (2) adverse financial performance, (3) new products, and

EXHIBIT 18.5   Suitability of Basic MNC Organizational Structures to Corporate Concerns

| | Level of Suitability | | | |
Area of Corporate Concern	International Division	Worldwide Product Division	Area Division	Matrix
Rapid growth	Medium	High	Medium	High
Diversity of products	Low	High	Low	High
High technology	Medium	High	Low	High
Few experienced managers	High	Medium	Low	Low
Close corporate control	Medium	High	Low	High
Close government relations	Medium	Low	High	Medium
Resource allocation				
Product considerations should dominate	Low	High	Low	Medium
Geographic considerations should dominate	Medium	Low	High	Medium
Functional considerations should dominate	Low	Medium	Low	High
Relative cost	Medium	Medium	Low	High

Source: Reprinted by permission of *Harvard Business Review*. An exhibit from "Reorganizing Your Worldwide Business" by J. William Widing, Jr., May–June 1973, p. 159. Copyright © 1973 by the President and Fellows of Harvard College; all rights reserved.

(4) changes in the external environment (for example, political upheaval in the country). Suppose a company has recently entered international markets through filling infrequent export orders. The work involved has amounted to clerical functions handled by an experienced clerk in the sales department. Over the years, as sales grew, the nature of the foreign business changed, requiring a variety of managerial decisions.[5] This triggered a structural reorganization. An international division was established that handled all matters related to business outside the U.S. As another example, Hartford-based Aetna Inc. reconstructed its organization into global units to create more cross-selling opportunities for its business, promote a greater sharing of expertise, and show investors the value of all its operations, not just healthcare. Thus, its existing units: Aetna U.S. Healthcare, Aetna Services, and Aetna International were reorganized into two units—Global Health and Global Financial Services.

Management of Reorganization

Reorganization changes the status quo and established patterns of doing things. People within the organization may not have the capacity or willingness to adjust to structural changes. They may, therefore, resist changes. Such resistance can lead to disruption of intergroup and intragroup working relationships. For example, the domestic organization may neglect work strictly meant for international business. Resistance especially becomes a problem when reorganization calls for dilution of the responsibility and authority of an executive or group that hitherto wielded great influence and performed well.

To ensure organizational harmony, the change must be gradual, not revolutionary.[6] Nor can structural change be imposed unilaterally. More people than just those likely to be affected should be consulted before finalizing the reorganization; for example, it may be necessary to persuade senior management of the need for reorganization.

New Perspectives on Organization: Corporate Networking

As MNCs become ever larger through foreign acquisitions, joint ventures, or direct investments overseas, the traditional ways of organizing just do not work for them, and no amount of tinkering can change that fact. These companies tend to be technology oriented; they need to stay flexible, respond quickly to technological advances, and become or remain product innovators.[7]

Such companies have decided that the only way they can accommodate their needs is to adopt a radical system of organizing people and work, called *corporate networking*. This can best be characterized as an "anti-organization" approach, in that its designers are consciously seeking to break through the constraints imposed by all the conventional organizational structures.

In a networked company, employees around the globe create, produce, and sell the firm's products through a carefully cultivated system of interrelationships. Middle-level managers from R&D, marketing, distribution, and other functions discuss common problems and try to accommodate one another. Flexibility is valued over conformity; therefore, information does not necessarily travel along present organizational routes or chains of command as it does in other organization systems. Marketing people in France might speak directly to manufacturing people in Singapore without going through the home office in, say, the U.S. According to proponents of the network approach, these lateral relationships spur innovation, new-product development, and better quality control. They believe it is the only way a company can be truly innovative in today's bureaucratic world. Networking puts greater decision-making responsibility in the hands of middle managers, who are not required to clear every detail and event with higher-ups. The idea is to substitute cooperation and coordination, which are in everyone's interest, for strict control and supervision.

Corporate networks require the various groups to stay in close contact with each other. Their success hinges on fast, reliable communication. It is no coincidence that networks have become popular at a time when electronic mail, facsimiles, teleconferencing, and other advanced telecommunications techniques have become accessible, inexpensive, and increasingly recognized as extremely valuable management tools.[8]

Pioneering work on network organization has been done by Christopher Bartlett and Sumantra Ghoshal.[9] They classify companies involved in foreign business into four categories: multinational, global, international, and transnational. The first three categories represent traditional organization, while *transnational* refers to networking organization. Key characteristics of each type of traditional organization are as follows:

- *Multinational:* strong local presence through sensitivity and responsiveness to national differences.
- *Global:* cost advantages through centralized global-scale operations.
- *International:* use of parent company knowledge and capabilities through worldwide diffusion and adaptation.

The multinational organization is decentralized. Control from headquarters is informal and personal, overlaid with simple financial controls. Top executives consider overseas operations independent profit centers that are part of the parent company's portfolio. This structure allows local organizations to tailor products to their home markets and helps firms avoid trade barriers.

Being sensitive and responsive to national differences gives an MNC advantages over competitors, but it has drawbacks, too. Because an MNC is so decentralized, knowledge developed within each unit rarely reaches the rest of the company. Efficiency also suffers, since duplication is inherent in the structure and economies of scale are not fully exploited.

The multinational model was frequently adopted by companies prior to World War II, when communications technology was in its infancy and national markets varied dramatically. Overseas operations incapable of operating independently of the home office were not effective in that environment. In some cases, World War II actually forced companies to use a multinational structure when overseas subsidiaries were cut off from the parent company.

The global organization model is almost a mirror image of the multinational model. Highly centralized, the global organization considers overseas operations delivery pipelines to the global market. The corporate headquarters is a central hub maintaining tight controls over decision resources and information. Global companies consider the world one global market. They centralize production and operations, enabling economies of scale and cost advantages but making them less responsive to local needs and more susceptible to tariffs and trade barriers.

The global organization model is typical of many Japanese companies. *Group behavior* and *interpersonal harmony* are strongly emphasized in Japanese culture. These cultural characteristics contributed to the adoption of the global organization model by many Japanese firms.

The international organization represents a "coordinated federation." Assets, resources, and responsibilities are decentralized, but headquarters still coordinates many activities. Formal planning and control systems allow central management to coordinate overseas operations.

The control inherent in this system facilitates the transfer of knowledge and skills from the parent company to overseas divisions. Transferred knowledge can be adapted to meet local market needs. Decentralization with tight controls allows the international organization to capture some of the advantages of both the global and multinational models without the disadvantages. Yet, the international organization does not fully gain the advantages of global-scale economies or responsiveness that the other two models respectively have.

The international model often is adopted by companies with strong domestic positions. These companies move into overseas markets and produce miniature models of the home organization. Overseas operations are given flexibility to adapt to local markets, but strong control and coordination are maintained by headquarters.

Bartlett and Ghoshal argue that until recently, most worldwide industries presented relative one-dimensional strategic requirement.[10] In each industry, either responsiveness, efficiency, or knowledge transfer was crucial, and companies that possessed the matching structure were rewarded. Thus, if the strategic requirement of the industry was *responsiveness* (e.g., branded packaged products), a company following the multinational model found a good fit. Similarly, for companies in industries requiring strategic *efficiency* (e.g., consumer electronics), the global model was appropriate, while the international model was suitable for companies in industries where *transfer of knowledge* was a dominant strategic requirement (e.g., telecommunications switching).

In the 1980s success in global industries depended not just on one dimension (responsiveness or efficiency or leveraging of parent company knowledge and competencies), but on all three at the same time. This need led to a new model of organization, the *transnational structure.* The transnational model, or *network organization,* draws on the strengths of the three traditional models as a means to achieve global competitiveness. Instead of making a blanket centralization or decentralization decision, the transnational organization makes selective decisions. Some operations and resources are centralized while others are decentralized. These decisions are made so that the entire company gains from the proper spread of resources and control.

The structure relies on interdependencies to integrate all company units while allowing them to concentrate on their strengths and maintain the independence necessary for responsiveness. For example, if Division X has a strength in precision manufacturing technology, that will be its focus. Other divisions will depend on Division X for its expertise. However, precision manufacturing will not be monopolized by Division X.

The transnational configuration develops its strengths from three fundamental characteristics: dispersion, specialization, and interdependencies. New consumer trends, tech-

es varies from
ordinarily the de-
on, the relative impor-
he location of the MNC's

The extent and pattern of decentralization of authority
situation to situation. Empirical work on the subje
gree of delegation rests on the following factor that is deeply affected by local fac-
tance of international business and the ing decisions is therefore decentralized in
home base, and the nature of the ind her's study of what kinds of decisions are
study involved the local management of the
U.S.–based consumer durable goods compa-

Type of Decision Marketi ne insight was responsible for 86 percent of the advertis-
tors. Primary authorit e isions of isions, and 61 percent of the channel decisions.
favor of host co perations re involved, local management often retained a
made by who that local ese decisions. As far as product design was con-
Western E found that loca the parent organization.

nies. Ayl ns, 74 percent of fandt and James M. Hulbert generally substantiates
ing where other or conducted among 63 U.S., European, Canadian, and
Even voice in th azil. They concluded that, of the three major marketing
strong decisio pricing—product-related decisions sustained the most
cerned, A sim Forty-five percent of the 63 subsidiaries involved replied
Aylme guidance regarding product design specifications. Forty-
making brand-name decisions. These two areas require ex-

nological advar...
ability to se...
achieve...
tra...

company is asking pe...
outside their countr...
since ICI's stronger...
The payoff is...
and have warring...
son responsible fo...
The profits will...
steam out of t...
quicker—decis...
different mark...
introductions...
A globa...
was all Brit...
Among the...
Britis...
is an Aus...
a comm...
couldn'...
the En...
haps...
Forg...
to t...
ahe...

So...

Delegating Decision-...

Organizat...
not econom...
all of the trem...
ment level. On...
pletely separate b...
lated investments...
also to each other's su...
Determining the...
tradeoffs between contro...
of decentralization that ma...
ble to quantify either benefit...

never...
as any t...
billion a ye...
other products...

In 1983 ICI...
establish worldwi...
strongest ones. Wi...
nine new business...
Delaware—ICI is g...
home. A factory in...
answers to a boss in...

To avoid overlap...
most important mark...
in defense industries,...
the market.

The strategic shift...
Britain by 10,000 to 55,...
hard on people who have...

Internat...
Industries: A N...

perial Chemi...
erve cente...
abanorld's...
ss units. The...
focused activi...
adquartered ou...
nt a year in the...
roducing advanc...
d the world, labs...
research went to...
vent to the sout...

duced its ma...
or taken off...
have such...

Factors That Affect Delegation

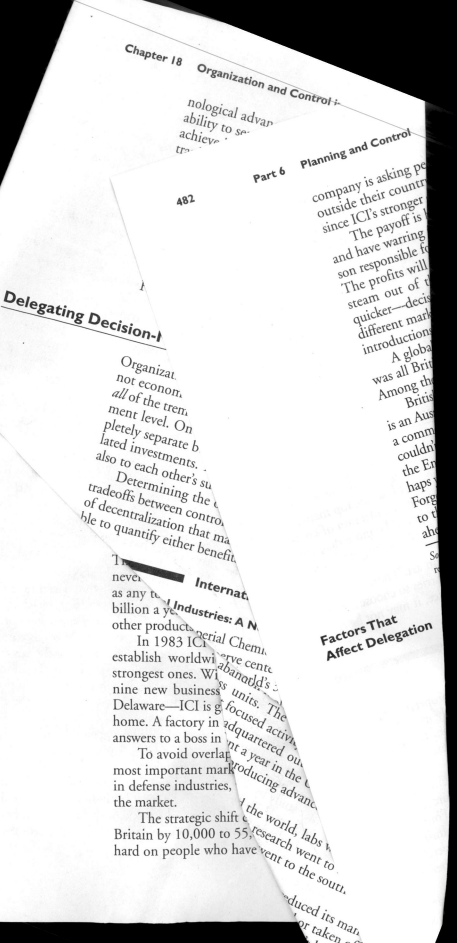

tensive financial investment. For this reason the home office exercised greater control in any decisions made. Decisions concerning price guidelines received a minimal amount of assistance. Greater autonomy to the subsidiary was permitted because it was recognized that local management has a better knowledge of the competitive situation in the area and is more in tune with how customers and the local market will react to price changes (see International Marketing Highlight 18.3).

Relative Importance of International Business and Size of Affiliates The relative importance of the firm's international operations and that of the local affiliates' position within the firm are two important organizational forces that affect the delegation of authority.[13] The frequency of higher management participation in local decision making is affected by the firm's international sales as a percentage of total sales—the higher the sales, the greater the frequency of top management participation in local decision making. For example, in Aylmer's research in one company with 50 percent international sales, top management was directly involved with the major marketing decisions. By contrast, the policy decisions of another company, where international sales accounted for less than 10 percent of total sales, were delegated to local management.

The size of an affiliate also affects the delegation of authority. The larger the affiliate, the greater the authority shared with local management. In the case of smaller affiliates, parent company management more often imposes decisions on local management.[14]

■■■■■■■■■■ **International Marketing Highlight 18.3** ■■■■■■■■■

Managing a Global Business

Cray Research's organizational approach is designed to suit its product line. The supercomputer industry that it has pioneered epitomizes global business in its purest form, much like the large commercial airframe industry in which Boeing is the world leader. Worldwide installations and clients number in the low hundreds at most. The price tag on a supercomputer is high, averaging $12 million to $15 million. Each sale is a discrete event that moves through a complex and time-consuming cycle lasting anywhere from one and one-half to four years. And each purchase decision commits the buyer for a long period of time.

The focal point of the operation is Chippewa Falls, Wisconsin, the site of the company's research and development and manufacturing facilities, where Cray invites customers to visit. It sets prices centrally, and each sales contract is signed directly by Cray U.S. and the individual customer, regardless of location.

Cray's country organizations handle marketing, sales, and service functions and derive a commission on sales and revenues from service contracts. Sensitive, however, to the value that country managers can add, Cray allows them room for decisions in some areas. For example, the country manager has greater control over the marketing of used equipment in his territory, can determine trade-in credit for upgrades, and sets service fees.

In addition, Cray recognizes that country managers are key frontline players in dealing with customers. To enhance their status, it has the managers of six leading country subsidiaries report to internal boards of directors, which include their peers from various functions and U.S. regions and are chaired by executive vice presidents. This reporting relationship encourages collaborative behavior. Country managers also have direct access to Cray's CEO. Country managers are, however, expected to meet specific financial and technical criteria, both set centrally.

Source: Winning in the World Market (New York: American Business Conference, Inc., 1987), pp. 34–35.

Location of MNC's Home Base The delegation of decision-making authority to subsidiaries varies among MNCs of different nations.[15] According to Jacques Picard, U.S. subsidiaries of European corporations enjoy more autonomy than subsidiaries of U.S. corporations in Europe for the following reasons (see International Marketing Highlight 18.4):[16] First, many European companies are understaffed at the top executive level relative to U.S. companies; therefore, not enough managerial attention and time can be given to the subsidiaries. Also, before modern telecommunications were developed, many European companies were already exporting a large portion of their production and were establishing sales subsidiaries overseas because their own local markets were too small. Lack of rapid telecommunications caused most decisions to be made at the local level.

The American multinational corporations' tendency to control may stem from the fact that when they expanded after World War II, the overseas markets were very small compared to the domestic market.[17]

Nature of the Industry The degree of delegation is affected also by the nature of the industry. For example, high centralization is more likely for firms in nonfood categories than those in the food category. In general, the nature of a company's products has an important influence on the delegation of authority to overseas affiliates. Consider the following observation:

> Food products . . . are generally perceived to be . . . "culture-bound"; this means they often become part of a national culture and their use pattern and meaning to consumers vary considerably from one country to the other. Coffee is an old product—350 years old in Europe, so local patterns and traditions surrounding coffee have been built up over many years. As a result, local taste preferences vary considerably from country to country, and even within a country; the café au lait of France and Switzerland, the thin slightly acid taste of Americans, the strong espresso in the small cup in Italy, coffee as a strong milk modifier in England and Australia, the smooth rich acidic taste of the Germans and the Scandinavians.[18]

Avon Products organization arrangements in Latin America further illustrates this point. Unlike many other MNCs operating in the region, Avon does not have a Mercosur or even a South American headquarters. Instead, each country manager reports to an overall Latin American regional manager in Mexico City, who in turn reports to executives in New York.[19]

This structure allows each country manager to tailor decisions to his own market rather than having to coordinate programs and projects with other Avon offices. Although all subsidiaries must adhere to Avon's operating standards, they enjoy a great deal of autonomy with regard to advertising, marketing and product choice. This leeway permits quicker and more accurate pricing decisions.

■■■ International Marketing Highlight 18.4 ■■■

How Japanese Firms Delegate

According to a white paper on Japanese international trade, the widest range of autonomy allowed by Japanese parent companies to their local operations is in decisions on promotion and performance rating systems (in line with adjustment of personnel management to local cultures), supply sources for raw materials and parts, production and inventory volumes, and marketing strategy. The authority most zealously guarded by Japanese corporate headquarters was in the appointment of officers and in decisions on corporate finances (e.g., dividend payouts, long-term fund raising, capital expansions), research and development plans, and plant and equipment investments or expansions.

nological advances, and competitive strategies can develop anywhere in the world. The ability to sense and respond to these changes provides a competitive advantage, which is achieved through *dispersed assets*. Also, *specialization* of national operations allows the transnational company to capture minimum-scale efficiencies while retaining a dispersed structure. The current world competitive situation demands that company units engage in collaborative information sharing and problem solving, cooperative resource sharing, and collective implementation. That is, a transnational organization must employ relationships built on *interdependencies*.

The transnational organization requires highly flexible coordination processes to cope with both short-term shifts in specific role assignments and long-term realignments of basic responsibilities and reporting relationships. Furthermore, it must be capable of modifying roles and relationships on a decision-by-decision basis (see International Marketing Highlight 18.2).

Delegating Decision-Making Authority to Foreign Subsidiaries

Organizations are seldom totally centralized or decentralized. Complete centralization is not economical in most instances because of the administrative impossibility of making *all* of the tremendous number of decisions that would have to be made at the top management level. On the other hand, complete decentralization implies a collection of completely separate businesses, which is also undesirable. Subunits should be more than isolated investments. They should contribute not only to the success of the corporation but also to each other's success as well.

Determining the optimal degree of delegation amounts to an art. There are always tradeoffs between control and delegation. Ideally, top management tries to choose a degree of decentralization that maximizes benefits over costs. Yet, in practice, it may not be feasible to quantify either benefits or costs.

■■■■■■■■   **International Marketing Highlight 18.2**   ■■■■■■■■

Imperial Chemical Industries: A Network Corporation

The archaic name [of Imperial Chemical Industries (ICI)] is entirely appropriate: The sun never sets on ICI's far-flung nerve centers, and the company has probably moved as near as any to being truly global. The world's 38th-largest industrial corporation, ICI sells $21 billion a year of pharmaceuticals, film, polymers, agricultural chemicals, explosives, and other products.

In 1983 ICI began to abandon its traditional country-by-country organization and establish worldwide business units. The company concentrated its resources on its strongest ones. Within each, it focused activity where the most strength lay. Four of the nine new business units are headquartered outside Britain. Two are in Wilmington, Delaware—ICI is growing 20 percent a year in the U.S. but only 2 percent to 3 percent at home. A factory in Britain or Brazil producing advanced materials or specialty chemicals answers to a boss in Wilmington.

To avoid overlapping research around the world, labs were given lead roles near the most important markets. Advanced materials research went to Phoenix to be near clients in defense industries, while leather dye research went to the south of France, the heart of the market.

The strategic shift created wrenching changes. ICI reduced its manufacturing jobs in Britain by 10,000 to 55,000; other people were transferred or taken off pet projects. It's hard on people who have built national empires and now don't have such freedom. The company is asking people to be less nationalistic and more concerned with what happens outside their country. The upheaval has been especially worrisome to British employees, since ICI's stronger growth rate elsewhere attracts more resources.

The payoff is better decision making. Before, each territory would work up projects and have warring factions competing in London for the same money. Now with one person responsible for a global product line, it becomes immaterial where a project is located. The profits will be the same. When you start operating in this manner, it takes a lot of steam out of the defense of fiefdoms. In pharmaceuticals, for example, better—and quicker—decision making has helped ICI reduce the time lag in introducing new drugs to different markets from half a dozen years to one or two. ICI hopes eventually to make the introductions simultaneous.

A global company needs a world view at the top. Until 1982, ICI's 16-person board was all British. Now it includes two Americans, a Canadian, a Japanese, and a German. Among the 180 top people in the company, 35 percent are non-British.

British or non-British, they may go anywhere. The new chairman of ICI Americas Inc. is an Australian who also has worked for ICI in Britain and Canada. He quickly learned that a common language is no insurance against cultural shocks. When he went to England, he couldn't get any respect with his direct Australian manner, so he learned the oblique ways of the English. For example, he says, if an English boss reacts to a pet project by saying, "Perhaps you ought to think about this a little more," what he really means is "You must be mad. Forget it." In the U.S., he had to unlearn the lesson. He told a manager, "Perhaps you ought to think about this a little more." The manager took him literally. Asked why he had gone ahead, the man replied, "Well, I thought about it, like you said, and the idea got better."

Source: Jeremy Main, "How to Go Global—And Why," *Fortune,* August 28, 1989, p. 70. © 1989 Time Inc. All rights reserved.

Factors That Affect Delegation   The extent and pattern of decentralization of authority in overseas affiliates varies from situation to situation. Empirical work on the subject has indicated that ordinarily the degree of delegation rests on the following factors: the type of decision, the relative importance of international business and the size of the affiliates, the location of the MNC's home base, and the nature of the industry.

Type of Decision Marketing is a polycentric function that is deeply affected by local factors. Primary authority for international marketing decisions is therefore decentralized in favor of host country management. R. J. Aylmer's study of what kinds of decisions are made by whom provides some insights.[11] This study involved the local management of the Western European operations of nine major U.S.–based consumer durable goods companies. Aylmer found that local management was responsible for 86 percent of the advertising decisions, 74 percent of the pricing decisions, and 61 percent of the channel decisions. Even where other organization levels were involved, local management often retained a strong voice in the final outcome of these decisions. As far as product design was concerned, decisions primarily rested with the parent organization.

A similar study by William K. Brandt and James M. Hulbert generally substantiates Aylmer's findings.[12] Their study was conducted among 63 U.S., European, Canadian, and Japanese subsidiaries located in Brazil. They concluded that, of the three major marketing areas—product, promotion, and pricing—product-related decisions sustained the most intervention from headquarters. Forty-five percent of the 63 subsidiaries involved replied that they received home office guidance regarding product design specifications. Forty-seven percent received help in making brand-name decisions. These two areas require extensive financial investment. For this reason the home office exercised greater control in any decisions made. Decisions concerning price guidelines received a minimal amount of assistance. Greater autonomy to the subsidiary was permitted because it was recognized that local management has a better knowledge of the competitive situation in the area and is more in tune with how customers and the local market will react to price changes (see International Marketing Highlight 18.3).

Relative Importance of International Business and Size of Affiliates The relative importance of the firm's international operations and that of the local affiliates' position within the firm are two important organizational forces that affect the delegation of authority.[13] The frequency of higher management participation in local decision making is affected by the firm's international sales as a percentage of total sales—the higher the sales, the greater the frequency of top management participation in local decision making. For example, in Aylmer's research in one company with 50 percent international sales, top management was directly involved with the major marketing decisions. By contrast, the policy decisions of another company, where international sales accounted for less than 10 percent of total sales, were delegated to local management.

The size of an affiliate also affects the delegation of authority. The larger the affiliate, the greater the authority shared with local management. In the case of smaller affiliates, parent company management more often imposes decisions on local management.[14]

■■■■■■■■■ International Marketing Highlight 18.3 ■■■■■■■■■

Managing a Global Business

Cray Research's organizational approach is designed to suit its product line. The supercomputer industry that it has pioneered epitomizes global business in its purest form, much like the large commercial airframe industry in which Boeing is the world leader. Worldwide installations and clients number in the low hundreds at most. The price tag on a supercomputer is high, averaging $12 million to $15 million. Each sale is a discrete event that moves through a complex and time-consuming cycle lasting anywhere from one and one-half to four years. And each purchase decision commits the buyer for a long period of time.

The focal point of the operation is Chippewa Falls, Wisconsin, the site of the company's research and development and manufacturing facilities, where Cray invites customers to visit. It sets prices centrally, and each sales contract is signed directly by Cray U.S. and the individual customer, regardless of location.

Cray's country organizations handle marketing, sales, and service functions and derive a commission on sales and revenues from service contracts. Sensitive, however, to the value that country managers can add, Cray allows them room for decisions in some areas. For example, the country manager has greater control over the marketing of used equipment in his territory, can determine trade-in credit for upgrades, and sets service fees.

In addition, Cray recognizes that country managers are key frontline players in dealing with customers. To enhance their status, it has the managers of six leading country subsidiaries report to internal boards of directors, which include their peers from various functions and U.S. regions and are chaired by executive vice presidents. This reporting relationship encourages collaborative behavior. Country managers also have direct access to Cray's CEO. Country managers are, however, expected to meet specific financial and technical criteria, both set centrally.

Source: Winning in the World Market (New York: American Business Conference, Inc., 1987), pp. 34–35.

Location of MNC's Home Base The delegation of decision-making authority to subsidiaries varies among MNCs of different nations.[15] According to Jacques Picard, U.S. subsidiaries of European corporations enjoy more autonomy than subsidiaries of U.S. corporations in Europe for the following reasons (see International Marketing Highlight 18.4):[16] First, many European companies are understaffed at the top executive level relative to U.S. companies; therefore, not enough managerial attention and time can be given to the subsidiaries. Also, before modern telecommunications were developed, many European companies were already exporting a large portion of their production and were establishing sales subsidiaries overseas because their own local markets were too small. Lack of rapid telecommunications caused most decisions to be made at the local level.

The American multinational corporations' tendency to control may stem from the fact that when they expanded after World War II, the overseas markets were very small compared to the domestic market.[17]

Nature of the Industry The degree of delegation is affected also by the nature of the industry. For example, high centralization is more likely for firms in nonfood categories than those in the food category. In general, the nature of a company's products has an important influence on the delegation of authority to overseas affiliates. Consider the following observation:

> Food products . . . are generally perceived to be . . . "culture-bound"; this means they often become part of a national culture and their use pattern and meaning to consumers vary considerably from one country to the other. Coffee is an old product—350 years old in Europe, so local patterns and traditions surrounding coffee have been built up over many years. As a result, local taste preferences vary considerably from country to country, and even within a country; the café au lait of France and Switzerland, the thin slightly acid taste of Americans, the strong espresso in the small cup in Italy, coffee as a strong milk modifier in England and Australia, the smooth rich acidic taste of the Germans and the Scandinavians.[18]

Avon Products organization arrangements in Latin America further illustrates this point. Unlike many other MNCs operating in the region, Avon does not have a Mercosur or even a South American headquarters. Instead, each country manager reports to an overall Latin American regional manager in Mexico City, who in turn reports to executives in New York.[19]

This structure allows each country manager to tailor decisions to his own market rather than having to coordinate programs and projects with other Avon offices. Although all subsidiaries must adhere to Avon's operating standards, they enjoy a great deal of autonomy with regard to advertising, marketing and product choice. This leeway permits quicker and more accurate pricing decisions.

■■■■■■■■■ International Marketing Highlight 18.4 ■■■■■■■■■

How Japanese Firms Delegate

According to a white paper on Japanese international trade, the widest range of autonomy allowed by Japanese parent companies to their local operations is in decisions on promotion and performance rating systems (in line with adjustment of personnel management to local cultures), supply sources for raw materials and parts, production and inventory volumes, and marketing strategy. The authority most zealously guarded by Japanese corporate headquarters was in the appointment of officers and in decisions on corporate finances (e.g., dividend payouts, long-term fund raising, capital expansions), research and development plans, and plant and equipment investments or expansions.

Further, measurements must preserve a proper balance between immediate results and long-term objectives. A higher rate of return in Indonesia may be desirable in light of the economic and political instability threatening foreign investment in that country. However, such a target may be unrealistic because of foreign-exchange losses, import restrictions, and other impediments. Many companies are willing to accept a poor performance in the present in exchange for expected future profitability dependent upon a continued presence in the market.

Controlling Multinational Operations

Controls are defined as checkpoints used to verify performance progress by comparison with some standard. Often the standard is established by top management in the planning process. The control and analysis process becomes more difficult as a corporation's size increases, lengthening the distance between top management and marketing operations. In a changing environment, information must come swiftly to ensure quick action. This timing factor has led toward tighter controls of foreign subsidiaries by multinational corporations. It has been observed that if Union Carbide Corp. had maintained tighter control over its Indian subsidiary, the Bhopal tragedy might not have happened.[21]

A second factor favoring stricter controls is the completion of the EU's 1992 internal market program. EU countries represent a single market without any barriers. As a consequence, U.S. firms have wisely relocated plants and reorganized distribution and marketing functions in the EU countries. However, control must go hand in hand with expansion. Tight control should ensure consistency in product and marketing performance.

The third reason for adoption of strict controls is the correction of unsatisfactory performance by subsidiaries. Sometimes such failure is caused by a subsidiary manager's incompetence. Whatever the reason, control over subsidiaries should provide standards for achievement that result in improved performance.

Further, since an MNC typically has several foreign subsidiaries in different parts of the world, a good control system is important to ensure that these subsidiaries move together toward a common goal, spelled out by the corporate strategic plan. A poor control system can make the task of evaluation and adjustment very cumbersome. General Motors Corp., for example, operates in 17 European countries. Its European operations have been hurt by the corporation's lack of a coherent strategy and strong management. Its Adam Opel subsidiary in West Germany often has been pitted against its Vauxhall Motors Ltd. unit in Britain. In the absence of proper controls, both companies lost money. Consequently, in early 1986 GM decided to overhaul the organization and impose new control procedures in Europe.[22]

A good control system is also vital in evaluating the performance of top management in each subsidiary. Since the environmental conditions surrounding each subsidiary differ, it is impossible to use a completely standard system of evaluation. Some managers are forced to operate under far more severe conditions (cultural, economic, political) than others. A good control system allows for consideration of these variant factors in order to measure the true progress of an operation. Finally, a good control system permits better strategic planning and implementation of the planning.

Financial Measures of Performance

A number of financial measures of performance are relied upon by MNCs. Some of the more popular measures are income or profit contributions, cash flow, and performance relative to a budget. All agree that no single measure of performance is adequate in and of itself. An ideal measure of the true economic benefit of a subsidiary would require comparing the performance of the entire MNC with and without that subsidiary—a difficult if not impossible accomplishment particularly when there are many interrelated subsidiaries in the multinational network. As a practical alternative, corporations rely on a combination of different measures to assess the performance of their operations, both domestic and overseas.[23]

Budgets as Indicators of Performance Companies rely heavily on budgets to compare forecasts of the unit's results with actual results. The variance between the two is then analyzed to evaluate performance and to determine areas in need of improvement. A major problem in the use of budgets for performance evaluation is the setting of realistic, attainable numerical goals.

Income or Profit Contribution Accounting-based *net income* of a foreign operation is a logical and readily available index of performance. However, it can be an inaccurate measure of performance because profits can be manipulated, especially in the short run. For example, elimination of such staff functions as research may improve the profit picture for the purpose of performance evaluation, but in the long run, such cuts can also hurt profit performance. Moreover, net income is not a useful measure for evaluating managerial performance because it typically reflects allocation of corporate headquarters' costs, which are beyond the control of the foreign manager.

Profit contribution is a better measure of managerial success than net income. Profit contribution is unit operating revenues less all expenses directly traceable to the unit, and this figure is more likely to include items under the manager's control. The major limitation of profit contribution is that it omits the unit's share of headquarters' costs. Both net income and profit contribution neglect the investment base required to generate earnings.

Return on Investment (ROI) Evaluation by *return on investment (ROI)* is frequently used because it is believed that the ultimate test of performance is the relationship of profit to invested capital. ROI is computed by dividing the net income by the net assets. Controversy exists over which items should be included in the profits (numerator) and the investment base (denominator), and how they should be measured.

As far as marketing is concerned, different factors affect ROI differently. Empirical work by Susan P. Douglas and C. Samuel Craig provides interesting insights on this issue.[24] Overall they found that, at least in the short run, increased expenditure on marketing mix variables depressed levels of ROI. However, in European markets, high price in conjunction with new product development and expenditure on advertising was positively related to ROI, while salesforce and other marketing type expenditures were negatively related to ROI. In other foreign markets, the authors found little effect of marketing mix variables on ROI, and only superior-quality products could be related to ROI. They conclude that the consequent ambiguity can be explained by the fact that the effectiveness of different types of promotional activity may vary from one market to another.

Douglas and Craig's work failed to reinforce the opinion popularly held in the U.S. that overseas market share leads to profitability, as little correlation was found between market shares and ROI in European or other foreign markets. This result, however, may be due to manipulation of transfer pricing, where creative accounting is used to show losses in high-tax countries and profits in low-tax areas. In addition, the level of investment (joint venture, wholly owned subsidiary) may serve to obscure any relationship between ROI and marketing strategy.

Residual Income The *residual income* is equal to a foreign operation's net income less an investment carrying charge equal to the unit's investment base multiplied by the cost of capital. A benefit of using residual income as a measurement is that it relates income to the investment costs of producing that income. Also, suboptimal decisions are not made with regard to investments, as may happen with ROI. But residual income is subject to the same measurement problems associated with ROI.

Cash Flow Depreciation plus net income (after taxes) equals *cash flow*. Benefits of the cash flow approach as a measure of profitability and performance are its familiarity to executives as a method and its compatibility with a capital budgeting framework. The cash flow computation for the foreign subsidiary should include the returns to the rest of the corporate system rendered by the activities of the foreign operation. In addition, differential taxes levied on the foreign subsidiary, the cost of transferring funds back to the parent, and funds that can be repatriated to the parent should be included in the derivation.

Nonfinancial Measures

Long-range profitability depends not only on the figures in the budget but also on what lies behind the figures. A wide range of nonfinancial aspects, some quantifiable, some not, ultimately affect profits, although they may not show up in short-term profit statements. To be effective, these nonfinancial measures should be defined as clear and precise objectives with definite times of completion. For example, if a subsidiary plans to introduce in November a new product that has been successful elsewhere, a nonfinancial objective for that product might state that by April a market study of specific dimensions must be completed.

Management should develop a checklist of meaningful measures that it intends to use to rate the relative performance of affiliates. From marketing's standpoint, one of the most important nonfinancial measures is *market penetration.* For many products, particularly for consumer products, many companies use market penetration as a yardstick to measure how well business is doing in a given market. A given percentage of the market is required to support the necessary level of promotion for a product to sell effectively and generally obtain a high enough level of visibility to make an overall impression on the consumer.

Measuring market penetration can best be done by comparing company sales with the market as a whole. After the size of the potential market has been estimated, the percentage of available business actually captured by the subsidiary should be calculated for total sales and for sales by product. When compared with forecast sales, these figures will give a good measure of how aggressive local management has been and where weak spots in the product line are holding back the overall effort. Of course, market penetration should be appropriately qualified by the impact of other factors such as degree of competition, local and foreign; impact of substitute products; treatment of export sales in view of local laws or incentives, production costs, or tariff position; weighting of captive sales to the total sales effort; and level of the sales effort (wholesale, retail, ultimate consumer).[25]

Evaluation of promotional effort must be basically qualitative, since it is difficult to establish a valid relationship between sales performance and advertising and promotion expenses. Further, the suitability of promotional effort to the local market is most often the prime factor in evaluating effectiveness. Suitability of the product to the market may also have a significant effect on the marketing effort. Consumer preference evaluation, as well as social and cultural acceptance of the product, is especially important in areas where these factors may differ considerably from American norms. The subsidiary's staff is responsible for recommending and marketing the product that will best suit the local market.

Development of new products is closely linked to product suitability, as the subsidiary must make recommendations from field experience as to product development trends in the market. An evaluation measure used by some firms is the *frequency and quality of new-product suggestions* from the field subsidiaries to the parent R&D department and of new promotion and sales techniques.

Distribution and service evaluation may be combined, since the distributor is often responsible for after-sale servicing. The most frequently listed factors for evaluation in this area are effective use of channels of distribution; attitudes of distributors, retailers, consumers; distributor performance; quality of after-sale servicing; and promptness in filling orders.

In all these areas, the following long-term judgment question should always be present: Have actions been taken during the period under analysis that will help or hinder sales performance in subsequent periods?

Conflicts and Their Resolution

In any organizational setup, conflicts are bound to arise between different groups. In the context of international marketing such conflicts usually emerge from differing parent corporation and subsidiary points of view.

One of the biggest problems subsidiaries encounter in the control process is that corporate decisions are made too slowly. Delays in receiving important and urgent decisions from headquarters cause companies to miss out on many opportunities. Subsidiary managers also find that too many reports have to be sent to headquarters. In most cases, they feel nobody reads these reports and that the importance of the information tends to be minimized. The result is that headquarters management often relies on information not from the subsidiary but from superficially formed impressions.[26]

Another aspect of the control problem is attributed to low levels of credibility in both headquarters and the subsidiary management. Corporate executives tend to disregard the local manager's recommendations. As a result, in highly centralized and controlled companies, local managers must resort to persuasion to get their ideas accepted at headquarters. On the other hand, local managers tend to disregard headquarters' directives and doubt the soundness of its decisions because local managers often are uninformed about the reasons for the decisions, or they cannot accept that a corporate executive is better informed or better qualified to make decisions. Thus, each distrusts the other's judgments and abilities.

Finally, one of the biggest problems in the control relationship is headquarters' lack of knowledge about conditions abroad. Most U.S. companies with foreign subsidiaries underestimate the importance of social, cultural, economic, and political conditions with which foreign subsidiaries must deal. Many companies are just not well informed about such conditions (see International Marketing Highlight 18.6).

■■■■■■■■■   **International Marketing Highlight 18.6**   ■■■■■■■■■

A Question of Culture

Bosses in France tend to be Napoleonic. Graduates as a rule of one of the elite Grandes Écoles, they are expected to be brilliant technical planners, equally adept at industry, finance, and government. They can be vulnerable to surprise when troops below fail to respond to orders from the top. Stiff hierarchies in big firms discourage informal relations and reinforce a sense of "them" and "us." Managers in Italy tend to be more flexible. Firms' rules and regulations (where they exist) are often ignored. Informal networks of friends and family contacts matter instead. Decision making tends to be more secretive than elsewhere, and what goes on in a meeting is often less important than what happens before and after.

This can shock Germans, who on the whole prefer to go by the book. Board members tend to have years of technical training and higher degrees. Rarely will a German manager move out of his special field before reaching board-level. This is in sharp contrast to Britain, where tomorrow's top managers tend to be spotted young and then sent rapidly through every department in the firm, giving them a broad, but not always thorough, overview of its operations. To avoid clashes between these strongly flavored national cultures, some European companies prefer Swedish or Swiss chief executives, who, it seems, are better blenders.

Source: The Economist, December 7, 1991, p. 64.

An empirical investigation by Ulrich E. Wiechmann and Lewis G. Pringle provides interesting insights into the problems that concern marketing executives of large U.S. and European multinationals and their subsidiaries worldwide.[27] In a nutshell, it is not primarily competition, political and legal pressure, nonavailability of channels, or differing social and cultural outlooks that bother marketing executives in corporate headquarters and their foreign subsidiaries. The worst problems are internal, those emerging from friction between two groups. For example, marketing executives at the headquarters may charge marketing managers in foreign subsidiaries with failure to formulate long-term strategy, while subsidiary managers are bothered by the parent company's overemphasis on short-term financial performance.

Summarized here are the major concerns of corporate marketing executives:

- Lack of qualified international personnel.
- Lack of strategic thinking and long-range planning at the subsidiary level.
- Lack of marketing expertise at the subsidiary level.
- Too little relevant communications between headquarters and the subsidiaries.
- Insufficient utilization of multinational marketing experience.
- Restricted headquarters control of the subsidiaries.

Subsidiaries' concerns are as follows:

- Excessive headquarters control procedures.
- Excessive financial and marketing constraints.
- Insufficient participation of subsidiaries in product decisions.
- Insensitivity of headquarters to local market differences.
- Shortage of useful information from headquarters.
- Lack of multinational orientation at headquarters.

Naturally, some conflict is inevitable, simply because the orientation of the two groups is different. The corporate people want detailed information on subsidiary operations to enable them to unify and integrate their far-flung operations. Subsidiary executives prefer less control and more authority and want to be treated as autonomous units. Some conflict and tension may be desirable to help avert obsolete approaches to management and to encourage continual dialogue between the parties. However, some problems need to be eliminated, including such common areas of concern as deficiencies in the communication process, overemphasis on short-term issues, and failure to utilize fully the corporation's experience overseas.

To resolve shortcomings, the first step is to articulate the problems. Then the causes of conflict should be established. For example, a subsidiary's short-term perspective may be related to unique competitive conditions in its market area. Finally, an appropriate solution should be found. The remedy for each cause will be different. The solution may range from open discussion between the corporation and its subsidiary to organizational changes. In any event, as a lasting solution to conflict resolution, foreign subsidiaries must be adequately involved in both strategy formulation and implementation processes.

Christopher Bartlett and Sumantra Ghoshal note,

> When Procter & Gamble launched Pampers in Europe, it directed the marketing strategy from European headquarters. The result: a big failure. The reason: P&G failed to take advantage of particular strengths of national units; country managers, bypassed in the planning, had no stake in the outcome.
>
> The failure led P&G to rethink the way it used local subsidiaries and to form the highly successful "Eurobrand teams," made up of line and staff officers of key national subsidiaries. Shouldering the load in marketing development with product configurations, advertising themes, and packaging, Eurobrand teams successfully introduced Vizir, a liquid detergent, in six countries within a year.
>
> In pushing new strategies like this, P&G and other successful MNCs diverge from traditional hierarchical structures in which the top formulates—and the national subunit simply implements—strategy and planning. By cooperating and co-opting capabilities, the parent's sales and market share get a big boost from the country unit's technical expertise, market knowledge, and competitive awareness—all without losing boundary-crossing benefits like scale economies.[28]

Summary

As the scope of a firm's international business changes, its organizational structure must be adequately modified in accordance with its tasks and technology and the external environment. There are four main ways of structuring an international organization: international division structure, geographic structure, product structure, and matrix structure. The organizational structure is affected by such factors as quality of management, diversity of product line, size of firm, subsidiaries' locations and their characteristics, and existence of regional blocks within the market. Each of the different structures has relative merits and demerits. An empirical study of international organizations shows that most firms follow a complex structure along the lines of the matrix organization. Added to that, firms have the international division or regional office to serve as a buffer between the corporate and host country management.

The choice of an appropriate organizational form for international marketing activities is dictated by such considerations as the relative importance of foreign markets vis-à-vis domestic markets, the evolutionary pattern of the firm's organizational structure, the nature of business and its related strategy, management's orientation (home country versus host country versus world orientation), and availability of qualified managers.

Business is conducted in a dynamic environment. As the environment undergoes change, there should be appropriate responsive change in the structure. Change is triggered by such factors as sales growth, adverse performance, introduction of new products, and changes in the external environment. The need for reorganization becomes noticeable as these causes articulate themselves in the form of specific indicators of organizational malaise—for example, conflict among divisions or duplication of administrative services, among many other signs of trouble. The change should be managed in such a way that organizational harmony continues to be maintained. Thus, consultations with people likely to be affected by the change and gradual introduction of change would be in order.

An important decision for international marketing executives to make at the headquarters level is how much decision-making authority will be delegated to subsidiary management. To the extent that marketing is a *polycentric* function subject to influence by local factors, the primary responsibility for marketing decisions is delegated to local management. However, product-related decisions remain largely the prerogative of the parent corporation's management with subsidiary management dominating in decisions of price, promotion, and distribution. The extent of authority delegation differs also according to parent corporation national identity. For example, U.S. multinationals as a group prefer greater centralization than do European or Japanese multinationals. Similarly, the nature of a product also influences authority delegation decisions.

Performance evaluation and control of foreign operations are linked with organizational structure. There are two types of performance evaluation measures, financial and nonfinancial. Financial techniques include measurements against budgets and balance sheet ratios. Nonfinancial measures include market penetration, affiliate export sales results, salesforce workload appraisals, and the general attitudes of distributors, dealers, and large customers toward the company.

Organizational conflicts are inevitable between corporate executives and subsidiary management. One empirical study on the subject showed that the worst problems are internal, emerging from friction between the two groups. For example, both groups charge each other with pursuing short-term orientations. While some of the conflicts can be expected and tolerated because of the different perspectives of their work situations, efforts by and large must be made to eliminate the underlying causes of conflicts. Improvements in the organizational structure can smooth the way.

Review Questions

1. What factors affect an organization structure in the context of international marketing?
2. What factors lead a company to opt for the matrix form of organization?
3. What criteria might a firm employ to determine an appropriate organization for structuring international business?
4. Differentiate between ethnocentric, polycentric, and geocentric orientations of international executives. How does each orientation affect organization structure?
5. What factors necessitate change in organizational design to accommodate international marketing?
6. To what extent are marketing decisions delegated to overseas subsidiaries' managers? What insights do empirical findings provide on this issue?
7. What different ways are there to integrate multinational marketing activities?
8. Discuss market penetration as a measure of performance evaluation in international marketing.

Creative Questions

1. Traditionally, subsidiaries have played a secondary role, doing what headquarters desired. Illustrate, with the help of an example, how subsidiaries could become a significant partner in global growth of the parent corporation.
2. What is relationship marketing? How could this concept work in international marketing? Illustrate with an example.

Endnotes

1. *See* William G. Egelhoff, "Strategy and Structure in Multinational Corporations: A Revision of the Stopford and Wells Model," *Strategic Management Journal* 9 (1988): 1–14.

2. Milton G. Halman, "Organization and Staffing of Foreign Operations of Multinational Corporations," a paper presented at

the Academy of International Business Meeting, New Orleans, October 25, 1980.

3. Stefan H. Robock, Kenneth Simmons, and Jack Zwick, *International Business and Multinational Enterprise*, 4th ed. (Homewood, IL: Irwin, 1989), pp. 270–272. *Also see* Gunnar Hedlund,

"Organization In-between: The Evaluation of the Mother-Daughter Structure of Managing Foreign Subsidiaries in Swedish Multinational Corporations," *Journal of International Business Studies*, Fall 1984, pp. 109–124.

4. *See* David K. Tse, Kam-hon Lee, Lean Vertinsky, and Donald A. Wehrung, "Does Culture Matter? A Cross-Cultural Study of Executives' Choice, Decisiveness, and Risk Adjustment in International Marketing," *Journal of Marketing*, October 1988, pp. 81–95. *Also see* Lane Kelley, Arthur Whatley, and Reginald Worthley, "Assessing the Effects of Culture on Managerial Attitudes: A Three-Culture Test," *Journal of International Business Studies*, Summer 1987, pp. 17–32.

5. Tarun Khanna and Krishna Palepu, "The Right Way to Restructure Conglomerates in Emerging Markets," *Harvard Business Review*, July–August 1999, pp. 125–135.

6. *See* Christopher A. Bartlett, "MNCs: Get Off the Organization Merry-Go-Round," *Harvard Business Review*, March–April 1983, pp. 138–146.

7. *See* "Building Tomorrow's Global Company," *Crossborder Monitor*, October 15, 1997, p. 12.

8. *See* Jeremy Main, "How to Go Global—And Why," *Fortune*, August 28, 1989, p. 70.

9. Christopher A. Bartlett and Sumantra Ghoshal, *Managing Across Borders: The Transnational Solution* (Boston: Harvard Business School Press, 1989).

10. Ibid.

11. R. J. Aylmer, "Who Makes Marketing Decisions in the Multinational Firm?" *Journal of Marketing*, October 1970, pp. 25–30. *Also see* Donna G. Goehle, *Decision Making in Multinational Corporations* (Ann Arbor, MI: University Research Press, 1980); and J. Michael Geringer and Louis Hebert, "Control and Performance of International Joint Ventures," *Journal of International Business Studies*, Summer 1989, pp. 235–254.

12. William K. Brandt and James M. Hulbert, "Headquarters Guidance in Marketing Strategy in the Multinational Subsidiary," *Columbia Journal of World Business*, Winter 1977, pp. 7–14. *Also see* Zada L. Martinez and David A. Ricks, "Multinational Parent Companies' Influence Over Human Resource Decisions of Affiliates: U.S. Firms in Mexico," *Journal of International Business Studies*, Fall 1989, pp. 465–488.

13. *See* Saeed Samiee, "Pricing in Marketing Strategies of U.S. and Foreign-Based Companies," *Journal of Business Research* 15 (1987): 17–30.

14. R. J. Aylmer, "Who Makes Marketing Decisions in the Multinational Firm?" *Journal of Marketing*, October 1970, pp. 25–30.

15. Stephen R. Gates and William G. Egelhoff, "Centralization in Headquarters—Subsidiary Relationships," *Journal of International Business Studies*, Summer 1986, pp. 71–92.

16. Jacques Picard, "How European Companies Control Marketing Decisions Abroad," *Columbia Journal of World Business*, Summer 1977, p. 120. *Also see* Hans Jansson, *Interfirm Linkages in a Developing Economy: The Case of Swedish Firms in India* (Uppsala, Sweden: Uppsala University, 1982); Charles Y. Young, "Demystifying Japanese Management Practices," *Harvard Business Review*, November–December 1984, p. 172.

17. Jacques Picard, op. cit., pp. 121–124.

18. Ulrich Wiechmann, "Integrating Multinational Marketing Activities," *Columbia Journal of World Business*, Winter 1974, p. 12.

19. "Avon Sticks to Its Formula," *Crossborder Monitor*, September 9, 1998, p. 8.

20. Joann S. Lublin, "Firms Ship Unit Headquarters Abroad," *The Wall Street Journal*, December 9, 1992, p. B1.

21. Thomas M. Gladwin and Ingo Walter, "Bhopal and the Multinational," *The Wall Street Journal*, January 16, 1985, p. 28.

22. "General Motors' Big European Overhaul," *Business Week*, February 10, 1986, p. 42.

23. Anthony E. Boardman, Daniel M. Shapiro and Aidan R. Vining, "The Role of Agency Costs in Explaining the Superior Performance of Foreign MNE Subsidiaries," *International Business Review*, Vol. 6, No. 3, 1997, pp. 295–318.

24. Susan P. Douglas and C. Samuel Craig, "Examining Performance of U.S. Multinationals in Foreign Markets," *Journal of International Business Studies*, Winter 1983, pp. 51–62.

25. David Norburn, Sue Birley, Mark Dunn, and Adrian Payne, "A Four-Nation Study of the Relationship Between Marketing Effectiveness, Corporate Culture, Corporate Values, and Market Orientation," *Journal of International Business Studies*, Third Quarter 1990, pp. 451–68.

26. Daniel E. Ding, "Control, Conflict, and Performance: A Study of U.S.—Chinese Joint Ventures," *Journal of International Marketing* No. 3 (1997): 31–45.

27. Ulrich E. Wiechmann and Lewis G. Pringle, "Problems that Plague Multinational Marketers," *Harvard Business Review*, July–August 1979, pp. 118–124.

28. Christopher A. Bartlett and Sumantra Ghoshal, "Tap Your Subsidiaries for Global Reach," *Harvard Business Review*, November–December 1986, p. ES26.

CHAPTER 19

Marketing Planning and Strategy for International Business

After studying this chapter, you should be able to

- ■ Describe perspectives of marketing planning at the corporate and subsidiary levels.

- ■ List the steps in achieving planning effectiveness.

- ■ Discuss the current and future role of the U.S. in light of emerging changes.

- ■ Name some strategic changes that MNCs are likely to face at the turn of the century.

The essence of international marketing management is the development of appropriate objectives, strategies, and plans that culminate in the successful realization of foreign market opportunities. The world marketplace experiences accelerating change that requires explicit statements of objectives and strategies reflecting changed opportunities and threats as they occur.

Business across national boundaries became a dominant factor in world commerce after World War II. Today, for a number of U.S. companies, as well as for many non–U.S. companies, sales and/or revenues from overseas exceed domestic business. In the 1960s U.S. corporations had an edge in many ways, but no longer. In such markets as automobiles, steel, watches, textile goods, and electronic equipment, there is fierce competition. In addition to multinational enterprises from Europe and Japan, corporations belonging to developing nations such as South Korea, China, Taiwan, Brazil, and India are increasingly participating in world markets, posing new forms of competition.

Currently MNCs are expanding at a rate of more than 10 percent a year, or twice the growth rate for gross world product. The prospect is that these business organizations will become even more important in the future. According to the projections of knowledgeable economists based on present trends, in the year 2005 the economy of the world will be more than half internationalized.

Although markets overseas are changing and the competition increasing, international markets nonetheless continue to offer attractive opportunities. Indeed, markets across national boundaries frequently offer higher rates of return than domestic markets. For example, in 1993 the profitability of U.S. investment was 5.5 percent in the U.S., 5.7 percent in Canada, 9.4 percent in Europe, 15.0 percent in Latin America, and 20.4 percent in Asia and the Pacific.[1] To make a mark in the international arena, though, a company needs to define its objectives clearly, choose appropriate strategies, and develop adequate plans to implement the chosen strategies.

The purpose of this chapter is fourfold. First, perspectives of international marketing planning and strategy are examined. This analysis is followed by a discussion of a short-term operations marketing plan. Next, concepts and procedures for developing and formulating international marketing strategy are studied. Finally, the unfolding environment likely to have an impact on international marketing in the future years is probed. This final section highlights the challenges that lie ahead for international marketing executives.

Dimensions of International Planning and Strategy

Planning practices for multinational markets are far behind those for domestic markets. This is particularly true of strategic planning. Theoretically, international marketing planning and strategy should involve both subsidiary and headquarters management. Further planning should focus on operational matters as well as strategic issues. Currently, however, most marketing planning among MNCs is operational and short-term. In a great many corporations, the effort amounts to a set of financial figures extrapolated for the next four to six quarters. In some cases, the plan is put together by the headquarters staff with meager inputs from the subsidiary. In other cases, the planning task is entirely delegated to subsidiary management, and the headquarters' review is skimpy and only ritualistic.

The challenge of successfully competing in the international field in the future will force corporations to become more systematic in planning efforts. Every industry must look ahead—1 year, 5 years, 10 years—and plan for (1) the future political, social, and economic environment; (2) the evolution of the particular industry; and (3) how the industry must change to meet the problems and opportunities it judges it will face.

Essentially, marketing planning at the subsidiary level is short-term planning related to the next 12 to 15 months and not strategic planning, which usually has a long-run focus. Conceptually, a subsidiary's planning efforts should be duly coordinated with those at headquarters. Characteristically, it should be from the bottom up and take into account the environmental realities surrounding its products and markets. In this effort, the parent corporation plays three roles. The first role involves facilitating linkage between corporate and subsidiary perspectives. This task amounts to providing corporate-wide inputs relative to overall mission and direction, both generally and with reference to the subsidiary/country market. The second role is to establish a worldwide planning system by developing planning procedures and communicating them to subsidiaries. An additional role that corporate headquarters must perform is that of catalyst in creating a planning culture among the subsidiary executives.

At headquarters, marketing planning focuses on coordination and approval of plans submitted by subsidiaries, as well as formulation of corporate-wide strategy. The strategy formulation in international business reflects not only the domestic experience of the company, but also management's orientation toward multinational business. Three management orientations were discussed in the previous chapter: ethnocentrism, polycentrism, and geocentrism. A company with a *geocentric perspective* tends to look at world markets as a whole, with no demarcation between domestic and international business. Its strategic focus is global. Following a *polycentric orientation,* the company establishes overseas subsidiaries that operate independently from each other. Each country follows its unique marketing strategy. An executive with an *ethnocentric orientation* views international business as secondary, a place to dispose of "surplus" products left over after fulfilling domestic demand. The differences in these approaches have been illustrated by choices of branding policy.

- *Ethnocentric approach.* Branding policy in overseas companies stresses the parent company as a unifying feature, but not necessarily the origin of the parent company.

- *Polycentric approach.* Each local company brands products on an independent basis, consistent with local country criteria.

- *Geocentric approach.* A worldwide branding policy exists only for those brands that are acceptable worldwide.

Planning at a Subsidiary Level

Presumably, an overseas subsidiary should undertake both short-term marketing planning as well as strategic planning. The following section examines conceptual designs for formulating subsidiary plans. Also addressed are the problems that hinder the planning process. Finally, suggestions are made to resolve the problem.

Short-Term Planning

A *short-term marketing plan* constitutes the core of an overseas subsidiary's planning effort. It is operationally, not strategically, oriented. The plan covers marketing operations usually for about a year.

The complexity of planning varies among companies. In some cases, it may amount to simple preparation of sales budgets. In more globally oriented firms, however, planning would involve multiple considerations to consolidate mutual interdependence between different overseas affiliates and the parent corporation.

The process of short-term marketing planning is depicted in Exhibit 19.1 The inputs for triggering the planning process are partly received from the parent corporation and partly generated within the subsidiary. The corporate headquarters shares with the subsidiary the perspectives of its mission and objective. This input helps the subsidiary to define its overall goals and specific marketing objectives. Headquarters, in order to establish homogeneity among different subsidiaries' plans, may prescribe a standard procedure for conducting the planning process. For example, a standard format may be required for sales forecasts or budgets. Additionally, the parent organization would provide the subsidiary an analysis of the shape of things to come in the environment.

The planning inputs gathered at the subsidiary level consist of external and internal factors. *External factors* are the emerging trends in the product/market environment (for example, competition, legislation to be enacted, demands shifts, and the like). *Internal factors* include past sales data and the scope of activities in other functional areas of business.

Equipped with this information, planning starts with a review of past sales and their extrapolation into the future. The extrapolated forecasts are duly revised in light of the planning inputs. For example, sales forecasts may need to be revised downward because of a newly established plant by a domestic competitor. Similarly, sales forecasts for a product/market may be increased if the subsidiary's production facilities expect to be able to manufacture an improved version of the product.

The final sales forecasts form the basis for generating action strategies and developing the marketing budget. *Action strategies* refer to the perspective to be pursued in different areas of the marketing mix—product, price, promotion, and distribution. The *marketing budget* would include sales revenues, gross margin, full details of selling and administrative expenses, promotional allocations, and other overheads. The budget may include data from the past one or two years to permit historical comparisons. The budget should be prepared in local currency as well as in U.S. dollars.

The marketing budget must be reviewed by the subsidiary management to add to and accommodate the company-wide outlook. For example, the subsidiary's controller office would supply the cash flow analysis. Similarly, the finance function would reflect the likely impact of the fluctuations in local currency value, and a capital-expenditure and working-capital plan would be appended. By itself, the marketing budget does not constitute a complete budget. A variety of other financial information must be included before it is ready for submission to the corporate management.

Once the subsidiary review is complete, the short-term marketing plan emerges. This is submitted to the parent corporation for examination together with the subsidiary budget and other related information. Usually the subsidiary plan and budget are presented to a corporate team in person. For a U.S. company, the meeting usually is held in the U.S. so the subsidiary executives have a chance to meet different corporate officers and visit various plants and facilities.

If the corporation is regionally organized, the subsidiary may present its plan and budget to the regional management. The regional management then assimilates all the plans within the region and makes a region-wide presentation to the corporate management.

Revisions may be demanded in the marketing plan or the accompanying budget. The subsidiary management can accept the revisions or defend its position by supplying appropriate information and arguments. Once a compromise is reached, the parent corporation approves the plan, and it becomes the basis for the subsidiary's operations in the next year.

Ideally, the short-term marketing plan should be initiated by the subsidiary management. Further, it should bear a close relation to the subsidiary's strategic plan, which should be appropriately linked to overall corporate strategy. In practice, however, it would

EXHIBIT 19.1 Framework for Short-Term Marketing Planning by Overseas Subsidiary

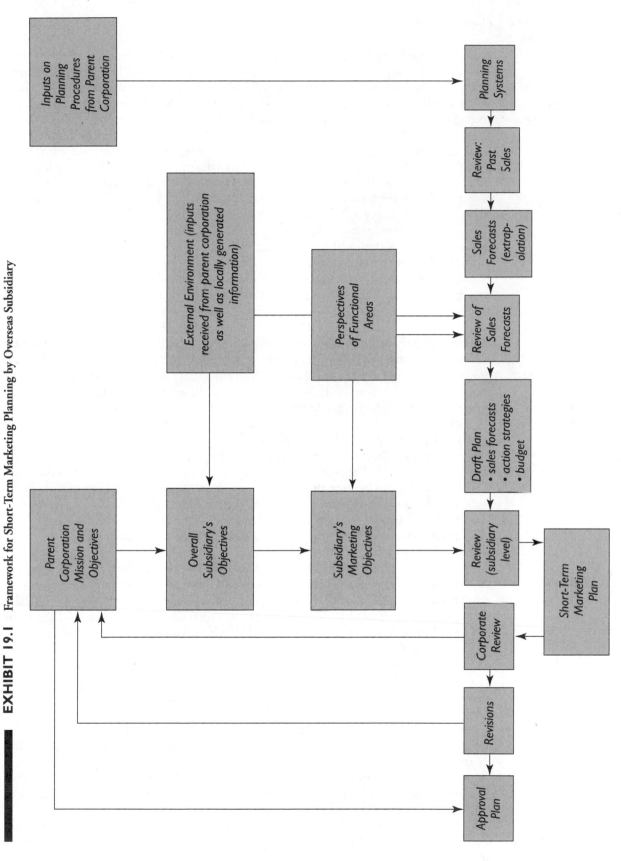

be naive to expect such a systematic effort, for two reasons. First, the state of the art may not permit drawing plans in a smooth, sequential manner. Second, lack of necessary data and proper management orientation impede adherence to a conceptually sound system. For example, corporate management with an ethnocentric orientation would want the corporate way of planning adopted without consideration of the local environment.

Strategic Planning

Very few subsidiaries practice *strategic market planning*. Anything beyond short-term planning mainly consists of longer-term extrapolations of the same plan. The lack of a true strategic perspective can be explained by two factors. First, the art of strategic planning is still emerging, and its articulation at the subsidiary level can be difficult among MNCs. Second, many MNCs consider strategic planning to be the prerogative of the corporation and discourage subsidiary involvement. Although the resultant centralization of strategic planning at headquarters may appear reasonable, it poses one crucial problem: Centrally developed strategic plans tend to consider the entire world to be similar; thus, standardized strategies are formulated for all markets. Inevitably, such strategies fail in those markets that differ from the home market in significant ways, and many do.

Process of Strategic Market Planning Two basic factors in strategic planning are markets and competition. Surrounding these factors are the sociocultural, technological, political, and regulatory concerns, unique to each market. Strategic market planning should begin with customer analysis and end with differential marketing programs tailored to meet buyer needs, giving due consideration to environmental influences.

After a thorough analysis of buyer needs and expectations, the department of research and development (R&D) should be asked to create a customized product as necessary. Strategic directions for introducing new products and penetrating new markets should be developed. The customization may involve simple adaptation of package design or size, or it may require an entirely new version of the product. The remaining ingredients of the marketing mix should be custom-designed similarly.

Once the strategy is approved by the parent corporation, implementation of the program begins. The implementation of a strategy may take years, and in the process several go/no-go decisions are required.

In the development of different market-related strategies, the impact of emerging environmental trends ought to be incorporated. For example, wage rates in Germany rose proportionally to productivity increases, constituting one of the strengths of the German economy, until 1991 and 1992, when wage rates increased by an average of 12 percent each year but productivity increased less than half that amount.[2] Under those circumstances, little could be realized in substantial price increases. Naturally, a complete study of competitive conditions was required to determine how much prices could be raised.

Problems of Strategic Market Planning Among the problems encountered in a subsidiary's planning process is the lack of adequate information. Both the subsidiary and the parent corporation can be blamed for this problem. Subsidiaries often lack the knowledge and resources to scan the environment systematically and gather adequate information from the external environment. Furthermore, internal information may not be adequately organized. Even more troublesome is the fact that available information on national trends and so on is often outdated, particularly in such emerging countries as Thailand, Brazil and China, which are changing fast.

As far as headquarters is concerned, there may not even be a worldwide marketing information system in place. Thus, information at headquarters from different subsidiaries and different groups is neither collected nor disseminated properly.

Another problem is that sometimes information is poorly coordinated. Despite an abundance of data, the right information may be impossible to locate. Conceivably, headquarters could request information from a subsidiary that headquarters itself had made available.

Lack of an established planning system is still another hindrance to strategic planning. Emphasis on day-to-day matters by headquarters sometimes discourages the establishment of such a planning system at the subsidiary level. In some cases, the planning system that exists is too complex and unnecessarily cumbersome. Thus, a major portion of marketing managers' time in subsidiary companies may be spent in responding to the needs of the parent corporation.

Also, if the plan is adhered to as a rigid instrument of control, it could lead to intracompany fighting and manipulations to ensure meeting cost and revenue projections. Such fighting leads to rivalries, which are obviously counterproductive. Manipulations result in a distorted picture of performance.

The easiest problem to solve concerns the scarcity of trained managers. Subsidiaries often lack trained personnel to undertake planning, but this problem can be mitigated through training arranged by the parent corporation.

Seeking Planning Effectiveness

Effective planning at the subsidiary level should be encouraged through the setting of objectives, the training of planning professionals, the development of planning and communications systems and a cordial, collaborative attitude among all the people involved. The core of these measures is cooperation between the subsidiary and the parent corporation (see International Marketing Highlight 19.1).

Objective Setting The subsidiary's objectives must not be directives from the home office, nor be defined solely by the subsidiary itself in isolation from corporate direction. Rather, the objectives should be jointly set so that both corporate-wide perspectives and conditions peculiar to the subsidiary environment are weighed in arriving at the subsidiary objectives.

Cadre of Planning Professionals The corporation should develop a cadre of international strategic planning professionals. Such professionals should have awareness and insight into the country or region whose planning they coordinate. In other words, marketing planning at headquarters should not be entrusted to finance people who examine strictly in terms of set formulas and cutoff points. The planners at headquarters should be sensitive to the varying environment of each subsidiary before passing judgment on its financial performance.

Planning and Communication Systems Traditionally, MNCs have pursued standardized strategies worldwide. For example, if a corporate decision is made to increase market share for a particular product, that decision must be carried out globally. Standardization, however, ignores the realities of the marketplace in subsidiaries. The problem may be solved in two ways: (1) by overhauling the planning system to take into account the marketing environment of each subsidiary, or (2) by developing appropriate databases through effective communication between the subsidiary and the home office.

Collaborative Attitudes Both the subsidiary and the parent corporation should develop an attitude of cordiality toward each other. Neither can do an adequate job of marketing planning on its own. They should collaborate with each other, with the parent playing the staff role and the subsidiary assuming the line responsibility for marketing planning. This way, headquarters would be able to bring its systems capability to the planning while the subsidiary would contribute its deep knowledge of the marketplace.

Marketing Planning at the Corporate Level

Corporate management mainly plays two planning-related roles. First, it provides various informational inputs to the subsidiaries and reviews and approves their plans. Second, it develops a corporate-wide strategic plan, which may be either one global strategic plan covering both domestic and international markets or two separate strategic plans, one each for domestic and international business. Presumably, companies with an ethnocentric or polycentric orientation would follow the latter course. Geocentrically oriented firms, however, would consider global markets as one market and would not make a distinction between domestic and international business.

Corporate headquarters' role in the planning efforts of subsidiaries has been examined in the previous section. Studied in this section are different aspects of an MNC's strategic planning activity. Strategic planning among corporations became a popular topic and began to receive emphasis in the 1970s. Initial efforts at strategic planning, as might be expected, were limited to domestic business. Strategic planning in international business is still in the developmental state. Thus, overall experience in strategic planning for worldwide business is limited.

International Marketing Highlight 19.1

Planning Activities at the Subsidiary Level

Grand Metropolitan monitors the effectiveness of subsidiary marketing programs annually, but evaluation is conducted at the sector level more frequently, and at the local level sales and marketing activity is often measured on a monthly basis.

At the start of each company year, long-term (i.e., four-year) objectives are updated and agreed upon and short-term objectives reviewed. (Long-term overall objectives are set by the individual sectors working in conjunction with representatives from the corporate planning department, but specific marketing tasks remain the exclusive province of the relevant sector managers.) Short-term marketing performance is judged by reference to these short- and long-term goals at regular intervals by local management and by sector management, both of which formally review progress at the end of each quarter.

In the autumn, each sector reviews its strategy and if necessary revises it. This review is finalized at the corporate center in December. Local marketing decisions are then amended in the light of any changes that have been agreed to. The review at this time is concerned with strategic concepts rather than specific quantified business objectives. These issues are settled at the subsequent set of meetings that take place in the spring, at which quantified objectives are agreed for actions consequent upon previously agreed strategies. The final step in the process is the submission and agreement of annual plans at local, sector, and corporate levels. This takes place in August/September.

Source: Marketing Strategies for Global Growth and Competitiveness (New York: Business International, no date), p. 74.

Strategic marketing planning constitutes only a part of the corporate strategic plan. *The true role of strategic marketing planning is to influence the behavior of the competitors and the evolution of the market to the advantage of the corporation.*

Stated differently, *marketing strategy is the concept of changing the competitive environment.* Thus, a marketing strategy statement includes a description of the new competitive equilibrium to be created, the cause-and-effect relationships that will bring it about, and the logical steps to support the course direction. A strategic marketing plan specifies the sequence and timing of the steps that will alter competitive status.

Against today's background of mounting labor costs, sluggish growth in home markets, shifting exchange rates, and rising nontariff barriers abroad, international strategy becomes increasingly significant (see International Marketing Highlight 19.2). Moreover, shrinking profit margins from domestic operations impel MNCs more strongly than ever to make explicit strategy statements. Marketing figures prominently in these statements.[3]

Two related developments appear to signal the continued importance of strategic planning for international business. First, companies that derive a major portion of their sales and profit from overseas activities and look at markets abroad for future growth must depend on a well-prepared strategy to pursue appropriate paths. Second, giving the changing patterns of competition, strategic planning is a critical factor for maintaining leverage in overseas markets.

International Marketing Highlight 19.2

Singapore Airlines—The Flying Beauty

It may be the world's 15th largest carrier, but Singapore Airlines is consistently the most profitable. In the year ending March 31, 1991, it made a net profit of S$913 million ($513 million) on sales of S$4.9 billion. Its balance sheet shows a mere S$438 million in long-term debt and a cool S$2.1 billion in cash. The carrier has the youngest fleet of any big airline—the average age of its 46 aircraft is less than five years. It is also the winner of countless awards for service.

The contrast with American and European airlines, many of which began to hemorrhage cash during the Gulf War and have yet to recover, could hardly be starker. This raises two intriguing questions: How has a tiny city-state with a population of under 3 million, and thus no automatic reservoir of passengers for its national carrier, managed to create a global airline? And can Singapore Airlines maintain its edge?

The recipe for success as described by Joseph Pillay, the airline's chairman since its formation in 1972, looks deceptively simple: "Our mission remains inviolable: offer the customer the best service that we are capable of providing; cut our costs to the bone; and generate a surplus to continue the unending process of renewal."

What has saved this from becoming just another empty mission statement is Singapore Airlines' relentless investment. The most important are the 747-400s, which carry more people and fly farther than earlier versions of the jumbo. They also use 35 percent less fuel. Lower running costs and the ability to fly nonstop, a key factor in attracting high-yield business travelers, create bigger profits. These enable Singapore Airlines to pay cash for its aircraft. Another benefit of this virtuous circle is that aircraft can be sold before they are too old.

Source: The Economist, December 14, 1991, p. 74.

Planning Process

The process for international strategic planning is depicted in Exhibit 19.2. The process consists of sequential steps to be followed. These steps are basic to strategic planning, irrespective of management's attitudinal orientation (see International Marketing Highlight 19.3).

The process begins with the firm's commitment to go international. A corporation enters overseas markets to pursue long-term profitable growth. As growth prospects in the domestic market diminish, international markets provide a strategic alternative. Or sometimes companies opt for international business in response to an invitation by a foreign interest. The decision to go or not go international must be based on such considerations

EXHIBIT 19.2   Process of Strategic Marketing Planning at the Corporate Level

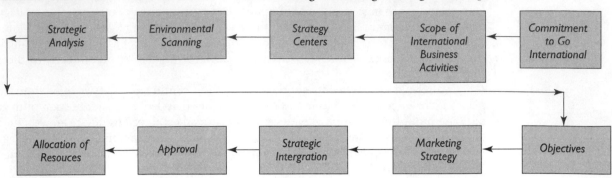

as corporate mission and objectives, long-term opportunity potential, analysis of strengths and weaknesses, management philosophy, opportunities at home, and financial implications of foreign entry.

The decision to enter international markets may be an open decision, or it may be relative to specific countries. The decision should be based on a complete examination of the economic, cultural, political, and business environment of the host countries.[4] It would be an arduous task to analyze a vast amount of data (assuming it is available) pertaining to different countries. As a shortcut, therefore, companies often choose countries that satisfy basic criteria such as GNP per capita, growth rate, and market size.

International Marketing Highlight 19.3

How IBM Approaches Global Strategic Planning

IBM has developed an approach to global strategic planning that takes into account the divergence between headquarters and regions. The approach revolves around its unique needs and corporate culture. These include parallel planning process, the ability to direct and leverage the immense resources of the organization worldwide, the ability of corporate planners to promote cultural cross-fertilization and act as "broker" of creative ideas, and the use of global models to promote common goals.

The core of IBM's strategic planning process resides within the divisions. Each geographic and functional division generates its own strategic plan on an annual cycle, coordinated by the corporate planning office. The cycle culminates in "commitment plans," which comprise a five-year strategic plan and a two-year detailed business plan. The plans represent both a blueprint for the division's response to regional market needs and opportunities and a financial commitment to the corporation. There's a qualitative and a quantitative dimension and the latter becomes the measurement for the following year.

Concurrent with the commitment plan cycle, a "top-down" planning mechanism provides direction from senior management. A series of strategic planning conferences is attended by 20 top executives. The strategies emerging from these conferences are often far-reaching in their implications for the organization. An example is the company's commitment to the concept of "market-driven quality" in the late 1980s. Although the concept sounds general, it has had implications for every part of the vast organization. It has affected not only the marketing and production techniques, but the very way in which IBM measures its own progress. This sets the overall framework, defines the business, and establishes a long-range intent.

A third critical dimension to the planning process is product planning. Within IBM, there is a separate framework for technology-driven planning of new products and service concepts, where the time frame may be as long as a decade. A continual exchange takes place between the technological research function and the corporate and divisional strategies, providing input on customer needs or "systems imperatives" on the one hand and defining the "art of the doable" on the other. The technology community provides major input to the corporate and divisional planning processes.

Source: Business International, May 28, 1990, pp. 169–170.

GE's strategy on this matter, as described by Linda Grant, is interesting:

> Many companies today pursue a one-size-fits-all approach to global manufacturing and marketing. GE, however, believes that formula is too crude to mine the riches it seeks. The company has launched a successful strategy it calls "smart bombing." Here's how it works in Asia: GE executives examine each country's idiosyncrasies microscopically, then tailor a mix of products, brands, manufacturing facilities, marketing, and retail approaches to wring the best performance from each. They measure factors such as the quality and strength of local competitors, the market's growth potential, and the availability of skilled labor. Their unyielding goal: to generate the handsomest returns possible on the smallest investment possible.[5]

Chapter 8, on economic environment, presents a framework for selecting international markets for making investments. This same framework is relevant in the strategic decision process.

Strategy Centers or Strategic Business Units (SBUs)

After overseas product/market matches are established, the next step is to reorganize the different parts of the business that would be involved internationally into *strategy centers* or *strategic business units* (SBUs), self-contained businesses that meet three criteria: (1) they have a set of clearly defined external competitors, (2) their managers are responsible for developing and implementing their own strategies, and (3) their profitability can be measured in real income rather than in artificial dollars posted as transfer payments between divisions. Once SBUs are identified, appointments of SBU heads should be made.

The steps discussed so far are the purview of top management. Such work should be undertaken at the highest level with analytical support provided by corporate staff. It should be strongly emphasized that SBUs do not replace the traditional organizational lines. The operations continue to be planned and implemented as in the past. Over and above the traditional organization, however, SBU structure is created for determining strategy. Thus, an SBU may be established around products/markets in different divisions in different countries. For example, a company may manufacture color television sets in one country, while in another country radios and stereos are manufactured as a part of the home entertainment division. For strategy development purposes, television sets, radios, and stereo equipment may be considered as one SBU.

Strategic planning analysis from that point on is undertaken at the SBU level. In a large multiproduct, multimarket company, strategy cannot be developed at the top management level because it would be too complex a task for one office to examine the perspectives of all products/markets. Each SBU conducts opportunity analysis of the different products/markets under its control. This analysis can be accomplished by using the growth-share matrix product portfolio approach discussed next.

Growth-Share Matrix Product Portfolio Approach

The *growth-share matrix product portfolio* approach is based on the assumption that the firm with the highest market share relative to its competitors should be able to produce at the lowest cost. Conversely, firms with a low market share relative to competition will be high-cost producers. By comparing relative market share positions (high/low) with market growth rates (high/low), the firm can position its different businesses on a two-by-two matrix. Using these two dimensions, growth and market share, businesses can then be classified into four categories: stars, cash cows, question marks, and dogs. Businesses in each category exhibit different financial characteristics and offer different strategic choices.

Stars High-growth market leaders are called **stars**. They generate large amounts of cash, but the cash they generate from earnings and depreciation is more than offset by the cash that must be put back into these businesses in the form of capital expenditures and increased working capital. Such heavy reinvestment is necessary to fund the capacity increases and inventory and receivable investment that go along with market share gains. Thus, star products represent probably the best profit opportunity available to a company, and their competitive position must be maintained.

Cash Cows The **cash cows** are characterized by low growth and high market share. They are net providers of cash. Their high earnings coupled with their depreciation represent high cash inflows, while they need very little in the way of reinvestment. Thus, these products generate large cash surpluses, which help to pay dividends and interest, provide debt capacity, supply funds for R&D, meet overheads, and also make cash available for investment in other products.

Question Marks Products that are in growth markets but have a low share are categorized as **question marks**. Because of growth, these products require more cash than they are able to generate on their own, since they have a low share of the market. If nothing is done to change its market share, the question mark will simply absorb large amounts of cash in the short run and later, as growth slows down, will become a *dog* (discussed next). Thus, unless something is done to change its future outlook, a question mark remains a cash loser throughout its existence and ultimately becomes a *cash trap*.

What can be done to make a question mark more viable? One alternative is to gain market share increases for it. Since the business is growing, it can be funded to dominance so that it may become a star, and later a cash cow when growth slows down. The other strategy is to divest the business. Outright sale is more desirable

Dogs Products with low market share and in a low growth position are called **dogs**. Their poor competitive position condemns them to poor profits. Because growth is low, there is little potential for gaining sufficient share to achieve a viable cost position. Therefore, further investment in the business is rigorously avoided. An alternative is to convert dogs into cash, if there is an opportunity to do so.

The usage of the product portfolio framework for performing opportunity analysis in the context of international business is illustrated in Exhibit 19.3.[6] The top half of the figure shows product/market portfolios of competitors A and B. Competitor A is a market leader. In the U.S. and Canada, its business has reached maturity, while in Europe it has a solid position. The cash cow position in the U.S. and Canada should generate extra cash for investment in the star markets of Europe. Competitor A has an insignificant position in Brazil and no entry in the Japanese market. On the other hand, B is a smaller competitor, but it occupies a dominant position in the two fast-growing and potentially large markets of Japan and Brazil. It is quite conceivable that in the future, B may generate more total units sales than A and thus seek lower costs through greater scale effects. The cost leadership may make B more competitive also even in mature markets (the U.S.

EXHIBIT 19.3 Strategic Analysis Using the Product Portfolio Approach

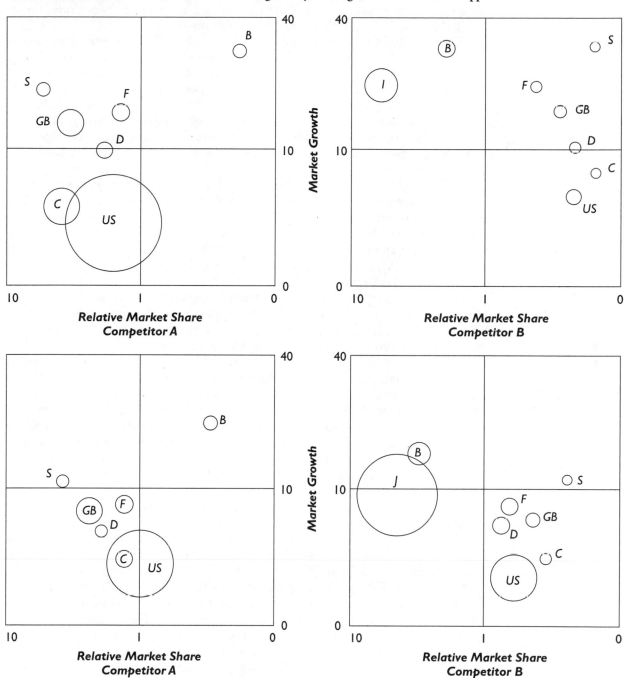

(B = Brazil, C = Canada, D = Germany, F = France, GB = Great Britain, J = Japan, S = Spain, US = United States)

Source: Jean-Claude Larre', "The International Product-Market Portfolio," in Subhash C. Jain, ed., *Research Frontiers in Marketing: Dialogues and Direction*, Educators' Conference Proceedings (Chicago: American Marketing Association, 1978), p. 278

and Canada), which currently are A's stronghold. In brief, if competitor A does not take adequate strategic measures in its illustrated position, in five years its position is quite likely to be as depicted as in the bottom half of Exhibit 19.3.

Following the BCG approach, a company may conduct an opportunity analysis by (1) analyzing its current international product/market portfolios, (2) analyzing the competitors' current international product/market portfolio, and (3) projecting its own and the competitors' future international product/market portfolios. The analysis may then be used to define objectives of each product/market. For example, competitor A in Exhibit 19.3 may set an objective to enter the Japanese market. Likewise, objective(s) may be set to make a major commitment to the Brazilian market. Essentially, a product/market objective should be stated either in terms of growth rate, market share, or profitability.

Once objectives have been specified, alternative strategy options are generated. The preferred strategy will usually have a focus on one of the areas of the marketing mix, product, price, promotion, or distribution. For example, the preferred strategy may be to reduce prices to maintain market share. Here the emphasis of the strategy is on pricing. Thus, pricing would be labeled as the *core strategy,* the area of primary concern. However, in order to make an integrated marketing decision, appropriate changes may have to be made in the product, promotion, and distribution areas. The strategic perspective in these areas can be called *supporting strategies.*

The strategic perspectives of each product/market will be consolidated into an SBU strategic plan. It is quite conceivable that in some cases an SBU consists of just one product/market. In that case, the product/market would represent the plan of the SBU. The strategic plans of worldwide SBUs are reviewed at the corporate level for the purpose of integration and to develop a corporate-wide posture to achieve synergies and realize tradeoffs.

Here again, the same product portfolio framework can be used. Different SBUs can be positioned in the matrix. Based on the matrix position, the role of each SBU can be determined and resources allocated accordingly. Thus, an SBU positioned as a cash cow may be expected to generate surplus cash. No new investments would be planned for such an SBU. On the other hand, a question mark SBU may be designated for conversion into a star, which would qualify it for new investments. Once that is accomplished, different SBU plans are approved, and a corporate-wide strategic plan is formulated, after which resources are allocated.

Exhibit 19.4 illustrates the Ford Motor Company's international matrix.[7] Like the product portfolio approach just discussed, this *multifactor matrix* has two dimensions in this case, "country attractiveness" and "competitive strengths." But each of these dimensions is based on a variety of factors. It is this multifactor characteristic that differentiates the Ford approach from the product portfolio one.

Also shown in Exhibit 19.4 are the appropriate strategies to adopt based on the position of a country on the matrix. For example, countries positioned in the top left portion of the matrix provide the best opportunity for growth, so the MNC should seriously consider investing in them. Countries falling in the right bottom area of the matrix promise little growth, so the company might consider harvesting or divesting its interests there. Countries in the middle offer some opportunity, but caution is needed, and therefore selective strategies should be employed.

Country attractiveness is determined based on market size, market growth, government regulation, and economic and political stability. These factors are combined using a single linear scale as follows:

Country attractiveness = market size + 2 × market growth + (0.5 × price control/regulation + 0.25 × homologation requirements + 0.25 × local content and compensatory export requirements) + (0.35 × inflation + 0.35 × trade balance + 0.3 × political factors).

EXHIBIT 19.4   Multifactor Matrix for Plotting Products

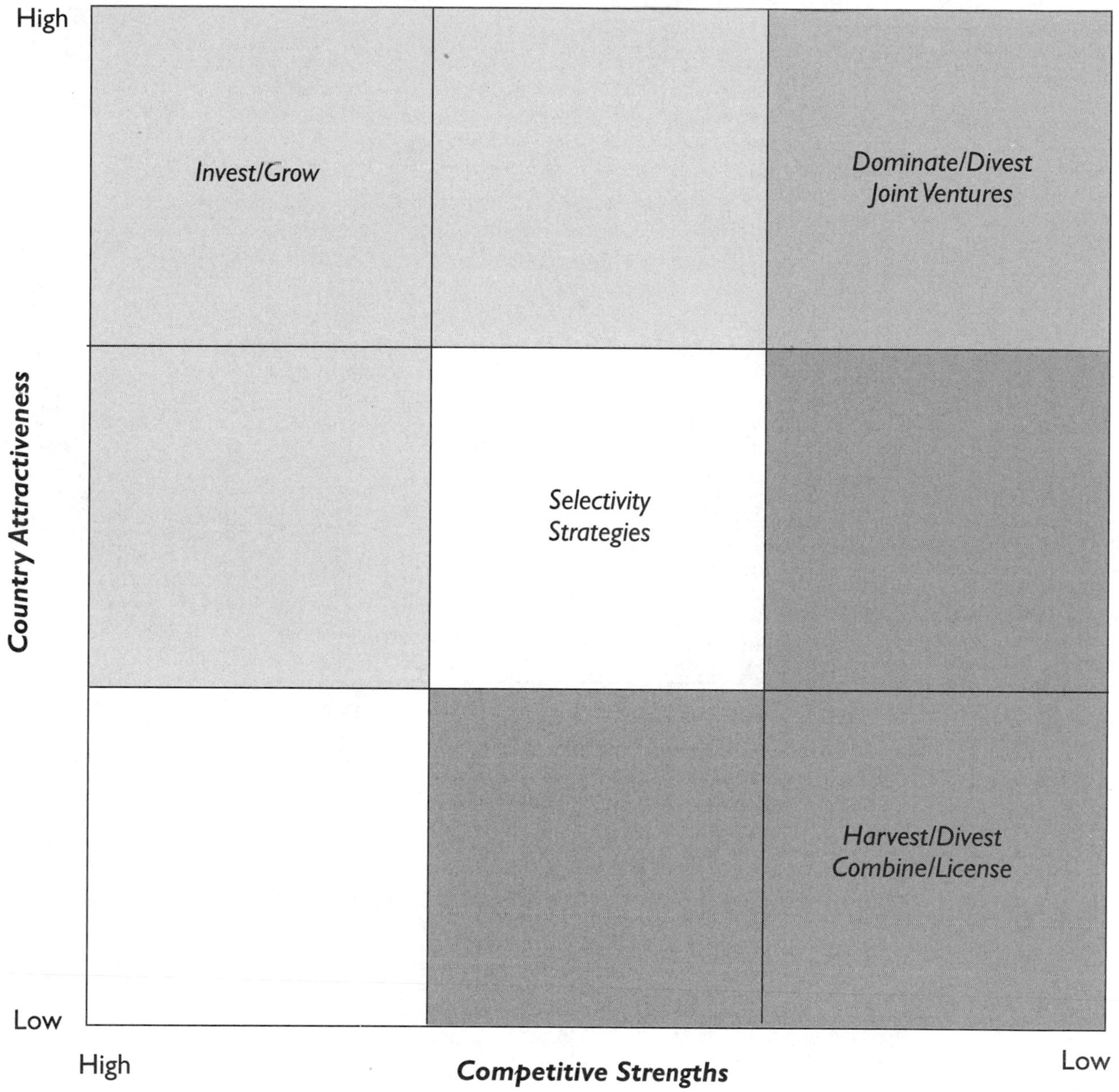

The weights are based on Ford's strategic planning perspective. Another company may use different weights.

Competitive strength is computed using the four factors of market share, product fit, contribution margin, and market support in the following manner:

Competitive strength = (0.5 × absolute market share + 0.5 industry position) × 2 + product fit + (0.5 × profit per unit + 0.5 × profit percentage of net deal cost) + market support.

Exhibit 19.5 shows the position of different countries on the matrix developed using the ratings that were computed based on country attractiveness and competitive strength

EXHIBIT 19.5   European Matrix

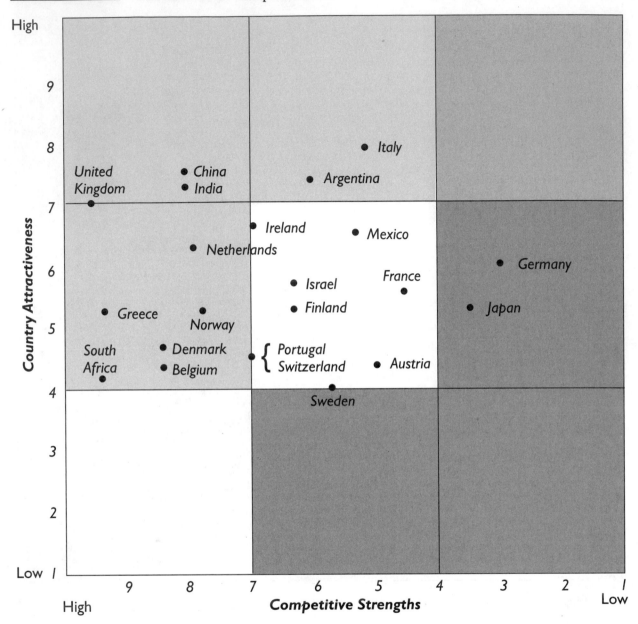

scores. The invest/grow countries indicate where the company must make a strong commitment. The harvest/divest position refers to countries where harvesting profits or selling the business may be generally appropriate. The dominate/divest joint venture position represents a difficult strategic choice, because the firm is competitively weak but the market is appealing. The final decision demands a careful analysis of investment requirements and other available options.

Essentially, as is done with the product portfolio approach, the multifactor matrix approach offers guidelines for strategy formulation in international market environments. A company may position its products or country markets on the matrix to study their present standing. The future direction of different countries also can be developed, assuming no changes are made in the strategy. The future perspective may be compared with the corporate mission to identify gaps between what is desired and what may be expected if no measures are taken now. Filling these gaps will require making strategic moves for different countries. Once strategic alternatives for an individual country have been identified, the final choice of a strategy will be based on the scope of the overall corporation vis-à-vis the matrix. For example, a country's prospects along the diagonal may appear good, but business in this country should not be funded in preference to a business in the "high-high" cell.

The strategic planning process just discussed is equally relevant to smaller companies. For example, a small company mainly involved overseas through exporting may use the product portfolio framework to strategically choose markets where it should lay greater emphasis. Similarly, it may position its overseas distributor on the matrix to determine their relative importance and decide the amount of headquarters support that should be allocated to each.

Information Scanning and Monitoring

MNCs, today more than ever before, are profoundly sensitive to social, economic, political, and technological changes. Each company must scan and monitor relevant changes in the environment to meet these challenges. The scanned information must be analyzed for its impact on marketing strategy. Finally, the impact should be absorbed through appropriate changes in marketing strategy.

The scanning system ought to be comprehensive and include monitoring in several different areas: political, governmental, economic, social, demographic, technological, markets, and resources. Many people will be necessary for whatever monitoring system is developed, because the results must be assessed systematically. Issues considered to be most vital to a company should be followed by action plans stating what the firm is going to do in each area: nothing, gather more data, change product lines, go into new business opportunities, build a defense, or whatever. The monitoring system must be custom-designed for the particular needs of a company.

The development of a system for monitoring diverse and critical areas is an important management task that requires not only the assembly of information, but also the translation of information into whatever meaning it has for the company—opportunities to be grasped or threats to be averted.[8] The resultant system may simply be an organized way for a group of assigned monitors to abstract and process information in cross-disciplinary modes and define the meanings for the company; or the system may involve the use of some of the predictive methods available (for example, delphi and cross-impact studies).

There are many organizations (for example, Business International Corporation, The Futures Group, and SRI International) and a variety of published sources with information on different areas that is pertinent to monitoring the international business scene. Some of these sources of information have been mentioned in previous chapters. For example, Chapter 4, on marketing research, discussed data sources appropriate for demographic monitoring. Chapter 3, on market segmentation, identified different ways of classifying market segments, a valuable tool for monitoring. Chapter 10, on political environments, noted organizations active in rating countries as political risks.

Achieving Planning Effectiveness

A previous section examined the problems that hinder effective marketing planning at the subsidiary level—similar problems complicate the planning effort at the parent level.

These problems can be categorized as the *management type* (poor definition of planning roles, unclear expectations from planning, short-run perspective, insensitivity to foreign conditions, resistance to headquarters direction, cultural bias against forward planning, local market myopia, and "doctoring" of data), and the *planning type* (oversophistication for subsidiary, overformalization, standardized criteria for evaluation, insufficient data support for subsidiary, scarce market data, unreliable or outdated information, inadequate information system, and unskilled planners).

The problem may exist either at headquarters or at the foreign subsidiary. The genesis of these problems are unwillingness to change, lack of adequate and timely information, and poor communications. While some problems must be tolerated as constraints because of complexity of planning in MNCs, others can be solved, or at least minimized, by streamlining the system and encouraging mutual understanding of others' roles and viewpoints. The planners at headquarters can play a unique role in smoothing the functioning of the planning activity.

In order for planning professionals at headquarters to be effective, they should serve as agents for bringing corporate direction and subsidiary goals together. For example, the headquarters planners should provide information about techniques and factual data related to international decisions to top management. Planners should find ways of reconciling corporate needs and host country requirements.

New Emphasis on Global Strategic Market Planning

After reaching a peak of popularity in the 1970s and 1980s, global strategic market planning declined in importance in the 1990s. Currently however, strategic planning once more is becoming significant, but with a difference.[9]

As restructuring and efficiency improvements give way to the goal of value creation through growth, executives are realizing they once again need a long-term strategy. One driver of this reassessment is the process of globalization. International businesses, if they are to be more than loosely affiliated national enterprises, must coordinate their efforts in areas such as product development, marketing and supply chain integration.

Another driver is the changing nature of planning. Gone are the days when strategy consisted solely of a series of discrete actions or transactions—enter these market channels, acquire that company and so on. Now, strategy is much more about building the internal capabilities to respond to change and integrate flexibility into the firm.

Formerly, strategic market planning was often conducted by a dedicated team, placing emphasis on analytical rigor and "getting the right answer." The strategic market planning process today is moving beyond analysis and assuming responsibility for creating commitment to a shared vision. Strategists today need to play a greater role in facilitating plan development and encouraging operational managers to contribute to the process. Managers thus become more likely to commit to the plans that arise.

The need for a participative process has never been stronger. Yet, whereas the perfect strategic market planning process might involve a series of off-site meetings to build a shared position, this is rarely feasible for large MNCs. The tension between the need for participation and the complexity of managing multi-location global businesses lies at the root of the need to rethink the planning process.

Traditional approaches emphasize industry structure and customer requirements, and ways to satisfy these requirements better—or at lower cost—than competitors. However, the rapid pace of change in many sectors requires more than what traditional approaches offer. Today companies may also need to define a clear, shared vision for the future business in terms of the capabilities to be built, either alone or with alliance partners. Developing such a vision requires thinking about potential future worlds and the company's possible position in them.

For example, one MNC selling a mature consumer product in 100 countries introduced a process for exchanging information about market position, competitor activity, and customer needs at an international level. This enabled the organization to coordinate strategic crossborder initiatives. Although the resulting strategies were largely rooted in the past and present, the value generated by addressing strategic decisions at a global level at all was huge.

In contrast, a global research-based supplier of high-tech products focused its efforts on brainstorming future market, technological, and competitive developments. It developed a radically new approach to both of its main customer segments and identified the need for several significant acquisitions and alliances. These are now being implemented.

One of the primary responsibilities of strategic market planning, as always, is resource allocation. In this area *value-based management (VBM)* techniques can make a major contribution. At the corporate level, strategies can be improved by evaluating them in terms of their likely effect on value creation for shareholders, customers, and staff. For individual businesses and teams, drivers of value may also be identified and used to improve local decision making.

Much of the work in establishing effective strategic market planning focuses on determining the mechanics of the process and implementing them. Among the important issues included in this area are ensuring that correct and comparable data are gathered and that participants know the timetable and are able to attend key meetings.

The right leadership style is also important: a balance has to be struck between top-down direction and realistic, implementable plans developed by managers close to the markets. One company suffered from superficial business planning in that top management insisted that the strategic numbers be consistent with the business plan numbers for the following year. Any attempt to create a more adventurous plan would inevitably lead to targets being increased, so managers had learned to "play safe" and quench any innovative ideas they might have.

An approach that sometimes works in such cases is to set nonfinancial strategic targets, such as building a new capability, breaking into a new distribution channel, or overtaking a competitor in a given time frame, leaving aside financial targets linked to the next year's budget and annual plan.

To avoid having the mechanics of the strategic planning process become too burdensome, companies should try to create a consultative process. This process will enable the various parts of the organization to understand what they need from each other and from the head office, as well as what the head office really needs from the markets and the different corporate functions.

In addition, although many planning activities fit into an annual planning cycle, some businesses and issues have a different time horizon. For example, a computer technology company found that many of its markets change so rapidly that nine months into the year its annual strategic plan becomes irrelevant. The company now creates plans that extend only a few months into the future.

In the new strategic market planning process, the roles and responsibilities of the participants may include the delivery of timely and accurate information (by the local businesses), setting of direction and approval of plans (by senior management) or the working through of the financial implications (by the financial department).

The role of the central strategic market planning unit itself may be reduced to managing the mechanics of the process. In other cases it may extend to providing specialist advice, coaching, or even becoming a resource for information gathering and analysis to support decision making. Critical to the success of the unit, however, is ensuring that other parts of the business share expectations about what role the strategic market planning function is expected to play.

Epilogue

This section concludes not only this chapter but also this book, and therefore it seems appropriate to include an overview of American business and trade across national boundaries. A projection of things to come indicates many challenges for international marketers in future years.

For much of the World War II postwar period, international trade and finance occupied only a minor role in the U.S. economy. Exports and imports were a small percentage of U.S. GNP as compared with the significant, and sometimes dominant, role played by foreign trade in most other industrial economies. Since the driving forces behind the U.S. economy were primarily domestic, policy initiatives by governments of other countries were thought to have only a small impact on the course of this country's economic growth and prosperity.

In addition, during the same period, the U.S. trading position was believed strong, particularly in capital goods, transportation, scientific equipment, and other high-technology industries. Concern among Europeans focused on fears of a growing and perhaps permanent "technological gap" between themselves and the U.S. U.S. direct investment abroad was increasing continuously and rapidly, accounting for a significant portion of the world's production and exports and giving rise to large-scale development of the world's production and distribution systems to serve world markets. The U.S. dollar was the key international reserve currency, and although the U.S. balance-of-payments deficits were becoming a permanent feature of the postwar period, their size generally was not thought to cause major disequilibrating problems for the world economy. Indeed, the main issue was how best to manage aid, trade, and investment without straining the absorbing capabilities of foreign economies.

The U.S. was the dominant force in the world economy at the end of World War II and for approximately two decades thereafter. It took the lead in restructuring the world's economic and political systems and in fostering the postwar trend toward greater international economic and political integration through both its domestic and foreign policies and programs. Its active participation in the United Nations, the International Monetary Fund (IMF), the International Bank for Reconstruction and Development (World Bank), the General Agreement on Tariffs and Trade or GATT (now WTO), and other postwar international organizations has shown the U.S. leadership and its commitment to global cooperation. Although U.S. foreign sector activities in the past have had relatively little effect on the U.S. economy, its trade, investment, and monetary policies and programs were essential to the economic and political interests of the free world.

New International Realities

The current situation presents a marked contrast to the post–World War II period. The issues and problems confronting the world economy have grown in number, size, and complexity, with profound implications for U.S. international competitiveness. Although both the rate of economic growth and the domestic and international economic policies and programs of the U.S. continue to exert a strong influence on the economies of the industrialized and the developing world, U.S. economic prosperity now is inexorably linked with economic and political developments occurring in other countries. Consider the following comments:

> U.S. exports and imports as a percentage of GNP and as a proportion of the total output of goods rose markedly in the 1970s and early 1980s and will continue to rise in relation to greater international interdependence. For some U.S. industries, exports and imports constitute a considerable percentage of total domestic output, and for a growing number of industries, changes in merchandise trade patterns can result in a significant number of gains or losses in domestic employment opportunities. For example, in 1997, (1) one out of every five jobs in the manufacturing sector depended on exports; (2) for each of those jobs an additional one was created in a supporting industry; (3) over 10.5 million domestic jobs depended on U.S. exports; (4) approximately 60 percent of U.S. imports were either essential minerals (for example, chromium, man-

ganese, cobalt, and tin) or products that could not be readily produced domestically; and (5) one out of every three dollars of U.S. corporate profits was derived from international activities.[10]

Although U.S. technological gains have been impressive, the technological accomplishments of its main trading partners—particularly Japan, the Federal Republic of Germany, and the United Kingdom—and the high-technology manufacturing capabilities of the advanced developing countries—South Korea, India, Brazil, and Taiwan—have resulted in both a consistent narrowing of the so-called technological gap and greater competition among manufacturers of high-technology products.[11]

Record-setting United States balance-of-payment deficits have led to declines in the value of the U.S. dollar, whether measured as severe in relation to key foreign currencies or as moderate on a trade-weighted basis. As a result, concern developed, both at home and abroad, that the U.S. economy would no longer be competitive in world markets and that the stability of the world monetary arrangements had been severely and perhaps permanently affected. The depreciated U.S. dollar and persistent trade deficits with certain industrialized countries showed the United States that it was no longer free to pursue economic policies with internal rather than external considerations in mind. Indeed, they were symptomatic of a need for the United States to coordinate economic policies with those of other large industrialized countries.[12]

These examples show not only that U.S. policies and programs have profound effects on other countries, but also that the U.S. has become more vulnerable to developments in other countries. Clearly, the world is becoming increasingly interdependent, economically and politically. An important feature of this growing economic interdependence—and a measure of it—is the degree to which economic developments in one country (particularly those of the U.S.) are increasingly transmitted via market forces, or spillover, into other countries. In turn, this leads to foreign trade (and other) feedback effects that have an impact on U.S. domestic economic activity (see International Marketing Highlight 19.4).

Current and Future U.S. Role

As the foregoing discussion indicates, the U.S. has an enormous stake in economic and political interdependence. On the one hand, it is no longer insulated from international market developments with regard to terms of trade, price, availability of energy, fulfillment of raw materials requirements, and other relevant factors. On the other hand, the U.S. is the largest exporter and importer of goods and services, and the world's largest foreign investor. In addition, it is becoming the world's greatest host for foreign direct and portfolio investment and is a significant developer and exporter of high technology. The extent of U.S. leadership in restructuring the world's international economic system is likely to be a function of its perceptions of its current and future competitive strength. The central questions are, what is the current international competitive position of U.S. industries and how can U.S. competitiveness be improved through public and private policies?

U.S. corporations face a strategic challenge. Competition from Europe, Japan, and elsewhere is becoming insurmountable. As the global market adapts and evolves, competition will further intensify. To cope with worldwide competition, U.S. companies must place renewed emphasis on marketing strategy. At the same time, the U.S. government should adopt policies that enhance, not hinder, corporate efforts in their struggle against foreign competition.

■■■■■■■■■■ **International Marketing Highlight 19.4** ■■■■■■■■■■

How Do You Compare with Mexican Workers?

Dario Sanchez Delgado
26, married, two children
Work: Welder at Chrysler plant in Toluca, Mexico
Seniority: 5 years
Pay: $1.75 an hour
Benefits: Mandated profit-sharing, extra vacation pay, a one-cent lunch
Education: Junior High School

Michael Schultz
36, married, one child
Work: Welder at Chrysler's Michigan, plant, Sterling Heights
Seniority: 17 years
Pay: $16 an hour
Benefits: Paid vacation, full health care, bonus at Christmas, income protection for layoffs
Education: High School, working on an associate's degree

Source: Business Week, March 16, 1992, p. 100.

Strategic Challenges for Multinational Corporations

The following review considers some of the important factors affecting the competitive position of U.S. multinationals in world markets and suggests positive courses of action.[13]

Management of Foreign-Dominated Liquid Assets MNCs conduct business in a number of foreign currencies. The exchange rates of these currencies are subject to great upheavals, with far-reaching consequences for earnings. These changes result from disturbances in international, social, political, and economic environments. Thus, in addition to protecting their business from competitive inroads, the management of foreign funds has an impact in other areas—for example, the decision on the best currency mix to maintain on a short-term basis.

Expansion or Growth Policies Traditionally, U.S. corporations have pursued expansion or growth overseas as an important corporate objective. Growth per se, however, may be problematic. The trade deficits of many countries (both among industrialized and developing nations) and a common desire among nations for self-sufficiency may render achievement of perpetual growth in foreign markets difficult. Even where opportunities abound, an entry should be clearly earmarked with the possibility of retrenchment or exit forced through economic nationalism or other political reasons. For example, it may become virtually impossible to raise capital in a host country, the traditional source of long-term funding, and that would certainly block growth (see International Marketing Highlight 19.5).

■■■■■■■■■■ **International Marketing Highlight 19.5** ■■■■■■■■■■

MNCs Focus on Growth

The strategic thinking of top executives planning for the twenty-first century is dominated by global growth and the improvement of shareholder value through innovation, operational agility, and customer-focused knowledge management systems.

Global strategies for the new millennium spotlights a major turnaround among multinationals: they are moving away from the belt-tightening, cost-control strategies of the late 1980s and early 1990s and looking instead to growth as the key to success. Moreover, the components of growth strategies—especially among larger, more profitable organizations—reflect a more aggressive posture in global markets through enterprise transformation, "organic" improvements (i.e., developing the existing business) and strategic business alliances rather than acquisitions alone.

A recent study on the subject showed

- Growth is the most important objective of international organizations, along with creation of shareholder value.

- The components of strategies designed to foster growth are increasingly, globalization, innovation and business alliances. Strategies for "confronting no-traditional competitors" loom ever larger.

- Operationally, customer service continues as the leading objective, but organizational flexibility and agility, new product development and workforce management are becoming more important, while cost reduction is declining in significance.

- *Business process reengineering (BPR)* and other high-priority technological issues today will be less critical in the years ahead.

- The development of knowledge management systems—and their extension to customers and business partners—has become the number one IT issue for 2001.

- While many firms will continue to use acquisitions as a means of growth, most think the future lies in organic growth Business alliances are still seen as the more important strategy.

Source: Crossborder Monitor, December 9, 1998.

Decentralization of the Production Process For both political and economic reasons, more and more industries may follow the strategic lead of the electronics industry and seek component specialization over product specialization. If not all components of a product can be efficiently manufactured by an MNC in one host country, the MNC may opt for specialization in a few components while depending on other sources for others. The decentralization of the production process is attractive to host nations because local involvement in the manufacture of the product would be encouraged.

Automation of Assembly Lines In advanced countries especially, many routine tasks on the assembly line might be performed by robots, Japan is way ahead in this area. The U.S. will probably move in the same direction in the coming years. Such automation of assembly lines should result in substantial cost reductions and uniformity in product quality, which in turn should affect favorably the U.S. competitive position in the world markets.[14]

Corporate-Labor Relationships The developing nations' MNCs, with the abundance of cheap labor in their factories, may emerge as a newly significant competitive force. This new competition is likely to have a far-reaching impact on corporate-labor relationships in the industrialized countries. Increased understanding and harmony between the traditional adversaries will become necessary for mutual survival. The change in labor-management agreements for the U.S. auto industry bears testimony to the emergence of this trend.

Globalization of Consumer Tastes Another interesting phenomenon concerns the development of a common worldwide preference for a variety of consumer goods. The global craze for designer jeans and fast foods illustrates the point.[15] However, the commonality of demand does not mean that the same marketing mix strategies will be effective in every overseas market. The marketing strategies must be appropriately customized to the local customs and traditions.

The world marketplace, as we approach the new century, will be quite different from what it was in the past. Although opportunities should abound, international marketers will need new strategic perspectives to capitalize successfully on these opportunities. The big growth and profits may not come from traditional policies and strategies. Corporations will need to develop new marketing strategies that not only enhance their competitiveness but also fit the needs of the future.[16]

Businesses as Citizens Environmental issues such as waste disposal and pollution are becoming ever more important. Businesses will be expected to play an important role in solving these problems (see International Marketing Highlight 19.6). In addition, improvement in the quality of education will be another significant social issue affecting the organizations. It is commonly believed that business can make a very useful contribution to basic literacy skills.[17]

People Power In the 1990s, a dramatic convergence of demographic, technological, competitive, and global forces is likely to shift power from employers to employees, from the boardroom to the workplace, where value is added and wealth is created.[18] Throughout North America, Europe, and Asia, these forces will converge in a strikingly similar manner—the power of the twenty-first century will be *people power.*

Shared Services Centers (SSCs) Rapidly gaining momentum worldwide are shared service centers (SSCs). An SSC is a separate unit, sited in a centralized location, into which a company bundles its supporting processes and nonstrategic activities. In addition to basic economy-of-scale savings, an SSC in theory eliminates much of the distraction of managing replicated business functions across the region, allowing in turn greater focus on strategic operations and on the core business.[19]

Having expanded massively across the region, giving little thought to the duplication of support processes and staff in each new country, companies are now realizing the need to hasten new administrative and decision-making efficiencies and rein in back-office costs. New technologies are fueling the process: the Internet and better telecoms infrastructure across the region are helping companies communicate more quickly, effectively, and safely with branch offices.

Companies tend to kick off an SSC with finance functions. Overtime, an SSC can expand to engulf other processes as varied as administration, human resources and IT services.

▰▰▰▰▰▰ International Marketing Highlight 19.6 ▰▰▰▰▰▰

Enlightened Capitalism

The London-based Body Shop, with 14 outlets in the U.S., puts environmental concerns at its core and in the process finds its way to the green in the customers' pockets. The skin- and hair-care stores display literature on ozone depletion next to sunscreens and fill their windows with information on issues like global warming. Every employee is assigned to spend half a day each week on activist work. Customers get discounts if they bring their old bottles back to the store for recycling. In 1988, the chain collected over a million signatures in Britain on a petition asking Brazil's president to save the rain forests. In 13 years, the Body Shop has opened 420 stores in 38 countries.

Source: Fortune, February 12, 1990, p. 50.

Summary

Effective global marketing calls for a systematic planning effort and an explicit statement of strategy. The need for a planned perspective has never been greater than in the highly competitive and changing world marketplace of today. No longer do the favorable conditions that once welcomed American business prevail. In the aftermath of the economic turbulence of the 1970s and 1980s, a simple extension of domestic business overseas cannot suffice. And the future has never held promises that the past will return. Therefore, adequate strategic planning is essential to business success abroad.

Planning in the area of marketing must be undertaken both at the subsidiary and headquarters levels. An overseas subsidiary should engage in both short-term and strategic planning, Essentially, short-term planning involves reviewing past performance, making sales forecasts, and developing or revising marketing strategies to achieve the objectives.

The next step is a budget, itemizing the various programs in the marketing strategy in monetary terms. The plan is then submitted to the corporation for approval. Usually the chief executive of the subsidiary presents the plan to the corporation at a meeting held in at corporate headquarters. Plan approval follows after revisions recommended by the corporation have been incorporated. Often the planning activity is conducted according to systems and procedures spelled out by corporate headquarters to foster homogeneity in the planning efforts of different subsidiaries.

Strategic planning is usually an exercise in long-term projections of sales and related matters. Both parent corporation and subsidiary share the blame for poor strategic planning. Although the parent company may consider strategy development to be its prerogative, the subsidiary should take initiative in this direction as well. Various problems that hinder effective planning at the subsidiary level can be avoided or ameliorated by certain methods of planning, such as objective setting, forming a cadre of planning professionals, establishing an appropriate planning and communication system, and encouraging a collaborative attitude between parent and subsidiary.

At the corporate level, the major emphasis is on strategic planning. In addition, the corporation reviews and approves the plans of subsidiaries. The corporate-level strategic planning process begins with a commitment to international business. This commitment is followed by a delineation of the scope of its overseas business and the identification of strategy centers and/or strategic business units. A strategic business unit (SBU) may be defined as a stand-alone business with identifiable independence from other businesses of the corporation in terms of competition, prices, substitutability of product, style/quality, and impact of product withdrawal.

Strategy development efforts center on an SBU with a review of the environment and an analysis of the business' strategic role. Objectives of the SBU are set, and appropriate marketing strategies outlined. Strategies of different SBUs are reviewed and incorporated by the corporate people. Once the SBU plans have been approved, resources are allocated, and the strategic plan becomes the guideline for direction and decision making.

The concept of product portfolio helps determine an appropriate role for each business and review and integrate SBU perspectives at the corporate level.

Worldwide strategic planning development is still rudimentary. This lack of sophistication may be attributed in part to the relatively new development of the art of strategic planning. Strategic planners can play a key role in improving the planning perspectives of their corporations.

An overview of the emerging international marketing environment reveals eight strategic challenges to come (or continue): management of foreign-dominated liquid assets, expansion or growth policies, decentralization of the production process, automation of assembly lines, reevaluation of corporate-labor relationships, globalization of consumer tastes, the role of businesses as citizens, and the shift of power from employers to employees.

Review Questions

1. What type of planning is mainly conducted by overseas subsidiaries? What input does the parent corporation supposedly provide in their planning effort?
2. Why do many foreign subsidiaries fail to undertake strategic planning? Discuss.
3. What problems hinder a good planning job at the subsidiary level?
4. Why is strategic planning an important activity for an MNC?
5. How can a product portfolio framework apply in the international strategic planning process?
6. What role can strategic planners play in streamlining the planning activity? How?

7. Briefly list the environments/areas that MNCs should scan. Why is such scanning necessary?

8. Summarize the strategic challenges that MNCs are likely to face in the future years.

Creative Questions

1. Traditionally, strategic planning has been the purview of the parent corporation while subsidiaries concentrated on short-term planning. However, since subsidiaries have a better knowledge of local conditions, should they not be doing the strategic planning for their future? Discuss the pros and cons of the transfer of strategic planning responsibility to subsidiaries.

2. There are 3 billion people in Asia. Half of them are under age 25. Examine how such demographic changes are likely to open new opportunities in Asia.

Endnotes

1. *Transnationals,* October 1995, p. 10.

2. "Ready To Take on the World," *The Economist,* January 15, 1994, p. 65.

3. Bronislaw J. Verhage and Eric Waarts, "Marketing Planning for Improved Performance: A Comparative Analysis," *International Marketing Review,* Summer 1988, pp. 20–30. *Also see* Martin Van Mesdag, "Winning It in Foreign Markets," *Harvard Business Review,* January–February 1987, pp. 71–74.

4. *See* Leslie M. Dawson, "Multinational Strategic Planning for Third World Markets," *Journal of Global Marketing,* Spring 1988, pp. 29–50.

5. Linda Grant, "GE's Smart Bomb Strategy," *Fortune,* July 23, 1997, p. 109.

6. Jean-Claude Larréché, "The International Product-Market Portfolio," in Subhash C. Jain, ed., *Research Frontiers in Marketing: Dialogues and Directions,* Educators' Conference Proceedings (Chicago: American Marketing Association, 1978), pp. 276–281.

7. Gilbert D. Harrell and Richard O. Kiefer, "Multinational Market Portfolio in Global Strategy Development," *International Marketing Review* 10, no.1 (1993): 60–72. *Also see* Subhash C. Jain, *op. cit,* pp. 271–280. *Also see* Susan P. Douglas and C. Samuel Craig, "Global Portfolio Planning and Market Interconnectedness," *Journal of International Marketing* 4, no. 1 (1996): pp. 93–110; and Carl Arthur Solberg, "A Framework for Analysis of Strategy Development in Globalizing Markets," *Journal of International Marketing* 5, no., 1 (1997): 9–30.

8. Sumantra Goshal, "Environmental Scanning in Korean Firms: Organizational Isomorphism in Action," *Journal of International Business Studies,* Spring 1988, pp. 69–86.

9. Braxton Associates, Deloitte & Touche Consulting Group, 1998.

10. "Current International Trade Position of the United States," *Business America,* March 1998, pp. 30–32.

11. Norihiko Shirouzu, "Korean Auto Makers Seeking to Tiptoe into Japan's Market," *Asian Wall Street Journal Weekly,* October 3, 1988, p.4.

12. Graham Hooley and Josef Beracs, "Marketing Strategies for the 21st Century: Lessons from the Top Hungarian Companies," *Journal of Strategic Marketing,* September 1997, pp. 143–166. *Also see* John K. Ryans, Jr. "Global Marketing," *Marketing Management,* Winter 1999, pp. 44–47.

13. William Lazer, "Changing Dimensions of International Marketing Management—The New Realities," *Journal of International Marketing* 1, no. 3 (1993): 93–103.

14. "The Responsive Factory," *Business Week,* Enterprise 1993, p. 48. *Also see* Keichi Ohmae, *Triad Power* (New York: The Free Press, 1985), chapter 2.

15. Hajo Riesenbeck and Anthony Freeling, "How Global Are Global Brands?" *The McKinsey Quarterly,* 4 (1991): 3–18.

16. William U. Lewis and Marvin Harris, "Why Globalization Must Prevail," *The McKinsey Quarterly,* 2 (1992): 114–131. *Also see* Benjamin R. Barber, "Jihad *vs.* McWorld," *The Atlantic,* March, 1992, pp. 53–55, 58–63; and Jeffrey E. Garten, "Globalism Doesn't Have to Be Cruel," *Business Week,* February 9, 1998, p. 26.

17. *See* Rosabeth Moss Kanter, "Transcending Business Boundaries: 12,000 World Managers View Change," *Harvard Business Review,* May–June 1991, pp. 151–164. *Also see* "Summit to Save the World," *Time,* June 1, 1992, p. 42.

18. "MNCs of Year 2000: Corporate Strategies for Success," *Crossborder Monitor,* March 23, 1994, p. 1.

19. "MNCs New Mantra," *Country Monitor,* July 7, 1999, p. 3.

Cases

Case 1: Kodak vs. Fuji

In the fall of 1997, Mr. George Fisher, CEO of Eastman Kodak Company, was meeting his top marketing executives to formulate the strategy to contain Fuji Photo Film Co. from making further inroads in the U.S. film market.

For some years now Fuji and Kodak have been battling it out in overseas film markets. But in the United States the picture was quite different. Kodak and Fuji treated that market like a cozy, mutually profitable duopoly. Both enjoyed fat margins. Kodak controlled over 80% of the American film market, and distant No. 2 Fuji always priced its film just a little bit lower.

Then, in spring 1997, Fuji began slashing prices by as much as 25%. Fuji's explanation was that Costco, one of its five largest distributors in the United States, ditched Fuji for Kodak and the company got stuck with 2.5 million rolls of film. Fuji unloaded the film at a steep discount to other distributors. When consumers saw that the familiar red, white, and green boxes were a dollar or two cheaper, they snapped them up. Over the past year Fuji increased its share of the U.S. film market to nearly 16% from 10%, while Kodak's share took an unprecedented tumble from 80% to just under 75%.

Fuji executives deny that they intended to start a price war. Yet its prices were still hanging low now that the excess inventory had been worked off. Whatever the case, for the first time in its long history, Kodak could no longer take its home market for granted.

Eastman Kodak Company

The Eastman Kodak Company was established in 1884 in Rochester, New York. In 1997 the company still overwhelmingly dominated the $2.7 billion U.S. amateur film market. The Kodak brand remained solid gold, and its quality was not in dispute. But Fuji's gains in the United States were ominous, especially because the Japanese film company was already poised to surpass Kodak on a global basis, particularly in Asia, where film sales were growing at 20% a year or more. (Worldwide, Fuji and Kodak were neck and neck, with about a third of the market each.) Alex Henderson, managing director of technology research at Prudential Securities Inc. in New York, who had been watching the two companies for 12 years, believed that if current trends held, Fuji would overtake Kodak by 1999. "When that happens," said Henderson, "Kodak will go from being Coke to being Pepsi. That's a very damning thing." Worse yet, he expected that in the United States, Fuji would continue to creep up on Kodak by a rate of about 2% a year.

Fuji Photo Film Company

The Fuji Photo Film Company was established in Japan in 1909. In 1997, financially, Fuji was a very strong company, giving it more flexibility to cut prices. Fuji's sales in 1996 were a record $11 billion, and profits were a near-record $757 million; at the same time, Fuji had a net cash position of about $4.5 billion and access to incredibly cheap borrowing—around 2.5%—thanks to Japan's record-low interest rates. Kodak had more than $1 billion in short- and long-term debt and was in the midst of a sales and profit slide, not to mention impending restructuring write-offs likely to run $1 billion or more. And Kodak could not borrow at much under 7%. Fuji could afford a showdown, but Kodak could not.

Marketplace

Kodak and Fuji had been slugging it out for three equally important parts of the consumer photo business. Those little yellow and green film boxes were the most obvious part to the man in the street, but Fuji and Kodak also manufactured photographic paper, mostly for sale to big photo-processing laboratories and small retail developers. To ensure a market for their paper, both companies had invested heavily in the third line of business—developing—by buying up big film-processing companies across the United States. Fuji's deep pockets had enabled it to make acquisitions like the estimated $400 million purchase in 1996 of Wal-Mart's six wholesale photo labs, a move that in one swoop gave it about 15% of the U.S. photo-processing market.

Fuji's long-term strategy was to transplant as much film and paper production as possible onto U.S. soil. That kept costs down, reduced nettlesome trade disputes, and made Fuji's factories more responsive to local market demands. In 1987, just 3.5% of Fuji's production was outside Japan; now the figure was 31%, and the move offshore was accelerating. In April 1997, Fuji opened a highly automated, $300 million photographic paper plant in Greenwood, South Carolina, which was already producing about 20% of the photo paper consumed in North America. Later in 1997, Fuji was scheduled to open an equally high-tech, $200 million film plant in Greenwood. According to industry sources, it would not take much time or investment to double the plants' capacities should Fuji need it.

Competition

Fuji was one of the leanest and meanest of Japan's big companies. Led for the past 17 years by no-nonsense Chairman and CEO Minoru Ohnishi, Fuji was cutting white-collar overhead long before it started to become fashionable in Japan. In the past ten years the company's sales nearly doubled worldwide, but its staffing in Japan remained almost flat. Ohnishi tried to maintain a sense of crisis by reminding staff that Kodak was still out front. "He likes to constantly cut costs in order to anticipate a rainy day," says a consultant, "so that there will be less pain down the road." Or more likely, greater market share.

Fuji's aggressive tactics had sometimes earned it charges of unfair trading practices. In the early 1990s, the U.S. Commerce Department investigated charges that the Japanese company dumped photographic paper in the U.S. market. Fuji managed to dodge import duties by agreeing to raise prices to levels just above the going rate. (Fuji subsequently lost most of its 20% market share but bounced back when it opened its paper plant in Greenwood and bought out Wal-Mart's processing labs.) And the World Trade Organization was expected to rule soon on U.S. allegations that the government of Japan worked with Fuji to exclude competitors from the Japanese market, which Fuji dominated with a 70% market share. A decision was expected in spring 1998, though it was not likely to affect either company's business.

Ironically, Fuji got its big break in the American market thanks to Kodak. The company opened its first office in the United States in 1958, in the Empire State Building, but it only began selling film there in 1970, when it was one of several relative minnows—among the others were GAF, Agfa, and 3M—swimming in Kodak's pond. Then in 1984, the Olympics came to Los Angeles. Olympic czar Peter Ueberroth believed that Kodak was the natural choice to be the exclusive film sponsor, but Kodak wouldn't bite. Even after Ueberroth visited Rochester to make his pitch, Kodak refused to pay just $1 million, far below the $4 million floor for sponsorships that Ueberroth had established. So he approached Fuji, which in those days was still barely known in the U.S. market. Ohnishi said yes on the spot and eventually committed around $7 million. No marketing investment ever brought better returns. Within months of becoming a sponsor, Fuji landed 50,000 new distribution outlets. "Salespeople said that accounts that didn't used to return their calls were suddenly calling them," says Tom Shay, head of corporate communications for Fuji USA and a 26-year Fuji veteran. "The Olympics completely changed the way people looked at us."

Since then, Fuji had built a reputation for price, quality, and sharp marketing. It had won a strong following among professional photographers, some of whom raved over the film's luminous blues and greens. Its acceptance in the professional world had given Fuji a lot of cachet with amateur shutterbugs. Fuji also adopted a hipper, more technologically oriented marketing image to differentiate itself from a Kodak style that was sentimental. In 1993, Fuji ran a highly successful, award-winning TV campaign obliquely directed at Kodak. The killer line: "Pictures should be nostalgic; your film shouldn't." Fuji's current slogan also painted the company as forward looking: "You can see the future from here."

In technology too, Fuji had shown that it could set the pace by consistently spending about 7% of sales on R&D. In 1986, Fuji was the first to introduce the disposable camera, a product that had been a huge boon for both Kodak and Fuji. Fuji also worked with Kodak and other companies to introduce a new 24mm "advanced photo system" film—which used a new generation camera, a hybrid of digital and traditional systems. In Japan, the launch was a great success, thanks to Fuji's ensuring that the cameras and processing were readily available. APS already accounted for about 10% of the color-negative film market in Japan. "Fuji's greatest strength is that they always make sure that consumers are ready to buy their new products, and they actually get the products to the consumers," remarked Toby Williams, an analyst at SBC Warbug in Tokyo. By contrast, Kodak flubbed the U.S. introduction of its advanced photo system, called Advantix.

If Kodak and Fuji had one thing in common, it was their vulnerability as photography moves into the digital age. In 1997 alone, market watchers expected to see 1.8 million digital cameras sold worldwide, and that number would grow sharply as quality improved and prices dropped. That posed three big issues for film companies: One was the danger—still much in dispute—that film sales would soften as digital cameras made by companies like Sony, Canon, and Casio took up a bigger share of the market. Another was a challenge on the photographic paper and processing side from Canon, Epson, and Hewlett-Packard. Their latest generation ink-jet printers produced high-quality prints of digital images on plain and coated paper. (Fuji just launched one of its own.) Both Kodak and Fuji were working on ways to add value to digital photography—such as a service that lets customers order prints directly over the Internet—but those ideas were untested.

Finally, Kodak and Fuji had jumped into the digital camera business themselves. But they were in a mob of nearly two dozen camera, computer, and consumer electronics companies trying to get into the same space. One thing was sure: The companies that won in digital photography would need marketing and product smarts, technology, and, not least, money. Fuji, it seems, had them all.

Case 2: **Curtis Automotive Hoist***

In September 1990, Mark Curtis, president of Curtis Automotive Hoist (CAH), had just finished reading a feasibility report on entering the European market in 1991. CAH manufactured surface automotive hoists, a product used by garages, service stations, and other repair shops to lift cars for servicing. The report, prepared by CAH's marketing manager, Pierre Gagnon, outlines the opportunities in the European Economic Community and the entry options available.

Mr. Curtis was not sure if CAH was ready for this move. While the company had been successful in expanding sales into the U.S. market, Mr. Curtis wondered if this success could be repeated in Europe. He thought that with more effort, sales could be increased in the United States. On the other hand, there were

some positive aspects to the European idea. He began reviewing the information in preparation for the meeting the following day with Mr. Gagnon.

Curtis Automotive Hoist

Mr. Curtis, a design engineer, had worked for eight years for the Canadian subsidiary of a U.S. automotive hoist manufacturer. During those years, he had spent considerable time designing an above-ground (or surface) automotive hoist. Although Mr. Curtis was very enthusiastic about the unique aspects of the hoist, including a scissor lift and wheel alignment pads, senior management expressed no interest in the idea. In 1980, Mr. Curtis left the company to start his own business with the express purpose of designing and manufacturing the hoist. He left with the good wishes of his previ-

* This case is printed here with the permission of the author, Gordon H. G. McDougall of Wilfrid Laurier University, Québec.

ous employer, who had no objections to his plans to start a new business.

Over the next three years, Mr. Curtis obtained financing from a venture capital firm, opened a plant in Lachine, Québec, and began manufacturing and marketing the hoist, called the Curtis Lift.

From the beginning, Mr. Curtis had taken considerable pride in the development and marketing of the Curtis Lift. The original design included a scissor lift and a safety locking mechanism that allowed the hoist to be raised to any level and locked in place. As well, the scissor lift offered easy access for the mechanic to work on the raised vehicle. Because the hoist was fully hydraulic and had no chains or pulleys, it required little maintenance. Another key feature was the alignment turn plates that were an integral part of the lift. The turn plates meant that mechanics could accurately and easily perform wheel alignment jobs. Because it was a surface lift, it could be installed in a garage in less than a day.

Mr. Curtis continually made improvements to the product, including adding more safety features. In fact, the Curtis Lift was considered a leader in automotive lift safety. Safety was an important factor in the automotive hoist market. Although hoists seldom malfunctioned, when they did, it often resulted in a serious accident.

The Curtis Lift developed a reputation in the industry as the "Cadillac" of hoists; the unit was judged by many as superior to competitive offerings because of its design, the quality of the workmanship, the safety features, the ease of installation, and the five-year warranty. Mr. Curtis held four patents on the Curtis Lift, including the lifting mechanism on the scissor design and a safety locking mechanism. A number of versions of the product were designed that made the Curtis Lift suitable (depending on the model) for a variety of tasks, including rustproofing, muffler repairs, and general mechanical repairs.

In 1981, CAH sold 23 hoists and had sales of $172,500. During the early years, the majority of sales were to independent service stations and garages specializing in wheel alignment in the Québec and Ontario market. Most of the units were sold by Mr. Gagnon, who was hired in 1982 to handle the marketing side of the operation. In 1984, Mr. Gagnon began using distributors to sell the hoist to a wider geographic market in Canada. In 1986, he signed an agreement with a large automotive wholesaler to represent CAH in the U.S. market. By 1989, the company sold 1,054 hoists and had sales of $9,708,000 (Exhibit 1). In

1989, about 60% of sales were to the United States with the remaining 40% to the Canadian market.

EXHIBIT I Curtis Automotive Hoist—Selected Financial Statistics (1987 to 1989)

	1989	1988	1987
Sales	$9,708,000	$7,454,000	$6,218,000
Cost of Sales	6,990,000	5,541,000	4,540,000
Contribution	2,718,999	1,913,000	1,678,000
Marketing expenses*	530,000	510,000	507,000
Administrative expenses	840,000	820,000	810,000
Earnings before tax	1,348,000	583,000	361,000
Units sold	1,054	847	723

*Marketing expenses in 1989 included advertising ($70,000), four salespeople ($240,000), and a marketing manager and three sales support staff ($220,000).
Source: Company records.

Industry

Approximately 49,000 hoists were sold each year in North America. Typically hoists were purchased by an automotive outlet that serviced or repaired cars, including new car dealers, used car dealers, specialty shops (for example, muffler shops, transmission, wheel alignment), chains (for example, Firestone, Goodyear, Canadian Tire), and independent garages. It was estimated that new car dealers purchased 30% of all units sold in a given year. In general, the specialty shops focus on one type of repair, such as mufflers or rustproofing, while "nonspecialty" outlets handle a variety of repairs. While there was some crossover, in general, CAH competed in the specialty shop segment and, in particular, those shops that dealt with wheel alignment. This included chains, such as Firestone and Canadian Tire as well as new car dealers (for example, Ford) who devote a certain percentage of their lifts to the wheel alignment business, and independent garages who specialized in wheel alignment.

The purpose of a hoist was to lift an automobile into a position where a mechanic or service person could easily work on the car. Because different repairs required different positions, a wide variety of hoists had been developed to meet specific needs. For example, a muffler repair shop required a hoist that allowed the mechanic to gain easy access to the underside of the car. Similarly, a wheel alignment job required a hoist that offered a level platform where the wheels could be adjusted as well as providing easy access for the mechanic. Mr. Gagnon estimated that 85% of CAH's sales were to the wheel alignment market to service centers such as Firestone, Goodyear, and Canadian Tire, and to independent garages that specialized in wheel alignment. About 15% of sales were made to customers who used the hoist for general mechanical repairs.

Firms purchasing hoists were part of an industry called the automobile aftermarket. This industry was involved in supplying parts and service for new and used cars, and was worth over $54 billion at retail in 1989, while servicing the approximately 11 million cars on the road in Canada. The industry was large and diverse; there were over 4,000 new car dealers in Canada, over 400 Canadian Tire stores, over 100 stores in each of the Firestone and Goodyear chains, and over 200 stores in the Rust Check chain.

The purchase of an automotive hoist was often an important decision for the service station owner or dealer. Because the price of hoists ranged from $3,000 to $15,000, it was a capital expense for most businesses.

For the owner/operator of a new service center or car dealership the decision involved determining what type of hoist was required, then what brand would best suit the company. Most new service centers or car dealerships had multiple bays for servicing cars. In these cases, the decision would involve what types of hoists were required (for example, in-ground, surface). Often, more than one type of hoist was purchased, depending on the service center/dealership needs.

Experienced garage owners seeking a replacement hoist (the typical hoist had a useful life of 10 to 13 years) would usually determine what products were available and then make a decision. If the garage owners were also mechanics, they would probably be aware of two or three types of hoists but would not be very knowledgeable about the brands or products currently available. Garage owners or dealers who were not mechanics probably knew very little about hoists. The owners of car or service dealerships often bought the product that was recommended and/or approved by the parent company.

Competition

Sixteen companies competed in the automotive lift market in North America: four Canadian and twelve

U.S. firms. Hoists were subject to import duties. Duties on hoists entering the U.S. market from Canada were 2.4% of the selling price; from the U.S. entering Canada the import duty was 7.9%. With the advent of the Free Trade Agreement in 1989, the duties between the two countries would be phased out over a 10-year period. For Mr. Curtis, the import duties had never played a part in any decisions: The fluctuating exchange rates between the two countries had a far greater impact on selling prices.

A wide variety of hoists were manufactured in the industry. The two basic types of hoists were in-ground and surface. As the names imply, in-ground hoists required that a pit be dug "in-ground" where the piston that raised the hoist was installed. In-ground hoists were either single-post or multiple-post, were permanent, and obviously could not be moved. In-ground lifts constituted approximately 21% of total lift sales in 1989 (Exhibit 2). Surface lifts were installed on a flat surface, usually concrete. Surface lifts, compared to in-ground lifts, were easier to install and could be moved, if necessary. Surface lifts constituted 79% of total lift sales in 1989. Within each type of hoist (for example, post-lift surface hoists), there were numerous variations in terms of size, shape, and lifting capacity.

EXHIBIT 2 North America Automotive Lift Sales, by Type (1987 to 1989)

	1987	1988	1989
In-ground			
Single-post	5,885	5,772	5,518
Multiple-post	4,812	6,625	5,075
Surface			
Two-post	27,019	28,757	28,923
Four-post	3,892	3,162	3,745
Scissor	2,170	2,258	2,316
Other	4,486	3,613	3,695
Total	48,234	50,187	49,272

Source: Company records.

The industry was dominated by two large U.S. firms, AHV Lifts and Berne Manufacturing, who together held approximately 60% of the market. AHV Lifts, the largest firm with approximately 40% of the market and annual sales of about $60 million, offered a complete line of hoists (that is, in-ground and surface) but focused primarily on the in-ground market and the two-post surface market. AHV Lifts was the only company that had its own direct sales force; all other companies used (1) only wholesalers or (2) a combination of wholesalers and company sales force. AHV Lifts offered standard hoists with few extra features and competed primarily on price. Berne Manufacturing, with a market share of approximately 20%, also competed in the in-ground and two-post surface markets. It used a combination of wholesalers and company salespeople and, like AHV Lifts, competed primarily on price.

Most of the remaining firms in the industry were companies that operated in a regional market (for example, California or British Columbia) and/or offered a limited product line (for example, four-post surface hoist).

Curtis had two competitors that manufactured scissor lifts. AHV Lift marketed a scissor hoist that had a different lifting mechanism and did not include the safety locking features of the Curtis Lift. On average, the AHV scissor lift sold for about 20% less than the Curtis Lift. The second competitor, Mete Lift, was a small regional company with sales in California and Oregon. It had a design that was very similar to the Curtis Lift but lacked some of its safety features. The Mete Lift, regarded as a well-manufactured product, sold for about 5% less than the Curtis Lift.

Marketing Strategy

As of early 1990, CAH had developed a reputation for a quality product backed by good service in the hoist lift market, primarily in the wheel alignment segment.

The distribution system employed by CAH reflected the need to engage in extensive personal selling. Three types of distributors were used: a company sales force, Canadian distributors, and a U.S. automotive wholesaler. The company sales force consisted of four salespeople and Mr. Gagnon. Their main task was to service large "direct" accounts. The initial step was to get the Curtis Lift approved by large chains and manufacturers and then, having received the approval, to sell to individual dealers or operators. For example, if General Motors approved the hoist, then CAH could sell it to individual General Motors dealers. CAH sold directly to the individual dealers of a number of large accounts, including General Motors, Ford, Chrysler, Petro-Canada, Firestone, and Goodyear. CAH had been successful in obtaining manufacturer approval from the big three automobile manufacturers in both Canada and the United States. CAH had also received approval from service companies such as Canadian Tire and Goodyear. To date, CAH had not been rejected by any major account but, in some cases, the approval process had taken over four years.

In total, the company sales force generated about 25% of the unit sales each year. Sales to the large "direct" accounts in the United States went through CAH's U.S. wholesaler.

The Canadian distributors sold, installed, and serviced units across Canada. These distributors handled the Curtis Lift and carried a line of noncompetitive automotive equipment products (for example, engine diagnostic equipment, wheel balancing equipment) and noncompetitive lifts. These distributors focused on the smaller chains and the independent service stations and garages.

The U.S. wholesaler sold a complete product line to service stations as well as manufacturing some equipment. The Curtis Lift was one of five different types of lifts that the wholesaler sold. Although the wholesaler provided CAH with extensive distribution in the United States, the Curtis Lift was a minor product within the wholesaler's total line. While Mr. Gagnon did not have any actual figures, he thought that the Curtis Lift probably accounted for less than 20% of the total lift sales of the U.S. wholesaler.

Both Mr. Curtis and Mr. Gagnon felt that the U.S. market had unrealized potential. With a population of 248 million people and over 140 million registered vehicles, the U.S. market was over 10 times the size of the Canadian market (population of 26 million, approximately 11 million vehicles). Mr. Gagnon noted that the six New England states (population over 13 million), the three largest mid-Atlantic states (population over 32 million), and the three largest mid-Eastern states (population over 32 million) were all within a day's drive of the factory in Lachine. Mr. Curtis and Mr. Gagnon had considered setting up a sales office in New York to service these states, but they were concerned that the U.S. wholesaler would not be willing to relinquish any of its territory. They had also considered working more closely with the wholesaler to encourage it to "push" the Curtis Lift. It appeared that the wholesaler's major objective was to sell a hoist, not necessarily the Curtis Lift.

CAH distributed a catalog-type package with products, uses, prices, and other required information for both distributors and users. In addition, CAH advertised in trade publications (for example, *Service Station & Garage Management*), and Mr. Gagnon traveled to trade shows in Canada and the United States to promote the Curtis Lift.

In 1989, Curtis Lifts sold for an average retail price of $10,990 and CAH received, on average, $9,210 for each unit sold. This average reflected the mix of sales through the three distribution channels: (1) direct (where CAH received 100% of the selling price), (2) Canadian distributors (where CAH received 80% of the selling price), and (3) the U.S. wholesaler (where CAH received 78% of the selling price).

Both Mr. Curtis and Mr. Gagnon felt that the company's success to date was based on a strategy of offering a superior product that was primarily targeted to the needs of specific customers. The strategy stressed continual product improvement, quality workmanship, and service. Personal selling was a key aspect of the strategy; salespeople could show customers the benefits of the Curtis Lift over competing products.

The European Market

Against this background, Mr. Curtis had been thinking of ways to continue the rapid growth of the company. One possibility that kept coming up was the promise and potential of the European market. The fact that Europe would become a single market in 1992 suggested that it was an opportunity that should at least be explored. With this in mind, Mr. Curtis asked Mr. Gagnon to prepare a report on the possibility of CAH entering the European market. The highlights of Mr. Gagnon's report follow.

History of the European Community

The European Community (EC) stemmed from the 1953 Treaty of Rome in which five countries decided it would be in their best interest to form an internal market. These countries were France, Spain, Italy, West Germany, and Luxembourg. By 1990, the EC consisted of 12 countries (the additional seven were Belgium, Denmark, Greece, Ireland, the Netherlands, Portugal, and the United Kingdom) with a population of over 325 million people.[1] In 1992, virtually all barriers

(physical, technical, and fiscal) in the EC were scheduled to be removed for companies located within the EC. This would allow the free movement of goods, persons, services, and capital.

In the last five years many North American and Japanese firms had established themselves in the EC. The reasoning for this was twofold. First, these companies regarded the community as an opportunity to increase global market share and profits. The market was attractive because of its sheer size and lack of internal barriers. Second, in 1992, companies that were established within the community were subject to protection from external competition via EC protectionism tariffs, local contents, and reciprocity requirements. EC protectionism tariffs were only temporary and would be removed at a later date. It would be possible for companies to export to or establish in the community after 1992, but there was some risk attached.

Market Potential

The key indicator of the potential market for the Curtis Lift hoist was the number of passenger cars and commercial vehicles in use in a particular country. Four countries in Europe had more than 20 million vehicles in use, with West Germany having the largest domestic fleet of 30 million vehicles, followed in order by France, Italy, and the United Kingdom (Exhibit 3). The number of vehicles was an important indicator because the more vehicles in use meant a greater number of service and repair facilities that needed vehicle hoists and potentially the Curtis Lift.

An indicator of the future vehicle repair and service market was the number of new vehicle registrations. The registration of new vehicles was important, as this maintained the number of vehicles in use by replacing cars that had been retired. Again, West Germany had the most new cars registered in 1988 and was followed in order by France, the United Kingdom, and Italy.

Based primarily on the fact that a large domestic market was important for initial growth, the selection of

EXHIBIT 3
Number of Vehicles (1988) and Population (1989)

Country	Vehicles in Use (Thousands)		New Vehicle Registrations (Thousands)	Population (Thousands)
	Passenger	Commercial		
West Germany	28,304	1,814	2,960	60,900
France	29,970	4,223	2,635	56,000
Italy	22,500	1,897	2,308	57,400
United Kingdom	20,605	2,915	2,531	57,500
Spain	9,750	1,750	1,172	39,400

a European country should be limited to the "Big Four" industrialized nations: West Germany, France, the United Kingdom, or Italy. In an international survey companies from North America and Europe ranked European countries on a scale of 10 to 100 on market potential and investment site potential. The results showed that West Germany was favored for both market potential and investment site opportunities while France, the United Kingdom, and Spain placed second, third, and fourth, respectively. Italy did not place in the top four in either market or investment site potential. However, Italy had a large number of vehicles in use, had the second-largest population in Europe, and was an acknowledged leader in car technology and production.

Little information was available on the competition within Europe. There was, as yet, no dominant manufacturer, as was the case in North America. At this time, there was one firm in Germany that manufactured a scissor-type lift. The firm sold most of its units within the German market. The only other available information was that 22 firms in Italy manufactured vehicle lifts.

Investment Options

Mr. Gagnon felt that CAH had three options for expansion into the European market: Licensing option was a real possibility as a French firm had expressed an interest in manufacturing the Curtis Lift.

In June 1990, Mr. Gagnon had attended a trade show in Detroit to promote the Curtis Lift. At the show, he met Phillipe Beaupre, the marketing manager for Bar Maisse, a French manufacturer of wheel alignment equipment. The firm, located in Chelles, France, sold a range of wheel alignment equipment throughout Europe. The best-selling product was an electronic modular aligner that enabled a mechanic to utilize a sophisticated computer system to align the wheels of a car. Mr. Beaupre was seeking a North American distributor for the modular aligner and other products manufactured by Bar Maisse.

At the show, Mr. Gagnon and Mr. Beaupre had a casual conversation in which each explained what their respective companies manufactured; they exchanged company brochures and business cards, and both went on to other exhibits. The next day, Mr. Beaupre sought out Mr. Gagnon and asked if he might be interested in having Bar Maisse manufacture and market the Curtis Lift in Europe. Mr. Beaupre felt the lift would complement Bar Maisse's product line and the licensing would be of mutual benefit to both parties. They agreed to pursue the idea. Upon his return to Lachine, Mr.

Gagnon told Mr. Curtis about these discussions, and they agreed to explore this possibility.

Mr. Gagnon called a number of colleagues in the industry and asked them what they knew about Bar Maisse. About half had not heard of the company, but those who had commented favorably on the quality of its products. One colleague, with European experience, knew the company well and said that Bar Maisse's management had integrity and would make a good partner. In July, Mr. Gagnon sent a letter to Mr. Beaupre stating that CAH was interested in further discussions and enclosed various company brochures, including price lists and technical information on the Curtis Lift. In late August, Mr. Beaupre responded stating that Bar Maisse would like to enter a three-year licensing agreement with CAH to manufacture the Curtis Lift in Europe. In exchange for the manufacturing rights, Bar Maisse was prepared to pay a royalty rate of 5% of gross sales. Mr. Gagnon had not yet responded to this proposal.

A second possibility was a joint venture. Mr. Gagnon had wondered if it might not be better for CAH to offer a counterproposal to Bar Maisse for a joint venture. He had not worked out any details, but Mr. Gagnon felt that CAH would learn more about the European market and probably make more money if they were an active partner in Europe. Mr. Gagnon's idea was a 50–50 proposal where the two parties shared the investment and the profits. He envisaged a situation where Bar Maisse would manufacture the Curtis Lift in their plant with technical assistance from CAH. Mr. Gagnon also thought that CAH could get involved in the marketing of the lift through the Bar Maisse distribution system. Further, he thought that the Curtis Lift, with proper marketing, could gain a reasonable share of the European market. If that happened, Mr. Gagnon felt that CAH was likely to make greater returns with a joint venture.

The third option was direct investment where CAH would establish a manufacturing facility and set up a management group to market the lift. Mr. Gagnon had contacted a business acquaintance who had recently been involved in manufacturing fabricated steel sheds in Germany. On the basis of discussions with his acquaintance, Mr. Gagnon estimated the costs involved in setting up a plant in Europe at: (1) $250,000 for capital equipment (welding machines, cranes, other equipment), (2) $200,000 in incremental costs to set the plant up, and (3) carrying costs to cover $1,000,000 in inventory and accounts receivable. While the actual costs of renting a building for the factory would depend on the site location, he estimated that annual building rent including heat, light, and insurance would be about $80,000. Mr. Gagnon recognized these estimates were guidelines but he felt that the estimates were probably within 20% of actual costs.

The Decision

As Mr. Curtis considered the contents of the report, a number of thoughts crossed his mind. He began making notes concerning the European possibility and the future of the company.

- If CAH decided to enter Europe, Mr. Gagnon would be the obvious choice to head up the direct investment option or the joint venture option. Mr. Curtis felt that Mr. Gagnon had been instrumental in the success of the company to date.

- While CAH had the financial resources to go ahead with the direct investment option, the joint venture would spread the risk (and the returns) over the two companies.

- CAH had built its reputation on designing and manufacturing a quality product. Regardless of the option chosen, Mr. Curtis wanted the firm's reputation to be maintained.

- Either the licensing agreement or the joint venture appeared to build on the two companies' strengths; Bar Maisse had knowledge of the market and CAH had the product. What troubled Mr. Curtis was whether this apparent synergy would work or whether Bar Maisse would seek to control the operation.

- It was difficult to estimate sales under any of the options. With the first two (licensing and joint venture), it would depend on the effort and expertise of Bar Maisse; with the third option, it would depend on Mr. Gagnon.

- CAH's sales in the U.S. market could be increased if the U.S. wholesaler would "push" the Curtis Lift. Alternatively, the establishment of a sales office in New York to cover the eastern states could also increase sales.

As Mr. Curtis reflected on the situation he knew he should probably get additional information—but it wasn't obvious exactly what information would help him make a "yes" or "no" decision. He knew one thing for sure—he was going to keep his company on a "fast growth" track, and at tomorrow's meeting he and Mr. Gagnon would decide how to do it.

Endnote

1. As of September 1990, West Germany and East Germany were in the process of unification. East Germany had a population of approximately 17 million people.

Case 3: **Farggi***

It was early 1995 and Margarita Farga, Farggi's marketing director, was turning over in her mind the situation of her company's different businesses. The Farga/Farggi Corporation was a group of family companies, whose annual sales were expected to amount to between 2.8 and 3.0 billion pesetas in 1995 (1 U.S. dollar = 130 Spanish pesetas).

From its humble beginnings as a small traditional cake and pastry shop in 1957, the company had expanded and diversified. By the end of 1994, it had three traditional cake shops operating under the name Farga. It also manufactured and sold ice cream and frozen cakes for the catering market under the Farggi brand name.

However, its latest "great leap forward" had been in 1993, when it started to manufacture and market luxury ice cream for sale in Farggi stores—either owned by the company or franchised—and in supermarkets and other nonexclusive shops. As a result of the latter activity, their positioning was now very similar to that of the famous Häagen Dazs ice creams. In fact, it was rumored that someone had heard an unidentified Häagen Dazs manager say that, of all its competitors in the entire world, Farggi had been the one most able to adapt its concept, positioning, and way of selling premium ice cream with the greatest speed and precision.

In July 1993, the first exclusive Farggi Tub's & Ice Cream parlour was opened in Barcelona's upmarket Paseo de Gracia and, by the end of 1994, 13 such parlours had been opened, 5 owned by the company and 8 franchises.

---

*This case was prepared by Professor Lluis Renart and Francisco Parés, lecturer at IESE, Barcelona, Spain. Copyright © 1995, IESE. Reprinted by permission.

While she reviewed everything that had been achieved so far, Margarita tried to think what her company's action priorities should be, both in the short and in the medium term. Jesús Farga, her father and the company's president, insisted that all these questions needed to be clearly defined, as the future consolidation of the company depended on it.

History of the Company

In 1957, Jesús Farga opened a traditional food retail store on Mayor de Gracia Street in Barcelona, near Plaza Lesseps. About five years later, after attending occupational training courses in cake making, he turned his food shop into a cake shop, keeping the same name, Farga. With the cake shop operating, he married Magdalena Bertrán and had four children: Elena, Margarita, Lluís, and Eduardo.

About five years after that, Jesús Farga opened his second cake shop, on the Paseo de San Gervasio, in a neighborhood with a higher socioeconomic level, manufacturing and selling fresh cakes and pastry.

The First Diversification: Tartas y Helados Farga

With both cake shops operating at full capacity, in the late 1960s, Jesús Farga started to sell cakes outside of his shops, delivering them frozen to nearby cafeterias and restaurants, where they were thawed in a refrigerator or at room temperature before being served to customers. Jesús Farga and his employees managed to perfect their formulas and processes to such a point that it was impossible for the end customers in the restaurants and cafeterias to tell that the cakes they were eating had been frozen and thawed beforehand.

The transportation and delivery service was carried out by José Manuel Garrido. In the course of time, he was to become one of Jesús Farga's right-hand men and, in 1994, he was still sales director. Also at about that time, Farga started to make and sell ice cream.

Thus, slowly but surely, a second business activity, separate from that of the retail stores, came into being and consolidated itself under the name of Tartas y helados Farga. Legally, both activities continued to be a single business activity owned by Jesús Farga.

The Farggi Brand

In spite of the excellent performance of both activities (sales in the cake and pastry stores, and the sale of frozen cakes and ice creams by delivery to cafeterias and restaurants), close monitoring of the second of these two lines of business convinced Jesús Farga of the need to use a different brand name.

Shortly before, during a trip to Italy, his friends and travelling companions had jokingly called him "Comendatore Farggi." Jesús decided to use his own Italianized name to give a distinctive identity to his second business activity.

When, in 1974, he started to use the name Farggi, the business's name was extended to Farggi: Tartas, Helados y Sorbetes de Lujo (Farggi: Luxury Cakes, Ice Creams and Sorbets), to prevent any connotation of a second, lower-quality brand name.

The First Factory in Badalona

In 1975, Jesús moved production to a factory measuring just under 1,000 square meters in Badalona. One of the innovations at that time was the production and sale of individual portions of frozen cake and ice cream, with the same luxury quality.[1]

Jesús Farga observed with satisfaction that when he sold portions of ice cream or cake of between 100 and 150 ml, priced by the portion and in a market niche which he had practically all to himself, his sales revenues were substantially higher than when he sold by the litre. Although the production process had a somewhat higher skill and labour content, his margins improved considerably.

With the opening of the new factory in Badalona and due to the sudden economic downturn as a result of the oil crisis, Jesús Farga decided to legally reform his business as a limited company under the name Lacrem, S.A. At the same time, he brought his brother-in-law into the business as financial director and minority shareholder. For many years, the company's management team consisted of Jesús Farga, Miguel Bertrán, and José Manuel Garrido.

As a result of the increase in production capacity, the company was now able to sell its products virtually throughout Catalonia, although still basically focused on the catering sector.

Farggi's products and salesmen consistently used the image of the Farga cake retail stores as their reference point, quality guarantee, and visiting card. This enabled them to gain entry in restaurants and cafeterias with relative ease, smoothing their path in a market that was coveted by many other companies. Farga's guarantee also gave them a solid argument for defending higher sales prices.

Often, the "secret weapon" used by Farggi's salesmen and distributors was to get a foot in a new customer's door by first offering him the more typical frozen cake products, that is, apple, chocolate, almond cakes, and the like. Once the restaurant or cafeteria had become a customer for the cakes and trusted the salesman, the service, the products and Farggi in general, the salesmen gradually introduced new articles, particularly ice creams.

This process was also facilitated by the fact that Farggi always differentiated itself from its possible competitors in the way it did things: It offered higher quality products, with a more craftlike appearance and a more attractive presentation, a more extensive and creative collection, and so forth. So it was usual for restaurants and cafeterias always to have some Farggi products in stock.

As regards to distribution and logistics, Farggi had its own distribution organization, delivering directly to the restaurants in Barcelona and its metropolitan area. In the rest of Catalonia, Farggi sold through independent distributors.

These distributors were almost always small local companies, enabling distribution to be fragmented into small units. The distributors were required to have their own warehouse, equipped with cold-storage chambers suitable for handling frozen products, a fleet of delivery vehicles, and a minimum sales team. However, they were not required to work exclusively for Farggi, so it was common for Farggi's distributors to distribute other brands of ice cream such as Frigo, Camy, or Marisa, which targeted other market segments and/or with less demanding quality requirements.

When it started to sell through distributors, Farggi offered them a 28% discount on ice creams and a 26% discount on cakes, applied on their own direct sales price, so that the distributor could sell to its restaurant customers at the same prices that Farggi would have charged if they had been direct customers. Following an "oil stain" strategy, distribution was gradually extended to other parts of Spain, using the same system of independent distributors.

The New Factory in Montgat and the Third Cake Shop in the Avenida Diagonal In Barcelona

In 1982–1983, the new Montgat factory was opened.[2] With a floor area of 8,000 square meters, it completely replaced the previous Badalona factory, which was closed. With the new factory operating, both capacity and service were improved.

Almost at the same time, Jesús Farga had the opportunity to rent premises on the prestigious Avenida Diagonal, in Barcelona, between the Paseo de Gracia and the Rambla de Cataluña, where it opened its third Farga cake shop, with restaurant service. A veritable

flagship, it consisted of a ground floor, a mezzanine, and two basements where the kitchen and the workshop were installed—in total, about 1,500 square meters, in one the best locations in Barcelona.

After opening the new factory in Montgat, Farga's turnover amounted to about 400 million pesetas between the three cake shops, whose work force now stood at 45 employees. For its part, the Farggi business was billing another 600 million pesetas, with 60 employees and 18 independent distributors. With its present distribution network its ice creams and frozen cakes now reached cities as far afield as Madrid, Malaga and Corunna.

The new shop, large and well-located, enhanced the reflected glory of the Farga cake shops that was projected on the Farggi brand, and increased general brand awareness.

The years up until 1987–1988 were the company's period of greatest prosperity. It had excellent sales margins and was able to sell without any major marketing or advertising efforts, as it was virtually the sole player in the high quality ice-cream and frozen cake segment in Spain.

Farggi was, and defined itself as, "Luxury cakes, ice creams and desserts for restaurants." A single product concept, with about 250 products or stock keeping units, serving a single market: the catering trade.

Competition Gets Tougher and It Becomes Necessary to Install Freezer Cabinets in Restaurants

Unfortunately for Farggi, in the late 1980s and early 1990s, the big Spanish ice-cream companies, many of them owned by multinationals, started to develop their own ad hoc product lines for the catering segment.

Companies such as La Menorquina (previously Marisa), Frigo, and Miko started to launch products with formats (sizes and appearance) similar to those of Farggi, although without seeking to position themselves on the same high quality level. They sold at lower prices, with advertising backing, and provided the restaurants with menu cards showing the desserts.

One of the consequences of the stiffening in competition was a fashion whereby a manufacturer had to install a freezer cabinet on deposit in the restaurant in order to be able to sell ice cream to it. Each freezer cost the ice-cream manufacturer about 100,000 pesetas. The restaurants' order of priorities when buying ice cream now became: freezer-price-quality-service.

Faced with this new market situation, Farggi had to invest considerable sums in installing freezers: 40

million pesetas in 1989, 70 million pesetas in 1990, and between 80 and 100 million pesetas in 1991.

An Offer to Buy Farggi

In 1989–1990, Camy (Nestlé) started talks with a view to buying Farggi. At that time, Farggi was billing about 800 million pesetas and the entire group, including the cake shops, had a turnover of about 1.5 billion pesetas. It appears that the purchase offer was considerably above this figure and was therefore very tempting. Finally, it was decided to turn the offer down.

The Second Generation Joins the Company

In June 1989, Margarita Farga, the second daughter of Jesús Farga and Magdalena Bertrán, graduated in business studies from ESADE. Immediately afterwards, she went to Boston, United States of America, where she stayed until March 1990, following an extension management studies course at the renowned Harvard Business School. Margarita would be the first daughter to join the company.

In addition to her formal studies, Margarita recalled having accompanied her father on many business trips; he had made her visit supermarkets and restaurants in various countries in order to find out about the prices, the products sold, who bought them and how, and other details.

First Awareness of the Existence of Häagen Dazs

When she was in Boston, Margarita first saw a Häagen Dazs ice-cream parlour:

> I was struck by the fact that it sold a much more expensive ice cream and that it used the word "luxury." The containers seemed very unsightly to me, but when I tried the ice cream, I realized that it tasted different, although I did not know why.

Another detail that caught her attention was that Häagen Dazs also sold ice cream on a stick. In Spain, this sort of ice folly or Popsicle had traditionally been little more than "a chunk of ice with some sort of flavoring" (usually orange or lemon), and occupied the lowest quality segments; one did not think of an ice folly as a "luxury" product.

The Häagen Dazs stores that Margarita saw seemed unappealing to her, and also fairly empty, in spite of the fact that they sold a good product which could be served with toppings. In her opinion, they lacked "a touch of European design," which would give them more class.

Margarita's reaction could be summed up by saying that she noticed and appreciated the containers[3] and

the presentation of the ice creams, their taste and the variety of flavors offered, the use of the word "luxury" and of the color gold in the materials and designs (although accompanied by other decorative details in black which she did not find so pleasing). At the same time, the stores, which she felt could be improved on in several respects, showed her "what Farggi would like to be when it was grown up," as a commercial mechanism for reaching the end consumer more directly (selling ice cream for consumption in the store itself or strolling along the street, or to take home).

Although Margarita felt that "it could be done even better," she was well aware that in Spain the few retailers who specialized in the sale of ice cream were almost without exception open only in summer, with inadequate fluorescent lighting, white tiles on the walls, and, as the only form of decoration, posters showing the various ice creams on sale and rows of glasses upside down on the shelves. With very few exceptions, the stores were independent, family-run businesses. Consequently, the staff usually wore no uniform, or else each person wore his own; and obviously, each store used its own name and had its own sign, with very poor quality lettering.

For Margarita, the concept of the Häagen Dazs–type ice-cream parlour was "love at first sight." However, if she was to introduce similar ice-cream parlours in her own country, the first problem would be to find the way to make them viable throughout the year, since up until then ice-cream consumption in Spain had always been highly seasonal, falling to almost zero during the winter.[4] Also, unlike in the United States, there was very little ice-cream consumption at home.

Margarita invited her parents to visit her, among other reasons so that they could see the Häagen Dazs ice-cream parlours and share with her all these opinions and concerns. Jesús Farga decided that the matter had to be looked into in greater depth and that the first thing to do was to thoroughly analyze the product. So, when he went back to Barcelona, he took several samples of ice-cream with him in his hand luggage.

By then, Farggi's ice cream was already being manufactured without stabilizers and with low air content. This was stated in the sales brochures as features indicative of its high quality.

The results of the analyses carried out in Barcelona showed that half a litre of Häagen Dazs weighed about 470 grammes, while the same volume of Farggi ice cream weighed between 300 and 350 grammes, and the ice creams of the major domestic brands weighed between 200 and 250 grammes. This was because Farggi had always sold ice cream with a low air content; in fact, every 100 litres of solid ingredients used to make Farggi ice cream yielded only about 150 litres of ice cream. From the same quantity of solid ingredients the major Spanish brands might obtain about 200 litres of finished ice cream ready for consumption. Another significant difference was that the Häagen Dazs ice creams (and most of the North American ice creams) had a fat content of 16%, whereas the norm in Spain was 5% to 6%, including Farggi.

Margarita Returns to Barcelona

By the time Margarita returned to Barcelona in March 1990 and joined the company as head of marketing, Farggi's managers had realized that if in previous years they had grown at annual rates of up to 30%, now they were growing more slowly and they had to invest more to obtain that growth. Also, because of the economic recession, restaurants were buying less, which made it even more difficult to recoup the investment in freezer cabinets, which the company bought on a lease.

The first thing Margarita did was to spend six months riding in the delivery trucks, crossing Barcelona from one end to the other, accompanying the company's salesmen and visiting distributors throughout Spain. This enabled her to acquire a certain degree of authority both inside and outside the company.

At about this time, it was also observed that the company's mousse cakes were very popular and had relatively little competition. Furthermore, in the course of his travels to other European countries, Jesús Farga had noticed that this was a widely accepted product in many of the more developed countries' markets. They were sold frozen in supermarkets in somewhat smaller sizes than those normally sold by Farggi to Spanish restaurants.

Concerns in 1991[5]

By 1991, the entire management team in Farggi was reflecting on what seemed to them to be their chief strategic dilemma: whether to try to maintain growth in the catering market or to try to expand their market by entering another distribution channel with products for consumption in the home. All were aware that they had to find something that would enable them to achieve two objectives at the same time: to preserve and improve their image, and to sustain and improve the company's profitability.

One of the fruits of this search for new openings was the idea of launching frozen cakes targeted at the home consumption market, to be sold in supermarkets, select food shops, and the like, offering to install a Farggi freezer cabinet. They would be the first to launch this type of product in Spain.

It seemed to them that the traditional cake shop, although it continued to play a very important role, had probably entered a phase of gradual decline.

An extensive survey was carried out of the supply of frozen cakes in Europe and the United States. While the frozen cakes made and sold by Farggi on the catering market measured 26 cm in diameter and 4.5 cm in height, the new cakes for home consumption would measure 19 cm in diameter and 3 cm in height, giving a net weight of 550 grammes. However, being mousse cakes, that is, with a light, airy body, it was considered that they were large enough to serve between six and eight portions.

A range of nine flavors was defined: five mousse flavors and four cheesecake flavors.[6] Following the serving recommendations for the products used by the catering market, on the packs of these cakes for home consumption it was clearly stated that they should not be eaten frozen but that they should be taken out of the freezer about two hours before serving to allow them to thaw. The names Pastimús and Cheesecake de Farggi were registered as trademarks, and all the other details regarding finish, formulas, processes, packaging, and so forth were defined.

Farggi's sale price to the retailer was set at 920 pesetas, plus VAT, per unit, so that retailers, in turn, could sell them to the public at 1,300 pesetas per unit, that is, with a gross margin of 380 pesetas. This retail sale price was higher than that of the ice-cream bars and frozen cakes sold by the major national ice-cream manufacturers, but significantly lower than a fresh cake bought in a traditional cake shop.

Everyone was aware that, in some way which was still not clear at that time, the mousse cakes were laying the foundation for opening the distribution channel to ice cream for home consumption. Consequently, in 1991, it was decided to build a new cold storage chamber with a capacity of 10,000 cubic metres on a piece of land adjoining the Montgat factory. With this decision, Farggi took a step forward, anticipating future needs, whereas in the past its decisions to increase production and storage capacity had almost always been reactive, that is to say, they had not expanded capacity until they had first created the market and the need.

First Contact with Häagen Dazs

In June 1991, Lluis Farga, Jesús Farga's third child and Margarita's brother, graduated in economics. Then, like his sister, he went to Harvard University to take an extension management course. Once there he, too, was fascinated by the quality of North American premium ice cream and, like Margarita, insisted that Farggi should start to make and sell it in Spain.

During a visit made by his father, they decided to make an appointment with Häagen Dazs in order to explore the possibility of doing something together in Spain. The meeting took place at the end of 1991 and was rather cold. The Häagen Dazs executive they spoke to told them that any matter related to a European market should be discussed at Häagen Dazs' European headquarters in Paris.

In January 1992, they had another meeting with a senior Häagen Dazs manager in Paris, but there did not seem to be any possibility of collaboration between the two companies. In fact, the only clear impression they got from the meeting was that Häagen Dazs had not yet decided whether or not to try to penetrate the Spanish market.

While in Paris, Jesús Farga visited the Häagen Dazs parlour in the Av. Victor Hugo and saw the improvements they had made in the appearance of the parlour, giving it more class. Jesús Farga traveled on to Brussels and London, where he observed and gathered information on the Häagen Dazs parlours open there.

In March 1992, the Alimentaria (Food Industry Trade Fair) was held in Barcelona. Farggi was present with a stand of its own, where they were visited by the manager responsible for Häagen Dazs parlours in all Europe. He told them that Häagen Dazs was about to open their first ice-cream parlour in Barcelona and that he wished to explore the possibilities of cooperation between the two companies.

In August 1992, while the Olympic Games were in full swing in Barcelona, the first Häagen Dazs ice-cream parlour was opened at number 85 in the centrally-located and classy Rambla de Cataluña. On their packaging it was stated that the product was manufactured in France and imported by Helados Häagen Dazs, S.A.

Meanwhile, the Pastimús Project . . .

A few months earlier, in January 1992, Farggi had vigorously launched the frozen cakes Pastimús and Cheesecake on the Spanish market, targeting the home consumption market.

In a period of only three months, they installed about 300 freezer cabinets in supermarkets and other select food shops in Barcelona and the surrounding area, where Farggi continued to have direct physical distribution, and a further 500 freezers, through its distributors, in the rest of Spain.

The new range of frozen cakes for home consumption was readily accepted by this kind of retailer. However, the sales volume grew at a rate substantially lower than forecast. Farggi's managers considered that this was because fresh cakes were withstanding the incursion better than expected, and that the habit of buying their cakes fresh in the cake shops, rather than in supermarkets and food shops such as bakeries, delicatessens, or frozen food shops, was deeply ingrained in the public.

In any case, the market and customer surveys seemed to indicate that the low turnover was not due to the product itself, which people liked when they bought and tried it. They thought that perhaps it was because the Farggi trademark, traditionally centered on the catering market, was not sufficiently well known and did not have enough strength to persuade the final consumers to try the new cakes.

The lower turnover of frozen cakes for home consumption led Farggi to speed up the project to launch the ice cream—which was to be displayed in the same freezers—as soon as possible in order to recoup the heavy investment made in freezer cabinets. However, it should be pointed out that, at that time, Farggi's managers had not yet decided whether the launching of ice creams through the freezers already installed in retail outlets would be accompanied by the opening of exclusive Farggi ice-cream parlours or not.

Further Contact with Häagen Dazs: Possible Cooperation in Logistics

In September 1992, that is, right after having opened their first Häagen Dazs parlour in the Rambla de Cataluña, in Barcelona, the multinational company's management took the initiative to contact Farggi again in order to explore the possibility of the Spanish company taking care of the physical distribution of its ice creams to the freezer cabinets it intended to install in supermarkets throughout Catalonia.

In the ensuing discussions, Häagen Dazs' managers provided the necessary detailed information on the number and foreseeable location of their freezers, the expected turnover, ice cream SKU numbers, restocking frequencies, and so forth to enable Farggi's managers to study the foreseeable workload volumes, compatibility with their delivery schedules, and so on.

For their part, Farggi's managers informed them of the areas and types of outlets that they could cover with their logistics distribution system, including the fact, which apparently seemed to be completely new to Häagen Dazs, that they were already distributing their frozen cakes in bakeries, delicatessens, and the like, in addition to selling in supermarkets.

Margarita Farga remarked:

> I had my eyes and ears wide open because they were telling me the story I had dreamed of doing with our brand. The fact is that we were very unsure whether we should agree to carry out the physical distribution of Häagen Dazs. We knew that the company belonged to the extremely powerful Grand Metropolitan Group and its enormous economic potential inspired a certain amount of awe.

The talks went on, with both parties exploring the project's viability until, on a certain day in November 1992, something unexpected happened:

> We had already explored all the data and details of the proposed cooperation—said Margarita—and we were relatively close to an agreement. But at that moment, the Häagen Dazs manager we mainly spoke with—a delightful person and very competent—possibly carried away by his enthusiasm at the way things were starting to come together, exclaimed, "Fantastic, we'll install the first Häagen Dazs freezers in the three Farga cake shops!" That sentence, no doubt uttered with the best of intentions, made something snap inside us. It came as a thunderbolt! As if suddenly a veil had fallen from our eyes and it was crystal clear to us what we should not do!

There were at least another three reasons against closing the physical distribution agreement. First, Häagen Dazs only offered to pay Farggi 13% on its list price to the retailer, while the latter, just for selling the product to the public, had a gross margin of more than 38% on the retail sale price.[7]

Furthermore, in the event that Farggi were to physically distribute Häagen Dazs ice creams outside of the metropolitan area of Barcelona, that is, outside of its direct distribution area, the money received would have to be shared in some way between Farggi and its 30 independent distributors.[8] In any case, taking into account the direct costs of storage, delivery, administration, and control, Farggi estimated that 13% was not a very good rate for them.

The second, and perhaps most important and decisive reason against a logistics cooperation between Farggi and Häagen Dazs, was that José Manuel Garrido, Farggi's sales director, was never quite sure that the distribution of Häagen Dazs products was really compatible with the delivery of Farggi products, from the commercial and image viewpoints (signage on the vans, etc.).

Finally, Farggi's managers also thought that, if they acted merely as a logistics service for storage and delivery, any time that Häagen Dazs received a more attractive offer from another logistics company, they could decide to discontinue their relationship with Farggi, which could leave Farggi with excess storage and transport capacity, which it would not be easy to reoccupy.

In the end, the negotiations were broken off and, almost without giving it a second thought, Farggi's management team took the momentous decision: "We must open our own Farggi parlours as soon as possible!" Initially, the plan was to open five Farggi-owned ice-cream parlours, the first of which had to be open by June 1993 to gain maximum benefit from the summer season. They knew that they would need bank financing for this. Consequently, right from the start, they planned and executed the entire project on the understanding that subsequent growth of the number of exclusive Farggi parlours would be by franchising.

Farggi's managers were well aware that both Farggi, through its Farga cake shops, and Häagen Dazs created and developed their image through establishments that bore their name. Thus, one of the key success factors would be to get customers to buy the luxury ice cream in the supermarket thanks to the memory and image they took away from their visit to the exclusive ice-cream parlour.

A Few More Months of Frenetic Activity: The Design of Farggi Tub's & Ice Cream

Once the decision to open their own parlours had been made, Farggi began a frantic race against time. Numerous operational details concerning the new ice-cream parlours and the range of ice cream had to be decided.

They designed a new logo with the Farggi brand name and considered different names for their new establishments (they did not want to call them ice-cream parlours). They did not know what name to give their ice-cream containers either.

Finally, they decided that the formal name would be *Farggi Tub's & Ice Cream*.[9] Generally, they referred to them as their shops.

In addition, they had to resolve, decide, and define a large number of operational details, such as the following:

1. Find a container manufacturer who could supply food-quality printed cardboard tubs. Apparently,

there was no such manufacturer in Spain. It was also difficult to find a suitable supplier of plastic lids for the tubs. Then, the tub had to be "dressed," that is, its decoration had to be designed so that it conveyed the idea of luxury ice cream, using gold and navy blue, which became the corporate livery.

However, there was another problem: The tub manufacturer—which was not a Spanish company—stipulated minimum runs of 100,000 units for each model or type of decoration. The solution was to print and manufacture a standard or universal tub model, that is, a preprinted base to which two labels would be added: one on the tub front or side, with the name of the flavor (and stamped with the outline of the object defining the flavor, for example, a strawberry), and another with the barcode, which would be stuck on the tub base. Likewise, it was decided to buy lids made of white plastic, to which a round sticker was added. Initially, and on a temporary basis, these labels would have to be stuck on by hand, which would slow down and increase the cost of the production process. The primary goal was to get the product on the market as soon as possible. These production details could be improved at a later date.

2. Define the range of ice-cream flavors to sell. Then, develop the corresponding formulas and production processes. For this purpose, besides using the knowledge and experience of Farggi's production and management team, numerous trips were made to the United States to make contact with various manufacturers of machinery for making ice cream. Jesús Farga also contacted experts in formulas and production processes for North American–style ice cream.

During these months, Farggi's management team and technical and production staff, with outside help as and when necessary, developed the formulas and processes for the 25 flavors[10] that made up the new range of ice cream for sale both in Farggi's exclusive ice-cream parlours and through the 800 freezer cabinets that were already installed in supermarkets and other nonexclusive food shops to sell the Pastimús and Cheesecake frozen cakes.

Establishing the formulas and production processes for the new range of ice cream involved serious technical difficulties because Farggi wanted to use only absolutely natural ingredients and because the new ice cream had to meet the following specifications: about 16% fat content (instead of the 5% to 6% that was usual in Spain, even in the ice cream previously manufactured by Farggi), a very low air content, and no stabilizers or artificial coloring.

In fact, so great were the technical difficulties that the formulas and processes were not considered to have been finalized until June 1993, when the opening of the first Farggi ice-cream parlour was imminent.

These formulas produced ice cream that was very similar to Häagen Dazs ice cream. On the other hand, both company's premium ice cream was clearly different from any other ice cream manufactured at that time in Spain.

3. It was necessary to purchase, install, and start up a number of new machines in the Montgat factory in order to manufacture and package the new types of ice cream.

4. It was also difficult to find a manufacturer who could supply the 9.5-litre cardboard cylinders that were required as bulk containers for use in the glass-fronted freezer cabinets in the Farggi parlours, for serving to the public in individual scoops. In Spain, the normal size was 5 litres, but Farggi's managers wanted them bigger, so that they would not have to be changed so often and so that they would fit better in the freezer cabinet.

5. Much to their surprise, they also found that there was no Spanish manufacturer capable of supplying freezer cabinets with the machines and thermostats needed to keep the ice cream precisely between $-18°C$ and $-20°C$. This was an essential detail, not only to keep the ice cream in perfect condition (manufactured with a high milk solids content), but also to ensure that the consumer would find it cold enough when he ate it. Finally, after a hard search, they managed to locate a manufacturer of freezer cabinets in the United States, to whom they sent their first orders.

However, a surprising incident occurred: When these freezer chests were ready, the North American manufacturer shipped them to Europe. When Farggi's managers asked for the address and telephone number of the collection point, they discovered to their horror that the North American manufacturer had assumed that they were Häagen Dazs licensees and had sent the freezer chests to the Häagen Dazs warehouse in Paris! So, in March 1993, Häagen Dazs found out that Farggi was planning to open its own ice-cream parlours.

6. The interior of the freezer cabinets installed in the retail outlets where the frozen cakes were being

sold had to be redesigned so that they could also be used to store the new tubs in such a way that customers could help themselves directly from the freezer.

7. A large number of decisions had to be taken regarding the range of products to be sold in the Farggi ice-cream parlours, the functional design of the parlours, and their decoration. For example, one of the key decisions was whether only ice creams would be served, as seemed to be the case in Häagen Dazs, or whether coffee, soft drinks, and pastries would also be served. If coffee was to be served, the establishment's decoration depended, among other things, on whether the coffee machine would be located in a place where it was visible to the public, as in most bars and cafeterias, or not. If they served coffee and pastries, would the typical bar counter be installed or would they only be served to take away or to eat sitting at the tables?

There was never any doubt that portions of Pastimús and Cheesecake would be served in Farggi's parlours, and this feature would clearly differentiate them from Häagen Dazs.

In the end, it was decided that coffee, soft drinks, and pastries would be served, in addition to ice creams and cakes. There were at least two reasons for this decision: On the one hand, Farggi's managers were continually concerned about ensuring their parlours' commercial and economic viability during the winter months, when ice-cream consumption drops off considerably. In fact, the thought process followed by Farggi's management team had been the following: "Our growth will necessarily depend on granting franchises. Therefore, inevitably, the exclusive Farggi parlours must be profitable for our future franchisees. Consequently, the parlours and the range of products served in them must be designed so that they make good business sense in their own right, even if we stay with the idea that most of their sales should be ice creams."

Secondly, by offering and serving combinations of scoops of ice-cream with portions of cake (possibly with toppings, such as whipped cream, melted chocolate, caramel sauce, or other fruit sauces), the aim was to inspire consumers to imitate them and prepare similar dessert combinations in their own homes, after purchasing the ingredients in the Farggi parlours or from the freezers at the supermarkets. As Margarita Farga added, ". . . by this means, we wanted to get the final consumer to identify with 'the sweet world of Farggi.'"

8. It was also decided that they would manufacture and sell three varieties[11] of premium ice cream on sticks, to be called baronets, a name that was unique in Spain.

9. Having established the products and services to be sold in their own parlours, they printed menus so that customers wishing to consume the products sitting at the establishment's tables could choose in complete comfort and ask the waiters to bring them what they wanted.

10. As regards to the decoration of the first Farggi parlour, it was necessary to contact a number of contractors and interior decorators. One of the prerequisites was that these companies should be organizations large enough to be able to fit out and decorate other exclusive Farggi parlours (either owned by Farggi or franchised) in any part of Spain. Also, right from the start, there was a serious and persistent effort to define designs that used standard measurements and specifications, so that they could easily be reproduced in other premises of a different size, in different locations and with different floor layouts.

The idea was that Farggi parlours would have two parts: The entrance had always to be "very Farggi," with a more striking and direct style of decoration, lighting, and signage. Further inside, on the other hand, in what Farggi's managers called the "tea room," the style of decoration would be softer and more flexible, and could vary from one parlour to another, although they would always use fine materials such as marble and wood.

11. The last three important decisions were, first, to run a number of blind tests of the ice cream developed at the Montgat factory, comparing it with Häagen Dazs ice cream. Farggi's managers reached the conclusion that, at least when the test was carried out blind—that is, when the customer did not know which brand of ice cream he or she was tasting—the result was a draw between the two companies. In actual fact, what happened was that with certain flavors there was a preference for the ice cream of one manufacturer, while in other flavors there was a preference for the ice cream of the other manufacturer. And there was a third group of flavors where there was no significant preference in either direction.

Encouraged by this result, Farggi's managers then decided that their ice cream would be sold at exactly the same retail price as Häagen Dazs products, both in their parlours and in the freezer cabinets installed in supermarkets and other sales outlets. First, this would give them the same (substantial!) unit margins that Häagen Dazs enjoyed. Second, selling at lower prices could have been interpreted by the consumers as an indication that Farggi's ice creams were lower quality. Finally, they did not have any wish or intention to start a hypothetical price war with Häagen Dazs.[12]

The final decision concerned the location of their first parlour. After considering various options as regards to site, size, and rent, it was decided that their first parlour would be at number 94 of the stately Paseo de Gracia, a few yards along the street from Gandí's world-famous building, La Pedrera, and a few blocks from the first Häagen Dazs parlour on the Rambla de Cataluña.

The First Farggi Tub's & Ice Cream Parlour Is Opened

The first Farggi parlour opened its doors to the public in July 1993, almost one year after Häagen Dazs opened its first parlour. A few months later, in November of the same year, the second Farggi parlour was opened in the Rambla de Cataluña, barely three blocks away from the first Häagen Dazs parlour and on the same side of the street. A few weeks later, on December 2, the third parlour was opened in the L'Illa Diagonal shopping centre, on the Avenida Diagonal.

These three parlours were owned and operated by Farggi[13]—that is, the necessary investments had been made by the company itself and they were run by Farggi personnel. Responsibility for the day-to-day management and supervision of the parlours was assigned to Marcos Serra. Eduardo Farga was made responsible for planning and initiating relationships with franchisees: identification of future franchisees, negotiation, implementation, start-up, and monitoring.

On his return from the United States, Lluís Farga had also joined the company as Assistant Sales Director, with direct responsibility for the distribution of Farggi products in supermarkets and other types of nonexclusive food shops. His first task was to study the performance of each of the freezers where frozen mousse cakes were sold. Any freezer that did not reach certain minimum sales levels was reinstalled in a different shop.

The opening of these first three Farggi-owned parlours—true flagships for Farggi Tub's Ice Cream—attracted a lot of attention, and the company started to receive unsolicited requests to open franchised Farggi parlours.

This fitted in perfectly with the company's intentions and plans, since they had all been aware, right from the start of the new project, that franchises would be indispensable if they were to continue growing at a high enough rate. Indeed, opening the first three parlours had required an investment of about 140 million pesetas, which the company had financed with bank loans.

Therefore, in early 1994, on the basis of the experience acquired during the first months of operation of the three Farggi-owned parlours, and other sources of information, Margarita Farga drew up an operating manual running to more than 200 pages detailing, from A to Z, the operation of a Farggi parlour.

The First Franchised Farggi Parlour Is Opened; the Other Parlours Opened in 1994

With the manual now available, in February 1994 the owner of a restaurant that was a customer for Farggi products opened the first franchised Farggi parlour in Vilanova i la Geltrú.[14]

The agreement initially took the form of a precontract, while Elena Farga, who had a degree in law and worked in a law firm unrelated to the company, worked against the clock to draw up a highly detailed franchise contract that eventually ran to over 40 pages.

In May 1994, the fourth Farggi-owned parlour was opened in the Port Olímpic in Barcelona. A trial run had been carried out beforehand by opening a corner franchise, almost a window franchise, in El Túnel del Port, one of the many restaurants in the area. In view of the enormous success of the window, it was decided to open the parlour while maintaining the corner franchise. This double sale in the same area was still operating at the time this case was written.

In May 1994, the seventh exclusive sales outlet was opened (the third of the franchised outlets) in Conde de Penalver Street in Madrid, near the El Corte Ingles department store. In this case, the licensee was Farggi's own distributor in Madrid.

In June, the fifth Farggi-owned parlour was opened in the heart of Barcelona: the Plaza de Cataluña. Located between El Corte Inglés and the head of the Ramblas, Barcelona's most famous boulevard, this parlour would benefit from high visibility and high pedestrian traffic. With this parlour, Farggi's management team had a certain sensation of having achieved, in barely one year and a half, the objective that they had set themselves in November 1992 of opening five

Farggi-owned parlours. They were frankly pleased with the impact they had had in Barcelona and on the ice-cream market.

In the same month, the fourth franchised parlour was opened in Salou, a well-known coastal town located a few kilometres to the south of Tarragona. Finally, in the next few months, another three franchised parlours were opened: in the port of Mataró, in Malaga, and in Calella de Palafrugell, on the Costa Brava.

Thus, the first full year of activity of Farggi Tub's & Ice Cream (July 1993 through July 1994) ended with 12 parlours open: five Farggi-owned in the city of Barcelona and seven franchises (one corner franchise in Barcelona's Port Olímpic, four in towns on the Catalonian coast, one in Madrid and another in Malaga). After the summer, in September 1994, a second franchised parlour was opened in Madrid (Pintor Sorolla, Santa Engracia).

In order to make sure that the franchisees properly complied with the conditions contained in Farggi's manual, an independent company that specialized in the control and monitoring of food franchises was hired. This company used the "mystery buyer" method, which basically consists of visiting the establishments without any prior announcement or identification to verify the level and quality of service to customers, the establishment's cleanliness and appearance, and other details.

New Parlours That Would Be Opened in 1995 and After

In February 1995, the third Farggi franchised parlour was opened in Madrid. A further nine new franchised Farggi parlours were scheduled: in the Maremagnum shopping and entertainment complex in the port of Barcelona; in the Calle del Pi, also in Barcelona; in Vic (province of Barcelona); in L'Escala (province of Gerona); in Benidorm (province of Alicante); in Puerto Banús (province of Malaga); in Marbella (province of Malaga); in Lloret de Mar (province of Barcelona); in Corunna; in Las Arenas, near Bilbao; and in Ciutadella, in Menorca.

In short, if these plans worked out, by the end of 1995, Farggi would have a chain of 25 exclusive ice-cream parlours, five owned by the company itself and located in the city of Barcelona, and 20 franchises.

By the end of the fifth year of operations, Eduardo Farga expected to have about 100 exclusive Farggi parlours open, of which 90 would be franchises and perhaps 10 Farggi-owned.

Evolution of the Sale of Farggi Products in Supermarkets and Other Types of Nonexclusive Shops for Home Consumption

The first Farggi products for consumption at home had been the Pastimús and Cheesecake cakes, which were distributed and sold frozen, but were to be eaten after thawing. They had been introduced in early 1992 by installing about 800 freezer cabinets in supermarkets and other types of retailer.

Even back then, Farggi's management team had guessed that this range of cakes would eventually be complemented with another range of ice cream to be eaten at home, possibly taken from or based on the range of Farggi ice cream sold to restaurants.

Unfortunately, sales of this range of frozen cakes were growing at a much slower rate than expected. Margarita Farga attributed this slowness to the need to induce and allow time for a double change in the end customers' purchasing and eating habits, since, in Spain, it was not the custom for people to buy frozen cakes in the supermarket. Normally, people either ate fresh cakes bought in a traditional cake shop, or ice-cream bars and frozen cakes bought in supermarkets and eaten while still frozen.

In spite of this difficulty, Farggi had never advertised its frozen mousse cakes in the mass media.

As a result of all this, sales of the Pastimús and Cheesecake range in some of the freezers were just above 100,000 pesetas per freezer per year, at Farggi's selling prices to the retailer. Although this was a minimum figure, the company's managers admitted that the project would only have been profitable in the long term. There were even cases where some freezers had to be relocated, installing them in restaurants and cafeterias.

Throughout 1992, these freezers were installed in various kinds of sales outlets. From November 1992 onward, the attention of Farggi's management team was concentrated on preparing the launch of Farggi Tub's & Ice Cream, so little attention was paid to the Pastimús and Cheesecake range during that period.

Of course, these cakes were included in the range of products to be sold in the Farggi ice-cream parlours. However, once the first Farggi parlour had been opened in Paseo de Gracia, modifications were made to the freezers' shelving so as to be able to display the ice-cream tubs in them, starting with the freezers installed in Barcelona. At the same time, Farggi's sales teams re-opened negotiations with some supermarket chains with a view to relaunching the installation of new freezer cabinets, which would sell the ice-cream tubs and the Farggi frozen mousse cakes right from the start.

Like Häagen Dazs, Farggi's policy was first to open an exclusive Farggi parlour in a city, so as to create the product's image, and then start distributing ice cream in supermarkets through the freezer cabinets. Of course, Farggi had the advantage in that a large number of freezers had already been installed.

Consequently, all that was needed in order to expand the product range was to change the inside shelving and obtain the retailer's agreement, which was relatively easy as the sales turnover of a Farggi freezer cabinet increased very substantially, almost always to about 500,000 pesetas per year, at Farggi prices to the retailer.

Although both Farggi and Häagen Dazs maintained a discreet silence regarding their costs and margins, a number of experts in ice-cream manufacture indicated that, even taking into account the fact that both brands used only top quality natural ingredients, the cost of the raw materials and packaging would probably not be more than 35% of their sale price for tubs and pints to retailers.

Generally speaking, although both had started in Barcelona, there was relatively little confrontation between Farggi and Häagen Dazs, first because both were still in an early phase of market entry; second because Farggi already had a large installed base of freezer cabinets; and third because both realized that they could coexist perfectly, sharing presence in many supermarkets and even in smaller shops.

In spite of this, there were a few clashes. For example, Farggi managed to be present in all the Caprabo supermarkets (55 points of sale), whereas Häagen Dazs would only be present in the 15 largest, sharing presence with Farggi. In those supermarkets where both brands' freezers were installed side by side, their sales volumes were very similar.

On the other hand, in the Pizza Hut chain, even though Farggi had managed to get its foot in first, in March 1994 Häagen Dazs became sole supplier of ice cream. However, Farggi remained as a cake supplier for Pizza Hut, so the business relationship was not broken. Much the same thing happened in the Pans & Company sandwich chain, which bought ice cream from Häagen Dazs and cakes from Farggi.

In August 1993, Farggi signed a contract with the Barcelona Football Club for the exclusive sale of ice cream in its sports facilities. The purpose of this contract was to create brand impact and enable a large number of people to taste Farggi's products. Minitubs (100 ml) and baronets were sold from 25 carts at 350 pesetas each. The contract would run for three years, with Farggi paying 15 million pesetas a year.

Meanwhile, Häagen Dazs . . .

Farggi's managers believed that, by the end of 1994, Häagen Dazs had about 25 parlours operating, of which two were actually owned by the company: one in the Rambla de Cataluña in Barcelona and the other in the centre of Madrid.

As regards to distribution, it was estimated that they had about 600 freezer cabinets installed in Barcelona and a further 400 in Madrid, mainly in relatively small outlets, but with presence in some supermarket and hypermarket chains. The physical distribution in the Barcelona area was carried out by La Menorquina, although this relationship seemed to have ended by the end of 1994. In other parts of Spain, they used the services of professional frozen product logistics companies.

In June 1994, Häagen Dazs had introduced a range of four varieties of ice cream under the name Exträas, which it sold in its parlours but not in supermarkets. This range had a distinctive presentation and seemed to have achieved a relative success.

By the end of 1994, one or two Häagen Dazs franchisees had raised the possibility with Farggi of changing flags and joining its chain.

Main Strategic Dilemmas Facing the Farga/Farggi Group in Early 1995

In early 1995, Margarita Farga, as Farggi's marketing director, was reflecting on what had been done so far and what had been achieved. To help her organize her thoughts about the Farga/Farggi Group's business activities, she sometimes used the following branch system:

Farga/Farggi Group:
1. Farga traditional cake shops
2. Farggi businesses
2.1 Farggi products sold to restaurants
2.2. Farggi products sold to retail shops
2.2.1. Sold to nonexclusive shops (supermarkets, etc.)
2.2.2. Sold to the exclusive Farggi parlours
2.2.2.1. Farggi-owned parlours
2.2.2.2. Franchised parlours

Some of her thoughts and concerns about each of these "branches of the Farga/Farggi tree" were the following: On the one hand, the three Farga cake shops (item 1) were carrying on as usual, with 37 years of professional and trade experience, as upmarket establishments making fresh cakes and high-quality pastries, sold directly to the public either for consumption on the premises or to take home. There did not seem to be any intention of modifying their activities or increasing the number of such establishments.

On the other hand, there were all the Farggi products (item 2). First among these, both for historical reasons of "order of appearance" and because of its basic economic importance, was the sale of ice cream and frozen cake to restaurants and cafeterias (item 2.1), which was still the group's largest business in terms of sales: Excluding sales by the Farga cake shops, it had accounted for 60% of total ice-cream and frozen cake sales under the Farggi brand name in 1994.

Margarita was aware that, since November 1992, this business 2.1 had been somewhat neglected as a result of the strategic priority given by all the company's personnel to designing and starting up the Farggi Tub's Ice Cream project. Consequently, it seemed to her that the time had come to redefine and refocus it strategically, both as a brand and as regards to its product range or collection.

Restaurants and cafeterias were a mature market, but one in which some fast food chains were growing rapidly. However, during 1993 and 1994, Margarita had not had the impression that Farggi's customary competitors in this field (Frigo, Camy, Menorquina, Avidesa, etc.) were introducing any striking novelties.

In third place was business 2.2, that is, the sale of Farggi products in shops and parlours for consumption at home, for consumption on the premises, or for consumption on the street (impulse sale). It seemed clear to Margarita that Farggi's management team's chief achievement during the previous three years (1992–1994) had been the creation of a relatively complex strategic platform for the sale of Farggi ice cream and frozen cake for consumption in Farggi ice-cream parlours and at home. Over a period of three years, they had taken this business from zero to 40% of the total sales of Farggi products, that is, of the total of business 2 in 1994.

According to a market survey carried out in September 1994, their only competitor in this business 2.2, in the opinion of a sample of final consumers in Barcelona, was Häagen Dazs. It seemed that Farggi and Häagen Dazs were the only two ice-cream brands that had really succeeded in positioning and consolidating themselves in the high-quality, premium-price segment of the ice-cream market in Spain. However, at the same time, it seemed obvious to her that both luxury ice-cream brands competed with the major brands, such as Frigo, Camy, Avidesa, Miko, and so on, given that the

consumer, when buying ice cream, had to decide whether he wanted high-quality ice cream at a high price or medium-quality ice cream at a medium price.

As regards to sales in nonexclusive shops (item 2.2.1), by the end of 1994, Farggi was distributing its ice-cream tubs and frozen cakes (Pastimús and Cheesecake) in Catalonia, Madrid, and Malaga through 800 freezer cabinets installed in supermarkets and other retail sales outlets. Farggi's management team were of the opinion that, in these three areas, the market was still a long way from being saturated and that in Catalonia, Madrid, and Malaga–Costa del Sol, they could install up to a maximum of 6,000 freezers.

It was also their intention to expand the distribution of Tub's and frozen cakes as new exclusive Farggi parlours were opened in other locations; the parlours would create the brand image, in each location, paving the way for sales in nonexclusive shops. The brand image was also needed to justify the price premium of Farggi ice cream, which was sold to the public in supermarkets at 675 pesetas for half a litre, whereas the usual price for Frigo, Camy, and Miko ranged between 400 and 450 pesetas per litre, although they often ran promotions during which the price could be reduced to as little as 350 pesetas per litre.

By the end of 1994, Farggi had about 80 applications to open new franchised Farggi parlours, so Margarita was sure that there would be no obstacle to growth due to lack of parlours. However, depending on the rate at which new parlours were opened and the market size and potential of each town or city in which they were to be opened, a limiting factor might be their financial capacity to invest in the purchase of freezer cabinets. By the end of 1994, each freezer cost 150,000 pesetas. The upside of this was that, thanks to the sale of Tub's and cakes in the same freezer, sales figures exceeding 600,000 pesetas per freezer per year were being achieved, at Farggi's sales prices to the retailer. In a large supermarket, the figure could easily be double this amount. When Farggi sold to retailers through its local distributor, it granted the distributor a 20% discount, giving a net billing for Farggi per freezer of 480,000 pesetas/year. Even so, with such figures, it was possible to depreciate a freezer over a reasonable period of five years, financing them by credit lines or leasing operations.

Finally, as regards to sales in exclusive Farggi parlours (item 2.2.2.), a distinction had to be made between Farggi-owned parlours and franchised parlours.

As stated earlier, by the end of 1994, Farggi had five parlours of its own (item 2.2.2.1), all of them located in the city of Barcelona. The parlours in Paseo de Gracia, Rambla de Cataluña, and L'Illa had been operating for barely a year. Port Olímpic and Plaza de Cataluña, which were opened in mid-1994, had only been going for a few months and had yet to pass the acid test of the winter season.

In Margarita Farga's opinion, these five Farggi-owned parlours were "perfect as flagships," that is, to create the necessary Farggi image: (a) to sell Tub's in the supermarkets; (b) to promote sales of new franchises; and (c) to generate a good image, in general, with a very broad range of groups and audiences, such as gastronomic journalists, retailers, financial institutions, and so on. Their profitability was in some cases "very high," while in others she considered it to be "satisfactory."

The company's immediate plans were not to open any more Farggi-owned parlours, except in cities or streets which might be considered strategic, that is, necessary for the process of creating or strengthening the company's image.

There could perhaps be a middle road, consisting of having part-owned parlours, in which Farggi would share ownership of the parlour with a local partner.

As regards to the franchised parlours (item 2.2.2.2), one point that had to be remembered was that some of them were seasonal, that is, they were open to the public only for about six months. Such was the case of the parlours in Salou, Calella, and Mataró. It appeared that the seasonal parlours, located in coastal resorts, were extremely profitable. Other parlours were open all the year round: Madrid and Malaga. The key profitability factor for these parlours would be their performance during the difficult winter months.

At least until the end of 1994, these franchised parlours did not pay any royalties nor had they made any initial down payment to buy their franchising rights when they signed the contract. Farggi obtained its profits from the captive sale to its franchisees of five products or groups of products:

1. ice cream, in 9.5-litre packs ("bulks"), which they resold by the scoop
2. ice cream in tubs for taking away
3. Pastimús and Cheesecake frozen cakes for taking home whole.
4. frozen cakes for selling in the parlour in portions.
5. various complementary articles, such as paper napkins, cone wafers and paper cups for serving the balls of ice cream, toppings and sauces, uniforms, and so forth.

The margin—that is, the difference between the purchase price from Farggi and the selling price to the public in the parlour—was very high, being about 65% of the retail price. To put it the other way round, the cost of the products sold to the public was 35% of the selling price. Of course, the parlour owner had to pay the rent, wages, and social security, financial expenses (if any), electricity, water, and to amortize the machinery and facilities, etc.

Farggi required that parlours which were to be open all year round should have a minimum surface area of 100 square metres. A parlour of this size required investments of about 20 to 25 million pesetas in machinery, equipment, and decoration.

In the case of parlours that were open only during the summer season, Farggi allowed them to be smaller, with a minimum of about 50 square metres. The investment to fit out an ice-cream parlour of this size usually ran to between 12 and 15 million pesetas.

Some Financial Information

Being a family-owned company, Lacrem, S.A. did not publish its balance sheets. Traditionally, it had always made a profit, which had enabled it to finance its growth from self-generated funds. Exceptionally, in 1993, the company had recorded a negative cash flow. But cash flow had been moderately positive again in 1994. The economic forecasts for 1995 and 1996 were for a strong increase in cash flow, which, should this in fact be the case, would enable the company to progressively decrease its level of indebtedness, open new Farggi-owned parlours, or buy more freezer cabinets.

As marketing director, Margarita had a relatively modest budget of about 25 or 30 million pesetas, which she used to carry out typical marketing activities, such as local promotional events when new parlours were opened, tasting events, preparing the new menus for the company's parlours, a number of public relations activities, and so on.

The Group's turnover, that is, Lacrem, S.A.'s turnover plus the final turnover (sales to the public) of the five Farggi-owned parlours, less Lacrem, S.A.'s billing to these five parlours (so as not to count twice), was expected to double between 1993 and 1995, as follows:

	1992	+5%
	1993	−15%
	1994	+40%
Forecast	1995	+30%
Forecast	1996	+30%

The investments in the factory had amounted to about 350 million pesetas, and total investments in Farggi-owned parlours and freezer cabinets had amounted to another 350 million pesetas.

By the end of 1994, for all its sales activities, including sales to restaurants and cafeterias, the company had an installed base of about 3,000 freezer cabinets and a further 2,000 top-opening freezer chests, used by restaurants and cafeterias to store their stocks of Farggi products.

Some Questions About the Future

Faced with this situation, Margarita Farga was turning over a number of questions in her mind. For example:

- Who were they really competing against? Against Häagen Dazs? Against the traditional big ice-cream companies: Frigo, Camy, and so on? Against the traditional cake shops? Or were they perhaps expanding the market; that is, were they expanding consumption among people who would not otherwise eat ice cream?

- How quickly should they grow? In which cities or geographical areas? Farggi was already receiving a large number of franchise applications from outside of Spain. Should it start to internationalize itself? If so, which countries should it go to first? Should they open directly in other countries or reach an agreement with a master franchiser who would be given exclusive rights for an entire country?

- Were five Farggi-owned parlours enough or should they try and open more? Should they maintain a certain percentage or proportion of Farggi-owned parlours out of the total number of exclusive Farggi parlours?

- Would it be enough to open exclusive parlours to create the necessary image? Or should they also run advertising campaigns in the mass media? In the case of the latter, what should be their positioning and message? It was clear that such advertising would have to promote high-quality, premium-price products, but should they aim for an adult positioning like Häagen Dazs? Or would a more family-style positioning be better, with advertisements showing children with their parents and/or grandparents? Or perhaps a "for gourmets of all ages" positioning?

- What things should they try to do like Häagen Dazs and what things should they do differently in order to achieve a distinct, differentiated image? For example, on the subject of ice-cream flavors, should they make "international flavors" or should they differentiate themselves by creating flavors more in tune with the Spanish palate?

- In short, what were the key success factors of Farggi Tub's & Ice Cream? What things could Farggi do that Häagen Dazs could not or did not want to do? And, looking at it the other way round, what things could Häagen Dazs do that Farggi could not do, or at least could not do so well? What things could both of them do with more or less equal cost-effectiveness, that is, without any differential competitive advantages on either side?

- Finally, Farggi's management team were aware of a significant dilemma: (a) They could either go on alone, self-financing their growth, in which case they might not be able to keep up with Häagen Dazs and other competitors might appear in the same segment;[15] (b) or else it might be better to allow a nonfamily investor to come in with a view to accelerating their market penetration at home and abroad.

No doubt, this list of questions was not exhaustive, and what most worried Margarita was the possibility that she might have left out some key decision in this maze of decisions and opportunities.

Endnotes

1. Individual portions of sorbet or ice cream were already common in Spain, but only in the impulse sale market segments and/or in the medium quality segments.

2. Small coastal town located to the north of Barcelona and adjoining Badalona.

3. For example, she observed that, in the United States in general, round tubs were generally accepted as indicating that the ice-cream they contained was higher quality and were labeled "super premium," whereas the lower-quality lower-price ice creams were sold in square-shaped packs.

4. According to some estimates by industry sources, in 1989, 80% of ice-cream consumption in Spain took place between May and October. The statistics indicated that ice-cream consumption in Spain was about 3 litres per inhabitant per year, whereas in the United States it was about 15 litres.

5. Throughout this case, we call these shops "nonexclusive retail stores" because they sell Farggi products together with other food products, possibly including other ice-cream brands.

6. Mousse of fresh pears with truffled chocolate; fresh lemon; vanilla and Irish coffee; dairy cream and fresh strawberries; and chocolate with walnuts. The cheesecake flavors were bitter orange, cranberries, pineapple, and raspberries. In total, they had nine stock keeping units (SKUs).

7. A food shop equipped with a freezer cabinet (belonging to Häagen Dazs) bought the ice cream at 440 pesetas plus 6% VAT and resold it to the public at 675 pesetas, that is, with a gross

margin of 235 pesetas per 500 ml tub. From the supermarket's point of view, this was not only an excellent gross margin in absolute terms but was even more so when the fast turnover and small area occupied by the freezer in the shop (approx. 1 square metre) were worked into the calculation.

8. The logistics process that had been designed would have been the following: Häagen Dazs would be responsible, on the one hand, for placing its ice cream (manufactured in France) in Farggi's central cold-storage warehouse in Montgat, which would act as a central warehouse. On the other hand, Häagen Dazs, through its own team of sales representatives, would carry out all the initial sales work with the supermarkets and would install the freezer cabinets. It would then notify the new customer to Farggi, who would serve the initial order to load the freezer. From then on, Farggi's delivery/salesperson would visit the sales outlet at least twice a week. At each visit, he would verify stock status, replace the sold articles, place the ice cream inside the freezer, and obtain the retailer's signature on the delivery note, which detailed what had been delivered at each visit. Farggi's delivery person would not collect payment but would hand in the signed delivery notes at his operations base, at the end of the day's work, for verification, control, and subsequent despatch to Häagen Dazs, which would issue the corresponding invoice and would take care of collecting payment (apparently, it was Häagen Dazs' intention to only issue one monthly invoice, summarizing everything that had been delivered to a particular shop during each calendar month). In return for its cooperation in this process, Farggi would receive 13% of Häagen Dazs's selling price to the retailer. It was estimated that the average order per visit and delivery would be at least about 12 to 14 pints (500-ml tubs). In autumn 1992, Häagen Dazs's selling price to the retailer was 440 pesetas (plus 6% VAT) per "pint." Consequently, Farggi's average revenue per visit would have been 13% of this amount, or about 744 pesetas per visit made by its own delivery personnel (13 pints sold per visit × 440 pesetas/pint × 13%).

Obviously, the more successful and better-accepted Häagen Dazs ice cream became, the higher the average sale per visit. At that time, Häagen Dazs had only installed three freezers, but it intended to initiate an aggressive sales and freezer installation campaign as soon as it had solved the physical distribution issue.

9. Tub's is a registered trademark of Farggi.

10. Of these 25 flavours, at least three were typically Spanish and therefore had no Häagen Dazs counterpart: milk meringue streaked with cinnamon, mandarin sorbet, and Spanish nougat.

11. Swiss chocolate with black chocolate, vanilla with mild chocolate and almonds, and vanilla with milk chocolate.

12. This price policy would be continued during the following months. Farggi accepted a role as price "follower" with respect to Häagen Dazs, so that when Häagen Dazs took the initiative to increase prices, Farggi followed suit, raising prices by the same amount.

13. All Farggi parlours are exclusive; that is, they only sell products made by Farggi. In this text, we use the expression "Farggi-owned parlours" to refer to the parlours in which the investment and operation are Farggi's responsibility, using the expression "franchised parlours" when the investment and operation are the responsibility of an independent licensee, although always under Farggi's control and supervision.

14. A coastal town with about 40,000 inhabitants located about 40 km south of Barcelona.

15. On February 5, 1995, the newspaper *Expansión* published an article stating that the North American ice-cream company Ben & Jerry's had recruited Robert Holland as its new CEO. The article closed by quoting Holland, an ex-McKinsey consultant, as saying, "We will be in Europe next year." According to the same article, Ben & Jerry's sales in 1993 totaled 140 million dollars, with a net income of 7.2 million U.S. dollars.

EXHIBIT 1   Farggi: The Spanish Ice-Cream Market

The Spanish ice-cream market had a total volume of almost 182 million litres (some 48 million U.S. gallons) in 1994. According to industry sources, this figure includes only "industrial" ice cream, manufactured by companies which were members of the Asociación Española de Fabricantes de Helados. Therefore, to obtain the real total market volume, one should add to the above figure a further 20 to 25 million litres of homemade ice cream or made by small artisan-like manufacturers, plus some 20 to 25 million litres manufactured by small industrial companies which were not members of the above-mentioned Asociación.

Bearing in mind that Spain has a permanent population of some 40 million, the annual consumption of ice cream would be around 5 litres per person. It may be considered to be even less than that, bearing in mind that Spain received some 60 million tourists and visitors in 1994.

According to industry sources, the total market may be broken down in the following manner:

1. Some 42% of the total market would be made up of products classified as impulse; that is, sold in individual portions, individually packed or wrapped, frequently sold by street or beach stands or vendors, or from ice-cream freezers located at the door of bars, supermarkets or miscellaneous food retailers. The most common products in this category would be prepackaged ice-cream cones, small cups, and ice lollies or Popsicles. It may be necessary to clarify that this classification refers to product categories, and not to how or where it is consumed. In other words, whether an impulse product, as described above, is bought at a bar or in a restaurant, if it is a product in an individual portion, individually packaged, it continues to be classified as impulse.

   In the last few years, formats of impulse products have appeared in the market, such as ice-cream sandwiches, or small ice-cream bars, such as Crunch by Nestlé, or frozen Mars bars.

2. A further 11% of the total market is made up of home consumption products. These are frequently packaged in one-litre packs, such as the product ranges of La Cremería (Nestlé), Carte d'Or (Frigo), or Etiqueta Negra (Miko). We would also find in this group the large ice-cream bars or blocks that have to be cut into smaller individual portions for consumption, as well as frozen cakes or confections, such as Gala, Comtessa, crocanti, or whisky frozen cakes. We also find here multipacks containing several portions usually sold as impulse, but in a special multiple pack to be sold in supermarkets and food stores, to be consumed at home.

3. A further 11% of the total market is made up of products sold in restaurants, cafeterias, and food service outlets. This product category is made up of larger ice-cream bars or blocks for restaurants (intended to be cut into individual portions just before serving), and also ice cream prepared by the manufacturer in individual portions to be sold in restaurants, mostly as desserts: individual portions with fruit, or packaged in ceramic terrines, bonbons, tartuffi, small cartons or plastic cups for food service cafeterias, and so on.

4. Finally, the remaining 25% of the total market is defined as blocks and bulks. This product category would be made up of ice cream in large bars or blocks, sold directly to consumers using the same freezers out of which impulse products are sold to the public. We would also find here the large ice-cream carton cylinders of 2, 4, and even 6 litres each, out of which ice-cream parlours or restaurants serve cones or cups by the ball. These ice-cream balls will be eaten at the restaurant, or while walking in the street. These portions are never individually packed, and are meant to be consumed immediately. Maybe as much as 50% of the volume sold in this way is really an impulse purchase, that is, bought and consumed without any previous planning on the part of the consumer.

Industry sources estimated that ice-cream consumption by impulse and in restaurants and cafeterias amounted to some 75% of the total market, while ice cream consumed at home would account for only around 25% of the total volume. These same sources expected that consumption at home would increase in the immediate future, attaining maybe some 40% total market volume by the year 2000.

Some observers said that the Spanish market had witnessed a significant improvement in the average quality of ice cream. The traditional water-based ice lollies or Popsicles had given way to richer and more nutritive products. It was estimated that maybe some 50% of the total Spanish ice-cream market was now manufactured with milk fats, while the other 50% was manufactured using modern and advanced vegetable fats.

Regarding the main competitors and their products, FRIGO (Unilever) had been the traditional leader in the Spanish ice-cream market for many years, with a market share of around 30% (Source: *El País-Negocios*, July 2, 1995, p. 5). In 1993, Frigo had had a total turnover of some 27,780 million pesetas (1 US$ = 130 Spanish pesetas), of which 87% had been by its ice-cream division, while the other 13% had been in frozen foods (*Fomento*, October, 1994, p. 260). According to *IP mark* (September 16–30, 1995, p. 45), Frigo was said to have spent around 1,100 million pesetas on media advertising in 1994.

But Frigo's leadership had just been lost to Nestlé. After a premature announcement in August 1994, in March 1995 Nestlé-Camy had finally bought Avidesa and Miko. According to Carina Farreras (*La Vanguardia*, July 22, 1995, "Economía y Negocios," p. 7), Nestlé would now be the new leader of the Spanish ice-cream market with a total market share of around 40%, with its three brands Camy, Avidesa, and Miko. According to the same issue of *IP mark*, Nestlé had spent some 900 million pesetas on media advertising to promote their ice cream in 1994 (presumably, just to promote their Camy brand). However, sources close to Nestlé indicated that their media spending in that year was close to 350 million pesetas.

In other words, some 70% of the total Spanish ice-cream market would now be jointly held by Nestlé (Camy + Avidesa + Miko) and Unilever (Frigo). TLC Beatrice-La Menorquina would be the third contender, with a total turnover of some 12,800 million pesetas in 1993 (*Fomento*, October 1994, page 259). This turnover was slightly less than the 13,950 million pesetas sold in 1993 by Helados y Congelados, S.A. (Conelsa-Miko), recently acquired by Nestlé. However, Beatrice Foods and its partner Mr. Delfín Suárez also owned Interglás, S.A. (Kalise), which had a turnover of 7,800 million pesetas in 1993, including yoghurt.

Finally, the U.S. market was estimated to be worth between 3.2 and 3.3 billion US$. Out of these, the super premium segment had a share of about 11%. In the last few years, the total U.S. market was said to have grown at an annual rate of about 3.5%, while the super premium segment would have grown faster.

The two major competitors in the super premium segment were Häagen Dazs and Ben & Jerry's, with some 40% each. The remaining 20% was in the hands of other super premium brands such as Frutsen Gladge, Steve's Home-made, some "ethnic" brands such as Goya, or private brands such as Dag's Select, owned by D'Augostino supermarkets.

Case 4: Hatfield Graphics, Inc.

In the spring of 1990, Mark Hunt, senior vice president of marketing at Hatfield Graphics, Inc. (HGI), was preparing an evaluation of the corporation's progress in penetrating overseas markets. While Hatfield's sales had been very respectable in their well-established European subsidiaries, Hunt was anxious to see the firm evaluate, penetrate, and develop some of the previously ignored markets in other parts of the world. He was particularly interested in China and the Eastern European countries, because he believed that these countries represented potentially large untapped markets for Hatfield products, especially in light of the lack of competition there. Hunt began to review the possible strategies the company could adopt to capture these markets.

Company Background

Hatfield Graphics, Inc., was organized in 1945. Headquartered in New Haven, Connecticut, it conducted its business through two principal subsidiaries: (1) the Hatfield Scientific Instrument Company, a manufacturer of computer-controlled drafting and plotting systems and turnkey interactive computer graphic design (IDS) and data management systems (DMS), and (2) Hatfield Garment Technology, Inc., a manufacturer of computer-controlled fabric cutting systems. In addition, the company owned about 54% interest in Ashi Engineering Development, Ltd., of Beersheba, Israel, whose principal products were electronic medical and dental instruments. The company's total sales in 1989 amounted to $148 million.

	1985	1986	1987	1988	1989
Drafting Systems	58%	55%	59%	54%	42%
Cutting Systems	30	22	30	25	32
IDS and DMS	8	8	7	17	23
Other	4	5	4	4	3
Total	100%	100%	100%	100%	100%

HGI's Businesses

Hatfield designed, manufactured, marketed, and serviced different computer-controlled drafting and cutting systems and provided software for its systems. Its principal businesses fell into three categories: drafting systems, cutting systems, and IDS and DMS. Following is the sales history of the company for five years.

Drafting Systems Hatfield's computer-controlled drafting systems were used primarily to produce finished engineering drawings and graphic artwork many times faster and more accurately than a draftsman could do the same work. A drafting system was composed of a control unit and a plotter. The control unit was computer programmed to receive instructions from an input device, such as a magnetic tape reader, and to process the information and issue commands to drive the plotter. The plotter was an electromechanical device that moved the drafting tool over the drafting medium. Hatfield produced a variety of plotters of different sizes, speeds, and accuracy. Computer-controlled drafting systems were used to produce engineering drawings in an array of industries including the automotive, aerospace, shipbuilding, mapmaking, garment, and electronic industries. The price of such drafting systems, including control software and various accessories, ranged from $50,000 to $500,000. Hatfield had been engaged in the production of computer-controlled drafting systems for 15 years.

Cutting Systems Hatfield produced computer-controlled cutting systems that provided quick and accurate cutting of a wide variety of fabrics for different industries. Multiple layers of material spread on a long table and compressed by a patented vacuum system were cut to the desired shape by a computer-controlled cutterhead containing a reciprocating knife. Depending on the particular application, the user realized significant savings in materials and cutting and sewing operations, and there was a significant improvement in productivity. A typical cutter system was priced anywhere from $325,000 to $550,000.

Interactive Design and Data Management Systems A typical IDS consisted of a mini-computer, a keyboard, a cathode ray tube display, and other devices such as a plotter and applications software. A primary function of an IDS was the preparation and recording of data involved in the design process. In manufacturing industries, a design begins with the creation of a mathematical model of a tangible item, such as a mechanical part. The IDS provided the means for a design engineer to construct a mathematical model of the part easily and quickly, to view the part in the form of a graphic display, and to make engineering changes. From this design data, an IDS could produce documents, such as engineering drawings and layouts, on microfilm, paper, or vellum, as well as generate bills for materials. Using the final design data, manufacturing engineers could use the IDS to generate numerical control tapes for automatic operation of the machine tools used to produce the part.

The IDS could be used by all industries and businesses requiring graphic design. In addition to designing mechanical products such as those found in the aerospace and automotive industries, IDS could be used in architectural design, mapmaking, design of printed circuit boards, electrical schematics, tooling design, plant layout, and various other applications.

Hatfield's DMS provided flexibility by linking several IDS into a single "distributed" interactive graphics system. This networking, which used the DMS computer, permitted different engineering and manufacturing groups to share a common design data base as well as the computing and data storage resources. The DMS also could be linked together and to large mainframe computers, thus providing very large storage and data management capacity and computer power to run complex analysis programs for an IDS. The software of Hatfield's DMS provided full security of the design data, so that only persons with appropriate clearance had access to the data.

Hatfield's IDS and DMS were available in a large number of configurations, permitting each system to be tailored to a customer's particular requirements.

Research and Development

Hatfield had major research and development programs in effect, in both hardware and software. The objective of these programs was to create new products and improve, as well as modify, existing products for Hatfield's present customers. Research and development expenditures amounted to $3,270,000 in 1989. The company held more than 200 U.S. and more than 150 foreign patents.

Marketing

Hatfield's products were sold to end-users primarily through Hatfield's direct sales force in the United States, through wholly owned subsidiaries in Western Europe, and through independent sales representatives in other areas. The Western European subsidiaries were headquartered in Belgium, Germany, and the United Kingdom, with sales personnel in other significant European countries. The subsidiaries served as sales representatives on a commission basis. Hatfield also had 54% interest in an Israeli company. In 1988, the company entered into agreements with Yokogawa Electric Works Ltd., Tokyo, which gave Yokogawa the exclusive right to manufacture and sell Hatfield's IDS and DMS in Japan, Korea, and Singapore.

Hatfield first began foreign sales and support activities through a combination of foreign sales agents and sales representatives. This gave Hatfield fast inroads into foreign markets because of its agents' and representatives' familiarity with the language, local industry, and business customs. Technical support and service for each sale, however, were handled by domestic personnel until local people could be trained as service personnel, usually employees of a subsidiary.

The first overseas offices, located in the United Kingdom and Brussels, were designed along the lines of the domestic sales organization. Each office operated independently and had both sales and service responsibility for its respective territory. Office staff were primarily composed of home nationals. Unfortunately, it was not long before serious personnel problems developed. Many employees complained of ambiguity in the channels of command and were unclear as to whether their loyalties were to the home office or the parent.

In view of these problems, Hatfield established wholly owned subsidiaries totally staffed by locals. The nationals naturally spoke the local language and were thought to be much more skilled in local sales techniques. They were also expected to have a competitive advantage over other foreign manufacturers because of their ability to deal on a local manufacturer to local customer basis.

Each overseas subsidiary was designed to support full sales, service, and manufacturing activities. Despite these capabilities, Hatfield conducted all manufacturing in the United States. Hunt explained:

> Back when we set up our subsidiaries, the cost of manufacturing overseas was lower due to a rather depressed wage scale. In addition, the U.S. dollar was overvalued relative to other currencies. However, the forecasts were for overseas wage rates to eventually climb beyond those in the United States and for the dollar to realign itself at a much lower level. For example, the average hourly wage rates in the United States were currently $17 to $18 with associated fringe benefits of 30 to 40 percent of total salary. Average hourly wages in Germany, by comparison, were $19 to $19.50 with fringe benefits amounting to 50 to 60 percent of salary.

Competition

Hatfield competed with a variety of companies, some of which were larger and had greater monetary resources. In the computer-controlled drafting systems, however, Hatfield was the major supplier in the United States, and one of the major suppliers in the Western European market. In other businesses, the company position was among the major competitors. Approximately 12 companies offered turnkey interactive computer graphic design systems. Of those, Applican, Inc., Autotrol Technology Corporation, Calma Company, and ComputerVision Corporation were the formidable competitors.

Expansion into International Markets

According to Hunt, three ingredients are essential in marketing products overseas:

1. The entire corporation must make a commitment to export the product overseas. Exports of your product must be recognized as a vital part of your business and as a major growth area in the future. Anything less than a full, long-term emotional commitment to overseas markets will not be profitable for the company.
2. The product must offer something useful to the market you are entering. It must either be seriously looking for the product you are offering or be developed by proving to the end-user the benefits of the product.
3. The product must be adapted to its target market. Environmental differences, such as the different power requirements in Europe, require that the product be modified in order to be accepted by the user.

Hatfield first became involved in foreign markets through unsolicited orders from large European electronics firms looking to acquire the high-technology products that Hatfield manufactured and that were not available in their own countries. As these orders became a more significant part of Hatfield's total sales revenue, the company began to develop aggressively a sales and service organization to address the needs of these foreign customers.

The prospect of an established overseas market for Hatfield's products had many attractive characteristics. One of the most appealing of these was the potential for effectively lowering its per-unit research and development costs through increased unit sales. Since Hatfield's products were highly specialized and required the most exact engineering, development costs were high and represented a substantial initial investment. An overseas market would allow the company to increase substantially their return on this investment.

The overseas market also offered an avenue by which they could increase the sales life expectancy of their products. "Many countries have not experienced the rapid advances in technology that we have in the United States," Hunt commented. "Some products considered nearly obsolete by our standards are thought to be state-of-the-art in foreign markets."

Finally, many industries that were the prime users of Hatfield products were growing at a much faster rate overseas than in the United States. The European market for so-called systems products, for example, was estimated to be growing at 20% per year.

Future International Markets for Hatfield Products

Hunt discussed the possibilities for future expansion of Hatfield's sales overseas. Continued growth could be expected in the well-established European market, although at a declining rate. With this forecast, Hatfield was considering the possibilities for development of a number of new markets, particularly those in China and the Eastern European countries.

Chinese Market China, as described by Hunt, would provide Hatfield with an outlet for his company's software and marketing systems within the nation's large garment industry. The Chinese garment industry, unlike its European counterparts, did not have a need for Hatfield's fast, accurate garment cutters because of China's abundant, cheap labor resource. Materials, however, were constantly in short supply and very expensive, accounting for 85% of the total cost of each garment. The China market, therefore, seemed a likely candidate for Hatfield's AM-1 marker grading systems, which automatically arranged and marked materials for manual cutting operations. In addition, Mr. Hunt felt that the market offered great potential when viewed against several other criteria.

A primary consideration was the overall size of the Chinese marketplace. The country, with a population of approximately one billion people (the largest in the world), had a workforce that increased by 20 million annually. The Chinese government was also supporting a national modernization program for specific industries. The garment industry, while not an immediate high priority in that program, hoped to gain increased government support over the next three to ten years. Hunt, therefore, foresaw an overall increase in demand for Hatfield products in China over the long term.

Eastern European Countries The Eastern European countries offered rich potential markets for Hatfield's products. Romania, in particular, had expressed interest in Hatfield equipment. U.S. and Romanian government regulations and red tape, however, caused extremely long and frustrating sales transactions. In a previous sale in 1981, the Romanian and U.S. governments delayed a signed order for three years. When the order was finally approved, Hatfield was obligated to manufacture a then-obsolete piece of equipment at great expense and little profit. Despite these admitted difficulties, Hunt felt that Hatfield was in a strong financial position to explore possibilities in the post-communist Eastern European countries, which promised a vast potential in the coming years.

How to Proceed

While the China and Eastern European markets appeared attractive, Hunt was not sure what entry strategy would be most desirable to make inroads into these markets. In addition, he wondered what information should be gathered to determine entry routes.

Case 5: PBS (A) and PBS (B)*

Richard Kuba had brought a decision to his board of directors. A joint venture proposal between První Brěnská Strojíma (PBS), of which he was the general manager, and Asea Brown Boveri (ABB), the Swiss-Swedish engineering company, was on the table. Kuba had worked more than a year on these negotiations. A majority of his board members had been opposed to a joint venture with ABB and had initially rejected it. Now ABB had a new proposal to offer. Kuba and his board would reconsider the joint venture decision in a new board meeting. It was the board's decision to make, and it would not be easy.

As the general director (chief executive officer) of a sizable Czech company struggling to make the transition from central planning to market economy, Kuba was in uncharted managerial waters. He believed that PBS had to take a decisive step to adapt to the challenge of international competition in the post-Soviet era. He felt responsible for the welfare of his employees and fellow managers, and he had a sense of national duty. PBS, a power plant equipment engineering and manufacturing company, had a continuous history from its founding in 1814 (the company name means "First Brno Machinery") through two world wars and the recently ended communist period. Now PBS once again had to adapt in order to survive.

---

* This case was prepared by Stanley D. Nollen, Karen L. Newman, and Jacqueline M. Abbey, Georgetown University. It is printed here with permission from the *Case Research Journal* and the authors.

PBS

The Company's Business

At the time of the Velvet Revolution, PBS's principle business was the manufacture of turbines and boilers, which accounted for a large majority of its revenue. (See Exhibit 1 for a description of the change in government and general business conditions under central.) The company also built complete power and heating plants, serviced and reconstructed old plants, and manufactured miscellaneous industrial parts. The company listed its product lines as follows:

> Turbines: Steam turbines for industrial heating and power plants, small to mid-size gas turbines, turbochargers, and accessories
>
> Boilers: Oil-fired, gas-fired, and coal-burning industrial boilers and accessories
>
> Power plants: Complete power and heating plants made on a turnkey basis; service and reconstruction of existing plants
>
> Other products: Burners, heaters, railcar shock absorbers, power plant measurement and regulation instruments, gas meters, castings, and forgings.

In 1992, PBS booked orders worth Kč 4,857 million (about $175 million) (Exhibit 2) and earned revenue of Kč 3,472 million (about $125 million). Profit was Kč 365 million ($13 million). The level of employment was just under 8,000 and falling steadily (Exhibit 3).

▬▬▬▬▬▬▬   **EXHIBIT I**   Business Under Central Planning and the Velvet Revolution

The Czechoslovak economy was nearly totally state-owned and mostly closed to trade and investment with the West from 1946 until the end of 1989. Most industries had only a few large enterprises, and in many instances they were monopoly producers of individual products. This meant that enterprises were typically very big (relative to the size of the market) and specialized in the production of just one product or a narrow product line. Enterprises in an industry were typically combined under a single "koncern." PBS was part of the Škoda Koncern group of companies, which consisted of Škoda Plzen (a heavy machinery maker with 30,000 employees), PBS (10,000 employees), CKD (a maker of railroad cars with 4,000 employees), SES (a Slovak company with 8,000 employees), and several smaller companies. Škoda Koncern was organized differently from most other Czech industrial groups insofar as it did not separate research and engineering into an enterprise apart from manufacturing units. Each company was a standalone enterprise.

The needs of the Soviet Union shaped the production program of many enterprises. Producers in centrally planned economies typically were only manufacturing plants (an enterprise was termed a "statni podnik" or state plant). They were producers, but they did not do other business functions such as marketing and finance. Distribution and sales were handled by separate state-owned trading companies, research and development was either centralized or assigned to a separate enterprise, and capital investment decisions were made by the state. Banks disbursed funds and collected "profits" but did not make lending decisions. There were no capital markets.

The goal of the firm that all managers understood was to meet the production plan set by the central ministry. Successful managers were those who could skillfully negotiate a favorable plan and who knew how to produce the required quantity. Another goal imposed on firms by the state was to provide employment for everyone. There was little concern about costs, prices, money, or profits. Most managers were technically trained, and all top managers were necessarily members of the Communist Party; selection depended on political as well as business considerations.

Enterprises were centralized and hierarchical and typically had a functional organizational structure in which the production function was the biggest and most important. Other functions usually included a technical function, a commercial function (this was mainly order-filling and shipping), an economy function (mainly financial record-keeping), a personnel function, and others depending on the company's type of business. Large enterprises during the socialist era typically provided a wide range of housing, recreation, education, and medical services to their employees.

The Velvet Revolution occurred in late November of 1989 in Czechoslovakia, a few months after the fall of the Berlin Wall. The name, Velvet Revolution, comes from the fact that the existing Communist government resigned without bloodshed, after massive peaceful demonstrations in Prague, giving way to a democracy almost overnight. The first post-Communist government was led by Václav Havel, a playwright who had been imprisoned under the former regime for his political views. Havel, though inexperienced in government, was a strong symbol of the moral underpinnings of the Velvet Revolution and the future for Czechoslovakia. One of the first orders of business was rapid transformation of the economy (one of the ten largest in the world between World Wars I and II) from the most thoroughly state-owned of all Soviet bloc economies to a market economy based on private ownership of property. Many of the people who rose to power in companies had been active in the "Prague Spring" of 1968, a period of liberalization. The reforms were put down by an invasion of troops and tanks from Russia and other Soviet client states in August 1968. Many business leaders who sympathized with Prague Spring reforms were demoted.

The company's headquarters and most of its manufacturing facilities were in Brno, where it had made steam turbines for 90 years and gas turbines for 35 years. Four plants were located in smaller towns in Moravia, dating from post–World War II years. The plant in Trebič made boilers and accessories (burners, heaters), and the plant in Mikulov made blades for turbines. The plant in Velká Bítě made turbochargers and had received most of the new capital investment that came to PBS from the central planning authorities

EXHIBIT 2 PBS Sales Booked by Product Line from 1990 to 1992 (Kč million current)

Product	1990	1991	1992
Total sales	1,484	3,307	4,857
Turbines	527	1,080	782
Steam turbines	234	270	557
Gas turbines	63	54	27
Turbochargers	230	756	198
Boilers	549	724	1,823
Industrial boilers	415	563	1,099
Piping	134	161	724
Assemblies	85	288	299
Repairs	171	191	162
Central heating equipment	68	111	119
Aircraft equipment	101	14	18
Other (see text)	282	898	1,653

Notes: Freeing of prices in 1991 resulted in price inflation in Czechoslovakia of 58% in that year. Gas turbines includes expansion turbines.
Source: První Brněnská Strojíma (PBS), *Annual Report 1992*

EXHIBIT 3 Selected Financial and Operating Data for PBS, 1990–1992 (Kč million current except where indicated otherwise)

Variable	1990	1991	1992
Total revenue	2,052	3,412	3,472
Production revenue	1,842	3,207	3,255
Profit	224	369	365
Total assets	3,338	5,399	6,187
Fixed assets	2,246	2,688	2,972
Trade receivables	377	1,411	1,635
Trade payables	322	814	857
Bank loans	752	1,107	931
Exports as percent of booked sales—to COMECON	20	19	10
Exports as percent of booked sales—worldwide	24	28	53
Employees (number)	9,564	8,857	7,946
Labor productivity (Kč 000 revenue per employee)	215	385	437
Average monthly wages (Kč)	3,629	4,410	5,299

Notes: Data include the Velká Bíteš plant. Figures for revenue in this table do not match sales figures in Exhibit 2 because the figures in Exhibit 2 represent sales orders booked, not revenue received.
Source: První Brněnská Strojíma (PBS), *Annual Report 1992,* and communication with PBS managers.

during the 1980s. This plant's output was exported mostly to the Soviet Union until its breakup in 1991; this business then fell by 80%. The plant in Oslavany made a variety of products and parts, such as railcar shock absorbers, nuts, bolts, and screws that were not central to PBS's main turbine and boiler businesses.

By 1992, PBS had begun to concentrate on environmentally friendly power plant and heating plant systems. Much of its recent boiler business was to overhaul and reconstruct existing boilers to meet higher regulatory standards.

In precommunist Czechoslovakia, PBS was a leader in the power generation equipment industry, with a reputation for good products and service. The early years of central planning were economically satisfactory as well. However, relative competitive decline set in at PBS after the "normalization" that followed Prague Spring in 1968. Investment in plant and equipment and new technology was insufficient for over 20 years. By 1992, PBS product quality was below Western standards, concern for the customer was low, and employee willingness to take initiative was lagging.

Yet PBS was better off than many other Czech companies that also suffered from little investment, aging capital equipment, and outdated products. Unlike most companies during central planning, PBS had its own engineering capabilities in-house, and as a result

had developed its own coal-fired boiler and steam turbine technology. In addition, PBS had a long-standing but small turnkey business. It not only made boilers and turbines, but it also did all the work necessary to construct or reconstruct complete electric power generation plants and steam heating plants. PBS was not just a manufacturing plant.

Distribution

Before 1989, PBS used two state trading companies for export sales: Škoda export and Technoexport. Exports accounted for about one-quarter of PBS business, about three-quarters of which went to Soviet Bloc countries. Domestic sales of turbines and boilers were uncomplicated, partly because the product was tailor-made; also, there were few potential customers, orders were big, and there were no direct domestic competitors. PBS customers were the contractors that built the power plants or end users (usually companies or city governments) if PBS did the project on a turnkey basis.

Employee Wages and Production Costs

Wage rates at PBS as in all Czech companies were quite low—an average of Kč 5,400 per month in 1992 (about $190). The skill level of the workforce was very good. However, productivity was also quite low because, PBS managers asserted, of the lack of investment in recent years. However, PBS did not have a production cost advantage compared to German companies. As Kuba said,

> We figured the German company's hourly rate for value added to engineer and produce turbine blades. We added up their wage rates and rental rates and depreciation rates, but we excluded the price of raw materials and parts they purchased from outside suppliers. Then we did the same calculation for ourselves. We found that our hourly rate was one-third of theirs. But then we looked at how long it took the Germans to make the turbine blades compared to how long it took us. It turned out that the German company used one-third the time that our company used. So our production costs were about the same as theirs.

Managers

The top managers at PBS were mostly technically educated (as expected in Czech industrial companies), and most had been employed at PBS for their entire careers. Richard Kuba, the first post-revolution general manager, fit this pattern.

Richard Kuba joined PBS in 1965 after graduating from Brno Technical University, where he studied power generation and turbine design. Early in his career he spent some time in PBS's turnkey business. In 1968 Kuba began to attend economics courses from the Prague School of Economics, but when Prague Spring was crushed and tighter government control was reasserted, he dropped his studies.

Kuba's ascent to the upper levels of PBS management was slow because he chose not to join the Communist Party. Despite his refusal to join the Party he was given the opportunity to travel abroad and work with foreign customers in Bulgaria, Romania, Sweden, and Syria. After completing graduate studies in power grid management in 1989, he was promoted to director of the engineering department in the power plant division. His promotion to general manager in 1990 at the age of 47 (he was selected by the head of Škoda Konzern) came as a surprise, even to Kuba himself.

Corporate Culture

The PBS corporate culture was influenced strongly by the requirements of central planning. PBS was the monopoly producer of boilers and turbines in its size range (small to medium sizes) in the Czech Republic. There was no competition. Producing to meet a plan was the most important criterion of success. Cost control did not matter, and costs and prices were determined by central planners rather than market forces.

The workforce was dominated by engineers. Boilers and turbines were over-engineered to stand up under extremely adverse conditions. Building a tough, sturdy, long-lasting product was far more important than building efficiently. PBS collaborated with the local technical university on research and development and took pride in its ability to design sophisticated equipment. More employees than necessary worked for PBS, a function of the government's full-employment policy. The enterprise was driven by production and engineering concerns. Employees were more excited about a well-engineered boiler than financial results.

The Investment and Finance

During the years of central planning, investment decisions from the Czechoslovak government were heavily influenced by the needs of major national or Soviet projects (e.g., the development of nuclear energy or the construction of a natural gas pipeline). Profits earned by enterprises were remitted to the State and new investment capital came from the State, but there was no linkage between the two. In the case of PBS, most of the investment that came to it went into the outlying plants, especially the plant at Velká Bíteš which made turbochargers, mainly for the Soviet Union. However, these investments were of little value in 1992 because they were designed for the Soviet market that diminished so rapidly and dramatically. Conversion of these plants to meet Western needs was difficult and costly because of differences in product specifications.

Interest rates were quite high in Czechoslovakia during this time, even in real terms, and loanable funds were very scarce. Short-term finance was also difficult to obtain, and a liquidity crisis ensued during 1992 and 1993. Since trade credit was scarcely available, many companies responded by simply not paying their bills. In PBS's case, trade receivables at their worst exceeded payables by a factor or two, and were Kč 1,635 million ($57 million) at the end of 1992, just below half of that year's sales revenue (Exhibit 3).

Privatization

The Czechoslovak government's objective for privatization was to transfer most of the country's large enterprises to widespread private ownership quite quickly.

EXHIBIT 4   PBS Organization Chart (Partial) in 1989

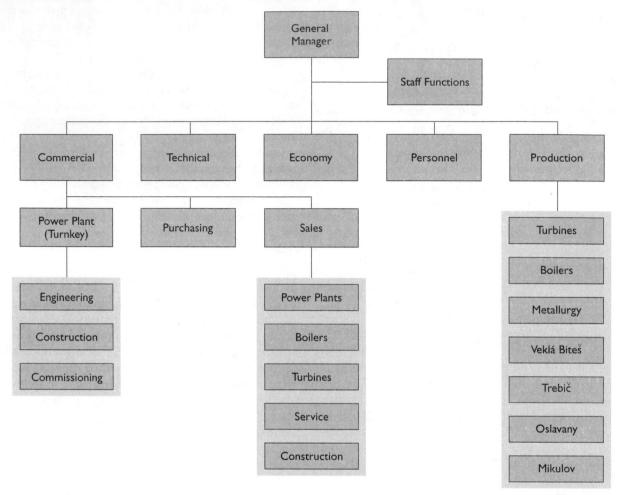

Source: První Brněnská Strojíma (PBS), *Annual Report 1991,* and communication with PBS managers.

Because local citizens did not have the financial resources to "buy the economy" overnight, much of it was "given away." Under voucher privatization, each adult citizen was entitled to buy a book of vouchers containing 1,000 points for Kč 1,000 (which in early 1992 was an average week's wages). The voucher holder could bid for shares of individual companies or spend voucher points on mutual funds that in turn bought shares of companies. Other methods of privatization included auction (for small companies), tender offers (usually with conditions attached about future employment levels), management buyouts, direct sale to a predetermined buyer, transfer at no cost to a municipality, and restitution to the family from which property had been confiscated by the State.

PBS was converted to the legal form of a joint stock company to become PBS a.s. in 1991. All of the shares in the company were owned by the National Property Fund (NPF), which was the Czech government agency established to hold shares of enterprises until they could be sold to private buyers. The company, which had the usual functional structure of large enterprises in centrally planned economies (Exhibit 4), reorganized into a divisional structure of product-centered businesses (Exhibit 5). The Ministry of Industry put PBS a.s. into the first wave of voucher privatization in 1992. Thirty-six percent of PBS a.s. shares were purchased by individuals and investment funds; 60% remained with the NPF; and 4% were set aside for restitution, which was the standard practice. The fact

EXHIBIT 5   PBS Organization Chart in 1992

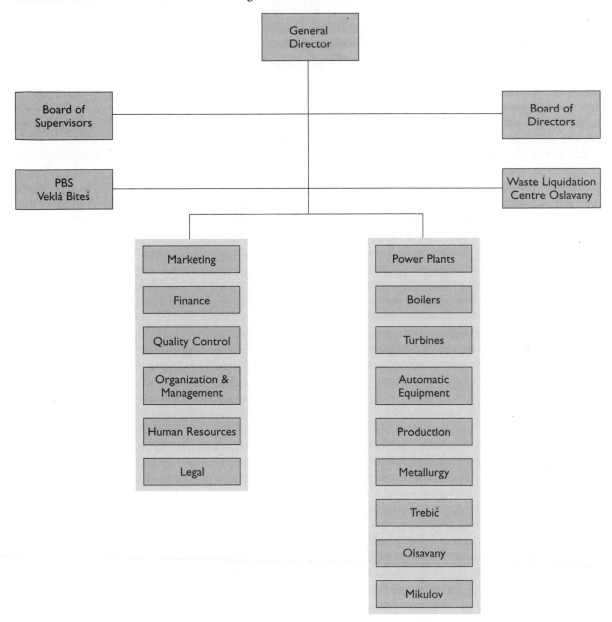

Source: První Brněnská Strojíma (PBS), *Annual Report 1992.*

that the NPF held the majority of PBS shares meant that privatization was not complete and that further ownership changes would occur.

The Search for a New Business Strategy

To successfully make the transition from central planning and become competitive in world markets, PBS managers proposed two different types of strategies. PBS had been an industry leader before the central planning era. Some managers believed it could regain this position through increased efficiency and product innovation. These people, who included most of the deputy general directors and department heads, placed their hopes for PBS in an ambitious new business strategy that called for maintaining independence and becoming more competitive by increasing quality standards, cutting production costs, producing products to meet international environmental standards, improving the fuel efficiency of products, and creating a climate for change within the company.

Financing this strategy, however, was a problem. There was very little capital available from Czech banks in the form of multiyear loans at reasonable interest rates, and PBS had not met with success in finding affordable financing from Western banks.

Other managers believed the choice was to decide which among several alternative relationships with other companies was best. They thought a go-it-alone approach could not succeed. the range of possibilities included some type of technology licensing or manufacturing link with a foreign company, some type of marketing agreement, a strategic alliance of some sort that would have technology transfer gains for PBS, the establishment of a joint venture with a foreign or domestic company, or purchase by a foreign or domestic company. When several Western companies—including General Electric, GEC-Alsthom, Deutsche Babcock, Siemens, and ABB—discussed business relationships with PBS beginning in 1991, PBS management listened, but only reluctantly.

The Joint Venture Negotiations

Points of View and Kuba's Role

When foreign companies initially discussed partnership proposals with PBS, managers were ambivalent. They knew they needed capital to modernize, to gain access to Western technology, and to get assistance in developing export markets. But they also had a strong wish to remain independent and not lose their brand name. PBS was, according to the Czechoslovak Ministry of Privatization, the "family silver." Most managers were unwilling to consider breaking up the company or entering into a relationship that rendered PBS "just an equipment manufacturer." Many of the initial partnership proposals from Western companies would have led to one or both of these unattractive outcomes. Some PBS managers declared that the company had operated successfully for nearly two centuries and could survive without any Western equity partners. The trend toward environmentally clean power plants and heating plants by itself would bring substantial new business to PBS's repair and reconstruction unit. The PBS order book was full in 1991. Maybe no foreign partner was needed.

Richard Kuba, however, thought differently. He knew that PBS did not have the latest technology. He discovered that Western companies could deliver a product in 25% less time than PBS could. While Kuba thought that PBS could upgrade its technology by itself, it would take more than five years because the investment capital was not available. With a foreign partner, it would go faster. In addition, turnover among young engineers at PBS was making internal technology development harder.

Kuba also believed PBS did not have the market economy experience to implement the company's strategy for improving its international competitiveness. In 1991 and 1992, he visited several PBS customers in foreign countries such as Pakistan and Iran.

> They knew about Škoda Plzen and Škodaexport, but not about us. Škoda Plzen had ten businesses. If one of their businesses fails, they have nine others. We had one, and we had no name. . . . There are four big international companies—General Electric, Siemens, ABB, and Mitsubishi—that control a big majority of the world market. There are tens of smaller companies like us, and some will not survive.

Kuba thought PBS was not diversified, so if its one business failed, the company failed. He learned that world markets did not know his product. These facts, he believed, were as important as the need for technology updates.

The Czechoslovak economy, with economic reforms initiated in January 1990, was still getting worse. Industrial production had fallen about 40% since the Velvet revolution, and GDP was off 26% (Exhibit 6). An upturn in business conditions was not predicted until 1994.

Kuba came to believe that it would be necessary to bring in a foreign investor, for both technological and market reasons.

> I was not enthusiastic about bringing in a foreign investor, but I knew that we had to do it if we wanted to keep the company whole and not split it up. To keep the company together was more important than keeping it independent.

Although the company could survive for several more years on the strength of its existing assets, order book, workforce, and customer base, he thought that only a strong Western partner could ensure that PBS would flourish and remain the pride of Czechoslovakia.

As was common practice in the centrally-planned Czechoslovakian economy, the general director of PBS decided most issues of company policy himself within the framework of the five-year plan. In 1992, Kuba

EXHIBIT 6 Economic Conditions in Czechoslovakia, 1989–1992

Variable	1989	1990	1991	1992
Gross domestic product, real % change[a]	0.7	−3.5	−15.0	−7.1
Industrial production, real % change	0.9	−3.7	−23.1	−12.4
Consumer price inflation, %	1.4	10.0	57.8	11.5
Interest rate %[b]	5.5	6.2	15.4	13.9
Exchange rate, Kč/$, annual average	15.1	18.0	29.5	28.3
Unemployment rate, %	na	0.3	6.8	7.7

Notes:
[a] Net material product
[b] Lending rate to state enterprises
Sources: Economist Intelligence Unit, *Country Report: Czech Republic and Slovakia,* 2nd Quarter 1993, 2nd Quarter 1990. London 1993, 1990.
International Monetary Fund, *International Financial Statistics,* March 1994. Washington DC, 1996, 1994.

was, in theory, accountable to a board of directors elected by the shareholders of PBS and to the state. In practice, however, these bodies had little experience with corporate governance. Committing the assets of PBS to a venture with a Western company that meant a foreign ownership stake was a controversial decision with major ramifications. Kuba expected to be criticized no matter which course the company chose. Therefore he would not make this decision alone.

The International Finance Corporation

At the recommendation of the Ministry of Industry, which was keenly interested in the fate of PBS, Kuba met with advisors from the International Finance Corporation (IFC), the consulting arm of the World Bank. The first meeting occurred in March 1992. Kuba was impressed with the work the IFC advisors had done earlier in the Czech Republic, particularly in facilitating the conclusion of Škoda Plzeň's joint venture negotiations. Kuba hired the IFC to structure a tender process and oversee negotiations for a joint venture.

The IFC advisors made two important recommendations to Kuba. First, PBS should secure government approval to enter into a joint venture with a Western partner in advance of negotiations. This would ensure that PBS, not the state, would be the ultimate decision maker. PBS acted on this recommendation immediately.

Second, the IFC advised that PBS should separate its turbine, boiler, and turnkey businesses from its other activities. Only by packaging the core businesses together, without adding in peripheral businesses and unrelated assets of dubious value, would PBS attract a Western partner. The advisors explained that they were trying to create an auction-like situation, and in order to do that they had to package the most valuable parts of the company separate from the rest. Though most managers and board members were very skeptical, Kuba convinced them to allow the IFC advisors to restructure the company on paper in order to find the best potential partners.

Kuba remained noncommittal throughout the discussions, supporting the IFC advisors and facilitating negotiations but always in the name of "exploring options." He communicated that he was willing to take a risk to improve the company's prospects, but he did not challenge the sometimes passionate objections of his fellow managers to the need for a foreign investor in the company.

As the discussions continued, General Electric proposed to license technology to PBS, but General Electric would have imposed conditions that were unattractive and would not have invested any equity. The other potential partners fell into secondary positions. Siemens, GEC Alsthom, and Deutsche Babcock did not put forward sufficiently comprehensive proposals, or they did not offer enough technology transfer. The remaining contender was ABB.

ABB

ABB, formed by the merger in 1988 of Asea of Sweden and Brown Boveri of Switzerland, was one of the world's major engineering and industrial equipment companies. It had revenue of $29.6 billion in 1992 and net income of $505 million, which gave it a return on equity of 11.8% (from ABB Web site http://www.abb.ch/abbgroup/investor). The company, with 213,000 employees, came out on top of both the 1994 and 1995 Financial Times—Price Waterhouse polls of European executives as the most respected company in the world (*Financial Times,* September 19, 1995).

The ABB corporate culture was more market- and efficiency-oriented than PBS's. Operating throughout the world in competitive markets, ABB's emphasis was on high quality at the right price. The customer dictated technical specifications as much as design engineers in ABB. ABB was accustomed to competing against other industry giants on big contracts. The firm was lean, renowned for having one of the smallest corporate staffs of any firm its size. Subsidiaries generally were given semi-exclusive rights to a geographic area, but if the subsidiary failed to win bids or failed to make a profit, its geographic area might be changed or it might be sold.

ABB had five main businesses: industrial and building systems, power generation, power transmission and distribution, transportation, and financial services. The power generation business, into which PBS's business would fall, was the second largest of ABB's businesses, accounting for one-quarter of all ABB revenue. This business had experienced rapid growth; it had nearly tripled its revenue since 1988, despite declining prices. ABB's main competitors in its main businesses were Siemens of Germany, GEC Alsthom of Britain and France, Mitsubishi of Japan, and General Electric of the United States.

ABB was an example of a truly global corporation. The company had product-oriented business units with worldwide responsibilities ranging from design through manufacturing to marketing and customer service. ABB had a very small headquarters group in Zurich, and dozens of wholly-owned or majority-owned companies on six continents.

ABB was no stranger to negotiating foreign joint ventures. Its approach to negotiations—which emphasized relationship-building, patient persistence, and resolving issues one at a time—had been honed through experience. In the power generation business, its corporate strategy was to locate the complete range of boiler production, turbine production, and power plant design activities into each of several ABB companies around the world rather than to separate boilers from turbines and put them in different companies. This approach allowed ABB to reduce the high costs of engineering labor and to compete in the high-value-added turnkey plant market.

Drawn by the country's skilled workforce, low relative labor costs, proximity to Western Europe, and successful conservative government, the company began investing in the Czech Repbulic in 1991. PBS would be the fourth and largest of seven Czech companies in the ABB network; other acquisitions had already been made in Poland, Hungary, and Romania.

In particular, ABB identified four main attractions of a joint venture with PBS:

1. ABB expected the market for power plants in the Czech Republic and in other central and east European countries to develop over time and become large, stimulated by the effort to clean up old plants; ABB wanted to be a "local" company inside this market.

2. ABB needed to develop a low-cost export platform—to export components to other ABB companies and to export complete products to other countries. Low-cost east European components could be combined with high-cost German or Swedish components to make an attractive total product package.

3. PBS had boilers and turbines in one company (one location), while ABB did not have boiler capacity in Europe. (It is easier to build a power plant if boiler and turbine production are located together because they frequently communicate with each other.)

4. PBS had considerable installed capacity to service; this would provide good short-run business even though the Czech Republic was not a major growth market in the power plant business at present.

ABB gave no thought to a licensing arrangement. According to an ABB negotiator,

> It is not the ABB way. We wanted equity. Anyway, in this case, we wanted just about the whole company, and that is not as easy to license as, say, the production of gas turbines like General Electric does. . . . We wanted to develop the power generation business in east and central Europe, and that required the hands-on management that only a controlling interest in a joint venture allowed.

The ABB team made it clear that they sought to buy into both the turbine and boiler businesses and to expand the turnkey operations. The other bidders were interested in smaller segments of the business. The ABB team's desire to incorporate both the turbine and boiler business made it more attractive to PBS management. ABB presented opportunities for technology transfers, training, market access, and investment capital that could build up PBS instead of simply absorbing it.

ABB sent representatives from its Power Ventures unit to negotiate the deal. Their task was to establish the joint venture and to manage its startup. The representatives had contact with PBS management and employees at different levels. Meetings with ABB's top corporate executives, including a lunch in Zurich with

Percy Barnevik, the chief executive officer, were arranged for Kuba. ABB also engaged the head of its Prague office to emphasize to PBS management the advantages that ABB offered as a joint venture partner and ABB's vision for creating with PBS an efficient engineering firm capable of serving the turbine, boiler, and turnkey markets using advanced technologies and creative engineering solutions. ABB recognized PBS's capabilities in coal-fired power plants and intended to keep the joint venture a full-fledged company, not just a manufacturing plant. ABB also included environmental indemnifications in its offer. Substantial sums were invested in developing and presenting the pitch.

Among all potential Western partners, only ABB was seemingly unfazed by PBS's lack of unified commitment to the concept of a joint venture. ABB sought to identify specific concerns of PBS management and responded with detailed presentations.

The Decision

After several months of negotiations, PBS managers had all the information needed to make a decision and several proposals before them to consider, the most attractive of which was from ABB. The meeting of the PBS board to decide on the proposals was held in late December 1992; it lasted 12 hours and became contentious. Everyone realized the gravity of the situation.

The board members returned to the issue of whether PBS should enter into a joint venture with a large Western partner. Strong concerns were voiced; many of the managers had worked for PBS for decades and feared that PBS was inviting ruin by surrendering its independence. They feared the intrusion of Western management. They saw the joint venture proposals as giving up, and they weren't ready to do that. Finally, after several hours, one member stood up and said "I'm going to say what I think everyone else is afraid to say—we don't like it. We don't want a deal." The board took a poll and decided that PBS should reject all joint venture proposals.

After the poll, the IFC advisors addressed the board for a further six hours, emphasizing that PBS's negotiating position was not likely to improve with time. Its market position would decline in the absence of needed investment and technology improvement. Further, if they simply broke off negotiations with the companies courting them now, they should expect that any future discussions on cooperation would meet with a much less favorable response. In short, PBS's negotiating leverage would steadily decrease over time and eventually, given its economic prospects, the company would be forced to accept a much less desirable arrangement than was currently available. The time to form a joint venture was now or never; the company needed to decide now whether it would pursue its business objectives without a foreign partner or tell the existing bidders why their proposals were not satisfactory and invite revised bids. After further deliberation, the board resolved to solicit improved bids.

ABB responded quickly with a multifaceted approach, directing its attention not only to the board members but also to managers at lower levels and employees whose voices they knew could flow upward to persuade board members to change their minds in favor of a deal. Several ABB executives and engineers arrived in Brno the weekend following the marathon board meeting to address the issues that PBS had identified as most troublesome. They arranged to meet with employees at several different levels in order to hear and address the most common concerns. They believed it was important to provide a formal avenue for these employees to express their fears and reservations.

The ABB team presented a new proposal within a few days. A new board meeting was scheduled in which a decision would be made.

PBS (B): The ABB PBS Joint Venture in Operation

The PBS board meeting to make the decision whether to accept the ABB proposal for a joint venture lasted 18 hours. In the end, the PBS board voted in favor and the joint venture was agreed. Several legal and contractual issues were quickly resolved, and the deal was signed in late December 1992.

Structure and Organization

ABB První Brněnská Strojíma Brno, Ltd. (ABB PBS) was a joint venture in which ABB had a 67% stake and PBS a.s. had a 33% stake. The PBS share was determined nominally by the value of the land, plant and equipment, employees, and goodwill. ABB contributed cash and specified technologies, and assumed some of the debt of PBS. The new company started operations on April 15, 1993.

The ABB PBS company was a joint venture in its formal structure and governance. PBS a.s. had seats on the board, had part ownership, and was a supplier to the joint venture. The core operations of PBS a.s. were its Brno-based power generation business, its experience with turnkey operations, and its engineering and manufacturing capabilities with its customer base of installed equipment. The joint venture included the turnkey power plant business, boilers, and turbines (but not turbochargers). All of the PBS facilities in Brno and the outlying plant in Mikulov that made turbine blades went into the joint venture (refer to Exhibit 5). In sum, about 4,000 employees from PBS a.s. went to the joint venture; about 3,400 remained in PBS a.s. About 80% of the revenue of PBS a.s. became part of the joint venture.

Profit was to be divided in 2/3–1/3 shares according to ownership when it was earned and distributed; initial plans called for reinvestment of all profits and no dividends paid out to corporate parents.

ABB PBS was organized by product lines: power plants, turbines, boilers, and external services (the latter was added in 1995). Centralized functions such as marketing, finance, human resources, quality control, and information systems reported vertically to the general director and were matrixed horizontally with the business units or product divisions. The internal service division (maintenance) served the four product divisions. Each product division also had some of the same functions (Exhibit 7).

ABB PBS was assigned geographic regions as its market territories by the ABB power generation segment and used the ABB selling network in these territories. Other ABB companies in the same lines of business had other territories, so head-to-head competition among ABB sister companies for the same customers was minimized.

The ABB regional selling network assisted ABB PBS to identify business opportunities. ABB PBS was the prime contractor for projects that were obtained. For turbines and boilers that were not part of a turnkey project, or in cases in which another ABB company was the primary contractor, ABB PBS participated as a subcontractor. ABB PBS had its own vice president for export sales and an export sales force for direct selling as well as selling in cooperation with the ABB regional network.

In the domestic market, ABB PBS continued to use its own sales force and customer contacts. There were two domestic competitors, Škoda Turbiny (a company in the Škoda Koncern) and Vitkovice, whose principal business was steel.

Business Results

Financial Performance

Business for the joint venture in its first two full years was good in most aspects. Orders received in 1994, the first full year of the joint venture's operation, were the highest in the history of PBS. Orders received in 1995 increased 7% over 1994 in nominal terms. Revenues for 1995 were 2 1/2 times those in 1994 (Exhibit 8). The company was profitable in 1995 and ahead of 1994's results with a rate of return on assets of 2.3% and a rate of return on sales of 4.5% (Exhibit 9).

The 1995 results showed substantial progress toward meeting the joint venture's strategic goals adopted in 1994 as part of a five-year plan. One of the goals was that exports should account for half of total orders by 1999. (Exports had accounted for more than a quarter of the PBS business before 1989, but most of this business disappeared when the Soviet Union collapsed.) In 1995 exports increased as a share of total orders to 28%, up from 16% the year before.

The external service business, organized and functioning as a separate business for the first time in 1995, did not meet expectations. It accounted for 5% of all orders and revenues in 1995, below the 10% goal set for it. The retrofitting business, which was expected to be a major part of the service business, was disappointing for ABB PBS, partly because many other small companies began to provide this service in 1994 (including some started by former PBS employees who took their knowledge of PBS-built power plants with them). However, ABB PBS managers hoped that as the company introduced new technologies, these former employees would gradually lose the ability to perform these services and that the retrofit and repair service business would return to ABB PBS.

ABB PBS dominated the Czech boiler business with 70% of the Czech market in 1995, but managers expected this share to go down in the future as new domestic and foreign competitors appeared. Furthermore, the West European boiler market was actually declining because environmental laws caused a surge of retrofitting to occur in the mid-1980s, leaving less business in the 1990s. Accordingly, ABB PBS boiler orders were flat in 1995.

Top managers at ABB PBS regarded business results to date as respectable, but they were not satisfied with the company's performance. Cash flow was not as good as expected. Cost reduction had to go further.

EXHIBIT 7   ABB PBS Organizational Chart in 1995

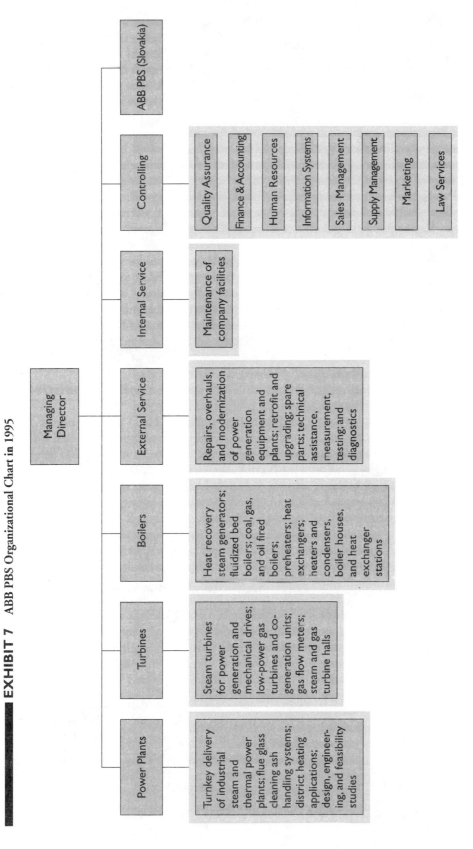

Source: ABB PBS Annual Report 1995.

EXHIBIT 8   Orders and Revenues for ABB PBS Businesses in 1994 and 1995

Business	1994 Kč million	1994 % of total	1995 Kč million	1995 % of total
Power plants				
Revenue	490	23	3,062	52
Orders	3,230	49	3,687	47
Turbines				
Revenue	707	34	1,118	19
Orders	938	14	1,389	18
Boilers				
Revenue	900	43	1,353	23
Orders	2,439	37	2,452	31
Services	(not reported			
Revenue	separately in		314	5
Orders	1994)		381	5
Total	2,097	100	5,847	100
	6,607	100	7,909	100

Notes: Kč are in nominal terms. The sum of revenues and orders across businesses in this table exceeds the total revenue and orders figures reported in the income statement data in Exhibit 9; the percent distributions in this table are figured on the sum of revenues and orders in this table.
Source: ABB První Brněnská Strojíma s.r.o., *1995 Business Report* and *1994 Business Report.*

"The more we succeed, the more we see our shortcomings," said one official.

Restructuring

The first round of restructuring was largely completed in 1995, the last year of the three-year restructuring plan. Plant logistics, information systems, and other physical capital improvements were in place. The restructuring included:

- Renovating and reconstructing workshops and engineering facilities
- Achieving ISO 9001 for all four ABB PBS divisions (awarded in 1995)
- Transfer of technology from ABB (this was an ongoing project)
- Installation of an information system
- Management training, especially in total quality assurance and the English language
- Implementing a project management approach

A notable achievement of importance to top management in 1995 was a 50% increase in labor productivity, measured as value added per payroll crown. However, in the future ABB PBS expected its wage rates to go up faster than West European wage rates

(Czech wages were increasing about 15% per year), so it would be difficult to maintain the ABB PBS unit cost advantage over West European unit cost.

The Technology Role for ABB PBS

The joint venture was expected from the beginning to play an important role in technology development for part of ABB's power generation business worldwide. PBS a.s. had engineering capability in coal-fired steam boilers, and that capability was expected to be especially useful to ABB as more countries became concerned about air quality. (When asked if PBS really did have leading technology here, a boiler engineering manager remarked, "Of course we do. We burn so much dirty coal in this country, we have to have better technology.")

However, the envisioned technology leadership role for ABB PBS had not been realized by mid-1996. Richard Kuba, the ABB PBS managing director, realized the slowness with which the technology role was being fulfilled, and he offered his interpretation of events:

> ABB did not promise to make the joint venture its steam boiler technology leader. The main point we wanted to achieve in the joint venture agreement was for ABB PBS to be recognized as a full-fledged company, not just a factory. . . . We were slowed down on our technology plans

EXHIBIT 9 Selected Income Statement, Balance Sheet, and Other Operating Data for ABB PBS, 1994 and 1995 (Kč million current)

Variable	1994	1995
Revenue	1,999	5,015
Orders received	6,208	7,088
R & D expenditure	29	64
Investment	435	388
Total assets	5,115	9,524
Fixed assets	1,773	2,186
Trade receivables	451	509
Trade payables	197	817
Bank loans	690	710
Equity	1,130	1,110
Exports (percent of orders)	16%	28%
Employees (number)	3,600	3,235
Labor productivity (value added/salaries)*	Kč 109/Kč	Kč 163/Kč

Note:
* Value added is revenue minus purchased inputs. The labor productivity figures are not meaningful as absolute numbers but rather are used for overtime comparisons.
Sources: ABB První Brněnská Strojíma s.r.o., *1995 Business Report* and *1994 Business Report.*

because we had a problem keeping our good, young engineers. The annual employee turnover rate for companies in the Czech Republic is 15 or 20 percent, and the unemployment rate is zero. Our engineers have many other good entrepreneurial opportunities. Now we've begun to stabilize our engineering workforce. The restructuring helped. We have better equipment and a cleaner and safer work environment. . . . We also had another problem, which is a good problem to have. The domestic power plant business turned out to be better than we expected, so just meeting the needs of our regular customers forced some postponement of new technology initiatives.

ABB PBS had benefited technologically from its relationship with ABB. One example was the development of a new steam turbine line. This project was a cooperative effort among ABB PBS and two other ABB companies, one in Sweden and one in Germany. Nevertheless, technology transfer was not the most important early benefit of the ABB relationship. Rather, one of the most important gains was the opportunity to benchmark the joint venture's performance against other established Western ABB companies on variables such as productivity, inventory, and receivables.

Management Issues

The toughest problems that ABB PBS faced in the early years of the joint venture were management issues. There were two: How to relate to ABB sister companies in other countries and how to transform the human capital of the company.

Relationships with Other ABB Companies

Managing a joint venture company was always difficult, and joining a global corporation compounded the start-up challenges. The Czech managers at ABB PBS had to learn fast. One set of problems arose from the relationship of ABB PBS to its ABB sister companies. Richard Kuba and his colleagues were accustomed to working together with other companies on big projects; before the Velvet Revolution, PBS worked with other companies in the Škoda group. But ABB was different. Cooperation coexisted with competition, and that was outside Kuba's experience. Sibling rivalry among companies was very much a fact of business life, he discovered. Kuba related an unhappy episode about his company's unfamiliarity with these business relationships. He said:

> We underestimated the cultural differences between Czechs and other West European people. We have to learn how to say "no." We have to be better in claim management. We have to fight more in order to succeed in this environment.

This fact of corporate life was confirmed by Erik Fougner, the ABB country manager in the Czech Republic, who also noted that excess capacity in Europe caused the older ABB companies to be particularly anxious about the arrival of the Czech newcomer. Some were concerned that there would not be room for three ABB power generation industry companies in Europe in the future.

Human Capital Transformation

The physical and organizational restructuring of ABB PBS was nearly completed by 1996. The transformation of the thinking and behavior of employees had just begun. The ways that were adaptive, or at least tolerated, under central planning would not succeed in a competitive market economy. Changing employees' "mentality"—the term used by Czech managers—was human capital restructuring. It was proving very difficult to do, and it was going very slowly.

In several respects, ABB PBS was nicely positioned to accomplish human capital restructuring. The top management of the joint venture was stable; it was thoroughly Czech but with a keen awareness of the mentality issues; and the ABB parent company tried to offer assistance in a variety of ways. Czech management was supported by two or three expatriates taking non-executive positions in project management, supply management, and workshop planning.

The ABB PBS managers believed a background of knowledge of local history, culture, and business practices was essential. These Czech managers, as in most Czech companies, knew they had to change the attitudes and behaviors of their employees. Richard Kuba said,

> It is easy to change the structure of the company, and it is easy to change the facilities, but it is not easy to change people's minds. . . . Employees don't yet understand the consequences of their actions. They don't take responsibility. There is low unemployment so they can leave and get a less stressful job instead of taking responsibility here.

ABB PBS had never laid off any employees for lack of work. Managers appreciated the good reputation this brought the company, but they also wondered if it dampened employees' motivation to work hard. Without the threat of layoff, would managers' human resource initiatives be followed?

Fougner, a Norwegian located in Prague since 1992, saw the same "mentality" problem:

> This is a bigger challenge than I thought it would be. The first level of change in Czech companies comes easily. To make nice new offices and new factory layouts is quite simple. But the transfer of real human resource learning is slow. . . . Responsibility and initiative are poor because it was not rewarded for two generations in these formerly centrally planned economies. Under central planning, you were given a task, you did it, and nothing bad would happen to you. The tasks themselves were compartmentalized—I did mine and you did yours. I did my duty so I'm okay. Even managers did not see the whole picture and could not take responsibility for it. The functional organization of companies [with the archetypal "functional chimneys"] made it worse.

What could be done? The company took three approaches. At the corporate level, ABB PBS tried to instill a sense of mission. The annual report for 1995 noted the efforts of top management to find agreement on corporate goals and values in order to strengthen employee identification with the company.

ABB, the parent company, tried to assist, but did not want to send too many expatriates to ABB PBS. Rather, local managers had to bring about the mentality changes themselves. ABB loaned some of the people from its internal consulting unit to the joint venture on a part-time basis. Their job was to train the (local) trainers and to sit beside the production and engineering managers and supervisors and work through attitude change material with them. Line managers were the ones who would implement the human capital restructuring, not personnel managers.

The compensation system was the third line of attack. Before the Velvet Revolution, factory-worker pay at PBS was based on a piece rate system that was surprisingly common in the Czech Republic. However, it was badly manipulated so that it did not motivate workers to raise output. Real or imagined equipment problems or shortages of parts—both of which occurred frequently—would excuse workers from meeting desired rates of output, or workers would stockpile output and then slack off. The system fostered the attitude among some workers that "you get a wage to show up, and anything extra you do gets you extra pay." This attitude reflected working conditions under communism where wages were an entitlement rather than a payment for labor services rendered.

ABB PBS introduced a new incentive pay scheme that was not without its problems. Employees were accustomed to stability and predictability in earnings. Another problem was that the time horizon for the incentive pay was too long—year-long profit-sharing schemes were too distant for production workers because they could not see the link between their performance and their reward that far ahead. The scheme was modified in 1996 to reintroduce some smaller discretionary bonuses that were granted when the bonus-worthy work took place.

The Future

The ABB PBS joint venture was only three years old in the spring of 1996. By that time, the legal privatization of industry in the Czech Republic was essentially completed. The first five years of the transition from central planning to market economy for Czech companies was over. This meant that some of the most extreme external stresses on companies, such as loss of markets and lack of finance, were behind them. The Czech economy appeared to be strong and growing (Exhibit 10).

By 1996, most of the major restructuring of ABB PBS was completed. Most of the easier internal changes had been made. Plant and equipment had been improved, and product quality was in good shape. Richard Kuba and his colleagues had accomplished a lot, but they were not satisfied. Some of the hard

EXHIBIT 10 Economic Conditions in Czech Republic, 1993–1995

Variable	1993	1994	1995
Gross domestic product, real % change	−0.9	2.6	4.6
Industrial production, real % change	−5.3	2.3	9.0
Consumer price inflation, %	20.8	10.0	8.9
Interest rate, %	14.1	13.1	12.8
Exchange rate, Kč/$, annual average	29.3	28.8	26.3
Unemployment rate, %	3.5	3.2	3.0

Sources: Economist Intelligence Unit, *Country Report: Czech Republich and Slovakia,* 1st Quarter 1996; 2nd Quarter 1994. International Monetary Fund, *International Financial Statistics,* March 1996, January 1994. Washington DC, 1996, 1994.

changes were yet to be made, and the outlook for the company was mixed.

Doing business in competitive Western markets was much more rugged than Kuba expected. Financial results were sufficient given the difficult business conditions the company faced, but they were not good enough for a mature market economy. Kuba knew there was overcapacity in the industry worldwide. There were tons of relatively small companies like his, and some of them would not survive. Belonging to the ABB network had advantages of course, but it also brought problems. Cooperation with ABB sister companies in marketing and technology was mirrored by competition and sibling rivalry with companies from cultures with which Kuba and his colleagues were unfamiliar. Internally, the transformation of ABB PBS's considerable human capital required renewed focus. Kuba could not rest easily yet.

Case 6: Colgate-Palmolive Company

The Colgate-Palmolive Company represented a textbook case on how to succeed in developing countries. A combination of marketing strategy and iron-fisted discipline had kept the company growing despite fierce competition. For example, in 1995, a full 50% of its sales and profits came from the developing world, where population and earnings capacity were growing faster than elsewhere in the world, with the consumption of personal care products rising at a furious rate.

Despite its superb performance in the past, Colgate-Palmolive's charismatic CEO, Reuben Mark, was fully conscious of the emerging competition in the developing world, where almost one billion people were expected to come in the market within the next decade. To continue to excel in that market, he must revamp the company's marketing strategy.

Colgate's Marketing Razzmatazz

The scene was a makeshift stage in a small village that was really not much more than a clearing in the dense Papua New Guinea jungle. A troupe of traveling performers was acting out live commercials. "Up and down. Round and round. That's the way to brush your teeth," they sang, while hopping up and down and twirling around the stage.

This unusual way was the Colgate-Palmolive Company's method of educating consumers and providing them with product samples. "In 1900, we were going into New York City schools and teaching kids how to brush their teeth," said Colgate's John Steel, a genial Australian who was Colgate's senior vice president for global marketing and sales. "We have guidelines on sampling, selling, and down-market distribution, but it takes local knowledge to execute them efficiently."

In the past decade, Colgate's global sales had risen 140%, from a bit under $3.5 billion to more than $8.36 billion. This at a time when erstwhile competitors such as Anglo-Dutch Unilever, Germany's Henkel, France's L'Oréal, and the United States' Procter and Gamble, all much larger companies, had been pushing aggressively into Colgate's developing world markets. To achieve that kind of growth without sacrificing profits (Colgate's operating profits consistently hover at about 13% of sales) in the face of such fierce opposition had taken a unique marketing razzmatazz with the single aim of making Colgate's global brands even more powerful. "Our equity is in our brand franchises worldwide," declares

Mark. "Our earnings capacity is based entirely on the value of our brands."

How do you measure something as intangible as brand value? One way is to look at how deeply embedded a product is in the minds of the consumers. Another way to quantify brand value is by measuring how much money a company must spend over time on advertising to generate a given payback in sales. The less it needs to spend, the more likely that consumers are firmly wedded to its brand. According to *Brandweek* magazine's "Superbrands '96" issue, in merchandise categories where Colgate was one of the top five brands, the company consistently got a greater dollar return on its U.S. advertising expenditures than its competitors.

Take toothpaste for instance. Part of Colgate's oral care group, it was the only area where Colgate had absolute global leadership. While Procter & Gamble's Crest was number one in sales inside the United States to Colgate's number two, Colgate got $7.30 in sales for every dollar spent on advertising, versus $5.70 for Crest. That was a 28% greater return. In bath soap, Colgate did even better. Unilever's market-leading Dove generated $10.12 in U.S. sales for every dollar of advertising. But each ad dollar spent promoting Colgate's fifth-place Irish Spring generated a whopping $23.91 in sales, a difference of more than 130%.

If there was one reason why Colgate was able to generate such consistent success, it was because the company had learned how to stay tightly focused on marketing strategies and objectives. It did this with what was called a bundle book. To an outsider, a bundle book would look like an ordinary white loose-leaf binder. In reality, the bundle book was everything that Colgate knew about any given brand. Each one contained, down to the smallest details, all that one of Colgate's country or regional managers needed to know about how to effectively market a particular product, including the product attributes, its formulas, ingredient sourcing information, market research, pricing positions, graphics, even advertising, public relations, and point-of-sale materials.

With a bundle book, a Colgate manager in any one of the 206 countries and territories where Colgate sold products could project the Colgate brand exactly like one of his or her counterparts. "As the smallest among our major competitors," remarked Steel, "we are trying to make sure that we maximize our resources. By having very tightly controlled brands, we can leverage across borders rapidly."

What he meant was that, by using a highly centralized management style, Colgate could introduce new products at an extremely rapid clip, which was critical in a world where markets were fragmenting into smaller and smaller niches. "Ten years ago, we had two variants of toothpaste and so did Procter in the United States," noted Steel, who had worked for Colgate since 1949. "Today, we have about 15 variants. We now get about one-third of our sales from products that weren't on the market five years ago." And Steel credited Colgate's ability to rapidly launch new products to its disciplined approach to marketing, which often meant "sending a bundle book out via e-mail so that it reaches all of our operations overnight if we have an important issue to get to them."

Competition

Colgate had been selling products in Latin America, Asia Pacific, and Europe since the 1920s, so keeping its brands strong was relatively easy when it was the only major game in town. But since the late 1980s, companies such as Procter & Gamble, Unilever, and Henkel had more aggressively gone after Colgate-dominated markets, especially in the Third World. P&G was coming after them in a lot of product categories in Third World countries now, and they weren't before. The reason was that growth opportunities in most product categories were much greater outside the United States and Western Europe.

But a strong, long-established market leadership won't keep a company from worrying much when a much larger competitor begins to muscle in. To put it in the proper perspective, Colgate had been growing steadily for more than a decade. But the company's $8 billion in worldwide sales for 1995, while a 10% increase over 1994, was small potatoes when compared to Procter & Gamble's 1995 sales of $33 billion and Unilever's almost $50 billion. Procter & Gamble's diaper business overseas was probably as large as Colgate's entire international operations, and it was probably growing as fast as Colgate's entire business.

So the task facing Colgate was how to prosper in the face of competition from some of the largest consumer products companies in the world. Colgate's solution was two pronged. First, the company decided to focus on five core business areas—oral care, personal care, household surface care, fabric care, and pet nutrition. "We tried being all things to all people and it didn't work," explained Steel. So beginning in the late 1970s and ending about a decade later, Colgate sold off many businesses, including Hebrew National Foods and Riviana Rice, and now was unwavering in its focus on core businesses.

The second thing Colgate did was develop its bundle book strategy as a means of communicating its plans and ensuring sales consistency around the world. The first bundle book was done in 1985 for Colgate tartar control toothpaste. Since then, the company had produced several hundred for new products developed internally as well as those it had purchased, even for entire product categories such as bleach and baby care.

Global Marketing

Colgate realized that to be a major player it had to have global brands and it had to market globally.

But what makes a brand global? Product consistency and a uniform communications message. Currently, Colgate had about 20 products that it sold in 50 major markets, its dividing line between a regional and a global brand. Six of them—Colgate toothpaste, Palmolive soap, Mennen deodorant, Ajax household cleaners, Hills pet foods, and StaSoft fabric softener (also sold under the brand names Soupline and Suavitel)—account for two-thirds of the company's sales. Colgate also had a large number of regional brands, such as Protex antibacterial soap, Axion dishwashing liquid, and Softsoap, which were starting to go global.

"We can leverage our technology better if we have global and not regional businesses," opined Steel.

As the number of its global brands increased, Colgate was experiencing efficiencies in other areas as well. Recently, the company consolidated all of its advertising at Young & Rubicam, one of the world's largest ad agencies. While Y&R was headquartered in New York City, only a few blocks away from Colgate, much of Colgate's advertising was developed by Y&R offices outside the United States. Protex creative came from Latin America, the fabric softener ads were developed in France, and the campaign for Colgate Total, a recent, globally launched antibacterial toothpaste, was created in Italy.

Going global also meant that Colgate had to price and size its products according to the requirements of each market. To ensure that consumers in the developing world could buy Colgate's products, the company had instituted what Steel called "Trigger-point marketing." The idea was to provide the consumer with sophisticated products at affordable prices. "We have to look at the economics of these countries and then market our products at those levels," noted Steel. "Trigger-point marketing lets us get products like toothpaste, fabric softener, or shampoo to emerging consumers. We're able to offer them one-shot sachets of shampoo or bleach they can then dilute."

So far, it was all paying off handsomely for Colgate-Palmolive. What changes, if any, the company should introduce in its marketing strategy to continue to be effective in the future was the question that Mark and Steel must think out.

Case 7: **Currency Concepts International**[*]

Dr. Karen Anderson, Manager of Planning for Century Bank of Los Angeles, settled down for an unexpected evening of work in her small beach apartment. It seemed that every research project Century had commissioned in the last year had been completed during her ten-day trip to Taiwan. She had brought three research reports home that evening to try to catch up before meeting with the banks' Executive Planning Committee the next day.

* This case is printed with the permission of the author, Grady D. Bruce of the California State University, Fullerton.

Possibly because the currency-exchange facilities had been closed at the Taiwan Airport when she first arrived, Dr. Anderson's attention turned first to a report on a project currently under consideration by one of Century Bank's wholly owned subsidiaries, Currency Concepts International (CCI). The project concerned the manufacture and installation of currency-exchange automatic teller machines (ATMs) in major foreign airports.

CCI had been responsible for the development of Century Bank's very popular ATM ("money machine"), now installed in numerous branches of the bank, as well as in its main location in downtown Los Angeles. The current project was a small part of CCI and Century Bank's plan to expand electronic banking services worldwide.

As she started to review the marketing research effort of Information Resources, Inc., she wondered what she would be able to recommend to the Executive Planning Committee the next day regarding the currency-exchange project. She liked her recommendations to be backed by solid evidence, and she looked forward to reviewing results of the research performed to date.

Activities of Information Resources, Inc.

Personnel of Information Resources, Inc., had decided to follow three different approaches in investigating the problem presented to them: (1) review secondary statistical data; (2) interview companies that currently engage in currency exchange; and (3) conduct an exploratory consumer survey of a convenience sample.

Secondary Data

The review of secondary data had three objectives:

1. To determine whether the number of persons flying abroad constitutes a market potentially large enough to merit automated currency exchange
2. To isolate any trends in the numbers of people flying abroad
3. To determine whether the amount of money that these travelers spend abroad is sizable enough to provide a potential market for automated currency exchange.

The U.S. Department of Transportation monitors the number of people traveling from U.S. airports to foreign airports. These statistics are maintained and categorized as follows: citizen and noncitizen passengers, and civilian and military passengers. Since this study was concerned only with Americans who travel abroad, only citizen categories were considered. Furthermore, since American military flights do not utilize the same foreign airport facilities as civilian passenger flights, the military category was also excluded. The prospect that non-Americans might also use these facilities causes the statistics to be somewhat conservative. The figures, for 1978, were summed for each foreign airport; the results

EXHIBIT 1 American Citizens Flying Abroad in 1978 to Foreign Ports of Entry with Over 25,000 Arrivals

Europe	3,725,952
Caribbean	1,930,756
Central America	1,356,496
South America	301,347
Far East	516,861
Oceania	133,584

Note: Included in these area totals are all ports of entry that receive more than 25,000 passengers annually (68 per day). Ports of entry with lower through-put rate were excluded.
Source: Based on data provided in U.S. Department of Transportation, *United States International Air Travel Statistics,* 1978, Washington, D.C.

EXHIBIT 2 Most Frequented Foreign Ports of Entry from All American Ports

Port	Passengers
1. London, England	1,420,285
2. Mexico City, Mexico	641,054
3. Frankfurt, Germany	446,166
4. Hamilton, Bermuda	378,897
5. Nassau, Bahamas	361,791
6. Tokyo, Japan	320,827
7. Freeport, Bahamas	309,288
8. Paris, France	295,823
9. Rome, Italy	272,186
10. Acapulco, Mexico	226,120

Source: Based on data provided in U.S. Department of Transportation, *United States International Air Travel Statistics,* 1978, Washington, D.C.

by geographical area are shown in Exhibit 1. The top ten gateway cities from all American ports are shown in Exhibit 2.

The second objective, to determine any growth trends in air travel, was addressed by studying the number of Americans flying abroad in the last five years. Exhibit 3 shows the number of American travelers flying to various geographic areas and the associated growth rates in each of those areas. Europe, clearly, has the greatest number of travelers; and, although it did not show the greatest percentage growth in 1978, it does have the largest growth in absolute numbers. Generally, growth rates in overseas air travel have been good for the last four years; at this time, these trends appear to be positive from the standpoint of a potential market.

EXHIBIT 3 Growth in Number of Americans Flying Abroad 1974–1978 (Thousands)

	1974	% Change	1975	% Change	1976	% Change	1977	% Change	1978
European and Mediterranean	3,325	(4.2)	3,185	10.6	3,523	11.3	3,920	5.2	4,105
Western Europe	3,118	(4.1)	2,990	10.0	3,245	6.9	3,663	6.9	3,914
Caribbean and Central America	2,147	(3.8)	2,065	6.6	2,201	—	2,203	7.4	2,365
South America	423	5.7	447	(2.5)	436	10.8	483	6.6	515
Other Areas	572	14.9	657	12.2	737	6.4	784	2.7	805
Total	9,585	8.5	9,344	36.9	10,142	39.7	11,053	28.8	11,704

Source: U.S. Department of Commerce, *Survey of Current Business,* June 1979, Washington, D.C.

EXHIBIT 4 Per Capita Spending by Americans Traveling Abroad 1974–1978

	1974	% Change	1975	% Change	1976	% Change	1977	% Change	1978
Europe	542	11.1	602	1.3	610	—	612	17.2	717
Caribbean and Central America	319	19.4	381	(6.6)	356	—	359	4.5	375
South America	494	9.5	541	(1.7)	532	(1.1)	526	12.9	594
Other Areas	786	1.9	802	0.9	809	3.7	839	20.0	1,007
All Areas	489	12.6	547	—	545	1.8	555	14.6	635

Source: U.S. Department of Commerce, *Survey of Current Business,* June 1979, Washington, D.C.

However, there are also some potential problems on the horizon. As the world's energy situation increasingly worsens, there is the possibility of significant decreases in international travel.

In order to address the third objective, whether the amount of money spent by American travelers abroad constitutes a potential market, per capita spending was examined. Exhibit 4 shows per capita spending, by geographic area, for the last five years as well as yearly percentages of growth. The category that includes the Far East, "other areas," shows the highest per capita spending. This may be the result of the relatively low prices found in the Far East.

Europe shows the second-highest figures for per capita spending; this area also exhibited strong growth in the last year. These figures indicate that Americans are spending increasing amounts of money abroad; even when inflation is taken consideration, these figures are positive.

Information Resources, Inc. concluded, therefore, that Europe holds the greatest market potential for introduction of the new system. As Dick Knowlton, co-ordinator of the research team, said, "Not only are all of the statistics for Europe high, but the short geographic distances between countries can be expected to provide a good deal of intra-area travel."

Company Interviews

In an attempt to better understand the current operations of currency exchange in airports, four major firms engaged in these activities were contacted. While some firms were naturally reluctant to provide information on some areas of their operations, several were quite cooperative. These firms, and a number of knowledgeable individuals whose names surfaced in initial interviews, provided the information that follows.

In both New York and Los Angeles, there was only one bank engaged in airport currency exchange: Deak-Perera. American Express, Bank of America, and Citibank, as well as Deak-Perera, were engaged in airport currency exchange in a variety of foreign locations. Approval of permits to engage in airport currency exchange activity rests with the municipal body that governs the airport and is highly controlled. It appears that foreign currency exchange was a highly profitable venture. Banks make most of their profits on the spread in exchange rates, which are posted daily.

Both Citibank and Bank of America indicated that they attempt to ensure their facilities' availability to all flights. The more profitable flights were found to be those that were regularly scheduled, rather than chartered. The person most likely to use the facilities was the vacationer rather than the businessperson. Neither bank could give an exact figure for the average transaction size; estimates ranged from $85 to $100.

It was the opinion of bank employees, who dealt with travelers on a daily basis, that the average traveler was somewhat uncomfortable changing money in a foreign country. They also believed it to be particularly helpful if clerks at the exchange counter converse with travelers in their own language. A number of years ago Deak attempted to use a type of vending machine to dispense money at Kennedy Airport. This venture failed; industry observers felt that absence of human conversation and assurance contributed to its lack of success.

Most of the exchanges perform the same types of services, including the sale of foreign currency and the sale of travelers checks. The actual brand of travelers checks sold varies with the vendors.

American Express has recently placed automated travelers check dispensers in various American airports. This service is available to American Express card holders and the only charge is 1% of the face value of the purchased checks; the purchase is charged directly to the customer's checking account. As yet, the machines have not enjoyed a great deal of use, although American Express has been successful in enrolling its customers as potential users.

Methods of payment for currency purchases are similar at all exchanges. Accepted forms of payment include actual cash, travelers checks, cashier checks drawn on local banks, and Master Charge or Visa cards. When a credit card is used to pay for currency purchase, there is a service charge added to the customer's bill, as with any cash advance.

Traveler Interviews

To supplement and complement the statistical foundation gained by reviewing secondary data sources, the consumer interview portion of the study was purposefully designed to elicit qualitative information about travelers' feelings toward current and future forms of exchanging currency. Approximately 60 American travelers were interviewed at both the San Francisco and Los Angeles International Airports, due to the accessibility of these locations to Information Resources' sole location. An unstructured, undisguised questionnaire was developed to assist in channeling the interview toward specific topics (see Appendix at the end of this case). Questions were not fixed and the question order was dependent on the respondent's answers. Basically, the guide served to force the interview conversation around the central foreign currency exchange theme. The interviews were conducted primarily in the arrival/departure lobbies of international carriers and spanned four weeks, beginning in mid-December 1979. A deliberate attempt was made to include as many arriving as departing passengers to neutralize the effect of increasing holiday traffic. Additionally, to reduce interviewer bias, three different interviewers were used. Interviews were intentionally kept informal. And Dick Knowlton cautioned the interviewers to remain objective and "not let your excitement over the product concept spill over into the interview and bias the responses."

The interviews were divided almost evenly between those who favored the concept and those who did not. Those who did perceive value in the concept tended also to support other innovations such as the automated teller machine and charging foreign currency on credit cards. Those who would not use the currency exchange terminals wanted more human interaction and generally did not favor automation in any form; a fair proportion also had previous problems exchanging foreign currency. However, even those who did not favor the currency exchange idea did seem to prefer the system of having 24-hour availability of the machines, and of using credit cards to get cash under emergency situations.

The respondents represent a diverse group of individuals ranging in age from 18 to 80 years, holding such different positions as oil executive, photographer, homemaker, and customs officer. Primarily bound for Europe, Canada, and Mexico, the interviewees were mainly split between pleasure-seekers and those on business. Only three individuals interviewed were part of tour groups, and of these three, only one had previously traveled abroad. The majority of the others had been out of the United States before and had exchanged currency in at least one other country. Many had exchanged currency in remote parts of the world, including Morocco, Brazil, Australia, Japan, Tanzania, and Russia. Only five individuals had not exchanged money in airports at one time or another. The majority had obtained foreign currency in airports and exchanged money in airports primarily in small denominations for use in taxi cab fares, bus fares, phones, and airport gift shops, as well as for food, tips, and drinks. Most respondents agreed a prime motive for exchanging money in airports was the security of having local currency.

Exchanging currency can become a trying ordeal for some individuals. They fear being cheated on the exchange rate; they cannot convert the foreign currency into tangible concepts (for example, "How many yen should a loaf of bread cost?"); they dislike lines and associated red tape; and many cannot understand the rates as posted in percentages. Most individuals exchange money in airports, hotels, or banks, but sometimes there are no convenient facilities at all for exchanging currency.

People like to deal with well-known bank branches, especially in airports, because they feel more confident about the rate they are receiving. However, major fears of individuals are that many exchange personnel will not understand English and that they will be cheated in the transaction. Furthermore, a few people mentioned poor documentation when they exchange currency in foreign airports.

The travelers were divided as to whether they exchange currency before or after they arrive in the foreign country, but a few said that the decision depended on what country they were entering. If a currency, such as English pounds, could easily be obtained from a local bank before leaving the United States, they were more likely to exchange before leaving. However, in no case would the traveler arrange for currency beyond a week in advance. Most preferred to obtain the foreign currency on relatively short notice—fewer than three days before the trip. Of the individuals on tours, none planned to obtain currency in the foreign airport. Apparently, the tour guide had previously arranged for the necessary transportation from the airport to the hotels, and there would be only enough time to gather one's luggage and find the bus before it would depart, leaving no time to enjoy the facilities of the airport which required foreign currency. All three tour individuals did mention that they planned to obtain foreign currency once they arrived at the hotel. All individuals mentioned that they had secured their own foreign currency, but a few of the wives who were traveling with their husbands conceded that their spouses usually converted the currency in the foreign airport.

Very few of the interviewees had actually used an automated teller machine, but the majority had heard of or seen the teller machines on television. Those who had used the automated machines preferred their convenience and were generally satisfied with the terminal's performance. Many of those who had not used the automated teller machines mistrusted the machine and possible loss of control over their finances. Concerns about security and problems with the machines breaking down were also expressed. One woman described the teller machines as being "convenient, but cold." Apparently, many people prefer having human interaction when their money is concerned.

As noted earlier, approximately 30 of the respondents would favor the exchange terminals over their normal airport currency exchange routine, while the same number would have nothing to do with the machines. However, the majority of potential users qualified their use by such features as competitive rates, knowing the precise charges, or knowing they could get help if something went wrong. Individuals who indicated no preference were included in the favorable category, simply because they would not refuse to try the machine. Most of the indifferent people seemed to indicate they would try such a machine if some type of introductory promotional offer was included, such as travel information, currency tips, or a better rate.

With virtual unanimity, the respondents felt that 24-hour availability made the currency exchange machines more attractive, yet that alone would not persuade the dissenters to use the terminals. Some individuals felt that a machine simply could not give the travel advice that could be obtained at the currency exchange booths.

The opportunity to charge foreign currency against a major credit card, such as Master Charge or Visa, was a definite plus in the minds of most respondents. One individual clearly resented the idea, however, feeling that he would "overspend" if given such a convenient way to obtain cash. Respondents offered a number of suggestions concerning implementations of the product concept and a number of specific product features:

1. Add information about the country.
2. Provide small denominations, and include coins
3. Have it communicate in English
4. Put in travelers checks to get cash
5. Put in cash to get foreign currency
6. Post rates daily
7. Keep rates competitive and post charges
8. Have television screen with person to describe procedure
9. Place the machines in hotels and banks
10. Have a change machine nearby that can convert paper money

11. Place machine near existing currency exchange facilities for convenience when normal lines become long
12. Demonstrate how to use the machine
13. Use all bank credit cards

Appendix: Interview Guide for International Travelers (U.S. Citizens)

These interviews should remain as informal as possible. The object is not to obtain statistically reliable results, but to get ideas that will help to stimulate research. These questions are not fixed; the order, however, is sometimes dependent on answers the respondents give. Introduce yourself

1. Are you going to be traveling to a foreign country? Arriving from a foreign country? A U.S. resident?
2. Where is/was your final destination?
3. Why are you traveling (business, pleasure, a tour)?
4. How often do you travel outside of the United States?
5. Have you ever exchanged currency in a foreign country. (If no, go to #6.) Where? Does anything in particular stand out in your mind when you exchanged currency?
6. Have you ever changed money in an airport? (If no, go to #7.)
7. Where do you plan to exchange currency on this trip?
8. Where do you change money normally?
9. Have you ever had any problems changing currencies? Explain circumstances.
10. Normally, would you change money before entering a country or after you arrive? If before, how long in advance? Where? (Probe.)
11. Are you familiar with automated teller machines that banks are using? (If not, explain.) Have you used one of these machines?
12. What are your feelings toward these machines?
13. If a currency exchange terminal, similar to an automated teller machine, was placed in your destination airport, would you use the machine or follow your normal routine?
14. Would 24-hour availability make the currency exchange machines more attractive? Would you use the terminals at night?
15. None of the currency exchange machines currently exists. What features or services could be provided so that you might choose to use a terminal rather than other currency exchange facilities?
16. If you could charge the foreign currency received to a major credit card, such as Master Charge or Visa, would you be more likely to use the machine?
17. Demographics—age range (visual), occupation, gender. Traveling alone?

Case 8: **Outback Goes International**[*]

In early 1995 Outback Steakhouse enjoyed the position as one of the most successful restaurant chains in the United States. Entrepreneurs Chris Sullivan, Bob Basham, and Tim Gannon, each with more than 20 years' experience in the restaurant industry, started Outback Steakhouse with just two stores in 1988. In 1995 the company was the fastest-growing U.S. steakhouse chain, with over 200 stores throughout the United States.

Outback achieved its phenomenal success in an industry that was widely considered as one of the most competitive in the United States Fully 75% of entrants into the restaurant industry failed within the first year. Outback's strategy was driven by a unique combination of factors atypical of the foodservice industry. As Chairman Chris Sullivan put it, "Outback is all about a lot of different experiences that has been recognized as entrepreneurship." Within six years of commencing operations, Outback was voted as the best steakhouse chain in the country. The company also took top honors, along with the Olive Garden, as America's favorite restaurant. In December of 1994, Outback was awarded *Inc's* prestigious Entrepreneur of the Year award. In 1994 and early 1995 the business press hailed the company as one of the biggest success stories in corporate America in recent years.

In late 1994 Hugh Connerty was appointed president of Outback International. In early 1995 Connerty,

* This case was prepared by Marilyn L. Taylor and Madelyn Gengelbach, University of Missouri at Kansas City; George M Puia, Indiana State University, and Krishnan Ramaya, University of Southern Indiana. It is printed here with their permission.

a highly successful franchisee for Outback, explained the international opportunities facing Outback Steakhouse as it considered its strategy for expansion abroad:

> We have had hundreds of franchise requests from all over the world. [So] I took about two seconds for me to make that decision [to become President of Outback International]. . . . I've met with and talked to other executives who have international divisions. All of them have the same story. At some point in time the light goes off and they say, "Gee we have a great product. Where do we start?" I have traveled quite a bit on holiday. The world is not as big as you think it is. Most companies who have gone global have not used any set strategy.

Despite his optimism, Connerty knew that the choice of targeted markets would be critical. Connerty wondered what strategic and operational changes the company would have to make to assure success in those markets.

History of Outback Steakhouse, Inc.

Chris Sullivan, Bob Basham, and Tim Gannon met in the early 1970s shortly after they graduated from college. The three joined Steak & Ale, a Pillsbury subsidiary and restaurant chain, as management trainees as their first post-college career positions. During the 1980s Sullivan and Basham became successful franchisees of 17 Chili's restaurants in Florida and Georgia with franchise headquarters in Tampa, Florida.[1] Meanwhile Tim Gannon played significant roles in several New Orleans restaurant chains. Sullivan and Basham sold their Chili's franchises in 1987 and used the proceeds to fund Outback, their start-from-scratch entrepreneurial venture. They invited Gannon to join them in Tampa in fall 1987. The trio opened their first two restaurants in Tampa in 1988.

The three entrepreneurs recognized that in-home consumption of meat, especially beef, had declined.[2] Nonetheless, upscale and budget steakhouses were extremely popular. The three concluded that people were cutting in-home red meat consumption, but were still very interested in going out to a restaurant for a good steak. They saw an untapped opportunity between high-priced and budget steakhouses to serve quality steaks at an affordable price.

Using an Australian theme associated with the outdoors and adventure, Outback positioned itself as a place providing not only excellent food but also a cheerful, fun, and comfortable experience. The company's Statement of Principles and Beliefs referred to employees as "Outbackers" and highlighted the importance of hospitality, sharing, quality, fun, and courage.

Catering primarily to the dinner crowd,[3] Outback offered a menu that featured specially seasoned steaks and prime rib. The menu also included chicken, ribs, fish, and pasta entrees in addition to the company's innovative appetizers.[4] CFO Bob Merritt cited Outback's food as a prime reason for the company's success. As he put it:

> One of the important reasons for our success is that we took basic American meat and potatoes and enhanced the flavor so that it fit with the aging population. . . . Just look at what McDonalds and Burger King did in their market segment. They [have] tried to add things to their menu that were more flavorful [for example] McDonalds put the Big Mac on the menu. . . . as people age, they want more flavor. . . . higher flavor profiles. It's not happenstance. It's a science. There's too much money at risk in this business not to know what's going on with customer taste preferences.

The company viewed suppliers as partners in the company's success and was committed to work with suppliers to develop and maintain long-term relationships. Purchasing was dedicated to obtaining the highest quality ingredients and supplies. Indeed, the company was almost fanatical about quality. As Tim Gannon, vice president and the company's chief chef, put it, "We don't tolerate less than the best." One example of the company's quality emphasis was its croutons. Restaurant kitchen staff made the croutons daily on site. The croutons had 17 different seasonings, including fresh garlic and butter. The croutons were cut by hand into irregular shapes so that customers would recognize they were handmade. At about 40% of total costs, Outback had one of the highest food costs in the industry. On Friday and Saturday nights customers waited up to two hours for a table. Most felt that Outback provided exceptional value for the average entrée price of $15 to $16.

Outback focused not only on the productivity and efficiency of "Outbackers" but also their long-term well-being. Executives referred to the company's employee commitment as "tough on results, but kind with people." A typical Outback restaurant staff consisted of a general manager, an assistant manager, and a kitchen manager plus 50 to 70 mostly part-time hourly employees. The company used aptitude tests, psychological profiles, and interviews as part of a the employee selection process. Every applicant interviewed with two managers. The company placed emphasis on creating an entrepreneurial climate where learning and personal growth were strongly emphasized. As Chairman Chris Sullivan explained:

I was given the opportunity to make a lot of mistakes and learn, and we try to do that today. We try to give our people a lot of opportunity to make some mistakes, learn, and go on.

In order to facilitate ease of operations for employees, the company's restaurant design devoted 45% of restaurant floor space to kitchen area. Wait staff were assigned only three tables at any time. Most Outback restaurants were only open 4:30 to 11:30 p.m. daily. Outback's wait staff enjoyed higher income from tips than in restaurants that also served lunch. Restaurant management staff worked 50 to 55 hours per week, in contrast to the 70 or more common in the industry. Company executives felt that the dinner-only concept had led to effective utilization of systems, staff, and management. "Outbackers" reported that they were less worn out working at Outback and that they had more fun than when they worked at other restaurant companies.

Outback executives were proud of their "B-locations (with) A-demographics" location strategy. They deliberately steered clear of high-traffic locations targeted by companies that served a lunch crowd. Until the early 1990s most of the restaurants were leased locations, retrofits of another restaurant location. The emphasis was on choosing locations where Outback's target customer would be in the evening. The overall strategy payoff was clear. In an industry where a sales-to-investment ratio of 1.2-to-1 was considered strong, Outback's restaurants generated $2.10 for every $1 invested in the facility. The average Outback restaurant unit generated $3.4 million in sales.

In 1995 management remained informal. Headquarters were located on the second floor of an unpretentious building near the Tampa airport. There was no middle management—top management selected the joint venture partners and franchisees who reported directly to the president. Franchisees and joint venture partners in turn hired the general managers at each restaurant.

Outback provided ownership opportunities at three levels of organization: at the individual restaurant level, through multiple-store arrangements (joint venture and franchise opportunities), and through a stock ownership plan for every employee. Health insurance was also available to all employees, a benefit not universally available to restaurant industry workers. Outback's restaurant-level general managers' employment and ownership opportunities were atypical in the industry. A restaurant general manager invested $25,000 for a 10% ownership stake in the restaurant, a contract for five years in the same location, a 10% share of the cash flow from the restaurant as a yearly bonus, opportunity for stock options, and a 10% buyout arrangement at the end of five years. Outback store managers typically earned an annual salary and bonus of over $100,000 as compared to an industry average of about $60,000 to $70,000. Outback's management turnover of 5.4% was one of the lowest in its industry, in which the average was 30% to 40%.

Community involvement was strongly encouraged throughout the organization. The corporate office was involved in several nonprofit activities in the Tampa area, and also sponsored major national events such as the Outback Bowl and charity golf tournaments. Each store was involved in community participation and service. For example, the entire proceeds of an open house held just prior to every restaurant opening went to a charity of the store manager's choice.

Early in its history the company had been unable to afford any advertising. Instead, Outback's founders relied on their strong relationships with local media to generate public relations and promotional efforts. One early relationship developed with Nancy Schneid, who had extensive experience in advertising and radio. Schneid later became Outback's first vice president of marketing. Under her direction, the company developed a full-scale national media program that concentrated on television advertising and local billboards. The company avoided couponing and its only printed advertising typically came as part of a package offered by charity or sports events.

Early financing for growth had come from limited partnership investments by family members, close friends, and associates. The three founders' original plan did not call for extensive expansion or franchising. However, in 1990 some friends, disappointed in the performance of several of their Kentucky-based restaurants, asked to franchise the Outback concept. The converted Kentucky stores enjoyed swift success. Additional opportunities with other individuals experienced in the restaurant industry arose in various parts of the country. These multistore arrangements were in the form of franchises or joint ventures. Later in 1990 the company turned to a venture capital firm for financing for a $2.5 million package. About the same time, Bob Merritt joined the company as CFO. Merritt's previous IPO[5] experience helped the company undertake a quick succession of three highly successful public equity offerings. During 1994 the price of the company's stock ranged from $22.63 to a high $32.00. The company's income statements, balance sheets, and a summary of the stock price performance appear as Exhibits 1, 2, and 3, respectively.

EXHIBIT I   Outback Steakhouse, Inc. Consolidated Statements of Income

	Years Ended December 31,		
	1994	1993	1992
Revenues	$451,916,000	$309,749,000	$189,217,000
Cost and Expenses			
Cost of revenues	175,618,000	121,290,000	73,475,000
Labor and other related expenses	95,476,000	65,047,000	37,087,000
Other restaurant operating expenses	93,265,000	64,603,000	43,370,000
General & administrative expenses	16,744,000	12,225,000	9,176,000
(Income) from oper. of unconsol. affl.	(1,269,000)	(333,000)	
	379,834,000	262,832,000	163,108,000
Income From Operations	72,082,000	46,917,000	26,109,000
Non-operating Income (Expense)			
Interest income	512,000	1,544,000	1,428,000
Interest expense	(424,000)	(369,000)	(360,000)
	88,000	1,175,000	1,068,000
Income Before Elimination			
Minority Partners Interest and Income Taxes	72,170,000	48,092,000	27,177,000
Elimination of Minority Partners' Interest	11,276,000	7,378,000	4,094,000
Income Before Provision for Income Taxes	60,894,000	40,714,000	23,083,000
Provision for Income Taxes	21,602,000	13,922,000	6,802,000
Net Income	$39,292,000	$26,792,000	$16,281,000
Earnings Per Common Share	$0.89	$.061	$0.39
Weighted Average Number of			
Common Shares Outstanding	43,997,000	43,738,000	41,504,000
Pro Forma:			
Provision for Income Taxes	22,286,000	15,472,000	8,245,000
Net Income	$38,608,000	$25,242,000	$14,838,000
Earnings Per Common Share	$0.88	$0.58	$0.36

Outback's International Rollout

Outback's management believed that the U.S. market could accommodate at least 550 to 600 Outback steakhouse restaurants. At the rate the company was growing (70 stores annually), Outback would near the U.S. market's saturation within 4 to 5 years. Outback's plans for longer-term growth hinged on a multipronged strategy. The company planned to roll out an additional 300 to 350 Outback stores, expand into the lucrative Italian dining segment through its joint venture with the successful Houston-based Carrabbas Italian Grill, and develop new dining themes.

At year-end 1994 Outback had 164 restaurants in which the company had direct ownership interest. The company had six restaurants which it operated through joint ventures in which the company had a 45% interest. Franchises operated another 44 restaurants. Outback operated the company-owned restaurants as partnerships in which the company was general partner.

The company owned from 81% to 90%. The remainder was owned by the restaurant managers and joint venture partners. The six restaurants operated as joint ventures were also organized as partnerships in which the company owned 50%. The company was responsible for 50% of the costs of these restaurants.

The company organized the joint venture with Carrabbas in early 1993. The company was responsible for 100% of the costs of the new Carrabbas Italian Grills although it owned a 50% share. As of year end 1994 the joint venture operated ten Carrabbas restaurants.

The franchised restaurants generated 0.8% of the company's 1994 revenues as franchise fees. The portion of income attributable to restaurant managers and joint venture partners amounted to $11.3 million of the company's $72.2 million 1994 income.

By late 1994 Outback's management had also begun to consider the potential of non-U.S. markets for the Outback concept. As Chairman Chris Sullivan put it:

EXHIBIT 2   Outback Steakhouse, Inc. Consolidated Balance Sheets

	December 31				
Assets	1994	1993	1992	1991	1990
Current Assets					
Cash and cash equivalents	$18,758,000	$24,996,00	$60,538,000	$17,000,700	$2,983,000
Short-term municipal securities	4,829,000	6,632,000	1,316,600		
Inventories	4,539,000	3,849,000	2,166,500	1,020,800	319,200
Other current assets	11,376,000	4,658,000	2,095,200	794,900	224,100
Total current assets	39,502,000	40,135,000	66,116,700	18,816,400	3,526,300
Long-term municipal securities	1,226,000	8,903,000	7,071,200		
Property, fixtures and equipment, net	162,323,000	101,010,000	41,764,500	15,479,000	6,553,200
Investments in and advances to unconsolidated affiliates	14,244,000	1,000,000			
Other assets	11,236,000	8,151,000	2,691,300	2,380,700	1,539,600
	$228,531,000	$159,199,000	$117,643,700	36,676,100	11,619,100

Liabilities and Stockholders' Equity					
Current Liabilities					
Accounts payable	$10,184,000	$1,053,000	$3,560,200	643,800	666,900
Sales tax payable	3,173,000	2,062,000	1,289,500	516,800	208,600
Accrued expenses	14,961,000	10,435,000	8,092,300	2,832,300	954,800
Unearned revenue	11,862,000	6,174,000	2,761,900	752,800	219,400
Current portion of long-term debt	918,000	1,119,000	326,600	257,000	339,900
Income taxes payable			369,800	1,873,200	390,000
Total current liabilities	41,098,000	20,843,000	16,400,300	6,875,900	2,779,600
Deferred income taxes	568,000	897,000	856,400	300,000	260,000
Long-term debt	12,310,000	5,687,000	1,823,700	823,600	1,060,700
Interest of minority partners in consolidated partnerships	2,255,000	1,347,000	1,737,500	754,200	273,000
Total Liabilities	56,231,000	28,774,000	20,817,900	8,753,700	4,373,300
Stockholders Equity					
Common stock, $0.01 par value, 100,000,000 shares authorized for 1994 and 1993; 50,000,000 authorized for 1992 42,931,344 and 42,442,800 shares issued and outstanding as of December 31, 1994 and 1993, respectively. 39,645,995 shares issued and outstanding as of December 31,1992.	429,000	425,000	396,500	219,000	86,300
Additional paid-in capital	83,756,000	79,429,000	74,024,500	20,296.400	4,461,100
Retained earnings	88,115,000	50,571,000	22,404,800	7,407,000	2,698,400
Total stockholders' equity	172,300,000	130,425,000	96,825,800	27,922,400	7,245,800
	$228,531,000	$159,199,000	$117,643,700	36,676.100	11,619,100

We can do 500–600 (Outback) restaurants, and possibly more over the next five years. . . . [However] the world is becoming one big market, and we want to be in place so we don't miss that opportunity. There are some problems, some challenges with it, but at this point there have been some casual restaurant chains that have gone [outside the United States] and their average unit sales are way, way above the sales level they enjoyed in the United States. So

EXHIBIT 3   Outback Steakhouse, Inc. Selected Financial and Stock Data

Year	Systemwide Sales	Co Revenues	Net Income	EPS	Co. Stores	Franchises & JVS	Total
1988	$2,731	$2,731	$47	0.01	2	0	2
1989	13,328	13,328	920	0.04	9	0	9
1990	34,193	34,193	2,260	0.08	23	0	23
1991	91,000	91,000	6,064	0.17	49	0	49
1992	195,508	189,217	14,838	0.36	81	4	85
1993	347,553	309,749	25,242	0.58	124	24	148
1994	548,945	451,916	38,608	0.88	164	50	214

Outback Stock Data

1991	High	Low
Second Quarter	$4.67	$4.27
Third Quarter	6.22	4.44
Fourth Quarter	10.08	5.50
1992		
First Quarter	13.00	9.17
Second Quarter	11.41	8.37
Third Quarter	16.25	10.13
Fourth Quarter	19.59	14.25
1993		
First Quarter	22.00	15.50
Second Quarter	26.16	16.66
Third Quarter	24.59	19.00
Fourth Quarter	25.66	21.16
1994		
First Quarter	29.50	23.33
Second Quarter	28.75	22.75
Third Quarter	30.88	23.75
Fourth Quarter	32.00	22.63

the potential is there. Obviously, there are some distribution issues to work out, things like that. But we are real excited about the future internationally. That will give us some potential outside the United States to continue to grow as well.

In late 1994 the company began their international venture by appointing Hugh Connerty as president of Outback International. Connerty, like Outback's three founders, had extensive experience in the restaurant industry. Prior to joining Outback he developed a chain of successful Hooter's restaurants in Georgia. He used the proceeds from the sale of these franchises to fund the development of his franchise of Outback restaurants in Northern Florida and Southern Georgia. Connerty's success as a franchisee was well recognized. Indeed, in 1993 Outback began to award a large crystal

trophy with the designation "Connerty Franchisee of the Year" to the company's outstanding franchisee.

Much of Outback's growth and expansion were generated through joint venture partnerships and franchising agreements. Connerty commented on Outback's franchise system:

> Every one of the franchisees lives in their areas. I lived in the area I franchised. I had relationships that helped with getting permits. That isn't any different than the rest of the world. The loyalties of individuals that live in their respective areas [will be important]. We will do the franchises one by one. The biggest decision we have to make is how we pick that franchise partner. . . . That is what we will concentrate on. We are going to select a person who has synergy with us, who thinks like us, who believes in the principles and beliefs.

Outback developed relationships very carefully. As Hugh Connerty explained:

> Trust . . . is foremost and sacred. The trust between [Outback] and the individual franchisees is not to be violated. . . . Company grants franchises one at a time.[6] It takes a lot of trust to invest millions of dollars without any assurance that you will be able to build another one.

However, Connerty recognized that expanding abroad would present challenges. He described how Outback would approach its international expansion.

> We have built Outback one restaurant at a time. . . . There are some principles and beliefs we live by. It almost sounds cultish. We want international to be an opportunity for our suppliers. We feel strongly about the relationships with our suppliers. We have never changed suppliers. We have undying commitment to them and in exchange we want them to have undying commitment to us. They have to prove they can build plants [abroad].

He explained:

> I think it would be foolish of us to think that we are going to go around the world buying property and understanding the laws in every country, the culture in every single country. So the approach that we are going to take

is that we will franchise the international operation with company-owned stores here and franchises there so that will allow us to focus on what I believe is our pure strength, a support operation.

U.S. Restaurants in the International Dining Market

Prospects for international entry for U.S. restaurant companies in the early 1990s appeared promising. Between 1992 and 1993 alone international sales for the top 50 restaurant franchisers increased from US $15.9 billion to US $17.5 billion. Franchising was the most popular means for rapid expansion. Exhibit 4 provides an overview of the top U.S. restaurant franchisers, including their domestic and international revenues and number of units in 1993 and 1994.

International expansion was an important source of revenues for a significant number of players in the industry. International growth and expansion in the U.S. restaurant industry over the 1980s and into the 1990s was largely driven by major fast food restaurant chains. Some of these companies—for example, McDonald's, Wendy's, Dairy Queen, and Domino's pizza—were public and free-standing. Others, such as Subway, and Little Caesars, remained private and free-standing. Some of the largest players in international markets were subsidiaries of major consumer products firms such as PepsiCo[7] and Grand Metropolitan PLC.[8] In spite of the success enjoyed by fast food operators in

non-U.S. markets, casual dining operators were slower about entering international markets. (See Appendix A for brief overviews of the publicly available data on the top ten franchisers and casual dining chains that had ventured abroad as of early 1995.)

One of the major forces driving the expansion of the U.S. foodservice industry was changing demographics. In the U.S. prepared foods had become the fastest-growing category because they relieved the cooking burdens on working parents. By the early 1990s, U.S. consumers were spending almost as much on restaurant fare as for prepared and nonprepared grocery store food. U.S. food themes were very popular abroad. U.S. food themes were common throughout Canada as well as Western Europe and East Asia. As a result of the opening of previously inaccessible markets like Eastern Europe, the former Soviet Union, China, India, and Latin America, the potential for growth in U.S. food establishments abroad was enormous.

In 1992 alone, there were more than 3,000 franchisers in the United States operating about 540,000 franchised outlets—a new outlet of some sort opened about every 16 minutes. In 1992, franchised business sales totaled $757.8 billion, about 35 % of all retail sales. Franchising was used as a growth vehicle by a variety of businesses, including automobiles, petroleum, cosmetics, convenience stores, computers, and financial services. However, food service constituted the franchising industry's largest single group. Franchised restaurants generally performed better than

EXHIBIT 4   Top 50 U.S. Restaurant Franchises Ranked by Sales (in Millions)

Rank	Firm	Total Sales		International Sales		Total Stores		International Stores	
		1994	1993	1994	1993	1994	1993	1994	1993
1	McDonald's	$25,986	$23,587	$11,046	$9,401	$15,205	$13,993	$5,461	$4,710
2	Burger King	7,500	6,700	1,400	1,240	7,684	6,990	1,357	1,125
3	KFC	7,100	7,100	3,600	3,700	9,407	9,033	4,258	3,905
4	Taco Bell	4,290	3,817	130	100	5,615	4,634	162	112
5	Wendy's	4,277	3,924	390	258	4,411	4,168	413	377
6	Hardee's	3,491	3,425	63	56	3,516	3,435	72	63
7	Dairy Queen	3,170	2,581	300	290	3,516	3,435	628	611
8	Domino's	2,500	2,413	415	275	5,079	5,009	840	550
9	Subway	2,500	2,201	265	179	9,893	8,450	944	637
10	Little Caesar	2,000	2,000	70	70	4,855	4754	155	145
Average of firms 11–20		1,222	1,223	99	144	2,030	1,915	163	251
Average of firms 21–30		647	594	51	26	717	730	37	36
Average of firms 31–40		382	358	7	9	502	495	26	20
Average of firms 41–50		270	257	17	23	345	363	26	43

(continued)

Non-Fast Food in Top 50

Rank	Firm	Total Sales		International Sales		Total Stores		International Stores	
		1994	1993	1994	1993	1994	1993	1994	1993
11	Denny's	$1,779	$1,769	$63	$70	$1,548	$1,515	$58	$63
13	Dunkin Donuts	1,413	1,285	226	209	3,453	3,047	831	705
14	Shoney's	1,346	1,318	0	0	922	915	0	0
15	Big Boy	1,130	1,202	100	0	940	930	90	78
17	Baskin-Robbins	1,008	910	387	368	3,765	3,562	1,300	1,278
19	T.G.I. Friday's	897	1,068	114	293	314	Na	37	Na
20	Applebee's	889	609	1	0	507	361	2	0
21	Sizzler	858	922	230	218	600	666	119	116
23	Ponderosa	690	743	40	38	380	750	40	38
24	Int'l house of Pancakes	632	560	32	29	657	561	37	35
25	Perkins	626	588	12	10	432	425	8	6
29	Outback Steakhouse	549	348	0	0	Na	Na	Na	Na
30	Golden Corral	548	515	1	0	425	425	2	1
32	TCBY Yogurt	388	337	22	15	2,801	2,474	141	80
37	Showbiz/Chuck E. Cheese	370	373	7	8	332	Na	8	Na
39	Round Table Pizza	357	340	15	12	576	597	29	22
40	Western Sizzlin	337	351	3	6	281	Na	2	Na
41	Ground Round	321	310	0	0	Na	Na	Na	Na
42	Papa John's	297	Na	0	Na	632	Na	0	Na
44	Godfather's Pizza	270	268	0	0	515	531	0	0
45	Bonanza	267	327	32	47	264	Na	30	Na
46	Village Inn	266	264	0	0	Na	Na	Na	Na
47	Red Robin	259	235	27	28	Na	Na	Na	Na
48	Tony's Roma	254	245	41	36	Na	Na	Na	Na
49	Marie Callender	251	248	0	0	Na	Na	Na	Na

Na: Not ranked in the top 50 for that category
Source: "Top 50 Franchises," *Restaurant Business,* November 1, 1995, pp. 35–41)

free-standing units. For example, in 1991 franchised restaurants experienced per-store sales growth of 6.2% versus an overall restaurant industry growth rate of 3.0%. However, despite generally favorable sales and profits, franchisor-franchisee relationships were often difficult.

Abroad franchisers operated an estimated 31,000 restaurant units. The significant increase in restaurant franchising abroad was driven by universal cultural trends, rising incomes, improved international transportation and communication, rising educational levels, increasing number of women entering the work force, demographic concentrations of people in urban areas, and the willingness of younger generations to try new products.[9] However, there were substantial differences in these changes between the United States and other countries and from country to country.

Factors Impacting Country Selection

Outback had not yet formed a firm plan for its international rollout. However, Hugh Connerty indicated the preliminary choice of markets targeted for entry:

> This year will be Canada. . . . Then we'll go to Hawaii. . . . Then we'll go to South America and then develop our relationships in the Far East, Korea, Japan, . . . the Orient. At the second year we'll begin a relationship in Great Britain and from there a natural progression throughout Europe. But we view it as a very long-term project. I have learned that people think very different than Americans.

There were numerous considerations which U.S. restaurant chains had to take into account when determining which non-U.S. markets to enter. Some of these factors are summarized in Exhibit 5. Issues

EXHIBIT 5   Factors Affecting Companies' Entry into International Markets

External Factors

Country Market Factors

Size of target market, competitive structure—atomistic, oligopolistic to monopolistic, local marketing infrastructure (distribution, etc.)

Country Production Factors

Quality, quantity and cost of raw materials, labor, energy, and other productive agents in the target country as well as the quality and cost of the economic infrastructure (transportation, communications, port facilities and similar considerations)

Country Environmental Factors

Political, economic, and sociocultural character of the target country—government policies and regulations pertaining to international business

Geographical distance—impact on transportation costs

Size of the economy, absolute level of performance (GDP per capita), relative importance of economic sectors—closely related to the market size for a company's product in the target country.

Dynamics including rate of investment, growth in GDP, personal income, changes in employment. Dynamic economies may justify entry modes with a high break-even point even when the current market size is below the break-even point.

Sociocultural factors—cultural distance between home country and target country societies. Closer the cultural distance, quicker entry into these markets, e.g., Canada.

Home Country Factors

Big domestic market allows a company to grow to a large size before it turns to foreign markets. Competitive structure. Firms in oligopolistic industries tend to imitate the actions of rival domestic firms that threaten to upset competitive equilibrium. Hence, when one firm invests abroad, rival firms commonly follow the lead. High production costs in the home country is an important factor.

Internal Factors

Company Product Factors

Products that are highly differentiated with distinct advantages over competitive products give sellers a significant degree of pricing discretion.

Products that require an array of pre- and post-purchase services makes it difficult for a company to market the product at a distance.

Products that require considerable adaptation.

Company Resource/Commitment Factors

The more abundant a company's resources in management, capital, technology, production skills, and marketing skills, the more numerous its entry-mode options. Conversely, a company with limited resources is constrained to use entry modes that call for only a small resource commitment. Size is therefore a critical factor in the choice of an entry mode. Although resources are an influencing factor, it must be joined with a willingness to commit them to foreign market development. A high degree of commitment means that managers will select the entry mode for a target from a wider range of alternative modes than managers with a low commitment.

The degree of a company's commitment to international business is revealed by the role accorded to foreign markets in corporate strategy, the status of the international organization, and the attitudes of managers.

Source: Franklin Root, *Entry Strategies for International Markets.* Lexington MA: D.C. Health (1987)

regarding infrastructure and demographics are expanded below. Included are some of the difficulties that U.S. restaurant companies encountered in various countries. Profiles of Canada, South Korea, Japan, Germany, Mexico, and Great Britain appear as Appendix B and Tables B1 through B18.

Infrastructure

A supportive infrastructure in the target country is essential. Proper means of transportation, communication, basic utilities such as power and water, and locally available supplies are important elements in the decision to introduce a particular restaurant concept. A restaurant must have the ability to get resources to its location. Raw materials for food preparation, equipment for manufacture of food served, employees, and customers must be able to enter and leave the establishment. The network that brings these resources to a firm is commonly called a supply chain.

The level of economic development is closely linked to the development of a supportive infrastructure. For example, the U.S. International Trade Commission said:

> Economic conditions, cultural disparities, and physical limitations can have substantial impact on the viability of foreign markets for a franchise concept. In terms of economics, the level of infrastructure development is a significant factor. A weak infrastructure may cause problems in transportation, communication, or even the provision of basic utilities such as electricity. . . . International franchises frequently encounter problems finding supplies in sufficient quantity, of consistent quality, and at stable prices. . . . Physical distance also can adversely affect a franchise concept and arrangement. Long distances create communication and transportation problems, which may complicate the process of sourcing supplies, overseeing operations, or providing quality management services to franchisees. [10]

Some food can be sourced locally, some regionally or nationally, and some must be imported. A country's transportation and distribution capabilities may become an element in the decision of the country's suitability for a particular restaurant concept.

Sometimes supply chain issues require firms to make difficult decisions that affect the costs associated with the foreign enterprise. Family Restaurants inc. encountered problems providing brown gravy for its CoCo's restaurants in South Korea. "If you want brown gravy in South Korea," said Barry Krantz, company president, "you can do one of two things. Bring it over, which is very costly. Or, you can make it yourself. So we figure out the flavor profile, and make it in the kitchen." Krantz concedes that a commissary is "an expensive proposition but the lesser of the two evils."[11]

In certain instances a country may be so attractive for long-term growth that a firm dedicates itself to creating a supply chain for its restaurants. An excellent illustration is McDonald's expansion into Russia in the late 1980s:

> Supply procurement has proved to be a major hurdle, as it has for all foreign companies operating in Russia. The problem has several causes: the rigid bureaucratic system, supply shortages caused by distribution and production problems, available supplies not meeting McDonald's quality standards. . . . To handle these problems, McDonald's scoured the country for supplies, contracting for such items as milk, cheddar cheese, and beef. To help ensure ample supplies of the quality products it needed, it undertook to educate Soviet farmers and cattle ranchers on how to grow and raise those products. In addition, it built a $40 million food-processing center about 45 minutes from its first Moscow restaurant. And because distribution was (and still is) as much a cause of shortages as production was, McDonald's carried supplies on it's own trucks.[12]

Changing from one supply chain to another can affect more than the availability of quality provisions—it can affect the equipment that is used to make the food served. For example:

> Wendy's nearly had its Korean market debut delayed by the belatedly discovered problem of thrice-frozen hamburger. After being thawed and frozen at each step of Korea's cumbersome three-company distribution channel, ground beef there takes on added water weight that threw off Wendy's patty specifications, forcing a hasty stateside retooling of the standard meat patty die used to mass-produce its burgers.[13]

Looking at statistics such as the number of ports, airports, quantity of paved roads, and transportation equipment as a percentage of capital stock per worker can give a bird's eye view of the level of infrastructure development.

Demographics

Just like the domestic market, restaurants in a foreign market need to know who their customers will be. Different countries will have different strata in age distribution, religion, and cultural heritage. These factors can influence the location, operations, and menus of restaurants in the country.

A popular example is India, where eating beef is contrary to the beliefs of the 80% of the population that is Hindu.[14] Considering that India's population is nearly one billion people, companies find it hard to ignore this market even if beef is a central component of the firm's traditional menu. "We're looking at serving mutton patties," says Ann Connolly, a McDonald's spokeswoman.[15]

Another area where religion plays a part in affecting the operation of a restaurant is the Middle East. Dairy Queen expanded to the region and found that during the Islamic religious observance of Ramadan no business was conducted; indeed, the windows of shops were boarded up.[16]

Age distribution can affect who should be the target market. "The company [McDonald's in Japan] also made modifications [not long after entering the market], such as targeting all advertising to younger people, because the eating habits of older Japanese are very difficult to change."[17] Age distribution can also impact the pool of labor available. In some countries over 30% of the population is under 15 years old; in other countries over 15% is 65 and older. These varying demographics could create a change in the profile for potential employees in the new market.

Educational level may be an influence on both the buying public and the employee base Literacy rates vary, and once again this can change the profile of an employee as well as who comprises the buying public.

Statistics can help compare countries using demographic components like literacy rates, total population and age distribution, and religious affiliations.

Income

Buying power is another demographic that can provide clues to how the restaurant might fare in the target country, as well as how the marketing program should position the company's products or services. Depending on the country and its economic development, the firm may have to attract a different segment than in the domestic market. For example in Mexico

> Major U.S. firms have only recently begun targeting the country's sizable and apparently burgeoning middle class. For its part, McDonald's has changed tactics from when it first entered Mexico as a prestige brand aimed almost exclusively at the upper class, which accounts for about 5 percent of Mexico's population of some 93 million. With the development of its own distribution systems and improved economies of scale McDonald's lately has been slashing prices to aid its penetration into working-class population strongholds. "I'd say McDonald's pricing now in Mexico is 30 percent lower, in constant dollar terms, than when we opened in '85," says Moreno [Fernando Moreno, now international director of Peter Piper Pizza], who was part of the chain's inaugural management team there.[18]

There are instances where low disposable income does not translate to a disinterest in dining out in a Western-style restaurant. While Americans dine at fast food establishments such as McDonald's one or two

tiems per week, lower incomes in the foreign markets make eating at McDonald's a special, once-a-month occurrence. "These people are not very wealthy, so eating out at a place like McDonald's is a dining experience."[19] China provides another example:

> At one Beijing KFC last summer, [the store] notched the volume equivalent of nine U.S. KFC branches in a single day during a $1.99 promotion of two piece meal with a baseball cap. Observers chalk up that blockbuster business largely to China's ubiquitous "spoiled-brat syndrome" and the apparent willingness of indulgent parents to spend one or two months' salaries on splurges for the only child the government allows them to rear.[20]

Statistics outlining the various indexes describing the country's gross domestic product, consumer spending on food, consumption and investment rates, and price levels can assist in evaluating target countries.

Trade Law

Trade policies can be friend or foe to a restaurant chain interested in expanding to other countries. Trade agreements such as NAFTA (North American Free Trade Agreement) and GATT (General Agreement on Tariffs and Trade) can help alleviate the ills of international expansion if they achieve their aims of "reducing or eliminating tariffs, reducing non-tariff barriers to trade, liberalizing investment and foreign exchange policies, and improving intellectual property protection. . . . The recently signed Uruguay Round Agreements [of GATT] include the General Agreement on Trade in Services (GATS), the first multilateral, legally enforceable agreement covering trade and investment in the services sector. The GATS is designed to liberalize trade in services by reducing or eliminating governmental measures that prevent services from being freely provided across national borders or that discriminate against firms with foreign ownership."[21]

Franchising, one of the most popular modes for entering foreign markets, scored a win in the GATS agreement. For the first time franchising was addressed directly in international trade talks. However, most countries have not elected to make their restrictions on franchising publicly known. The U.S. International Trade Commission pointed out:

> Specific commitments that delineate barriers are presented in Schedules of Commitments (Schedules). As of this writing, Schedules from approximately 90 countries are publicly available. Only 30 of these countries specifically include franchising in their Schedules. . . . The remaining two-thirds of the countries did not schedule commitments on franchising. This means that existing restrictions

are not presented in a transparent manner and additional, more severe restrictions may be imposed at a later date. Among the 30 countries that addressed franchising in the Schedules, 25 countries, including the United States, have committed themselves to maintain no limitations on franchising except for restrictions on the presence of foreign nationals within their respective countries.[22]

Despite progress, current international restaurant chains have encountered a myriad of challenges because of restrictive trade policies. Some countries make the import of restaurant equipment into their country difficult and expensive. The Asian region possesses "steep tariffs and [a] patchwork of inconsistent regulations that impede imports of commodities and equipment."[23]

Outback's Growth Challenge

Hugh Connerty was well aware that there was no mention of international opportunities in Outback's 1994 annual report. The company distributed that annual report to shareholders at the April, 1995 meeting. More then 300 shareholders packed the meeting to standing room only. During the question and answer period a shareholder had closely questioned the company's executives as to why the company did not pay a dividend. The shareholder pointed out that the company made a considerable profit in 1994. Chris Sullivan responded that the company needed to reinvest the cash that might be used as dividends in order to achieve the targeted growth. His response was a public and very visible commitment to continue the company's fast-paced growth. Connerty knew that international opportunities had the potential to play a critical role in that growth. His job was to help craft a strategy that would assure Outback's continuing success as it undertook the new and diverse markets abroad.

Appendix A: Profiles of Casual Dining and Fast Food Chains[24]

This appendix provides summaries of the 1995 publicly available data on (1) the two casual dining chains represented among the top 50 franchisers that had operations abroad (Applebee's and T.G.I. Friday's/Carlson Companies, Inc.) and (2) the top ten franchisers in the restaurant industry all of which are fast food chains (Burger King, Domino's, Hardee's, International Dairy Queen, Inc., Little Caesars, McDonalds, Pepsico including KFC, Taco Bell and Pizza Hut, Subway, and Wendy's).

(1) Casual Dining Chains with Operations Abroad

Applebee's

Applebee's was one of the largest casual dining chains in the United States. It ranked twentieth in sales and thirty-sixth in stores for 1994. Like most other casual dining operators, much of the company's growth had been fueled by domestic expansion. Opening in 1986, the company experienced rapid growth and by 1994 had 507 stores. The mode of growth was franchising, but in 1992 management began a program of opening more company-owned sites and buying restaurants from franchisees. The company positioned itself as a neighborhood bar and grill and offered a moderately priced menu including burgers, chicken, and salads.

In 1995 Applebee's continued a steady program of expansion. Chairman and CEO Abe Gustin set a target of 1,200 U.S. restaurants and had also begun a slow push into international markets. In 1994 the company franchised restaurants in Canada and Curacao, and signed an agreement to franchise 20 restaurants in Belgium, Luxembourg, and the Netherlands.

Year	1989	1990	1991	1992	1993	1994
Sales*	29.9	38.2	45.1	56.5	117.1	208.5
Net Income*	0.0	1.8	3.1	5.1	9.5	16.9
EPS ($)	(0.10)	0.13	0.23	0.27	0.44	0.62
Stock Price— Close ($)	4.34	2.42	4.84	9.17	232.34	13.38
Dividends ($)	0.00	0.00	0.01	0.02	0.03	0.04
Employees	1,149	1,956	1,714	2,400	46,600	8,700

*$m ** 1994: Debt ratio 20.1%; ROE 19.2; Cash $17.2m; Current ratio 1.13; LTD $23.7

T.G.I. Friday's/Carlson Companies, Inc.

T.G.I. Friday's was owned by Carlson Companies, Inc., a large, privately held conglomerate that had interests in travel (65% of 1994 sales), hospitality (30%) plus marketing, employee training and incentives (5%). Carlson also owned a total of 345 Radisson Hotels and Country Inns plus 240 units of Country Kitchen International, a chain of family restaurants.

Most of Carlson's revenues came from their travel group. The company experienced an unexpected surprise in 1995 when U.S. airlines announced that they would put a cap on the commissions they would pay to book U.S. flights. Because of this change, Carlson decided to change their service to a fee-based arrangement and expected sales to drop by US $100 million in 1995. To make up for this deficit, Carlson began to focus on building their hospitality group of restaurants and hotels through expansion in the U.S. and overseas. The company experienced significant senior management turnover in the early 1990s and founder Curtis Carlson, age 80, had announced his intention to retire at the end of 1996. His daughter was announced as next head of the company.

T.G.I. Friday's grew 15.7% in revenue and 19.4% in stores in 1994. With 37 restaurants overseas, international sales were 12.7% of sales and 11.8% of stores systemwide. Carlson operated a total of 550 restaurants in 17 countries. About one-third of overall sales came from activities outside the United States.

Year	1985	1986	1987	1988	1989
Sales*	.9	1.3	1.5	1.8	2.0

Year	1990	1991	1992	1993	1994
Sales*	2.2	2.3	2.9	2.3	2.3

* $b; no data available on income; excludes franchisee sales

(2) The Top Ten Franchisers in the Restaurant Industry

Burger King

In 1994 Burger King was number two in sales and number four in stores among the fast food competitors. Burger King did not have the same presence in the global market as McDonald's and KFC. For example, McDonald's and KFC had been in Japan since the 1970's. Burger King opened its first Japanese locations in 1993. By that time, McDonald's already had over 1,000 outlets there. In 1994 Burger King had 1,357 non-U.S. stores (17.7% of systemwide total) in 50 countries, and overseas sales (18.7%) totaled $1.4 billion USD.

Burger King was owned by British food and Spirits conglomerate Grand Metropolitan PLC. Among the company's top brands were Pillsbury, Green Giant, and Haagen-Dazs. Grand Met's situation had not been bright during the 1990's, with the loss of major distribution contracts like Absolute vodka and Grand Marnier liqueur, as well as sluggish sales for its spirits in

major markets. Burger King was not a stellar performer, either, and undertook a major restructuring in 1993 to turn the tide including reemphasis on the basic menu, cuts in prices, and reduced overhead. After quick success, BK's CEO James Adamson left his post in early 1995 to head competitor Flasgston Corporation.

Year	1985	1986	1987	1988	1989
Sales*	5,590	5,291	4,706	6,029	9,298
Net Income*	272	261	461	702	1,068
EPS($)	14	16	19	24	28
Stock Price—					
Close ($)	199	228 225	215	314	329
Dividend/Share ($)	5.0	5.1	6.0	7.5	8.9
Employees (K)	137	131	129	90	137

Year	1990	1991	1992	1993	1994
Sales*	9,394	8,748	7,913	8,120	7,780
Net Income*	106,943 2	616	412	450	
EPS($)	32	33	28	30	32
Stock Price—					
Close ($)	328	441	465	476	407
Dividend/Share ($)	10.2	11.4	12.3	13.0	14.0
Employees (K)	138	122	102	87	64

* Millions of Sterling; 1994: debt ratio 47.3%; R.O.E. 12.4%; Cash (Ster.) 986M; LTD (Ster.) 2,322M.
1994 Segments sales (profit): North America: 62%(69%); U.K. & Ireland 10%(10%); Africa & Middle East 2%(1%); Other Europe: 21% (18%); Other Countries: 5%(2%)
Segment Sales (Profits) by Operating Division: Drinks 43%(51%); Food 42%(26%); Retailing 14%(22%); Other 1%(1%).

Domino's

Domino's Pizza was eighth in sales and seventh in stores in 1994. Sales and store unit growth had leveled off; from 1993 to 1994 sales grew 3.6%, and units only 1.4%. The privately held company registered poor performance in 1993, with a 0.6% sales decline from 1992. Observers suggested that resistance to menu innovations contributed to the share decline. In early 1990s the company did add deep dish pizza and buffalo wings.

Flat company performances and expensive hobbies were hard on the owner and founder Thomas Monaghan. He attempted to sell the company in 1989 but could not find a buyer. He then replaced top management and retired from business to pursue a growing interest in religious activities. Company performance began to slide, and the founder emerged from retirement to retake the helm in the early 1990s. Through extravagant purchases of the Detroit Tigers, Frank Lloyd Wright pieces, and antique cars, Monaghan put the company on the edge of financial ruin. He sold off many of his holdings (some at a loss), reinvested the funds to stimulate the firm, and once again reorganized management.

Despite all its problems, Domino's had seen consistent growth in the international market. The company opened its first foreign store in 1983 in Canada. Primary overseas expansion areas were Eastern Europe and India. By 1994 Domino's had 5,079 stores with 823 of these in 37 major international markets. International brought in 17% of 1994 sales. Over the next 10 to 15 years the company had contracts for 4,000 additional international units.[25] These units would give Domino's more international than domestic units. International sales were 16.6% of total, and international stores were 16.5% of total in 1994.

Years	1985	1986	1987	1988	1989
Sales*	1,100	1,430	2,000	2,300	2,500
Stores	2,841	3,610	4,279	4,858	5,185
Employees (K)	NA	NA	NA	NA	NA

Years	1990	1991	1992	1993	1994
Sales*	2,600	2,400	2,450	2,200	5,079
Stores	5,342	5,571	5,264	5,369	5,079
Employees (K)	100	NA	NA	NA	115

* $000,000

Hardee's

Hardee's was number six in sales and eleven in stores for 1994. In 1981 the large diversified Canadian company, Imasco, purchased the chain. Imasco also owned Imperial Tobacco (Player's and du Maurier, Canada's top two sellers), Burger Chef, two drug store chains, the development company Genstar, and CT Financial.

Hardee's had pursued growth primarily in the United States. Of all the burger chains in the top 10 franchises, Hardee's had the smallest international presence, with 72 stores generating, US $63 million (1.8% and 2.0% of sales and stores, respectively) in 1994.

Hardee's sales grew by about 2% annually for 1993 and 1994. A failed attempt by Imasco to merge their

Roy Roger's restaurants into the Hardee's chain forced the parent company to maintain both brands. Hardee's attempted to differentiate from the other burger chains by offering an upscale burger menu, which received a lukewarm reception by consumers.

Year	1985	1986	1987	1988	1989
Sales*	3,376	5,522	6,788	7,311	8,480
Net income*	262	184	283	314	366
EPS ($)	1.20	0.78	1.12	1.26	1.44
Stock Price—Close ($)	13.94	16.25	12.94	14.00	18.88
Dividends ($)	0.36	0.42	0.48	0.52	0.56
Employees (K)	NA	NA	NA	NA	190

Year	1990	1991	1992	1993	1994
Sales*	9,647	9,870	9,957	9,681	9,385
Net income*	205	332	380	409	506
EPS ($)	1.13	0.64	0.68	0.74	0.78
Stock Price—Close ($)	13.81	18.25	20.63	20.06	19.88
Dividends ($)	0.64	0.64	0.68	0.74	0.78
Employees (K)	190	180	NA	200	200

* $M – all $ in Canadian; 1994: Debt ratio: 38.4%; R.O.E. 16.1%; Current ratio: 1.37; LTD(M): $1,927; 1994 Segment Sales (Operating Income): CT Financial Services 47% (28%); Hardee's 32%(11%); Imperial Tobacco 16%(0%); Shoppers Drug Mart 2% (9%); Genstar Development 1% (2%)

International Dairy Queen, Inc.

Dairy Queen was one of the oldest fast-food franchises in the United States: The first store was opened in Joilet, Illinois in 1940. By 1950, there were over 1,100 stores, and by 1960 Dairy Queen had locations in 12 countries. Initial franchise agreements focused on the right to use the DQ freezers, an innovation that kept ice cream at the constant 23 degrees (F) necessary to maintain the soft consistency. In 1970 a group of investors bought the franchise organization; but the group has been only partly successful in standardizing the fast food chain. In 1994 a group of franchisees filed an antitrust suit in an attempt to get the company to loosen its control on food supply prices and sources. DQ franchises cost $30,000 initially plus continuing payments of 4% of sales.

The company's menu consisted of ice cream, yogurt, and Brazier (hamburgers and other fast food) items. Menu innovations had included Blizzard (candy and other flavors mixed in the ice cream). The company had also acquired several companies, including the Golden Skillet (1981), Karmelkorn (1986), and Orange Julius (1987).

In 1994, Dairy Queen ranked number seven in sales and six in stores. By that same year the company had expanded its presence into 19 countries with 628 stores and US $300 million in international sales. 1994 was an excellent year for DQ: Sales were up 22.8% over 1993. This dramatic change (1993 scored an anemic 3.0% gain) was fueled by technology improvements for franchisees and international expansion. In 1992 Dairy Queen opened company-owned outlets in Austria, China, Slovenia, and Spain. DQ announced in 1995 that they had a plan to open 20 stores in Puerto Rico over a four-year period.

Years	1985	1986	1987	1988	1989
Sales*	158	182	210	254	282
Net income*	10	12	15	20	23
EPS($)	0.33	0.42	0.51	0.70	0.83
Stock Price—Close ($)	5.20	7.75	8.00	11.50	14.75
Dividends ($)	-0-	-0-	-0-	-0-	-0-
Employees (K)	430	459	503	520	549

Years	1990	1991	1992	1993	1994
Sales*	287	287	296	311	341
Net income*	27	28	29	30	31
EPS($)	0.97	1.05	1.12	1.79	1.30
Stock Price—Close ($)	16.58	21.00	20.00	18.00	16.25
Dividends ($)	-0-	-0-	-0-	-0-	-0-
Employees (K)	584	592	672	538	564

*$M; 1994: Debt ratio 15.3%; R.O.E. 24.4%; Current ratio 3.04; LTD $23M.
1994 Restaurants: U.S. 87%; Canada 9%; Other 4%; Restaurants by type: DQ's: franchised by company: 62%; franchised by territorial operators 27%; foreign 3%; Orange Julius: 7%; Karmelkorn 1%, Golden Skillet less than 1%; Sales by source: Good supplies & equipment to franchises 78%; service fees 16%; franchise sales & other fees 3%; real-estate finance & rental income 3%.

Little Caesar's

Little Caesar's ranked tenth in sales and eighth in stores for 1994. Sales growth had slowed to halt: A 1992–93 increase of 12.2% evaporated into no increase for 1993–94.

These numbers were achieved without a significant overseas presence. Of the top ten franchises, only Hardee's had a smaller number of stores in foreign lands. Little Caesar's received 3.5% of sales from foreign stores. Only 3.2% of the company's stores were in non-U.S. locations, namely, Canada, Czech and Slo-

vak Republics, Guam, Puerto Rico, and the United Kingdom.

Year	1985	1986	1987	1988	1989
Sales	340	520	725	908	1,130
# of stores	900	1,000	1,820	2,000	2,700
Employees	18,000	26,160	36,400	43,600	54,000

Year	1990	1991	1992	1993	1994
Sales	1,400	1,725	2,050	2,150	2,000
# of stores	3,173	3,650	4,300	5,609	4,700
Employees	63,460	73,000	86,000	92,000	95,000

McDonald's

At the top in 1994 international sales and units, McDonald's Inc. was the most profitable retailer in the United States during the 1980s and into the 1990s. The company opened its first store in California in 1948, went public in 1965, and by 1994 had over 20% of the U.S. fast food business. McDonald's opened its first international store in Canada in 1967. Growing domestic competition in the 1980s gave impetus to the company's international expansion. By 1994 there were over 15,000 restaurants under the golden arches in 79 countries. The non-U.S. stores provided about one-third of total revenues and half of the company's profits. McDonald's planned to open 1,200 to 1,500 new restaurants in 1995—most outside the United States. International markets had grown into an attractive venue for the burger giant because there was "less competition, lighter market saturation, and high name recognition" in international markets.

The company's growth was fueled by aggressive franchising. In the early 1990s two-thirds of the McDonald's locations were franchised units and franchisees remained with the company an average of 20 years. McDonald's used heavy advertising ($1.4B in 1994) and frequent menu changes and other innovations (1963: Filet-O-Fish sandwich and Ronald McDonald; 1968 Big Mac and first TV ads; 1972: Quarter Pounder, Egg McMuffin (breakfast); 1974: Ronald McDonald House; 1975: drive thru; 1979: Happy Meals; 1983: Chicken McNuggets; 1986: provided customers with list of products' ingredients; 1987: salads; 1980s "value menus"; 1991: McLean DeLuxe, a low-fat hamburger (not successful) and experimentation with decor and new menu items at local level; 1993: first restaurants inside another store

(Wal-Mart)). The company planned to open its first restaurants in India in 1996 with menus featuring chicken, fish sandwiches, and vegetable nuggets. There would be no beef items.

From 1993 to 1994, McDonald's grew 10.2% in sales and 8.7% in stores. Because of their extensive experience in international markets, international sales had grown to 42.5% of their total revenues, and half its profits. Indeed, McDonald's was bigger than the 25 largest full-service chains put together.

Taco Bell was fourth in sales and fifth in stores of the top 50 franchises in 1994. This ranking had been achieved with minimal international business to date. Taco Bell and US $130 million sales and 162 stores internationally. The company attempted to enter the Mexican market in 1992 with a kiosk and cart strategy in Mexico City. The venture did not fare well, and Taco Bell soon pulled out of Mexico.[26] In 1994, international revenues were 3.0% of sales and 2.9% of stores were international locations.

Years	1985	1986	1987	1988	1989
Sales*	3,695	4,144	4,894	5,566	6,142
Net income*	433	480	549	656	727
EPS($)	0.56	0.63	0.73	0.86	0.98
Stock Price—					
Close ($)	9.00	10.16	11.00	12.03	17.25
Dividends ($)	0.10	0.11	0.12	0.14	0.16
Employees (K)	148	159	159	169	176

Years	1990	1991	1992	1993	1994
Sales*	6,640	6,695	7,133	7,408	8,321
Net income*	802	860	959	1,083	1,224
EPS($)	1.10	1.18	1.30	1.46	1.68
Stock Price—					
Close ($)	14.56	19.00	24.38	28.50	29.25
Dividends ($)	0.17	0.18	0.20	0.21	0.23
Employees (K)	174	168	166	169	183

* $M; 1994: Debt ratio 41.2%; R.O.E.: 20.7%; Cash: $180M; Current ratio: 0.31; LTD $2.9M; Market Value: $20B

Year	1985	1986	1987	1988	1989
Sales*	8,057	9,291	11,485	13,007	15,242
Net income*	544	458	595	762	901
EPS($)	0.65	0.58	0.76	0.97	1.13
Stock Price—					
Close ($)	8.06	8.66	11.11	13.15	21.31
Div./Share ($)	0.15	0.21	0.22	0.25	0.31
Employees (K)	150	214	225	235	266

Year	1990	1991	1992	1993	1994
Sales*	17,803	19,608	21,970	25,021	28,474
Net income*	1,007	1,080	1,302	1,588	1,784
EPS($)	1.35	1.35	1.61	1.96	2.22
Stock Price—					
Close ($)	26.00	22.88	3.40	40.88	36.25
Div./Share ($)	0.37	0.44	0.50	0.58	0.68
Employees (K)	308	338	372	423	471

* $m; 1994: Debt ratio: 48.1%; R.O.E.: 27.0%; cash(M) $1,488; Current ratio: 0.96; LTD (M) $8,841
1994 Segment Sales (Operating Income): Restaurants: 37% (22%); Beverages 34% (37%); Snack foods 29% (41%)

Pepsico: KFC and Taco Bell—Also Includes Pizza Hut (latter is not in the top 50)

Pepsico owned powerful brand names such as Pepsi-Cola and Frito-Lay, and was also the world's number one fast food chain with its ownership of KFC, Taco Bell, and Pizza Hut.

KFC was third in sales and stores of the top 50 franchises in 1994. Active in the international arena since the late 1960s, KFC had been a major McDonald's competitor in non-U.S. markets. In 1994, the company had US $3.6 billion in sales and 4,258 stores in other countries. McDonald's had been commonly number one in each country it entered, but KFC had been number two in international sales and had the number-one sales spot in Indonesia. In 1994, KFC international revenues were 50.7% of sales with 45.3% of stores in international locations.

Subway

Founded more than 29 years before, Subway remained privately held in 1994.[27] The company had experienced explosive growth during the 1990s. It ranked ninth in sales and second in stores for 1994. Sales grew 13.6% from 1993 to 1994, and 26% from 1992 to 1993. Stores grew 17.1% from 1993 to 1994, and 15.3% from 1992 to 1993. In 1994, Subway overtook KFC as the number-two chain in number of stores behind McDonald's. The company attributed its growth at least partially to an exceptionally low-priced and well-structured franchise program. In addition store sizes of 500 to 1500 square feet were small. Thus, the investment for a Subway franchise was modest.

The company's growth involved a deliberate strategy. The formula involved no cooking on site, except for the baking of bread. The company promoted the "efficiency and simplicity" of its franchise and advertised its food and "healthy, delicious, (and) fast." The company advertised regularly on TV with a $25M budget and planned to increase that significantly. All stores contributed 2.5% of gross sales to the corporate advertising budget. Subway's goal was to equal or exceed the number of outlets operated by the largest fast food company in every market that it entered. In most cases the firm's benchmark was burger giant McDonald's.

International markets played an emerging role in Subway's expansion. In 1994, international sales were 10.6% of sales, compared to 8.9% the previous year. International stores were 9.5% of total in 1994, and 7.5% in 1993. Subway boasted a total of 9,893 stores in all 50 states and 19 countries.[28]

Wendy's

Wendy's was number five in sales and number nine in stores for 1994. In 1994, after 25 years of operation, Wendy's had grown to 4,411 stores. This growth had been almost exclusively domestic until 1979, when Wendy's ventured out of the United States and Canada to open its first outlets in Puerto Rico, Switzerland, and West Germany. Wendy's granted J.C. Penney the franchise rights to France, Belgium, and Holland, and had one store opened in Belgium by 1980.

Wendy's still saw opportunities for growth in the United States. Industry surveys had consistently ranked Wendy's burgers number one in quality, but poor in convenience (Wendy's had one store for every 65,000 people while McDonald's, in contrast, had one for every 25,000). Growth was driven primarily by franchising. In 1994 71% of the stores were operated by franchisees and 29% by the company. Company restaurants provided 90% of total sales while franchise fees provided 8%. The company had made menu and strategic changes at various points in its history. For example in 1977 the company first began TV advertising; 1979 introduced its salad bar; 1985 experimented with breakfast; 1986 and 1987 introduced Big Classic and SuperBar buffet (neither very successful); 1990 grilled chicken sandwich and 99 cent Super Value Menu items; and 1992 packaged salads.

Wendy's planned to add about 150 restaurants each year in foreign markets. With a presence of 236 stores in 33 countries in 1994, international was 9.1% of sales and 9.4% of stores in 1994.

Years	1985	1986	1987	1988	1989
Sales*	1,126	1,140	1,059	1,063	1,070
Net income*	76	(5)	4	29	24
EPS ($)	0.82	(0.05)	0.04	0.30	0.25
Stock Price—					
Close ($)	13.41	10.25	5.63	5.75	4.63
Div./Share ($)	0.17	0.21	0.24	0.24	0.24
Employees (K)	40	40	45	42	39

Years	1990	1991	1992	1993	1994
Sales*	1,011	1,060	1,239	1,320	1,398
Net income*	39	52	65	79	97
EPS ($)	0.40	0.52	0.63	0.76	0.91
Stock Price—					
Close ($)	6.25	9.88	12.63	17.38	14.38
Div./Share ($)	0.24	0.24	0.24	0.24	0.24
Employees (K)	35	39	42	43	44

*SM; 1994: Debt ratio 36.6%; R.O.E. 5.2%; Current ratio 0.98; LTD(M) $145

Appendix B: Country Summaries[28]

Canada

In the 1990s Canada was considered an ideal first stop for U.S. businesses seeking to begin exporting. Per capita output, patterns of production, market economy, and business practices were similar to U.S. practices. U.S. goods and services were well received in Canada: 70% of all Canadian imports were from the United States. Canada's market conditions were stable, and U.S. companies continued to see Canada as an attractive option for expansion.

Canada had one of the highest real growth rates among the OECD during the 1980s, averaging about 3.2%. The Canadian economy softened during the 1990s, but Canadian imports of U.S. goods and services were expected to increase about 5% in fiscal year 1996.

Although Canada sometimes mirrored the United States, there are significant cultural and linguistic differences from the U.S. and between the regional markets in Canada. These differences were evident in the mounting friction between the English- and French-speaking areas of Canada. The conflict had potential for splitting of territory between the factions, slicing Canada into two separate countries. The prospect of this outcome left foreign investors tense.

Germany

In the mid-1990s Germany was the largest economy in Europe, and the fifth-largest overall importer of U.S. goods and services. Since reunification in 1990, the eastern part of Germany had continued to receive extensive infusions of aid from western Germany, and these funds were only just beginning to show an impact. The highly urbanized and skilled West German population enjoyed a very high standard of living with abundant leisure time. In 1994, Germany emerged from a recession and scored a GDP of US $2 trillion.

A unique feature of Germany was the unusually even distribution of both industry and population— there was no single business center for the country. This was a challenge for U.S. firms. They had to establish distribution networks that adequately covered all areas of the country. In Germany there was little opportunity for regional concentration around major population centers, as in the United States.

The country was a good market for innovative high tech goods and high-quality food products. Germans expected high quality goods, and would reject a less expensive product if quality and support were not in abundance. Strongest competition for U.S. firms were the German domestic firms not only because of their home-grown familiarity of the market, but also because of the consumers' widely held perception that German products were "simply the best."

A recurring complaint from Germans was the prevalent "here today, gone tomorrow" business approach of American firms. Germans viewed business as a long term commitment to support growth in markets, and did not always receive the level and length of attention necessary from U.S. companies to satisfy them.

Conditions in the former area of East Germany were not the doomsday picture often painted, nor were they as rosy as the German government depicts. It would take 10 to 15 years for the eastern region of the country to catch up to the western region in terms of per capita income, standard of living, and productivity.

Japan

Japan had the second largest economy in the world. Overall economic growth in Japan over the past 35 years had been incredible: 10% average annual growth during the 1960s, 5% in the 1970s and 1980s. Growth ground to a halt during the 1990s due to tight fiscal policy. The government tightened fiscal constraints in order to correct the significant devaluation of the real estate markets. The economy posted a 0.6% growth in 1994 largely due to consumer demand. The overall economic outlook remained cloudy, but the outlook for exports to Japan remained positive.

Japan was a highly homogeneous society with business practices characterized by long-standing close relationships among individuals and firms. It took time for Japanese businessmen to develop relationships and for non-Japanese business people the task of relationship-building in Japan was formidable. It was well known that Japan's market was not as open as the U.S. but the U.S. government had mounted multifaceted efforts to help U.S. business people to "open doors". While these efforts were helpful, most of the responsibility in opening the Japanese market to U.S. goods or services remained with the individual firm. Entering Japan was expensive and generally required four things: (1) financial and management capabilities and a Japanese-speaking staff residing within the country, (2) modification of products to suit Japanese consumers, (3) a long term approach to maximizing market share and achieving reasonable profit levels, and (4) careful monitoring of Japanese demand, distribution, competitors, and government. Despite the challenges of market entry, Japan ranked as the second-largest importer of U.S. goods and services.

Historically Japanese consumers were conservative and brand conscious, although the recession during the 1990s nurtured opportunities for "value" entrants. Traditional conformist buying patterns were still prominent, but more individualistic habits were developing in the younger Japanese aged 18 to 21. This age cohort had a population of 8 million people and boasted a disposable income of more than US $35 billion.

Japanese consumers were willing to pay a high price for quality goods. However, they had a well-earned reputation for having unusually high expectations for quality. U.S. firms with high-quality, competitive products had to be able to undertake the high cost of initial market entry. For those that were willing, Japan could provide respectable market share and attractive profit levels.

Mexico

Mexico had experienced a dramatic increase in imports from the United States since the late 1980s. During 1994 the country experienced 20% growth over 1993. In 1994, Mexico's peso experienced a massive devaluation brought on by investor anxiety and capital flight. Although the Mexican government implemented tight fiscal measures to stabilize the peso, their efforts could not stop the country from plunging into a serious recession.

Inflation rose as a result of the austerity policies and it was expected to be between 42% and 54% in 1995. Negative economic growth was anticipated in 1995 as well. The U.S. financial assistance package (primarily loans) provided Mexico with nearly US $50 billion and restored stability to the financial markets by mid-1995. The government was taking measures to improve the country's infrastructure. Mexico's problems mask that its government had, on the whole, practiced sound economic fundamentals.

Mexico was still committed to political reform despite the current economic challenges. After ruling the government uninterrupted for 60 years, the PRI party had begun to lose some seats to other political parties. Mexico was slowly evolving into a multiparty democracy.

Despite the economic misfortunes of recent years, Mexico remained the United State's third-largest trading partner. Mexico still held opportunities for U.S. firms able to compete in the price-sensitive recessionary market. Mexico had not wavered on the NAFTA agreement since its ratification, and in the mid-1990s 60% of U.S. exports to Mexico entered duty free.

South Korea

South Korea had been identified as one of the U.S. Department of Commerce's 10 "Big Emerging Markets." The country's economy overcame tremendous obstacles after the Korean War in the 1950s left the country in ruins. The driving force behind South Korea's growth was export-led development and energetic emphasis on entrepreneurship. Annual real GDP growth from 1986 to 1991 was over 10%. This blistering pace created inflation, tight labor markets, and a rising current account deficit. Fiscal policy in 1992 focused on curbing inflation and reducing the deficit. Annual growth, reduced to a still enviable 5% in 1992, rose to 6.3% in 1993. Fueled by exports, 1994's growth was a heady 8.3%. South Korea's GDP was larger than Russia, Australia, or Mexico.

The American media had highlighted such issues as student demonstrations, construction accidents, and North Korean nuclear problems and trade disputes. Investors needed to closely monitor developments related to North Korea. However, the political landscape in South Korea had been stable enough over the 1980s to fuel tremendous economic expansion. The country was undertaking significant infrastructure improvements. Overall, South Korea was a democratic republic with an open society and a free press. It was a modern, cosmopolitan, fast-paced, and dynamic country with abundant business opportunities for savvy American businesses.

There had been staggering development of U.S. exports to South Korea: US $21.6 billion in 1994 and over US $30 billion expected in 1995. While South Korea was 22 times smaller than China in terms of population, it imported two times more U.S. goods and services than China in 1994!

Although South Korea ranked as the United State's sixth-largest export market, obstacles for U.S. firms still remained. Despite participation in the Uruguay Round of GATT and related trade agreements, customs clearance procedures and regulations for labeling, sanitary standards, and quarantine often served as significant non-tariff barriers.

The United Kingdom (or Great Britain)

The United Kingdom (UK) was the United States' fourth-largest trading partner and the largest market for U.S. exports in Europe. Common language, legal heritage, and business practices facilitated U.S. entry into the British market.

The United Kingdom had made significant changes to their taxation, regulation, and privatization policies that changed the structure of the British economy and increased its overall efficiency. The reward for this disciplined economic approach had been sustained, modest growth during the 1980s and early 1990s. GDP grew 4.2% in 1994, the highest level in six years. The United Kingdom trimmed its deficit from US $75 billion in fiscal 1994 to US $50 billion in fiscal 1995.

The United Kingdom had no restrictions on foreign ownership and movement of capital. There was a high degree of labor flexibility. Efficiencies had soared in the United Kingdom and in the mid-1990s the country boasted the lowest real per unit labor cost of the Group of Seven (G7) industrialized countries.

The United Kingdom's shared cultural heritage and warm relationship with the United States translated into the British finding U.S. goods and services as attractive purchases. These reasons, coupled with

British policy emphasizing free enterprise and open competition, made the United Kingdom the destination of 40% of all U.S. investment in the European Union.

The U.K. market was based on a commitment to the principles of free enterprise and open competition. Demand for U.S. goods and services was growing. The abolition of many internal trade barriers within the European Common Market enabled European-based firms to operate relatively freely. As a result, U.S. companies used the United Kingdom as a gateway to the rest of the European Union. Of the top 500 British companies, one in eight was a U.S. affiliate. Excellent physical and communications infrastructure combined with a friendly political and commercial climate were expected to keep the United Kingdom as a primary target for U.S. firms for years to come.

Endnotes

1. All three Outback founders credited casual dining chain legend and mentor Norman Brinker with his strong mentoring role in their careers. Brinker played a key role in all of the restaurant chains Sullivan and Basham were associated with prior to Outback.

2. American consumption of meat declined from the mid-1970s to the early 1990s primarily as a result of health concerns about red meat. In 1976 Americans consumed 131.6 pounds of beef and veal, 58.7 pounds of pork, and 12.9 pounds of fish. In 1990 the figures had declined to 64.9 pounds of beef and veal, 46.3 of pork, and 15.5 of fish. The dramatic decrease was attributed to consumer attitudes toward a low-fat, healthier diet. Menu items that gained in popularity were premium baked goods, coffees, vegetarian menu items, fruits, salsa, sauces, chicken dishes, salad bars, and spicy dishes. [George Thomas Kurian, *Datapedia of the United States* 1790–10000 (Maryland: Bernan Press, 1994) pp. 113.]

3. Outback's original Henderson Blvd. (Tampa, Florida) restaurant was one of the few open for lunch. By 1995 the chain had also begun to open in some locations for Sunday lunch or for special occasions such as Mother's Day lunch.

4. Outback's signature trademark was its best-selling "Aussie-Tizer," the "Bloomin' Onion." The company expected to serve nine million "Bloomin' Onions" in 1995.

5. Merritt had worked as CFO for another company which had come to the financial markets with its IPO (initial public offering).

6. Outback did not grant exclusive territorial franchises. Thus, if an Outback franchisee did not perform the company could bring additional franchisees into the area. Through 1994 Outback had not had territorial disputes between franchisees.

7. Pepsico owned Kentucky Fried Chicken, Taco Bell, and Pizza Hut.

8. Grand Met owned Burger King.

9. Ref. AME 76 (KR).

10. "Industry and Trade Summary: Franchising," U.S. International Trade Commission, Washington, DC, 1995, pp. 15–16

11. "World Hunger," *Restaurant Hospitality,* November 1994, p. 97.

12. *International Business Environments and Operations,* seventh edition, 1995, pp. 117–119.

13. "U.S. restaurant chains tackle challenges of Asian expansion," *Nation's Restaurant News,* February 14, 1994, p. 36.

14. *CIA World Factbook,* India, 1995.

15. "Big McMuttons," *Forbes,* July 17, 1995, p. 18.

16. Interview with Cheryl Babcock, Professor, University of St. Thomas, October 23, 1995.

17. "Franchise management in East Asia," *Academy of Management Executive,* Vol. 4, No. 2, 1990, p. 79.

18. "U.S. operators flock to Latin America," *Nation's Restaurant News,* October 17, 1994, p. 47.

19. Interview with Cheryl Babcock, Professor, University of St. Thomas, October 23, 1995.

20. "U.S. restaurant chains tackle challenges of Asian expansion," *Nation's Restaurant News,* February 14, 1994, p. 36.

21. "Industry and Trade Summary: Franchising," U.S. International Trade Commission, Washington, DC, 1995, p. 30.

22. Ibid.

23. "U.S. restaurant chains tackle challenges of Asian expansion," *Nation's Restaurant News,* February 14, 1994, p. 36.

24. Unless otherwise noted the information from this appendix was drawn from "Top 50 Franchisers," *Restaurant Business,* November 1, 1995, pp. 35–41 and *Hoover's Company Profile Database,* 1996, The Reference Press, Inc., Austin, TX (from American Online Service) various company listings.

25. "Big News Over There!," *Restaurants and Institutions,* July 1, 1994.

26. "US Operators Flock to Latin American," *Nation's Restaurant News,* November 17, 1994.

27. There is, thus, no publicly available financial data on Subway.

28. Subway's site on the Internet, accessed March 24, 1996.

29. Note: The material in this appendix is adapted from the Department of Commerce Country Commercial Guides and the *CIA World Fact Book.*

Case 9: **California Foods Corporation**

In early 1990, the international marketing manager at California Foods Corporation (CFC), Lois Verbrugge, was considering how to react to the continuing decline of CFC grape juice sales in the Puerto Rican market. In 1989, the marketing staff in the international division estimated that sales of CFC grape juice had fallen off by approximately 30% from the previous year. To determine why this loss of volume had taken place, extensive consumer research was utilized. But, as of February, Ms. Verbrugge and her staff had not come up with any clear-cut remedies for CFC's problems in the Puerto Rican market.

Company Background

CFC was a wholly owned subsidiary of the Federation of Grape Growers' Associations. The federation purchased the California Foods Corporation in 1956 as part of a strategy to integrate its business forward into the processing and distribution of grape products. CFC continued in 1990 to operate as an agribusiness largely as it had in 1956. The federation supplied the grapes, and CFC handled all processing and marketing of the products. CFC's sales had increased every year since the takeover by the federation. CFC was generally considered the foremost leader in the juice industry. It set the standards for progressive marketing techniques and new product development for the industry. With sales reaching a quarter billion dollars in 1989, the growers and CFC were the largest grape growing, processing, and marketing enterprise in the world.

Originally, CFC had produced only grape-related products: grape jams, grape jelly, frozen grape concentrate, grape drink, and grape preserves. In recent years, however, CFC had expanded to include nongrape products, too. Between 1970 and 1982, CFC introduced 36 new products. In 1990, CFC incorporated a complete line of fruit juices with a selection of fruit drinks and a line of fruit-flavored preserves.

CFC's International Division

CFC distributed an assortment of products to foreign markets with the majority of sales derived from juices and fruit drinks. It marketed its products to over 40 countries. Major markets included Puerto Rico, Mexico, and Japan. CFC products were distributed by food brokers and distributors to retail stores and food service institutions. In 1988, the International Division experienced record sales and greater than expected profitability. Sales slipped slightly during 1989, largely the result of sales erosion in the Puerto Rican market.

The Juice and Drinks Market in Puerto Rico

Most of the juice consumption in Puerto Rico was composed of imported products. Some of the more popular brands competing for market share were CFC, Seneca, Pueblo, and Grand Union. There was only one domestic grape juice producer, selling under the name Richy. Richy had been in business for a few years, but its impact on the market had been minimal. Exhibit 1

EXHIBIT 1   Juices and Drinks Imported into Puerto Rico

	Thousands of Cases (not Equivalents)			Percent of Change
	1987	1988	1989	1988–1989
Fruit juices				
Vegetable juice	20.6	23.4	23.9	+2.1
Tomato juice	45.5	21.2	26.3	+24.6
Apple juice	84.5	109.0	105.6	−3.1
Citrus juice	203.5	198.7	183.4	−7.7
Nectars	—	5.0	1.8	−64.0
Pineapple juice	22.5	22.9	29.1	+27.1
Prune juice	25.8	23.3	29.5	+26.6
Grape juice—CFC	569.1	586.5	412.1	−29.7
Grape juice—other	40.6	37.1	26.6	−28.3
Fruit drinks				
RJR	114.1	161.0	116.3	−27.8
Borden*	92.9	124.4	132.6	+6.6
Miscellaneous/ all others†	260.5	296.4	356.0	+20.4
Fruit juice—frozen and concentrated				
Citrus Central	184.8	236.6	219.5	−7.2
CFC	34.4	23.4	32.5	+33.2
Miscellaneous/all others	378.1	431.5	499.8	+15.8

* Includes Orange Burst instant breakfast drink, Wyler's ades.
† Includes Tang powdered grape and orange drinks.
Source: Maritime Reports (Washington, D.C.: U.S. Government Printing Office, 1990).

EXHIBIT 2   Consumption Results of Sample of Puerto Rican Grape Juice Users During 1988 and 1989

Juices	Previous Users (n = 45)				Current CFC Users (n = 155)			
	More	The Same	Less	Don't Use	More	The Same	Less	Don't Use
Orange	57.7%	28.9%	11.1%	2.3%	43.5%	42.2%	11.7%	2.6%
Grape	13.3	37.8	24.5	24.5	38.9	47.4	13.0	0.7
Pineapple	22.2	26.7	33.3	17.8	23.3	29.9	31.1	15.7
Grapefruit	15.6	11.1	51.2	22.1	5.2	16.9	45.4	32.5
Fruit drinks	47.7	20.0	33.5	26.8	13.6	29.2	23.3	33.9
Fruite nectar	20.0	35.6	26.7	17.7	13.6	30.5	30.5	25.4
Powdered drinks	31.1	17.8	24.4	26.7	9.1	32.5	34.4	24.0

outlines the imported volumes of juices and drinks into Puerto Rico over the last three years. As the table reveals, grape juice imports (California Foods' and others) were declining rather sharply. Still, the grape juice market was by far the largest juice market in Puerto Rico.

The fruit drink category was quite large too and was growing, especially the miscellaneous/all-others subgroup, which included Tang's imported powdered grape and orange drinks. Because many Puerto Ricans equated powdered grape with grape juice, it was possible that at least some of CFC grape juice's volume loss could be traceable to these imports, although no hard evidence existed.

Frozen concentrates represented another competing group that was large and had shown strong growth in the preceding three years. Again, the miscellaneous/all others subgroup had shown steady growth. Perhaps some of CFC grape juice's loss could be attributable to a shift of sales across generic categories.

CFC's Entry into Puerto Rico

CFC's first experience in Puerto Rico came in the 1950s when it introduced CFC grape juice. At that point, grape juice was practically unheard of by the majority of Puerto Ricans. Despite this, the introduction was a resounding success and CFC grape juice became the best-selling juice in Puerto Rico.

Rumour had it that CFC grape juice's success was traceable to the Puerto Rican belief that grape juice was good for men's virility and for women's hemoglobin during their menstrual cycles. Pseudomedicinal drinks were concocted by mixing egg with grape juice. The resulting mixture was referred to as an "egg punch." To take advantage of this seemingly unique consumer behavior, CFC launched an "egg punch" campaign in 1985. One television spot showed a young Puerto Rican man at a disco drinking an egg punch and subsequently departing with an attractive young woman. Print advertising featured a mother nursing her newborn and copy expounding the nutritional value of grape juice.

Grape juice was indeed CFC's biggest seller in Puerto Rico. Sales for 1989 were 412,000 cases. Frozen concentrated grape juice accounted for sales of 32,000 cases during 1989. Other CFC products were Calfood fruit drink, California instant powdered grape drink, CFC grape soda, and CFC strawberry soda.

Consumer Research

In order to ascertain the causes for CFC's rapid decline in grape juice sales, an "Awareness, Usage, and Attitude Study" was compiled in February 1990 to update the marketing department's understanding of Puerto Rican grape juice consumers. Two hundred personal interviews were done with people who had used grape juice during the previous two years. The study was administered by a Puerto Rican consulting group. Results are listed in Exhibit 2.

The results of the study showed that the demand for orange juice had increased tremendously since 1988. In both current and previous studies, users of CFC grape juice were drinking much more orange juice by 1990. In addition, the percentage of respondents who did not use orange juice was practically nil.

Current users of CFC juice continued to drink large quantities of grape juice, as the figures reveal. In fact, 86% of all CFC users said that they drank as much, or more, grape juice in 1989 as they had previously. However, among the previous CFC users, there were many more who had decreased their consumption of grape juice than had increased it. Therefore, it was implied that they were not switching from one grape juice brand to another, but drinking more orange juice instead. Over 57% of previous CFC users drank more orange juice by 1990 than they had in early 1988.

The main motive for the purchase of grape juice by mothers in the sample was because their children had asked for and/or liked it. The study also revealed that Puerto Ricans perceived grape juice to be both tasty and nutritious. On the negative side, respondents who were buying less grape juice had a variety of reasons for not buying it; most notably, very high price and preference for other juices were mentioned.

It was discovered that previous CFC users replaced grape juice with three other types of beverages: other canned juices (pineapple, orange, grapefruit), natural juices (orange, grapefruit, tamarind, lemon), and carbonated drinks (Pepsi, Coca-Cola, and the like).

Researchers had asked the question "Why aren't you using more CFC grape juice?" The most frequent response indicated that CFC's price was too high and that the respondents tried to buy products that were more economical. Secondary reasons suggested that they did not like the taste and preferred other flavors to grape. Exhibit 3 summarizes consumers' reasons for buying either less or no grape juice in general and of CFC's in particular.

CFC had performed a similar consumer study in 1985 to determine grape juice drinkers' attitudes toward CFC grape juice. One section of the 1985 questionnaire involved consumers' opinions of the characteristics of CFC grape juice. Likewise, part of the 1990 survey was devoted to similar questioning. In both studies, respondents rated CFC grape juice on the basis of eight criteria, on a scale from 1 to 6. The figures in Exhibit 4 represent average ratings for each of the product characteristics.

Both studies seemed to suggest that CFC grape juice had been, and still was, well regarded in the Puerto Rican market. There had not been too much change in the general opinion that CFC grape juice was a good-tasting, nutritious, high-quality product. In

EXHIBIT 3 Respondents' Reasons for Not Buying Grape Juice

	Reasons for No Longer Serving Grape Juice	Reasons for No Longer Serving CPC Grape Juice
High price	22.6%	23.2%
Only use it occasionally	9.7	4.4
Prefer other flavors	29.0	22.2
Harmful to stomach/diet	12.9	10.3
Prefer natural juices	16.1	6.7
Not accustomed to using it	NA	8.9
Prefer powdered drinks	NA	8.7
Other	9.7	15.6
Total	100.0%	100.0%

EXHIBIT 4 Averaged Ratings of CFC Grape Juice (Scale of 1 to 6)

	1990 Study (n = 200)	1985 Study (n = 200)
Sweetness	4.95	3.96
Taste	4.96	4.73
Economy	3.86	3.47
Nutrition	5.06	5.24
Naturalness	4.91	5.05
Best for children	4.97	4.92
Best for adults	4.88	4.74
Quality	5.13	5.17

consumers' minds even the price had become more reasonable in relation to the generally stormy economic conditions. So, what seems to be the problem with CFC grape juice in the Puerto Rican market?

The study data appeared to support the notion that CFC grape juice is held in high esteem in Puerto Rico, yet a solution to CFC's sales problem was needed. With this in mind, Ms. Verbrugge arranged a meeting with Jeff Hartman, Market Research Manager, to discuss and review the situation. Ms. Verbrugge wanted to examine the problem in more detail and was prepared to commit additional funds for marketing research. Before making any decision, however, she wanted Mr. Hartman's assessment of the situation.

Case 10: Chivaly International

In early 1991, Martin Creich, product manager for Chivaly International's urethane foam product division, was considering a recommendation that the firm establish a regional sales office in Singapore. Since marketing its products in Indonesian markets in 1984, Chivaly had captured 10% of the urethane foam market. By establishing a sales office in Singapore, Creich could foresee increasing the Indonesian market share for Chivaly's urethane foam to 25% and expanding into Malaysian and Thai markets. In addition, a regional sales office would strengthen Chivaly's competitive posture, allowing the firm to conduct sales directly to distributors and commission agents.

Before presenting his recommendations to top management, Creich wanted to compile necessary information to support his decision.

Chivaly Corporation

Chivaly was a major manufacturer of chemicals, metals, flax-based papers, cellophane, sports equipment, and home building products. Incorporated in South Dakota in 1892, the firm had since established its executive offices in Oklahoma City.

Urethane foam, a part of the chemical division, had been marketed since 1949 and was one of the world's most adaptable products. It was used primarily as cushioning material in chairs, beds, spring mattresses, auto upholstery, and other products that needed foam cushioning. As a result of the product's adaptability, its major chemical component, tuluene dusocyanate (TDI), had become one of the world's largest chemical commodities. Chivaly was also a large producer of TDI, supplying the chemical division with adequate proportions of the commodity for urethane foam production.

Urethane foam was produced for the firm's worldwide markets in two plants located in Lake Charles, Louisiana, and in Mansville, West Virginia. Each plant separately produced more than 50,000 tons of urethane foam per year. Production inefficiencies resulted if either plant fell below the standard 50,000-ton level.

From a process standpoint, urethane foam was a difficult chemical to produce. The product's toxic and lethal components made production and process controls vital steps in manufacturing. Orders were shipped directly from each plant to Chivaly's distributors throughout the world.

International Markets

In 1990, approximately 16% of Chivaly's $2 billion in sales were derived from international markets. By 2000, the company planned to obtain a significant portion of its sales and profits from its overseas businesses. Management believed that investing substantial sums of capital to establish sales offices around the world would help the firm strengthen its international presence. Chivaly already had established offices in Mexico City, Caracas, Dublin, London, Paris, Frankfurt, Johannesburg, Madrid, Cape Town, and Sydney.

Chivaly's entry into specific foreign markets was a result of thorough market analyses. Specifically, the firm performed market profiles and market attractiveness analyses that considered pertinent factors such as target markets, resource requirements, cultural factors, and personnel requirements. After such basic information had been gathered, corporate representatives then traveled to the targeted countries to meet with regional sales representatives, who helped gather further information based on questionnaires distributed to local contacts. The corporate representatives then used this information to formulate a final area profile with analyses and recommendations, eventually determining which markets were most attractive. This process determined which consumers, commission agents, and distributors were to be used if the market proved profitable.

Indonesian Operations

Chivaly entered the Indonesian market in 1984, selling urethane foam on a freight-alongside basis through a Japanese trading company. The trading company, in turn, sold the urethane to local companies in Indonesia. Chivaly's entry into the Indonesian market was haphazard. Initially, the firm knew nothing about the market or how their product was sold. As Chivaly's Indonesian operation grew, the firm established sales representatives in the region, providing a direct link to the market.

The Indonesian market was heavily influenced by corruption. Indonesians expected "royalty payments" in exchange for special treatment and favors. Chivaly representatives, however, had been instructed to refrain from participating in these payments. To avoid this situation, Chivaly sought clients whose executives were American-educated and familiar with Western business procedures.

Indonesia's cultural environment also restricted the way foreign firms could do business. For example, Indonesians preferred to do business with local people; therefore, Chivaly hired a large number of local people as sales representatives.

Chivaly also sold its urethane foam through local distributors. Sales were volume oriented, and long-term business relationships were valued more than short-term profits. Because American companies concentrated on profits, firms would often lose their distributors and commission agents. Asians also refused to wage price wars and, more often than not, refused to sell any product at a price higher than that of their competitors.

Indonesia had few political constraints; however, Chivaly was prohibited from opening regional offices in the country unless a majority of the subsidiary was owned by nationals. Chivaly also was prevented from purchasing and stockpiling urethane foam in local warehouses, which was a major factor in establishing an office in Singapore. As a free-trade zone, Singapore adopted a laissez-faire attitude toward free enterprise.

Chivaly's major Indonesian competitor was the German firm Bayer. Chivaly also competed on a smaller scale with Dow Chemical and BASF. There was little product differentiation among these suppliers. Factors that provided the competitive edge included service, local relationships, and the strength of letters of credit.

Bayer was the largest producer of urethane in the world, while Chivaly ranked second. As the first company to enter the Indonesian urethane foam market, Bayer had captured roughly 45% of the Indonesian market, with sales of over 7,500 tons of urethane.

Bayer's German production facilities provided the firm with huge production capacity and economies of scale. The firm used its extensive distribution network to distribute its full line of urethane foam chemical components to Indonesian markets. However, Bayer did not adapt to cultural factors. Sales representatives maintained a strict European attitude in business affairs, which proved a handicap in Indonesia.

There was little advertising in the urethane foam business. Sales were made strictly through sales contacts. Prices were based on open market demand. In 1990, the price for urethane foam components was $1,550 a ton.

Competitors often mislabeled chemicals for shipment to get cheaper freight rates. Because TDI was a Poison B chemical that caused several health hazards, the word *Tylene* was often painted over the TDI label in Indonesia. Tylene was a comparatively harmless chemical and could be shipped at lower freight rates. Chivaly made sure its products were always represented in the correct manner.

By 1990, Chivaly had captured 10% of the Indonesian market, but management believed they were underpricing their product. To combat its price problem, Chivaly wanted to achieve two objectives: (1) to sell 4,000 tons of TDI and (2) to increase its urethane foam market share to 25 percent. Management felt that the Singapore office would fulfill these objectives.

Case 11: U.S. Automakers in Asia*

To U.S. automakers, Asia looked as California must have to the prospectors of 1849: a place to strike it rich. Weary of competing in the slow-growing, overcrowded markets of North America and Western Europe, they cheered at the thought of millions of potential customers who had yet to buy their first Cavalier, Explorer,

or Jeep. General Motors, Ford, and Chrysler executives were streaming into cities like Shanghai, Manila, and Kuala Lumpur to negotiate with government officials and meet with potential dealers, and scout locations for parts depots and assembly plants. It had been said that there would be ten million units of worldwide automotive growth in the next ten years and the vast majority of that growth would be in Asia. Exhibit 1 shows the vehicle sales in Asia.

---

* This case was prepared in spring 1997 before Chrysler merged with Mercedes-Benz.

EXHIBIT 1 Vehicle Sales in Asia (in Millions)

Country	1990	1996	2002
China	0.3	1.0	2.1
India	0.2	0.7	1.0
Thailand	0.2	0.6	0.8
Taiwan	0.5	0.5	0.6
Malaysia	0.1	0.4	0.5
Indonesia	0.2	0.4	0.4
Philippines	0.1	0.4	0.4
Hong Kong	0.1	0.1	0.2
Singapore	0.1	0.1	0.2
Vietnam	0.1	0.1	0.1

Source: The Economist, April 18, 1998, p. 56.

Different Strategies

Having abandoned manufacturing in Asia in the years before World War II, U.S. automakers were planning a huge sales offensive and their first local production in half a century. Each company was pursuing a separate strategy. GM, the most ambitious, was setting up an integrated Asian production system that utilized its vast parts-making operations as well as its affiliation with Japanese automakers Isuzu and Suzuki. Ford, meanwhile, was pursuing what it called a "reasoned approach" that relied on alliances with local partners in select markets like Vietnam and India. Chrysler wanted to manufacture in only a few countries; its primary focus was exporting vehicles built in North America.

Problems Ahead

With everyone trying to mine the same rich vein, some of the prospectors were bound to come up empty-handed. Asia was dominated by Japanese automakers, who had been propelled by the declining yen and in 1997 controlled 80% of the market; superaggressive South Korean manufacturers also were making a big push. Another problem for the U.S. companies was that Asian markets tilted toward small cars that were less profitable than larger models and sporty trucks.

As Americans built up their manufacturing capabilities in Asia, oversupply could squeeze margins to the vanishing point. GM and Ford each hoped to win 10% of Asian sales by early in the next century, versus less

than 1% each in 1997. Autofacts, a Pennsylvania consulting firm, estimated that over the next five years, five million units of manufacturing capacity would be added to the 23 million already in place. But since sales would not keep pace, 30% of the capacity would be unused. The excess capacity would mean more widespread price cutting and sharply lower profits than if supply and demand were better balanced.

Yet the prospect of so many car buyers overwhelmed the doubters. Like most business people, automakers were optimists who fell in love with their cars and believed they were better than anyone else's. They were not concerned about overcapacity, because it had been a fact of life for years. Ignoring Asia would be psychologically devastating to U.S. manufacturers. It would also allow competitors to reap windfall profits from an uncontested market.

China and India were the ultimate prizes in Asia, but their economies and infrastructures were so underdeveloped that it would be years before auto sales took off. Japan and Korea were dominated by their respective auto industries and protected by a variety of formal and informal regulations. So Detroit's first battles would be fought in six countries of Southeast Asia: Indonesia, Malaysia, the Philippines, Singapore, Thailand, and Vietnam.

Southeast Asian Market

For U.S. manufacturers, doing business in Southeast Asia would be vastly more complicated than anything they had experienced before. Governments delighted in throwing up obstacles to foreign competitors. Malaysia and Indonesia had encouraged the development of locally owned auto industries and tried to squeeze out foreign interlopers. Vietnam had licensed 14 foreign automakers to compete for the market, after originally saying it would license only four. By 2000, Vietnam could have the capacity to build 135,000 cars, but sales were expected to reach only 45,000.

U.S. automakers last tried to dent Southeast Asian markets in the 1960s with a ship 'em and sell 'em policy: They pulled out because Asians' enthusiasm for V-8 powered, left-hand-drive Detroit iron ebbed with the Vietnam War. The Japanese quickly arrived to fill the vacuum. After establishing a beachhead with models exported from Japan, they began building a local manufacturing presence. The Japanese realized much earlier than the U.S. companies did that rapid growth in Asia made it imperative to be there. They would be extremely difficult competition.

With their ambitious goals for market share gains, GM and Ford would have to take business away from the Japanese, which they had historically found difficult to do. Further, the Japanese had an advantage because they were better at flexible manufacturing. They also had 30 years of experience managing in a local context, brand-name recognition, skilled labor, and first-comer advantages in distribution and supplier networks.

The Koreans would be formidable competitors, too. They had very competent technology, their quality was good, and they were aggressive and committed to growth.

Thinking globally did not come naturally to U.S. manufacturers, who tended to be preoccupied with North America. The Japanese were much more effective at adapting to foreign markets. Building cars in Malaysia was not the same as starting up a line in Michigan. Workers and management had to be recruited and trained and the payback could be long.

Competing in Thailand

Each market presented its own obstacles—along with a few opportunities. Fewer than 1.5 million vehicles were sold in Southeast Asia in 1996—about one-tenth of the number sold in the United States Yet Thailand was the most attractive, with some 560,000 sales in 1996. Its market was nearly 50 times larger than Vietnam's, the smallest, and ten times larger than Singapore's, the second smallest. Indonesia, the Philippines, and Malaysia ranked second, third, and fourth in sales.

So intense was activity in Thailand that by 2000 it would have the capacity to produce more cars that the rest of Southeast Asia combined. After GM and Ford decided in 1996 to build regional assembly plants there, the United States dubbed Thailand the "Detroit of Asia." The "Nagoya of Asia" would be more appropriate. Japanese manufacturers had established robust assembly, parts, and distribution networks in Thailand, and seven Japanese companies controlled 91% of the market.

Thailand had a population of 60 million, and its economy had grown faster than any other in the world for the past ten years, though a slowdown in exports and consumer spending caused the rate to sag in 1996 to 6.7%. Fast growth hadn't helped stabilize the Thai government, however, which turned over every couple

of years. Primarily farmers and laborers, Thais had been trading in bicycles for motorbikes and, increasingly, motorbikes for cars. Vehicle purchases had more than doubled since 1990. Still, only one new vehicle was sold there in 1996 for every 100 people (vs. one in 20 for the United States). To put it another way, Thailand had a lot of potential.

Because of high luxury taxes on passenger cars—between 35.75% and 50%—pickup trucks made by Toyota, Isuzu, and Mitsubishi outsold cars 2 to 1. Pickups functioned as cargo haulers, family sedans, even minibuses; ten or more men commuting to work frequently crammed into the back of a truck without benefit of seat belts, or, for that matter, seats.

Besides imposing steep taxes on cars, the Thai government unofficially controlled their prices. Manufacturers must file the prices of new cars three weeks before they go on sale. In 1996, government officials decreed that the $15,000 Honda City was overpriced by 16,000 baht, or $625, because of too much corporate overhead. In addition to lowering their prices, Honda had to pay rebates to 150 customers.

Sometimes it seemed as if all Thailand's cars and trucks were stuck in the same traffic jam. Road construction hadn't kept up with the traffic growth, and cars must compete for space with bicycles and motorbikes. Congestion was legendary in Bangkok, where many roads terminate in dead ends because of the city's network of rivers and canals. To beat the traffic, young female office workers rode to work sidesaddle on the backs of motorbike taxis. As a Toyota executive noted: "Without traffic jams, Bangkok would be paradise."

Thai car-buyers were very style conscious, and their trend-seeking habits made the market hard to predict, even for locals. The mood changed every week. Every car company had to keep close watch. Styling and price were the two key factors. Status counted too. In a country were cellular telephones had become fashion accessories, Mercedes-Benz outsold Volvo, Volkswagen, Opel, Ford, and Peugeot.

Dealerships in Thailand had their own unique flavor. At Honda's landmark seven-story outlet in Bangkok, the largest in Asia, 80% of the salespeople were women. No dickering on price was allowed, and taxes drove up the final tab astronomically. A Honda Accord, nearly identical to the one sold in the United States except for the location of the steering wheel, sold for $35,520, about a 50% premium.

Japanese manufacturers had been building cars in Thailand for nearly two decades. The government kept entry requirements simple, and Thai wages were dirt cheap. The minimum wage set by the government for an auto worker was 10,000 baht a month, or $20 a day—about one-tenth the wage in Japan. Engineers earned up to $30 a day, or $600 a month. Generous benefits included family medical care, free bus transportation to and from work, a uniform, lunch, and 12 vacation days.

The flip side of cheap wages was high turnover and short supply. Thailand had one of the lowest rates of secondary and college education in Asia. According to the Japanese Chamber of Commerce in Thailand, there were 11,000 openings a year for new engineers, but only 6,000 Thai engineers a year graduating to fill them. Wages were rising at a rate of 10% a year. Managing the local labor force required a small army of expatriates, who were considered more expensive than the locals. Honda employed 43 at one of its plants and said they cost $200,000 a year each—as much as 35 Thais.

To cope with the labor shortage, job training was as critical for automakers as steel buying. Toyota had invested $20 million in a training center outside Bangkok, where it could provide instruction to thousands of workers annually. But the automakers' recruitments and job training would have a hard time keeping up with their planned increases in production. Nissan was increasing capacity at its plant 50%, to 140,000 cars and trucks a year. Mitsubishi had moved its pickup-truck production from Japan to Thailand's eastern seaboard. Toyota spent $350 million to build a second assembly plant in Thailand, boosting its capacity to 200,000 units. Honda opened a new Thai auto-assembly plant in April 1996, raising capacity to 80,000 units.

To tour a Japanese auto plant in Thailand was to marvel at the efficient substitution of labor for machinery—and at times to be appalled at the disregard for worker safety. Because wages were low, workers instead of machines performed such functions as body welding and assembly. Nobunari Matsushita, president of Honda Cars Manufacturing (Thailand), noted the handwork produced high-quality Hondas. But productivity at Honda's plant was 10% to 15% lower than in Japan because, according to Matsushita, Thai workers were less diligent than their Japanese counterparts. "Generally speaking, the Japanese worker arrives earlier and prepares for his job ahead of time, and then stays to clean up after his shift, says Matsushita. "That's not the case here. The Japanese worker performs ten operations and ten quality checks in one cycle. The Thai worker also performs ten processes, but only three to four quality checks."

To solidify their hold on Southeast Asia, the Japanese were beginning to produce cars engineered specifically for the market. In January, Toyota launched its "affordable family car" called Soluna, which was about the size of a subcompact Tercel. Honda had already begun selling a durable low-cost sedan called the City. Depending on one's point of view, the City was either a clever, economical solution to developing markets or, as competitors say, a stripped-down Civic. But it was solidly built and would undoubtedly satisfy American buyers if it were sold in the United States.

The Thai government required local content of 60% for pickup trucks and 54% for passenger cars, so developing a reliable network of suppliers was critical to manufacturing success. Because Thai suppliers were so much less sophisticated and efficient than Japanese suppliers, companies like Honda had imported their own. Of its 107 suppliers, 70 were joint venture operations with Japanese companies. One of the best known was Stanley Electric, which began selling headlights and other electrical parts to Honda's motorcycle factories in 1980; now Stanley supplied every Japanese auto manufacturer in Thailand.

Stanley's president, Akihiro Nakamura was eager for business from U.S. automakers. But he said they should be prepared for adverse conditions in Thailand that included floods "every so often." He also said that GM and Ford might have trouble finding enough suppliers: "Many parts manufacturers have apprehensions about increasing capacity for new customers. In addition, local Thai suppliers have no experience dealing with the Big Three."

Undeterred, U.S. manufacturers were arriving in Thailand en masse. Chrysler had the most modest goals. In its only Asian assembly operations, it built right-hand-drive Jeep Cherokees, which were taxed as cars, in tiny quantities. It sold 3,000 Jeeps in 1996 and was now adding small production runs of the Jeep Grand Cherokee. Starting this year, Chrysler would also begin importing subcompact Neons and Voyager minivans.

Ford had far more ambitious plans to invest $500 million in a pickup-truck plant in the eastern seaboard region, 72 miles south of Bangkok. Production would begin in 1999. The plant was conceived as a joint venture with Mazda, which was now controlled by Ford, and the 135,000 trucks built there annually would be badged as both Fords and Mazdas. Beginning in 1999, Ford would follow Toyota and Honda in building a new small car at the plant designed exclusively for Asia.

A year and a half of study preceded Ford's decision to locate in Thailand. David L. Snyder, who headed the project, said the company talked to its top 100 suppliers about supporting operations in Thailand as well as elsewhere in Asia; it was also forming two new companies to manufacture components. "Putting a lot of capacity in place at one time produces a lot of risks," admitted Snyder. "But there are prospects for attractive returns."

After investigating 12 countries in its search for an Asian production center, GM finally chose a site right next to Ford's in Thailand. Its $750 million plant, which would have a capacity of 100,000 cars expandable to 150,000, would build a version of the subcompact Open Astra. GM was making the right moves, such as setting up a human resource operation to groom local managers. But Asia boss Donald Sullivan was not promising a quick payoff. Noted he: "The nature of the business in Asia is tougher. Profits are thinner, startup costs are higher, and there is more competition from the Japanese and Koreans. So the payback is longer." He estimated that it would take eight to ten years for GM to recover its investment.

Conclusion

In Southeast Asia, then, its *déjà vu* all over again for U.S. automakers: They were waging another war against the heavily armed Japanese. Japanese companies got to Southeast Asia first, and as always they were more concerned with gaining market share and holding on for the long haul than they were with profits or return on capital. After several years of concerted efforts in Japan, GM, Ford, and Chrysler still had a combined market share of just 3%. Southeast Asia should be easier—though not by much—because its markets were more open and national competitors were fewer.

Daunting as Asia was, U.S. automakers had no choice but to be there. Investing more in North America, where returns were less than the cost of capital, was throwing good money after bad. Acquisitions were out of style. Unless the Big Three wanted to deliberately liquidate, they must explore new markets, and Asia was the biggest market of all.

Case 12: Nestlé (Ghana) Ltd.*

It was January 1995 and Pierre Charles had just taken up his new position of marketing director of Nestlé's subsidiary in Ghana in West Africa. A native of Switzerland, he had never been to Africa. In fact, apart from reports that periodically crossed his desk at headquarters in Vevey, Switzerland, he was not very familiar with developing country environments. His education and work experience had all been in Switzerland. Prior to taking up the appointment, Pierre took the opportunity to review conditions in Ghana and Nestlé's operations in that country. It was important that he do well in the new job since that would enhance his career prospects in the international division.

As he reviewed the available information, he was struck by how different the Ghanaian environment was from what he was used to. Economic and political conditions were like nothing he had experienced. The infrastructure for marketing was totally different. For example, it was impossible to get reliable information on such crucial factors as market shares, market segments,

distributor volumes, and other market data. Conducting market research was also a major task primarily because of deficiencies in postal and telephone systems. Yet, marketing managers were expected to design effective strategies and maintain profitable positions. It appeared to him that he had to quickly adjust to this environment in order to maximize his effectiveness. Fortunately he spoke English, the official language of Ghana, so language problems would be minimized. In particular, he had to assess the situation and make decisions about expanding operations, maintaining competitive position, and above all, maintaining profit margins. He did not have a whole lot of time because competitive pressures were mounting, and the economic and political situation was changing rapidly. Underlying all of this was a need to prioritize possible courses of action.

Nestlé (Ghana) Operations

Nestlé (Ghana) was a joint venture between Nestlé A.S. (a Swiss multinational corporation) and the state-owned National Investment Bank (NIB). The joint

---

* This case was prepared by Franklyn A. Manu and Ven Sriram, Morgan State University. It is printed here with permission from the *Case Research Journal* and the authors.

venture was established in 1971 with Nestlé S.A. owning 51%. In the mid-1970s, the then ruling military government of Ghana, the National Redemption Council (NRC), pursuing an indigenization strategy, acquired 55% of the shares.

The government of current President Rawlings reverted to a 49% share in 1993, held by the National Investment Bank (NIB). These changes in ownership structure reflected the country's shift from a nationalistic philosophy involving state participation in leading enterprises to a reluctant push towards privatization. Nestlé was very interested in acquiring the shares held by NIB.

The company had stated capital of 1 billion cedis (about US$1.05 million) and 600 employees, 350 more than normal Nestlé standards in its other subsidiaries for that level of capitalization. Annual sales were currently about 25 billion cedis (about US$26.3 million). The company had four main product lines: canned and powered milk, powdered cocoa drinks, coffee, and Maggi spice cubes. It had one factory in the industrial port city of Tema, some 20 miles from the capital Accra, and this was Nestlé's only milk-processing plant in West Africa. The subsidiary had been set a growth target of 5% in Swiss francs but had actually averaged a rate of 12% in recent years, compared to 5% for Nestlé worldwide. Exhibit 1 provides performance data for Nestlé (Ghana).

Nestlé (Ghana) was headed by a managing director who oversaw a three-division structure—Marketing, Production, and Finance and Administration. The managing director and the plant engineer were typically appointed by Nestlé S.A., which had a management contract to run Nestlé (Ghana). These appointees had usually been white expatriates. As of January 1995, the managing director, director of marketing, sales manager, and plant engineer positions were filled by white expatriates. The remaining positions were mostly filled by Ghanaians. The company had a six-member board of directors, four appointed by Nestlé's S.A. and two appointed by the NIB.

The Republic of Ghana

Political History

The Republic of Ghana lay on the western coast of Africa. It had an area of 92,000 square miles and had an estimated population of 15.5 million in 1991. The country had experienced a chequered political history since independence was gained from the British in

EXHIBIT 1 Nestlé Operating Results (Billions of Cedis)

	1993	1992
Sales	19.3	14.7
Operating Profit	2.7	1.9
Net Profit	2.5	1.8
Fixed Costs	4.9	3.4
Variable Costs	11.6	8.4
Total Assets	11.8	9.9
Total Equity	5.7	4.2
Liabilities (Short Term)	4.0	2.2
Liabilities (Medium Term)	1.8	1.7
Dividends	1.7	1.5

1993: US$1 = 699.30 cedis
1992: US$1 = 437.09 cedis

Source: Nestlé 1993 Annual Report.

1957. Military regimes had run the country for 21 of the years since independence. The current civilian government of President Rawlings, which won the latest elections in 1992, was an offshoot of a military regime, the Provisional National Defence Council (PNDC), which overthrew the previous civilian democratic government of the People's National Party in 1981. The rule of then Flight-Lieutenant Rawlings' PNDC was characterized by suppression of human rights, including imprisonment and execution of alleged opponents. The period was also marked by many attempts to overthrow the PNDC regime. Political and ethnic tensions increased and continue currently, even though Rawlings won the 1992 presidential election with 58% of the vote, a result certified by international observers despite incidents of irregularities. Other political parties refused to accept the results and boycotted the parliamentary elections. This resulted in a situation in which Rawlings and his allies won 199 out of 200 seats in the Parliament, with the remaining seat going to a political independent. Independent media consistently attacked government policies and personalities while the state-owned media consistently supported them. Allegations of corruption and ethnic bias had been leveled against the government. Of particular concern were the upcoming 1996 presidential and parliamentary elections. The government and opposition parties had serious disagreements over revision of the voters' register and issuance of identity cards, with the opposition parties threatening violence if the elections were not fair.

Economy

Economically, Ghana was in the lower tier of developing countries and classified as a least developed country (LDC) by international development agencies because its per capita annual income was US$400. Quite prosperous at independence, the country had declined precipitously as a result of economic mismanagement, political instability, brain drain, and corruption. The World Bank and other external donors were currently funding an economic recovery program (ERP) which appeared to be pulling the economy out of the doldrums. Gross national product (GNP) was about $7 billion or $400 per capita and growing at around 1.2% per annum in real terms. Gross domestic product (GDP) was growing at about 3.2% in real terms. Consumer prices increased by an average of 10% in 1992 and 16% in 1993. Inflation had averaged 40% per annum since 1985.

Agriculture contributed about 49% of GDP and was growing at an annual average of 1.2%. Forty-nine percent of the labor force was employed in this sector. Industry (including mining, manufacturing, construction and power) contributed 17% of GDP and employed 13% of the labor force. Industrial GDP had been growing at an annual average of 3.7% in recent times. While mining had shown the greatest growth (17.7%) in the industrial sector, manufacturing remained the largest component of the sector. It contributed 10% of national GDP, growing at a rate of 4.1% per annum, and employed 11% of the labor force.

Ghana had merchandise trade and balance of payments deficits in the five years prior to 1995. Principal exports were cocoa, gold, and timber, growing at 5% per annum. Major imports were machinery, transport equipment, basic manufactures, and petroleum. External debt was about $4.3 billion and debt-service was equal to 30% of exports of goods and services.

Discussions with other Nestlé managers familiar with Ghana brought out the following additional information:

- Inflation was higher than official estimates.
- Foreign exchange availability was low.
- Cedi would continue to depreciate.
- There was a high level of currency instability.
- Nestlé had very little commitment to exports.
- No price controls existed.
- Interest rates were currently high (around 30%) but were expected to come down to 25%.

- Government regulations were not very burdensome. Sales taxes, for example, had declined from 35% to 15%. Potential problems were expected though from current government attempts to implement a value-added tax (VAT).
- Money supply was expected to rise dramatically as the government launched its campaign for the 1996 election.
- Nestlé had few labor problems even though there might be general labor unrest.

Exhibit 2 provides selected statistics and information on Ghana.

The Cocoa Beverage Market

The size of Ghana's cocoa beverage market was estimated at 4,500 tons and growing slowly. It was forecast to grow at approximately 5% per annum through 1997. Cocoa beverages were primarily a breakfast drink. Information on market segments relating to beverage consumption was unavailable. However, most marketers in Ghana used a classification scheme based on socioeconomic status (SES) to segment markets. The scheme, and the methodology underlying it, is shown in Exhibit 3. It was not exactly clear how these socioeconomic segments impacted on product consumption or purchase. Other types of segmentation data were nonexistent or were highly proprietary.

The market could, however, be divided into three categories based on the product.

1. The Premium Segment: Brands in this category included malt in addition to the basic cocoa powder, sugar, and milk. Leading brands were Milo, Bournvita, and Ovaltine.
2. Mass Market: Brands in this category did not contain malt, thus reducing their costs considerably. Leading brands were Chocolim, Drinking Chocolate, Richoco, and Golden Tree.
3. Institutional Market: Products aimed at this segment contained basic unsweetened cocoa powder supplied to school, hospitals, the armed forces, and so on.

Nestlé's (Ghana) Products

Nestlé's powdered cocoa drinks consisted of Milo and Chocolim. Milo came in a 450-gram tin size with 24 tins to a carton. Tin for making the containers was supplied by headquarters and was rapidly becoming a

![EXHIBIT 2 Selected Information on Ghana]

EXHIBIT 2 Selected Information on Ghana

1. Average Exchange Rate (Cedis per US$)

1990	326.33
1991	367.83
1992	437.09
1993	699.30
1994	950.00

2. Money Supply ('000 Million Cedis at 31 December)

1990	271.64
1991	345.49
1992	525.93
1993	664.67

Average annual growth, 1980–91: 43%

Sources: International Monetary Fund's International Financial Statistics and World Bank Tables, 1995.

3. Cost of Living (Consumer Price Index. Base: 1980 = 100)

	1990	1991	1992
Food	2,711	2,955	3,261
Clothing and Footwear	4,371	5,052	5,488
Rent, Fuel, and Light	5,802	8,373	10,097
All Items (incl. others)	3,575	4,219	4,644

Source: United Nations Economic Commission for Africa (UNECA)—African Statistical Yearbook.

4. Communications Media

	1989	1990	1991
Radios ('000s)	NA	4,000	4,150
TVs ('000s)	211	225	235
Telephones ('000s)	83	84	85

Newspapers	Circulation
Daily:	
Daily Graphic	100,000
Ghanaian Times	40,000
Pioneer	100,000
Other Major:	
Chronicle	60,000
Mirror	90,000
Spectator	165,000
Standard	50,000

5. Income Distribution (% Share of Income)

Lowest 20%	2nd Quintile	3rd Quintile	4th Quintile	Highest 20%	Highest 10%
7.0	11.3	15.8	21.8	44.1	29.0

6. Education

	Primary School	Secondary School	Higher Education
1. Student Population	1.95m (1990)	805,000 (1990)	16,350 (1981)

2. Government Expenditure: 65 billion cedis (1990), i.e., 26% of total spending

Sources: (4, 5, and 6): United Nations Economic and Social Council (UNESCO), Statistical Yearbook and UNECA, African Statistical Yearbook.

7. Population

	1970–75	1980–85	1989–94
Urban % of Population	30.1	32.3	35.8
Urban Population Growth Rate	2.9	4.3	4.0

Access to Safe Water (% of population)

Total	35	49.2	55.7
Urban	86	72.0	93.0
Rural	14	39.0	39.0

Source: World Bank—Social Indicators of Development, 1995.

Age Profile of Population:

0–14	=	45%
15–29	=	26.4%
30–44	=	14.6%
45–59	=	8.1%
60–74	=	4.1%
75 plus	=	1.8%

Annual growth rate of population estimated at 3.1% for 1990–95 and 3.04% for 1995–2000.

Source: Encyclopedia of the Third World, 4th ed, Volume 1 (1992). George Thomas Kurian (ed).

major cost component in the production process. Consideration was being given to the introduction of a 200-gram soft plastic pack. Chocolim was sold in a 500-gram soft plastic pack with 40 packs to a carton. The two products were quite similar, with a cocoa base, added milk, and pre-sweetened. Chocolim did not contain malt and this made it cheaper. Sixty percent of the company's powdered beverage sales came from Milo and 40% from Chocolim. Milo was introduced into Ghana from another Nestlé subsidiary. It was formulated by an Australian, Thomas Maynee, about 60 years ago and was extremely popular in Africa and Southeast Asia. Annual worldwide sales are 90,000 tons, worth about $430 million from the 30 countries

████████████ **EXHIBIT 3**   An Approach to Market Segmentation: Determining the Socioeconomic Status (SES) of Respondents

The following process was used to determine the socioeconomic status (SES) of respondents.

Step 1: Scoring of Variables

1. Highest Education in Household	Score
None	4
Primary	3
Secondary	2
Post-secondary/University/Higher	1

2. Occupation of Chief Wage Earner

Professional/Managerial/Large-Scale Entrepreneur	1
Artisans/Skilled/Technician/Civil Servant/Teacher	2
Semi-Skilled/Small Trader/Clerical	2
Manual Labour	3
Agricultural Worker/Farmer/Hunter	3
Not Working/Student/Housewife	4

3. Consumer Durable Ownership

Telephone	2
Bicycle	1
Television (if any)	2
Video Recorder	2
Refrigerator	2
Car/truck	2
Kerosene Stove	1
Gas/Electric Stove (Cooker)	2
House	2
Radio	1

*Maximum durables score possible = 17

Durables Score Range	Recorded Score
0–5	3
6–11	2
12–17	1

Step 2: Importance Weighting of Variable Categories

	Weighting
Education	3
Occupation	2
Consumer Durables	1

Step 3: Application of Formula to Each Respondent Individually

Formula: (Weight × scores)
Total SES score for each respondent = (3 × education score) + (2 × occupation score) + (1 × consumer durables score)

Determination of SES Group	Score Range
Class A/B	6–10
Class C	11–14
Class D	15–20
Class E	21–24

Possible scoring range = 6–24

Source: Market Research International (Ghana)—private communication.

in Nestlé's strategy was to ensure high awareness of its brands and widespread distribution.

Competition

Finding information on competitors' activities was one of the most difficult aspects of designing marketing strategy in Ghana. Industry and brand level data were hard to come by. Nestlé managers estimated their share of the cocoa beverage market at 80% based on research by a firm which tracked sales in a sample of retailers in addition to tracking consumption. Other observers, however, believed Nestlé's share was closer to 55%. Major competitors for Nestlé were Bournvita and Richoco, manufactured by Cadbury (Ghana) with an estimated 20% to 40% market share, and imported Ovaltine.

Originally known as Cadbury and Fry (England), Cadbury entered Ghana in 1910 to source cocoa beans for its own chocolate-making plants in England. Processing of cocoa beans started in 1963, with a cocoa-based drink introduced soon after. Cadbury (Ghana) was 100% owned by Cadbury Schweppes (U.K.) and had 120 employees. Of estimated 1994 sales of 4 billion cedis, 70% was derived from cocoa beverages and the remainder from sugar confectioneries (e.g. Hacks and Trebor) and Kwench, a fruit-flavored noncarbonated drink. Cocoa beverage capacity of Cadbury averaged 2,000 tons per annum with profit margins of about 35%. In 1990 Cadbury started a major diversification away from cocoa beverages and into sugar confectioneries. The company hoped to have the latter contributing 51% of sales by 1997. Introduction of Richoco in 1990 to exploit a gap in the lower end of the

where it is marketed. Chocolim was locally developed in 1981–82.

Milo was the premier brand and was targeted to the high end of the market, while Chocolim was aimed at rural areas and low-end urban segments. In terms of age, Milo was targeted toward 10- to 18-year-olds but with a focus on mothers as decision makers. The thrust

EXHIBIT 4 Leading Brands and Prices of Selected Powdered Cocoa Beverages at a Leading Supermarket in Accra (January 9, 1995)

Company	Brand	Composition	Pack Size	Price (Cedis)
Nestlé	Milo	Malt extract, milk, sugar, cocoa powder, ethyl vanillin	200g soft pack	850
Nestlé	Milo	Malt extract, milk, sugar, cocoa powder, ethyl vanillin	450g can	2,400
Nestlé	Chocolim	Cocoa powder, milk, sugar, vegetable fat, mineral salts, vitamins	500g soft pack	1,300
Cadbury	Bournvita	Malt extract, sugar, glucose syrup, fat-reduced cocoa, dried skimmed milk, dried egg	450 plastic jar	2,200
Cadbury	Drinking Chocolate	Sugar, skimmed milk powder, cocoa flavorings	500g soft pack	1,050
Cadbury	Richoco	Cocoa, sugar, milk, mineral salts	1kg soft pack	2,800
Cocoa Processing Company (CPC)	Golden Tree Vitaco Instant Drinking Chocolate	Cocoa powder, sugar; skimmed milk powder, lecithin, vanillin	350g soft pack	980
NABB Brothers	Ovaltine (Imported)	Barley and malt extract, skimmed milk powder, whey powder, vegetable fat, sugar, sodium bicarbonate, potassium bicarbonate	200g can	2,700
NABB Brothers	Ovaltine (Imported)	Barley and malt extract, skimmed milk powder, whey powder, vegetable fat, sugar, sodium bicarbonate, potassium bicarbonate	400g can	4,250
NABB Brothers	Ovaltine (Imported)	Barley and malt extract, skimmed milk powder, whey powder, vegetable fat, sugar, sodium bicarbonate, potassium bicarbonate	1,200g can	11,500
Unknown (Imported from France)	Petit de Jeuner		400g box	2,800
Unknown (Imported from France)	Instantane		400g plastic jar	2,800

market and good relations with distributors reflected Cadbury's strong marketing skills. For example, Cadbury went to a 1-kg package for Richoco, which enabled retailers to repackage, thus increasing the latter's margins by 40%.

Another competitor, though on a much smaller scale, was the state-owned Cocoa Processing Company (CPC) which made Golden Tree Vitaco Instant Drinking Chocolate. CPC was strongest in the institutional market, where it had a cost advantage (estimated 23% lower) because it supplied the basic cocoa powder to other firms. The company also made Golden Tree Chocolates, which had won many awards in European and Japanese competitions.

An additional category of competition came from imports, the most prominent of which was Ovaltine, marketed by NABB Brothers, a leading distributor of supermarket products. Volume of imports was low, about 2% of the market, and there were no statistics on brand volumes. It was believed that these imports were either smuggled or evaded taxes and could therefore be sold at lower prices than domestically produced brands. The major brands, their composition, packaging, and prices are shown in Exhibit 4. Milo was the leader in the premium category, while Golden Tree was strongest in the institutional market. Richoco was believed to lead Chocolim by about 5% to 10% market share in the mass market. Exhibit 5 indicates available

████████   **EXHIBIT 5**   Imports of
Cocoa Powder*

Period	Imports (CIF value in cedis)	Cedi/Kg
January–May 1991	27,971,505	837.75
January–December 1992	66,379,420	1159.24
January–September 1993	15,559,184	1098.73
January–May 1994	28,920,619	3748.62

* Cocoa powder, containing added sugar or other sweetening matter.
Source: Government of Ghana Central Bureau of Statistics

████████   **EXHIBIT 6**   Local Production
of Cocoa Powder

Year	Production (kilograms)
1986	578,000
1987	665,000
1988	618,000
1989	557,000
1990	830,000
1991	1,078,000
1992	462,000
1993*	467,500

* Provisional
Source: Government of Ghana Central Bureau of Statistics

government statistics on imports. Exhibit 6 shows domestic production of cocoa powder.

Distribution Structure

"Ghana is fast becoming a nation of shopkeepers" was a popular joke in the country as economic liberalization gave the retail industry a very strong boost in urban areas. Most of the retail outlets were small and specialized in merchandise lines such as appliances, food and beverages, and clothing. Competition was intense; however, this had not shown up in price wars at the general retail level. Most outlets were standalone and there were very few retail chains. Stores were usually of the "mom and pop" variety found in the Western world. Additional retailing institutions included itinerant street hawkers, wooden kiosks, and "container" stores made from metal shipping containers. With no zoning laws, all the retailing forms were found in business districts as well as residential neighborhoods, making location extremely important. Nestlé had 100 regular distributors nationwide and a few other irregulars. Warehouses in Accra (the capital) and Tamale (in the northern part of the country) supplied these distributors. Some of the large distributors such as supermarkets and department stores were supplied directly from the plant at Tema. The biggest distributor was Unilever's G. B. Ollivant subsidiary. Nestlé also operated its own sales outlets in three of the biggest cities (Kumasi, Takoradi, and Tamale) outside of the capital Accra. Margins to distributors were nominally 7.5% but in reality they only made 2% to 3% because of serious price undercutting among them to gain sales. Some distributors were also granted a 21-day interest-free credit on supplied goods. The large distributors typically ordered in quantities of 15 to 20 million cedis (about US$16,000–$21,000), while the smaller ones ordered around 5 million cedis (about US$5,500). While officially Nestlé did not place any restriction on its distributors carrying competing lines, unofficially it frowned on the practice.

Promotion

Promotion in Ghanaian industries had become quite intense as the economy was liberalized and consumer goods flooded the market. Most of the promotional wars took the form of contests and advertising in all its forms. What was not so clear were the effects of such promotions. Some argued that different companies' promotions canceled each other out and consumers often postponed their purchases until there was a sales promotion in effect. Others argued that if a company's promotion was unique it would gain an edge. The problem with the latter view was that many of these promotions were easily imitated.

Nestlé used a combination of media advertising and sales promotions targeted at the youth for Milo. In particular, sports-based promotion was emphasized. The company sponsored highly popular youth soccer leagues for ages 10 to 18 years and for schools and colleges. It also sponsored tennis tournaments and a marathon race for all age groups. Another widely used sales promotion technique was wet sampling (i.e., free drinks) at the Ministry of Education Sports Department's events for school children. Total expenditure for promotion was about 150 million cedis (about US$150,800) and was estimated to grow by 10% to 15% per annum. Sixty percent of the budget went for nonmedia promotion while 40% covered media expenditures. This was the reverse of other Nestlé products. Media advertising promoted the themes of good health, growing up, and success as closely related and linked to drinking Milo. Another theme was that Milo contributed to success in sports, and success in sports contributed to success in life. As a policy, Nestlé did not use sports personalities because they switched product endorsements frequently and often had short popularity spans. Rather, Nestlé emphasized the use of ordinary people in its advertisements. This was despite the national and international popularity of Ghanaian stars like Azumah Nelson (world featherweight boxing champion), Abedi Pele (star midfielder in the French soccer league), and Tony Yeboah (star striker in the English soccer league). Advertising development was performed by Media Magique and Market Research Systems (MMRS) and the Advertising Design Agency (ADA), which focused on Milo.

Mass promotion in Ghana was particularly difficult given low levels of television and radio ownership as well as low circulation of print media. This meant that mass promotion was viable primarily in the urban areas, but the majority of people lived in rural areas. Companies had to use the more expensive sponsorship approach in the latter areas. The rural areas were also places where ethnic differences, particularly language, were most pronounced. This required the use of many languages and dialects in local sponsorship programs and activities.

Pricing

Nestlé's brands were sold at premiums of 5% to 10% over competitors' because of its perceived better quality. With declining real incomes, products were becoming less affordable. There was also increasing price pressure from imports that were flooding the market as a result of import liberalization. (Prices of the major brands in the country are shown in Exhibit 4.) Ghana had a long history of government-controlled prices for consumer goods, and it was only since the late 1980s that companies had been really free to set their own prices. As a result, people were quite sensitive to price changes and were said to have long-term negative perceptions of companies that were perceived to engage in price gouging. Such incidents also attracted negative press coverage. On the other hand though, rapid increases in inflation and the fast-falling cedi were exerting upward pressure on costs of production and reducing profit margins. Distributors therefore raised their prices frequently in an attempt to keep up with inflation. This often had unintended consequences on the pricing strategy of manufacturers who often had to reduce their margins to keep their products affordable.

Conclusion

As Pierre pondered all this information he realized the complexity of the task ahead of him and wondered what his focus should be. There was increasing competition in the market, the external economic and political environment was increasingly hostile and risky, and yet there was clearly insufficient information to make decisions in the manner to which he was accustomed. While he could argue that nothing should be done until a marketing information system was put in place, reality indicated that some responses had to be made soon in order to compete effectively and maintain profitability. In the long term, issues relating to new product introductions, further market penetration, market data, diversification, and contingency planning would have to be addressed. Foremost in his mind was the sequence of actions to pursue. Could he put everything on hold while he launched a comprehensive marketing research effort to provide appropriate information? What if, in the meantime, Nestlé's strong position was adversely affected by competition and the political/economic environment?

Case 13: EQ Bank

On October 20, 1988, Michael Banks, political risk manager of EQ Bank in New York, was approached by Daniel Whitman, president of Enviro-systems, to arrange financing for the construction of a refuse recycling facility to be built in Senegal, Africa. This project called for shipping human refuse from the eastern seaboard of the United States to the West African country, where the labor-intensive job of sorting would take advantage of the lower wage rate. The bulk of the refuse was to be sorted into recyclable components such as metals, glass, and plastic; the remainder was to be shredded, sterilized, and then seeded with a bacteria to ferment into a clean compost that would be superior to the local African soil. The human waste and some of the refuse was to be combined to produce methane. Both end products would be sold locally.

Banks was now preparing for a meeting, on November 15, 1988, with Joseph Gergacz, vice president of EQ's venture capital fund management division to discuss procedures for the project.

EQ Bank

EQ Bank, established in 1975, deals primarily in Africa. EQ Bank is a private nondeposit bank whose personnel see themselves as deal makers. They buy and sell a wide variety of African products, for both import and export. They also find buyers and suppliers for African manufacturers and provide financial services and capital. Their variety of clients include private businesses, state-owned firms, governments, and international agencies that deal with Africa.

The company is divided into EQ Trade, EQ Aviation, EQ Capital Markets, and EQ Bank. These four units can operate separately or in concert depending on the needs of the client.

The import-export trade division is based on the belief that Africa's future depends on advanced technology and improving methods of production. To this end EQ Trade helps by providing a conduit for knowledge as well as products. It also encourages worldwide purchases of African products. They are manufacturers' agents for mining equipment (drills, bores, dump trucks, heavy earth moving machinery), surface transportation (fishing vessels, oil-field service vessels, railway locomotives and rolling stock, buses, commercial lorries, tractor-trailers), and commercial and general aviation (new and used aircraft, aircraft parts, ground service). They offer financial support in the form of supplier credit lines, short-term bridge financing, and currency hedging. They also act as consultants giving advice on markets, product information, and economic development assistance agency packages. The latter involves products that qualify for special treatment under bilateral or multilateral institutions providing grant or concession financing for development projects.

EQ Aviation is a worldwide network of airplanes, parts, and aviation services. Its personnel can provide the equipment to operate an airport and the expertise to form an airline.

EQ Capital Markets provides general managerial, financial, and technical skills in support of a wide variety of economic and business activities in Africa. Personnel in this division advise on mergers, acquisitions, divestitures, and joint ventures. They often counsel senior executives of African government ministries, financial institutions, state-owned enterprises, and private firms. They help corporations expand capital, structure debt and equity, and, in general, work to present the enterprise to the financial markets effectively and efficiently.

Through its affiliation with the Hong Kong Bank Group and other contacts in financial centers, EQ Capital Markets works to match capital with worthwhile projects in need of funds. It is also working to establish financial institutions in Africa.

Through its close relationship with African finance ministers and commercial banks, EQ Capital Markets is in an ideal situation to participate in debt-for-equity and debt-for-debt swaps—a practice personnel like to call debt arbitrage.

EQ Bank is the original EQ company. This merchant banking division concentrates most of its activities in trade and capital equipment financing. It is a registered Bahamian bank, and its personnel pride themselves on being able to create a variety of specialized financing structures tailored to specific client needs. They offer a variety of offshore banking services, including foreign currency exchange, hedging, interest rate futures, and interest rate swaps, all performed under the Bank Secrecy Act of the Bahamas.

The projects at EQ Bank were given to teams that had specific knowledge on the business aspects as well as a strong background in the region of Africa involved. With respect to the refuse conversion project, Banks worked with a Senegal and an Ivory Coast national. They were required to report their progress to their superior; however, when questioned on reporting procedures, Banks stated that he "reports occasionally, and sometimes not at all."

Banks had spent two years in the Peace Corps after graduating from Stanton College with a degree in philosophy. He then earned a master's degree in international affairs from Columbia University. After working for Chase Manhattan Bank for 16 months, he returned to his undergraduate university and taught for one year. He then came to EQ Bank and has been there for almost two years. He is a humanitarian and always stresses how he and his company are in business to help Africa, not just to make money.

The Rubbish

Currently the United States is producing 200 million tons of rubbish per year and it is disposed of by either landfall, incineration, or recycling. Burying is the cheapest and accounts for 90% of American disposal;

however, this is likely to decrease in the future. Americans are voting to keep the smelly dump sites away from their homes and environmentalists are constantly campaigning to eliminate them altogether. Environmentalists are armed with many cases of poisoned land—completed dump sites where the rubbish is producing methane, thus making the land unusable.

Landfill sites are also being exhausted. One-third have closed since 1980, and more than half the cities on the East Coast will exhaust their sites by 2000. In New York 14 sites have closed in the past ten years and now most of the city's 24,000 tons of trash per day is put into the Fresh Kills landfill on Staten Island. This site produces 5 million cubic feet of methane per year, enough to heat 50,000 homes. As landfill sites fill up, municipalities have looked to other locations. The notorious garbage barge, the *Mobro,* publicized this crisis when it spent two months in the summer of 1987 meandering around the Caribbean looking for a dump site for its 3,100 tons of New York's trash before returning home with it.

Incineration has the advantage of reducing the rubbish to ash, greatly decreasing the volume, and generating energy that by law, the local utility must buy. At this time there are several domestic American companies operating profitable incineration plants.

The major drawback to incineration is pollution. The smoke plume can contain hydrogen chloride and dioxin if the smokestack is not equipped with expensive scrubbing equipment. This added cost increases the incinerator's burning charge by almost 50%. However, not all states require such equipment and many believe that in the long run this will give incinerators a black eye. Also, the ash, which still must be disposed of, often contains dioxin and heavy metals. The introduction of these contaminants can be reduced with an extensive sorting of the input but this, too, is very expensive.

In other parts of the world recycling is a major solution to the problem of rubbish disposal. In Japan, for example, more than half of the waste paper is recycled and in Germany nearly 40% of the glass is recycled. Yet Americans only recycle 28% of their aluminum, 27% of their paper, and 10% of their glass. This seems to be a product of capitalism, as the sale of recycled material will not pay for the cost of collecting and reprocessing it in a free market.

The cost of landfills is estimated to be from $40 to $60 per ton and incineration is between $70 and $120 per ton. This implies that a net gain to society would occur if a subsidy of up to $40 per ton were made—potentially a politically dangerous move. But even if such a subsidy were granted, recycling only affects specific components and is only as effective as the consumers make it.

The newest approach to disposal problems comes from companies like Enviro-systems. Their system of converting rubbish into fertilizer by shredding, sterilizing, and seeding the waste with bacteria is already in use in France, producing 800,000 tons a year, and another plant in Pompano Beach, Florida, will open soon.

The Project

The people at Enviro-systems estimate that with the cheaper labor in Africa they will be able to collect, transport, and process rubbish for $70 per ton. This low cost is due mainly to the wage rate in Senegal, which is approximately $10 per day.

Senegal was selected not only for its low wage rate but also because it had a relatively stable dictatorship government that had been in power for the past 20 years. Furthermore, the country was in an economic decline, so the prospect of employing 700 to 800 people should outweigh the undesirable aspects of foreign rubbish processing.

The beauty of recycling is that the accepting country is paid to receive rubbish from municipalities and private collection agencies as well as being paid for the recycled product.

Enviro-systems estimates that it will require $25 million to build the collection site in the United States and the facility in Africa, which will have a 4,000-ton-per-day capacity. They would also like to purchase a 10,000-ton vessel for transporting the rubbish. They believe the project will be very profitable; in fact, they predict making $378 million over the first six years.

The demand for fertilizer and methane in Africa is quite strong, and even though other disposal techniques are being explored, their impact on the demand for disposal is expected to be minimal. If the system is operational soon and the company lands some long-term contracts, the profit predictions may be fulfilled.

EQ Bank's Problem

To obtain financing EQ Bank must first convince the host country, Senegal, that the project will be beneficial to its society and not harmful to its environment. To help in this, Banks was trying to get endorsements from environmental organizations such as Greenpeace and the EPA. As a backup and bartering chip, he was also looking at nearby countries that would be acceptable.

EQ Bank then had to convince lenders of the viability of the project. Banks was planning to solicit funds from the World Bank, a very conservative donor group. In order to get funds from the World Bank, Banks knew that he would need to prove the soundness of the project both financially and environmentally, especially the latter. This aspect worried Banks, who did not have a technical background and was not quite sure what to look for or how to prove the system's safety. This is where the competition comes into play.

The Competition

Many of the large investment banking houses on Wall Street saw refuse recycling projects as a means to accomplish two goals. First, as the statistics presented above illustrate, there is a growing demand for this kind of facility, and investment bankers saw this project as a new niche in the market. They were working to de-velop a small staff of experts who understood the problems associated with installing such a facility and with environmental legislation, lobbying, and environmental engineering.

Secondly, this was an ideal opportunity to improve their public image. With all the negative publicity coming out of the insider trading scandals, firms like the former Drexel Burnham were eager to be involved in projects that were considered to be in the best interest of the country.

The Meeting

It is now the beginning of November, and Banks and his cohorts have approximately two weeks to formulate a strategy and gather the appropriate data to support it.

Case 14: Kellogg in Europe

Arnold G. Langbo, President and Chief Operating Officer of Kellogg, Inc. and President of Kellogg International, was uneasy as he read the 1990 annual market analysis coming out of Europe. Since late 1989, for the first time in their sixty-plus-year presence in Europe, Kellogg of Battle Creek, Michigan, had a formidable opponent in the ready-to-eat cereal market there. Nestlé, S.A. of Switzerland had formed a joint venture with Kellogg's biggest competitor, General Mills. Cereal Partners Worldwide (CPW, as the new enterprise was called) was out to cut into Kellogg's 51% share of cereal sales outside the United States.

The U.S. market for cereals was mature. There was little growth, high competition, with more than 200 brands to choose from, under heavy attack from the private label brands and their lower prices. These private labels targeted many of Kellogg's core products such as Corn Flakes and Frosted Flakes. When Kellogg raised its U.S. prices 3% in 1990, Corn Flakes was not involved.

General Mills had already chipped away at Kellogg's market share in the United States. From 1987 to 1990, Kellogg saw its share in the market fall from 41.2% to 37.5%, while General Mills' share of the $6.9 billion dollar industry had risen from 21.2% to 23.8% (Exhibit 1). The only other share growth was seen in the private label segment of the industry. And now it appeared that the Big G of General Mills was aiming for Kellogg International.

Langbo knew that beyond Europe were the markets of Latin America and the East. While Kellogg already had a more than 90% share in Brazil, the Japanese marketplace was going to be much more difficult to master. In Japan they were accustomed to eating something warm and soft for breakfast, and to change that into a taste for a cold, crisp cereal was going to take tremendous marketing skills. The society was deeply entrenched in tradition, but was not impenetrable, as the presence of McDonald's and Kentucky Fried Chicken attested to.

Kellogg could not afford to tackle those obstacles while still worrying about losing market share in Europe. No, Cereal Partners Worldwide would have to be put in its place and fast.

Langbo called in Holger U. Birkigt, Vice President and Director, Continental European Operations, and Thomas A. Knowlton, Vice President and Managing Director of Kellogg Company of Great Britain, to discuss the situation.

Kellogg of Battle Creek

Kellogg was founded in 1906, focusing on the manufacture of nutritious, ready-to-eat breakfast cereal made from corn. Nutrition and good taste had always been their trademark, and at the height of their kingdom, in the 1950s, they had attained a 45% market share in the United States.

EXHIBIT 1 Percent of U.S. Market in Pounds

Company	1987	1988	1989	1990	1991
Kellogg	41.2%	41.4%	39.7%	37.5%	38.8%
General Mills	21.2	21.1	23.4	24.3	23.8
Post/General Foods	13.2	12.2	10.9	11.3	11.2
Quaker Oats	7.5	8.1	7.9	7.4	7.4
Ralston Purina	5.6	5.2	5.6	6.1	4.7
Nabisco	5.4	5.2	4.8	4.4	3.4
Private Labels	3.6	4.3	5.2	6.5	7.4
Others	2.3	2.5	2.5	2.5	3.3

EXHIBIT 2 Ready-to-Eat Cereal Sales Growth—Germany

Year	Growth (%)
1988	15
1989	16.5
1990	16
1991*	27

* First Quarter

EXHIBIT 3 Ready-to-Eat Cereal Sales Growth—Great Britain

Year	Growth (%)
1988	9
1989	12
1990	11
1991*	10

* First Quarter

Through the 1970s, the market grew rapidly and became increasingly competitive. Women were joining the workforce in record numbers, and the lure of a quick, healthy breakfast for the family caused cereal sales to soar.

Kellogg had not been prepared for what came in the 1980s. Health experts everywhere were touting the benefits of oat bran as a preventative against heart disease and certain cancers. With 80% of their products made from corn, Kellogg saw their market share slip away. They were slow to respond to this phenomenon, and competitors such as General Mills, with 40% of their cereals oat-based, grew.

The oat-based cereals that Kellogg did develop came too late and at a great cost to the company. From 1985 to 1990 the number of cereals on the American shelves increased by 52%. Customers had over 200 names to choose from and the new ones from Kellogg were lost in the avalanche.

In 1990, the U.S. market was growing at a relatively slow 0.2% annually. Market share could only be gotten at a competitor's loss, which could be quite expensive in an industry where the cost of introducing a new product had risen from $5 million in the 1970s to $30 to $40 million in the 1990s. Langbo knew the answer lay in the underdeveloped markets overseas, where current growth rates were 8% to 9% annually and were expected to continue for some time to come. After all, he thought, ready-to-eat breakfast cereals were currently marketed to less than half of the world's population.

Kellogg International

Kellogg had been a player in the European breakfast market since 1922, when Kellogg's Corn Flakes were introduced in London. A production facility was built in 1938, and the cereal giant from Battle Creek, Michigan, set down its roots and began to expand, crossing over to the Continent in the 1950s.

Kellogg had to create their market in most of Europe. The consumption of cereal for breakfast was traditional only in Britain and Ireland, where a big, American-style breakfast was the norm. In France, for instance, croissants and sweet rolls were more common, and in some countries, meat and cheese were the first meal of the day. Kellogg had always felt that being first in markets like these would help secure a first-place position in the market.

Kellogg had been somewhat successful in developing the cereal market throughout most of Europe. The market was expanding, but there were still drastic differences in consumption among consumers in different European countries. In Great Britain, for instance, the average consumer ate 13 pounds of cereal a year, which even exceeded U.S. consumption of 10 pounds annually. In France and Germany, however, consumption levels in 1989 were 2 pounds per person. Exhibits 2 and 3 show the growth in sales in Germany and Great Britain. The significantly higher growth rate in Germany can be attributed to this lower consumption per capita. It was clear to Langbo that there was still plenty of room for growth in this market.

Kellogg had production facilities in several locations throughout Europe poised to accept increased production as sales increased. Their distribution channels were also up to the task. All that was needed was the demand.

In 1990, Kellogg products were distributed in 130 countries worldwide, a distribution exceeded only by Coca-Cola. If this trend continued, international sales were expected to top domestic sales by 1992.

Kellogg International was organized as a subsidiary of Kellogg, with Langbo as its president, reporting to C.E.O. William E. LaMothe. Each international operating manager in turn reported to Langbo. With the pending retirement of LaMothe, Langbo was considering an organizational change, giving each manager more responsibility and authority in their respective areas of control, since they each had unique characteristics.

Cereal Partners Worldwide

In 1989, Nestlé approached General Mills with an offer that they found impossible to turn down: Create a joint venture combining their individual strengths to tap into the rapidly expanding ready-to-eat cereal market in Europe. They had first approached Quaker Oats with their offer of a joint venture, but had been rejected.

The products would be the same that General Mills sold elsewhere, but would carry the Nestlé name, which was well known in Europe. Initially they would be manufactured in Nestlé production facilities, using General Mills' knowledge and technology. Nestlé would also provide the distribution channels and access to the local markets. This mix of General Mills' collection of products, technology, and knowledge of the cereal business along with Nestlé's distribution network, name recognition, and knowledge of the European market was creating quite a wave in the European marketplace.

CPW entered the European market with much fanfare and its requisite advertising. All this hoopla had caused an increase in overall cereal consumption and as such, was helpful to Kellogg's bottom line. In 1990, although Kellogg's market share had remained steady at 51.2%, total sales in Europe had increased by 6.5% and were expected to continue their upward climb.

To counter CPW's emergence as a competitor, Kellogg had thus far introduced products that were nearly identical to those launched by Cereal Partners. Cereals such as Golden Crackles competed with General Mills' Golden Grahams. Honey Nut Loops, made by Kellogg, was launched to compete with Big G's biggest seller, Cheerios. Kellogg even went so far as to introduce a cereal called Golden Oatmeal Crisp, akin to General Mills' Oatmeal Crisp, which they marketed in the United States. Although it helped soften the blow, this strategy gave Kellogg the appearance of being a follower, not the leader that they were accustomed to being. While this strategy might prove beneficial in the short term, the Battle Creek giant needed a defense that would protect its market position against all competitors.

Kellogg's Name Recognition

The Kellogg name had always been associated with quality and nutrition. In order to project this image worldwide, the company had been a leader in product labeling, had sponsored nutrition workshops with health professionals, been a corporate sponsor of the Olympics, and had even entered into a comarketing arrangement with the French government to preach the benefits of a good breakfast.

The Kellogg name was well known throughout Europe and was perceived by many people in England to be an English corporation. This would give them the "home court" advantage on the battlefield.

Market

In 1990, Kellogg was the number-one seller of cereal in much of Europe (Exhibit 4). Sales were growing at an alarming rate and showed no signs of ebbing. Even countries in Eastern Europe were discovering ready-to-eat cereals, and Kellogg was planning to open production facilities in Latvia in late 1991. There were still areas where consumption was low enough to warrant a special effort by the company, and Birkigt thought they should concentrate their efforts there. Some of these markets, such as Spain and France, were virtually untouched. Birkigt pointed to Kellogg's popularity in these countries (Exhibit 5), saying that Kellogg had the market share; what they needed to do was develop the market.

EXHIBIT 4 Top Sellers in Europe, December 1990

Company	U.K.	France	W. Germany	Italy
Kellogg	42%	54%	42%	42%
Quaker	7	16	—	18
Nabisco	8	—	—	4
Nestlé	—	12	—	—
Wheatabix	14	—	—	6
Banania	—	9	—	—
CPC	—	—	8	—

EXHIBIT 5 Top Ten Brands in Selected Markets as of March 1991

Great Britain	France	Spain
1. Corn Flakes*	1. Chocopic	1. Smacks*
2. Wheatabix	2. CPW Country	2. Coco Pops*
3. Frosted Flakes*	Store*	3. Corn Flakes*
4. Rice Krispies*	3. Coco Pops*	4. All Bran*
5. All Bran*	4. Smacks*	5. Frosted
6. Bran Flakes*	5. Frosted Flakes*	Flakes*
7. Crunchy Nut*	6. Corn Pops*	6. Corn Pops*
8. CPW Shredded	7. Quaker Cruesli	7. CPW
Wheat	8. Extra*	Chocapic
9. Sugar Puffs	9. Corn Flakes*	8. Krispies*
10. Fruit n' Fibre	10. Rice Krispies*	9. Rice Krispies*
		10. Chocos*

* Denotes a Kellogg cereal

This growth could be attributed to several things: the ever-increasing number of women in the workforce who are attracted to the convenience of the product; Europeans traveling to the United States and bringing their newly developed tastes for cereal back home (in fact, for many years some of Kellogg's products were sold in Europe in specialty import stores); and the development of commercial television, making advertising more profitable.

Kellogg had answered the growing demand by continually introducing new products in the different countries. Each product was slightly different in each country, making it impossible for Kellogg to take advantage of the economies of scale, or to market a truly global product. Changes had been made recently to eliminate the differences, with Kellogg's Corn Flakes consistent across borders, and Frosted Flakes and Rice Krispies almost there.

Marketing efforts were also becoming global. Tony the Tiger now hawks Frosted Flakes all over the world, and Toucan Sam of Fruit Loops fame is fast becoming a household character.

All this gave Kellogg a solid base from which to defend their cereal kingdom on the Continent. But CPW is a worthy opponent and Langbo felt that further steps in streamlining production, distribution, and marketing were warranted.

Entrenchment

Knowlton questioned whether the constant introduction of new products in a developing market such as Europe was prudent. He was already hearing rumblings from distributors that the store managers did not want to devote any more shelf space to cereal. If a new product went up, an old one came down. Kellogg had also suffered severe financial setbacks from recent flops such as Big Mixx and SW Graham in the United States and Raisin Splitz and Toppas abroad. Maybe concentrating on a few core products, creating consistency in manufacture and marketing, would give them the solid growth everyone wanted.

Case 15: **The Gillette Company**

In April 1998, Gillette unveiled a revolutionary advance in shaving: The Mach3. Gillette had spent 15 years and $750 million in developing this product. The Mach3 was the company's biggest and most important new product since Sensor, and the company hoped it would have a similar effect. Eight years ago, Gillette was losing its grip on the razor market to cheap throwaways and facing the fourth in a succession of hostile takeover bids. Sensor saved the company on both counts. Today, Gillette was vastly stronger. Its market capitalization had jumped from $3 billion in 1986 to $66.1 billion in 1998, putting it among America's 30 biggest companies. The company, however, was concerned about the higher price tag of the Mach 3 and the impact it might have in its foreign markets.

Gillette's future might not exactly be on a razor's edge—it had 71% of the North American and European market for razors and blades. The company, whose consumer brands included Duracell batteries, Oral-B toothbrushes and Parker and Waterman pens, was beloved by management consultants. But investors had begun to fret about slowing growth, lackluster sales, and an imminent change in top management. Growth had slowed in the hugely profitable razors division, partly because Schick, its smaller rival, had recently launched a new razor of its own. In August 1997, the mildest of profit warnings was enough to send the shares tumbling nearly 20%, although they had since recovered.

Gillette had an unusual approach to innovation in the consumer-products business. Most such companies tweaked their offerings in response to competition or demand. Gillette, launched a new product only when it had made a genuine technical advance. To make the Mach3, Gillette had found a way to bond diamond-hard carbon to slivers of steel. Michael Hawley, the company's chief operating officer, boasted that it "will blow the doors off other technology."

But razors were not the only products where the company's researchers beavered away at innovation. Duracell Ultra, due to be launched in May 1998, was an alkaline battery designed to last 50% longer than its rivals in devices that needed a lot of power, such as palmtop computers and personal CD players. The company also promised in late 1998 a "universally new, remarkable" toothbrush, which abandoned the usual practice of stapling the filaments through the brush head.

At heart, Gillette liked to think of itself as a giant research laboratory. It spent 2.2% of sales on Research & Development, twice as much as the average consumer-products company. "We manage ourselves like a pharmaceutical company," remarked Mr. Zeien, the chairman of the company. "The people working on our toothbrushes are Ph.D.s in polymer chemicals." Like a drugs company, Gillette had a product pipeline: The successor to the Mach3 was already being developed. It does better than the pharmaceutical industry on another measure: Almost half of its $10 billion sales in 1997 came from products introduced in the past five years, more than SmithKline Beecham or Johnson & Johnson could boast. Mr. Zeien expected to maintain that, helped by more than 20 big products launched in 1998 alone.

Marketing Strategy

Gillette's marketing strategy was equally unique. The slower growth that scared Wall Street in 1997 was caused partly by Gillette's decision to run down stocks of its Sensor and Atra shavers ahead of this week's launch. While most rivals would consider this suicidal, Gillette used the strategy to ramp up prices of new products. Mach3 would sell for around 35% more than SensorExcel, which itself was 60% more expensive than Atra, its predecessor. Duracell Ultra cost 20% more than a conventional battery. Mr. Zeien insisted that premium prices did not matter: "People never remember what they used to pay. But they do want to feel they are getting value for money." Perhaps; but shavers might nick themselves at the thought of paying a hefty $1.60 a blade for the Mach3.

Gillette's emphasis on refining the manufacturing process was much admired by management gurus. Few companies were as good at combining new products with new ways of making them. It gave the company a huge advantage over the competition. Three-quarters of the $1 billion spent on the Mach3 had gone on 200 new pieces of dedicated machinery, designed in-house, which would churn out 600 blade cartridges a minute, tripling the current speed of production. This meant, according to Gillette calculations, the investment would pay for itself within two years. The fact that the company spent more on new production equipment than on new products was one reason why Gillette regularly hit its target of reducing manufacturing costs by 4% a year.

Another difference between Gillette and most other consumer-products companies was that it did not tailor its products to local tastes. That gave it vast economies of scale in manufacturing. Those were mirrored on the distribution side, where it usually broke into new markets with razors and them pumped its batteries, pens, and toiletries through the established sales channels. The impact on margins was dramatic: The company's operating margin, currently a fat 23%, was rising by a percentage point a year.

And Gillette's products obviously had global appeal. In 1997, 70% of the company's sales were outside America. More than 1.2 billion people now used at least one of its products every day, compared with 800 million in 1990. The company had sliced into developing markets: It had 91% of the market for blades in Latin America and 69% in India, measured by value. It would love to shave China, too, but the trouble there was the Chinese beard, or lack of it: "If they shake their heads, they don't need to shave," commented a Gillette executive. Gillette might therefore rely on the Chinese passion for gadgets such as pagers, and lead its push into that market with Duracell.

Future Perspectives

The biggest question concerning Gillette's future was not technical but human. Much of the company's recent success must be put down to Mr. Zeien. When he took over, Gillette's name was on everything from sun-

---

Most men spend a few precious morning minutes reluctantly dragging a razor across their skin. Cuts and razor burn are all part of the raw deal as they scrape their faces up to 700 times per shave, chopping way 27 (8.2 meters) of hair over a life time. Scientists at Gillette's "world shaving headquarters" in Boston had spent 15 years and $750 million developing their latest response. Unveiled in New York on April 8, 1998, in a presentation worthy of a NASA space launch, complete with images of jet engines shattering sound barriers, the new razor had a name to match: Mach3.

Such high-tech allusions were appropriate. The Mach3 was covered by 35 patents, astonishing for something as commonplace as a razor. Its three spring-mounted blades were some 10% thinner at the tip than the two blades of its predecessor, SensorExcel. They were toughened with diamond-like carbon from the semiconductor industry and this was bonded on to the steel with niobium, a rare tin alloy normally used in super-conducting magnets. John Bush, vice-president of Gillette's research and development, likened the reduced drag to cutting down a tree with an ax rather than a wedge. Since irritated skin was the shaver's main complaint and most men blamed their razors rather

than themselves for cuts and rashes, this looked like a genuine improvement.

There was, boasted Gillette folk, another bonus: productivity. Each stroke with the new razor took off around 40% more stubble than before. Imagine 40 million working American males saving one minute a day this way. That could add up to 7 million working days a year—assuming they did not dawdle over breakfast instead.

Of course, all this innovation came with a catch. Gillette expected customers to pay almost $7 for a Mach3 with two spare blade cartridges—a 35% premium to SensorExcel, currently the priciest razor on the market. The company had a successful history of persuading shoppers to trade up. However, it risked arousing the same complaints as Microsoft, whose customers grumbled about the relentless cycle of software upgrades they had to make. Shavers could slice through stubble just as easily if they only soaked their chins in hot water for two minutes first. That changes whiskers from inflexible copper wire to the pliability of aluminum. The Mach3 offered a state-of-the-art shave, but for the cost-conscious a hot shower and a plastic disposable might be just the thing.

---

glasses to watches to calculators. He forced a focus on a few world-leading products. But he was now past normal retirement age and had been persuaded to stay on the board for another year with the lure of new stock options. Investors worried about his heir-apparent, Mr. Hawley, who was 60 and had a very different management style. Compared with the clear-thinking, strategic Mr. Zeien, whose ability to communicate had been a hit on both Wall Street and in the company, Mr. Hawley came across rather as a strong operational manager.

Mr. Hawley acknowledged their different styles. "Al is an architect first, then a builder; he has a new concept, and then worries about how to make it work. I would flip it for me. My experience has been building and expanding. I see myself as a catalyst, helping to make something new from what we have."

But Gillette's global sensibilities were ingrained in the culture. This was not a cult of personality. But the new shaving system, with so much invested in it, had to prove a success.

Case 16: **IKEA**

Most successful retailers find it hard to go global while remaining true to themselves. Yet Sweden's IKEA succeeded in the United States by carefully adapting its strategies to the unique requirements of the market. Successful though the outcome had been, toward the end of 1994, IKEA's American experience posed wider

questions for the whole firm's future. Could it adapt its retailing concept to local peculiarities without compromising the Swedish identity at the heart of its marketing and brand image? Could it continue to control costs if it was forced to dilute the uniformity of its product range? And as the firm's operations became ever more global, could IKEA retain the intimate corporate culture that was an important part of its success?

Going Global

As store chains struck out beyond their home markets, they often had to change the formula that had previously guaranteed success. This happened to many types of business, but retailers were particularly close to customers. They must, therefore, move especially fast to adapt to local peculiarities. The trick was to do so without destroying the very thing that made them successful in the first place.

As the world's most competitive retail market, the United States had a well-deserved reputation: a graveyard for foreign retailers—and especially for Europe's nonfood retailers. Even Britain's Marks and Spencer had struggled to make a success of its acquisition of Brooks Brothers. Four years ago it looked as if IKEA might suffer a similar fate.

But the Swedish firm had been going from success to success in America. Its secret seemed to be a classic example of the difficult art of "change management": IKEA draped itself in the stars-and-stripes by adapting but not destroying its original formula. Meanwhile, its experience in America persuaded it to remix its recipe elsewhere.

IKEA Venturing Out of Sweden

It was not hard to see why IKEA was initially so confident about America. In the decade after it opened its first non-Scandinavian outlet, in Switzerland in 1973, the furnishing chain's vast out-of-town warehouse stores decked out in Sweden's blue and yellow colors had marched triumphantly across much of Europe. Its formula was based on re-inventing the furniture-retailing business. Traditionally, selling furniture was a fragmented affair, shared between department stores and small, family-owned shops. All sold expensive products for delivery up to two months after a customer's order.

IKEA's approach trimmed costs to a minimum while still offering service. It started with a global sourcing network, which in 1995 stretched to 2,300 suppliers in 67 countries. An IKEA supplier gained long-term contracts and received technical advice and leased equipment. In return, IKEA demanded an exclusive contract and low prices. IKEA's designers worked closely with suppliers to build savings into products from the outset.

IKEA displayed its enormous range of more than 10,000 products in cheap out-of-town stores. It sold most of its furniture as knocked-down kits, for customers to take home and assemble themselves. The firm reaped huge economies of scale from the size of each store and the big production runs made possible by selling the same furniture all around the world.

This allowed the firm to match rivals on quality, while undercutting them by up to 30% on price. An IKEA store, with its free crèche and Scandinavian café, was supposed to be a "complete shopping destination" for value-conscious, car-borne consumers. IKEA had forced both customers and suppliers to think about value in a new way in which customers were also suppliers (of time, labor, information, and transportation), suppliers were also customers (of IKEA's business and technical services), and IKEA itself was not so much a retailer as the central star in a constellation of services.

U.S. Entry

Initially, IKEA's successful and apparently flexible system hit problems in America. In 1985, IKEA opened a 15,700-square-meter (169,000 sq. ft.) warehouse store outside Philadelphia. At first, with the dollar at around SKr8.6, it was quite easy to make money. Six more shops (five on the East Coast and one in Los Angeles) followed in as many years.

But things had started to go wrong. By 1989, the American operation looked to be in deep trouble. In each new European country it entered, the company had normally broken into profit after two or three years with its third or fourth store. In America, it was still losing money. And this could not be blamed wholly on a slowdown in the economy and a weak furniture market.

Many people visited the stores, looked at the furniture, and left empty-handed. Customers complained of long queues and constant non-availability of stock. Imitators were benefiting from the marketing effort IKEA had made in introducing Americans to Scandinavian design. Worst of all, since it was still making many of its products in Sweden, IKEA's cherished reputation was threatened as the dollar's value dropped to SKr5.8 by 1991.

Another retailer might at that point have sought a dignified exit. IKEA, it had been claimed, never considered that option. "If you're going to be the world's best furnishing company you have to show you can succeed in America, because there's so much to learn here," remarked Goran Carstedt, who took over North American operations in 1990.

Its perseverance paid off. IKEA's American operation had finally turned around. Since 1990, sales had tripled, to $480 million in 1994, and the company made a profit beginning 1995. In December 1991, IKEA purchased Stor, an imitator with four shops in the Los Angeles area. In October it opened its thirteenth American store, a franchised outlet in Seattle.

U.S. Marketing Strategy

To achieve success in the United States, IKEA had to revise several of its central tenets. The most basic was that it could sell the same product in the same way in Houston as it could in Helsingborg. IKEA took this approach to such extremes that its advertising deliberately stressed not only its clean Scandinavian design, but its blue-and-yellow Swedishness.

IKEA had cheerfully broken several of the rules of international retailing: Enter a market only after exhaustive study; cater for local tastes as much as possible; gain local expertise through acquisition, joint ventures, or franchising. "We don't spend much money or time on studies. We use our eyes and go out and look, and say it will probably do quite well here. Then we may adapt, but quite often we stick to our opinions," noted Anders Moberg, IKEA's chief executive.

This iconoclasm had paid off in Europe, but it helped to get the firm in trouble in America. In 1989 and 1990, Mr. Moberg himself spent much time in the American stores, talking to customers. "We were behaving like all Europeans, as exporters, which meant we were not really in the country," he said. "It took us time to learn this."

Unapologetically, European products jarred with American tastes and sometimes physiques. Swedish beds were narrow and measured in centimeters. IKEA did not sell the matching bedroom suites that Americans liked. Its kitchen cupboards were too narrow for the large dinner plates needed for pizza. Its glasses were too small for a nation that piled them high with ice: Mr. Carstedt noticed that Americans were buying the firm's flower vases as glasses.

So IKEA's managers decided to adapt. The firm started selling king- and queen-sized beds, in inches, as part of complete suites. After noticing that customers were inspecting IKEA's bedroom chests, and then walking away without buying, Mr. Carstedt worked out that because Americans used them to store sweaters in, they wanted the drawers in the chests to be an inch or two deeper. Sales of the chests immediately increased by 30% to 40%. In all, IKEA redesigned around a fifth of its product range in America; its kitchen units were next on the list.

The firm changed its American operations in other ways, too. "When we went in, we hadn't planned a clear strategy of how to supply the American market at low cost," Mr. Moberg admitted. That meant, for example, that it was shipping sofas from Europe, adding to costs and problems of stock availability.

Now 45% of the furniture in the American stores was produced locally, up from 15% in 1990. This helped the firm to cut prices in its American stores for three years running. And because Americans hated queuing, the firm installed new cash registers that speeded throughput by 20%, and altered store layout. It offered a more generous returns policy than in Europe, and a next-day delivery service.

Managing Growth Through Making Changes Within the Corporate Culture

Hard on the heels of its American difficulties, overall sales growth slackened thanks to slower than expected growth in Eastern Europe and recession in Sweden and Germany, IKEA's two largest markets. The firm reacted with intense soul-searching. In 1992–93, it opened only six new stores, compared with 16 the previous year.

One problem was that IKEA had become lax about costs. *Sweden Business*, a newsletter, estimated that costs excluding the purchase of goods climbed from 30% of sales in the late 1980s to 37.5% by the fiscal year 1991–92. Mr. Moberg was still trying to return them to 30%. This involved cutting the amount of time it took to develop new products and, over three years, trimming 10% of the workforce at the firm's Swedish product-development and purchasing center.

Another problem imposed by growth was the management of an increasingly complex global supply chain, one that led to glitches in quality control and stock availability. The firm had begun random checks on goods as soon as it received them; it had also taken equity stakes in some East European suppliers to help improve quality.

In making these adjustments, IKEA could draw on an egalitarian culture forged by its founder, Ingvar Kamprad (who remained the chairman of its supervisory board despite having recently admitted to a youthful flirtation with a Nazi group, saying that he "bitterly regretted it"). Fast decision-making was helped by a management structure that was as ruthlessly flat as the firm's knocked-down furniture kits, with only four layers separating Mr. Moberg from the checkout or warehouse worker. Even senior managers must share secretaries and travel economy class.

The firm described itself as a learning and problem-solving organization that trusted the institution of its staff. Insiders were much exercised about how this problem-solving culture could thrive beyond its Swedish roots. In recent years, Mr. Kamprad had held annual seminars for managers on the firm's corporate culture. Experience with globalization forced managers to adapt in three important ways in order to maintain the firm's antibureaucratic culture.

The first change involved giving more autonomy to Mr. Carstedt than his European counterparts enjoyed. "You can't steer America from Europe," noted Mr. Moberg. The second decision was characteristically unconventional: In 1992 IKEA abolished internal budgets. "We realized that our business planning system was getting to heavy; we can use the time saved for doing other things better," Mr. Moberg said. Now each region must merely keep within a fixed ratio of costs to turnover.

Lastly, to encourage IKEA to stay lean in the absence of stock-market pressures—the firm remained private, with ownership vested in a Dutch charitable foundation—Mr. Kamprad had created internal competition: In 1992 he bought Habitat's British and French stores (which were separately managed), and he had split off franchise rights into Inter IKEA Systems. Although IKEA itself had first refusal over new markets, the idea was that it must show it could do a better job than franchises would.

Lessons Learned from the U.S. Experience

IKEA's contortions should frighten all would-be globalists. They show how even an adaptable system based on what Mr. Moberg called "permanent evolution" could not prevent teething troubles in a major market. But unlike many foreign venturers, IKEA started with the advantages of being both unconventional and rich. As Vanessa Cohen, a retailing consultant at Cooper's & Lybrand pointed out, IKEA did comply with at least one of the rules of international retailing: Its strong balance sheet in Europe enabled it to absorb its initial American loses.

So far, the results of IKEA's reorganization are encouraging. At 8.35 billion guilders ($4.5 billion) its sales for the year to August in 1997 grew by 6%. IKEA did not reveal its profits, but outsiders estimated its 1993 net profit margin at 6% to 7%, a creditable figure given recession in core European markets. Exhibit 1 shows the company sales by country/region. Exhibit 2 identifies its suppliers by country/region. The firm

EXHIBIT 1   IKEA's Sales by Region, 1994 (Year ending August 31)

Country/Region	Sales
Germany	29.6%
United States	14.2
Belgium, Britain, Denmark, Holland, Norway	21.9
Austria, France, Italy, Switzerland	20.5
Sweden	11.1
Eastern Europe	1.6
Austria	1.1
	100%

Source: Company reports.

EXHIBIT 2   IKEA's Purchases by Region, 1994 (Year Ending August 31)

Country/Region	Purchases
Nordic countries	33.0%
Europe	30.0
Far East	19.5
Eastern Europe	13.0
United States/Canada	4.5
	100%

Source: Company reports

claimed that in the year to August in 1994, 116 million customers—equivalent to 2% of the world's population—visited its 108 wholly owned stores, spread across 18 countries (another 15 stores, mainly in the Middle East, Hong Kong, and Spain, are franchised).

On November 4, 1994, IKEA announced that it planned to move into China, where it would open up ten stores in the "foreseeable future." In making this move, the firm was sticking to its tradition of jumping into big new markets feet first, as it did in America: IKEΛ's managers stress that it was easier to make changes to the product range once critical volume had been achieved.

But IKEA also would take to China other lessons from America. It already set up the bones of a supply network in the country. Above all, the firm was tilting toward a more decentralized system of managing. In America, the result was that IKEA's Swedish identity was evolving into "a new alloy", according to Mr. Carstedt. "It's still blue and yellow, but mixing in the stars and stripes." Expect a red star to join IKEA's multi-colored galaxy.

Case 17: **NOVA Biomedical and the Iran Deal**[*]

Jim Means, Vice President of International Operations for NOVA Biomedical, pulled out the three-week-old *Boston Globe* article again. When he first saw that President Clinton was imposing a new embargo on Iran, he assumed that humanitarian products would be excluded. "To my knowledge, humanitarian goods have always been exempted from embargoes . . . U.S. firms are allowed to export humanitarian goods into Cuba and Iraq, why are they being excluded from doing so to Iran?" asked Jim. NOVA's lawyers had evaluated the embargo order and verified that it imposed a complete ban of all trade, including humanitarian goods. It was May 31, 1995, and the whole $1.1 million deal with Iran was in jeopardy. After cultivating a lucrative new Iranian market for a number of years, Jim saw the opportunity slipping from his grasp. Jim noted:

> NOVA does $70 million in sales a year, so $1.1 million isn't going to break us, but this was just the beginning of a much larger opportunity. Iran is a virgin market, and we could gain a first mover advantage, especially considering all the restrictions and barriers for doing business in Iran. Not only did I expect Iran to buy more of our product in the future, but just providing the supplies to support the initial order would generate $300,000 annually for at least the next 10 years.

The barriers were indeed steep. Although NOVA had received the purchase order for 70 NOVA Biomedical Blood Analyzers from the Iranian Ministry of Health early in the year (January 8, 1995), it had taken five months to receive an irrevocable and transferable letter of credit (dated May 29, 1995). Doing business with Iran was complicated and time consuming. But now, after they had diligently completed all the necessary steps to consummate the transaction, President Clinton imposed an embargo on Iran that was to be effective June 6. That didn't leave enough time to manufacture and deliver the 70 analyzers. Not only was the company losing $1.1 million in immediate sales but also the additional $300,000 in subsequent yearly supplies to support the blood analyzers. But it wasn't even the lost revenue that disturbed Jim so much as it was the reasons behind the embargo and the perceived effectiveness of the ban.

History of Iran and Its Relationship with the United States

Officially known as the Islamic Republic of Iran, the country is located in southwestern Asia and covers an area of 634,724 square miles (1,643,958 square kilometers). Iran is strategically located bordering the Azerbaijan and Armenian Republics and the Caspian Sea on the north, Pakistan and Afghanistan on the east, the Persian Gulf and the Gulf of Oman on the south, and Iraq and Turkey on the west. Teheran, the capital city, is located in the north-central part of the country; over 10,000,000 people live in greater metropolitan Teheran.

The estimated 65,000,000 population of Iran consists of several diverse ethnic groups. The majority of the people are Iranians, historically known as Persians. Kurds, Lurs, and Bakhtiyari tribes, and Baluchis are among the most important ethnic minorities. There is also a small group of Arabs in the south and southwestern party of the country. The Armenians, with a different ethnic heritage, have maintained their linguistic identity. Ethnic Turks constitute another small minority although, for historical reasons, Turkish language and dialects are spoken by over one-fourth of the Iranian people. The official language of the country is Farsi, which is an Indo-European language.

The vast majority of Iranians are Shiite Muslims, which is the official state religion. The Kurds, Turkmans, and Arabs are Sunnite Muslims, with other major religious minorities including Christians, Jews, Bahais, and Zoroastrians. A sizable number of Iranian religious minorities, mostly Jews and Bahais, fled the country after the 1979 revolution.

Modern Political History

In 1921, Reza Khan, a low-ranking officer in the Iranian Army, took advantage of the hardship brought on Iranians because of World War I and came to power in a coup. In 1925, he deposed the last Qajar ruler and declared himself shah (king) of the country. Prior to Reza Shah's coup, after many years of revolutionary struggle, Iranians had been able to start the foundations of a genuine democratic system by adopting Iran's first constitution and establishing the Majlis, the Iranian representative assembly, in 1906. Through a system called *constitutional monarchy,* the constitution provided very limited power for the ruling king. But both Reza Khan and later his successor, Mohammad Reza Shah, subverted both the constitution and the

---

[*] This case was prepared by Golpira Eshghi, Bentley College, and Andrew Zacharakis, Babson College. It is printed here with permission from the *Case Research Journal* and the authors.

assembly. The successive American government's role in maintaining the status quo is the primary reason for current tensions between the two countries.

In 1941, Allied forces from the United States, Great Britain, and the Soviet Union—who had occupied strategic parts of Iran—forced Reza Shah, who was thought of as supporting Nazi Germany, to abdicate the throne in favor of his son, Mohammad Reza Shah Pahlavi. After the war, the Soviets continued to occupy the northern province of Azerbaijan. The United States government played a crucial role in forcing the Russians to withdraw from the province. This was the beginning of the roller-coaster relationship between Iran and the United States.

Perhaps the most defining incident in diplomatic relations between Iran and the United States is the CIA's role in the 1953 military coup in Iran, which consolidated the Shah's power. In 1951, Prime Minister Muhammad Mossadeq, a passionate nationalist and the most popular political figure in modern Iranian history, announced that the Iranian oil industry, dominated by British oil companies, was nationalized. However, Mossadeq's attempts to create an independent oil industry were unsuccessful since the United States joined the United Kingdom in supporting the British oil interests through a British naval blockade of Iranian oil. Because Iran's economy was greatly dependent on oil revenues, the boycott started to put pressure on Mossadeq, forcing him out of office in 1953. Within a short period, popular pressure brought him back into power, and the Shah fled the country. However, the CIA brought back the Shah through a military coup which was engineered and financed by the U.S. government. Mossadeq was arrested, tried, and sentenced to life in prison, but due to his enormous popularity and old age, he was put under house arrest until his death.

After the 1953 military coup, the United States played a much more active role in Iranian political and economic affairs. Muhammad Reza Shah, with his power consolidated, purged all political and religious opposition. From 1953 until 1978, no independent political parties were allowed in Iran. In 1975, the Shah created his own political party, Rastakhiz (the National Resurgence Party) and announced that membership in the party was basically mandatory for all Iranians.

The rise in crude oil prices in the international markets combined with a significant rise in volume of oil exports from Iran provided resources for the Shah to embark on large-scale modernization and Westernization programs in the 1960s and 1970s. American firms had the lion's share of these projects. For example,

American oil companies had a 40% share of the Iranian Oil Consortium, and total U.S. exports (merchandise and service, including arms) was about $5 billion. Iran's exports to the United States in 1978 amounted to $5 billion. In addition, by 1977, the flow of U.S. foreign direct investment to Iran was about $200 million annually, with more than 60,000 Americans residing in Iran. In sum, a year before the Islamic revolution, Iran was the largest trading partner for the United States in all of the Middle East and North Africa.

The Shah's modernization programs, however, had mixed results. On the one hand, there was real progress in building the infrastructure of the country. Most of the relatively modern highways in the country were projects which were started in the 1970s. But the 1963 land reform (the White Revolution), which was an attempt to take power from feudal families, had a significant negative impact on the social structure of the country. The distribution of land to almost 2 million farmers created a large number of small and inefficient farms. When the financial resources of the landlords disappeared and no government support existed to substitute for it, large numbers of disparate peasants migrated to the cities. These new poor urban dwellers, who did not benefit from the material gains of the Shah's economic programs, found the ever-increasing presence of Western culture offensive and unacceptable. Given their traditional religious and cultural values, these groups were among the strongest supporters of the religious uprisings in the mid- to late 1970s. Despite the strong military and SAVAK (Shah's secret service said to be organized and trained by the CIA), there were signs of mass dissatisfaction by the mid-1970s. In the absence of any form of free speech and legal formats to express political opinions, thousands of cases of acts of urban terrorism occurred in Iran. While the Shah publicly attributed these acts to the "Islamic Marxists," an analysis of several hundred Iranians arrested for terrorist activity between 1972 and 1976 indicated that 90% of them were professional men and women with a middle-class origin.

By 1976, the declining oil revenues, inflation, and budget deficits were putting a halt to some of the modernization projects. Under pressure from Jimmy Carter, who was advocating some political freedoms under his human rights policy, the Shah implemented a very modest opening of the political system. With a perception of relative freedom, hundreds of thousands of Iranians from the educated to the peasants, as well as factory workers and others, took to the streets and demonstrated against the government. There were also economic boycotts and strikes, which basically brought the system to a halt.

Throughout the mass demonstrations, the U.S. government continued its unconditional support of the Shah. In December 1977, to show his support, President Jimmy Carter traveled to Iran. In his address to the Shah at a New Year's Party he said: "Iran, under the great leadership of the Shah, is an island of stability in one of the most troubled areas of the world. This is a great tribute to you, Your Majesty, and to your leadership, and to the respect, admiration, and love which your people give to you."

By early 1979 the country was in total disarray. The Shah's government collapsed and he fled the country. In the absence of any real political alternative, the religious opposition had taken over the leadership of the revolution. A few days after the Shah's departure, Ayatollah Ruhollah Khomeni, an exiled Shiah leader, returned to Teheran from Paris. Shortly after his arrival, the Iranian military announced their support of the revolutionary forces. With the support of the military, Ayatollah Khomeni announced the establishment of the Islamic Republic of Iran. The U.S. government was one of the first to officially recognize the new regime in the country.

While the diplomatic relations of Iran and the United States had definitely deteriorated with the change of government in Iran, it had not totally collapsed. The two governments maintained their respective embassies, although both refrained from sending ambassadors.

In the early years of the revolution, fundamentalist Muslim codes were enacted and Western, particularly American, influence was suppressed. In addition, there were several factions within the ruling group who had extremely opposing views on the issue of relations with the United States.

In November 1979, a group of young revolutionaries attacked the U. S. embassy and took 66 U.S. citizens as hostages. For over a year, 55 U.S. citizens were kept in Iran (the rest had been released for different reasons). To this date, television images of blind-folded American hostages being carried away by their Iranian captors in the midst of an angry mob shouting anti-U.S. slogans symbolizes Iranian attitudes toward the United States, even though the overwhelming majority of ordinary Iranians may not have approved of the hostage-taking act. In repeated interviews, the hostage takers claimed that their act was in retaliation against the continued support of the deposed Shah by the American government. A few hours after President Reagan was inaugurated, the hostages were freed. The hostage crisis was the final blow to the already fragile relationship between the two countries.

The 1995 Economic Embargo Against Iran

In the 15-year period from the end of the hostage crisis to the imposition of trade sanctions in May 1995, there were no formal diplomatic relations between Iran and the United States. From 1980 to 1988, Iran was involved in a bloody war with Iraq, which took an enormous toll on human life and economic infrastructure of the country. Throughout these years, each country accused the other of irresponsible behavior. The United States, on the other hand, was frustrated with Iran's continued support of the anti-Israel groups (Palestinian Hammas and Hizbollah in Lebanon) and their terrorist activities. In 1987, President Reagan issued an executive order that banned all imports from Iran, including oil. In addition, with the exception of food, farm machinery, and a few other categories, other exports to Iran required a license from the Department of Commerce. In spite of all these restrictions, the trade between the two countries showed signs of improvement. From 1980 to 1992, Iran's merchandise imports from the United States increased almost 500%, from $142 million to $822 million. Oil industry-related machinery and equipment, chemical and gas turbines, and medical equipment constituted the bulk of exports to Iran.

While the 1987 executive order banned imports of Iranian crude to the United States, American oil companies continued to lift Iranian oil to non-U.S. refineries. In 1992, Exxon, with a 20% share, was the largest lifter of Iranian oil.

The political tensions between the two countries, however, kept mounting. In 1994, there were fresh accusations of Iranian efforts to start manufacturing nuclear weapons and derail the delicate Arab-Israeli peace process. With support from the new Republican majority in both the House and the Senate, led by Newt Gingrich and Senator Alfonse D'Amato, President Clinton signed a bill passed in May 1995 that would ban all trade with Iran (see Exhibit 1). The trade embargo, which was to go into effect on June 6, 1995, would prevent American companies and their foreign subsidiaries from doing any business with Iran.

At the time that the embargo was being debated, American lawmakers expected the European Union and other U.S. major allies to follow suit and impose similar embargoes. In fact, congressional leaders had threatened to impose stricter sanctions on Iran unless

EXHIBIT I   Text of Executive Order Banning Trade with Iran (Transcript)

By the authority vested in me as President by the Constitution and the laws of the United States of America, including the International Emergency Economic Powers Act (50 U.S.C. 1701 et seq.) (IEEPA), the National Securities Act (50 U.S.C. 1601 et seq.), section 505 of the International Security and Development Cooperation Act of 1985 (22 U.S.C. 2349aa-9) (ISDCA), and section 301 of title 3, United States Code:

I, WILLIAM J. CLINTON, President of the United States of America, in order to take steps with respect to Iran in addition to those set forth in Executive Order No. 12957 of 15 March, 1995, to deal with the unusual and extraordinary threat to the national security, foreign policy, and economy of the United States referred to in that order, hereby order:

Section 1. The following are prohibited, except to the extent provided in regulations, orders, directives, or licenses that may be issued pursuant to this order, and notwithstanding any contract entered into or any license or permit granted prior to the effective date of this order:

(a) the importation into the United States, or the financing of such importation, of any goods or services of Iranian origin, other than Iranian-origin publications and material imported for news publications or news broadcast dissemination;

(b) except to the extent provided in section 203 (b) of IEEPA (50 U.S.C. 1702(b)), the exportation from the United States to Iran, the Government of Iran, or to any entity owned or controlled by the Government of Iran, or the financing of such exportation, of any goods, technology (including technical data or other information subject to the Export Administration Regulations, 15 CFR Parts 768-799 (1994) (the "EAR")), or services;

(c) the reexportation to Iran, the government of Iran, or to any entity owned or controlled by the government of Iran, of any goods or technology (including technical data or other information) exported from the United States, the exportation of which to Iran is subject to export license application requirements under any United States regulations in effect immediately prior to the issuance of this order, unless, for goods, they have been (i) substantially transformed outside the United States, or (ii) incorporated into another product outside the United States and constitute less than 10% by value of that product exported from a third country;

(d) except to the extent provided in section 203(b) of IEEPA (50 U.S.C. 1702(b)), any transaction, including purchase, sale, transportation, swap, financing, or brokering transactions, by a United States person relating to goods or services of Iranian origin or owned or controlled by the Government of Iran;

(e) any new investment by a United States person in Iran or in property (including entities) owned or controlled by the Government of Iran;

(f) the approval or facilitation by a United States person of the entry into or performance by an entity owned or controlled by a United States person of a transaction or contract (i) prohibited as to United States persons by subsection (c), (d), or (e) above, or (ii) relating to the financing of activities prohibited as to United States persons by those subsections, or of a guaranty of another person's performance of such transaction or contract; and (g) any transaction by any United States person or within the United States that evades or avoids, or has the purpose of evading or avoiding, or attempts to violate, any of the prohibitions set forth in this order.

Section 2. For the purposes of this order:

(a) the term "person" means an individual or entity;

(b) the term "entity" means a partnership, association, trust, joint venture, corporation, or other organization;

(c) the term "United States person" means any United States citizen, permanent resident alien, entity organized under the laws of the United States (including foreign branches), or any person in the United States;

(d) the term "Iran" means the territory of Iran and any other territory or marine area, including the exclusive economic zone and continental shelf, over which the government of Iran claims sovereignty, sovereign rights or jurisdiction, provided that the government of Iran exercises partial or total *de facto* control over the area or derives a benefit from economic activity in the area pursuant to international arrangements; and

(e) the term "new investment" means (i) a commitment or contribution of funds or other assets, or (ii) a loan or other extension of credit.

Section 3. The Secretary of the Treasury, in consultation with the Secretary of State, is hereby authorized to take such actions, including the promulgation of rules and regulations, the requirement of reports, including reports by United States persons on oil transactions engaged in by their foreign affiliates with Iran or the Government of Iran, and to employ all powers granted to the President by IEEPA or ISDCA as may be necessary to carry out the purposes of this order. The Secretary of the Treasury may redelegate any of these functions to other officers and agencies of the United States government. All agencies of the United States government are hereby directed to take all appropriate measures within their authority to carry out the provisions of this order.

Section 4. The Secretary of the Treasury may not authorize the exportation or re-exportation to Iran, the government of Iran, or an entity owned or controlled by the Government of Iran of any goods, technology or services subject to export license application requirements of another agency of the United States government, if authorization of the exportation or reexportation by that agency would be prohibited by law.

Section 5. Sections 1 and 2 Executive Order No. 12613 of October 29, 1987, and sections 1 and 2 of Executive Order NO. 12957 of March 15, 1995, are hereby revoked to the extent inconsistent with this order. Otherwise, the provisions of this order supplement the provisions of Executive Orders No. 12613 and 12957.

Section 6. Nothing contained in this order shall create any right or benefit, substantive or procedural, enforceable by any party against the United States, its agencies or instrumentalities, its officers or employees, or any other person.

Section 7. The measures taken pursuant to this order are in response to actions of the Government of Iran occurring after the conclusion of the 1981 Algiers Accords, and are intended solely as a response to those later actions.

Section 8. (a) This order is effective at 12:01 a.m., eastern daylight time, on May 7, 1995, except that (i) section I(b), (c), and (d) of this order shall not apply until 12:01 a.m., eastern daylight time, on June 6, 1995, to trade transactions under contracts in force as of the date of this order if such transactions are authorized pursuant to federal regulations in force immediately prior to the date of this order (existing trade contracts), and (ii) letters of credit and other financing agreements with respect to existing trade contracts may be performed persuant to their terms with respect to underlying trade transactions occurring prior to 12:01 a.m., eastern daylight time, on June 6, 1995.

(b) This order shall be transmitted to the Congress and published in the *Federal Register.*

Clinton agreed to discuss the embargo in a G-7 meeting. In reality, there was little support for an American unilateral embargo from America's economic allies. Members of the European Union, which traded $14 billion in oil and other goods with Iran in 1993, stated that they did not support unilateral embargoes, and Canada and Australia stated that they would continue their trade with Iran. In the June 1995 meeting of the Group of Seven countries, the subject of the Iranian embargo was not even discussed.

In the United States itself, the issue of using economic sanctions to influence political actions of other nations had been hotly debated. Supporters argued that deteriorating economic conditions put pressure on the sanctioned country and limited its ability to support terrorism. On the other hand, others questioned the effectiveness of sanctions in penalizing governments. An editorial in *Oil and Gas Journal* stated:

> Nonsense. Terrorism is cheap. Extremists can always find enough money for their treachery. Heavy-handed behavior by wealthy nations only assures them of support from desperate and disaffected people, many of them have no other option. For this reason, commercial embargoes imposed to fight terrorism are self-defeating. They hurt not only the powerful few but the struggling many. By fostering mass desperation, they inflame reactionary impulses.

Economic embargoes were also opposed on competitive grounds. As the Iranian case indicates, it is rare for economically developed countries to be able to agree on a multilateral embargo against a particular "enemy." In the age of globalization of trade and investment, frequently the true losers in an embargo are companies and citizens of the country imposing the sanctions. Other companies from the rest of the world may even gain more in the absence of their major competitors. In the special case of Iran, U.S. allies have very strong economic ties with the country. For some of them, like Japan, Iran is the largest supplier of crude oil. In addition, the deterioration of their political relations with Iran has never been nearly as bad as it has been for the United States. Consequently, they have been very reluctant to participate in economic boycotts against Iran. Finally, some had concerns about ethical implications of embargoes, especially when medical equipment and supplies were included.

The Industry

The medical diagnostic device industry was fragmented and global in nature. Companies tended to be of medium size and relatively focused in a particular area of expertise. The few larger firms that existed in this industry often evolved from a conglomeration of several related companies. For example, Orion Research (where many of NOVA's founders previously worked) was acquired by Analytical Technology, Inc. (ATI), in 1989. Shortly thereafter, ATI acquired Harvard (1990), Russell (1991), and Cahn Instruments (1991). Although all of these firms could broadly be classified as producers of laboratory products, each focused on different equipment. As such, each company operated somewhat autonomously from the parent ATI and the other subsidiaries.

The overall blood diagnostic and supplies market was $2.5 billion worldwide. The blood gas equipment and supplies market (NOVA's segment) was approximately $500 million. The industry experienced rapid growth of over 10% annually during the 1980s. That rapid growth had slowed somewhat, and the market was currently growing at about 5% per year.

Technology transfer from research institutions was often key for a firm's success. As with NOVA, this transfer often occurred when scientists left academia or other firms to start their own ventures. As with any technology industry, a key success factor was technological innovation. Products had relatively short life cycles. NOVA, for example, expected its products to become obsolete within five years. If a firm was to remain competitive, it had to strive for continuous innovation.

NOVA's History

A group of six engineers and scientists led by Frank Manganaro started NOVA biomedical in 1976. At the time, the group could little imagine that this new company would become an international player selling products to over 45 countries worldwide. The founders met while working for Orion Research of Cambridge, Massachusetts. Orion Research, founded in 1962, manufactured electrolytic conductivity instruments. Orion's process control instruments were primarily used in industry, but they also had applications in the medical field. Frank, however, recognized that Orion was not committed to the healthcare sector. He saw a need for quick and efficient blood analyzing and built a team of founders that quickly developed a product. Within a year, NOVA sold its first product.

The Product

NOVA Biomedical produced a line of blood analyzers that hospitals use to test for a variety of gases and chemical analytes in blood. For example, the machines tested for glucose levels (blood sugar level), ionized calcium levels (an indicator of cardiac function), and lactic levels (determine how well oxygen is being absorbed into the tissue). Such analyses provided physicians with timely information that could be used to assess the patient's condition and allowed surgeons to closely monitor patients during intrusive operations, such as heart surgery and other life-threatening procedures. Although commonly used in intensive care units (ICUs) and other outside labs associated with hospitals, NOVA Blood Analyzers were also being used at race tracks.

A common problem with horse racing was that trainers were often tempted to dope their horses to give them an edge. One such method was to give the horse a "milkshake," which was a bicarbonate soda solution injected into the horse prior to race time. The milkshake gave the horse added energy, yet dissipated within hours after the race, making it difficult to catch violators. However, a NOVA Biomedical Stat Analyzer could detect the milkshake within minutes of conducting the test. The machine was used by the Meadowlands, New Jersey, track to prevent such unfair advantages. Offending horses were "scratched," and repeat offenders were banned from the track.

Jim Means noted NOVA's competence for producing high-quality and technologically advanced products:

> NOVA is on the leading edge in product R&D. Our NOVA Stat Profile product has many competitive advantages over competitor offerings. The Stat Profile series can measure up to eleven tests with one blood sample whereas competitor machines often measure only one critical care test. Imagine that you are a hospital administrator. Would you want to purchase and support one NOVA Stat Series machine or arrange to buy and support several different machines from a variety of other companies to accomplish the same tasks that the lone NOVA product can do? Better yet, imagine that you are a patient in a hospital that needs some blood work. Would you like the doctor to draw blood once for the NOVA product to conduct a full analysis, or would you like the doctor to take several blood samples to conduct individual tests on a number of different machines? The number of tests that one of our NOVA machines can assess, as well as the speed of receiving results, gives NOVA a competitive advantage.

(See Exhibit 2 for a list of NOVA innovations.) From both the doctor and patient perspective, NOVA's multiple testing capability was preferred. Another competitive edge for NOVA was the speed with which results were derived. Doctors could get a complete analysis in 90 seconds. Competitors' machines often required hours. This speed made the NOVA machine the market leader in ICU units, where speed was often a necessity. NOVA commanded a 40% market share in U.S. ICUs. When factoring in labs and other uses for the an-

EXHIBIT 2
Nova Biomedical Biosensor Firsts

1978	First practical biosensor for Ionized calcium
1980	First biosensor to measure chloride in blood
1984	First biosensor to measure total calcium
1985	First biosensor to measure hematocrit by ISE/ conductivity
1988	First biosensor to directly measure whole blood glucose
1990	First biosensor to measure lithium
1991	First biosensor to measure BUN (urea)
1993	First biosensor to directly measure whole blood lactate
1994	First biosensor to measure Ionized magnesium
1995	First biosensor to measure total CO_2 in whole blood
1995	First biosensor to directly measure creatinine

Source: NOVA Biomedical Sales Brochure.

alyzer, NOVA's overall North American market share was 20%. The number of tests and the speed directly contributed to NOVA's lowest cost per test claim.

Such advantages did not come cheaply. The typical NOVA Stat Profile analyzer was priced at $42,000. Even so, the sales price barely covered the large R&D and manufacturing costs, especially since these high-tech products suffered from rapid obsolescence. The average life of a high-tech blood analyzer was no more than five years in affluent countries such as the United States. Iran, on the other hand, might extend the life of the machines to more than 10 years due to the high cost of replacing them with newer, more advanced machines. Since the profit margin was so slim, NOVA's success derived from the bundled nature of its sales. Jim observed:

> This is a razor and razor blade business. The hardware is basically a means of selling testing kits. NOVA testing kits aren't transferable to competitor products and their testing kits aren't transferable to our product. Thus, once a hospital commits to NOVA, the switching costs are too high. They become a long-term customer.

Since the Iranian market was unpenetrated, it was especially attractive to NOVA and its competitors.

The Company

Although the company had suffered some setbacks, the overall success of the firm was admirable. After gaining its first sale in 1977 and its first international sale shortly thereafter, the private company had grown to over $70 million in revenue with over 500 employees worldwide. NOVA Biomedical had recognized the importance of the international market from day one. In fact, Jim

Means joined the company in 1983 to identify and target potential international markets. Jim was uniquely qualified to grow NOVA's international operations. Fluent in several languages including Spanish and French, Jim had held several international positions prior to joining NOVA. Largely because of Jim's efforts, NOVA Biomedical derived over 40% of its finished-good sales from international sources (which doesn't include that portion of NOVA's large OEM sales that eventually ended up in international markets).

Four of the original seven founders were still active in the privately held company. Frank Manganaro was President; Dr. Young was Senior Vice President of R&D; James Fowler was Senior Vice President of Engineering; and Jack Driscoll was President of a sister company, HNU. These four individuals fostered a team-oriented culture that was flexible and able to respond to new situations quickly. Visitors termed the firm's Waltham, Massachusetts, 210,000-square-foot facility (where 400 or the 500 employees worked) quite impressive. The wide-open facility housed R&D, manufacturing, and all support functions under one roof. Every employee, including Manganaro and other senior executives, was accessible. There were few offices. Most management personnel, including Jim Means and other vice presidents, used open cubicles.

The manufacturing area was situated in the middle of all the support functions so that it was only a short stroll between the lowest-level employees and the highest-level managers. Jim discussed the benefits of this open layout.

> The physical layout of our facility fosters open communication. In turn, open communications fosters process and product innovations. Those closest to the manufacturing process know that they can talk to any manager about changes that should be made. Hourly production workers often recognize shortcuts or improvements in assembly processes that managers may never see. Likewise, the sales people directly communicate new product ideas to R&D personnel—quite unusual for high-technology companies.

NOVA's culture enhanced its ability to be flexible. In addition, NOVA's just-in-time process allowed the firm to custom tailor machines for the end user by including only the tests that the buyer deemed most important. Most U.S. customers preferred the higher-end machines that conducted the most possible tests. However, such machines were expensive and some of the tests weren't as critical as others. NOVA could modify its machines according to the needs of its customers, especially in newly emerging countries where financial resources were at a premium. Since machines were made to order, NOVA did not maintain an inventory of finished products.

Moreover, NOVA's just-in-time process also meant that they did not keep shells or other work-in-process machines could be quickly adapted to customer orders.

International Operations

The blood analyzer market was global in nature. Wherever hospitals used advanced surgical techniques, such as open heart surgery, there was a need for blood analysis. Industrialized and newly emerging countries all needed such equipment. Japan, Germany, and France comprised NOVA's top three international outlets, but the demand in many newly emerging countries (such as Korea, India, etc.) provided numerous opportunities for NOVA. Most countries in Europe, Eastern Europe, former Soviet Republics, the Far East, Australia, and Latin America had a need for blood analysis. Hospitals in many middle Eastern countries, including Egypt, Bahrain, and Israel, utilized NOVA products. Thus, NOVA analyzers were on every continent in the world, except Antarctica. NOVA typically entered a new market by using a foreign export agent. If the market became important in terms of revenue generated, NOVA often established a subsidiary (as they had done in Germany and France).

Iran, on the other hand, was one of the few Middle Eastern countries where NOVA did not have a significant presence. In fact, Iran was still a relatively virgin market in that none of NOVA's competitors had established any significant presence either. The deal with Iran would remedy that situation . . . if it went through. NOVA had out-maneuvered its rivals for the contract, but even these carefully laid plans might not be enough in the end.

NOVA's rivals within this segment of blood analysis were:

1. Ciba Corning Diagnostics (Medfield, MA), a subsidiary of Chiron Diagnostics. As its name indicated, it was related to part of the large Swiss conglomerate Ciba-Geigy, which maintained a 49.5% interest in Chiron. In addition to blood analytic devices, Chiron was also actively involved in vaccinations and the development of DNA technology. Annual revenues in 1994 were approximately $454 million. Ciba Corning currently had 30% of the world blood gas analysis market (also 30% of the North American market). Although Chiron could potentially tap into its parent to fund massive R&D on blood analytic devices, it seemed that most of its focus was on the vaccination side of its business. Ciba Corning was also making overtures to the Iranian market.

2. Radiometer (Denmark). Founded in 1935, Radiometer was a pioneer in blood gas analysis. Initially, the company produced measurement equipment for the radio industry. By 1937, the company had developed equipment to measure the acidity of liquids. During the polio epidemic of the 1950s, Dr. Poul Astrup, chief of the laboratory at the Epidemic Hospital in Copenhagen, discovered that blood pH could provide critical information to save lives. In 1954, Radiometer developed the first commercial blood gas apparatus. Thereafter, the company continued to develop their expertise in the blood diagnostic arena. At the time of the case, the company maintained a 30% worldwide market share (20% in North America).

3. AVL Verwaltungsgesellschaft mbH (Austria). AVL had 20% of the worldwide market and 10% of the North American market.

4. Instrumentation Laboratory (I.L.) (Spain). This company had a factory and research center in Lexington, Massachusetts. I.L. commanded 10% of the worldwide market, as well as 10% of the North American market.

All of the firms were involved in global operations.

The Iranian Deal

NOVA Biomedical's interest in the Iranian medical devices market dated back to the early 1990's. Jim recalled:

> We knew back in 1991 . . . that the state of the art in surgery was advancing in Iran. We wanted to be part of it. Our traditional markets in the U.S. and most other developed countries were maturing, while markets in developing countries were in the introductory or early growth stages which means they weren't ready for our sophisticated products. The Iranian market, on the other hand, was especially promising. It is the largest potential market in the Middle East with a population of over 65 million, yet the least exploited. There just aren't any remaining markets where a company can place seventy units in one major transaction.

In addition, NOVA was already present in all neighboring countries including Turkey, Saudi Arabia, United Arab Emirates (but not Iraq, which had its own problems with the global community). Thus, NOVA knew how to do business in countries with governments and cultures similar to that of Iran.

With Iran's potential in mind, Jim assigned his area manager in Vienna to further develop the opportunity. Although the market was lucrative, the manager could afford to devote no more than 5% of his time to Iran.

The Iran market was lucrative but risky. I didn't want to devote a lot of time and resources to a deal that could potentially self-destruct so I instructed the Vienna manager to "bootstrap" this thing together.

By May of 1995, the area manager had made strong progress and it looked as if the deal would be consummated.

Iran was still suffering from the effects of a long war with Iraq, but the economic and social conditions were gradually improving. A shortage of foreign currencies made imports of some products into the country virtually impossible. However, medical-related devices were considered to be necessities; therefore, it was not too difficult to secure government approval of credit transfers. In fact, many large hospitals in Iran were government owned and operated, and such close contact with government officials meant that hospitals were very high on the pecking order for expensive imported goods. Even though relations between Iran and the United States had been strained, the U.S. government allowed the export of humanitarian goods into the country prior to Clinton's recent embargo. Jim had felt especially good about the Iran deal. It filled in another piece of the Middle East market for NOVA. If NOVA could somehow manage the embargo, the deal would be another success story in NOVA's 20-year history.

Entry Strategy

When entering a foreign market, firms have a number of options. Companies can either export products, establish a licensing agreement with a manufacturer in the target country, pursue a joint venture with a partner in the target country, or establish a foreign branch or subsidiary. In the early stages of entry into Iran, NOVA took a very conservative approach. They contacted a reputable Iranian distributor and developed a modest export business. Later, the European director for NOVA traveled to Iran to learn firsthand about the Iranian market for blood analyzers. The director helped the Iranian distributor to develop this business and made contacts with several physicians and clinical chemists who were interested in NOVA's line of equipment. In fact, NOVA developed advertisements in Iran's official language, Farsi, to support their distributor's efforts. In order to demonstrate the superiority of NOVA's products, the company invited a group of Iranian doctors and lab chemists to travel to the United States, where they toured NOVA's facilities in Waltham, Massachusetts, and also observed the equipment in use at the Brigham and Women's Hospital in Boston.

We escalated our commitment to the market when we submitted the bid for the seventy Pro Stat Analyzers. We awarded the existing distributor exclusive rights to the Iranian market. The distributor hired technical support personnel and sent them to the U.S. for training on NOVA products. Our Iranian distributor was very committed. He initiated several additional meetings, including meeting us at several international trade shows.

In the process if developing the Iranian market, NOVA was concerned mostly with market/competitive condition and financial risk. Timing was critical since competition, mostly European, also was working hard to break into the Iranian market. It was important for NOVA to be among the first in the emerging Iranian market. They also had concerns that there was substantial financial risk (nonpayment) in selling to a country with balance-of-payments problems, but Jim and his staff were not overly concerned with political risk.

We felt it was critical to secure an irrevocable letter of credit in the Iran case. Other American firms had been quite active and successful in the medical hospital area in Iran. We could not even envision that there would be political problems, although considering the rocky relationship between our governments [U.S. and Iran], we should have kept that in the back of our mind. Even if we had suspected a complete embargo was in the foreseeable future, we would have preceded as we did, because it was a bulk order with guaranteed payment.

Given the nature of NOVA's products, they seemed to be on the priority list of the Iranian government. Furthermore, NOVA was only exporting to the Iranian market, so there was no risk of nationalization of property and investment. As far as the American government's actions were concerned, the hostage crisis had been over for almost 14 years, and medical products, due to their humanitarian nature, were not on the black list of exports to Iran.

In late 1994, NOVA biomedical won a public tender offer, organized by the Iranian Ministry of Health, involving seventy NOVA biomedical blood testing analyzers and a one-year supply of consumables. The total value of the deal was $1.1 million f.o.b. Boston. The company expected to sell at least another $1.2 million worth of consumables in the next four years.

From the company's perspective, the deal-making process was rather smooth. The purchase order was received on January 8, 1995, but it took almost five months to secure the funding in Iran. On May 29, 1995, an irrevocable confirmed letter of credit for the amount of the deal was opened in NOVA Biomedical's favor.

Jim was pleased with the progress on the Iran deal. All the pieces were falling into place, albeit slowly.

NOVA had established a close, supportive working relationship with an Iranian partner. Payment was secured through the letter of credit. Everything was in place. Yet, as Jim learned, conducting business with Iran can be trying, especially considering the past history between the United States and Iran.

The Decision

Many in the United States perceived that Iran supported the Palestinian Hammas and the Hizbollah rebels in Lebanon. With strong support from Congressman Newt Gingrich, Senator Alfonse D'Amato, and the Republican-controlled Congress, President Clinton extended the existing Iranian oil ban, effective in one week (June 6), to include all trade between the two countries. Jim was distraught. America's new policy directly impacted NOVA. Jim reflected:

> Iran was dismayed by the embargo and they thought that NOVA was purposely withholding its products. One official accused us of "not wanting to deal." Besides the negative impact on our firm, I wonder whether the embargo is even good policy. Unilateral embargoes diminish the U.S. government's credibility, not only with Iran, but with other countries in the region. Germany and Japan are deemed reliable suppliers, because their companies aren't subject to political whims.

In addition, Jim questioned whether the embargo would have the desired effect, especially since the United States was the only country imposing it. Should humanitarian products be included in such a ban? Did the United States have the moral high ground in this all-encompassing ban?

Jim Means and NOVA were at a crossroads. Regardless of how they personally felt about the embargo, they needed to take action or let the Iran deal fall apart.

Although these questions played in the back of Jim's mind, he realized there was little he or NOVA Biomedical could do to lift the embargo. The more immediate question was whether NOVA could beat the clock. What steps could they take to meet the June 6 deadline? Was there a way to extend the deadline? Did NOVA have any other options, or was the Iran deal over before it began? Jim laid out his alternatives:

1. Try to build as many analyzers as possible within one week. Only 10 machines could conceivably be produced in that short time frame, even if NOVA had all the parts in inventory. However, NOVA used a JIT process, so it would be difficult to produce even a fraction of the order. Moreover, it would mean delaying other orders.
2. NOVA could lobby the U.S. Treasury Department (the agency responsible for enforcing embargoes) for an extension. NOVA had a completed contract and its product was purely humanitarian. Extensions were not unheard of in such circumstances, but NOVA estimated it needed a minimum of six months to consummate the deal. It was unclear whether the Treasury Department would grant such a lengthy exemption.
3. NOVA could try to bypass the embargo by sourcing the product through a third party in another country. The embargo was unilateral, meaning that only the United States was imposing the action. NOVA could conceivably source through a European country, but such an action violated the embargo. Jim wondered if bypassing the embargo would be ethical.
4. NOVA could forgo the business and cut its losses. Jim hated to give up the first-mover advantage, but it might be better than expending time and resources to overcome the embargo.

In addition to the current dilemma, the recent developments with the Iranian transaction might signal potential problems with other NOVA deals. NOVA was actively seeking or currently involved in such volatile countries as China and India. Could U.S. policy come into play again? What could or should NOVA do to prepare for or counteract such legislation? It had been a bad week, and there were a lot of decisions that Jim had to make—and make quickly.

Case 18: **The Clondike Works**

In March 1989, Robert Lenore, an executive in the International Division of the Clondike Works, was faced with deciding what tactics the company could employ against a Taiwanese manufacturing company that was exporting counterfeit products labeled with the Clondike name. Among many products, the company was most concerned about power-lock tape rules, of which it had lost 50% of its sales to the Taiwanese competitor.

The Taiwanese firm had duplicated the tape lock and sold it with either the Clondike name or a close facsimile for $2.00 to $2.50 below the Clondike price. Clondike's biggest customers for the power tape lock were in the Middle East, and during the previous two years the sales there had dropped over 50%. Mr. Lenore expressed deep concern over what could be done to rectify this situation.

The Clondike Works

In 1840, James and Patrick Clondike earned a reputation for manufacturing quality hardware products with Yankee craftsmanship. This reputation for quality continued to grow over the years, and Clondike always stood behind the quality of its work. For example, Clondike "Life Span" hinges were guaranteed for the life of the building in which they were installed. Over 10,000 of these hinges were used in the twin towers of the World Trade Center in New York City.

As the company's product lines grew, so did its quality control capability. New techniques and procedures, and new instruments and controls had been added to ensure that Clondike's reputation for quality could keep pace with the nation's growing technological sophistication. Because of its high standards, "Clondike" was the preferred name in tools, as well as builder's hardware. During the 1970s, the company registered tremendous growth. Its sales increased from $1 billion in 1981 to $1.8 billion in 1988. Earnings in 1988 amounted to about 6% of sales. The company was headquartered in Newton, Massachusetts.

Product Lines

Clondike manufactured and sold over 20,000 products. These products were divided into three product lines: consumer products ("do-it-yourselfers"), industrial products, and construction and maintenance products. The "do-it-yourselfer" (DIY) industry was seen as a major strategic thrust for Clondike works. Products in this category were introduced to enable the consumers to do everyday repair work, simple construction, and other types of improvements. The products in the DIY line were grouped into five categories: hand tools, hardware, drapery hardware, garden tools, and automatic garage door openers. DIY products accounted for about 42% of Clondike's sales. Industrial products were categorized into five groups: air tools, electrical tools, hand tools, hydraulic tools, and systems. Clondike's industrial products, sold worldwide, contributed about 35% toward the company's sales. Construction and maintenance products were divided into five categories: hand tools,

electrical tools, hardware, doors, and hydraulic tools, and provided 23% of Clondike's sales.

Clondike International

International sales accounted for more than 42% of Clondike's total business. Besides the United States, Clondike had manufacturing operations in nine countries—England, France, Germany, Italy, Australia, Colombia, Brazil, Guatemala, and Mexico. The company had sales offices in 33 countries around the globe. International sales of the company's products began through overseas representation 50 years ago. The steady sales growth of Clondike's products in overseas markets was based largely upon the customer's approval of Clondike quality

Internationally, the company was extremely diversified, which added to its strengths and protected it against currency fluctuations. For example, during the 1970s when the U.S. dollar was very strong, U.S. products were more expensive compared with products of countries whose currencies were weak against the dollar. Thus, the distributors in Europe found it to their advantage to source out of England, France, or Germany. During the 1980s, the U.S. dollar was weak and U.S. products were in great demand on the export market because they were cheaper. Many Middle Eastern orders, which formerly had gone to England or Europe, began coming to the United States because of the difference in currency values, and Clondike was able to make the best of the situation.

Competition from Taiwan

Clondike's 3-meter, 1-1/2-inch-wide, 10-foot power lock was sold all over the world. "Power lock" is a Clondike trademark registered in the United States. Its reproduction and sale throughout the Middle East, Africa, and Asia by the Taiwanese manufacturers were illegal. Originally the quality of the Taiwanese product had been inferior to the Clondike product, but in recent years the reproduction had been improved to a level comparable to the Clondike product.

The Taiwanese manufacturers capitalized on Clondike packaging and its logo and name to sell their product by outright use of the word *Clondike* on a label and package that duplicated Clondike's. In some instances, the Clondike logo was utilized by simply rearranging the design, colors, and background. In other cases, the imitation product was stamped with a look-alike "Clondike" name—minus the "e." In most ways, it was difficult to distinguish between the reproduction and Clondike's product. The only discernible difference was the stamped USA logo on the original products. Most dealers overseas exhibited the forged product side-by-side with the original product, and customers could not distinguish between the two, except by the prices.

Customer Loyalty

Clondike experienced customer losses based solely on price criteria. Sales had dropped over 50% in the previous two years in the firm's primary market—the Middle East, Far East, and Nigeria. In addition, costly labor and high overhead costs placed constraints on Clondike's ability to compete with the Taiwanese producer. Clondike's experience was comparable to the U.S. automotive industry's competition from the Japanese in the 1980s, whose labor costs were $10 to $12 per hour compared with U.S. costs of $14 to $16 per hour. Because of a similar discrepancy, the Taiwanese were able to offer quality goods, manufactured with cheap labor at prices well below their U.S. competition.

In an effort to compete with the Taiwanese on a price basis, Clondike attempted to supply the Middle East with tape locks produced in England, France, and Mexico. However, customer loyalty to the U.S.-made product discouraged the purchase of products manufactured elsewhere. Foreign customers were intrigued with the prestige of buying a product manufactured in the United States. Clondike's attempt to sell a less-expensive product proved unsuccessful, and it returned to supplying foreign dealers from the United States.

The Effects of International Politics, Economics, and Legislation

In early 1988, Clondike tried to take legal action against the Taiwanese firm. It proved to be a difficult task. There are no international courts and no enforceable laws. Legal action, therefore, had to be pursued through either the U.S. or the Taiwanese courts. Of basic importance to international legal action are (1) the cooperation given by the foreign government and (2) the strength of the company's representation in the foreign country.

Cooperation from the Taiwanese government was negligible for economic reasons. At the time, Taiwan was experiencing a difficult period of economic growth and development. The increase in its exports had a positive influence on its balance of payments. Therefore, the manufacturing and exporting of Taiwanese tape locks were good for the economy, even if they were illegally manufactured. Also, export was the only market for counterfeit products since selling them within Taiwan would result in court action for patent infringement.

Politically, Taiwan and United States were no longer staunch allies. The United States had withdrawn its ambassador to Taiwan, and the UN had expelled the Taiwanese representative. Such political actions precluded any cooperation from the Taiwanese government. As Mr. Lenore pondered the facts, he realized a decision had to be made regarding what action Clondike would take against Taiwanese counterfeiting. Part of the answer, he realized, was to stay in the market rather than pull out altogether. Also, there was reassurance in the idea that 50% of something was better than 50% of nothing.

Case 19: All Shave in Saudi Arabia*

On a hot summer day in 1990, Mike Lacey lay on his bed and watched as the fan went around. He felt whipped and didn't really know what to do next. All week he had been trying to influence Mustafa Almin, and he had no more effect than the fan was having on the heat of Riyadh. Three years ago the All Shave Company, of which Mike was Middle Eastern manager, had been very successful exporting razors and blades to Saudi Arabia. Then, in the face of possible import restrictions, the company had turned over its business to a new com-

pany financed by the Almin family. The family members were leading Saudi industrialists who had built a fortune on the production of steel products, like picks and shovels, and were then interested in expanding to new fields. All Shave received a minority interest in the new business in return for its trade name and technical aid.

The contract with the Almin family had also specified that they would "actively promote All Shave products." Mike thought that it was clearly understood that this meant continuing the aggressive promotion that had been used in Saudi Arabia to build the company's sales in the 1970s from nothing to a high level. Under Almin management, however, All Shave sales had dropped steadily. It was soon evident that the Almins were not

* This case is printed here with the permission of the authors, Ellen Cook, Philip Hunsaker, and Mohammed Ali Alireza of the University of San Diego.

pushing sales, and in visits and correspondence, the company applied increasing pressure for more activity.

When nothing happened, Mike finally decided he would go to Saudi Arabia and stay until he could find a way to get the Almins moving. That was over six weeks ago. After spending the first month in the field, Mike had worked up a detailed program designed to reestablish All Shave's market position. He had found All Shave products were being sold from Almin warehouses with virtually no sales effort and that promotion was limited to a few newspaper advertisements and a scattering of posters distributed by the Almin family's industrial sales reps. No additional salespeople had been added for All Shave accounts. The selling activity fell far short of All Shave's former program and that of its leading competitor.

For the past week, Mike had been trying to convince Mustafa Almin, the 60-year-old head of the family, to adopt a better program. But he had argued in vain. Mike had pointed to the low sales volume and the Almins' limited program, which he pointed out did not meet their agreement. He had supported his proposals in the greatest detail, arguing particularly that All Shave's previous success and the present results achieved by their competition proved that strong promotion was worthwhile.

Mustafa Almin expressed appreciation for Mike's interest and efforts but had agreed to nothing. He explained that a sales drop was inevitable with the change to the Saudi manufacturer. Although sales were lower, the company was making a reasonable profit. He said that to fulfill the contract terms he had undertaken newspaper advertising even though he did not believe in it. He felt its blatant character reflected on the prestige of the Almin family name.

Mustafa Almin believed that a good product was its own best advertisement and on that basis the Almin family had built a great business. He also observed that the closest competitor sold a higher-quality blade than All Shave and it was quite probable that this, rather than promotion, accounted for their success. In any case, several British concerns in related fields did very little advertising, and since they had been in India for many years, Mr. Almin felt their approach to the market was probably sounder.

Mike found it hard to counter these arguments. He was sure he was right, and equally sure that Mr. Almin was a very competent businessman who should be able to see the logic of Mike's proposals. He had great respect and liking for Mr. Almin, and he believed that once Almin grasped the value of promotion, he would do great things for All Shave in Saudi Arabia.

But how could he convince him?

Mustafa Almin settled himself to relax before the evening meal and reflected for a moment on the events of the past week. He had spent a great deal of time with the boy from the United States. He was a good boy, full of energy and ideas. He wished he could do something to help him. He drove so hard, and for what? This whole arrangement with the All Shave Company had turned out rather differently from what the Almins had expected. The product was good, and left to themselves, his family could develop it into a good business, as they had with the rest of their operations.

But they were not left to themselves. Instead, there had been constant pushing and arguing. These people from the United States never seemed to be satisfied with anything. Now they sent this young man who scarcely knew Saudi Arabia to tell the Almins how to run their business. It was not pleasant at all. He hoped the young man would give up soon.

Case 20: **Seagram Co.**

In 1997, executives at Seagram Co. were reviewing how to implement their decision to establish operations in China.

Chinese Market

China was no stranger to orange juice. Oranges, after all, had been a staple fruit of China for more than four millennia, though the juice is mostly quaffed at banquets and by children. In 1996, the country ranked as the world's number three producer of citrus after Brazil and the United States, growing 8 million tons of oranges each year. Seagram's Tropicana Beverage Group estimated sales in China of pure juices was a relatively minuscule $100 million annually, but that number was growing by one-third each year.

Seagram was planning to enter China with a $55 million joint venture with the Chongqing Three Gorges

Construction Group to squeeze orange juice in south-western China. Under the agreement signed in November 1996, Seagram would build a technology center, seedling nursery, and demonstration grove, providing technical assistance to help farmers design groves, raise trees, and do soil analysis; the Chinese group would oversee and help finance as many as 40,000 farm families to plant more than one million orange trees. Both sides would share the costs of constructing a juice-processing factory.

Even with the current financial crisis rocking Asia, the company was determined to push ahead with the orange-juice project.

Company's Interest in China

Mr. Edgar Bronfman started thinking about producing orange juice in China in 1992, when he first tasted a China-made version of the beverage during lunch with a Chinese official and proclaimed it "fabulous." He said, "I was determined that Tropicana would find a great future in China."

Unfortunately for him, executives at Tropicana didn't share his enthusiasm. Wary of international expansion, especially into a business morass like China, they resisted. Tropicana, which Montréal-based Seagram acquired in 1988, had $2.1 billion in global sales in 1997 and boasted a 41% share of the U.S. market for fresh juice, but its business had remained focused largely on the United States. The Brandenton, Florida, company rang up three-quarters of its beverage sales in North America and sourced virtually all of its oranges in its own backyard in Florida.

"Initially, there was no other support for this," noted Roger Knight, managing director of Tropicana Asia Pacific. Every year when Mr. Bronfman visited China, he would ask if Tropicana had come up with a project. "Everyone would stare at his shoes," remarked one Seagram executive.

Seagram already sold orange juice from concentrate in China under the Dole juice brand, which it acquired in 1995. In summer 1998, it was planning to introduce the Tropicana brand in three Chinese cities, including in Beijing at an entertainment and retail center called "The Universal Experience" that Seagram's Universal Studios unit was opening. But because the beverage would be shipped from Florida in pure-juice form, it would be sold for a hefty $5 a liter, triple U.S. prices, and would be marketed mainly to expatriates, hotels, and nightclubs. The hope was that once orange-juice production was up and running in China, Tropicana could lower the price of its product by at least half.

By 1995, Mr. Bronfman was fed up with the inaction. And after sending Seagram associates on a dozen scouting trips to find the perfect site in China for an orange project, the company settled on Zhongxian.

Situated high above the muddy waters of the Yangtze, the region's lush mountains slope at a gentle incline and offer good drainage. The sun rarely shines here, but temperatures are mild, as in Florida. Just as important, the area had been included in China's Three Gorges Dam project, a gargantuan undertaking to harness the Yangtze. More than one million peasants, many from Zhongxian, faced resettlement because of the damming, and authorities eagerly welcomed any job-generating investments.

Problems Ahead

Plenty of roadblocks loomed, as the company grappled with China's poor transportation system, inefficient distribution networks and the challenges of converting thousands of traditional, small-time farmers to growing citrus the Tropicana way.

Such hurdles had kept many agricultural investors out of China. Utilized foreign investment—those investments that had actually been channeled into a project—in agriculture totaled $152 million for the first nine months of 1997, accounting for just 1% of all utilized overseas investment in China. While those projects included a handful of large ventures, like Minneapolis-based Cargill Inc.'s animal-feed mills or the chicken farms of Thailand's CP Group, most remained small in scale.

The realities of investing in China's agriculture sector were on harsh display here. Tucked high in the hills, the project site was a day's travel by boat and car from the central city of Chongqing. Peasants lived and farmed as they had for centuries, lugging buckets of water using shoulder poles and terracing small squares of rice paddy that draped the mountains like patchwork. "There's a lot to do," said Steven Schafer, general manager of Tropicana Beverages Greater China Ltd. Phone lines were few. Modern toilet facilities were nonexistent until local officials erected a port-a-potty in honor of Mr. Bronfman's arrival.

Winning Over Farmers

Seagram was betting that multinational highways would proliferate by the time the processing plant was operational in 2005, to allow for easy transport of the juice out to cities on the coast. But it was basically a crap shoot, and there was a lot of concern then, and still some now, over the remoteness of the area.

The biggest challenge would be winning over the Chinese farm families who would grow the oranges Tropicana planned to squeeze. Many of the farmers had planted *jin-cheng,* a local type of orange, for years as a cheap side crop without fertilizer or watering either. Such neglect had resulted in diseased trees and yields of one-fifth to one-tenth of those in Florida. Tropicana would have to persuade the farmers not only to switch to growing Valencia and Hamlin oranges (the base for Tropicana orange juice), but also to water, fertilize, and otherwise tend the trees regularly, an expensive proposition that wouldn't see any returns for five years.

Chinese farmers were very risk-averse. All the company could do was show people it worked, provide the resources, and hope they would believe and do it.

Case 21: **Carvel in Beijing**[*]

In April 1995 Greg Demadis, Director of Business Development for Carvel Corporation, was returning to the People's Republic of China to plot the next stage of development for the American company's fledgling interests in the Pacific Rim. As the representative of Carvel U.S., Demadis was already making his fourth trip to Asia in six months.

After fact-finding stops in Hanoi and Seoul, Demadis planned to proceed on to Beijing, where six months earlier the Carvel Beijing joint venture had opened its doors to Chinese consumers. Despite moderate success and growth since the venture's grand opening, Demadis felt that the company was facing its most serious challenge to date.

With summer quickly approaching, sales for the Carvel Ice Cream Bakery line would face its first upward spike in what is an inherently cyclical business. The inescapable truth in the ice-cream business is that the best marketing is a hot, sunny day. Having had six months to introduce the product to Chinese consumers, Demadis felt it was crucial for the company to take advantage of its first-mover status to establish the brand as the premium ice-cream cake and novelty company against which all subsequent competition would be compared. Accordingly, Demadis had to defend his position to market the product as a premium ice cream demanding a premium price. Inherent in the corporate long-term marketing strategy was the need to establish the brand as a premium product to which a Chinese rank and file with increasing disposable income would aspire. However, by April, retail sales remained flat and wholesale sales were sluggish. This slow growth would deprive the company of the capital needed to fuel more regional and, eventually, national growth.

Phil Fang (yang Dengsheng), the Taiwanese general manager of the Beijing operation, faced similar pressure. Slow sales had reduced the company's opportunity to break from the myriad of small brands and establish itself as the first truly national brand in China. Moreover, with Baskin & Robbins, Carvel's main rival in the United States, already with a longer, if small, presence in Beijing, and with other Western companies planning to enter the market, Fang also felt the pressure to expand the company as much as possible. Additionally, Fang must aggressively promote Carvel in Beijing.

First, as a Taiwanese manager of a three-part joint venture, Fang was pulled by each partner's differing business perspectives. Moreover, the cultural complexities of being a Taiwanese manager for an American firm in mainland China further complicated his role. Most important, though, Fang had questioned the American management's decision to price and market the product as strictly an American ice cream. At times, Fang felt that the Americans did not appreciate the complexities and subtleties of doing business in China. Now, as the company faced its first summer sales period, Fang would have to make some long-lasting business decisions.

Each manager quietly felt he understood the problem. Demadis believed that the product was by far the best quality ice cream in Beijing; the company simply needed to improve the marketing and retailing of the product. He wanted Carvel Beijing to increase the

---

[*] This case was prepared by Bill Bambara, graduate student, and Professor Subhash C. Jain for class discussion. © by the Center for International Business Education and Research, School of Business Administration, University of Connecticut, 1997.

product's price and, in turn, its perceived value. De-madis feared entering a pricing spiral would establish the product as a commodity solely marketed on price. In the end, he was confident that once Beijing natives tasted and recognized the product, the brand was sure to explode in the market.

Phil Fang, however, felt that there was more to the equation than better marketing. Fang believed that certain pricing and product line changes might be needed before Chinese consumers would really take to the new brand. Time was running out for Carvel to seize its unique opportunity to establish the first national brand of ice cream in the People's Republic of China.

Company History

Carvel Corporation had one of the oldest and most en-dearing histories of all the ice cream companies in the United States. In 1934 Tom Carvel, a Greek immi-grant, parlayed a flat tire on his ice-cream truck into what would become a multimillion-dollar franchise business. As the story had it, after a flat tire forced Tom Carvel into an abandoned parking lot one summer af-ternoon in 1934, Mr. Carvel quickly realized he could sell far more product in a stationary location than he ever could in the streets of Hartsdale, New York. Mr. Carvel soon borrowed $100 and opened the first Carvel Ice Cream store.

Mr. Carvel used a combination of fresh ice cream and innovative products and manufacturing techniques to establish himself as the local, family-oriented ice-cream parlor in the New York city area. In 1947, Mr. Carvel franchised his first store and proceeded to be-come one of the pioneers in fast food franchising. In fact, it was only after Tom Carvel refused his partner-ship offer that Ray Kroc used Mr. Carvel's store design as the model for his McDonald's chain.

Throughout the 1960s and 1970s, the gravely-voiced Mr. Carvel used his folksy and savvy style to dominate the greater New York area. By standardizing procedures and providing franchisees with exclusive product designs and marketing material, Mr. Carvel expanded all along the East coast. By the early 1980s, there were over 800 Carvel stores in operation along the East Coast and in some Midwestern states such as Ohio and Wisconsin. Included in the company chain were over 40 stores in California. However, by the mid 1980s, the recession and the strain on Tom Carvel to manage his business began to take its effect

on the franchise. Sales and quality control began to decline, and events forced Mr. Carvel to consider changes.

In 1989, at age 88, and faced with diminishing sales and increasing store closures, Tom Carvel reluc-tantly sold his company to Investcorp, a Bahrainian-based investment banking group. The Investcorp strat-egy centered on acquiring previously gainful companies whose profitability had diminished in recent years due to recession. Following that strategy, between 1988 and 1992 Investcorp had purchased Macy's, Sax Fifth Av-enue, Tilecorp, and Carvel.

By infusing new capital and bringing in a new management team headed by CEO Steve Fellingham, the former president of Kentucky Fried Chicken, In-vestcorp focused on growth and revamping Carvel's listless image. Management was forced, however, to walk a fine line between creating a new, vibrant image for Carvel and alienating long-time, loyal customers who had grown up with Mr. Carvel's occasionally awk-ward but always folksy style.

In 1992, Carvel introduced the Ice Cream Bakery concept to its customers. Under this program, the company continued to offer long-time favorites such as Cookie Puss and Fudgie the Whale, but also intro-duced a new product line that featured specialty cakes and novelty ice-cream treats for special occasions. By focusing on creating Carvel ice cream as a bakery dessert item, Carvel hoped to reduce both the cyclical sale pattern of the company and the perception that an ice cream cake was only for special occasions. To this end, Carvel instituted its current mission statement:

> Working together, we will make Carvel the leading choice for unique, quality frozen desserts be consistently exceeding customer expectations.

In 1993, the company initiated its grocery store program, in which Carvel displayed its own dedicated freezers in the bakery departments of supermarkets up and down the East coast. By 1994, in the face of industry-wide declines, Carvel decided it was time to bring its Ice Cream Bakery to the People's Republic.

Carvel in Asia

It was Steve Fellingham who decided to bring Carvel to China. Having already successfully completed a mar-keting coup by introducing KFC to China in 1978, Fellingham hoped to repeat the success of the past. After an initial backing from Investcorp of $4 million, Fellingham negotiated a joint venture in which Carvel Corporation established two new enterprises. These two new enterprises were Carvel Asia, headed by Tony Wang (Wang Da Dong), and Carvel Beijing, headed by Phil Fang. Exhibit 1 shows Carvel's organizational arrangements in Asia.

In this arrangement, Investcorp and Carvel Corporation provided 51% and 49%, respectively, of the capital financing for Carvel Asia. Carvel Asia then provided 50% of the equity for Carvel Beijing. Wang Meng, president and owner of New Continent Dairy, a local dairy and producer of low-end ice cream in Beijing, contributed 30% of the capital financing for Carvel Beijing. Li Shiqing, representing the government's Beijing Food Industry Association, provided the final 20% investment in Carvel Beijing.

At the same time, within Carvel Asia there were two other regional franchises. First, Carvel had agreed to franchise the regional rights to Shandong Province to a group of investors headed by Andrew Tsui. Second, Carvel had also agreed to franchise the national rights to Taiwan to the CP Group, which in turn had named Bob Yein as general manager of Carvel Taiwan.

By creating both regional partners and joint venture partners, Carvel U.S. attempted to meet two objectives. First, in Carvel Beijing, Carvel U.S. hoped to create a training and marketing base from which to expand into other areas in China. Second, by having regional franchises in Shandoug Province and Taiwan, Carvel hoped to jump-start its presence in Asia and generate much-needed cash flow to fuel the growth of Carvel Beijing. To that end, it was the success and crowds of Carvel Beijing that concerned both Greg Demadis and Phil Fang.

Political and Economic Developments

After the end of the Cultural Revolution and the death of Mao Ze-dong in 1976, China had embarked on a continual but vacillating course toward free market reforms. As has been the case in China since Mao declared the People's Republic from atop Qian Men Gate in 1949, China had experienced intermittent periods of moderate reform and growth in the midst of hardline backlash and recidivism. Mao's Great Leap Forward, the Cultural Revolution, illustrated the tentative and at times reactionary road to reform the Communist government had followed. For this reason alone, business ventures in China today were far from secure.

Since the succession of Deng Xiaoping as the head of the Communist Party in 1978, however, the

EXHIBIT I Carvel's Organizational Arrangements in Asia

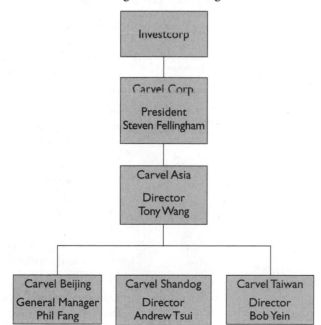

potential of the China market was as tangible now as it had ever been in the country's 5,000-year history. With his endorsement of "socialism with Chinese characteristics" policy in 1978, the Communist government had taken steady but reluctant steps forward, improving the business climate in China. In particular, reforms in the area of telecommunication infrastructure, business and copyright law, and financial structures had led to increased foreign investment in China. The foreign investment, in turn, had led to significant changes in the socioeconomic structure of China. According to a recent Gallop poll,[1] several facts reflected this change:

- China's population was currently 1.2 billion, nearly 20% of the world population.

- Gross national product reached $410 billion in 1994 and was expected to grow at a national average of 10% to 14% in 1995. The eastern and southern regions experienced growth of 20% to 30% in 1994.

- Annual inflation averaged 20% and peaked at 27% in some major cities in 1994. The Communist government had targeted 1995's annual inflation rate at 9%.

- Export volume grew at an average annual rate of 12% between 1980 and 1993. China ranked as the world's eighth-largest exporter in 1993, up from twenty-sixth in 1980.

- China attracted $33.8 billion in foreign investment in 1994; in 1993 foreign investment totaled $27 billion.

The growth had a positive impact on increasing per capita income. The 10 cities with the highest per capita monthly income in 1994 were:

- Guangthou, ¥416[2]
- Shanghai, ¥338
- Beijing, ¥274
- Nanjing, ¥255
- Wuhan, ¥234
- Tianjin, ¥212
- Chongqing, ¥201
- Xian, ¥189
- Shenyang, ¥174
- Harbin, ¥169

In short, the apparent stability and growth in the Chinese economy continued to offer good opportuni-

ties for profitable business, but political uncertainty still clouded the future. First, the ailing health of paramount Communist leader Deng had set the stage for another succession struggle in the Party. Chinese history was replete with fractious and problematic succession battles, and financial circles remained cautious about the political fallout after Deng. Second, while the Communist government continued to court foreign investment with assurances of improved business conditions in China, recent events reflected the inherent risk in the Chinese market. In particular, the Communist government's recent summary decision on McDonald's lease on its celebrated Chang An Avenue store reflected this intrinsic risk. Although the government cited legal clauses in the lease agreement, the move caused shockwaves in the business community trying to establish long-term commitments in China. It was under these conditions that Carvel Beijing began operations in 1994.

Carvel Beijing

By April of 1995, Phil Fang's operations had grown to include one factory, two retail stores, and seventeen outside accounts. Fang carried out cake production at the factory, and used the stores and outside accounts to merchandise the product and do small decorations and personalizing. Exhibit 2 lists these stores and outlets. Fang classified his outlets according to the following schedule:

- **A-Type Stores**—These were individual retail stores that had a large holding freezer called a *shock box,* Taylor ice cream machines, and customer seating. A-type stores were able to make and decorate cakes (i.e., East Four store).

- **B-Type Stores**—These stores were like A-type stores but could not produce cakes. B-type stores could decorate cakes, though (i.e., West Four store).

- **C-Type Stores**—These stores had no customer seating but had Taylor ice cream machines. They were generally mini-stores found inside in the food court areas of large department stores. C-type stores also had FPD-5s (display freezers) and could do small decorations (i.e., Chang An and Baisheng department stores).

- **Counter Stores**—These sites used CMCT freezers to sell cakes and novelties. They also had menu boards and were similar to the grocery store outlets in the United States.

EXHIBIT 2
Carvel in Beijing: Channel Outlets

	Account Name	Account Type
1	East Four	A
2	West Four	B
3	Baisheng Department Store	C
4	Chang An Department Store	C
5	Chengxiang Department Store	Counter
6	Fuxing Department Store	Ice Cream Bakery
7	Beicheng Department Store	Retail
8	Canyou Department Store	Retail
9	Chaoyang Department Store	Retail
10	Friendship Hotel	Retail
11	Landao Department Store	Retail
12	Shangan Department Store	Retail
13	Anbao Restaurant	Wholesale
14	Apollo Club	Wholesale
15	Golden Song KTV	Wholesale
16	Minzu Hotel	Wholesale
17	Songhe Hotel	Wholesale
18	Xidan Shopping Center	Wholesale
19	Xingzuo Department Store	Wholesale

- **Ice Cream Bakeries** These sites concentrated on cake sales. They were generally located inside the bakery and food court areas of department stores and used FPD-5s and rollhards to market the cakes. Ice cream bakeries had the capability to decorate cakes on site. They did not have Taylor ice cream machines, however.

- **Retail Outlets**—These sites used pushcarts or small rollhards. Some of the current retail outlet sites could become Ice cream bakeries or C-type stores if space permitted.

- **Wholesale Outlets**—These were large accounts that bought in huge quantities and sold the product to different vendors in their areas as well as retailed on their premises.

- **Factory**—The Beijing factory had the following equipment:
    four Taylor 771 ice-cream machines
    two large walk-in shock boxes
    one walk-in cooler
    twelve PF IK 4-foot rollhards, small ware, and utensils to maintain three shifts of production

The factory was located on the southwest side of Beijing, a fact that caused delivery trouble in the dense Beijing traffic. However, the production and storage capacity of the facility was larger than most of the American plants. Moreover, the company's dairy, the New Continent Dairy, was located directly beside the factory. This created tremendous ease and integration for mix production. The potential of the factory was tremendous but still untapped.

The East Four store was the first outlet to open in October 1994. This large store almost exactly resembled an American store and was used as the showpiece of the joint venture's appearance in China. But flat sales had yet to justify the large outlay to build the store. Because of decreasing cash flow, finances began to force Fang away from outlets that demanded large initial costs, such as A-type stores. Instead, Fang had begun to concentrate on C-type stores to improve sales volume and cash flow. For the same reason, Fang had recently decided to suspend cake production at the East Four store. Instead, all production took place at the factory in order to reduce the idle capacity there. Demadis and the district manager, Li Qunsheng, had questioned the efficacy of this decision. Although there was little doubt that the factory needed to increase production to justify costs, both Demadis and Li agreed it was better to maintain the flexibility of the East Four production.

As for the structure within Carvel Beijing, Fang had organized his staff as shown in Exhibit 3. Fang hoped to increase retail sales through the various outlets under Li's control. While Demadis did not disagree with this strategy, he did think that wholesale markets were underdeveloped. He felt that in order to justify the costs of the factory, more emphasis should be placed on the wholesale operations of Cao Donghui.

Demadis based this thinking on the success of the grocery store program in the United States. In general, the cost of opening a retail outlet included the cost of several machines. Depending on the type of outlet, an average retail opening would include some or all of the following equipment:

Item	Cost
Taylor 771 or 770 Ice Cream Machine	$11,806
FPD-5 Freezer Cabinet	2,760
CMCT-4 Rollhard Freezer	2,550
MasterBilt Rollhard	2,350
T-50 Glass-Door Upright Freezer	3,460
TM-6 Display Freezer	3,850
Hackney Bros. VC 12-32 Vendcart	3,710

EXHIBIT 3   Carvel in Beijing: Organizational Structure

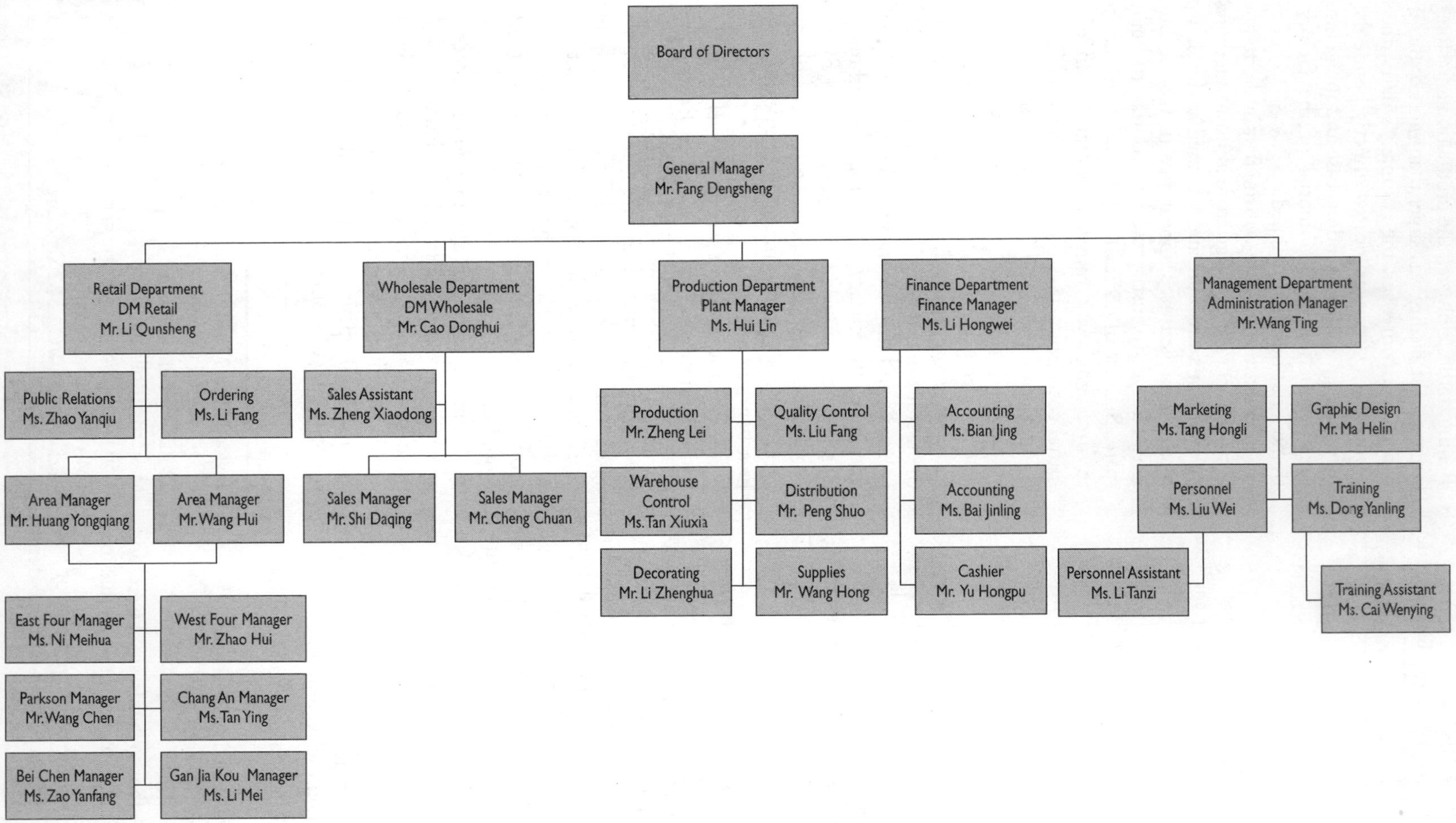

- Board of Directors
  - General Manager
    Mr. Fang Dengsheng
    - Retail Department
      DM Retail
      Mr. Li Qunsheng
      - Public Relations
        Ms. Zhao Yanqiu
      - Ordering
        Ms. Li Fang
      - Area Manager
        Mr. Huang Yongqiang
      - Area Manager
        Mr. Wang Hui
        - East Four Manager
          Ms. Ni Meihua
        - West Four Manager
          Mr. Zhao Hui
        - Parkson Manager
          Mr. Wang Chen
        - Chang An Manager
          Ms. Tan Ying
        - Bei Chen Manager
          Ms. Zao Yanfang
        - Gan Jia Kou Manager
          Ms. Li Mei
    - Wholesale Department
      DM Wholesale
      Mr. Cao Donghui
      - Sales Assistant
        Ms. Zheng Xiaodong
      - Sales Manager
        Mr. Shi Daqing
      - Sales Manager
        Mr. Cheng Chuan
    - Production Department
      Plant Manager
      Ms. Hui Lin
      - Production
        Mr. Zheng Lei
      - Quality Control
        Ms. Liu Fang
      - Warehouse Control
        Ms. Tan Xiuxia
      - Distribution
        Mr. Peng Shuo
      - Decorating
        Mr. Li Zhenghua
      - Supplies
        Mr. Wang Hong
    - Finance Department
      Finance Manager
      Ms. Li Hongwei
      - Accounting
        Ms. Bian Jing
      - Accounting
        Ms. Bai Jinling
      - Cashier
        Mr. Yu Hongpu
    - Management Department
      Administration Manager
      Mr. Wang Ting
      - Marketing
        Ms. Tang Hongli
      - Graphic Design
        Mr. Ma Helin
      - Personnel
        Ms. Liu Wei
        - Personnel Assistant
          Ms. Li Tanzi
      - Training
        Ms. Dong Yanling
        - Training Assistant
          Ms. Cai Wenying

Source: Company records.

Also included in the cost of retail operations were labor, rent, and a royalties fee. This fee was a percentage of the gross sales that Carvel paid to the location's management and could range from 5% to 20% of gross sales. On the other hand, wholesale accounts could be established for just the cost of a T-50, TM-6, or vendcart. Moreover, since these sites took less space and were self-serving, Carvel could save on both rent and labor.

Phil Fang agreed that the sales department had to pursue wholesale accounts. However, high rent locations such as Chang An nearly doubled the sales of East Four. Such high-volume locations provided much needed exposure, and he continued to pursue such additional affordable locations. In addition, Fang felt the pressure of trying to explain the fact that in China, the concept of *guan xi* (meaning *relations* or *connections*) went a long way in determining what sites Carvel could enter. On many occasions, it was necessary to have personal recommendations from local business or government leaders before Carvel could assume locations. Though Fang agreed that wholesale accounts were a very cost-effective way to increase sales, they might not be the most economically or politically feasible way to increase sales at this time.

Operations

The operations of running an ice-cream store parallel those of any fast food chain except for the fact that product handling is more critical to ice-cream production than it is for other food products. Simply stated, whereas hamburgers can be reheated, a melted cake must be scrapped. For that reason time, temperature, and quality control are the key factors in producing ice-cream products.

There are two key elements that Tom Carvel added to ice-cream making, and Carvel Corporation still followed his innovations. The first was the concept of overrun. Simply put, overrun is the process of forcing air into the ice cream as it is being beaten and frozen in the ice cream machine. It is Tom Carvel's patented DL and DH ice cream machine series that first introduced this concept to ice cream production, and it is this high overrun that gives Carvel ice cream its traditional creamy texture. In addition, higher overrun translates into lower unit costs, since adding air to the ice-cream mix increases the total output of the mix.

Secondly, Tom Carvel combined creamy ice cream and various molds to create assorted shaped ice cream cakes. Such cakes as Fudgie the Whale and Hug Me Bear became standards at all Carvel stores. In fact, although Carvel always had much competition with its standard ice-cream offerings of cups, cones, and fountain products, none if its major competition ever challenged Carvel's standing as the preeminent ice cream cake. For that reason, it is this concept on which Carvel Corporation capitalized to create its new line of desserts and novelties. In fact, in 1993 Carvel introduced its new Everything Should Be Made of Ice Cream slug line as a way to leverage its standing as the preeminent ice-cream cake company.

Ice-Cream Mix

The actual production of ice cream and ice-cream cakes begins with the ice-cream mix. The foundation of Carvel's success had always been the quality and creamy texture of Tom Carvel's patented mix formula.

There are two pasteurization processes that distinguish the mix itself. In both processes, the ingredients are the same and the processing steps are very similar. In high-temperature short-time (HTST) processing, however, pasteurization occurs by heating the mix to 180°F and maintaining that temperature for 20 seconds. HTST pasteurization kills most of the bacteria and produces a mix with a shelf life of 10 to 12 days.

In ultra-high temperature (UHT) processing, pasteurization occurs by heating the mix to 285°F and maintaining that temperature for five seconds. The fundamental difference between the two processes is that UHT processing is an entirely closed system in which the mix is never exposed to the outside environment.

UHT processing had several advantages. First, it produced a mix with a shelf life of 90 days. Second, it preserved the mix's natural flavor without causing any residual cooked flavors. Currently, the mix being produced for Carvel Beijing was HTST mix.

New Continent Dairy produced Carvel Beijing's mix. The dairy, located directly next to Carvel Beijing's factory, used an HTST process and currently produced one 75-gallon batch per week at a cost of ¥10 per kilogram.

Electricity Needs and Temperature

Clearly the ability to maintain the product at cold temperatures was vital throughout the production process of the ice cream. Once the product begins to melt, its creaminess and smoothness are lost. In particular, placing a melting cake or novelty back in the shock box caused ice to form on the product. The result was a blander, less tasty ice cream.

In the same respect, a dependable supply of electricity was also crucial. Rollhards, ice-cream machines, and shock boxes produced large surges and drains on electricity. Carvel Beijing's operations had already experienced several power problems in both its retail stores and factory.

Product Inputs

Because of the wide product line offered by Carvel, the inputs necessary to produce Carvel's product line were extensive. In particular, Carvel used a variety of food products, especially fruit fillings, flavorings, and syrups. Carvel also used an assortment of baked items, including cones, cookies, and cannoli shells. Finally, Carvel included a variety of nuts and confectionery toppings on its products.

In the same light, Carvel also used a wide selection of cake boxes and packaging to produce the product line. Combined with the numerous cleaning products and production tools and utensils, Carvel had a tremendous amount of inputs to manage in order to produce its product line. For the time being, most of these items were being imported from the United States at a relatively high cost, an issue both Fang and Demadis must address.

Product Delivery

Product delivery was the most crucial link in Carvel's production process. Because of the nature of the product, poorly designed delivery systems could negate otherwise perfect production lines and operations systems.

Carvel Beijing improved its delivery systems tremendously since the opening of operations. Currently, finished cakes are placed in Styrofoam boxes that hold nearly ten cakes. Two small refrigerated trucks then transport these Styrofoam boxes to the accounts. However, the current capacity of the trucks is only 150 cakes. As the company grows, it will need greater and more flexible delivery capacity.

Quality Control

Because of the nature of ice cream, quality control and sanitation standards are particularly important. Like milk, Carvel's mix and ice cream must be monitored at all levels of production to ensure that the company provides its customers with a tasty and safe product. Unlike flour-based cakes, ice-cream cakes must be kept at continually low temperatures, and they require that decoration be done in short intervals. As mentioned earlier, melting ice cream is both unattractive and unsanitary, and electric supply and maintenance are a priority.

There are several factors in the Beijing environment that exacerbate quality control efforts. The first is the inordinate amount of dust, pollution, and coal ash found in the city. This dust makes it particularly difficult to keep floors and work surface areas clean.

Secondly, the water supply in Beijing is not potable. Therefore, it must be boiled and filtered before it can be used in any products. Like its electrical needs, Carvel must continually monitor water quality.

Finally, American management had a difficult time adapting to the traditional Chinese cultural aversion to waste. Especially when working with dairy products, at times it was necessary to throw out questionable products or utensils. Carvel also used several single-use items in its production process for sanitation reasons. For their part, the Chinese resisted certain procedures and standards as too costly or wasteful.

To this end, Carvel Beijing instituted strict quality control standards and a continual internal inspection program. Weekly bacteria reports were done on the mix batches, and biweekly coliform counts were checked in the retail outlets.

Financial Review

Financially, Phil Fang did not anticipate reaching break-even sales until 1996, and the company's slow start in 1995 jeopardized even that prediction. His biggest problem continued to be slow sales growth and slow customer attachment to the high-margin cakes. As the income statement for 1994 in Exhibit 4 depicts, Carvel Beijing operated at a net loss of nearly ¥1,070,000 in 1994.

For 1995, Fang had requested an additional $800,000 from the joint venture partners and set the following objectives for the year:

- Sales of ¥13 million
- 100,000 cakes sold
- 68 total sales outlets by year end

As mentioned earlier, the company's poor cash flow forced Fang to reconsider his growth strategy. He would not be able to count on large retail stores like in the United States. Instead, he planned on operating many smaller outlets that would demand less initial cash investment. His budgeted breakdown for pro-

EXHIBIT 4 Carvel in Beijing: Net Income Statement 1994

Revenues	
Sales	¥320,065
Other revenue	0
Total revenue	320,065

Expenses	
Costs of goods sold	
Mix	98,100
Commissary	63,780
Labor	126,099
Total cost of goods sold	287,979

Operating Expenses	
Administrative expenses	407,000
Store operating expenses	642,456
Advertising expenses	9,868
Total operating expenses	1,059,324

Gross Margin	(1,027,238)
Depreciation	42,325
Net Income 1994	(¥ 1,069,563)

Note: The exchange rate as of April 1, 1995 was ¥ 8.41/US$1.00.
Source: Company records

jected outlets by the end of 1995 underlined this strategy. By the calendar and fiscal year end of 1995, Fang aimed to have the following outlet distribution:

A & B-Type Stores	2
C-Type Stores	11
Counter Stores	15
Ice-Cream Bakeries	20
Retail Outlets	20
Wholesale Accounts	10

These goals, however, were jeopardized by continual negative cash flow, which in February 1995 totaled ¥400,000.

Clearly, as the projected budget for 1995 in Exhibit 5 shows, nearly 60% of Fang's investment from the joint venture partners would go toward rent and the purchase of new equipment. In fact, by April Fang had already realized that the cash crunch he was under was

EXHIBIT 5 Carvel in Beijing: Projected Budget 1995

	US$	¥ *
Outstanding Invoices		
Invoice #66586	$23,288	¥195,619
Invoice #66262	5,333	44,796
Invoice #68302	1,650	13,860
Invoice #68300	905	7,600
Invoice #68301	35,375	297,151
Total current invoices	66,551	559,025
Cash Flow Needs		
Factory annual rent	$113,095	¥950,000
Office annual rent	27,381	230,000
East Four annual rent	26,190	220,000
West Four annual rent	13,095	110,000
Subtotal rent	179,762	1,510,000
Inventory overhead	71,429	600,000
Total current cash flow needs	251,190	2,110,000
Plant & Equipment Needs		
5 KDC-47	$10,150	¥85,260
15 FPD-5	42,525	357,210
15 CMCT-4	36,765	308,826
9 Taylor 770	82,197	690,455
Subtotal equipment	171,637	1,441,751
Custom tax on equipment (50%)	85,819	720,875
Refurbishment of 9 C-Type stores	85,819	720,875
60 rollhards	28,571	240,000
2 delivery trucks	45,238	380,000
Total P&E Needs	$406,265	¥3,412,626
Total Cash Needs 1995	**$724,006**	**¥6,081,651**

Exchange Rate = ¥8.4/US$1.00
Source: Company records

going to force him to revise his budget plans or to request more capital from the joint venture partners. Fang's projected 1995 profit & loss statement in Exhibit 6 reveals several factors that contributed to this problem.

Customs and Import Duties

Customs taxes and regulations presented the single largest day-to-day problem for Phil Fang. Since nearly

■■■■■■ **EXHIBIT 6**   Carvel in Beijing:
Projected Net Income Statement
1995 (in Thousands of ¥)

Revenues	¥13,000
Sales	
Sales discounts and allowances	1,170
Net sales before tax	11,830
Sales tax	1,710
Net sales	10,120
Expenses	
Costs of goods sold	
Mix	2,600
Commissary	1,820
Packaging	1,170
Labor	1,200
Total costs of goods sold	6,790
Operating expenses	
Administrative expenses	1,560
Store operating expenses	2,280
Expenses	
Advertising expenses	180
Total operating expenses	4,020
EBITDA	**(690)**
Depreciation	540
Renovation expenses	850
Other expenses	30
Projected Net Income 1995 (¥2,110)	

Source: Company records.

909 of all his input products were shipped from the United States, arranging for delivery through the complicated and fluid world of Chinese customs was critical. Currently, according to the import license that the government had issued Carvel Beijing, Fang was only allowed to import a certain amount of products each year. In general, tariff rates averaged 50% of the net value of the item as listed on the original shipping invoice. However, some items, such as syrups, whip topping powder, and cones, could have tariff rates as high as 80% of their original value. For 1995, Fang faced potential tariffs of 100% unless Carvel could negotiate a better license or use *guan xi* to arrange a more palatable agreement.

Consequently, Fang's projected cost of goods sold as a percent of sales was roughly 48%. He realized he would have to reduce the man hours and capital spent to receive products from the United States if he were to achieve the aggressive goals he had established. Clearly, he must begin to locally source as much of his inputs as he could. He had begun to check on local producers of refrigeration equipment, and local manufacturers were already producing several new packaging materials for the cakes.

Demadis had established this priority to source goods locally, but both he and Fang were wary of the quality standards of these goods. Especially since the product was still in its introduction period, both Fang and Demadis wanted to ensure that the public's first impression of the product was one of quality.

Mix

After labor, mix production represented the largest expense Fang faced. Currently, mix production represented 45% of the cost of goods sold and nearly 20% of total projected sales. New Continent Dairy, a partner in the joint venture, presently charged Carvel Beijing ¥41.81 per gallon of mix and was averaging batch rounds of 3,000 gallons per month.

Fang predicted that as sales increased with the weather, he would be using 12,000 gallons in July and 30,000 gallons total for the first six months of the year. This fact, combined with the fact that New Continent still produced mix for its own ice-cream brand, had lead Fang to believe there were economies of scale in the mix production cycle that could lower his mix expense. In short, Fang would like Wang Meng, president of New Continent, to share those scale economies with Carvel Beijing. However, because of the political nature of the issue, Fang had few options to pursue in this matter.

Fang and Demadis were currently planning the conversion of New Continent's Dairy facilities from HTST to UHT. In order to convert the plan, Carvel Beijing would have to purchase a new filler, holding tank, and vacuum pump at a cost of nearly $100,000. Fang was searching to defray some of this cost by locally sourcing some of the pipe fitting and tank assembly parts. Once completed, Carvel's UHT system would be the first in China and would have tremendous potential as Carvel expanded in the region. By creating 90-day mix in Beijing, Carvel could centralize mix production throughout its chain and potentially create other lines of mix for other companies. Fang was hopeful that this conversion would allow him to work with Wang Meog to reduce the cost of Carvel Beijing's mix.

Labor

Another of the financial restraints facing Fang was labor. Oddly enough, although relatively inexpensive labor was one of the chief reasons firms expanded into China, labor was not the leveraged competitive advantage it first appeared to be. First, although the average employee at Carvel Beijing earned ¥800 per month, there were other, hidden costs involved. In particular, for each employee, Carvel Beijing must pay a 17% government payroll tax; also, the government also required the company to set aside an additional 32% of each employee's salary in a special account for health care, training, and child care costs. Ultimately, these costs raised labor expense to 149% of their actual cost.

Secondly, the government imposed a luxury payroll tax of 5% to 20% for each employee earning over ¥1,000 per month, of which there were four at Carvel Beijing. With inflation running at 16% in 1994 and projected at 9% in 1995, Fang must consider ways to reduce labor cost.

Finally, the fact that Carvel Beijing was a foreign joint venture in China encouraged employees to expect relatively higher wages than domestic companies offered. With over 60 employees to manage, Fang often found himself busy with this wage issue. He often questioned the validity of the advantage of cheap Chinese labor.

Sales

Sales growth continued to be a major problem for the new franchise. By beginning operations in October, management had run the risk of starting the new venture in what was traditionally the slowest period of the year for Carvel. Consequently, Fang and Demadis were still unable to identify the cause of the slow sales with any real certainty. As the sales figures below demonstrate, sales were actually increasing both in gross and relative terms. However, the true potential for the operation remained unclear. The following sales summary clarifies this point:

	December	January	February
East Four Store	¥57,222	73,424	77,305
West Four Store	24,127	30,421	35,585
Chang An Dept. Store	79,351	128,147	119,167
Parkson Store Dept. Store	NA	44,609	78,320
Wholesale Accounts	73,360	94,455	72,040
Total	234,060	371,056	382,417

These sales figures followed the traditional sales cycle of the American stores. Except for several spikes around the six major holidays (Valentine's Day, Easter, Mother's Day, Father's Day, Thanksgiving and Christmas), weather had historically driven sales volume in the United States.

To combat this cycle, Carvel U.S. has introduced various measures to dispel the notion that ice-cream cakes were only for special occasions and warm weather. The success of the grocery store program in the United States had reinforced the theory that a push-oriented sales program would help remind customers that ice-cream cakes were a tasty treat all year round.

Demadis felt this was exactly the strategy to apply in China. Solid marketing could introduce Carvel's traditional American ice-cream experience to unfamiliar Chinese consumers. An aggressive push campaign for outside accounts would create brand awareness and drive sales.

Fang, however, felt that there were other market forces at work. In particular, Fang believed that the conventional Carvel approach did not appeal to the traditional Chinese consumers. Such cakes as rainbows and baboon cakes did not attract the typical Chinese consumer, who expected a more elaborate, Chinese design on cakes. According to Phil Fang it was a reluctant, unfamiliar consumer, that was behind the slow sales.

Both Fang and Demadis agreed that slow sales and negative cash flow limited their options to grow the business. Analysis of the accounting information confirmed the difficulty the retail stores had on covering their costs. On the other hand, the success of the Chang An and Parkson stores confirmed the fact that Carvel could produce a profit in Beijing. Furthermore, despite continuing losses, Fang and Demadis both agreed that the East Four and West Four stores were necessary for the chain to project a positive image in the city of Beijing. What remained to be determined was how best to improve their performance.

Meanwhile, Wang Meng presented Phil Fang with a new option to increase wholesale sales. Recently, he had constructed 6,000 new vendcarts in order to merchandise his product in Beijing and Tianjin. These carts closely resembled the color and design of the Carvel vendcarts, and Weng Meng was willing to let Fang use the 4,000 Beijing carts to sell Carvel novelties along with New Continent ice cream. It was a tough decision for Fang to make.

On one hand, Fang could not argue with the economies of this proposal. Wang Meng had bought his carts domestically at a cost of ¥4,000 per cart. Currently,

Fang was importing Carvel carts from the United States at a cost of ¥35,000 plus the added cost of ¥15,000 in customs tax. Wang Meng expected a return of nearly ¥30,000 per month per cart. Faced with such tight cash flow, even a small percentage of these sales offered Fang the opportunity to meet his budget and concentrate on plans for the rest of the business. On the other hand, Fang faced harsh opposition from Demadis on this point. Besides the apparent conflict of interest and appearance of impropriety, Demadis strongly argued that selling Carvel products alongside cheaper-quality New Continent products would severely harm the long-term status and positioning of the product. Especially with so many first-time buyers during the summer, Demadis felt selling Carvel alongside New Continent would confuse customers and jeopardize his strategy to develop the line as a premium product from America. This was an issue that both had yet to agree upon.

Finally, part of the problem Fang was having centered on the lack of any centralized cost accounting and transfer pricing systems. This lack of accurate and centralized information hampered efforts to determine the cause of high costs. One of the goals Fang had set for 1995 was to improve the internal and corporate reporting of information.

Product Line

Carvel Corporation offered a wide variety of ice-cream products. The company's fundamental product, though, remained its soft-serve ice cream and fountain line. Included in this category were

- cups and cones
- shakes
- floats
- sundaes
- hard ice cream—soft ice cream that is frozen in the shock box in tubs so that it can be scooped and served as traditional ice cream.

In order to promote the everyday nature of the business, though, management had introduced numerous new products over the last three years. Included in this category were novelty ice creams.

Carvel classified novelty products as individual ice-cream treats that were more premium than the traditional soft-serve and fountain offerings. The following is a sample of Carvel's novelty line:

- **Flying Saucer**—Carvel's original round ice cream sandwich

- **Brownie**—a cube of chocolate ice cream with layers of chocolate fudge and walnuts
- **Ice Cream Cannoli**—a real cannoli shell filled with soft-serve ice cream and toppings
- **Truffle**—a ball of vanilla ice cream filled with cherries, almonds, and chocolate chips inside a chocolate shell

Management felt that these novelties would greatly renew and invigorate the brand's name and image, but Carvel's traditional cake line remained the high-margin product that had the greatest impact on sales. Carvel's traditional line of cakes all had the same recipe. Each cake was made with one layer of vanilla ice cream, one layer of chocolate ice cream, and a chocolate crunch cookie center. The cakes were frosted with a vanilla whip frosting and decorated in several fashions, including roses, balloons, and rainbows. Cakes differed, however, in size, shape, and weight. In particular, Carvel's traditional cake line included

- **Dessert Cake**—a 6" round cake weighing 21 ounces
- **Small Round Cake**—an 8" round cake weighing 43 ounces
- **Large Round Cake**—a 10" round cake weighing 66 ounces
- **Small Sheet Cake**—an 8"×12" square cake weighing 85 ounces
- **Large Sheet Cake**—a 10"×14" square cake weighing 156 ounces

It was Carvel's cake line that distinguished it from all the other offerings in Beijing. In particular, Carvel's classic cake line aimed to offer customers more variety than the traditional chocolate and vanilla cakes. This line included

- **Mint Chocolate Chip Cake**—mint and chocolate ice cream with a chocolate cookie crunch middle, decorated with mint frosting, fudge, and chocolate chips
- **Sinfully Chocolate Cake**—chocolate ice cream with a fudge and cookie crunch center, decorated with chocolate mousse topping, hot fudge, and chocolate candy shards
- **Strawberry and Cream Atop**—strawberry and vanilla ice cream with a vanilla cookie crunch center, topped with vanilla frosting and whole strawberries
- **Cappuccino Coffee Cake**—coffee ice cream with a chocolate crunch center, topped with

mocha frosting, walnuts, and vanilla cookie crunch

These cakes continued to sell well in the United States, particularly in the grocery store program. Carvel also offered various shaped cakes, including the following:

- **Cookie Puss**—a clown-shaped face with an ice cream cone nose and cookie eyes
- **Fudgie the Whale**—a chocolate whale cake with fudge frosting
- **Hug Me the Bear**—chocolate and vanilla ice cream bear cake with a cookie crust

- **Holiday Cakes**—including Santa, heart-shaped cakes, and turkey cakes

Finally, Carvel offered both sugar-free and fat-free frozen yogurt and a fat-free ice cream. To date, however, these products had not been introduced to China.

Product Line Sales

With such a wide product line, Fang had tried to introduce as many items as he could to the Beijing customers. However, he soon realized that certain products were not selling. Exhibit 7 illustrates the breakdown of product sales over the course of the first four months of operations.

EXHIBIT 7   Carvel in Beijing: Sales Breakdown (in Units Sold)

Item	November	December	January	February
Small Round Cake	14	123	162	186
Large Round Cake	1	520	17	94
Small Sheet Cake	0	121	64	37
Large Sheet Cake	2	21	10	2
Small Heart Cake	14	74	148	162
Large Heart Cake	9	118	102	68
Dessert Cake	27	134	237	335
Hug Me Bear Cake	42	180	304	265
Fudgie the Whale Cake	8	29	13	33
Cookie Puss Cake	6	22	21	29
Santa Cake	13	89	48	20
Football Cake	0	0	0	0
Bunny Cake	0	0	32	39
Carvel Log	0	0	29	49
Sinfully Chocolate Cake	20	144	293	228
Fudge Drizzle Cake	27	61	132	85
Strawberry and Cream Cake	21	62	123	132
Mint Chocolate Chip Cake	16	33	72	41
Cappuccino Coffee Cake	0	1	72	43
Truffle	0	0	96	343
Brownie	370	744	878	739
Dream Bar	274	592	751	651
Neapolitan	18	819	757	582
Blondie	320	538	637	501
Chocolate Flying Saucer	59	106	134	921
Vanilla Flying Saucer	56	76	89	82
Strawberry Flying Saucer	19	79	93	78
Deluxe Flying Saucer	73	103	147	110
Vanilla Mini Sundae	98	1388	2635	1927
Strawberry Mini Sundae	88	1407	720	0
Van-Straw Mini Sundae	120	1853	3616	4627

Source: Company records

Fang drew several conclusions from the sales data. First, some cakes, such as the Sinfully Chocolate and Strawberry and Cream cakes, had strong sales, while the Cappuccino Coffee cakes and Mint Chocolate Chip cakes had very slow sales. Fang felt that such relatively exotic cakes simply did not appeal to Chinese, who were accustomed to traditional vanilla, chocolate, and strawberry flavors. Demadis, on the other hand, continued to assert that consumer awareness was the issue, not consumer taste. Second, Fang also noticed that Hug Me Bear cakes continued to show strong sales numbers, but Cookie Puss and Fudgie the Whale cakes were sluggish. Again, he concluded that such traditional Chinese shapes such as the bear were inherently strong sellers, while American-style cakes such as Cookie Puss simply seemed too exotic and too foreign. Third, Fang had to face frequent comments from customers that the ice cream, and, consequently, the ice-cream mix, was too sweet. Fang knew that Chinese traditionally did not like very sweet desserts, and he feared that traditional American tastes might not appeal to the broad spectrum of Chinese consumers. Changing the mix formula might increase sales, but Demadis strongly opposed tampering with the traditional success of the company in any form.

Finally, Fang felt that pricing was both driving strong cup and cone sales and inhibiting relatively slow cake sales. For this reason, Fang had serious doubts about the pricing strategy established last October.

Pricing

Before Carvel Beijing opened its doors in October, Demadis and Fang had to discuss the pricing strategy for the company. Demadis argued that prices should be at least as high as what he considered the company's chief competitor, Baskin & Robbins. Demadis based his rationale on the fact that Carvel was virtually unknown in Beijing, and consequently, management had the unique opportunity to create whatever image and market position it wanted for the company. He argued that Carvel Beijing should be seen as a premium ice cream that was not priced out of the range of the typical Beijing resident; nevertheless, it should be priced high enough to make people consider it a product of quality and prestige.

Fang, however, maintained that such a long-term approach to pricing would suffocate short-term sales and consequently nullify the long-term benefit of such a strategy. Fang considered his chief competition Walls and Bud's, both of which offered novelty cups and cones throughout the city for roughly ¥4.

Both men presented their arguments in an early October meeting. Demadis argued that since Baskin & Robbins presented the most significant long-term threat to the Beijing ice-cream market, Carvel had to price its product in line with them. At that time, Baskin & Robbins was asking ¥9 for an ice-cream cone. Demadis felt that by pricing Carvel's product below that would send the wrong, initial signal to the customers.

Fang argued that the future of the Beijing market lay in understanding the Chinese consumer, who was not ready to purchase ice-cream cones that represented, on average, nearly 25% of a day's pay. Fang contended that Carvel should price more in line with Walls and Bud's, both of which had been in the market longer than Baskin & Robbins and had experienced annual growth and profits.

In the end, the two decided on a cost-plus strategy that considered the following costs:

- Mix cost: 4¢/oz.
- Duty on commissary: 50% to 80%
- Freight charge: 10%
- Carvel surcharge: 10%
- East Four rent: ¥210,000 per year
- Taxes: 17%

Ultimately, Fang and Demadis agreed that Carvel's standard 3-h ounce small cone in the East Four store should be priced at ¥9. However, they disagreed on the issue of soft and hard ice cream prices. Fang wanted to price soft-serve cones at ¥7 and hard ice cream cones at ¥9. Demadis felt that pricing one higher than the other gave customers the impression that one ice cream cone was better than the other, when in fact they were both made from the same soft-serve ice cream. In the United States, Demadis argued, hard and soft serve ice cream were always priced the same.

As for the rest of the product line, Fang again applied a modified cost-plus strategy. However, since his cost accounting system had not been established, he had to use what cost information he had together with the production costs that Carvel U.S. had determined for American production. Although both men agreed they would have to review these prices once Chinese cost figures were available, they were willing to go along with the above approach to determine prices. The following table lists the available cost and retail price information for Carvel Beijing.

Item	Production Cost	Retail Sale Price
Large Heart	¥30	¥130
Dessert	12	49
Hard Ice Cream Cone (scoop)	1.5/ 3.0/ 4.5	8/ 15/ 20
Small Cone	1.5	7
Small Cup	1.5	10
Hug Me Bear	23	69
Cookie Puss	25	99
Fudgie the Whale	32	99
Sinfully Chocolate	18	69
Strawberry & Cream	17	69

By April, however, Fang had to reconsider his costs and sales prices. It was clear that he had to reduce costs. This he could accomplish by continuing to source inputs locally and increase volume and his economies of production.

What was uncertain, though, was whether these prices made Carvel products unreachable to Chinese consumers. After six months, Fang felt that slow sales had forced him to examine the decision whether to stick with the original pricing strategy, or whether to redefine his product through price cuts.

Advertising

The basic drive behind the advertising campaigns both in China and the United States was to use fountain and novelty products to drive cake sales. Cake sales by far had the most margin, and it was in cake production that Carvel had its most leveraged competitive advantage. Clearly, if Carvel were to succeed in China, it had to do so on the back of cake sales.

Fang had several avenues to explore to promote his product. Among the options and costs to consider were:

Television

- 5-second commercial three times per day for seven days—¥4,000
- 15-second commercial three times per day for seven days—¥10,000
- 30-second commercial three times per day for seven days—¥15,000

Radio

- 5-second commercial three times per day for seven days—¥1,000

- 15-second commercial three times per day for seven days—¥3,500
- 30-second commercial three times per day for seven days—¥5,000

Billboards—¥10,000 per month

Bus placards—¥40,000 for one bus on one bus line for six months

Newspapers

- 150-word ad—¥2,000 per month
- color ad on front cover—¥5,000 per month

Magazines

- local biweekly magazine—¥3,000
- local monthly magazine—¥5,500

Before making his decision, Fang wanted to examine media-related information, as shown in Exhibit 8, available from the Gallup Poll.

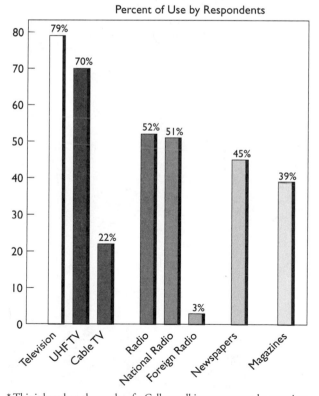

EXHIBIT 8
Carvel in Beijing: Media Usage*

Percent of Use by Respondents

Television 79%, *UHF TV* 70%, *Cable TV* 22%, *Radio* 52%, *National Radio* 51%, *Foreign Radio* 3%, *Newspapers* 45%, *Magazines* 39%

* This is based on the results of a Gallup poll in response to the question: Which of the following did you read, see or listen to yesterday?
Source: Company records

Consumer Market in China

The recent Gallup Poll provided interesting insights into the burgeoning consumer market in China. The most striking fact to emerge was that Chinese consumers were very intelligent shoppers who valued quality and long life in their purchases. For example, only 29% of consumers bought on price alone, whereas 63% bought on quality.

EXHIBIT 9 Carvel in Beijing: Popular Brand Names in China

Rank	Company	Percent
1	Hitachi—a	65%
2	Coca Cola—b	62
3	Panasonic—a	60
4	Toshiba—a	58
5	Qing Dao Beer—e	56
6	Toyota—a	54
7	Mickey Mouse—b	51
8	Marlboro—b	47
9	Suzuki—a	44
10	Honda	42
11	Pepsi Cola—b	42
12	Kodak—b	42
13	Sanyo—a	42
14	Boeing—b	42
15	Fuji—a	41
16	Nestlé—c	40
17	Mitsubishi—a	40
18	Mercedes Benz—c	39
19	Head and Shoulders—b	36
20	Gold Star—d	36
21	Sharp—a	35
22	Philips—c	34
23	Sony—a	33
24	Volkswagen—c	33
25	Hilton—b	33
26	Samsung—d	31
27	Nissan—a	26
28	NEC—a	26
29	Casio—a	25
30	Peugeot—c	22

Legend:
a = Japanese companies
b = American companies
c = European companies
d = Korean companies
e = Chinese companies

Source: Company records

As for consumer tastes in food, the survey revealed that, as expected, rice, tea, and pasta were the most common foods in the Chinese household. However, 17% of those polled had dairy products in their house, and 13% regularly kept frozen foods at home.

The Gallup Poll also indicated that Chinese were very well aware of foreign brand names. The respondents were read a list of over 100 brand names and were asked whether they had heard of names. Forty-four of the names were those of American-based companies or brands, 25 were Japanese, 17 were European, and the other 14 were from other nations. Exhibit 9 lists the 30 most popular brand names in China, of which 14 are Japanese, 8 American, 5 European, 2 Korean, and only 1 Chinese.

Exhibit 10 shows the Gallup Poll information relative to fast food and soft drinks. Kentucky Fried Chicken was the most widely recognized fast food chain in China; McDonald's, Burger King, and Pizza Hut were also very recognizable throughout China. However, as the survey concluded, the most telling fact about these findings was the following:

> As has been the case for almost every measure, urbanization is the factor most affecting brand recognition levels. Those living in urban areas are much more likely to recognize brand names than are people nationwide, and residents of the largest nine cities are still more able to recognize brand names than are urban residents in general.

EXHIBIT 10 Carvel in Beijing: Brand Recognition of Fast Food and Soft Drinks

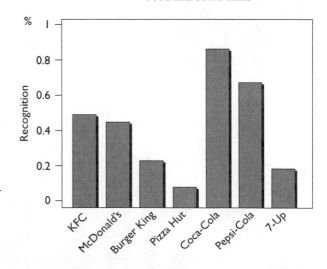

Source: Company records

Finally, the Gallup Poll revealed some telling information on buying habits in China. For example, in response to the question, "On average, about how much do you and your household spend per month on the following items?" considerable differences were found between large cities, urban areas, and the country as a whole (see Exhibit 11).

Competition

Carvel Beijing faced a very fragmented market in Beijing. Generally speaking, several domestic and international companies had penetrated the market and achieved moderate brand awareness. However, no brand had yet to break from the pack and establish itself as the market leader in ice cream. The following breakdown describes the most dominant of these fragmented players:

- **Walls**—Walls was a Holland-based company and one of the market leaders in Europe and Australia. In Beijing, Walls' product line was limited to cups, cones, and various other novelty treats. Mainly their distribution was limited to roughly 3,000 rollhards from which they sold novelty ice creams, namely cups and cones. Walls was also available in several supermarkets.

  As one of the first Western ice creams in Beijing, Walls still enjoyed the benefits of its first-mover status. Beijing customers still considered Walls to be the preeminent Western ice cream in Beijing, simply due to the breadth and duration of its presence. On average, Walls sold its products for ¥4, but recently it had raised its prices to ¥5. It was estimated that Carvel had taken much of its market share from Walls.

- **Bud's**—Bud's was a San Francisco–based ice cream company that enjoyed a wide presence and brand awareness in Beijing. Although only a regional brand in the United States, in China Bud's enjoyed the reputation of being the preeminent American brand because it was the first American brand to appear in the People's Republic of China. To date, in a country where consumers still prized a company's tradition and longevity, both Baskin & Robbins and Carvel had not yet been able to dispel Bud's image.

  Like Walls, Bud's did not have any retail store outlets. Instead, Bud's sold only from nearly 600 rollhards scattered throughout Beijing's markets and supermarkets. Bud's only

Item	National Response	Urban Response	Largest 9 Cities
Food, including eating out	¥22.10	¥38.00	¥53.10
Family savings	11.40	17.00	20.50
Clothing	5.60	9.00	10.00
Child's education	4.70	7.00	9.10
Home, rent, and electricity	4.30	8.20	9.80
Daily goods (non-food)	3.50	4.80	5.60
Entertainment	1.30	3.20	4.50
Medical	2.30	4.00	4.00

EXHIBIT 11 Carvel in Beijing: Spending Habits in China

Source: Company records.

produced cup and cone products, and its prices matched those of Wall's. Small cups were ¥4.2, hard ice cream was ¥6, and pints sold for ¥23.

- **Baskin & Robbins**—Baskin & Robbins represented the most significant long-term competition to Carvel Beijing for several reasons. First, Baskin & Robbins was Carvel's chief rival in the United States and its products enjoyed a more national brand awareness than Carvel's. Second, Baskin & Robbins was the only competitor in Beijing that produced an all-ice-cream cake and had retail stores in which to promote them. Finally, Baskin & Robbins had a longer and broader presence in Beijing and appeared to have the positioning strategy that Carvel had targeted.

  Baskin & Robbin's presence was mainly limited to its two retail stores. Like Carvel, Baskin & Robbins offered its customers a true ice-cream parlor experience. While Carvel's cakes were of better quality, Baskin & Robbins relied on its tradition of hard ice-cream cones and fountain products to drive sales. Currently, Baskin & Robbins charged ¥9 for a single-scoop ice-cream cone and ¥107 for a cake comparable to Carvel's small round. Baskin & Robbins did not have any wholesale outlets at this time.

- **Meadow Gold**—Meadow Gold was a locally produced product with high market saturation. Meadow Gold's product quality was much lower than the above competitors, but the company's rollhards were in twice as many outlets as Walls, and the company sold its products through a number of channels: local stores, supermarkets, and on the street.

Concentrating on only novelty products, Meadow Gold charged only ¥2 to ¥3 for its product line of cups and cones.

- **New Continent**—As a venture partner in Carvel Beijing, New Continent was also a strong domestic player in the novelty side of the market. Generally speaking, New Continent competed along side of Meadow Gold for market share and sales, and produced novelty products in the same factory that produced Carvel Beijing's ice-cream mix. Most of New Continent's prices were ¥2 or lower.

New Continent, though, had clearly used its partnership with Carvel to project itself deeper into the Beijing market. The company had come out with awning and vendcart styles that closely resembled the colors and logos of Carvel. Also, with nearly 6,000 vendcarts on order, New Continent would clearly redefine the lower end of the ice-cream market in Beijing.

Finally, New Continent had also begun to open mini stores along the same lines as Carvel's Chang An and Parkson outlets. The company was also considering bringing out a new line of ice cream cakes that would compete on price with Carvel's and Baskin & Robbin's products.

Substitute Products

Beijing residents enjoyed a wide variety of dessert products. Beside ice cream products, there were numerous bakeries that offered a variety of traditional Chinese designed cakes and pastries. These flour-based cakes were richly designed with traditional Chinese figures and styles and sold on average from ¥100 to ¥250 for an ornate wedding cake.

Other traditional treats included pastries with a sweetened jelly or fruit paste filling. Chinese also enjoyed various types of traditional dried fruits, and they often ended each meal with a platter of fresh fruit and tea. There were also many styles of Chinese and Western candies. Furthermore, a traditional sweet treat called *suan niu nai* (literally meaning *sour milks*), a yogurt-like product, was sold throughout the city for ¥1.5. Chinese of all status enjoyed *suan niu nai* at all hours of the day, but it was more closely associated with the less affluent segments of society.

Finally, the growth of McDonald's, Burger King and Kentucky Fried Chicken had presented Carvel with other possible substitute products. More and more consumers were trying these fast food giants' own desserts, such as apple pies, shakes, and their own ice cream cups and sundaes.

In short, there was a wide variety of dessert and snack treats from which Chinese consumers could choose. What concerned Phil Fang, though, was that all these alternative treats were cheaper and more widely recognized than his product line.

Conclusion

On April 30, 1995, Phil Fang gathered his management team together to perform a SWOT analysis of Carvel Beijing. They concluded that Carvel Beijing was operating under the following conditions:

Strengths

- Carvel had the best ice-cream cake in Beijing and one of the best ice creams.
- Carvel had received positive reviews from its customers.
- Training and operations had progressed well and the company was ready to increase production.

Weaknesses

- Vaguely defined management roles and objectives hampered definitive marketing policies.
- Inability to source inputs locally continued to hamper the bottom line.
- Too many potential customers still did not know of Carvel Beijing.

Opportunities

- Carvel was looking into involving the foreign embassy community in its sales promotions as a means of increasing both sales and potential outside business contracts.
- The approaching summer allowed Carvel to have a seasonal grand opening to reintroduce the brand to first-time customers.
- Wang Meng's offer to use 6,000 New Continent vendcarts offered Carvel the opportunity to increase greatly the brand's exposure at minimal cost.

Threats

- The cash flow and sales problems threatened to scuttle the proposed business plan for 1995.
- The competition, including Wang Meng, were quickly realizing the potential of ice-cream cakes in Beijing, and Carvel's competitive advantage in this area would be challenged.

- The dynamic political and economic environment in China presented inherent uncertainty.

Having done this analysis, Fang had to plot his strategy for the rest of 1995 and beyond. More important, he had to make some very tough decisions on where he wanted to position Carvel Beijing as it entered its first and, arguably, most important summer in Beijing. Among the most pressing issues he had to face were

- how to price the product: competitively or as premium product

- how to design and position the cakes: as American products or as more traditional Chinese products

- how to confront the financial problems: with short-term or long-term policies

- how to respond to Wang's vendcart proposal

- how to produce the mix: as the original American mix or as a less sweet mix more appealing to traditional Chinese tastes.

What complicated these decisions were the problems associated with a multinational joint venture: issues of personality, culture, and the joint venture agreement itself. In the end, though, it was Phil Fang who would have to overcome these challenges and seize upon the unique chance to create the first truly national brand of ice cream in the People's Republic of China.

Endnotes

1. The Gallup Organization of Princeton, New Jersey, recently completed the first nationwide survey of consumer behavior in the PRC. To complete this survey, Gallup interviewed 3,400 Chinese citizens in each of the country's provinces except Tibet. The sample represents the entire adult population 18 years of age and older. All interviews were conducted in person in the applicant's home between May 2 and September 15, 1994. The interview included over 400 questions and required more than one hour to complete.

2. The exchange rate as of April 1, 1995 was US$/8.41.

Case 22:   Hewlett-Packard: DesignJet Online[*]

At the beginning of September 1997, Ignacio Fonts, marketing director of the Barcelona Division of Hewlett-Packard Española, S.A., had a number of decisions to make regarding the start-up of the www.designjet-online.hp.com project, a relationship marketing program that would allow HP to communicate on an interactive basis with the users of its large-format printers.

Hewlett-Packard (HP) was a multinational company with a presence in more than 120 countries worldwide whose activities included the manufacture and sale of personal and business computing products. In Europe it has 11 manufacturing sites, including one in the town of Sant Cugat del Vallès, near Barcelona (Spain), where it designed and manufactured large-format printers for the world market. HP was the undisputed world leader in this product category, with a market share of over 50%.

The Barcelona Division (HP-BCD) already had a Web presence[1] at www.hp.com/go/designjet, but this new proposal would signify a major change. Fonts had

to carefully consider all the implications. The target visitors of the new Web site would not be the general public, nor even potential customers; rather, the site would be very specifically aimed at existing users of the approximately 500,000 HP large-format printers in use around the world. However, of those 500,000 machines, only around 50,000 had been identified and registered.

For the first time, HP-BCD would try to interact directly with the end users of its large-format printers scattered around the world, and at the same time offer them new technical support tools. As the project advanced, the situation turned out to be considerably more complicated than expected.

One of Fonts' concerns was that, for the project to succeed, it was vital to get the Technical Support Organization and the Territorial Sales Organization involved (both operated at a global level and with total independence within HP). It was vital that they accepted the new Web site as a useful marketing tool that served their interests and did not see it as an intrusion into their respective areas of responsibility.

Fonts had just returned from his summer holiday and had a meeting with his team planned for the coming Monday. At that meeting they would have to decide

[*] This case was prepared by Professors Lluís G. Renart and José Antonio Segarra, and Lecturer Francesc Parés at IESE, University of Navarra, Spain. It is printed here with permission. Copyright © 1999, IESE.

whether or not to go ahead and set up the new site. If they chose to go ahead, they would have to decide on the definitive content of the site, the measures that would have to be taken to ensure it operated smoothly, and which of them should take on the task of launching and maintaining the site.

While he prepared the agenda for the meeting, Fonts recalled his initial enthusiasm for the new interactive Web site project. Now, however, as the moment of truth when they would have to decide whether to go ahead and develop the project drew nearer, he felt vaguely apprehensive. If they set up the new Web site, they would make it possible for any end user of a large-format printer to start talking directly to "the manufacturer." This meant that various departments within the HP organization, both within Fonts' direct area of responsibility and beyond it, would have to respond effectively if the service was to generate added value for the customer.

Fonts thought that if any part of the HP organization was not properly prepared, or not set up, to communicate appropriately with the end users and as a consequence they could not guarantee a good response capacity, it might be better to postpone the project or limit its scope, so as not to harm the currently excellent image of either HP Barcelona Division or its products, not only internally, within HP, but throughout the world market.

Large-Format Printers

In 1997 there had for several years been a number of computer programs capable of creating and manipulating images by computer. CAD (Computer Assisted Design) and other similar applications were regularly used by architects, engineers, and graphic designers to create two- and three-dimensional drawings. For example, an architect could use her computer to draw the classic two-dimensional planes (plans and elevations) and also three-dimensional perspective views of the future building.

Large-format printers were a type of computer peripheral capable of printing the designs created on screen onto paper or other similar media at widths of more than 1 meter and almost unlimited length.

The earliest users of large-format printers were the pioneers of CAD in the fields of engineering and architecture. Later, graphic designers started to experiment, generating and printing large poster-size images. Initially, the CAD market had used plotters, which could print large formats but were limited to line drawings and so could not print large shaded areas (patterns or halftones) or solid color, which were often needed in graphic design.

In 1997, however, most manufacturers had stopped using the term" plotter" for their machines, using the term "printer" instead. The performance of the machines had improved considerably and some models were capable of producing near-photo-quality prints.

There were different types of large-format printer, using different printing technologies. On the one hand, there were the electrostatic printers, which were more robust and were recommended for jobs that required high capacity. But their high purchase price made them unsuitable for many graphic design applications.

For high-quality and short runs, large-format inkjet printers were used. The main drawbacks of these machines were the need for frequent cartridge changes and the slow printing speed. Many ink cartridge manufacturers were developing pigmented inks with special substrates and laminated systems to extend the durability of the prints. Increasing the printing speed, however, was not so easy. The main problem facing the manufacturers in this sector was the productivity of their printers.

Some professional large-format printers could print at higher speeds using film and offset techniques. However, this system involved using some kind of intermediate printing plate and so was extremely expensive if only a small number of copes was required. Inkjet printers were therefore the best choice for short runs, or for situations where the page design might have to be changed after the first few copies had been printed.

All of HP's large-format printers used the inkjet printing system.

The purchasing process of large-format inkjet printers differed in important respects from that of the usual small desktop printers, which were regarded as consumer items. Large-format printers required an investment of between $2,000 and $12,000, depending on the model and the features, to which the user would have to add a sizeable budget for consumables. Basically, there were two product ranges, each with a wide spectrum of features and prices: the purely technical printers for printing plans and drawings, and the graphic printers that could print spectacular images.

The decisive purchasing factors were quality and printing speed, based above all on reliability and robustness. For the end users it was particularly important that the printer worked smoothly, without unevenness between one print and another, making as little noise as possible, and if necessary for many hours at a stretch. Printing jobs often had to be done in a rush, just before the deadline for delivery of a project.

If a printer broke down, a technician had to go to the user's premises to repair it. Normally repairs were carried out on the spot and often consisted of minor adjustments, either to the software or to the hardware. If a major part or component (printheads, electronic components, paper cutter, etc.) had to be changed, the work could be scheduled with the customer for a future date and carried out on site. Only very rarely did the printer have to be transported to a repair shop.

Large-format printers had a long useful life of over 10 years, but in practice they became out of date within five years, owing to technological obsolescence resulting from the rapid pace of innovation.

They were sold with a one-year warranty which included maintenance labor, parts and components, and even call-out. After that, the customer could choose from a range of alternative maintenance programs, which ranged from extending the initial warranty period from one to three years at a cost of between $500 and $2,400 (depending on the model) to simply paying the cost of the repair each time technical assistance was required.

When customers needed a large-format printer, they tended to go to their regular computer equipment supplier and to think the decision over much more carefully than they would normally do in the case of conventional office computing equipment.

HP had some exclusive distributors that sold only HP brand equipment and that specialized in supplying engineering offices. HP protected them by means of a preferential discount policy. Most of its distributors, however, were multibrand and sold to all types of customers.

If a particular market warranted it, HP would have one or two large-format printer specialists in that country's sales organization, who would visit the distributors and respond to any requests for help from end users.

Exhibits 1, 2, and 3 show some models of large-format inkjet printers developed and manufactured by HP Barcelona Division for the world market. As can be seen, the different models were sold under names that consisted of the expression "HP DesignJet," which was common to all, followed by a number or combination of numbers and letters, such as "HP DesignJet 450" and "HP DesignJet 750C Plus."

The World Market for Large-Format Printers

The CAD market (made up mainly of engineers and architects) had a wide installed base of large-format printers. It had matured very considerably, mainly because almost all the engineering offices of architectural and engineering firms already had one or more large-format printers, or at least a plotter, and the number of new firms needing CAD equipment was growing only very slowly. Also, the motivation to buy a new high-quality graphic printer was low, as there was no demand for spectacular improvements in performance or print quality in this sector. This was, therefore, basically a replacement market segment.

In contrast, the graphic design segment of large-format printer users had gown rapidly, and continued to do so. Customers in this segment could appreciate the cost reductions and the enhanced print quality and performance offered by large-format inkjet printers. Higher printing speeds and a more robust design had stimulated the demand for this type of printer. Advertising agencies, poster producers, industrial designers, interior designers, printers, design schools, design departments in companies, and so on were increasingly adopting this type of printer.

In the graphic design market segment there were two types of purchaser: companies that used the printers in-house, and print service providers, (i.e. shops open to the public where anyone who could create a graphic design on-screen could go to get it printed, paying a price per copy according to the shop's price list).

For graphic designers who worked in companies where not a lot of printing was done, or that for reasons of cost and low usage decided not to purchase a large-format printer of their own, the print shops were a good solution. These shops were precisely the sort of customers that bought the top-of-the-range large-format printers, that is the machines that cost upward of $10,000.

In 1997 the main suppliers of large-format printers in the world were as follows:

With Focus On	Graphic Applications	Graphic and CAD Applications
HP		XXXXXX
ENCAD	XXXXXX	
CAL COMP		XXXXXX
XEROX		XXXXX
SCITEX	XXXXXX	
EPSON	XXXXXX	
MUTOH	XXXXXX	
ROLAND	XXXXXX	
SELEX		XXXXXX

EXHIBIT I   Hewlett-Packard DesignJet Online: Lower Price Range of Large-Format Printers

	HP DesignJet 430 Black-only printer for individuals or small workgroups	HP DesignJet 450C Colour printer for individuals or small workgroups	HP DesignJet 455CA Plug-and-play PostScript language-compatible colour printer for small work groups
	For engineers and architects	For mechanical engineers, architects, GIS professionals, retailers, and office workgroups	For graphic designers and advertising agencies
Print Quality	• Superior line quality • 600-dpi addressable black	• Superior line quality and superior graphics for maps, renders and images • 600-dpi addressable black and 300-dpi colour	• Superior line quality and near-photographic quality images, graphics and signs • 600-dpi addressable black and 300-dpi colour
Print Time* **A1-size (unless otherwise stated)**	Black line drawings in about 1.5 minutes (Fast mode) Black line drawings in about 3.5 minutes (Normal mode)	Black line drawings in about 1.5 minutes (Fast mode) Colour line drawings in about 4 minutes (Normal mode) Colour images in about 18 minutes (Best mode)	Black line drawings in about 1.5 minutes (Fast mode) Colour line drawings in about 4 minutes (Normal mode) Colour images in about 18 minutes (Best mode)
Memory, Standard **Memory, Maximum**	4 MB 36 MB	4 MB 36 MB	4 MB 36 MB
Languages, Standard **Languages, Optional**	HP-GL/2, HP-GL, HP RTL	HP-GL/2, HP-GL, HP RTL	PostScript® language compatible (for Macintosh PowerPC), HP-GL/2, HP-GL, HP RTL
Interfaces, Standard **Interfaces, Optional**	IEEE-1284 compatible, RS-232-C HP JetDirect EX Plus and EX Plus3 external network interfaces	IEEE-1284 compatible, RS-232-C HP JetDirect EX Plus and EX Plus3 external network interfaces	HP JetDirect EX Plus external network interface IEEE-1284 compatible, RS-232-C HP JetDirect EX Plus3 external network interface
Highlights	• HP ZoomSmart scaling technology for large-format output from Windows applications • Microsoft® Windows® and AutoCAD™ drivers included • Optional colour upgrade kit • Optional rollfeed with integrated auto cutter • Tabletop design with optional legs	• HP ZoomSmart scaling technology for large-format output from Windows applications • Microsoft Windows and AutoCAD drivers included • Optional rollfeed with integrated auto cutter • Tabletop design with optional legs	• Software PostScript RIP for Macintosh graphics applications • HP ZoomSmart scaling technology for large-format output from Windows applications • Microsoft Windows and AutoCAD drivers included • Rollfeed with integrated auto cutter • Tabletop design with optional legs
Warranty	One-year with free on-site service	One-year with free on-site service	One-year with free on-site service
Model Number	C4714A (A0)/C4713A (A1)	C44716A (A0)/C4715A (A1)	C6081A (A0)/C6080A (A1)

* Print time specifications quoted are on HP Coated Paper (HP BrightWhite for 1050C/1055CM). Line drawing: Cadalyst 4775, Images: full coverage. HP DesignJet CP Series can be significantly faster when used with a productivity-tuned RIP. All specifications subject to change without notice.

███████████ **EXHIBIT 2**   Hewlett-Packard DesignJet Online: Middle Range of Large-Format Printers

HP DesignJet 750 Plus Value-packed colour printer for small to medium workgroups	HP DesignJet 1050C Premium-performance, colour printer for medium to large workgroups	HP DesignJet 1055CM Premium-performance, plug-and-play PostScript colour printer for medium to large workgroups
For mechanical engineers and architects	For mechanical engineers, architects, GIS professionals, retailers, and office workgroups	For mechanical engineers, architects, GIS professionals, retailers, and office workgroups
• Superior line quality and superior graphics for renders and images • True 600-dpi black and 300-dpi colour • Addressable 600-dpi for colour lines	• Best line quality and near-photo-quality graphics for maps, renders, images, and signs • True 600-dpi black and colour • Addressable 1200-dpi for black lines	• Best line quality and near-photo-quality graphics for maps, renders, images, and signs • True 600-dpi black and colour • Addressable 1200-dpi for black lines

Black line drawings in about
  1.5 minutes (Fast mode)
Colour line drawings in about
  4 minutes (Normal mode)
Colour images in about
  8 minutes (Best mode)
	Black and colour line drawings in about
	  45 seconds or about 35 m^2/hr (Draft mode)
	Colour line drawings in about 2 minutes, or
	  13 m^2/hr (Normal mode)
	Colour images in about 4 minutes or about
	  6.5 m^2/hr (Best mode)
		Black and colour line drawings in about
		  45 seconds or about 35 m^2/hr (Draft mode)
		Colour line drawings in about 2 minutes, or
		  13 m^2/hr (Normal mode)
		Colour images in about 4 minutes or about
		  6.5 m^2/hr (Best mode)

8 MB 72 MB	16 MB 128 MB, 2 GB hard disk	32 MB, 2 GB hard disk 128 MB
HP-GL/2, HP-GL, HP RTL Adobe® PostScript® Level 2™	HP-GL/2, HP-GL, HP RTL, CALS G4 Adobe PostScript 3	HP-GL/2, HP-GL, HP RTL, CALS G4 Adobe PostScript 3
HP JetDirect network interface cards, IEEE-1284 compatible, RS-232-C	HP JetDirect network interface cards, IEEE-1284 compatible	HP JetDirect network interface cards, IEEE-1284 compatible
• Queuing, nesting, rollfeed and autocutter for unattended printing • Network-ready • HP ZoomSmart scaling technology for large-format output from Windows applications • MicroSoft Windows and AutoCAD drivers included • Automatic cartridge alignment • Optional Adobe PostScript level 2 support • TIFF and JPEG support available for UNIX	• Revolutionary printheads with JetExpress technology for faster printing • Modular ink system featuring up to 350 ml ink cartridges • Up to 300 ft media rolls support • Dual paper feed system for easier media loading • Queuing, nesting, rollfeed and autocutter • Network-ready • HP ZoomSmart scaling technology for large- format output from Windows applications • MicroSoft Windows and AutoCAD drivers included • TIFF and JPEG support available for UNIX • Automatic printhead alignment • Optional Adobe PostScript 3 support	• Revolutionary printheads with JetExpress technology for faster printing • Modular ink system featuring up to 350 ml ink cartridges • Up to 300 ft media rolls support • Dual paper feed system for easier media load- ing • Queuing, nesting, rollfeed and autocutter • Network-ready • HP ZoomSmart scaling technology for large- format output from Windows applications • MicroSoft Windows and AutoCAD drivers included • TIFF and JPEG support available for UNIX • Automatic printhead alignment • Adobe PostScript 3 support • PANTONE®* certified
One-year with free on-site service	One-year with free on-site service	One-year with free on-site service
C4709B (A0)/C4708B (A1)	C6074A (A0)	C6075A (A0) * Pantone, Inc.'s check-standard trademark for colour

HP was the undisputed leader in large-format printers, with a market penetration in 1996 of more than 50% of the installed base. None of its competitors had as much as 20% of a world market estimated to be worth some $1 billion per year at manufacturers' selling prices.

HP's competitors in the large-format printer market were generally companies with more specific products for specialist uses, such as large-format printers for printing on fabric used as weather sheeting to cover scaffolding during renovation work on buildings in large cities, which was used as a gigantic advertising medium.

EXHIBIT 3   Hewlett-Packard DesignJet Online: High-End Large-Format Printers

HP DesignJet 2000CP Photo-quality colour printer	HP DesignJet 2500CP Photo-quality, plug-and-play PostScript colour printer	HP DesignJet 3000CP Photo-quality, extra-wide (1.37 m) colour printer	HP DesignJet 3500CP Photo-quality, extra-wide (1.37 m), plug-and-play PostScript colour printer
For print service providers, graphic designers, retailers, office workgroups, and GIS professionals	For print service providers, graphic designers, retailers, office workgroups, and GIS professionals	For print service providers, graphic designers, retailers, office workgroups, and GIS professionals	For print service providers, graphic designers, retailers, office workgroups, and GIS professionals
• Best photo-quality images with brilliant, accurate colours and smooth, subtle tones • True 600-dpi black and colour	• Best photo-quality images with brilliant, accurate colours and smooth, subtle tones • True 600-dpi black and colour	• Best photo-quality images with brilliant, accurate colours and smooth, subtle tones • True 600-dpi black and colour	• Best photo-quality images with brilliant, accurate colours and smooth, subtle tones • True 600-dpi black and colour
7.7 m²/hr (Fast mode) 3.9 m²/hr (Normal mode) 1.6 m²/hr (Best mode)	7.7 m²/hr (Fast mode) 3.9 m²/hr (Normal mode) 1.6 m²/hr (Best mode)	8.6 m²/hr (Economy mode) 4.3 m²/hr (Productivity mode) 1.7 m²/hr (Photo mode)	8.6 m²/hr (Economy mode) 4.3 m²/hr (Productivity mode) 1.7 m²/hr (Photo mode)
8 MB 68 MB	36 MB; 4.3 GB hard disk 68 MB; 4.3 GB hard disk	12 MB 68 MB	36 MB; 4.3 GB hard disk 68 MB; 4.3 GB hard disk
HP-GL/2, HP RTL	Adobe PostScript 3, HP-GL/2, HP RTL	HP-GL/2, HP RTL	Adobe PostScript 3, HP-GL/2, HP RTL
IEEE-1284 compatible HP JetDirect network interface cards	HP JetDirect network interface cards, IEEE-1284 compatible	IEEE-1284 compatible HP JetDirect network interface cards	HP JetDirect network interface cards, IEEE-1284 compatible
• Large-capacity ink system prints up to 186 m² between dye-based ink system changes • Requires external RIP solution or supplied Microsoft Windows or AutoCAD drivers • Optional take-up reel • Indoor and UV ink sets • Automatic printhead alignment • 24 months outdoor and 5 years indoor warranty with 3M™ MCS™ • TIFF and JPEG support available for UNIX	• Large-capacity ink system prints up to 186 m² between dye-based ink system changes • Can also be used with an external RIP • Optional take-up reel • Indoor and UV ink sets • Adobe PostScript 3 standard • AutoCAD and Microsoft Windows drivers included • Network-ready • Automatic printhead alignment • Automatic colour calibration; PANTONE certified; SWOP, Eurostandard and TOYO colour emulation • 24 months outdoor and 5 years indoor warranty with 3M™ MCS™ • TIFF and JPEG support available for UNIX	• Large-capacity ink system prints up to 186 m² between dye-based ink system changes • Requires external RIP solution or supplied Microsoft Windows or AutoCAD drivers • Standard take-up reel • Indoor and UV ink sets • Automatic printhead alignment • 24 months outdoor and 5 years indoor warranty with 3M™ MCS™ • TIFF and JPEG support available for UNIX	• Large-capacity ink system prints up to 186 m² between dye-based ink system changes • Can also be used with an external RIP • Standard take-up reel • Indoor and UV ink sets • Adobe PostScript 3 standard • AutoCAD and Microsoft Windows drivers included • Network-ready • Automatic printhead alignment • Automatic colour calibration; PANTONE certified; SWOP, Eurostandard and TOYO colour emulation • 24 months outdoor and 5 years indoor warranty with 3M™ MCS™ • TIFF and JPEG support available for UNIX
One-year with free on-site service	One year with free on-site service	One-year with free on-site service	One-year with free on-site service
C4703A (91 cm paper width) HP DesignJet 2000CP printer not upgradeable to HP DesignJet 2500CP printer	C4704A (91 cm paper width)	C4723A (1.37 m paper width) HP DesignJet 3000CP printer not upgradeable to HP DesignJet 3500CP printer	C4724A (1.37 m paper width)

Basically, HP maintained one entry barrier that gave it a competitive advantage in the sector: its constant investment in Research and Development aimed at continuous improvement, which could only be justified economically by having an excellent market share.

Hewlett-Packard (HP)

In 1997, HP was a multinational present in some 120 countries, with more than 120,000 employees and net revenue of more than $40 billion. It is specialized in the manufacture and sale of personal and business computing products, peripherals, products for the world of electronics, test and measurement products, networking products, medical electronic equipment, chemical analysis, handheld calculators, and electronic components.

It had 141 sales and support offices spread across 27 countries which, together with 95 national distributors, supported a network of more than 600 retail distributors.

HP had 111 manufacturing centers in Europe, one of which was the facility in Sant Cugat del Vallès in the province of Barcelona (Spain). (See Exhibit 4 for further information on the company.)

HP's Operations in Spain

In this section, by way of example, we shall explain the organization of HP in Spain. Our aim is to introduce the situation of HP Barcelona Division in the context of the company's activities in Spain, and also to describe how the HP organization worked in a country in which the company engaged directly in sales and technical support activities.

Under a single legal identity (HP Española, S.A.), there were three distinct operational organizations, each with different functional relationship to the parent.

First, the Territorial Sales Organization was responsible for selling all of Hewlett-Packard's product lines in Spain. It had its head office in Madrid. Its global headquarters was located in Geneva (Switzerland).

The Territorial Sales Organization was responsible for developing and strengthening the network of local distributors or agents, some of which were exclusive HP agents who sold to large companies or specialists, though most were shops selling computer equipment for office use. HP had specialized area managers and sales engineers for particular products if the market warranted it. In Spain there were two specialist sales representatives for large-format printers who visited the agents and called on potential customers with them. They also conducted training activities focused on market knowledge and sales techniques.

Besides maintaining the network of distributors and agents, the Territorial Sales Organization was responsible for implementing the entire marketing plan for Spain, following general guidelines laid down by each product division though adapting them to its market. Thus, it was the Territorial Sales Organization that decided on prices, promotional and advertising campaigns, and so on, and kept in touch with the local market. Each product division, through its marketing department, would suggest marketing campaigns and

plans, even prices, but ultimately each country was responsible for its own decisions and for the results of HP's general sales plan.

Second, there was the Technical Support Organization, also with its head office in Madrid, but reporting to its own headquarters in Boise (Idaho). It was responsible for providing technical assistance for all the products and equipment of all of HP's product divisions established in Spain. It had technicians and specialized workshops to attend to the needs of the users of the equipment. It also organized the official technical assistance services through associated technical service centers. Besides, carrying out repairs under warranty, which were charged to the corresponding product division, it offered its customers maintenance plans and charged for all its services, including those provided by telephone, when the products and equipment were out of warranty.

The Territorial Sales Organization and the Technical Support Organization coexisted in all those countries in which HP had a direct market presence. In other countries, or in smaller or less developed territories, their functions were performed by one or more independent importer-distributors.

In Spain, the third operational organization was HP Barcelona Division (HP-BCD). Located in Sant Cugat del Vallès, Barcelona, HP-BCD designed and manufactured large-format printers, reporting to HP Inkjet Products Group[2], with its headquarters in San Diego (California).

Organizations Legally Integrated in Hewlett-Packard Española, S.A.		
Territorial Sales Organization	**Technical Support Organization**	**Barcelona Division**
• Deployed on territorial lines	• Deployed on territorial lines	• Design and manufacture of large-format printers for the world market
• Multiproduct	• Multiproduct	
• Headquarters in Geneva (Switzerland)	• Headquarters in Boise (Idaho)	• Headquarters in San Diego (California)

HP Barcelona Division (HP-BCD)

Founded in 1985, HP-BCD was responsible for performing the research and development, marketing, and

EXHIBIT 4   Hewlett-Packard DesignJet Online

Information on HP

In 1997, Hewlett-Packard was one of the world's largest computer companies and a leading manufacturer of test and measurement products. The company's more than 29,000 products were used by people for personal use and in industry, business, engineering, science, medicine, and education.

It also made networking products, medical electronic equipment, systems for chemical analysis, portable computers, and semiconductor products.

HP was among the top 20 in the *Fortune 500* list. It had net revenue of $42.9 billion in fiscal 1997. More than 56% of its business came from outside the United States, and more than two-thirds of that was from Europe.

Other principal markets were Japan, Canada, Australasia, the Far East, and Latin America. HP ranked among the top 10 U.S. exporters. It was number five among *Fortune's* Most Admired Companies and number ten among *Fortune's* Best Companies to Work for in America.

With it headquarters in Palo Alto, California, HP employed more than 120,000 people, of whom some 69,000 worked in the United States. It had major sites in 28 U.S. cities and in Europe, Asia Pacific, Latin America, and Canada. The company sold its products and services through about 600 sales and support offices and distributorships in more than 120 countries, and through resellers and retailers.

Started in a Garage

HP was founded in 1939 by Bill Hewlett and Dave Packard. The company's first product, built in a Palo Alto garage, was an audio oscillator—an electronic test instrument used by sound engineers. One of HP's first customers was Walt Disney Studios, which purchased eight oscillators to develop and test and innovative sound system for the classic movie *Fantasia.*

In 1997, HP's test-and-measurement instruments, as well as systems and related services, were used by engineers and scientists to design, manufacture, operate, and repair electronic equipment, including global telecommunications networks.

Other principal markets for HP instruments and systems were the aerospace/defense, automotive, consumer electronics, computer, semiconductor, and components industries, and scientific research programs.

Medical, Analytical and Semiconductor Products

In the early 1960s, HP extended its electronics technology to the fields of medicine and analytical chemistry. In 1997, the range of HP medical equipment included ultrasound heart scanners and patient monitoring systems that were used in hospitals and clinics around the world. HP computer equipment was used in both the clinical and the administrative areas. HP's expertise helped health care organizations improve patient care and reduce overall costs.

HP analytical instruments analyzed the chemical components of liquids and gases. They were used in the chemical, energy, pharmaceutical and food industries, and in environmental monitoring, medicine, bio-science, and university research.

HP was extending the frontiers of fiber-optic, wireless, and visual communications through its more than 9,000 components in products that helped people communicate quickly, reliably, and cost-effectively.

Computers and Computer Systems

In 1997, most of HP's revenue came from computers—ranging in size from palmtops to super-computers—plus peripherals and services.

HP was one of the fastest-growing and largest personal computer manufacturers in the world. In addition, HP manufactured and serviced networking products to help customers connect HP computers, as well as those of other manufacturers.

HP introduced its first computer in 1966 to gather and analyze data from HP electronic instruments. The company branched into business computing in the 1970s with the HP 3000 midrange computer, launching a new era of distributed data processing, taking computers out of computer rooms and making them accessible to people throughout an organization.

HP was the leader in UNIX® and Windows NT® systems, both successfully integrated in today's business world. HP helped its customers to maximize the productivity of their computing resources while reducing costs.

In 1997, HP acquired Verifone, a leader in electronic commerce solutions. HP currently had preeminent technology in Internet payment systems, where it remained the leader in security, enterprise solutions, service, and support.

HP was one of the best computer service companies, with 35 assistance centers and with offices in more than 120 cities. It also offered a broad range of management consulting services and financial services to give its customers efficient access to information technologies.

World Leader in Printers

HP was the leading supplier that set the technology standards, in performance and in reliability, both in laser printers and in small- and large-format inkjet printers, scanners, and black-and-white or color desktop printers.

Research and Development

The company's central research facility ranked as one of the leading research centers in the world. At its headquarters in Palo Alto, as well as in laboratories in the United Kingdom, Japan, and Israel, researchers developed and applied leading-edge technologies that supported HP's current businesses and created new opportunities for the company. In 1997, between HP Labs and some 70 product divisions, HP invested $3.1 billion in R&D.

Entrepreneurial Environment

The company's entrepreneurial flexibility was fostered by a decentralized organization that gave business units consid-erable decision-making authority. Collaboration with other companies and technology alliances allowed HP to extend leading computing, instrument and communications solutions to many industries.

A Unique Culture

HP's management practices were based on a belief that people are committed to doing a good job and are capable of making sound decisions. Seven corporate objectives provided a framework for group and individual goal-setting in which all employees participated. HP's culture was one of openness and informality. Employees shared in HP's success—which their efforts made possible—through regular cash profit-sharing and stock-purchase programs.

Generous Philanthropist

Because HP considered science and math competence vital in preparing people for the future, it was among the leading contributors to education. In 1997, HP donated $46.7 million in equipment and cash to education. This was 67% of the company's total philanthropic contributions of nearly $61.4 million.

More information about Hewlett-Packard is available from the HP Communications Department, 3000 Hanover Street, Palo Alto, CA 94304-1185. HP's World Wide Web address is *http://www.hp.com.*

---

manufacturing functions for the entire range of HP large-format printers for the entire world market. It also manufactured a range of HP inkjet products for Europe.

Asked about the printers designed and manufactured at Sant Cugat, Ignacio Fonts replied in the following terms:

> With our large-format, photo-quality printers, our goal is to fuse art and technology in a way that will enable graphic designers, architects, engineers, geographers, etc. to express their ideas and feelings through computer-assisted designs of extraordinary quality and size.

In 1997, HP-BCD had around 1,250 employees. Most of them were directly involved in the production processes, which for most of the year were carried out in four shifts (three shifts per day plus Saturdays and Sundays).

The General Management of HP-BCD oversaw six departments:

- Research and Development (R&D)
- Marketing
- Finance
- Human Resources
- Production
- Internal Services

With exports of more than Pta 90,000 million, HP-BCD was one of Spain's largest exporters of computer products.

The Marketing Department at HP-BCD

Under Ignacio Fonts' management the Marketing Department at HP-BCD designed and monitored the global marketing strategy for the products manufactured by HP-BCD. It employed around 70 people. It was responsible for applying the funds corresponding to the total marketing campaign budget for large-format printers, and negotiated with each country the specific campaigns each wanted to run.

As can be seen from the organization chart in Exhibit 5, the Marketing Department was organized in four sections.

Product Marketing

This section had two main functions:

1. Propose new products, which involved visiting customers and distributors to detect new needs, adding whatever qualitative data were needed
2. Work closely with the R&D Department to ensure that products under development matched the established specifications

Market Development

The task of this section was to develop the market for HP-BCD's products. It had to give each Territorial Sales Organization guidelines on

- Communication: advertising, publications, public relations campaigns, and so on
- Prices: suggest a price level for each country (normally a price band)
- Promotions: design special promotions. (For example, the Renewal Plan, whereby an old large-format printer would be accepted in part exchange for a new one, with a variable discount depending on the age of the machine to be replaced, whether it was an HP machine or not, etc. This plan had recently been accepted by a large number of countries with great success.)
- Product: suggest what accessories should be included as standard

Technical Support

This third section of the Marketing Department was responsible for developing easy and effective technical support or assistance systems to be used by the Technical Support Organization in each country.

The local Technical Support Organization in each country (reporting to Boise, Idaho) provided on-site technical assistance for all types of HP equipment. The Technical Support section of the Marketing Department at HP-BCD, however, dealt exclusively with large-format printers and acted only through the Technical Support Organization of each country.

The Technical Support section of the Marketing Department at HP-BCD also trained repair technicians (support engineers), both those employed by HP and those employed by the distributors, monitored warranties, and even resolved technical problems that were too complex for the Technical Support Organizations to handle. For example, when a customer used a printer in very special conditions (unusual software environment, special print media, etc.), the Technical Support Organization might not be able to respond appropriately, and this would bring to light limitations of the product under extreme conditions of use. By studying and classifying the technical problems that emerged it was possible to design and propose improvement plans for the development of future generations of printers.

Strategic Planning

The main task of this section was to supply Marketing Management with information and data relating to sales and marketing. To do this it closely monitored data on sales, installed customer base, reasons for purchasing HP products, and competition at world level. It was also responsible for planning sales and negotiating targets with Territorial Sales Organizations.

The Origins of the New Web Site Project

In January 1997, a group of managers from the Marketing Department at HP-BCD discussed the possibility of communicating directly with the end users of HP's large-format printers. There were some 500,000 of these printers scattered around the world and, as we have already said, the users were not the typical small printer (DIN A4) customers. They consisted mainly of architects, engineers, and graphic designers who had chosen an HP large-format printer but who could equally be regular customers if other brands of computers more specialized in graphics solutions, such as Apple Com-

EXHIBIT 5   Hewlett-Packard DesignJet Online: Organization Chart of the Marketing Department of HP Barcelona Division (HP-BCD)

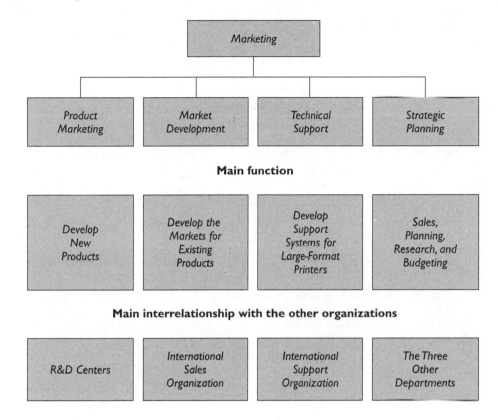

The Focus Groups

Before proceeding with the idea, six focus groups were organized with end users (two in Germany, two in the United States, and two in the United Kingdom), and the project was explained to them.

The reaction of the participants in the focus group was unanimous: What most concerned them was technical assistance. They were not satisfied with the attention they received. They had difficulty obtaining the appropriate drivers[4]. There was a certain amount of interest in hearing about the launch of new products, but what they really wanted was immediate and effective attention to their everyday operating problems.

The Web Site Project

From the outset, the possibility of using the World Wide Web as the channel for communicating directly with end users had been considered, but this idea had been discarded on the grounds that many end users did not have Internet access and so would effectively be excluded.

puter. It was quite possible, therefore, that these users were working in very diverse computing environments[3], often unlike that of a typical user of HP products.

The idea of offering this group of users a tool to communicate directly and at any time with HP-BCD, whereby HP-BCD could inform them of new products and offer them consumables and other equipment, seemed an excellent marketing opportunity. The initial idea was to publish a printed newsletter, in various languages, that would be mailed to all end users of HP large-format printers.

This new channel of communication would be complementary to the messages that were already being sent through HP distributors and the sales and technical support organizations, and to the advertising messages and news that the end users of large-format printers received through the traditional mass media.

The problem was that only 50,000 end users had registered when they purchased their large-format printer, so HP-BCD did not have a complete and unified database, at product level, that gave the names and addresses of the end users of the printers.

However, in light of the comments from the focus groups and the realization that HP needed to be capable of giving an integral response, that is, involving not only the Marketing Department at HP-BCD but also the various support and sales organizations, the pros and cons of using electronic media rather than print were reconsidered.

When it was found that in the United States, in 1996, around 70% of the users of large-format printers of any brand had Internet access, and that in 1997 in the world as a whole the figure was 55%, the idea of using paper was definitely abandoned and developing a new Web site was seen as the best alternative.

After a number of brainstorming sessions involving various departments at Sant Cugat, the project began to take shape. It was assigned to Joan Miró, from Strategic Planning, who in a report dated July 1997 summed up the conclusions reached so far:

Description of the Designjet project

Target of the programme: Users of HP Designjet printers (not retailers or potential customers). We already have a generic web site for HP Designjet printers, but it is aimed at promoting sales; it is not targeted at current users, which we regard as our "installed base".

Definition of the programme's main objectives:

- Stimulate and speed up renewal of the installed base.
- Increase HP's involvement in the sale of consumables.
- Strengthen and increase the loyalty of our customers.
- Increase our knowledge of the market.

The main criterion for including services in this web site will be whether they offer anything that may be considered to be "of value" to the end user. For example, the birthday card that El Corte Inglés department store or the Red Cross send to patrons is not what our programme is about. Giving our users access to a list of telephone numbers for Technical Assistance, on the other hand, is of much greater "value" to them.

Another important feature of the programme is its interactive nature: We must allow the users of our printers to talk to us and ask us questions, and we must talk to them, proactively and continuously, whenever possible.

Services included in the programme

For your eyes only
This service will inform users directly of the appearance of any new HP product. Registered users will receive an e-mail on the date of launch of the new product and will be able to visit the web site if they want more information.

HP Designjet speaking!
Online discussion forum for users. HP will not take part in the discussion. The messages will be 100% from users. In the future, when the necessary internal resources are available, we will have to try to reply to all the messages.

Feedback
Users will send in messages about the products and the solutions that HP offers.

HP will reply, thanking each user for the message, but it will not give a personalized reply. In the future, if the volume of messages allows it, we should try to develop a team capable of answering them.

Quarterly newsletter ("Big Impressions")
Quarterly publication by HP to keep its customers informed of important events in their business or field of activity. Registered users will receive an e-mail containing a list of the subjects covered in each newsletter as it is published, and will be able to visit the web site if they want to read the full text of the articles.

Success Stories
Users will be able to share their positive experiences with their Designjets. Each month, the best story will be rewarded with an HP polo shirt.

Warranty Status
Information on the coverage provided by the HP warranty.

Technical Assistance Information
List of Technical Assistance services available at HP.

Contact addresses and telephone numbers for all countries.

Diagnostics for Designjets
Online tool for breakdowns. (An interactive tool enabling users to resolve some technical problems affecting their printers for themselves.)

Pass the word on!
Whereby users invite a colleague to visit the web site. (Positive word-of-mouth advertising—"member invites member".)

Driver Upgrades
Users will be able to download the latest versions of the drivers for HP Designjets.

Besides all the above-mentioned services, HP will at regular intervals send users an e-mail containing:

- Information on new products and drivers
- Update on the content of the web site
- Newsletter: list of articles
- General news: Y2K effect. printing the new Euro symbol, etc.

Under the plan, it is estimated that each user will receive around 10 e-mails per year.

The Budget

The preliminary budget for printing the newsletter on paper had been put at $1 million per year. The same budget was maintained for the Web site project.

More than 50% of this amount was earmarked for the development and subsequent maintenance of the computer program. The rest would be devoted to promotional material and other derivative costs.

The figure of $1 million, though large, was acceptable within HP-BCD's general marketing budget. The main problem therefore lay in assessing what impact the success or failure of the project might have on HP-BCD's excellent image, and the additional cost of any corrective measures that might have to be taken in the future.

How to Get the Rest of the HP Organization Involved

Although HP-BCD had assigned two people full-time to the project—and planned to continue to do so—there were other people in HP, outside the Barcelona Division, that needed to be actively involved.

Joan Miró explained:
Initially, there was no plan to reply to the e-mails from users. But we'd like the Technical Support Organization to e-mail a reply to all the messages that come in via the Web site. We'd also like them to inform any users of large-format printers that contact them by telephone about the online project and publicize it.

And we'd like the Territorial Sales Organizations throughout the world to publicize the Web site and inform people about it in all their publications. Also, we'd like them to pass on to us any recent information that may be of interest to their users, so that we can keep the site up-to-date and attractive.

What all these ideas that emerged during the various stages of development of the project amounted to was an organizational challenge. The project would require the collaboration of a large part of the structure of HP. It went beyond the sphere of responsibility of the Marketing Department of HP-BCD.

The Reaction of HP's and Other Organizational Units

The Technical Support Organization, which was responsible for Technical Assistance, had its headquarters in the United States, was totally independent, and had its own budgets.

The collaboration of the Technical Support Organization was vital. The Web site was supposed to improve customer satisfaction, so what was needed was not just an attractive array of "pull"[5] information (Web site) such as self-solve tools, a driver library, FAQs, and so on, but also, given the customers' professional expertise, "push" messages (e-mail) giving "tailored" solutions to specific problems.

"The Web site had to be connected to specific support groups that would answer the customers' e-mails in 24 hours free of charge," said Joan Miró.

If we didn't do it that way, we'd be creating an image of HP that was at odds with the image we aimed to convey through the web site. And what's more, all of this had to be done in a variety of languages. Initially, we thought of using 6 languages: English German, French, Italian, Portuguese and Spanish. It was not just a question of translating the content of the web site: we also had to be able to reply to any ("push" or "pull") message in any of these languages.

And she went on:
The Technical Support Organization was willing to make an organizational effort and support the programme, but they didn't know how to get over a problem that they shared with the Support teams in a lot of other countries. The problem was that they charged for the technical assistance they provided, even if it was provided by telephone. We at HP-BCD said that our programme had to be free of charge; we argued that the Internet had created a low-cost standard, and we couldn't charge customers for the service.

One thing was clear: large-format printers accounted for only 3.5% of the Technical Support Organization's revenue. The technical solutions they offered were fairly standard. In the short term, and looking only at large-format printers, the Technical Support Organization's financial results were not going to be seriously affected if they did not charge for the assistance they provided over the Internet. But they wouldn't, and couldn't, allow this to become a precedent for other HP products, and stop charging for their services.

IF HP-BCD wanted the Technical Support Organization to give its approval, it had to convince them that they would continue to charge for the services they provided outside the Web site, even though customers might find out about the difference, depending on what channel of communication and what HP product they used.

It was also important to bear in mind that some distributors had their own profitable technical assistance organizations, whose interests the Web site could conceivably damage.

With the Territorial Sales Organization the problem was even more complicated. Being close to the customer in each territory, it welcomed the idea of giving better service. But who would decide the content of the marketing messages to be sent to end users? HP-BCD? And would HP-BCD tell the users what it wanted when it was wanted?

For the Territorial Sales Organization it was very important that their permission be sought first. The problem was how.

How could they impose territorial limits on the Web site? How could the new channel of communication be coordinated with the marketing and sales campaigns in each individual country? They could not all be expected to keep their marketing actions perfectly synchronized and unanimous.

And what about the distributors? Until then each distributor had had its own customers. HP did not have much direct contact with them, to the point where, as we mentioned earlier, HP had only 10% of the end users of its large-format printers registered. How would the distributors react to the project? Should they be consulted? Would they feel threatened?

The Decision

Ignacio Fonts was in no doubt that it would be difficult to secure the formal approval of all the organizations affected. He also fully realized that, to work well, the project would require sufficient financial and human resources, and a great effort of coordination and communications, both internal and external.

He was convinced that HP-BCD, and he himself as marketing director, had the power and the resources to set up the new Web site. But the risks, both internal and external, were not to be underestimated.

Was it worth the effort? HP-BCD's Marketing Department issued guidelines for large-format printers to all the Territorial Sales and Technical Support Organizations, and they adapted the guidelines to the circumstances in their country, But they had never been directly in touch with their customers before, and this prompted some reservations.

Within the Marketing Department itself, Fonts was not even sure who should take on the task of developing and maintaining the Web site. Initially, the project had been assigned to Strategic Planning, which normally carried out "staff" functions for the other sections. But should Strategic Planning continue to be in charge of the development or start-up of the new project?

All the heads of the four sections of the Marketing Department basically agreed that the new project should go ahead, but their opinions did not coincide exactly, as can be seen from the following comments:

Product Marketing:	"There's no doubt that it may be a very effective tool for our work. It's essential for us to know our customers' future needs, and this project will help us achieve that. Even before we launch a new project, when we do the beta test[6] it will be easy for us to identify the users we want to test our prototypes. Right now, it's difficult for us to find the most appropriate users for our tests."
Market Development:	"Essentially, it's a tool for developing the market and our department. The culture of horizontal and vertical communication is very well established in HP. Deciding what relationship we should have with other departments and divisions is a challenge for us; although we don't have the means or experience of communicating as intensely as this, communication has always been part of our job."
Technical Support:	"It's very clearly a question of improving the satisfaction of the users of our printers, and we've always played a key role in that. We need to ensure that the Support units get involved at an international level. It may not depend on us alone, but, judging by the results of the focus groups, we are undoubtedly one of the keys to success."
Strategic Planning:	"The web site is a window through which users will be able to make contact with HP, and they won't be familiar with our internal organization. They'll want answers, and we'll try to ensure that the messages we receive are answered by those in our organization responsible for doing so, whatever department or division they belong to. Coordinating between different departments is part of my regular job."

"Creating ideas is easy up to a point, but making them work is more difficult," thought Fonts. "Are we about to jeopardize the prestige of HP-BCD? Are there any changes we ought to make?"

And even, would the new Web site be appreciated by the users? Would they value all the services offered?

If the services were not well received, would they be able to change their mind and back out, once the site had been launched and publicized?

All these doubts crowded into Fonts' mind as he prepared the meeting with the heads of his department and drew up a list of the subjects that would have to be discussed before deciding whether or not to give the project his final approval.

HP-BCD Marketing Department Meeting
Monday, September 8, 1997
Room GD-124, 9:30 A.M.
Project: DesignJet-Online

- Analysis of costs, risks and benefits of the project
- Key success factors. Ways to measure and ensure success.
- Internal marketing plan: How to secure the collaboration of the territorial organizations.

- Approval or modification of Web site content.
- Evaluation of subsequent budget and organizational forecasts.
- Responsibility for Web site development and maintenance.

Endnotes

1. By "Web presence" we mean a site that merely offered information about the company and its products.
2. The Sant Cugat factory also manufactured small-format inkjet printers for conventional applications for the whole of Europe.
3. By "diverse environments" we mean the operating systems of other makes of computer.
4. Small software programs needed to adapt peripherals to a particular environment.
5. Referring to the transmission of pre-installed messages that any user could access.
6. Name given to the testing process using experimental machines installed on future users' premises.

Case 23: The Kellogg Company

In 1990, Peter A. Horekens, marketing director for Kellogg Company, was faced with the problem of developing a market for ready-to-eat cereals in the Latin American region. Although Kellogg had no competition in the ready-to-eat cereal market in this region, they also had no market. Latin Americans did not eat breakfast as the Americans did. This problem was especially prominent in Brazil. To create a market and increase sales in this region, Horekens had to create a nutritious breakfast habit among the Brazilians.

Company Background

Kellogg Company, headquartered in Battlecreek, Michigan, was founded in 1906 by W. K. Kellogg to "help people help themselves." This focus had remained intact throughout the company's history. The company continued to operate successfully with sales in 1990 amounting to $3,215 million.

Scope of Business

The Kellogg Company manufactured and marketed a wide variety of convenience foods, with ready-to-eat cereals topping the list. Other products included frozen and fresh-baked pies, toaster pastries, soups, soup bases, seasonings, tea, frozen waffles, dessert mixes, and snack items. The company's products were manufactured in 18 countries and distributed in 130 countries.

Kellogg subsidiaries included Mrs. Smith's Frozen Foods, Inc., Salada Company, and Fearn International Inc. Mrs. Smith's was a leader in the frozen food industry, and the product line included pies, desserts, entrees, and frozen waffles sold under the Eggo brand. Salada Company sold tea bags and other tea products. Fearn International produced quality food service items marketed under the brand name LeGout. The company also produced products for school service and health care markets. In addition, efforts had been concentrated on expansion into delicatessens and restaurant chains.

Kellogg engaged in a variety of supporting activities, including grain milling and carton printing.

Distribution of products was handled through brokers and distributors, as well as through its own sales force. Jobbers—independent and chain store warehouses—made Kellogg products available in retail stores, restaurants, and feeding institutions worldwide. Ready-to-eat cereals were sold principally to the grocery trade for sale to consumers.

Kellogg faced intense competition in each of the consumer food areas in which it was engaged from manufacturers who offered products similar in nature or a variety of alternatives.

Kellogg research and development objectives were designed to generate new and improved products, processing methods, and packaging to keep ahead of the competition. Research and development budgeting allowed for this stress on innovation and new product development. Existing and new products were supported through increased budgets for advertising and promotion. Budgets were also increased to modernize and expand production facilities to meet the increased demand for Kellogg products and to keep costs down.

Kellogg had spent heavily and continued to increase its spending to stay at the top of its primary market—the ready-to-eat cereal market. But competition in the domestic market had led Kellogg to seek new markets. Among these, Latin America was at the top of the list. The primary market within Latin America was Brazil.

International Market

In 1990, Kellogg International operations accounted for 42% of Kellogg Company's sales of more than $3 billion. International operations were divided into four segments: Canada, the United Kingdom and Europe, Afro-Australasia, and Latin America. Among the products sold overseas were ready-to-eat cereals, frozen pizzas, drink products, entrees, snacks, desserts, and pharmaceuticals. The ready-to-eat cereal sales made up the majority of international sales.

In most of these foreign markets, Kellogg controlled more than half of the ready-to-eat cereal market. The United Kingdom was by far Kellogg's largest market. Internationally, sales in the ready-to-eat cereal market continued to increase, although in the past few years the competition also had increased. But in Latin America, consumption of ready-to-eat cereals was negligible.

The Latin American Market

The Latin American market, mainly Mexico and Brazil, showed great potential as a Kellogg's ready-to-eat cereal market. The demographics fit the ready-to-eat market; the only problem was Latin Americans did not eat the traditional American-style breakfast.

The Latin American market included a growing number of families with children. The population mix was becoming younger. The developing economy enabled consumers to spend more of their income on food. Kellogg wanted to increase sales in this Latin American region, especially Brazil, but consumers had turned their backs on the American-style breakfast. How was Kellogg to create a nutritious breakfast habit among the Brazilians?

The company asked J. Walter Thompson, Kellogg's advertising agency, to help instill the breakfast habit in Brazil. According to Horekens, "In general, Brazilians do what people in *novelas* do." *Novelas* are Brazilian soap operas. J. Walter Thompson tried to advertise Kellogg ready-to-eat cereal and instill the breakfast habit by advertising within a soap opera. The first experience of advertising within a soap opera failed; the advertisement portrayed a boy eating the cereal out of a package.

Kellogg wanted to teach the Brazilians how to eat a complete, nutritious breakfast, not just Kellogg's cereal. The commercial did not work because it made Kellogg ready-to-eat cereal seem more like a snack than a major part of a complete breakfast. Thus, they needed the cereal to be eaten in a bowl with milk along with other foods to make a complete breakfast.

The company believed that the growing population in this region would reinforce the importance of grains as a basic food source. The 1990 population in Brazil was 165 million, which made it the sixth most populated country in the world. The population was estimated to grow to 210 million by 2000. Within this population growth was an increase in the number of women of childbearing age, which further supported Kellogg's potential for a successful cereal market. The structure of the population in Brazil in 1990 was

- 37% of the population under age 15
- 48% of the population under age 20
- 12% of the population over age 50
- 6% of the population over age 60

These figures showed that the population of Brazil better fit the market for a ready-to-eat cereal, with the increasing number of children and elderly people as the two largest cereal-consuming segments.

The "cult of the family" continued to be the most important institution in the formation of the Brazilian society. This cultural ideal was reflected in the ways they conceptualized and evaluated the range of personal and social relations. This seemed to be the way Kellogg would have to demonstrate the importance of a nutritional breakfast—by playing up the family and its importance.

Through the use of the *novelas,* Kellogg made a second attempt to teach the Brazilians the importance of breakfast. Most Brazilian families watched these soap operas, composed mostly of family scenes. In their commercials, Kellogg opted for scenes that showed the family at the breakfast table. One member of the family, usually the father, took the cereal box,

poured the cereal, and then added milk. This scene represented a complete "Kellogg" breakfast in a way that Brazilians could relate to. The advertisement focused first on nutrition, then on flavor, and finally on ease of preparation. As a result of this campaign, sales in Brazil increased. Kellogg controlled 99.5% of the ready-to-eat cereal market in Brazil; however, per capita cereal consumption was less than one ounce or several spoonfuls per Brazilian annually, even after advertising.

Although Kellogg controlled the market, there was not much of a market to control. Brazilians had begun to eat breakfast, but Horekens was not sure whether sales would continue to increase.

How can Kellogg further convince the Brazilians of the importance of eating a nutritious breakfast in order to establish a long-term market?

Case 24: Avon Products, S.A. de C.V.

In 1990, Philip Evans, marketing manager in the international division of Avon Products, Inc., met with his colleagues to consider long-range marketing strategy for Latin America, especially Mexico. A decidedly profitable market, Mexico and the rest of Latin America accounted for almost 15% of Avon's worldwide sales. The problem confronting Avon executives was how to sustain the growth rate it had generated in the past.

Company Background

Avon Products, Inc., a diversified company, included the Avon Division, Mallinckrodt, Inc., Tiffany & Co., and a direct-mail division.

The Avon division was the world's largest direct-selling business. Its two principal industry segments were the manufacture and sale of cosmetics, fragrances, and toiletries; and of fashion jewelry and accessories. Avon Products, Inc., sales in 1989 amounted to $4 billion, of which over 42% were from operations outside the United States. Operating profits from international business in 1989 amounted to about 53%. Net sales in 1989 from Latin American operations were $545.6 million. Of the total corporate-wide operating profits

of $600 million in 1989, $81.6 million were generated in Latin America.

Avon's international division was formed in 1949 when the company expanded the distribution and sales force to Canada. By late 1954, the company expanded its operations to include Puerto Rico and Venezuela. During the ensuing years, international operations grew at a rapid pace, first to Europe and Latin America and then to the far East and Africa.

In Mexico, the company had a wholly owned subsidiary under the name of Avon Products, S.A. de C.V., headquartered in Mexico City. The Mexican subsidiary had three manufacturing laboratories and five distribution branches covering Mexico and the rest of Latin America.

Avon had captured its largest international market share in Latin America, where competition had been less fierce than in other markets. In Mexico, the results had been truly phenomenal, largely because Latin hospitality blended well with the Avon approach. The Latins were much more apt to invite Avon representatives into their homes. Whereas U.S. representatives, on an average in each two-week campaign, won orders from fewer than 30 customers, Mexican representatives, in each three-week campaign, averaged 54 customers.

Products

The two principal businesses of Avon Products, S.A. de C.V., were the manufacture and sale of (1) cosmetics, fragrances, and toiletries, and (2) fashion jewelry and accessories. The products were sold directly to customers in their homes by Avon representatives, following the method used since Avon's founding in the United States in 1886. The company sold more than 650 products. Although the range of products sold in foreign countries was not as extensive as that sold in the United States, most of the products were substantially the same as those marketed domestically. The products marketed in Mexico were categorized as follows:

- *Fragrance and bath products for women.* These products consisted of perfumes, colognes, sachets, fragrance candles, pomanders, lotions, soaps, and powders. They were marketed in a number of fragrance lines, each based on a particular scent and packaging theme.

- *Makeup, skin-care, and other products for women.* These products included makeup items such as lipsticks, mascaras, and eye shadows; skin-care products; nail and hand-care items; and hair-care products such as shampoos, conditioners, and brushes.

- *Men's toiletry products.* Men's toiletries included colognes, after-shave lotions, shaving creams, talc, and soaps marketed in a number of fragrance lines, each based on a particular scent and packaging theme.

- *Daily need, children's, and teen products.* Daily need items included deodorants, antiperspirants, oral hygiene products, and household products such as room sprays. Children's and teen products included fragrance products and novelty products for young children.

- *Fashion jewelry and accessories.* The line included rings, earrings, bracelets, and necklaces for women, men, and children. Women's items accounted for most of the sales.

In Mexico, Avon cosmetics were affordable, medium-priced products that appealed to both women at home and the small number of women who worked outside the home.

Avon packaging consisted of glass and chrome bottles and ceramic jars tailored to meet the tastes of its primary market, the vast middle class.

Product Distribution

In Mexico and elsewhere in Latin America, Avon's cosmetics, fragrances, and toiletries were sold by a sizeable sales force. The sales force consisted of women known as *representatives de Avon* (Avon representatives). They served as independent dealers and not as agents or employees of the company. They purchased products directly from the company and sold them directly to the residents of their communities.

With some exceptions in rural areas, each representative was responsible for one territory. Unlike U.S. sales territories, in Mexico there were 200 homes in an average territory. But like in the United States, Mexican representatives called on homes in their territories, selling primarily through the use of brochures highlighting new products and specially priced items for each three-week sales campaign. Product samples, demonstration products, makeup color charts, and complete sales catalogs were also used. The representatives forwarded orders every three weeks to a distribution center located just outside Mexico City. Each representative's orders were processed and assembled by Avon and delivered to her home using local delivery services.

Over the long term, Avon S.A. had planned for a 10% growth in its sales force—a key determinant in keeping earnings growing at a healthy pace. The company's main method of building a sales force was to shrink the size of sales territories once an area was covered. This tactic served to intensify sales efforts.

Avon's long-term prospect for recruiting representatives looked particularly bright in Mexico, since neighborhoods were receptive to door-to-door selling. Both personal contacts and local advertising were used to recruit representatives.

As a local manager noted:

Avon's coverage in Mexico was excellent. We were in every small town and village, as well as in the big cities. Sixty-five percent of Mexico's population is under the age of 25. We are a very young people and a very young country. As the younger generation's buying power increases, we will have many opportunities to create new products that are attractive to them.

Product Promotion

Avon directed its sales promotion and sales development activities toward giving direct-selling assistance to its representatives. This was done by making available such aids as product samples and demonstration products, as well as the Avon brochure. Avon sought to motivate its representatives through the use of special prize programs that rewarded superior sales performance. Periodic sales meetings were conducted by the district manager to which representatives were invited. The meetings were designed to keep representatives alert to the product line changes, to explain sales techniques, and to give recognition to representatives' superior performance. Mexican representatives took particular pride in receiving recognition for sales achievements, and because of that, management favored an increase in promotional activities in developing future strategy.

An additional promotional tool was introduced in Mexico in 1988—a program called "Opportunity Unlimited." Under this program, top-performing representatives, who qualified as group sales leaders, had the opportunity to earn commissions by stimulating sales increases in their groups or representatives. Representatives could continue to earn commissions as group sales leaders as long as they stimulated sales increases. This program anticipated that group sales leaders would increase group sales by such methods as searching for new representatives, training new representatives, and motivating and assisting established representatives. Mexico was a testing ground for "Opportunity Unlimited." If the program proved successful there, the company planned to introduce it in other foreign markets.

Product Manufacture

Avon S.A. manufactured and packaged almost all of its cosmetics, fragrances, and toiletries products. Although most of the Mexican products were based on U.S. products, Avon S.A. developed several of its own fragrances based on Mexican tastes. Packages, consisting of containers and packaging components, were designed by U.S.-based Avon and manufactured in Mexico.

The fashion jewelry line was generally developed by Avon's U.S. staff and manufactured in Puerto Rico and Ireland or by several independent manufacturers in the United States and shipped to the Mexican distribution center.

Mexican Cosmetics Market

The cosmetics market in Mexico was segmented by product and by final user. Men, women, and children used different products. Similarly, Mexicans of Indian heritage required different products than did those of Spanish descent. However, in both the groups, most products were purchased by women. So the focus of the industry was on women between the ages of 18 and 65. On an average, women spent $35 per capita annually on cosmetics for themselves and their families.

As Mexican society became more liberal, it was anticipated that teenagers (16–18) would become frequent users of a limited number of cosmetics. Avon had produced a line of cosmetics for U.S. teenagers called "Color World," which was promoted as "not your mother's makeup." Test marketing was being done with this age group in Mexico to survey acceptance of the line.

Mexican men, especially in the cities, tended to purchase more colognes and after-shave lotions than their U.S. counterparts. They preferred products with a musky, masculine scent. Avon believed that this segment would continue to grow annually throughout the 1990s.

Competition

Avon faced competition from two sources: Max Factor, a U.S. firm with a subsidiary located in Mexico City, and Bella, a Mexican firm also based in Mexico City. Unlike Avon, these companies concentrated their retail distribution through supermarkets, department stores, and pharmacies. Of the two competitors, Bella concerned Avon the most.

Bella manufactured and marketed a full line of products in the medium-level price range. Its highly segmented and differentiated products were aimed at women with either light or dark complexions. Bella sales concentrated in the larger cities, such as Mexico City, Mazatlán, Veracruz, and Oaxaca. The large-city market was estimated to be about $424 million in 1989 and was expected to grow 12% annually in coming years.

Promotion was aimed at "La Bella Mujer Mexican"—the beautiful Mexican woman. Focused on ethnic pride, Bella maintained that their line of cosmetics was custom-made for the different complexions of Mexican women. As an attack on Avon's direct selling, Bella incorporated the use of catalog sales. A large number of households were mailed a seasonal catalog displaying the full line of products. Consumers placed their orders with a central distribution center, but the orders were delivered in person by a sales representative, who could then solicit additional orders. In the long run, Avon S.A. saw this as a threat to their door-to-door method.

Issues Confronting Management

Despite its healthy incursion into Mexico, the prospects for long-term growth for Avon, S.A. de C.V., appeared hazy, largely because the company faced a major turning point in the years ahead. Its expansion was derived primarily from its ability to move into, and then saturate, vacant territories in its sales network. As mentioned previously, once a territory was covered, Avon simply divided it into smaller areas and added new representatives to canvass customers on a more concentrated basis.

Such so-called downsizing had been occurring since the late 1950s when Mexican representatives were supposed to cover some 400 to 500 households. Naturally, very few managed to do this, so when the company started reducing the territories to 250 to 300, there was little impact on representatives' earnings potential. The impact on the company's earnings, however, was tremendous. This strategy allowed Avon S.A. to more than triple its sales force over a 15-year period.

By 1992, Avon S.A. expected to have completed a planned conversion to 100-home territories in Mexico, from a then-current level of 150-home territories. Once this was accomplished, Avon S.A. was unsure about going lower. It became apparent that if Avon S.A. wanted to grow with the population and keep ahead of the rate of inflation, it must find other ways to build sales.

One alternative was to add new lines of products, particularly those that could be tailor-made to the Mexican market. But U.S.-based Avon executives were afraid that these new products would hurt existing products. Evans and his colleagues realized that planning was needed if Avon S.A. was to sustain growth and maintain profits in the future.

Case 25: Connecticut Corporation (Japan)

In late 1988, John Lindstrom, director of marketing for the International Beverage Division of Connecticut Corporation (CC), was faced with deciding what action should be taken to increase the market share for Bleinheau Vodka in Japan. Three strategies were open to him:

1. Increase promotional efforts on behalf of Bleinheau in Japan, and streamline distribution.
2. License Suntory, Japan's largest liquor producer, to manufacture, label, and sell Bleinheau in Japan.
3. Remove Bleinheau from the Japanese market.

Connecticut Corporation entered the market in Japan in 1981 by licensing out Black Velvet Whiskey to the Suntory Company. In this arrangement, CC gave Suntory the rights to produce, label, and sell Black Velvet in return for 10% of the profits. In 1985, however, CC opened up branch headquarters in Tokyo to export Bleinheau and other CC beverage products, such as Black and White Scotch, Wild Turkey, Club Cocktails, Grand Marnier cognac, and United Vintners wines from the United States and distribute them in Japan.

Because vodka was not yet popular in the Japanese spirit market, Bleinheau had not yet been able to gain the distribution and market share it wanted. Mr. Lindstrom believed that with the increasing popularity of Western-style drinks, vodka would soon gain the acceptance of the Japanese public.

Corporate Background

Connecticut Corporation is a multinational corporation, headquartered in Springfield, Massachusetts. In 1987, the firm's worldwide sales of $1,921,879,000 were divided among three categories. The following table shows the approximate percentage of sales attributed to each.

Category of Business	Percentage of Sales
Beverage operations	57%
Food operations	24
International operations	19
Total	100%

Connecticut International was responsible for the overseas manufacture and export, as well as the marketing, of all products sold by CC outside the United States. Those products included the ones that were part of the Food Group, both owned and franchised operations of Southern Fried Chicken, A-1 Steak Sauce, and Ortega Taco Sauce and Taco Shells, and the ones that were part of the Beverage Operations, such as Bleinheau Vodka, Yukon Jack Whiskey, Black Velvet Whiskey, Irish Mist Liqueur, Arrow Brand Liquors, Lancer Wines, Inglenook Wines, and Club Cocktails.

Connecticut International's beverage operations were divided into two parts: Connecticut de Brazil, which included only the manufacturing, exporting/importing, and marketing in Brazil, and the Connecticut International Beverage Group, which housed, among others, Connecticut in Japan.

Marketing Environment

A study done by Steven Young, marketing research manager for Connecticut in Japan, showed the following facts about the environment the company faced in Japan:

- The overall spirits market environment in Japan is attractive. Although GNP will grow at a slower rate than it has in the past 30 years, it will outstrip the United States and other major industrialized nations. This should mean substantial discretionary income. This coupled with increased urbanization should contribute to the growth of quality spirits. Besides, the post–World War II population has been drinking more in the Western fashion, suggesting that vodka should gain in popularity.

- Because economic activity is contracting, unemployment is at the highest levels since 1946.

- Competition is strengthening. This is especially true of the domestic competition such as Suntory.

- The percentage of the population on the high and upper-middle income segments has increased.

- The consumer economy is relatively healthy as both disposable income and personal consumption expenditures are attractive to other countries. Also, recent trends in household expenditures favor increased consumption of services and nondurable goods at the expense of durable goods.

- Per capita alcoholic beverage consumption continues to increase rapidly along with disposable income, yet is still far from saturation in comparison with other developed/underdeveloped countries.

- Media costs are the highest in the world and increasing.

- Domestic competitors such as Suntory tend to ignore profitability to achieve market share. This attitude fosters dumping. An example is the market for Scotch, which had a reputation as an expensive, high-quality item. Suntory began dumping, and now Scotch is no longer part of the high-quality market for gift giving and other such occasions for which Scotch traditionally has been used.

In summary, because of the size of its population, its stability, and its track record, Japan represented an attractive, although challenging, market with long-term economic prospects. In keeping with Japan's growth-oriented economy and tradition of following America, it would be reasonable to expect that the alcoholic beverage market, particularly the quality spirits market, would experience continued real growth in the foreseeable future, perhaps at a somewhat slower pace.

Advertising and Promotion

Whereas U.S. laws prohibited the advertising of hard liquor on television, it was not so in Japan. Therefore, a large part of Connecticut's advertising for Bleinheau in Japan was done through television and cinema media. Other forms of advertising media used by Connecticut Japan included posters and billboards, which showed different drinks that could be made with Connecticut products (including Bleinheau) and explained how to make them. In addition, the company provided various freestanding point-of-purchase displays for use in distribution centers where liquor was sold.

The copy used in all advertising centered around the idea of Bleinheau having "world popularity," especially of being "big in the United States," because anything considered popular in the United States has great appeal to the Japanese, especially the younger generation.

In addition to advertising, there were several types of promotion for Bleinheau.

1. Merchandise giveaways were directed at the dealers who supplied the bars and other types of wholesalers.

2. Bleinheau was directed to the general public through "Bleinheau Nights" in local night clubs and bars. On these nights, Bleinheau offered discounts on all drinks made with Bleinheau vodka. The company also had giveaways such as T-shirts and glasses with "Bleinheau" printed on them.

3. Tie-ins with other products were used. A tie-in was done with Canada Dry. In areas where Canada Dry had a strong market share, consumers would buy a six-pack of Canada Dry and get a bottle of Bleinheau at a very low price. In markets where Bleinheau held a strong position, the purchase of a bottle of Bleinheau entitled the consumer to a free bottle of Canada Dry.

Distribution

The distribution system in Japan was much different from that in the United States. To distribute their products in Japan, Connecticut had to work through a complicated multitiered distribution system. This system had been in a gradual state of change for years because overlapping and the sheer size of the distribution system had resulted in a profit squeeze, with some middle levels being forced to accept lower margins and even being bypassed in some cases. This trend was expected to continue in the 1990s.

Connecticut at that time had approximately 20% distribution in Japan. This had been achieved through five major wholesalers and 17 secondary wholesalers. The problem lay in the fact that, while wholesalers were ultimately credited for every sale, they aggressively sold only their proprietary brands.

Competition

Connecticut's competition came not only from other rivals in the vodka market, but from all spirits marketers. For example, Scotch whiskey was very popular in Japan, holding over 75% of the spirits market through 1987. Vodka, on the other hand, had not yet become a popular drink in Japan.

In both the spirits market as a whole and the vodka market by itself, Connecticut's major competition came from the Suntory Company. In the vodka market, Nikka was Connecticut's second-biggest competitor.

Suntory Company Suntory was the largest producer and seller of domestic spirits in Japan, as well as a major importer of whiskey into Japan. Suntory held the number one position in national whiskeys and had entries in all the spirits categories. Further, Suntory held the number-one position in vodka with a 57% market share (mostly through licensing from companies outside Japan). Suntory's strategy, however, was not aimed at this market, but instead at putting all its resources into maintaining its market share in whiskey.

Nikka Nikka provided the only other strong competition in the vodka market in Japan, with an 18% market share. Assuming the anticipated activity in white spirits materialized, Nikka was expected to be second in market share in the domestic field, behind Suntory.

Other Brands Of the remaining 25% of the market, Connecticut's Bleinheau held 18% and the other 17% belonged to several domestic and imported brands.

The Japanese Consumer

Alcoholic beverage consumption was well accepted in Japan, but usage, penetration, and frequency (especially in regard to wine) were still low. For example, the Japanese rarely drank during the day. Central to this was the increased consumption of Western spirits occasioned by Westernization after World War II. Just as with products, traditions, and fashion, what was popular in the United States often was very attractive to the Japanese. Examples included blue jeans, golf, and tennis. The popularity of Westernized bars and nightclubs also was increasing. The incidence of alcoholic beverage consumption ("drank last week") was increasing among women but stable among men, as the following table shows.

	Drinking Population				
	1979	1981	1983	1985	1987
Male	26.8%	25.2%	26.5%	26.2%	25.8%
Female	8.0	9.0	10.5	11.5	11.8
Total	34.8	34.2	37.0	37.7	37.6

Except for a few imported brands, the Japanese had little brand familiarity and/or loyalty with respect to alcoholic beverages. The Japanese consumer, however, was responsive to advertising and its creation of "in-ness," as shown with the growth of gin in 1981–1982, when it was heavily advertised, and its subsequent deterioration when advertising support was pulled. The trendsetters in Japan were a small group of the post–World War II generation who were the most-traveled, best-educated, and affluent. The following table summarizes trends in liquor consumption in Japan.

Trends in Served Market in Japan (in Thousands of Cases)			
	1980	1987	1994†
Scotch whiskey	199	2,719	4,792
Vodka	25	43	320
Cognac	56	237	651
Others*	198	377	1,251
Total served market	478	3,376	7,014

* Including gin, rum, tequila, bourbon, and Canadian whiskey.
† Projected.

Case 26: FedEx and UPS in China—Competing with Contrasting Strategies

Just how "American" should you be when doing business many cultures away from home?

Rarely have two rivals offering similar services answered that question so differently as have Federal Express Corp. and United Parcel Service of America, Inc.

FedEx was trying to paint China red, white, and blue, following the same frontal-assault strategy it employed in the United States in the 1970s and in Europe in the 1980s. While promoting itself with jarring, Western-style advertising, FedEx was pouring out money to acquire its own air routes, fly its own aircraft into and out of China and, in partnership with an aggressive local company, built a huge network of purple and orange trucks and distribution centers.

"We're the largest all-cargo carrier in the world and as a result we've got a pretty good formula for attacking any market," noted T. Michael Glenn, executive vice president for marketing at FedEx's parent, FDX Corp. "Whether it's China or Japan or Germany, it really doesn't make any difference."

UPS, by contrast, hopes that Chinese customers won't even notice that it was made in America. Its advertising was understated and old-fashioned even by Chinese standards. Its freight lands in China packed into leased space in the underbellies of planes operated by a Hong Kong airline, Dragonair, or other regional carriers. To deliver packages on the ground, UPS followed the traditional approach for foreign freight companies in China, piggybacking on the operations of Sinotrans, a vast, labyrinthine, government-owned transportation company.

"We're a quiet company," remarked Charles Adams, UPS's top executive in Asia. "Sometimes we're the student, and sometimes we're the teacher."

How the giants of the U.S. delivery business were forging ahead in China was more than a case study on differing corporate styles. Their strategies, which tracked what they did all across Asia, vividly illustrated two radically different approaches to questions faced by almost any U.S. company striving to expand overseas: Do we partner with entrenched competitors or tackle them head-on? Do we risk the capital to build our own manufacturing and distribution systems or lease someone else's? Who are our customers, the locals or our multinational accounts? How much do we risk to build future market share?

Is There a Winning Strategy?

The jury was still out for both FedEx and UPS. Neither was discussing market share or disclosing specific financial results in China. But each said its operations were growing and profitable, and each contended that its approach was better.

In the spring of 1998, UPS executives, buffered by their lower spending from much of the turmoil in Asia, had been quietly congratulating themselves on the apparent wisdom of their low-risk approach. As freight traffic slowed in the region, UPS had simply reduced the space it leased on other companies' planes.

"Because of the investment (FedEx) made, they're almost stuck in that market," remarked Joseph M. Pyne, UPS's vice president for marketing. "That's the plan they have to live with. We're looking at the market and moving with it in China."

Meanwhile, at FedEx, currency devaluations elsewhere in Asia had cut profits by more than $20 million during the first six months of 1998. On March 25, 1998, the company posted its first quarterly loss on international operations since 1996, largely because of the high costs attributable to its extensive air network in Asia, coupled with declining cargo volume and revenue in the region. Nevertheless, FedEx noted China remained "a bright spot." Air-freight volumes from troubled Asian nations to China declined, but China's exports were still strong, remarked Michael L. Drucker, FedEx's top executive in Asia.

FedEx added that, despite the expense, its "build it and they will come" strategy was paying off in the market share. Estimates vary, but according to Air Cargo Management Group, a Seattle consultancy, FedEx had captured 13% of the express market in China, excluding Hong Kong, while UPS trailed with less than 5%. "We knew it was risky when we built so much capacity, but we're staying. And that has just got to have a long-term payoff," noted the FedEx's chief financial officer.

The payoff was critical for both companies. Although both were still small players in China, each with less than half the express-freight market share of at least 30% held by DHL International Ltd., a long-established Brussels-based company, both viewed China as the industry's most important emerging market. China's demand for time-definite express freight—the high-profit sector they crave—was projected to grow as much as 20% a year through 2002, far faster than the worldwide air-freight market. Currently, China's air-cargo market was the world's fifth largest, and its embryonic express sector was valued at $400 million a year.

"It's hard to be unmindful of a 1.2 billion-person country that arguably has the most entrepreneurial, merchant-oriented people in the world," said Frederick W. Smith, FedEx's founder, chairman and chief executive officer.

FedEx's Culture

FedEx's approach to that market reflected its personality at home. The company, and Mr. Smith, liked sizzle. With $12 billion in annual revenue, FedEx prided itself on having blitzkrieged the U.S. freight business by inventing overnight delivery in the 1970s. It called itself a "global evangelist" for high-tech, just-in-time deliveries. Its U.S. ad campaigns had long poked fun at competitors and warned business executives of certain humiliation if they used any other delivery company.

FedEx pursued that strategy in China, even at the risk of seeming cheeky. Last year, it ran a ubiquitous print ad in Asia showing the tail of a FedEx plane parked in front of the Forbidden City—a cherished array of imperial buildings that was off limits to the public for 500 years. "Call FedEx," the ad said. "It's almost forbidden not to."

"I don't know that I agree that there's a sort of Chinese way and an American way," Mr. Smith noted. "I think there is an establishment way . . . and China at the moment is a country that is very entrepreneurial in nature. We are more consonant with the new China."

Nonetheless, the FedEx style seemed to annoy some companies that expected a certain tone in the formal face-to-face sales pitches traditional in China. "I know they're one of the biggest companies in the U.S.A., but that doesn't matter here," said Li Ping, an executive at Chinatex Cotton Yarns & Fabrics Import & Export Corp. in Beijing. "The personal relationship matters most here. You have to talk to customers and make them feel good. . . . They haven't sent anyone here; so we don't do business with them."

FedEx was not worried. Instead of chasing the established Chinese business clique, it was focusing first on multinational corporations with Chinese operations that already used FedEx elsewhere. It also was targeting expanding Chinese entrepreneurs whom FedEx believed would readily adopt its mantra about cutting-edge manufacturing and delivery techniques.

For those customers who valued a highly controlled distribution system and constant information about the status of shipments, FedEx's philosophy was appealing. Wang Fazhang, a manager at Siemens Technology Development Corp. of Beijing, a unit of Siemens AG of Germany, noted using FedEx cut the delivery time for medical-equipment spare parts from Europe to three days from 28.

To achieve such results, FedEx was trying to leapfrog rivals in China and all across Asia by spending millions to build a network much like the one it operated in the United States. That investment started in 1988 with its $880 million acquisition of Flying Tiger Line Inc.; FedEx mostly wanted the cargo carrier's Asian routes, including a coveted but long-unused link between Japan and China. In 1995, FedEx paid Evergreen International Aviation Inc. $67.5 million, according to Evergreens' regulatory filings, to buy the only operating authority currently permitting a U.S. cargo carrier to fly directly into China.

Much Cheaper Cargo

Using that authority, FedEx flew an MD-11, laden with up to 170,000 pounds of freight into Beijing and Shanghai four times a week. For now, FedEx filled much of the plane with cheap air cargo, for which it charged as little as $2 a pound and made at best, a slim profit. As more manufacturing operations in China adopted just-in-time manufacturing systems, however, FedEx believed that the bulk freight would shift to high profitable small-package services, for which the company charged up to $30 a pound. FedEx promised delivery of packages from the United States to China in three days, but often they arrived in just two days. Deliveries from China to the United States frequently arrived overnight.

In more than a dozen major cities in China, FedEx's operations, trucks, and employees looked identical to those in the United States. In scores of other cities, FedEx packages were delivered in aqua-blue trucks and painted with the logos of both FedEx and its Chinese affiliate.

UPS Style

The 91-year-old UPS, with its giant, mostly ground-based U.S. delivery network and annual revenue of about $22.46 billion, was hewing to its long history of keeping a low profile. Until recent years, the company, owned mostly by its managers and retirees, eschewed any marketing at all, even at home. Its boldest advertising moves had been sponsorship of the Olympic games in 1996 and 1998.

So in China, UPS was doing as the Chinese do. Its marketing sought to build relationships discreetly, on Chinese terms—even though it, too, felt multinationals were the core of its initial customer base here.

Monica Yan, an ad executive at China Guoxin Information Corp., switched to UPS from the state-run express-mail service after a UPS account executive came calling at her dank basement office in Beijing. "She came here and explained to me how UPS could be more convenient and not cost so much money, so I decided to use her company," Ms. Yan noted.

In promoting itself, UPS emphasized its global network and stability, virtues that ring true for many Chinese. It also nurtured a Chinese customer base outside China, sponsoring Chinese New Year celebrations in Toronto and Vancouver, where many recent immigrants lived. A six-week UPS television campaign in China showed a motorized three-wheeler moving down a runway, followed by a larger van, a truck and then a 747. "Their ads show lots of planes and trucks, with a very big worldwide network," said Chen Bin, a manager of a state-owned logistics company in Beijing. "The image is not American" but "more worldwide."

Investing just a fraction of what FedEx had put into Asia, UPS had gradually expanded along with demand, trading some market share for more-limited risk. Meanwhile, it felt it could catch up whenever the market was ripe.

So Big Brown operated without a single aircraft in China. It offered "total brown" service—packages were picked up by workers in brown UPS uniforms, driving brown trucks—in Beijing, Shanghai, and only one other Chinese city, Guangzhou.

Lacking its own air service, UPS could not offer customers in China the range of logistical services that FedEx could. But UPS, while avoiding the cheap air cargo that FedEx depended upon to fill out its aircraft, could still skim from the cream of the business, the lucrative document and small-package sector. The upshot: UPS could deliver a one-pound package or document from the United States to major Chinese cities in the same time FedEx promised, three days, at a price of about $47. For now, UPS executives felt that was plenty.

"If the situation changes in five to 10 years, then maybe we'll want our own planes" in China, UPS's Mr. Adams noted. "But that's not a priority now."

Case 27:   PSA Peugeot Citroën*

The PSA Group included two general car manufacturing companies: Automobiles Peugeot and Automobiles Citroën. The two were linked by strong technological, industrial, and financial synergies, although each marque kept its identity, and its own marketing and sales. In 1994 the PSA group was the third-largest car manufacturer in Europe, with 12.8% market share.

The year 1994 showed improved performance of PSA, after difficulties in 1993: Profitability rose from a Ffr1 billion loss to profits of Ffr3.1 billion, and the sales turnover increased from Ffr145.4 billion to Ffr166.2 billion (95% of which was in car manufacturing). PSA employed 139,800 people and manufactured 1,989,000 vehicles, of which two-thirds were sold outside France in 150 countries and 22,000 sales locations. With export sales of Ffr74.9 billion, the group was the main French exporter.

The PSA Group

In 1976 Peugeot, a family-owned company, took over Citroën. Then in 1978 it took over the European subsidiaries of Chrysler. At the beginning of the 1990s, the group (Peugeot and Citroën) was controlled by the Peugeot family, who owned 22.7% of the equity, the largest other shareholder being Michelin. The rest of the equity was held by financial institutions and individual stockholders.

From 1980 to 1984 the PSA Group went through financial difficulties, its net debts rising to Ffr33.1 billion and its equity dropping to Ffr5.3 billion in 1984. In 1983, the group lost Ffr2.6 billion. The renaissance of PSA came with the hiring of a new top manager, Jacques Calvet, and with the growth in the European market (+4 per cent per year on average) between 1985 and 1989. Jacques Calvet became président directeur général of Peugeot, then président directeur général of Citroën in 1983 and président du directoire of the holding company in 1984. Formerly he had been directeur du trésor at the French Ministry of Finance and president of the Banque Nationale de Paris. Experts believed that his skills and the rigor of his management

were at the center of the recovery of the PSA Group. Losses were cut as early as 1984, and debts were reduced starting from 1987. At the end of 1989, the company announced net profits of Ffr10.3 billion (a net margin of 6.7% of turnover); the sales turnover was about Ffr153 billion and debts had been reduced to Ffr1.9 billion.

Substantial progress in production methods was also achieved: productivity improvement was about 72% between 1982 and 1987 (the best European performance according to the consulting company Luvigsen Associates), and 60% during the period 1985 to 1989. High investments were made to rationalize manufacturing and to develop the company's range of products.

In 1986, Jacques Calvet announced an ambitious goal for PSA: to become the leading car manufacturer in the European market in terms of number of vehicles sold. However, the aim of dominant market share was postponed with the recession of the Western European market and the unexpected opening of the Eastern European market, which was more favorable to competitors based in Germany (Volkswagen and GM-Opel). Indeed, from 1990 to 1993, with the economic recession, the European car market decreased and sales and profits of the PSA Group slowly declined before the 1994 revival.

Exhibit 1 gives the main financial indicators of PSA between 1990 and 1994, and Exhibit 2 gives information on the two main companies of the group, Automobiles Peugeot and Automobiles Citroën.

---

* This case was prepared by Roland Calori, Philippe Very, and Michel Berthelier, professors at the Group ESC Lyon. The authors would like to thank the PSA Group for its support in writing the case study. It is intended as a basis for class discussion and not as illustration of either good or bad management practice. © R. Calori, P. Very, and M. Berthelier, 1996. It is reproduced here with the permission of the authors.

EXHIBIT I
PSA Group: Main Consolidated Financial Data

	1994	1993	1992	1991	1990
Net sales	166.2	145.4	155.4	160.2	160
Cash flow	15.2	8.3	13.7	15.4	16.2
Investments (tangible assets)	10.5	11.3	13.8	15.5	15.2
Net profit	3.1	(−1.4)	3.4	5.5	9.3
Shareholder's equity	53.5	50.5	53.1	51.7	47.2
Net financial debts	7.6	16.7	14.3	9.4	8.3
Earnings per share (Ffr)	62	(−28)	67	111	185

Note: Figures in million of French francs unless stated.
Source: Adapted from annual report, 1994.

![EXHIBIT 2] **EXHIBIT 2**   The Two Main Companies of the PSA Group:
Automobiles Peugeot and Automobile Citroën

Automobiles Peugeot			Automobiles Citroën		
Group's holding: 100% (fully by Peugeot SA) Plants in: Sochaux-Montebélard, Mulhouse, Poissy, Ryton (UK), and Villaverde (Spain). Plants in: Dijon, Lille, Saint-Étienne, Sept-Fons, Vesoul, Valenciennes, and Villers la Montagne.			Group's holding: 100% (fully by Peugeot SA) Production sites in: Aulnay, Rennes, Vigo (Spain), and Mangualde (Portugal). Plants in: Asnières, Caen, and Charleville		
	1994	**1993**		**1994**	**1993**
Economic Data			*Economic Data*		
Production (in number of vehicles)	1,202,200	1,058,100	Production (in number of vehicles)	787,800	693,500
Sales (in number of vehicles)	1,209,200	1,061,900	Sales (in number of vehicles)	779,600	702,000
Employees			*Employees*		
Company	41,900	43,800	Company	28,900	29,900
Group	69,200	73,000	Group	45,700	46,800
Consolidated financial data (Ffr m)			*Consolidated financial data (Ffr m)*		
Net sales	101,778	89,968	Net sales	70,653	64,592
Working capital provided from operations	7,545	3,102	Working capital provided from operations	4,416	1,540
Net income	1,394	(958)	Net income	184	(2,341)
Stockholder's equity	30,644	29,318	Stockholder's equity	4,757	4,637
Capital expenditures	6,047	5,758	Capital expenditures	3,240	3,456
Dividend	280		Dividend		

Source: Annual report, 1994.

Markets

Western European market shares fluctuated depending on two main factors: significant changes in relative prices and the success of new models. The top management of the PSA Group was preoccupied with the price war that had been taking place since 1990. They were also concerned with monetary fluctuations within Europe, particularly with the competitive devaluations of sterling, the peseta and the Italian firs (about 38% since 1992), which had upset sales at the beginning of the 1990s. PSA and several other car manufacturers were looking forward to the possibility of a single European currency. As Jacques Calvet remarked in the annual stockholders' meeting in June 1995:

> For Europe, which is now truly a single market, the worst wounds have come from within, with the break-down of the European Monetary System and competitive devaluations, notably of the Italian lira. Europe will not hold up long if there is not a rapid solution to this problem.

Moreover, new competitors were emerging. The market share of Korean car manufacturers in Europe (about 3% in 1994) was growing, particularly in the low-priced segment.

The Eastern European markets had stagnated at around 1 million vehicles a year and experts forecast a maximum of 1.5 million vehicles by the year 2000. The Russian market was estimated at around 2 million vehicles and moderate growth was expected.

The North American market grew in 1992 (5%) and in 1993 (7.3%), and it represented 16.5 million vehicles in 1994. Light trucks (minivans, pick-ups, four-wheel-drives) represented 40% of sales, with a high growth. General Motors, Ford, and Chrysler had a 73% market share, compared to the Japanese 23%, and the European car manufacturers, 2.7%. PSA had left the U.S. market in 1985, since it could not establish a significant position in this highly competitive environment (on average the price of cars in the United States was 30% lower than in Europe).

The Japanese market showed signs of revival in 1994 (an increase of 1%) after three years of decline. It represented 6.6 million vehicles. In this market, dominated by Toyota (with a 41% market share), imports from foreign OECD countries were marginal. German manufacturers together exported 121,000 vehicles in 1994, Americans exported 37,000 vehicles, and the French sold 6,800 units.

The African and Middle East markets remained marginal (stable at around a total of 1 million vehicles a year). Two other zones experienced high growth: South America (2.8 million vehicles a year, with a 6% annual growth) and Asia (apart from Japan), which represented annual sales of 4.8 million vehicles (with a 9% annual growth).

Exhibit 3 shows the breakdown of the sales of the PSA Group in the world, and Exhibit 4 gives the breakdown of market share for the group in Europe.

At the annual stockholders' meeting in June 1995, Jacques Calvet commented on the 1994 performance of PSA as follows:

> The market share of Peugeot and Citroën in Western Europe, 12.8 percent, as compared to 12.1 percent in 1992 and 12.4 percent in 1993, has grown significantly. This commercial dynamism results both from the deployment of our ranges of vehicles . . . and from the favorable evolution of European markets: those where Peugeot and Citroën have a high share have evolved more favorably than the European average.

The Strategy of PSA

Jacques Calvet chose to be chairman of Automobiles Peugeot and chairman of Automobiles Citroën in order to stimulate synergies between the two companies, which had kept their own culture for several years after the merger. Peugeot and Citroën were both involved in the main segments of the market and adopted parallel market positioning (see Exhibit 5). Automobiles Peugeot had a 7.7% market share in Western Europe (18.7% in France) and Automobiles Citroën had a

EXHIBIT 3 Worldwide Sales of the PSA Group (Passenger Cars and Light Commercial Vehicles, 000s)

	1994	1993	1992
Western Europe			
France			
Peugeot	430	328	437
Citroën	304	250	270
F5A Peugeot Citroën	734	577	707
Other Western European countries			
Peugeot	585	544	617
Citroën	416	399	459
PSA Peugeot Citroën	1,000	942	1,076
Outside Western Europe			
Eastern Europe			
Peugeot	14	20	15
Citroën	8	10	6
PSA Peugeot Citroën	22	30	21
Africa			
Peugeot	24	22	31
Citroën	9	7	8
PSA Peugeot Citroën	34	29	39
America			
Peugeot	99	71	59
Citroën	11	8	8
PSA Peugeot Citroën	110	79	67
Asia-Pacific area			
Peugeot	40	59	57
Citroën	21	19	15
PSA Peugeot Citroën	61	79	72
Special registrations			
Peugeot	19	18	19
Citroën	10	9	13
PSA Peugeot Citroën	19	28	33
Total Worldwide			
Peugeot	1,209	1,062	1,235
(including small collections)	(40)	(42)	(27)
Citroën	780	702	779
PSA Peugeot Citroën	1,989	1,764	2,014

Source: Annual report 1994.

6.1% market share in Western Europe (12.4% in France).

Some other competitors also had more than one marque. The Volkswagen Group had several, with Scat

EXHIBIT 4 European Sales of the PSA Group: Share of Passenger Car Registrations (%)

	1994	1993	1992
France	31.1	29.7	30.4
Austria	7.8	7.5	7.0
Belgium-Luxembourg	43.7	13.6	14.2
Denmark	14.8	14.8	12.3
Finland	8.4	6.9	5.7
Germany	4.5	5.1	4.5
Greece	11.3	11.5	11.2
Ireland	7.0	6.9	6.7
Italy	7.0	6.7	7.1
Netherlands	12.1	13.1	11.0
Norway	8.9	8.0	7.5
Portugal	13.3	14.0	16.2
Spain	19.9	20.3	20.7
Sweden	4.6	4.3	33.2
Switzerland	7.9	7.9	6.6
United Kingdom	12.1	12.6	11.8
Total Europe	12.8	12.4	12.1
Europe outside France	9.2	9.8	8.8

Note: Does not include light commercial vehicle registrations.
Source: Annual report, 1994.

and Skoda at the low end of the market, Volkswagen as a generalist, and Audi at the top end of the market. The Fiat Group had Ferrari at the very top of the market,

Alfa Romeo, Fiat, itself and Lancia. Other car manufacturers such as Renault had only one marque.

At PSA, the standardization of vehicles was relatively high between the two product lines, about 50% of the components being common. These were the nonvisible components—engines, gearboxes, and so on—while the elements of the car that could be seen were different. Joint purchasing of components through Sogedac, a group company (with an annual sales turnover of Ffr80 billion), was seen as a source of competitive benefit by the company.

Part of the R&D expenses were also shared: Thanks to the two parallel model ranges, synergies in R&D had increased, particularly in the early phases of new product development. For instance, the Citroën XM and the Peugeot 605 were developed by a single technical platform (multifunctional project team). Innovations concerning new materials and new methods were shared. Industrial teams also worked together on international operations.

Differences and separation between the two marques were apparent in product design and style, the development of production processes, and marketing and sales, with two distinct dealer networks competing with each other. There was no intention to merge the two distribution networks, since executives believed the weaker marque could be disadvantaged (a problem which occurred when Peugeot took over Chrysler-Simca in 1979). Besides, the view was that merging the two independent distribution networks could give an

EXHIBIT 5
Group Production of Peugeot and Citroën Models (Number of Vehicles)

Sector	Peugeot Model	Peugeot 1994	Citroën Model	Citroën 1994
Mini	106	340,800	AX	198,700
Super mini	205	146,600		
Lower medium	306	380,850	ZX	251.600
	309	300		
Upper medium	405	214,300	Xantia	214,700
	504 Paykan	45,550	BX	100
	505	9,600		
Executive	605	19,050	XM	20,600
"Monospace"	806	10,900	Evasion	7,200
Utitlity and miscellaneous	J5, J9, Boxer	34,050	C15, C25 C35, Jumper	94,900
Total		1,202,000	Total	787,800

Source: Annual report, 1994.

opportunity for foreign competitors to take over dealer networks.

Such a strategy required a significant effort to renew the range of models of the two companies. In order to renew eight basic models (four Peugeot and four Citroën) every six years, PSA would have to launch one or two new models every year. On average the investment to launch a new model was estimated at around Ffr10 billion.

The PSA Group was the world leader in diesel cars with 957,400 vehicles in 1994, and had a significant competitive advantage in this domain. It sold diesel engines to Rover and Ford. In general, French car manufacturers PSA and Renault had a particularly strong position in diesel cars, with a 38% market share in Western Europe. The top management of PSA argued that diesel engines consumed less and cheaper fuel, produced less pollution, and were more reliable and long lasting than petrol engines. The proportion of diesel cars was very low in Japan and in the United States, but it was significant and growing in Europe, particularly where the taxation of fuel was not unfavorable (see Exhibit 6).

Renewal

Since the beginning of the 1990s, a particular effort was made to launch new models and renew existing models. In 1994 PSA launched the 806 Monospace (Peugeot) and its brother, the Evasion (Citroën). At Peugeot the 605 was restyled and re-engined, and new versions of the 306 (a cabriolet and a tricorps), and new utility vehicles (Boxer and 205 van) were launched. At Citroen the XM was restyled and re-engined, new versions of the ZX (Break) and the Xantia (Active) were produced, and a new utility vehicle (Jumper) was launched. Advertising and promotional budgets were increased so as to rejuvenate the image: warm and relaxed for Citroen, humorous and lively for Peugeot. Peugeot reinvested in the Formula 1 Grand Prix and won eight podiums in 1994 with the McLaren team; they also won super tourism competitions with the 405. Citroen won the world rally championship for the second time with its ZX.

The cooperation between Peugeot and Citroen was crucial in order to share the efforts in renewing products. For years PSA also cooperated with Renault in the development and manufacture of components as well as in research on environmentally friendly cars. At the beginning of the 1990s, the cooperation with Fiat was

EXHIBIT 6 Percentages of Diesel Cars in the Main EEC Countries

	1990	1994
France	33.0	47.6
Germany	9.8	16.6
Italy	7.3	8.7
United Kingdom	6.4	21.7
Netherlands	10.9	12.0
Belgium-Luxembourg	31.8	41.4
Spain	14.7	28.2
European-Union (12 countries)	14.2	23.1

Source: PSA.

strengthened in order to share the development and manufacturing of a monospace. In 1994 the Sevelnord plant at Valenciennea (France) started to manufacture the monospace for the four companies: Peugeot 806, Citroën Evasion, Fiat Ulysse, and Lancia Zeta. Sevelnord, a 60/60 joint venture between PSA and Fiat, required a Ffr6 billion investment and was to produce 130,000 vehicles a year. The same type of cooperation was set up in Italy in order to share the manufacturing of small utility vehicles: Peugeot Boxer, Citroën Jumper, and Fiat Ducat. Sevelsud was to manufacture 190,000 vehicles a year. The top management of PSA viewed such focused alliances at the best way to compete in new market niches.

From 1988 to 1990 PSA spent 3.5% of its turnover on research and development. In 1994 the budget for R&D was Ffr7.2 billion, representing 3.8% of the consolidated turnover, a high percentage compared to other European competitors, but lower than the Japanese Toyota and Honda (both around 5%). Most of the 9,200 persons employed in R&D worked for the two marques: on the development of new models, on market-driven technological innovations, or on manufacturing technologies and methods. For instance, PSA participated in a joint European program, Prometheus, to improve road traffic in Europe with the help of electronic systems. The group was also active in joint European programs for the recycling of vehicles. The improvement of subsystems such as diesel engines and suspensions was also seen as a priority: For instance, the launch of the Xantia Activa in 1994 as based on a new system of active suspensions.

The electric car was one of the top research priorities for PSA. In 1991, PSA was the first car manufacturer to sell electric vehicles for urban use (to Electricite

Opel with Hindustan (objective: 12,000 vehicles), and Volkswagen with Eicher Motors (objective: 30,000 vehicles of the Golf 4 and Audi). At the end of 1993, PSA had signed an agreement with Premier Automobile Ltd. (the number two in India) to manufacture the Peugeot 309 in Kalyan, starting from 1995. After a Ffr1 billion investment, the objective of the joint venture PAL Peugeot Ltd. was to produce 60,000 vehicles a year. In the South American continent, Peugeot and Citroën had significant positions in Argentina (with a 16% market share) and in Chile (8,000 vehicles in 1994). The industrial presence of Peugeot in Argentina through the Sevel joint venture was a key success factor in the context of the new Mercosur free-trade agreement in this zone. Peugeot and Citroen had just established sales subsidiaries in Brazil, and sales grew from 3,000 vehicles in 1993 up to 10,300 in 1994.

Finally the top management of PSA was studying the opportunity of a comeback in the North American market. Like several other European car manufacturers, PSA had been pushed out of the U.S. market in the late 1980s. At the time, it distributed the 505 and the 405 through a limited number of megadealers, in the East Coast, the West Coast, and the Southeast. A study conducted in 1994 recommended the following:

- Specific vehicles were needed (given the local norms and preferences).

- A complete sales network was needed (because cars travel all around the country).

- At least two and up to four models were needed in order to feed the sales network.

- It was necessary to have local production (given the evolution of the U.S. dollar and the relatively low cost of manpower in this zone); plants could be located in the United States of America, in Canada, or in Mexico (Volkswagen had plants in Mexico; BMW and Mercedes had plants in South Carolina).

- Such an investment was estimated at around Ffr20 billion in four years, and the next high cycle of the U.S. market was expected in the year 2000 (after the 1994–1995 high cycle).

Challenges for 1995–2000

Within Western Europe the top management of PSA was concerned with the decrease in consumption, as shown by the estimation of sales for 1995. Price differentials between European countries, mainly due to competitive devaluation, stimulated the development of parallel distribution channels (for instance, the price of French cars in Italy was 30% lower than in France for some models). This situation, combined with increased competition in a mature market, was driving down prices. Moreover, according to the EEC-Japan agreement, the competition with the Japanese would be free in Europe starting from the year 2000, and Korean competitors were expected to sell about 1 million vehicles in Europe by the end of the twentieth century.

Finally, the chairmanship of Jacques Calvet was supposed to come to an end in 1997, although some believed that, given his success as the head of PSA, he would continue. Indeed, the market value of the group had been multiplied by 15 in ten years, with the Peugeot family keeping control of the company.

In June 1995 Jacques Calvet concluded his address to the annual stockholders' meeting as follows:

> The challenges facing us are clear. The economic and monetary environment and the intense competition in our markets are serious threats. On the other hand, the Group's forward looking attitude and our employees' strong commitment to achieving our objectives—which I greatly appreciate—are precious, even crucial strengths. As a result we can face the future with confidence

Appendix: Additional Information on Europe's Car Industry

Europe's Car Dynasties at a Crossroads

They are the glittering royalty of the European auto industry: the Agnellis of Italy's Fiat, the Peugeots of France, and the Quandts of Germany's BMW. Now after generations of adamant control and independence, all three dynasties are suddenly at a crossroads as the auto industry gets crunched by global consolidation.

Day by day, it's harder to fathom that Fiat, P and BMW can go it alone following the Dai AG and Chrysler Corp. deal, which set ￼ ping world-wide. In its aftermath, N raced into the arms of Renault SA sorbed Volvo Cars, and Gener Saab Automobile.

In Europe, talk abo overdrive. Amid s would buy contro tions—a rumor so fa board member said yes.

de France and to local government authorities and public institutions). The market was estimated by executives to be around 250,000 vehicles in Europe by 1995. The large-scale manufacturing and sale of the electric Peugeot 106 and Citroën AX was planned to start in 1996. The electric car was to become the second family car, for driving short distances mainly in towns. The PSA executives believed they were three years ahead of competition in this domain. The group co-operated with several townships so as to implant the necessary infrastructure to provide power for recharging batteries. PSA also launched the 'tulip' project, a system of electric car rental for the town. Small two seater Tulip cars would be rented by subscribers in several places in a town, and batteries would be recharged in a number of parking places with an electric terminal. The system was experimented with in Tours at the end of 1995, and PSA decided to continue its further development.

Productivity and Effectiveness

Investment was particularly high at the beginning of the 1990s, about Ffr15 billion a year in 1990 and 1991. It represented about 9.5% of the sales turnover, one of the highest ratios of the industry, and was financed internally rather than through borrowing. Investments are aimed at renewing the product range. They are also aimed at continuing the modernization of the industrial assets of the group, in order to improve productivity, flexibility, efficiency, and the quality of the products' (annual report, 1990). With the crisis in 1993, investment was reduced; however, in 1994 it still represented Ffr10.5 billion.

On average, productivity was improved by 10% cent a year during this period, with a 12% improvement in 1994 compared to 1993. Reductions in costs were vital. Jacques Calvet stated that the market reversals in 1990 and 1991 and the price war made them even more so.

Purchases represented 58% of production costs in 1994. Cost cutting on procurement was a priority for the Sogedac, and productivity points were implemented with suppliers. On average, suppliers increased their added value ratio by 5% a year.

In PSA's plants the number of hierarchical levels was reduced and a price controller was named for each . His or her role was to validate suggestions for simplifications and cost cutting, many of which came from the workers (128,755 suggestions in 1994 compared to 78,434 in 1991).

The forecasts for the in Africa,
continuation of this opportuni
and forecasts at PSA exceptions
long term. Indeed, pt). The furth
tween 1984 and 199 resentation
workers rose from 10 uding Turke
nicians from 9% to of the group
visors and managers was limited to
developed an ambiti
more than 4% of tl was too compet
2% in 1984).   PSA: 6,600 vehi
                      market was attract

The Internatio expected in the ye
                   d and dominated
Europe   undai). On the oth
                      growing in Malaysi
PSA had industrial 4,500), and in Thai
In 1994, about 80 panese car manufac-
France. Indeed, Fr et shares and strong
country in terms o cal suppliers (for in-
España (with 205 a gines and electrical
and Citroën España and transmissions in
tured at Vigo) repr Indonesia, steering
tion. Peugeot Talb ed activities in Sin-
Kingdom), manuf less structured and
306 after 1993 (76 million vehicles in
about 3 per cent of locally. In this mar-
Portugal manufact ore active, particu-
venture with PSA had a joint venture
vehicles. Automol zhou Peugeot Auto-
roën made 87% of e 45,000 vehicles a
pean market was s duction was around
particularly the la was a project to ex-
German market, the 405 (150,000
tried to strengthen Citroën Automobile
work of dealers. troën ZXs in 1994
chronically loss-n ew plants were be-
production had ri an in order to pro-
to 116,600 in 199 apacity to 150,000
decline of the Bri
improving its UK individuals belong-
roën as the main in India, and the
                   cted to become a
The relations year 2000. The In-
France and the by Maruti, a joint
more complex as dian state, which
Research and de rly with the small
product marketir tional competitors
cies were also de partners: Mercedes
to particular imp the local DCM,
between the head

deed considering a deal.

"Fiat is being courted heavily," said Franzo Grande Stevens, who is also a confidante of the Agnelli family. "It will take some time to consider the offers. However, probably by the end of this year, we will have to decide on the partner and whether to make an alliance."

Auto makers in Europe have enough capacity to build 5.4 million light vehicles, or 33% more than are expected to be produced this year, according to the PriceWaterhouseCooper's Autofacts consulting group. With so much capacity oversupply, industry executives say, not everybody can make money.

Adding to the competitive pressure are the enormous costs developing new technologies such as fuel-cell and hybrid electric-propulsion systems.

In this environment, Fiat, PSA Peugeot Citroën and Bayerische Motoren Werke AG look vulnerable. Despite such fabulous brands as Ferrari, Maserati, Alfa Romeo, and Lancia, Fiat's auto operations are too small, too centered on Italy. Competitive new products have helped Peugeot lately, but its concentration in Southern Europe and in the less-profitable market segments have hurt. And BMW, with one of the world' great brands, is hobbled by its loss-making British Rover Group unit.

Still, each of these companies would be a prize for any global giant. The families that will decide the fates of the European national treasures have much in common. They are fabulously wealthy. All are secretive. And family members play an active role in running each of the car companies.

The Agnellis and Fiat

Gianni Agnelli, honorary chairman of Fiat and patriarch of the clan that owns the auto group, has often been described as the uncrowned king of Italy.

The charming, 78-year-old auto mogul has long enjoyed unparalleled political and economic clout in Italy, where Fiat's activities represent nearly 4% of gross national product and the family is revered as one of Europe's leading industrial dynasties. But it is precisely the issue of family ownership that has hamstrung the 100-year-old company in recent years, leaving the Agnellis grappling now with a painful decision over whether to cede control of their beloved empire.

Since it foundation in 1899 by Mr. Agnelli's grandfather, Fiat has both driven and dominated the industrial development of Italy. In 1950, Fiat developed the Ciquecento, the subcompact that embodied the postwar return to prosperity for millions of Ital-

ians. As it diversified into everything from defense to construction, Fiat went unchallenged as the country's leading industrial company right up through the 1970s. "What's good for Fiat is good for Italy," goes a popular saying.

The Agnellis' clout extends well beyond cars. They own Turin's largest newspaper and hold a sizeable stake in Italy's leading daily, *Corriere della Sera,* where the nomination of any new director must have the blessing of Mr. Agnelli. The Fiat owner also has veto power over the top spot at Italy's most prestigious business daily, *Il Sole-24 Ore.*

The family also owns Juventus, Italy's powerhouse soccer team, as well as a popular ski resort in the Alps. They once helped sponsor a sailboat in the America's Cup and were instrumental in Turin's winning bid for the 2006 Winter Olympics.

In the 1980s, the Agnellis had created a scandal after dumping their loss-making steel business on the state for a sum that has since remained secret. "A wise government must take into consideration what the biggest private company in the country thinks," says Foreign Trade Minister Piero Fassino. "Helping Fiat is in the interest of the entire country."

More recent years have seen Fiat—which once held more than 60% of the Italian market and was Europe's leading car group—come under increasing pressure. Profits have been slipping, and family control has proven to be a major obstacle. The Agnellis' emotional attachment to the car business and their reluctance to give up control, according to sources close to Fiat, helped quash two past merger possibilities—one with Ford in 1985 and the other with Chrysler in 1990.

"The obsession for control has played a role in the decline of Fiat, [and] has also failed to increase shareholders value," says Salvatore Bragantini, a top official at stock-market regulator Consob.

Sources close to the family say their control is again the major wild card as to the partner and type of deal the group would eventually make. The family was left without a clear heir apparent with the tragic death several years ago of Mr. Agnelli's young nephew, who was being groomed to take the helm. About two years ago, Mr. Agnelli chose his beloved 23-year-old grandson, John Elkann, to represent the family in the future and the university student has already started shadowing Fiat's top management.

Mr. Agnelli will find it tough to make a choice that could end the clan's association with the company, people close to the family say, and the Agnellis are keenly aware of the social and political pressures to retain Fiat's Italian identity.

The Quandts and BMW

In an era of auto-industry consolidation, BMW is widely seen as too small to last alone. But any attempt to take over BMW will run squarely up against a seemingly unmovable object—the Quandt family, Matriarch Johanna, 73, and her two children Stefan, 33, and Susanne, 37, own 46.6% of BMW's shares.

Much to the disappointment of acquisitive care executives on both sides of the Atlantic, the Quandts so far have refused to entertain overtures from buyers. "There is a very emotional bridge between the family and the company," says family spokesman Thomas Gauly. "They won't sell."

Unlike Europe's other auto families, the Quandts entered the game late, taking a stake in BMW in 1959. With BMW facing bankruptcy and a takeover by rival Daimler-Benz AG, Herbert Quandt rode to the rescue, buying up the floundering company and making himself the hero throughout Bavaria. More importantly, he established BMW's formula for success—building affordable, sporty, high-quality cars.

Today, Stefan and Susanne sit on BMW's supervisory board. Stefan studied economics and engineering at Karlsruhe University, worked in Hong Kong and the U.S., and now owns a pharmaceutical and design company, Delton AG, with sales of 1.3 billion marks. Susanne studied business in Switzerland and in the U.S. at Harvard. She now has a 51.1% stake in Altana, a publicly traded pharmaceutical and chemical company with sales of 31 billion marks.

Estimates of their wealth vary considerably, but they are generally considered the richest family in Germany and among the 10 wealthiest in the world.

Although the children do not have any specific responsibilities on the board, people knowledgeable about BMW say their presence is felt everywhere, from seemingly routine daily decisions to boardroom dramas such as that played out last February. That was when BMW Chairman Bernd Pischetsrieder was summoned to the supervisory board to explain his plans for rescuing the company's loss-making Rover cars unit.

Although Pischetsrieder won high marks for his management of the BMW brand, the Quandts were tired of waiting for a return at Rover and pressed Mr. Pischetsrieder to explain himself. He couldn't, and in a stunning move, was shown the door.

Rover has lost money ever since BMW bought it in 1994. BMW has promised that the British company will break even by 2002.

While the BMW brand continues to sell strongly, company officials say Rover is likely to report a loss slightly wider than 1998's 1.87 billion-mark shortfall. In 1998, the entire BMW group's net income fell 27.5% to 903 million marks. The company's share price has slipped over the last 12 months.

The Peugeots

The Peugeot family, which founded the car maker more than a century ago, is one of France's wealthiest. Last year, the French magazine *le Nouvel Economist* estimated the clan was worth 13.2 billion francs.

The extended Peugeot family, now comprising about 100 people, controls a 25.1% stake in the car maker and 37.4% of its voting rights. Four family members hold seats on the company's supervisory board, while another six have operating jobs within the company.

Peugeot's Chief Executive Officer, Jean-Martin Folz, has said the company and the family want to remain independent but use alliances with other auto makers to achieve economies of scale for certain new products or technologies.

An effort to sign DaimlerChrysler as a partner on a new small-car project merely extended a long line of cooperative agreements. The first one, dating back three decades, is a joint venture with Renault to build engines and engine components. Along with Fiat, Peugeot designs and makes commercial vans and minivans. It recently expanded a partnership with Ford to develop and produce diesel engines and forged an agreement with supplier Valeo SA to jointly develop components.

Publicly, the Peugeot family is standing behind this strategy. No family members have spoken out on this issue. But in an *Automotive News Europe* interview in June, supervisory board president Pierre Peugeot was quoted as saying, "In order for a company to work well, it needs to not have any problem with control of its capital. I believe in continuity because the car industry needs a long-term approach. I think that Michelin and Ford (families) have the same philosophy."

Meanwhile, Peugeot is pushing to bolster its market position. Fueled by hot products and a strong home market, the French car maker boosted European car sales last year by 11.6%, and overtook GM to become Europe's second-largest car maker, after Volkswagen

AG. The spunky new 206 model introduced in 1998 took off and the company sold 554,000 of them worldwide, increasing production from 2,000 cars a day to 3,000 over the course of the year to keep up with demand.

	Fiat	Peugeot	BMW
• **Key Family Members**	Founder's grandson and honorary Chairman Gianni Agnelli. Umberto Agnelli, former deputy chairman of Fiat and currently CEO of the family's holding company IFIL. Umberto shares in major decisions, but elder brother Gianni has the final say.	Supervisory board members: Pierre Peugeot, president; Roland Peugeot, president d'honneur; Robert Peugeot, director of innovation; Bertrand Peugeot, vice-president of quality.	Herbert Quandt (died 1982), Johanna Quandt, family matriarch, and children, Stefan and Susanne, who sit on BMW's supervisory board.
• **Total Controlled by the Family**	30% through two family holding companies. Another 10% is in the hands of longtime allies. The family tightly controls the board.	Extended Peugeot family controls 37.4% of stock voting rights.	46.6%, with Johanna's share of 16.7%, Stefan's 17.4%, and Susanne's 12.5%.
• **Signature Cars**	The classic Cinquecentro, which was Italy's first mass-produced car and a symbol of the country's post-war reconstruction. The Punto, Fiat's modern-day battle horse, is a subcompact aimed largely at developed markets and represents about a quarter of its worldwide production.	Peugeot 206	BMW 3-Series
• **Strengths and Weaknesses**	The Fiat group's sprawling reach goes well beyond cars and gives the Agnelli family enormous power in Italy. But the money-losing Fiat car business is overly dependent on the small-car segment. Fiat has invested heavily in emerging markets but lacks presence in the U.S.	Hot new models made Peugeot No. 2 in European sales last year, outpacing General Motors. Profits are up. But Peugeot lacks global reach. France and Spain account for 45% of car sales.	BMW's strength is in the BMW luxury brand name. Its major weakness is the money-losing British Rover Cars unit.

Case 28:   ABB in China: 1998*

"I want to make ABB a company that encourages and demands innovation from all of its employees, and a company that creates the environment in which team-work and innovation flourish," declared ABB's CEO Göran Lindahl. In seeking new growth, CEO Göran Lindahl was moving out of the long shadow of his predecessor Percy Barnevik. The former CEO of ABB, Percy Barnevik was arguably one of the most successful international managers in Europe.

ABB, the world leader in electrical engineering, is a US$35 billion electrical engineering group, with companies all over the globe. It operates primarily in the fields of reliable and economical generation, transmission, and distribution of electrical energy.[1] Much has been written about the worldwide company. In 1996 ABB was ranked in the top 40 of *Fortune* 500. Recently, the company announced their newest reorganization that would make the company more up-to-date with the global world, the current CEO, Göran Lindahl, said.[2] Göran Lindahl took over from Percy Barnevik as CEO in 1997 of the technology giant ABB, and the pressure from the shareholders and the market was mounting.

ABB had different priorities in different markets. Western Europe and North America were the company's biggest markets. However, the high-potential markets were the Middle East, Africa, Latin America, and Asia. These markets were growing fast and ABB expected to have half of its customers in these regions not long into the twenty-first century. The priority is on building local manufacturing, engineering, and other forms of added value. ABB wanted to integrate these operations into the global networks to get full synergy effects and scale economies.

During 1998 the industrial production in OECD countries, in which ABB performed about 75% of its total business, continued to grow, although at a slower pace than the strong growth rates. Overall, industrial production in Europe was lower than the year before,

but still high compared to historical levels. Economic activity in North America was slowing and in Latin America high interest rates were delaying the financial closing of projects in an environment of reduced economic activity. The Indian economy was slowing, also due to reduced exports as a result of its strong currency compared to others in the region. Southeast Asia was gradually stabilizing at a low level with reduced consumption and investments.

As a result of the ongoing economic uncertainty, overall global demand was forecast to remain soft in the near future. ABB expected to benefit, thanks to its well-established local presence around the world, from higher demand in various industries and world markets. Appropriate cost cutting, continued selective tendering, and successful working capital reduction programs were expected to contribute positively to ABB Group results. The company recognized that the world market is rapidly changing and increasingly unpredictable. Its efforts had paid off and the Group had positioned itself for future growth in "the world's most dynamic market over a long term—China."[3]

The interest in China was growing steadily, and companies in Japan, the Western European countries, the United States, and elsewhere viewed the China market as having enormous potential. With a population of a billion and a growing economy, it appeared worthwhile to make a major effort to gain a foothold in the market.[4] On the one hand, China represents a huge and largely untapped market. The Chinese market alone is potentially bigger than that of the United States, the European Community, and Japan combined. On the other hand, China's new firms are proving to be very competitive, and China's culture is quite different from that of the West. However, in the China market the growth levels remain good for enterprises such as Procter & Gamble, Motorola, Nestlé, and ABB. The Appendix at the end of this case summarizes perspectives of these firms in the Chinese market. A lot of worldwide companies suffering from the financial crisis in the rest of Southeast Asia regard the China market as a lifeboat. Nevertheless, concerns remained about currency devaluation which might drag China down into the crisis. Yet China seemed unshakable, and analysts were still calling China the country of the future.[5] Thus, the changes in China were creating both opportunities and threats for established worldwide companies. According to *Management Today*, China

* This case was prepared by Suzanne Uhlen at Lund University (Sweden), under the supervision of Professor Michael Lubatkin (University of Connecticut), during her six months of field study in China. The case is to serve as a basis for classroom discussion rather than to illustrate either effective or ineffective handling of an administrative situation.

Due to concerns related to the translation of this case from the Swedish language to English, it has been edited to appear in this publication only.

will be one of the top 10 economies in the world by the year 2010.[6]

Chinese Influence

> China will enter the next century as the rising power in Asia after two decades of astonishing economic growth that has transformed the country and that has given rise to new challenges.[7]

Many cities in China have more than 5 million inhabitants. Its economy is growing faster than that of any other country in almost three decades.[8] China is not like other developing countries: In some areas, such as home electronics,[9] its development has surpassed development in Western countries, while in other areas China lags far behind.

Chinese culture and society stretch back more than five thousand years. Its cultural heritage of philosophy, science and technology, societal structures, and traditional administrative bureaucracy are unique.[10] It is no wonder, then, that conflicts often occur between Chinese and foreign cultures. Foreign managers are accustomed to other values and norms, some of which may hardly be acceptable in China.[11]

Dagens Industri has noticed a trend in the semi-annual reports of worldwide companies:[12] The more focus that the companies have put on basic industry, the more the Asian crisis tends to affect them. However, China may save these companies and others, especially those companies operating in the infrastructure business.[13] When the Cold War ended, China's economic growth began to stabilize and the people demanded a speedy reconstruction. The country began to enjoy strategic latitude for the first time in 200 years, and it no longer faced the threat of aggression.[14] This has enabled the country to focus on economic developments in its domestic and foreign policies. According to Professor Yahuda, China's leaders also have come to base their legitimacy on providing conditions of stability in which people can look forward to continued high levels of prosperity. The need for economic development is fuelled by many other factors, such as providing employment for a population that increases by some 15 million people a year. Additionally, there are significant regional inequalities that can only be addressed by further economic development.[15]

China is expected to evolve into a hybrid system of authoritarianism, democracy, socialism, and capitalism. Also recognized are the internal problems the country faces, such as environmental disasters, political struggles, and tensions between the emerging entrepreneurial economy and the vast parts of China still under state control.[16] Today China receives more direct investment and foreign aid than any other developing country. Many companies are eager to establish a presence in China, which, it is argued, attracts more than its share of investments.[17] However, ". . . Westerners cannot expect to know how China will develop and need to expect that the Chinese will always be different from them. Instead of trying to change China, they should look for positive steps that take their differences into account."[18]

According to China's Premier Zhu Rongji, China is indeed the largest market in the world. Due to duplicate construction, some areas experience oversupply, but the premier states that the market is far from saturated.[19] Since China opened up its doors to the outside world in the late 1970s, a large number of foreign investors enjoyed high return on their investments, while others have failed. Some keys to ensuring success in business in China, according to *China Daily*, include:[20]

- Look to the long term in the China market. Competition is intensifying and market exploitation needs time and patience. Foreign companies eager to get a quick return are usually disappointed at the results.

- Employ locals. They are familiar with the local business environment.

- Stay aware of changes in policies and regulation. China is in a process of transforming from a planned economy to a market economy. Various policies and regulations are being revised and replaced, while new ones are being issued. Foreign investors must keep informed of the ongoing changes.

- Undertake practical market research. Due to social, economic, and cultural differences, practical and down-to-earth market research is a must before and during investment in China.

Chinese Cultural Influence

China has a strong tradition of respect for age, hierarchy and authority.[21] This originates from the Confucian concept of *li* (rite, proprietary), which plays an important role in social position. *Li* can be seen today in China's traditional bureaucracy and in vertical decision making relationships, as well as in corruption which is acceptable in such a cultural context.[22]

The family is viewed as an essential social unit and there is a strong tendency to promote the collective or the group. Members of the family or group must maintain harmonious relationships which are seen as more important than the individual.[23] Thus, the family or clan norms are adopted as the formal code of conduct, and members are bound to these standards. In modern China, business and industrial enterprises are perceived as an extension of the family system.[24]

The concept of "face" (*mianzi*) is also very important. As Ju noted, the general idea of *mianzi* is related to "a reputation achieved through getting on in life through success and ostentation".[25] Mianzi also serves to enhance harmony within the family or group, so that only the positive is expressed publicly and any conflicts remain private.[26] Hong has found that *mianzi* plays an important role in social relationships and organizational behavior.[27] However, Yuan points out that there are two sides to this concept.[28] The first includes the individual's moral character and the strong fear of losing this limits a person's behavior. The second aspect of *mianzi* involves assertions about a person, which is not seen quite as serious as loss of face.[29]

The importance of personal relations (*guanxi*) is the fourth characteristic. According to Hong, persons with *guanxi* usually share a common birthplace, lineage, surname, or experience, such as attending the same school, working together, or belonging to the same organization.[30] A comparative study of decision-making in China and Britain has revealed that Chinese managers use their personal *guanxi* more widely to exchange information, negotiate with planning authorities, and accelerate decision-making processes than managers from British firms.[31] Because this *guanxi* network transmits information, and because contacts and cooperation are built on trust, it is very serious if that trust is broken. When trust is broken the whole network soon knows about the incident, and the person involved will have a hard time doing business again.[32]

ABB has been doing business on the China market since 1919, but it was not until 1979 that ABB established its first permanent office there. Almost 11 years later, energy companies started to realize there were billions to be had from the booming demand for electricity in Asia.[33] More recently, the emerging Asian market has slowed down due to the financial crisis in the area. At the moment it seems like China is the only country not affected by this financial crisis, and consequently, many companies are now trying to be successful in China.

ABB seems to be in a good position on the Chinese market due to good performance, delivery, autonomy, and its good name. Today the company has nine representative offices and 15 joint ventures, and the number of employees has grown in four years from approximately 1,000 to 6,000 employees in China.

Local Roots

ABB's strategy is to use its global strength to support the needs of its local customers around the world. However, in China, ABB has a fairly high import duty on its products, which limits how much the company can sell. The idea of setting up local production in China was to increase the market share, due to the fact that most Chinese customers do not have foreign currency[34] and are consequently forced to buy locally produced goods with the currency. ABB localized in China not to achieve lower production costs—locally supplied components are actually more expensive in China than elsewhere—it was to be closer to the local market, and therefore facilitate a few local modifications to the products and provide shorter delivery times to the customer.

The phrase "think global, act local" reflects ABB's fundamental idea of strong local companies working together across borders to gain economies of scale in many areas.[35] In spite of ABB claims to be able to respond swiftly and surely to market conditions,[36] some of its products in China are not truly adapted to the local market. Most of the products are designed for the IEC—international standard association based in Europe. The company manufactures products, which have to be tested according to different norms and standards. For example, North America ABB follows the ANSI-standard and in Canada ABB follows the CSA-standard.

However, some of ABB's products would not pass a type test based on Chinese standards. That is not because the quality is too low; on the contrary the quality of ABB products is sometimes too high. The quality of some of the products has evolved far beyond the requirements of Chinese standards which are based on what the local manufacturer can produce—therefore these ABB products cannot meet the standards. As one ABB manager in China stated:

> We are not going to redesign our products in order to meet the standards for the obvious reasons, why should we take our quality out, why shall we take the advances out. It does become an issue from time to time. Chinese

are very risk averse, if we have not done the type test in China. It is more to cover themselves in case something goes wrong.

Other managers felt that even though ABB tried to adapt the products to Chinese local standards their customers regard Western standards as superior and were actually asking for the superior product. The Chinese customers are seen as tough and sometimes demand more tests than ABB's products have gone through. Another reason put forward that feasibility studies are insufficient. This delays the work when new information has to be collected about market conditions. This aspect originates from the speed of changes in China and the companies difficulty in catching up with what is going on.

However, when the so-called type tests of the product have been done, the company cannot change the design due to the high costs involved. Some critics say ABB should adapt more to the Chinese situation, but the company cannot change technical design, because the tests would have to be done all over again. Of course, it is different from product to product—for some of the products, as one manger said,

> We have to adapt to the configurations the customers want, because they might go to the competitor.

Still in most cases, ABB companies in China are not allowed to change the products other than according to agreements with the licensee, which state that ABB's technology partners[37] oversee quality and performance. ABB definitely does not want different product performance from different countries. The products must have the same descriptions, so that they are seen as the same product all over the world. Consequently the local ABB company can only make a few modifications to the standard product for the specific customer and cannot change the technology involved. The technology partners have a few alternatives that meet the demands of the Chinese customers, and these products are also tested but do not necessarily meet the Chinese standards.

The local ABB company tries to follow the ABB Group's policy, to be close to the customer and responsive to his or her needs.[38] In China, however, contracts are not commonly used, and this frequently obstructs satisfying the many customer demands.

> They keep on saying this is China and you should adapt to the Chinese way: OK, if you want to buy a Chinese product that's fine, but this is our product—here are the terms and conditions. You can't just give in to that; otherwise you will kill your company, because they expect

you to accept unlimited liability and lifetime warranty and the risks to which you would expose your company would eventually lead to its shutting down, so you just cannot do that.

ABB believes that closeness to the customer is the best guarantee that local requirements are met.[39] However, the headquarters in Zurich has also set up rules about the kind of contracts that subsidiaries may sign. In China the concept of contracts is rather new, and many Chinese customers do not want these contracts. So some ABB companies in China do not use the standard ABB contract and are actually responsive to the customers' needs. When another ABB company comes to the same customer to set up a standard contract, the customer refers them to the previous ABB company who did not seem to find the contract necessary. The confused customer asks:

> Why do you then have to use a standard contract when the other ABB didn't?

Profit Centers

ABB's strategy is to take full advantage of its economies of scale while being represented by some 5,000 entrepreneurial profit centers that are attentive to every local customer. These profit centers are quite independent and have to stand on their own economically. In addition, the individual company's profit can easily be compared to revenue. In other words, the individual ABB company is measured on its own performance and needs, of course, to make a profit when selling products or parts, even though it is within the ABB Group. The profit centers are efficient and allow the organization to act relatively fast, enabling the company to be sensitive and responsive to potential problems. Each company has a fair amount of autonomy, which in turn makes it flexible in the decision-making process. Even though ABB brochures state that the profit-centers strategy enables the easy transfer of know-how across borders,[40] the direction is pretty much one-way—from the technology partners, business areas, and country level to the subsidiary, rather than two-way.

Some conflicts of interest have occurred, due to the fact, for example, that the local ABB company and all other licensees are more or less dependent on their licensors in Europe.[41] In the local ABB company's case one of their technology partners is measured, like everyone else, on its performance and on its profit. If it gives the local ABB company support, it will cost the former money, and likewise, if it sells the local ABB company components, it wants to make a profit. The consequence is that it charges the local ABB company 25%–100% over the cost of its parts.

> So in the end you end up calling them as little as possible and we end up buying parts from local suppliers that probably we should not buy from local suppliers. And we reduce our quality. They have great profit figures, we have some profit figures but there are some real serious problems along the way.

The technology partner argues that the prices are high because it has to buy from its supplier and then sell to the local ABB company. This of course makes the products more expensive, and also because the technology partners pay for the "type tests" and all the product development.[42]

These conflicts have been occurring for a long time within ABB, but nobody has yet found a solution. It is difficult for a company like ABB, which is working with so many different products, markets, and cultures, to have anything other than sole profit centers. If the profit centers did not aim for a profit when selling within the ABB Group, the companies would no longer be independent companies. Nonetheless, between these independent companies with profit centers there are some extreme examples:

> Our partner in Y-country was selling the finished product in China before. Now he sells the parts to the joint venture in China and wants to charge more for the parts than he did for the finished product, and that is because it is in his interest and he will be evaluated on his performance. If he does not do that, his profits will be too low and he will be blamed for it. So he has got to do what he has got to do. That is what he is motivated to do and that is what he is going to do.

To some extent the technology partners are even selling indirectly to the Chinese market using unofficial agents to avoid a high import tax and to slip under China's high market price. ABB China has tried to put a stop to these agents and they are trying to force ABB companies to use only two official channels for ABB goods into the Chinese market—those produced by the local ABB company and those directly imported from a technology partner.

Structure

ABB is a huge enterprise with dispersed business areas, which encompass three segments: Power Generation, Transmission & Distribution, and Industrial Building Systems. However, this has recently been changed and divided into six segments. Before the reorganization, every country had a national ABB head office with a country management that dealt with all the company business in that particular country. The other dimension of the matrix structure reflects the clustering of the activities of the enterprise into 36 business areas (BAs). Each business area represents a distinct worldwide product market. Simply put, each BA is responsible for worldwide market allocation and the development of a worldwide technical strategy for that specific product line. Additional responsibilities for the BA are to coordinate who shall supply or deliver where, and to work as a referee in potential disagreements between companies within the ABB Group.

However, in China as in most developing countries, there is no BA in place and the decision-making power of the country management is consequently closer at hand. As a result, the decision-making power tends to rest more with the country level than the BA level. Disagreements between licensees in Western countries and subsidiaries in China have been and are occurring, due to different business orientations. The local subsidiary in China has two or more licensors in Western countries, from which they buy components. Some of the licensees sold these components themselves before the local subsidiary was set up in China. In some cases the licensee feels that the market in China was taken from them and that they therefore can only compensate for potentially lost sales by charging the Chinese subsidiary a higher price. If the disagreeing partner seeks the BA as a referee in this kind of case, the following happens:

> The BA are looking at the global business—we can increase our global business if we set up a joint venture in China. But the technology partner can't increase their business if we set up a joint venture in China. If we set up a joint venture in China the technology partner wants to increase its business also; they are going to do some work, and of course want something for it. The BA is really powerless to push those along.

To date, the licensors have also been paying for all the technology development, which is, from their point of view, the reason for charging a higher price. Because the enterprise is divided into 5,000 profit centers and because each of these profit centers must make a profit when selling a component or product, coordination and cooperation between the licensors and the local Chinese subsidiary has suffered.

For example, the licensor in Germany may not inform the licensee in China about quality problems. When the local ABB company suggests changes to the licensor, the licensor will evaluate the changes on the basis of benefits to itself. The licensor, of course, is going to invest in areas beneficial to itself first or charge the local ABB company extra. The consequences are thus:

> We have had some things that would really help us here in China. But I don't even bother, because I know the reaction.

Over 80% of what the Centers of Excellence produce is for export,[43] which makes it especially important that the partners of the licensor can manage challenges and opportunities that emerge. However, the BA divides the world markets into areas in which specific ABB companies are a so-called first source.[44] Between some of the licensors and the local ABB company this has resulted in disputes. For example:

> We are responsible for the Peoples Republic of China's market and are supposed to be the sole source (or rather first source) because we have the expertise for this market. Our technology partner in X country quotes into this market on a regular basis, does not inform us, and competes against us, and takes orders at a lower prices. This can destroy our position in the marketplace.

According to the licensor they do not quote in the local ABB company's market because if a final customer has foreign currency, they prefer imported products. The licensor argues that it does not go into the Chinese market and offer its products, but rather gets inquiries from ABB in Hong Kong and delivers to them. Hong Kong in turn sells the products directly to the Chinese customer after having increased the original price up to the market price, which is often several times higher in China than in Europe, for example. ABB China may decide that the Hong Kong coordinated sales force should sell the local ABB company's products on the Chinese market, among imported products and products locally produced by the joint venture.

The technology is owned today by the centers of excellence in Europe or so-called licensors, which are also paying for all the product development. ABB has chosen these licensees as the company's world source of this specific technology. These units are responsible for developing new products, and look after the quality by arranging technical seminars about the technology and by keeping special technology parts—so-called noble parts at only their factory. This strategic decision enables the company to guard against competitors copying their products. Consequently, these parts will not be localized or purchased in China. However, for one product group (THS) there has been an organizational change, including the establishing of a unit called CHTET, which will own all new technology that is developed and pay for product development. This change involves all product groups.

Multicultural

The current fashion, exemplified by ABB, is for the firms to be "multicultural multinationals," which means the company must be sensitive to national differences.[45] Barnevik believed that a culturally diverse set of managers could be a source of strength. According to Barnevik, managers should not try to eradicate these differences and establish a uniform managerial culture; rather, they should seek to understand cultural differences, to empathize with the views of people from different cultures, and to make compromises for such differences. Barnevik believes that the advantage of building a culturally diverse cadre of global managers is to improve the quality of managerial decision making.[46]

ABB in China is typified by a culturally diverse set of managers with a mixture of managerial ideas, derived from their national backgrounds, values, and methods of working. Whether a manager is going to be influenced and absorb the new climate depends on which stage in personal development the manager has reached. As one manager said:

> If you are close to being retired you might not change so much, there isn't much point. But you can't work in the same way as you do at home—it just wouldn't work.

According to another manager, ABB is an international company with a strong Scandinavian influence. However, this really depends on where the ABB company is located. In China the ABB culture is influenced by Chinese culture, by the environmental circumstances, and by the laws. The environment is stricter in China than it is, for example, in Europe, because there are more rules. In spite of that, the managers do not feel that the result is a subculture of the ABB culture rather it is a mixture of managers from different cultures— "we are a multidomestic company."

The companies in China see the top level of the ABB management as far away from the daily life at the subsidiary level in China. Or as one manager expressed it "between that level and here, it's like the Pacific Ocean." All the managers argue, though, that what the top level, including Barnevik and Lindahl,[47] says sounds very good and that is how it should be. Some managers expressed this difference:

Sounds like I'm working for a different ABB than these guys are. What they talk about is really good and that is how it should be. But then when I sit back and go into the daily work and say that's not at all how it is. Somewhere along the line something gets lost between the theory and ideas at that level which is quite good. But when you get down to the working level and have to make it work something really gets lost along the way.

Transferred Personnel

The BA with its worldwide networks has recommended, after suggestions from local offices, who is going to be sent to China or any other country, but incountry company finally decides who should go. This person must be able to fit into the system in China, due to the high costs involved: it is estimated that each transferred employee costs the company about $250,000 a year.

ABB is supported not only by its coordinating executive committee but also by an elite cadre of 500 global managers, which the top management shifts through a series of foreign assignments. Their job is to knit the organization together, to transfer expertise around the world, and to expose the company's leadership to differing perspectives.[48]

ABB in China is not yet a closely tied country unit, for several reasons. Firstly, most of the transferees' contacts are back in the home country. These expatriates argue, that the home office does not understand how difficult it can be to work abroad and that they need support—"sometimes it just feels like I'm standing in the desert screaming," one expatriate said. The home office, on the other hand, often feels that the expatriates can be a burden because they need so much support. The home office also helps select candidates, along with the BA, to a foreign placement, even though it is argued they have little or no knowledge of what it is like to work in the country.

The expatriates say that they are stationed in China on assignments for a relatively short time period and are thus less able to build up informal networks. The few contact persons the managers have will eventually return home and there is no formal way to contact the replacement person. LOTUS notes, a computer-based network of managers worldwide is deficient in building the preferred strong country unit within China. Finally, the managers do not feel that they can take the time, or the effort, to establish informal networks if these have to be rebuilt due to the replacement of these expatriates every two to three years. (A worldwide policy within the company limits the expatriates to operating as such for not more than five years at a time.) This executives have questioned, saying that

> It is during the first year you learn what is going on and get into your new clothes. During the second year you get to know the people and the system, the third year you apply what you learned, and the fourth year you start to make some changes—and this is very specific for developing countries.

Three years ago the transferees did not get any information or education before being sent out to ABB's subsidiaries in China. Now with about 100 transferees of 25 different nationalities in China, this has changed to some degree, but still it is mostly up to the individual to prepare and acclimatize. Within the worldwide corporation there is no formal training; it is up to the home office of the transferees to prepare managers for foreign assignments. Some argue that "you could never prepare for the situation in China anyway, so any education wouldn't help." Others say that this has resulted in a lot of problems with transferred managers, which results in even higher costs for the company if the manager fails.

When it is time for the expatriate to return to the home office, he or she may feel unsure of having a job back home. It is very important for the expatriate to have as close contact with the home office as possible and to make use of the free trips home offered by the company.

The Chinese Challenge

ABB wants to send out managers with 10 to 15 years of experience. However, this is difficult, when the company is in a rural area and most managers with 10 to 15 years' experience have families who may not want to move to these areas. Sometimes a manager gets sent to China when the company does not want to fire him.

> So instead they send the manager to where the pitfalls are greater and challenges bigger and potential risks are greater.

After being located in China, the task of adapting to the new environment, whether a rural area or a big city, is difficult. Most expatriates have strong feelings about living in and adapting to the new environment in China. Newly arrived managers seem to enjoy the respect they get from the Chinese, which several managers delightedly expressed:

> I love it here, and how could you not, you get a lot of respect just because you're a foreigner and life is just pleasant.

Some managers dislike the situation to a great extent and a number have asked to leave because their expectations about the situation in China have not been fulfilled.[49]

Some country-specific problems are how to teach Chinese employees to work in teams. The ABB promotes teamwork and active participation among its employees,[50] but Chinese employees have a hard time working in a group, for cultural and historical reasons. Some of the local ABB companies have failed to introduce team working, ad hoc groups, and the like successfully, because they have rushed things:

> Here in China the management needs to encourage the teamwork a little bit, because it is a little against the culture and the nature of the people. This it not a question of lack of time for the managers, but I do not think we have the overall commitment to do it. Some of us feel strongly that we should, others that we can't.

Another problem is that management made up of transferees simply does not have the understanding or the commitment to teach local employees the company values, resulting in poor quality.

ABB has a great advantage over other worldwide companies due to its priority of building deep local roots by hiring and training local managers who know their local markets.[51] Replacing expatriates with local Chinese employees, a certain number of years, demonstrates this commitment to having a local profile. However, the Chinese employees come from an extremely different system , so it takes quite a long time for the former to learn Western management practices. To ease this problem and to teach Western management style, ABB China, among other companies, has recently arranged training for its Chinese employees with good management potential at a business school in Beijing. This is unusual because in developed countries, employees are responsible for their own development.[52] ABB ran their own school in Beijing, but this school had to close due to the profit center philosophy: Even the school had to charge ABB China for teaching their employees.

ABB also regularly sends about 100 local Chinese employees to an ABB company in a Western country every year. After several employees quit after the training, ABB instituted a so-called service commitment, in which the employee (or new employer) agrees to pay back the training investment if he or she quits or agrees to continue working for ABB for a certain number of years. The problem with local employees quitting after training has been experienced in other developing countries in Asia, such as in India and Thailand. The personnel turnover rate, approximately 22% within ABB China, reflects the fact that many local employees are aiming for the experience of working for an international company such as ABB and then move on to another job, which might be better paid.

However, by having local employees, the local ABB company is responsive to local conditions and sensitive to important cultural objectives such as the Chinese *guanxi*.[53] Local employees handle customer contact because expatriate employees are usually only stationed for a few years at one location and are consequently not able to build up strong connections with customers.

Reorganization

ABB is a decentralized organization, with delegated responsibility and decision-making authority allowing it to respond quickly to customers' requirements. In the core of this complex organization are two principles: decentralization of responsibility and individual accountability. These principles have been in operation at ABB since the Percy Barnevik days.[54] Decentralization is so highly developed the expatriate[55] managers have more responsibility than they would normally have in a Western company. However, in other respects the organization may be too centralized; for example, country managers must approve all overseas travel by employees.

According to ABB brochures, the greatest efficiency gains lie in improving the way people work together.[56] Within ABB China, however, companies with overlapping products or similar products often do not exchange information or coordinate marketing strategies. While managers usually receive up to 100 e-mails from other ABB employees a day, effective informal communication between ABB companies operating in China is lacking. The distances are large and accordingly, organizing a meeting demands greater efforts than in almost any other country in the world.

According to former CEO, Percy Barnevik, the purpose of a matrix organization is to make the company more bottom heavy than top heavy: "Clean out the headquarters in Zurich and send everybody out, have independent companies operating in an entrepreneurial manner." These entrepreneurial business units have the freedom and motivation to run their own business with a sense of personal responsibility.[57]

However, the result of matrix organization in China is that the ABB, subsidiaries must meet both ABB China's objectives (the country level) and the business areas objectives. ABB China objectives measure how the different companies are performing within China, while the BA measure how the specific products are performing on a worldwide basis and what the profitability is for the products. Each BA has a financial controller, and as does each country level:

> Rarely are the two coordinated, nor do they meet. So you end up with one set of objectives from each . . . Duplication! Which one shall you follow?

According to the *ABB Mission Book,* the roles in the two dimensions of the ABB matrix must be complementary.[58] This means that both the individual company and headquarters must be flexible and strive for extensive communication. This is the way to avoid the matrix interchange becoming cumbersome and slow. It is seen to be the only way to "reap the benefits of being global (economies of scale, technological strength, etc.) and of being multidomestic (a high degree of decentralization and local roots in the countries in which we operate)."

For many years ABB was widely regarded as an exemplary European company, yet it is undergoing its second major restructuring within four years. CEO Göran Lindahl's restructuring is aimed at making the organization faster and more cost efficient.[59] Due to the demands of the global market, ABB is getting rid of the regional structure and concentrating more on specific countries. The reorganization has basically dismantled one half of the matrix: the country management. Henceforth, BAs will manage their businesses on a worldwide basis so there will no longer be a conflict between BA's and country management's objectives. At the same time, segments are being split up (many BAs form a segment) to make them more manageable (e.g., the Transmission & Distribution segment has been split into two segments: Transmission and Distribution). The general managers of the individual joint ventures and other units will only have one manager, who has a global view of the business. In China, this also means dismantling the Hong Kong organization as well as the Asia Pacific organization.

According to Göran Lindahl, the reorganization will prepare ABB for a much faster rate of change on the markets and enable it to respond more effectively to the demands of globalization. It is seen as an aggressive strategy to create a platform for future growth.

Future Vision

CEO Göran Lindahl was appointed in 1997 to be the new president and chief executive of ABB. He believes the future can be forecasted with creativity, imagination, ingenuity, innovation—action based not on what was, but on what could be. The corporate culture needs to be replaced by globalizing leadership and corporate values. ABB is focusing on this by creating a unified organization across national, cultural, and business borders.

On the path toward the next century, ABB is going to focus on several essential elements: a strong local presence; a fast and flexible organization; the best technology and products available; and excellent local managers who know the business culture, are able to cross national and business borders easily, and who can execute your strategy faster than the competition.[60]

> We are living in a rapidly changing environment, and our competitors will not stand still. In the face of this great challenge and opportunity, enterprises that adapt quickly and meet customer needs will be the winner, and this is the ultimate goal of ABB.[61]

Appendix

Motorola

Facing problems in Russia during the glasnost error, Motorola declared that China was the country with the best growth market. Consequently, Motorola established their first representative office in China in 1987; they have grown rapidly ever since. Today, China generates more than 10% of Motorola's sales.

Motorola has found that modernization in China happens quickly; all their competitors are now present in the country, but Motorola is still predicting that China will be the market leader in Asia. Customers have high expectations of Motorola products is offering, because the products are regarded to be very expensive. Indeed, Motorola is growing *too* fast:

> The problem we have is that Motorola is growing very fast; it is like chasing a speeding train and trying to catch up with it.

Presently, Motorola has 12,000 Chinese employees and 200 expatriates in China; its goal is to have the Chinese employees take over the jobs of the expatriates. The expatriates are sent out on assignments for two to three years, with the possibility of renewal limited to a maximum of six years. High demands are made of the expatriates, especially concerning teaching teamwork to local employees. This is very important within the company because all the strategy planning is done in teams. When the contract time for the expatriate has expired the following is expressed:

You have done your job when the time comes and you have left the company and everything is working smoothly, but if everything is falling apart, you are a failure as an expatriate and have not taught a successor.

However, progress has been made in developing the company's local employees. Motorola has set up training abroad. The training is preferably held within China, with rotation assignments and training at Motorola University. This company university was set up in 1994 when the company found that the Chinese universities did not turn out sufficiently well-trained students. Within the company there is, however, a requirement that every employee worldwide shall have at least 40 hours of training, possibly to be exceeded in China. There must be a combination of good training and mentor development to get successful people. Motorola admits that they did make a mistake by not providing enough training for foreign expatriates before they came to China. They have noticed that overseas Chinese often do not fit into the system well, even though they speak Chinese:

You get more understanding if you look like a foreigner and make some mistakes than if you don't. Overseas Chinese are measured through other standards than other foreigners.

Other problems the company is facing concerning expatriation are that some expatriates just cannot handle the situation in China. If an expatriate fails, this has to be handled with care, otherwise the person loses face on returning to the home office. The company also has pointed out that they need expatriates with 10 to 15 years of experience in order to teach the local employees the company values and to transfer company knowledge. However, the people that are willing to move to China are the younger employees with less than five years of experience.

The expatriates are often responsible for transferring technical knowledge and getting projects started, especially in the case of the newly set up Center of Excellence in Tianjin, where $750 million was invested. This was Motorola's first manufacturing research laboratory outside the United States; all together, the company has invested $1.1 billion in China and plans to invest another $1 to 1.5 million. Motorola has also set up two branches of its training universities to educate customers, suppliers, and government officials, as well as its own employees. The money invested in China is from the earnings within the whole enterprise, in the belief that the Chinese market is going to be huge. CEO Gary Tucker says:

Motorola has come to your country hoping never to leave. . . . We manufacture in China because this is where our market is. We profit by going to a lot of countries around the world and then doing well in that country.

The strategy in China is to expand through joint ventures. Thus it is important that the Chinese partners bring something of value, which means that the partners have to be approved by the CEO. It is argued that the company has become "so decentralized that it has become bad," and that the company desires to reorganize more along customer than product lines. A practical reorganization has taken place to move everybody operating in Beijing to the same newly built headquarters. Entrepreneurial activities are also of importance, but difficult in practice due to problems of financial motivation and autonomy.

Motorola phones and pagers in China have Chinese characters. In 1987 when Motorola started selling pagers it thought there would not be a big market because the telephone net was not well established, but then the company invented codebooks, which enabled two-way communication. Fortunately this also worked in Hong Kong, Singapore, and Taiwan. After five years of operation in China, the company has not yet been able to put down deep roots in the market. Nevertheless, the investments in the country and efforts to make the company "Chinese" one have led to deep localization and made the company's position unshakable. To show how serious it is about putting down deep roots in China, Motorola has invested huge sums in environmental protection, providing scholarships to students, building labs at universities, and donating money to primary schools in rural areas.[62]

Motorola's worldwide organization is a pyramid, with the corporate management at the top and business units underneath—"then put the apex at the bottom." The corporate office works as the glue that holds the organization together. In 1997 Motorola conducted a reorganization to better reflect the global nature of its business.[63] The coordination is safeguarded by this new formal structure. However, the informal information flow, mostly through e-mails, is probably overused. A manager may get approximately 70 to 100 a day, of which less than 30% are really useful:

Some days it feels like we have all these opportunities and we do not really communicate.

All the controllers or general managers in the joint ventures get together quarterly to solve problems and support each other. Information exchange is encouraged, but no system has been developed to track what is going on in the six districts in China where the company is operating. Competition between units is a common problem, resulting in customer confusion. The matrix organization exacerbates the problem:

> We do not have the answers, because if we are too centralized then we miss new opportunities. How do you encourage creativity and yet keep people from competing with each other?

Motorola key beliefs or guiding principles come from the role model and father figure of the company, Galvin: "uncompromising integrity and constant respect for people—that is what makes us Motorola." This is the principal code of conduct that Motorola practices, which managers must reread and sign every two years.

Motorola management believes that they "obviously" have to change the way the company does things to accommodate the Chinese market; such as show face, build relations, and go to ceremonial meetings. They must make sure their partners are reliable, that the business makes sense, and that it is legal. However, Motorola looks the same all over the world, but the expatriates and their families have made an effort to adapt to Chinese norms.

China is a very difficult environment for a huge company like Motorola to be operating in:

> . . . because they would like to control the system and everything takes a long time because they will make sure that you are not cheating. You must be able to work with all the people that come from different departments and to let them trust you. Ordinary things like getting water, electricity etc, is a huge problem. Doing business in the Chinese system is a challenge and therefore creates pressure because you get frustrated.

Procter & Gamble

Procter & Gamble is China's largest international employer. Procter & Gamble (P&G), has approximately 5,000 Chinese employees and 100 expatriates spread over 11 joint ventures and wholly-owned enterprises in the country. This success has also been paying off by *Fortune* magazine's "World's Most Admired Companies" ranking. Currently, the biggest market for the company is China, where new companies are being established. Before establishing companies in China, P&G did a feasibility study. As with most other feasibility studies done in China, the information was outdated before it was a year old, and P&G people were criticized for not having sufficient knowledge about the country's specific situation.

The expatriates sent to China for the P&G account seemed to be unprepared. The company makes continuous efforts to put different cultural backgrounds together. Its own cultural values are consistent all over the world, but its expatriates come from a wide variety of cultural backgrounds and their culture is colored by their management style. This mixture of management styles can confuse local Chinese employees.

Expatriate sales people get a year of orientation training and language training. In line with the demand for localization P&G is decreasing the number of expatriates it employs. Expatriates, who are mostly three to four levels up in the organization are expensive, so one of P&G's key strategies is to develop local employees. Everybody who is an expatriate for P&G has a sponsor back home, a contact. People are also encouraged to go home once a year at the company's expense. There is no official limit, but most expatriates are on a three-year contract. The expatriate network is not yet an issue; however, the expatriates are said to be a very close group—"we are all in this together and we have a common vision."

The optimal goal for P&G is to develop the organization so that it can be a Chinese-run company. Today, everything is made in the Chinese P&G factories for internal use and the company has opened up a research center in Beijing, in cooperation with a prominent university.[64] If this works in China, the company wants to apply these ideas in the rest of the world.

Counterfeits are the greatest competition for P&G in China. Customers often cannot distinguish counterfeit products from real ones. P&G sold in China are not as high quality as those it markets in Western countries because Chinese customers cannot afford higher-quality products for better value. Nevertheless, the company is trying to offer the consistency of quality the Chinese consumers are willing to pay for.

The Chinese P&G organization has fewer management layers than its other organizations and decision-making takes less time. Because the company evolved very quickly and the market is so dynamic, it has not had the time to implement the layers "only tried to understand the market." The Chinese P&G organization is by all accounts more efficient, and P&G may implement what it has learned in China in other countries. A reorganization is taking place at the global level in P&G to include a reward system and to make the company more flexible.[65]

In China *guanxi* is difficult for expatriates to establish, so the company relies on the local staff. Local employees get an immense amount of education at P&G's own school. Expatriates are explicitly responsible for dealing with company principles, values, and all the technical specifics for P&G, which means the expatriates "are so in to running the business that sometimes the coaching of the locals is not possible."

Another challenge Procter & Gamble faces in China is dealing with the government. The company dealt with this by hiring a sophisticated government-relations manager who reports not only to the head of operations in China but also to the chief executive of the company.[66]

Nestlé

In the early 1980s China asked the world's largest food company—Nestlé—to build "milk streets" in the country. China was unfamiliar with how to produce milk and turned to Nestlé, whose core business is actually milk powder. From that time the company has grown in China and now has almost 4,000 employees, 200 of them foreigners.

Nestlé began as a Swiss company.[67] During World War I, Nestlé gave their local managers increasing independence to avoid disruptions in distribution.[68] This resulted in many of Nestlé's operations being established far from their headquarters in Switzerland.

The company believed that consumers' taste was very local and that there were no synergy effects to be gained by standardizing the products. In 1993 the company started to rethink this belief due to the increasing competition in the industry. Nestlé has acquired several local brands, influenced by their own country culture, which has caused Nestlé to standardize where it is possible.[69]

Although Nestlé is growing in China, they are not getting as much margin as they would like. In maintaining high quality of their products they have had to lower margins in order to be competitive, which is not always profitable. So why is Nestlé in China?

> It is because China is a large country and if you have a company that is present in more than 100 countries, you see it as a *must* for all international companies to be present there. We supply all over the world and it is our obligation to bring food to the people—which is the Company's priority.

Nestlé entered China with the intent of staying for the long term. Nestlé's overall approach is "Think global and act local!" The company's strategy is guided by several fundamental principles, such as the following:

Nestlé's existing products will grow through innovation and renovation while maintaining a balance in geographic activities and product lines.[70]

Its local Chinese employees—get a few days education on the Nestlé culture, but the expatriates have less training. It is up to the home country to decide whether it is necessary to train expatriates before sending them on their three-year foreign assignment. However, the leadership talent is highly valued within the company and consequently Nestlé has developed courses for this. The managers can independently develop their leadership talent without any connection with the specific company style or culture. Community centers have been developed to help expatriates with their contacts, to support expatriates psychologically, and even to offer language training.

In 1997 Nestlé published "The Basic Nestlé Management and Leadership Principles," aimed at making "the Nestlé spirit" generally known throughout the organization through discussions, seminars, and courses.[71] According to the CEO of Nestlé China, Theo Klauser, this publication is the key to the corporate culture that started the company's international expansion 130 years ago.[72]

Nestlé China has developed a specific structure based on its joint venture configuration. The information flow is seen as easy and smooth between the company's three regions in China. Communication is limited to a very high level, because the company believes it is not necessary to get all levels involved. As an example, one unit in China takes care of all the marketing. At the same time each Nestlé company in China is responsible for its own turnover rate, making each more flexible and decentralized. Quite unique for a worldwide company, Nestlé does not have any external e-mail network, and this is believed to concentrate the flow of information within the company.

A major challenge for Nestlé in China is building long-term relationships that will help establish Nestlé as the country's leading food company. It also needs to improve profitability. Legal difficulties are also more important than in any other country. Finally, Nestlé is challenged by the speed of change:

> Change happens every couple of months here—that is how the environment is; a lot of employees come from other more stable countries and sometimes find it difficult with all the changes. Change is how things are in China—it is normal. It is when something doesn't change, that is when you get worried! It is expected to change! Different from other countries where changes can be difficult to get.

Endnotes

1. 100 years of experience ensures peak technology today, ABB STAL AB, Finspong.

2. *Dagens Industri*, August 13, 1998, p. 25.

3. ibid.

4. Usunier, Jean-Claude, *Marketing Across Cultures*.

5. *Dagens Industri*, July 2, 1998.

6. *Management Today*, April 1996, by David Smith, p. 49.

7. Ahlquist, Magnus, ed.; *The recruiters guide to China*, preface by Professor Michael Yahuda.

8. *Bizniz*, Sept. 30, 1997.

9. Examples include VCD player, CD-ROM player, mobile telephones, beepers, and video cameras.

10. Garten, Jeffrey E., "Opening the Doors for Business in China," *Harvard Business Review*, May–June, 1998, pp. 160–172.

11. *Månadens Affärer*, Nov. 11, 1996.

12. *Dagens Industri* August 19, 1998.

13. ibid.

14. Ahlquist, Magnus, ed.; *The recruiters guide to China*, preface by Professor Michael Yahuda.

15. ibid.

16. Garten, Jeffrey E., "Opening the doors for business in China," *Harvard Business Review*, May–June, 1998, pp. 167–171.

17. See *The Economist* (*www.economist.com*) October 1998.

18. Hong Yung Lee, "The implications of reform for ideology, state, and society in China," *Journal of International Affairs*, vol. 39, no. 2, pp. 77–90.

19. An interview with Premier Zhu Rongji in *China Daily*, March 20, 1998, p. 2.

20. *China Daily Business Weekly*, vol. 18, no. 5479, March 29–April 4, 1998, p. 2.

21. Hoon-Halbauer, Sing Keow. *Management of Sino-Foreign Joint Ventures. Working Paper,* Lund University, 1997.

21. Yuan Lu. *Management Decision-Making in Chinese Enterprises. Working Paper,* Lund University, 1997.

22. ibid.

23. Ma, Jun. *Intergoveral relations and economic management in China.*

24. Laaksonen, Oiva. *Management in China during and after Mao in enterprises, government, and party.*

25. Ju, Yanan. *Understanding China*, p. 45.

26. Hwang, Quanyu; *Business decision-making in China.*

27. Hong Yung Lee, "The implications of reform for ideology, state, and society in China," *Journal of International Affairs*, vol. 39, no. 2, pp. 77–90.

28. Yuan Lu. *Management Decision-Making in Chinese Enterprises.*

29. Yuan Lu. *Management Decision-Making in Chinese Enterprises.*

30. Hong Yung Lee, "The implications of reform for ideology, state, and society in China," *Journal of International Affairs*, vol. 39, no. 2, pp. 77–90.

31. Yuan Lu. *Management Decision-Making in Chinese Enterprises.*

32. *Månadens Affärer*, Nov. 11, 1996.

33. *The Economist*, Oct. 28, 1995.

34. Because China's still a closed country, Chinese people cannot get foreign currency, except in in very limited amounts.

35. ABB, "The art of being local," ABB Corporate Communications Ltd., printed in Switzerland.

36. "You can rely on the power of ABB," ABB Asea Brown Boveri Ltd., Department CC-C, Zurich.

37. Technology partner (in this case) is the Center of Excellence (CE), licensors.

38. ABB's Mission, Values, and Policies.

39. HV Switchgear, ABB, ABB Business Area H.V. Switchgear, Printed in Switzerland.

41. Licensing is defined here as a form of external production where the owner of technology or proprietary right (licensor) agrees to transfer this to a joint venture in China, which is responsible for local production (licensee).

42. During the study this has changed to some degree due to a unit called CHTET being introduced.

43. http://www.abb.se/swg/switchgear/index.html, November 1997.

44. First source: You are the first source, but if you cannot meet the customers requirements the second source steps in.

45. *The Economist*, Jan. 6, 1996.

46. ibid.

47. Göran Lindahl is the present CEO, Chairman of the Board.

48. *The Economist*, Jan. 6, 1996.

49. There are two common, but false expectations expatriates have when coming to China. They believe they are going to make a lot of money or are going to experience the old Chinese culture, not the culture of China today.

50. ABB's Mission, Values, and Policies, Zurich, 1991.

51. ABB, "The art of being local," ABB Corporate Communications Ltd. Printed in Switzerland.

52. ABB's Mission, Value, and Policies, Zurich, 1991.

53. *Guanxi* Connections, relations.

54. ABB set up its first office, a representative office, in 1979.

55. Expatriate: A person who has a working placement outside the home country.

56. "You can rely on the power of ABB," ABB Asea Brown Boveri Ltd., Department CC-C, Zurich.

57. "You can rely on the power of ABB," ABB Asea Brown Boveri Ltd., Department CC-C, Zurich.

58. ABB's Mission, Values, and Policies.

59. *Dagens Industri*, August 13, 1998, p. 25.

60. "Meeting the challenges of the future," Presentation to the Executives Club of Chicago, October 16, 1997.

61. "You can rely on the power of ABB," ABB Asea Brown Boveri Ltd., Department CC-C, Zurich.

62. Garten, Jeffrey E. "Opening the doors for business in China," *Harvard Business Review*, May–June, 1998, pp. 174–175.

63. Motorola Annual Report 1997.

64. Qinghua University.

65. Procter & Gamble Annual Report 1998.

66. Garten, Jeffrey E. "Opening the doors for business in China," *Harvard Business Review*, May–June, 1998, pp. 173–175.

67. http://www.Nestlé.com/html/home.html, September 1998.

68. Quelch, J. A. and Hoff, E. J. "Customizing global marketing," *Harvard Business Review*, May–June, No. 3, pp. 59–60.

69. Brorsson, Skarsten, Torstensson; *Marknadsföring på den inre markanden—Standardisering eller Anpassning*. Thesis at Lund University, 1993.

70. http://www.Nestlé.com/html/h2h.html, September 1998.

71. Nestlé Management Report 1997.

72. Interview with Theo Klauser, *Metro*, July, 1998, p. 27.

Case 29: **Barossa Winery**[*]

Mr. George Steen, marketing manager for the Barossa Winery, had just been given an interesting assignment: to evaluate the feasibility of launching a major export drive. The Barossa Winery, an Australian producer of quality table wines, had experienced rapid growth in the early 1980s, but in 1986 and 1987 sales and profits had slowed considerably. At a strategy meeting held in early July 1988, the senior management group, which included Mr. Steen, decided that a growth opportunity existed in export markets and Mr. Steen agreed to prepare a feasibility study for the next strategy meeting.

As Mr. Steen sat in his office, Mr. Tony Clark, the general manager, came in and they began discussing the assignment. Mr. Steen said, "There will never be a better opportunity for us to get into foreign markets in a big way. The world has now heard of Australia because of *Crocodile Dundee* and the Bicentennial Celebration; we've got a very favorable exchange rate; and we produce great wines." Mr. Clark replied, "I agree, it's a good opportunity for growth and we've got the capacity of doing it and making a profit. I know our wines are as good and, in some instances, better than comparable European wines, but the consumer doesn't know that." Mr. Steen replied, "That's true, but we only need a small share of any one of a number of markets to sell a large volume of wine. I think it's a matter of selecting one or two markets and going after them." Mr. Clark responded, "You are probably right, but I'm more cautious. I'll be very interested in hearing what you recommend. Our future growth may depend on your report."

The Company

The Barossa Winery, located in the Barossa Valley of South Australia, was started in the early 1960s by a winemaker, Mr. Rolf Mann, who had obtained a degree in viticulture from a well-regarded French school and emigrated to Australia. Since 1970, the firm had captured numerous awards every year at national and regional wine shows for both its red and white wines. By 1980, the company had established a solid reputation in Australia as a consistent producer of high-quality premium table wines.

The company was also known for its marketing skills. Mr. Steen, who joined the company in 1976, instituted various marketing initiatives including a series of labels that were regarded by many industry analysts as exceptional in terms of communicating the quality of the wines and "standing out" among the many competitive brands. As well, Mr. Steen established a distribution system that resulted in the prominent display of the company's products in many retail outlets. Finally, many of the advertising campaigns prepared for the Barossa Winery were judged as innovative and had contributed to the recognition and acceptance of the company's brands.

These efforts had resulted in rapid growth for the company. Between 1980 and 1985 sales increased from $18,500,000 to $33,900,000 and profits before tax from $1,600,000 to $3,100,000 (Exhibit 1). However, in 1986 and 1987 sales grew more slowly and profits were unchanged. Company officials felt that recent results were due, in part, to a slowdown in the growth of both the overall market and the table wine market

---

[*] This case is printed here with the permission of the author, Gordon H. G. McDougall of Wilfrid Laurier University, Canada.

EXHIBIT 1 Barossa Winery—Selected Company Statistics (1980–1987)

	1980	1981	1982	1983	1984	1985	1986	1987
Profit and loss statement (in $000,000)								
Sales	$17.5	20.6	23.6	26.8	30.5	33.9	35.3	36.8
Cost of goods sold	11.7	13.8	15.6	17.9	20.8	23.2	24.4	25.7
Gross margin	5.8	6.8	8.0	8.9	9.7	10.7	10.9	11.1
Marketing expenses	3.0	3.5	3.9	4.5	4.8	5.5	5.7	5.8
Profit before tax	$1.6	1.8	2.4	2.6	2.9	6.1	3.0	3.1
Sales by volume								
(000 litres)	4,120	4,520	4,830	4,950	5,210	5,680	5,800	5,900
(000 cases)[a]	468	502	537	550	579	631	644	656
Average selling price per case ($)	37.40	41.00	44.00	48.70	52.70	53.70	54.80	56.10
Export statistics								
Export sales (000 litres)	84.2	122.0	115.9	158.4	187.6	215.8	237.8	336.3
Export sales (000 cases)	9.4	13.6	12.9	17.6	20.8	24.0	26.4	37.4
Average selling price/case ($)[b]	$31.80	34.90	37.40	41.40	44.80	45.60	46.60	56.00
Export sales ($000)[c]	$298.9	474.6	482.5	728.6	931.8	1094.4	1230.2	2094.4
Consumer price index	100.0	109.8	120.8	135.5	148.7	160.9	176.7	186.0

[a] One case equals 9 L (12 bottles containing 750 mL each).
[b] Up to 1987 detailed sales records on prices were not kept. Company officials estimated that between 1980 and 1986 the average selling price per case was approximately 15% less than the domestic price per case.
[c] It was estimated that marketing expenses and administration and overhead amounted to 3% of sales for export versus around 8% for domestic sales.
Note: These numbers are in Canadian dollars.
Source: Company records.

(Exhibit 2). As well, increased competition in the quality premium bottled table wine market had led to price discounting by some wineries. As a policy, the Barossa Winery did not engage in price discounting.

With respect to export activity, up to now the company could best be described as a passive exporter. While George Steen had made one overseas trip in the past two years (the trip covered stops in the United States, Canada, and the United Kingdom) to "drum up" some business with wine importers, no explicit export strategy had been established. In fact, the company's export sales had been generated by wine importers who had approached the Barossa Winery.

The interest of those wine importers (primarily from the United Kingdom) in Barossa Winery products was due to the increasing recognition by many knowledgeable buyers of the quality of Australian and the company's wines. In the early 1980s, wine experts from the United Kingdom visited Australia and sampled numerous wines. Upon their return home, many wrote glowing reports on the quality of these wines, including Barossa Winery's products.

In 1987, the company exported 37,400 cases of wine valued at $2,094,400, an increase of 42% in volume and 70% in dollar value compared to 1986 (Exhibit 1). In fact, 1987 was the first year the company received the same average price for its wine in both the domestic and export markets. In prior years it was estimated (no records had been kept) that export sales generated a price per case of approximately 15% less than the average price received in the domestic market.

The Australian Wine Industry

In many ways, the Australian wine industry is similar to other world wine markets. The first requirement for producing good wines was to have the appropriate climate and soil conditions. Many regions of Australia had these conditions and produced wine grapes, including such classics as Cabernet Sauvignon, Grenache, and Pinot Noir for red wines, and Clare, Rhine Riesling, and Traminer for white wines. Most medium- and large-sized wineries in Australia made a complete range of wines, each with their own individuality. The Barossa Winery made six different white wines with two brands, Barossa Chardonnay and Barossa Rhine Riesling, making up over 80% of the company's white wine sales. The company produced five different red wines and, again, two brands, Barossa Cabernet Sauvignon and Barossa Hermitage, accounted for the majority of sales. Dry white wines accounted for 85% of total company sales.

EXHIBIT 2   Australian Wine Market—Selected Statistics (1980–1987) (000 Liters)

	1980	1981	1982	1983	1984	1985	1986	1987
Total wine sales	245,040	262,872	278,595	293,582	305,802	320,478	325,183	329,952
Table	160,867	179,278	197,904	216,948	227,805	245,400	253,045	258,231
Fortified[a]	45,587	45,868	45,189	43,027	42,587	38,617	36,819	36,246
Sparkling[b]	29,915	29,577	27,749	27,022	29,021	31,277	30,413	30,098
All other[c]	8,671	8,158	7,753	6,585	6,389	5,182	4,907	5,378
Table wine sales by variety								
Dry white	121,093	138,016	155,310	172,334	175,341	179,286	171,780	176,227
Sweet white	3,497	3,912	4,529	4,929	10,060	20,840	36,936	34,657
Red rose	27,667	29,258	30,362	31,856	34,480	37,805	37,188	40,192
Rose	8,610	8,091	7,706	7,830	7,924	7,466	7,140	7,155
Table wine sales by package								
Soft pack—white	51,148	69,525	84,680	103,585	111,486	137,675	140,788	138,787
Bottled—white	34,300	36,709	39,368	38,644	36,278	39,559	38,851	41,7436
Soft pack—red	7,451	8,871	11,263	12,787	14,425	16,191	16,927	17,659
Bottled—red	11,507	12,455	12,252	12,657	14,058	16,779	16,838	19,004
All other[d]	56,461	51,718	50,341	49,275	51,558	35,196	39,641	41,038

[a] Includes sherry and dessert wines.
[b] Includes champagne and carbonated wines.
[c] Includes flavored and vermouth.
[d] Includes white, red, and rose sold in bulk and in bottles over one liter in size.
Source: Australian Wine and Brandy Corporation.

A second requirement for producing good wines was to have a skilled winemaker. Mr. Mann had quickly established a reputation throughout Australia for producing high-quality wines on a consistent basis. He was renowned for his ability to purchase the finest grapes (the company did not own any vineyards, but instead purchased its grapes from among the over 4,000 grape growers in Australia), and he used the latest technology in producing many award-winning wines.

The third requirement was the ability to market the company's wines. Few, if any, product categories offered the consumer as wide a choice of varieties and brands as the wine category. For example, one of the large wholesalers of beer, wine, and spirits in Australia listed 577 brands of bottled table wines, including 256 red wines and 273 white wines. Most of these listed wines would be supplied by the 50 medium to large wineries in Australia.

Retail liquor outlets would not carry the complete range of wines offered by a wholesaler, but a typical outlet would handle at least 100 different brands of red and white bottled table wines. This large selection meant that marketing was critical in getting a brand known and recognized by consumers. While wine connoisseurs understood the differences between the varieties and brands of wines, these consumers constituted a very small percentage of the wine-buying public. A second group, who knew a reasonable amount about wines and could identify the major and some minor brands, tended to purchase the majority of the bottled table wines.

In terms of quantity, most table wine in Australia was sold in two- or four-liter casks to consumers who were relatively price sensitive. Retail liquor outlets in Australia could advertise and offer beer, wine, and spirits at any price. A consumer could purchase a four-liter cask of average-quality Riesling for about $7.00 on sale (regular price $10.00) or a 750 mL bottle of slightly higher quality Riesling for $3.50 on sale (regular price of $6.50). As shown in Exhibit 2, soft pack or cask sales of table wine constituted about 61% of total table wine sales, while bottled table wines constituted about 24% of total table wine sales by volume.

A further indication of the price sensitivity of the market was the impact of government taxation policies on the level of wine consumption. In late 1984, a 10% tax was placed on wines, and in 1985 the tax was increased to 20%. As shown in Exhibit 2, the total market growth rate, which averaged 5% between 1980 and 1984, declined to 1.5% in 1985.

On a broader scale, the consumption of wine in Australia appeared to have peaked in 1985 at 21 liters per capita. This compared to per-capita consumption of 9 liters in 1970, 12 liters in 1975, and 17 liters in 1980.

Against this backdrop, the Barossa Winery competed in the bottled table wine markets. Its target market was the relatively sophisticated wine drinker who was somewhat knowledgeable about wines and was likely to drink wine with his or her evening meal two or more times a week. Within this target market, the Barossa Winery competed with virtually all the wineries in Australia, as this was the most profitable segment. However, only a few companies, such as Wolf Blass and Leasingham, had been as successful as the Barossa Winery within this segment. While no market data were available, some industry observers felt that Wolf Blass and Leasingham were increasing their share of the market at a faster rate than the Barossa Winery.

The World Wine Industry

On a worldwide basis, the wine market was dominated by the European Community (EC) and within the community, by three countries, France, Italy, and Spain. The EC vineyards accounted for approximately 27% of the total area of the world under vines, 38% of the world's grapes, and 60% of the world's production of wines. Because of price supports within the EC for the wine industry in the past, the EC countries typically produced more wine than could be consumed within the EC. Consequently, there was considerable pressure to export wine. Due to declining consumption within the EC countries and revised price support policies, in recent years the production of wine by EC nations had declined (Exhibit 3). However, a surplus of wine was still produced within the EC, and the countries collectively exported over 4 billion liters of wine annually. Exporting of wine was encouraged by governments, as the EC provided export refunds and subsidies for table wine exported outside the EC.

Australian Wine Imports and Exports

Between 1980 and 1985 only a small portion (about 3%) of Australia's total wine production was exported. In the 1985–86 period exports increased to 11 million liters, and in 1986–87 exports rose to 21 million liters (Exhibit 4). This was due primarily to a more favorable exchange rate, as the Australian dollar had fallen sharply against most foreign currencies (Exhibit 5). Two other factors also contributed to this increase. First, the Chernobyl nuclear incident (a nuclear reactor that exploded

EXHIBIT 3   World Wine Market Selected Data (000,000 Liters)

	Production			Exports	Imports	Per Capita Consumption (Liters)	
	1983–84	1984–85	1985–86	1986	1985	1983	1985
France	6,855	6,436	7,015	1,189	701	85	80
Italy	8,228	7,090	6,258	1,803	n/a	91	85
Spain	3,247	3,625	3,277	731	n/a	57	48
Portugal	845	850	855	152	n/a	89	87
West Germany	1,340	889	540	292	962	27	26
Greece	525	503	478	140	n/a	44	43
United Kingdom	—	—	—	—	580	9	10
Total EC	21,040	19,393	18,423	4,307	2,243	—	—
Europe—All others (incl. U.S.S.R)	7,031	6,692	5,804	—	—	—	—
United States	1,476	1,670	1,810	—	519	8	9
Australia	396	451	480	11	8	20	21
Canada	47	50	50	—	140	9	10
Africa, Latin America, and South Africa	3,312	2,931	3,124	—	—	—	—
All others	1,002	918	981	—	—	—	—
Total	34,304	32,105	30,6726	4,318	2,910		

Source: Australian Wine and Brandy Corporation.

EXHIBIT 4 Australian Wine Imports and Exports (1986–1987)

	Imports			Exports		
	Liters (000)	Value ($000)	Value/ Liter ($)	Liters (000)	Value ($000)	Value/ Liter ($)
Champagne	1,134	19,628	17.31	370	1,484	4.01
Table wine	4,852	14,084	3.52	18,627	37,967	2.04
All others	1,573	4,899	3.11	2,236	5,170	2.22
Total	7,559	41,611	5.50	21,323	44,621	2.09

	Exports from Australia by Destination (000 Liters or $000)								
	Champagne		Table Wine		All Others		Total		Value/ Liter
	L	Value	L	Value	L	Value	L	Value	
United States	36	$171	2,455	$9,029	422	$1,255	2,913	$10,455	$3.39
United Kingdom	34	122	2,190	6,775	96	352	2,320	7,249	3.12
Sweden	—	—	5,223	5,257	—	—	5,223	5,257	1.01
New Zealand	183	611	1,054	3,397	177	540	1,414	4,548	3.22
Canada	—	—	1,228	3,017	791	1,283	2,019	4,300	2.13
Hong Kong	28	149	527	1,009	108	246	663	1,404	2.12
Fiji	14	67	230	426	72	136	316	629	1.99
All other	75	364	5,720	9,057	660	1,358	6,455	10,779	1.67
Total	370	$1,484	18,627	$37,967	2,326	$5,170	21,323	$44,621	$2.09

* Largest imports (in 1000 L) come from Italy (2,714), France (1,981), and Portugal (777).

EXHIBIT 5 Exchange Rates (Units of Foreign Currency per $ Australian)

June	United States Dollar	Canadian Dollar	U.K. Pound Sterling	West German Mark	French Franc	Italian Lira	Trade Weighted Index*
1984	0.86	1.14	0.64	2.40	7.36	1,477.13	79.2
1985	0.67	0.91	0.51	2.03	6.19	1,294.40	65.0
1986	0.68	0.94	0.44	1.48	4.73	1,019.90	56.3
1987	0.72	0.96	0.45	1.31	4.40	955.48	56.6
1988	0.81	0.99	0.44	0.99	3.97	1,099.32	56.8

*Trade-weighted index of average value of the Australian dollars compared with currencies of Australia's trading partners. May 1970 index, 100.
Source: Reserve Bank of Australia, *Bulletin,* Publication No. NBP 4521

in Ukraine in 1986, spreading nuclear waste across Europe) had raised concern in a number of countries (particularly in Scandinavia) about contamination of European grapes. Second, there was a growing awareness in many countries of the quality of Australian wines.

The vast majority of Australian wine exports were table wines, and most of these exports went to seven countries, with the United States, the United Kingdom, and Canada being three of the largest markets. The value per liter of export sales varied considerably by country. At the lower end, Sweden purchased wine in bulk (it was shipped from Australia in large containers) at a value per liter of $1.01. The wine was bottled and

sold by the Swedish liquor control board. At the upper end, all of the wine exported to the United States was in bottle form at an average price to the exporter of $3.59 per liter.

The Export Decision

In preparing the report, Mr. Steen first considered the possible countries where the Barossa Winery could achieve significant sales. Based on a preliminary screening, he decided to limit his investigation to the three countries that he felt offered a good potential for the company's products: Canada, the United States, and the United Kingdom.

Canada

Canada was an attractive market because the domestic wine industry was not well developed and was not recognized as producing quality wines (Exhibit 6). The marketing of wine and spirits in Canada was strictly controlled by the 10 provincial governments, and most sales were made through government liquor stores. In March 1988, the Australian Wine and Brandy Corporation sponsored a tour of the listing agents for the 10 liquor control boards of Canada. The agents visited the major wine-growing areas and sampled many of the wines available for export. The main objective of the tour was to acquaint the agents with the quality, variety, and availability of Australian wines.

The two major drawbacks to the Canadian market were the difficulties in getting a general listing and the restrictions placed on marketing activities. Australian wines would compete against all other wine-producing countries for listings. It was estimated that up to 1,000 listing requests were received by each of the 10 boards every year and a selection committee might list 75 new wines. Chances of acceptance were improved by a personal visit to present the listing application. Primarily, it was felt that price (within a given quality range) was the dominant criterion in getting accepted on the list. Government restrictions placed on marketing activities (for example, no price discounting, restrictions as to the amount and type of advertising, no point-of-purchase displays) made it difficult to develop brand awareness and trial by consumers.

In preparing his report Mr. Steen obtained information on the largest Australian wine exporter's operations in Canada (Hardy's Wines). It was rumored that Hardy's held somewhat over 40% share of the Canadian table wine market for Australian wines. As well, Hardy's was thought to have about a 50% share of the "all other" wines category. It had achieved this position by spending approximately $200,000 each year in Canada. Hardy's had two full-time employees, one in Ontario and one in Québec (total costs for both employees including salaries, office space, cars, and expenses were $100,000) and the company spent about

---

EXHIBIT 6　　Fact Sheet on Canada

- Canadian consumption of wine, particularly imported wine, is increasing despite severe marketing restrictions. The import and retailing of all alcoholic beverages is controlled by individual provincial monopolies, as are all aspects of product marketing (for example, advertising, sampling).

- Import licensing as such is not required. However, distribution is controlled by the provincial government liquor monopolies, who will only list a brand if convinced it will achieve the required sales volume.

- Import duties are $12 Canadian per imperial gallon (one imperial gallon equals 4.546 liters). Excise taxes are $0.35 Canadian per liter. Federal sales taxes are 12% on the landed duty and excise paid value. As of June 1988, import duties in Australian dollars would be $2.64 per liter, excise duties would be $0.35 per liter, and federal sales tax would be $1.14 per liter.

- No major difficulties in terms of certification, packaging, etc. However, with respect to labels, the label information must be in English and French.

- Canada produces less than one-half of its wine requirements, and Canada's climate is not conducive to grape growing.

- Prices to the provincial monopolies should be quoted in Canadian dollars CIF (cost, insurance, freight). Each province arbitrarily sets the retail price of a product by applying a fixed markup to the landed cost (C$CIF). For example, Alberta has a markup of 55%; British Columbia has a markup of 50% on B.C.-produced table wines, 110% on other Canadian-produced table wines, and 120% on imported wines; Ontario has a markup of 58% on Ontario-produced table wines, 98% on other Canadian-produced table wines, and 123% on imported wines; Québec has a markup of 80% on Québec-produced table wines, 114% on other Canadian-produced table wines, and 120% on imported table wines.

- Distribution of all wine and spirits sold in Canada is controlled by government monopolies and/or liquor boards. Each of the 10 provinces has its own liquor board. Since each province will stock a limited range of wines out of the hundreds of different types and brands available, it establishes a price list giving the names of those wines available for sale. However, even when a wine is listed, it will probably not be available in every store.

- The majority of Canada's 26 million people reside in Ontario, Québec, British Columbia, and Alberta.

Source: Australian Wine and Brandy Corporation, *Export Market Grid.*

$100,000 on all types of promotions, including visits by the Australian export manager. The two employees spent the majority of their time making regular calls on the liquor board head offices, checking stocks, and calling on individual liquor stores to ensure that the product was available. As well, the employees would have the product on hand at any wine tastings within the provinces. A further important duty was to encourage Canadian wine writers for newspapers and magazines to write about Hardy's Wines. Hardy's also employed agents in Alberta and British Columbia who received a 10% commission plus up to 5% more for expenses.

Most Australian wine producers who exported to Canada used agents to perform the marketing function. The agents worked on a commission basis (usually 10% of the landed cost in Canada) and their prime role was to obtain product exposure. This could be done by convincing restaurants and hotels to include the product on wine lists, by conducting tastings, and by obtaining good press for the product. Agents could be valuable because the need for personal selling was considerable in Canada. Wine consumption in Canada had been increasing and per capita consumption had risen from 6.3 liters per year in 1976 to 10 liters in 1985. Over 50% of the wine sold in Canada was imported and over 80% of that came from the wine-producing countries of the EC. Some well-known European brands such as Blue Nun, Black Tower, and Mateus had substantial sales in Canada. Of the 140,000,000 liters of wine imported to Canada in 1985, 90% were table wines.

United States

By Australian standards, the magnitude of the U.S. market was staggering (Exhibit 7). Imports of table wine alone were about 313 million liters in 1986, most of it coming from Italy (48%), France (30%), and West Germany (11%). The Italian wine imports tended to be lower-priced ($1.52/liter on average), while the French imports were relatively high-priced ($4.43/liter). The German imports ($2.89/liter) were close to the average of all imports ($3.09/liter).[1] In 1986, the Australian share of the U.S. table wine market was estimated at 0.06%.

The top-selling import brands in the U.S. market included Riunite from Italy (8,500,000 cases), Blue Nun from Germany (1,000,000 cases), and Mateus from Portugal (800,000 cases). It was estimated that the wholesale prices per case for these brands were: Riunite $19.35 ($2.15/liter), Blue Nun $33.12 ($3.68/liter), and Mateus $21.30 ($2.37/liter). Promotion expenditures for many of the imported wines were extensive, and while total expenditures were not available it was estimated that Riunite spent over $12 million in television advertising and Blue Nun spent approximately $2.4 million in radio advertising.

With respect to markets, the top 10 markets for table wine in the United States accounted for 65% of all sales. The New York metropolitan area had sales of 5.9 million cases of imported table wine, and Detroit (ninth-ranked) had sales of 550,000 cases in 1986.

EXHIBIT 7   Fact Sheet on the United States

- The U.S. consumption of wine, both domestic and imported, has been increasing, and the absolute size of the market is one of the most attractive in the world. Estimated sales for 1988 are 2 billion liters.
- Import licenses may only be held by U.S. citizens.
- Import duties on table wines are $0.375 per U.S. gallon (one U.S. gallon = 3.785 liters). Excise taxes are US$0.17 per U.S. gallon. As of June 1988, import duties in Australian dollars would be $0.12 per liter and excise taxes would be $0.06 per liter.
- No major difficulties in terms of certification, packaging, labeling, etc.
- Seventy-two percent of the table wine sold in the United States was produced in California, 24% was imported, and 4% was produced by other states in 1986.
- The U.S. market, because of its size and complexity, should be treated on a state-by-state basis. The sale of alcoholic beverages is controlled by state organizations, the degree of authority ranging from minimal licensing requirements to complete control of retail outlets. There are 18 "monopoly" states that operate in a similar manner to Canada. Most of the larger states, including California and New York, are nonmonopoly states. The nonmonopoly states operate in a similar manner to the Australian system. In these states, the product can only enter the United States through a licensed importer, who, in turn, can only then sell to a wholesaler. A direct sale to the retailer or consumer level is not permitted. Importers' or agents' margins range from 10% to 25% of landed cost, wholesalers' around 15% to 30% and retailers' 30% to 40%.
- In 1968, the majority of table wines sold in the United States retailed in Australian dollars between $3.40 and $5.25 (69%); $5.26 and $7.10 (15%); and $7.11 and $9.26 (9%).

Source: Australian Wine and Brandy Corporation, *Export Market Grid.*

Selection of an agent or importer was obviously an important consideration. Numerous spirit agents were available, ranging from small companies that specialized in a few product lines in one area of the country to national distributors that had a vast product line and covered the entire country.

Marketing activities for wine companies, particularly in the nonmonopoly states, could be extensive and include advertising, in-store promotions, and price specials. Many U.S. wine producers, particularly from California, had established well-known brand names and were recognized as producing quality wines.

United Kingdom

The third market under consideration was the United Kingdom (Exhibit 8). In the past few years, per capita wine consumption in the United Kingdom had increased and stood at ten liters in 1985. A review of the U.K. wine market in 1986 noted that Australia had less than 2% of the table wine market.

The U.K. market was very competitive, and extensive advertising, point-of-purchase displays, and price specials were used at the retail level to promote individual brands.

The major drawback for any exporter in developing the U.K. market was the potential threat that import regulations for wines might be changed. In the past France had engaged in certain activities that "changed the rules," resulting in a new set of regulations that disrupted the marketing activities of exporters to the EC.

Most of the larger and some of the medium-sized Australian wine producers had entered the export market by focusing first on the United Kingdom. For example, one of the largest Australian producers, Orlando Wines, had been very active in the United Kingdom. Orlando regarded the United Kingdom as an important market. As one executive of Orlando stated: "If you can be successful in the United Kingdom, it will stand you in good stead in other export markets." Orlando had established its own company in the United Kingdom and the subsidiary performed the role of the importer. The export marketing manager visited the United Kingdom four times a year, spending two weeks on each visit. His main activities were to motivate the distributor of the company's brands and to discuss the brands with wine writers, if possible. The distributor was a medium-sized wholesaler who sold to retail liquor chains, primarily in the London area. While no figures were available on Orlando's export sales it was estimated that in 1988, its sales into the U.K. market would be approximately 40,000 cases.

Orlando did some advertising in both consumer and trade magazines in the United Kingdom. In a recent issue of *Decanter* (a consumer magazine targeted at wine buffs) Orlando had a full-page ad emphasizing the quality of its brands and stated, "They [the two brands] compare beautifully with similar wines from France, yet only cost around half as much."

Another company that was actively involved in export marketing was Wolf Blass, a well-known, medium-sized producer of quality wines. In 1985, it set up distributorships with agents in both the United States and the United Kingdom. Wolf Blass was one of the few companies that received the same price of wine in both the domestic and export markets (in 1987, the average

---

■■■■■ EXHIBIT 8   Fact Sheet on the United Kingdom

- The U.K. consumption of wine has been increasing and all wine consumed in the United Kingdom is imported. The United Kingdom is a member of the EC.
- Import licenses can be easily obtained, although there are major difficulties in complying with various EC requirements for import.
- Import duties on table wines entering the EC are £8.58 per hundred liters. It should be noted that wines entering the EC must exceed a minimum threshold price. Excise taxes in the United Kingdom are £0.980/liter on table wine. As well, a value added tax of 15% is placed on all products. As of June 1988, import duties in Australian

dollars would be $0.20 per liter; excise taxes would be $2.23 per liter; and the value added tax would be $1.34 per liter.
- Considerable efforts are required to comply with EC standards with respect to certification, packaging, and labeling. In particular, an EC analysis certificate that describes the wine's characteristics, including actual alcohol strength, total dry extract, total acidity, and residual sugar, must be completed (the analysis can be done in Australia) and meet EC requirements.
- In 1985, the United Kingdom imported 580 million liters of wine, most of it from member countries of the EC.

Source: Australian Wine and Brandy Corporation, *Export Market Grid.*

price received was approximately $65 per case). In selecting the distributors in both the United States and the United Kingdom, Wolf Blass had decided on large agents to give them access to the markets they wanted. In 1987, Wolf Blass had sold a total of 50,000 cases in the export market, but it was not clear whether it had made any profits. Some experts felt that the money Wolf Blass invested to develop the export markets (estimated annual marketing expenditures for both major markets were $600,000) had been substantial and that no profits would be obtained for at least four years.

Preliminary Cost Data

Mr. Steen prepared some rough calculations on the costs of getting a case of wine to each of the three markets and what it might sell for at retail (Exhibit 9).

EXHIBIT 9 Estimated Retail Price of a Case of Barossa Wine in the Three Markets

	United Kingdom	United States	Canada
Barossa Winery price	$ 56.00	$ 56.00	$ 56.00
Transport to destination[a]	2.55	2.85	2.85
Landed cost	58.55	58.85	58.85
Import duties and excise tax[b]	21.90	1.60	26.90
Other taxes[b]	12.05	—	10.30
Landed cost with duties/taxes	92.50	60.45	96.05
Importer/agent margin[c]	27.75	9.10	9.60
Importer price	120.25	69.55	105.65
Wholesale margin[d]	—	13.90	—
Wholesale price	120.25	83.45	105.65
Retail margin[e]	60.15	29.20	64.75
Retail price	180.40	112.65	170.40
Bottle price (750 mL)	$ 15.00	$ 9.40	$ 14.20

Assumptions:
[a] It costs $347 to ship a container from the Barossa Valley to Port Adelaide. On average, a container holds 1,000 cases. One case contains 9 L or 12 bottles (750 mL) Port Adelaide to U.K. is $2,200 per container; to U.S. or Canada, approximately $2,500.
[b] Based on information in fact sheets.
[c] Importer margin in U.K. ranges from 25% to 40% of landed cost (assume 30% for estimation purposes); in U.S. range is 10% to 25% (assume 15%); in Canada agents average 10%.
[d] Wholesale margins in U.S. range from 15% to 30% (assume 20%).
[e] Retail margins in U.K. are about 50%; in U.S. from 30% to 40% (assume 35%); in Canada, range from 55% to 123% of landed cost (assume 110%).

With respect to costs of production, Mr. Steen had read a recent newspaper article on the costs of wine and was surprised at how close those costs were to those of the Barossa Winery. As shown in Exhibit 10, the production cost for a 750 mL bottle of good-quality Chardonnay was $3.02. By the time the consumer purchased it, the price was $11.08. While the cost of grapes for some of the other varieties of wines could be considerably less (for example, $600 per metric ton for Semillon), most of the price of a bottle of wine ($8.06 per the example) was made up of margins and taxes.

Mr. Steen also worked out some preliminary estimates of what it would cost to actively enter all three export markets. In terms of personnel, the cost of an export sales manager was about $60,000 and if the manager made six overseas trips a year, this expense would be about $100,000. One or two sales clerks might be required at a cost of $30,000 each. Preparation of custom requirements, including documentation, obtaining label approvals, and sending samples could cost up to $30,000. Promotion costs were difficult to estimate, but they could exceed $100,000 for expenditures on wine tastings and shows for both the

EXHIBIT 10 Typical Cost Structure of a Bottle/Case of Wine (In AUST$)

	Per Bottle	Per Case
Product*	$ 1.61	
Packaging	10.7	
Bottling	.22	
Transportation	.12	
Total production cost	3.02	$ 36.24
Manufacturer margin (50% of costs)	1.50	
Price to wholesaler	4.52	54.24
Wholesaler margin (25%)	1.13	
Wholesaler price before taxes	5.65	
Federal tax (20%)	1.13	
Wholesaler price after federal tax	6.78	
State tax (9%)	.61	
Wholesaler price after taxes	7.39	88.68
Retailer margin (50%)	3.69	
Retail price	11.08	132.96

* Based on premium chardonnay fruit at a price per metric ton of $1,200. One metric ton will produce 744 bottles of 750 mL wine. A case contains 12 bottles (9 L).

public and the trade, advertising expenditures for consumers and the trade, and public relations.

A portion of these expenditures could be recovered from the federal government through the Export Market Development Grant. Firms engaged in export marketing were eligible (for the first five years) to receive up to 70% of certain export costs, including printing of special labels, preparation and printing of point-of-sale material, a portion of the cost of any personnel who were located in the export market, air travel, and a portion of accommodation expenses for managers visiting the export markets, samples, and expenses related to wine trade shows. While it was difficult to estimate the precise proportion of costs that would be recovered, depending on the type of expenditure, Barossa Winery could receive up to $100,000 each year.

Although the Barossa Winery had not aggressively pursued the export market, Mr. Steen was quick to capitalize on any export opportunity that was presented. For example, if a British importer expressed interest in any of the company's products, Mr. Steen, or a member of the marketing group, would provide free samples, information on the wines, and product availability. If an importer placed an order, Mr. Steen ensured that the order was shipped as quickly as possible with proper documentation. As Mr. Steen once joked to a colleague, "We may not go after the export business, but if anybody comes to us, we'll offer better service and support than any other winery in Australia."

Mr. Steen was pleased with the growth of exports in the past few years, but he was concerned about the tenuous nature of the business. While the export business had experienced steady growth, the source of sales often changed substantially on a yearly basis. For example, sales to the United Kingdom had been made through two different U.K. importers in the past three years. Between 1981 and 1984, Star Importers, a U.K. importer who specialized in Australian wines, had purchased up to 10,000 cases of Barossa Wines in a given year. In late 1984, Star Importers switched their major buying from Barossa to a competitive winery in New South Wales. In 1985, the Reid Company, another U.K. importer, began buying Barossa Wines, and in 1987 purchased 18,000 cases for the U.K. market.

Similarly, the company had been approached in the past five years by six different U.S. importers. The Barossa Winery had conducted business with all six (sales in a given year to any one of the importers ranged from 400 to 4,500 cases) over the years and in 1987 sold a total 9,000 cases through four importers to the U.S. market. Two sales agents in Canada (who have been importing the product for about four years) had generated sales of about 800 cases in Ontario and Alberta. As well, the company had sold about 10,000 cases to the "rest of the world" through two Australian exporters. These two firms approached Australian wine producers and obtained products that they would sell to distributors at the wholesale or retail level in other countries. As far as Mr. Steen could tell, the two exporters who sold Barossa Wines had most of their sales in New Zealand, Micronesia, and the Far East (for example, Japan, Taiwan, Thailand, Hong Kong).

Mr. Steen realized that the Barossa Winery did not have strong links with these importers or exporters in that no formal contracts were signed with any of them in terms of an exclusive agreement. In all cases, both parties were free to buy from or sell to anyone. Further, the company had little expertise in exporting, as most of the work and all of the marketing was done by the importer or exporter. In the final analysis, Mr. Steen felt that the company's success to date had been a combination of good service, good prices, and good-quality wine.

The Decision

Having gathered the preliminary data, Mr. Steen began thinking about the report. He was not certain what he should recommend. On the one hand, export sales were growing with little effort and expense on the company's part. Possibly with a little more effort, sales could be increased without going "full speed ahead" into exporting. On the other hand, the tenuous nature of the company's relationship with its exporters suggested that some action should be taken.

Mr. Steen knew that the senior management group was expecting a report that contained specific recommendations including whether the Barossa Winery should aggressively enter the export market and, if so, how many markets to enter. As well, the group would expect to receive details of the proposed strategy Mr. Steen would pursue for the next three years in the export area. With these thoughts in mind, Mr. Steen began writing the report.

Endnote

1. Value at foreign export port exclusive of shipping costs and taxes.

Case 30: MacDermid, Inc.

In 1990, Buzz Fanning, technical liaison for MacDermid, Inc., was sent to Korea to investigate MacDermid's loss of market share in the Korean market. MacDermid was an international specialty chemical company that supplied the metal finishing, printed circuit board, and microelectronics industries. The majority of sales in the Far East were for the printed circuit board (PC) market. In a two-year period, MacDermid had gone from a 30% to 50% market share to a 10% market share in the Korean PC market. Fanning was charged with regaining MacDermid's market share and its leadership position in Korea.

Background of the Company

MacDermid, Inc., was founded on February 2, 1922, in Waterbury, Connecticut, by Archie J. MacDermid, a Scottish immigrant. MacDermid's first product was Metex Metal Cleaner #1 for the metal finishing industry. Metex was an alkaline metal soak and electrolytic cleaner that was used to clean brass and other metals. The thriving brass industry in Connecticut provided a large market for MacDermid. In 1930 MacDermid moved its manufacturing facilities to a new location in Waterbury. This plant still serves as MacDermid's primary manufacturing facility in the United States.

In 1938 Harold Leever joined MacDermid as a research chemist. Leever later served as the second of only three MacDermid presidents and subsequently as chairman of the board. It was Leever's innovative and insightful ideas that led MacDermid to be a world leader in specialty chemicals for the metal finishing, printed circuit board, and microelectronics industries.

Leever began changing the company when he developed Anodex, a reverse-current alkaline cleaner. Anodex could be used to clean steel and this opened the automotive market to MacDermid. With this, MacDermid became a national marketer.

Leever also developed the philosophy of "sales and service." This philosophy merged research and sales by requiring that research conducted in Waterbury start from and serve the customer's needs. This philosophy still works at MacDermid today.

During the 1940s and 1950s, MacDermid introduced some industry firsts. Cyanide bright copper addition agents eliminated dull finishes and the need for buffing procedures. Dry acid salt replaced the more hazardous liquid acids thus providing environmental improvements. Metal strippers allowed customers to salvage scrapped electroplated parts. Metex Acid Salt M-629 was a refinement of the original salt and provided a longer life and a better adhesion of plated metals. Chromate conversion coatings improved corrosion resistance and appearance. The 1950s also saw the construction of another MacDermid manufacturing facility located in Ferndale, Michigan. MacDermid had emerged as an innovator and market leader in the metal finishing industry. This reputation would help propel the company into new markets.

By 1954, Leever had earned the position of president of MacDermid. Archie MacDermid remained active in the company until 1959 when he retired. With $3 million in sales, 75 employees, and 50 products, Archie offered ownership of the company to the employees. The employees bought 29,000 of Archie's shares for $961,640. This allowed control of the company to remain with those who had helped make it successful.

Leever introduced the concept of "Complete Cycle Responsibility," which then became company policy. This policy stated that every MacDermid representative will accept responsibility for satisfactory operation of a complete processing cycle.

In the 1960s MacDermid began to develop and market chemicals for a new industry that was very significant in size—the electronics industry. Printed circuit boards are an essential component of this market. Chemicals are used to clean, coat, etch, strip, and protect printed circuit boards. MacDermid's first product in this market was alkaline etchant. This eliminated the need for hazardous chromic acids and ferric chloride and thus improved working conditions and worker safety.

In 1966 a public stock offering of 20% of the 510,456 outstanding shares was made. By this time, MacDermid had also begun to compete internationally, with $200,000 in overseas sales. A 50/50 joint venture with Occidental Petroleum Corporation was formed and called MOSA. MOSA was responsible for worldwide manufacturing and distribution of proprietary chemicals. This agreement was terminated in 1983.

In 1977, MacDermid had $42 million in sales, 440 employees, and 500 specialty chemicals. There were manufacturing plants in Connecticut, Michigan, California, Missouri, England, and Spain, and a research facility in Tel Aviv, Israel. There were sales and service operations throughout the world. It was in this growing environment that Arthur J. LoVetere was made the third and current president of MacDermid.

LoVetere joined MacDermid when he was eighteen as a summer worker. He continued his association with MacDermid as he earned his BS in chemical engineering and his MBA. In 1963, after receiving his MBA, LoVetere began as a technical sales representative for the mid-Atlantic. By 1966, LoVetere was the company's youngest regional sales manager at age 27. In 1973 he became vice president of marketing and by 1975 he was vice president and chief operating officer. In 1977 he was made president and chief executive officer. LoVetere believed in management by participation. Although LoVetere was now responsible for daily operations, Leever remained as an active participant in the company and chairman of the board.

Under LoVetere, the company continued to expand its operations by acquisitions and entry into international markets. In 1978 MacDermid had 6,000 customers in the United States and Canada. Products were marketed in Europe by 25 sales representatives located throughout England, Germany, the Netherlands, Spain, and Switzerland. Proprietary products were manufactured and sold in Australia, Italy, and on a limited basis in Japan. MacDermid purchased the Plating Systems Division of 3M. This acquisition provided manufacturing, distribution networks, and a basis for overseas business that were extremely valuable, especially in the Far East.

In 1980, the Employee Stock Ownership Plan was instituted, continuing the tradition of employee ownership. Employee ownership was now 40% with retirees, friends, and families of employees constituting another 25%.

By 1990, MacDermid had $106 million in sales, 800 employees, 1,000 products, and served 23 countries. The company was still characterized as an innovator and industry leader. There was no rigid organizational chart and the "MacDermid Spirit" was evident to anyone who came in contact with a MacDermid employee. In 1986, a 2,500-square-foot manufacturing plant was built in Taiwan.

Products—PC Market

MacDermid had a full line of products to service the PC industry. Products included Metex activators, accelerators, acid cleaners and acid salts, electrocleaners, strippers, antitarnish coating, circuit board tapes, polymer thick films, solder pastes, resists and masks, and etch resists and inks. These products are used in such applications as communication systems, television, video and sound recorders, compact discs, microwaves, radios, industrial automation and robotics, computer system electronics, navigation electronics, and medical instrumentation and monitoring devices. MacDermid was considered one of the major competitors in this market. It was the only specialty chemical company with direct operations in every major market in the world.

Competition

Shiplee Corporation of Germany was MacDermid's major competitor. Shiplee was privately owned and had a significant market share. Their claim to success was consistent quality. Shiplee competed with MacDermid in most major markets in the world.

Korean Market

MacDermid was well established in Japan, Korea, Singapore, Hong Kong, and Taiwan. MacDermid had its own manufacturing facility in Taiwan and used contract manufacturers in Japan. For 13 years, the Korean market had been served by MacDermid out of its Japanese division. The Japanese fully controlled the market. The Korean market had become significantly large due to the government's commitment to the electronics industry. However, because of the loss of one major account, MacDermid's market share had dropped to 10%. There was considerable animosity between the Koreans and the Japanese. A brief history lesson highlights the fact that the Japanese invaded Korea during World War II. In addition, the cultural, political, and economic differences between the two nations further increased the friction.

The Korean market was serviced by Japanese salesmen. There was no local representation. The price charged by the Japanese division was twice that available in the United States. This was primarily due to the strength of the yen. In 1990, the Korean sales volume was $40,000 per year.

The Korean government had recently mandated a balance of trade. Currently, there was an excess of imports from Japan and an excess of exports to the United States and Hong Kong. The Korean customers were requesting to deal directly with the U.S. division, which would result in a better balance with the United States and Japan (i.e., fewer imports from Japan and more imports from the United States). MacDermid's Japanese employees furiously fought this option. They would lose a large percentage of sales if they lost the Korean market. Buzz was challenged with finding a solution to this complicated international problem.